CHAPTERS 1 TO 13

Accounting

Charles T. Horngren Series in Accounting

- AUDITING: AN INTEGRATED APPROACH, 7E
  Arens/Loebbeck
- KOHLER'S DICTIONARY FOR ACCOUNTANTS, 7E
  Copper/Ljiri
- FINANCIAL STATEMENT ANALYSIS, 2E
  Foster
- GOVERNMENTAL AND NONPROFIT ACCOUNTING: THEORY AND PRACTICE, 5E
  Freeman/Shoulders
- FINANCIAL ACCOUNTING, 3E
  Harrison/Horngren
- COST ACCOUNTING; A MANAGERIAL EMPHASIS, 9E
  Horngren/Foster/Datar
- ACCOUNTING, 4E
  Horngren/Harrison/Bamber
- CASES IN FINANCIAL REPORTING, 2E
  Hirst/McAnally
- PRINCIPLES OF FINANCIAL AND MANAGEMENT ACCOUNTING: A SOLE PROPRIETORSHIP APPROACH, 2E
  Horngren/Harrison/Robinson
- INTRODUCTION TO FINANCIAL ACCOUNTING, 7E
  Horngren/Sundem/Elliot
- INTRODUCTION TO MANAGEMENT ACCOUNTING, 11E
  Horngren/Sundem/Stratton
- BUDGETING, 6E
  Welsch/Hilton/Gordon

CHAPTERS 1 TO 13

FOURTH EDITION

Accounting

- **CHARLES T. HORNGREN**
  Stanford University

- **WALTER T. HARRISON, JR.**
  Baylor University

- **LINDA SMITH BAMBER**
  University of Georgia

Annotations by
Betsy Willis   Becky Jones
Baylor University

PRENTICE-HALL
Upper Saddle River, New Jersey 07458

Executive Editor: *Annie Todd*
Executive Editor: *Deborah Hoffman Emery*
Development Editor: *Bruce Kaplan*
Senior Editorial Assistant: *Jane Avery*
Assistant Editor: *Natacha St. Hill*
Editor in Chief: *P.J. Boardman*
Director of Development: *Stephen Deitmer*
Executive Marketing Manager: *Beth Toland*
Book Production: *Progressive Publishing Alternatives*
Production Editor: *Carol Lavis*
Managing Editor: *Bruce Kaplan*
Senior Manufacturing Supervisor: *Paul Smolenski*
Manufacturing Manager: *Vincent Scelta*
Design Director: *Pat Smythe*
Interior Design: *Lorraine Castellano*
Cover Design: *Deborah Chused*
Composition: *TSI Graphics*
Cover Art/Photo: *Marjorie Dressler*

A Simon & Schuster / A Viacom Company
Upper Saddle River, New Jersey 07548

Printed in the United States of America
10 9 8 7 6 5 4 3 2

ISBN 0-13-082305-8

Prentice Hall International (UK) Limited, London
Prentice Hall of Australia Pty. Limited, Sydney
Prentice Hall of Canada Inc., Toronto
Prentice Hall Hispanoamericano, S.A., Mexico
Prentice Hall of India Private Limited, New Delhi
Prentice Hall of Japan, Inc., Tokyo
Simon & Schuster Asia Pte. Ltd., Singapore
Editora Prentice Hall do Brasil, Ltda., Rio de Janeiro

To Betsy Willis and Becky Jones for their wisdom on learning and teaching over a 10-year period and to Michael Bamber for his insight on business practices and ethical issues in management accounting.

Photo Credits

4 Bob Daemmrich/Stock Boston; **5** Bob Daemmrich/Stock Boston; **9** Courtesy of Boeing Commercial Airline Group; **10** Coca-Cola, the Red Disk Icon, the Contour Bottle design, and the Dynamic Ribbon device are registered trademarks of The Coca-Cola Company; **42** Courtesy of Land's End; **43** Courtesy of Land's End; **46** B.G. Graphics; **59** R. Lord/The Image Works; **67** Teri Stratford; **90** Andrea McGinty, Chairman: It's Just Lunch, Inc.; **91** Andrea McGinty, Chairman: It's Just Lunch, Inc.; **92** Stephen Simpson/FPG International; **94** Newman Brown/Monkmeyer Press; **101** Frank LaBua/Simon & Schuster/PH College; **136** Courtesy Motorola Pager Division; **137** Courtesy Motorola Pager Division; **145** Sotographs/Gamma-Liaison, Inc.; **152** Courtesy of International Business Machines Corporation. Unauthorized use not permitted; **155** Courtesy of International Business Machines Corporation. Unauthorized use not permitted; **180** Rudi Von Briel/Photo Edit; **181** Rudi Von Briel/Photo Edit; **184** Jeff Greenberg/PhotoEdit; **194** Joseph Heider/Simon & Schuster/PH College; **244** Capece/Monkmeyer Press; **245** Capece/Monkmeyer Press; **247** Chuck Pefley/Stock Boston; **255** Reprinted with permission of Consumers Digest, Inc.; **288** Michael Rosenfeld/Tony Stone Images; **289** Michael Rosenfeld/Tony Stone Images; **293** M. Antman/The Image Works; **294** SuperStock, Inc.; **311** Nancy Richmond/The Image Works; **334** Frank LaBua/Simon & Schuster/PH College; **335** Frank LaBua/Simon & Schuster/PH College; **339** J. Albertson/Stock Boston; **357** Frank LaBua/Simon & Schuster/PH College; **376** Steven Peters/Tony Stone Images; **377** Steven Peters/Tony Stone Images; **389** Courtesy of Owens Corning; **396** Simon Wolfe/The Stock Market; **418** Zigy Kaluzny/Gamma Liaison, Inc.; **419** Zigy Kaluzny/Gamma Liaison, Inc.; **422** Zigy Kaluzny/Tony Stone Images; **435** Tony Stone Images; **442** John McDermott/Tony Stone Images; **462** Courtesy American Airlines; **463** Courtesy American Airlines; **467** M. Farrell/The Image Works; **474** Courtesy of International Business Machines Corporation. Unauthorized use not permitted.; **506** Rob Lewine/The Stock Market; **507** Rob Lewine/The Stock Market; **519** Jean-Marc Giboux/Gamma-Liaison, Inc.; **542** Dennis M. Gottlieb/The Stock Market; **543** Dennis M. Gottlieb/The Stock Market; **549** Courtesy Kimberly Clark/Corporation-©°KCC; **582** Michael Quackenbush/The Image Bank; **583** Michael Quackenbush/The Image Bank; **592** Michael Newman/PhotoEdit; **624** Courtesy Chrysler Corporation; **625** Courtesy Chrysler Corporation; **642** Courtesy Quality Dining, Inc.; **645** Bonnie Kamin/PhotoEdit; **672** Courtesy Saturn Media Center; **673** Courtesy Saturn Media Center; **681** Reinhold Spiegler/Reinhold Spiegler Photography; **687** Teri Stratford; **692** Teri Stratford; **712** John Gajda/FPG International; **713** John Gajda/FPG International; **720** James Blank/FPG International; **721** Courtesy Northrop Grumman Corporation; **736** Adam Butler/The Image Works; **770** Tony Stone Images; **771** Tony Stone Images; **772** Teri Stratford; **782** Courtesy Rubbermaid Incorporated; **816** Courtesy Dell Computer Corporation; **817** Courtesy Dell Computer Corporation; **820** Rob Crandall/Stock Boston; **834** Steve Maines/Stock Boston; **858** Courtesy of Dell Computer Corporation; **859** Courtesy of Dell Computer Corporation; **864** Courtesy La-Z-Boy Incorporated; **880** Steve Dunwell/The Image Bank; **902** Reagan Bradshaw/Bradshaw Studio; **903** Reagan Bradshaw/Bradshaw Studio; **904** Courtesy General Mills; **923** Michael Jarrett Studio/Courtesy of U.S. Divers; **948** Al Richmond/Grand Canyon Railway; **949** Al Richmond/Grand Canyon Railway; **965** Courtesy of Deere & Company; **990** Courtesy of the Ritz-Carlton Hotel Company, L.L.C.; **991** Courtesy of the Ritz-Carlton Hotel Company, L.L.C.; **999** Jean Marc Barey/Agence Vandystadt/Photo Researchers, Inc.; **1009** Courtesy of Ford Motor Company, Detroit; **1034** Ralf-Finn Hestoft/SABA Press Photos, Inc.; **1035** Ralf-Finn Hestoft/SABA Press Photos, Inc.; **1037** Sylvan Pools/Marketing Group/Courtsey Anthony & Sylvan Pools; **1045** Courtesy of Thomson Consumer Electronics, Inc.; **1076** Bob Daemmrich/Photo, Inc.; **1077** Bob Daemmrich/Photo, Inc.; **1081** Chris Jones/The Stock Market; **1095** Courtesy of Intel Corporation; **1120** Courtesy of Deer Valley Resort; **1121** Courtesy of Deer Valley Resort; **1131** Gary Wagner/Stock Boston

About the Authors

Charles T. Horngren is the Edmund W. Littlefield Professor of Accounting, Emeritus, at Stanford University. A graduate of Marquette University, he received his MBA from Harvard University and his Ph.D. from the University of Chicago. He is also the recipient of honorary doctorates from Marquette University and DePaul University.

A Certified Public Accountant, Horngren served on the Accounting Principles Board for six years, the Financial Accounting Standards Board Advisory Council for five years, and the Council of the American Institute of Certified Public Accountants for three years. For six years, he served as a trustee of the Financial Accounting Foundation, which oversees the Financial Accounting Standards Board and the Government Accounting Standards Board.

Horngren is a member of the Accounting Hall of Fame.

A member of the American Accounting Association, Horngren has been its President and its Director of Research. He received its first annual Outstanding Accounting Educator Award.

The California Certified Public Accountants Foundation gave Horngren its Faculty Excellence Award and its Distinguished Professor Award. He is the first person to have received both awards.

The American Institute of Certified Public Accountants presented its first Outstanding Educator Award to Horngren.

Horngren was named Accountant of the Year, Education, by the national professional accounting fraternity, Beta Alpha Psi.

Professor Horngren is also a member of the Institute of Management Accountants, where he has received its Distinguished Service Award. He was a member of the Institute's Board of Regents, which administers the Certified Management Accountant examinations.

Horngren is the author of other accounting books published by Prentice-Hall: *Cost Accounting: A Managerial Emphasis*, Ninth Edition, 1997 (with George Foster and Srikant Datar); *Introduction to Financial Accounting*, Seventh Edition, 1999 (with Gary L. Sundem and John A. Elliott); *Introduction to Management Accounting*, Eleventh Edition, 1999 (with Gary L. Sundem and William O. Stratton); and *Financial Accounting*, Third Edition, 1998 (with Walter T. Harrison, Jr.).

Horngren is the Consulting Editor for the Charles T. Horngren Series in Accounting.

Walter T. Harrison, Jr. is Professor of Accounting at the Hankamer School of Business, Baylor University. He received his B.B.A. degree from Baylor University, his M.S. from Oklahoma State University, and his Ph.D. from Michigan State University.

Professor Harrison, recipient of numerous teaching awards from student groups as well as from university administrators, has also taught at Cleveland State Community College, Michigan State University, the University of Texas, and Stanford University.

A member of the American Accounting Association and the American Institute of Certified Public Accountants, Professor Harrison has served as Chairman of the Financial Accounting Standards Committee of the American Accounting Association, on the Teaching/Curriculum Development Award Committee, on the Program Advisory Committee for Accounting Education and Teaching, and on the Notable Contributions to Accounting Literature Committee.

Professor Harrison has lectured in several foreign countries and published articles in numerous journals, including *The Accounting Review*, *Journal of Accounting Research*, *Journal of Accountancy*, *Journal of Accounting and Public Policy*, *Economic Consequences of Financial Accounting Standards*, *Accounting Horizons*, *Issues in Accounting Education*, and

Journal of Law and Commerce. He is coauthor of *Financial Accounting, Third Edition, 1998* (with Charles T. Horngren and *Accounting, Fourth Edition* (with Charles T. Horngren and Linda S. Bamber) published by Prentice Hall. Professor Harrison has received scholarships, fellowships, research grants or awards from Price Waterhouse & Co., Deloitte & Touche, the Ernst & Young Foundation, and the KPMG Peat Marwick Foundation.

Linda Smith Bamber is Professor of Accounting at the J.M. Tull School of Accounting at the University of Georgia. She graduated summa cum laude from Wake Forest University, where she was a member of Phi Beta Kappa. She is a certified public accountant. For her performance on the CPA examination, Professor Bamber received the Elijah Watt Sells Award in addition to the North Carolina Bronze Medal. Before returning to graduate school, she worked in cost accounting at RJR Foods. She then earned an MBA from Arizona State University, and a Ph.D. from The Ohio State University.

Professor Bamber has received numerous teaching awards from The Ohio State University, the University of Florida, and the University of Georgia, including selection as Teacher of the Year at the University of Florida's Fisher School of Accounting.

She has lectured in Canada and Australia in addition to the U.S., and her research has appeared in numerous journals, including *The Accounting Review*, *Journal of Accounting Research*, *Journal of Accounting and Economics*, *Journal of Finance*, *Contemporary Accounting Research*, *Auditing: A Journal of Practice and Theory*, *Accounting Horizons*, *Issues in Accounting Education*, and *CPA Journal.* She provided the annotations for the *Annotated Instructor's Edition* of Horngren, Foster, and Datar's *Cost Accounting: A Managerial Emphasis*, Seventh, Eighth, and Ninth Editions.

A member of the Institute of Management Accounting, the American Accounting Association (AAA), and the AAA's Management Accounting Section and Financial Accounting and Reporting Section, Professor Bamber has chaired the AAA New Faculty Consortium Committee, served on the AAA Council, the AAA Research Advisory Committee, the AAA Corporate Accounting Policy Seminar Committee, the AAA Wildman Medal Award Committee, the AAA Nominations Committee, and has chaired the Management Accounting Section's Membership Outreach Committee. She served as Associate Editor of *Accounting Horizons*, and will serve as editor of *The Accounting Review* from 1999 to 2002.

cross training

PRENTICE HALL BUSINESS PUBLISHING

Charles T. Horngren
Stanford University

Walter T. Harrison, Jr.
Baylor University

Linda Smith Bamber
University of Georgia

fourth edition

accounting

AUTHOR LETTER

ACCOUNTING 4/E

exercise. motivation. stamina. commitment.

Going the Distance.

Teaching introductory accounting today is a lot like training athletes. It requires a careful warmup, focus on specific topics and ideas, regular doses of motivation, and a cooling-off period when "the big picture" is clearly evident. Helping your students develop and master these skills is what **ACCOUNTING 4/E** *is all about.*

- **Exercise** - *always key to any athlete's performance, we offer a wealth of assignment material, now including new Daily Exercises, Team Projects, and Internet Exercises.*
- **Motivation** - *your students will see how accounting principles are actually used in a variety of well-known companies including NIKE, Dell Computer, and McDonald's through a unique series of On Location! Videos, in-text Internet Tours, and new Decision Guidelines.*
- **Stamina** - *an athlete has to start and finish the race strongly. So too must a principles text offer balanced, comprehensive coverage of both financial and managerial topics. New coauthor Linda Smith Bamber has added her talents and expertise to the management accounting chapters.*
- **Commitment** - *as athletes commit to a regular training regimen and you commit to your students, we commit to providing you with the best available text and package. Prentice Hall, our publisher, commits to giving you the best service available by providing forums like PHASE (Prentice Hall Accounting Seminars for Educators) and customer services like the toll-free Accounting and Taxation Hotline (1-800-227-1816).*

We believe that **ACCOUNTING 4/E** *offers an unprecedented teaching and learning system for your accounting students. We invite you to learn more about how our new training program can challenge your students to "just do it." If you have any suggestions or questions, we'd like to hear from you.*

Charles T. Horngren
Stanford University

Walter T. Harrison, Jr.
Baylor University

Linda Smith Bamber
University of Georgia

Chapter 1
ACCOUNTING AND THE BUSINESS ENVIRONMENT

1. Prologue on Careers in Accounting.
2. Expanded focus on the statement of cash flows throughout the text.

Chapter 2
RECORDING BUSINESS TRANSACTIONS

1. The accounting equation shows the link between the journal entry and the ledger accounts, and from Chapter 1 to Chapter 2.

Chapter 3
MEASURING BUSINESS INCOME: THE ADJUSTING PROCESS

1. T-accounts show transaction effects on the accounting equation.

Chapter 4
COMPLETING THE ACCOUNTING CYCLE

1. New visuals for the work sheet.
2. Classified balance sheet provided for the sole proprietor running example.

Chapter 5
MERCHANDISING OPERATIONS AND THE ACCOUNTING CYCLE

1. Clear separation of the perpetual and the periodic inventory systems.
2. New visuals, speedbumps, and learning tips.
3. New section on accrual accounting and cash flows for a merchandising entity.

Chapter 6
ACCOUNTING INFORMATION SYSTEMS: SPECIAL JOURNALS, CONTROL ACCOUNTS, AND SUBSIDIARY LEDGERS

1. Streamlined coverage of accounting systems.
2. New section on the general journal's role in an accounting information system.
3. New coverage of the credit memorandum and the debit memorandum.

Chapter 7
INTERNAL CONTROL, MANAGING CASH, AND MAKING ETHICAL JUDGMENTS

1. Revised focus on controlling and managing cash.
2. New section on how owners and managers use the bank reconciliation.
3. New emphasis on cash budgeting.

Chapter 8
ACCOUNTS AND NOTES RECEIVABLE

1. Streamlined section on accounting for uncollectible receivables.
2. New section on reporting receivables transactions on the statement of cash flows.

Chapter 9
ACCOUNTING FOR MERCHANDISE INVENTORY

1. New material on cost of goods sold and gross margin; ethical issues in inventory accounting; and reporting inventory transactions on the statement of cash flows.

Chapter 10
ACCOUNTING FOR PLANT ASSETS, INTANGIBLE ASSETS, AND RELATED EXPENSES

1. New sections on capitalizing the cost of interest, research and development costs, and ethical issues in accounting for plant assets and intangibles.
2. New material on reporting plant asset transactions on the statement of cash flows.

Chapter 11

CURRENT LIABILITIES AND PAYROLL ACCOUNTING

1. New coverage of accounting for notes payable issued at a discount, and unearned revenue.
2. New summary of payroll liabilities.
3. New section on ethical issues in reporting current and contingent liabilities.

Chapter 12

ACCOUNTING FOR PARTNERSHIPS

1. New section on the different types of partnerships: general, limited, and S corporations.
2. New visuals throughout the chapter.

Chapter 13

CORPORATE ORGANIZATION, PAID-IN CAPITAL, AND THE BALANCE SHEET

1. New section on ethical considerations in accounting for the issuance of stock.
2. Streamlined coverage of accounting for income taxes by corporations.

Chapter 14

RETAINED EARNINGS, TREASURY STOCK, AND THE INCOME STATEMENT

1. Accounting equation added to help students learn that stock dividends and stock splits do not affect total stockholders' equity.
2. New section on reporting comprehensive income covers FASB Statement 130.

Chapter 15

LONG-TERM LIABILITIES

1. New graphs show the movements of interest expense and bon carrying amount over the life of a bond issue.
2. New section on reporting long-term liability transactions on t statement of cash flows.

Chapter 16

ACCOUNTING FOR INVESTMENTS AND INTERNATIONAL OPERATIONS

1. New section on short-term trading investments.
2. Moved section on preparing consolidated financial statements to an appendix.
3. New section on reporting comprehensive income (FASB Statement 130) and on reporting investment transactions on the statement of cash flows.

Chapter 17

PREPARING AND USING THE STATEMENT OF CASH FLOW.

1. New coverage on how the statement of cash flows is prepared from the income statement plus the comparative balance sheet.
2. Expanded coverage of the indirect method of reporting cash flows from operating activities.
3. New section on using cash-flow information in investment and credit analysis.

Chapter 18

FINANCIAL STATEMENT ANALYSIS

1. New section on benchmarking versus an industry average and benchmarking versus a key competitor.
2. New section on Economic Value Added.

Chapter 19

INTRODUCTION TO MANAGEMENT ACCOUNTING

1. New introductory chapter covers service plus merchandising and manufacturing companies.
2. New second half of the chapter covers modern business environment topics such as the shift towards a service economy, competing in the global marketplace, and quality.
3. New section on ethics, with two dilemmas for students to solve and inclusion of the standards of Ethical Conduct for Management Accountants.

Chapter 20

JOB COSTING

1. New separate chapter provides a more complete treatment of job costing.
2. New introductory section contrasts job costing and process costing.
3. New section on job costing in a non-manufacturing company.

Chapter 21

PROCESS COSTING

1. New time lines diagram process cost accounting and show the difference between FIFO and Weighted Average Costing.

Chapter 22

COST-VOLUME-PROFIT ANALYSIS AND THE CONTRIBUTION MARGIN APPROACH TO DECISION MAKING

1. New comparison of variable costing and absorption costing shows how managers use these methods.

Chapter 23

THE MASTER BUDGET AND RESPONSIBILITY ACCOUNTING

1. New section on budgeting for a service company.
2. New section on the allocation of indirect costs to departments.

Chapter 24

FLEXIBLE BUDGETS AND STANDARD COSTS

1. New section on common pitfalls to avoid in price and efficiency variance computations.
2. Streamlined overhead variance analysis.

Chapter 25

ACTIVITY-BASED COSTING AND OTHER TOOLS FOR COST MANAGEMENT

1. Expanded coverage of activity-based costing with a running example contrasting the traditional system and an activity-based costing system; a discussion of when activity-based costing is most likely to pass the cost-benefit test; and a new section on warning signs to identify a broken cost system.
2. Quality discussion expanded with NEW assignment material.

Chapter 26

SPECIAL BUSINESS DECISIONS AND CAPITAL BUDGETING

1. New - Two themes are now woven through the shorter-term decisions: focus on relevant information and use a contribution margin approach.

NEW CO-AUTHOR LINDA SMITH BAMBER

LINDA SMITH BAMBER CRAFTED A MORE INTUITIVE APPROACH TO MANAGERIAL ACCOUNTING, USING NEW REAL-WORLD EXAMPLES - LIKE DELL COMPUTER!

Seeing is believing. When your students see how well-known companies like NIKE use accounting each and every day, they'll appreciate the importance of being well trained in class. Using **ACCOUNTING 4/E**, *your students will benefit from the Daily Exercises, Team Projects, and other valuable learning assignment materials. Our On Location! Custom Case Videos are linked to chapter-opening stories to help you motivate your students. Each video profiles a company, showing how today's leading businesses employ accounting information to drive business decisions.*

on location!

Cross-training sure works for NIKE. Five "On-Location" segments were shot at NIKE headquarters in Beaverton, OR.

- **Accounting and Its Environment**
- **Accounting Cycle**
- **How Accounting Systems Support Management**
- **Accounting for Endorsement Contracts**
- **Performance Evaluation and the Role of Accounting**

On Location companies include McDonald's, General Motors, May Department Stores, Home Depot, and more.

your students' **performance**

guarantee

Just like beginning athletes question the value of a good warm-up, your non-major students may wonder how accounting is relevant to their field of study.

Our **Decision Guidelines** *make procedures relevant by showing the student* ***who*** *is likely to use the information and* ***how*** *it will be used.*

DECISION	GUIDELINE		
Has a transaction occurred?	If the event affects the entity's financial position and can be reliably recorded - Yes		
	If either condition is absent - No		
Where to record the transaction?	In the journal, the chronological record of transactions		
What to record for each transaction?	Increases and/or decreases in all the accounts affected by the transaction		
How to record an increase/decrease in the following accounts?	Rules of debit and credit:		
		Increase	**Decrease**
Asset		Debit	Credit
Liability		Credit	Debit
Owners' equity		Credit	Debit
Revenue		Credit	Debit
Expense		Debit	Credit
Where to store all the information for each account?	In the ledger, the book of accounts and their balances		
Where to list all the accounts and their balances?	In the trial balance		
Where to report the Results of operations?	In the income statement (revenue - expenses = net income or net loss)		
Financial position?	In the balance sheet (assets = liabilities + stockholders' equity)		

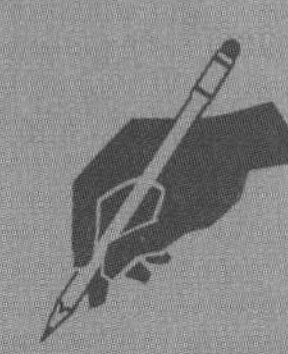

SELECTED EXERCISES AND PROBLEMS ARE LINKED TO PRENTICE HALL SPREADSHEET STUDENT SOFTWARE AND PHAS GENERAL LEDGER SOFTWARE PACKAGES. WRITING ASSIGNMENTS ARE INCLUDED IN THE END-OF-CHAPTER MATERIAL IN EVERY CHAPTER.

NEW!! Thinking It Over *segments ask students to reflect on concepts they have just learned; in-text answers provide immediate feedback*

NEW!! Working It Out *exercises give students additional practice putting concepts and techniques to work; again, in-text answers provide immediate feedback*

Concept Links *point students back to previous discussion of topics for those who want, or need, the review*

Infographics *help students understand concepts by providing interesting visual displays of often difficult material: one picture is worth a thousand words*

Concept Highlights *provide summaries of key concepts that students can use for review*

Mid-Chapter and End-of-Chapter Summary Problems *help students work with key chapter material discussed up to that point, while fully worked-out solutions let them test their understanding*

GETTING YOUR STUDENTS TO THE FINISH LINE

Our problems are your solutions

Extensive market research told us accounting instructors want a greater variety of different problems and exercises. So we added New assignment material to each chapter.

New **Daily Exercises** *include a whole new set of assignments on single topics, perfect for day-to-day drills.*

New **Team Projects** *provide collaborative learning cases in every chapter*

New **Internet Exercises** *are featured in nearly every chapter and are often tied to the chapter-opening story, and in some cases, the accompanying "On Location!" video.*

Mid-Chapter and End-of-Chapter Summary Problems *are provided with worked-out solutions*

Group A & B Problems *provide homework alternatives*

Decision Cases *have been expanded from the previous edition*

Ethical Cases *appear in each chapter*

DAILY EXERCISE • CHAPTER 5

DE 5-18 Contrasting accounting income and cash flows (Objective 4)

Lands' End, the catalog merchant, reported the following for the year ended January 31, 1997 (as adapted, with amounts in millions):

Cash payments for financing activities	$ 28
Cash payments to suppliers	$ 573
Cash collections from customers	$1,118
Cost of sales	$ 609
Selling, general, and administrative expenses	$ 424
Cash payments for investing activities	$ 18
Net sales revenue	$1,119

As an investor, you wonder which was greater, Lands' End (a) gross margin, or (b) the company's excess of cash collections from customers over cash payments to suppliers. Compute both amounts to answer this real-world question.

DE 5-19 Computing cost of goods sold in a periodic inventory system (Objective 6)

At January 31, 1996, The May Department Stores Company had merchandise inventory of $2,134 million. During the year May purchased inventory costing $8,472 million, including freight in. At January 31, 1997, May's inventory stood at $2,380 million.

1. Compute May's cost of goods sold as in the periodic system.
2. Compare your cost-of-goods-sold figure to Exhibit 5-1, page xxx. The two amounts should be equal. Are they?

INTERNET EXERCISE • CHAPTER 17

Statement of Cash Flows — Compaq

This innovative company started operations at the beginning of the personal computer revolution in 1982. During their first year, Compaq had sales of $111 million — a U.S. business record. Now it is a Fortune 100 company and the number one supplier of PCs in the world with sales exceeding $20 billion.

The computer industry is highly competitive, especially for PC manufacturers, as many customers consider the PC to be a commodity. Numerous PC manufacturers have come and gone, but Compaq has strengthened its leadership position year after year. The Statement of Cash Flows demonstrates the Company's financial strength.

REQUIRED:

1. Go to http://www.compaq.com. This is Compaq's home page where visitors can purchase a computer over the Internet as well as read Compaq's webzine and learn about the company.
2. Click **Inside Company** and then **Investor Relations** to find Compaq's corporate information. The financial statements are located in the section **SEC documents**.
3. The Statement of Cash Flows provides sources and uses of cash by Compaq.

a. Does Compaq use the Direct or Indirect method in calculating Cash provided by Operating Activities?

b. For the most recent year, what is Net Income and Cash Provided by Operating Activities? These are measures of Compaq's operating activities. Why are these two numbers different?

c. Compare the differences between Cash Received from Customers and Cash Paid to Suppliers and Employees for the past three years. Given the competitive environment of the PC market, what are possible reasons for this trend?

d. Why does Compaq report a "Reconciliation of net income to net cash provided by (used by) operating activities" at the end of the Statement of Cash Flows?

e. Did Compaq have any material non-cash transactions? Explain.

f. Compare Compaq's Purchases of Property, Plant, and Equipment to its Depreciation and Amortization for the past three years. Comment on Compaq's expected future growth opportunities as it relates to this data.

The NIKE Annual Report financials are included in an end-of-text appendix. The entire NIKE Annual Report is shrink-wrapped to the text so students can identify with a real Annual Report. Financial Statement Cases, based on NIKE, are at the end of financial accounting chapters.

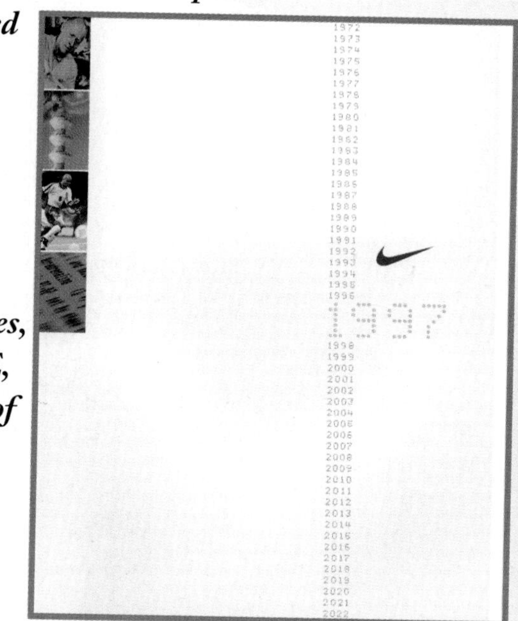

Our new in-text guided **Internet Tours** *build active learning skills, show beginning students accounting resources available on the Internet, and introduce students to the tools used by accounting professionals.*

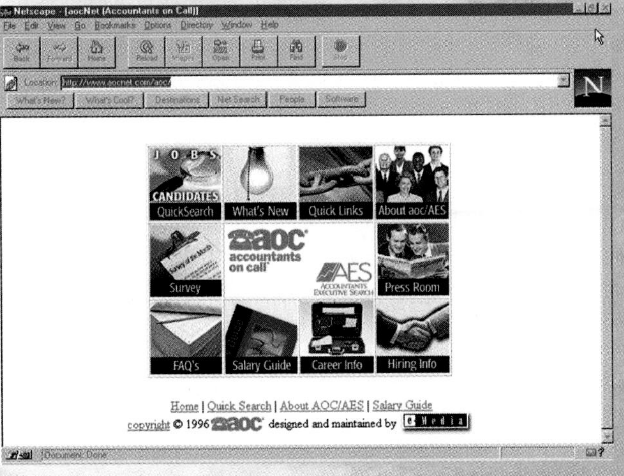

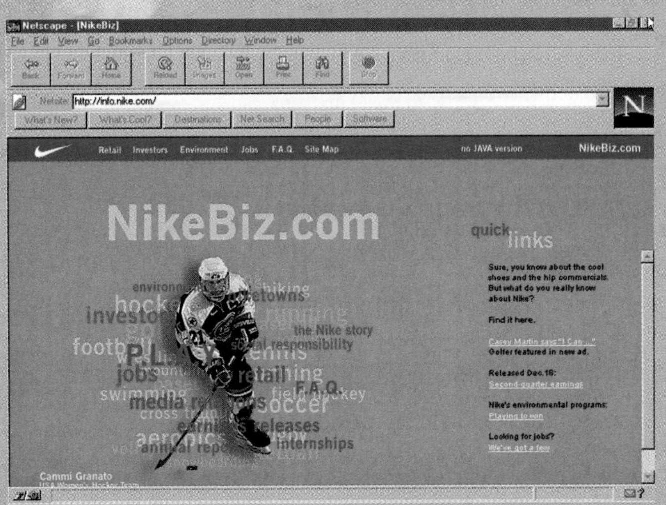

Prentice Hall's Learning on the Internet Partnership (PHLIP) located at **www.prenhall.com/phbusiness** offers the most expansive Internet-based textbook support currently available for Business and Economics faculty and their students. PHLIP resources include:

PHLIP

Student Study Hall *lets students use conference and chat room functions. An accounting instructor monitors student questions and provides timely responses. It's like having an "Online Instructor!"*

Interactive Study Guide *provides chapter-by-chapter questions and exercises tied to chapter objectives. Students get immediate feedback and receive a grade on what they've completed. Students can also take "Self-Test" Quizzes to see how well they've mastered the chapter material.*

Hotlinks *are provided for real companies discussed in the text as well as to pertinent areas on the Rutgers Accounting Web (RAW).*

Learning Assessment *sections allow students to see their strengths with different types of material.*

Practice Tests *let students test their knowledge before they get the "real thing" in the classroom.*

Faculty Lounge *provides a wealth of resources for the instructor:*

- *the ability to download only those supplements you need*
- *teaching tips*
- *transition notes if you have used other texts*
- *sample syllabi*
- *check figures*
- *links to Prentice Hall software support*
- *links to Prentice Hall's Accounting and Taxation Hotline*

and much more...

What's New | Study Hall | Faculty Lounge | Help!?!

Home Page | Global Info | Research Area | Feedback

GET YOUR STUDENTS CONNECTED TO THE INTERNET

TECHNOLGY SOLUTIONS

accounting made easy

CD-ROM

This self-paced computerized tutorial program teaches students accounting procedures and concepts in short, self-paced units; pretests student understanding; and then ties all the material together with case studies at the end. The CD-ROM is available in two levels:

Level 1 covers accounting basics such as business organization, accounting information, financial statements, the accounting equation, general ledger, and basic business transactions.

Level 2 focuses on accounting procedures to cover the following areas: recording transactions, posting transactions, adjustments, and completing the accounting cycle.

- Easy-to-use instructions are given in the program
- Self-paced software program allows students to learn accounting procedures on their own
- Dialogue boxes refer the students back to the appropriate topic in ***ACCOUNTING 4/E*** when they give incorrect answers
- On-screen and audio responses provide instant feedback
- All concepts are tied together by a comprehensive, end-of-module case

CAREER PATHS IN ACCOUNTING CD-ROM

Winner of the New Media INVISION Gold Award in Education

This CD-ROM provides students with a dynamic, interactive job-search tool. It includes workshops in career planning, resume writing, and interviewing skills. Students can learn the latest market trends, facts about the accounting profession, and the skills they need to land a job. The CD also provides salary information, video clips on specific jobs, and profiles and interviews with accounting professionals.

ACCOUNTING 4/E

software specifically designed for students:

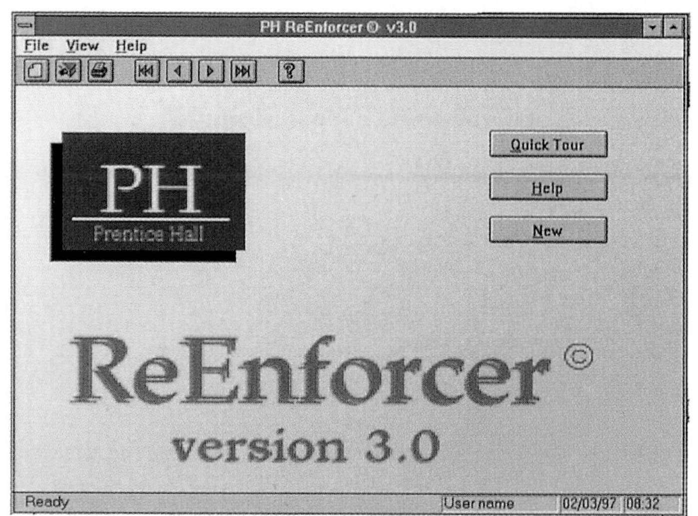

PH Re-Enforcer Tutorial Software 3.0 for Windows. *This enhanced interactive tutorial allows students to work through accounting problems to reinforce concepts and skills covered in the text. Users can work through multiple choice questions, short exercises, vocabulary games, and case problems using multimedia graphics and a computer tutorial based on objective and/or difficulty level.*

A Teacher's Edition allows instructors to edit, change, and add existing or additional material.

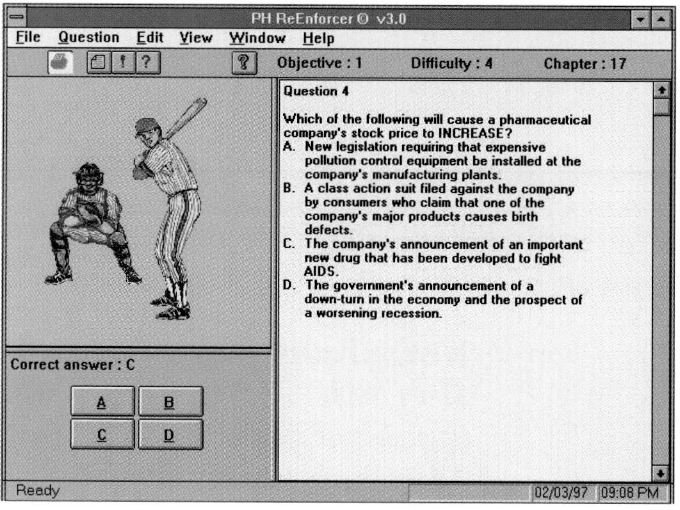

Also available:

- *Prentice Hall Accounting Software (PHAS): A General Ledger Package*
- *New, Improved Spreadsheet Templates*

  Quick Tours are part of the Prentice Hall Accounting Software (PHAS) 2.0 and the PH Re-Enforcer Tutorial Software 3.0. The Quick Tours provide students with quick and easy practice drills that demonstrate how to use the program.
- *Prentice Hall's Software Training Video teaches students and instructors how to use Prentice Hall's software products.*

Surfing for Success in Business *introduces students to the Internet and more specifically, the many useful ways to extract and use accounting information from the World Wide Web.*

The Presentation Manager *is a user-friendly program that organizes the Instructor's Manual, custom Video footage, PowerPoint slides, Teaching Transparencies, PHAS General Ledger Program, and the PH ReEnforcer© Tutorial Software under one convenient instructional tool. This powerful resource can help instructors create a powerful classroom presentation.*

INSTRUCTORS

STUDENTS

SUPPLEMENTS

our core teaching aids

Instructor's Manual and Video Guide
On Location! Video Library
Accounting Tutorial Videos
Teaching Transparencies
Solution Transparencies
PHLIP Website support for both instructors and students
Solutions Manual
Test Item File - Prentice Hall Custom Test Software
PH Professor: A Classroom Presentation on PowerPoint

For The Student

Working Papers
Study Guide
Spreadsheet Templates with Solutions
Accounting Made Easy CD-ROM
PHAS: General Ledger Software
PH Re-Enforcer
Accounting Tutorial Videos
PHLIP Website support

Plus...

New Tutorial Video Library by Beverly Amer, Northern Arizona University, provides detailed instruction on important topics in accounting principles, while demonstrating key concepts with sample problems from the book. Tied to the text these video segments are perfect for students who miss class or need additional review.

REVIEWERS OF ACCOUNTING, 4/E

Frank Aquilino, Montclair State University
John R. Blahnik, Lorain County Community College
Thomas M. Bock, Berkeley College (NYC)
Marianne Bradford, University of Tennessee
Kathleen M. Brenan, Ashland University
Robert C. Brush, Cecil Community College
Eric Carlsen, Kean College of New Jersey
Betty Chavis, California State University, Fullerton
Siu N. Chung, Los Angeles Valley College
Marilynn Collins, John Carroll University
Robert D. Collmier, Bloomfield College
Joan E. Cook, Milwaukee Area Technical College
David Erlach, Queens College of CUNY
William E. Faulk, Northwestern Michigan College
Mary A. Flanigan, Longwood College
James S. Gale, Northern Virginia Community College
Kathleen H. Gandy, Catonsville Community College
George F. Gardner, Bemidji State University
Sally W. Gilfillan, Longwood College
Jane Green, Valley College
Steven C. Hall, Widener University
Douglas S. Hamilton, Berkeley College (West Paterson, NJ)
William H. Harvey, Henry Ford Community College
Daniel G. Hertz, Montana State University
Jay Hollowell, Commonwealth College
Patricia H. Holmes, Des Moines Area Community College
Zachary E. Holmes, Oakland Community College
Richard C. Jarvies, Fayetteville Technical Community College
Fred Jex, Macomb Community College
Betty T. Johns, Dundalk Community College
Thomas Kam, Hawaii Pacific University
N. Leroy Kauffman, Western Carolina University
Frank J. Kopczynski, University of New Hampshire
William G. Lasher, Jamestown Community College
Heidi H. Meier, Cleveland State University
Barbara A. Moreira, Berkeley College (Waldwick, NJ)
Harold Moreland, Pacific Lutheran University
M. Salah Negm, Prince George's Community College
Linda Hayden Overstreet, Hillsborough Community College
Frank N. Paliotta, Berkeley College (NYC)
LaVonda Ramey, Schoolcraft College
Carla Rich, Pensacola Junior College
Victoria S. Rymer, University of Maryland
Wayne M. Schell, Christopher Newport University
Richard W. Schrader, North Dakota State University
Robert Shepherd, San Jose State University
Sue Singer, Western Maryland College
Carolyn Streuly, Marquette University
Kim Tarantino, California State University, Fullerton
Robert R. Wennagel, College of the Mainland
Beulah Winfrey, College of the Ozarks

CONTRIBUTIONS

ENSURING QUALITY

Our thanks to you and your colleagues who contributed to the development of Accounting, 4/E...

Focus Group Participants
John Blahnik, Lorain County Community College
Kay Carnes, Gonzaga University
Joan E. Cook, Milwaukee Area Technical College
Judith M. Cook, Grossmont College
Michael Farina, Cerritos College
Bob Garrett, American River College
Shirley Glass, Macomb Community College
Janet Grange, Chicago State University
William Harvey, Henry Ford Community College
Sherry Hellmuth, Elgin Community College
Anthony W. Jackson, Governor's State College
Sam Lanzafame, Bryant & Stratton
Lawrence Lease, Shasta College
Dennis Ludden, Moraine Valley Community College
Dan Lux, Salt Lake Community College
Linda Spotts Michael, Maple Woods Community College
LaVonda Ramey, Schoolcraft College
Mary Ston, Oakland Community College
George Tutt, Spokane Community College
Karen Walton, John Carroll University
Martin E. Ward, DeVry Institute of Technology

Special thanks to Thelma Blake and Terry L. Sofsky, students at Harford Community College in Maryland, for giving extensive student feedback.

SUPPLEMENT AUTHORS/REVIEW

Instructor's Manual and Video Guide
Betsy Willis, Baylor University
Becky Jones, Baylor University
Beverly Amer, Northern Arizona University

Solutions Manual
Charles T. Horngren, Stanford University
Walter T. Harrison, Jr., Baylor University
Linda Smith Bamber, University of Georgia

Test Item File
Alice B. Sineath, Forsyth Technical Community College

Working Papers
Ellen Sweatt, DeKalb College

PH Professor: A Classroom Presentation on PowerPoint
Olga Quintana, University of Miami

On Location! Video Library
Accounting Tutorial Videos
Beverly Amer, Northern Arizona University

Solutions Transparencies
Charles T. Horngren, Stanford University
Walter T. Harrison, Jr., Baylor University
Linda Smith Bamber, University of Georgia

Study Guide
Stephen Schaefer, Contra Costa Community College

Spreadsheet Templates with Solutions
Albert Fisher, Community College of Southern Nevada

Technical Reviewers
John R. Blahnik, Lorain County Community College
Carolyn Streuly, Marquette University
Barbara Mull, Harford Community College

Solutions Manual Technical Reviewers:
Thomas Hoar, Houston Community College
Kathleen Brenan, Ashland University
Carolyn Streuly, Marquette University

PowerPoint Reviewers:
Jean Insinga, Middlesex Community College
Anita Ellzey, Harford Community College

Test Item File Reviewers:
Thomas M. Carment, Northeastern State University
Richard C. Jarvies, Fayetteville Technical Community College
Thomas Hoar, Houston Community College

Contributors to the First, Second, and Third Editions

Salvador D. Aceves, Napa Valley College
John Blahnick, Lorain County Community College
Nina Brown, Tarrant County Junior College
Kurt H. Buerger, Angelo State University
Glenn Bushnell, DeAnza College
Eric Carlson, Kean College of New Jersey
Wallace P. Carroll, J. Sargeant Reynolds Community College
Darrel W. Davis, University of Northern Iowa
S. T. Desai, Cedar Valley College
James Emig, Villanova University
Kevin Feeney, Southern Connecticut State University
Carl J. Fisher, Foothill College
Jessica Frazier, Eastern Kentucky University
Marilyn Fuller, Paris Junior College
Roger Gee, San Diego Mesa College
Lucille Genduso, Nova University
James Genseal, Joliet Junior College
Barbara Gerrity, Berkeley School of Westchester
Gloria Grayless, Sam Houston State University
Ann Gregory, South Plains College
Deborah Halik, Ivy Technical College
Jim Hansen, North Dakota State University
Saad Hassanein, Marymount University
Jimmie Henslee, El Centro College
Cynthia Holloway, Tarrant County Junior College
Andrew Hrechek, Seton Hall University
Jean Insinga, Middlesex Community College
Tyronne James, Southern University of New Orleans
Fred Jex, Macomb Community College
Mary Thomas Keim, California State University - Bakersfield
Nancy L. Kelly, Middlesex Community College
Randy Kidd, Penn Valley Community College
Raymond L. Larson, Appalachian State University
Cathy Larson, Middlesex Community College
Linda Lessing, SUNY College of Technology - Farmingdale
Lola Locke, Tarrant County Junior College
Catherine Lumbattis, Southern Illinois University
Paul Mihalek, University of Hartford
Graham Morris
Bruce Neumann, University of Colorado - Denver
Alfonso R. Oddo, Niagara University
Linda Overstreet, Hillsborough Community College
Robert Palmer, Troy State University
Patrick M. Premo, St. Bonaventure University
Karen Russom, North Harris College
Sherry Shively, Johnson County Community College
Kathleen Simione, Quinnipiac College
Dorothy Steinsapir, Middlesex Community College
Gracelyn Stuart, Palm Beach Community College
Diane Tanner, University of North Florida
Katherene Terrell, University of Central Oklahoma
Cynthia Thomas, Central Missouri State University
John Vaccaro, Bunker Hill Community College
Paul Waite, Niagara Community College
Martin Ward, DeVry Institute of Technology
James Weglin, North Seattle Community College
Bill Wempe, Wichita State University
Dale Westfall, Midland College
Joseph Zernik, Ivy Technical College

English-as-a-Second-Language Reviewer

Zhu Zhu, Phoenix College

Focus Group Participants

Richard Ahrens, Los Angeles Pierce College
Charles Alvis, Winthrop University
Juanita Ardevany, Los Angeles Valley College
Patricia Ayres, Arapahoe Community College
Carl Ballard, Central Piedmont Community College
Maria Barillas, Phoenix College
Dorcus Berg, Wingate College
Angela Blackwood, Belmont Abbey College
Gary R. Bower, Community College of Rhode Island
Jack Brown, Los Angeles Valley College
Virginia Brunell, Diablo Valley College
James Carriger, Ventura College
Stan Carroll, New York City Technical College
Janet Cassagio, Nassau Community College
Lester Chadwick, University of Delaware
Stanley Chu, Borough of Manhattan Community College
Kerry Colton, Aims Community College
Shaun Crayton, New York City Technical College
Susan Crosson, Santa Fe Community College
Donald Daggett, Mankato State University
Joneal W. Daw, Los Angeles Valley College
Lyle E. Dehning, Metropolitan State College
Wanda DeLeo, Winthrop University
Jim Donnelly, Bergen Community College
Bruce England, Massasoit Community College
Dave Fellows, Red Rocks Community College
Roger Gee, San Diego Mesa College
Martin Ginsberg, Rockland Community College
Earl Godfrey, Gardner Webb University
Edward S. Goodhart, Shippensburg University
Jean Gutmann, University of Southern Maine
Ralph W. Hernandez, New York City Technical College
Carl High, New York City Technical College
Mary Hill, University of North Carolina - Charlotte
Jean Insinga, Middlesex Community College
Bernard Johnson, Santa Monica College
Diane G. Kanis, Bergen Community College
John Keelan, Massachusetts Bay Community College
Mary Thomas Keim, California State University - Bakersfield
Cynthia Kreisner, Austin Community College
Raymond L. Larson, Appalachian State University
Cathy Larson, Middlesex Community College
Linda Lessing, SUNY College of Technology - Farmingdale
Angela Letourneau, Winthrop University
Frank Lordi, Widener University
Audra Lowray, New York City Technical College
Grace Lyons, Bergen Community College
Edward Malmgren, University of North Carolina - Charlotte
Paola Marocchi, New York City Technical College
Larry McCarthy, Slippery Rock University
Linda Spotts Michael, Maple Woods Community College
Greg Mostyn, Mission College
Kitty Nessmith, Georgia Southern University
Lee Nicholas, University of Northern Iowa
Terry Nunnelly, University of North Carolina - Charlot
Alfonso R. Oddo, Niagara University
Al Partington, Los Angeles Pierce College
Lynn Mazzola Paluska, Nassau Community College
Juan Perez, New York City Technical College
Ronald Pierno, University of Missouri
Geraldine Powers, Northern Essex Community Colle
Harry Purcell, Ulster County Community College
John Ribezzo, Community College of Rhode Island
Rosemarie Ruiz, York University
Stephen Schaefer, Contra Costa College
Parmar Sejal, Bergen Community College
Lynn Shoaf, Belmont Abbey College
Walter J. Silva, Roxbury Community College
Leon Singleton, Santa Monica College
David Skougstad, Metropolitan State College
Paul Sunko, Olive-Harvey College
Chandra Taylor, New York City Technical College
Phillip Thornton, Metropolitan State College
John L. Vaccaro, Bunker Hill Community College

Prentice Hall Accounting and Taxation Services Hotline:

When you call Prentice Hall's unique Accounting and Taxation Services Hotline you'll be able to speak directly to one of our Accounting and Taxation Service Specialists, Monday through Friday, during normal business hours (E.S.T.). Otherwise, you may leave a message and your call will be returned promptly. Our specialists can provide you with information on text instock dates, supplements, software, and much more. Plus, they'll process your Accounting and Taxation orders. Keep this toll-free number on hand — it's your direct link to satisfaction for all your adoption needs!

Accounting and Taxation Service Hotline Number 1-800-227-1816

Accounting and Taxation Service Hotline E-Mail: christopher_smerillo@prenhall.com

Accounting Software Technical Support Line: 1-800-875-4118

The Prentice Hall Accounting Seminars for Educators (PHASE):

Prentice Hall sponsors a series of seminars for professors to get together, share information, and learn from the experts. Contact your local Prentice Hall sales representative, or e-mail the Accounting and Taxation Hotline for information concerning upcoming seminar dates and locations.

The Prentice Hall Accounting Faculty Directory

Compiled by James R. Hasselback. Published by Prentice Hall since 1978, this has become the most frequently cited reference in professional and academic material. This listing of the Deans and Accounting Faculty from over 900 four-year schools presents their names, addresses, telephone/fax/e-mail, as well as degree and area of specialization, and is updated annually.

Beth Toland
Executive Marketing Manager

Annie Todd
Executive Editor

P.J. Boardman
Editor in Chief

Deborah Hoffman Emry
Executive Editor

Eve Adams
Advertising Art Director

Jane Avery
Senior Editorial Assistant

Elaine Oyzon-Mast
Editorial Assistant

Robert Prokop
Senior Marketing Assistant

Bruce Kaplan
Development Editor

Stephen Deitmer
Director of Development

Pat Smythe
Design Manager

Natacha St. Hill
Assistant Editor

Iain MacDonald
Accounting Sales Director

Kris King
Sales Director

Dana Simmons
Sales Director

Julia Meehan
Event Marketing Manager

Janet Ferruggia
Marketing Communications Director

Brian Kibby
Director of Marketing

Brief Contents

PART ONE

The Basic Structure of Accounting 4

1 Accounting and the Business Environment 4
2 Recording Business Transactions 42
3 Measuring Business Income: The Adjusting Process 90
4 Completing the Accounting Cycle 136
5 Merchandising Operations and the Accounting Cycle 180
6 Accounting Information Systems: Special Journals, Control Accounts, and Subsidiary Ledgers 244

PART TWO

Accounting for Assets and Liabilities 288

7 Internal Control, Managing Cash, and Making Ethical Judgments 288
8 Accounts and Notes Receivable 334
9 Accounting for Merchandise Inventory 376
10 Accounting for Plant Assets, Intangible Assets, and Related Expenses 418
11 Current Liabilities and Payroll Accounting 462

PART THREE

Accounting for Partnerships and Corporate Transactions 506

12 Accounting for Partnerships 506
13 Corporate Organization, Paid-In Capital, and the Balance Sheet 542

Appendixes

A NIKE, Inc. Annual Report A-1
B Present-Value Tables and Future-Value Tables B-0

Glossary G-0

Indexes I-1

Company Index I-1
Subject Index I-4

Check Figures CF-1

Contents

Prologue **Careers in Accounting 1**
Private Accounting 2
Public Accounting 2

PART ONE

The Basic Structure of Accounting 4

1 Accounting and the Business Environment 4
Accounting—The Basis for Business Decisions 6
The Users of Accounting Information: Decision Makers 6
Financial Accounting and Management Accounting 7
The History and Development of Accounting 8
Ethical Considerations in Accounting and Business 8
Types of Business Organizations 9
Standards of Professional Conduct 9
Accounting Concepts and Principles 10
The Entity Concept 10
The Reliability (Objectivity) Principle 11
The Cost Principle 11
The Going-Concern Concept 11
The Stable-Monetary-Unit Concept 12
The Accounting Equation 12
Assets and Liabilities 12
Owner's Equity 13
Accounting for Business Transactions 14
Evaluating Business Transactions 18
The Financial Statements 18
Financial Statement Headings 20
Relationships Among the Financial Statements 20
***Decision Guidelines: Major Business Decisions* 23**
Summary Problem for Your Review 23
Summary of Learning Objectives 25
Accounting Vocabulary/Questions/Daily Exercises/Exercises/Problems/Cases 26
Internet Tour: Financial Accounting 40
Video Series: NIKE (Accounting Environment)

2 Recording Business Transactions 42
The Account 44
Assets 44
Liabilities 45
Owner's Equity 45
Double-Entry Accounting 46
The T-Account 46
Increases and Decreases in the Accounts 47
Recording Transactions in the Journal 49
Flow of Accounting Data 51
Transferring Information (Posting) from the Journal to the Ledger 51
Transaction Analysis, Journalizing, and Posting to the Accounts 52
Accounts after Posting 54
The Trial Balance 54
Correcting Trial Balance Errors 54
***Mid-Chapter Summary Problem for Your Review* 55**
Details of Journals and Ledgers 56
Posting from the Journal to the Ledger 57

The Four-Column Account Format: An Alternative to the T-Account Format **58**
Charts of Accounts in the Ledger **59**
The Normal Balance of an Account **60**
Expanding the Accounting Equation with Two Categories of Additional Owner's Equity Accounts: Revenues and Expenses **60**
Expanded Problem Including Revenues and Expenses **62**
Transaction Analysis, Journalizing, and Posting **62**
Ledger Accounts after Posting **66**
Trial Balance **66**
Decision Guidelines: Analyzing and Recording Transactions **66**
Using Accounting Information for Quick Decision Making **67**
Summary Problem for Your Review **68**
Summary of Learning Objectives **70**
Accounting Vocabulary/Questions/Daily Exercises/Exercises/Problems/Cases **70**
Appendix: Typical Charts of Accounts for Different Types of Businesses **87**
Video Series: Land's End (Part 1)

3 **Measuring Business Income: The Adjusting Process** **90**
Net Income, the Income Statement, and Adjusting Entries **92**
Accrual-Basis Accounting versus Cash-Basis Accounting **92**
The Accounting Period **93**
The Revenue Principle **94**
The Matching Principle **95**
The Time-Period Concept **95**
Adjusting the Accounts **96**
Prepaids (Deferrals) and Accruals **97**
Prepaid Expenses **97**
Depreciation of Plant Assets **99**
Accrued Expenses **101**
Accrued Revenues **103**
Unearned Revenues **104**
Summary of the Adjusting Process **105**
The Adjusted Trial Balance **106**
Preparing the Financial Statements from the Adjusted Trial Balance **108**
Relationships among the Three Financial Statements **109**
Ethical Issues in Accrual Accounting **111**
Decision Guidelines: Measuring Business Income: The Adjusting Process **111**
Summary Problem for Your Review **112**
Summary of Learning Objectives **115**
Accounting Vocabulary/Questions/Daily Exercises/Exercises/Problems/Cases **116**
Appendix: Alternative Treatment of Accounting for Prepaid Expenses and Unearned Revenues **133**
Prepaid Expenses **133**
Prepaid Expense Recorded Initially as an Expense **133**
Unearned (Deferred) Revenues **134**
Unearned (Deferred) Revenue Recorded Initially as a Revenue **134**
Video Series: It's Just Lunch

4 **Completing the Accounting Cycle** **136**
The Accounting Cycle **138**
Accounting Work Sheet **138**
Mid-Chapter Summary Problem for Your Review **142**
Completing the Accounting Cycle **143**
Preparing the Financial Statements **143**
Recording the Adjusting Entries **144**
Closing the Accounts **145**
Postclosing Trial Balance **148**
Correcting Journal Entries **149**
Classification of Assets and Liabilities **150**
Assets **150**
Liabilities **150**
A Real Classified Balance Sheet **151**
Different Formats of the Balance Sheet **153**
Using Accounting Information in Decision Making: Accounting Ratios **153**
Current Ratio **153**
Debt Ratio **154**
Decision Guidelines: Completing the Accounting Cycle **155**
Summary Problem for Your Review **156**
Summary of Learning Objectives **158**
Accounting Vocabulary/Questions/Daily Exercises/Exercises/Problems/Cases **159**
Internet Exercise **176**

Appendix: Reversing Entries: An Optional Step **177**
Video Series: NIKE (Accounting Cycle)

5 Merchandising Operations and the Accounting Cycle 180

What Are Merchandising Operations? **182**
The Operating Cycle of a Merchandising Business **183**
Inventory Systems: Perpetual and Periodic **184**
Purchasing Merchandise in the Perpetual Inventory System **185**
Using the Purchase Invoice: A Basic Business Document **185**
Taking Discounts from Purchase Prices **185**
Recording Purchase Returns and Allowances **187**
Recording Transportation Costs: Who Pays? **187**
Alternative Procedures for Purchase Discounts, Returns and Allowances, and Transportation Costs **189**
Selling Inventory and Recording Cost of Goods Sold **189**
Offering Sales Discounts and Sales Returns and Allowances **191**
Mid-Chapter Summary Problem for Your Review **192**
Adjusting and Closing the Accounts of a Merchandising Business **194**
Adjusting Inventory Based on a Physical Count **194**
Preparing and Using the Work Sheet of a Merchandising Business **194**
Preparing the Financial Statements of a Merchandising Business **197**
Journalizing the Adjusting and Closing Entries for a Merchandising Business **198**
Income Statement Formats: Multi-Step and Single-Step **200**
Multi-Step Income Statement **200**
Single-Step Income Statement **200**
Using the Financial Statements for Decision Making: Two Key Ratios **200**
The Gross Margin Percentage **201**
The Rate of Inventory Turnover **201**
Accrual Accounting and Cash Flows for a Merchandising Entity **202**
Measuring Cost of Goods Sold and Inventory Purchases in the Periodic Inventory System **203**
Decision Guidelines: Merchandising Operations and the Accounting Cycle **205**
Summary Problem for Your Review **206**
Summary of Learning Objectives **209**
Accounting Vocabulary/Questions/Daily Exercises/Exercises/Problems/Cases **209**
Supplement: Accounting for Merchandise in a Periodic Inventory System **228**
Recording the Purchases of Inventory **228**
Purchasing Merchandise in the Periodic Inventory System **228**
Recording Purchase Returns and Allowances **229**
Recording Transportation Costs **229**
Recording the Sale of Inventory **229**
Cost of Goods Sold **229**
Adjusting and Closing the Accounts in a Periodic Inventory System **229**
Preparing and Using the Work Sheet in a Periodic Inventory System **232**
Preparing the Financial Statements of a Merchandising Business **233**
Journalizing the Adjusting and Closing Entries in a Periodic Inventory System **235**
Summary Problem for Your Review **237**
Supplement Exercises/Supplement Problems **240**
Video Series: May Department Stores

6 Accounting Information Systems: Special Journals, Control Accounts, and Subsidiary Ledgers 244

Features of an Effective Accounting Information System **246**
Control **246**
Compatibility **246**
Flexibility **246**
Favorable Cost/Benefit Relationship **246**
Components of a Computerized Accounting System **247**
The Three Stages of Data Processing: A Comparison of Computerized and Manual Accounting Systems **247**

Designing an Accounting System: The Chart of Accounts 248
Classifying Transactions: Computerized and Manual Systems 249
Menu-Driven Accounting Systems 249
Preparing Accounting Reports 250
Summary of the Accounting Cycle: Computerized and Manual 251
Integrated Accounting Software 251
Spreadsheets 251
Special Journals 252
Special Accounting Journals 252
Using the Sales Journal 253
Using the Cash Receipts Journal 256
Using the Purchases Journal 258
Using the Cash Disbursements Journal 260
The General Journal's Role in an Accounting Information System 262
The Credit Memorandum—The Document for Recording Sales Returns and Allowances 262
The Debit Memorandum—The Business Document for Recording Purchase Returns and Allowances 263
Balancing the Ledgers 264
Using Documents as Journals in a Manual Accounting System 264
Blending Computers and Special Journals in an Accounting Information System 264
Decision Guidelines: Using Special Journals and Control Accounts 265
Summary Problem for Your Review 266
Summary of Learning Objectives 267
Accounting Vocabulary/Questions/Daily Exercises/Exercises/Problems/Cases 268
Internet Exercise 284
Video Series: NIKE (Accounting Systems)
Comprehensive Problems for Part One 284

PART TWO

Accounting for Assets and Liabilities 288

7 Internal Control, Managing Cash, and Making Ethical Judgments 288
Internal Control 290
Establishing an Effective System of Internal Control 291
The Limitations of Internal Control 295
Using the Bank Account as a Control Device 295
The Bank Reconciliation 296
How Owners and Managers Use the Bank Reconciliation 302
Mid-Chapter Summary Problem for Your Review 303
Internal Control over Cash Receipts 304
Internal Control over Cash Disbursements *(Payments)* 306
Controls over Payment by Check 306
Petty Cash Disbursements 307
Using a Budget to Manage Cash 309
International Focus 311
Reporting Cash on the Balance Sheet 311
Ethics and Accounting 312
Corporate and Professional Codes of Ethics 312
Ethical Issues in Accounting 312
Decision Guidelines: Framework for Making Ethical Judgments 313
Ethics and External Controls 314
Summary Problem for Your Review 315
Summary of Learning Objectives 316
Accounting Vocabulary/Questions/Daily Exercises/Exercises/Problems/Cases 316
Appendix: The Voucher System 332

8 Accounts and Notes Receivable 334
Receivables: An Introduction 336
The Types of Receivables 336
Establishing Internal Control over the Collection of Receivables 337
Decision Guidelines: Controlling, Managing, and Accounting for Receivables 338
Managing the Collection of Receivables: The Credit Department 338
Accounting for Uncollectible Accounts (Bad Debts): The Allowance Method 339
Estimating Uncollectibles 340
Using the Percent of Sales and the Aging Methods Together 342
Writing Off Uncollectible Accounts 343
The Direct Write-Off Method 344
Recoveries of Uncollectible Accounts 344
Credit-Card and Bankcard Sales 344
Credit Balances in Accounts Receivable 345

Mid-Chapter Summary Problem for Your Review **346**
Notes Receivable: An Overview **346**
Identifying a Note's Maturity Date **347**
Computing Interest on a Note **347**
Accounting for Notes Receivable **348**
Recording Notes Receivable **348**
Accruing Interest Revenue **349**
Discounting a Note Receivable **349**
Contingent Liabilities on Discounted Notes Receivable **351**
Dishonored Notes Receivable **351**
Reporting Receivables and Allowances: Actual Company Reports **352**
Using Acounting Information for Decision Making **353**
Acid-Test (or Quick) Ratio **353**
Days' Sales in Receivables **354**
Reporting Receivables Transactions on the Statement of Cash Flows **355**
Decision Guidelines: Accounting for Receivables Transactions **356**
Computers and Accounts Receivable **357**
Summary Problem for Your Review **357**
Summary of Learning Objectives **358**
Accounting Vocabulary/Questions/Daily Exercises/Exercises/Problems/Cases **358**
Internet Exercise **375**

9 Accounting for Merchandise Inventory 376
The Basic Concept of Inventory Accounting **379**
Inventory Systems **379**
Perpetual Inventory System **380**
Periodic Inventory System **382**
Comparing the Perpetual and Periodic Inventory Systems **382**
Cost of Goods Sold (Cost of Sales) and Gross Margin (Gross Profit) **383**
How Owners and Managers Use the Cost-of-Goods-Sold Model **383**
Gross Margin (Gross Profit) **384**
Computing the Cost of Inventory **384**
Inventory Costing Methods **385**
Income Effects of FIFO, LIFO, and Weighted-Average Cost **387**
The Income Tax Advantage of LIFO **387**
GAAP and Practical Considerations: A Comparison of Inventory Methods **388**
Mid-Chapter Summary Problem for Your Review **390**
Perpetual Inventory Records under FIFO, LIFO, and Weighted-Average Costing **391**
Accounting Principles and Their Relevance to Inventories **392**
Consistency Principle **392**
Disclosure Principle **393**
Materiality Concept **393**
Accounting Conservatism **393**
Lower-of-Cost-or-Market Rule **394**
Effects of Inventory Errors **395**
Ethical Issues in Inventory Accounting **396**
Estimating Inventory **397**
Gross Margin (Gross Profit) Method **397**
Internal Control over Inventory **398**
Reporting Inventory Transactions on the Statement of Cash Flows **398**
Decision Guidelines: Guidelines for Inventory Management **399**
Summary Problem for Your Review **400**
Summary of Learning Objectives **401**
Accounting Vocabulary/Questions/Daily Exercises/Exercises/Problems/Cases **402**

10 Accounting for Plant Assets, Intangible Assets, and Related Expenses 418
Types of Assets **420**
Measuring the Cost of Plant Assets **421**
Land **421**
Buildings **422**
Machinery and Equipment **422**
Land and Leasehold Improvements **422**
Construction in Progress and Capital Leases **422**
Capitalizing the Cost of Interest **423**
Lump-Sum (or Basket) Purchases of Assets **424**
Capital Expenditures versus Revenue Expenditures **425**
Measuring the Depreciation of Plant Assets **426**
The Causes of Depreciation **427**
Measuring Depreciation **427**
Depreciation Methods **427**
Comparing the Depreciation Methods **431**

Mid-Chapter Summary Problem for Your Review 432
The Relationship Between Depreciation and Income Taxes 433
Depreciation for Partial Years 434
Changing the Useful Life of a Depreciable Asset 435
Using Fully Depreciated Assets 436
Disposal of Plant Assets 437
Selling a Plant Asset 437
Internal Control of Plant Assets 439
Exchanging Plant Assets 439
Accounting for Natural Resources and Depletion 440
Accounting for Intangible Assets and Amortization 441
Ethical Issues in Accounting for Plant Assets and Intangibles 443
Decision Guidelines: Accounting for Plant Assets and Related Expenses 444
Reporting Plant Asset Transactions on the Statement of Cash Flows 444
Summary Problem for Your Review 445
Summary of Learning Objectives 446
Accounting Vocabulary/Questions/Daily Exercises/Exercises/Problems/Cases 446
Video Series: Home Depot

11 **Current Liabilities and Payroll Accounting** 462
Current Liabilities of Known Amount 464
Accounts Payable 464
Short-Term Notes Payable 465
Short-Term Notes Payable Issued at a Discount 466
Sales Tax Payable 467
Current Portion of Long-Term Debt 468
Accrued Expenses (Accrued Liabilities) 469
Payroll Liabilities 469
Unearned Revenues 470
Current Liabilities That Must Be Estimated 471
Estimated Warranty Payable 471
Estimated Vacation Pay Liability 472
Income Tax Payable (for a Corporation) 473
Contingent Liabilities 473
Ethical Issues in Accounting for Current and Contingent Liabilities 474
Decision Guidelines: Accounting for Current and Contingent Liabilities, Including Payroll 475
Mid-Chapter Summary Problem for Your Review 476
Accounting for Payroll 477
Gross Pay and Net Pay 477
Payroll Deductions 477
Required Payroll Deductions 478
Optional Payroll Deductions 479
Employer Payroll Taxes 479
Employer FICA Tax 479
State and Federal Unemployment Compensation Taxes 479
Payroll Entries 480
The Payroll System 481
Payroll Register 481
Payroll Bank Account 483
Payroll Checks 483
Earnings Record 483
Recording Cash Disbursements for Payroll 484
Net Pay to Employees 484
Payroll Taxes and Payroll Deductions to the Government 484
Benefits 487
Internal Control over Payroll 487
Controls for Efficiency 487
Controls for Safeguarding Payroll Disbursements 488
Reporting Payroll Expense and Liabilities 488
Decision Guidelines: Accounting for Payroll 489
Summary Problem for Your Review 490
Summary of Learning Objectives 490
Accounting Vocabulary/Questions/Daily Exercises/Exercises/Problems/Case 491
Video Series: America West
Comprehensive Problems for Part Two 504

PART THREE

Accounting for Partnerships and Corporate Transactions 506

12 **Accounting for Partnerships** 506
Characteristics of a Partnership 508

Different Types of Partnerships **510**
General Partnerships **510**
Limited Partnerships **510**
Initial Investments by Partners **511**
Sharing Partnership Profits and Losses **512**
Sharing Based on a Stated Fraction **512**
Sharing Based on Capital Contributions **513**
Sharing Based on Capital Contributions and on Service **514**
Sharing Based on Salaries and on Interest **515**
Partner Drawings **516**
Admission of a Partner **516**
Admission by Purchasing a Partner's Interest **517**
Admission by Investing in the Partnership **517**
Withdrawal of a Partner **521**
Withdrawal at Book Value **522**
Withdrawal at Less than Book Value **522**
Withdrawal at More than Book Value **523**
Death of a Partner **523**
Liquidation of a Partnership **523**
Sale of Noncash Assets at a Gain **524**
Sale of Noncash Assets at a Loss **525**
Partnership Financial Statements **525**
Decision Guidelines: Accounting for Partnerships **527**
Summary Problem for Your Review **528**
Summary of Learning Objectives **529**
Accounting Vocabulary/Questions/Daily Exercises/Exercises/Problems/Cases **529**
Internet Exercise **541**

13 Corporate Organization, Paid-In Capital, and the Balance Sheet 542
Corporations: An Overview **544**
Characteristics of a Corporation **544**
Organization of a Corporation **545**
Capital Stock **546**
Stockholders' Equity **547**
Paid-in Capital Is Received from the Stockholders **547**
Retained Earnings Are Earned from the Customers **547**
Corporations May Pay Dividends to the Stockholders **548**
Stockholders' Rights **548**
Classes of Stock **548**
Common and Preferred Stock **548**
Par Value, Stated Value, and No-Par Stock **549**
Issuing Stock **549**
Issuing Common Stock **550**
Issuing Preferred Stock **553**
Ethical Considerations in Accounting for the Issuance of Stock **553**
Donations Received by a Corporation **554**
Review of Accounting for Paid-in Capital **554**
Decision Guidelines: Reporting Stockholders' Equity on the Balance Sheet **555**
Mid-Chapter Summary Problem for Your Review **556**
Accounting for Cash Dividends **557**
Dividend Dates **557**
Dividends on Preferred and Common Stock **557**
Dividends on Cumulative and Noncumulative Preferred Stock **558**
Convertible Preferred Stock **559**
Different Values of Stock **559**
Market Value **559**
Redemption Value **560**
Liquidation Value **560**
Book Value **560**
Evaluating Operations: Rate of Return on Total Assets and Rate of Return on Common Stockholders' Equity **562**
Return on Assets **562**
Return on Equity **562**
Accounting for Income Taxes by Corporations **563**
Decision Guidelines: Dividends, Stock Values, Evaluating Operations, & Accounting for Income Tax **565**
Summary Problem for Your Review **566**
Summary of Learning Objectives **567**
Accounting Vocabulary/Questions/Daily Exercises/Exercises/Problems/Cases **567**
Video Series: IHOP

Appendixes A-1

A NIKE, Inc. Annual Report **A-1**
B Present-Value Tables and Future-Value Tables **B-0**

Glossary G-0

Indexes I-1

Company Index I-1

Subject Index I-4

Check Figures CF-1

CHAPTERS 1 TO 13

Accounting

PROLOGUE

Careers in Accounting

Every organization uses accounting. The corner store keeps accounting records to measure its success in business. The largest corporations need accounting to keep track of their locations, employees, and transactions. Why is accounting so important? Because it is impossible to physically observe a business in its entirety. Accounting helps an organization understand its business in the same way a model helps an architect construct a building. The model helps the manager get a handle on the organization as a whole without drowning in its details.

Accounting offers exciting career opportunities. Accounting careers are usually divided into two areas: private accounting and public accounting.

Private Accounting

Private accountants work for a single business, such as a local department store, the McDonald's restaurant chain, or the Eastman Kodak Company. Charitable organizations, educational institutions, and government agencies also employ private accountants. The chief accounting officer usually has the title of controller, treasurer, or chief financial officer (CFO). Whatever the title, this person usually carries the status of a vice president. Accountants who have met certain professional requirements in the area of management accounting are designated as *certified management accountants (CMAs).*

Private accountants perform a wide variety of services:

- *Cost accounting* analyzes a business's costs to help managers control expenses. Cost accounting records guide managers in pricing their products and services to achieve greater profits. Also, cost accounting information shows management when a product is not profitable and should be dropped.
- *Budgeting* sets sales and profit goals and develops detailed plans (called *budgets*) for achieving those goals. Some of the most successful companies in the United States have been pioneers in the field of budgeting—Procter & Gamble and General Electric, for example.
- *Information systems design* identifies the organization's information needs, both internal and external. Using flow charts and manuals, systems designers develop and implement an information system to meet those needs.
- *Internal auditing* is performed by a business's own accountants. Large organizations—Motorola, Bank of America, and 3M among them—maintain a staff of internal auditors. These accountants evaluate the firm's accounting and management systems to improve operating efficiency and to ensure that employees follow company policies.

Public Accounting

Public accountants serve the general public and collect professional fees for their work, much as doctors and lawyers do. Public accountants are a small fraction (about 10%) of all accountants. Accountants who have met certain professional requirements in law, auditing, and accounting are designated as *certified public accountants (CPAs).*

Like private accountants, public accountants provide many valuable services:

- *Auditing* is one of the accounting profession's most important services. In conducting an audit, CPAs from outside a business examine the business's financial statements. If the CPAs believe that these documents are a fair and accurate presentation of the business's operations, they submit a professional opinion stating that the firm's financial statements are in accordance with generally accepted accounting principles. Why is the audit so important? Creditors want assurance that the facts and figures submitted by borrowers are reliable. Stockholders, who have invested in the company, need to know that the financial picture management shows them is complete. Government agencies also need accurate information from businesses.
- *Tax accounting* has two aims: complying with the tax laws and minimizing the company's tax bill. Because federal income tax rates run as high as 39.6% for individuals and 35% for corporations, reducing the company's tax bill is an important management consideration. Accountants prepare tax returns and plan business transactions to minimize taxes. CPAs advise individuals on what type of investments to make and on how to structure their transactions.
- *Management consulting* is a catchall term describing the wide scope of advice CPAs provide to help managers run a business. As CPAs conduct audits, they look deep into a business's operations. With the insights they gain, they often make suggestions for improvements in the business's management structure and accounting systems.

Some public accountants pool their talents and work together within a single firm. Most public accounting firms are called *CPA firms* because most of their professional employees are CPAs. CPA firms vary greatly in size. Most are small businesses, but many are large partnerships. Exhibit P-1 gives data on the largest U.S. accounting firms.

Exhibit P-2 shows the accounting positions within public accounting firms and other organizations. Note the upward movement of accounting personnel, as indicated by the arrows. In particular, note how accountants may move from positions in public accounting firms to similar or higher positions in industry and government. This is a frequently traveled career path. Because accounting deals with all facets of an organization—such as purchasing, manufacturing, marketing, and distribution—it provides an excellent basis for gaining broad business experience.

During this term, you will learn how to use accounting to make business decisions. Consider a career in accounting as you work through this first course.

EXHIBIT P-1
The Largest U.S. Accounting Firms

			Personnel			Revenue		Fee Split*		
Rank, 1997	Firm	Headquarters	Offices	Partners	Total Employees	$ Million	% Change Over Previous Year	A&A	Tax	MAS
1	Andersen Worldwide	Chicago	94	1,575	38,924	4,511.0	17%	31	15	54
2	Ernst & Young	New York	89	1,933	23,072	3,571.0	20%	39	22	39
3	Deloitte & Touche	Wilton, Conn.	106	1,556	19,764	2,925.0	14%	40	19	41
4	KPMG Peat Marwick	New York	121	1,515	16,065	2,530.0	9%	40	19	41
5	Coopers & Lybrand**	New York	115	1,241	16,826	2,115.0	11%	43	21	36
6	Price Waterhouse**	New York	94	963	15,203	2,020.0	14%	37	23	40
7	H & R Block Tax Services†	Kansas City, MO	8,400	8,323	84,000	750.4	14%	0	100	0
8	Grant Thornton	New York	48	285	2,697	266.0	11%	45	30	25
9	McGladrey & Pullen	Davenport, Iowa	66	388	2,816	251.1	9%	47	32	21
10	BDO Seidman	New York	40	223	1,633	211.0	4%	53	27	20

*A&A = Accounting and auditing
Taxes = Income and other taxes
MAS = Management advisory services
**Coopers & Lybrand and Price Waterhouse are in the process of merging.
†H&R Block, unlike the other accounting firms, is not organized as a partnership.

Source: Adapted from *Accounting Today* (March 17–April 6, 1997), p. 28.

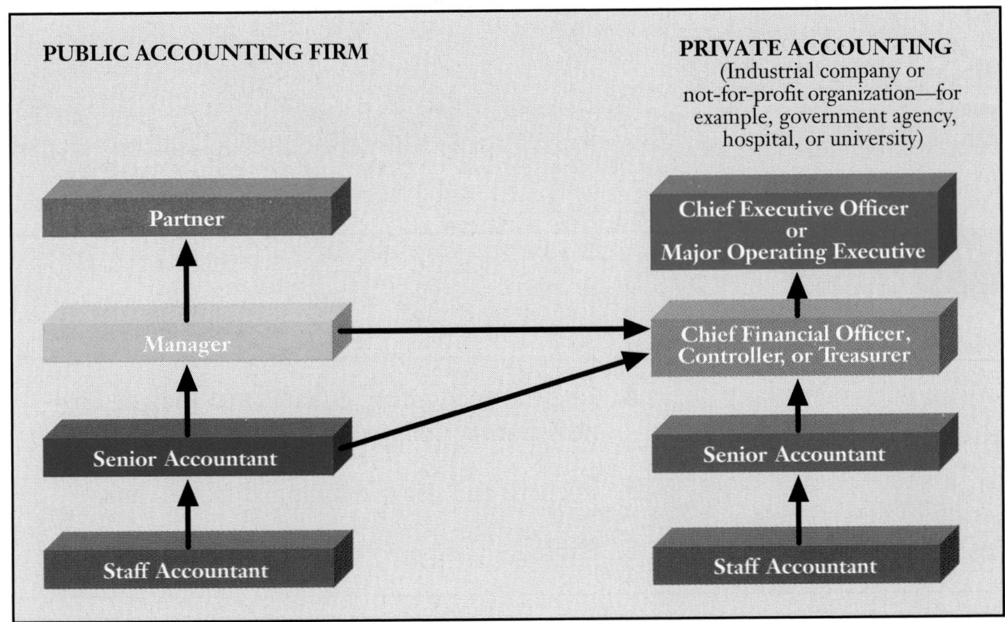

EXHIBIT P-2
Accounting Positions within Organizations

CHAPTER 1

Accounting and the Business Environment

LEARNING OBJECTIVES

After studying this chapter, you should be able to

1. Use accounting vocabulary for decision making
2. Apply accounting concepts and principles to business situations
3. Use the accounting equation to describe an organization's financial position
4. Use the accounting equation to analyze business transactions
5. Prepare and use the financial statements
6. Evaluate the performance of a business

> *"Accounting may not be what you think it is. You are probably already using basic accounting skills without even knowing it!"*
>
> MEGAN THOMAS, OWNER OF HELPING HAND

Can you start a successful business with $50 or less? Believe it or not, you can. Like many college students, Megan Thomas of Atlanta, Georgia, needed to earn some extra money. A business major at the University of Georgia, she had only $50 to work with. She'd gained experience working for a catering firm, so she decided to start her own business, offering her services as a helping hand at parties. She would set up for a party, serve the food, and clean up afterward—do everything but cook the food—for $10 an hour. Thomas named her company Helping Hand. She spent $20 to have advertising fliers printed and $18 to purchase aprons. Within two months she had assisted at eight parties and earned $200. With her earnings she bought matching skirts and shirts to use as uniforms.

During the summer, Thomas averaged ten jobs a month. She hired two high school students at $8 an hour and earned $300 a month. By September, she had paid $200 in business expenses and had earned $900—enough to pay off her car and have $100 left over. Along the way, Megan Thomas gained valuable experience from advertising her services, dealing with both clients and employees, and maintaining the finances of her business.

What role does accounting play in this situation? Megan Thomas had to decide how to organize her company. Helping Hand is a proprietorship—a single-owner company—with Thomas as the owner. As her business grows, she may consider joining forces with a fellow student to form a partnership. If she wants to expand the business after graduation, she could choose to incorporate—that is, to form a corporation. In this chapter, we discuss all three forms of business organizations: proprietorships, partnerships, and corporations.

How well did Thomas's business, Helping Hand, perform? In common usage, we might say that during its first year Helping Hand "made" $900. This means that for the year, Helping Hand earned a profit of $900 after all expenses were paid. *Earnings* and *profit* are accounting terms that mean the same thing. *Expenses* is another key accounting term. In this chapter, we explain these terms and introduce the financial statements that businesses use to report their financial affairs.

You may already know various accounting terms and relationships, because accounting affects people's behavior in many ways. This first accounting course will sharpen your focus by explaining how accounting works. As you progress through this course, you will see how accounting helps people like Megan Thomas—and you—achieve business goals.

Objective 1

Use accounting vocabulary for decision making

Accounting—The Basis for Business Decisions

Accounting. The information system that measures business activities, processes that information into reports, and communicates the results to decision makers.

Financial Statements. Business documents that report on a business in monetary amounts, providing information to help people make informed business decisions.

Accounting is the information system that measures business activities, processes that information into reports, and communicates the results to decision makers. Accounting is often called "the language of business." The better you understand this language, the better your business decisions will be, and the better you can manage the financial aspects of living. A recent survey indicates that business managers believe it is more important for college students to learn accounting than any other business subject. Personal financial planning, education expenses, loans, car payments, income taxes, and investments are based on the information system that we call accounting. A key product of an accounting system is a set of financial statements. **Financial statements** report on a business in monetary amounts, providing information to help people make informed business decisions. Is my business making a profit? Should I hire assistants? Am I earning enough money to pay my rent? Answers to business questions like these are based on accounting information.

Please don't mistake bookkeeping for accounting. *Bookkeeping* is a procedural element of accounting, just as arithmetic is a procedural element of mathematics. Increasingly, people are using computers to do detailed bookkeeping—in households, businesses, and organizations of all types. Exhibit 1-1 illustrates the role of accounting in business. The process starts and ends with people making decisions.

The Users of Accounting Information: Decision Makers

Decision makers need information. The more important the decision, the greater the need for information. Virtually all businesses and most individuals keep accounting records to aid in making decisions. In the following sections, we discuss some of the people and groups who use accounting information.

INDIVIDUALS People such as you use accounting information in their day-to-day affairs to manage bank accounts, evaluate job prospects, make investments, and decide whether to rent or to buy a house.

BUSINESSES Business managers use accounting information to set goals for their organizations, to evaluate progress toward those goals, and to take corrective action if necessary. Decisions based on accounting information may include which building to purchase, how much merchandise to keep on hand, and how much cash to borrow. Megan Thomas needed to know how much she could spend on advertising and on supplies for her helping-hand business.

EXHIBIT 1-1
The Accounting System: The Flow of Information

INVESTORS Investors provide the money a business needs to begin operations. Megan Thomas was able to start Helping Hand by investing only $50 in the business. To decide whether to invest in a company, potential investors evaluate what income they can expect from their investment. This means analyzing the financial statements of the business and keeping up with developments in the business press—for example, *The Wall Street Journal* and *Business Week*.

CREDITORS Before making a loan, creditors (lenders) such as banks determine the borrower's ability to meet scheduled payments. This evaluation includes a report on the borrower's financial position and a prediction of future operations, both of which are based on accounting information.

GOVERNMENT REGULATORY AGENCIES Most organizations face government regulation. For example, the *Securities and Exchange Commission (SEC)*, a federal agency, requires businesses to disclose certain financial information to the investing public.

TAXING AUTHORITIES Local, state, and federal governments levy taxes on individuals and businesses. Income tax is figured using accounting information. Businesses determine their sales tax from accounting records that show how much they have sold.

NONPROFIT ORGANIZATIONS Nonprofit organizations—such as churches, hospitals, government agencies, and colleges, which operate for purposes other than profit—use accounting information in much the same way that profit-oriented businesses do.

OTHER USERS Employees and labor unions make wage demands based on their employer's reported income. Consumer groups and the general public are also interested in the amount of income businesses earn. Newspapers report "improved profit pictures" of companies as the nation emerges from economic downturns. Such news, based on accounting information, is related to our standard of living.

Financial Accounting and Management Accounting

Users of accounting information are a diverse group. They may be categorized as *external users* or *internal users*. This distinction allows us to classify accounting into two fields—financial accounting and management accounting.

Financial accounting focuses on information for people outside the firm. Creditors and outside investors, for example, are not part of the day-to-day management of the company. Likewise, government agencies and the general public are external users of a firm's accounting information. Chapters 2 through 18 of this book deal primarily with financial accounting.

Management accounting focuses on information for internal decision makers, such as top executives, department heads, college deans, and hospital administrators. Chapters 19 through 26 cover management accounting.

Financial Accounting. The branch of accounting that focuses on information for people outside the firm.

Management Accounting. The branch of accounting that focuses on information for internal decision makers of a business, such as top executives.

The History and Development of Accounting

Accounting has a long history. Some scholars claim that writing arose in order to record accounting information. Account records date back to the ancient civilizations of China, Babylonia, Greece, and Egypt. The rulers of these civilizations used accounting to track the costs of labor and materials used in building structures such as the great pyramids. The need for accounting has existed as long as there has been business activity.

In the Industrial Revolution of the nineteenth century, the growth of corporations spurred the development of accounting. Because corporation owners—the stockholders—do not manage the business they own, managers have had to create accounting systems to report to the owners how well their business is doing. Because accurate information is important to investment decisions, society needs a way to ensure that business information is reliable.

Financial Accounting Standards Board (FASB). The private organization that determines how accounting is practiced in the United States.

Certified Public Accountant (CPA). A licensed accountant who serves the general public rather than one particular company.

Certified Management Accountant (CMA). A licensed accountant who works for a single company.

In the United States, a private organization called the **Financial Accounting Standards Board (FASB)** determines how accounting is practiced. The FASB works with the SEC, the American Institute of Certified Public Accountants (AICPA), and the Institute of Management Accountants (IMA), two large professional organizations of accountants. **Certified public accountants,** or **CPAs,** are accountants who are licensed to serve the general public rather than one particular company. **Certified management accountants,** or **CMAs,** are licensed accountants who work for a single company. The relationships among the SEC, the FASB, the AICPA, and the IMA, and the rules that govern them (generally accepted accounting principles, or GAAP) are diagrammed in Exhibit 1-2. (Start with the public sector at the top.) The prologue at the beginning of this book explains the work of CPAs and CMAs.

Ethical Considerations in Accounting and Business

Ethical considerations pervade all areas of accounting and business. Consider a current situation that is challenging the ethical conduct of accountants.

Tobacco companies are defendants in a large number of lawsuits. The managers of Philip Morris, RJR Nabisco, and American Brands have reason to downplay these lawsuits for fear that investors will stop buying their stock and that banks will stop lending money to them. Should Philip Morris, RJR Nabisco, and American Brands disclose this sensitive information? Accounting guidelines require companies to describe such lawsuits in their financial statements. And each company's auditor is required to state whether the company's disclosures are adequate.

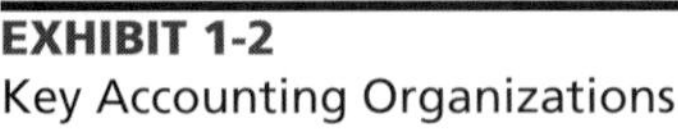
EXHIBIT 1-2
Key Accounting Organizations

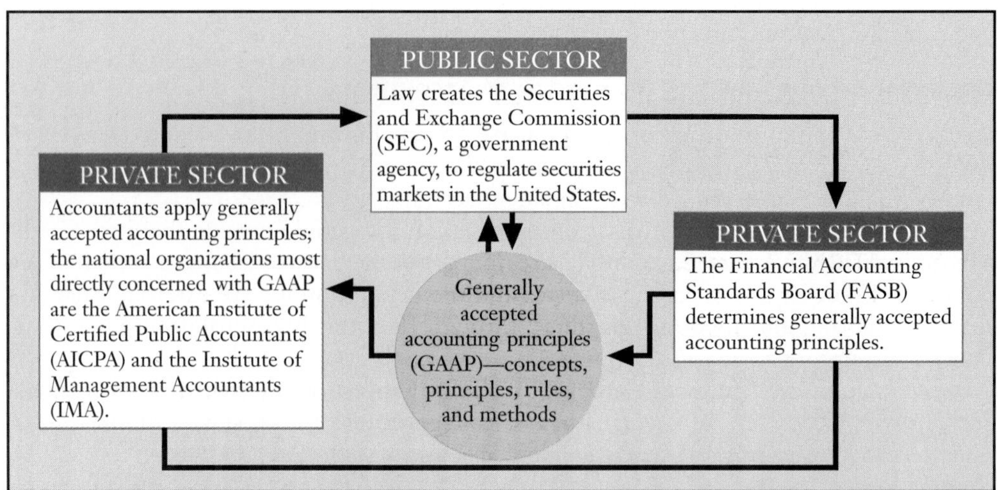

By what criteria do accountants address questions that challenge their ethical conduct? The AICPA, other professional accounting organizations, and most large companies have codes of ethics that bind their members and employees to high levels of ethical conduct.

Standards of Professional Conduct

The AICPA's Code of Professional Conduct for Accountants was adopted by its members to provide guidance to CPAs in performing their professional duties. Ethical standards in accounting are designed to produce accurate information for decision making. The preamble to the Code states: "[A] certified public accountant assumes an obligation of self-discipline above and beyond the requirements of laws and regulations...[and] an unswerving commitment to honorable behavior, even at the sacrifice of personal advantage."

The opening paragraph of the Standards of Ethical Conduct of the Institute of Management Accountants (IMA) states: "Management accountants have an obligation to the organizations they serve, their profession, the public, and themselves to maintain the highest standards of ethical conduct." The Ethical Standards include sections on competence, confidentiality, integrity, objectivity, and resolution of ethical conflict. The requirements for a high level of professional conduct are similar to those in the AICPA code.

Most corporations also set standards of ethical conduct for their employees. For example, The Boeing Company, a leading manufacturer of aircraft, has a highly developed set of business conduct guidelines. In the introduction to those guidelines, the chairperson of the board and the chief executive officer state: "We owe our success as much to our reputation for integrity as we do to the quality and dependability of our products and services. This reputation is fragile and can easily be lost."

"The Boeing Company, a leading manufacturer of aircraft, has a highly developed set of business conduct guidelines."

Types of Business Organizations

A business takes one of three forms of organization and, in some cases, accounting procedures depend on which form the organization takes. Therefore, you should understand the differences among the three types of business organizations: proprietorships, partnerships, and corporations.

PROPRIETORSHIPS A **proprietorship** has a single owner, called the proprietor, who is generally also the manager. Megan Thomas's company, Helping Hand, started out as a proprietorship. Proprietorships tend to be small retail establishments or individual professional businesses, such as those of physicians, attorneys, and accountants. From the accounting viewpoint, each proprietorship is distinct from its proprietor. Thus the accounting records of the proprietorship do *not* include the proprietor's personal financial records.

Proprietorship. A business with a single owner.

PARTNERSHIPS A **partnership** joins two or more individuals together as co-owners. Each owner is a partner. Helping Hand would become a partnership if Thomas takes on a partner. Many retail establishments, as well as some professional organizations of physicians, attorneys, and accountants, are partnerships. Most partnerships are small or medium-sized, but some are gigantic, exceeding 2,000 partners. Accounting treats the partnership as a separate organization, distinct from the personal affairs of each partner.

Partnership. A business with two or more owners.

CORPORATIONS A **corporation** is a business owned by **stockholders,** or *shareholders*, people who own stock (shares of ownership) in the business. A business becomes a corporation when the state approves its articles of incorporation. A corporation is a legal entity, an "artificial person" that conducts its business in its own name. Like the proprietorship and the partnership, the corporation is an organization with an existence separate from its owners.

Corporation. A business owned by stockholders; it begins when the state approves its articles of incorporation. A corporation is a legal entity, an "artificial person," in the eyes of the law.

Stockholder. A person who owns stock in a corporation. Also called a **shareholder.**

Corporations differ significantly from proprietorships and partnerships in one very important way. If a proprietorship or a partnership cannot pay its debts, lenders can take

Concept Highlight

EXHIBIT 1-3
Comparison of the Three Forms of Business Organization

	Proprietorship	Partnership	Corporation
1. Owner(s)	Proprietor—there is one owner	Partners—there are two or more owners	Stockholders—there are generally many owners
2. Life of organization	Limited by owner's choice or death	Limited by owners' choices or death	Indefinite
3. Personal liability of owner(s) for business debts	Proprietor is personally liable	Partners are personally liable	Stockholders are not personally liable
4. Accounting status	The proprietorship is separate from the proprietor	The partnership is separate from partners	The corporation is separate from the stockholders

the owners' personal assets—cash and belongings—to satisfy the business's obligations. But if a corporation goes bankrupt, lenders cannot take the personal assets of the stockholders. This *limited personal liability* of stockholders for corporate debts partly explains why corporations are the dominant form of business organization: People can invest in corporations with limited personal risk.

"The Coca-Cola Company, for example, has 1.3 billion shares of stock owned by over 500,000 stockholders."

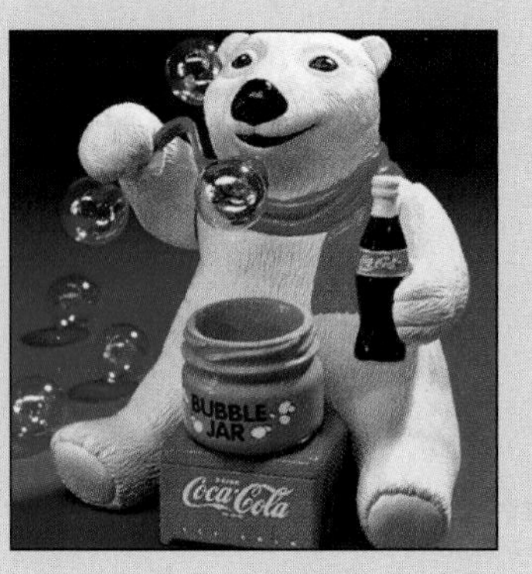

Another factor in corporate growth is the division of ownership into individual shares. The Coca-Cola Company, for example, has 1.3 billion shares of stock owned by over 500,000 stockholders. An investor with no personal relationship either to the corporation or to any other stockholder can become a co-owner by buying 30, 100, 5,000, or any number of shares of its stock. For many corporations, the investor can sell the stock at any time. It is usually harder to sell out of a proprietorship or a partnership than to sell out of a corporation.

Exhibit 1-3 summarizes the differences among the three types of business organization.

Accounting for corporations includes some unique complexities. For this reason, we initially focus on proprietorships. We cover partnerships in Chapter 12 and begin our discussion of corporations in Chapter 13.

Objective 2

Apply accounting concepts and principles to business situations

Accounting Concepts and Principles

Generally Accepted Accounting Principles (GAAP). Accounting guidelines, formulated by the Financial Accounting Standards Board, that govern how accountants measure, process, and communicate financial information.

Accounting practices follow certain guidelines. The rules that govern how accountants measure, process, and communicate financial information fall under the heading GAAP, which stands for **generally accepted accounting principles.** GAAP is the "law" of accounting—rules for conducting behavior in a way acceptable to the majority of people.

GAAP rests on a conceptual framework written by the FASB. *The primary objective of financial reporting is to provide information useful for making investment and lending decisions.* To be useful, information must be relevant, reliable, and comparable. Accountants strive to meet those goals in the information they produce. This course will expose you to the generally accepted methods of accounting. We begin the discussion of GAAP in this section and introduce additional concepts and principles as needed throughout the book. The major elements of generally accepted accounting principles can be found on the front endsheets, just after the front cover.

■ Daily Exercise 1-3

Entity. An organization or a section of an organization that, for accounting purposes, stands apart from other organizations and individuals as a separate economic unit.

The Entity Concept

The most basic concept in accounting is that of the **entity.** An accounting entity is an organization or a section of an organization that stands apart from other organizations and individuals as a separate economic unit. From an accounting perspective, sharp boundaries are drawn around each entity so as not to confuse its affairs with those of other entities.

Consider Megan Thomas, the owner of Helping Hand. Suppose that her bank account shows a $2,000 balance at the end of the year. Only $1,200 of that amount came from the business's operations. The other $800 was a gift from her parents. Thomas follows the entity concept, so she will account for the money generated by the business—one economic unit—separately from the money she received from her family, a second economic unit. This separation makes it possible to view Helping Hand's financial position clearly.

Suppose Thomas disregards the entity concept and treats the full $2,000 as a product of Helping Hand's operations. She will be misled into believing that the business has produced more cash than it has. Steps needed to make the business more successful may not be taken.

Consider Toyota, a huge organization with several divisions. Toyota management evaluates each division as a separate accounting entity. If sales in the Lexus division are dropping drastically, Toyota should identify the reason. But if sales figures from all divisions of the company are analyzed as a single amount, then management will not know that the company is not selling enough Lexus automobiles. Thus the entity concept also applies to the parts of a large organization—in fact, *to any entity that needs to be evaluated separately.*

In summary: The transactions of different entities should *not* be accounted for together. Each entity should be evaluated separately.

The Reliability (Objectivity) Principle

Accounting records and statements are based on the most reliable data available so that they will be as accurate and useful as possible. This guideline is the *reliability principle*, also called the *objectivity principle*. Reliable data are verifiable. They may be confirmed by any independent observer. For example, Megan Thomas's $18 purchase of aprons is supported by a paid invoice. This is objective evidence of her cost of the aprons. Ideally, accounting records are based on information that flows from activities documented by objective evidence. Without the reliability principle, accounting records would be based on whims and opinions, and would be subject to dispute.

Suppose you want to open a stereo shop. To have a place for operations, you transfer a small building to the business. You believe the building is worth $155,000. To confirm its cost to the business, you hire two real estate professionals, who appraise the building at $147,000. Which is the more reliable estimate of the building's value? It is the real estate appraisal of $147,000, because it is supported by external, independent, objective observation. The business should record the building cost as $147,000.

The Cost Principle

The *cost principle* states that acquired assets and services should be recorded at their actual cost (also called *historical cost*). Even though the purchaser may believe the price paid is a bargain, the item is recorded at the price paid in the transaction and not at the "expected" cost. Suppose your stereo shop purchases stereo equipment from a supplier who is going out of business. Assume that you get a good deal on this purchase and pay only $2,000 for merchandise that would have cost you $3,000 elsewhere. The cost principle requires you to record this merchandise at its actual cost of $2,000, not the $3,000 that you believe the equipment is worth.

The cost principle also holds that the accounting records should maintain the historical cost of an asset for as long as the business holds the asset. Why? Because cost is a reliable measure. Suppose your store holds the stereo equipment for six months. During that time, stereo prices increase, and the equipment can be sold for $3,500. Should its accounting value—the figure "on the books"—be the actual cost of $2,000 or the current market value of $3,500? According to the cost principle, the accounting value of the equipment remains at actual cost, $2,000.

The Going-Concern Concept

Another reason for measuring assets at historical cost is the *going-concern concept*, which holds that the entity will remain in operation for the foreseeable future. Most firm resources—such as supplies, land, buildings, and equipment—are acquired to use rather than to sell. Under the going-concern concept, accountants assume that the business will remain in operation long enough to use existing resources for their intended purpose.

To understand the going-concern concept better, consider the alternative, which is to go out of business. A store that is holding a Going-Out-of-Business Sale is trying to sell all its holdings. In that case, the relevant measure is current market value. Going out of business, however, is the exception rather than the rule.

The Stable-Monetary-Unit Concept

We think of a loaf of bread and a month's rent in terms of their dollar value. In the United States, accountants record transactions in dollars because the dollar is the medium of exchange. British accountants record transactions in pounds sterling, and Japanese accountants record transactions in yen.

Unlike the value of a liter, a mile, or an acre, the value of a dollar or of a Mexican peso changes over time. A rise in the general price level is called *inflation.* During inflation, a dollar will purchase less milk, less toothpaste, and less of other goods. When prices are stable—when there is little inflation—a dollar's purchasing power is also stable.

Accountants assume that the dollar's purchasing power is relatively stable. The *stable-monetary-unit concept* is the basis for ignoring the effect of inflation in the accounting records. It allows accountants to add and subtract dollar amounts as though each dollar has the same purchasing power as any other dollar at any other time. In South America, where inflation rates are often high, accountants make adjustments to report monetary amounts in units of current buying power—a very different concept.

Working It Out You are considering the purchase of land for future expansion. The seller is asking $50,000 for land that cost her $35,000. An appraisal shows a value of $47,000. You first offer $44,000. The seller counter-offers with $48,000, and you agree on a price of $46,000.

What dollar value for this land is reported on your financial statements? Which accounting concept or principle guides your answer?

Answer: According to the *cost principle*, assets and services should be recorded at their actual cost. You paid $46,000 for the land. Therefore, $46,000 is the cost to report on your financial statements.

Objective 3

Use the accounting equation to describe an organization's financial position

The Accounting Equation

Financial statements tell us how a business is performing and where it stands. They are the final product of the accounting process. But how do we arrive at the items and amounts that make up the financial statements? The most basic tool of accounting is the **accounting equation.** This equation presents the resources of the business and the claims to those resources.

Accounting Equation. The most basic tool of accounting, presenting the resources of the business and the claims to those resources: Assets = Liabilities + Owner's Equity.

Assets and Liabilities

Assets are the economic resources of a business that are expected to be of benefit in the future. Cash, office supplies, merchandise, furniture, land, and buildings are examples.

Asset. An economic resource that is expected to be of benefit in the future.

Liability. An economic obligation (a debt) payable to an individual or an organization outside the business.

Owner's Equity. The claim of a business owner to the assets of the business. Also called **capital.**

Claims to those assets come from two sources. **Liabilities** are *outsider* claims, which are economic obligations—debts—payable to outsiders. These outside parties are called *creditors.* For example, a creditor who has loaned money to a business has a claim—a legal right—to a part of the assets until the business pays the debt. *Insider* claims to the business's assets are called **owner's equity,** or **capital.** These are the claims held by the owners of the business. Owners have a claim to the entity's assets because they have invested in the business. The $50 that Megan Thomas invested in Helping Hand is an example. Owner's equity is measured by subtracting liabilities from assets.

The accounting equation shows the relationship among assets, liabilities, and owner's equity. Assets appear on the left-hand side of the equation. The legal and economic claims against the assets—the liabilities and owner's equity—appear on the right-hand side of the equation. As Exhibit 1-4 shows, the two sides must be equal:

Economic Resources *Claims to Economic Resources*
Assets = Liabilities + Owner's Equity

EXHIBIT 1-4
The Accounting Equation

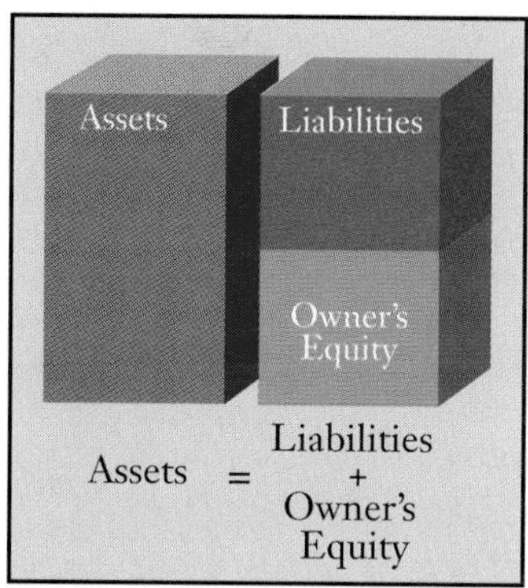

Let's take a closer look at the elements that make up the accounting equation. Suppose you run Top Cut Meats, which supplies beef to McDonald's and other restaurants. Some customers pay you in cash when you deliver the meat. Cash is an asset. Other customers buy on credit and promise to pay you within a certain time after delivery. This promise is also an asset because it is an economic resource that will benefit you in the future, when you receive cash from the customer. To Top Cut Meats, this promise is an **account receivable.** A written promise for future collection is called a **note receivable.**

McDonald's promise to pay you for the meat it purchases on credit creates a debt for McDonald's. This liability is an **account payable** of McDonald's—the debt is not written out. Instead, it is backed up by the reputation and the credit standing of McDonald's. A written promise of future payment is called a **note payable.**

Learning Tip: All receivables are assets. All payables are liabilities.

■ Daily Exercise 1-1

Owner's Equity

Owner's equity is the amount of an entity's remaining assets after the liabilities are subtracted. For this reason, owner's equity is often called *net assets*. We often write the accounting equation to show that the owner's claim to business assets is a *residual*, something that is left over after subtracting the liabilities.

Assets − Liabilities = Owner's Equity

The purpose of business is to increase owner's equity through **revenues,** which are amounts earned by delivering goods or services to customers. Revenues increase owner's equity because they increase the business's assets but not its liabilities. As a result, the owner's share of business assets increases. Exhibit 1-5 shows that owner investments and revenues increase the owner's equity of the business.

Exhibit 1-5 also indicates the types of transactions that decrease owner's equity. **Owner withdrawals** are those amounts removed from the business by the owner. Withdrawals are the opposite of owner investments. **Expenses** are decreases in owner's equity that occur from using assets or increasing liabilities in the course of delivering goods and services to customers. Expenses are the cost of doing business and are the opposite of revenues. Expenses include

- office rent
- salaries of employees
- newspaper advertisements
- utility payments for light, electricity, gas, and so forth
- interest
- insurance
- property taxes

Account Receivable. A promise to receive cash from customers to whom the business has sold goods or for whom the business has performed services.

Note Receivable. A written promise for future collection of cash.

Account Payable. A liability backed by the general reputation and credit standing of the debtor.

Note Payable. A written promise of future payment.

Revenue. Amounts earned by delivering goods or services to customers. Revenues increase owner's equity.

Owner Withdrawals. Amounts removed from the business by an owner.

Expense. Decrease in owner's equity that occurs from using assets or increasing liabilities in the course of delivering goods or services to customers.

■ Daily Exercise 1-2

■ Daily Exercise 1-4

EXHIBIT 1-5
Transactions That Increase or Decrease Owner's Equity

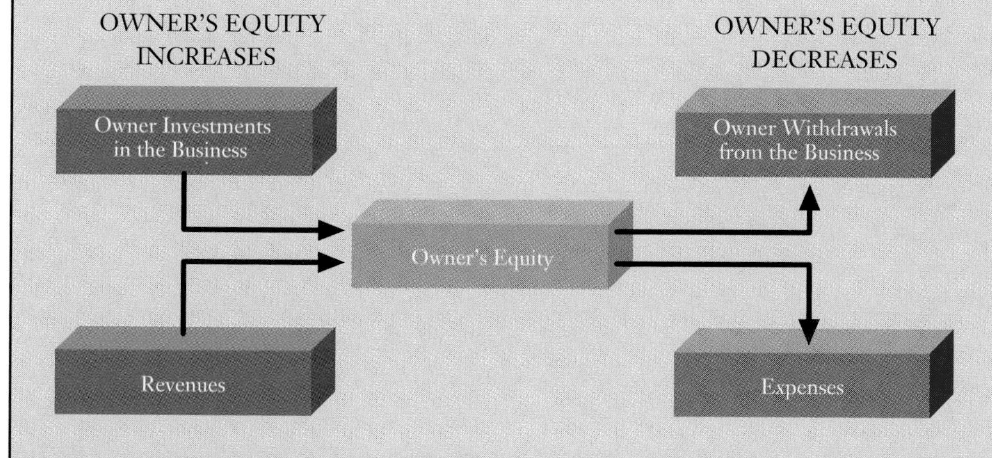

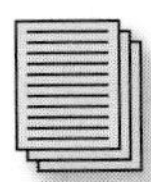

Working It Out

1. If the assets of a business are $174,300 and the liabilities total $82,000, how much is the owner's equity?
2. If the owner's equity in a business is $22,000 and the liabilities are $36,000, how much are the assets?

Answers: To answer both these questions, use the accounting equation:

Assets − Liabilities = Owner's Equity

1. Plug in the amounts given: $174,300 for assets and $82,000 for liabilities.

	Assets =	**Liabilities +**	**Owner's Equity**
	$174,300 =	$82,000 +	X
$174,300 – $82,000 =			X
	$92,300 =		X

2. Plug in the amounts given: $22,000 for owner's equity and $36,000 for liabilities.

Assets	**=**	**Liabilities +**	**Owner's Equity**
X	=	$36,000 +	$22,000
X	=	$58,000	

Accounting for Business Transactions

Objective 4

Use the accounting equation to analyze business transactions

Transaction. An event that affects the financial position of a particular entity and can be reliably recorded.

In accounting terms, a **transaction** is any event that *both* affects the financial position of the business entity *and* can be reliably recorded. Many events may affect a company, including (1) elections, (2) economic booms and downturns, (3) purchases and sales of merchandise inventory, (4) payment of rent, (5) collection of cash from customers, and so on. But an accountant records only events with effects that can be measured reliably as transactions.

Which of these events would an accountant record? The answer is events (3), (4), and (5), because their dollar amounts can be measured reliably. The accountant would not record events (1) and (2) because the dollar effects of elections and economic trends on a particular entity cannot be measured reliably.

To illustrate accounting for business transactions, let's assume that Gary Lyon has recently become a CPA and opens his own accounting practice. Because the business has a single owner, it is a proprietorship. We will now consider 11 events and analyze each in terms of its effect on the accounting equation of Gary Lyon's accounting practice. Transaction analysis is the essence of accounting.

TRANSACTION 1: STARTING THE BUSINESS Gary Lyon invests $50,000 of his money to begin the business. Specifically, he deposits $50,000 in a bank account entitled Gary Lyon, CPA. The effect of this transaction on the accounting equation of the Gary Lyon, CPA, business entity is

	Assets		**Liabilities +**	**Owner's Equity**	**Type of Owner's Equity Transaction**
	Cash	=		**Gary Lyon, Capital**	
(1)	+50,000			+50,000	*Owner investment*

For every transaction, the amount on the left side of the equation must equal the amount on the right side. The first transaction increases both the assets (in this case, Cash) and the owner's equity of the business (Gary Lyon, Capital). The transaction involves no liabilities of the business because it creates no obligation for Lyon to pay an outside party. To the right of the transaction, we write "Owner investment" to keep track of the reason for the effect on the owner's equity of the business. This transaction is identical to Megan Thomas's $50 investment to start Helping Hand.

TRANSACTION 2: PURCHASE OF LAND Lyon purchases land for a future office location, paying cash of $40,000. The effect of this transaction on the accounting equation is

	Assets		Liabilities + Owner's Equity	Type of Owner's Equity Transaction
	Cash +	Land	Gary Lyon, Capital	
(1)	50,000		50,000	*Owner investment*
(2)	−40,000 +	40,000		
Bal.	10,000	40,000	50,000	
	50,000		50,000	

The cash purchase of land increases one asset, Land, and decreases another asset, Cash, by the same amount. After the transaction is completed, Lyon's business has cash of $10,000, land of $40,000, no liabilities, and owner's equity of $50,000.

■ Daily Exercise 1-6

Learning Tip: Note that the sums of the balances (which we abbreviate Bal.) on both sides of the equation are equal. This equality must always exist.

TRANSACTION 3: PURCHASE OF OFFICE SUPPLIES Lyon buys stationery and other office supplies, agreeing to pay $500 within 30 days. This transaction increases both the assets and the liabilities of the business. Its effect on the accounting equation is

	Assets			Liabilities + Owner's Equity	
	Cash +	Office Supplies +	Land	Accounts Payable +	Gary Lyon, Capital
Bal.	10,000		40,000		50,000
(3)		+500		+500	
Bal.	10,000	500	40,000	500	50,000
	50,500			50,500	

The asset affected is Office Supplies, and the liability is an account payable. (Recall that the term *payable* signifies a liability.) Because Lyon is obligated to pay $500 in the future but signs no formal promissory note, we record the liability as an Account Payable, not as a Note Payable.

■ Daily Exercise 1-5

TRANSACTION 4: EARNING OF SERVICE REVENUE Gary Lyon earns service revenue by providing professional accounting services for his clients. Assume he earns $5,500 and collects this amount in cash. The effect on the accounting equation is an increase in the asset Cash and an increase in Gary Lyon, Capital, as follows:

	Assets			Liabilities +	Owner's Equity	Type of Owner's Equity Transaction
	Cash +	Office Supplies +	Land	Accounts Payable +	Gary Lyon, Capital	
Bal.	10,000	500	40,000	500	50,000	
(4)	+ 5,500				+ 5,500	*Service revenue*
Bal.	15,500	500	40,000	500	55,500	
	56,000			56,000		

This revenue transaction caused the business to grow, as shown by the increases in total assets and in the sum of total liabilities plus owner's equity. A company that sells goods to customers is a merchandising business. Its revenue is called *sales revenue.* By contrast, Gary Lyon and Megan Thomas perform services for clients; their revenue is called *service revenue.*

■ Daily Exercise 1-7

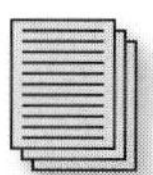

Working It Out Lyon's accounting practice has now completed four business transactions. Answer these questions about the business:

1. How much in total assets does Lyon's business have to work with?
2. How much of the total assets does Lyon actually own? How much does the business owe outsiders?

Answers

1. Look at the balances under the Assets heading for transaction 4. Lyon's business owns three assets: Cash ($15,500), Office Supplies ($500), and Land ($40,000). By adding these amounts, we see that Lyon's business has $56,000 in total assets.
2. Recall that *owner's equity* represents the owner's claim to the assets of the business. Lyon's owner's equity is $55,500.
   Liabilities are the amounts that a business owes to outsiders. After transaction 4, the company owes $500 in liabilities.

TRANSACTION 5: EARNING OF SERVICE REVENUE ON ACCOUNT Lyon performs services for a client who does not pay immediately. In return for his accounting services, Lyon receives the client's promise to pay the $3,000 amount within one month. This promise is an asset to Lyon, an account receivable because he expects to collect the cash in the future. In accounting, we say that Lyon performed this service *on account*. When the business performs service for a client or a customer, the business earns revenue regardless of whether it receives cash immediately or expects to collect cash later. This $3,000 of service revenue is as real an increase in the wealth of Lyon's business as the $5,500 of revenue that he collected immediately in transaction 4. Lyon records an increase in the asset Accounts Receivable and an increase in owner's equity as follows:

	Assets					Liabilities +	Owner's Equity	Type of Owner's Equity Transaction
	Cash +	Accounts Receivable +	Office Supplies +	Land		Accounts Payable +	Gary Lyon, Capital	
Bal.	15,500		500	40,000	=	500	55,500	
(5)		+3,000					+ 3,000	*Service revenue*
Bal.	15,500	3,000	500	40,000		500	58,500	
	59,000					59,000		

TRANSACTION 6: PAYMENT OF EXPENSES During the month, Lyon pays $2,700 in cash expenses: office rent, $1,100; employee salary, $1,200 (for a part-time assistant); and total utilities, $400. The effects on the accounting equation are

	Assets					Liabilities +	Owner's Equity	Type of Owner's Equity Transaction
	Cash +	Accounts Receivable +	Office Supplies +	Land		Accounts Payable +	Gary Lyon, Capital	
Bal.	15,500	3,000	500	40,000		500	58,500	
(6)	− 1,100				=		− 1,100	*Rent expense*
	− 1,200						− 1,200	*Salary expense*
	− 400						− 400	*Utilities expense*
Bal.	12,800	3,000	500	40,000		500	55,800	
	56,300					56,300		

Because expenses have the opposite effect of revenues, they cause the business to shrink, as shown by the smaller balances of total assets and total owner's equity.

Each expense should be recorded in a separate transaction. Here, for simplicity, they are listed together. We could record the cash payment in a single amount for the sum of the three expenses, $2,700 ($1,100 + $1,200 + $400). In all cases the "balance" of the equation holds, as we know it must.

Businesspeople, Gary Lyon included, run their businesses with the objective of having more revenues than expenses. An excess of total revenues over total expenses is called **net income, net earnings,** or **net profit.** If total expenses exceed total revenues, the result is a **net loss.**

Net Income. Excess of total revenues over total expenses. Also called **net earnings** or **net profit.**

Net Loss. Excess of total expenses over total revenues.

TRANSACTION 7: PAYMENT ON ACCOUNT Lyon pays $400 to the store from which he purchased $500 worth of office supplies in transaction 3. In accounting, we say that he pays $400 *on account*. The effect on the accounting equation is a decrease in the asset Cash and a decrease in the liability Accounts Payable as follows:

	Assets					Liabilities +	Owner's Equity
	Cash	+ Accounts Receivable	+ Office Supplies	+ Land		Accounts Payable +	Gary Lyon, Capital
Bal.	12,800	3,000	500	40,000	=	500	55,800
(7)	− 400					−400	
Bal.	12,400	3,000	500	40,000		100	55,800
	55,900					55,900	

The payment of cash on account has no effect on the asset Office Supplies because the payment does not increase or decrease the supplies available to the business.

TRANSACTION 8: PERSONAL TRANSACTION Lyon remodels his home at a cost of $30,000, paying cash from his personal funds. This event is *not* a transaction of Gary Lyon's business. It has no effect on Lyon's accounting practice and therefore is not recorded by the business. It is a transaction of the Gary Lyon *personal* entity, not the Gary Lyon, CPA, *business* entity. We are focusing solely on the business entity, and this event does not affect it. This transaction illustrates the application of the *entity concept*.

TRANSACTION 9: COLLECTION ON ACCOUNT In transaction 5, Gary Lyon performed service for a client on account. Lyon now collects $1,000 from the client. We say that Lyon collects the cash *on account*. Lyon will record an increase in the asset Cash. Should he also record an increase in service revenue? No, because Lyon already recorded the revenue when he earned it in transaction 5. The phrase "collect cash on account" means to record an increase in Cash and a decrease in the asset Accounts Receivable. The effect on the accounting equation is

	Assets					Liabilities +	Owner's Equity
	Cash	+ Accounts Receivable	+ Office Supplies	+ Land		Accounts Payable +	Gary Lyon, Capital
Bal.	12,400	3,000	500	40,000	=	100	55,800
(9)	+ 1,000	−1,000					
Bal.	13,400	2,000	500	40,000		100	55,800
	55,900					55,900	

Total assets are unchanged from the preceding transaction's total. Why? Because Lyon merely exchanged one asset for another. Also, total liabilities and owner's equity are unchanged.

■ Daily Exercise 1-8

TRANSACTION 10: SALE OF LAND An individual approaches Lyon about selling a parcel of land owned by the Gary Lyon, CPA, business entity. Lyon and the other person agree to a sale price of $22,000, which is equal to Lyon's cost of the land. Lyon's business sells the land and receives $22,000 cash. The effect on the accounting equation is

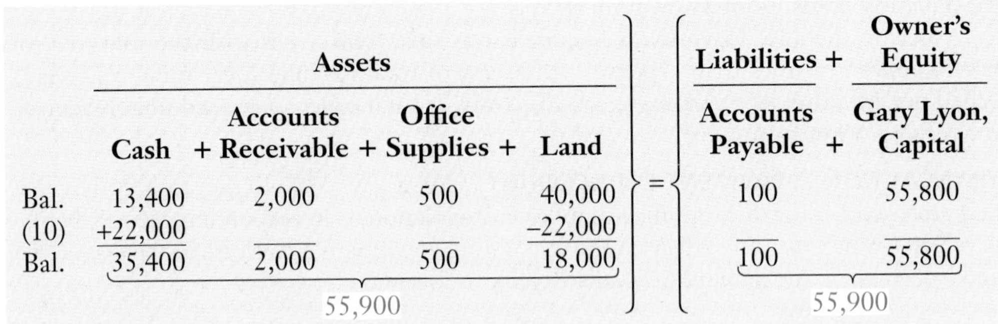

	Assets					Liabilities +	Owner's Equity
	Cash	+ Accounts Receivable	+ Office Supplies	+ Land		Accounts Payable +	Gary Lyon, Capital
Bal.	13,400	2,000	500	40,000	=	100	55,800
(10)	+22,000			−22,000			
Bal.	35,400	2,000	500	18,000		100	55,800
	55,900					55,900	

TRANSACTION 11: WITHDRAWING OF CASH Lyon withdraws $2,100 cash from the business for personal use. The effect on the accounting equation is

	Assets					Liabilities +	Owner's Equity	Type of Owner's Equity Transaction
	Cash	+ Accounts Receivable	+ Office Supplies	+ Land		Accounts Payable +	Gary Lyon, Capital	
Bal.	35,400	2,000	500	18,000	=	100	55,800	
(11)	− 2,100						− 2,100	*Owner withdrawal*
Bal.	33,300	2,000	500	18,000		100	53,700	
	53,800					53,800		

Lyon's withdrawal of $2,100 cash decreases the asset Cash and also the owner's equity of the business. *The withdrawal does not represent a business expense because the cash is used for personal affairs unrelated to the business.* We record this decrease in owner's equity as Withdrawals or as Drawings. The double underlines below each column indicate a final total.

Evaluating Business Transactions

Exhibit 1-6 summarizes the 11 preceding transactions. Panel A lists the details of the transactions, and Panel B presents the analysis. As you study the exhibit, note that every transaction maintains the equality

Assets = Liabilities + Owner's Equity

Thinking It Over Why does Gary Lyon, or anyone else, go into business? If you could identify only one reason, what would it be? How does accounting serve to meet this need?

Answer: Gary Lyon went into business to earn a profit—and thereby to make a living. Lyon hopes his accounting revenues exceed his expenses to provide an excess—a net income. Accounting tells him how much income he has earned and how much cash and other assets his business has and how much in liabilities the business owes.

The Financial Statements

Objective 5

Prepare and use the financial statements

Once the analysis of the transactions is complete, what is the next step in the accounting process? How does a business present the results of the analysis? We now look at the *financial statements*, which are formal reports of an entity's financial information. The primary financial statements are the (1) income statement, (2) statement of owner's equity, (3) balance sheet, and (4) statement of cash flows.

PANEL A—Details of transactions

(1) Lyon invested $50,000 cash in the business.
(2) Paid $40,000 cash for land.
(3) Bought $500 of office supplies on account.
(4) Received $5,500 cash from clients for accounting service revenue earned.
(5) Performed accounting service for a client on account, $3,000.
(6) Paid cash expenses: rent, $1,100; employee salary, $1,200; utilities, $400.
(7) Paid $400 on the account payable created in transaction 3.
(8) Remodeled his personal residence. This is *not* a transaction of the business.
(9) Collected $1,000 on the account receivable created in transaction 5.
(10) Sold land for cash at its cost of $22,000.
(11) Withdrew $2,100 cash for personal expenses.

PANEL B—Analysis of transactions

	Assets				=	Liabilities +	Owner's Equity	Type of Owner's Equity Transaction
	Cash +	Accounts Receivable +	Office Supplies +	Land		Accounts Payable +	Gary Lyon, Capital	
(1)	+50,000						+50,000	*Owner investment*
Bal.	50,000						50,000	
(2)	−40,000			+40,000				
Bal.	10,000			40,000			50,000	
(3)			+500			+500		
Bal.	10,000		500	40,000		500	50,000	
(4)	+ 5,500						+ 5,500	*Service revenue*
Bal.	15,500		500	40,000		500	55,500	
(5)		+3,000					+ 3,000	*Service revenue*
Bal.	15,500	3,000	500	40,000	=	500	58,500	
(6)	− 1,100						− 1,100	*Rent expense*
	− 1,200						− 1,200	*Salary expense*
	− 400						− 400	*Utilities expense*
Bal.	12,800	3,000	500	40,000		500	55,800	
(7)	− 400					−400		
Bal.	12,400	3,000	500	40,000		100	55,800	
(8)	Not a transaction of the business							
(9)	+ 1,000	−1,000						
Bal.	13,400	2,000	500	40,000		100	55,800	
(10)	+22,000			−22,000				
Bal.	35,400	2,000	500	18,000		100	55,800	
(11)	− 2,100						− 2,100	*Owner withdrawal*
Bal.	33,300	2,000	500	18,000		100	53,700	
	53,800					53,800		

Concept Highlight

EXHIBIT 1-6
Analysis of Transactions of Gary Lyon, CPA

INCOME STATEMENT The **income statement** presents a summary of an entity's revenues and expenses for a specific period of time, such as a month or a year. The income statement, also called the **statement of earnings** or **statement of operations,** is like a video of the entity's operations—it presents a moving financial picture of business operations during the period. The income statement holds perhaps the most important single piece of information about a business—its *net income*, revenues minus expenses. If expenses exceed revenues, a net loss results for the period.

Income Statement. Summary of an entity's revenues, expenses, and net income or net loss for a specific period. Also called the **statement of operations** or the **statement of earnings.**

STATEMENT OF OWNER'S EQUITY The **statement of owner's equity** presents a summary of the changes that occurred in the entity's *owner's equity* during a specific time period, such as a month or a year. Increases in owner's equity arise from investments by the

Statement of Owner's Equity. Summary of the changes in an entity's owner's equity during a specific period.

owner and from net income earned during the period. Decreases result from owner withdrawals and from a net loss for the period. Net income or net loss comes directly from the income statement. Owner investments and withdrawals are capital transactions between the business and its owner, so they do not affect the income statement.

Balance Sheet. List of an entity's assets, liabilities, and owner's equity as of a specific date. Also called **the statement of financial position.**

BALANCE SHEET The **balance sheet** lists all the entity's assets, liabilities, and owner's equity as of a specific date, usually the end of a month or a year. The balance sheet is like a snapshot of the entity. For this reason, it is also called the **statement of financial position.**

Statement of Cash Flows. Reports cash receipts and cash disbursements during a period.

STATEMENT OF CASH FLOWS The **statement of cash flows** reports the amount of cash coming in (*cash receipts*) and the amount of cash going out (*cash payments* or *disbursements*) during a period. Business activities result in either a net cash inflow (receipts greater than payments) or a net cash outflow (payments greater than receipts). The statement of cash flows shows the net increase or decrease in cash during the period and the cash balance at the end of the period. We will cover the statement of cash flows in greater depth in Chapter 17.

Financial Statement Headings

Each financial statement has a heading giving the name of the business (in our discussion, Gary Lyon, CPA), the name of the particular statement, and the date or time period covered by the statement. A balance sheet taken at the end of year 19X4 would be dated December 31, 19X4. A balance sheet prepared at the end of March 19X7 is dated March 31, 19X7.

An income statement or a statement of owner's equity covering an annual period ending in December 19X5 is dated "Year Ended December 31, 19X5." A monthly income statement or statement of owner's equity for September 19X9 has in its heading "Month Ended September 30, 19X9," "For the Month Ended September 30, 19X9," or "For the Month of September 19X9." Income is meaningless unless identified with a particular time period.

Computers and software programs have had a significant impact on the preparation of the financial statements. Financial statements can be produced instantaneously after the data from the financial records are entered into the computer. Of course, any errors that exist in the financial records will be passed on to the financial statements. For this reason, the person responsible for analyzing the accounting data is important to the accuracy of the financial statements.

Relationships Among the Financial Statements

Objective 6

Evaluate the performance of a business

Exhibit 1-7 illustrates all four financial statements. Their data come from the transaction analysis in Exhibit 1-6, which covers the month of April 19X1. Study the exhibit carefully, because it shows the relationships among the four financial statements. Specifically, observe the following in Exhibit 1-7:

1. The *income statement* for the month ended April 30, 19X1
   a. Reports all revenues and all expenses during the period. Expenses are listed in decreasing order of amount, with the largest expense first.
   b. Reports *net income* of the period if total revenues exceed total expenses, as in the case of Gary Lyon's accounting practice for April. If total expenses exceed total revenues, a *net loss* is reported instead.
2. The *statement of owner's equity* for the month ended April 30, 19X1
   a. Opens with the owner's capital balance at the beginning of the period.
   b. Adds *investments by the owner* and adds net income (or subtracts net loss, as the case may be). Net income (or net loss) comes directly from the income statement, (see arrow ① in Exhibit 1-7).
   c. Subtracts withdrawals by the owner. The parentheses around withdrawals indicate a subtraction.
   d. Ends with the owner's capital balance at the end of the period.
3. The *balance sheet* at April 30, 19X1, the end of the period
   a. Reports all assets, all liabilities, and owner's equity of the business at the end of the period.
   b. Reports that total assets equal the sum of total liabilities plus total owner's equity.

EXHIBIT 1-7
Financial Statements of Gary Lyon, CPA

- Daily Exercise 1-9
- Daily Exercise 1-10
- Daily Exercise 1-11
- Daily Exercise 1-12
- Daily Exercise 1-13
- Daily Exercise 1-14
- Daily Exercise 1-15
- Daily Exercise 1-16
- Daily Exercise 1-17
- Daily Exercise 1-18

GARY LYON, CPA
Income Statement
Month Ended April 30, 19X1

Revenue		
Service revenue		$8,500
Expenses:		
Salary expense	$1,200	
Rent expense	1,100	
Utilities expense	400	
Total expenses		2,700
Net income		$5,800

GARY LYON, CPA
Statement of Owner's Equity
Month Ended April 30, 19X1

Gary Lyon, capital, April 1, 19X1	$ 0
Add: Investments by owner	50,000
Net income for the month	5,800
	55,800
Less: Withdrawals by owner	(2,100)
Gary Lyon, capital, April 30, 19X1	$53,700

GARY LYON, CPA
Balance Sheet
April 30, 19X1

Assets		Liabilities	
Cash	$33,300	Accounts payable	$ 100
Accounts receivable	2,000	**Owner's Equity**	
Office supplies	500		
Land	18,000	Gary Lyon, capital	53,700
		Total liabilities and	
Total assets	$53,800	owner's equity	$53,800

GARY LYON, CPA
Statement of Cash Flows*
Month Ended April 30, 19X1

Cash flows from **operating** activities:		
Receipts:		
Collections from customers ($5,500 + $1,000)		$ 6,500
Payments:		
To suppliers ($1,100 + $400 + $400)	$ (1,900)	
To employees	(1,200)	(3,100)
Net cash inflow from operating activities		3,400
Cash flows from **investing** activities:		
Acquisition of land	$(40,000)	
Sale of land	22,000	
Net cash outflow from investing activities		(18,000)
Cash flows from **financing** activities:		
Investment by owner	$ 50,000	
Withdrawal by owner	(2,100)	
Net cash inflow from financing activities		47,900
Net increase in cash		$33,300
Cash balance, April 1, 19X1		0
Cash balance, April 30, 19X1		$33,300

*Chapter 17 explains how to prepare this statement.

c. Reports the owner's ending capital balance, taken directly from the statement of owner's equity (see arrow ②).

4. The *statement of cash flows* for the month ended April 30, 19X1
   a. Reports cash flows from three types of business activities (*operating, investing,* and *financing* activities) during the month.

      - *Operating activities* bring in revenues and the related cash collections from customers. They also include the payment of expenses.
      - *Investing activities* purchase and sell assets that the business uses for operations.
      - *Financing activities* are the receipts of cash from people who finance the organization, and also payments back to those people.

      Each category of cash-flow activities includes both cash receipts, which are positive amounts, and cash payments, which are negative amounts (denoted by parentheses). Each category results in a net cash inflow or a net cash outflow for the period. We discuss these categories in detail in later chapters.
   b. Reports a net increase in cash during the month and ends with the cash balance at April 30, 19X1. This is the amount of cash to report on the balance sheet (see arrow ③).

Thinking It Over Study Exhibit 1-7, which gives the financial statements of Gary Lyon's accounting practice at April 30, 19X1, end of the first month of operations. Answer these questions for Lyon.

1. What was the result of business operations for the month of April—a profit or a loss, and how much? Which financial statement provides this information?
2. How much revenue did the business earn during April? What was the business's largest expense? How much were total expenses?
3. Is the income statement dated, at the last day of the period or for the entire period? Why?
4. How much owner capital did the business have at the beginning of April? At the end of April? Identify all the items that changed owner capital during the month, along with their amounts. Which financial statement provides this information?
5. How much cash does the business have as it moves into the next month—that is, into May 19X1? Which financial statement provides this information?
6. How much do clients owe the accounting practice at April 30? Is this an asset or a liability for Lyon's accounting practice? What does Lyon call this item?
7. How much does the business owe outsiders at April 30? Is this an asset or a liability of Lyon's accounting practice? What does Lyon call this item?
8. How is the balance sheet dated? Why is it dated this way? Why does the balance sheet's date differ from the date on the income statement?

Answers

1. From the income statement: Net income = $5,800.
2. From the income statement: Total revenue = $8,500. Salary was the largest expense, at $1,200. Total expenses = $2,700.
3. The income statement is dated "Month Ended April 30, 19X1." The income statement is dated for the entire period because the revenues and the expenses occurred *during* the month, not at the end of the month. The income statement reports on the business's operations during the whole span of the period.
4. From the statement of owner's equity:
   Beginning owner capital = $0   Ending owner capital = $53,700
   Increases: Investment by owner = $50,000; Net income for the month = $5,800
   Decrease: Withdrawal by owner = $2,100
5. From the balance sheet: Cash = $33,300.
6. Clients owe the business $2,000, which is an *asset* called Accounts Receivable.
7. The business owes outsiders $100 for a *liability* called Accounts Payable.
8. The balance sheet is dated April 30, 19X1, which means at midnight on April 30. The balance sheet is dated at a single moment in time (in this case, April 30, 19X1) to show the amount of assets, liabilities, and owner's equity the business had on that date. The balance sheet is like a snapshot, while the income statement provides a moving picture of the business through time.

The Decision Guidelines feature summarizes the chapter in terms of some decisions that businesspeople must make. A Decision Guidelines feature appears in each chapter of this book. They serve as useful summaries of the decision-making process and its foundation in accounting information.

DECISION GUIDELINES — Major Business Decisions

DECISION	GUIDELINES
How to organize the business?	If a single owner—a *proprietorship.* If two or more owners, but not incorporated—a *partnership.* If the business issues stock to stockholders—a *corporation.*
What to account for?	Account for the business, a separate entity apart from its owner *(entity concept).* Account for transactions and events that affect the business and can be measured objectively *(reliability principle).*
How much to record for assets and liabilities?	Actual historical amount *(cost principle).*
How to organize the various effects of a transaction?	The accounting equation: ASSETS = LIABILITIES + OWNER'S EQUITY
How to measure profits and losses?	Income statement: REVENUES – EXPENSES = NET INCOME (or NET LOSS)
Did owner's equity increase or decrease?	Statement of owner's equity: Beginning capital + Owner investments + Net income (or – Net loss) – Owner withdrawals = Ending capital
Where does the business stand financially?	Balance sheet (accounting equation): ASSETS = LIABILITIES + OWNER'S EQUITY
Where did the business's cash come from? Where did cash go?	Statement of cash flows *Operating activities* Net cash inflow (or outflow) + *Investing activities* Net cash inflow (or outflow) + *Financing activities* Net cash inflow (or outflow) = Net increase or (decrease) in cash

SUMMARY PROBLEM FOR YOUR REVIEW

Jill Smith opens an apartment-location business near a college campus. She is the sole owner of the proprietorship, which she names Campus Apartment Locators. During the first month of operations, July 19X1, Smith engages in the following transactions:

a. Smith invests $35,000 of personal funds to start the business.
b. She purchases on account office supplies costing $350.
c. Smith pays cash of $30,000 to acquire a lot next to the campus. She intends to use the land as a future building site for her business office.
d. Smith locates apartments for clients and receives cash of $1,900.
e. She pays $100 on the account payable she created in transaction (b).
f. She pays $2,000 of personal funds for a vacation.
g. She pays cash expenses for office rent, $400, and utilities, $100.
h. The business sells office supplies to another business for its cost of $150.
i. Smith withdraws cash of $1,200 for personal use.

REQUIRED

1. Analyze the preceding transactions in terms of their effects on the accounting equation of Campus Apartment Locators. Use Exhibit 1-6 as a guide, but show balances only after the last transaction.
2. Prepare the income statement, statement of owner's equity, and balance sheet of the business after recording the transactions. Use Exhibit 1-7 as a guide.

SOLUTION

REQUIREMENT 1

PANEL A—Details of transactions

a. Smith invested $35,000 cash to start the business.
b. Purchased $350 of office supplies on account.
c. Paid $30,000 to acquire land as a future building site.
d. Earned service revenue and received cash of $1,900.
e. Paid $100 on account.
f. Paid for a personal vacation, which is not a transaction of the business.
g. Paid cash expenses for rent, $400, and utilities, $100.
h. Sold office supplies for cost of $150.
i. Withdrew $1,200 cash for personal use.

PANEL B—Analysis of transactions

	Assets				Liabilities +	Owner's Equity	Type of Owner's Equity Transaction
	Cash	**+ Office Supplies +**	**Land**		**Accounts Payable +**	**Jill Smith, Capital**	
(a)	+35,000					+35,000	*Owner investment*
(b)		+350			+350		
(c)	−30,000		+30,000	=			
(d)	+ 1,900					+ 1,900	*Service revenue*
(e)	− 100				−100		
(f)	Not a transaction of the business						
(g)	− 400					− 400	*Rent expense*
	− 100					− 100	*Utilities expense*
(h)	+ 150	−150					
(i)	− 1,200					− 1,200	*Owner withdrawal*
Bal.	5,250	200	30,000		250	35,200	
	35,450				35,450		

REQUIREMENT 2

Financial Statements of Campus Apartment Locators

CAMPUS APARTMENT LOCATORS
Income Statement
Month Ended July 31, 19X1

Revenue:		
Service revenue		$1,900
Expenses:		
Rent expense	$400	
Utilities expense	100	
Total expenses		500
Net income		1,400

CAMPUS APARTMENT LOCATORS
Statement of Owner's Equity
Month Ended July 31, 19X1

Jill Smith, capital, July 1, 19X1	$ 0
Add: Investments by owner	35,000
Net income for the month	1,400
	36,400
Less: Withdrawals by owner	(1,200)
Jill Smith, capital, July 31, 19X1	$35,200

CAMPUS APARTMENT LOCATORS
Balance Sheet
July 31, 19X1

Assets		**Liabilities**	
Cash	$ 5,250	Accounts payable	$ 250
Office supplies	200	**Owner's Equity**	
Land	30,000		
		Jill Smith, capital	35,200
		Total liabilities and	
Total assets	$35,450	owner's equity	$35,450

Summary of Learning Objectives

1. *Use accounting vocabulary for decision making.* Accounting is an information system for measuring, processing, and communicating financial information. As the "language of business," accounting helps a wide range of decision makers.

2. *Apply accounting concepts and principles to analyze business situations.* *Generally accepted accounting principles (GAAP)* guide accountants in their work. The three basic forms of business organization are the proprietorship, the partnership, and the corporation. Whatever the form, accountants use the entity concept to keep the business's records separate from other economic units. Other important guidelines are the *reliability principle*, the *cost principle*, the *going-concern concept*, and the *stable-monetary-unit concept.*

3. *Use the accounting equation to describe an organization's financial position.* In its most common form, the accounting equation is

Assets = Liabilities + Owner's Equity

4. *Use the accounting equation to analyze business transactions.* A transaction is any event that both affects the financial position of a business entity and can be reliably recorded. Transactions affect a business's assets, liabilities, and owner's equity. Therefore, transactions are often analyzed in terms of their effect on the accounting equation.

5. *Prepare and use the financial statements.* The *financial statements* communicate information for decision making by an entity's managers, owners, and creditors and by government agencies. The *income statement* summarizes the entity's operations in terms of revenues earned and expenses incurred during a specific period. Total revenues minus total expenses equal net income. The *statement of owner's equity* reports the changes in owner's equity during the period. The *balance sheet* lists the entity's assets, liabilities, and owner's equity at a specific time. The *statement of cash flows* reports the cash coming in and the cash going out during the period.

6. *Evaluate the performance of a business.* High net income indicates success in business; net loss indicates a bad business year.

Accounting Vocabulary

Like many other subjects, accounting has a special vocabulary. It is important that you understand the following terms. They are explained in the chapter and also in the glossary at the end of the book.

account payable *(p. 13)*
account receivable *(p. 13)*
accounting *(p. 6)*
accounting equation *(p. 12)*
asset *(p. 12)*
balance sheet *(p.20)*
capital *(p. 12)*
certified management accountant (CMA) *(p. 8)*
certified public accountant (CPA) *(p. 8)*
corporation *(p. 9)*
entity *(p. 10)*
expense *(p. 13)*
financial accounting *(p. 7)*
Financial Accounting Standards Board (FASB) *(p. 8)*
financial statements *(p. 6)*
generally accepted accounting principles (GAAP) *(p. 10)*
income statement *(p. 19)*
liability *(p. 12)*
management accounting *(p. 7)*
net earnings *(p. 17)*
net income *(p. 17)*
net loss *(p. 17)*
net profit *(p. 17)*
note payable *(p. 13)*
note receivable *(p. 13)*
owner's equity *(p. 12)*
owner withdrawals *(p. 13)*
partnership *(p. 9)*
proprietorship *(p. 9)*
revenue *(p. 13)*
statement of cash flows *(p. 20)*
statement of earnings *(p. 19)*
statement of financial position *(p. 20)*
statement of operations *(p. 19)*
statement of owner's equity *(p. 20)*
stockholder *(p. 9)*
transaction *(p. 14)*

Questions

1. Distinguish between accounting and bookkeeping.
2. Identify five users of accounting information, and explain how they use it.
3. Name two important reasons for the development of accounting.
4. What organization formulates generally accepted accounting principles? Is this organization a government agency?
5. Identify the owner(s) of a proprietorship, a partnership, and a corporation.
6. Why do ethical standards exist in accounting? Which organization directs its standards toward independent auditors? Which organization directs its standards more toward management accountants?
7. Why is the entity concept so important to accounting?
8. Give four examples of accounting entities.
9. Briefly describe the reliability principle.
10. What role does the cost principle play in accounting?
11. If *assets = liabilities + owner's equity*, then how can liabilities be expressed?
12. Explain the difference between an account receivable and an account payable.
13. What role do transactions play in accounting?
14. Give a more descriptive title for the balance sheet.
15. What feature of the balance sheet gives this financial statement its name?
16. Give another title for the income statement.
17. Which financial statement is like a snapshot of the entity at a specific time? Which financial statement is like a video of the entity's operations during a period of time?
18. What information does the statement of owner's equity report?
19. Give a synonym for the owner's equity of a proprietorship.
20. What piece of information flows from the income statement to the statement of owner's equity? What information flows from the statement of owner's equity to the balance sheet? What balance sheet item is explained by the statement of cash flows?

Daily Exercises

Explaining assets, liabilities, owner's equity
(Obj. 1)

DE1-1 Shortly after starting Colorado Express Company, you realize the need for a bank loan in order to purchase office equipment. In evaluating your loan request, the banker asks about the assets and liabilities of your business. In particular, she wants to know the amount of your owner's equity. In your own words, explain the differences among *assets, liabilities,* and *owner's equity.* What is the mathematical relationship among assets, liabilities, and owner's equity?

Explaining revenues, expenses
(Obj. 1)

DE1-2 Arlington Farms Apartments have been open for one year, and the owner wants to know the amount of the business's profit (net income) or net loss for the year. First, she must identify the revenues earned and the expenses incurred by the business during the year. What are *revenues* and *expenses?* How do revenues and expenses enter into the determination of net income or net loss? Review the definitions on page 13 and Exhibit 1-7 on page 21.

Applying accounting concepts and principles
(Obj. 2)

DE1-3 Suppose you are starting a business, On-Point Delivery Service, that will provide delivery services for law firms in your city. In organizing the business and setting up its accounting records, consider the following:

1. Should you account for your personal assets and personal liabilities along with the assets and the liabilities of the business, or should you keep the two sets of records separate? Why? Which accounting concept or principle provides guidance?

2. In keeping the books of the business, you must decide the amount to record for assets purchased and liabilities incurred. At what amount should you record assets and liabilities? Which accounting concept or principle provides guidance?

Using the accounting equation **(Obj. 3)**

DE1-4 You begin On-Point Delivery Service by investing $6,000 of your own money in a business bank account. Before starting operations, you borrow $10,000 cash by signing a note payable to Southside Bank. Write the business's accounting equation (page 13) after completing these transactions.

Using the accounting equation **(Obj. 3)**

DE1-5 Chuck McElravy owns Common Grounds Coffee House, near the campus of Manatee College. The business has cash of $2,000 and furniture that cost $8,000. Debts include accounts payable of $1,000 and a $6,000 note payable. How much equity does McElravy have in the business? Using McElravy's figures, write the accounting equation (page 13) of Common Grounds Coffee House.

Analyzing transactions **(Obj. 4)**

DE1-6 Review transaction 2 of Gary Lyon, CPA, on page 14. In that transaction, Lyon's business purchased land for $40,000. To buy the land, Lyon was obligated to pay for it. Why, then, did he record no liability in this transaction?

Analyzing transactions **(Obj. 4)**

DE1-7 Study Gary Lyon's transaction 4 on page 15. Lyon recorded revenue he earned from providing professional services for clients. Suppose the amount of revenue earned in transaction 4 was $7,500 instead of $5,500. How much are the business's cash and total assets after the transaction? How much is Gary Lyon, Capital?

Analyzing transactions **(Obj. 4)**

DE1-8 Review transaction 9 of Gary Lyon, CPA, on page 17. Lyon collected cash from a client for whom he had provided professional services earlier. Why did Lyon not record any revenue in transaction 9?

Preparing a balance sheet **(Obj. 5)**

DE1-9 Return to Gary Lyon's first business transaction on page 14. Lyon deposited $50,000 in a business bank account to start his accounting practice (assume Lyon started on April 2, 19X1). Prepare the Lyon business's balance sheet on April 2, 19X1, immediately after the first transaction. The figures are given on page 14, and Exhibit 1-7 (page 21), shows the format of the balance sheet.

Note: This exercise illustrates that financial statements can be prepared at any time. Usually, however, they are prepared at the end of the accounting period.

Preparing the financial statements **(Obj. 5)**

DE1-10 Examine Exhibit 1-6 on page 19. The exhibit summarizes the transactions of Gary Lyon, CPA, for the month of April 19X1. Suppose Lyon has completed the first seven transactions only and needs a bank loan on April 21, 19X1. The vice president of the bank requires financial statements to support all loan requests.

Prepare the income statement, statement of owner's equity, and balance sheet that Gary Lyon would present to the banker after completing the first seven transactions on April 21, 19X1. Exhibit 1-7, page 21, shows the format of these financial statements.

Format of the income statement **(Obj. 5)**

DE1-11 Gary Lyon wishes to know how well his business performed during April. The income statement in Exhibit 1-7, page 21, helps answer this question. Write the formula for the income statement as an equation: $X - Y = Z$. What are X, Y, and Z?

Using the financial statements **(Obj. 5)**

DE1-12 Examine Exhibit 1-7 on page 21. The exhibit gives the financial statements of Gary Lyon, CPA, at the end of the business's first month of operations. Focus on the arrows that chart the flow of information from statement to statement, and then answer these questions:

1. Which statement measures net income or net loss? Into which other statements does net income flow? That is, where is net income's final resting place in the financial statements?
2. Which statement lists the assets, liabilities, and owner's equity of the business? Which of these elements is most directly affected by net income?

Evaluating performance **(Obj. 6)**

DE1-13 Return to Exhibit 1-7 on page 21, which gives the financial statements of Gary Lyon, CPA, at April 30, 19X1. Suppose Gary Lyon's accounting practice paid Salary Expense of $2,000 for April instead of the actual amount of $1,200.

1. What would be the amount of the business's net income or net loss for April?
2. What would be the amount of Gary Lyon's capital at April 30?
3. What would be the ending amount of cash at April 30?

Using the statement of cash flows **(Obj. 5)**

DE1-14 Exhibit 1-17, page 21, gives the statement of cash flows of Gary Lyon, CPA, for the month of April. Study the exhibit and answer these questions to solidify your understanding of the accounting process and the financial statements:

1. The statement of cash flows is organized in terms of three categories of *activities*. What are the three main categories of cash-flow activities?
2. Why do you think collections from customers is an operating activity? Why is the acquisition of land an investing activity? Why is the business's receipt of cash from the investment by owner a financing activity? Answer in your own words.
3. How does the statement of cash flows relate to the balance sheet?

Preparing the income statement
(Obj. 5)

DE1-15 On-Point Delivery Service has just completed operations for the year ended December 31, 19X3. This is the third year of operations for the company. As the proprietor of the business, you want to know how well the business performed during the year. You also wonder where the business stands financially at the end of the year. To address these questions, you have assembled the following data:

Salary expense	**$32,000**	**Insurance expense**	**$ 4,000**
Accounts payable	**7,000**	**Service revenue**	**91,000**
Owner, capital,		**Accounts receivable**	**17,000**
December 31, 19X2	**13,000**	**Supplies expense**	**1,000**
Supplies	**2,000**	**Cash**	**5,000**
Withdrawals by owner	**36,000**	**Fuel expense**	**6,000**
Rent expense	**8,000**		

Prepare the income statement of On-Point Delivery Service for the year ended December 31, 19X3. Follow the format shown in Exhibit 1-7, page 21. The income statement will measure the business's performance for the year.

Preparing the statement of owner's equity
(Obj. 5)

DE1-16 Use the data in Daily Exercise 1-15 to prepare the statement of owner's equity of On-Point Delivery Service for the year ended December 31, 19X3. Follow the format in Exhibit 1-7. Compute net income from the data in Daily Exercise 1-15.

Preparing the balance sheet
(Obj. 5)

DE1-17 Use the data in Daily Exercise 1-15 to prepare the balance sheet of On-Point Delivery Service at December 31, 19X3. The year-end balance sheet will show where the business stands financially at the end of the year. Follow the format in Exhibit 1-7, page 21. Owner's equity (Owner, capital) at December 31, 19X3, is $17,000.
Note: Daily Exercise 1-18 should be used in conjunction with Daily Exercises 1-15, 1-16, and 1-17.

Evaluating performance
(Obj. 6)

DE1-18 Review the On-Point Delivery Service financial statements that you prepared for Daily Exercises 1-15, 1-16, and 1-17. Use the statements to evaluate the business's performance by answering these questions:

1. The income statement gives the results of operations. Did the business earn a profit or suffer a loss? The owner had hoped to earn at least $30,000. Will he be pleased or disappointed about the business's performance during the year?
2. The statement of owner's equity reveals whether the owner's capital increased or decreased during the year—and why. Did On-Point Delivery Service's equity increase or decrease? Is this a good sign or a bad sign about the company? State your reason.
3. The balance sheet reports the financial position of the business. Which are greater, total assets or total liabilities? By how much? What is the name of the difference between assets and liabilities? Is the financial position of On-Point Delivery Service strong or weak? Give your reason.

Exercises

Explaining the income statement and the balance sheet
(Obj. 1)

E1-1 Max and Leah Butler publish a travel magazine. In need of cash, they ask City Bank & Trust for a loan. The bank's procedures require borrowers to submit financial statements to show likely results of operations for the first year and likely financial position at the end of the first year. With little knowledge of accounting, Max and Leah don't know how to proceed. Explain to them the information provided by the statement of operations (the income statement) and the statement of financial position (the balance sheet). Indicate why a lender would require this information.

Business transactions
(Obj. 2)

E1-2 For each of the following items, give an example of a business transaction that has the described effect on the accounting equation:

a. Increase one asset and decrease another asset.
b. Decrease an asset and decrease owner's equity.
c. Decrease an asset and decrease a liability.
d. Increase an asset and increase owner's equity.
e. Increase an asset and increase a liability.

Transaction analysis
(Obj. 2)

E1-3 Irwin Enterprises, a proprietorship (Lance Irwin, owner), experienced the following events. State whether each event (1) increased, (2) decreased, or (3) had no effect on the total assets of the business. Identify any specific asset affected.

a. Irwin increased his cash investment in the business.
b. Paid cash on accounts payable.
c. Purchased machinery and equipment for a manufacturing plant; signed a promissory note in payment.
d. Performed service for a customer on account.
e. Irwin withdrew cash from the business for personal use.
f. Received cash from a customer on account receivable.
g. Irwin used personal funds to purchase a swimming pool for his home.
h. Sold land for a price equal to the cost of the land; received cash.
i. Borrowed money from the bank.
j. Cash purchase of land for a future building site.

E1-4 Compute the missing amount in the accounting equation for each entity:

Accounting equation (Obj. 3)

	Assets	Liabilities	Owner's Equity
Company A	$?	$61,800	$84,400
Company B	45,900	?	34,000
Company C	81,700	59,800	?

E1-5 Campbell Soup Company started 19X5 with total assets of $4,992 million and total liabilities of $3,003 million. At the end of 19X5, Campbell's total assets stood at $6,315 million, and total liabilities were $3,847 million.

Accounting equation (Obj. 4, 5)

REQUIRED

1. Did the owners' equity of Campbell Soup increase or decrease during 19X5?By how much?
2. Identify two possible reasons for the change in owners' equity of Campbell Soup during the year.

E1-6 Laser Optics' balance sheet data at May 31, 19X2, and June 30, 19X2, follow:

Accounting equation (Obj. 4, 5)

	May 31, 19X2	June 30, 19X2
Total assets	$150,000	$195,000
Total liabilities	109,000	131,000

Following are three assumptions about investments and withdrawals by the owner of the business during June. For each assumption, compute the amount of net income or net loss of the business during June 19X2.

REQUIRED

1. The owner invested $10,000 in the business and made no withdrawals.
2. The owner made no additional investments in the business but withdrew $11,000 for personal use.
3. The owner invested $48,000 in the business and withdrew $6,000 for personal use.

E1-7 Indicate the effects of the following business transactions on the accounting equation. Transaction (*a*) is answered as a guide.

Transaction analysis (Obj. 4)

a. Received cash of $35,000 from the owner, who was investing in the business.
   Answer: Increase asset (Cash)
   Increase owner's equity (Capital)
b. Paid monthly office rent of $500.
c. Paid $700 cash to purchase office supplies.
d. Performed legal service for a client on account, $2,000.
e. Purchased on account office furniture at a cost of $500.
f. Received cash on account, $900.
g. Paid cash on account, $250.
h. Sold land for $12,000, which was our cost of the land.
i. Performed legal service for a client and received cash of $780.

E1-8 Pamela Daftary opens a medical practice. During the first month of operation, May, her practice, entitled Pamela Daftary, M.D., experienced the following events.

Transaction analysis; accounting equation (Obj. 2, 4)

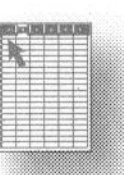

May 6	Daftary invested $80,000 in the business by opening a bank account in the name of Pamela Daftary, M.D.
9	Daftary paid cash for land costing $65,000. She plans to build an office building on the land.
12	She purchased medical supplies for $2,000 on account.
15	Daftary officially opened for business.
15–31	During the rest of the month, she treated patients and earned service revenue of $8,000, receiving cash.

May 15–31 She paid cash expenses: employees' salaries, $1,400; office rent, $1,000; utilities, $300.

28 She sold supplies to another physician for the cost of those supplies, $500.

31 She paid $1,500 on account.

REQUIRED

Analyze the effects of these events on the accounting equation of the medical practice of Pamela Daftary, M.D. Use a format similar to that of Exhibit 1-6, with headings for Cash; Medical Supplies; Land; Accounts Payable; and Pamela Daftary, Capital.

Business organization, transactions, and net income
(Obj. 1, 2, 3, 4)

E1-9 The analysis of the transactions in which Metzger Leasing engaged during its first month of operations follows. The company buys equipment that it leases out to earn revenue. The owner of the business made only one investment to start the business and no withdrawals.

	Cash	+	Accounts Receivable	+	Lease Equipment	=	Accounts Payable	+	Owner Capital
a.	+ 50,000								+50,000
b.	– 750				+ 750				
c.					+100,000		+100,000		
d.			+500						+ 500
e.	– 1,000								– 1,000
f.	+ 5,600								+ 5,600
g.	+ 150		–150						
h.	– 10,000						– 10,000		

REQUIRED

1. Describe each transaction of Metzger Leasing.
2. If these transactions fully describe the operations of Metzger Leasing during the month, what was the amount of net income or net loss?

Business organization, balance sheet
(Obj. 1, 2, 5)

E1-10 The balances of the assets and liabilities of FASTAX Service as of September 30, 19X2, follow. Also included are the revenue and expense figures of this tax-preparation business for September.

Delivery service revenue	$9,100	Office equipment	$15,500
Accounts receivable	4,900	Supplies	600
Accounts payable	1,750	Note payable	6,000
H. Dry, capital	?	Rent expense	500
Salary expense	2,000	Cash	750

REQUIRED

1. What type of business organization is FASTAX Service? How can you tell?
2. Prepare the balance sheet of FASTAX Service as of September 30, 19X2.
3. What does the balance sheet report—financial position or operating results? Which financial statement reports the other information?

Income statement
(Obj. 2, 5)

E1-11 The assets, liabilities, owner's equity, revenues, and expenses of Quasar Import Service at December 31, 19X3, the end of its first year of business, have the following balances. During the year, V. Quasar, the owner, invested $15,000 in the business.

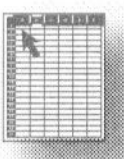

Office furniture	$ 35,000	Note payable	$30,000
Utilities expense	6,800	Rent expense	24,000
Accounts payable	3,300	Cash	3,600
V. Quasar, capital	27,100	Office supplies	4,800
Service revenue	181,200	Salary expense	49,000
Accounts receivable	9,000	Salaries payable	2,000
Supplies expense	4,000	Property tax expense	1,200

REQUIRED

1. Prepare the income statement of Quasar Import Service for the year ended December 31, 19X3. What is the result of Quasar's operations for 19X3?
2. What was the amount of the proprietor's withdrawals during the year?

Evaluating the performance of a real company
(Obj. 6)

E1-12 This exercise will help you learn to use the actual data of a well-known company.

The 19X6 annual report of Toys "Я" Us reported net sales revenue of $9,427 million. Total expenses for the year were $9,279 million. Toys "Я" Us ended the year with total assets of $6,738 million, and the company owed debts totaling $3,306 million at year end.

During the preceding year, 19X5, Toys "Я" Us earned net income of $532 million. At year-end 19X5, Toys "Я" Us reported total assets of $6,571 million and total liabilities of $3,142 million.

REQUIRED

1. Compute Toys "Я" Us's net income for 19X6. Did net income increase or decrease from 19X5 to 19X6, and by how much?
2. Did Toys "Я" Us's owners' equity increase or decrease during 19X5? By how much?

3. Toys "Я" Us management strives for a steady increase in net income and owners' equity. How would you rate Toys "Я" Us's performance for 19X6—excellent, fair, or poor? Give your reason.

Preparing a statement of cash flows **(*Obj. 5*)**

E1-13 During 19X4, Lands' End, Inc., the catalog merchant located in Dodgeville, Wisconsin, experienced the following cash flows:

	Millions
Collections from customers	$867
Payments to suppliers and employees	846
Purchases of assets	16
Dividend payments to owners (same as withdrawals by owner)	6
Cash balance, beginning of year	23

REQUIRED

Prepare the statement of cash flows of Lands' End, Inc., for the year. Follow the format of the statement of cash flows in Exhibit 1-7, page 21.

CHALLENGE EXERCISE

Using the financial statements **(*Obj. 5*)**

E1-14 Compute the missing amounts for each of the following companies.

	Red Co.	White Co.	Blue Co.
Beginning:			
Assets	$110,000	$ 50,000	$ 90,000
Liabilities	50,000	20,000	60,000
Ending:			
Assets	$160,000	$ 70,000	$?
Liabilities	70,000	35,000	80,000
Owner's Equity:			
Investments by owner	$?	$ 0	$ 10,000
Withdrawals by owner	100,000	40,000	70,000
Income Statement:			
Revenues	$430,000	$210,000	$400,000
Expenses	320,000	?	300,000

Beyond the Numbers

Analyzing a loan request **(*Obj. 1, 3*)**

BN1-1 As an analyst for Lakewood Bank, it is your job to write recommendations to the bank's loan committee. Nippon Sales Company has submitted these summary data to support the company's request for a $400,000 loan.

Income Statement Data:	19X5	19X4	19X3
Total revenues	$890,000	$830,000	$820,000
Total expenses	640,000	570,000	540,000
Net income	$250,000	$260,000	$280,000
Statement of Owner's Equity Data:	**19X5**	**19X4**	**19X3**
Beginning capital	$380,000	$400,000	$390,000
Add: Net income	250,000	260,000	280,000
	630,000	660,000	670,000
Less: Withdrawals	(290,000)	(280,000)	(270,000)
Ending capital	$340,000	$380,000	$400,000
Balance Sheet Data:	**19X5**	**19X4**	**19X3**
Total assets	$730,000	$700,000	$660,000
Total liabilities	$390,000	$320,000	$260,000
Total owner's equity	340,000	380,000	400,000
Total liabilities and owner's equity	$730,000	$700,000	$660,000

REQUIRED

Analyze these financial statement data to decide whether the bank should lend $400,000 to Nippon Sales Company. Consider the performance of net income and ending capital from year to year, and the changes in total liabilities in making your decision. Write a one-paragraph report to the bank's loan committee.

Transaction analysis, effects on financial statements **(*Obj. 4*)**

BN1-2 Camp Penuel conducts summer camps for children with disabilities. Jim and Virginia Campbell operate the camp as their life work near Gainesville, Texas. Because of the nature of its business, the camp experiences many unusual transactions. Evaluate each of the following transactions in terms of its effect on Camp Penuel's income statement and balance sheet.

1. A camper suffered an injury that was not covered by insurance. Camp Penuel paid $800 for the child's medical care. How does this transaction affect the camp's income statement and balance sheet?
2. Camp Penuel sold land adjacent to the camp for $190,000, receiving cash of $50,000 and a note receivable for $140,000. When purchased five years earlier, the land cost Camp Penuel $120,000. How should the camp account for the sale of the land?
3. One camper's father is a physician. Camp Penuel allows this child to attend camp in return for the father's serving part-time in the camp infirmary for the two-week term. The standard fee for a camp term is $1,000. The physician's salary for this part-time work would be $1,000. How should Camp Penuel account for this arrangement?
4. A tornado damaged the camp dining hall. The cost to repair the damage will be $8,000 over and above what the insurance company will pay.

ETHICAL ISSUES

ETHICAL ISSUE 1. The oil spill of the Exxon *Valdez* tanker off the coast of Alaska continues to plague Exxon, the giant petroleum company. More than ten years later, Exxon's financial statements still report the accident's effects on the company. At the time of the accident, it appeared that the damage to Exxon could be gigantic. Generally accepted accounting principles require companies to report in their financial statements the effects of potential losses that the company might suffer as a result of past events.

REQUIRED

1. Suppose you are the chief financial officer (CFO) responsible for the financial statements of Exxon Corporation. What ethical issue would you face as you consider what to report in Exxon's annual report about the *Valdez* oil spill? What is the ethical course of action for the Exxon's CFO to take in this situation?
2. What are some of the negative consequences to Exxon of not telling the truth? What are some of the negative consequences to Exxon of telling the truth?

ETHICAL ISSUE 2. The board of directors of Ultramar Corporation is meeting to discuss the past year's results before releasing financial statements to the public. The discussion includes this exchange:

Lisa Todd, company president:	"Well, this has not been a good year! Revenue is down and expenses are up—way up. If we don't do some fancy stepping, we'll report a loss for the third year in a row. I can temporarily transfer some land that I own into the company's name, and that will beef up our balance sheet. Ralph, can you shave $500,000 from expenses? Then we can probably get the bank loan that we need."
Ralph Nettle, company chief accountant:	"Lisa, you are asking too much. Generally accepted accounting principles are designed to keep this sort of thing from happening."

REQUIRED

1. What is the fundamental ethical issue in this situation?
2. Discuss how Lisa Todd's proposals violate generally accepted accounting principles. Identify the specific concept or principle involved.

Problems (GROUP A)

Entity concept, transaction analysis, accounting equation
(Obj. 2, 4)

P1-1A Gwen Blake practiced law with a partnership for ten years after graduating from law school. Recently she resigned her position to open her own law office, which she operates as a proprietorship. The name of the new entity is Gwen Blake, Attorney. Blake experienced the following events during the organizing phase of her new business and its first month of operations. Some of the events were personal and did not affect the law practice. Others were business transactions and should be accounted for by the business.

July	1	Blake sold 1,000 shares of Eastman Kodak stock, which she had owned for several years, receiving $68,000 cash from her stockbroker.
	2	Blake deposited in her personal bank account the $68,000 cash from sale of the Eastman Kodak stock.
	3	Blake received $150,000 cash from her former partners in the law firm from which she resigned.
	5	Blake deposited $100,000 cash in a new business bank account entitled Gwen Blake, Attorney.
	6	A representative of a large company telephoned Blake and told her of the company's intention to transfer its legal business to the new entity of Gwen Blake, Attorney.

July 7 Blake paid $550 cash for letterhead stationery for her new law office.
9 Blake purchased office furniture for the law office, agreeing to pay the account payable, $9,500, within three months.
23 Blake finished court hearings on behalf of a client and submitted her bill for legal services, $3,000. She expected to collect from this client within one month.
30 Blake paid office rent, $1,900.
31 Blake withdrew $3,500 cash from the business for personal living expenses.

REQUIRED

1. Classify each of the preceding events as one of the following:
   a. A business transaction to be accounted for by the proprietorship of Gwen Blake, Attorney.
   b. A business-related event but not a transaction to be accounted for by the proprietorship of Gwen Blake, Attorney.
   c. A personal transaction not to be accounted for by the proprietorship of Gwen Blake, Attorney.
2. Analyze the effects of the above events on the accounting equation of the proprietorship of Gwen Blake, Attorney. Use a format similar to Exhibit 1-6.

Balance sheet
(Obj. 2, 5)

P1-2A The bookkeeper of Dole Editorial Service prepared the balance sheet of the company while the accountant was ill. The balance sheet contains numerous errors. In particular, the bookkeeper knew that the balance sheet should balance, so he plugged in the owner's equity amount needed to achieve this balance. The owner's equity amount, however, is not correct. All other amounts are accurate.

DOLE EDITORIAL SERVICE
Balance Sheet
Month Ended October 31, 19X7

Assets		**Liabilities**	
Cash	$ 3,400	Notes receivable	$14,000
Insurance expense	300	Interest expense	2,000
Land	31,500	Office supplies	800
Salary expense	3,300	Accounts receivable	2,600
Office furniture	6,700	Note payable	21,000
Accounts payable	3,000	**Owner's Equity**	
Utilities expense	2,100		
		Owner's equity	9,900
Total assets	$50,300	Total liabilities	$50,300

REQUIRED

1. Prepare the correct balance sheet, and date it correctly. Compute total assets, total liabilities, and owner's equity.
2. Identify the accounts that should *not* be presented on the balance sheet and state why you excluded them from the correct balance sheet you prepared for requirement 1.

Balance sheet, entity concept
(Obj. 2, 3, 5)

P1-3A Raj Imani is a realtor. He buys and sells properties on his own, and he also earns commission as a real estate agent for buyers and sellers. He organized his business as a proprietorship on March 10, 19X2. Consider the following facts as of March 31, 19X2:

a. Imani had $10,000 in his personal bank account and $6,000 in his business bank account.
b. Office supplies on hand at the real estate office totaled $1,000.
c. Imani's business had spent $15,000 for an Electronic Realty Associates (ERA) franchise, which entitled Imani to represent himself as an ERA agent. ERA is a national affiliation of independent real estate agents. This franchise is a business asset.
d. Imani owed $33,000 on a note payable for some undeveloped land that had been acquired by his business for a total price of $60,000.
e. Imani owed $65,000 on a personal mortgage on his personal residence, which he acquired in 19X1 for a total price of $90,000.
f. Imani owed $950 on a personal charge account with Sears.
g. Imani had acquired business furniture for $12,000 on March 26. Of this amount, Imani's business owed $6,000 on open account at March 31.

REQUIRED

1. Prepare the balance sheet of the real estate business of Raj Imani, Realtor, at March 31, 19X2.
2. Identify the personal items that would not be reported on the balance sheet of the business.

Business transactions and analysis
(Obj. 4)

P1-4A Colonial Shell Oil Company was recently formed. The balance of each item in the company's accounting equation follows for April 4 and for each of the nine business days given:

	Cash	Accounts Receivable	Supplies	Land	Accounts Payable	Owner's Equity
Apr. 4	$3,000	$7,000	$ 800	$11,000	$3,800	$18,000
9	6,000	4,000	800	11,000	3,800	18,000
14	4,000	4,000	800	11,000	1,800	18,000
17	4,000	4,000	1,100	11,000	2,100	18,000
19	5,000	4,000	1,100	11,000	2,100	19,000
20	3,900	4,000	1,100	11,000	1,000	19,000
22	9,900	4,000	1,100	5,000	1,000	19,000
25	9,900	4,200	900	5,000	1,000	19,000
26	9,700	4,200	1,100	5,000	1,000	19,000
28	4,600	4,200	1,100	5,000	1,000	13,900

REQUIRED

Assuming that a single transaction took place on each day, describe briefly the transaction that was most likely to have occurred beginning with April 9. Indicate which accounts were increased or decreased and by what amount. No revenues or expense transactions occurred on these dates.

Income statement, statement of owner's equity, balance sheet
(Obj. 5)

P1-5A The amounts of (a) the assets and liabilities of Inkjet Supply Co. as of December 31, 19X4, and (b) the revenues and expenses of the company for the year ended on that date follow. The items are listed in alphabetical order.

Accounts payable	**$12,000**	**Note payable**	**$ 31,000**
Accounts receivable	**3,000**	**Property tax expense**	**2,000**
Building	**56,000**	**Rent expense**	**14,000**
Cash	**1,000**	**Salary expense**	**38,000**
Equipment	**21,000**	**Service revenue**	**104,000**
Interest expense	**4,000**	**Supplies**	**7,000**
Interest payable	**1,000**	**Utilities expense**	**3,000**
Land	**8,000**		

The beginning amount of Jana Sneller, Capital, was $41,000, and during the year Sneller withdrew $32,000 for personal use.

REQUIRED

1. Prepare the income statement of Inkjet Supply Co. for the year ended December 31, 19X4.
2. Prepare the company's statement of owner's equity for the year ended December 31, 19X4.
3. Prepare the company's balance sheet at December 31, 19X4.
4. Answer these questions about the company.
   a. Was the result of operations for the year a profit or a loss? How much?
   b. Did Sneller, the owner of the business, drain off all its earnings for the year, or did she build the company's capital during the period? How would her actions affect the company's ability to borrow in the future?
   c. How much in total economic resources does the company have as it moves into the new year? How much does the company owe? What is the dollar amount of Sneller's equity interest in the business at the end of the year?

Transaction analysis, accounting equation, financial statements
(Obj. 4, 5)

P1-6A Dan Lutz owns and operates an interior design studio called Lutz Design Studio. The following amounts summarize the financial position of his business on April 30, 19X5:

	Assets				=	**Liabilities**	+	**Owner's Equity**
	Cash +	**Accounts Receivable +**	**Supplies +**	**Land**	=	**Accounts Payable**	+	**Dan Lutz, Capital**
Bal.	1,720	2,240		24,100		5,400		22,660

During May 19X5, the following events occurred.

a. Lutz received $12,000 as a gift and deposited the cash in the business bank account.
b. Paid off the beginning balance of accounts payable.
c. Performed services for a client and received cash of $1,100.
d. Collected cash from a customer on account, $750.
e. Purchased supplies on account, $720.

f. Consulted on the interior design of a major office building and billed the client for services rendered, $5,000.
g. Invested personal cash of $1,700 in the business.
h. Recorded the following business expenses for the month:
   (1) Paid office rent—$1,200.
   (2) Paid advertising—$660.
i. Sold supplies to another interior designer for $80 cash, which was the cost of the supplies.
j. Withdrew cash of $1,400 for personal use.

REQUIRED

1. Analyze the effects of the preceding transactions on the accounting equation of Lutz Design Studio. Adapt the format of Exhibit 1-6.
2. Prepare the income statement of Lutz Design Studio for the month ended May 31, 19X5. List expenses in decreasing order by amount.
3. Prepare the statement of owner's equity of Lutz Design Studio for the month ended May 31, 19X5.
4. Prepare the balance sheet of Lutz Design Studio at May 31, 19X5.

Problems (GROUP B)

Entity concept, transaction analysis, accounting equation
(Obj. 2, 4)

P1-1B Rod Richey practiced law with a partnership for five years after graduating from law school. Recently he resigned his position to open his own law office, which he operates as a proprietorship. The name of the new entity is Rod Richey, Attorney. Richey experienced the following events during the organizing phase of his new business and its first month of operations. Some of the events were personal and did not affect his law practice. Others were business transactions and should be accounted for by the business.

Feb. 4	Richey received $80,000 cash from his former partners in the law firm from which he resigned.
5	Richey deposited $60,000 cash in a new business bank account entitled Rod Richey, Attorney.
6	Richey paid $300 cash for letterhead stationery for his new law office.
7	Richey purchased office furniture for his law office. He agreed to pay the account payable, $7,000, within six months.
10	Richey sold 500 shares of IBM stock, which he and his wife had owned for several years, receiving $75,000 cash from his stockbroker.
11	Richey deposited the $75,000 cash from sale of the IBM stock in his personal bank account.
12	A representative of a large company telephoned Richey and told him of the company's intention to transfer its legal business to the new entity of Rod Richey, Attorney.
18	Richey finished court hearings on behalf of a client and submitted his bill for legal services, $5,000. Richey expected to collect from this client within two weeks.
25	Richey paid office rent, $1,000.
28	Richey withdrew $1,000 cash from the business for personal living expenses.

REQUIRED

1. Classify each of the preceding events as one of the following:
   a. A business transaction to be accounted for by the proprietorship of Rod Richey, Attorney.
   b. A business-related event but not a transaction to be accounted for by the proprietorship of Rod Richey, Attorney.
   c. A personal transaction not to be accounted for by the proprietorship of Rod Richey, Attorney.
2. Analyze the effects of the above events on the accounting equation of the proprietorship of Rod Richey, Attorney. Use a format similar to that in Exhibit 1-6.

Balance sheet
(Obj. 2, 5)

P1-2B The bookkeeper of Forté Publishing Co. prepared the balance sheet of the company while the accountant was ill. The balance sheet contains numerous errors. In particular, the bookkeeper knew that the balance sheet should balance, so he plugged in the owner's equity amount needed to achieve this balance. The owner's equity amount, however, is not correct. All other amounts are accurate.

FORTÉ PUBLISHING CO.
Balance Sheet
Month Ended July 31, 19X3

Assets		Liabilities	
Cash	$12,000	Accounts receivable	$ 3,000
Office supplies	1,000	Service revenue	68,000
Land	44,000	Property tax expense	800
Salary expense	2,500	Accounts payable	9,000
Office furniture	10,000	**Owner's Equity**	
Note payable	16,000		
Rent expense	4,000	Owner's equity	8,700
Total assets	$89,500	Total liabilities	$89,500

REQUIRED

1. Prepare the correct balance sheet, and date it correctly. Compute total assets, total liabilities, and owner's equity.
2. Identify the accounts that should *not* be presented on the balance sheet and state why you excluded them from the correct balance sheet you prepared for requirement 1.

Balance sheet, entity concept
(Obj. 2, 3, 5)

P1-3B Celina Garcia is a realtor. She buys and sells properties on her own, and she also earns commissions as a real estate agent for buyers and sellers. She organized her business as a proprietorship on November 24, 19X4. Consider the following facts as of November 30, 19X4:

a. Garcia owed $45,000 on a note payable for some undeveloped land that had been acquired by her business for a total price of $100,000.
b. Garcia's business had spent $20,000 for a Century 21 real estate franchise, which entitled her to represent herself as a Century 21 agent. Century 21 is a national affiliation of independent real estate agents. This franchise is a business asset.
c. Garcia owed $80,000 on a personal mortgage on her personal residence, which she acquired in 19X1 for a total price of $120,000.
d. Garcia had $10,000 in her personal bank account and $12,000 in her business bank account.
e. Garcia owed $1,800 on a personal charge account with Neiman-Marcus Department Store.
f. Garcia acquired business furniture for $17,000 on November 25. Of this amount, her business owed $6,000 on open account at November 30.
g. Office supplies on hand at the real estate office totaled $1,000.

REQUIRED

1. Prepare the balance sheet of the real estate business of Celina Garcia, Realtor, at November 30, 19X4.
2. Identify the personal items that would not be reported on the balance sheet of the business.

Business transactions and analysis
(Obj. 4)

P1-4B Trevelli Company was recently formed. The balance of each item in the company's accounting equation is shown for October 10 and for each of the nine following business days.

	Cash	Accounts Receivable	Supplies	Land	Accounts Payable	Owner's Equity
Oct. 10	$ 8,000	$4,000	$1,000	$ 8,000	$4,000	$17,000
11	13,000	4,000	1,000	8,000	4,000	22,000
12	6,000	4,000	1,000	15,000	4,000	22,000
15	6,000	4,000	3,000	15,000	6,000	22,000
16	5,000	4,000	3,000	15,000	5,000	22,000
17	7,000	2,000	3,000	15,000	5,000	22,000
18	16,000	2,000	3,000	15,000	5,000	31,000
19	13,000	2,000	3,000	15,000	2,000	31,000
22	11,000	2,000	5,000	15,000	2,000	31,000
23	3,000	2,000	5,000	15,000	2,000	23,000

REQUIRED

Assuming that a single transaction took place on each day, describe briefly the transaction that was most likely to have occurred, beginning with October 11. Indicate which accounts were increased or decreased and by what amount. No revenue or expense transactions occurred on these dates.

Income statement, statement of owner's equity, balance sheet
(Obj. 5)

P1-5B Presented below are the amounts of (a) the assets and liabilities of Far Side Talent Search as of December 31, and (b) the revenues and expenses of the company for the year ended on that date. The items are listed in alphabetical order.

Accounts payable	**$ 19,000**	**Note payable**	**$ 85,000**
Accounts receivable	**12,000**	**Property tax expense**	**4,000**
Advertising expense	**13,000**	**Rent expense**	**23,000**
Building	**170,000**	**Salary expense**	**63,000**
Cash	**10,000**	**Salary payable**	**1,000**
Equipment	**20,000**	**Service revenue**	**184,000**
Interest expense	**9,000**	**Supplies**	**3,000**
Land	**60,000**	**Insurance expense**	**2,000**

The beginning amount of Chris Wilke, Capital, was $150,000, and during the year Wilke withdrew $50,000 for personal use.

REQUIRED

1. Prepare the entity's income statement for the year ended December 31 of the current year.
2. Prepare the company's statement of owner's equity for the year ended December 31.
3. Prepare the company's balance sheet at December 31.
4. Answer these questions about the company:
   a. Was the result of operations for the year a profit or a loss? How much?
   b. Did Wilke, the owner of the business, drain off all its earnings for the year, or did he build the company's capital during the period? How would his actions affect the company's ability to borrow in the furture?
   c. How much in total economic resources does the company have as it moves into the new year? How much does the company owe? What is the dollar amount of Wilke's equity interest in the business at the end of the year?

Transaction analysis, accounting equation, financial statements **(Obj. 4, 5)**

P1-6B Courtney Rolfe owns and operates an interior design studio called Rolfe Interiors. The following amounts summarize the financial position of her business on August 31, 19X2:

	Assets							=	Liabilities	+	Owner's Equity
	Cash	+	Accounts Receivable	+	Supplies	+	Land	=	Accounts Payable	+	Courtney Rolfe, Capital
Bal.	1,250		1,500				12,000		8,000		6,750

During September 19X2, the following events occurred.

a. Rolfe inherited $20,000 and deposited the cash in the business bank account.
b. Performed services for a client and received cash of $700.
c. Paid off the beginning balance of accounts payable.
d. Purchased supplies on account, $1,000.
e. Collected cash from a customer on account, $1,000.
f. Invested personal cash of $1,000 in the business.
g. Consulted on the interior design of a major office building and billed the client for services rendered, $2,400.
h. Recorded the following business expenses for the month:
   (1) Paid office rent—$900.
   (2) Paid advertising—$100.
i. Sold supplies to another business for $150 cash, which was the cost of the supplies.
j. Withdrew cash of $1,100 for personal use.

REQUIRED

1. Analyze the effects of the preceding transactions on the accounting equation of Rolfe Interiors. Adapt the format of Exhibit 1-6.
2. Prepare the income statement of Rolfe Interiors for the month ended September 30, 19X2. List expenses in decreasing order by amount.
3. Prepare the entity's statement of owner's equity for the month ended September 30, 19X2.
4. Prepare the balance sheet of Rolfe Interiors at September 30, 19X2.

Applying Your Knowledge

DECISION CASES

Using financial statements to evaluate a request for a loan **(Obj. 1, 2, 6)**

CASE 1. The proprietors of two businesses, A.C. Schmidt Company and Donna Samuels Executive Search, have sought business loans from you. To decide whether to make the loans, you have requested their balance sheets.

A.C. SCHMIDT COMPANY Balance Sheet August 31, 19X4			
Assets		**Liabilities**	
Cash	$ 9,000	Accounts payable	$ 12,000
Accounts receivable	14,000	Note payable	18,000
Merchandise inventory	85,000	Total liabilities	30,000
Store supplies	500	**Owner's Equity**	
Furniture and fixtures	9,000		
Building	82,000	A.C. Schmidt, capital	183,500
Land	14,000	Total liabilities	
Total assets	$213,500	and owner's equity	$213,500

DONNA SAMUELS EXECUTIVE SEARCH Balance Sheet August 31, 19X4			
Assets		**Liabilities**	
Cash	$ 11,000	Accounts payable	$ 3,000
Accounts receivable	4,000	Note payable	168,000
Office supplies	1,000	Total liabilities	171,000
Office furniture	56,000	**Owner's Equity**	
Land	169,000		
		Donna Samuels, capital	70,000
		Total liabilities	
Total assets	$241,000	and owner's equity	$241,000

REQUIRED

1. Solely on the basis of these balance sheets, to which entity would you be more comfortable lending money? Explain fully, citing specific items and amounts from the balance sheets.
2. In addition to the balance sheet data, what other information would you require? Be specific.

Using accounting information **(*Obj. 1, 2, 3, 4, 5*)**

CASE 2. A friend learns that you are taking an accounting course. Knowing that you do not plan a career in accounting, the friend asks you why you are "wasting your time." Explain to the friend:

1. Why you are taking the course.
2. How accounting information is used and will be used
   a. In your personal life.
   b. In the business life of your friend, who plans to be a farmer.
   c. In the business life of another friend who plans a career in sales.

FINANCIAL STATEMENT CASES

Identifying items from a company's financial statements **(*Obj. 4*)**

CASE 1. This and similar problems in later chapters focus on the financial statements of a real company—NIKE, Inc., which is famous for sporting goods. As you work each problem, you will build your confidence in understanding and using the financial statements of real companies.

Refer to the NIKE financial statements in Appendix A at the end of the book.

REQUIRED

1. How much in cash (including cash equivalents) did NIKE, Inc., have on May 31, 1997?
2. What were the company's total assets at May 31, 1997? At May 31, 1996?
3. Write the company's accounting equation at May 31, 1997, by filling in the dollar amounts:

   Assets = Liabilities + Stockholders' Equity

   NIKE treats Redeemable Preferred Stock as a liability.
4. Identify total revenue for the year ended May 31, 1997. How much did total revenue increase or decrease in fiscal year 1997?
5. How much net income or net loss did NIKE experience for the year ended May 31, 1997? Was the year ended May 31, 1997, a good year or a bad year compared to the preceding year? State your reasons.

CASE 2. Obtain the annual report of a company of your choosing. Annual reports are available in various forms, including the original document in hard copy available in libraries and computerized databases that are available by visiting the company's Web site. Answer the following questions about the company. Concentrate on the current year in the annual report you select, except as directed for particular questions.

Identifying items from a company's financial statements
(Obj. 4)

REQUIRED

1. How much in cash (which may include cash equivalents) did the company have at the end of the current year? At the end of the preceding year? Did cash increase or decrease during the current year? By how much?
2. What were total assets at the end of the current year? At the end of the preceding year?
3. Write the company's accounting equation at the end of the current year by filling in the dollar amounts:

Assets = Liabilities + Owners' (or Stockholders') Equity

4. Identify net sales revenue for the current year. The company may label this as Net sales, Sales, Net revenue, or other title. How much was the corresponding revenue amount for the preceding year?
5. How much net income or net loss did the company experience for the current year? For the preceding year? Evaluate the current year's operations in comparison with the preceding year.

Team Projects

PROJECT 1. You are promoting a rock concert in your area. Your purpose is to earn a profit, so you will need to establish the business. Assume you organize as a proprietorship.

REQUIRED

1. Make a detailed list of ten factors you must consider to establish the business.
2. Describe ten of the items your business must arrange in order to promote and stage the rock concert.
3. Prepare your business's income statement, statement of owner's equity, and balance sheet on August 31, 19XX, immediately after the rock concert and, before you have had time to pay all the business's bills and to collect all receivables. Use made-up amounts, and include a complete heading for each financial statement. For the income statement and the statement of owner's equity, assume the period is the three months ended August 31, 19XX.
4. Assume that you will continue to promote rock concerts if the venture is successful. If it is unsuccessful, you will terminate the business within three months after the concert. Discuss how you will evaluate the success of your venture and how you will decide whether to continue in business.

PROJECT 2. You are opening a pet kennel. Your purpose is to earn a profit, so you will need to establish the business. Assume you organize as a proprietorship.

1. Make a detailed list of ten factors you must consider to establish the business.
2. Identify ten or more transactions that your business will undertake to open and operate the kennel.
3. Prepare the kennel's income statement, statement of owner's equity, and balance sheet at the end of the first month of operations before you have had time to pay all the business's bills. Use made-up figures and include a complete heading for each financial statement. Date the balance sheet as of August 31, 19XX.
4. Discuss how you will evaluate the success of your business and how you will decide whether to continue its operation.

INTERNET TOUR ▪ FINANCIAL ACCOUNTING

The Internet: Why?

Most people have heard of the Internet, even if they have not yet experienced it. The Internet is a worldwide structure linking computers across the globe.

Your knowledge of the Internet may come from three sources: communication (e-mail), business transactions (buying CDs over the Internet), and information (researching a paper). Perhaps you have sent or received electronic mail. Many universities are in the process of converting their systems to widespread Internet usage so that every student has an electronic mail address and easy access. When up and working, students can communicate over the Internet with their teachers or with each other, collaborating on homework assignments or team projects.

You may be familiar with the Internet because you have bought things over it. Though the extent of business transactions over the Internet is still small, this will change as security improves and people become more comfortable with making purchases electronically. Catalogue retailers such as Lands' End and L. L. Bean have witnessed a growing volume of business over the Internet. In fact, the bookseller Amazon.com is a purely electronic business.

The full power of the Internet can be seen in its third function: as an information provider. This is where it stands out as a vital tool for business persons. The Internet provides masses of convenient and timely information.

The Starting Point: Accounting on the Internet via The Rutgers Accounting Web (RAW)

The starting point for your tour of the accounting resources over the Internet should be the Rutgers Accounting Web (RAW). You access this by going to

http://www.rutgers.edu/accounting

The RAW plays such an important role for the accounting profession because of the extent of the information it provides — almost everything you want can be found by starting here, from recent statements made by the Financial Accounting Standards Board to Security and Exchange Commission filings made by public companies to career

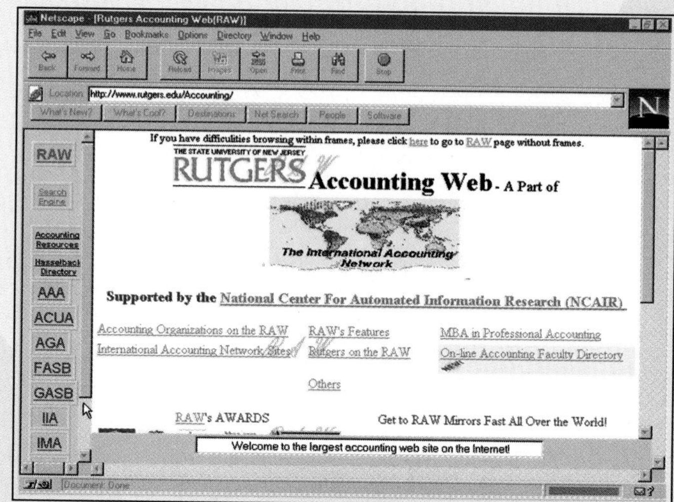

opportunities with the big accounting firms. The Rutgers Accounting Web holds a wealth of riches.

When you arrive at the Rutgers Accounting Web's home page, click on **RAW's Features.** On the next page that comes up, click on **Accounting Resources on the Internet.** You will notice a large number of destinations. Let's try one, with one warning. Contents and addresses often change on web sites, so be prepared to do a little sleuthing at times.

Governing Boards

Let's go to the Financial Accounting Standards Board home page. Click on the FASB box, and then click on **Table of Contents.** What kinds of information are avail-

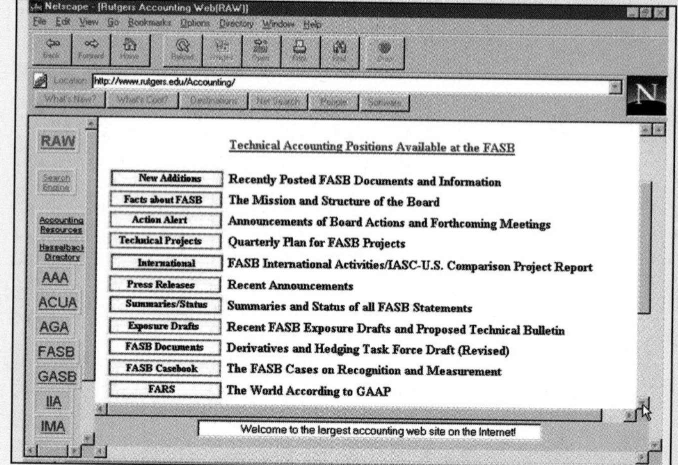

able for the financial accountant? From the home page, you can obtain and read all FASB statements. But there is more to this home page than a simple reference feature. Note that you can also see recent pronouncements and exposure drafts of pronouncements in process. This lets you see potential changes in accounting rules.

For example, you can call up the draft made by the Derivatives and Hedging Task Force. You will learn more about derivatives and hedging later. For now, just recognize that this is a pressing issue in financial reporting.

Edgar

The Securities and Exchange Commission regularly receives filings of financial information from public companies. Rather than wait for a company to mail you its quarterly or annual report, you can retrieve these electronically through the SEC's EDGAR database. EDGAR stands for Electronic Data Gathering, Analysis, and Retrieval system. Again, you can access this through the RAW, or go to

http://www.sec.gov/edgarhp.htm

Here you have a wealth of information in a convenient, cost-efficient, and timely format.

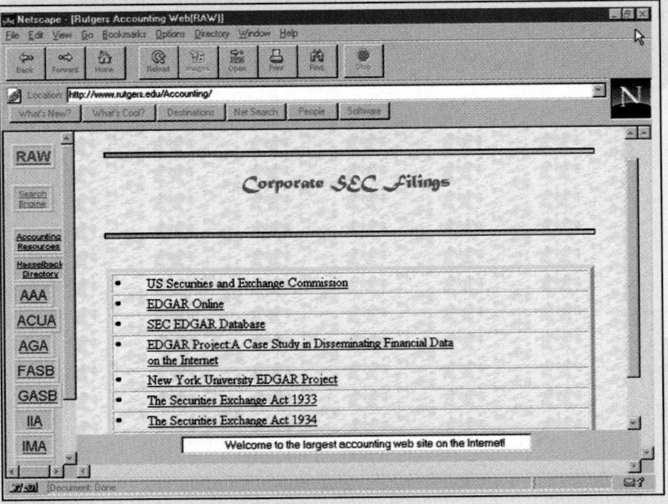

Individual Companies

While you can stay within the confines of the RAW and obtain lots of information on financial reporting standards and individual companies, it is usually worth it to go directly to a company itself. Many public companies have web sites that provide product information and financial information. Think of it this way: A public company may release results in a press announcement and then mail more complete results to individual shareholders and interested parties; by putting these results on its Web site, individual parties can gain immediate access to this information. For example, by going to

http://www.NIKE.com

you can reach NIKE's home page and then go to NIKE's financial statements by clicking on **NIKEbiz.** The latest quarterly earnings report is often linked to this business opening page. You can view the latest annual report by clicking the **Investors** button.

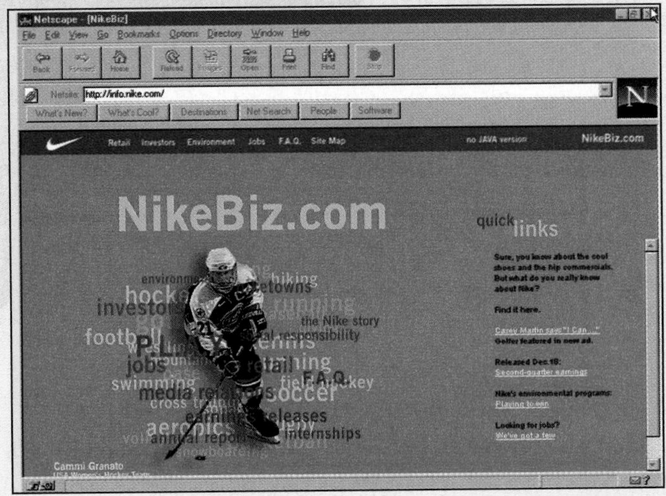

The Internet is ideally suited to provide financial information quickly, conveniently, and inexpensively. But there is more to the Internet than this — from career information to guidelines for making ethical decisions. Continue your tour on page 856 at the end of Chapter 19 to see what other riches await you on the Internet. ■

CHAPTER 2

Recording Business Transactions

LEARNING OBJECTIVES

After studying this chapter, you should be able to

1. Define and use key accounting terms: *account*, *ledger*, *debit*, and *credit*
2. Apply the rules of debit and credit
3. Record transactions in the journal
4. Post from the journal to the ledger
5. Prepare and use a trial balance
6. Set up a chart of accounts for a business
7. Analyze transactions without a journal

> *I want everything that appears in the Lands' End annual report to help the potential shareholder or the active shareholder to understand the business.*
>
> —CHARLOTTE LA COMB, MANAGER, INVESTOR RELATIONS, LANDS' END

Like all other companies, Lands' End—the well-known direct-marketing company—represents itself to outsiders through its financial statements. But the accounting information is also used internally. Lands' End managers at all levels use financial statement data for decision making. For example, when you phone Lands' End with an order, the company can tell you whether the goods are available because the accounting records show the amount of inventory on hand. And how does the company know when its liabilities are due and how much to pay for them? Again, the accounting records provide the information.

Chapter 1 introduced transaction analysis and the financial statements. But that chapter did not show how the financial statements are prepared. Chapters 2, 3, and 4 cover the accounting process that results in the financial statements.

Chapter 2 discusses the processing of accounting information as it is done in practice. Throughout this and the next two chapters, we continue to illustrate accounting procedures with service businesses, such as Gary Lyon, CPA, a law practice, or a sports franchise like the Chicago Bulls. In Chapter 5, we move into merchandising businesses such as Macy's and Wal-Mart. All these businesses use the basic accounting system that we illustrate in this book.

By learning how accounting information is processed, you will understand where the facts and figures reported in the financial statements come from. This knowledge will increase your confidence as you make decisions. It will also speed your progress in your business career.

Objective 1

Define and use key accounting terms: *account, ledger, debit,* and *credit*

The Account

Account. The detailed record of the changes that have occurred in a particular asset, liability, or owner's equity during a period. The basic summary device of accounting.

Ledger. The book of accounts.

In Chapter 1, p. 12, we learned that the accounting equation is the accountant's most basic tool. It measures the assets of the business and the claims to those assets.

The basic summary device of accounting is the **account,** the detailed record of the changes that have occurred in a particular asset, liability, or owner's equity during a period of time. For convenient access to the information, accounts are grouped in a record called the **ledger.** In the phrases "keeping the books" and "auditing the books," *books* refers to the ledger. Today the ledger usually takes the form of a computer listing.

Accounts are grouped in three broad categories, according to the accounting equation:

ASSETS = LIABILITIES + OWNER'S EQUITY

Assets

Assets are economic resources that benefit the business and will continue to do so in the future. Most firms use the following asset accounts.

CASH The Cash account shows the cash effects of a business's transactions. Cash includes money and any medium of exchange that a bank accepts at face value, such as bank account balances, paper currency, coins, certificates of deposit, and checks. Successful companies such as Lands' End usually have plenty of cash. Most business failures result from a shortage of cash.

NOTES RECEIVABLE A business may sell its goods or services in exchange for a *promissory note,* which is a written pledge that the customer will pay a fixed amount of money by a certain date. The Notes Receivable account is a record of the promissory notes the business expects to collect in cash. A note receivable offers more security for collection than a mere account receivable does.

ACCOUNTS RECEIVABLE A business may sell its goods or services in exchange for an oral or implied promise of future cash receipt. Such sales are made on credit ("on account"). The Accounts Receivable account contains these amounts. Most sales in the United States and in other developed countries are made on account receivable.

PREPAID EXPENSES A business often pays certain expenses in advance. A *prepaid expense* is an asset because the business avoids having to pay cash in the future for the specified expense. The ledger holds a separate asset account for each prepaid expense. Prepaid Rent, Prepaid Insurance, and Office Supplies are accounted for as prepaid expenses.

LAND The Land account is a record of the cost of land a business owns and uses in its operations. Land held for sale is accounted for separately—in an investment account.

BUILDING The cost of a business's buildings—office, warehouse, garage, and the like—appear in the Building account. Lands' End owns buildings that house its company headquarters in Dodgeville, Wisconsin. Buildings held for sale are separate assets accounted for as investments.

EQUIPMENT, FURNITURE, AND FIXTURES A business has a separate asset account for each type of equipment—Office Equipment and Store Equipment, for example. The Furniture and Fixtures account shows the cost of this asset, which is similar to equipment.

We will discuss other asset categories and accounts as needed. For example, many businesses have an Investments account for their investments in the stocks and bonds of other companies.

Liabilities

Recall that a *liability* is a debt. A business generally has fewer liability accounts than asset accounts because a business's liabilities can be summarized under relatively few categories.

NOTES PAYABLE The Notes Payable account is the opposite of the Notes Receivable account. Notes Payable represents the amounts that the business must pay because it signed promissory notes to borrow money or to purchase goods or services.

ACCOUNTS PAYABLE The Accounts Payable account is the opposite of the Accounts Receivable account. The oral or implied promise to pay off debts arising from credit purchases appears in the Accounts Payable account. Such a purchase is said to be made on account. All companies, including Lands' End, have accounts payable.

ACCRUED LIABILITIES An *accrued liability* is a liability for an expense that has not been paid. Accrued liability accounts are added as needed. Taxes Payable, Interest Payable, and Salary Payable are liability accounts of most companies.

Owner's Equity

The owner's claim to the assets of the business is called *owner's equity*. Lands' End started out as a proprietorship when Gary Comer launched the business out of his garage. In a proprietorship or a partnership, owner's equity is split into separate accounts for the owner's capital balance and the owner's withdrawals.

CAPITAL The Capital account shows the owner's claim to the assets of the business, whether it is Gary Comer, the founder of Lands' End or Gary Lyon, CPA. After total liabilities are subtracted from total assets, the remainder is the owner's capital. Amounts received from the owner's investments in the business are recorded directly in the Capital account. The Capital balance equals the owner's investments in the business plus its net income and minus net losses and owner withdrawals over the entire life of the business.

See the statement of owner's equity in Chapter 1, p. 21.

WITHDRAWALS When Gary Lyon, CPA, withdraws cash or other assets from the business for personal use, the business's assets and owner's equity decrease. The amounts taken out of the business appear in a separate account entitled Gary Lyon, Withdrawals, or Gary Lyon, Drawing. If withdrawals were recorded directly in the Capital account, the amount of owner withdrawals would not be highlighted and decision making would be more difficult. The Withdrawals account shows a *decrease* in owner's equity.

REVENUES The increase in owner's equity created by delivering goods or services to customers or clients is called *revenue*. The ledger contains as many revenue accounts as needed. Gary Lyon's CPA practice would need a Service Revenue account for amounts earned by providing accounting services for clients. If a business lends money to an outsider, it will need an Interest Revenue account for the interest earned on the loan. If the business rents a building to a tenant, it will need a Rent Revenue account.

EXPENSES Expenses use up assets or create liabilities in the course of operating a business. Expenses have the opposite effect of revenues; they *decrease* owner's equity. A business needs a separate account for each type of expense, such as Salary Expense, Rent Expense, Advertising Expense, and Utilities Expense. Businesses of all sizes strive to minimize their expenses in order to maximize net income—whether they be Lands' End or Gary Lyon, CPA.

Exhibit 2-1 shows how asset, liability, and owner's equity accounts can be grouped in the ledger.

■ Daily Exercise 2-1

EXHIBIT 2-1
The Ledger (Asset, Liability, and Owner's Equity Accounts)

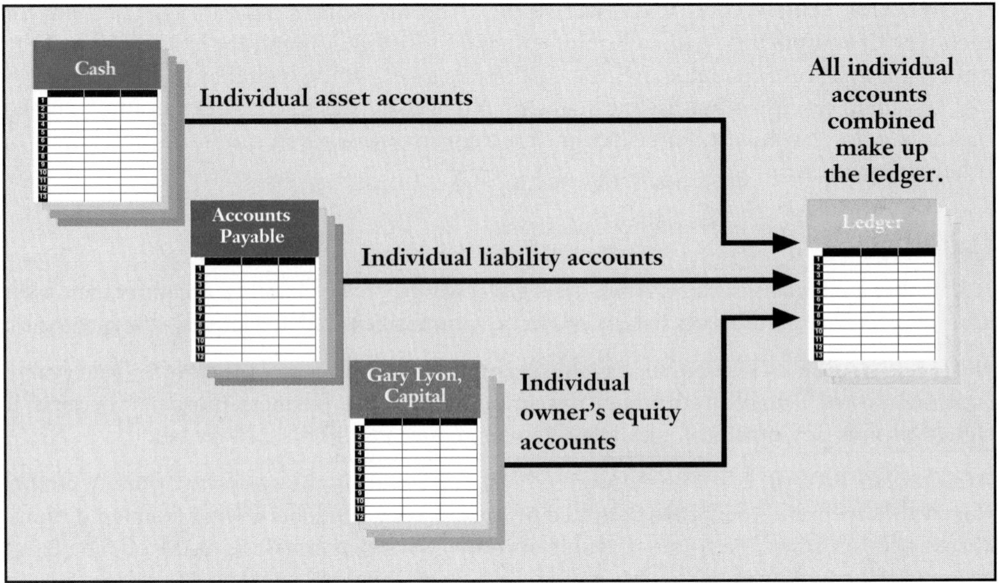

PUTTING SKILLS TO WORK

THE KEY TO LONG-TERM GROWTH IN BUSINESS

Bill Neely, the founder of B.G. Graphics, a computer graphics and desktop publishing company in Silver Spring, Maryland, likens revenues and expenses to a foot race. "No person can win a 26-mile race by sprinting," says Neely. "The runner is spending energy (expenses) to obtain speed and distance (revenues). But he or she should be aiming for the revenue of endurance instead."

Neely, a Howard University graduate, established his company when he was a sophomore. The journalism major bought his first computer system with money he had received from a scholarship. By using the computer to provide graphic design services, Neely was able to *make* money (revenue).

Within two years, B.G. Graphics' gross income was $80,000, and its expenses were $38,000. With net income of $42,000, Neely was able to spend $12,000 for a more powerful computer and expand his services.

"The businessperson is faced with tough decisions," says Neely. "Each purchase must be analyzed in terms of which expense will result in the fastest and greatest amount of revenue. The key to attaining success in business is vision—learning to purchase only assets that are essential to the business's long-term growth."

Bill Neely of B.G. Graphics

Double-Entry Accounting

Accounting is based on a *double-entry system*, which means that we record the *dual effects* of a business transaction. *Each transaction affects at least two accounts*. For example, Gary Lyon's $50,000 cash investment in his accounting practice increased both the Cash account and the Capital account of the business. It would be incomplete to record only the increase in the entity's cash without recording the increase in its owner's equity.

Consider a cash purchase of supplies. What are the dual effects of this transaction? The purchase (1) decreases cash and (2) increases supplies. A purchase of supplies on credit (1) increases supplies and (2) increases accounts payable. A cash payment on account (1) decreases cash and (2) decreases accounts payable. All transactions have at least two effects on the entity.

The T-Account

How do we record transactions? The account format used most widely is called the *T-account* because it takes the form of the capital letter "T." The vertical line in the

T-account divides the account into its left and right sides. The account title rests on the horizontal line. For example, the Cash account of a business appears in the following T-account format:

Cash	
(Left side) *Debit*	(Right Side) *Credit*

The left side of the account is called the **debit** side, and the right side is called the **credit** side. Often beginners in the study of accounting are confused by the words *debit* and *credit*. To become comfortable using them, remember that

Debit. The left side of an account.

Credit. The right side of an account.

Debit = Left side
Credit = Right side

Even though *left side* and *right side* are more descriptive, the terms *debit* and *credit* are deeply entrenched in business.[1] Debit and credit are abbreviated as follows:

- Dr = Debit
- Cr = Credit

Increases and Decreases in the Accounts

The account type determines how increases and decreases in it are recorded. For any given account, all increases are recorded on one side, and all decreases are recorded on the other side. Increases in *assets* are recorded on the left (debit) side of the account. Decreases in assets are recorded on the right (credit) side. Conversely, increases in *liabilities* and *owner's equity* are recorded by *credits*. Decreases in liabilities and owner's equity are recorded by *debits*. These are the *rules of debit and credit*.

Objective 2

Apply the rules of debit and credit

Learning Tip: In everyday conversation, we may praise someone by saying, "She deserves credit for her good work." In your study of accounting, forget this general usage. Remember that *debit means left side* and *credit means right side*. Whether an account is increased or decreased by a debit or a credit depends on the type of account.

In a computerized accounting system, the computer interprets debits and credits as increases or decreases by account type. For example, a computer reads a debit to Cash as an increase to that account and an increase to Accounts Payable as a credit.

This pattern of recording debits and credits is based on the accounting equation:

ASSETS = LIABILITIES + OWNER'S EQUITY

■ Daily Exercise 2-2

Assets are on the opposite side of the equation from liabilities and owner's equity. Therefore, increases and decreases in assets are recorded in the opposite manner from those in liabilities and owner's equity. And liabilities and owner's equity, which are on the same side of the equal sign, are treated in the same way. Exhibit 2-2 shows the relationship between the accounting equation and the rules of debit and credit.

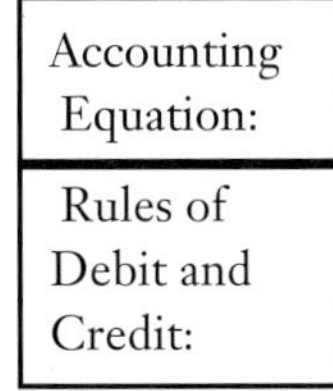

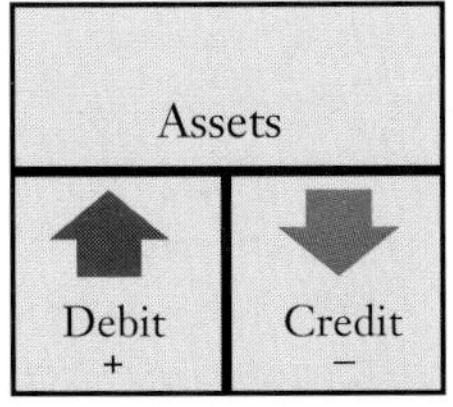

=

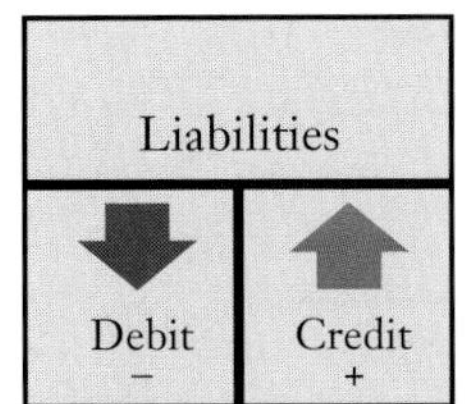

+

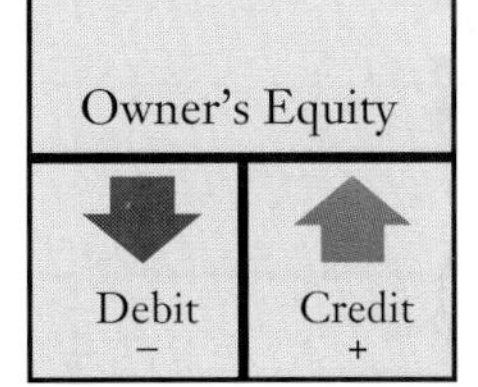

EXHIBIT 2-2
The Accounting Equation and the Rules of Debit and Credit (The Effects of Debits and Credits on Assets, Liabilities, and Owner's Equity)

To illustrate the ideas diagrammed in Exhibit 2-2, reconsider the first transaction from Chapter 1. Gary Lyon invested $50,000 in cash to begin his accounting practice. The business received $50,000 cash from Lyon and gave him the owner's equity in the business. We are accounting for the business entity, Gary Lyon, CPA. Which accounts of the business are affected? By what amounts? On what side (debit or credit)? The answer: The business's Assets and Capital would increase by $50,000, as the following T-accounts show.

[1]The words *debit* and *credit* have a Latin origin (*debitum* and *creditum*). Luca Pacioli, the Italian monk who wrote about accounting in the 15th century, used these terms.

ASSETS	=	LIABILITIES	+	OWNER'S EQUITY
Cash				**Gary Lyon, Capital**
Debit for Increase, 50,000 |				| Credit for Increase, 50,000

Notice that Assets = Liabilities + Owner's Equity *and* that total debit amounts = total credit amounts. Exhibit 2-3 illustrates the accounting equation and Gary Lyon's first three transactions.

The amount remaining in an account is called its *balance*. The first transaction gives Cash a \$50,000 debit balance and Gary Lyon, Capital a \$50,000 credit balance.

Thinking It Over Can you prepare a balance sheet for Gary Lyon's accounting practice after the first transaction on April 2, 19X1? Can you prepare an income statement?

Answer

GARY LYON, CPA
Balance Sheet
April 2, 19X1

Assets		Liabilities	
Cash	\$ 50,000	None	
		Owner's Equity	
		Gary Lyon, capital	\$50,000
		Total liabilities and	
Total assets	\$50,000	owner's equity	\$50,000

You could not yet prepare an income statement because the business has experienced no revenues or expenses.

The second transaction is a \$40,000 cash purchase of land. This transaction affects two assets: Cash and Land. It decreases (credits) Cash and increases (debits) Land, as shown in the T-accounts:

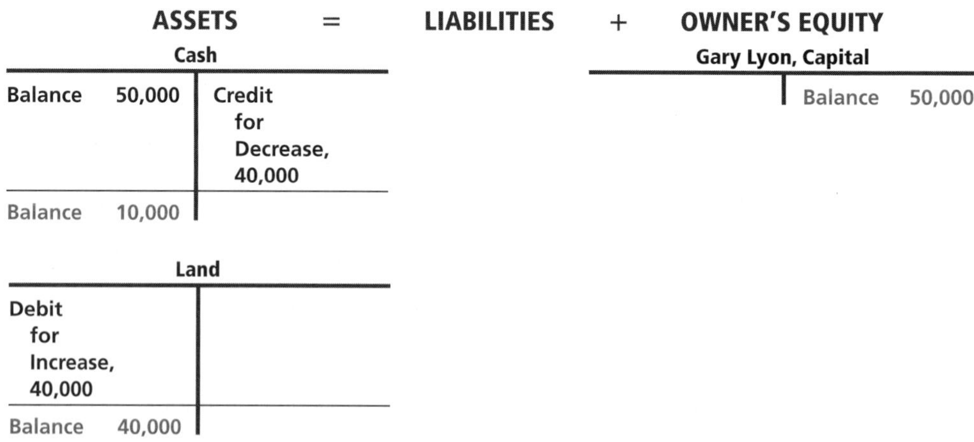

ASSETS		=	LIABILITIES	+	OWNER'S EQUITY
Cash					**Gary Lyon, Capital**
Balance 50,000	Credit for Decrease, 40,000				Balance 50,000
Balance 10,000					
Land					
Debit for Increase, 40,000					
Balance 40,000					

After this transaction, Cash has a \$10,000 debit balance (\$50,000 debit amount minus \$40,000 credit amount), Land has a debit balance of \$40,000, and Capital has a \$50,000 credit balance, as shown here and in the middle section of Exhibit 2-3 (labeled transaction 2).

Transaction 3 is a \$500 purchase of office supplies on account. This transaction increases the asset Office Supplies and the liability Accounts Payable, as shown in the following accounts and in the right side of Exhibit 2-3 (labeled transaction 3):

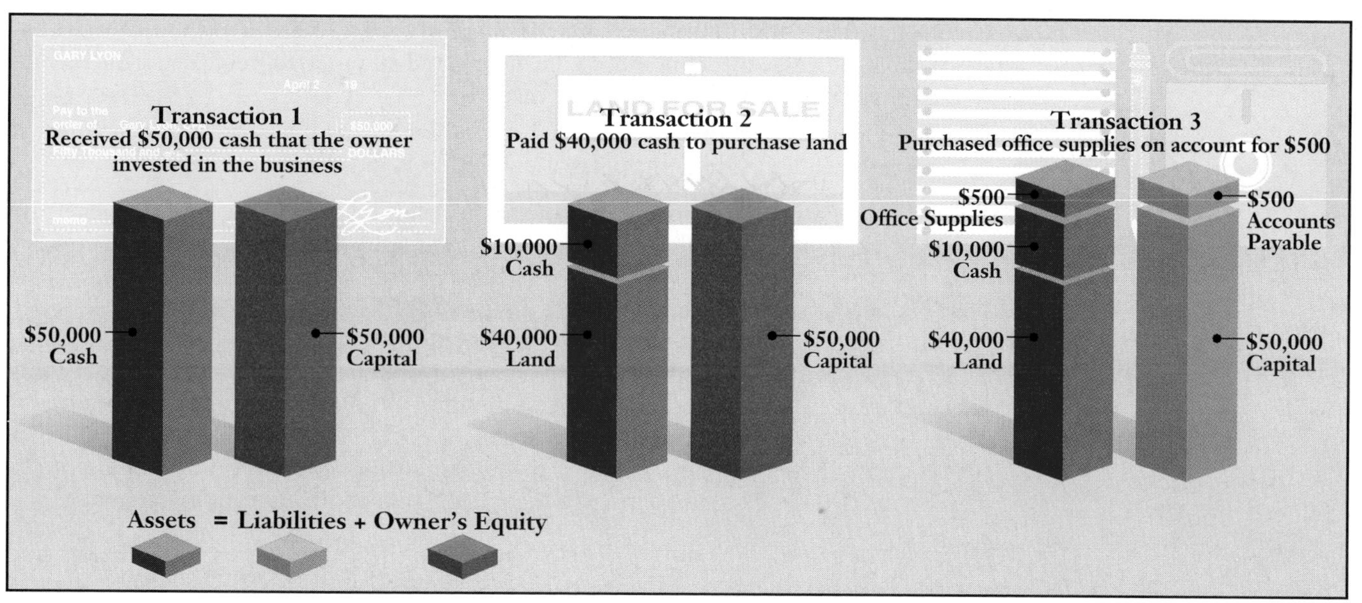

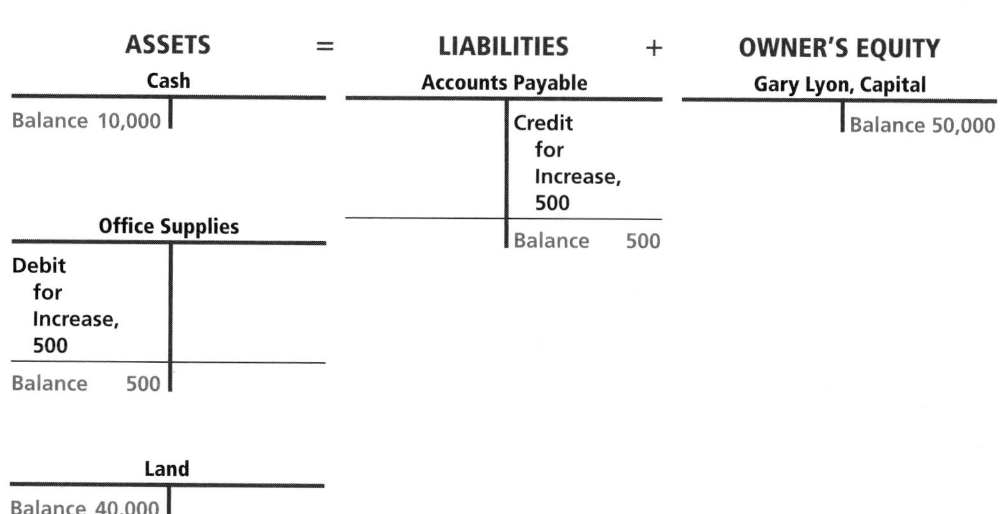

EXHIBIT 2-3
The Accounting Equation and the First Three Transactions of the Business Entity, Gary Lyon, CPA

We create accounts as they are needed. The process of creating a new T-account in preparation for recording a transaction is called *opening the account*. For transaction 1, we opened the Cash account and the Gary Lyon, Capital account. For transaction 2, we opened the Land account and for transaction 3, we opened Office Supplies and Accounts Payable.

Learning Tip: In all transactions, total debits must equal total credits.

We could record all transactions directly in the accounts, as we have shown for the first three transactions. However, that way of accounting does not leave a clear record of each transaction. You may have to search through all the accounts to find both sides of a particular transaction. To save time, accountants keep a record of each transaction in a *journal* and then transfer the information from the journal into the accounts.

Recording Transactions in the Journal

Objective 3
Record transactions in the journal

In practice, accountants record transactions first in a **journal,** which is a chronological record of the entity's transactions. The journalizing process follows four steps:

1. Identify the transaction from source documents, such as bank deposit slips, sale receipts, and check stubs.
2. Specify each account affected by the transaction and classify it by type (asset, liability, or owner's equity).

Journal. The chronological accounting record of an entity's transactions.

3. Determine whether each account is increased or decreased by the transaction. Using the rules of debit and credit, determine whether to debit or credit the account to record its increase or decrease.
4. Enter the transaction in the journal, including a brief explanation for the journal entry. The debit side of the entry is entered first and the credit side last.

Step 4, "Enter the transaction in the journal," means to record the transaction in the journal. This step is also called "making the journal entry" or "journalizing the transaction."

These four steps are completed in a computerized accounting system as well as in a manual system. In step 4, however, the journal entry is generally entered into the computer by account number, and the account name is then listed automatically. Most computer programs replace the explanation in the journal entry with some other means of tracing the entry back to its source documents.

Let's apply the four steps to journalize the first transaction of the accounting practice of Gary Lyon, CPA—the business's receipt of Lyon's $50,000 cash investment in the business.

Step 1. The source documents are Lyon's bank deposit slip and $50,000 check, which is deposited in the business bank account.

Step 2. The accounts affected by the transaction are *Cash* and *Gary Lyon, Capital.* Cash is an asset account. Gary Lyon, Capital is an owner's equity account.

Step 3. Both accounts increase by $50,000. Therefore, Cash, the asset account, is increased (debited) and Gary Lyon, Capital, the owner's equity account, is increased (credited).

Step 4. The journal entry is

Date	Accounts and Explanation	Debit	Credit
Apr. 2[a]	Cash[b]	50,000[d]	
	Gary Lyon, Capital[c]		50,000[e]
Received initial investment from owner.[f]			

The journal entry includes (a) the date of the transaction; (b) the title of the account debited (placed flush left); (c) the title of the account credited (indented slightly); the dollar amounts of the (d) debit (left) and (e) credit (right)—dollar signs are omitted in the money columns; and (f) a short explanation of the transaction.

Learning Tip: To get off to the best start when analyzing a transaction, first pinpoint its effects (if any) on cash. Did cash increase or decrease? Then find the transaction's effect on other accounts. Typically, it is easier to identify the effect that a transaction has on cash than to identify the effects on other accounts.

The journal offers information that the ledger accounts do not provide. Each journal entry shows the complete effect of a business transaction. Consider Gary Lyon's initial investment. The Cash account shows a single figure, the $50,000 debit. We know that every transaction must also have a credit, so in what account will we find the corresponding $50,000 credit? In this illustration, we know that the Capital account holds this figure. But imagine the difficulties you would face trying to link debits and credits for hundreds of transactions—without a separate record of each transaction. The journal solves this problem and presents the full story for each transaction. Exhibit 2-4 shows how Journal page 1 looks after Lyon has recorded the first transaction.

EXHIBIT 2-4
The Journal

Journal — **Page 1**

Date	Accounts and Explanation	Debit	Credit
Apr. 2	Cash	50,000	
	Gary Lyon, Capital		50,000
	Received initial investment from owner.		

PANEL A—Journal Entry:

Accounts and Explanation	Debit	Credit
Cash	50,000	
Gary Lyon, Capital		50,000
Received initial investment from owner.		

PANEL B—Posting to the Ledger:

Cash	
50,000	

Gary Lyon, Capital	
	50,000

EXHIBIT 2-5
Journal Entry and Posting to the Ledger

Transferring Information (Posting) from the Journal to the Ledger

Posting means transferring the amounts from the journal to the accounts in the ledger. Debits in the journal are posted as debits in the ledger, and credits in the journal are posted as credits in the ledger. The initial investment transaction of Gary Lyon is posted to the ledger, as shown in Exhibit 2-5. Computers perform this tedious task quickly and without error. In these introductory discussions, we temporarily ignore the date of each transaction to focus on the accounts and their dollar amounts.

Posting. Transferring of amounts from the journal to the ledger.

Objective 4

Post from the journal to the ledger

Flow of Accounting Data

Exhibit 2-6 summarizes the flow of accounting data from a business transaction all the way through the accounting system to the ledger. In the pages that follow, we continue the example of Gary Lyon, CPA, and account for six of the business's early transactions. Keep in mind that we are accounting for the business entity, Gary Lyon, CPA. We are *not* accounting for Lyon's *personal* transactions.

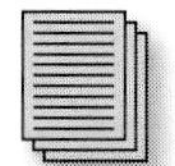

Working It Out Prepare the journal entry to record a $1,600 payment on account.

1. Identify the accounts.
2. Are these accounts increased or decreased? Should they be debited or credited?
3. Make the journal entry, with an explanation.

Answers

1. The company paid $1,600 on account. The accounts affected are Cash and Accounts Payable.

Answer is continued on the next page.

Concept Highlight

EXHIBIT 2-6
Flow of Accounting Data from the Journal to the Ledger

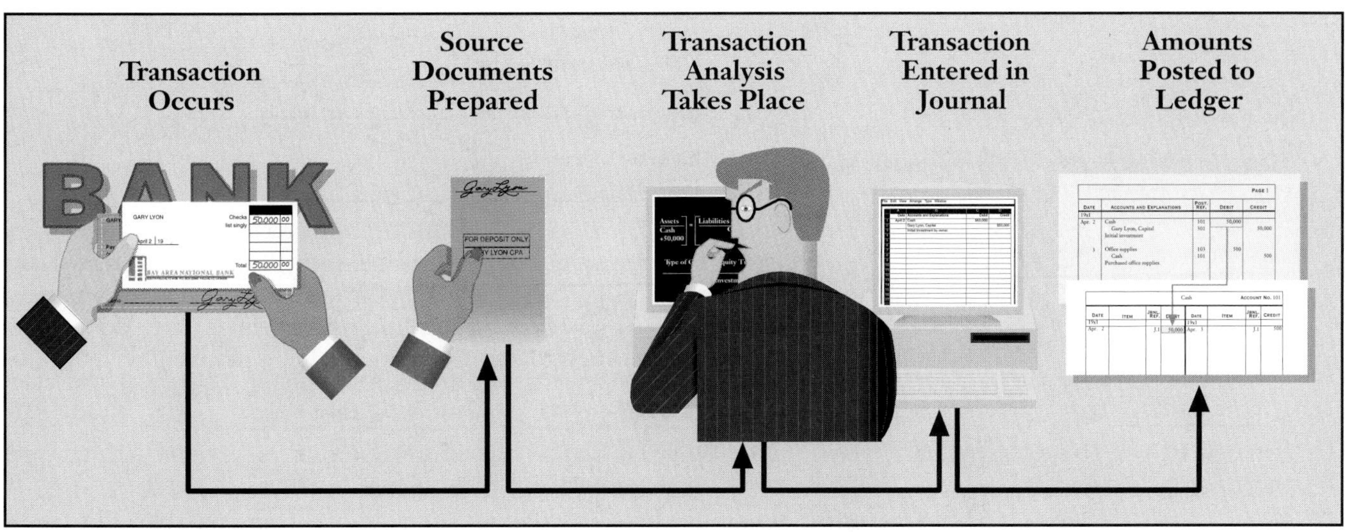

2. Cash (an asset) decreases by $1,600. Accounts Payable (a liability) decreases by the same amount.

   To record a decrease in an asset, we use a credit. To record a decrease in a liability, we use a debit. Review Exhibit 2-2.

3. The journal entry is

Accounts Payable	1,600	
Cash		1,600
Made payment on account.		

Transaction Analysis, Journalizing, and Posting to the Accounts

1. *Transaction Analysis* The business received $50,000 cash that Lyon invested to begin his accounting practice. The business increased its asset cash; to record this increase, debit Cash. The business also increased its owner's equity; to record this increase, credit Gary Lyon, Capital.

Journal Entry

Cash	50,000	
Gary Lyon, Capital		50,000
Received initial investment from owner.		

Accounting Equation

ASSETS	=	LIABILITIES	+	OWNER'S EQUITY
Cash				Gary Lyon, Capital
+50,000	=	0	+	50,000

The journal entry records the same information that you learned by using the accounting equation in Chapter 1. Both accounts—Cash and Gary Lyon, Capital—increased because the business received $50,000 cash and gave Lyon $50,000 of capital (owner's equity) in the business.

Ledger Accounts

Cash		Gary Lyon, Capital	
(1) 50,000			(1) 50,000

2. *Transaction Analysis* Lyon paid $40,000 cash for land as a future office location. The purchase decreased the business's cash; therefore, credit Cash. The purchase increased the entity's asset land; to record this increase, debit Land.

Journal Entry

Land	40,000	
Cash		40,000
Paid cash for land.		

Accounting Equation

ASSETS		=	LIABILITIES	+	OWNER'S EQUITY
Cash	Land				
−40,000	+40,000	=	0	+	0

This transaction increased one asset, land, and decreased another asset, cash. The net effect on the business's total assets was zero, and there was no effect on liabilities or owner's equity. We use the term *net* in business to mean an amount after a subtraction.

■ Daily Exercise 2-3

Ledger Accounts

Cash		Land	
(1) 50,000	(2) 40,000	(2) 40,000	

3. *Transaction Analysis* Lyon purchased $500 office supplies on account payable. The credit purchase of office supplies increased this asset, so we debit Office

Supplies. The purchase also increased the liability accounts payable; to record this increase, credit Accounts Payable.

Journal Entry

Office Supplies	500	
Accounts Payable		500
Purchased office supplies on account.		

Accounting Equation

ASSETS	=	LIABILITIES	+	OWNER'S EQUITY
Office Supplies		Accounts Payable		
+500	=	+500	+	0

Ledger Accounts

Office Supplies			
(3)	500		

Accounts Payable			
		(3)	500

4. *Transaction Analysis* He paid $400 on the account payable created in transaction 3. The payment decreased the asset cash; therefore, credit Cash. The payment also decreased the liability, accounts payable, so we debit Accounts Payable.

Journal Entry

Accounts Payable	400	
Cash		400
Paid cash on account.		

Accounting Equation

ASSETS	=	LIABILITIES	+	OWNER'S EQUITY
Cash		Accounts Payable		
–400	=	–400	+	0

Ledger Accounts

Cash			
(1)	50,000	(2)	40,000
		(4)	400

Accounts Payable			
(4)	400	(3)	500

5. *Transaction Analysis* Lyon and his wife remodeled their residence with personal funds and a loan from Nations Bank. This is not a transaction of the accounting practice, so no journal entry is made on the business's books.

6. *Transaction Analysis* Lyon withdrew $2,100 cash for personal living expenses. The withdrawal decreased the entity's cash; therefore, credit Cash. The transaction also decreased the owner's equity of the entity. Decreases in the owner's equity of a proprietorship that result from owner withdrawals are debited to a separate owner's equity account entitled Withdrawals. Therefore, debit Gary Lyon, Withdrawals.

Journal Entry

Gary Lyon, Withdrawals	2,100	
Cash		2,100
Withdrawal of cash by owner.		

Accounting Equation

ASSETS	=	LIABILITIES	+	OWNER'S EQUITY
				Gary Lyon, Withdrawals
Cash				
–2,100	=	0		–2,100

Ledger Accounts

Cash			
(1)	50,000	(2)	40,000
		(4)	400
		(6)	2,100

Gary Lyon, Withdrawals			
(6)	2,100		

Each journal entry posted to the ledger is keyed by date or by transaction number. In this way, any transaction can be traced from the journal to the ledger and back to the journal. This linking allows you to locate any information you may need for decision making.

Accounts after Posting

We next show how the accounts look when the amounts of the preceding transactions have been posted. The accounts are grouped under the accounting equation's headings.

Each account has a balance, denoted *Bal.* An account balance is the difference between the account's total debits and its total credits. For example, the balance in the Cash account is the difference between the total debits, \$50,000, and the total amount of the credits, \$42,500 (\$40,000 + \$400 + \$2,100). Thus the cash balance is \$7,500. The balance amounts are not the same as journal entries posted to the accounts, so we set an account balance apart from the transaction amounts by horizontal lines. The final figure in an account below the horizontal line is the balance of the account after the transactions have been posted.

ASSETS = LIABILITIES + OWNER'S EQUITY

ASSETS

Cash

(1)	50,000	(2)	40,000
		(4)	400
		(6)	2,100
Bal.	7,500		

Office Supplies

(3)	500		
Bal.	500		

Land

(2)	40,000		
Bal.	40,000		

LIABILITIES

Accounts Payable

(4)	400	(3)	500
		Bal.	100

OWNER'S EQUITY

Gary Lyon, Capital

		(1)	50,000
		Bal.	50,000

Gary Lyon, Withdrawals

(6)	2,100		
Bal.	2,100		

If the sum of an account's debits is greater than the sum of its credits, that account has a debit balance, as the Cash account does here. If the sum of its credits is greater, that account has a credit balance, as Accounts Payable does.

The Trial Balance

Objective 5

Prepare and use a trial balance

A **trial balance** is a list of all the accounts with their balances—assets first, followed by liabilities and then owner's equity—taken from the ledger. Before computers, the trial balance provided a check on accuracy by showing whether the total debits equal the total credits. The trial balance is still useful as a summary of all the accounts and their balances. A trial balance may be taken at any time the postings are up to date. The most common time is at the end of the accounting period. Exhibit 2-7 is the trial balance of the ledger of Gary Lyon's accounting practice after the first six transactions have been journalized and posted.

Trial Balance. A list of all the ledger accounts with their balances.

Correcting Trial Balance Errors

In a trial balance, the total debits and total credits should be equal. If they are not equal, then accounting errors exist. Computerized accounting systems eliminate most errors because the journal amounts are posted precisely as they have been journalized. But computers cannot *eliminate* all errors because humans sometimes input the wrong data.

Many out-of-balance conditions can be detected by computing the difference between total debits and total credits on the trial balance. Then perform one or more of the following actions:

1. Search the trial balance for a missing account. For example, suppose the accountant omitted Gary Lyon, Withdrawals, from the trial balance in Exhibit 2-7. The total amount of the debits would be \$48,000 (\$50,100 – \$2,100). Trace each account from the ledger to the trial balance, and you will locate the missing account.
2. Search the journal for the amount of difference. For example, suppose the total credits on Gary Lyon's trial balance equal \$50,100 and total debits are \$49,900. A \$200 transaction may have been recorded incorrectly in the journal or posted incorrectly to the ledger. Search the journal for a \$200 transaction.

GARY LYON, CPA Trial Balance April 30, 19X1		
	Balance	
Account Title	Debit	Credit
Cash	$ 7,500	
Office supplies	500	
Land	40,000	
Accounts payable		$ 100
Gary Lyon, capital		50,000
Gary Lyon, withdrawals	2,100	
Total	$50,100	$50,100

EXHIBIT 2-7
Trial Balance

- Daily Exercise 2-4
- Daily Exercise 2-14

3. Divide the difference between total debits and total credits by 2. A debit treated as a credit, or vice versa, doubles the amount of error. Suppose Gary Lyon posted a $300 credit as a debit. Total debits contain the $300, and total credits omit the $300. The out-of-balance amount is $600. Dividing the difference by 2 identifies the $300 amount of the transaction. Then search the journal for a $300 transaction and trace to the account affected.
4. Divide the out-of-balance amount by 9. If the result is evenly divisible by 9, the error may be a *slide* (example: writing $61 as $610) or a *transposition* (example: treating $61 as $16). Suppose Gary Lyon wrote his $2,100 Withdrawals balance as $21,000 on the trial balance—a slide-type error. Total debits would differ from total credits by $18,900 ($21,000 – $2,100 = $18,900). Dividing $18,900 by 9 yields $2,100, the correct amount of withdrawals. Trace this amount through the ledger until you reach the Gary Lyon, Withdrawals account with a balance of $2,100. Computer-based systems avoid such errors.

A warning: Do not confuse the trial balance with the balance sheet. Accountants prepare a trial balance for their internal records. The company reports its financial position—both inside and outside the business—on the balance sheet, a formal financial statement. And remember that the financial statements are the focal point of the accounting process. The trial balance is merely a step in the preparation of the financial statements.

SUMMARY PROBLEM FOR YOUR REVIEW — MID-CHAPTER

On August 1, 19X5, Liz Shea opens Shea's Research Service. She will be the owner of the proprietorship. During the entity's first ten days of operations, the business completes these transactions:

a. To begin operations, Shea deposits $40,000 of personal funds in a bank account entitled Shea's Research Service. The business receives the cash and gives Shea capital (owner's equity).
b. Shea pays $30,000 cash for a small building to be used as an office for the business.
c. Shea purchases office supplies for $500 on account.
d. Shea pays cash of $6,000 for office furniture.
e. Shea pays $150 on the account payable she created in transaction (c).
f. Shea withdraws $1,000 cash for personal use.

REQUIRED

1. Journalize these transactions. Key the journal entries by letter. The accounting equation analysis is not required.
2. Post the entries to the ledger.
3. Prepare the trial balance of Shea's Research Service at August 10, 19X5.

SOLUTION

REQUIREMENT 1

	Accounts and Explanation	Debit	Credit
a.	Cash	40,000	
	Liz Shea, Capital		40,000
	Received initial investment from owner.		
b.	Building	30,000	
	Cash		30,000
	Purchased building for an office.		
c.	Office Supplies	500	
	Accounts Payable		500
	Purchased office supplies on account.		
d.	Office Furniture	6,000	
	Cash		6,000
	Purchased office furniture.		
e.	Accounts Payable	150	
	Cash		150
	Paid cash on account.		
f.	Liz Shea, Withdrawals	1,000	
	Cash		1,000
	Withdrew cash for personal use.		

REQUIREMENT 2

ASSETS

Cash

Debit	Credit
(a) 40,000	(b) 30,000
	(d) 6,000
	(e) 150
	(f) 1,000
Bal. 2,850	

Office Furniture

Debit	Credit
(d) 6,000	
Bal. 6,000	

Office Supplies

Debit	Credit
(c) 500	
Bal. 500	

Building

Debit	Credit
(b) 30,000	
Bal. 30,000	

LIABILITIES

Accounts Payable

Debit	Credit
(e) 150	(c) 500
	Bal. 350

OWNER'S EQUITY

Liz Shea, Capital

Debit	Credit
	(a) 40,000
	Bal. 40,000

Liz Shea, Withdrawals

Debit	Credit
(f) 1,000	
Bal. 1,000	

REQUIREMENT 3

SHEA'S RESEARCH SERVICE
Trial Balance
August 10, 19X5

Account Title	Balance Debit	Balance Credit
Cash	$ 2,850	
Office supplies	500	
Office furniture	6,000	
Building	30,000	
Accounts payable		$ 350
Liz Shea, capital		40,000
Liz Shea, withdrawals	1,000	
Total	$40,350	$40,350

Details of Journals and Ledgers

To focus on the main points of journalizing and posting, we purposely omitted certain essential data. In practice, the journal and the ledger provide additional details that create a "trail" through the accounting records for future reference. For example, a supplier may bill us twice for the same item we purchased on account. To prove we paid the bill, we would search the accounts payable records and work backward to the journal entry that recorded our payment. To see how this process works, let's take a closer look at the journal and the ledger.

DETAILS IN THE JOURNAL Exhibit 2-8, Panel B, presents a widely used journal format. The journal page number appears in the upper right corner. As the column headings indicate, the journal displays the following information:

1. The *date*, which indicates when the transaction occurred. The year appears only when the journal is started or when the year has changed. For our purposes, the year appears with an X in the third, or decade's, position. Thus, 19X1 is followed by 19X2, and so on. The date of the transaction is recorded for every transaction.
2. The *account title* and explanation of the transaction, as in Exhibit 2-4.
3. The *posting reference*, abbreviated Post. Ref. How this column helps the accountant will become clear when we discuss the details of posting.
4. The *debit* column, which shows the amount debited.
5. The *credit* column, which shows the amount credited.

DETAILS IN THE LEDGER Exhibit 2-8, Panel C, presents the ledger in T-account format. Each account has its own record in the illustrative ledger. Our example shows Gary Lyon's Cash account, Office Supplies account, and Capital account. These accounts maintain the basic format of the T-account but offer more information—for example, the account number at the upper right corner. Each account has its own identification number.

The column headings identify the ledger account's features:

1. The date.
2. The item column. This space is used for any special notation.
3. The journal reference column, abbreviated Jrnl. Ref. The importance of this column will become clear when we discuss the mechanics of posting.
4. The debit column, with the amount debited.
5. The credit column, with the amount credited.

Posting from the Journal to the Ledger

We know that posting means transferring information from the journal to the ledger accounts. But how do we handle the additional details that appear in the journal and the ledger formats that we have just seen? Exhibit 2-8 illustrates the steps in full detail. Panel A lists two transactions of the business entity, Gary Lyon, CPA; Panel B presents the journal; and Panel C shows the ledger.

The posting process includes four steps. After recording the transaction in the journal:

Arrow ①—Copy (post) the transaction **date** from the journal to the ledger.

Arrow ②—Copy (post) the journal page number from the journal to the ledger. We use several abbreviations:

Jrnl. Ref. means Journal Reference. **J.1** refers to Journal page 1.

This step indicates where the information in the ledger came from: Journal page 1.

Arrow ③—Copy (post) the dollar amount of the debit **($50,000)** from the journal as a debit to the same account (Cash) in the ledger. Likewise, post the dollar amount of the credit (also **$50,000**) from the journal to the appropriate account in the ledger. Now the ledger accounts have their correct amounts.

Arrow ④—Copy (post) the account number **(101)** from the ledger back to the journal. This step indicates that the $50,000 debit to Cash has been posted to the Cash account in the ledger. Also, copy the account number **(301)** for Gary Lyon, Capital, back to the journal to show that the $50,000 amount of the credit has been posted to the ledger.

Post. Ref. is the abbreviation for Posting Reference.

After posting, you can prepare the trial balance, as we discussed earlier.

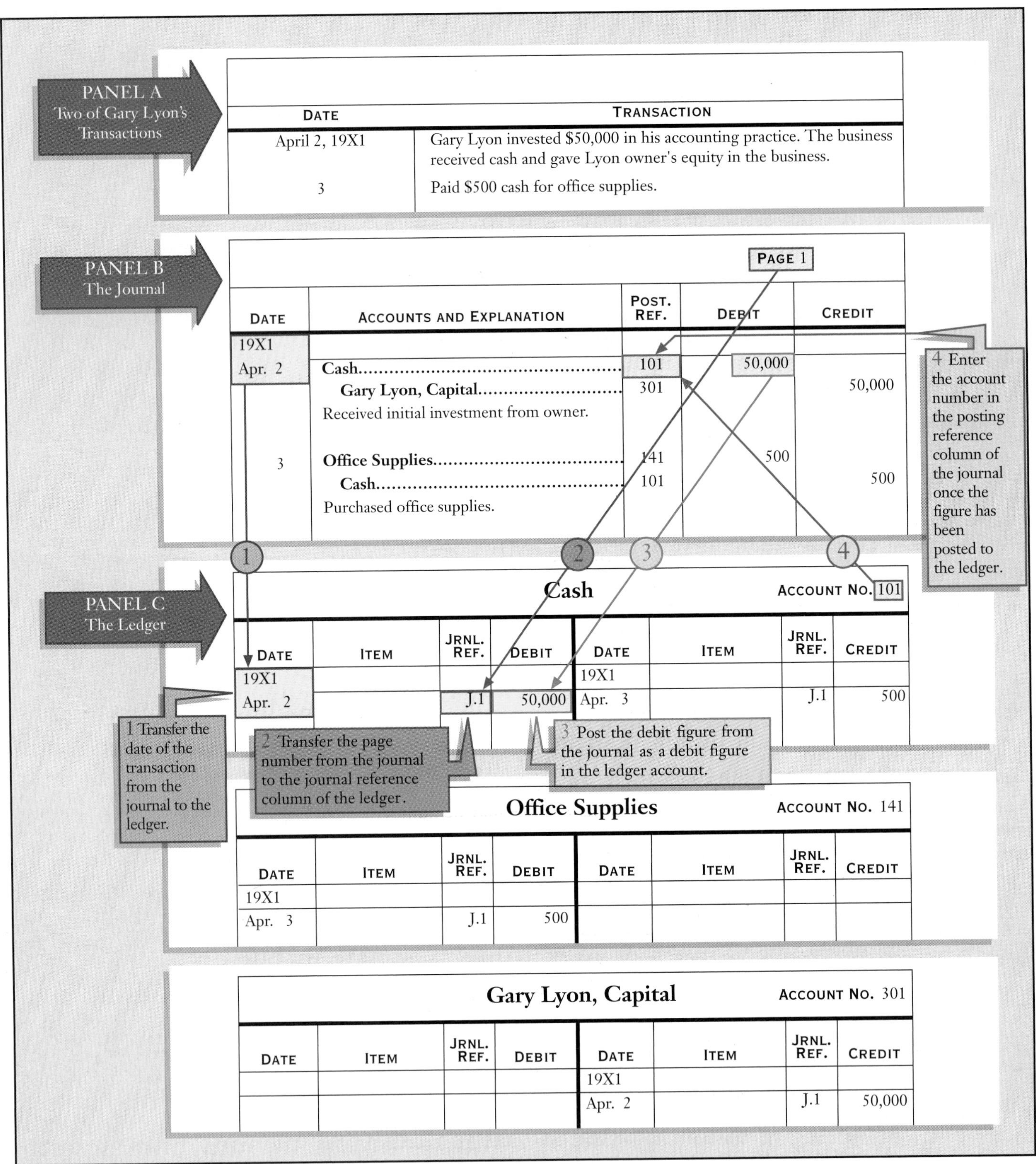

EXHIBIT 2-8
Details of Journalizing and Posting

The Four-Column Account Format: An Alternative to the T-Account Format

The ledger accounts illustrated in Exhibit 2-8 are in the two-column T-account format, with the debit column on the left and the credit column on the right. The T-account clearly distinguishes debits from credits and is often used for illustrative purposes that do not require much detail.

Account Cash					Account No. 101	
		Jrnl.			Balance	
Date	Item	Ref.	Debit	Credit	Debit	Credit
19X1						
Apr. 2		J.1	50,000		50,000	
3		J.1		500	49,500	

EXHIBIT 2-9
Account in Four-Column Format

Another standard format has four amount columns, as illustrated for the Cash account in Exhibit 2-9. The first pair of amount columns are for the debit and credit amounts posted from individual entries, as just discussed. The second pair of amount columns are for the account's balance. This four-column format keeps a running balance in the account. For this reason, it is used more often in practice than the two-column format. In Exhibit 2-9, Cash has a debit balance of $50,000 after the first transaction is posted and a debit balance of $49,500 after the second transaction.

Chart of Accounts in the Ledger

Objective 6

Set up a chart of accounts for a business

As you know, the ledger contains the business's accounts grouped under these headings:

1. Balance sheet accounts: Assets, Liabilities, and Owner's Equity
2. Income statement accounts: Revenues and Expenses

To keep track of their accounts, organizations have a **chart of accounts,** which lists all the accounts in the ledger and their account numbers. These account numbers are used as posting references, as illustrated by arrow 4 in Exhibit 2-8. This numbering system makes it easy to locate individual accounts in the ledger.

Chart of Accounts. List of all the accounts and their account numbers in the ledger.

Accounts are identified by account numbers with two or more digits. Assets are often numbered beginning with 1, liabilities with 2, owner's equity with 3, revenues with 4, and expenses with 5. The second, third, and higher digits in an account number indicate the position of the individual account within the category. For example, Cash may be account number 101, which is the first asset account. Accounts Receivable may be account number 111, the second asset account. Accounts Payable may be number 201, the first liability account. All accounts are numbered by this system.

We learned in Chapter 1, p. 20, that balance sheet amounts report the assets, liabilities, and owner's equity of an entity as of a specific date. The income statement amounts report the revenues and expenses of the entity for a specific period of time.

Organizations with many accounts use lengthy account numbers. For example, the chart of accounts of Yankelovich-Clancy-Shulman, a leading marketing research firm, uses five-digit account numbers. Exhibit 2-10 lists some of Yankelovich's asset accounts. The assignment material reflects the variety found in practice.

The chart of accounts for Gary Lyon, CPA, appears in Exhibit 2-11. Notice the gap in account numbers between 111 and 141. Gary Lyon realizes that at some later date he may need to add another category of receivables—for example, Notes Receivable, which he might number 121.

". . . the chart of accounts of Yankelovich-Clancy-Shulman, a leading marketing research firm, uses five-digit account numbers."

Account Number	Account Title
10100	Cash Chase [cash in Chase Manhattan Bank]
10130	Cash—Petty Cash [cash on hand]
10200	Accounts Receivable—Trade
10300	Accounts Receivable— Rent
10520	Prepaid Insurance
10530	Prepaid Rent
11110	Furniture & Fixtures
11140	Machinery & Equipment

EXHIBIT 2-10
Partial Chart of Accounts of Yankelovich-Clancy-Shulman

Balance Sheet Accounts:

Assets	Liabilities	Owner's Equity	
101 Cash	201 Accounts Payable	301 Gary Lyon, Capital	
111 Accounts Receivable	231 Notes Payable	311 Gary Lyon, Withdrawals	
141 Office Supplies		**Income Statement Accounts (part of Owner's Equity):**	
151 Office Furniture		**Revenues**	**Expenses**
191 Land		401 Service Revenue	501 Rent Expense
			502 Salary Expense
			503 Utilities Expense

EXHIBIT 2-11
Chart of Accounts—Accounting Practice of Gary Lyon, CPA

The chapter appendix starting on page 87 gives two expanded charts of accounts that you will find helpful as you work through this course. The first chart lists the typical accounts of a large *service* proprietorship, such as Gary Lyon's accounting practice after a period of growth. The second chart is for a *merchandising* corporation, one that sells a product rather than a service. The third chart gives some accounts that a *manufacturing* company uses. You will be using these accounts in Chapters 19–26. Study the service proprietorship chart of accounts now, and refer to the other charts of accounts as needed later.

The Normal Balance of an Account

■ Daily Exercise 2-5

An account's *normal balance* appears on the side of the account—debit or credit—where *increases* are recorded. That is, the normal balance is on the side that is positive. For example, Cash and other assets usually have a debit balance (the debit side is positive and the credit side negative), so the normal balance of assets is on the debit side. Assets are called *debit-balance accounts*. Conversely, liabilities and owner's equity usually have a credit balance, so their normal balances are on the credit side. They are called *credit-balance accounts*. Exhibit 2-12 illustrates the normal balances of assets, liabilities, and owner's equity.

An account that normally has a debit balance may occasionally have a credit balance, which indicates a negative amount of the item. For example, Cash will have a temporary credit balance if the entity overdraws its bank account. Similarly, the liability Accounts Payable—normally a credit-balance account—will have a debit balance if the entity overpays its account. In other instances, the shift of a balance amount away from its normal column indicates an accounting error. For example, a credit balance in Office Supplies, Office Furniture, or Buildings indicates an error because negative amounts of these assets cannot exist.

As we saw earlier in this chapter, owner's equity contains several accounts. In total, these accounts show a normal credit balance. An individual owner's equity account with a normal credit balance represents an *increase* in owner's equity. An owner's equity account that has a normal debit balance represents a *decrease* in owner's equity.

Expanding the Accounting Equation with Two Categories of Additional Owner's Equity Accounts: Revenues and Expenses

■ Daily Exercise 2-15

The owner's equity category includes the two income statement accounts Revenues and Expenses because revenues and expenses make up net income or net loss, which flows into owner's equity. As we have discussed, *revenues* are increases in owner's equity that result from delivering goods or services to customers in the course of operating the business. *Expenses* are decreases in owner's equity that occur from using assets or increasing liabilities in the course of operations. Therefore, the accounting equation may be expanded as shown in Exhibit 2-13. Revenues and expenses appear in parentheses to high-

Assets		=	Liabilities		+	Owner's Equity	
Normal Bal. Debit				Normal Bal. Credit			Normal Bal. Credit

EXHIBIT 2-12
Normal Balances of the Balance Sheet Accounts

light the fact that their net effect—revenues minus expenses—equals net income, which increases owner's equity. If expenses are greater than revenues, the net effect of operations is a net loss, which decreases owner's equity.

We can now express the rules of debit and credit in final form, as shown in Exhibit 2-14, Panel A. Panel B shows the *normal* balances of the five types of accounts: *Assets; Liabilities;* and *Owner's Equity* and its subparts, *Revenues* and *Expenses.* All of accounting is based on these five types of accounts. **You should not proceed until you have learned the rules of debit and credit and the normal balances of the five types of accounts.**

Working It Out Computing the missing amounts in each of the following T-accounts.

1.

Cash	
Bal. 10,000	
20,000	13,000
Bal. ?	

2.

Accounts Receivable	
Bal. 12,800	
45,600	?
Bal. 23,500	

3.

Annie Todd, Capital	
	Bal. ?
22,000	56,000
	15,000
	Bal. 73,000

Answers

1. The ending balance (X) is, for Cash:

$$X = \$10,000 + \$20,000 - \$13,000$$
$$X = \$17,000$$

2. We are given the beginning and ending balances.
We can compute the credit entry as follows for Accounts Receivable:

$$\$12,800 + \$45,600 - X = \$23,500$$
$$\$12,800 + \$45,600 - \$23,500 = X$$
$$X = \$34,900$$

3. The Capital account has an ending credit balance of \$73,000. We can figure the beginning credit balance, as follows:

$$X + \$56,000 + \$15,000 - \$22,000 = \$73,000$$
$$X = \$73,000 - \$56,000 - \$15,000 + \$22,000$$
$$X = \$24,000$$

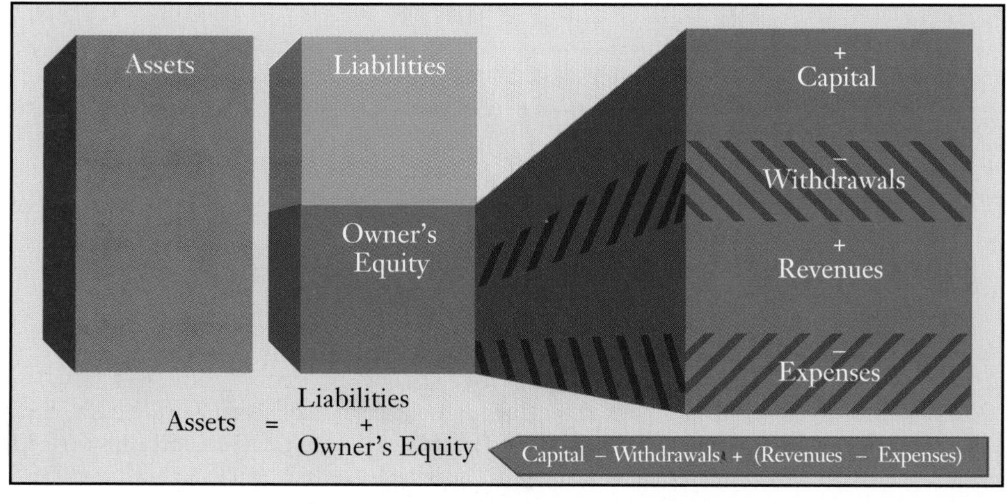

EXHIBIT 2-13
Expansion of the Accounting Equation

Concept Highlight

EXHIBIT 2-14
Expanded Rules of Debit and Credit and the Normal Balance of Accounts

■ Daily Exercise 2-6

PANEL A—Rules of Debit and Credit:

Assets		=	Liabilities		+	Capital	
Debit for Increase	Credit for Decrease		Debit for Decrease	Credit for Increase		Debit for Decrease	Credit for Increase

Withdrawals	
Debit for Increase	Credit for Decrease

Revenues	
Debit for Decrease	Credit for Increase

Expenses	
Debit for Increase	Credit for Decrease

PANEL B—Normal Balances:

Assets	Debit	
Liabilities		Credit
Owner's Equity—overall		Credit
Capital		Credit
Withdrawals	Debit	
Revenues		Credit
Expenses	Debit	

Expanded Problem Including Revenues and Expenses

Let's account for the revenues and expenses of the law practice of Sara Nichols, Attorney, for the month of July 19X1. We follow the same steps illustrated earlier in this chapter: Analyze the transaction, journalize, post to the ledger, and prepare the trial balance.

Transaction Analysis, Journalizing, and Posting

1. *Transaction Analysis* Sara Nichols invested $10,000 cash in a business bank account to open her law practice. The business received the cash and gave Nichols owner's equity. The business's asset cash is increased; therefore, debit Cash. The owner's equity of the business increased, so credit Sara Nichols, Capital.

Journal Entry

Cash	10,000	
Sara Nichols, Capital		10,000
Received investment from owner.		

Accounting Equation

ASSETS	=	LIABILITIES	+	OWNER'S EQUITY
Cash				Sara Nichols, Capital
+10,000	=	0	+	10,000

Ledger Accounts

Cash	
(1) 10,000	

Sara Nichols, Capital	
	(1) 10,000

2. *Transaction Analysis* Nichols performed service for a client and collected $3,000 cash. The asset cash is increased, so debit Cash. The revenue account Service Revenue is increased; credit Service Revenue.

Journal Entry

Cash	3,000	
Service Revenue		3,000
Performed service and received cash.		

Accounting Equation

ASSETS	=	LIABILITIES	+	OWNER'S EQUITY	+	REVENUES
Cash						Service Revenue
+3,000	=	0			+	3,000

Ledger Accounts

Cash			Service Revenue	
(1) 10,000				(2) 3,000
(2) 3,000				

3. *Transaction Analysis* Nichols performed service for a client and billed the client for $500 on account receivable. This means the client owes the business $500, and Nichols expects to collect the $500 later. The asset accounts receivable is increased; therefore, debit Accounts Receivable. Service revenue is increased; credit Service Revenue.

Journal Entry

Accounts Receivable	500	
Service Revenue		500
Performed service on account.		

Accounting Equation

ASSETS	=	LIABILITIES	+	OWNER'S EQUITY	+	REVENUES
Accounts Receivable						Service Revenue
+500	=	0			+	500

Ledger Accounts

Accounts Receivable			Service Revenue	
(3) 500				(2) 3,000
				(3) 500

4. *Transaction Analysis* Nichols earned $700 service revenue by performing legal service for a client. The client paid Nichols $300 cash immediately. Nichols billed the remaining $400 to the client on account receivable. The assets cash and accounts receivable are increased; therefore, debit both of these asset accounts. Service revenue is increased; credit Service Revenue for the sum of the two debit amounts.

Journal Entry

Cash	300	
Accounts Receivable	400	
Service Revenue		700
Performed service for cash and on account.		

Accounting Equation

ASSETS		=	LIABILITIES	+	OWNER'S EQUITY	+	REVENUES
Cash	Accounts Receivable						Service Revenue
+300	+400	=	0			+	700

Note: Because this transaction affects more than two accounts at the same time, the entry is called a *compound entry*. **No matter how many accounts a compound entry affects—there may be any number—total debits must equal total credits.**

■ Daily Exercise 2-7

Ledger Accounts

Cash		Accounts Receivable		Service Revenue	
(1) 10,000		(3) 500			(2) 3,000
(2) 3,000		(4) 400			(3) 500
(4) 300					(4) 700

5. *Transaction Analysis* Nichols paid the following cash expenses: office rent, $900; employee salary, $1,500; and utilities, $500. The asset cash is decreased; therefore, credit Cash for the sum of the three expense amounts. The following expenses are increased: Rent Expense, Salary Expense, and Utilities Expense. Each should be debited separately.

Journal Entry

Rent Expense	900	
Salary Expense	1,500	
Utilities Expense	500	
Cash		2,900
Paid cash expenses.		

Accounting Equation

ASSETS	=	LIABILITIES	+	OWNER'S EQUITY	–	EXPENSES		
						Rent Expense	Salary Expense	Utilities Expense
Cash –2,900	=	0				–900	–1,500	–500

Note In practice, the business would record these three transactions separately. To save space, we can record them together in a compound journal entry.

Ledger Accounts

Cash

(1)	10,000	(5)	2,900
(2)	3,000		
(4)	300		

Rent Expense

(5)	900		

Salary Expense

(5)	1,500		

Utilities Expense

(5)	500		

6. *Transaction Analysis* Nichols received a telephone bill for $120 and will pay this expense next week. Utilities expense is increased, so debit this expense. The liability accounts payable is increased, so credit Accounts Payable.

Journal Entry

Utilities Expense	120	
Accounts Payable		120
Received utility bill.		

Accounting Equation

ASSETS	=	LIABILITIES	+	OWNER'S EQUITY	–	EXPENSES
		Accounts Payable				Utilities Expense
0	=	+120			–	120

Ledger Accounts

Accounts Payable

		(6)	120

Utilities Expense

(5)	500		
(6)	120		

7. *Transaction Analysis* Nichols collected $200 cash from the client established in transaction 3. The asset cash is increased, so debit Cash. The asset accounts receivable is decreased; credit Accounts Receivable.

Journal Entry

Cash	200	
Accounts Receivable		200
Received cash on account.		

Accounting Equation

ASSETS		=	LIABILITIES	+	OWNER'S EQUITY
Cash	Accounts Receivable				
+200	–200	=	0	+	0

Note — This transaction has no effect on revenue; the related revenue was accounted for in transaction 3.

Ledger Accounts

Cash				Accounts Receivable			
(1)	10,000	(5)	2,900	(3)	500	(7)	200
(2)	3,000			(4)	400		
(4)	300						
(7)	200						

Learning Tip: Recording an expense does not necessarily involve a credit to cash. In transaction 6, the expense is recorded now, but the cash will be paid later. Likewise, a debit to cash does not always mean revenue. Transaction 7 records cash collected on a receivable (the revenue was recorded in transaction 3).

8. *Transaction Analysis* — Nichols paid the telephone bill that was received and recorded in transaction 6. The asset cash is decreased; credit Cash. The liability accounts payable is decreased; therefore, debit Accounts Payable.

Journal Entry

Accounts Payable	120	
Cash		120
Paid cash on account.		

Accounting Equation

ASSETS	=	LIABILITIES	+	OWNER'S EQUITY
Cash		Accounts Payable		
−120	=	−120	+	0

Note — This transaction has no effect on expense because the related expense was recorded in transaction 6.

Ledger Accounts

Cash				Accounts Payable			
(1)	10,000	(5)	2,900	(8)	120	(6)	120
(2)	3,000	(8)	120				
(4)	300						
(7)	200						

9. *Transaction Analysis* — Nichols withdrew $1,100 cash for personal use. The asset cash decreased; credit Cash. The withdrawal decreased owner's equity; therefore, debit Sara Nichols, Withdrawals.

Journal Entry

Sara Nichols, Withdrawals	1,100	
Cash		1,100
Withdrew cash for personal use.		

Accounting Equation

ASSETS	=	LIABILITIES	+	OWNER'S EQUITY
Cash				Sarah Nichols, Withdrawals
−1,100	=	0		−1,100

Ledger Accounts

Cash				Sara Nichols, Withdrawals			
(1)	10,000	(5)	2,900	(9)	1,100		
(2)	3,000	(8)	120				
(4)	300	(9)	1,100				
(7)	200						

- Daily Exercise 2-8
- Daily Exercise 2-9
- Daily Exercise 2-10
- Daily Exercise 2-11

Ledger Accounts after Posting

ASSETS

Cash

(1)	10,000	(5)	2,900
(2)	3,000	(8)	120
(4)	300	(9)	1,100
(7)	200		
Bal.	9,380		

Accounts Receivable

(3)	500	(7)	200
(4)	400		
Bal.	700		

LIABILITIES

Accounts Payable

(8)	120	(6)	120
		Bal.	0

OWNER'S EQUITY

Sara Nichols, Capital

		(1)	10,000
		Bal.	10,000

Sara Nichols, Withdrawals

(9)	1,100		
Bal.	1,100		

REVENUE

Service Revenue

		(2)	3,000
		(3)	500
		(4)	700
		Bal.	4,200

EXPENSES

Rent Expense

(5)	900		
Bal.	900		

Salary Expense

(5)	1,500		
Bal.	1,500		

Utilities Expense

(5)	500		
(6)	120		
Bal.	620		

Trial Balance

■ Daily Exercise 2-12
■ Daily Exercise 2-13

To prepare the trial balance, we list and summarize the balances from the ledger accounts.

SARA NICHOLS, ATTORNEY
Trial Balance
July 31, 19X1

Account Title	Balance Debit	Balance Credit
Cash	$ 9,380	
Accounts receivable	700	
Accounts payable		$ 0
Sara Nichols, capital		10,000
Sara Nichols, withdrawals	1,100	
Service revenue		4,200
Rent expense	900	
Salary expense	1,500	
Utilities expense	620	
Total	$14,200	$14,200

Now you have seen how to record business transactions. Post to the ledger accounts, and prepare a trial balance. Solidify your understanding of the accounting process by reviewing the Decision Guidelines feature.

DECISION GUIDELINES — Analyzing and Recording Transactions

DECISION	GUIDELINES
• Has a transaction occurred?	If the event affects the entity's financial position and can be reliably recorded—*Yes* If either condition is absent—*No*
• Where to record the transaction?	In the *journal,* the chronological record of transactions
• What to record for each transaction?	Increases and/or decreases in all the accounts affected by the transaction

(continued)

DECISION GUIDELINES *(continued)*

	Rules of debit and credit:	
• How to record an increase/decrease in a (an)	Increase	Decrease
Asset	Debit	Credit
Liability	Credit	Debit
Owner's Equity	Credit	Debit
Revenue	Credit	Debit
Expense	Debit	Credit
• Where to store all the information for each account?	In the *ledger*, the book of accounts and their balances	
• Where to list all the accounts and their balances?	In the *trial balance*	
• Where to report the Results of operations?	In the income statement (revenues − expenses = net income or net loss)	
Financial position?	In the balance sheet (assets = liabilities + owner's equity)	

Thinking It Over Review the chapter opening story and concentrate on Lands' End's need for financial statement information. How do the procedures covered in this chapter help Lands' End convince bank lenders that the business is stable?

Answer: The final product of the accounting process is a set of financial statements. The Lands' End accounting records will generate the income statement and balance sheet that banks require of businesses before lending them money.

Using Accounting Information for Quick Decision Making

Objective 7

Analyze transactions without a journal

Often businesspeople make decisions without taking the time to follow all the steps in an accounting system. For example, suppose Lands' End needs more warehouse space to meet customer demand. The company can either purchase a warehouse building for $700,000, or it can rent a building at an overall cost of $100,000. The decision whether to buy or rent the building will depend on the decision's financial and other effects on the company.

". . . can either purchase a warehouse building for $700,000, or it can rent a building at an overall cost of $100,000."

The Lands' End vice president does not need to record in the journal all the transactions that would be affected by his decision. After all, the company has not completed a transaction yet. But the vice president does need to know how the decision will affect Lands' End. If he knows accounting, he can visualize how the ledger accounts would be affected. The following accounts summarize the immediate effects of renting or purchasing the warehouse building.

■ Daily Exercise 2-16

Rent the Building

Cash		Rent Expense	
	100,000	100,000	

Buy the Building

Cash		Building	
	700,000	700,000	

Immediately the Lands' End vice president can see that buying the building will require more cash. But he can also see that he will obtain the building as an asset. This may motivate him to borrow cash and buy the building. A low cash balance may lead to renting.

Companies do not actually keep their records in this short-cut fashion. But a decision maker who needs information immediately can quickly analyze the effect of a set of transactions on the company's financial statements.

SUMMARY PROBLEM FOR YOUR REVIEW

The trial balance of Tomassini Computer Service Center on March 1, 19X2, lists the entity's assets, liabilities, and owner's equity on that date.

Account Title	Balance Debit	Balance Credit
Cash	$26,000	
Accounts receivable	4,500	
Accounts payable		$ 2,000
Larry Tomassini, capital		28,500
Total	$30,500	$30,500

During March, the business engaged in the following transactions:

- **a.** Borrowed $45,000 from the bank and signed a note payable in the name of the business.
- **b.** Paid cash of $40,000 to a real estate company to acquire land.
- **c.** Performed service for a customer and received cash of $5,000.
- **d.** Purchased supplies on credit, $300.
- **e.** Performed customer service and earned revenue on account, $2,600.
- **f.** Paid $1,200 on account.
- **g.** Paid the following cash expenses: salaries, $3,000; rent, $1,500; and interest, $400.
- **h.** Received $3,100 on account.
- **i.** Received a $200 utility bill that will be paid next week.
- **j.** Withdrew $1,800 for personal use.

REQUIRED

1. Open the following accounts, with the balances indicated, in the ledger of Tomassini Computer Service Center. Use the T-account format.
   Assets—Cash, $26,000; Accounts Receivable, $4,500; Supplies, no balance; Land, no balance
   Liabilities—Accounts Payable, $2,000; Note Payable, no balance
   Owner's Equity—Larry Tomassini, Capital, $28,500; Larry Tomassini, Withdrawals, no balance
   Revenues—Service Revenue, no balance
   Expenses—(none have balances) Salary Expense, Rent Expense, Utilities Expense, Interest Expense
2. Journalize the preceding transactions. Key journal entries by transaction letter.
3. Post to the ledger.
4. Prepare the trial balance of Tomassini Computer Service Center at March 31, 19X2.
5. Compute the net income or net loss of the entity during the month of March. List expenses in order from the largest to the smallest.

SOLUTION

REQUIREMENT 1

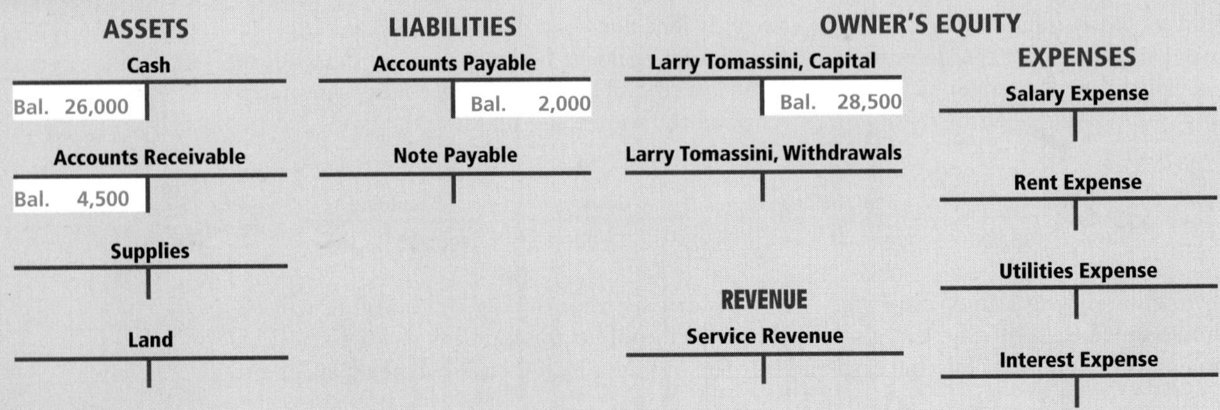

REQUIREMENT 2

	Accounts and Explanation	Debit	Credit
a.	Cash	45,000	
	Note Payable		45,000
	Borrowed cash on note payable.		
b.	Land	40,000	
	Cash		40,000
	Purchased land for cash.		
c.	Cash	5,000	
	Service Revenue		5,000
	Performed service and received cash.		
d.	Supplies	300	
	Accounts Payable		300
	Purchased supplies on account.		
e.	Accounts Receivable	2,600	
	Service Revenue		2,600
	Performed service on account.		
f.	Accounts Payable	1,200	
	Cash		1,200
	Paid cash on account.		
g.	Salary Expense	3,000	
	Rent Expense	1,500	
	Interest Expense	400	
	Cash		4,900
	Paid cash expenses.		
h.	Cash	3,100	
	Accounts Receivable		3,100
	Received cash on account.		
i.	Utilities Expense	200	
	Accounts Payable		200
	Received utility bill.		
j.	Larry Tomassini, Withdrawals	1,800	
	Cash		1,800
	Withdrew cash for personal use.		

REQUIREMENT 3

ASSETS

Cash

	Debit		Credit
Bal.	26,000	(b)	40,000
(a)	45,000	(f)	1,200
(c)	5,000	(g)	4,900
(h)	3,100	(j)	1,800
Bal.	31,200		

Accounts Receivable

	Debit		Credit
Bal.	4,500	(h)	3,100
(e)	2,600		
Bal.	4,000		

Supplies

	Debit		Credit
(d)	300		
Bal.	300		

Land

	Debit		Credit
(b)	40,000		
Bal.	40,000		

LIABILITIES

Accounts Payable

	Debit		Credit
(f)	1,200	Bal.	2,000
		(d)	300
		(i)	200
		Bal.	1,300

Note Payable

	Debit		Credit
		(a)	45,000
		Bal.	45,000

OWNER'S EQUITY

Larry Tomassini, Capital

	Debit		Credit
		Bal.	28,500

Larry Tomassini, Withdrawals

	Debit		Credit
(j)	1,800		
Bal.	1,800		

REVENUE

Service Revenue

	Debit		Credit
		(c)	5,000
		(e)	2,600
		Bal.	7,600

EXPENSES

Salary Expense

	Debit		Credit
(g)	3,000		
Bal.	3,000		

Rent Expense

	Debit		Credit
(g)	1,500		
Bal.	1,500		

Utilities Expense

	Debit		Credit
(i)	200		
Bal.	200		

Interest Expense

	Debit		Credit
(g)	400		
Bal.	400		

REQUIREMENT 4

TOMASSINI COMPUTER SERVICE CENTER Trial Balance March 31, 19X2		
	Balance	
Account Title	Debit	Credit
Cash	$31,200	
Accounts receivable	4,000	
Supplies	300	
Land	40,000	
Accounts payable		$ 1,300
Note payable		45,000
Larry Tomassini, capital		28,500
Larry Tomassini, withdrawals	1,800	
Service revenue		7,600
Salary expense	3,000	
Rent expense	1,500	
Interest expense	400	
Utilities expense	200	
Total	$82,400	$82,400

REQUIREMENT 5

Net income for the month of March		
Revenue:		
Service revenue		$7,600
Expenses:		
Salary expense	$3,000	
Rent expense	1,500	
Interest expense	400	
Utilities expense	200	
Total expenses		5,100
Net income		$2,500

Summary of Learning Objectives

1. ***Define and use key accounting terms:* account, ledger, debit, *and* credit.** *Accounts* can be viewed in the form of the letter "T." The left side of each T-account is its *debit* side. The right side is its *credit* side. The *ledger,* which contains a record for each account, groups and numbers accounts by category in the following order: assets, liabilities, and owner's equity (and its subparts, revenues and expenses).

2. ***Apply the rules of debit and credit.*** *Assets* and *expenses* are increased by debits and decreased by credits. *Liabilities, owner's equity,* and *revenues* are increased by credits and decreased by debits. An account's *normal balance* is the side of the account—debit or credit—in which increases are recorded. Thus the normal balance of assets and expenses is a debit, and the normal balance of liabilities, owner's equity, and revenues is a credit. The Withdrawals account, which decreases owner's equity, normally has a debit balance. Revenues, which are increases in owner's equity, have a normal credit balance. Expenses, which are decreases in owner's equity, have a normal debit balance.

3. ***Record transactions in the journal.*** The accountant begins the recording process by entering the transaction's information in the *journal,* a chronological list of all the entity's transactions.

4. ***Post from the journal to the ledger.*** *Posting* means transferring the amounts from the journal to the *ledger* accounts. Posting references are used to trace amounts back and forth between the journal and the ledger.

5. ***Prepare and use a trial balance.*** The *trial balance* is a summary of all the account balances in the ledger. When *double-entry accounting* has been done correctly, the total debits and the total credits in the trial balance are equal.

6. ***Set up a chart of accounts for a business.*** A chart of accounts lists all the accounts in the ledger and their account numbers. Larger entities often use lengthy account numbers.

7. ***Analyze transactions without a journal.*** Decision makers must often make decisions without a complete accounting system. They can analyze the transactions without a journal.

Accounting Vocabulary

account *(p. 44)*
chart of accounts *(p. 59)*
credit *(p. 47)*
debit *(p. 47)*
journal *(p. 49)*
ledger *(p. 44)*
posting *(p. 51)*
trial balance *(p. 54)*

Questions

1. Name the basic summary device of accounting. What letter of the alphabet does it resemble? Name its two sides.
2. Is the following statement true or false? Debit means decrease and credit means increase. Explain your answer.
3. Write two sentences that use the term *debit* differently.
4. What are the three *basic* types of accounts? Name two additional types of accounts. To which one of the three basic types are these two additional types of accounts most closely related?
5. Suppose you are the accountant for Smith Courier Service. Keeping in mind double-entry bookkeeping, identify the *dual effects* of Mary Smith's investment of $10,000 cash in her business.
6. Briefly describe the flow of accounting information.
7. To what does the *normal balance* of an account refer?
8. Indicate the normal balance of the five types of accounts.

Account Type	Normal Balance
Assets	________
Liabilities	________
Capital	________
Revenues	________
Expenses	________

9. What does posting accomplish? Why is it important? Does it come before or after journalizing?
10. Label each of the following transactions as increasing owner's equity (+), decreasing owner's equity (–), or as having no effect on owner's equity (0). Write the appropriate symbol in the space provided.
    ___ a. Investment by owner
    ___ b. Revenue transaction
    ___ c. Purchase of supplies on credit
    ___ d. Expense transaction
    ___ e. Cash payment on account
    ___ f. Withdrawal by owner
    ___ g. Borrowing money on a note payable
    ___ h. Sale of service on account
11. What four steps does posting include? Which step is the fundamental purpose of posting?
12. Rearrange the following accounts in their logical sequence in the ledger:

Notes Payable	Cash
Accounts Receivable	Jane East, Capital
Sales Revenue	Salary Expense

13. What is the meaning of this statement? Accounts Payable has a credit balance of $1,700.
14. Jack Brown Campus Cleaners launders the shirts of customer Bobby Baylor, who has a charge account at the cleaners. When Bobby picks up his clothes and is short of cash, he charges it. Later, when he receives his monthly statement from the cleaners, Bobby writes a check on Dear Old Dad's bank account and mails the check to Jack Brown. Identify the two business transactions described here. Which transaction increases Jack Brown's owner's equity? Which transaction increases Jack Brown's cash?
15. Explain the difference between the ledger and the chart of accounts.
16. Why do accountants prepare a trial balance?
17. What is a compound journal entry?
18. The accountant for Bower Construction Company mistakenly recorded a $500 purchase of supplies on account as a $5,000 purchase. He debited Supplies and credited Accounts Payable for $5,000. Does this error cause the trial balance to be out of balance? Explain your answer.
19. What is the effect on total assets of collecting cash on account from customers?
20. What is the advantage of analyzing transactions without the use of a journal? Describe how this "journal-less" analysis works.
21. Briefly summarize the similarities and differences between manual and computer-based accounting systems in terms of journalizing, posting, and the preparation of a trial balance.

Daily Exercises

DE2-1 There are three broad categories of accounts: assets, liabilities, and owner's equity. *Using key terms (Obj. 1)*

1. Give a short (one- or two-word) synonym for an *asset* and a *liability*. Then list several individual assets and several specific liabilities.
2. Owner's equity is more complex than assets and liabilities. What is the definition of *owner's equity?* Suppose your assets total $3,000 and your liabilities are $1,000. How much is your owner's equity?
3. Identify two categories of transactions that *increase* owner's equity. Name two categories of transactions that *decrease* owner's equity. This concept is discussed beginning on page 45.

DE2-2 Review basic accounting definitions by completing the following crossword puzzle. *Using key terms (Obj. 1)*

Down:

1. Records an increase in an asset or an expense.
4. Economic resource of an entity.

Across:

2. Assets – Liabilities = Owner's ________.
3. A debt.
5. Records an increase in a liability or owner's equity.

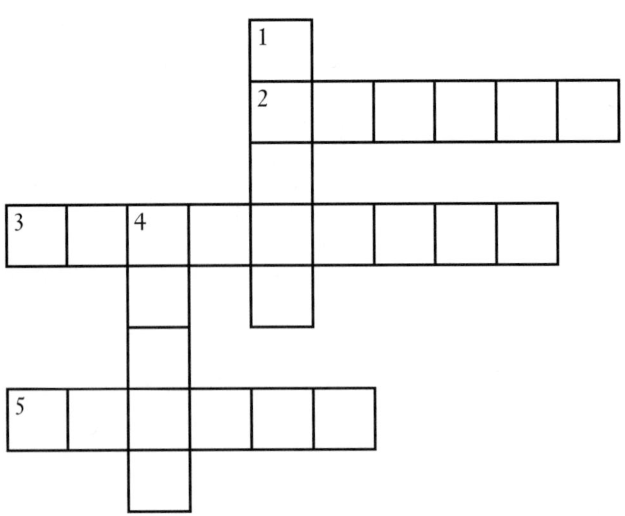

Explaining an asset versus an expense
(Obj. 1)

DE2-3 Kathryn Shafer opened an architectural firm and immediately paid $15,000 for equipment to be used in the business. Was Shafer's payment an expense of the business? If not, what did Shafer acquire? Explain your reasoning after reviewing the definitions of *assets* on page 44 and *expenses* on page 45.

Using key terms
(Obj. 1)

DE2-4 Understanding basic concepts is essential for success in accounting. Tighten your grip on the accounting process by filling in the blanks to review the definitions of key terms.

Madelyn Albritton, an introductory accounting student, is describing the accounting process for a friend who is a philosophy major. Madelyn states, "The basic summary device in accounting is the **account,** which can be represented by the letter ________. The left side of an account is called the ________ side, and the right side is called the ________ side.

"We record transactions first in a ________. Then we post (transfer the data) to the accounts in the ________. It is helpful to list all the accounts with their balances on a ________ ________."

Using accounting terms
(Obj. 1)

DE2-5 Accounting has its own vocabulary and basic relationships. Match the accounting terms at left with the corresponding definition or meaning at right.

___	1. Receivable	A. Using up assets in the course of operating a business
___	2. Capital	B. Always a liability
___	3. Debit	C. Revenues – Expenses
___	4. Expense	D. Grouping of accounts
___	5. Net income	E. Owner's equity in the business
___	6. Ledger	F. Record of transactions
___	7. Posting	G. Always an asset
___	8. Normal balance	H. Left side of an account
___	9. Payable	I. Side of an account where increases are recorded
___	10. Journal	J. Transferring data from the journal to the ledger

Explaining the rules of debit and credit
(Obj. 2)

DE2-6 Jeff Stanberry, a recent graduate, is tutoring Dennis Liu, who is taking introductory accounting. Jeff explains to Dennis that *debits* are used to record increases in accounts and *credits* record decreases. Dennis is confused and seeks your advice.

- When are debits increases? When are debits decreases?
- When are credits increases? When are credits decreases?

Exhibit 2-14, page 62, gives the full rules of debit and credit.

Recording transactions
(Obj. 3)

DE2-7 Monica Peres opened a medical practice in Tucson, Arizona. Record the following transactions in the journal of Monica Peres, M.D. Include an explanation with each journal entry.

June 1	Peres invested $64,000 cash in a business bank account to start her medical practice. The business received the cash and gave Peres owner's equity in the business.
2	Purchased medical supplies on account, $9,000.
2	Paid monthly office rent of $4,000.
3	Recorded $5,000 revenue for service rendered to patients. Received cash of $2,000 and sent bills to patients for the remainder.

DE2-8 After operating for several months, Monica Peres, M.D., completed the following transactions during the latter part of October:

Recording transactions (Obj. 3)

Oct. 15 Borrowed $50,000 from the bank, signing a note payable.
22 Performed service for patients on account, $4,000.
30 Received cash on account from patients, $1,000.
31 Received a utility bill, $200, which will be paid during November.
31 Paid monthly salary to nurse, $3,000.
31 Paid interest expense of $2,500 on the bank loan.

Journalize the transactions of Monica Peres, M.D. Include an explanation with each journal entry.

DE2-9 The accounting records of all businesses include three basic categories of accounts: assets, liabilities, and owner's equity. In turn, owner's equity is divided into the following categories: capital, withdrawals, revenues, and expenses. Identify which categories of accounts—including the subparts of owner's equity—have a normal debit balance and which categories of accounts have a normal credit balance. Exhibit 2-14, Panel B, on page 62, gives the normal balance in each category of account.

Normal account balances (Obj. 2)

DE2-10 Lisa Khoury purchased supplies on account for $2,000. Two weeks later, Khoury paid $1,500 on account.

Journalizing transactions; posting (Obj. 3, 4)

1. Journalize the two transactions on the books of Lisa Khoury. Include an explanation for each transaction.
2. Open the Accounts Payable account and post to Accounts Payable. Compute the balance, and denote it as *Bal.*
3. How much does Khoury owe after both transactions? In which account does this amount appear?

DE2-11 Grant Tobias performed legal service for a client who could not pay immediately. Tobias expected to collect the $3,000 the following month. A month later, Tobias received $2,000 cash from the client.

Journalizing transactions; posting (Obj. 3, 4)

1. Record the two transactions on the books of Grant Tobias, Attorney. Include an explanation for each transaction.
2. Open these accounts: Cash; Accounts Receivable; Service Revenue. Post to all three accounts. Compute each account's balance, and denote as *Bal.*
3. Answer these questions based on your analysis:
   a. How much did Tobias earn? Which account shows this amount?
   b. How much in total assets did Tobias acquire as a result of the two transactions? Show the amount of each asset.

Note: Daily Exercise 2-12 should be used in connection with Daily Exercise 2-7.

DE2-12 Use the June transaction data for Monica Peres, M.D., given in Daily Exercise 2-7.

Posting; preparing a trial balance (Obj. 4, 5)

1. Open the following T-accounts of Monica Peres, M.D.: Cash; Accounts Receivable; Medical Supplies; Accounts Payable; Monica Peres, Capital; Service Revenue; Rent Expense.
2. After making the journal entries in Daily Exercise 2-7, post from the journal to the ledger. No dates or posting references are required. Take the balance of each account, and denote it as *Bal.*
3. Prepare the trial balance, complete with a proper heading, at June 3, 19X8. Use the trial balance on page 56 as a guide.

DE2-13 Intel Corporation, famous for the Pentium© processor, reported the following summarized data at December 31, 1996. Accounts appear in no particular order; dollar amounts are in billions.

Preparing a trial balance (Obj. 5)

Revenues	**$21**	**Other liabilities**	**$ 6**
Other assets	**20**	**Cash**	**4**
Accounts payable	**1**	**Expenses**	**16**
Capital	**12**		

Prepare the trial balance of Intel Corporation at December 31, 1996. List the accounts in their proper order, as on page 56.

DE2-14 Sara Nichols, Attorney, prepared the business's trial balance on page 66. Suppose Nichols made two errors in preparing the trial balance, as follows:

Correcting a trial balance (Obj. 5)

Error 1—Nichols erroneously listed Accounts Receivable of $700 as a credit rather than as a debit.
Error 2—Nichols erroneously listed Service Revenue as a credit balance of $42,000 rather than the correct amount of $4,200.

Consider each error separately.

1. For each error, compute the incorrect trial balance totals for total debits and total credits.
2. Refer to the discussion of correcting trial balance errors on page 54 and show how to correct each error.

Setting up a chart of accounts
(Obj. 6)

DE2-15 Mid-Cities Apartment Locators helps college students locate apartments because Dardanelle Community College has no student housing on campus. Kirk Lang, the owner of Mid-Cities Apartment Locators, is setting up the business's chart of accounts after making an initial investment of cash in the business.

Lang will perform apartment locator services for clients on account. His office will need some supplies, a computer (equipment), and furniture. Lang has borrowed money by signing a note payable to the bank. The business will also purchase on account some of the things it needs.

Expenses of the business will include rent, utilities, and advertising.

Prepare the chart of accounts for Mid-Cities Apartment Locators, including three-digit account numbers. Use Exhibit 2-11, page 60, as a guide.

Analyzing transactions without a journal
(Obj. 7)

DE2-16 Erika Wolens established Sports Depot, a health club, with an initial cash investment of $80,000. The business immediately purchased equipment on account for $30,000.

1. Open the following T-accounts on the books of Sports Depot: Cash; Equipment; Accounts Payable; Erika Wolens, Capital.
2. Record the first two transactions of Sports Depot directly in the T-accounts without using a journal.
3. Compute the balance in each account and show that total debits equal total credits.

Exercises

Using accounting vocabulary
(Obj. 1)

E2-1 Your employer, Amgen Enterprises, has just hired an office manager who does not understand accounting. Amgen's trial balance lists Cash of $51,000. Write a short memo to the office manager, explaining the accounting process that produced this listing on the trial balance. Mention *debits, credits, journal, ledger, posting,* and *trial balance.*

Using debits and credits with the accounting equation
(Obj. 1, 2)

E2-2 *Link Back to Chapter 1 (Accounting Equation).* The Coca-Cola Company is famous worldwide for soft drinks. At the end of 1995, Coca-Cola had total assets of $15 billion and liabilities totaling $10 billion.

REQUIRED

1. Write the company's accounting equation, and label each element as a debit amount or a credit amount.
2. Coca-Cola's total revenues for 1995 were $15 billion, and total expenses for the year were $12 billion. How much was Coca-Cola's net income (or net loss) for 1995? Write the equation to compute Coca-Cola's net income, and indicate which element is a debit amount and which element is a credit amount. Does net income represent a net debit or a net credit? Does net loss represent a net debit or a net credit? Review Exhibit 1-7, page 21, if needed.
3. During 1995, the owners of Coca-Cola withdrew $2 billion in the form of dividends (same as owner Withdrawals). Did the dividends represent a debit amount or a credit amount?
4. Considering both Coca-Cola's net income (or net loss) and dividends for 1995, by how much did the company's owners' equity increase or decrease during 1995? Was the increase in owners' equity a debit amount or a credit amount?

Analyzing and journalizing transactions
(Obj. 2, 3)

E2-3 Analyze the following transactions in the manner shown for the December 1 transaction of Telemark Cellular. Also record each transaction in the journal. Explanations are not required.

Dec.	1	Paid utilities expense of $700. (*Analysis:* The expense utilities expense is increased; therefore, debit Utilities Expense. The asset cash is decreased; therefore, credit Cash.)		
	1	Utilities Expense	700	
		Cash		700
	5	Borrowed $7,000 cash, signing a note payable.		
	10	Performed service on account for a customer, $1,600.		
	12	Purchased office furniture on account, $800.		
	19	Sold for $74,000 land that had cost this same amount.		

Dec. 24 Purchased building for $140,000; signed a note payable.
27 Paid the liability created on December 12.

Applying the rules of debit and credit ***(Obj. 2)***

E2-4 Refer to Exercise 2-3 for the transactions of Telemark Cellular.

REQUIRED

1. Open the following T-accounts with their December 1 balances: Cash, debit balance $6,000; Land, debit balance $74,000; Toni Steere, Capital, credit balance $80,000.
2. Record the transactions of Exercise 2-3 directly in the T-accounts affected. Use the dates as posting references. Journal entries are not required.
3. Compute the December 31 balance for each account, and prove that total debits equal total credits.

Journalizing transactions ***(Obj. 3)***

E2-5 Wellness Health Club engaged in the following transactions during March 19X3, its first month of operations:

Mar. 1 Lou Stryker invested $45,000 of cash to start the business.
2 Purchased office supplies of $200 on account.
4 Paid $40,000 cash for a building to use as a future office.
6 Performed service for customers and received cash, $2,000.
9 Paid $100 on accounts payable.
17 Performed service for customers on account, $1,600.
23 Received $1,200 cash from a customer on account.
31 Paid the following expenses: salary, $1,200; rent, $500.

REQUIRED

Record the preceding transactions in the journal of Wellness Health Club. Key transactions by date and include an explanation for each entry, as illustrated in the chapter. Use the following accounts: Cash; Accounts Receivable; Office Supplies; Building; Accounts Payable; Lou Stryker, Capital; Service Revenue; Salary Expense; Rent Expense.

Posting to the ledger and preparing a trial balance ***(Obj. 4, 5)***

E2-6 Refer to Exercise 2-5 for the transactions of Wellness Health Club.

REQUIRED

1. After journalizing the transactions of Exercise 2-5, post the entries to the ledger, using T-account format. Key transactions by date. Date the ending balance of each account Mar. 31.
2. Prepare the trial balance of Wellness Health Club at March 31, 19X3.

Describing transactions and posting ***(Obj. 2, 3)***

E2-7 The journal of Rosenberg & Associates includes the following transaction entries for August 19X6.

Journal				**Page 5**
Date	**Accounts and Explanation**	**Post. Ref.**	**Debit**	**Credit**
Aug. 2	Cash		18,000	
	Marvin Rosenberg, Capital			18,000
5	Cash		15,000	
	Note Payable			15,000
9	Supplies		270	
	Accounts Payable			270
11	Accounts Receivable		2,630	
	Sales Revenue			2,630
14	Rent Expense		4,200	
	Cash			4,200
22	Cash		1,400	
	Accounts Receivable			1,400
25	Advertising Expense		350	
	Cash			350
27	Accounts Payable		270	
	Cash			270
31	Utilities Expense		220	
	Accounts Payable			220

REQUIRED

1. Describe each transaction.
2. Post the transactions to the ledger using the following account numbers: Cash, 110; Accounts Receivable, 120; Supplies, 130; Accounts Payable, 210; Note Payable, 230; Marvin Rosenberg, Capital, 310; Sales Revenue, 410; Rent Expense, 510; Advertising Expense, 520;

Utilities Expense, 530. Use dates, journal references, and posting references as illustrated in Exhibit 2-8. You may write the account numbers as posting references directly in your book unless directed otherwise by your instructor.

3. Compute the balance in each account after posting. Prepare Rosenberg & Associates' trial balance at August 31, 19X6.

Journalizing transactions ***(Obj. 3)***

E2-8 The first five transactions of Chirac Security Company have been posted to the company's accounts as follows:

Cash	
(1) 50,000	(3) 42,000
(4) 7,000	(5) 6,000

Supplies	
(2) 400	

Equipment	
(5) 6,000	

Land	
(3) 42,000	

Accounts Payable	
	(2) 400

Note Payable	
	(4) 7,000

Jacques Chirac, Capital	
	(1) 50,000

REQUIRED

Prepare the journal entries that served as the sources for the five transactions. Include an explanation for each entry as illustrated in the chapter.

Preparing a trial balance ***(Obj. 5)***

E2-9 Prepare the trial balance of Chirac Security Company at April 30, 19X4, using the account data from Exercise 2-8.

Preparing a trial balance ***(Obj. 5)***

E2-10 The accounts of Allergan Company follow with their normal balances at December 31, 19X4. The accounts are listed in no particular order.

Account	Balance
Mario Allergan, capital	$48,800
Advertising expense	650
Accounts payable	4,300
Sales commission revenue	22,000
Land	29,000
Note payable	45,000
Cash	5,000
Salary expense	6,000
Building	65,000
Rent expense	2,000
Mario Allergan, withdrawals	6,000
Utilities expense	400
Accounts receivable	5,500
Supplies expense	300
Supplies	250

REQUIRED

Prepare the company's trial balance at December 31, 19X4, listing accounts in proper sequence, as illustrated in the chapter. For example, Supplies comes before Building and Land. List the expense with the largest balance first, the expense with the next largest balance second, and so on.

Correcting errors in a trial balance ***(Obj. 5)***

E2-11 The trial balance of PacifiCare Enterprises at March 31, 19X9, does not balance:

Cash	**$ 4,200**	
Accounts receivable	**2,000**	
Supplies	**600**	
Land	**66,000**	
Accounts payable		**$23,000**
Jan Ekberg, capital		**41,600**
Service revenue		**9,700**
Salary expense	**1,700**	
Rent expense	**800**	
Utilities expense	**300**	
Total	**$75,600**	**$74,300**

Investigation of the accounting records reveals that the bookkeeper

a. Recorded a $400 cash revenue transaction by debiting Accounts Receivable. The credit entry was correct.
b. Posted a $1,000 credit to Accounts Payable as $100.
c. Did not record utilities expense or the related account payable in the amount of $200.
d. Understated Jan Ekberg, Capital, by $400.

Prepare the correct trial balance at March 31, complete with a heading. Journal entries are not required.

REQUIRED

E2-12 Open the following T-accounts: Cash; Accounts Receivable; Office Supplies; Office Furniture; Accounts Payable; Nick Loren, Capital; Nick Loren, Withdrawals; Service Revenue; Salary Expense; Rent Expense.

Recording transactions without a journal ***(Obj. 7)***

Record the following transactions directly in the T-accounts without using a journal. Use the letters to identify the transactions. Take the balance of each account.

a. Loren opened an accounting firm by investing $12,400 cash and office furniture valued at $5,400.
b. Paid monthly rent of $1,500.
c. Purchased office supplies on account, $800.
d. Paid employee's salary, $1,800.
e. Paid $400 of the account payable created in transaction (c).
f. Performed accounting service on account, $1,700.
g. Withdrew $2,000 for personal use.

E2-13 After recording the transactions in Exercise 2-12, prepare the trial balance of Nick Loren, CPA, at May 31, 19X7.

Preparing a trial balance ***(Obj. 5)***

E2-14 Medtronic Medical Supply began when Elaine Peugeot invested $35,000 cash in a business bank account. During the first week, the business purchased supplies on credit for $8,000 and paid $12,000 cash for equipment. Peugeot later paid $6,000 on account.

Analyzing transactions without a journal ***(Obj. 7)***

REQUIRED

1. Open the following T-accounts: Cash; Supplies; Equipment; Accounts Payable; Elaine Peugeot, Capital.
2. Record the four transactions described above directly in the T-accounts without using a journal.
3. Compute the balance in each account, and show that total debit balances equal total credit balances after you have recorded all the transactions. The T-accounts on page 54 provide a guide for your answer.

Continuing Exercise

Exercise 2-15 is the first exercise in a sequence that begins an accounting cycle. The cycle is completed in Chapter 5.

E2-15 Alvin Derring completed these transactions during the first half of December:

Recording transactions and preparing a trial balance ***(Obj. 2, 3, 4, 5)***

Dec. 2 Invested $12,000 to start a consulting practice, Alvin Deering, Consultant.
2 Paid monthly office rent, $500.
3 Paid cash for a Dell computer, $3,000. The computer is expected to remain in service for five years.
4 Purchased office furniture on account, $3,600. The furniture should last for five years.
5 Purchased supplies on account, $300.
9 Performed service for a client and received cash for the full amount of $800.
12 Paid utility expenses, $200.
18 Performed consulting service for a client on account, $1,700.

REQUIRED

1. Open T-accounts in the ledger: Cash; Accounts Receivable; Supplies; Equipment; Furniture; Accounts Payable; Alvin Deering, Capital; Alvin Deering, Withdrawals; Service Revenue; Rent Expense; Utilities Expense; and Salary Expense.
2. Journalize the transactions. Explanations are not required.
3. Post to the T-accounts. Key all items by date, and denote an account balance as Bal. Formal posting references are not required.
4. Prepare a trial balance at December 18. In the Continuing Exercise of Chapter 3, we will add transactions for the remainder of December and will prepare a trial balance at December 31.

CHALLENGE EXERCISES

E2-16 The owner of Northeast Financial Services needs to compute the following summary information from the accounting records:

Computing financial statement amounts without a journal ***(Obj. 7)***

a. Net income for the month of March.
b. Total cash paid during March.

c. Cash collections from customers during March.
d. Cash paid on a note payable during March.

The quickest way to compute these amounts is to analyze the following accounts:

Account	Balance Feb. 28	Balance Mar. 31	Additional Information for the Month of March
a. Owner, Capital	$ 9,000	$15,000	Withdrawals, $4,000
b. Cash	5,000	3,000	Cash receipts, $61,000
c. Accounts Receivable	24,000	26,000	Revenues on account, $55,000
d. Note Payable	13,000	16,000	New borrowing on a note payable, $9,000

The net income for March can be computed as follows:

Owner, Capital

Debit		Credit		
		Feb. 28 Bal.	9,000	
March Withdrawals	4,000	March Net Income	×	= $10,000
		March 31 Bal.	15,000	

Use a similar approach to compute the other three items.

Analyzing accounting errors
(Obj. 2, 3, 4, 5)

E2-17 Felix Hart has trouble keeping his debits and credits equal. During a recent month, he made the following errors:

a. In journalizing a receipt of cash for service revenue, Hart debited Cash for $900 instead of the correct amount of $1,900. Hart credited Service Revenue for $900, the incorrect amount.
b. Hart posted a $700 utility expense as $70. The credit posting to Cash was correct.
c. In preparing the trial balance, Hart omitted a $20,000 note payable.
d. Hart recorded a $120 purchase of supplies on account by debiting Supplies and crediting Accounts Payable for $210.
e. In recording a $400 payment on account, Hart debited Supplies and credited Accounts Payable.

REQUIRED

1. For each of these errors, state whether the total debits equal total credits on the trial balance.
2. Identify any accounts with misstated balances, and indicate the amount and direction of the error (such as account balance too high or too low).

Beyond the Numbers

Identifying the accounts of a new business
(Obj. 6)

BN2-1 Tom O'Brien asks your advice in setting up the accounting records for his new business. The business will be a photography studio and will operate in a rented building. O'Brien will need office equipment and cameras. The business will borrow money on notes payable to buy the needed equipment. O'Brien will purchase on account photographic supplies and office supplies. Each asset has a related expense account, some of which have not yet been discussed. For example, equipment wears out (depreciates) and thus needs a depreciation account. As supplies are used up, the business must record a supplies expense.

The business will need an office manager. O'Brien anticipates paying this person a weekly salary of $300. Other expenses will include advertising and insurance.

O'Brien will want to know which aspects of the business are the most, and the least, profitable, so he will need a separate service revenue account for portraits, school pictures, and weddings. He will let his better customers open accounts receivable with the business.

REQUIRED

List all the accounts the photography studio will need, starting with the assets and ending with the expenses. Indicate which accounts will be reported on the balance sheet and which accounts will appear on the income statement.

ETHICAL ISSUE

Caritas, a charitable organization in Encino, California, has a standing agreement with Encino State Bank. The agreement allows Caritas to overdraw its cash balance at the bank when donations are running low. In the past, Caritas managed funds wisely and rarely used this privilege. Don Hunter has recently become the president of Caritas. To expand operations, Hunter acquired office equipment and spent large amounts for fundraising. During Hunter's presidency, Caritas has maintained a negative bank balance of approximately $14,000.

REQUIRED

What is the ethical issue in this situation? State why you approve or disapprove of Hunter's management of Caritas funds.

Problems (GROUP A)

Analyzing a trial balance (Obj. 1)

P2-1A *Link Back to Chapter 1 (Balance Sheet, Income Statement).* The owner of Medtech Company is selling the business. He offers the following trial balance to prospective buyers. Your best friend is considering buying Medtech Company. She seeks your advice in interpreting this information. Specifically, she asks whether this trial balance is the same as a balance sheet and an income statement. She also wonders whether Medtech is a sound business. After all, the company's accounts are in balance.

MEDTECH COMPANY Trial Balance December 31, 19X4		
Cash	$ 7,000	
Accounts receivable	11,000	
Prepaid expenses	4,000	
Land	31,000	
Accounts payable		$ 31,000
Note payable		20,000
Abe Gianela, capital		33,000
Abe Gianela, withdrawals	21,000	
Service revenue		72,000
Wage expense	48,000	
Rent expense	14,000	
Advertising expense	13,000	
Supplies expense	7,000	
Total	$156,000	$156,000

REQUIRED

Write a short note to answer your friend's questions. To aid her decision, state how she can use the information on the trial balance to compute Medtech's net income or net loss for the current period. State the amount of net income or net loss in your note. Refer to Exhibit 1-7, page 21, if needed.

Analyzing and journalizing transactions (Obj. 2, 3)

P2-2A Christine Eccles practices medicine under the business title Christine Eccles, M.D. During May, her medical practice engaged in the following transactions:

May 1 Eccles deposited $35,000 cash in the business bank account. The business gave Eccles owner's equity in the business.
5 Paid monthly rent on medical equipment, $700.
9 Paid $22,000 cash to purchase land for an office site.
10 Purchased supplies on account, $1,200.
19 Paid $1,000 on account.
22 Borrowed $20,000 from the bank for business use. Eccles signed a note payable to the bank in the name of the business.
30 Revenues earned during the month included $6,000 cash and $5,000 on account.
30 Paid employees' salaries ($2,400), office rent ($1,500), and utilities ($400).
30 Withdrew $4,000 from the business for personal use.

Eccles' business uses the following accounts: Cash; Accounts Receivable; Supplies; Land; Accounts Payable; Notes Payable; Christine Eccles, Capital; Christine Eccles, Withdrawals; Service Revenue; Salary Expense; Rent Expense; Utilities Expense.

REQUIRED

1. Analyze each transaction of Christine Eccles, M.D., as shown for the May 1 transaction:

   May 1 The asset Cash is increased. Increases in assets are recorded by debits; therefore, debit Cash. The owner's equity is increased. Increases in owner's equity are recorded by credits; therefore, credit Christine Eccles, Capital.

2. Journalize each transaction. Explanations are not required.

Journalizing transactions, posting to T-accounts, and preparing a trial balance (Obj. 2, 3, 4, 5)

P2-3A Ray LeBeau opened a law office on January 2 of the current year. During the first month of operations, the business completed the following transactions:

Jan. 2 LeBeau deposited $40,000 cash in the business bank account Ray LeBeau, Attorney.
3 Purchased supplies, $500, and furniture, $2,600, on account.
4 Performed legal service for a client and received cash, $1,500.
7 Paid cash to acquire land for a future office site, $22,000.
11 Defended a client in court and billed the client for $800.
15 Paid secretary's salary, $650.
16 Paid for the furniture purchased January 3 on account.
18 Received partial payment from client on account, $400.
19 Prepared legal documents for a client on account, $900.
29 Received $1,800 cash for helping a client sell real estate.
31 Paid secretary's salary, $650.
31 Paid rent expense, $700.
31 Withdrew $2,200 for personal use.

REQUIRED

Open the following T-accounts: Cash; Accounts Receivable; Supplies; Furniture; Land; Accounts Payable; Ray LeBeau, Capital; Ray LeBeau, Withdrawals; Service Revenue; Salary Expense; Rent Expense.

1. Record each transaction in the journal, using the account titles given. Key each transaction by date. Explanations are not required.
2. Post the transactions to the ledger, using transaction dates as posting references in the ledger. Label the balance of each account *Bal.*, as shown in the chapter.
3. Prepare the trial balance of Ray LeBeau, Attorney, at January 31 of the current year.

Journalizing transactions, posting to accounts in four-column format, and preparing a trial balance
(Obj. 2, 3, 4, 5)

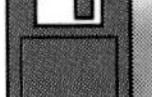

P2-4A The trial balance of the law practice of John Koch, Attorney, at November 15, 19X3, follows.

JOHN KOCH, ATTORNEY
Trial Balance
November 15, 19X3

Account Number	Account	Debit	Credit
11	Cash	$ 3,000	
12	Accounts receivable	8,000	
13	Supplies	600	
14	Land	35,000	
21	Accounts payable		$ 4,600
31	John Koch, capital		40,000
32	John Koch, withdrawals	2,300	
41	Service revenue		7,100
51	Salary expense	1,800	
52	Rent expense	1,000	
	Total	$51,700	$51,700

During the remainder of November, Koch completed the following transactions:

Nov. 16 Collected $4,000 cash from a client on account.
17 Performed tax service for a client on account, $1,700.
21 Paid on account, $2,600.
22 Purchased supplies on account, $200.
23 Withdrew $2,100 for personal use.
23 Used personal funds to pay for the renovation of private residence, $55,000.
24 Received $1,900 cash for legal work just completed.
30 Paid rent, $700.
30 Paid employees' salaries, $2,400.

REQUIRED

1. Record the transactions that occurred during November 16 through 30 on page 6 of the journal. Include an explanation for each entry.
2. Post the transactions to the ledger, using dates, account numbers, journal references, and posting references. Open the ledger accounts listed in the trial balance together with their balances at November 15. Use the four-column account format illustrated in the chapter (Exhibit 2-9). Enter *Bal.* (for previous balance) in the Item column, and place a check mark (✓) in the journal reference column for the November 15 balance of each account.
3. Prepare the trial balance of John Koch, Attorney, at November 30, 19X3.

P2-5A ⬅ *Link Back to Chapter 1 (Income Statement).* The trial balance for Matson Financial Services does not balance. The following errors were detected:

Correcting errors in a trial balance **(Obj. 2, 5)**

- **a.** The cash balance is understated by $400.
- **b.** Rent expense of $200 was erroneously posted as a credit rather than a debit.
- **c.** The balance of Advertising Expense is $300, but it is listed as $400 on the trial balance.
- **d.** A $600 debit to Accounts Receivable was posted as $60.
- **e.** The balance of Utilities Expense is understated by $60.
- **f.** A $1,300 debit to the Withdrawal account was posted as a debit to Emily Matson, Capital.
- **g.** A $100 purchase of supplies on account was neither journalized nor posted.
- **h.** A $5,600 credit to Service Revenue was not posted.
- **i.** Office furniture should be listed in the amount of $1,300.

MATSON FINANCIAL SERVICES
Trial Balance
October 31, 19X1

Cash	$ 3,800	
Accounts receivable	2,000	
Supplies	500	
Office furniture	2,300	
Land	46,000	
Accounts payable		$ 2,800
Note payable		18,300
Emily Matson, capital		29,500
Emily Matson, withdrawals	3,700	
Service revenue		4,900
Salary expense	1,300	
Rent expense	600	
Advertising expense	400	
Utilities expense	200	
Total	$60,800	$55,500

REQUIRED

1. Prepare the correct trial balance at October 31. Journal entries are not required.
2. Prepare Matson Financial Services' income statement for the month ended October 31, 19X1, to determine whether the business had a net income or a net loss for the month. Refer to Exhibit 1-7, page 21, if needed.

P2-6A Jay Irani started Irani Catering Service, and during the first month of operations (January, 19X7), he completed the following selected transactions:

Recording transactions directly in the ledger, preparing a trial balance **(Obj. 2, 5, 7)**

- **a.** Irani began the business with an investment of $15,000 cash and a van (automobile) valued at $13,000. The business gave Irani owner's equity in the business.
- **b.** Borrowed $25,000 from the bank; signed a note payable.
- **c.** Paid $32,000 for food-service equipment.
- **d.** Purchased supplies on account, $400.
- **e.** Paid employee's salary, $1,300.
- **f.** Received $500 for a catering job performed for customers.
- **g.** Performed service at a wedding on account, $3,300.
- **h.** Paid $100 of the account payable created in transaction (d).
- **i.** Received an $800 bill for advertising expense that will be paid in the near future.
- **j.** Received cash on account, $1,100.
- **k.** Paid the following cash expenses:
  - **(1)** Rent, $1,000.
  - **(2)** Insurance, $600.
- **l.** Withdrew $2,600 for personal use.

REQUIRED

1. Open the following T-accounts: Cash; Accounts Receivable; Supplies; Food-Service Equipment; Automobile; Accounts Payable; Note Payable; Jay Irani, Capital; Jay Irani, Withdrawals; Service Revenue; Salary Expense; Rent Expense; Advertising Expense; Insurance Expense.
2. Record the transactions directly in the T-accounts without using a journal. Use the letters to identify the transactions.
3. Prepare the trial balance of Irani Catering Service at January 31, 19X7.

Note: Problem 2-7A should be used in conjunction with Problem 2-6A.

Preparing the financial statements
(Obj. 5)

P2-7A ⇐ *Link Back to Chapter 1 (Income Statement, Statement of Owner's Equity, Balance Sheet).* Refer to Problem 2-6A. After completing the trial balance in Problem 2-6A, prepare the following financial statements for Irani Catering Service:

1. Income statement for the month ended January 31, 19X7.
2. Statement of owner's equity for the month ended January 31, 19X7.
3. Balance sheet at January 31, 19X7.

Draw the arrows linking the statements. If needed, use Exhibit 1-7, page 21, as a guide for preparing the financial statements.

Problems (GROUP B)

Analyzing a trial balance
(Obj. 1)

P2-1B ⇐ *Link Back to Chapter 1 (Balance Sheet, Income Statement).* The owner of Gallop Polling Service is selling the business. He offers the trial balance shown here to prospective buyers. Your best friend is considering buying Gallop Polling Service. He seeks your advice in interpreting this information. Specifically, he asks whether this trial balance is the same as a balance sheet and an income statement. He also wonders whether Gallop must be a sound business. After all, the company's accounts are in balance.

GALLOP POLLING SERVICE Trial Balance December 31, 19X8		
Cash	$ 12,000	
Accounts receivable	27,000	
Prepaid expenses	4,000	
Land	81,000	
Accounts payable		$ 35,000
Note payable		32,000
Ron Gallop, capital		30,000
Ron Gallop, withdrawals	48,000	
Service revenue		134,000
Rent expense	26,000	
Advertising expense	3,000	
Wage expense	23,000	
Supplies expense	7,000	
Total	$231,000	$231,000

REQUIRED

Write a short note to answer your friend's questions. To aid his decision, state how he can use the information on the trial balance to compute Gallop's net income or net loss for the current period. State the amount of net income or net loss in your note. Refer to Exhibit 1-7, page 21, if needed.

Analyzing and journalizing transactions
(Obj. 2, 3)

P2-2B Century City Theater Company owns movie theaters in the shopping centers of a major metropolitan area. Its owner, David Andes, engaged in the following business transactions:

Feb.	1	Andes invested $100,000 personal cash in the business by depositing that amount in a bank account entitled Century City Theater Company. The business gave Andes owner's equity in the company.
	2	Paid $50,000 cash to purchase land for a theater site.
	5	Borrowed $220,000 from the bank to finance the construction of the new theater. Andes signed a note payable to the bank in the name of Century City Theater Company.
	7	Received $20,000 cash from ticket sales and deposited that amount in the bank. (Label the revenue as Sales Revenue.)
	10	Purchased theater supplies on account, $1,700.
	15	Paid employee salaries, $2,800, and rent on equipment, $1,800.
	15	Paid property tax expense on theater building, $1,200.
	16	Paid $800 on account.
	17	Withdrew $6,000 from the business for personal use.

Century City uses the following accounts: Cash; Supplies; Land; Accounts Payable; Notes Payable; David Andes, Capital; David Andes, Withdrawals; Sales Revenue; Salary Expense; Rent Expense; Property Tax Expense.

REQUIRED

1. Analyze each business transaction of Century City Theater Company, as shown for the February 1 transaction:

   Feb. 1 The asset Cash is increased. Increases in assets are recorded by debits; therefore, debit Cash. The owner's equity of the entity is increased. Increases in owner's equity are recorded by credits; therefore, credit David Andes, Capital.

2. Journalize each transaction. Explanations are not required.

P2-3B Martin Dodd opened a law office on September 3 of the current year. During the first month of operations, the business completed the following transactions:

Journalizing transactions, posting to T-accounts, and preparing a trial balance ***(Obj. 2, 3, 4, 5)***

Sep. 3 Dodd transferred $25,000 cash from his personal bank account to a business account entitled Martin Dodd, Attorney. The business gave Dodd owner's equity in the business.
4 Purchased supplies, $200, and furniture, $1,800, on account.
6 Performed legal services for a client and received $4,000 cash.
7 Paid $15,000 cash to acquire land for a future office site.
10 Defended a client in court, billed the client, and received her promise to pay the $600 within one week.
14 Paid for the furniture purchased September 4 on account.
15 Paid secretary's salary, $600.
17 Received partial payment from client on account, $500.
20 Prepared legal documents for a client on account, $800.
28 Received $1,500 cash for helping a client sell real estate.
30 Paid secretary's salary, $600.
30 Paid rent expense, $500.
30 Withdrew $2,400 for personal use.

Open the following T-accounts: Cash; Accounts Receivable; Supplies; Furniture; Land; Accounts Payable; Martin Dodd, Capital; Martin Dodd, Withdrawals; Service Revenue; Salary Expense; Rent Expense.

REQUIRED

1. Record each transaction in the journal, using the account titles given. Key each transaction by date. Explanations are not required.
2. Post the transactions to the ledger, using transaction dates as posting references in the ledger. Label the balance of each account *Bal.*, as shown in the chapter.
3. Prepare the trial balance of Martin Dodd, Attorney, at September 30 of the current year.

P2-4B The trial balance of the accounting practice of Laura Loeb, CPA, is dated February 14, 19X3:

Journalizing transactions, posting to accounts in four-column format, and preparing a trial balance ***(Obj. 2, 3, 4, 5)***

LAURA LOEB, CPA
Trial Balance
February 14, 19X3

Account Number	Account	Debit	Credit
11	Cash	$ 2,000	
12	Accounts receivable	8,000	
13	Supplies	800	
14	Land	18,600	
21	Accounts payable		$ 3,000
31	Laura Loeb, capital		25,000
32	Laura Loeb, withdrawals	1,200	
41	Service revenue		7,200
51	Salary expense	3,600	
52	Rent expense	1,000	
	Total	$35,200	$35,200

During the remainder of February, Loeb completed the following transactions:

Feb. 15 Loeb collected $2,000 cash from a client on account.
16 Performed tax services for a client on account, $900.
20 Paid on account, $1,000.
21 Purchased supplies on account, $100.
21 Withdrew $1,200 for personal use.
21 Paid for a swimming pool for private residence, using personal funds, $13,000.
22 Received cash of $5,100 for consulting work just completed.
28 Paid rent, $800.
28 Paid employees' salaries, $1,600.

REQUIRED

1. Record the transactions that occurred during February 15 through 28 in page 3 of the journal. Include an explanation for each entry.
2. Open the ledger accounts listed in the trial balance, together with their balances at February 14. Use the four-column account format illustrated in the chapter (Exhibit 2-9). Enter *Bal.* (for previous balance) in the Item column, and place a check mark (✓) in the journal reference column for the February 14 balance in each account. Post the transactions to the ledger using dates, account numbers, journal references, and posting references.
3. Prepare the trial balance of Laura Loeb, CPA, at February 28, 19X3.

Correcting errors in a trial balance (Obj. 2, 5)

P2-5B *Link Back to Chapter 1 (Income Statement).* The following trial balance for Cincinnati Landscaping Service does not balance:

CINCINNATI LANDSCAPING SERVICE
Trial Balance
June 30, 19X2

Cash	$ 2,000	
Accounts receivable	10,000	
Supplies	900	
Equipment	3,600	
Land	46,000	
Accounts payable		$ 4,000
Note payable		22,000
Margo Schotte, capital		31,600
Margo Schotte, withdrawals	2,000	
Service revenue		6,500
Salary expense	2,100	
Rent expense	1,000	
Advertising expense	500	
Utilities expense	400	
Total	$68,500	$64,100

The following errors were detected:

a. The cash balance is understated by $700.
b. The cost of the land was $43,000, not $46,000.
c. A $200 purchase of supplies on account was neither journalized nor posted.
d. A $2,800 credit to Service Revenue was not posted.
e. Rent expense of $200 was erroneously posted as a credit rather than a debit.
f. The balance of Advertising Expense is $600, but it was listed as $500 on the trial balance.
g. A $300 debit to Accounts Receivable was posted as $30.
h. The balance of Utilities Expense is overstated by $70.
i. A $900 debit to the Withdrawals account was posted as a debit to Margo Schotte, Capital.

REQUIRED

1. Prepare the correct trial balance at June 30. Journal entries are not required.
2. Prepare the company's income statement for the month ended June 30, 19X2, in order to determine Cincinnati Landscaping Service's net income or net loss for the month. Refer to Exhibit 1-7, page 21, if needed.

Recording transactions directly in the ledger, preparing a trial balance (Obj. 2, 5, 7)

P2-6B Paul Maher started a consulting service and during the first month of operations (September 19X3) completed the following selected transactions:

a. Maher began the business with an investment of $2,000 cash and a building valued at $60,000. The business gave Maher owner's equity in the business.
b. Borrowed $30,000 from the bank; signed a note payable.
c. Purchased office supplies on account, $1,300.
d. Paid $18,000 for office furniture.
e. Paid employee's salary, $2,200.
f. Performed consulting service on account for client, $5,100.
g. Paid $800 of the account payable created in transaction (c).
h. Received a $600 bill for advertising expense that will be paid in the near future.
i. Performed consulting service for customers and received cash, $1,600.
j. Received cash on account, $1,200.
k. Paid the following cash expenses:
   (1) Rent on land, $700.
   (2) Utilities, $400.
l. Withdrew $3,500 for personal use.

REQUIRED

1. Open the following T-accounts: Cash; Accounts Receivable; Office Supplies; Office Furniture; Building; Accounts Payable; Note Payable; Paul Maher, Capital; Paul Maher, Withdrawals; Service Revenue; Salary Expense; Advertising Expense; Rent Expense; Utilities Expense.
2. Record each transaction directly in the T-accounts without using a journal. Use the letters to identify the transactions.
3. Prepare the trial balance of Maher Consulting Service at September 30, 19X3.

Note: Problem 2-7B should be used in conjunction with Problem 2-6B.

Preparing the financial statements ***(Obj. 5)***

P2-7B *Link Back to Chapter 1 (Income Statement, Statement of Owner's Equity, Balance Sheet).* Refer to Problem 2-6B. After completing the trial balance in Problem 2-6B, prepare the following financial statements for Maher Consulting Service:

1. Income statement for the month ended September 30, 19X3.
2. Statement of owner's equity for the month ended September 30, 19X3.
3. Balance sheet at September 30, 19X3.

Draw the arrows linking the statements. If needed, use Exhibit 1-7, page 21, as a guide for preparing the financial statements.

Applying Your Knowledge

DECISION CASES

Recording transactions directly in the ledger, preparing a trial balance, and measuring net income or loss ***(Obj. 2, 5, 7)***

CASE 1. You have been requested by a friend named Vijay Karan to give advice on the effects that certain transactions will have on his business. Time is short, so you cannot journalize the transactions. Instead, you must analyze the transactions without the use of a journal. Karan will continue the business only if he can expect to earn monthly net income of $4,000. The following transactions have occurred during March:

a. Karan deposited $5,000 cash in a business bank account to start the company.
b. Borrowed $4,000 cash from the bank and signed a note payable due within one year.
c. Paid $300 cash for supplies.
d. Paid cash for advertising in the local newspaper, $800.
e. Paid the following cash expenses for one month: secretary's salary, $1,400; office rent, $400; utilities, $300; interest, $50.
f. Earned service revenue on account, $5,300.
g. Earned service revenue and received $2,500 cash.
h. Collected cash from customers on account, $1,200.

REQUIRED

1. Open the following T-accounts: Cash; Accounts Receivable; Supplies; Notes Payable; Vijay Karan, Capital; Service Revenue; Salary Expense; Advertising Expense; Rent Expense; Utilities Expense; Interest Expense.
2. Record the transactions directly in the accounts without using a journal. Key each transaction by letter.
3. Prepare a trial balance at March 31, 19X9. List expenses with the largest amount first, the next largest amount second, and so on. The business name is Karan Apartment Locators.
4. Compute the amount of net income or net loss for this first month of operations. Would you recommend that Karan continue in business?

Using the accounting equation
(Obj. 2)

CASE 2. Answer the following questions. Consider each question separately.

1. Explain the advantages of double-entry bookkeeping over single-entry bookkeeping to a friend who is opening a used book store.
2. When you deposit money in your bank account, the bank credits your account. Is the bank misusing the word *credit* in this context? Why does the bank use the term credit to refer to your deposit, and not *debit?*
3. Your friend asks, "When revenues increase assets and expenses decrease assets, why are revenues credits and expenses debits and not the other way around?" Explain to your friend why revenues are credits and expenses are debits.

FINANCIAL STATEMENT CASES

Journalizing transactions for a company
(Obj. 2, 3)

CASE 1. This problem helps develop skill in recording transactions by using a company's actual account titles. Refer to the NIKE, Inc., financial statements in Appendix A. Assume that NIKE completed the following selected transactions during October 1998:

Oct.	5	Earned sales revenue on account, $60,000.
	9	Borrowed $500,000 by signing a note payable (long-term debt).
	12	Purchased equipment on account, $50,000.
	17	Paid $100,000, a current maturity of a long-term debt, plus interest expense of $8,000.
	19	Earned sales revenue and immediately received cash of $16,000.
	22	Collected the cash on account that was earned on October 5.
	24	Paid rent of $24,000 for three months in advance (debit Prepaid Rent).
	28	Received a home-office electricity bill for $1,000, which will be paid in November (this is an administrative expense).
	30	Paid off half the account payable created on October 12.

REQUIRED

Journalize these transactions, using the following account titles taken from the financial statements of NIKE Inc.: Cash; Accounts Receivable; Prepaid Expenses; Equipment; Current Portion of Long-Term Debt; Accounts Payable; Long-Term Debt; Sales Revenue; Selling and Administrative Expense; Interest Expense. Explanations are not required.

Journalizing transactions for a company
(Obj. 2, 3)

CASE 2. Obtain the annual report of a company of your choosing. Assume that the company completed the following selected transactions during May of the current year:

May	3	Borrowed $350,000 by signing a short-term note payable (may be called Short-Term Debt or other account title).
	5	Paid rent for six months in advance, $4,600 (debit Prepaid Rent).
	9	Earned sales revenue on account, $74,000.
	12	Purchased equipment on account, $33,000.
	17	Paid a telephone bill $300 (this is Selling Expense).
	19	Paid $90,000 of the money borrowed on May 3.
	26	Collected half the cash on account from May 9.
	30	Paid the account payable from May 12.

REQUIRED

1. Journalize these transactions, using the company's actual account titles taken from its annual report. Explanations are not required.
2. Open a ledger account for each account that you used in journalizing the transactions. (For clarity, insert no actual balances in the accounts.) Post the transaction amounts to the accounts, using the dates as posting references. Take the balance of each account.
3. Prepare a trial balance.

Team Project

Contact a local business and arrange with the owner to learn what accounts the business uses.

REQUIRED

1. Obtain a copy of the business's chart of accounts.
2. Prepare the company's financial statements for the most recent month, quarter, or year. You may use either made-up account balances or balances supplied by the owner.

If the business has a large number of accounts within a category, combine related accounts and report a single amount on the financial statements. For example, the company may have several cash accounts. Combine all cash amounts and report a single Cash amount on the balance sheet.

You will probably encounter numerous accounts that you have not yet learned. Deal with these as best you can. The chart of accounts given in the appendix to this chapter will be helpful.

Keep in mind that the financial statements report the balances of the accounts listed in the company's chart of accounts. Therefore, the financial statements must be consistent with the chart of accounts.

APPENDIX to Chapter 2

Typical Charts of Accounts for Different Types of Businesses

(FOR BUSINESSES DISCUSSED IN CHAPTERS 1–12)

Service Proprietorship

Assets

Cash
Accounts Receivable
Allowance for Uncollectible Accounts
Notes Receivable, Short-Term
Interest Receivable
Supplies
Prepaid Rent
Prepaid Insurance
Notes Receivable, Long-Term
Land
Furniture
Accumulated Depreciation—Furniture
Equipment
Accumulated Depreciation—Equipment
Building
Accumulated Depreciation—Building

Liabilities

Accounts Payable
Notes Payable, Short-Term
Salary Payable
Wage Payable
Employee Income Tax Payable
FICA Tax Payable
State Unemployment Tax Payable
Federal Unemployment Tax Payable
Employee Benefits Payable
Interest Payable
Unearned Service Revenue
Notes Payable, Long-Term

Owner's Equity

Owner, Capital
Owner, Withdrawals

Revenues and Gains

Service Revenue
Interest Revenue
Gain on Sale of Land (or Furniture, Equipment, or Building)

Expenses and Losses

Salary Expense
Payroll Tax Expense
Insurance Expense for Employees
Rent Expense
Insurance Expense
Supplies Expense
Uncollectible Account Expense
Depreciation Expense—Furniture
Depreciation Expense—Equipment
Depreciation Expense—Building
Property Tax Expense
Interest Expense
Miscellaneous Expense
Loss on Sale (or Exchange) of Land (Furniture, Equipment, or Building)

Service Partnership

Same as Service Proprietorship, except for Owners' Equity:

Owners' Equity

Partner 1, Capital
Partner 2, Capital
Partner *N*, Capital

Partner 1, Drawing
Partner 2, Drawing
Partner *N*, Drawing

Merchandising Corporation

Assets

Cash
Short-Term Investments (Trading Securities)
Accounts Receivable
Allowance for Uncollectible Accounts
Notes Receivable, Short-Term
Interest Receivable
Inventory
Supplies
Prepaid Rent
Prepaid Insurance
Notes Receivable, Long-Term
Investments in Subsidiaries
Investments in Stock (Available-for-Sale Securities)
Investments in Bonds (Held-to-Maturity Securities)
Other Receivables, Long-Term
Land
Land Improvements
Furniture and Fixtures
Accumulated Depreciation—Furniture and Fixtures
Equipment
Accumulated Depreciation—Equipment
Buildings
Accumulated Depreciation—Buildings
Organization Cost
Franchises
Patents
Leaseholds
Goodwill

Liabilities

Accounts Payable
Notes Payable, Short-Term
Current Portion of Bonds Payable
Salary Payable
Wage Payable
Employee Income Tax Payable
FICA Tax Payable
State Unemployment Tax Payable
Federal Unemployment Tax Payable
Employee Benefits Payable
Interest Payable
Income Tax Payable
Unearned Sales Revenue
Notes Payable, Long-Term
Bonds Payable
Lease Liability
Minority Interest

Stockholders' Equity

Preferred Stock
Paid-in Capital in Excess of Par—Preferred
Common Stock
Paid-in Capital in Excess of Par—Common
Paid-in Capital from Treasury Stock Transactions
Paid-in Capital from Retirement of Stock
Retained Earnings
Foreign Currency Translation Adjustment
Treasury Stock

Revenues and Gains

Sales Revenue
Interest Revenue
Dividend Revenue
Equity-Method Investment Revenue
Unrealized Holding Gain on Trading Investments
Gain on Sale of Investments
Gain on Sale of Land (Furniture and Fixtures, Equipment, or Buildings)
Discontinued Operations—Gain
Extraordinary Gains

Expenses and Losses

Cost of Goods Sold
Salary Expense
Wage Expense
Commission Expense
Payroll Tax Expense
Insurance Expense for Employees
Rent Expense
Insurance Expense
Supplies Expense
Uncollectible Account Expense
Depreciation Expense—Land Improvements
Depreciation Expense—Furniture and Fixtures
Depreciation Expense—Equipment
Depreciation Expense—Buildings
Organization Expense
Amortization Expense—Franchises
Amortization Expense—Leaseholds
Amortization Expense—Goodwill
Income Tax Expense
Unrealized Holding Loss on Trading Investments
Loss on Sale of Investments
Loss on Sale (or Exchange) of Land (Furniture and Fixtures, Equipment, or Buildings)
Discontinued Operations—Loss
Extraordinary Losses

Manufacturing Corporation

Same as Merchandising Corporation, except for Assets and Expenses:

Assets	Expenses (Contra Expenses If Credit Balance)
Inventories:	Direct Materials Price Variance
Materials Inventory	Direct Materials Efficiency Variance
Work in Process Inventory	Direct Labor Price Variance
Finished Goods Inventory	Direct Labor Efficiency Variance
	Manufacturing Overhead Flexible Budget Variance
	Manufacturing Overhead Production Volume Variance

CHAPTER 3

Measuring Business Income: The Adjusting Process

LEARNING OBJECTIVES

After studying this chapter, you should be able to

1. Distinguish accrual-basis accounting from cash-basis accounting

2. Apply the revenue and matching principles

3. Make adjusting entries at the end of the accounting period

4. Prepare an adjusted trial balance

5. Prepare the financial statements from the adjusted trial balance

A1. Account for a prepaid expense recorded initially as an expense

A2. Account for an unearned (deferred) revenue recorded initially as a revenue

> “*None of my competitors had the low-tech, high level of personal service I was looking for.*”
>
> —ANDREA MCGINTY, FOUNDER, IT'S JUST LUNCH

Disappointed by blind dates and personal ads, Andrea McGinty started her own dating service. She also found a lucrative career.

In 1991, Andrea McGinty's fiancé walked out on her five weeks before the wedding, so it was back to the singles scene. One blind date threw a pizza against the wall when she got up to leave. There *had* to be a more civilized way to meet interesting people, McGinty thought. Wouldn't it be nice if a dating service could arrange prescreened lunch dates for busy professionals like herself? "Lunch is over in an hour, and you don't have to kiss goodnight," she dreamed.

McGinty made her dream a reality. Her company, It's Just Lunch, now has 6,000 customers and chalked up $4.5 million in revenues in 1996. McGinty charges $675 to arrange eight dates. Lunch is extra, dutch treat. "These are people who work long hours in fast-track careers. They need help with their social lives," says McGinty.

The business is a money-making machine, netting $400,000 after taxes in 1996 on revenues of $4.5 million. *Source:* Based on Suzanne Oliver, "Yuppie Yenta," Forbes (March 25, 1996), pp. 102–103.

What do we mean when we say that It's Just Lunch *nets* $400,000 per year? The business earns net income, or profit, of $400,000 per year, as reported on its income statement. The business's revenues consist of service-revenue fees of $675 earned by arranging eight lunch dates for a client. What are the business's expenses? Advertising, computer data searches, mailings to clients, and office expenses (such as employee salaries, rent, and supplies). It's Just Lunch operates in much the same way as Gary Lyon, CPA, the accountant whose business we studied in Chapters 1 and 2.

Whether the business is It's Just Lunch, Gary Lyon CPA, or Lands' End, the profit motive increases the owners' drive to carry on the business. As you study this chapter, consider how important net income is to a business.

Net Income, the Income Statement, and Adjusting Entries

How does a business know whether it is profitable? At the end of each accounting period, the entity prepares its financial statements. The period may be a month, three months, six months, or a full year. It's Just Lunch is typical. The company reports on a quarterly basis—at the end of every three months, with annual financial statements at the end of each year.

Whatever the length of the period, the end accounting product is the financial statements. And the most important single amount in these statements is the net income or net loss—the profit or loss—for the period. Net income captures much information: total revenues minus total expenses for the period. A business that consistently earns net income adds value to its owners, its employees, its customers, and society.

The trial balance, introduced in Chapter 2, p. 54, lists the ledger accounts and their balances.

An important step in financial statement preparation is the trial balance. The account balances in the trial balance include the effects of the transactions that occurred during the period—cash collections, purchases of assets, payments of bills, sales of assets, and so on. To measure its income, however, a business must do some additional accounting at the end of the period to bring the records up to date. This process is called *adjusting the books*, and it consists of making special entries called *adjusting entries*. This chapter focuses on these adjusting entries to show how to measure business income.

Objective 1

Distinguish accrual-basis accounting from cash-basis accounting

The accounting profession has concepts and principles to guide the measurement of business income.[1] Chief among these are the concepts of accrual-basis accounting, the accounting period, the revenue principle, and the matching principle. In this chapter, we apply these (and other) concepts and principles to measure the income and prepare the financial statements of Gary Lyon's business for the month of April.

Accrual-Basis Accounting versus Cash-Basis Accounting

Accrual-Basis Accounting. Accounting that records the impact of a business event as it occurs, regardless of whether the transaction affected cash.

Cash-Basis Accounting. Accounting that records transactions only when cash is received or paid.

There are two widely used bases of accounting: the accrual basis and the cash basis. In **accrual-basis accounting,** an accountant records the impact of a business event as it occurs. When the business performs a service, makes a sale, or incurs an expense, the accountant enters the transaction into the books, whether or not cash has been received or paid. In **cash-basis accounting,** the accountant does not record a transaction until cash is received or paid. *Cash receipts are treated as revenues, and cash payments are handled as expenses in a pure cash-basis accounting system.*

". . . the Plaza Hotel uses accrual-basis accounting to match the expenses and related revenues in a given fiscal period."

Suppose a client paid the Plaza Hotel in New York City $15,000 on October 1, 1998, for a three-month stay to begin November 1, 1998. Exhibit 3-1 shows how the hotel would record revenues by the two accounting methods over the three-month period November 1, 1998, through January 31, 1999. In actual practice, the Plaza Hotel uses accrual-basis accounting to match the expenses and related revenues in a given fiscal period.

[1] *FASB Statement No. 130, Reporting Comprehensive Income* (June 1997) requires companies with certain elements of income to report both net income and other comprehensive income. The elements of other comprehensive income are discussed in later chapters.

$1000 = $1,000 Effect on Revenue of $15,000 Collected in Advance

ACCRUAL-BASIS ACCOUNTING
Revenue is recorded when it is earned.

Total $15,000

Nov. 30, '98 | Month Ended Dec. 31, '98 | Jan. 31, '99
1998 | 1999

CASH-BASIS ACCOUNTING
Revenue is recorded when cash is received.

Total $15,000

Nov. 30, '98 | Month Ended Dec. 31, '98 | Jan. 31, '99
1998 | 1999

EXHIBIT 3-1
Accrual-Basis Accounting versus Cash-Basis Accounting for $15,000 of Revenue

■ Daily Exercise 3-1

GAAP requires that a business use the accrual basis. This means that the accountant records revenues as they are *earned* and expenses as they are *incurred*—not necessarily when cash changes hands.

Using accrual-basis accounting, It's Just Lunch records revenue when it sells dating services to a client, not when it collects cash later. Gary Lyon records revenue when he performs services for a client on account. Lyon has earned the revenue, and his efforts have generated an account receivable from the client for whom he did the work. By contrast, if Gary Lyon used cash-basis accounting, he would not record revenue at the time he performed the service. He would wait until he received cash.

Why does GAAP require that businesses use the accrual basis? Because accrual accounting provides a more complete portrayal of operating performance and financial position. Suppose Gary Lyon's accounting period ends after he earned some revenue but before he has collected the money. If he uses the cash-basis method, his financial statements would not report this revenue or the related account receivable. As a result, the financial statements would be misleading. Revenue on the income statement and the asset Accounts Receivable on the balance sheet would be understated, and thus his business would look less successful than it actually is. If he wants to get a bank loan to expand his practice, the understated revenue and asset figures might hurt his chances.

Using accrual-basis accounting, Gary Lyon treats expenses in a like manner. For instance, salary expense includes both amounts paid to employees and any amount owed to employees but not yet paid.

Under cash-basis accounting, a business records salary expense only when it actually pays the employee. Suppose Gary Lyon owed his secretary a salary, and the financial statements were drawn up before Lyon paid. Expenses and liabilities would be understated, so the business would look more successful than it really is. This incomplete information would *not* give potential creditors an accurate accounting.

■ Daily Exercise 3-2

Learning Tip: You can distinguish cash and accrual accounting this way:
Cash basis: Record revenue when you receive cash, regardless of when the service was performed or the sale made. Record expenses when you pay cash, regardless of when the expense was incurred.
Accrual basis: Forget cash flow. Record revenue when you make a sale or perform a service. Record expenses when the business uses goods or services. Revenues and expenses may not coincide with cash flows.

Clearly, accrual-basis accounting provides more complete information than cash-basis accounting does. This difference is important because the more complete the data, the better equipped decision makers are to reach conclusions about the firm's financial health and future prospects. Four concepts used in accrual-basis accounting are the accounting period, the revenue principle, the matching principle, and the time-period concept.

The Accounting Period

The only way to know for certain how successfully a business has operated is to close its doors, sell all its assets, pay the liabilities, and return any leftover cash to the owners.

This process, called *liquidation*, is the same as going out of business. Obviously, it is not practical for accountants to measure business income in this manner. Instead, businesses need periodic reports on their progress. Accountants slice time into small segments and prepare financial statements for specific periods.

The most basic accounting period is one year, and virtually all businesses prepare annual financial statements. For about 60% of large companies in a recent survey, the annual accounting period runs the calendar year from January 1 through December 31. Other companies use a *fiscal year*, which ends on some date other than December 31. The year-end date is usually the low point in business activity for the year. Retailers are a notable example. For instance, J.C. Penney Company uses a fiscal year ending on January 31 because the low point in Penney's business activity falls during January after the Christmas sales. J.C. Penney does more than 30% of its yearly sales during November and December, but only 5% in January. A company's fiscal year can end on any date.

". . . J.C. Penney Company uses a fiscal year ending on January 31 because the low point in Penney's business activity falls during January after the Christmas sales."

Managers and investors cannot wait until the end of the year to gauge a company's progress. Companies therefore prepare financial statements for *interim* periods, which are less than a year. Managers want financial information often, so monthly statements are common. A series of monthly statements can be combined for quarterly and semiannual periods. Most of the discussions in this book are based on an annual accounting period, but the procedures and statements can be applied to interim periods as well.

Objective 2

Apply the revenue and matching principles

The Revenue Principle

The **revenue principle** tells accountants (1) *when* to record revenue by making a journal entry, and (2) the *amount* of revenue to record. When we speak of "recording" something in accounting, we mean make an entry in the journal. That is where the accounting process starts.

Revenue, defined in Chapter 1, p. 13, is the increase in owner's equity from delivering goods and services to customers in the course of operating a business.

Revenue Principle. The basis for recording revenues; tells accountants when to record revenue and the amount of revenue to record.

■ Daily Exercise 3-3

The general principle guiding *when* to record revenue says to record revenue once it has been earned—but not before. In most cases, revenue is earned when the business has delivered a completed good or service to the customer. The business has done everything required by the agreement, including transferring the item to the customer. Exhibit 3-2 shows two situations that provide guidance on when to record revenue. The first situation illustrates when *not* to record revenue—because the client merely states her plans. Situation 2 illustrates when revenue should be recorded—after Gary Lyon has performed a service for the client.

The general principle guiding the *amount* of revenue says to record revenue equal to the cash value of the goods or the service transferred to the customer. Suppose that in order to obtain a new client, Gary Lyon performs accounting service for the price of $500. Ordinarily, Lyon would have charged $600 for this service. How much revenue

EXHIBIT 3-2
Recording Revenue: The Revenue Principle

should Lyon record? The answer is $500, because that was the cash value of the transaction. Lyon will not receive the full value of $600, so that is not the amount of revenue to record. He will receive only $500 cash, which pinpoints the amount of revenue he has earned.

The Matching Principle

The **matching principle** is the basis for recording expenses. Recall that expenses—such as rent, utilities, and advertising—are the costs of operating a business. Expenses are the costs of assets that are used up and liabilities that are increased in the earning of revenue. The matching principle directs accountants to (1) identify all expenses incurred during the accounting period, (2) measure the expenses, and (3) match the expenses against the revenues earned during that same span of time. To match expenses against revenues means to subtract the expenses from the revenues in order to compute net income or net loss. Exhibit 3-3 illustrates the matching principle.

An expense, defined in Chapter 1, p. 13, is a decrease in owner's equity that occurs from using assets or increasing liabilities in the course of operating a business.

Matching Principle. The basis for recording expenses. Directs accountants to identify all expenses incurred during the period, to measure the expenses, and to match them against the revenues earned during that same span of time.

There is a natural link between revenues and some types of expenses. Accountants follow the matching principle by first identifying a period's revenues and the expenses that can be linked to particular revenues. For example, a business that pays sales commissions to its sales personnel will have commission expense if the employees make sales. If they make no sales, the business has no commission expense. *Cost of goods sold* is another example. If there are no sales of Ford automobiles, Ford Motor Company has no cost of goods sold.

■ Daily Exercise 3-4
■ Daily Exercise 3-5

Other expenses are not so easy to link with particular sales. For example, monthly rent expense occurs regardless of the revenues earned during the period. The matching principle directs accountants to identify those types of expenses with a particular time period, such as a month or a year. If Gary Lyon employs a secretary at a monthly salary of $1,900, the business will record salary expense of $1,900 for each month.

How does Gary Lyon account for a transaction that begins in April but ends in May? How does he bring the accounts up to date for preparing the financial statements? To answer these questions, accountants use the time-period concept.

The Time-Period Concept

Managers, investors, and creditors make decisions daily and need periodic readings on the business's progress. Therefore, accountants prepare financial statements at regular intervals.

The **time-period concept** ensures that accounting information is reported at regular intervals. It interacts with the revenue principle and the matching principle to underlie the use of accruals. To measure income accurately, companies update the revenue and expense accounts immediately before the end of the period. Hawaiian Airlines, Inc., provides an example of an expense accrual. At December 31, 1996, Hawaiian Airlines recorded employee compensation of $2.5 million that the company owed its workers for unpaid services performed before year end. The company's accrual entry was

Time-Period Concept. Ensures that accounting information is reported at regular intervals.

1996			
Dec. 31	Salary and Wage Expense................	2,500,000	
	Salary and Wage Payable.........		2,500,000
	Accrued salary expense.		

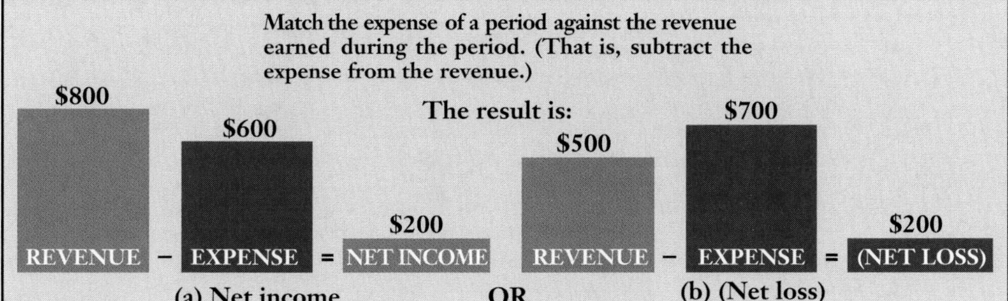

EXHIBIT 3-3
Recording Expenses: the Matching Principle

■ Daily Exercise 3-6

This entry serves two purposes. First, it assigns the expense to the proper period. Without the accrual entry at December 31, total expenses of 1996 would be understated, and as a result, net income would be overstated. The expense would incorrectly fall in 1997 when the company pays the next payroll. Second, the accrual entry records the liability for the balance sheet at December 31, 1996. Without the accrual entry, total liabilities would be understated.

At the end of the accounting period, companies also accrue revenues that have been earned but not collected. The remainder of the chapter discusses how to make the adjusting entries to bring the accounts up to date.

Adjusting the Accounts

Objective 3

Make adjusting entries at the end of the accounting period

At the end of the period, the accountant prepares the financial statements. This end-of-period process begins with the trial balance, which lists the accounts and their balances after the period's transactions have been recorded in the journal and posted to the accounts in the ledger. We saw how to prepare the trial balance in Chapter 2.

Exhibit 3-4 is the trial balance of Gary Lyon's accounting practice at April 30, 19X1. This *unadjusted trial balance* includes some new accounts that we will explain in this section. It lists most, but not all, of the revenues and expenses of Lyon's accounting practice for the month of April. These trial balance amounts are incomplete because they omit certain revenue and expense transactions that affect more than one accounting period. That is why the trial balance is *unadjusted*. In most cases, however, we refer to it simply as the trial balance, without the label "unadjusted."

Under cash-basis accounting, there would be no need for adjustments to the accounts because all April cash transactions would have been recorded. However, the accrual basis requires adjusting entries at the end of the period in order to produce correct balances for the financial statements. To see why, consider the Supplies account in Exhibit 3-4.

Lyon's accounting practice uses supplies in providing accounting services for clients during the month. This reduces the quantity of supplies on hand and thus constitutes an expense, just like salary expense or rent expense. Gary Lyon does not bother to record this expense daily, and it is not worth the effort to record supplies expense more than once a month. It is time-consuming to make hourly, daily, or even weekly journal entries to record the expense for the use of supplies. So how does Lyon account for supplies expense?

By the end of the month, the Supplies balance of $700 on the unadjusted trial balance (Exhibit 3-4) is not correct. The unadjusted balance represents the amount of supplies on hand at the start of the month plus any supplies purchased during the month. This balance fails to take into account the supplies used (*supplies expense*) during the accounting period. It is necessary, then, to subtract the month's expenses from the amount

EXHIBIT 3-4
Unadjusted Trial Balance

GARY LYON, CPA
Unadjusted Trial Balance
April 30, 19X1

Cash	$24,800	
Accounts receivable	2,250	
Supplies	700	
Prepaid rent	3,000	
Furniture	16,500	
Accounts payable		$13,100
Unearned service revenue		450
Gary Lyon, capital		31,250
Gary Lyon, withdrawals	3,200	
Service revenue		7,000
Salary expense	950	
Utilities expense	400	
Total	$51,800	$51,800

of supplies listed on the trial balance. The resulting new adjusted balance will measure the cost of supplies that are still on hand at April 30, say $400. This is the correct amount of supplies to report on the balance sheet—$400. Adjusting the entry will bring the supplies account up to date.

Adjusting entries assign revenues to the period in which they are earned and expenses to the period in which they are incurred. Adjusting entries also update the asset and liability accounts. They are needed to (1) properly measure the period's income on the income statement, and (2) bring related asset and liability accounts to correct balances for the balance sheet. Adjusting entries, which are the key to accrual-basis accounting, are made before the financial statements are prepared. The end-of-period process of updating the accounts is called *adjusting the accounts, making the adjusting entries,* or *adjusting the books.*

Adjusting Entry. Entry made at the end of the period to assign revenues to the period in which they are earned and expenses to the period in which they are incurred. Adjusting entries help measure the period's income and bring the related asset and liability accounts to correct balances for the financial statements.

A large company uses accounting software to print out a trial balance. For example, Occidental Petroleum (OXY), a large oil company, has its own accounting software that prints a monthly trial balance. The accountants then analyze the amounts on the trial balance. This analysis results in the adjusting entries that OXY posts to update its ledger accounts. OXY's trial balance has now become the company's *adjusted* trial balance. This chapter shows the adjusting process as it moves from the trial balance to the adjusted trial balance.

Two basic types of adjustments are *prepaids* and *accruals.*

Prepaids (Deferrals) and Accruals

In a *prepaid*-type adjustment, the cash transaction occurs before the related expense or revenue is recorded. Prepaids are also called *deferrals* because the recording of the expense or the revenue is deferred until after cash is paid or received. *Accrual*-type adjustments are the opposite of prepaids. For accruals, we record the expense or revenue before the related cash settlement.

Adjusting entries can be further divided into five categories:

1. Prepaid expenses
2. Depreciation of plant assets
3. Accrued expenses
4. Accrued revenues
5. Unearned revenues

The core of this chapter is the discussion of these five types of adjusting entries on pages 97–104. Study this material carefully because it is the most challenging topic in all of introductory accounting.

Prepaid Expenses

Prepaid expenses are advance payments of expense. The category includes miscellaneous assets that typically expire or are used up in the near future. Prepaid rent and prepaid insurance are prepaid expenses. They are called "prepaid" expenses because they are expenses that are paid in advance. Salary expense and utilities expense, among others, are typically *not* prepaid expenses because they are not paid in advance. All companies, large and small, must make adjustments regarding prepaid expenses. For example, McDonald's Corporation, the restaurant chain, must contend with such prepayments as rents, packaging supplies, and insurance.

Prepaid Expense. Advance payments of expenses. A category of miscellaneous assets that typically expire or are used up in the near future. Examples include prepaid rent, prepaid insurance, and supplies.

Learning Tip: Prepaid expenses are assets, not expenses.

PREPAID RENT Landlords usually require tenants to pay rent in advance. This prepayment creates an asset for the renter, who has purchased the future benefit of using the rented item. Suppose Gary Lyon prepays three months' rent on April 1, 19X1, after negotiating a lease for his business office. If the lease specifies monthly rental amounts of $1,000, the entry to record the payment for three months is a debit to the asset account, Prepaid Rent, as follows:

Apr. 1	Prepaid Rent ($1,000 × 3)........................	3,000	
	Cash..		3,000
	Paid three months' rent in advance.		

After posting, Prepaid Rent appears as follows:

ASSETS

Prepaid Rent			
Apr. 1	3,000		

The trial balance at April 30, 19X1, lists Prepaid Rent as an asset with a debit balance of \$3,000. Throughout April, the Prepaid Rent account maintains this beginning balance, as shown in Exhibit 3-4. But \$3,000 is *not* the amount to report for Prepaid Rent on Gary Lyon's balance sheet at April 30. Why?

At April 30, Prepaid Rent should be adjusted to remove from its balance the amount of the asset that has been used up, which is one month's worth of the prepayment. By definition, the amount of an asset that has expired is *expense*. The adjusting entry transfers one-third, or \$1,000 (\$3,000 × 1/3), of the debit balance from Prepaid Rent to Rent Expense. The debit side of the entry records an increase in Rent Expense, and the credit records a decrease in the asset Prepaid Rent:

Apr. 30	Rent Expense (\$3,000 × 1/3).........	1,000	
	Prepaid Rent..........................		1,000
	To record rent expense.		

After posting, Prepaid Rent and Rent Expense appear as follows:

ASSETS

Prepaid Rent			
Apr. 1	3,000	Apr. 30	1,000
Bal.	2,000		

→

EXPENSES

Rent Expense			
Apr. 30	1,000		
Bal.	1,000		

Correct asset amount: \$2,000 → **Total accounted for: \$3,000** ← **Correct expense amount: \$1,000**

The full \$3,000 has been accounted for: Two-thirds measures the asset, and one-third measures the expense. Recording this expense illustrates the matching principle.

The same analysis applies to a prepayment of three months of insurance premiums. The only difference is in the account titles, which would be Prepaid Insurance and Insurance Expense instead of Prepaid Rent and Rent Expense. In a computerized system, the adjusting entry crediting the prepaid account and debiting the expense account could be established to recur automatically in each accounting period until the prepaid account has a zero balance.

The chapter appendix shows an alternative treatment of prepaid expenses. The end result on the financial statements is the same as illustrated here.

SUPPLIES Supplies are accounted for in the same way as prepaid expenses. On April 2, Gary Lyon paid cash of \$700 for office supplies:

Apr. 2	Supplies...............................	700	
	Cash.............................		700
	Paid cash for supplies.		

Assume that Lyon purchased no additional supplies during April. The April 30 trial balance, therefore, lists Supplies with a \$700 debit balance, as shown in Exhibit 3-4. But Lyon's April 30 balance sheet should *not* report supplies of \$700. Why?

During April, Lyon used supplies in performing services for clients. The cost of the supplies used is the measure of *supplies expense* for the month. To measure supplies expense during April, Gary Lyon counts the supplies on hand at the end of the month. This is the amount of the asset (the economic resource) still available to the business. Assume the count at April 30 indicates that supplies costing \$400 remain. Subtracting the \$400 of supplies on hand at the end of April from the cost of supplies available during April (\$700) measures supplies expense during the month (\$300).

Cost of asset available during the period	–	Cost of asset on hand at the end of the period	=	Cost of asset used (expense) during the period
$700	–	**$400**	=	**$300**

The April 30 adjusting entry to update the Supplies account and to record the supplies expense for the month debits the expense and credits the asset, as follows:

Apr. 30	Supplies Expense ($700 – $400).........	300	
	Supplies		300
	To record supplies expense.		

After posting, the Supplies and Supplies Expense accounts appear as follows:

■ Daily Exercise 3-7

ASSETS

Supplies

Apr. 2	700	Apr. 30	300
Bal.	400		

→

EXPENSES

Supplies Expense

Apr. 30	300		
Bal.	300		

Correct asset amount: $400 → **Total accounted for: $700** ← **Correct expense amount: $300**

The Supplies account then enters the month of May with a $400 balance, and the adjustment process is repeated each month.

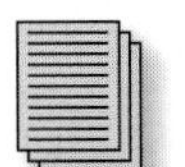

Working It Out At the beginning of the month, supplies were $5,000. During the month, the company purchased $7,800 of supplies. At month's end, $3,600 of supplies were still on hand.

1. What was the cost of supplies used during the month?
2. What is the ending balance of Supplies? Where is this item reported?
3. Make the adjusting entry to update the Supplies account at the end of the month.

Answers

1.

Beginning balance	$5,000
+ Purchases	7,800
– Ending balance	(3,600)
= Expense (Supplies used during the period).....	$9,200

2. The ending balance of Supplies is $3,600. This is the amount that should be reported on the balance sheet.

3.

Supplies Expense..........	9,200	
Supplies.................		9,200

Depreciation of Plant Assets

The logic of the accrual basis is probably best illustrated by how businesses account for plant assets. **Plant assets** are long-lived tangible assets—such as land, buildings, furniture, machinery, and equipment—used in the operations of the business. As one accountant said, "All assets but land are on a march to the junkyard." That is, all plant assets but land decline in usefulness as they age. This decline is an *expense* to the business. Accountants systematically spread the cost of each plant asset, except land, over the years of its useful life. This allocation of a plant asset's cost to expense over its useful life is called **depreciation.**

Plant Asset. Long-lived tangible assets—such as land, buildings, and equipment—used in the operations of a business.

Depreciation. The allocation of a plant asset's cost to expense over its useful life.

Learning Tip: An expense is recorded whenever a good or service is used. As plant assets are used, the portion of the cost that is used during the period is called *depreciation.*

SIMILARITY TO PREPAID EXPENSES The concept underlying accounting for plant assets and depreciation expense is the same as for prepaid expenses. In a sense, plant assets are merely large prepaid expenses that expire over a number of periods. With both prepaid expenses and plant assets, the business purchases an asset that wears out or is used up. As the asset is used, its cost is transferred from the asset account to the expense account. The major difference between prepaid expenses and plant assets is the length of time it takes for the asset to expire. Prepaid expenses usually expire within a year, while most plant assets remain useful for a number of years.

Consider Gary Lyon's accounting practice. Suppose that on April 3 Lyon purchased furniture on account for $16,500 and made this journal entry:

Apr. 3	Furniture	16,500	
	Accounts Payable		16,500
	Purchased office furniture on account.		

After posting, the Furniture account appears as follows:

ASSETS

Furniture		
Apr. 3	**16,500**	

Lyon believes the furniture will remain useful for five years and will be worthless at the end of its life. One way to compute the amount of depreciation for each year is to divide the cost of the asset ($16,500 in our example) by its expected useful life (five years). This procedure—called the *straight-line method*—computes annual depreciation of $3,300 ($16,500/5 years = $3,300 per year). Depreciation for the month of April is $275 ($3,300/12 months = $275 per month).

THE ACCUMULATED DEPRECIATION ACCOUNT Depreciation expense for April is recorded by the following entry:

Apr. 30	Depreciation Expense—Furniture	275	
	Accumulated Depreciation—Furniture		275
	To record depreciation on furniture.		

Accumulated Depreciation is credited instead of Furniture because the original cost of a plant asset (the furniture) should remain in the asset account as long as the business uses the asset. Accountants and managers can then refer to the Furniture account to see how much the asset cost. This information may be useful in a decision about whether to replace the furniture and how much to pay.

Accumulated Depreciation. The cumulative sum of all depreciation expense recorded for an asset.

The amount of depreciation is an *estimate*. Accountants use the **Accumulated Depreciation** account to show the cumulative sum of all depreciation expense recorded for the asset. The balance of the Accumulated Depreciation account increases over the life of the asset.

Contra Account. An account that always has a companion account and whose normal balance is opposite that of the companion account.

Accumulated Depreciation is a *contra asset* account, which means an asset account with a normal credit balance. A **contra account** has two distinguishing characteristics:

- A contra account has a companion account.
- A contra account's normal balance (debit or credit) is opposite that of the companion account.

In this case, Accumulated Depreciation is the contra account that accompanies Furniture. It appears in the ledger directly after Furniture. Furniture has a debit balance, and therefore Accumulated Depreciation, a contra asset, has a credit balance. *All contra asset accounts have credit balances.*

A business carries an accumulated depreciation account for each depreciable asset. If a business has a building and a machine, for example, it will carry the accounts Accumulated Depreciation—Building and Accumulated Depreciation—Machine.

After the depreciation entry has been posted, the Furniture, Accumulated Depreciation, and Depreciation Expense accounts of Gary Lyon, CPA, appear as follows:

ASSETS

Furniture		
Apr. 3	**16,500**	
Bal.	16,500	

CONTRA ASSET

Accumulated Depreciation—Furniture		
	Apr. 30	**275**
	Bal.	275

EXPENSES

Depreciation Expense—Furniture		
Apr. 30	**275**	
Bal.	275	

BOOK VALUE The balance sheet shows the relationship between Furniture and Accumulated Depreciation. The balance of Accumulated Depreciation is subtracted from the balance of Furniture. The resulting net amount of a plant asset (cost minus accumulated depreciation) is called its **book value,** or *net book value*, as shown here for Furniture:

Book Value (of a Plant Asset). The asset's cost minus accumulated depreciation.

Plant Assets:	
Furniture	**$16,500**
Less Accumulated depreciation.........	**(275)**
Book value..	**$16,225**

Suppose Lyon's accounting practice also owns a building that cost $48,000 and on which annual depreciation is $2,400 ($48,000/20 years). The amount of depreciation for one month would be $200 ($2,400/12), and the following entry records depreciation for April:

Apr. 30	Depreciation Expense—Building	200	
	Accumulated Depreciation—Building.........		200
	To record depreciation on building.		

■ Daily Exercise 3-8

The balance sheet at April 30 reports Lyon's plant assets as shown in Exhibit 3-5.

Exhibit 3-6 shows how Johnson & Johnson—makers of Band-Aids, Tylenol, and other health-care products—displayed Property, Plant, and Equipment in its annual report. Johnson & Johnson has real-estate holdings around the world; they are reported in line 1 of Exhibit 3-6. Line 2 includes the cost of buildings and the related equipment (air conditioners and elevators) in those buildings. The company's manufacturing machinery, office equipment, and furniture are given in line 3, and line 4 reports the cost of assets that are under construction.

"... Johnson & Johnson—makers of Band-Aids, Tylenol, and other health-care products—displayed Property, Plant, and Equipment in its annual report."

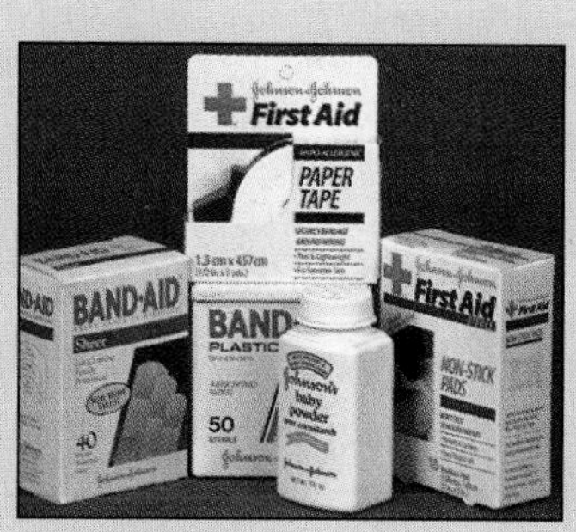

Johnson & Johnson's cost of plant assets was $8,175 million (cost principle). Of the total cost, Johnson & Johnson has depreciated a total of $2,979 million (matching principle). The book value of J&J's plant assets is therefore $8,175 – $2,979 = $5,196 million.

Thinking It Over Describe one similarity and one difference between (1) prepaid expenses and (2) plant assets and the related depreciation.

Answer

Similarity: For both prepaid expenses and plant assets, the business first pays cash; it records the expense later.

Difference: Prepaid expenses cover a shorter time period than plant assets and the related depreciation.

Now let's return to Gary Lyon's situation.

Accrued Expenses

Businesses incur many expenses before they pay cash. Payment is not due until later. Consider an employee's salary. The employer's salary expense and salary payable grow as the employee works, so the liability is said to *accrue*. Another example is interest expense

Plant assets:		
Furniture	$16,500	
Less Accumulated depreciation....................	275	$16,225
Building..	48,000	
Less Accumulated depreciation....................	200	47,800
Book value of plant assets		$64,025

EXHIBIT 3-5
Plant Assets on the Balance Sheet of Gary Lyon, CPA (April 30)

EXHIBIT 3-6
Johnson & Johnson's Reporting of Property, Plant, and Equipment

	Millions
(1) Land and land improvements	$ 344
(2) Buildings and building equipment............	2,611
(3) Machinery and equipment	4,217
(4) Construction in progress...........................	1,003
	8,175
Less Accumulated depreciation......................	2,979
	$5,196

Accrued Expense. An expense that the business has incurred but not yet paid.

on a note payable. Interest accrues as the clock ticks. The term **accrued expense** refers to an expense that the business has incurred but has not yet paid. Therefore, accrued expenses can be viewed as the opposite of prepaid expenses.

It is time-consuming to make hourly, daily, or even weekly journal entries to accrue expenses. Consequently, the accountant waits until the end of the period. Then an adjusting entry brings each expense (and related liability) up to date just before the financial statements are prepared.

Learning Tip: A prepaid expense is paid first and expensed later. An accrued expense is expensed first and paid later. Prepaids and accruals are opposites.

SALARY EXPENSE Most companies pay their employees at set times. Suppose Gary Lyon pays his employee a monthly salary of $1,900, half on the 15th and half on the last day of the month. Here is a calendar for April with the two paydays circled:

APRIL						
S	M	T	W	T	F	S
					1	2
3	4	5	6	7	8	9
10	11	12	13	14	(15)	16
17	18	19	20	21	22	23
24	25	26	27	28	29	(30)

Assume that if either payday falls on the weekend, Lyon pays the employee on the following Monday. During April, Lyon paid his employee's first half-month salary of $950 on Friday, April 15, and recorded the following entry:

Apr. 15	Salary Expense.........	950	
	Cash..................		950
	To pay salary.		

After posting, the Salary Expense account is

EXPENSES

Salary Expense		
Apr. 15	950	

The trial balance at April 30 (Exhibit 3-4) includes Salary Expense, with its debit balance of $950. This unadjusted balance of $950 is Lyon's salary expense for only the first half of April. Because April 30, the second payday of the month, falls on a Saturday, the second half-month amount of $950 will be paid on Monday, May 2. However, Lyon needs to record salary expense for the second half of April. Therefore, at April 30 Lyon makes an adjusting entry for additional *salary expense* and *salary payable* of $950 as follows:

Apr. 30	Salary Expense	950	
	Salary Payable		950
	To accrue salary expense.		

After posting, the Salary Expense and Salary Payable accounts are updated to April 30:

EXPENSES

Salary Expense

Apr. 15	950	
Apr. 30	950	
Bal.	1,900	

LIABILITIES

Salary Payable

	Apr. 30	950
	Bal.	950

■ Daily Exercise 3-9

The accounts at April 30 now contain the complete salary information for the month of April. The expense account has a full month's salary, and the liability account shows the portion that the business still owes at April 30. Lyon will record the payment of this liability on Monday, May 2.

This payment entry will not affect April or May expenses because the April expense was recorded on April 15 and April 30. May expense will be recorded in a like manner, starting on May 15. All accrued expenses are recorded with similar entries—a debit to the appropriate expense account and a credit to the related liability account.

Many computerized systems contain a payroll module. The adjusting entry for accrued salaries is automatically journalized and posted at the end of each accounting period.

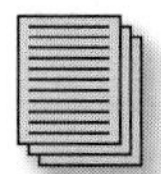

Working It Out Weekly salaries for a five-day workweek total $3,500, payable on a Friday. This month, April 30 falls on a Tuesday.

1. Which accounts require adjustment at April 30?
2. Make the adjusting entry.

Answers

1. To prepare its financial statements at Tuesday, April 30, the business must accrue *Salary Expense.* By the end of that day, the company owes its employees for two days' work. This liability is *Salary Payable.*

2.

Salary Expense ($3,500 × 2/5)	1,400	
Salary Payable		1,400

Accrued Revenues

■ Daily Exercise 3-10

In the same way that some expenses occur before the cash payment, businesses often earn revenue before they receive the cash. Collection occurs later. A revenue that has been earned but not yet received in cash is called an **accrued revenue.**

Accrued Revenue. A revenue that has been earned but not yet received in cash.

Assume that Gary Lyon is hired on April 15 by Garcia Construction Company to perform accounting services on a monthly basis. Under this agreement, Lyon will receive $500 monthly, with the first cash receipt on May 15. During April, Lyon will earn half a month's fee, $250, for work performed April 15 through April 30. On April 30, he makes the following adjusting entry in the journal of Gary Lyon, CPA:

Apr. 30	Accounts Receivable ($500 × 1/2)	250	
	Service Revenue		250
	To accrue service revenue.		

We see from the unadjusted trial balance in Exhibit 3-4 that Accounts Receivable has an unadjusted balance of $2,250. Service Revenues unadjusted balance is $7,000. Posting the April 30 adjusting entry has the following effects on these two accounts:

ASSETS			REVENUES		
Accounts Receivable			**Service Revenue**		
	2,250				7,000
Apr. 30	250			Apr. 30	250
Bal.	2,500			Bal.	7,250

This adjusting entry illustrates the revenue principle. Without the adjustment, Lyon's financial statements would be incomplete and misleading—they would understate Accounts Receivable and Service Revenue by $250 each. All accrued revenues are accounted for similarly—by debiting a receivable and crediting a revenue.

Working It Out Suppose that Gary Lyon's business holds a note receivable from a client. At the end of April, Lyon has earned $125 of interest revenue on the note.

1. Which accounts need to be adjusted at April 30?
2. Make the adjusting entry.

Answers

1. Earlier we saw that Lyon debits Accounts Receivable when he earns revenue that he has not yet received in cash. Here, Lyon is not earning service revenue. Rather, he is earning interest revenue, so we debit another account, *Interest Receivable*. We will credit another revenue account called *Interest Revenue*.
2.

Interest Receivable.............	125	
Interest Revenue.........		125

Now we turn to a different category of adjusting entries.

Unearned Revenues

Unearned revenue. A liability created when a business collects cash from customers in advance of doing work for the customer. The obligation is to provide a product or a service in the future. Also called **deferred revenue.**

Some businesses collect cash from customers in advance of doing work for them. Receiving cash in advance creates a liability called **unearned revenue** or deferred revenue. This obligation arises from receiving cash in advance of providing a product or a service. Only when the job is completed will the business have *earned* the revenue.

Suppose Baldwin Computing Service Center engages Lyon's services, agreeing to pay Lyon $450 monthly, beginning immediately. Suppose Baldwin makes the first payment on April 20. Lyon records the cash receipt and the related increase in liabilities as follows:

Apr. 20	Cash..	450	
	Unearned Service Revenue.........		450
	Received revenue in advance.		

After posting, the liability account Unearned Service Revenue appears as follows:

LIABILITIES		
Unearned Service Revenue		
	Apr. 20	450

Unearned Service Revenue is a liability because it represents Lyon's obligation to perform service for the client. The April 30 unadjusted trial balance (Exhibit 3-4) lists Unearned Service Revenue with a $450 credit balance prior to the adjusting entries. During the last ten days of the month—April 21 through April 30—Lyon will have *earned* one-third (10 days divided by April's total 30 days) of the $450, or $150. Therefore, Lyon makes the following adjustment to decrease the liability, Unearned Service Revenue, and to record an increase in Service Revenue, as follows:

Apr. 30	Unearned Service Revenue ($450 × 1/3)	150	
	Service Revenue		150
	To record service revenue that was collected in advance.		

This adjusting entry shifts $150 of the total amount of unearned service revenue from the liability account to the revenue account. After posting, the balance of Service Revenue is increased by $150, and the balance of Unearned Service Revenue is reduced by $150, to $300. Now, both accounts have their correct balances at April 30, as follows:

LIABILITIES

Unearned Service Revenue

Apr. 30	150	Apr. 20	450
		Bal.	300

REVENUES

Service Revenue

			7,000
		Apr. 30	250
		Apr. 30	150
		Bal.	7,400

Correct liability amount: $300 → **Total accounted for: $450** ← **Correct revenue amount: $150**

All types of revenues that are collected in advance are accounted for similarly.

■ Daily Exercise 3-11

An unearned revenue to one company is a prepaid expense to the company that made the payment. For example, suppose that two months in advance Xerox Corporation paid American Airlines $1,800 for the airfare of Xerox executives. To Xerox, the payment is Prepaid Travel Expense. To American Airlines, the receipt of cash creates Unearned Service Revenue. After the executives take the trip, American Airlines records the revenue and Xerox records travel expense.

Learning Tip: An unearned revenue is a liability, not a revenue. With all unearned revenue, cash is received before the work is performed or the goods are delivered.

Working It Out Consider the tuition you pay. Assume that one semester's tuition costs $500 and that you make a single payment at the start of the term. Can you make the journal entries to record the tuition transactions on your own books and on the books of your college or university?

Answer

	Your Entries on Your Books			Your College's Entries on Its Books		
Start of semester or quarter	Prepaid Tuition	500		Cash	500	
	Cash		500	Unearned Tuition Revenue		500
	Paid semester tuition.			Received revenue in advance.		
End of semester or quarter	Tuition Expense	500		Unearned Tuition Revenue	500	
	Prepaid Tuition		500	Tuition Revenue		500
	To record tuition expense.			To record unearned tuition revenue that has been earned.		

Exhibit 3-7 summarizes the timing of prepaid- and accrual-type adjusting entries. The chapter appendix shows an alternative treatment of unearned revenues.

Summary of the Adjusting Process

One purpose of the adjusting process is to measure business income (revenues and expenses) accurately. The other purpose of the adjusting process is to update the balance sheet accounts (assets and liabilities). All adjusting entries debit or credit:

- At least one *income statement* account, either a **Revenue** or an **Expense**

and

- At least one *balance sheet* account, either an **Asset** or a **Liability**

No adjusting entry debits or credits Cash because the cash transactions are recorded at other times. Exhibit 3-8 summarizes the adjusting entries.

PREPAIDS—The cash transaction occurs initially.

	Initially				Later		
Prepaid expenses	Pay cash and record an asset:			→	Record an expense and decrease the asset:		
	Prepaid Expense	XXX			Expense	XXX	
	Cash		XXX		Prepaid Expense.........		XXX
Unearned revenues	Receive cash and record unearned revenue:			→	Record a revenue and decrease unearned revenue:		
	Cash	XXX			Unearned Revenue.........	XXX	
	Unearned Revenue		XXX		Revenue		XXX

ACCRUALS—The cash transaction occurs later.

	Initially				Later		
Accrued expenses	Record (accrue) an expense and the related payable:			→	Pay cash and decrease the payable:		
	Expense..............................	XXX			Payable	XXX	
	Payable............................		XXX		Cash		XXX
Accrued revenues	Record (accrue) a revenue and the related receivable:			→	Receive cash and decrease the receivable:		
	Receivable...........................	XXX			Cash..............................	XXX	
	Revenue		XXX		Receivable...................		XXX

The authors thank Darrel Davis and Alfonso Oddo for suggesting this exhibit.

Concept Highlight

EXHIBIT 3-7
Prepaid- and Accrual-Type Adjustments

Recall from Chapter 2, p. 57, that posting is the process of transferring amounts from the journal to the ledger.

Exhibit 3-9 summarizes the adjusting entries of Lyon's business at April 30. Panel A briefly describes the data for each adjustment, Panel B gives the adjusting entries, and Panel C shows the accounts after they have been posted. The adjustments are keyed by letter.

The Adjusted Trial Balance

Objective 4

Prepare an adjusted trial balance

Adjusted Trial Balance. A list of all the ledger accounts with their adjusted balances, useful in preparing the financial statements.

This chapter began with the trial balance before any adjusting entries—the unadjusted trial balance (Exhibit 3-4). After the adjustments are journalized and posted, the accounts appear as shown in Exhibit 3-9, Panel C. A useful step in preparing the financial statements is to list the accounts, along with their adjusted balances, on an **adjusted trial balance.** This document has the advantage of listing all the accounts and their adjusted balances in a single place. Exhibit 3-10 shows the preparation of the adjusted trial balance.

Exhibit 3-10 is a *work sheet*. We will consider the work sheet further in Chapter 4. For now, simply note how clearly this format presents the data. The information in the Account Title column and in the Trial Balance columns is drawn directly from the trial balance. The two Adjustments columns list the debit and credit adjustments directly across from the appropriate account title. Each adjusting debit is identified by a letter in parentheses that refers to the adjusting entry. For example, the debit labeled (a) on the work sheet refers to the debit adjusting entry of $1,000 to Rent Expense in Panel B of Exhibit 3-9. Likewise for adjusting credits, the corresponding credit—labeled (a)—refers to the $1,000 credit to Prepaid Rent.

Concept Highlight

EXHIBIT 3-8
Summary of Adjusting Entries

	Type of Account	
Category of Adjusting Entry	**Debited**	**Credited**
Prepaid expense	Expense	Asset
Depreciation	Expense	Contra asset
Accrued expense	Expense	Liability
Accrued revenue	Asset	Revenue
Unearned revenue	Liability	Revenue

Adapted from material provided by Beverly Terry.

EXHIBIT 3-9
Journalizing and Posting the Adjusting Entries of Gary Lyon, CPA

PANEL A—Information for Adjustments at April 30, 19X1

(a) Prepaid rent expired, $1,000.
(b) Supplies on hand, $400.
(c) Depreciation on furniture, $275.
(d) Accrued salary expense, $950.
(e) Accrued service revenue, $250.
(f) Amount of unearned service revenue that has been earned, $150.

PANEL B—Adjusting Entries

(a) Rent Expense	1,000	
Prepaid Rent		1,000
To record rent expense.		
(b) Supplies Expense	300	
Supplies		300
To record supplies used.		
(c) Depreciation Expense—Furniture	275	
Accumulated Depreciation—Furniture		275
To record depreciation on furniture.		
(d) Salary Expense	950	
Salary Payable		950
To accrue salary expense.		
(e) Accounts Receivable	250	
Service Revenue		250
To accrue service revenue.		
(f) Unearned Service Revenue	150	
Service Revenue		150
To record revenue that was collected in advance.		

PANEL C—Ledger Accounts

ASSETS

Cash	
Bal. 24,800	

Accounts Receivable	
2,250	
(e) 250	
Bal. 2,500	

Supplies	
700	(b) 300
Bal. 400	

Prepaid Rent	
3,000	(a) 1,000
Bal. 2,000	

Furniture	
Bal. 16,500	

Accumulated Depreciation—Furniture	
	(c) 275
	Bal. 275

LIABILITIES

Accounts Payable	
	Bal. 13,100

Salary Payable	
	(d) 950
	Bal. 950

Unearned Service Revenue	
(f) 150	450
	Bal. 300

OWNER'S EQUITY

Gary Lyon, Capital	
	Bal. 31,250

Gary Lyon, Withdrawals	
Bal. 3,200	

REVENUE

Service Revenue	
	7,000
	(e) 250
	(f) 150
	Bal. 7,400

EXPENSES

Rent Expense	
(a) 1,000	
Bal. 1,000	

Salary Expense	
950	
(d) 950	
Bal. 1,900	

Supplies Expense	
(b) 300	
Bal. 300	

Depreciation Expense—Furniture	
(c) 275	
Bal. 275	

Utilities Expense	
Bal. 400	

■ Daily Exercise 3-12

GARY LYON, CPA
Preparation of Adjusted Trial Balance
April 30, 19X1

Account Title	Trial Balance		Adjustments		Adjusted Trial Balance	
	Debit	Credit	Debit	Credit	Debit	Credit
Cash	24,800				24,800	
Accounts receivable	2,250		(e) 250		2,500	
Supplies	700			(b) 300	400	
Prepaid rent	3,000			(a) 1,000	2,000	
Furniture	16,500				16,500	
Accumulated depreciation				(c) 275		275
Accounts payable		13,100				13,100
Salary payable				(d) 950		950
Unearned service revenue		450	(f) 150			300
Gary Lyon, capital		31,250				31,250
Gary Lyon, withdrawals	3,200				3,200	
Service revenue		7,000		(e) 250 (f) 150		7,400
Rent expense			(a) 1,000		1,000	
Salary expense	950		(d) 950		1,900	
Supplies expense			(b) 300		300	
Depreciation expense			(c) 275		275	
Utilities expense	400				400	
	51,800	51,800	2,925	2,925	53,275	53,275

EXHIBIT 3-10
Preparation of Adjusted Trial Balance

- Daily Exercise 3-13
- Daily Exercise 3-14
- Daily Exercise 3-15
- Daily Exercise 3-16

The Adjusted Trial Balance columns give the adjusted account balances. Each amount on the adjusted trial balance of Exhibit 3-10 is computed by combining the amounts from the unadjusted trial balance plus or minus the adjustments. For example, Accounts Receivable starts with a debit balance of $2,250. Adding the $250 debit amount from adjusting entry (e) gives Accounts Receivable an adjusted debit balance of $2,500. As we discussed at the outset of the chapter, Supplies begins with a debit balance of $700. After the $300 credit adjustment, its adjusted balance is $400. More than one entry may affect a single account, as is the case for Service Revenue. If an account is unaffected by the adjustments, it will show the same amount on both the unadjusted and the adjusted trial balances. In this example, this is true for Cash, Furniture, Accounts Payable, the Capital account, and the Withdrawals account.

Learning Tip: The differences between the amounts in the trial balance in Exhibit 3-4 and in the adjusted trial balance in Exhibit 3-10 result from the adjusting entries. If the adjusting entries were not given, you could determine them by computing the differences between the adjusted and the unadjusted amounts.

Preparing the Financial Statements from the Adjusted Trial Balance

Objective 5

Prepare the financial statements from the adjusted trial balance

The April financial statements of Gary Lyon, CPA, can be prepared from the adjusted trial balance. Exhibit 3-11 shows how the accounts are distributed from the adjusted trial balance to three of the four main financial statements. As we have seen throughout Chapters 1, 2, and 3, the income statement (Exhibit 3-12) comes from the revenue and expense accounts. The statement of owner's equity (Exhibit 3-13) shows why the owner's capital changed during the period. The balance sheet (Exhibit 3-14) reports the assets, liabilities, and owner's equity. You learned these relationships in Chapter 1.

The financial statements are best prepared in the order shown: the income statement first, followed by the statement of owner's equity, and then the balance sheet. The essential features of all financial statements are

EXHIBIT 3-11
Preparing the Financial Statements of Gary Lyon, CPA, from the Adjusted Trial Balance

Account Title	Adjusted Trial Balance Debit	Adjusted Trial Balance Credit	
Cash	24,800		Balance Sheet (Exhibit 3-14)
Accounts receivable	2,500		
Supplies	400		
Prepaid rent	2,000		
Furniture	16,500		
Accumulated depreciation		275	
Accounts payable		13,100	
Salary payable		950	
Unearned service revenue		300	
Gary Lyon, capital		31,250	Statement of Owner's Equity (Exhibit 3-13)
Gary Lyon, withdrawals	3,200		
Service revenue		7,400	Income Statement (Exhibit 3-12)
Rent expense	1,000		
Salary expense	1,900		
Supplies expense	300		
Depreciation expense	275		
Utilities expense	400		
	53,275	53,275	

Heading

- Name of the entity
- Title of the statement
- Date, or period, covered by the statement

Body of the statement

It is customary to list expenses in descending order by amount on the income statement, as shown in Exhibit 3-12. However, Miscellaneous Expense, a catchall account for expenses that do not fit another category, is usually reported last.

Relationships among the Three Financial Statements

The arrows in Exhibits 3-12, 3-13, and 3-14 illustrate the relationships among the income statement, the statement of owner's equity, and the balance sheet. Consider why the income statement is prepared first and the balance sheet last.

The relationships among the financial statements were introduced in Chapter 1, p. 21.

1. The income statement reports net income or net loss, figured by subtracting expenses from revenues. Because revenues and expenses are owner's equity accounts, their net amount is transferred to the statement of owner's equity. Note that net income in Exhibit 3-12, $3,525, increases owner's equity in Exhibit 3-13. A net loss would decrease owner's equity.
2. Capital is a balance-sheet account, so the ending balance in the statement of owner's equity is transferred to the balance sheet. This amount is the final balancing element of the balance sheet. To solidify your understanding of this relationship, trace the $31,575 figure from Exhibit 3-13 to Exhibit 3-14.

You may be wondering why the total assets on the balance sheet ($45,925 in Exhibit 3-14) do not equal the total debits on the adjusted trial balance ($53,275 in Exhibit 3-11). Likewise, the total liabilities and owner's equity ($45,925 in Exhibit 3-14) do not equal the total credits on the adjusted trial balance ($53,275 in Exhibit 3-11). The reason for these differences is that Accumulated Depreciation and Owner's Withdrawals are contra accounts. Recall that contra accounts are *subtracted* from their companion accounts on the balance sheet. But on the adjusted trial balance, contra accounts are *added* as a debit or a credit in their respective columns.

EXHIBIT 3-12
Income Statement

GARY LYON, CPA Income Statement Month Ended April 30, 19X1		
Revenue:		
Service revenue		$7,400
Expenses:		
Salary expense	$1,900	
Rent expense	1,000	
Utilities expense	400	
Supplies expense	300	
Depreciation expense	275	
Total expenses		3,875
Net income		$3,525

EXHIBIT 3-13
Statement of Owner's Equity

GARY LYON, CPA Statement of Owner's Equity Month Ended April 30, 19X1	
Gary Lyon, capital, April 1, 19X1	$31,250
Add: Net income	3,525
	34,775
Less: Withdrawals	(3,200)
Gary Lyon, capital, April 30, 19X1	$31,575

EXHIBIT 3-14
Balance Sheet

GARY LYON, CPA Balance Sheet April 30, 19X1				
Assets			**Liabilities**	
Cash		$24,800	Accounts payable	$13,100
Accounts receivable		2,500	Salary payable	950
Supplies		400	Unearned service	
Prepaid rent		2,000	revenue	300
Furniture	$16,500		Total liabilities	14,350
Less Accumulated				
depreciation	(275)	16,225	**Owner's Equity**	
			Gary Lyon, capital	31,575
			Total liabilities and	
Total assets		$45,925	owner's equity	$45,925

Working It Out Examine Gary Lyon's adjusted trial balance in Exhibit 3-10. Suppose Lyon forgot to record the $950 accrual of salary expense at April 30. What net income would his accounting practice then report for April? What total assets, total liabilities, and total owner's equity would the balance sheet have reported at April 30?

Answer: Omitting the salary accrual would produce these effects:

1. Net income on the income statement (Exhibit 3-12) would have been $4,475 ($3,525 + $950).
2. Total assets would have been unaffected by the error—$45,925, as reported on the balance sheet (Exhibit 3-14).
3. Total liabilities on the balance sheet (Exhibit 3-14) would have been $13,400 ($14,350 – $950).
4. Owner's equity (Gary Lyon, capital) would have been $32,525 ($31,575 + $950) on the balance sheet (Exhibit 3-14).

Ethical Issues in Accrual Accounting

Like most other aspects of life, accounting poses ethical challenges. At the most basic level, accountants must be honest in their work. Only with honest and complete information, including accounting data, can people expect to make wise decisions. An example will illustrate the importance of ethics in accrual accounting.

It's Just Lunch has done well as a business. Andrea McGinty is an excellent businesswoman. The company has opened offices in most major cities in the United States. Suppose that It's Just Lunch wishes to open an office in Nashville, Tennessee, and needs to borrow $100,000 for prepaid rent, office equipment, and so on. Assume that It's Just Lunch understated expenses in order to inflate net income as reported on the company's income statement. A banker could be tricked into lending money to It's Just Lunch. Suppose It's Just Lunch could not repay the loan, and the bank lost money—all because the banker relied on incorrect accounting information.

Accrual accounting provides several opportunities for unethical accounting. Recall from earlier in this chapter that depreciation is an estimated figure. No business can foresee exactly how long its buildings and equipment will last, so accountants must estimate these assets' useful lives. Accountants then record depreciation on plant assets over their *estimated* useful lives. A dishonest proprietor could buy a five-year asset and depreciate it over ten years. For each of the first five years, the company will report less depreciation expense and more net income than it should. People who rely on the company's financial statements, such as bank lenders, can be deceived into doing business with the company. You may reply, "But the company will be recording depreciation for the full ten years, including the last five years after the asset is worn out. Net income will be lower in the last five years, and this lower net income will offset the higher net income reported during the first five years." This is true, but the damage to the company's reputation from reporting too much net income too quickly will remain. Accounting information must be honest and complete—completely ethical—to serve its intended purpose. As you progress through introductory accounting, you will see other situations that challenge the ethics of accountants.

The cash basis of accounting poses fewer ethical challenges because either the company has the cash, or it does not. Therefore, the amount of cash a company reports is rarely disputed. By contrast, adjusting entries for accrued expenses, accrued revenues, and depreciation often must be estimated. Whenever there is an estimate, the accountant must deal with the temptation to rig the books to make the company look different from its true condition. Fortunately, accounting has a good reputation for honesty. Even with added ethical challenges, the accrual basis provides more complete accounting reports than the cash basis. That is why accounting relies on the accrual basis.

The Decision Guidelines feature provides a map of the adjusting process that leads to the adjusted trial balance.

DECISION GUIDELINES — Measuring Business Income: The Adjusting Process

DECISION	GUIDELINES
Which basis of accounting better measures business income (revenues – expenses)?	*Accrual basis,* because it provides more complete reports of operating performance
How to measure revenues?	Revenue principle
How to measure expenses?	Matching principle
Where to start with the measurement of income at the end of the period?	Unadjusted trial balance, usually referred to simply as the *trial balance*
How to update the accounts for preparation of the financial statements?	*Adjusting entries* at the end of the accounting period

(continued)

DECISION GUIDELINES *(continued)*

What are the categories of adjusting entries?	Prepaid expenses Depreciation of plant assets Accrued expenses Accrued revenues Unearned revenues
How do the adjusting entries differ from other journal entries?	**1.** Adjusting entries are usually made only at the end of the accounting period. **2.** Adjusting entries never affect cash. **3.** All adjusting entries debit or credit • At least one *income statement* account (a Revenue or an Expense) and • At least one *balance sheet* account (an Asset or a Liability)
Where are the accounts with their adjusted balances summarized?	*Adjusted trial balance,* which becomes the basis for preparing the financial statements

SUMMARY PROBLEM FOR YOUR REVIEW

The trial balance of State Service Company pertains to December 31, 19X3, which is the end of its year-long accounting period. Data needed for the adjusting entries include

a. Supplies on hand at year end, $2,000.
b. Depreciation on furniture and fixtures, $20,000.
c. Depreciation on building, $10,000.
d. Salaries owed but not yet paid, $5,000.
e. Accrued service revenue, $12,000.
f. Of the $45,000 balance of unearned service revenue, $32,000 was earned during the year.

REQUIRED

1. Open the ledger accounts with their unadjusted balances. Show dollar amounts in thousands, as shown for Accounts Receivable:

Accounts Receivable	
370	

2. Journalize State Service Company's adjusting entries at December 31, 19X3. Key entries by letter, as in Exhibit 3-9.
3. Post the adjusting entries.
4. Write the trial balance on a work sheet, enter the adjusting entries, and prepare an adjusted trial balance, as shown in Exhibit 3-10.
5. Prepare the income statement, the statement of owner's equity, and the balance sheet. Draw arrows linking these three financial statements.

STATE SERVICE COMPANY
Trial Balance
December 31, 19X3

Cash	$ 198,000	
Accounts receivable	370,000	
Supplies	6,000	
Furniture and fixtures	100,000	
Accumulated depreciation—furniture and fixtures		$ 40,000
Building	250,000	
Accumulated depreciation—building		130,000
Accounts payable		380,000
Salary payable		
Unearned service revenue		45,000
Capital		293,000
Owner's withdrawals	65,000	
Service revenue		286,000
Salary expense	172,000	
Supplies expense		
Depreciation expense—furniture and fixtures		
Depreciation expense—building		
Miscellaneous expense	13,000	
Total	$1,174,000	$1,174,000

SOLUTION

REQUIREMENTS 2 AND 3

(amounts in thousands)

ASSETS

Cash

Bal. 198	

Accounts Receivable

370	
(e) 12	
Bal. 382	

Supplies

6	(a) 4
Bal. 2	

Furniture and Fixtures

Bal. 100	

Accumulated Depreciation—Furniture and Fixtures

	40
	(b) 20
	Bal. 60

Building

Bal. 250	

Accumulated Depreciation—Building

	130
	(c) 10
	Bal. 140

LIABILITIES

Accounts Payable

	Bal. 380

Salary Payable

	(d) 5
	Bal. 5

Unearned Service Revenue

(f) 32	45
	Bal. 13

OWNER'S EQUITY

Capital

	Bal. 293

Owner's Withdrawals

Bal. 65	

REVENUE

Service Revenue

	286
	(e) 12
	(f) 32
	Bal. 330

EXPENSES

Salary Expense

172	
(d) 5	
Bal. 177	

Supplies Expense

(a) 4	
Bal. 4	

Depreciation Expense—Furniture and Fixtures

(b) 20	
Bal. 20	

Depreciation Expense—Building

(c) 10	
Bal. 10	

Miscellaneous Expense

Bal. 13	

REQUIREMENT 2

19X3

a. Dec. 31 Supplies Expense ($6,000 – $2,000) 4,000
Supplies 4,000
To record supplies used.

b. 31 Depreciation Expense—Furniture and Fixtures 20,000
Accumulated Depreciation—Furniture and Fixtures 20,000
To record depreciation expense on furniture and fixtures.

c.	31	Depreciation Expense—Building	10,000	
		Accumulated Depreciation—Building		10,000
		To record depreciation expense on building.		
d.	31	Salary Expense	5,000	
		Salary Payable		5,000
		To accrue salary expense.		
e.	31	Accounts Receivable	12,000	
		Service Revenue		12,000
		To accrue service revenue.		
f.	31	Unearned Service Revenue	32,000	
		Service Revenue		32,000
		To record service revenue that was collected in advance.		

REQUIREMENT 4

STATE SERVICE COMPANY
Preparation of Adjusted Trial Balance
December 31, 19X3
(amounts in thousands)

	Trial Balance		Adjustments		Adjusted Trial Balance	
	Debit	Credit	Debit	Credit	Debit	Credit
Cash	198				198	
Accounts receivable	370		(e) 12		382	
Supplies	6			(a) 4	2	
Furniture and fixtures	100				100	
Accumulated depreciation—furniture and fixtures		40		(b) 20		60
Building	250				250	
Accumulated depreciation—building		130		(c) 10		140
Accounts payable		380				380
Salary payable				(d) 5		5
Unearned service revenue		45	(f) 32			13
Capital		293				293
Owner's withdrawals	65				65	
Service revenue		286		(e) 12 (f) 32		330
Salary expense	172		(d) 5		177	
Supplies expense			(a) 4		4	
Depreciation expense—furniture and fixtures			(b) 20		20	
Depreciation expense—building			(c) 10		10	
Miscellaneous expense	13				13	
	1,174	1,174	83	83	1,221	1,221

REQUIREMENT 5

STATE SERVICE COMPANY
Income Statement
Year Ended December 31, 19X3
(amounts in thousands)

Revenue:		
Service revenue		$330
Expenses:		
Salary expense	$177	
Depreciation expense—furniture and fixtures	20	
Depreciation expense—building	10	
Supplies expense	4	
Miscellaneous expense	13	
Total expenses		224
Net income		$106

STATE SERVICE COMPANY
Statement of Owner's Equity
Year Ended December 31, 19X3
(amounts in thousands)

Capital, January 1, 19X3	$293
Add: Net income	106
	399
Less: Withdrawals	65
Capital, December 31, 19X3	$334

STATE SERVICE COMPANY
Balance Sheet
December 31, 19X3
(amounts in thousands)

Assets			Liabilities	
Cash		$198	Accounts payable	$380
Accounts receivable		382	Salary payable	5
Supplies		2	Unearned service revenue	13
Furniture and fixtures	$100		Total liabilities	398
Less Accumulated depreciation	60	40	**Owner's Equity**	
Building	$250			
Less Accumulated depreciation	140	110	Capital	334
Total assets		$732	Total liabilities and owner's equity	$732

Summary of Learning Objectives

1. *Distinguish accrual-basis accounting from cash-basis accounting.* In *accrual-basis accounting*, business events are recorded as they occur. In *cash-basis accounting*, only those events that affect cash are recorded. The cash basis omits important events such as purchases and sales of assets on account. It also distorts the financial statements by labeling as expenses those cash payments that have long-term effects, such as the purchases of buildings and equipment. Some small organizations use cash-basis accounting, but the generally accepted method is the accrual basis.

2. *Apply the revenue and matching principles.* Businesses divide time into definite periods—such as a month, a quarter, or a year—to report the entity's financial statements. The year is the basic *accounting period*, but companies prepare financial statements as often as they need the information. Accountants have developed the *revenue principle* to determine when to record revenue and the amount of revenue to record. Revenue is recorded once it has been earned, and not before. The *matching principle* guides the accounting for expenses. It directs accountants to match expenses against the revenues earned during a particular period of time.

3. *Make adjusting entries at the end of the accounting period.* *Adjusting entries* are a result of the accrual basis of accounting. Made at the end of the period, these entries update the accounts for preparation of the financial statements. Adjusting entries are divided into five categories: *prepaid expenses, depreciation, accrued expenses, accrued revenues,* and *unearned revenues.*

4. ***Prepare an adjusted trial balance.*** To prepare the *adjusted trial balance*, accountants enter the adjusting entries next to the *unadjusted trial balance* and compute each account's balance.

5. ***Prepare the financial statements from the adjusted trial balance.*** The adjusted trial balance can be used to prepare the financial statements. The three financial statements are related as follows: Income, shown on the *income statement*, increases the owner's capital, which also appears on the *statement of owner's equity*. The ending balance of capital is the last amount reported on the *balance sheet.*

Accounting Vocabulary

accrual-basis accounting *(p. 92)*
accrued expense *(p. 102)*
accrued revenue *(p. 103)*
Accumulated Depreciation *(p. 100)*
adjusted trial balance *(p. 106)*
adjusting entry *(p. 97)*
book value (of a plant asset) *(p. 101)*
cash-basis accounting *(p. 92)*
contra account *(p. 100)*
deferred revenue *(p. 104)*
depreciation *(p. 99)*
matching principle *(p. 95)*
plant asset *(p. 99)*
prepaid expense *(p. 97)*
revenue principle *(p. 94)*
time-period concept *(p. 95)*
unearned revenue *(p. 104)*

Questions

1. Distinguish accrual-basis accounting from cash-basis accounting.

2. How long is the basic accounting period? What is a fiscal year? What is an interim period?

3. What two questions does the revenue principle help answer?

4. Briefly explain the matching principle.

5. What is the purpose of making adjusting entries?

6. Why are adjusting entries made at the end of the accounting period, not during the period?

7. Name five categories of adjusting entries, and give an example of each.

8. Do all adjusting entries affect the net income or net loss of the period? Include the definition of an adjusting entry.

9. Why must the balance of Supplies be adjusted at the end of the period?

10. Manning Supply Company pays $1,800 for an insurance policy that covers three years. At the end of the first year, the balance of its Prepaid Insurance account contains two elements. What are the two elements, and what is the correct amount of each?

11. The title Prepaid Expense suggests that this type of account is an expense. If it is, explain why. If it is not, what type of account is it?

12. What is a contra account? Identify the contra account introduced in this chapter, along with the account's normal balance.

13. The manager of a Quickie-Pickie convenience store presents his entity's balance sheet to a banker to obtain a loan. The balance sheet reports that the entity's plant assets have a book value of $135,000 and accumulated depreciation of $65,000. What does *book value* of a plant asset mean? What was the cost of the plant assets?

14. Give the entry to record accrued interest revenue of $800.

15. Why is an unearned revenue a liability? Give an example.

16. Identify the types of accounts (assets, liabilities, and so on) debited and credited for each of the five types of adjusting entries.

17. What purposes does the adjusted trial balance serve?

18. Explain the relationship among the income statement, the statement of owner's equity, and the balance sheet.

19. Bellevue Company failed to record the following adjusting entries at December 31, the end of its fiscal year: (a) accrued expenses, $500; (b) accrued revenues, $850; and (c) depreciation, $1,000. Did these omissions cause net income for the year to be understated or overstated, and by what overall amount?

Daily Exercises

Accrual accounting versus cash-basis accounting for revenues
(Obj. 1)

DE3-1 Study Exhibit 3-1 and the related discussion on pages 92 and 93. Suppose the Plaza Hotel is preparing its income statement for the year ended December 31, 1998.

1. Identify the amount of revenue the Plaza Hotel would report on its *1998* income statement under (a) cash-basis accounting and (b) accrual-basis accounting.
2. How much revenue would the Plaza Hotel report on its *1999* income statement under (a) cash-basis accounting and (b) accrual-basis accounting?

Accrual accounting versus cash-basis accounting for expenses
(Obj. 1)

DE3-2 It's Just Lunch, the business featured at the beginning of this chapter, uses computer data bases to help its clients meet each other. Suppose It's Just Lunch paid $3,800 for a Dell computer. Review pages 92 and 93, and then describe how It's Just Lunch would account for the $3,800 expenditure under (a) the cash basis and (b) the accrual basis. State in your own words why the accrual basis is more realistic for this situation.

Applying the revenue principle
(Obj. 2)

DE3-3 Intel Corporation produces the Pentium© processor that is featured in many computers. Demand for Pentium© processors is very strong. Suppose Intel has completed production of 1,000 processor units that it expects to sell to IBM. Assume that Intel's cost to manufacture each processor is $160 and that Intel sells each processor for $400.

Apply the revenue principle to determine (1) when Intel should record revenue for this situation, and (2) the amount of revenue Intel should record for the sale of 1,000 Pentium© processors.

DE3-4 Return to the Intel Corporation situation described in DE3-3. Suppose that Intel has sold 1,000 Pentium© processors to IBM.

Applying the matching principle **(Obj. 2)**

What will Intel record in order to apply the matching principle? Give the name of the expense that Intel will record, and specify its amount.

DE3-5 Storage USA operates approximately 250 miniwarehouses across the United States. The company's headquarters are in Columbia, Maryland. During 1996, Storage USA earned rental revenue of $105 million and collected cash of $107 million from customers. Total expenses for 1996 were $61 million, of which Storage USA paid $59 million.

Applying the revenue and matching principles; accrual basis versus cash basis **(Obj. 1, 2)**

1. Using the data supplied here, apply the revenue principle and the matching principle to compute Storage USA's net income for 1996.
2. Identify the information that you did not use to compute Storage USA's net income. Give the reason for not using the information.

DE3-6 At December 31, 1996, Hawaiian Airlines recorded Salary and Wage Expense and Salary and Wage Payable of $2,500,000, as shown on page 95. Suppose Hawaiian Airlines paid $2,700,000 to its employees on January 3, 1997, the company's next payday after the end of the 1996 year.

Applying the matching principle and the time-period concept **(Obj. 2)**

1. Consider the salary and wage expense that Hawaiian Airlines accrued at December 31, 1996, and the related payment on January 3, 1997. Assuming no other expenses in this category, how much Salary and Wage Expense would Hawaiian Airlines report on its 1996 income statement? How much Salary and Wage Expense would the company report on its 1997 income statement?
2. Journalize Hawaiian Airlines' entry for payment of the payroll on January 3, 1997. Include the date and an explanation for the entry.

DE3-7 Answer the following questions.

Adjusting prepaid expenses **(Obj. 3)**

1. Prepaid expenses are discussed beginning on page 97. Focus on the accounting for prepaid rent. Assume that Lyon's initial $3,000 prepayment of rent on April 1 (page 97) was for six months rather than for three months. Give Gary Lyon's adjusting entry to record rent expense at April 30. Include the date of the entry and an explanation. Then post to the two accounts involved, and show their balances at April 30.
2. Refer to the supplies example on pages 98–99. Assume that Lyon's business has $100 of supplies on hand (rather than $400) at April 30. Give the adjusting entry, complete with date and explanation, at April 30. Post to the accounts and show their balances at April 30.

DE3-8 ⇐ *Link Back to Chapters 1 and 2 (Income Statement and Balance Sheet).* It's Just Lunch uses computers for data searches. Suppose that on May 1 the company paid cash of $36,000 for Gateway computers that are expected to remain useful for three years. At the end of three years, the computers' values are expected to be zero.

Recording depreciation **(Obj. 3)**

1. Make journal entries to record (a) purchase of the computers on May 1 and (b) depreciation on May 31. Include dates and explanations, and use the following accounts: Computer Equipment; Accumulated Depreciation—Computer Equipment; and Depreciation Expense—Computer Equipment.
2. Post to the accounts listed in requirement 1, and show their balances at May 31.
3. What is the equipment's book value at May 31?
4. Which account(s) listed in requirement 1 will It's Just Lunch report on the income statement for the month of May? Which account(s) will appear on the balance sheet of May 31? Show the amount to report for each account.

DE3-9 Suppose Gary Lyon borrowed $10,000 on August 1 by signing a note payable to First Interstate Bank. Lyon's interest expense for each month is $80. The loan agreement requires Lyon to pay August interest at the end of October, along with the interest that will accrue for September and October.

Accruing and paying interest expense **(Obj. 3)**

1. Make the same adjusting entry to record interest expense and interest payable at August 31, at September 30, and at October 31. Date each entry and include its explanation.
2. Post all three entries to the Interest Payable account. You need not take the balance of the account at the end of each month.
3. On which financial statement and under what category will Lyon report the interest payable? How much interest payable will Lyon report at August 31 and at September 30?

Accruing and receiving cash from interest revenue
(Obj. 3)

DE3-10 Return to the situation of Daily Exercise 3-9. Suppose you are accounting for the same transactions on the books of First Interstate Bank, which lent the money to Gary Lyon, CPA. Perform all three steps of Daily Exercise 3-9 for First Interstate Bank using its own accounts: Interest Receivable and Interest Revenue. (For requirement 2, post to the Interest Receivable account.)

Explaining unearned revenues
(Obj. 3)

DE3-11 Write a paragraph to explain why unearned revenues are liabilities rather than revenues. In your explanation, use the following actual example: Time Magazine collects cash from subscribers in advance and later mails the magazines to subscribers over a one-year period. Explain what happens to the unearned subscription revenue over the course of a year as Time mails the magazines to subscribers. Where (into what account) does the unearned subscription revenue go as Time mails magazines to subscribers? Give the adjusting entry that Time Magazine would make to record the earning of $10,000 of Subscription Revenue. Include an explanation for the entry, as illustrated in the chapter.

Contrasting the unadjusted and the adjusted trial balances
(Obj. 4)

DE3-12 Study the T-accounts in Exhibit 3-9, Panel C, on page 107. Focus on the Prepaid Rent account. Which amount in the Prepaid Rent account appeared on the *unadjusted* trial balance (Exhibit 3-10, page 108)? Which amount in the Prepaid Rent account will appear on the *adjusted* trial balance? Which amount will be reported on the balance sheet at April 30? Why will the balance sheet report this amount? Under what balance sheet category will Prepaid Rent appear?

Using the adjusted trial balance
(Obj. 4)

DE3-13 In the Adjustments columns of Exhibit 3-10, page 108, two adjustments affected Service Revenue.

1. Make journal entries for the two adjustments. Date the entries and include an explanation.
2. The journal entries you just made affected three accounts: Accounts Receivable; Unearned Service Revenue; and Service Revenue. Show how Gary Lyon, CPA, will report all three accounts in his business's financial statements at April 30. For each account, identify its (a) financial statement, (b) category on the financial statement, and (c) balance.

Explaining the adjusted trial balance
(Obj. 4)

DE3-14 Write a business memorandum to your supervisor explaining the difference between the unadjusted amounts and the adjusted amounts in Exhibit 3-10, page 108. Use Accounts Receivable in your explanation. If necessary, refer to the discussion of Accrued Revenues that begins on page 108.

Business memos are formatted as follows:

Date: ________

To: ________

From: ________

Subject: Difference between the *unadjusted* and the *adjusted* amounts on an adjusted trial balance

Preparing the balance sheet
(Obj. 5)

DE3-15 Refer to the adjusted trial balance in Exhibit 3-10, page 108.

1. Focus first on the *unadjusted* amounts. Compute the amount of **total assets** that Gary Lyon, CPA, would have reported on the balance sheet at April 30 if he had *not* made the adjusting entries at the end of the period. Also compute unadjusted **total liabilities.**
2. Now focus on the *adjusted* figures. Compute Lyon's total assets and total liabilities at April 30. Compare your totals to the balance sheet in Exhibit 3-14, page 110. Are they the same?
3. Why does a business need to make adjusting entries at the end of the period?

Preparing the income statement
(Obj. 5)

DE3-16 Refer to the adjusted trial balance in Exhibit 3-10, page 108.

1. Focus first on the *unadjusted* amounts. Compute the amount of **total revenues** that Gary Lyon, CPA, would have reported on the income statement for the month of April if he had *not* made the adjusting entries at the end of the period. Also compute unadjusted **total expenses.** Finally, determine the amount of **net income** Lyon would have reported if he had not adjusted the accounts.
2. Now focus on the *adjusted* figures. Compute Lyon's total revenues, total expenses, and net income for April. Compare your totals to the income statement in Exhibit 3-12, page 110. Are they the same?
3. Why does a business need to make adjusting entries at the end of the period?

Exercises

Cash basis versus accrual basis
(Obj. 1)

E3-1 Lexington Inn had the following selected transactions during January:

Jan.	1	Prepaid rent for three months, $2,700.
	5	Paid electricity expenses, $400.
	9	Received cash for the day's room rentals, $1,400.
	14	Paid cash for six television sets, $3,000.
	23	Served a banquet, receiving a note receivable, $1,200.
	31	Made the adjusting entry for rent (from Jan. 1).
	31	Accrued salary expense, $900.

Show how each transaction would be handled using the cash basis and the accrual basis. Under each column give the amount of revenue or expense for January. Journal entries are not required. Use the following format for your answer, and show your computations:

	Amount of Revenue or Expense for January	
Date	**Cash Basis**	**Accrual Basis**

Applying accounting concepts and principles
(Obj. 2)

E3-2 Identify the accounting concept or principle that gives the most direction on how to account for each of the following situations:

a. Expenses of the period total $4,300. This amount should be subtracted from revenue to compute the period's income.
b. Expenses of $1,200 must be accrued at the end of the period to measure income properly.
c. A customer states her intention to switch travel agencies. Should the new travel agency record revenue based on this intention? Give the reason for your answer.
d. The owner of a business desires monthly financial statements to measure the progress of the entity on an ongoing basis.

Applying accounting concepts
(Obj. 2)

E3-3 Write a memo to your supervisor explaining in your own words the concept of depreciation as it is used in accounting. Use the format for a business memo that is given with Daily Exercise 3-14.

Allocating prepaid expense to the asset and the expense
(Obj. 2, 3)

E3-4 Compute the amounts indicated by question marks for each of the following Prepaid Insurance situations. For situations 1 and 2, journalize the needed entry. Consider each situation separately.

	Situation			
	1	**2**	**3**	**4**
Beginning Prepaid Insurance	$ 300	$ 500	$ 900	$ 600
Payments for Prepaid Insurance during the year	1,400	?	1,100	?
Total amount to account for	?	?	2,000	1,300
Ending Prepaid Insurance	200	400	?	500
Insurance Expense	$?	$ 700	$1,400	$ 800

Journalizing adjusting entries
(Obj. 3)

E3-5 Journalize the entries for the following adjustments at December 31, the end of the accounting period.

a. Employee salaries owed for Monday and Tuesday of a five-day workweek; weekly payroll, $10,000.
b. Prepaid insurance expired, $300.
c. Interest revenue accrued, $4,400.
d. Unearned service revenue earned, $800.
e. Depreciation, $3,200.

Analyzing the effects of adjustments on net income
(Obj. 3)

E3-6 Suppose the adjustments required in Exercise 3-5 were not made. Compute the overall overstatement or understatement of net income as a result of the omission of these adjustments.

Journalizing adjusting entries
(Obj. 3)

E3-7 Journalize the adjusting entry needed at December 31 for each of the following independent situations.

a. On July 1, when we collected $6,000 rent in advance, we debited Cash and credited Unearned Rent Revenue. The tenant was paying for one year's rent in advance.
b. The business owes interest expense of $900, which it will pay early in the next period.
c. Interest revenue of $700 has been earned but not yet received. The business holds a $20,000 note receivable.
d. Salary expense is $1,000 per day—Monday through Friday—and the business pays employees each Friday. This year December 31 falls on a Wednesday.

e. The unadjusted balance of the Supplies account is $3,100. The cost of supplies on hand is $1,200.
f. Equipment was purchased last year at a cost of $10,000. The equipment's useful life is four years. Record the year's depreciation.
g. On September 1, when we prepaid $1,800 for a two-year insurance policy, we debited Prepaid Insurance and credited Cash.

Recording adjustments in T-accounts
(Obj. 3)

E3-8 The accounting records of Karl Umlauf, Architect, include the following unadjusted balances at May 31: Accounts Receivable, $1,000; Supplies, $600; Salary Payable, $0; Unearned Service Revenue, $400; Service Revenue, $4,700; Salary Expense, $1,200; Supplies Expense, $0. Umlauf's accountant develops the following data for the May 31 adjusting entries:

a. Supplies on hand, $100.
b. Salary owed to employee, $600.
c. Service revenue accrued, $350.
d. Unearned service revenue that has been earned, $200.

Open the foregoing T-accounts and record the adjustments directly in the accounts, keying each adjustment amount by letter. Show each account's adjusted balance. Journal entries are not required.

Adjusting the accounts
(Obj. 3, 4)

E3-9 The adjusted trial balance of Total Express Service is incomplete. Enter the adjustment amounts directly in the adjustment columns of the text. Service Revenue is the only account affected by more than one adjustment.

TOTAL EXPRESS SERVICE
Preparation of Adjusted Trial Balance
May 31, 19X2

	Trial Balance		Adjustments		Adjusted Trial Balance	
	Debit	Credit	Debit	Credit	Debit	Credit
Cash	3,000				3,000	
Accounts receivable	6,500				7,100	
Supplies	1,040				800	
Office furniture	32,300				32,300	
Accumulated depreciation		14,040				14,400
Salary payable						900
Unearned revenue		900				690
Capital		26,360				26,360
Owner's withdrawals	6,000				6,000	
Service revenue		11,630				12,440
Salary expense	2,690				3,590	
Rent expense	1,400				1,400	
Depreciation expense					360	
Supplies expense					240	
	52,930	52,930			54,790	54,790

Journalizing adjustments
(Obj. 3, 4)

E3-10 Make journal entries for the adjustments that would complete the preparation of the adjusted trial balance in Exercise 3-9. Date the entries and include explanations.

Preparing the financial statements
(Obj. 5)

E3-11 Refer to the adjusted trial balance in Exercise 3-9. Prepare Total Express Service's income statement and statement of owner's equity for the month ended May 31, 19X2, and its balance sheet on that date. Draw the arrows linking the three statements.

Preparing the financial statements
(Obj. 5)

E3-12 The accountant for Michael Gulig, Publisher, has posted adjusting entries (a) through (e) to the accounts at December 31, 19X2. Selected balance sheet accounts and all the revenues and expenses of the entity follow in T-account form.

Accounts Receivable

	Debit	Credit
	23,000	
(e)	4,500	

Supplies

Debit		Credit
4,000	(a)	1,000

Accumulated Depreciation Equipment

Debit		Credit
		5,000
	(b)	2,000

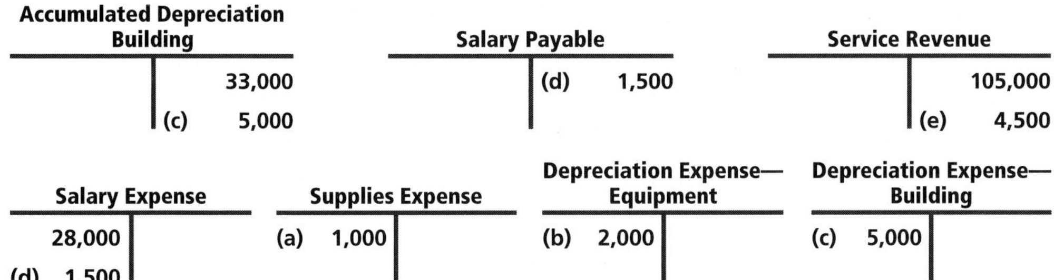

Accumulated Depreciation Building
33,000
(c) 5,000
Salary Payable
(d) 1,500
Service Revenue
105,000
(e) 4,500
Salary Expense
28,000
(d) 1,500
Supplies Expense
(a) 1,000
Depreciation Expense— Equipment
(b) 2,000
Depreciation Expense— Building
(c) 5,000

REQUIRED

1. Prepare the income statement of Michael Gulig, Publisher, for the year ended December 31, 19X2. List expenses in order from the largest to the smallest.
2. Were 19X2 operations successful? Give the reason for your answer.

Preparing the statement of owner's equity ***(Obj. 5)***

E3-13 24-Hour Copy Center began the year with capital of $105,000. On July 12, Eric Greer (the owner) invested $12,000 cash in the business. On September 26, he transferred to the company land valued at $70,000. The income statement for the year ended December 31, 19X5, reported a net loss of $28,000. During this fiscal year, Greer withdrew $1,500 monthly for personal use.

1. Prepare the copy center's statement of owner's equity for the year ended December 31, 19X5.
2. Did the owner's equity of the business increase or decrease during the year? What caused this change?

CONTINUING EXERCISE

Exercise 3-14 continues the Alvin Deering, Consultant, situation begun in Exercise 2-15 of Chapter 2.

Adjusting the accounts, preparing an adjusted trial balance, and preparing the financial statements ***(Obj. 3, 4, 5)***

E3-14 Refer to Exercise 2-15 of Chapter 2. Start from the trial balance and the posted T-accounts that Alvin Deering, Consultant, prepared for his business at December 18.

ALVIN DEERING, CONSULTANT
Trial Balance
December 18, 19XX

Account	Debit	Credit
Cash	$ 9,100	
Accounts receivable	1,700	
Supplies	300	
Equipment	3,000	
Furniture	3,600	
Accounts payable		$ 3,900
Alvin Deering, capital		12,000
Alvin Deering, withdrawals	—	
Service revenue		2,500
Rent expense	500	
Utilities expense	200	
Salary expense	—	
Total	$18,400	$18,400

Later in December, the business completed these transactions, as follows:

Dec. 21 Received $900 in advance for client service to be performed evenly over the next 30 days.
21 Hired a secretary to be paid $1,500 on the 20th day of each month. The secretary will begin work on January 1.
26 Paid for the supplies purchased on December 5.
28 Collected $600 from the consulting client on December 18.
30 Withdrew $1,600 for personal use.

REQUIRED

1. Open these additional T-accounts: Accumulated Depreciation—Equipment; Accumulated Depreciation—Furniture; Salary Payable; Unearned Service Revenue; Depreciation Expense—Equipment; Depreciation Expense—Furniture; Supplies Expense.
2. Journalize the transactions of December 21 through 30.
3. Post to the T-accounts, keying all items by date.
4. Prepare a trial balance at December 31. Also set up columns for the adjustments and for the adjusted trial balance, as illustrated in Exhibit 3-10.

5. At December 31, Deering gathers the following information for the adjusting entries:

   a. Accrued service revenue, $400.
   b. Earned a portion of the service revenue collected in advance on December 21.
   c. Supplies on hand, $100.
   d. Depreciation expense—equipment, $50; furniture, $60.
   e. Accrued expense for secretary's salary.

   Make these adjustments directly in the adjustments columns, and complete the adjusted trial balance at December 31. Throughout the book, to avoid rounding errors, we have based adjusting entries on 30-day months and 360-day years.
6. Journalize and post the adjusting entries. Denote each adjusting amount as *Adj.* and an account balance as *Bal.*
7. Prepare the income statement and the statement of owner's equity of Alvin Deering, Consultant, for the month ended December 31, and prepare the balance sheet at that date.

CHALLENGE EXERCISES

Computing the amount of revenue
(Obj. 3)

E3-15 Deng Pan Enterprises aids Chinese students upon their arrival in the United States. Paid by the Chinese government, Deng Pan collects some service revenue in advance. In other cases, he receives cash after performing relocation services. At the end of August—a particularly busy period—Deng Pan's books show the following:

	July 31	August 31
Accounts receivable	$1,900	$2,200
Unearned service revenue	1,200	300

During August, Deng Pan Enterprises received cash of $4,000 from the Chinese government. How much service revenue did the business earn during August? Show your work.

Computing cash amounts
(Obj. 3)

E3-16 For the situation of Exercise 3-15, take the service revenue of Deng Pan Enterprises as $5,900 during August. How much cash did the business collect from the Chinese government that month? Show your work.

Beyond the Numbers

Explaining why adjusting entries are needed
(Obj. 3)

BN3-1 Suppose a new management team is in charge of Pepco Inc., a fast-food company. Assume Pepco's new top managers rose through the company ranks in the sales and marketing departments and have little appreciation for the details of accounting. Consider the following conversation between two managers:

Lee Stice, President:	"I want to avoid the hassle of adjusting the books every time we need financial statements. Sooner or later we receive cash for all our revenues, and we pay cash for all our expenses. I can understand cash transactions, but all these accruals confuse me. If I cannot understand *our own* accounting, I'm fairly certain the average person who invests in our company cannot understand it either. Let's start recording only our cash transactions. I bet it won't make any difference to anyone."
Jan Bond, Chief Financial Officer:	"Sounds good to me. This will save me lots of headaches. I'll implement the new policy immediately."

Write a business memo to the company president giving your response to the new policy. Identify at least five individual items (such as specific accounts) in the financial statements that will be reported incorrectly. Will outside investors care? Use the format of a business memo given with Daily Exercise 3-14, page 118.

ETHICAL ISSUE

The net income of Collins, a department store, decreased sharply during 1999. Wayne Collins, owner of the store, anticipates the need for a bank loan in 2000. Late in 1999, Collins instructs his store's accountant to record a $7,000 sale of furniture to the Collins family, even though the goods will not be shipped from the manufacturer until January 2000. Collins also tells the accountant *not* to make the following December 31, 1999, adjusting entries:

Salaries owed to employees	$900
Prepaid insurance that has expired	400

REQUIRED

1. Compute the overall effect of these transactions on the store's reported income for 1999.

2. Why is Collins taking this action? Is his action ethical? Give your reason, identifying the parties helped and the parties harmed by Collins's action.
3. As a personal friend, what advice would you give the accountant?

Problems (GROUP A)

Cash basis versus accrual basis (Obj. 1, 2)

P3-1A Hillcrest Speech and Hearing Clinic experienced the following selected transactions during March:

Mar.	2	Prepaid insurance for March through May, $800.
	4	Paid gas bill, $400.
	5	Performed services on account, $1,000.
	9	Purchased office equipment for cash, $1,400.
	12	Received cash for services performed, $900.
	14	Purchased office equipment on account, $300.
	28	Collected $500 on account from March 5.
	29	Paid salary expense, $1,100.
	30	Paid account payable from March 14.
	31	Recorded adjusting entry for March insurance expense (see Mar. 2).
	31	Debited unearned revenue and credited revenue in an adjusting entry, $700.

REQUIRED

1. Show how each transaction would be handled using the cash basis and the accrual basis. Under each column, give the amount of revenue or expense for March. Journal entries are not required. Use the following format for your answer, and show your computations:

	Amount of Revenue or Expense for March	
Date	**Cash Basis**	**Accrual Basis**

2. Compute March net income or net loss under each method.
3. Indicate which measure of net income or net loss is preferable. Give your reason.

Applying accounting principles (Obj. 1, 2)

P3-2A Write a business memo to a new bookkeeper to explain the difference between the cash basis of accounting and the accrual basis. Mention the roles of the revenue principle and the matching principle in accrual-basis accounting. The format of a business memo follows.

Date:	______
To:	New Bookkeeper
From:	(Student Name)
Subject:	Difference between the cash basis and the accrual basis

Journalizing adjusting entries (Obj. 3)

P3-3A Journalize the adjusting entry needed on December 31, end of the current accounting period, for each of the following independent cases affecting La Salle Equipment Servicing.

a. Details of Prepaid Rent are shown in the account:

Prepaid Rent			
Jan.	1 Bal.	400	
Mar. 31		800	
Sept. 30		800	

La Salle pays office rent semiannually on March 31 and September 30. At December 31, part of the last payment is still an asset.

b. La Salle pays its employees each Friday. The amount of the weekly payroll is $4,000 for a five-day workweek, and the daily salary amounts are equal. The current accounting period ends on Monday.
c. La Salle has loaned money, receiving notes receivable. During the current year, the entity has earned accrued interest revenue of $737, which it will receive next year.
d. The beginning balance of Supplies was $2,680. During the year, the entity purchased supplies costing $6,180, and at December 31, the cost of supplies on hand is $2,150.
e. La Salle is servicing the air-conditioning system in a large building, and the owner of the building paid La Salle $12,900 as the annual service fee. La Salle recorded this amount as Unearned Service Revenue. Ferdinand La Salle, the owner, estimates that the company has earned one-fourth the total fee during the current year.

f. Depreciation for the current year includes Equipment, $3,850; Trucks, $10,320. Make a compound entry.

Analyzing and journalizing adjustments
(Obj. 3)

P3-4A Dayspring Construction Company's unadjusted and adjusted trial balances at April 30, 19X1, follow.

DAYSPRING CONSTRUCTION COMPANY
Adjusted Trial Balance
April 30, 19X1

	Trial Balance		Adjusted Trial Balance	
Account Title	**Debit**	**Credit**	**Debit**	**Credit**
Cash	6,180		6,180	
Accounts receivable	6,360		6,700	
Interest receivable			200	
Note receivable	4,100		4,100	
Supplies	980		290	
Prepaid rent	2,480		720	
Building	66,450		66,450	
Accumulated depreciation		16,010		17,290
Accounts payable		6,920		6,920
Wages payable				320
Unearned service revenue		670		110
Joseph Kent, capital		58,790		58,790
Joseph Kent, withdrawals	3,600		3,600	
Service revenue		9,940		10,840
Interest revenue				200
Wage expense	1,600		1,920	
Rent expense			1,760	
Depreciation expense			1,280	
Insurance expense	370		370	
Supplies expense			690	
Utilities expense	210		210	
	92,330	92,330	94,470	94,470

REQUIRED

Journalize the adjusting entries that account for the differences between the two trial balances.

Journalizing and posting adjustments to T-accounts; preparing the adjusted trial balance
(Obj. 3, 4)

P3-5A The trial balance of North Carolina Insurors at October 31, 19X2, and the data needed for the month-end adjustments follow.

NORTH CAROLINA INSURORS
Trial Balance
October 31, 19X2

Cash	$ 2,200	
Accounts receivable	14,750	
Prepaid rent	3,100	
Supplies	780	
Furniture	22,710	
Accumulated depreciation		$11,640
Accounts payable		1,940
Salary payable		
Unearned commission revenue		2,290
Will Harrison, capital		25,060
Will Harrison, withdrawals	2,900	
Commission revenue		8,400
Salary expense	2,160	
Rent expense		
Depreciation expense		
Advertising expense	730	
Supplies expense		
Total	$49,330	$49,330

Adjustment data:

a. Prepaid rent still in force at October 31, $400.
b. Supplies used during the month, $640.
c. Depreciation for the month, $900.
d. Accrued advertising expense at October 31, $320. (Credit Accounts Payable.)
e. Accrued salary expense at October 31, $180.
f. Unearned commission revenue still unearned at October 31, $2,000.

REQUIRED

1. Open T-accounts for the accounts listed in the trial balance, inserting their October 31 unadjusted balances.
2. Journalize the adjusting entries and post them to the T-accounts. Key the journal entries and the posted amounts by letter.
3. Prepare the adjusted trial balance.
4. How will the company use the adjusted trial balance?

Preparing the financial statements from an adjusted trial balance ***(Obj. 5)***

P3-6A The adjusted trial balance of Tradewind Travel Designers at December 31, 19X6, follows.

TRADEWIND TRAVEL DESIGNERS
Adjusted Trial Balance
December 31, 19X6

Cash	$ 1,320	
Accounts receivable	8,920	
Supplies	2,300	
Prepaid rent	1,600	
Office equipment	20,180	
Accumulated depreciation—office equipment		$ 4,350
Office furniture	37,710	
Accumulated depreciation—office furniture		4,870
Accounts payable		3,640
Property tax payable		1,100
Interest payable		830
Unearned service revenue		620
Note payable		13,500
Gary Gillen, capital		26,090
Gary Gillen, withdrawals	29,000	
Service revenue		124,910
Depreciation expense—office equipment	6,680	
Depreciation expense—office furniture	2,370	
Salary expense	39,900	
Rent expense	17,400	
Interest expense	3,100	
Utilities expense	2,670	
Insurance expense	3,810	
Supplies expense	2,950	
Total	$179,910	$179,910

REQUIRED

1. Prepare Tradewind's 19X6 income statement and statement of owner's equity and year-end balance sheet. List expenses in decreasing order on the income statement and show total liabilities on the balance sheet. Draw arrows linking the three financial statements.
2. a. Which financial statement reports Tradewind Travel's results of operations? Were operations successful during 19X6? Cite specifics from the financial statements to support your evaluation.
   b. Which statement reports the company's financial position? Does Tradewind's financial position look strong or weak? Give the reason for your evaluation.

Preparing an adjusted trial balance and the financial statements ***(Obj. 3, 4, 5)***

P3-7A The unadjusted trial balance of Jim Panther, Attorney, at July 31, 19X2, and the related month-end adjustment data follow.

JIM PANTHER, ATTORNEY Trial Balance July 31, 19X2		
Cash	$ 5,600	
Accounts receivable	11,600	
Prepaid rent	3,600	
Supplies	800	
Furniture	28,800	
Accumulated depreciation		$ 3,500
Accounts payable		3,450
Salary payable		
Jim Panther, capital		38,650
Jim Panther, withdrawals	4,000	
Legal service revenue		11,750
Salary expense	2,400	
Rent expense		
Utilities expense	550	
Depreciation expense		
Supplies expense		
Total	$57,350	$57,350

Adjustment data:

a. Accrued legal service revenue at July 31, $900.
b. Prepaid rent expired during the month. The unadjusted prepaid balance of $3,600 relates to the period July through October.
c. Supplies on hand at July 31, $400.
d. Depreciation on furniture for the month. The estimated useful life of the furniture is four years.
e. Accrued salary expense at July 31 for one day only. The five-day weekly payroll is $1,000.

REQUIRED

1. Using Exhibit 3-10 as an example, write the trial balance on a work sheet and prepare the adjusted trial balance of Jim Panther, Attorney, at July 31, 19X2. Key each adjusting entry by letter.
2. Prepare the income statement, the statement of owner's equity, and the balance sheet. Draw arrows linking the three financial statements.

Problems (GROUP B)

Cash basis versus accrual basis **(Obj. 1, 2)**

P3-1B Rigolosi Counseling Center had the following selected transactions during October:

Oct.	1	Prepaid insurance for October through December, $600.
	4	Performed counseling service on account, $1,000.
	5	Purchased office furniture on account, $150.
	8	Paid advertising expense, $300.
	11	Purchased office equipment for cash, $800.
	19	Performed counseling service and received cash, $700.
	24	Collected $400 on account for the October 4 service.
	26	Paid account payable from October 5.
	29	Paid salary expense, $900.
	31	Recorded adjusting entry for October insurance expense (see Oct. 1).
	31	Debited unearned revenue and credited revenue to adjust the accounts, $600.

REQUIRED

1. Show how each transaction would be handled using the cash basis and the accrual basis. Under each column, give the amount of revenue or expense for October. Journal entries are not required. Use the following format for your answer, and show your computations:

	Amount of Revenue or Expense for October	
Date	Cash Basis	Accrual Basis

2. Compute October net income or net loss under each method.
3. Indicate which measure of net income or net loss is preferable. Give your reason.

Applying accounting principles **(Obj. 2, 3)**

P3-2B As the controller of St. Hill Security Systems, you have hired a new bookkeeper, whom you must train. He objects to making an adjusting entry for accrued salaries at the end of the period. He reasons, "We will pay the salaries soon. Why not wait until payment to record the expense? In the end, the result will be the same." Write a business memo to explain to the bookkeeper why the adjusting entry for accrued salary expense is needed. The format of a business memo follows.

Date:	________
To:	New Bookkeeper
From:	(Student Name)
Subject:	Why the adjusting entry for salary expense is needed

Journalizing adjusting entries **(Obj. 3)**

P3-3B Journalize the adjusting entry needed on December 31, end of the current accounting period, for each of the following independent cases affecting Steiner Advertising Specialists.

a. Each Friday, Steiner pays its employees for the current week's work. The amount of the payroll is $4,000 for a five-day workweek. The current accounting period ends on Thursday.
b. Steiner has received notes receivable from some clients for professional services. During the current year, Steiner has earned accrued interest revenue of $170, which will be received next year.
c. The beginning balance of Art Supplies was $3,800. During the year, the entity purchased art supplies costing $12,530, and at December 31, the inventory of supplies on hand is $2,970.
d. Steiner designed an advertising campaign, and the client paid Steiner $36,000 at the start of the project. Steiner recorded this amount as Unearned Service Revenue. The ads will run on television over several months. Steiner estimates that the company has earned three-fourths of the total fee during the current year.
e. Depreciation for the current year includes: Office Furniture, $5,500; Building, $3,790. Make a compound entry.
f. Details of Prepaid Insurance are shown in the account:

Prepaid Insurance

Jan. 1 Bal.	1,200	
Apr. 30	1,800	
Oct. 31	1,800	

Steiner pays semiannual insurance premiums (the payment for insurance coverage is called a *premium*) on April 30 and October 31. At December 31, part of the last payment is still in force.

Analyzing and journalizing adjustments **(Obj. 3)**

P3-4B Todd Realty Company's unadjusted and adjusted trial balances at December 31, 19X7, follow.

TODD REALTY COMPANY
Adjusted Trial Balance
December 31, 19X7

Account Title	Trial Balance Debit	Trial Balance Credit	Adjusted Trial Balance Debit	Adjusted Trial Balance Credit
Cash	4,120		4,120	
Accounts receivable	8,260		14,090	
Supplies	1,090		280	
Prepaid insurance	2,600		2,330	
Office furniture	21,630		21,630	
Accumulated depreciation		8,220		10,500
Accounts payable		6,310		6,310
Salary payable				960
Interest payable				480
Note payable		12,000		12,000
Unearned commission revenue		1,840		1,160
Annie Todd, capital		13,510		13,510
Annie Todd, withdrawals	29,370		29,370	
Commission revenue		69,890		76,400
Depreciation expense			2,280	
Supplies expense			810	
Utilities expense	4,960		4,960	
Salary expense	26,660		27,620	
Rent expense	12,200		12,200	
Interest expense	880		1,360	
Insurance expense			270	
	111,770	111,770	121,320	121,320

REQUIRED

Journalize the adjusting entries that account for the differences between the two trial balances.

Journalizing and posting adjustments to T-accounts; preparing the adjusted trial balance
(Obj. 3, 4)

P3-5B The trial balance of Laser Printing Company at August 31 of the current year and the data needed for the month-end adjustments follow.

LASER PRINTING COMPANY
Trial Balance
August 31, 19X6

Cash	$ 7,100	
Accounts receivable	23,780	
Prepaid rent	2,420	
Supplies	1,180	
Furniture	19,740	
Accumulated depreciation		$ 3,630
Accounts payable		3,310
Salary payable		
Unearned service revenue		2,790
Emily Harrison, capital		39,510
Emily Harrison, withdrawals	5,350	
Service revenue		15,700
Salary expense	3,800	
Rent expense		
Depreciation expense		
Advertising expense	1,570	
Supplies expense		
Total	$64,940	$64,940

Adjustment data:

a. Unearned service revenue still unearned at August 31, $1,670.
b. Prepaid rent still in force at August 31, $620.
c. Supplies used during the month, $700.
d. Depreciation for the month, $400.
e. Accrued advertising expense at August 31, $610. (Credit Accounts Payable.)
f. Accrued salary expense at August 31, $550.

REQUIRED

1. Open T-accounts for the accounts listed in the trial balance, inserting their August 31 unadjusted balances.
2. Journalize the adjusting entries and post them to the T-accounts. Key the journal entries and the posted amounts by letter.
3. Prepare the adjusted trial balance.
4. How will the company use the adjusted trial balance?

Preparing an adjusted trial balance and the financial statements
(Obj. 3, 4, 5)

P3-6B The adjusted trial balance of Clement Antique Auctioneers at December 31, 19X8, follows.

CLEMENT ANTIQUE AUCTIONEERS
Adjusted Trial Balance
December 31, 19X8

Cash	$ 2,340	
Accounts receivable	41,490	
Prepaid rent	1,350	
Supplies	970	
Equipment	75,690	
Accumulated depreciation—equipment		$ 22,240
Office furniture	24,100	
Accumulated depreciation—office furniture		3,670
Accounts payable		13,600
Unearned service revenue		4,520
Interest payable		2,130
Salary payable		930
Note payable		45,000
C. Clement, capital		32,380
C. Clement, withdrawals	48,000	
Service revenue		195,790
Depreciation expense—equipment	11,300	
Depreciation expense—office furniture	2,410	
Salary expense	87,800	
Rent expense	12,000	
Interest expense	4,200	
Utilities expense	3,770	
Insurance expense	3,150	
Supplies expense	1,690	
Total	$320,260	$320,260

REQUIRED

1. Prepare Clement's 19X8 income statement and statement of owner's equity and year-end balance sheet. List expenses in decreasing order on the income statement and show total liabilities on the balance sheet. Draw arrows linking the three financial statements.
2. **a.** Which financial statement reports Clement's results of operations? Were 19X8 operations successful? Cite specifics from the financial statements to support your evaluation.
   b. Which statement reports the company's financial position? Does Clement's financial position look strong or weak? Give the reason for your evaluation.

Preparing an adjusted trial balance and the financial statements
(Obj. 3, 4, 5)

P3-7B Consider the unadjusted trial balance of TMS Landscaping at October 31, 19X2, and the related month-end adjustment data.

TMS LANDSCAPING
Trial Balance
October 31, 19X2

Cash	$ 6,300	
Accounts receivable	8,000	
Prepaid rent	4,000	
Supplies	600	
Equipment	27,000	
Accumulated depreciation		$ 3,000
Accounts payable		2,800
Salary payable		
Trent Stuckey, capital		36,000
Trent Stuckey, withdrawals	3,600	
Service revenue		9,400
Salary expense	1,400	
Rent expense		
Utilities expense	300	
Depreciation expense		
Supplies expense		
Total	$51,200	$51,200

Adjustment data:

a. Accrued service revenue at October 31, $2,000.
b. Prepaid rent expired during the month. The unadjusted prepaid balance of $4,000 relates to the period October 19X2 through January 19X3.
c. Supplies on hand October 31, $200.
d. Depreciation on equipment for the month. The equipment's expected useful life is five years.
e. Accrued salary expense at October 31 for one day only. The five-day weekly payroll is $2,000.

REQUIRED

1. Write the trial balance on a work sheet, using Exhibit 3-10 as an example, and prepare the adjusted trial balance of TMS Landscaping at October 31, 19X2. Key each adjusting entry by letter.
2. Prepare the income statement, the statement of owner's equity, and the balance sheet. Draw arrows linking the three financial statements.

Applying Your Knowledge

DECISION CASES

Valuing a business on the basis of its net income
(Obj. 4, 5)

CASE 1. Leslie Pechanek has owned and operated Pechanek Advertising since its beginning ten years ago. From all appearances the business has prospered. In the past few years, you have become friends with Pechanek and her husband through your church. Recently, Pechanek mentioned that she has lost her zest for the business and would consider selling it for the right price.

You are interested in buying this business and obtain its most recent monthly unadjusted trial balance, which follows.

PECHANEK ADVERTISING
Unadjusted Trial Balance
April 30, 19XX

Cash	$ 9,700	
Accounts receivable	7,900	
Prepaid expenses	2,600	
Computer equipment	201,300	
Accumulated depreciation		$ 18,600
Accounts payable		5,800
Salary payable		
Unearned advertising revenue		6,700
Leslie Pechanek, capital		187,400
Leslie Pechanek, withdrawals	7,000	
Advertising revenue		14,300
Rent expense		
Salary expense	3,400	
Utilities expense	900	
Depreciation expense		
Supplies expense		
Total	$232,800	$232,800

Revenues and expenses vary little from month to month, and April is a typical month. Your investigation reveals that the unadjusted trial balance does not include the effects of monthly revenues of $1,100 and monthly expenses totaling $2,100. If you were to buy Pechanek Advertising, you would hire a manager who would require a monthly salary of $3,000.

REQUIRED

1. The most you would pay for the business is 30 times the monthly net income *you could expect to earn* from it. Compute this possible price.
2. The least Pechanek will take for the business is her ending capital. Compute this amount.
3. Under these conditions, how much should you offer Pechanek? Give your reason.

Explaining the concepts underlying the accrual basis of accounting
(Obj. 1, 2)

CASE 2. The following independent questions are related to accrual-basis accounting.

1. It has been said that the only time a company's financial position is known for certain is when the company's assets are sold and its only asset is cash. Why is this statement true?
2. A friend suggests that the purpose of adjusting entries is to correct errors in the accounts. Is your friend's statement true? What is the purpose of adjusting entries if the statement is wrong?

3. The text suggested that furniture (and each other plant asset that is depreciated) is a form of prepaid expense. Do you agree? Why do you think some accountants view plant assets this way?

FINANCIAL STATEMENT CASES

Journalizing and posting transactions and tracing account balances to the financial statements
(Obj. 3, 5)

CASE 1. NIKE, Inc.—like all other businesses—makes adjusting entries prior to year end in order to measure assets, liabilities, revenues, and expenses properly. Examine NIKE's balance sheet, and pay particular attention to Prepaid Expenses and Accrued Liabilities (which includes Salary Payable and Interest Payable).

REQUIRED

1. Open T-accounts for Prepaid Expenses and Accrued Liabilities. Insert NIKE's balances (in thousands) at May 31, 1996. (Example: Prepaid Expenses, $94,427)
2. Journalize the following transactions for the current year, ended May 31, 1997. Key entries by letter. Explanations are not required.

   Cash transactions (amounts in thousands):

   a. Paid prepaid expenses, $75,917.
   b. Paid the May 31, 1996, accrued liabilities (use a single Accrued Liabilities account).

   Adjustments at May 31, 1997 (amounts in thousands):

   c. Prepaid expenses expired, $13,286. (Debit Administrative Expense)
   d. Accrued Liabilities, $570,504. (Debit Selling Expense.)
   e. Depreciation expense (obtain the 1997 amount from the statement of cash flows).

3. Post to the Prepaid Expenses account and the Accrued Liabilities account. Then these accounts agree with the corresponding amounts reported in the May 31, 1997, balance sheet.

Adjusting the accounts of a company
(Obj. 2, 3)

CASE 2. Obtain the annual report of a company of your choosing. Assume that the company accountants *failed* to make four adjustments at the end of the current year. For illustrative purposes, assume that the amounts reported in the company's balance sheet for the related assets and liabilities are *incorrect.*

Adjustments omitted:

a. Depreciation of equipment, $800,000.
b. Salaries owed to employees but not yet paid, $230,000.
c. Prepaid rent used up during the year, $100,000.
d. Accrued sales (or service) revenue, $140,000.

REQUIRED

1. Compute the correct amounts for the following balance sheet items:
   a. Book value of plant assets
   b. Total liabilities
   c. Prepaid expenses
   d. Accounts receivable
2. Compare the amount of net income or net loss that the company would have reported if the accountants had recorded these transactions properly. Ignore income tax.

Team Project

Return to the chapter introduction, which describes Andrea McGinty's business, It's Just Lunch. Suppose your group is opening an It's Just Lunch office in your area. You must make some important decisions—where to locate, how to advertise, and so on—and you must also make some accounting decisions. For example, what will be the end of your business's accounting year? How often will you need financial statements to evaluate operating performance and financial position? Will you use the cash basis or the accrual basis? When will you account for the revenue that the business earns? How will you account for the expenses?

REQUIRED

Write a report (or prepare an oral presentation, as directed by your professor) to address the following considerations:

1. What is likely to be the low point in the business's operations? This is ordinarily the end of the accounting year.
2. Will you use the cash basis or the accrual basis of accounting? Give a complete description of your reasoning.
3. How often do you want financial statements? Why? Discuss how you will use each financial statement.

4. What kind of revenue will you earn? When will you record it as revenue? How will you decide when to record the revenue?
5. Prepare a made-up income statement for It's Just Lunch for the Year ended December 31, 1996. List all the business's expenses, starting with the most important (largest dollar amount) and working through the least important (smallest dollar amount). Try to come as close as you can to the actual figures, as follows: Net revenues, $4,453,363; Net income, $410,566.
6. Using made-up dollar amounts, prepare all the adjusting entries your business will need at the end of the year. Identify the date of your adjustments.

APPENDIX to Chapter 3

Alternative Treatment of Accounting for Prepaid Expenses and Unearned Revenues

Chapters 1 through 3 illustrate the most popular way to account for prepaid expenses and unearned revenues. This appendix illustrates an alternative—and equally appropriate—approach to handling prepaid expenses and unearned revenues.

Prepaid Expenses

Prepaid expenses are advance payments of expenses. Prepaid Insurance, Prepaid Rent, Prepaid Advertising, and Prepaid Legal Cost are prepaid expenses. Supplies that will be used up in the current period or within one year are also accounted for as prepaid expenses.

When a business prepays an expense—rent, for example—it can debit an *asset* account (Prepaid Rent) as illustrated on page 97:

Aug. 1	Prepaid Rent..........	XXX	
	Cash		XXX

Alternatively, it can debit an *expense* account to record this cash payment:

Aug. 1	Rent Expense.........	XXX	
	Cash		XXX

Regardless of the account debited at the time of the prepayment, the business must adjust the accounts at the end of the period to report the correct amounts of the expense and the asset.

Prepaid Expense Recorded Initially as an Expense

Objective A1
Account for a prepaid expense recorded initially as an expense

Prepaying an expense creates an asset, as explained under the "Prepaid Rent" heading on page 97. However, the asset may be so short-lived that it will expire in the current accounting period—within one year or less. Thus the accountant may decide to debit the prepayment to an expense account at the time of payment. A $6,000 cash payment for rent (one year, in advance) on August 1 may be debited to Rent Expense:

19X6			
Aug. 1	Rent Expense.........	6,000	
	Cash................		6,000

At December 31, only five months' prepayment has expired (for August through December), leaving seven months' rent still prepaid. In this case, the accountant must transfer 7/12 of the original prepayment of $6,000, or $3,500, to the asset account Prepaid Rent. At December 31, 19X6, the business still has the benefit of the prepayment for January through July of 19X7. The adjusting entry at December 31 is

Adjusting Entries

19X6			
Dec. 31	Prepaid Rent ($6,000 × 7/12).........	3,500	
	Rent Expense		3,500

After posting, the two accounts appear as follows:

Prepaid Rent

19X6			
Dec. 31	Adj.	3,500	
Dec. 31	Bal.	3,500	

Rent Expense

19X6			19X6		
Aug. 1	CP	6,000	Dec. 31	Adj.	3,500
Dec. 31	Bal.	2,500			

CP = Cash payment entry Adj. = Adjusting entry

The balance sheet at the end of 19X6 reports Prepaid Rent of $3,500, and the income statement for 19X6 reports Rent Expense of $2,500 regardless of whether the business initially debits the prepayment to an asset account or to an expense account.

Unearned (Deferred) Revenues

Unearned (deferred) revenues arise when a business collects cash before earning the revenue. Unearned revenues are liabilities because the business that receives cash owes the other party goods or services to be delivered later.

Unearned (Deferred) Revenue Recorded Initially as a Revenue

Objective A2

Account for an unearned (deferred) revenue recorded initially as a revenue

Receipt of cash in advance creates a liability, as recorded on page 104. Another way to account for the receipt of cash is to credit a *revenue* account. If the business has earned all the revenue within the same period, no adjusting entry is needed at the end of the period. However, if the business earns only part of the revenue at the end of the period, it must make an adjusting entry.

Suppose on October 1, 19X2, a law firm records as revenue the receipt of cash for a nine-month fee of $7,200 received in advance. The cash receipt entry can be

19X2			
Oct. 1	Cash	7,200	
	Legal Revenue		7,200

At December 31, the attorney has earned only 3/9 of the $7,200, or $2,400, for the months of October, November, and December. Accordingly, the firm makes an adjusting entry to transfer the unearned portion (6/9 of $7,200, or $4,800) from the revenue account to a liability account, as follows:

Adjusting Entries			
19X2			
Dec. 31	Legal Revenue ($7,200 × 6/9)	4,800	
	Unearned Legal Revenue		4,800

The adjusting entry transfers the unearned portion (6/9, or $4,800) of the original amount to the liability account because the law firm still owes legal service to the client during January through June of 19X3. After posting, the total amount ($7,200) is properly divided between the liability account ($4,800) and the revenue account ($2,400), as follows:

Unearned Legal Revenue

Debit	Credit
	19X2
	Dec. 31 Adj. 4,800
	Dec. 31 Bal. 4,800

Legal Revenue

Debit	Credit
19X2	19X2
Dec. 31 Adj. 4,800	Oct. 1 CR 7,200
	Dec. 31 Bal. 2,400

CR = Cash receipt entry Adj. = Adjusting entry

The attorney's 19X2 income statement reports legal revenue of $2,400, and the balance sheet at December 31, 19X2, reports the unearned legal revenue of $4,800 as a liability, regardless of whether the business initially credits a liability account or a revenue account.

Appendix Exercises

Recording supplies transactions two ways ***(Obj. A1)***

E3A-1 At the beginning of the year, supplies of $1,690 were on hand. During the year, the business paid $5,400 cash for supplies. At the end of the year, the count of supplies indicates the ending balance is $1,360.

REQUIRED

1. Assume that the business records supplies by initially debiting an *asset* account. Therefore, place the beginning balance in the Supplies T-account, and record the above entries directly in the accounts without using a journal.
2. Assume that the business records supplies by initially debiting an *expense* account. Therefore, place the beginning balance in the Supplies Expense T-account, and record the above entries directly in the accounts without using a journal.

3. Compare the ending account balances under both approaches. Are they the same? Explain.

E3A-2 At the beginning of the year, the company owed customers $2,750 for unearned service collected in advance. During the year, the business received advance cash receipts of $10,000. At year end, the unearned revenue liability is $3,700.

Recording unearned revenues two ways ***(Obj. A2)***

REQUIRED

1. Assume that the company records unearned revenues by initially crediting a *liability* account. Open T-accounts for Unearned Service Revenue and Service Revenue, and place the beginning balance in Unearned Service Revenue. Journalize the cash collection and adjusting entries, and post their dollar amounts. As references in the T-accounts, denote a balance by Bal., a cash receipt by CR, and an adjustment by Adj.
2. Assume that the company records unearned revenues by initially crediting a *revenue* account. Open T-accounts for Unearned Service Revenue and Service Revenue, and place the beginning balance in Service Revenue. Journalize the cash collection and adjusting entries, and post their dollar amounts. As references in the T-accounts, denote a balance by Bal., a cash receipt by CR, and an adjustment by Adj.
3. Compare the ending balances in the two accounts. Explain why they are the same or different.

Appendix Problem

P3A-1 Diebolt Sales and Service completed the following transactions during 19X4:

Recording prepaid rent and rent revenue collected in advance two ways ***(Obj. A1, A2)***

Oct. 1 Paid $3,000 store rent covering the six-month period ending March 31, 19X5.
Dec. 1 Collected $3,200 cash in advance from customers. The service revenue will be earned $800 monthly over the period ending March 31, 19X5.

REQUIRED

1. Journalize these entries by debiting an asset account for Prepaid Rent and by crediting a liability account for Unearned Service Revenue. Explanations are unnecessary.
2. Journalize the related adjustments at December 31, 19X4.
3. Post the entries to the ledger accounts, and show their balances at December 31, 19X4. Posting references are unnecessary.
4. Repeat requirements 1 through 3. This time debit Rent Expense for the rent payment and credit Service Revenue for the collection of revenue in advance.
5. Compare the account balances in requirements 3 and 4. They should be equal.

CHAPTER 4

Completing the Accounting Cycle

LEARNING OBJECTIVES

After studying this chapter, you should be able to

1. Prepare an accounting work sheet
2. Use the work sheet to complete the accounting cycle
3. Close the revenue, expense, and withdrawal accounts
4. Correct typical accounting errors
5. Classify assets and liabilities as current or long-term
6. Use the current and debt ratios to evaluate a business

> *“People often ask, what’s the value of closing the books faster? Clearly, the value of information today is greater than the value of that same information tomorrow. The fast close provides time for more important functions, such as planning and analysis, and reduces overtime, thereby improving morale. It is a distinct competitive advantage.”*
>
> **KENNETH J. JOHNSON, CORPORATE VICE PRESIDENT AND CONTROLLER, MOTOROLA COMPANY**

Motorola Company, best known for its computer chips, cellular telephones, pagers, and other electronic products, was awarded the Malcolm Baldrige National Quality Award for total quality management. The U.S. Department of Commerce grants the Baldrige award, and Motorola won in the manufacturing category.

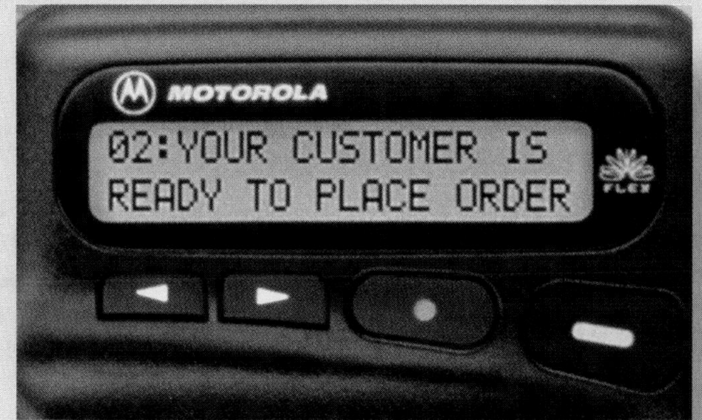

To compete in a changing economy, companies must get financial data to their managers fast. Motorola accomplishes this goal by rapidly *closing its books*—the process of preparing the accounts at the end of each period for recording the transactions of the next period. Motorola can close its accounts in just two days. Other companies take two to four weeks to assemble the same type of information; Motorola’s lightning-fast accounting system gives the company an edge over competitors.

In Chapter 3, we prepared the financial statements from an adjusted trial balance. That approach works well for quick decision making, but organizations of all sizes take the accounting process a step further. At the end of each period, after making the adjusting entries, they close their books. Whether the company is Motorola or Gary Lyon, CPA, the closing process follows the basic pattern outlined in this chapter. It marks the end of the *accounting cycle* for a given period.

The accounting process often uses a document known as the accountant's *work sheet.* There are many different types of work sheets in business—as many, in fact, as there are needs for summary data. Work sheets are valuable because they aid decision making.

The Accounting Cycle

Accounting Cycle. Process by which companies produce an entity's financial statements for a specific period.

The **accounting cycle** is the process by which companies produce their financial statements for a specific period of time. For a new business, the cycle begins with setting up (opening) the ledger accounts. Gary Lyon started his accounting practice on April 1, 19X1, so the first step in the cycle was to open the accounts. After a business has operated for one period, the account balances carry over from period to period. Therefore, the accounting cycle starts with the account balances at the beginning of the period. Exhibit 4-1 outlines the complete accounting cycle. The boldface items in Panel A indicate the new items that we will be discussing in this chapter.

The accounting cycle includes work performed at two different times:

- During the period—Journalizing transactions
  Posting to the ledger
- End of the period—Adjusting the accounts, including journalizing and posting
  Closing the accounts, including journalizing and posting
  Preparing the financial statements

The end-of-period work also readies the accounts for the next period. In Chapters 3 and 4, we cover the end-of-period accounting for a service business such as Gary Lyon, CPA. Chapter 5 then shows how a merchandising entity adjusts and closes its books.

Companies prepare financial statements on a monthly or a quarterly basis, and steps 1 through 6a in Exhibit 4-1 are adequate for statement preparation. Steps 6b through 7 can be performed monthly or quarterly but are necessary only at the end of the year.

Accounting Work Sheet

Objective 1

Prepare an accounting work sheet

Work Sheet. A columnar document designed to help move data from the trial balance to the financial statements.

Accountants often use a **work sheet,** a multicolumned document, to help move data from the trial balance to the financial statements. The work sheet summarizes the data for the statements. Listing all the accounts and their unadjusted balances helps identify the accounts that need adjustment. The work sheet aids the closing process by listing the ending adjusted balances for all accounts.

The work sheet is not part of the ledger or the journal, and it is not a financial statement. Therefore, it is not part of the formal accounting system. Instead, it is a summary device that exists for the accountant's convenience.

Exhibits 4-2 through 4-6 (see page 144) illustrate the development of a typical work sheet for the business of Gary Lyon, CPA. The heading at the top names the business, identifies the document, and states the accounting period. A step-by-step description of its preparation follows.

We introduced the adjusted trial balance in Chapter 3, p. 106.

Steps introduced in Chapter 3 to prepare the adjusted trial balance:

1. Print the account titles and their unadjusted ending balances in the Trial Balance columns of the work sheet, and total the amounts (Exhibit 4-2).
2. Enter the adjustments in the Adjustments columns, and total the amounts (Exhibit 4-3).
3. Compute each account's adjusted balance by combining the trial balance and adjustment figures. Enter the adjusted amounts in the Adjusted Trial Balance columns (Exhibit 4-4). Then compute the total for each column.

New steps introduced in this chapter:

4. Extend the asset, liability, and owner's equity amounts from the Adjusted Trial Balance to the Balance Sheet columns. Extend the revenue and expense amounts to the Income Statement columns. Total the statement columns (Exhibit 4-5).
5. Compute net income or net loss as the difference between total revenues and total expenses on the income statement. Enter net income or net loss as a balancing amount on the income statement and on the balance sheet, and compute the final column totals (Exhibit 4-6).

Let's examine these steps in greater detail.

1. *Print the account titles and their unadjusted balances in the Trial Balance columns of the work sheet, and total the amounts.* Total debits must equal total credits, as shown in Exhibit 4-2. The account titles and unadjusted balances come directly from the ledger accounts before the adjusting entries are prepared. Accounts are grouped on the work sheet by category (assets, liabilities, owner's equity, revenues, and expenses) and are usually listed in the order they appear in the ledger (Cash first, Accounts Receivable second, and so on).

Concept Highlight

EXHIBIT 4-1
The Accounting Cycle

PANEL A

During the Period

1. Start with the account balances in the ledger at the beginning of the period.
2. Analyze and journalize transactions as they occur.
3. Post journal entries to the ledger accounts.

End of the Period

4. Compute the unadjusted balance in each account at the end of the period.
5. Enter the trial balance on the **work sheet,** and complete the work sheet (optional).
6. Using the adjusted trial balance or the full **work sheet** as a guide.
   a. Prepare the financial statements.
   b. Journalize and post the adjusting entries.
   c. Journalize and post the **closing entries.**
7. Prepare the **postclosing trial balance.** This trial balance becomes step 1 for the next period.

PANEL B

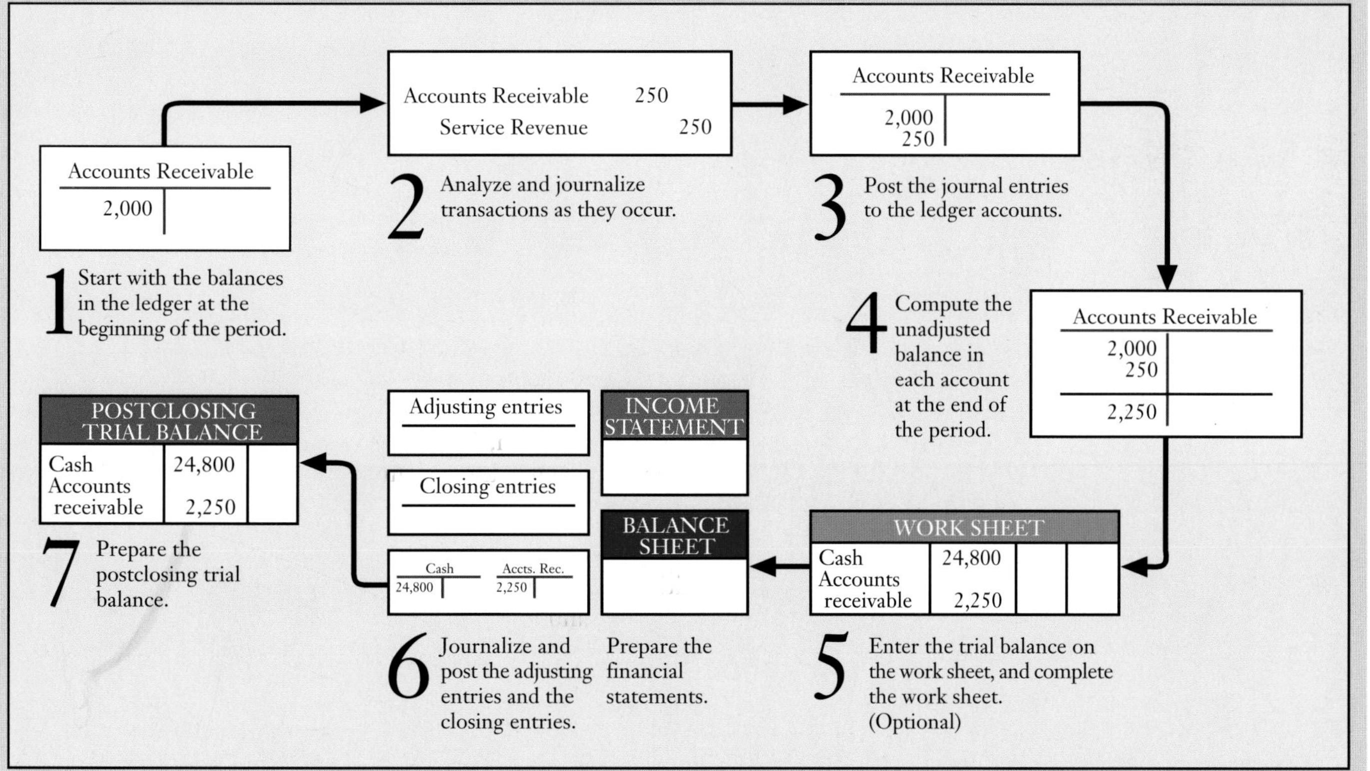

EXHIBIT 4-2
Trial Balance

GARY LYON, CPA
ACCOUNTING WORK SHEET
FOR THE MONTH ENDED APRIL 30, 19X1

	Trial Balance		Adjustments		Adjusted Trial Balance		Income Statement		Balance Sheet	
Account Title	**Dr.**	**Cr.**	**Dr.**	**Cr.**	**Dr.**	**Cr.**	**Dr.**	**Cr.**	**Dr.**	**Cr.**
Cash	24,800									
Accounts receivable	2,250									
Supplies	700									
Prepaid rent	3,000									
Furniture	16,500									
Accumulated depreciation										
Accounts payable		13,100								
Salary payable										
Unearned service revenue		450								
Gary Lyon, capital		31,250								
Gary Lyon, withdrawals	3,200									
Service revenue		7,000								
Rent expense										
Salary expense	950									
Supplies expense										
Depreciation expense										
Utilities expense	400									
	51,800	51,800								
Net income										

Write the account titles and their unadjusted ending balances in the Trial Balance columns of the work sheet, and total the amounts.

Accounts may have zero balances (for example, Depreciation Expense). All accounts are listed on the trial balance because they appear in the ledger. Electronically prepared work sheets list all the accounts, not just those with a balance.

2. *Enter the adjusting entries in the Adjustments columns, and total the amounts.* Exhibit 4-3 includes the April adjusting entries. These are the same adjustments that we used in Chapter 3 to prepare the adjusted trial balance.

■ Daily Exercise 4-1

We can identify the accounts that need to be adjusted by scanning the trial balance. Cash needs no adjustment because all cash transactions are recorded as they occur during the period. Consequently, Cash's balance is up to date.

Accounts Receivable is listed next. Has Gary Lyon earned revenue that he has not yet recorded? The answer is yes. At April 30, Lyon has earned $250 that he has not yet recorded because the cash will be received during May. Lyon debits Accounts Receivable and credits Service Revenue on the work sheet in Exhibit 4-3. A letter is used to link the debit and the credit of each adjusting entry.

By moving down the trial balance, Lyon identifies the remaining accounts that need adjustment. Supplies is next. The business has used supplies during April, so Lyon debits Supplies Expense and credits Supplies. The other adjustments are analyzed and entered on the work sheet as you learned in Chapter 3.

Listing the accounts in their proper sequence aids the process of identifying accounts that need to be adjusted. But suppose that one or more accounts are omitted from the trial balance. This account can always be written below the first column totals—$51,800. Assume that Supplies Expense was accidentally omitted and thus did not appear on the trial balance. When the accountant identifies the need to update the Supplies account, he or she knows that the debit in the adjusting entry is to Supplies Expense. In this case, the accountant can write Supplies Expense on the line beneath the amount totals and enter the debit adjustment—$300—on the Supplies Expense line. Keep in mind that the accounting work sheet is not the finished version of the financial statements, so the order of the accounts on the work sheet is not critical. Supplies Expense can be listed in its proper sequence on the income statement. After the adjustments are entered on the work sheet, the amount columns are totaled.

3. *Compute each account's adjusted balance by combining the trial balance and adjustment figures. Enter the adjusted amounts in the Adjusted Trial Balance columns.* Exhibit 4-4 shows the work sheet with the adjusted trial balance columns completed. Accountants perform this step as illustrated in Chapter 3. For example, the Cash balance is up to date, so it receives no adjustment. Accounts Receivable's adjusted balance of $2,500 is computed by adding the trial balance amount of $2,250 to the $250 debit adjustment. Supplies' adjusted balance of $400 is determined by subtracting the $300 credit adjustment from the unadjusted debit balance of $700. An account may receive more than one adjustment, as Service Revenue does. The column totals must maintain the equality of debits and credits.

■ Daily Exercise 4-2

4. *Extend (that is, transfer) the asset, liability, and owner's equity amounts from the Adjusted Trial Balance to the Balance Sheet columns. Extend the revenue and expense amounts to the Income Statement columns. Total the statement columns.* Every account is either a balance sheet account or an income statement account. The asset, liability, and owner's equity accounts go to the balance sheet, and the revenues and expenses go to the income statement. Debits on the adjusted trial balance remain debits in the statement columns, and credits remain credits. Each account's adjusted balance should appear in only one statement column, as shown in Exhibit 4-5.

■ Daily Exercise 4-3

Total the *income statement columns first*, as follows:

	Income Statement		
• Debits (Dr.)	Total expenses	= $3,875	Difference
• Credits (Cr.)	Total revenues	= $7,400	= $3,525

Then total the *balance sheet* columns of the work sheet:

	Balance Sheet	
• Debits (Dr.)	Total assets and withdrawals = $49,400	Difference = $3,525
• Credits (Cr.)	Total liabilities, owner's equity, and accumulated depreciation = $45,875	

At this stage, the column totals will probably not be equal.

■ Daily Exercise 4-4

5. *Compute net income or net loss as the difference between total revenues and total expenses on the income statement. Enter net income as a debit balancing amount on the income statement and as a credit amount on the balance sheet. Then compute the adjusted column totals.* Exhibit 4-6 presents the completed accounting work sheet, which shows net income of $3,525, computed as follows:

Revenue (total credits on the income statement).........	$7,400
Expenses (total debits on the income statement).........	3,875
Net income	$3,525

Net income of $3,525 is entered in the debit column of the income statement to balance with the credit column of the income statement, which totals $7,400. The net income amount is then extended to the credit column of the balance sheet, because an excess of revenues over expenses increases capital, and increases in capital are recorded by a credit. In the closing process, net income will find its way into the Capital account, as we shall soon see.

If expenses exceed revenues, the result is a net loss. In that event, net loss is printed on the work sheet. The loss amount should be entered in the *credit* column of the income statement and in the *debit* column of the balance sheet, because an excess of expenses over revenues decreases capital, and decreases in capital are recorded by a debit. After completion, total debits equal total credits in the Income Statement columns and in the Balance Sheet columns. The balance sheet columns are totaled at $49,400.

SUMMARY PROBLEM FOR YOUR REVIEW — MID-CHAPTER

The trial balance of State Service Company at December 31, 19X1, the end of its fiscal year, is as follows.

STATE SERVICE COMPANY
Trial Balance
December 31, 19X1

Cash	$ 198,000	
Accounts receivable	370,000	
Supplies.........	6,000	
Furniture and fixtures.........	100,000	
Accumulated depreciation—furniture and fixtures		$ 40,000
Building.........	250,000	
Accumulated depreciation—building		130,000
Accounts payable		380,000
Salary payable		
Unearned service revenue		45,000
Capital.........		293,000
Withdrawals.........	65,000	
Service revenues		286,000
Salary expense.........	172,000	
Supplies expense		
Depreciation expense—furniture and fixtures.........		
Depreciation expense—building.........		
Miscellaneous expense.........	13,000	
Total	$1,174,000	$1,174,000

Data needed for the adjusting entries include:

a. Supplies on hand at year end, $2,000.
b. Depreciation on furniture and fixtures, $20,000.
c. Depreciation on building, $10,000.
d. Salaries owed but not yet paid, $5,000.
e. Accrued service revenue, $12,000.
f. Of the $45,000 balance of Unearned Service Revenue, $32,000 was earned during 19X1.

REQUIRED

Prepare the accounting work sheet of State Service Company for the year ended December 31, 19X1. Key each adjusting entry by the letter corresponding to the data given.

SOLUTION

STATE SERVICE COMPANY
Work Sheet
Year Ended December 31, 19X1

	Trial Balance		Adjustments		Adjusted Trial Balance		Income Statement		Balance Sheet	
Account Title	**Dr.**	**Cr.**	**Dr.**	**Cr.**	**Dr.**	**Cr.**	**Dr.**	**Cr.**	**Dr.**	**Cr.**
Cash	198,000				198,000				198,000	
Accounts receivable	370,000		(e) 12,000		382,000				382,000	
Supplies	6,000			(a) 4,000	2,000				2,000	
Furniture and fixtures	100,000				100,000				100,000	
Accumulated depreciation—furniture and fixtures		40,000		(b) 20,000		60,000				60,000
Building	250,000				250,000				250,000	
Accumulated depreciation—building		130,000		(c) 10,000		140,000				140,000
Accounts payable		380,000				380,000				380,000
Salary payable				(d) 5,000		5,000				5,000
Unearned service revenue		45,000	(f) 32,000			13,000				13,000
Capital		293,000				293,000				293,000
Withdrawals	65,000				65,000				65,000	
Service revenue		286,000		(e) 12,000 (f) 32,000		330,000		330,000		
Salary expense	172,000		(d) 5,000		177,000		177,000			
Supplies expense			(a) 4,000		4,000		4,000			
Depreciation expense—furniture and fixtures			(b) 20,000		20,000		20,000			
Depreciation expense—building			(c) 10,000		10,000		10,000			
Miscellaneous expense	13,000				13,000		13,000			
	1,174,000	1,174,000	83,000	83,000	1,221,000	1,221,000	224,000	330,000	997,000	891,000
Net income							106,000			106,000
							330,000	330,000	997,000	997,000

Completing the Accounting Cycle

Objective 2

Use the work sheet to complete the accounting cycle

The work sheet helps organize accounting data and compute the net income or net loss for the period. It also aids in preparing the financial statements, recording the adjusting entries, and closing the accounts.

Preparing the Financial Statements

The work sheet shows the amount of net income or net loss for the period, but it is still necessary to prepare the financial statements. The sorting of accounts to the balance sheet and the income statement eases the preparation of the statements. The work sheet also provides the data for the statement of owner's equity. Exhibit 4-7 presents the April financial statements for the accounting practice of Gary Lyon, CPA (based on data from the work sheet in Exhibit 4-6).

The financial statements can be prepared directly from the adjusted trial balance; see p. 108. This is why completion of the work sheet is optional.

EXHIBIT 4-7
April Financial Statements of Gary Lyon, CPA

GARY LYON, CPA
Income Statement
Month Ended April 30, 19X1

Revenue:		
Service revenue		$7,400
Expenses:		
Salary expense	$1,900	
Rent expense	1,000	
Utilities expense	400	
Supplies expense	300	
Depreciation expense—furniture	275	
Total expenses		3,875
Net income		$3,525

GARY LYON, CPA
Statement of Owner's Equity
Month Ended April 30, 19X1

Gary Lyon, capital, April 1, 19X1	$31,250
Add: Net income	3,525
	34,775
Less: Withdrawals	(3,200)
Gary Lyon, capital, April 30, 19X1	$31,575

GARY LYON, CPA
Balance Sheet
April 30, 19X1

Assets			Liabilities	
Cash		$24,800	Accounts payable	$13,100
Accounts receivable		2,500	Salary payable	950
Supplies		400	Unearned service revenue	300
Prepaid rent		2,000	Total liabilities	14,350
Furniture	$16,500		**Owner's Equity**	
Less Accumulated depreciation	(275)	16,225	Gary Lyon, capital	31,575
			Total liabilities and	
Total assets		$45,925	owner's equity	$45,925

Recording the Adjusting Entries

The adjusting entries are a key element of accrual-basis accounting. The work sheet helps identify the accounts that need adjustments. But actual adjustment of the accounts requires journal entries that are posted to the ledger accounts; see Panel A of Exhibit 4-8. Panel B shows the postings to the accounts, with *Adj.* denoting an amount posted from an adjusting entry. Only the revenue and expense accounts are presented in the exhibit in order to focus on the closing process, which we discuss in the next section.

The adjusting entries may be recorded in the journal when they are entered on the work sheet, but it is not necessary to journalize them at the same time. Most accountants prepare the financial statements immediately after completing the work sheet. They can wait to journalize and post the adjusting entries just before they make the closing entries.

Delaying the journalizing and posting of the adjusting entries illustrates another use of the work sheet. Many companies journalize and post the adjusting entries (as in Exhibit 4-8)—only once annually—at the end of the year. The need for monthly or quarterly financial statements requires a tool like the work sheet. Accountants can use the work sheet to prepare monthly or quarterly statements without journalizing and posting the adjusting entries.

PANEL A—Journalizing: **Page 4**

Adjusting Entries

Apr. 30	Accounts Receivable	250	
	Service Revenue		250
30	Supplies Expense	300	
	Supplies		300
30	Rent Expense	1,000	
	Prepaid Rent		1,000
30	Depreciation Expense	275	
	Accumulated Depreciation		275
30	Salary Expense	950	
	Salary Payable		950
30	Unearned Service Revenue	150	
	Service Revenue		150

PANEL B—Posting the Adjustments to the Revenue and Expense Accounts:

REVENUE

Service Revenue

	7,000
	Adj. 250
	Adj. 150
	Bal. 7,400

EXPENSES

Rent Expense

Adj. 1,000	
Bal. 1,000	

Salary Expense

950	
Adj. 950	
Bal. 1,900	

Supplies Expense

Adj. 300	
Bal. 300	

Depreciation Expense

Adj. 275	
Bal. 275	

Utilities Expense

400	
Bal. 400	

Adj. = Amount posted from an adjusting entry Bal. = Balance

EXHIBIT 4-8
Journalizing and Posting the Adjusting Entries

Closing the Accounts

Closing the accounts is the end-of-period process that prepares the accounts for the next period. Closing the accounts consists of journalizing and posting the closing entries. Closing zeroes out the balances of the revenue and expense accounts in order to clearly measure the net income of each period separately from all other periods.

Closing the Accounts. Step in the accounting cycle at the end of the period that prepares the accounts for recording the transactions of the next period. Closing the accounts consists of journalizing and posting the closing entries to set the balances of the revenue, expense, and owner withdrawal accounts to zero.

Recall that the income statement reports only one period's net income. For example, net income for Burger King, Inc., for 1999 relates exclusively to 1999. At December 31, 1999, Burger King's accountants close the company's revenue and expense accounts for that year. Because the revenue and expense account balances relate to a particular accounting period (1999, in this case) and are therefore closed at the end of the period (December 31, 1999), the revenue and expense accounts are called **temporary (nominal) accounts** (see definition on p. 146). For example, Gary Lyon's balance of Service Revenue at April 30, 19X1, is $7,400. This balance relates exclusively to the month of April and must be zeroed out before Lyon starts accounting for the revenue that he will earn during May.

"... net income for Burger King, Inc., for 1999 relates exclusively to 1999."

The owner's withdrawal account—although not a revenue or an expense—is also a temporary account because it measures withdrawals for a specific period. The closing process applies only to temporary accounts.

Objective 3

Close the revenue, expense, and withdrawal accounts

To better understand the closing process, contrast the nature of the temporary accounts with the nature of the **permanent (real) accounts** (see definition on p. 146)—the assets, liabilities, and capital accounts. The asset, liability, and owner's capital accounts are *not* closed at the end of the period because their balances are not used to

Temporary Accounts. The revenue and expense accounts that relate to a particular accounting period and are closed at the end of the period. For a proprietorship, the owner withdrawal account is also temporary. Also called **nominal accounts.**

Permanent Accounts. Accounts that are *not* closed at the end of the period—asset, liability, and capital accounts. Also called **real accounts.**

Closing Entries. Entries that transfer the revenue, expense, and owner withdrawal balances from these respective accounts to the capital account.

measure income. Consider Cash, Accounts Receivable, Supplies, Buildings, Accounts Payable, Notes Payable, and Gary Lyon, Capital. These accounts do not represent business *activity* for a single period as do the revenues and expenses, which relate exclusively to one accounting period. Instead, the permanent accounts represent assets (resources), liabilities (debts), and capital that are on hand at a specific time. This is why their balances at the end of one accounting period carry over to become the beginning balances of the next period. For example, the Cash balance at December 31, 19X1, becomes the beginning balance for 19X2.

Closing entries transfer the revenue, expense, and owner withdrawal balances from their respective accounts to the capital account. As you know,

REVENUES	*increase*	owner's equity
EXPENSES and OWNER WITHDRAWALS	*decrease*	owner's equity

It is when we post the closing entries that the capital account absorbs the impact of the balances in the temporary accounts.

Income Summary. A temporary "holding tank" account into which revenues and expenses are transferred prior to their final transfer to the capital account.

As an intermediate step in the closing process, the revenues and the expenses are transferred first to an account entitled **Income Summary,** which collects in one place the total debit for the sum of all expenses and the total credit for the sum of all revenues of the period. The Income Summary account is like a temporary "holding tank" that is used only in the closing process. Then the balance of Income Summary is transferred to capital. The steps in closing the accounts of a proprietorship such as Gary Lyon, CPA, are as follows (the circled numbers are keyed to Exhibit 4-9).

① Debit each *revenue* account for the amount of its credit balance. Credit Income Summary for the sum of the revenues. This entry transfers the sum of the revenues to the *credit* side of Income Summary.

② Credit each *expense* account for the amount of its debit balance. Debit Income Summary for the sum of the expenses. This entry transfers the sum of the expenses to the *debit* side of Income Summary. It is not necessary to make a separate closing entry for each expense. In one closing entry, record one debit to Income Summary and a separate credit to each expense account.

③ Debit Income Summary for the amount of its *credit balance* (if there is a *net income*), and credit the Capital account. If there is a *net loss*, Income Summary has a *debit balance*. In that case, credit Income Summary for this amount, and debit Capital. This closing entry transfers the net income or loss from Income Summary to the Capital account.

■ Daily Exercise 4-5

④ Credit the *Withdrawals* account for the amount of its debit balance. Debit the Capital account of the proprietor. This entry transfers the withdrawal amount to the *debit* side of the Capital account. Withdrawals are not expenses and do not affect net income or net loss.

These steps are best illustrated with an example. Suppose Gary Lyon closes the books at the end of April. Exhibit 4-9 presents the complete closing process for Lyon's business. Panel A gives the closing journal entries, and Panel B shows the accounts after the closing entries have been posted.

The amount in the debit side of each expense account is its adjusted balance. For example, Rent Expense has a $1,000 debit balance. Also note that Service Revenue has a credit balance of $7,400 before closing. These amounts come directly from the adjusted balances in Exhibit 4-8, Panel B.

- Closing entry ① in Exhibit 4-9, transfers Service Revenue's balance to the Income Summary account. This entry zeroes out Service Revenue for April and places the revenue on the credit side of Income Summary.
- Closing entry ② zeroes out the expenses and moves their total ($3,875) to the debit side of Income Summary. At this point, Income Summary contains the net impact of April's revenues and expenses: a credit balance showing the month's net income ($3,525).

PANEL A—Journalizing: **Page 5**

		Closing Entries		
①	Apr. 30	Service Revenue..	7,400	
		Income Summary...........................		7,400
②	30	Income Summary	3,875	
		Rent Expense		1,000
		Salary Expense		1,900
		Supplies Expense		300
		Depreciation Expense......................		275
		Utilities Expense.............................		400
③	30	Income Summary ($7,400 – $3,875).........	3,525	
		Gary Lyon, Capital.........................		3,525
④	30	Gary Lyon, Capital....................................	3,200	
		Gary Lyon, Withdrawals		3,200

PANEL B—Posting:

Rent Expense

Adj. 1,000	
Bal. 1,000	Clo. 1,000

Salary Expense

950	
Adj. 950	
Bal. 1,900	Clo. 1,900

Supplies Expense

Adj. 300	
Bal. 300	Clo. 300

Depreciation Expense

Adj. 275	
Bal. 275	Clo. 275

Utilities Expense

400	
Bal. 400	Clo. 400

② (expense closings to Income Summary)

Income Summary

Clo. 3,875	Clo. 7,400
Clo. 3,525	Bal. 3,525

① (Service Revenue closing to Income Summary)

Service Revenue

	7,000
	Adj. 250
	Adj. 150
Clo. 7,400	Bal. 7,400

③ (Income Summary closing to Gary Lyon, Capital)

Gary Lyon, Withdrawals

Bal. 3,200	Clo. 3,200

④ (Withdrawals closing to Gary Lyon, Capital)

Gary Lyon, Capital

Clo. 3,200	31,250
	Clo. 3,525
	Bal. 31,575

Adj. = Amount posted from an adjusting entry Clo. = Amount posted from a closing entry Bal. = Balance

EXHIBIT 4-9
Journalizing and Posting the Closing Entries

- Closing entry ③ closes the Income Summary account by transferring net income ($3,525) to the credit side of Gary Lyon, Capital.[1]
- The last closing entry, entry ④, moves the owner withdrawals to the debit side of Gary Lyon, Capital, leaving a zero balance in the Withdrawals account.

The closing entries set all the revenues, the expenses, and the Withdrawals account back to zero. Now the owner's Capital account includes the full effects of April's revenues, expenses, and withdrawals. These amounts, combined with the beginning Capital balance, give the Gary Lyon, Capital account an ending balance of $31,575. Trace this ending Capital balance to the statement of owner's equity and also to the balance sheet in Exhibit 4-7.

- Daily Exercise 4-6
- Daily Exercise 4-7
- Daily Exercise 4-8
- Daily Exercise 4-9

[1]The Income Summary account is a convenience for combining the effects of the revenues and expenses before transferring their income effect to Capital. It is not necessary to use the Income Summary account in the closing process. Another way of closing the revenues and expenses makes no use of this account. In this alternative procedure, the revenues and expenses are closed directly to Capital.

CLOSING A NET LOSS What would the closing entries be if Lyon's business had suffered a net *loss* during April? Suppose expenses totaled $7,700 and all other factors were unchanged (revenues were $7,400, so Lyon's business suffered a net loss of $300 for April). Only closing entries ② and ③ would change. Closing entry ② would transfer expenses of $7,700 to the debit side of Income Summary, as follows:

Income Summary

Clo.	7,700	Clo.	7,400
Bal.	300		

Closing entry ③ would then credit Income Summary to close its debit balance and to transfer the net loss to Gary Lyon, Capital:

③	Apr. 30	Gary Lyon, Capital	300	
		Income Summary		300

After posting, these two accounts would appear as follows:

Income Summary

Clo.	7,700	Clo.	7,400
Bal.	300	Clo.	300

Gary Lyon, Capital

Clo.	300		31,250

Finally, the Withdrawals balance would be closed to Capital, as before.

Learning Tip: The double underline in an account means that the account has a zero balance; nothing more will be posted to it in the current period. The double line is drawn immediately after the closing entry is posted. In the general ledger, the account has a zero balance.

The closing process is fundamentally mechanical and is completely automated in a computerized system. Accounts are identified as either temporary or permanent. The temporary accounts are closed automatically by selecting that option from the software's menu. Posting also occurs automatically.

Postclosing Trial Balance

Postclosing Trial Balance. List of the ledger accounts and their balances at the end of the period after the journalizing and posting of the closing entries. The last step of the accounting cycle, the postclosing trial balance ensures that the ledger is in balance for the start of the next accounting period.

The accounting cycle ends with the **postclosing trial balance** (Exhibit 4-10). The postclosing trial balance is the final check on the accuracy of journalizing and posting the adjusting and closing entries. It lists the ledger's accounts and their adjusted balances after closing. This step shows where the business stands as it moves into the next accounting period. The postclosing trial balance is dated as of the end of the period for which the statements have been prepared.

The postclosing trial balance resembles the balance sheet. It contains the ending balances of the permanent accounts—the balance sheet accounts: the assets, liabilities,

EXHIBIT 4-10
Postclosing Trial Balance

■ Daily Exercise 4-15

GARY LYON, CPA
Postclosing Trial Balance
April 30, 19X1

Cash	$24,800	
Accounts receivable	2,500	
Supplies	400	
Prepaid rent	2,000	
Furniture	16,500	
Accumulated depreciation		$ 275
Accounts payable		13,100
Salary payable		950
Unearned service revenue		300
Gary Lyon, capital		31,575
Total	$46,200	$46,200

and capital. No temporary accounts—revenues, expenses, or withdrawal accounts—are included because their balances have been closed. The ledger is up to date and ready for the next period's transactions.

Learning Tip: Only permanent accounts should appear on the postclosing trial balance.

Correcting Journal Entries

Objective 4

Correct typical accounting errors

In Chapter 2, we discussed errors that affect the trial balance: treating a debit as a credit and vice versa; transpositions; and slides. Here we show how to correct errors in journal entries.

When a journal entry contains an error, the entry can be deleted and corrected—if the error is caught immediately. A computerized accounting system makes easy work of deleting an incorrect entry. When you delete the original entry, the posting is also cancelled. You can then record the correct entry and post it automatically.

If the error is detected after posting, the accountant must make a *correcting entry*. Suppose Gary Lyon paid $5,000 cash for furniture and erroneously debited Supplies as follows:

Incorrect Entry

May 13	Supplies	5,000	
	Cash		5,000
	Bought supplies.		

The debit to Supplies is incorrect, so it is necessary to make the following correcting entry:

Correcting Entry

May 15	Furniture	5,000	
	Supplies		5,000
	To correct May 13 entry.		

The credit to Supplies in the second entry offsets the incorrect debit of the first entry. The debit to Furniture in the correcting entry places the furniture's cost in the correct account. Now both Supplies and Furniture are correct. Cash was unaffected by the error because Cash was credited correctly in the entry to purchase the furniture.

- Daily Exercise 4-10
- Daily Exercise 4-11
- Daily Exercise 4-12

Working It Out Ann Kerrigan mistakenly recorded the collection of a $1,000 receivable as a debit to Cash and a credit to Service Revenue for $1,000.

1. Prepare the correcting entry.
2. Assume that Kerrigan's net income before the correction was $26,000. How much is her corrected net income?

Answers

1. First, ask yourself if any part of the entry is correct. The entry Kerrigan made was

Cash	1,000	
Service Revenue		1,000

The $1,000 debit to Cash is correct, because Cash increased by $1,000. However, the credit to Service Revenue is incorrect. The credit side of the entry needs to be fixed.

The incorrect credit to Service Revenue has mistakenly increased Service Revenue by $1,000. Therefore, the correcting entry needs to eliminate $1,000 from Service Revenue. To do this, we debit Service Revenue.

We also need to record the $1,000 decrease in Accounts Receivable. We do this by way of a $1,000 credit to that account. Thus, the correcting entry is

Service Revenue	1,000	
Accounts Receivable		1,000

2. To answer this question, remember that net income = revenues minus expenses. Because the incorrect entry inflated revenues by $1,000, it also inflated net income by $1,000. Thus we simply subtract $1,000 from the incorrect net income of $26,000, to get the correct net income figure of $25,000.

Classification of Assets and Liabilities

Objective 5

Classify assets and liabilities as current or long-term

On the balance sheet, assets and liabilities are classified as either *current* or *long-term* to indicate their relative liquidity. **Liquidity** is a measure of how quickly an item can be converted to cash. Cash is the most liquid asset. Accounts receivable is a relatively liquid asset because the business expects to collect the receivable in the near future. Supplies are less liquid than accounts receivable, and furniture and buildings are even less so.

Liquidity. Measure of how quickly an item can be converted to cash.

Users of financial statements are interested in liquidity because business difficulties often arise from a shortage of cash. How quickly can the business convert an asset to cash and pay a debt? How soon must a liability be paid? These are questions of liquidity. Balance sheets list assets and liabilities in the order of their relative liquidity.

Assets

Current Asset. An asset that is expected to be converted to cash, sold, or consumed during the next 12 months, or within the business's normal operating cycle if longer than a year.

Operating Cycle. Time span during which cash is paid for goods and services, which are then sold to customers from whom the business collects cash.

CURRENT ASSETS **Current assets** are assets that are expected to be converted to cash, sold, or consumed during the next 12 months or within the business's normal operating cycle if longer than a year. The **operating cycle** is the time span during which (1) cash is used to acquire goods and services, and (2) these goods and services are sold to customers, from whom (3) the business collects cash. For most businesses, the operating cycle is a few months. A few types of businesses have operating cycles longer than a year. Cash, Accounts Receivable, Notes Receivable due within a year or less, and Prepaid Expenses are current assets. Merchandising entities such as Kmart, Sears, and Motorola have an additional current asset, Inventory. This account shows the cost of the goods the business is holding for sale to customers.

Long-Term Asset. An asset other than a current asset.

Fixed Asset. Another name for property, plant, and equipment.

LONG-TERM ASSETS **Long-term assets** are all assets other than current assets. One category of long-term assets is **fixed assets,** another name for Property, Plant, and Equipment. Land, Buildings, Furniture and Fixtures, and Equipment are fixed assets. Of these, Gary Lyon has only Furniture.

Other categories of long-term assets include Available-for-Sale Investments, Held-to-Maturity Investments, and Other Assets (a catchall category for assets that are not classified more precisely). We discuss these categories in later chapters.

Liabilities

Financial statement users (such as creditors) are interested in the due dates of an entity's liabilities. Liabilities that must be paid the quickest create the greatest strain on cash. Therefore, the balance sheet lists liabilities in the order in which they are due to be paid. Knowing how much of a business's liabilities is current and how much is long-term helps creditors assess the likelihood of collecting cash from the entity. Balance sheets have two liability classifications, *current liabilities* and *long-term liabilities.*

Current Liability. A debt due to be paid with cash or with goods and services within one year or within the entity's operating cycle if the cycle is longer than a year.

CURRENT LIABILITIES **Current liabilities** are debts that are due to be paid with cash or with goods and services within one year or within the entity's operating cycle if the cycle is longer than a year. Accounts Payable, Notes Payable due within one year, Salary Payable, Unearned Revenue, and Interest Payable owed on notes payable are current liabilities.

Long-Term Liability. A liability other than a current liability.

■ Daily Exercise 4-13

LONG-TERM LIABILITIES All liabilities that are not current are classified as **long-term liabilities.** Many notes payable are long-term—payable after one year or the entity's operating cycle. Some notes payable are paid in installments, with the first installment due within one year, the second installment due the second year, and so on. In that case, the first installment would be a current liability, and the remainder long-term liabilities. For example, a $100,000 note payable to be paid $10,000 per year over

GARY LYON, CPA Balance Sheet April 30, 19X1				
Assets			**Liabilities**	
Current assets:			Current liabilities:	
Cash		$24,800	Accounts payable	$13,100
Accounts receivable		2,500	Salary payable	950
Supplies		400	Unearned service revenue	300
Prepaid rent		2,000	Total current liabilities	14,350
Total current assets		29,700	Long-term liabilities (None)	-0-
Long-term assets:			Total liabilities	14,350
Furniture	$16,500			
Less Accumulated			**Owner's Equity**	
depreciation	(275)	16,225	Gary Lyon, capital	31,575
			Total liabilities and	
Total assets		$45,925	owner's equity	$45,925

EXHIBIT 4-11
Classified Balance Sheet of Gary Lyon, CPA

ten years would include a current liability of $10,000 for next year's payment and a long-term liability of $90,000.

Thus far in this book we have presented the *unclassified* balance sheet of Gary Lyon, CPA. Our purpose was to focus on the main points of assets, liabilities, and owner's equity without the details of *current* assets, *current* liabilities, and so on. Exhibit 4-11 presents Lyon's classified balance sheet.

Lyon classifies each asset and each liability as current or long-term. He could have labeled long-term assets as *fixed assets.* The label "property, plant, and equipment" would not fit his business because it has no land, building, or equipment. Companies vary this terminology somewhat.

Compare Lyon's *classified* balance sheet in Exhibit 4-11 with the *unclassified* balance sheet in Exhibit 4-7. The classified balance sheet reports totals for current assets and current liabilities, which do not appear on the unclassified balance sheet. Also, Lyon has no long-term liabilities, so there are none to report on either balance sheet.

Thinking It Over Why is the classified balance sheet in Exhibit 4-11 more useful than an unclassified balance sheet (Exhibit 4-7) to (a) Gary Lyon and (b) a banker considering whether to lend $10,000 to Lyon?

Answer: A classified balance sheet indicates to (a) Lyon and (b) a banker

- Which of Lyon's liabilities, and the dollar amounts, that Lyon must pay within the next year
- Which of Lyon's assets are the most liquid and thus available to pay the liabilities
- Which assets and liabilities (and amounts) are long-term

Now let's examine a real company's classified balance sheet.

A Real Classified Balance Sheet

Exhibit 4-12 is an actual classified balance sheet of International Business Machines Corporation, better known as IBM. IBM labels its balance sheet as the Statement of Financial Position, a more descriptive title. The statement is labeled "Consolidated" because it reports the accounts of IBM and its component companies as well. Dollar amounts are reported in millions to avoid clutter. IBM reports on a calendar-year basis, ending each December 31. It is customary to present two or more years' statements together to let people compare one year with the other—1996 and 1995 in this case. For your understanding, we have added bracketed explanations for several accounts. The bracketed items do not appear on IBM's balance sheet.

You should be familiar with all but a few of IBM's account titles. Among the Current Assets are Marketable securities (also called Short-term investments), which are investments that IBM expects to sell within one year. These assets are very liquid, which

EXHIBIT 4-12
IBM's Classified Balance Sheet

INTERNATIONAL BUSINESS MACHINES CORPORATION AND SUBSIDIARY COMPANIES
Consolidated Statement of Financial Position (Adapted)

(Dollars in millions) At December 31:	1996	1995
Assets		
Current Assets:		
Cash and cash equivalents [such as money-market accounts]	$ 7,687	$ 7,259
Marketable securities, at cost, which approximates market	450	442
Notes and accounts receivable—trade	16,515	16,450
Other receivables	6,652	6,952
Inventories	5,870	6,323
Prepaid expenses and other current assets [such as supplies]	3,521	3,265
Total current assets	40,695	40,691
Plant, rental machines and other property	41,893	43,981
Less: Accumulated depreciation	(24,486)	(27,402)
	17,407	16,579
Investments and Other Assets:		
Software, less accumulated amortization (1996, $12,199; 1995, $11,276)	1,435	2,419
Investments and sundry assets	21,595	20,603
	$81,132	$80,292
Liabilities and Stockholders' Equity		
Current Liabilities:		
Taxes	$ 3,029	$ 2,634
Short-term debt	12,957	11,569
Accounts payable	4,767	4,511
Compensation and benefits payable	2,950	2,914
Deferred income [same as Unearned revenues]	3,640	3,469
Other accrued expenses and liabilities	6,657	6,551
Total current liabilities	34,000	31,648
Long-term debt [such as long-term notes payable]	9,872	10,060
Other liabilities [such as unearned revenue, long-term]	14,005	14,354
Deferred income taxes	1,627	1,807
Total Liabilities	59,504	57,869
Stockholders' Equity [Capital for a proprietorship]	21,628	22,423
	$81,132	$80,292

■ Daily Exercise 4-14

"IBM sells and leases out computer equipment and expects to collect cash on the notes and accounts receivable."

explains why they are listed before the receivables. IBM sells and leases out computer equipment and expects to collect cash on the notes and accounts receivable. "Trade" in the title of the receivables means that IBM obtained the receivables in the course of selling its goods, not from lending cash like a bank.

IBM reports plant assets as Plant, Rental Machines, and Other Property on its balance sheet. These assets cost IBM $41,893 million through the end of 1996 and had book value (that is, cost minus accumulated depreciation) of $17,407 million. The final asset category, Investments and Other Assets, includes IBM's Software, reported with its accumulated *amortization*, which is similar to accumulated depreciation on plant assets. At December 31, 1996, IBM had software with book value (cost minus accumulated amortization) of $1,435 million. IBM could have reported the asset software in the same way it reported the plant, rental machines, and other property, as follows:

For a review of plant assets, see Chapter 3, page 99.

Software	$13,634
Less: Accumulated amortization	(12,199)
	$ 1,435

IBM's Investments are the shares of stock that IBM owns in other companies. These investments are not current assets because IBM does not expect to sell them within one year of the balance sheet date. Sundry assets could be labeled Other Assets, a catchall category for items that are difficult to classify.

You should recognize all of IBM's current liabilities. Taxes could be labeled Taxes Payable. Short-Term Debt could be labeled Short-Term Notes Payable. Compensation and benefits could be listed as Salary and Wages Payable. IBM collects some revenues in advance from customers. This practice explains the account titled Deferred Income, which is another name for Unearned Revenues.

Unlike Gary Lyon, CPA, IBM does not provide a label for long-term assets. All assets besides the current assets are long-term. Likewise for liabilities, IBM reports three long-term liabilities: long-term debt, other liabilities, and deferred income taxes. How do we know the other liabilities and the deferred income taxes are long-term? They must be long-term because they are not current. Finally, IBM calls its owners' equity *stockholders' equity;* other corporations may call it shareholders' equity.

Different Formats of the Balance Sheet

The balance sheet of IBM shown in Exhibit 4-12 lists the assets at the top and the liabilities and owners' equity below. This arrangement is known as the *report format*. The balance sheet of Gary Lyon, CPA, presented in Exhibit 4-7 lists the assets at the left and the liabilities and the owner's equity at the right. This arrangement is known as the *account format*. These are the two formats companies use for their balance sheets.

Either balance-sheet format is acceptable. A recent survey of 600 companies indicated that 73% (436 companies) use the report format and only 27% (164 companies) use the account format.

Thinking It Over IBM reported less stockholders' equity at December 31, 1996, than at December 31, 1995. Why did stockholders' equity decrease? IBM's 1996 income statement reported net income of $5,429 million. Gary Lyon's statement of owner's equity in Exhibit 4-7 offers a clue.

Answer: Stockholders' equity decreased because during 1996, IBM paid out more to its owners than the amount of net income the company earned during the year. In fact, net payments to IBM's owners (similar to withdrawals) for 1996 totaled $6,224 million, as follows:

	Millions
IBM beginning stockholders' equity..........	$ 22,423
Add: Net income	5,429
	27,852
Less: IBM ending owners' equity...............	(21,628)
Payments to owners (withdrawals).............	$ 6,224

Trace ending stockholders' equity to the IBM balance sheet in Exhibit 4-12.

Using Accounting Information in Decision Making: Accounting Ratios

Objective 6

Use the current and debt ratios to evaluate a business

The purpose of accounting is to provide information for decision making. Chief users of accounting information include managers, investors, and creditors. A creditor considering lending money must predict whether the borrower can repay the loan. If the borrower already has a lot of debt, the probability of repayment is lower than if the borrower has a small amount of liabilities. To assess financial position, decision makers use ratios computed from the company's financial statements.

Current Ratio

One of the most widely used financial ratios is the **current ratio,** which is the ratio of an entity's current assets to its current liabilities:

Current Ratio. Current assets divided by current liabilities. Measures the company's ability to pay current liabilities from current assets.

$$\text{Current ratio} = \frac{\text{Total current assets}}{\text{Total current liabilities}}$$

The current ratio measures the company's ability to pay current liabilities with current assets. A company prefers to have a high current ratio, which means that the business has plenty of current assets to pay current liabilities. An increasing current ratio from period to period indicates improvement in financial position.

A rule of thumb: A very strong current ratio is 2.00, which indicates that the company has $2.00 in current assets for every $1.00 in current liabilities. A company with a current ratio of 2.00 would probably have little trouble paying its current liabilities. Most successful businesses operate with current ratios between 1.50 and 2.00. A current ratio of 1.00 is considered quite low. Lenders and investors would view a company with a current ratio of 1.50 or 2.00 as substantially less risky. Such a company could probably borrow money on better terms and also attract more investors.

Working It Out A company has current assets of $100,000 and current liabilities of $50,000. How will the payment of a $10,000 account payable affect the current ratio?

Answer: Before payment of the account payable, the current ratio is as follows:

$$\text{Current ratio} = \frac{\text{Total current assets}}{\text{Total current liabilities}} = \frac{\$100{,}000}{\$50{,}000} = 2.00$$

After payment of the account payable, total current assets decrease from $100,000 to $90,000, because $10,000 in cash was used to pay the liability, and cash is a current asset. Current liabilities decreased from $50,000 to $40,000. The new current ratio is

$$\text{Current ratio} = \frac{\$100{,}000 - \$10{,}000}{\$50{,}000 - \$10{,}000} = \frac{\$90{,}000}{\$40{,}000} = 2.25$$

Payment of the liability makes the company look better, as indicated by the increase in the current ratio.

Debt Ratio

Debt Ratio. Ratio of total liabilities to total assets. Tells the proportion of a company's assets that it has financed with debt.

A second aid to decision making is the **debt ratio,** which is the ratio of total liabilities to total assets:

$$\text{Debt ratio} = \frac{\text{Total liabilities}}{\text{Total assets}}$$

The debt ratio indicates the proportion of a company's assets that are financed with debt. This ratio measures a business's overall ability to pay both current and long-term debts—total liabilities.

A low debt ratio is safer than a high debt ratio. Why? Because a company with a small amount of liabilities has low required payments. Such a company is unlikely to get into financial difficulty. By contrast, a business with a high debt ratio may have trouble paying its liabilities, especially when sales are low and cash is scarce. When a company fails to pay its debts, the creditors can take the business away from its owner. The largest retail bankruptcy in history, Federated Department Stores, parent company of Bloomingdale's, was due largely to high debt during an economic recession in the retail industry. Federated was unable to weather the downturn and had to declare bankruptcy.

MANAGING BOTH THE CURRENT RATIO AND THE DEBT RATIO In general, a *high* current ratio is preferable to a low current ratio. *Increases* in the current ratio indicate improving financial position. By contrast, a *low* debt ratio is preferable to a high debt ratio. Improvement is indicated by a *decrease* in the debt ratio.

■ Daily Exercise 4-16
■ Daily Exercise 4-17

Financial ratios aid decision making. It is unwise, however, to place too much confidence in a single ratio or in any group of ratios. For example, a company may have a high current ratio, which indicates financial strength. It may also have a high debt ratio, which suggests weakness. Which ratio gives the more reliable signal about the company? Experienced lenders and investors examine a large number of ratios over several years to spot trends and turning points. They also consider other factors, such as the company's cash position and its trend of net income. No single ratio gives the whole picture about a company.

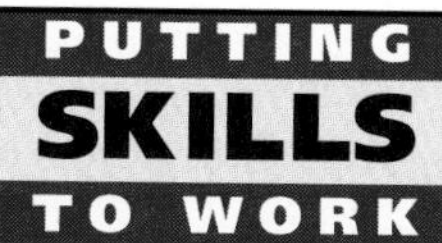

ACCOUNTING RATIOS: SHOULD A BANK GRANT A LOAN?

Suppose IBM, the company in Exhibit 4-12, needs a bank loan to finance the purchase of a new division. How would a bank evaluate IBM's financial position? This example shows two pieces of information a loan officer would consider.

EXCERPTS FROM IBM'S BALANCE SHEET

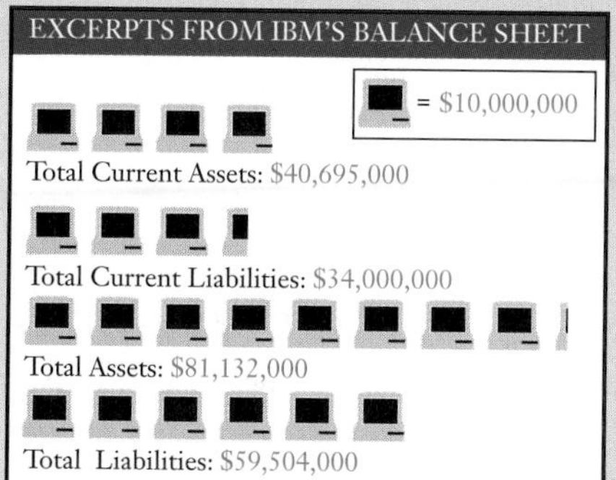

THE CURRENT RATIO

First, the bank would look at IBM's current ratio to determine the company's ability to pay current liabilities with current assets. IBM's current ratio was 1.20 at December 31, 1996:

$$\text{Current ratio} = \frac{\$40{,}695{,}000}{\$34{,}000{,}000} = 1.20$$

This ratio indicates that IBM has $1.20 of current assets with which to pay each $1.00 of its current liabilities. IBM is bordering on a risky position. One year earlier, at December 31, 1995, IBM's current ratio stood at 1.29 ($40,691,000/$31,648,000 = 1.29), which was a little better.

THE DEBT RATIO

The bank would want more information than just the current ratio before making a decision about a loan. It could also compute IBM's debt ratio to measure the company's ability to pay both current and long-term debts. From the balance sheet, IBM's debt ratio was 0.73 at December 31, 1996:

$$\text{Debt ratio} = \frac{\$59{,}504{,}000}{\$81{,}132{,}000} = 0.73$$

That figure is a little higher than the debt ratios of other successful companies. It is similar to IBM's debt ratio one year earlier, at December 31, 1995 ($57,869,000/$80,292,000 = 0.72).

THE FINAL DECISION

How would a loan officer use IBM's ratios? IBM's low current ratio and high debt ratio might worry the loan officer because they may signal difficulty for IBM in paying its debts. In fact, IBM has only recently rebounded from losses a few years back. If the bank did lend the money, it might place some restrictions on IBM. For example, the lender might charge a high interest rate and restrict IBM's payments to its owners. IBM's managers may feel some pressure to reduce the company's debt.

As you progress through the study of accounting, we will introduce key ratios used for decision making. Chapter 18 then summarizes all the ratios discussed in this book and provides a good overview of ratios used in decision making.

Now study the Decision Guidelines feature that summarizes what you have just learned in Chapter 4.

DECISION GUIDELINES — Completing the Accounting Cycle

DECISION	GUIDELINES
How (where) to summarize the effects of all the entity's transactions and adjustments throughout the period?	Accountant's *work sheet* with columns for • Trial balance • Adjustments • Adjusted trial balance • Income statement • Balance sheet
What is the last *major* step in the accounting cycle?	*Closing entries* for the *temporary accounts:* • Revenues } Income statement accounts • Expenses } • Owner's withdrawals
Why close out revenues, expenses, and owner withdrawals?	Because the *temporary accounts* have balances that relate only to one accounting period and do *not* carry over to the next accounting period.
Which accounts do not get closed out?	*Permanent (balance sheet) accounts:* • Assets • Liabilities • Owner's capital The balances of these accounts *do* carry over to the next period.

(continued)

DECISION GUIDELINES *(continued)*

How do businesses classify their assets and liabilities for reporting on the balance sheet?	*Current* (within one year or the entity's operating cycle if longer than a year) or *Long-term* (not current)
How do decision makers evaluate a company?	There are many ways, such as the company's net income or net loss on the income statement. Another way to evaluate a company is based on the company's *financial ratios.* Two key ratios: $$\text{Current ratio} = \frac{\text{Total current assets}}{\text{Total current liabilities}}$$ The *current ratio* measures the entity's ability to pay its current liabilities with its current assets. $$\text{Debt ratio} = \frac{\text{Total liabilities}}{\text{Total assets}}$$ The *debt ratio* shows the proportion of the entity's assets that are financed with debt. The debt ratio measures the entity's overall ability to pay its liabilities.

SUMMARY PROBLEM FOR YOUR REVIEW

Refer to the data in the Mid-Chapter Summary Problem for Your Review, presented on pages 142–143.

REQUIRED

1. Journalize and post the adjusting entries. (Before posting to the accounts, enter into each account its balance as shown in the trial balance. For example, enter the $370,000 balance in the Accounts Receivable account before posting its adjusting entry.) Key adjusting entries by *letter*, as shown in the work sheet solution to the mid-chapter review problem. You can take the adjusting entries straight from the work sheet on page 143.
2. Journalize and post the closing entries. (Each account should carry its balance as shown in the adjusted trial balance.) To distinguish closing entries from adjusting entries, key the closing entries by *number*. Draw arrows to illustrate the flow of data, as shown in Exhibit 4-9, page 147. Indicate the balance of the Capital account after the closing entries are posted.
3. Prepare the income statement for the year ended December 31, 19X1. List Miscellaneous Expense last among the expenses, a common practice.
4. Prepare the statement of owner's equity for the year ended December 31, 19X1. Draw an arrow to link the income statement to the statement of owner's equity.
5. Prepare the classified balance sheet at December 31, 19X1. Use the report form. All liabilities are current. Draw an arrow to link the statement of owner's equity to the balance sheet.

SOLUTION

REQUIREMENT 1

a.	Dec. 31	Supplies Expense	4,000	
		Supplies		4,000
b.	31	Depreciation Expense—Furniture and Fixtures	20,000	
		Accumulated Depreciation—Furniture and Fixtures		20,000
c.	31	Depreciation Expense—Building	10,000	
		Accumulated Depreciation—Building		10,000
d.	31	Salary Expense	5,000	
		Salary Payable		5,000
e.	31	Accounts Receivable	12,000	
		Service Revenue		12,000
f.	31	Unearned Service Revenue	32,000	
		Service Revenue		32,000

REQUIREMENT 2

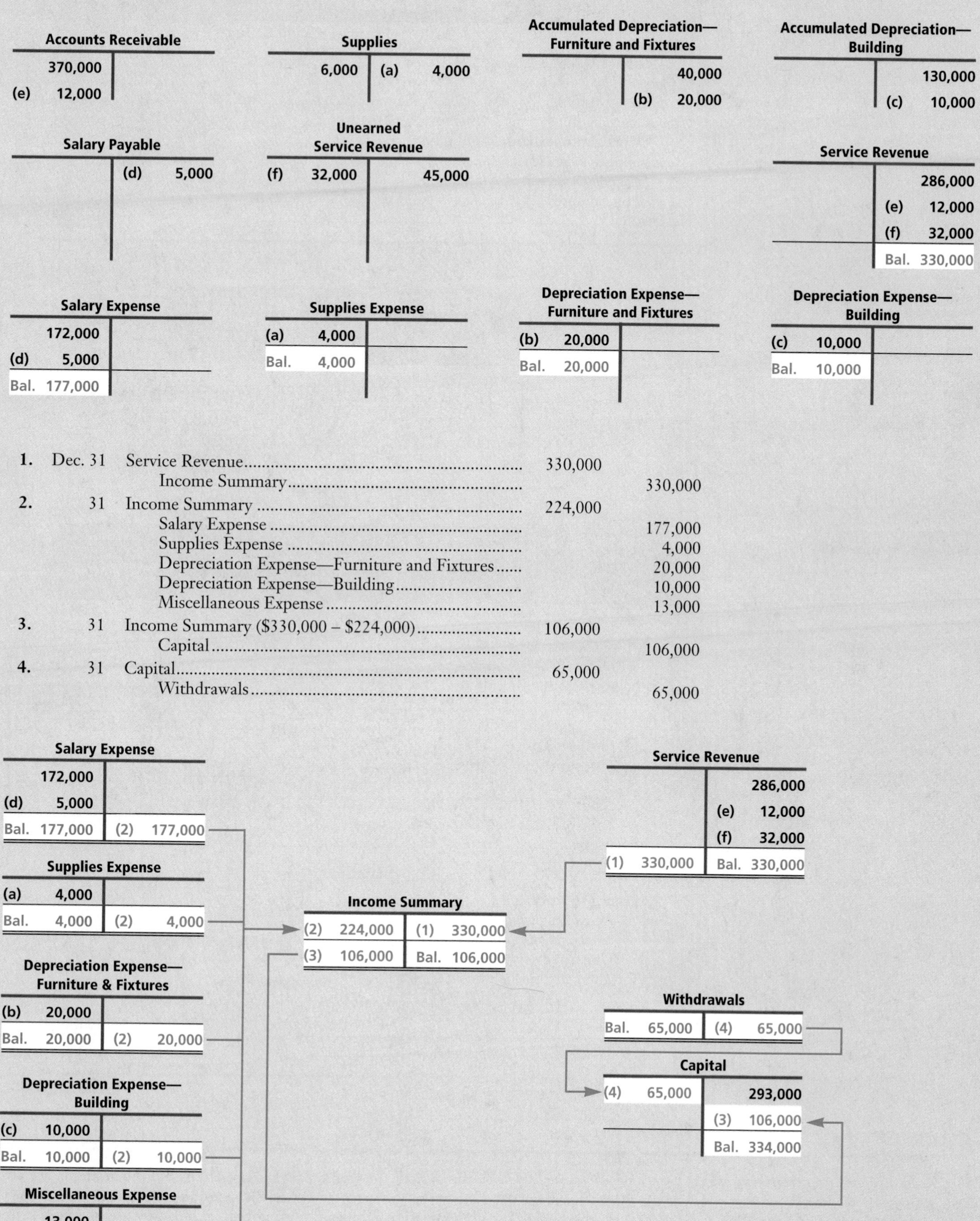

Accounts Receivable

Debit	Credit
370,000	
(e) 12,000	

Supplies

Debit	Credit
6,000	(a) 4,000

Accumulated Depreciation—Furniture and Fixtures

Debit	Credit
	40,000
	(b) 20,000

Accumulated Depreciation—Building

Debit	Credit
	130,000
	(c) 10,000

Salary Payable

Debit	Credit
	(d) 5,000

Unearned Service Revenue

Debit	Credit
(f) 32,000	45,000

Service Revenue

Debit	Credit
	286,000
	(e) 12,000
	(f) 32,000
	Bal. 330,000

Salary Expense

Debit	Credit
172,000	
(d) 5,000	
Bal. 177,000	

Supplies Expense

Debit	Credit
(a) 4,000	
Bal. 4,000	

Depreciation Expense—Furniture and Fixtures

Debit	Credit
(b) 20,000	
Bal. 20,000	

Depreciation Expense—Building

Debit	Credit
(c) 10,000	
Bal. 10,000	

	Date	Accounts	Debit	Credit
1.	Dec. 31	Service Revenue	330,000	
		Income Summary		330,000
2.	31	Income Summary	224,000	
		Salary Expense		177,000
		Supplies Expense		4,000
		Depreciation Expense—Furniture and Fixtures		20,000
		Depreciation Expense—Building		10,000
		Miscellaneous Expense		13,000
3.	31	Income Summary ($330,000 – $224,000)	106,000	
		Capital		106,000
4.	31	Capital	65,000	
		Withdrawals		65,000

Salary Expense

Debit	Credit
172,000	
(d) 5,000	
Bal. 177,000	(2) 177,000

Supplies Expense

Debit	Credit
(a) 4,000	
Bal. 4,000	(2) 4,000

Depreciation Expense—Furniture & Fixtures

Debit	Credit
(b) 20,000	
Bal. 20,000	(2) 20,000

Depreciation Expense—Building

Debit	Credit
(c) 10,000	
Bal. 10,000	(2) 10,000

Miscellaneous Expense

Debit	Credit
13,000	
Bal. 13,000	(2) 13,000

Income Summary

Debit	Credit
(2) 224,000	(1) 330,000
(3) 106,000	Bal. 106,000

Service Revenue

Debit	Credit
	286,000
	(e) 12,000
	(f) 32,000
(1) 330,000	Bal. 330,000

Withdrawals

Debit	Credit
Bal. 65,000	(4) 65,000

Capital

Debit	Credit
(4) 65,000	293,000
	(3) 106,000
	Bal. 334,000

REQUIREMENT 3

STATE SERVICE COMPANY Income Statement Year Ended December 31, 19X1		
Revenue:		
Service revenue		$330,000
Expenses:		
Salary expense	$177,000	
Depreciation expense—furniture and fixtures	20,000	
Depreciation expense—building	10,000	
Supplies expense	4,000	
Miscellaneous expense	13,000	
Total expenses		224,000
Net income		$106,000

REQUIREMENT 4

STATE SERVICE COMPANY Statement of Owner's Equity Year Ended December 31, 19X1	
Capital, January 1, 19X1	$293,000
Add: Net income	106,000
	399,000
Less: Withdrawals	(65,000)
Capital, December 31, 19X1	$334,000

REQUIREMENT 5

STATE SERVICE COMPANY Balance Sheet December 31, 19X1		
Assets		
Current assets:		
Cash		$198,000
Accounts receivable		382,000
Supplies		2,000
Total current assets		582,000
Long-term assets:		
Furniture and fixtures	$100,000	
Less Accumulated depreciation	(60,000)	40,000
Building	250,000	
Less Accumulated depreciation	(140,000)	110,000
Total assets		$732,000
Liabilities		
Current liabilities:		
Accounts payable		$380,000
Salary payable		5,000
Unearned service revenue		13,000
Total current liabilities		398,000
Owner's Equity		
Capital		334,000
Total liabilities and owner's equity		$732,000

Summary of Learning Objectives

1. ***Prepare an accounting work sheet.*** The *accounting cycle* is the process by which accountants produce the financial statements for a specific period of time. The cycle starts with the beginning account balances. During the period, the business journalizes transactions and posts them to the ledger accounts. At the end of the period, the trial balance is prepared, and the accounts are adjusted in order to measure the period's net income or net loss. Completion of the accounting cycle is aided by use of a *work sheet.* This multicolumned document summarizes the effects of all the period's activity.

2. *Use the work sheet to complete the accounting cycle.* The work sheet is neither a journal nor a ledger but merely a convenient device for completing the accounting cycle. It has columns for the trial balance, the adjustments, the adjusted trial balance, the income statement, and the balance sheet. It aids the adjusting process, and it is the place where the period's net income or net loss is first computed. The work sheet also provides the data for the financial statements and the *closing entries*. However, it is not a necessity. The accounting cycle can be completed from the less elaborate adjusted trial balance.

3. *Close the revenue, expense, and withdrawal accounts.* Revenues, expenses, and withdrawals represent increases and decreases in owner's equity for a specific period. At the end of the period, their balances are closed out to zero and, for this reason, they are called *temporary accounts*. Assets, liabilities, and capital are not closed because they are the *permanent accounts*. Their balances at the end of one period become the beginning balances of the next period. The final accuracy check of the period is the *postclosing trial balance*.

4. *Correct typical accounting errors.* Accountants correct errors by making correcting journal entries.

5. *Classify assets and liabilities as current or long-term.* The balance sheet reports *current* and *long-term assets* and *current* and *long-term liabilities*. It can be presented in *report format* or *account format*.

6. *Use the current and debt ratios to evaluate a business.* Two decision-making aids are the *current ratio* (total current assets divided by total current liabilities) and the *debt ratio* (total liabilities divided by total assets).

Accounting Vocabulary

accounting cycle *(p. 138)*
closing the accounts *(p. 145)*
closing entries *(p. 146)*
current asset *(p. 150)*
current liability *(p. 150)*
current ratio *(p. 153)*
debt ratio *(p. 154)*
fixed asset *(p. 150)*
Income Summary *(p. 146)*
liquidity *(p. 150)*
long-term asset *(p. 150)*
long-term liability *(p. 150)*
nominal account *(p. 145)*
operating cycle *(p. 150)*
permanent account *(p. 145)*
postclosing trial balance *(p. 148)*
real account *(p. 145)*
reversing entry *(p. 178)*
temporary account *(p. 145)*
work sheet *(p. 138)*

Questions

1. Identify the steps in the accounting cycle; distinguish those that occur during the period from those that are performed at the end.
2. Why is the work sheet a valuable accounting tool?
3. Name two advantages the work sheet has over the adjusted trial balance.
4. Why must the adjusting entries be journalized and posted if they have already been entered on the work sheet?
5. Why should the adjusting entries be journalized and posted before the closing entries are made?
6. Which types of accounts are closed?
7. What purpose is served by closing the accounts?
8. State how the work sheet helps with recording the closing entries.
9. Distinguish between permanent accounts and temporary accounts; indicate which type is closed at the end of the period. Give five examples of each type of account.
10. Is Income Summary a permanent account or a temporary account? When and how is it used?
11. Give the closing entries for the following accounts (balances in parentheses): Service Revenue ($4,700); Salary Expense ($1,100); Income Summary (credit balance of $2,000); Rhonda McGill, Withdrawals ($2,300).
12. Why are assets classified as current or long-term? On what basis are they classified? Where do the classified amounts appear?
13. Indicate which of the following accounts are current assets and which are long-term assets: Prepaid Rent, Building, Furniture, Accounts Receivable, Merchandise Inventory, Cash, Note Receivable (due within one year), Note Receivable (due after one year).
14. In what order are assets and liabilities listed on the balance sheet?
15. Identify an outside party that would be interested in whether a liability is current or long-term. Why would this party be interested in this information?
16. A friend tells you that the difference between a current liability and a long-term liability is that the two types are payable to different types of creditors. Is your friend correct? Define these two categories of liabilities.
17. Show how to compute the current ratio and the debt ratio. Indicate what ability each ratio measures, and state whether a high value or a low value is safer for each.
18. Capp Company purchased supplies of $120 on account. The accountant debited Supplies and credited Cash for $120. A week later, after this entry has been posted to the ledger, the accountant discovers the error. How should he correct the error?

Daily Exercises

Explaining items on the work sheet **(*Obj. 1*)**

DE4-1 ← *Link Back to Chapter 3 (Adjusting Entries).* Return to the trial balance in Exhibit 4-2, on the acetate between pages 140 and 141. In your own words, explain why at April 30 the following accounts must be adjusted:

a. Supplies
b. Prepaid rent
c. Accumulated depreciation
d. Salary payable
e. Unearned service revenue

Explain why these accounts do *not* need to be adjusted at April 30:

f. Cash
g. Furniture

Explaining items on the work sheet
(Obj. 1, 2)

DE4-2 ⟵ *Link Back to Chapters 1, 2, and 3 (Definitions of Accounts).* Examine the Adjusted Trial Balance columns of Exhibit 4-4, on the acetate between pages 140 and 141. Explain what the following items mean at April 30:

a. Accounts receivable
b. Supplies
c. Prepaid rent
d. Furniture
e. Accumulated depreciation
f. Accounts payable
g. Unearned service revenue
h. Service revenue
i. Rent expense

Comparing the work sheet and the adjusted trial balance
(Obj. 1, 2)

DE4-3 Study the completed work sheet (Exhbit 4-6) on the acetates between pages 140 and 141. How is the work sheet in Exhibit 4-2 similar to the adjusted trial balance that you learned in Chapter 3? How does the work sheet differ from the adjusted trial balance of Chapter 3 (Exhibit 3-10, page 108)?

Using the work sheet and closing entries
(Obj. 2, 3)

DE4-4 Consider the Income Statement columns and the Balance Sheet columns of the work sheet in Exhibit 4-6, on the acetate between pages 140 and 141. Answering the following questions will add to your understanding of the relationships among the accounts:

1. What balance does the Owner's Capital account have—debit or credit?
2. Which Income Statement account has the same type of balance as the Capital account?
3. Which Income Statement accounts have the opposite type of balance?
4. What do we call the difference between the total dollar amounts in the debit and credit columns of the Income Statement? Into what account is the difference figure closed?

Identifying accounts that need to be closed
(Obj. 3)

DE4-5 Examine Exhibits 4-2 and 4-4 on the acetates between pages 140 and 141. Answer this question about closing entries:

Exhibit 4-2, the (unadjusted) Trial Balance, lists all the accounts of the business entity Gary Lyon, CPA. Draw a horizontal line to separate the accounts that do *not* get closed out at the end of the period from those accounts that *do* get closed out. Identify the categories of accounts that *do* and do *not* get closed (assets, liabilities, and so on).

Making closing entries
(Obj. 3)

DE4-6 Study Exhibit 4-5 on the acetate between pages 140 and 141.

1. Journalize the closing entries for
   a. Owner's withdrawals
   b. Service revenue
   c. All the expenses (make a single closing entry for all the expenses)
2. Set up all the T-accounts affected by requirement 1 and insert their adjusted balances (denote as *Bal.*) at April 30. Also set up a T-account for Income Summary. Post the closing entries to the accounts, denoting posted amounts as *Clo.*
3. What is the ending balance of
   a. Gary Lyon, Capital?
   b. All the other accounts for which you set up T-accounts?

Analyzing the overall effect of the closing entries on the owner's capital account
(Obj. 3)

DE4-7 This exercise should be used in conjunction with Daily Exercise 4-6.

1. Return to Exhibit 4-5 on the acetate between pages 140 and 141. Without making any closing entries or using any T-accounts, compute the ending balance of Gary Lyon, Capital.
2. Trace Gary Lyon's ending capital balance to its two appropriate places in Exhibit 4-7 (page 144). In which financial statements do you find Gary Lyon, Capital? Where on each statement?

Making closing entries
(Obj. 3)

DE4-8 Sprint Corporation, the long-distance telecommunications company, reported the following items adapted from its financial statements at December 31, 1996 (amounts in millions):

Cash	**$ 1,150**	**Depreciation expense**	**$1,591**
Service revenue	**14,045**	**Other assets**	**1,882**
Accounts payable	**1,027**	**Interest expense**	**197**
Accounts receivable	**2,464**	**Long-term liabilities**	**5,119**

Make Sprint's closing entries, as needed, for these accounts.

Posting closing entries
(Obj. 3)

DE4-9 This exercise should be used in conjunction with Daily Exercise 4-8. Use the data in Daily Exercise 4-8 to set up T-accounts for those accounts that Sprint Corporation closed out at

December 31, 1996. Insert these account balances prior to closing, post the closing entries to these accounts, and show each account's final balance after closing. Denote a balance as *Bal.* and a closing entry amount as *Clo.* For posting to the T-accounts, you may ignore the Income Summary account.

DE 4-10 *Link Back to Chapter 3 (Correcting the Accounts).*

Making correcting entries **(Obj. 4)**

1. Suppose Gary Lyon, CPA, paid an account payable of $300 and erroneously debited Supplies. Make the journal entry to correct this error.
2. Assume Gary Lyon, CPA, made the following adjusting entry to record depreciation at April 30:

Depreciation Expense	275	
Furniture		275

Make the journal entry to correct this error.

3. In closing the books, Gary Lyon made this closing entry:

Income Summary	7,400	
Service Revenue		7,400

Make the journal entry to correct this error.

DE4-11 Magnum Enterprises, a software consulting company, purchased a file server software package from Microsoft Corporation. Magnum expensed this software asset by making the following entry at the time of purchase:

Making correcting entries **(Obj. 4)**

July 16	Supplies Expense	15,000	
	Cash		15,000
	Purchased software from Microsoft.		

At July 31, Magnum made the following adjusting entry to accrue salary expense:

July 31	Salary Expense	1,100	
	Accounts Payable		1,100
	Accrued salary expense.		

Make the journal entry to correct each error. Date the correcting entries at July 31, immediately after discovering the two errors.

DE4-12 This exercise should be used in conjunction with Daily Exercise 4-11. Use the Magnum Enterprises situation in Daily Exercise 4-11. Post Magnum's incorrect journal entries to the Supplies Expense T-account and to the Accounts Payable T-account. Ignore posting references. After making your correcting entries, post the correcting entries to all accounts affected. Then take the balance in all the T-accounts.

Posting correcting entries **(Obj. 4)**

What is the balance in

- Supplies Expense?
- Software?
- Accounts Payable?
- Salary Payable?

DE4-13 Lands' End had sales of $1,119 million during the year ended January 31, 1997, and total assets of $378 million at January 31, 1997, the end of the company's fiscal year. The financial statements of Lands' End reported the following (amounts in millions):

Classifying assets and liabilities as current or long-term **(Obj. 5)**

Sales revenue	**$1,119**	**Land and buildings**	**$ 72**
Inventory	**142**	**Accounts payable**	**77**
Long-term debt	**1**	**Operating expenses**	**424**
Receivables	**9**	**Accumulated depreciation**	**73**
Interest expense	**1**	**Accrued liabilities (such as Salary payable)**	**28**
Equipment	**99**		
Prepaid expenses	**17**		

Some of these account titles may be new to you, but you should be able to understand and use them.

1. Identify the assets (including contra assets) and liabilities.
2. Classify each asset and each liability as current or long-term.

Classifying assets and liabilities as current or long-term
(Obj. 5)

DE4-14 ⟸ *Link Back to Chapter 3 (Book Value).* Examine IBM's balance sheet in Exhibit 4-12 on page 152. Identify or compute the following amounts for IBM at December 31, 1996:

a. Total current assets
b. Total current liabilities
c. Book value of Plant, Rental Machines and Other Property (same as Fixed Assets; Plant and Equipment; or Property, Plant, and Equipment)
d. Total long-term assets
e. Total long-term liabilities (Deferred Income Taxes is a liability account.)

Preparing a postclosing trial balance
(Obj. 3)

DE4-15 After closing its accounts at December 31, 1996, Sprint Corporation had the following account balances (adapted) with amounts given in millions:

Property and equipment	**$10,464**	**Long-term liabilities**	**$5,119**
Cash	**1,150**	**Other assets**	**2,136**
Service revenue	**-0-**	**Accounts receivable**	**2,464**
Owners' equity	**8,520**	**Total expenses**	**-0-**
Other current assets	**739**	**Accounts payable**	**1,027**
Short-term notes payable	**200**	**Other current liabilities**	**2,087**

Prepare Sprint's postclosing trial balance at December 31, 1996. List accounts in proper order, as shown in Exhibit 4-10, page 148.

Computing and using the current ratio and the debt ratio
(Obj. 6)

DE4-16 This exercise should be used in conjunction with Daily Exercise 4-15. Use the postclosing trial balance that you prepared for Daily Exercise 4-15 to compute Sprint Corporation's current ratio and debt ratio.

1. How much in *current* assets does Sprint have for every dollar of *current* liabilities that it owes?
2. What percentage of Sprint's total assets are financial with debt?
3. What percentage of Sprint's total assets do the owners of the company actually own free and clear of debt?

Computing and evaluating the current ratio and the debt ratio
(Obj. 6)

DE4-17 Use Gary Lyon's classified balance sheet in Exhibit 4-11, page 151, to compute the current ratio and the debt ratio of Lyon's business at April 30.

1. How do Lyon's ratios compare to those of IBM, which are presented in the Putting Skills to Work feature on page 155? Based solely on these ratios, which business looks stronger? Why?
2. Do these two ratios tell the complete story of a company's financial position? What other factors should a lender consider in evaluating a business's ability to pay its debts?

Exercises

Preparing a work sheet
(Obj. 1)

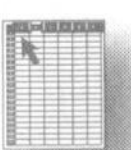

E4-1 The trial balance of Goldsmith Testing Service follows.

GOLDSMITH TESTING SERVICE
Trial Balance
September 30, 19X6

Cash	$ 3,560	
Accounts receivable	3,440	
Prepaid rent	1,200	
Supplies	3,390	
Equipment	32,600	
Accumulated depreciation		$ 2,840
Accounts payable		3,600
Salary payable		
L. Goldsmith, capital		36,030
L. Goldsmith, withdrawals	3,000	
Service revenue		7,300
Depreciation expense		
Salary expense	1,800	
Rent expense		
Utilities expense	780	
Supplies expense		
Total	$49,770	$49,770

Additional information at September 30, 19X6:

a. Accrued service revenue, $210.
b. Depreciation, $40.
c. Accrued salary expense, $500.
d. Prepaid rent expired, $600.
e. Supplies used, $1,650.

REQUIRED

Complete Goldsmith's work sheet for September 19X6.

Journalizing adjusting and closing entries **(Obj. 2, 3)**

E4-2 Journalize the adjusting and closing entries in Exercise 4-1.

Posting adjusting and closing entries **(Obj. 2. 3)**

E4-3 Set up T-accounts for those accounts affected by the adjusting and closing entries in Exercise 4-1. Post the adjusting and closing entries to the accounts; denote adjustment amounts by *Adj.*, closing amounts by *Clo.*, and balances by *Bal.* Double underline the accounts with zero balances after you close them, and show the ending balance in each account.

Preparing a postclosing trial balance **(Obj. 2, 3)**

E4-4 Prepare the postclosing trial balance in Exercise 4-1.

Identifying and journalizing entries **(Obj. 3)**

E4-5 From the following selected accounts from Tri-County Printers' ledger at June 30, 19X4, prepare the entity's closing entries:

Interest expense	**$ 2,200**	**Mel Nystrom, capital**	**$21,600**
Accounts receivable	**14,000**	**Service revenue**	**84,100**
Salary payable	**850**	**Unearned revenues**	**1,350**
Depreciation expense	**10,200**	**Salary expense**	**12,500**
Rent expense	**5,900**	**Accumulated depreciation**	**35,000**
Mel Nystrom, withdrawals	**40,000**	**Supplies expense**	**1,700**
Supplies	**1,400**	**Interest revenue**	**700**

What is Mel Nystrom, the owner's ending capital balance at June 30, 19X4?

Identifying and journalizing closing entries **(Obj. 3)**

E4-6 The accountant for Mackie Financial Services has posted adjusting entries (a) through (e) to the following selected accounts at December 31, 19X8. All the revenue, expense, and owner's equity accounts of the entity are listed here in T-account form.

Accounts Receivable

	Debit		Credit
	26,000		
(a)	3,500		

Supplies

	Debit		Credit
	4,000	(b)	2,000

Accumulated Depreciation—Furniture

	Debit		Credit
			5,000
		(c)	1,100

Accumulated Depreciation—Building

	Debit		Credit
			33,000
		(d)	6,000

Salary Payable

	Debit		Credit
		(e)	700

Ann Mackie, Capital

	Debit		Credit
			52,400

Ann Mackie, Withdrawals

	Debit		Credit
	61,400		

Service Revenue

	Debit		Credit
			111,000
		(a)	3,500

Salary Expense

	Debit		Credit
	26,000		
(e)	700		

Supplies Expense

	Debit		Credit
(b)	2,000		

Depreciation Expense—Furniture

	Debit		Credit
(c)	1,100		

Depreciation Expense—Building

	Debit		Credit
(d)	6,000		

REQUIRED

1. Journalize Mackie's closing entries at December 31, 19X8.
2. Determine Mackie's ending capital balance at December 31, 19X8.

Preparing a statement of owner's equity **(Obj. 3)**

E4-7 From the following accounts of Trautschold Locksmith Company, prepare the entity's statement of owner's equity for the year ended December 31, 19X9:

Rolf Trauschold, Capital

Date	Debit	Date	Credit
Dec. 31	42,000	Jan. 1	36,000
		Mar. 9	28,000
		Dec. 31	43,000

Rolf Trauschold, Withdrawals

Date	Debit	Date	Credit
Mar. 31	9,000	Dec. 31	42,000
Jun. 30	7,000		
Sep. 30	9,000		
Dec. 31	17,000		

Income Summary

Date	Debit	Date	Credit
Dec. 31	85,000	Dec. 31	128,000
Dec. 31	43,000		

Identifying and recording adjusting and closing entries
(Obj. 2, 3)

E4-8 The trial balance and income statement amounts from the August work sheet of Compassion Home Care follow.

Account Title	Trial Balance		Income Statement	
Cash	$ 3,100			
Supplies	2,400			
Prepaid rent	1,100			
Medical equipment	50,100			
Accumulated depreciation		$ 6,200		
Accounts payable		4,600		
Salary payable				
Unearned service revenue		4,400		
Alison Stiles, capital		35,800		
Alison Stiles, withdrawals	1,000			
Service revenue		11,700		$13,000
Salary expense	3,000		$ 3,800	
Rent expense	1,200		1,400	
Depreciation expense			300	
Supplies expense			400	
Utilities expense	800		800	
	$62,700	$62,700	6,700	13,000
Net income or net loss			6,300	
			$13,000	$13,000

REQUIRED

1. Journalize the adjusting and closing entries of Compassion Home Care at August 31.
2. How much net income or net loss did Compassion Home Care have for August? How can you tell?

Preparing a classified balance sheet
(Obj. 5, 6)

E4-9 Refer to Exercise 4-8.

REQUIRED

1. After solving Exercise 4-8, use the data in that exercise to prepare Compassion Home Care's classified balance sheet at August 31 of the current year. Use the report format.
2. Compute Compassion Home Care's current ratio and debt ratio at August 31. One year ago, the current ratio was 1.20 and the debt ratio was 0.30. Indicate whether Compassion's ability to pay its debts has improved or deteriorated during the current year.

Correcting accounting errors
(Obj. 4)

E4-10 Prepare a correcting entry for each of the following accounting errors:

a. Recorded the earning of $1,400 service revenue collected in advance by debiting Accounts Receivable and crediting Service Revenue.
b. Accrued interest revenue of $300 by a debit to Accounts Receivable and a credit to Interest Revenue.
c. Recorded a $2,000 cash purchase of supplies by debiting Supplies and crediting Accounts Payable.
d. Debited Supplies and credited Accounts Payable for a $2,900 purchase of office equipment on account.
e. Adjusted prepaid rent by debiting Prepaid Rent and crediting Rent Expense for $900. This adjusting entry should have debited Rent Expense and credited Prepaid Rent for $900.
f. Debited Salary Expense and credited Cash to accrue salary expense of $900.

Continuing Exercise

This exercise continues the Alvin Deering, Consultant, situation begun in Exercise 2-15 of Chapter 2 and continued to Exercise 3-14 of Chapter 3.

Closing the books, preparing a classified balance sheet, and evaluating a business
(Obj. 3, 5, 6)

E4-11 Refer to Exercise 3-14 of Chapter 3. Start from the posted T-accounts and the adjusted trial balance that Alvin Deering, Consultant, prepared for his accounting practice at December 31, at the top of the next page.

REQUIRED

1. Journalize and post the closing entries at December 31. Denote each closing amount as *Clo.* and an account balance as *Bal.*
2. Prepare a classified balance sheet at December 31.
3. If your instructor assigns it, complete the accounting work sheet at December 31.

ALVIN DEERING, CONSULTANT
Adjusted Trial Balance
December 31, 19XX

Account	Adjusted Trial Balance Debit	Adjusted Trial Balance Credit
Cash	$ 8,700	
Accounts receivable	1,500	
Supplies	100	
Equipment	3,000	
Accumulated depr.—equipment		$ 50
Furniture	3,600	
Accumulated depr.—furniture		60
Accounts payable		3,600
Salary payable		500
Unearned service revenue		600
Alvin Deering, capital		12,000
Alvin Deering, withdrawals	1,600	
Service revenue		3,200
Rent expense	500	
Utilities expense	200	
Salary expense	500	
Depreciation expense—equipment	50	
Depreciation expense—furniture	60	
Supplies expense	200	
Total	$20,010	$20,010

Challenge Exercise

Computing financial statement amounts (Obj. 2, 5)

E4-12 The unadjusted trial balance of Pinkston Security Couriers follows:

Account	Amount	Account	Amount
Cash	**$ 1,900**	**Accumulated depreciation—building**	**$14,900**
Accounts receivable	**7,200**	**Land**	**51,200**
Supplies	**1,100**	**Accounts payable**	**6,100**
Prepaid insurance	**2,200**	**Salary payable**	
Furniture	**8,400**	**Unearned service revenue**	**5,300**
Accumulated depreciation—furniture	**1,300**	**James Pinkston, capital**	**90,200**
James Pinkston, withdrawals	**46,200**	**Depreciation expense—building**	
Service revenue	**93,600**	**Supplies expense**	
Salary expense	**32,700**	**Insurance expense**	
Depreciation expense—furniture		**Utilities expense**	**2,700**
Building	**57,800**		

Adjusting data at the end of the year include the following:

a. Unearned service revenue that has been earned, $3,600.
b. Accrued service revenue, $1,700.
c. Supplies used in operations, $600.
d. Accrued salary expense, $1,400.
e. Insurance expense, $1,800.
f. Depreciation expense—furniture, $800; building, $2,100.

James Pinkston, the owner, has received an offer to sell the company. He needs to know the following information within one hour:

Net income for the year covered by these data.

REQUIRED

Without opening any accounts, making any journal entries, or using a work sheet, provide Pinkston with the requested information. Show all computations.

Ethical Issue

Link Back to Chapter 3 (Revenue Principle). Cash & Carry Carpets wishes to expand the business, and has borrowed $2 million from Tri-State Bank of Durango, Colorado. As a condition for making this loan, the bank requires that Cash & Carry maintain a current ratio at least 1.50 and a debt ratio no higher than 0.50.

Business has been good but not great. Expansion costs have brought the current ratio down to 1.40 and the debt ratio up to 0.51 at December 15. Cash & Carry's owner is considering what might happen if the business reports a current ratio of 1.40 to the bank. One course of action for Cash & Carry is to record in December some revenue that it will earn in January of next year. The contract for this job has been signed, and Cash & Carry will deliver the carpet to the customer during January.

REQUIRED

1. Journalize the revenue transaction, and indicate how recording this revenue in December would affect the current ratio and the debt ratio.
2. State whether it is ethical to record the revenue transaction in December. Identify the accounting principle relevant to this situation.
3. Propose a course of action that is ethical for Cash & Carry Carpets.

Problems (GROUP A)

Preparing a work sheet **(Obj. 1)**

P4-1A The trial balance of Amanda Blume Productions at May 31, 19X2, follows.

AMANDA BLUME PRODUCTIONS
Trial Balance
May 31, 19X2

Cash	$ 8,670	
Notes receivable	10,340	
Interest receivable		
Supplies	560	
Prepaid insurance	1,790	
Furniture	27,410	
Accumulated depreciation—furniture		$ 1,480
Building	53,900	
Accumulated depreciation—building		34,560
Land	18,700	
Accounts payable		14,730
Interest payable		
Salary payable		
Unearned service revenue		8,800
Note payable, long-term		18,700
Amanda Blume, capital		34,290
Amanda Blume, withdrawals	3,800	
Service revenue		16,970
Interest revenue		
Depreciation expense—furniture		
Depreciation expense—building		
Salary expense	2,170	
Insurance expense		
Interest expense		
Utilities expense	1,130	
Advertising expense	1,060	
Supplies expense		
Total	$129,530	$129,530

Additional data at May 31, 19X2:

a. Depreciation: furniture, $480; building, $460.
b. Accrued salary expense, $600.
c. Supplies on hand, $410.
d. Prepaid insurance expired during May, $390.

e. Accrued interest expense, $220.
f. Unearned service revenue earned during May, $4,400.
g. Accrued advertising expense, $60 (credit Accounts Payable).
h. Accrued interest revenue, $170.

Complete Blume's work sheet for May. Key adjusting entries by letter.

REQUIRED

Preparing financial statements from an adjusted trial balance; journalizing the adjusting and closing entries
(Obj. 2, 3, 6)

P4-2A The *adjusted* trial balance of Transamerica Brokerage Service at April 30, 19X2, after all adjustments, follows.

TRANSAMERICA BROKERAGE SERVICE Adjusted Trial Balance April 30, 19X2		
Cash	$ 1,370	
Accounts receivable	43,740	
Supplies	3,690	
Prepaid insurance	2,290	
Equipment	63,930	
Accumulated depreciation—equipment		$ 28,430
Building	74,330	
Accumulated depreciation—building		18,260
Land	20,000	
Accounts payable		19,550
Interest payable		2,280
Wages payable		830
Unearned service revenue		3,660
Note payable, long-term		69,900
William Bethke, capital		64,200
William Bethke, withdrawals	27,500	
Service revenue		98,550
Depreciation expense—equipment	6,900	
Depreciation expense—building	3,710	
Wage expense	32,810	
Insurance expense	5,370	
Interest expense	8,170	
Utilities expense	4,970	
Supplies expense	6,880	
Total	$305,660	$305,660

Adjusting data at April 30, 19X2, which have all been incorporated into the *adjusted* trial balance figures above, consist of

a. Unearned service revenue earned during the year, $4,180.
b. Supplies used during the year, $5,880.
c. Prepaid insurance expired during the year, $5,370.
d. Accrued interest expense, $1,280.
e. Accrued service revenue, $2,200.
f. Depreciation for the year: equipment, $6,900; building, $3,710.
g. Accrued wage expense, $830.

REQUIRED

1. Journalize the adjusting entries that would lead to the adjusted trial balance shown here. Also journalize the closing entries.
2. Prepare Transamerica's income statement and statement of owner's equity for the year ended April 30, 19X2, and the classified balance sheet on that date. Use the account format for the balance sheet.
3. Compute Transamerica's current ratio and debt ratio at April 30, 19X2. One year ago, the current ratio stood at 1.21 and the debt ratio was 0.82. Did Transamerica's ability to pay debts improve or deteriorate during fiscal year 19X2?

Taking the accounting cycle through the closing entries
(Obj. 2, 3)

P4-3A The unadjusted T-accounts of Prem Daftary, M.D., at December 31, 19X2, and the related year-end adjustment data follow.

Account	Debit	Credit
Cash	Bal. 29,000	
Accounts Receivable	Bal. 44,000	
Supplies	Bal. 6,000	
Equipment	Bal. 57,000	
Accumulated Depreciation		Bal. 12,000
Accounts Payable		Bal. 16,000
Salary Payable		
Unearned Service Revenue		Bal. 2,000
Note Payable, Long-Term		Bal. 40,000
Prem Daftary, Capital		Bal. 41,000
Prem Daftary, Withdrawals	Bal. 54,000	
Service Revenue		Bal. 130,000
Salary Expense	Bal. 36,000	
Supplies Expense		
Depreciation Expense		
Interest Expense	Bal. 5,000	
Insurance Expense	Bal. 10,000	

Adjustment data at December 31, 19X2:

a. Depreciation for the year, $5,000.
b. Supplies on hand, $2,000.
c. Accrued service revenue, $4,000.
d. Unearned service revenue earned during the year, $2,000.
e. Accrued salary expense, $4,000.

REQUIRED

1. Write the trial balance on a work sheet, and complete the work sheet. Key each adjusting entry by the letter corresponding to the data given. List all the accounts, including those with zero balances. Leave a blank line under Service Revenue.
2. Prepare the income statement, the statement of owner's equity, and the classified balance sheet in account format.
3. Journalize the adjusting and closing entries.
4. Did Daftary have a profitable year or a bad year during 19X2? Give the reason for your answer.

Completing the accounting cycle
(Obj. 2, 3)

P4-4A This problem should be used in conjunction with Problem 4-3A. It completes the accounting cycle by posting to T-accounts and preparing the postclosing trial balance.

REQUIRED

1. Using the Problem 4-3A data, post the adjusting and closing entries to the T-accounts, denoting adjusting amounts by *Adj.*, closing amounts by *Clo.*, and account balances by *Bal.*, as shown in Exhibit 4-9. Double underline all accounts with a zero ending balance.
2. Prepare the postclosing trial balance.

Completing the accounting cycle
(Obj. 2, 3, 5)

P4-5A The trial balance of Environmental Protection Services at October 31, 19X0, follows. The data needed for the month-end adjustments are as follows:

a. Unearned service revenue still unearned at October 31, $4,900.
b. Prepaid rent still in force at October 31, $2,000.
c. Supplies used during the month, $770.
d. Depreciation on equipment for the month, $250.
e. Depreciation on building for the month, $580.
f. Accrued salary expense at October 31, $310.

REQUIRED

1. Open the accounts listed in the trial balance, inserting their October 31 unadjusted balances. Also open the Income Summary account, number 33. Use four-column accounts. Date the balances of the following accounts October 1: Prepaid Rent, Supplies, Equipment, Accumulated Depreciation—Equipment, Building, Accumulated Depreciation—Building, Unearned Service Revenue, and David Kangas, Capital.
2. Write the trial balance on a work sheet and complete the work sheet of Environmental Protection Services for the month ended October 31, 19X0.
3. Prepare the income statement, the statement of owner's equity, and the classified balance sheet in report format.
4. Using the work sheet data, journalize and post the adjusting and closing entries. Use dates and posting references. Use 12 as the number of the journal page.
5. Prepare a postclosing trial balance.

ENVIRONMENTAL PROTECTION SERVICES Trial Balance October 31, 19X0			
Account Number	**Account Title**	**Debit**	**Credit**
11	Cash	$ 4,900	
12	Accounts receivable	15,310	
13	Prepaid rent	2,200	
14	Supplies	840	
15	Equipment	26,830	
16	Accumulated depreciation—equipment		$ 3,400
17	Building	68,300	
18	Accumulated depreciation—building		12,100
21	Accounts payable		7,290
22	Salary payable		
23	Unearned service revenue		5,300
31	David Kangas, capital		84,490
32	David Kangas, withdrawals	3,900	
41	Service revenue		12,560
51	Salary expense	1,840	
52	Rent expense		
53	Utilities expense	1,020	
54	Depreciation expense—equipment		
55	Depreciation expense—building		
56	Supplies expense		
	Total	$125,140	$125,140

Preparing a classified balance sheet in report format
(Obj. 5, 6)

P4-6A The accounts of Ernest Els, CPA, at March 31, 19X3, are listed in alphabetical order.

Accounts payable	**$14,700**	**Insurance expense**	**$ 600**
Accounts receivable	**11,500**	**Interest payable**	**300**
Accumulated depreciation—building	**47,300**	**Interest receivable**	**900**
Accumulated depreciation—furniture	**7,700**	**Note payable, long-term**	**3,200**
Advertising expense	**900**	**Note receivable, long-term**	**6,900**
Building	**55,900**	**Other assets**	**2,300**
Cash	**3,400**	**Other current liabilities**	**1,100**
Depreciation expense	**1,900**	**Prepaid insurance**	**600**
Ernest Els, capital, March 31, 19X2	**40,700**	**Prepaid rent**	**4,700**
Ernest Els, withdrawals	**31,200**	**Salary expense**	**17,800**
Furniture	**43,200**	**Salary payable**	**2,400**
		Service revenue	**71,100**
		Supplies	**3,800**
		Supplies expense	**4,600**
		Unearned service revenue	**1,700**

REQUIRED

1. All adjustments have been journalized and posted, but the closing entries have not yet been made. Prepare the company's classified balance sheet in report format at March 31, 19X3. Show totals for total assets, total liabilities, and total liabilities and owner's equity.
2. Compute Els's current ratio and debt ratio at March 31, 19X3. At March 31, 19X2, the current ratio was 1.28 and debt ratio was 0.32. Did Els's ability to pay debts improve or deteriorate during 19X3?

Analyzing and journalizing corrections, adjustments, and closing entries
(Obj. 3, 4)

P4-7A *Link Back to Chapter 2 (Accounting Errors).* The accountant of Reliance Estate Liquidators encountered the following situations while adjusting and closing the books at February 28. Consider each situation independently.

a. The company bookkeeper made the following entry to record a $310 credit purchase of supplies:

Feb. 26	Equipment	310	
	Accounts Payable		310

Prepare the correcting entry, dated February 28.

b. A $690 debit to Accounts Receivable was posted as $960.
  (1) At what stage of the accounting cycle will this error be detected?
  (2) Describe the technique for identifying the amount of the error.

c. The $1,620 balance of Utilities Expense was entered as $16,200 on the trial balance.
  (1) What is the name of this type of error?
  (2) Assume that this is the only error in the trial balance. Which will be greater, the total debits or the total credits, and by how much?
  (3) How can this type of error be identified?

d. The accountant failed to make the following adjusting entries at February 28:
  (1) Accrued service revenue, $1,400.
  (2) Insurance expense, $360.
  (3) Accrued interest expense on a note payable, $520.
  (4) Depreciation of equipment, $3,700.
  (5) Earned service revenue that had been collected in advance, $2,700.
  Compute the overall net income effect of these omissions.

e. Record each of the adjusting entries identified in item d.

Problems (GROUP B)

Preparing a work sheet
(Obj. 1)

P4-1B The trial balance of Associated General Contractors at July 31, 19X3, follows.

ASSOCIATED GENERAL CONTRACTORS
Trial Balance
July 31, 19X3

Cash	$ 21,200	
Accounts receivable	37,820	
Supplies	17,660	
Prepaid insurance	2,300	
Equipment	32,690	
Accumulated depreciation—equipment		$ 26,240
Building	42,890	
Accumulated depreciation—building		10,500
Land	28,300	
Accounts payable		22,690
Interest payable		
Wages payable		
Unearned service revenue		10,560
Note payable, long-term		22,400
Lane Stuart, capital		79,130
Lane Stuart, withdrawals	4,200	
Service revenue		20,190
Depreciation expense—equipment		
Depreciation expense—building		
Wage expense	3,200	
Insurance expense		
Interest expense		
Utilities expense	1,110	
Advertising expense	340	
Supplies expense		
Total	$191,710	$191,710

Additional data at July 31, 19X3:

a. Depreciation: equipment, $630; building, $370.
b. Accrued wage expense, $240.
c. Supplies on hand, $14,740.
d. Prepaid insurance expired during July, $500.
e. Accrued interest expense, $180.

f. Unearned service revenue earned during July, $4,970.
g. Accrued advertising expense, $100 (credit Accounts Payable).
h. Accrued service revenue, $1,100.

REQUIRED

Complete Associated General's work sheet for July. Key adjusting entries by letter.

Preparing financial statements from an adjusted trial balance; journalizing the adjusting and closing entries
(Obj. 2, 3, 6)

P4-2B The *adjusted* trial balance of Full Spectrum Color Laboratory at June 30, 19X9, after all adjustments, follows.

FULL SPECTRUM COLOR LABORATORY
Adjusted Trial Balance
June 30, 19X9

Cash	$ 19,350	
Accounts receivable	26,470	
Supplies	31,290	
Prepaid insurance	3,200	
Equipment	55,800	
Accumulated depreciation—equipment		$ 16,480
Building	114,900	
Accumulated depreciation—building		16,850
Land	30,000	
Accounts payable		38,400
Interest payable		1,490
Wages payable		770
Unearned service revenue		2,300
Note payable, long-term		97,000
Frank Santos, capital		68,390
Frank Santos, withdrawals	45,300	
Service revenue		139,860
Depreciation expense—equipment	7,300	
Depreciation expense—building	3,970	
Wage expense	21,470	
Insurance expense	3,100	
Interest expense	11,510	
Utilities expense	4,300	
Supplies expense	3,580	
Total	$381,540	$381,540

Adjusting data at June 30, 19X9, which have all been incorporated into the *adjusted* trial balance figures:

a. Depreciation for the year: equipment, $7,300; building, $3,970.
b. Supplies used during the year, $3,580.
c. Prepaid insurance expired during the year, $3,100.
d. Accrued interest expense, $690.
e. Accrued service revenue, $940.
f. Unearned service revenue earned during the year, $7,790.
g. Accrued wage expense, $770.

REQUIRED

1. Journalize the adjusting entries that would lead to the adjusted trial balance shown here. Also journalize the closing entries.
2. Prepare Full Spectrum Color Laboratory's income statement and statement of owner's equity for the year ended June 30, 19X9, and the classified balance sheet on that date. Use the account format for the balance sheet.
3. Compute Full Spectrum's current ratio and debt ratio at June 30, 19X9. One year ago, the current ratio stood at 1.01 and the debt ratio was 0.71. Did Full Spectrum's ability to pay debts improve or deteriorate during fiscal year 19X9?

Taking the accounting cycle through the closing entries
(Obj. 2, 3)

P4-3B The unadjusted T-accounts of Leslie LeCrone, Psychologist, at December 31, 19X2, and the related year-end adjustment data follow.

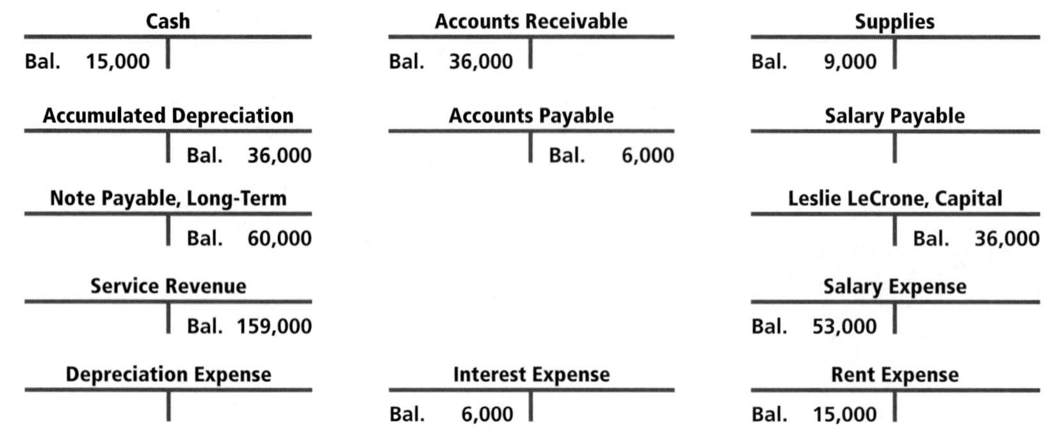

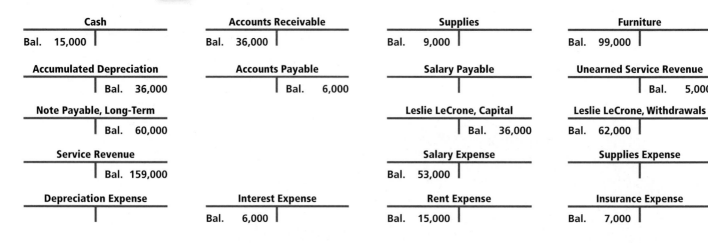

Account	Debit	Credit
Cash	Bal. 15,000	
Accounts Receivable	Bal. 36,000	
Supplies	Bal. 9,000	
Furniture	Bal. 99,000	
Accumulated Depreciation		Bal. 36,000
Accounts Payable		Bal. 6,000
Salary Payable		
Unearned Service Revenue		Bal. 5,000
Note Payable, Long-Term		Bal. 60,000
Leslie LeCrone, Capital		Bal. 36,000
Leslie LeCrone, Withdrawals	Bal. 62,000	
Service Revenue		Bal. 159,000
Salary Expense	Bal. 53,000	
Supplies Expense		
Depreciation Expense		
Interest Expense	Bal. 6,000	
Rent Expense	Bal. 15,000	
Insurance Expense	Bal. 7,000	

Adjustment data at December 31, 19X2:

a. Unearned service revenue earned during the year, $5,000.
b. Supplies on hand, $1,000.
c. Depreciation for the year, $9,000.
d. Accrued salary expense, $1,000.
e. Accrued service revenue, $2,000.

REQUIRED

1. Write the trial balance on a work sheet, and complete the work sheet. Key each adjusting entry by the letter corresponding to the data given. List all the accounts, including those with zero balances. Leave a blank line under Service Revenue.
2. Prepare the income statement, the statement of owner's equity, and the classified balance sheet in account format.
3. Journalize the adjusting and closing entries.
4. Did LeCrone have a profitable year or a bad year during 19X2? Give the reason for your answer.

Completing the accounting cycle
(Obj. 2, 3)

P4-4B This problem should be used in conjunction with Problem 4-3B. It completes the accounting cycle by posting to T-accounts and preparing the postclosing trial balance.

REQUIRED

1. Using the Problem 4-3B data, post the adjusting and closing entries to the T-accounts, denoting adjusting amounts by *Adj.*, closing amounts by *Clo.*, and account balances by *Bal.*, as shown in Exhibit 4-9. Double underline all accounts with a zero ending balance.
2. Prepare the postclosing trial balance.

Completing the accounting cycle
(Obj. 2, 3, 5)

P4-5B The trial balance of Town West Insurance Agency at August 31, 19X9, and the data needed for the month-end adjustments follow at the top of the next page.

Adjustment data:

a. Unearned commission revenue still unearned at August 31, $6,750.
b. Prepaid rent still in force at August 31, $1,050.
c. Supplies used during the month, $340.
d. Depreciation on furniture for the month, $370.
e. Depreciation on building for the month, $130.
f. Accrued salary expense at August 31, $460.

REQUIRED

1. Open the accounts listed in the trial balance and insert their August 31 unadjusted balances. Also open the Income Summary account, number 33. Use four-column accounts. Date the balances of the following accounts as of August 1: Prepaid Rent, Supplies, Furniture, Accumulated Depreciation—Furniture, Building, Accumulated Depreciation—Building, Unearned Commission Revenue, and Inge Wade, Capital.
2. Write the trial balance on a work sheet and complete the work sheet of Town West Insurance Agency for the month ended August 31, 19X9.

TOWN WEST INSURANCE AGENCY
Trial Balance
August 31, 19X9

Account Number	Account Title	Debit	Credit
11	Cash	$ 23,800	
12	Accounts receivable	15,560	
13	Prepaid rent	1,290	
14	Supplies	900	
15	Furniture	15,350	
16	Accumulated depreciation—furniture		$ 12,800
17	Building	89,900	
18	Accumulated depreciation—building		28,600
21	Accounts payable		4,240
22	Salary payable		
23	Unearned commission revenue		8,900
31	Inge Wade, capital		71,920
32	Inge Wade, withdrawals	4,800	
41	Commission revenue		27,300
51	Salary expense	1,100	
52	Rent expense		
53	Utilities expense	410	
54	Depreciation expense—furniture		
55	Depreciation expense—building		
56	Advertising expense	650	
57	Supplies expense		
	Total	$153,760	$153,760

3. Prepare the income statement, the statement of owner's equity, and the classified balance sheet in report format.
4. Using the work sheet data, journalize and post the adjusting and closing entries. Use dates and posting references. Use 7 as the number of the journal page.
5. Prepare a postclosing trial balance.

Preparing a classified balance sheet in report format
(Obj. 5, 6)

P4-6B The accounts of Doppler Travel Agency at December 31, 19X6, are listed in alphabetical order.

Account	Amount	Account	Amount
Accounts payable	**$ 5,100**	**Jill Doppler, capital, December 31, 19X5**	**$49,800**
Accounts receivable	**6,600**	**Jill Doppler, withdrawals**	**47,400**
Accumulated depreciation—building	**37,800**	**Note payable, long-term**	**27,800**
Accumulated depreciation—furniture	**11,600**	**Note receivable, long-term**	**4,000**
Advertising expense	**2,200**	**Other assets**	**3,600**
Building	**104,400**	**Other current liabilities**	**4,700**
Cash	**6,500**	**Prepaid insurance**	**1,100**
Commission revenue	**93,500**	**Prepaid rent**	**6,600**
Depreciation expense	**1,300**	**Salary expense**	**24,600**
Furniture	**22,700**	**Salary payable**	**3,900**
Insurance expense	**800**	**Supplies**	**2,500**
Interest payable	**600**	**Supplies expense**	**5,700**
Interest receivable	**200**	**Unearned commission revenue**	**5,400**

REQUIRED

1. All adjustments have been journalized and posted, but the closing entries have not yet been made. Prepare the company's classified balance sheet in report format at December 31, 19X6. Show totals for total assets, total liabilities, and total liabilities and owner's equity.
2. Compute Doppler's current ratio and debt ratio at December 31, 19X6. At December 31, 19X5, the current ratio was 1.52 and the debt ratio was 0.37. Did Doppler's ability to pay debts improve or deteriorate during 19X6?

Analyzing and journalizing corrections, adjustments, and closing entries
(Obj. 3, 4)

P4-7B *Link Back to Chapter 2 (Accounting Errors).* The accountant for Petsmart Veterinary Clinic, encountered the following situations while adjusting and closing the books at December 31. Consider each situation independently.

a. The company bookkeeper made the following entry to record a $2,000 credit purchase of office equipment:

Nov. 12	Office Supplies.....................	2,000	
	Accounts Payable		2,000

Prepare the correcting entry, dated December 31.

b. A $750 credit to Cash was posted as a debit.
(1) At what stage of the accounting cycle will this error be detected?
(2) Describe the technique for identifying the amount of the error.

c. The $39,000 balance of Equipment was entered as $3,900 on the trial balance.
(1) What is the name of this type of error?
(2) Assume that this is the only error in the trial balance. Which will be greater, the total debits or the total credits, and by how much?
(3) How can this type of error be identified?

d. The accountant failed to make the following adjusting entries at December 31:
(1) Accrued property tax expense, $200.
(2) Supplies expense, $1,090.
(3) Accrued interest revenue on a note receivable, $650.
(4) Depreciation of equipment, $4,000.
(5) Earned service revenue that had been collected in advance, $1,100.
Compute the overall net income effect of these omissions.

e. Record each of the adjusting entries identified in item d.

Applying Your Knowledge

DECISION CASES

Completing the accounting cycle to develop the information for a bank loan
(Obj. 3, 5)

CASE 1. One year ago, Peter Sandlin founded Sandlin Computing Service, and the business has prospered. Sandlin comes to you for advice. He wishes to know how much net income his business earned during the past year. He also wants to know what the entity's total assets, liabilities, and capital are. The accounting records consist of the T-accounts in the ledger, which were prepared by an accountant who has moved. The ledger at December 31 appears as follows:

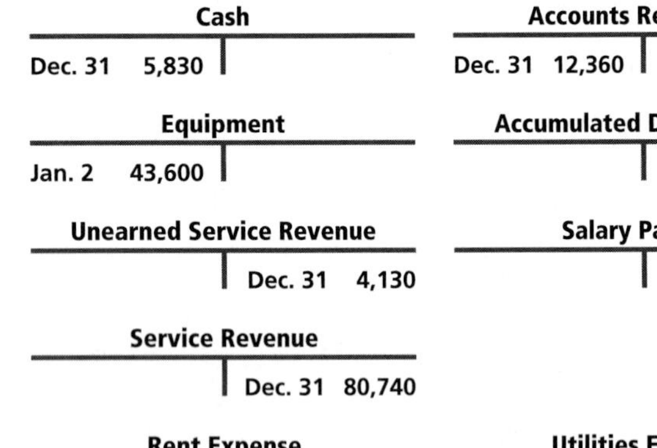

Account	Debit	Credit
Cash	Dec. 31 5,830	
Accounts Receivable	Dec. 31 12,360	
Prepaid Rent	Jan. 2 2,800	
Supplies	Jan. 2 2,600	
Equipment	Jan. 2 43,600	
Accumulated Depreciation		
Accounts Payable		Dec. 31 18,540
Unearned Service Revenue		Dec. 31 4,130
Salary Payable		
Peter Sandlin, Capital		Jan. 2 25,000
Peter Sandlin, Drawing	Dec. 31 43,420	
Service Revenue		Dec. 31 80,740
Salary Expense	Dec. 31 17,000	
Depreciation Expense		
Rent Expense		
Utilities Expense	Dec. 31 800	
Supplies Expense		

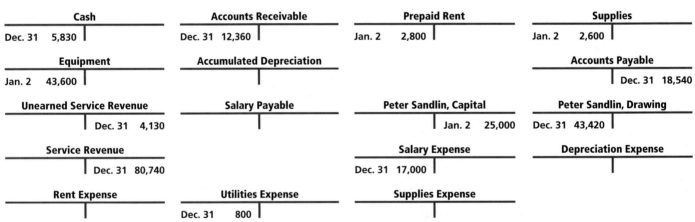

Sandlin indicates that at the year's end customers owe him $1,600 accrued service revenue, which he expects to collect early next year. These revenues have not been recorded. During the year, he collected $4,130 service revenue in advance from customers, but the business has earned only $600 of that amount. Rent expense for the year was $2,400, and he used up $2,100 of the supplies. Sandlin estimates that depreciation on equipment was $5,900 for the year. At December 31, he owes his employee $1,200 accrued salary.

Sandlin expresses concern that his withdrawals during the year might have exceeded the business's net income. To get a loan to expand the business, Sandlin must show the bank that his capital account has grown from its original $25,000 balance. Has it? You and Sandlin agree that you will meet again in one week.

REQUIRED

Prepare the work sheet and financial statements to answer Sandlin's questions.

CASE 2. You are preparing the financial statements for the year ended October 31, 19X5, for Jody Grant Dance Studio.

Finding an error in the work sheet (Obj. 1, 4)

- You began with the trial balance of the ledger, which balanced, and then made the required adjusting entries.
- To save time, you omitted preparing an adjusted trial balance.
- After making the adjustments on the work sheet, you extended the balances from the trial balance, adjusted for the adjusting entries, and computed amounts for the income statement and the balance sheet columns.

a. When you added the total debits and the total credits on the income statement, you found that the credits exceeded the debits by $10,000. According to your finding, did the business have a profit or a loss?

b. You took the balancing amount from the income statement columns to the debit column of the balance sheet and found that the total debits exceeded the total credits in the balance sheet. The difference between the total debits and the total credits on the balance sheet is $20,000. What is the cause of this difference? (Except for these errors, everything else is correct.)

FINANCIAL STATEMENT CASES

CASE 1. This problem, based on the balance sheet of NIKE, Inc., in Appendix A, will familiarize you with some of the assets and liabilities of that company. Use the NIKE balance sheet to answer the following questions.

Using a balance sheet (Obj. 5, 6)

REQUIRED

1. Which balance sheet format does NIKE, Inc., use?
2. Name the company's largest current asset and largest current liability at May 31, 1997.
3. Compute NIKE's current ratios and debt ratios at May 31, 1997, and May 31, 1996. NIKE treats Redeemable Preferred Stock as a liability. Did the ratio values improve, worsen, or hold steady during the fiscal year ended May 31, 1997? Refer to the income statement to explain your evaluation of the ratio values.
4. Under what category does NIKE report land, buildings, machinery, and equipment?
5. What was the cost of the company's plant assets at May 31, 1997? What was the amount of accumulated depreciation? What was the book value of the plant assets? The notes provide the information.

CASE 2. Obtain the annual report of a company of your choosing. Answer the following questions about the company.

Using a balance sheet (Obj. 5, 6)

REQUIRED

1. Which balance sheet format does the company use?
2. Name the company's largest asset and largest liability at the end of the current year and at the end of the preceding year.Name the largest *current* asset and the largest *current* liability at the end of the current year and at the end of the preceding year.
3. Compute the company's current ratio and debt ratio at the end of the current year and the current ratio and debt ratio at the end of the preceding year. Did these ratios improve, deteriorate, or hold steady during the current year? Does the income statement help to explain why the ratios changed? Give your reason.

Team Project

Jack Roberts formed a lawn service business as a summer job. To start the business on May 1, he deposited $1,000 in a new bank account in the name of the proprietorship. The $1,000 consisted of a $600 loan from his father and $400 of his own money. Jack rented lawn equipment, purchased supplies, and hired high school students to mow and trim his customer's lawns.

At the end of each month, Jack mailed bills to his customers. On August 31, he was ready to dissolve the business and return to Baylor University for the fall semester. Because he had been so busy, he had kept few records other than his checkbook and a list of amounts owed to him by customers.

At August 31, Jack's checkbook shows a balance of $1,640, and his customers still owe him $500. During the summer, he collected $5,200 from customers. His checkbook lists payments for supplies totaling $400, and he still has gasoline, weedeater cord, and other supplies that cost a total of $50. He paid his employees $1,900, and he still owes them $200 for the final week of the summer.

Jack rented some equipment from Ludwig Tool Company. On May 1, he signed a six-month lease on mowers and paid $600 for the full lease period. Ludwig will refund the unused portion of the prepayment if the equipment is in good shape. In order to get the refund, Jack has kept the mowers in excellent condition. In fact, he had to pay $300 to repair a mower that ran over a hidden tree stump.

To transport employees and equipment to jobs, Jack used a trailer that he bought for $300. He figures that the summer's work used up one-third of the trailer's service potential. The business checkbook lists an expenditure of $460 for cash withdrawals by Jack during the summer. Jack paid his father back during August.

REQUIRED

1. Prepare the income statement of Roberts Lawn Service for the four months May through August.
2. Prepare the classified balance sheet of Roberts Lawn Service at August 31.
3. Was Roberts's summer work successful? Give a detailed reason for your answer.

Internet Exercise MOTOROLA

Providing financial statement users with timely information has become increasingly important. Motorola excels in its ability to close its books and present financial information both to its own managers and to the financial community. This quick access to Motorola's latest results is yet another competitive advantage that distinguishes Motorola from its competition.

To prepare the year-end financial statements requires a substantial and coordinated effort by Motorola's accounting staff. Data must be gathered from Motorola's global activities, and numerous judgments and estimations must be made. A review of Motorola's financial statements can provide some insight into how the company closes its books.

REQUIRED

1. Go to Motorola's home page at **http://www.mot.com.**
2. Click on the **Inside Motorola** icon. This section provides the visitor with a vast amount of information concerning Motorola and its operations.
3. Click the **Annual Report** icon to see the company's financial data and reports.
   a. When does Motorola's fiscal year end?
   b. Locate Motorola's most recent year-end earnings release (that is, fourth quarter). This is located at the **Financial Reporting** page. How many days did Motorola take to announce its financial results to the public?
   c. What section of Motorola's trial balance work sheet, if any, does Motorola report on its financial statements?
   d. Which account on Motorola's balance sheet most likely was *not* affected by an adjusting journal entry?
   e. In preparing its financial statements does Motorola make a distinction between its current and long-term assets and liabilities? That is, does Motorola present a classified or unclassified balance sheet? Explain.

APPENDIX to Chapter 4

Reversing Entries: An Optional Step

Reversing entries are special types of entries that ease the burden of accounting after the adjusting and closing entries have been made at the end of a period. Reversing entries are used most often in conjunction with accrual-type adjustments such as accrued salary expense and accrued service revenue. *GAAP does not require reversing entries. They are used only for convenience and to save time.*

ACCOUNTING FOR ACCRUED EXPENSES

To see how reversing entries work, return to Gary Lyon's unadjusted trial balance at April 30 (Exhibit 4-2, page 140). Salary Expense has a debit balance of $950 for salaries paid during April. At April 30, the business still owes its employee an additional $950 for the last half of the month, so Lyon makes this adjusting entry:

Adjusting Entries

Apr. 30	Salary Expense................	950	
	Salary Payable.........		950

After posting, the accounts are updated at April 30.[2]

Salary Payable

Debit	Credit
	Apr. 30 Adj. 950
	Apr. 30 Bal. 950

Salary Expense

Debit	Credit
Paid during April CP 950	
Apr. 30 Adj. 950	
Apr. 30 Bal. 1,900	

After the adjusting entry,

- The April income statement reports salary expense of $1,900.
- The April 30 balance sheet reports salary payable of $950.

The $1,900 debit balance of Salary Expense is closed at April 30, 19X1, with this closing entry:

Closing Entries

Apr. 30	Income Summary...........	1,900	
	Salary Expense........		1,900

After posting, Salary Expense has a zero balance as follows:

Salary Expense

Debit	Credit
Paid during April CP 950	
Apr. 30 Adj. 950	
Apr. 30 Bal. 1,900	Apr. 30 Clo. 1,900

Zero balance

Assume for this illustration that on May 5, the next payday, Lyon will pay the $950 of accrued salary left over from April 30 plus $100 of salary for the first few days of May. Lyon's next payroll payment will be $1,050 ($950 + $100).

[2]Entry explanations used throughout this discussion are
Adj. = Adjusting entry CP = Cash payment entry—a credit to Cash
Bal. = Balance CR = Cash receipt entry—a debit to Cash
Clo. = Closing entry Rev. = Reversing entry

ACCOUNTING WITHOUT A REVERSING ENTRY

On May 5, the next payday, Lyon pays the payroll of $1,050 and makes this journal entry:

May 5	Salary Payable	950	
	Salary Expense	100	
	Cash		1,050

This method of recording the cash payment is correct. However, it wastes time because Lyon must refer to the adjusting entries of April 30. Otherwise, he does not know the amount of the debit to Salary Payable (in this example, $950). Searching the preceding period's adjusting entries takes time and, in business, time is money. To save time, accountants use reversing entries.

MAKING A REVERSING ENTRY

Reversing Entry. An entry that switches the debit and the credit of a previous adjusting entry. The reversing entry is dated the first day of the period after the adjusting entry.

A **reversing entry** switches the debit and the credit of a previous adjusting entry. *A reversing entry, then, is the exact opposite of a prior adjusting entry.* The reversing entry is dated the first day of the period that follows the adjusting entry.

To illustrate reversing entries, recall that on April 30, Lyon made the following adjusting entry to accrue Salary Payable:

Adjusting Entries

Apr. 30	Salary Expense	950	
	Salary Payable..........		950

The reversing entry simply reverses the debit and the credit of the adjustment:

Reversing Entries

May 1	Salary Payable	950	
	Salary Expense.........		950

Observe that the reversing entry is dated the first day of the new period. It is the exact opposite of the April 30 adjusting entry. Ordinarily, the accountant who makes the adjusting entry also prepares the reversing entry at the same time. Lyon dates the reversing entry as of the first day of the next period, however, so that it affects only the new period. Note how the accounts appear after Lyon posts the reversing entry:

Salary Payable

May 1	Rev.	950	Apr. 30	Bal.	950
		Zero balance			

Salary Expense

Apr. 30	Bal.	1,900	Apr. 30	Clo.	1,900
		Zero balance			
			May 1	Rev.	950

The arrow shows the transfer of the $950 credit balance from Salary Payable to Salary Expense. This credit balance in Salary Expense does not mean that the entity has negative salary expense, as you might think. Instead, the odd credit balance in the Salary Expense account is merely a temporary result of the reversing entry. The credit balance is eliminated on May 5, when Lyon pays the payroll and debits Salary Expense in the customary manner:

May 5	Salary Expense	1,050	
	Cash		1,050

Then this cash payment entry is posted as follows:

Salary Expense

May 5	CP	1,050	May 1	Rev.	950
May 5	Bal.	100			

Now Salary Expense has its correct debit balance of $100, which is the amount of salary expense incurred thus far in May. The $1,050 cash disbursement also pays the liability for Salary Payable so that Salary Payable has a zero balance, which is correct.

Appendix Problem

Using reversing entries

P4A-1 Refer to the data in Problem 4-5B, page 172.

REQUIRED

1. Open accounts for Salary Payable and Salary Expense. Insert their unadjusted balances at August 31, 19X9.
2. Journalize adjusting entry (f) and the closing entry for Salary Expense at August 31. Post to the accounts.
3. On September 5, Town West Insurance Agency paid the next payroll amount of $580. Journalize this cash payment, and post to the accounts. Show the balance in each account.
4. Using a reversing entry, repeat requirements 1 through 3. Compare the balances of Salary Payable and Salary Expense computed using a reversing entry with those balances computed without the reversing entry (as they appear in your answer to requirement 3).

CHAPTER 5

Merchandising Operations and the Accounting Cycle

LEARNING OBJECTIVES

After studying this chapter, you should be able to

1. Use sales and gross margin to evaluate a company
2. Account for the purchase and sale of inventory
3. Adjust and close the accounts of a merchandising business
4. Prepare a merchandiser's financial statements
5. Use the gross margin percentage and the inventory turnover ratio to evaluate a business
6. Compute cost of goods sold

SUPPLEMENT LEARNING OBJECTIVES

***S2.** Account for the purchase and sale of inventory

S3. Compute cost of goods sold

S4. Adjust and close the accounts of a merchandising business

S5. Prepare a merchandiser's financial statements

*Objectives S2 through S5 relate to the periodic inventory system.

> *"The May Department Stores Company is one of the country's leading department store companies, operating through eight regional divisions. Each division holds a leading position in its region."*
>
> MAY DEPARTMENT STORES ANNUAL REPORT, 1996

The May Department Stores Company, a major merchandising entity, operates more than 350 department stores across the United States. May's store divisions include:

- Lord & Taylor along the East Coast, Midwest, Texas and Louisiana
- Filene's in New England
- Hecht's and Strawbridge's along the East Coast
- Kaufmann's in Pennsylvania, Ohio, New York, and West Virginia
- Foley's in Texas, Oklahoma, Colorado, and New Mexico
- Robinsons-May in California, Arizona, and Nevada
- Famous-Barr and L.S. Ayres in Missouri, Indiana, and Illinois
- Meier & Frank in Washington and Oregon

The May Department Stores Company, headquartered in St. Louis, literally has the nation covered in merchandise. The company's income statement reports annual sales revenues of $12 billion and net income of almost $750 million. Assets total over $10 billion on the balance sheet.

What comes to mind when you think of *merchandising?* You probably think of the clothing that you purchase from a department store, the bread you buy at the grocery store, or the gas you purchase at your local service station. In addition to May Company, Wal-Mart, Sears, Exxon, and Best Buy are also merchandisers.

How do the operations of a Lord & Taylor store differ from those of the businesses we have studied so far? In the first four chapters, Gary Lyon, CPA, provided an illustration of a business that earns revenue by selling its services. Service enterprises include American Airlines, physicians, lawyers, CPAs, the Atlanta Braves baseball team, and the 12-year-old who cuts lawns in your neighborhood. A *merchandising entity* earns its revenue by selling products, called *merchandise inventory* or simply *inventory*.

This chapter demonstrates the central role of inventory in a business that sells merchandise. *Inventory* includes all goods that the company owns and expects to sell in the normal course of operations. Some businesses, such as Lord & Taylor department stores, Exxon stations, and Safeway grocery stores, buy their inventory in finished form, ready for sale to customers. Others, such as Sony, Hershey Foods, and Ford Motor Company, manufacture their own products. Both groups sell products rather than services.

We illustrate accounting for the purchase and sale of inventory, and we also illustrate how to adjust and close the books of a merchandiser. The chapter ends with an inventory model that managers use to determine how much inventory to purchase. The chapter covers two ratios that investors and creditors use to evaluate companies.

What Are Merchandising Operations?

Objective 1

Use sales and gross margin to evaluate a company

Exhibit 5-1 shows the income statement of The May Department Stores Company for a recent year. May's income statement differs from those of the service businesses discussed in previous chapters. For comparison, the exhibit also shows the income statement of Gary Lyon, CPA. The six highlighted items of May Department Stores are unique to merchandisers.

The amount that a business earns from selling merchandise inventory is called **sales revenue,** often abbreviated as **sales.** (**Net sales** equals sales revenue minus any sales returns and sales discounts.) The major revenue of a merchandising entity is sales revenue, which results from delivering inventory to customers. The major expense of a merchandiser is **cost of goods sold,** also called **cost of sales.** It represents the entity's cost of the goods (the inventory) that it sold to customers. While the inventory is held by a business, the inventory is an asset, an economic resource with future value to the company. When the inventory is sold, however, the inventory's cost becomes an expense to

Sales Revenue. The amount that a merchandiser earns from selling its inventory. Also called **sales.**

Net Sales. Sales revenue less sales discounts and sales returns and allowances.

Cost of Goods Sold. The cost of the inventory that the business has sold to customers, the largest single expense of most merchandising businesses. Also called **cost of sales.**

EXHIBIT 5-1
A Merchandiser's Income Statement Contrasted with the Income Statement of a Service Business

- Daily Exercise 5-1
- Daily Exercise 5-2
- Daily Exercise 5-3

THE MAY DEPARTMENT STORES COMPANY
Statement of Earnings (Adapted)

(Dollars in millions)	Year Ended January 31, 1997	1996
Revenues [such as Net sales revenue]	$12,000	$10,952
Cost of sales [same as Cost of goods sold]	8,226	7,461
Gross margin [same as Gross profit]	3,774	3,491
Selling, general, and administrative expenses	2,265	2,081
Interest expense	277	250
Other expenses	477	408
Total operating expenses	3,019	2,739
Net earnings (same as Net income)	$ 755	$ 752

GARY LYON, CPA
Income Statement
Year Ended December 31, 1997

Service revenue	$113,000
Expenses (listed individually)	42,000
Net income	$ 71,000

the seller. When Lord & Taylor sells you a shirt, the shirt's cost is expensed as cost of goods sold on May's books.

Net sales revenue minus cost of goods sold is called **gross margin** or **gross profit.**

Gross Margin. Excess of net sales revenue over cost of goods sold. Also called **gross profit.**

Net sales revenue (sometimes abbreviated as Sales)	−	Cost of goods sold (same as Cost of sales)	=	Gross margin (same as Gross profit)

or, more simply,

Sales	−	Cost of sales	=	Gross profit

Gross margin is a measure of business success. A sufficiently high gross margin is vital to a merchandiser. May's operations were quite successful during the year ended January 31, 1997. Sales increased by more than $1 billion, and the gross margin was up by over $280 million, as shown in Exhibit 5-1.

The following example will clarify the nature of gross margin. Suppose May's cost to purchase a man's shirt is $20 and May sells the shirt for $35. May's gross margin per unit is $15, computed as follows:

Sales revenue earned by selling one shirt	$35
Less: Cost of goods sold for the shirt	
(what the shirt cost May Department Stores)	(20)
Gross margin on the sale of one shirt	$15

The gross margin reported on May Department Stores' income statement, $3,774 million, is the sum of the gross margins on all the shirts and other products the company sold during its fiscal year.

The Operating Cycle of a Merchandising Business

A merchandising entity buys inventory, sells the goods to customers, and uses the cash to purchase more inventory and repeat the cycle. Exhibit 5-2 diagrams the operating cycle for *cash sales* and for *sales on account*.

For a cash sale—Panel A—the cycle is from cash to inventory, and back to cash. For a sale on account—Panel B—the cycle is from cash to inventory to accounts receivable and back to cash. In all lines of business, managers try to shorten the cycle in order to keep assets active. The faster the sale of inventory and the collection of cash, the higher the profits.

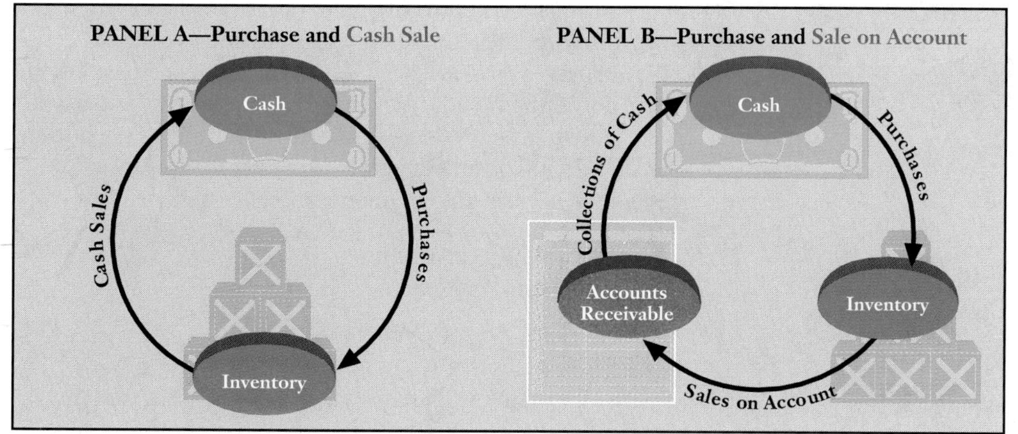

EXHIBIT 5-2
Operating Cycle of a Merchandiser

Inventory Systems: Perpetual and Periodic

Periodic Inventory System. An inventory accounting system in which the business does not keep a continuous record of the inventory on hand. Instead, at the end of the period the business makes a physical count of the on-hand inventory and uses this information to prepare the financial statements.

There are two main types of inventory accounting systems: the periodic system and the perpetual system. The **periodic inventory system** is used by businesses that sell relatively inexpensive goods. A grocery store without an optical-scanning cash register does not keep a daily running record of every loaf of bread and every can of pineapple that it buys and sells. The cost of recordkeeping would be overwhelming. Instead, grocers count their inventory periodically—at least once a year—to determine the quantities on hand. The inventory amounts are used to prepare the annual financial statements. Businesses such as office supply outlets, restaurants, and small department stores also use the periodic inventory system. The end-of-chapter supplement covers the periodic inventory system. That system is being used less and less as more businesses keep their inventory records by computer.

Perpetual Inventory System. The accounting inventory system in which the business keeps a running record of inventory and cost of goods sold.

Under the **perpetual inventory system,** the business maintains a running record of inventory and cost of goods sold. This system achieves control over expensive goods such as automobiles, jewelry, and furniture. The loss of one item would be significant, and this justifies the cost of a perpetual system. Computers reduce the time required to manage inventory and thus increase a company's ability to control its merchandise. But even under a perpetual system the business counts the inventory on hand at least once each year. The physical count establishes the correct amount of ending inventory and serves as a check on the perpetual records.

The following chart compares the periodic and perpetual systems:

Perpetual Inventory System	Periodic Inventory System
• Keeps a running record of all goods bought and sold.	• Does *not* keep a running record of all goods bought and sold.
• Inventory counted once a year.	• Inventory counted at least once a year.
• Used for all types of goods.	• Used for *inexpensive* goods.

COMPUTERIZED INVENTORY SYSTEMS A computerized inventory system can keep accurate, up-to-date records of the number of units purchased, the number of units sold, and the quantities on hand. Inventory systems are often integrated with accounts receivable and sales. For example, when May Department Stores orders shirts from Nautica, Nautica's computer checks warehouse records to see whether the shirts are in stock. If they are, Nautica enters the shipment into its computer, which multiplies the number of units shipped by the sale price. Nautica's computer then prints an invoice for May, and debits Accounts Receivable from May and credits Sales Revenue. The system also records Nautica's decrease in inventory.

"... in a perpetual system, the 'cash register' at a Wal-Mart or a Kmart store is a computer terminal that records the sale and also updates the company's inventory records."

The computer can keep up-to-the-minute records, so managers can call up current inventory information at any time. For example, in a perpetual system, the "cash register" at a Wal-Mart or a Kmart store is a computer terminal that records the sale and also updates the company's inventory records. Bar codes, which are scanned by a laser, are part of the perpetual inventory system. The lines of the bar coding represent coded data that keep track of each item. Because most businesses use them, we base our inventory discussions on the perpetual system.[1]

[1]For instructors who prefer to concentrate on the periodic inventory system, an overview starts on page 203 and a comprehensive treatment of that system begins on page 228. Follow Chapter Objectives S2 through S5 instead of 2 through 4.

Purchasing Merchandise in the Perpetual Inventory System

The cycle of a merchandising entity begins with the purchase of inventory, as Exhibit 5-2 shows. For example, a stereo center records the purchase of Sony compact disc (CD) players and other inventory acquired for resale, by debiting the Inventory account. A $500 purchase on account is recorded as follows:

Objective 2

Account for the purchase and sale of inventory

June 14	Inventory	500	
	Accounts Payable		500
	Purchased inventory on account.		

Learning Tip: The Inventory account should be used only for purchases of merchandise for resale. Purchases of any other asset are recorded in that asset account. For example, the purchase of supplies is debited to Supplies, not to Inventory.

Using the Purchase Invoice: A Basic Business Document

Business documents are the tangible evidence of transactions. As we trace the steps that Austin Sound Stereo Center, in Austin, Texas, takes in ordering, receiving, and paying for inventory, we will point out the roles that documents play in business.

1. Suppose Austin Sound wants to stock JVC brand CD players and speakers. Austin Sound prepares a *purchase order* and faxes it to JVC.
2. On receipt of the purchase order, JVC's computer scans its warehouse for the inventory that Austin Sound ordered. JVC ships the equipment and sends the invoice to Austin the same day. The **invoice** is the seller's request for cash from the purchaser. It is also called the *bill*.
3. Often the purchaser receives the invoice before the inventory arrives. Austin Sound does not pay immediately. Instead, Austin waits until the inventory arrives in order to ensure that it is the correct type and quantity ordered, and in good condition. After the inventory is inspected and approved, Austin Sound pays JVC the invoice amount.

Invoice. A seller's request for cash from the purchaser.

Exhibit 5-3 is an updated copy of an actual invoice from JVC to Austin Sound Stereo Center. From Austin Sound's perspective, this document is a *purchase invoice* (it is being used to purchase goods). To JVC, it is a *sales invoice* (it is being used to sell goods). Many companies buy and sell their goods electronically—with no invoices, no checks, and so on. Here we use actual documents to illustrate what is going on behind the scenes.

Taking Discounts from Purchase Prices

There are two major types of discounts from purchase prices: quantity discounts and cash discounts (called *purchase discounts*).

QUANTITY DISCOUNTS A *quantity discount* works this way: The larger the quantity purchased, the lower the price per item. For example, JVC may offer no discount for the purchase of only one or two CD players and charge the *list price*—the full price—of $200 per unit. However, JVC may offer the following quantity discount terms to persuade customers to buy more CD players:

Quantity	Quantity Discount	Net Price per Unit
Buy minimum quantity, 3 CD players	5%	$190[$200 – 0.05($200)]
Buy 4–9 CD players	10%	$180[$200 – 0.10($200)]
Buy more than 9 CD players	20%	$160[$200 – 0.20($200)]

Suppose that Austin Sound purchases five CD players from this manufacturer. The cost of each CD player is therefore $180. Purchase of five units on account would be recorded by debiting Inventory and crediting Accounts Payable for the net price of $900 ($180 per unit × 5 items purchased).

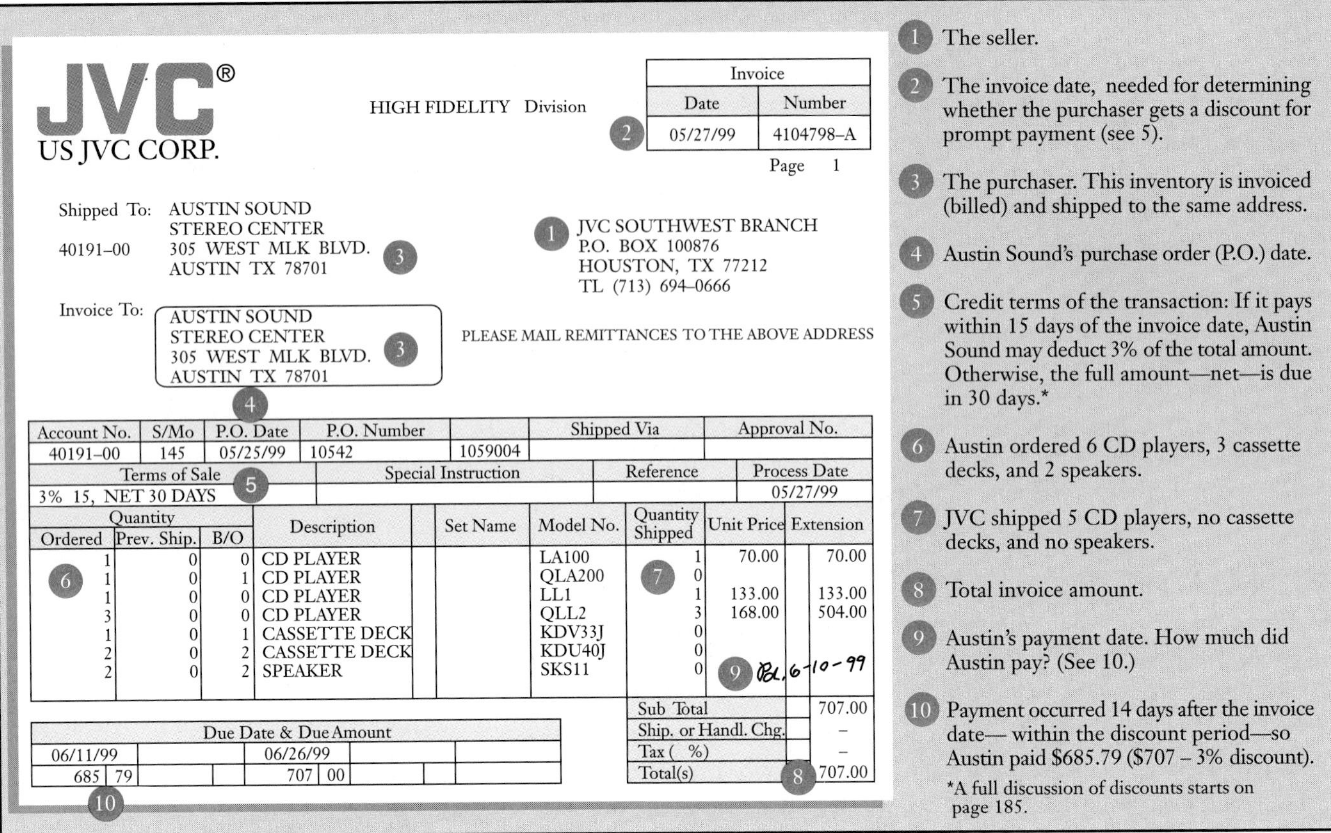

JVC®
US JVC CORP.

HIGH FIDELITY Division

Invoice	
Date	Number
05/27/99	4104798–A

Page 1

Shipped To: AUSTIN SOUND
STEREO CENTER
40191–00 305 WEST MLK BLVD.
AUSTIN TX 78701

JVC SOUTHWEST BRANCH
P.O. BOX 100876
HOUSTON, TX 77212
TL (713) 694–0666

Invoice To: AUSTIN SOUND
STEREO CENTER
305 WEST MLK BLVD.
AUSTIN TX 78701

PLEASE MAIL REMITTANCES TO THE ABOVE ADDRESS

Account No.	S/Mo	P.O. Date	P.O. Number		Shipped Via	Approval No.
40191–00	145	05/25/99	10542	1059004		

Terms of Sale	Special Instruction	Reference	Process Date
3% 15, NET 30 DAYS			05/27/99

Quantity Ordered	Prev. Ship.	B/O	Description	Set Name	Model No.	Quantity Shipped	Unit Price	Extension
1	0	0	CD PLAYER		LA100	1	70.00	70.00
1	0	1	CD PLAYER		QLA200	0		
1	0	0	CD PLAYER		LL1	1	133.00	133.00
3	0	0	CD PLAYER		QLL2	3	168.00	504.00
1	0	1	CASSETTE DECK		KDV33J	0		
2	0	2	CASSETTE DECK		KDU40J	0		
2	0	2	SPEAKER		SKS11	0	Pd. 6-10-99	

Due Date & Due Amount	
06/11/99	06/26/99
685 79	707 00

Sub Total	707.00
Ship. or Handl. Chg.	–
Tax (%)	–
Total(s)	707.00

1 The seller.

2 The invoice date, needed for determining whether the purchaser gets a discount for prompt payment (see 5).

3 The purchaser. This inventory is invoiced (billed) and shipped to the same address.

4 Austin Sound's purchase order (P.O.) date.

5 Credit terms of the transaction: If it pays within 15 days of the invoice date, Austin Sound may deduct 3% of the total amount. Otherwise, the full amount—net—is due in 30 days.*

6 Austin ordered 6 CD players, 3 cassette decks, and 2 speakers.

7 JVC shipped 5 CD players, no cassette decks, and no speakers.

8 Total invoice amount.

9 Austin's payment date. How much did Austin pay? (See 10.)

10 Payment occurred 14 days after the invoice date— within the discount period—so Austin paid $685.79 ($707 – 3% discount).

*A full discussion of discounts starts on page 185.

EXHIBIT 5-3
An Invoice

There is no Quantity Discount account, and there is no special accounting entry for a quantity discount. Instead, all accounting entries are based on the net price of a purchase after the quantity discount has been subtracted.

PURCHASE DISCOUNTS Many businesses also offer purchase discounts to their customers. A purchase discount is totally different from a quantity discount. A *purchase discount* is a reward for prompt payment. If a quantity discount is also offered, the purchase discount is computed on the net purchase amount after the quantity discount has been subtracted, further reducing the cost of the inventory.

JVC's credit terms of 3% 15, NET 30 DAYS can also be expressed as 3/15 n/30. This means that Austin Sound may deduct 3% of the total amount due if Austin pays within 15 days of the invoice date. Otherwise, the full amount—NET—is due in 30 days. Terms of simply n/30 mean that no discount is offered and that payment is due 30 days after the invoice date. Terms of *eom* usually mean that payment is due at the end of the current month. However, a purchase after the 25th of the current month on terms of *eom* can be paid at the end of the next month.

Let's use the Exhibit 5-3 transaction to illustrate accounting for a purchase discount. Austin Sound records this purchase on account as follows:

May 27	Inventory	707.00	
	Accounts Payable		707.00
	Purchased inventory on account.		

Austin Sound paid within the discount period, so its cash payment entry is

■ Daily Exercise 5-4

June 10	Accounts Payable	707.00	
	Cash ($707.00 × 0.97)		685.79
	Inventory ($707.00 × 0.03)		21.21
	Paid within discount period.		

Note the credit to Inventory. After Austin Sound has taken its discount, Austin Sound must adjust the Inventory account to reflect its true cost of the goods. In effect, this inventory cost Austin Sound $685.79 ($707.00 – the purchase discount of $21.21), as shown in the following Inventory account:

Inventory			
May 27	707.00	June 10	21.21
Bal.	685.79		

Alternatively, if Austin Sound pays this invoice after the discount period, it must pay the full invoice amount of $707. In that case, the payment entry is

June 29	Accounts Payable	707.00	
	Cash		707.00
	Paid after discount period.		

Without the discount, Austin Sound's cost of the inventory is the full amount of $707, as shown in the following T-account:

Inventory			
May 27	707.00		

Recording Purchase Returns and Allowances

Most businesses allow their customers to *return* merchandise that is defective, damaged in shipment, or otherwise unsuitable. But if the buyer chooses to keep the damaged goods, the seller may deduct an *allowance* from the amount the buyer owes.

Suppose the $70 CD player purchased by Austin Sound (top line of section 6 in Exhibit 5-3) was not the CD player Austin ordered. Austin returns the merchandise to the seller and records the purchase return as follows:

June 3	Accounts Payable	70.00	
	Inventory		70.00
	Returned inventory to seller.		

Now assume that one of the CD players was damaged in shipment to Austin Sound. The damage is minor, and Austin decides to keep the CD player in exchange for a $10 allowance from JVC. To record this purchase allowance, Austin Sound makes this entry:

June 3	Accounts Payable	10.00	
	Inventory		10.00
	Received a purchase allowance.		

The return and the allowance have two effects:

1. They decrease Austin Sound's liability, which is why we debit Accounts Payable.
2. They decrease the net cost of the inventory, which is why we credit Inventory.

Assume that Austin Sound has not paid its debt to JVC. After the return ($70) and the allowance ($10) transactions are posted, Austin Sound's accounts will show these balances:

Inventory			
May 27	707.00	June 3	70.00
		June 4	10.00
Bal.	627.00		

Accounts Payable			
June 3	70.00	May 27	707.00
June 4	10.00		
		Bal.	627.00

■ Daily Exercise 5-6
■ Daily Exercise 5-8
■ Daily Exercise 5-9

Austin Sound's cost of the *inventory* is $627, and Austin Sound owes JVC $627 on *account payable.*

Recording Transportation Costs: Who Pays?

The transportation cost of moving inventory from seller to buyer can be significant. The purchase agreement specifies FOB terms to indicate who pays the shipping charges. *FOB* means *free on board.* FOB governs (1) when legal title to the goods passes from seller to buyer, and (2) who pays the freight.

- Under FOB *shipping point* terms, title passes when the inventory leaves the seller's place of business—the shipping point. The buyer owns the goods while they are in transit and therefore pays the transportation cost.
- Under FOB *destination* terms, title passes when the goods reach the destination, so the seller pays the transportation cost.

Exhibit 5-4 summarizes FOB terms.

Working It Out Austin Sound purchases $1,000 of merchandise on account, with terms 2/10, n/30 on September 15. Austin returns $100 of merchandise for credit on September 20, then makes payment in full on September 25. Journalize these transactions.

Answer: Three separate journal entries are needed here. The initial purchase is recorded as follows:

Sep. 15	Inventory	1,000	
	Accounts Payable		1,000

The second entry decreases the payable and the inventory for the amount of the return, as follows:

Sep. 20	Accounts Payable	100	
	Inventory		100

The third entry records payment. The payable is now only $900, the $1,000 initial purchase minus the $100 merchandise return. Because Austin is paying within the discount period, it can take a 2% discount (terms are 2/10, net 30, and Austin is paying within ten days). This discount is $18 ($900 × 0.02). The cash payment thus becomes $882 ($900 – $18).

Total debits must always equal total credits. At this point, debits = $900 and credits = $882, so we must adjust the Inventory account for the $18 discount. The payment entry is

Sep. 25	Accounts Payable.................	900	
	Cash		882
	Inventory......................		18

FREIGHT IN FOB shipping point terms are most common, so the buyer generally pays the shipping cost. A freight cost that the buyer pays on an inventory purchase is called *freight in*. In accounting, the cost of an asset includes all costs incurred to bring the asset to its intended use. For inventory, cost therefore includes the

- *Net cost* after all discounts have been subtracted, plus
- *Freight* (transportation, or shipping) costs to be paid

To record the payment for freight in, the buyer debits Inventory and credits Cash or Accounts Payable for the amount. Suppose Austin Sound receives a $60 shipping bill directly from the freight company. Austin Sound's entry to record payment of the freight charge is

June 1	Inventory......................	60	
	Cash		60
	Paid a freight bill.		

EXHIBIT 5-4
FOB Terms

	FOB Shipping Point	FOB Destination
When does the title pass to the buyer?	Shipping point	Destination
Who pays the transportation cost?	Buyer	Seller

The freight charge increases the final cost of the inventory to $687, as follows:

Inventory			
May 27	707.00	June 3	70.00
June 1	60.00	June 4	10.00
Bal.	687.00		

Any discounts would be computed only on the account payable to the seller, not on the transportation costs, because the freight company offers no discount.

Under FOB shipping point terms, the seller sometimes prepays the transportation cost as a convenience and lists this cost on the invoice. The buyer can debit Inventory for the combined cost of the inventory and the shipping cost because both costs apply to the merchandise. A $5,000 purchase of goods, coupled with a related freight charge of $400, would be recorded as follows:

March 12	Inventory	5,400	
	Accounts Payable		5,400
	Purchased on account including freight.		

If the buyer pays within the discount period, the discount will be computed on the $5,000 merchandise cost, not on the $5,400. No discount is offered on transportation cost. For example, a 2% discount would be $100 ($5,000 × 0.02).

FREIGHT OUT The cost of freight charges paid to ship goods sold to customers is called *freight out.* Freight out is delivery expense, which is paid by the seller, not by the purchaser. Delivery expense is an operating expense for the seller. It is debited to the Delivery Expense account.

Alternative Procedures for Purchase Discounts, Returns and Allowances, and Transportation Costs

Some businesses keep detailed records of purchase discounts, returns and allowances, and transportation costs. For example, Austin Sound may receive defective CD players from an off-brand manufacturer. In recording purchase returns, Austin Sound can credit a special account, Purchase Returns and Allowances, which serves as a running record of the defective merchandise. The Purchase Returns and Allowances account carries a credit balance and is a contra account to Inventory. Freight In can be debited for transportation costs. Then, for reporting on the financial statements, these accounts can be combined with the Inventory account as follows to determine the total cost of inventory (amounts assumed):

Inventory		$35,000
Less: Purchase discounts	$(700)	
Purchase returns and allowances	(800)	(1,500)
Net purchases of inventory		33,500
Freight in		2,100
Total cost of inventory		$35,600

Selling Inventory and Recording Cost of Goods Sold

The sale of inventory may be for cash or on account, as Exhibit 5-2 shows.

CASH SALE Sales of retailers, such as grocery stores and restaurants, are often for cash. Cash sales of $3,000 would be recorded by debiting Cash and crediting Sales Revenue as follows:

Jan. 9	Cash	3,000	
	Sales Revenue		3,000
	Cash sale.		

To update the inventory records, the business also must decrease the Inventory balance. Suppose these goods cost the seller $1,900. An accompanying entry is needed to transfer the $1,900 cost of the goods—not their selling price of $3,000—from the Inventory account to Cost of Goods Sold as follows:

Jan. 9	Cost of Goods Sold	1,900	
	Inventory		1,900
	Recorded the cost of goods sold.		

The recording of cost of goods sold along with sales revenue is an example of the matching principle (Chapter 3, p. 95)—matching expense against revenue to measure net income.

Cost of goods sold (also called cost of sales) is the largest single expense of most merchandisers, such as May Department Stores, JVC, and Austin Sound. The Cost of Goods Sold account keeps a current balance throughout the period as transactions are journalized and posted.

After posting, the Cost of Goods Sold account holds the cost of the merchandise sold ($1,900 in this case):

Inventory			
Purchases (amount assumed)	50,000	Jan. 9	1,900

Cost of Goods Sold			
Jan. 9	1,900		

The computer automatically records the cost of goods sold entry when the cashier keys in the code number of the inventory that is sold. Optical scanners perform this task in most stores.

SALE ON ACCOUNT Most sales in the United States are made on account (on credit). A $5,000 sale on account is recorded by a debit to Accounts Receivable and a credit to Sales Revenue, as follows:

Jan. 11	Accounts Receivable	5,000	
	Sales Revenue		5,000
	Sale on account.		

If we assume that these goods cost the seller $2,900, the accompanying cost of goods sold and inventory entry is

Jan. 11	Cost of Goods Sold	2,900	
	Inventory		2,900
	Recorded the cost of goods sold.		

After the recording of the January 9 and 11 transactions, sales revenue is $8,000 ($3,000 + $5,000). Cost of goods sold totals $4,800 ($1,900 + $2,900).

The seller records the related cash receipt on account as follows:

Jan. 19	Cash	5,000	
	Accounts Receivable		5,000
	Collection on account.		

Thinking It Over Why is there no January 19 entry to Sales Revenue, Cost of Goods Sold, or Inventory?

Answer: On January 19, the seller merely receives one asset—Cash—in place of another asset—Accounts Receivable. The sales revenue, the related cost of goods sold, and the decrease in inventory for the goods sold were recorded on January 11. Examine the two entries on January 11.

Offering Sales Discounts and Sales Returns and Allowances

We just saw that purchase discounts and purchase returns and allowances decrease the cost of inventory purchases. In the same way, **sales discounts** and **sales returns and allowances,** which are contra accounts to Sales Revenue, decrease the net amount of revenue earned on sales.

Sales Discount. Reduction in the amount receivable from a customer, offered by the seller as an incentive for the customer to pay promptly. A contra account to Sales Revenue.

Sales Returns and Allowances. Decreases in the seller's receivable from a customer's return of merchandise or from granting the customer an allowance from the amount owed to the seller. A contra account to Sales Revenue.

Credit-balance account		Debit balance accounts				Credit subtotal (*not* a separate account)
Sales Revenue	−	Sales Discounts	−	Sales Returns and Allowances	=	Net sales revenue*

This equation is useful for calculating net sales. Note that sales discounts can be given on both goods and services.

Companies keep close watch on their customers' paying habits and on their own sales of defective and unsuitable merchandise. They maintain separate accounts for Sales Discounts and Sales Returns and Allowances. Now let's examine a sequence of the sale transactions of JVC. Assume JVC is selling to Austin Sound.

On July 7, JVC sells stereo components for $7,200 on credit terms of 2/10 n/30. These goods cost JVC $4,700. JVC's entries to record this credit sale and the related cost of the goods sold are

July 7	Accounts Receivable	7,200	
	Sales Revenue		7,200
	Sale on account.		

July 7	Cost of Goods Sold	4,700	
	Inventory		4,700
	Recorded the cost of goods sold.		

Assume that the buyer returns goods that sold for $600. JVC records the sales return and the related decrease in Accounts Receivable as follows:

July 12	Sales Returns and Allowances	600	
	Accounts Receivable		600
	Received returned goods.		

JVC receives the returned merchandise and updates the inventory records. JVC must also decrease cost of goods sold as follows (these goods cost JVC $400):

July 12	Inventory	400	
	Cost of Goods Sold		400
	Returned goods to inventory.		

Suppose JVC grants to the buyer a $100 sales allowance for damaged goods. Austin Sound gets to subtract $100 from the amount it will pay JVC. JVC journalizes this transaction by debiting Sales Returns and Allowances and crediting Accounts Receivable as follows:

July 15	Sales Returns and Allowances	100	
	Accounts Receivable		100
	Granted a sales allowance for damaged goods.		

*Often abbreviated as Net sales.

No inventory entry is needed for a sales allowance transaction because the seller receives no returned goods from the customer. Instead, JVC will simply receive less cash from the customer.

After the preceding entries are posted, all the accounts have up-to-date balances. Accounts Receivable has a $6,500 debit balance, as follows:

Accounts Receivable			
July 7	7,200	July 12	600
		15	100
Bal.	6,500		

On July 17, the last day of the discount period, JVC collects $4,000 of this receivable. Assume JVC allows customers to take discounts on all amounts JVC receives within the discount period. JVC's cash receipt is $3,920 [$4,000 – ($4,000 × 0.02)], and the collection entry is

- Daily Exercise 5-5
- Daily Exercise 5-7
- Daily Exercise 5-10

July 17	Cash	3,920	
	Sales Discounts ($4,000 × 0.02)	80	
	Accounts Receivable		4,000
	Cash collection within the discount period.		

Suppose that JVC collects the remainder, $3,000, on July 28. That date is after the discount period, so there is no sales discount. To record this collection on account, JVC debits Cash and credits Accounts Receivable for the same amount, as follows:

July 28	Cash	3,000	
	Accounts Receivable		3,000
	Cash collection within the discount period.		

In Exhibit 5-1, The May Department Stores Company—like most other businesses—reports only the net sales figure to the public. But May managers use the return and allowance data to track customer satisfaction and product quality.

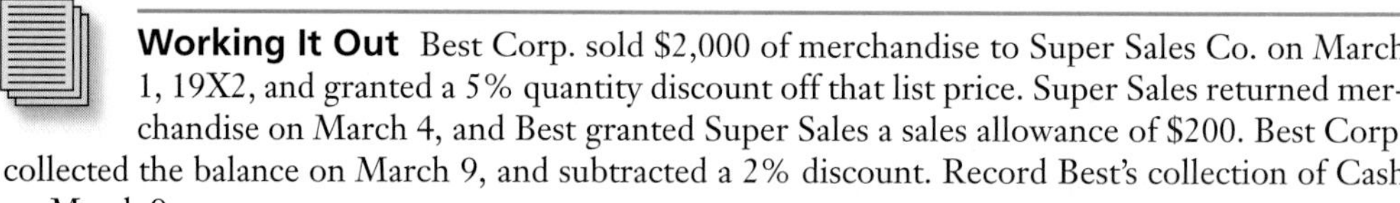

Working It Out Best Corp. sold $2,000 of merchandise to Super Sales Co. on March 1, 19X2, and granted a 5% quantity discount off that list price. Super Sales returned merchandise on March 4, and Best granted Super Sales a sales allowance of $200. Best Corp. collected the balance on March 9, and subtracted a 2% discount. Record Best's collection of Cash on March 9.

Answer

Cash	1,666[1]	
Sales Discounts ($1,700 × 0.02)	34	
Accounts Receivable ($2,000 – $100 – $200)		1,700

[1]$2,000 – .05($2,000) = $1,900
$1,900 – $200 = $1,700
$1,700 – .02($1,700) = $1,666

SUMMARY PROBLEM FOR YOUR REVIEW — MID-CHAPTER

Brun Sales Company engaged in the following transactions during June of the current year:

June 3	Purchased inventory on credit terms of 1/10 net eom (end of month), $1,610.
9	Returned 40% of the inventory purchased on June 3. It was defective.
12	Sold goods for cash, $920 (cost, $550).
15	Purchased goods of $5,100, less a $100 quantity discount. Credit terms were 3/15 net 30.
16	Paid a $260 freight bill on goods purchased.

June 18	Sold inventory on credit terms of 2/10 n/30, $2,000 (cost, $1,180).
22	Received damaged goods from the customer of the June 18 sale, $800 (cost, $480).
24	Borrowed money from the bank to take advantage of the discount offered on the June 15 purchase. Signed a note payable to the bank for the net amount.
24	Paid supplier for goods purchased on June 15, less all discounts.
28	Received cash in full settlement of the account from the customer who purchased inventory on June 18.
29	Paid the amount owed on account from the purchase of June 3, less the June 9 return.
30	Purchased inventory for cash, $900, less a quantity discount of $35.

REQUIRED

1. Journalize the preceding transactions. Explanations are not required.
2. Set up T-accounts and post the journal entries to show the ending balances in the Inventory and the Cost of Goods Sold accounts.
3. Assume that the note payable signed on June 24 requires the payment of $95 interest expense. Was borrowing funds to take advantage of the cash discount a wise or unwise decision?

SOLUTION

REQUIREMENT 1

Date	Accounts	Debit	Credit
June 3	Inventory	1,610	
	Accounts Payable		1,610
9	Accounts Payable ($1,610 × 0.40)	644	
	Inventory		644
12	Cash	920	
	Sales Revenue		920
12	Cost of Goods Sold	550	
	Inventory		550
15	Inventory ($5,100 – $100)	5,000	
	Accounts Payable		5,000
16	Inventory	260	
	Cash		260
18	Accounts Receivable	2,000	
	Sales Revenue		2,000
18	Cost of Goods Sold	1,180	
	Inventory		1,180
22	Sales Returns and Allowances	800	
	Accounts Receivable		800
22	Inventory	480	
	Cost of Goods Sold		480
24	Cash [$5,000 – 0.03($5,000)]	4,850	
	Note Payable		4,850
24	Accounts Payable	5,000	
	Inventory ($5,000 × 0.03)		150
	Cash ($5,000 × 0.97)		4,850
28	Cash [($2,000 – $800) × 0.98]	1,176	
	Sales Discounts [($2,000 – $800) × 0.02]	24	
	Accounts Receivable ($2,000 – $800)		1,200
29	Accounts Payable ($1,610 – $644)	966	
	Cash		966
30	Inventory ($900 – $35)	865	
	Cash		865

REQUIREMENT 2

Inventory

	Debit		Credit
June 3	1,610	June 9	644
15	5,000	12	550
16	260	18	1,180
22	480	24	150
30	865		
Bal.	5,691		

Cost of Goods Sold

	Debit		Credit
June 12	550	June 22	480
18	1,180		
Bal.	1,250		

REQUIREMENT 3

The decision to borrow funds was wise because the discount ($150) exceeded the interest paid on the amount borrowed ($95). Thus the entity was $55 better off as a result of its decision.

Adjusting and Closing the Accounts of a Merchandising Business

Objective 3

Adjust and close the accounts of a merchandising business

A merchandising business adjusts and closes the accounts much as a service entity does. The steps of this end-of-period process are the same: If a work sheet is used, the trial balance is entered, and the work sheet is completed to determine net income or net loss. The work sheet provides the data for journalizing the adjusting and closing entries and for preparing the financial statements.

Adjusting Inventory Based on a Physical Count

". . . virtually all businesses, such as the bookstore chain Barnes & Noble, Inc., take a physical count of inventory at least once each year."

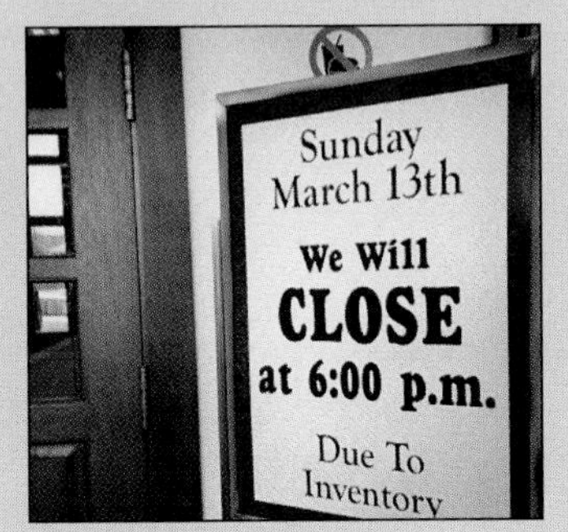

In theory, the Inventory account stays current at all times. However, the actual amount of inventory on hand may differ from what the books show. Theft losses and damage occur. Also, accounting errors can require adjustments to the Inventory Account. For this reason, virtually all businesses, such as the bookstore chain Barnes & Noble, Inc., take a physical count of inventory at least once each year. The most common time for a business to count its inventory is at the end of the fiscal year, before the financial statements are prepared. The business then adjusts the Inventory account to the correct amount on the basis of the physical count.

Exhibit 5-5, Austin Sound's trial balance at December 31, 19X6, lists a $40,500 balance for inventory. With no shrinkage—due to theft or error—the business should have on hand inventory costing $40,500. But on December 31, when Mr. Ernest, the owner of Austin Sound, counts the merchandise in the store, the total cost of the goods on hand comes to only $40,200. Austin Sound then records the $300 of inventory shrinkage with this adjusting entry:

Dec. 31	Cost of Goods Sold................................	300	
	Inventory ($40,500 – $40,200).........		300

This entry brings Inventory and Cost of Goods Sold to their correct balances. Austin Sound's December 31, 19X6, adjustment data, including this inventory information [item (b)], are given at the bottom of Exhibit 5-5.

The physical count can indicate that more inventory is present than the books show. Austin Sound may have made a purchase it did not record. This would be entered the standard way: Debit Inventory and credit Cash or Accounts Payable.

If the reason for the excess inventory cannot be identified, the business adjusts the accounts by debiting Inventory and crediting Cost of Goods Sold. To illustrate a merchandiser's adjusting and closing process, let's use Austin Sound's December 31, 19X6, trial balance in Exhibit 5-5. All the new accounts—Inventory, Cost of Goods Sold, and the contra accounts—are highlighted for emphasis. The additional data item (b) gives the ending inventory figure $40,200.

Preparing and Using the Work Sheet of a Merchandising Business

The Exhibit 5-6 work sheet is similar to the work sheets we have seen so far, but there are a few differences. This work sheet does not include adjusted trial balance columns. In most accounting systems, a single operation combines trial balance amounts with the adjustments and extends the adjusted balances directly to the income statement and balance sheet columns. Therefore, to reduce clutter, the adjusted trial balance columns are omitted.

This work sheet is slightly different from the one introduced in the Chapter 4 acetates following p. 138—it contains four pairs of columns, not five.

ACCOUNT TITLE COLUMNS The trial balance lists a number of accounts without balances. Ordinarily, these accounts are affected by the adjusting process. Examples include Interest Receivable, Wages Payable, and Depreciation Expense. The accounts are listed in

AUSTIN SOUND STEREO CENTER Trial Balance December 31, 19X6		
Cash	$ 2,850	
Accounts receivable	4,600	
Note receivable, current	8,000	
Interest receivable		
Inventory	40,500	
Supplies	650	
Prepaid insurance	1,200	
Furniture and fixtures	33,200	
Accumulated depreciation		$ 2,400
Accounts payable		47,000
Unearned sales revenue		2,000
Wages payable		
Interest payable		
Note payable, long-term		12,600
C. Ernest, capital		25,900
C. Ernest, withdrawals	54,100	
Sales revenue		168,000
Sales discounts	1,400	
Sales returns and allowances	2,000	
Interest revenue		600
Cost of goods sold	90,500	
Wage expense	9,800	
Rent expense	8,400	
Depreciation expense		
Insurance expense		
Supplies expense		
Interest expense	1,300	
Total	$258,500	$258,500

Additional data at December 31, 19X6:

a. Interest revenue earned but not yet collected, $400.
b. Inventory on hand, $40,200.
c. Supplies on hand, $100.
d. Prepaid insurance expired during the year, $1,000.
e. Depreciation, $600.
f. Unearned sales revenue earned during the year, $1,300.
g. Accrued wage expense, $400.
h. Accrued interest expense, $200.

EXHIBIT 5-5
Trial Balance

the order they appear in the ledger. If additional accounts are needed, they can be entered at the bottom of the work sheet, above the net income amount.

TRIAL BALANCE COLUMNS Examine the Inventory account in the trial balance. Inventory has a balance of $40,500 before the physical count at the end of the year. Cost of Goods Sold's balance is $90,500 before any adjustment based on the physical count. We shall assume that any difference between the Inventory amount on the trial balance ($40,500) and the correct amount based on the physical count ($40,200) is unexplained and should be debited or credited directly to Cost of Goods Sold.

ADJUSTMENTS COLUMNS The adjustments are similar to those discussed in Chapters 3 and 4. The adjustments may be entered in any order desired. The debit amount of each entry should equal the credit amount, and total debits should equal total credits. You should review the adjusting data in Exhibit 5-5 to reassure yourself that the adjustments are correct.

INCOME STATEMENT COLUMNS The income statement columns on the work sheet in Exhibit 5-6 contain adjusted amounts for the revenues and the expenses. Sales Revenue, for example, has an adjusted balance of $169,300.

AUSTIN SOUND STEREO CENTER
Accounting Work Sheet
Year Ended December 31, 19X6

Account Title	Trial Balance		Adjustments		Income Statement		Balance Sheet	
	Debit	Credit	Debit	Credit	Debit	Credit	Debit	Credit
Cash	2,850						2,850	
Accounts receivable	4,600						4,600	
Note receivable, current	8,000						8,000	
Interest receivable			(a) 400				400	
Inventory	**40,500**			**(b) 300**			**40,200**	
Supplies	650			(c) 550			100	
Prepaid insurance	1,200			(d) 1,000			200	
Furniture and fixtures	33,200						33,200	
Accumulated depreciation		2,400		(e) 600				3,000
Accounts payable		47,000						47,000
Unearned sales revenue		2,000	(f) 1,300					700
Wages payable				(g) 400				400
Interest payable				(h) 200				200
Note payable, long-term		12,600						12,600
C. Ernest, capital		25,900						25,900
C. Ernest, withdrawals	54,100						54,100	
Sales revenue		168,000		(f) 1,300		169,300		
Sales discounts	1,400				1,400			
Sales returns and allowances	2,000				2,000			
Interest revenue		600		(a) 400		1,000		
Cost of goods sold	**90,500**		**(b) 300**		**90,800**			
Wage expense	9,800		(g) 400		10,200			
Rent expense	8,400				8,400			
Depreciation expense			(e) 600		600			
Insurance expense			(d) 1,000		1,000			
Supplies expense			(c) 550		550			
Interest expense	1,300		(h) 200		1,500			
	258,500	258,500	4,750	4,750	116,450	170,300	143,650	89,800
Net income					53,850			53,850
					170,300	170,300	143,650	143,650

EXHIBIT 5-6
Accounting Work Sheet
■ Daily Exercise 5-11

The *income statement* column subtotals indicate whether the business had a net income or a net loss.

- Net income: Total credits > Total debits
- Net loss: Total debits > Total credits

Austin Sound's total credits of $170,300 exceed the total debits of $116,450, so the company earned a net income.

Insert the net *income* amount in the debit column to bring total debits into agreement with total credits. Insert a net *loss* amount in the credit column to equalize total debits and total credits. Net income or net loss is then extended to the opposite column of the balance sheet.

BALANCE-SHEET COLUMNS The only new item in the balance sheet columns is Inventory. The balance listed in Exhibit 5-6 is the ending amount of $40,200, as determined by the physical count of goods on hand at the end of the period.

Preparing the Financial Statements of a Merchandising Business

Exhibit 5-7 presents Austin Sound's financial statements.

EXHIBIT 5-7
Financial Statements of Austin Sound Stereo Center

AUSTIN SOUND STEREO CENTER
Income Statement
Year Ended December 31, 19X6

Sales revenue		$169,300	
Less: Sales discounts	$(1,400)		
Sales returns and allowances	(2,000)	(3,400)	
Net sales revenue			$165,900
Cost of goods sold			90,800
Gross margin			75,100
Operating expenses:			
Wage expense		10,200	
Rent expense		8,400	
Insurance expense		1,000	
Depreciation expense		600	
Supplies expense		550	20,750
Operating income			54,350
Other revenue and (expense):			
Interest revenue		1,000	
Interest expense		(1,500)	(500)
Net income			$ 53,850

- Daily Exercise 5-14
- Daily Exercise 5-15

AUSTIN SOUND STEREO CENTER
Statement of Owner's Equity
Year Ended December 31, 19X6

C. Ernest, capital, December 31, 19X5	$25,900
Add: Net income	53,850
	79,750
Less: Withdrawals	(54,100)
C. Ernest, capital, December 31, 19X6	$25,650

AUSTIN SOUND STEREO CENTER
Balance Sheet
December 31, 19X6

Assets				**Liabilities**	
Current:				Current:	
Cash		$ 2,850		Accounts payable	$47,000
Accounts receivable		4,600		Unearned sales revenue	700
Note receivable		8,000		Wages payable	400
Interest receivable		400		Interest payable	200
Inventory		40,200		Total current liabilities	48,300
Prepaid insurance		200		Long-term:	
Supplies		100		Note payable	12,600
Total current assets		56,350		Total liabilities	60,900
Plant:				**Owner's Equity**	
Furniture and fixtures	$33,200				
Less: Accumulated depreciation	(3,000)	30,200		C. Ernest, capital	25,650
Total assets		$86,550		Total liabilities and owner's equity	$86,550

- Daily Exercise 5-16

Objective 4

Prepare a merchandiser's financial statements

INCOME STATEMENT The income statement reports **operating expenses,** which are those expenses other than cost of goods sold that are incurred in the entity's major line of business—merchandising. Austin Sound's operating expenses include wage expense, rent, insurance, depreciation of furniture and fixtures, and supplies expense. In Exhibit 5-1, May Department Stores' total operating expenses are $3,019 million for the year ended January 31, 1997.

Operating Expenses. Expenses, other than cost of goods sold, that are incurred in the entity's major line of business. Examples include rent, depreciation, salaries, wages, utilities, property tax, and supplies expense.

Many companies report their operating expenses in two categories:

- *Selling expenses* are those expenses related to marketing the company's products—sales salaries; sales commissions; advertising; depreciation, rent, utilities, and property taxes on store buildings; depreciation on store furniture; delivery expense; and so on.
- *General expenses* include office expenses, such as the salaries of the company president and office employees; depreciation, rent, utilities, property taxes on the home office building; and office supplies.

May Department Stores (Exhibit 5-1) groups selling, general, and administrative expenses together for reporting on the income statement.

Gross margin minus operating expenses plus any other operating revenues equals **operating income,** or **income from operations.** Many people view operating income as an important indicator of a business's performance because it measures the results of the entity's major ongoing activities.

Operating Income. Gross margin minus operating expenses plus any other operating revenues. Also called **income from operations.**

Other Revenue. Revenue that is outside the main operations of a business, such as a gain on the sale of plant assets.

Other Expense. Expense that is outside the main operations of a business, such as a loss on the sale of plant assets.

The last section of Austin Sound's income statement is **other revenue and expense.** This category reports revenues and expenses that are outside the main operations of the business. Examples include gains and losses on the sale of plant assets (not inventory) and gains and losses on lawsuits. Accountants have traditionally viewed Interest Revenue and Interest Expense as "other" items because they arise from loaning money and borrowing money. These are financing activities that are outside the operating scope of selling merchandise. May Department Stores (Exhibit 5-1) lists Interest expense among the operating expenses, also a common practice.

The bottom line of the income statement is net income:

Net income = Total revenues and gains − Total expenses and losses

We often hear the term *bottom line* used to refer to a final result. *Bottom line* originated from the position of net income on the income statement.

STATEMENT OF OWNER'S EQUITY A merchandiser's statement of owner's equity looks exactly like that of a service business. In fact, you cannot determine whether the entity sells merchandise or services from looking at the statement of owner's equity.

BALANCE SHEET If the business is a merchandiser, the balance sheet shows inventory as a major current asset. In contrast, service businesses usually have no inventory at all or minor amounts of inventory.

To solidify your understanding of how the financial statements are prepared, you should trace the amounts in the work sheet (Exhibit 5-6) to the statements in Exhibit 5-7.

Journalizing the Adjusting and Closing Entries for a Merchandising Business

Exhibit 5-8 presents Austin Sound's adjusting entries, which are similar to those you have seen previously, except for the inventory adjustment [entry (b)]. The closing entries in the exhibit also follow the pattern illustrated in Chapter 4.

The adjusting and closing entries here are very similar to those discussed in Chapter 4, pp. 145 and 147. The closing entries also close the Cost of Goods Sold expense account for accumulating costs in the next period.

The *first closing entry* debits the revenue accounts for their ending balances. The offsetting credit of $170,300 transfers the sum of total revenues to Income Summary. This amount comes directly from the credit column of the income statement on the work sheet (Exhibit 5-6).

The *second closing entry* includes credits to Cost of Goods Sold, to the contra revenue accounts (Sales Discounts and Sales Returns and Allowances), and to the expense accounts. The offsetting $116,450 debit to Income Summary represents the amount of

Concept Highlight

EXHIBIT 5-8
Adjusting and Closing Entries for a Merchandiser

	Journal		
	Adjusting Entries		
a. Dec. 31	Interest Receivable	400	
	Interest Revenue		400
b. 31	Cost of Goods Sold	300	
	Inventory		300
c. 31	Supplies Expense ($650 – $100)	550	
	Supplies		550
d. 31	Insurance Expense	1,000	
	Prepaid Insurance		1,000
e. 31	Depreciation Expense	600	
	Accumulated Depreciation		600
f. 31	Unearned Sales Revenue	1,300	
	Sales Revenue		1,300
g. 31	Wage Expense	400	
	Wages Payable		400
h. 31	Interest Expense	200	
	Interest Payable		200
	Closing Entries		
1. Dec. 31	Sales Revenue	169,300	
	Interest Revenue	1,000	
	Income Summary		170,300
2. 31	Income Summary	116,450	
	Cost of Goods Sold		90,800
	Sales Discounts		1,400
	Sales Returns and Allowances		2,000
	Wage Expense		10,200
	Rent Expense		8,400
	Depreciation Expense		600
	Insurance Expense		1,000
	Supplies Expense		550
	Interest Expense		1,500
3. 31	Income Summary ($170,300 – $116,450)	53,850	
	C. Ernest, Capital		53,850
4. 31	C. Ernest, Capital	54,100	
	C. Ernest, Withdrawals		54,100

■ Daily Exercise 5-12
■ Daily Exercise 5-13

total expenses plus the contra revenues, which come from the debit column of the income statement on the work sheet.

The *last two closing entries* close net income from Income Summary to the Capital account and also close the owner Withdrawals into the Capital account. Study Exhibits 5-6, 5-7, and 5-8 carefully because they illustrate the entire end-of-period process that leads to the financial statements. As you progress through this book, refer to these exhibits to refresh your understanding of the adjusting and closing process for a merchandising business.

Learning Tip: Here is an easy way to remember the closing process. First look at the work sheet. Then

1. Debit all income statement accounts with a credit balance. Credit Income Summary for the total of all these debits.
2. Credit all income statement accounts with a debit balance. Debit Income Summary for the total of all these credits.
3. Take the balance in the Income Summary account. If the account has a debit balance, there is a net loss; credit Income Summary for that amount, and debit Capital. If Income Summary has a credit balance, there is a net income; debit Income Summary for that amount, and credit Capital.
4. Look at the debit balance of Withdrawals in the balance-sheet column. Credit Withdrawals for its balance, and debit Capital for the same amount.

Income Statement Formats: Multi-Step and Single-Step

For a review of balance sheet formats, see Chapter 4, p. 153.

We have seen that the balance sheet appears in two formats: the report format and the account format. There are also two basic formats for the income statement: *multi-step* and *single-step*. A recent survey of 600 companies indicated that 69% use the multi-step format and 31% use the single-step format.

Multi-Step Income Statement

Multi-step Income Statement. Format that contains subtotals to highlight significant relationships. In addition to net income, it presents gross margin and operating income.

The **multi-step format** contains subtotals to highlight significant relationships. In addition to net income, it also presents gross margin and operating income, or income from operations. This format communicates a merchandiser's results of operations especially well because gross margin and income from operations are two key measures of operating performance. The May Department Store Company in Exhibit 5-1 uses the multi-step format. The income statements presented thus far in this chapter have also been multi-step. Austin Sound's multi-step income statement for the year ended December 31, 19X6, appears in Exhibit 5-7.

Single-Step Income Statement

Single-Step Income Statement. Format that groups all revenues together and then lists and deducts all expenses together without drawing any subtotals.

The **single-step format** groups all revenues together and then lists and deducts all expenses together without drawing any subtotals. IBM and Wal-Mart use this format. The single-step format has the advantage of listing all revenues together and all expenses together, as shown in Exhibit 5-9. Thus it clearly distinguishes revenues from expenses. The income statements in Chapters 1 through 4 were single-step. This format works well for service entities because they have no gross margin to report.

Most published financial statements are highly condensed. Appendix A at the end of the book gives the income statement of NIKE, Inc. Of course, condensed statements can be supplemented with desired details.

Using the Financial Statements for Decision Making: Two Key Ratios

Objective 5

Use the gross margin percentage and the inventory turnover ratio to evaluate a business

Merchandise inventory is the most important asset to a merchandising business because it captures the essence of the entity. To manage the firm, owners and managers focus on the best way to sell the inventory. They use several ratios to evaluate operations.

EXHIBIT 5-9
Single-Step Income Statement

AUSTIN SOUND STEREO CENTER
Income Statement
Year Ended December 31, 19X6

Revenues:	
Net sales (net of sales discounts, $1,400, and returns and allowances, $2,000)	$165,900
Interest revenue	1,000
Total revenues	166,900
Expenses:	
Cost of goods sold	$ 90,800
Wage expense	10,200
Rent expense	8,400
Interest expense	1,500
Insurance expense	1,000
Depreciation expense	600
Supplies expense	550
Total expenses	113,050
Net income	$ 53,850

The Gross Margin Percentage

A key decision-making tool for a merchandiser is related to gross margin, which is net sales minus cost of goods sold. Merchandisers strive to increase the **gross margin percentage,** which is computed as follows:

Gross Margin Percentage. Gross margin divided by net sales revenue. A measure of profitability. Also called **gross profit percentage.**

For Austin Sound Stereo Center (Exhibit 5-7)

$$\text{Gross margin percentage} = \frac{\text{Gross margin}}{\text{Net sales revenue}} = \frac{\$75{,}100}{\$165{,}900} = 0.453 = 45.3\%$$

The gross margin percentage (also called the *gross profit percentage*) is one of the most carefully watched measures of profitability. A 45% gross margin means that each dollar of sales generates 45 cents of gross profit. On average, the goods cost the seller 55 cents. For most firms, the gross margin percentage changes little from year to year. A small increase may signal an important rise in income, and vice versa for a decrease.

Exhibit 5-10 compares Austin Sound's gross margin to that of both May Department Stores and Wal-Mart.

The Rate of Inventory Turnover

Owners and managers strive to sell inventory as quickly as possible because it generates no profit until it is sold. The faster the sales occur, the higher the income. The slower the sales, the lower the income. Ideally, a business could operate with zero inventory. Most businesses, however, including retailers such as May Department Stores and Austin Sound, must keep goods on hand for customers. **Inventory turnover,** the ratio of cost of goods sold to average inventory, indicates how rapidly inventory is sold. It is computed as follows:

Inventory Turnover. Ratio of cost of goods sold to average inventory. Measures the number of times a company sells its average level of inventory during a year.

For Austin Sound Stereo Center (Exhibit 5-7)

$$\text{Inventory turnover} = \frac{\text{Cost of goods sold}}{\text{Average inventory}}$$

$$= \frac{\text{Cost of goods sold}}{(\text{Beginning inventory} + \text{Ending inventory})/2} = \frac{\$90{,}800}{(\$38{,}600^* + \$40{,}200)/2} = \begin{array}{c}\text{2.3 times per year} \\ \text{(about every 159 days)}\end{array}$$

Inventory turnover is usually computed for an annual period, and the relevant cost-of-goods sold figure is the amount for the entire year. Average inventory is computed from the beginning and ending balances. Austin Sound's beginning inventory would be taken from the business's balance sheet at the end of the preceding year. A high turnover rate is preferable to a low turnover rate. An increase in the turnover rate usually means higher profits.

■ Daily Exercise 5-17
■ Daily Exercise 5-18

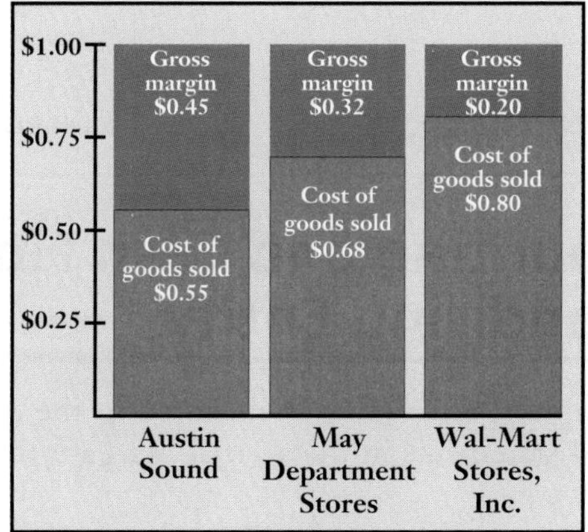

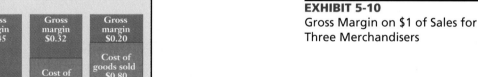

EXHIBIT 5-10
Gross Margin on $1 of Sales for Three Merchandisers

*Taken from balance sheet at the end of the preceding period.

EXHIBIT 5-11
Rate of Inventory Turnover for Three Merchandisers

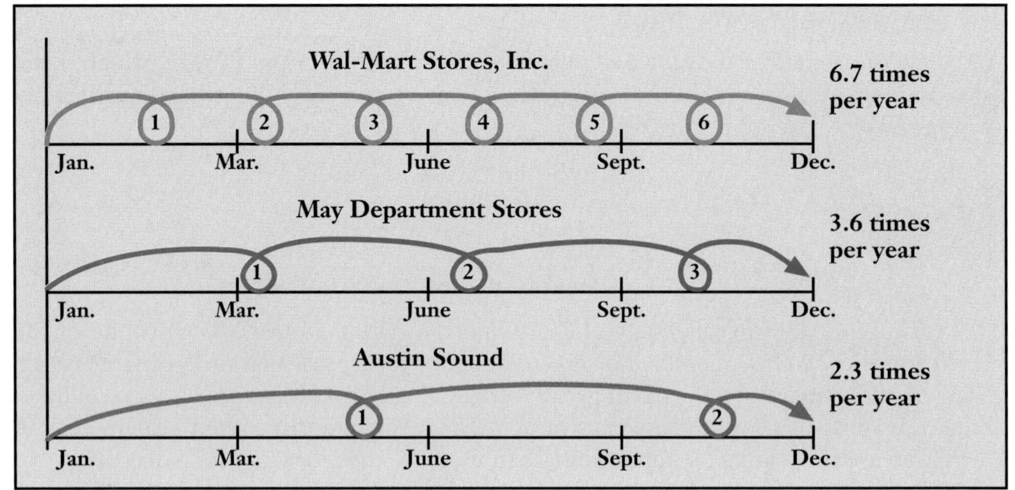

Inventory turnover varies from industry to industry. Grocery stores, for example, turn their goods over much faster than automobile dealers do. Drug stores have higher turnover than furniture stores do. Retailers of electronic products, such as Austin Sound, have an average turnover of 3.6 times per year. Austin Sound's turnover rate of 2.3 times per year suggests that Austin Sound is not very successful. Exhibit 5-11 compares the inventory turnover rate of Austin Sound, May Department Stores, and Wal-Mart Stores, Inc.

Exhibits 5-10 and 5-11 tell an interesting story. Wal-Mart sells a lot of inventory at a relatively low gross profit margin. Wal-Mart earns its profits by turning its inventory over rapidly—6.7 times during the year. May Department Stores sells more upscale merchandise and therefore turns its inventory over only 3.6 times per year.

Gross margin percentage and inventory turnover rate do not provide enough information to yield an overall conclusion about a merchandiser, but this example shows how owners and managers may use accounting information to evaluate a company.

Working It Out Calculate inventory turnover from the following data:

Beginning inventory	$ 2,350
Ending inventory	1,980
Cost of goods sold	15,310

Answer

$$\text{Inventory turnover} = \frac{\textbf{Cost of goods sold}}{\textbf{(Beginning inventory + Ending inventory)/2}}$$

Inventory turnover is

$$\frac{\$15{,}310}{(\$2{,}350 + \$1{,}980)/2} = \frac{\$15{,}310}{\$2{,}165} = 7.1 \text{ times per year}$$

Accrual Accounting and Cash Flows for a Merchandising Entity

As we saw in earlier chapters, accounting is anchored to the accrual basis. Two of the most important financial statements in the accrual basis are the income statement and the balance sheet.

- The *income statement* reports operating performance in terms of revenues, expenses, gross margin, and net income.
- The *balance sheet* reports financial position in terms of assets, liabilities, and owner's equity.

THE MAY DEPARTMENT STORES COMPANY Statement of Earnings (partial, adapted) Year Ended January 31, 1997	
Revenues	$12,000
Cost of sales	8,226

THE MAY DEPARTMENT STORES COMPANY Statement of Cash Flows (partial, adapted) Year Ended January 31, 1997	
Cash flows from Operating Activities:	
Receipts:	
Collections from customers	$11,628
Payments:	
To suppliers (for inventory)	(8,292)

EXHIBIT 5-12
Income Statement (partial, adapted) and Statement of Cash Flows (partial, adapted) of The May Department Stores Company (amounts in millions)

But the income statement and the balance sheet do not tell the complete financial story about a business.

Cash flows are also important because it takes cash to pay the bills. A company may earn a large amount of net income and have a good-looking balance sheet but go bankrupt because it is unable to pay its liabilities. How can this happen? The company may not be collecting cash from customers. The reason for all bankruptcies is simple: not enough cash. Cash is all-important in business.

In Chapter 1, we introduced the *statement of cash flows*, a required financial statement that is on the same level as the income statement and the balance sheet. The statement of cash flows (also called the cash-flow statement) reports the sources of the business's cash (cash receipts) and how the business spent its cash (cash payments). The statement of cash flows reports cash flows in three categories:

- Cash flows from *operating* activities
- Cash flows from *investing* activities
- Cash flows from *financing* activities

A merchandiser's purchases and sales of inventory are its most important *operating* transactions. Purchases require cash payments, and sales bring in cash receipts. Cash flows related to inventory purchases and sales are operating activities on the statement of cash flows. We discuss cash flows from investing and financing activities in later chapters.

Exhibit 5-12 shows the differences between the income statement and the statement of cash flows. The exhibit repeats the top part of The May Department Stores income statement that we saw in Exhibit 5-1. To the right is an adapted excerpt from the statement of cash flows of The May Department Stores Company.

Study the exhibit carefully. The income statement reports operating performance. The cash-flow statement reports cash flows. Revenues on the income statement are related to, but are *not* the same item as, Collections from customers on the statement of cash flows. Cost of goods sold (cost of sales), an expense on the income statement, is *not* the same as Payments to suppliers on the statement of cash flows.

As we move through this book, we will introduce topics from the statement of cash flows—one at a time. That way, you will be prepared to understand the various parts of the cash-flow statement when we cover it in Chapter 17.

Measuring Cost of Goods Sold and Inventory Purchases in the Periodic Inventory System

Objective 6
Compute cost of goods sold

The perpetual inventory accounting system that we have illustrated is designed to produce up-to-date records of inventory and cost of goods sold. That system provides the data for many decisions and for preparation of the financial statements. However, managers have other information needs that the perpetual inventory system does not meet. For example, the buyers for May Department Stores must know how much inventory to purchase in order to reach their goals.

Another computation of cost of goods sold—from the periodic inventory system—helps managers plan their purchases of inventory. The alternative computation of cost of

EXHIBIT 5-13
Measurement of Cost of Goods Sold in the Periodic Inventory System

■ Daily Exercise 5-19
■ Daily Exercise 5-20

Beginning inventory	$ 38,600
+ **Net purchases**	87,200*
+ Freight in	5,200
= Cost of goods available for sale	131,000
− Ending inventory	(40,200)
= Cost of goods sold	$ 90,800

*Computation of **Net purchases:**	
Purchases	$ 91,400
− Purchase discounts	(3,000)
− Purchase returns and allowances	(1,200)
= Net purchases	$ 87,200

goods sold is used so often in accounting that your education would be incomplete without it. We now turn to the alternative computation of cost of goods sold. The supplement at the end of the chapter covers the periodic inventory system in more detail.

Exhibit 5-13 gives the alternative computation of Austin Sound's cost of goods sold for 19X6.

Net Purchases. Purchases less purchase discounts and purchase returns and allowances.

Austin Sound began the year with some inventory. During the year, Austin Sound purchased more goods, also paying freight charges. The sum of these amounts make up Austin Sound's cost of goods available for sale. Note that **net purchases** equals purchases minus purchase discounts and purchase returns and allowances. Subtract ending inventory, and the result is cost of goods sold for the period. Exhibit 5-14 diagrams the alternative computation of cost of goods sold, with Austin Sound Stereo Center's amounts used for the illustration.

The Decision Guidelines feature summarizes some key decisions that a merchandising business must make. One key decision that the owner or manager of a merchandising business must make is

How much inventory should the business purchase in order to achieve its goals?

Here is how C. Ernest, the owner of Austin Sound, would decide how much inventory to buy (all numbers based on Exhibit 5-14):

■ Daily Exercise 5-21

1. Managers predict Cost of goods sold for the period	$ 90,800
2. Managers predict Ending inventory at the end of the period	40,200
3. Cost of goods available for sale = Sum of Ending inventory + Cost of goods sold	131,000
4. Subtract the period's beginning inventory	(38,600)
5. The difference is the amount of inventory to purchase (including Freight in) during the coming year	$ 92,400

EXHIBIT 5-14
T-Account Showing the Relationship Between the Inventory Account and Cost of Goods Sold in the Periodic Inventory System (Amounts for Austin Sound)

INVENTORY

Beginning balance	**38,600**		
Net purchases	**87,200**		
Freight in	**5,200**	**Cost of goods sold**	**90,800**
Ending balance	**40,200**		

This T-account shows that the *perpetual* and the *periodic* inventory systems compute the same amounts for ending inventory and for cost of goods sold:

- The *perpetual* system accumulates the balances of Inventory and Cost of Goods Sold throughout the period.
- The *periodic* system determines the correct amounts for Inventory and Cost of Goods Sold only at the end of the period.

The authors thank Betsy Willis for suggesting this exhibit.

DECISION GUIDELINES — Merchandising Operations and the Accounting Cycle

DECISION	GUIDELINES
How do merchandising operations differ from service operations?	• Merchandisers buy and sell *merchandise inventory* (often called inventory, or goods) • Service entities perform a *service.*
How do a merchandiser's financial statements differ from the financial statements of a service business?	**Balance sheet:** • Merchandiser has *inventory,* an asset. • Service business has no inventory.

Income statement:

Merchandiser

Sales revenue	$XXX
– Cost of goods sold	(X)
= Gross margin	$ XX
– Operating expenses	(X)
= Net income	$ X

Service Business

Service revenue	$XX
– Operating expense	(X)
= Net income	$ X

Statements of owner's equity:
No difference

DECISION	GUIDELINES
Which type of inventory system to use?	• *Perpetual system* shows the amount of inventory on hand (the asset) and the cost of goods sold (the expense) at all times. • *Periodic system* shows the correct balances of inventory and cost of goods sold only after a physical count of the inventory, which occurs at least once each year.
How do the adjusting and closing processes of merchandisers and service entities differ?	Very little. The merchandiser may have to *adjust* the Inventory account for spoilage and theft. The merchandiser must *close* the Cost of Goods Sold account. Service entities have no inventory to adjust or cost of goods sold to close.

How to format the merchandiser's income statement?

Multi-step format

Sales revenue	$XXX
– Cost of goods sold	(X)
= Gross margin	XX
– Operating expenses	(X)
+ Other revenues	X
= Net income	$ XX

Single-step format

Revenues:	
Sales revenue	$ XXX
Other revenues	X
Total revenues	XXXX
Expenses:	
Cost of goods sold	(X)
Operating expenses	(X)
Total expenses	(XX)
Net income	$ XX

How to evaluate inventory operations?

Two key ratios:

$$\text{Gross margin percentage*} = \frac{\text{Gross margin}}{\text{Net sales revenue}}$$

$$\text{Inventory turnover*} = \frac{\text{Cost of goods sold}}{\text{Average inventory}}$$

*In most cases—the higher, the better

How to determine the amount of cost of goods sold?

Can use the *cost of goods sold* model (assumed amounts):

Beginning inventory	$100
+ Net purchases and freight in	800
= Cost of goods available	900
– Ending inventory	(200)
= Cost of goods sold	$700

SUMMARY PROBLEM FOR YOUR REVIEW

The following trial balance and additional data are related to Jan King Distributing Company.

JAN KING DISTRIBUTING COMPANY Trial Balance December 31, 19X3		
Cash	$ 5,670	
Accounts receivable	37,100	
Inventory	60,500	
Supplies	3,930	
Prepaid rent	6,000	
Furniture and fixtures	26,500	
Accumulated depreciation		$ 21,200
Accounts payable		46,340
Salary payable		
Interest payable		
Unearned sales revenue		3,500
Note payable, long-term		35,000
Jan King, capital		23,680
Jan King, withdrawals	48,000	
Sales revenue		346,700
Sales discounts	10,300	
Sales returns and allowances	8,200	
Cost of goods sold	171,770	
Salary expense	82,750	
Rent expense	7,000	
Depreciation expense		
Utilities expense	5,800	
Supplies expense		
Interest expense	2,900	
Total	$476,420	$476,420

Additional data at December 31, 19X3:

a. Supplies used during the year, $2,580.
b. Prepaid rent in force, $1,000.
c. Unearned sales revenue still not earned, $2,400. The company expects to earn this amount during the next few months.
d. Depreciation. The furniture and fixtures' estimated useful life is 10 years, and they are expected to be worthless when they are retired from service.
e. Accrued salaries, $1,300.
f. Accrued interest expense, $600.
g. Inventory on hand, $65,800.

REQUIRED

1. Enter the trial balance on a work sheet and complete the work sheet.
2. Journalize the adjusting and closing entries at December 31. Post to the Income Summary account as an accuracy check on the entries affecting that account. The credit balance closed out of Income Summary should equal net income computed on the work sheet.
3. Prepare the company's multi-step income statement, statement of owner's equity, and balance sheet in account format. Draw arrows connecting the statements.
4. Compute the inventory turnover for 19X3. Inventory at December 31, 19X2, was $61,000. Turnover for 19X2 was 2.1. Would you expect Jan King Distributing Company to be more profitable or less profitable in 19X3 than in 19X2? Give your reason.

SOLUTION

REQUIREMENT 1

JAN KING DISTRIBUTING COMPANY
Accounting Work Sheet (Perpetual Inventory System)
Year Ended December 31, 19X3

Account Title	Trial Balance		Adjustments		Income Statement		Balance Sheet	
	Debit	Credit	Debit	Credit	Debit	Credit	Debit	Credit
Cash	5,670						5,670	
Accounts receivable	37,100						37,100	
Inventory	60,500		(g)5,300				65,800	
Supplies	3,930			(a) 2,580			1,350	
Prepaid rent	6,000			(b) 5,000			1,000	
Furniture and fixtures	26,500						26,500	
Accumulated depreciation		21,200		(d) 2,650				23,850
Accounts payable		46,340						46,340
Salary payable				(e) 1,300				1,300
Interest payable				(f) 600				600
Unearned sales revenue		3,500	(c)1,100					2,400
Note payable, long-term		35,000						35,000
Jan King, capital		23,680						23,680
Jan King, withdrawals	48,000						48,000	
Sales revenue		346,700		(c) 1,100		347,800		
Sales discounts	10,300				10,300			
Sales returns and allowances	8,200				8,200			
Cost of goods sold	171,770			(g) 5,300	166,470			
Salary expense	82,750		(e)1,300		84,050			
Rent expense	7,000		(b)5,000		12,000			
Depreciation expense			(d)2,650		2,650			
Utilities expense	5,800				5,800			
Supplies expense			(a)2,580		2,580			
Interest expense	2,900		(f) 600		3,500			
	476,420	476,420	18,530	18,530	295,550	347,800	185,420	133,170
Net income					52,250			52,250
					347,800	347,800	185,420	185,420

REQUIREMENT 2

Adjusting Entries

19X3			
Dec. 31	Supplies Expense	2,580	
	Supplies		2,580
31	Rent Expense	5,000	
	Prepaid Rent		5,000
31	Unearned Sales Revenue ($3,500 – $2,400)	1,100	
	Sales Revenue		1,100
31	Depreciation Expense ($26,500/10)	2,650	
	Accumulated Depreciation		2,650
31	Salary Expense	1,300	
	Salary Payable		1,300
31	Interest Expense	600	
	Interest Payable		600
31	Inventory ($65,800 – $60,500)	5,300*	
	Cost of Goods Sold		5,300

*Excess of inventory on hand over the balance in the Inventory account. This adjustment brings Inventory to its correct balance.

Closing Entries

19X3			
Dec. 31	Sales Revenue	347,800	
	Income Summary		347,800
31	Income Summary	295,550	
	Cost of Goods Sold		166,470
	Sales Discounts		10,300
	Sales Returns and Allowances		8,200
	Salary Expense		84,050
	Rent Expense		12,000
	Depreciation Expense		2,650
	Utilities Expense		5,800
	Supplies Expense		2,580
	Interest Expense		3,500
31	Income Summary ($347,800 – $295,550)	52,250	
	Jan King, Capital		52,250
31	Jan King, Capital	48,000	
	Jan King, Withdrawals		48,000

Income Summary

Clo.	295,550	Clo.	347,800
Clo.	52,250	Bal.	52,250

REQUIREMENT 3

JAN KING DISTRIBUTING COMPANY
Income Statement
Year Ended December 31, 19X3

Sales revenue		$347,800	
Less: Sales discounts	$(10,300)		
Sales returns and allowances	(8,200)	(18,500)	
Net sales revenue			$329,300
Cost of goods sold			166,470
Gross margin			162,830
Operating expenses:			
Salary expense		84,050	
Rent expense		12,000	
Utilities expense		5,800	
Depreciation expense		2,650	
Supplies expense		2,580	107,080
Income from operations			55,750
Other expense:			
Interest expense			3,500
Net income			$ 52,250

JAN KING DISTRIBUTING COMPANY
Statement of Owner's Equity
Year Ended December 31, 19X3

Jan King, capital, December 31, 19X2	$23,680
Add: Net income	52,250
	75,930
Less: Withdrawals	(48,000)
Jan King, capital, December 31, 19X3	$27,930

JAN KING DISTRIBUTING COMPANY Balance Sheet December 31, 19X3				
Assets			**Liabilities**	
Current:			Current:	
Cash		$ 5,670	Accounts payable	$ 46,340
Accounts receivable		37,100	Salary payable	1,300
Inventory		65,800	Interest payable	600
Supplies		1,350	Unearned sales revenue	2,400
Prepaid rent		1,000	Total current liabilities	50,640
Total current assets		110,920	Long-term:	
Plant:			Note payable	35,000
Furniture and fixtures	$26,500		Total liabilities	85,640
Less: Accumulated depreciation	(23,850)	2,650	**Owner's Equity**	
			Jan King, capital	27,930
			Total liabilities and	
Total assets		$113,570	owner's equity	$113,570

REQUIREMENT 4

$$\text{Inventory turnover} = \frac{\text{Cost of goods sold}}{\text{Average inventory}} = \frac{\$166,470}{(\$61,000 + \$65,800)/2} = 2.6$$

The increase in the rate of inventory turnover from 2.1 to 2.6 suggests higher profits in 19X3 than in 19X2.

Summary of Learning Objectives

1. ***Use sales and gross margin to evaluate a company.*** The major revenue of a merchandising business is *sales revenue*, or *sales*. The major expense is *cost of goods sold*. Net sales minus cost of goods sold is *gross margin*, or *gross profit*. This amount measures the business's success or failure in selling its products at a higher price than it paid for them.

2. ***Account for the purchase and sale of inventory.*** The *invoice* is the business document generated by a purchase or sale transaction. Most merchandising entities offer *discounts* to their customers and allow them to *return* unsuitable merchandise. They also grant *allowances* for damaged goods that the buyer chooses to keep. Discounts and Returns and Allowances are contra accounts to Sales Revenue.

The merchandiser's major asset is *inventory*. In a merchandising entity, the accounting cycle is from cash to inventory as the inventory is purchased for resale, and back to cash as the inventory is sold.

3. ***Adjust and close the accounts of a merchandising business.*** The end-of-period adjusting and closing process of a merchandising business is similar to that of a service business. In addition, a merchandiser adjusts inventory for theft losses, damage, and accounting errors.

4. ***Prepare a merchandiser's financial statements.*** The income statement may appear in the *single-step format* or the *multi-step format*. A single-step income statement has only two sections—one for revenues and the other for expenses—and a single income amount for net income. A multi-step income statement has subtotals for gross margin and income from operations. Both formats are widely used.

5. ***Use the gross margin percentage and the inventory turnover ratio to evaluate a business.*** Two key decision aids for a merchandiser are the *gross margin percentage* (gross margin/net sales revenue) and the *rate of inventory turnover* (cost of goods sold/average inventory). Increases in these measures usually signal an increase in profits.

6. ***Compute cost of goods sold.*** *Cost of goods sold* is the cost of the inventory that the business has sold. It is the largest single expense of most merchandising businesses. Cost of goods sold is the sum of the cost of goods sold amounts recorded during the period. In a periodic inventory system, Cost of goods sold = Beginning inventory + Purchases + Freight in − Ending inventory.

Accounting Vocabulary

cost of goods sold *(p. 182)*
cost of sales *(p. 182)*
gross margin *(p. 183)*
gross margin percentage *(p. 201)*
gross profit *(p. 183)*
gross profit percentage *(p. 201)*
income from operations *(p. 198)*
inventory turnover *(p. 201)*
invoice *(p. 185)*
multi-step income statement *(p. 200)*
net purchases *(p. 204)*
net sales *(p. 182)*
operating expenses *(p. 198)*
operating income *(p. 198)*
other expense *(p. 198)*
other revenue *(p. 198)*
periodic inventory system *(p. 184)*
perpetual inventory system *(p. 184)*
sales *(p. 182)*
sales discount *(p. 191)*
sales returns and allowances *(p. 191)*
sales revenue *(p. 182)*
single-step income statement *(p. 200)*

Questions

1. Gross margin is often mentioned in the business press as an important measure of success. What does gross margin measure, and why is it important?
2. Describe the operating cycle for (a) the purchase and cash sale of inventory, and (b) the purchase and sale of inventory on account.
3. Identify ten items of information on an invoice.
4. Indicate which accounts are debited and credited for (a) a credit purchase of inventory and the subsequent cash payment, and (b) a credit sale of inventory and the subsequent cash collection. Assume no discounts, returns, allowances, or freight.
5. Inventory costing $1,000 is purchased and invoiced on July 28 under terms of 3/10 n/30. Compute the payment amount on August 6. How much would the payment be on August 9? What explains the difference? What is the latest acceptable payment date under the terms of sale?
6. Inventory listed at $35,000 is sold subject to a quantity discount of $3,000 and under payment terms of 2/15 n/45. What is the net sales revenue on this sale if the customer pays within 15 days?
7. Name the new contra accounts introduced in this chapter.
8. Briefly discuss the similarity in computing supplies expense and computing cost of goods sold by the method shown in Exhibit 5-13 on page 204.
9. Why is the title Cost of Goods Sold especially descriptive? What type of account is Cost of Goods Sold?
10. Beginning inventory is $5,000, net purchases total $30,000, and freight in is $1,000. If ending inventory is $8,000, what is the cost of goods sold?
11. You are evaluating two companies as possible investments. One entity sells its services; the other is a merchandiser. How can you identify the merchandiser by examining the entities' balance sheets and income statements?
12. You are beginning the adjusting and closing process at the end of your company's fiscal year. Does the trial balance carry the final ending amount of inventory? Why or why not?
13. Give the adjusting entry for inventory if shrinkage is $9,100.
14. What is the identifying characteristic of the "other" category of revenues and expenses? Give an example of each.
15. Name and describe two formats for the income statements, and identify the type of business to which each format best applies.
16. List eight different operating expenses.
17. Which financial statement reports sales discounts and sales returns and allowances? Show how they are reported, using any reasonable amounts in your illustration.
18. Does a merchandiser prefer a high or a low rate of inventory turnover? Explain.
19. In general, what does a decreasing gross margin percentage, coupled with an increasing rate of inventory turnover, suggest about a business's pricing strategy?

Daily Exercises

Using sales, gross margin, and net income to evaluate a company ***(Obj. 1)***

DE5-1 Refer to Exhibit 5-1, page 182. Compare The May Department Stores Company operating performance for the years ended January 31, 1997 and 1996. Which year was better for the company's

- Sales?
- Gross margin?
- Net income?

For 1997, identify the title and the amount of May's

a. Gross revenue before subtracting any expenses
b. Excess of sales revenue over cost of goods sold
c. Bottom-line operating performance

Using sales, cost of goods sold, gross margin, and net income ***(Obj. 1)***

DE5-2 Compare the income statements of two merchandisers:

- The May Department Stores Company (Exhibit 5-1, page 182)
- Austin Sound Stereo Center (Exhibit 5-7, page 197)

For every item on the May income statement, give the title and the amount of the same item on Austin Sound's income statement. You can ignore May's three individual *expenses* and the related total of $3,019 million.

Using merchandising terminology ***(Obj. 1)***

DE5-3 Refer to The May Department Stores Company income statement in Exhibit 5-1, page 182. Give some alternative titles for the following items:

- Revenues
- Cost of sales
- Gross margin
- Net earnings

Recording purchase transactions ***(Obj. 2)***

DE5-4 Suppose a Lord & Taylor store purchases $25,000 of women's sportswear on account from Liz Claiborne, Inc. Credit terms are 2/10 net 30. Lord & Taylor pays electronically, and Liz Claiborne receives the money on the tenth day.

Journalize Lord & Taylor's (a) purchase and (b) payment transactions. What was Lord & Taylor's net cost of this inventory?
Note: Daily Exercise 5-5 covers this same situation for the seller.

Recording sales, cost of goods sold, and cash collections ***(Obj. 2)***

DE5-5 Liz Claiborne, Inc., sells $25,000 of women's sportswear to a Lord & Taylor store under credit terms of 2/10 net 30. Liz Claiborne's cost of the goods is $16,000, and Claiborne receives the appropriate amount of cash from Lord & Taylor on the tenth day.

Journalize Liz Claiborne's (a) sale, (b) cost of goods sold, and (c) cash receipt. How much gross margin did Liz Claiborne earn on this sale?
Note: Daily Exercise 5-4 covers the same situation for the buyer.

Recording purchase, purchase return, and cash payment transactions ***(Obj. 2)***

DE5-6 You may have shopped at The Gap. Suppose The Gap purchases 1,000 pairs of slacks on account for $30,000. Credit terms are 2/10 n/30. As part of this shipment, the supplier, Miralu Products of Hong Kong, shipped $6,000 worth of defective merchandise, which The Gap rejected and sent back to Miralu. The Gap then paid the balance within the discount period.

Journalize the following transactions for The Gap:

a. Purchase of inventory.
b. Return of defective goods.
c. Payment within the discount period.

Recording sale, sales return, and cash collection entries ***(Obj. 2)***

DE5-7 Refer to The Gap/Miralu Products situation in Daily Exercise 5-6. Record the three transactions on the books of the seller, Miralu Products. Assume Miralu keeps its records in U.S. dollars and that the goods cost Miralu $20,000. Miralu's transactions are

a. Sale of inventory and the related cost of goods sold.
b. The $6,000 sales return and the related receipt of defective goods (cost, $4,000) from the purchaser.
c. Collection of cash within the discount period.

Accounting for the purchase of inventory—quantity discount ***(Obj. 2)***

DE5-8 Toys "Я" Us purchases inventory from a variety of suppliers, including Mattel, Hasbro, and Tonka. Buying in large quantities, Toys "Я" Us receives a 10% quantity discount. Suppose Toys "Я" Us buys $100,000 worth of Lego toys on credit terms of 3/15 n/45. Unfortunately, the goods are damaged in shipment, so Toys "Я" Us returns $20,000 (original amount, before any discounts) of the merchandise to Lego.

How much must Toys "Я" Us pay Lego

a. After the discount period?
b. Within the discount period?

Recording purchase, purchase return, and cash payment transactions ***(Obj. 2)***

DE5-9 Refer to the Toys "Я" Us situation in Daily Exercise 5-8 and journalize the following transactions on the books of Toys "Я" Us:

a. Original purchase of the goods on May 6, 19X8.
b. Return of the damaged goods on May 13.
c. Payment on May 15. Before journalizing this transaction, it is helpful to post the first two transactions to the Accounts Payable T-account.

Explanations are not required.

Computing net sales and gross margin ***(Obj. 2)***

DE5-10 Intel Corporation, famous for the Pentium© processor that powers many personal computers, offers sales discounts to the computer companies to which Intel sells its products. Intel also allows its customers to return any defective processors. Suppose that during a recent period, Intel made sales of $800,000 on credit terms of 2/10 net 30. Assume that Intel received from customers sales returns of $12,000. Later, Intel collected cash within the discount period. Cost of goods sold for the period was $340,000 after all sales returns.

For this particular period, compute Intel's

a. Net sales revenue
b. Gross margin

Adjusting the accounts of a merchandiser ***(Obj. 3)***

DE5-11 Examine the work sheet of Austin Sound Stereo Center in Exhibit 5-6, page 196. Focus on adjusting entries (a) and (b). Which entry is exactly the same as for a service company? Which entry relates to a merchandiser only? Explain the reason for the merchandiser's adjusting entry.

Making closing entries ***(Obj. 3)***

DE5-12 Refer to the work sheet of Austin Sound Stereo Center in Exhibit 5-6, page 196. Based solely on the Income Statement columns of the work sheet, make two closing entries, as follows:

- Journalize the closing entry for the *first account* listed that must be closed at the end of the period.
- Journalize the closing entry for the *last account* listed on the work sheet (not net income, which is *not* an account).

All closing entries for revenues and expenses follow the pattern of the closing entries you just made. Now make the final two closing entries of Austin Sound Stereo Center:

- Journalize the closing entry for the Owner's Withdrawals account.
- Journalize the closing entry for net income.

Set up a T-account for the Owner's Capital account, and insert the balance from the work sheet. Then post your closing entries to the Capital account. Its ending balance should be the same as the amount reported on Austin Sound's balance sheet in Exhibit 5-7 on page 197. Is it?

Closing the accounts
(Obj. 3)

DE5-13 Refer to the income statement of The May Department Stores Company in Exhibit 5-1, page 182.

1. Identify every account on May's income statement that the company will close out at the end of the year. Make two closing entries for these accounts at January 31, 1997:
   - Close the revenue
   - Close the expenses
2. May's balance sheet reports the following selected accounts:
   - Merchandise inventories
   - Accounts payable
   - Land
   - Long-term debt
   - Other assets
   - Owners' equity

Which of these accounts does May close, if any?

Using a merchandiser's financial statements
(Obj. 4)

DE5-14 Examine the financial statements of Austin Sound Stereo Center in Exhibit 5-7, page 197. Identify every item, including subtotals and totals, that relates exclusively to a merchandiser and will not appear in the financial statements of a service entity.
Note: An early-payment discount, similar to a sales discount, can relate to a service entity because a service business can allow its customers to take a discount for early payment.

Preparing a merchandiser's income statement
(Obj. 4)

DE5-15 Dell Computer Corporation reported these figures in its January 31, 19X5 financial statements (adapted, and in millions):

Cash	**$ 43**	**Other assets (long-term)**	**$ 7**
Total operating expenses	**589**	**Other current liabilities**	**304**
Accounts payable	**447**	**Property and equipment**	**208**
Owners' equity	**652**	**Net sales revenue**	**3,475**
Long-term liabilities	**191**	**Other current assets**	**596**
Inventory	**293**	**Accounts receivable**	**538**
Cost of goods sold	**2,737**	**Accumulated depreciation**	**91**

Prepare Dell Computer's multi-step income statement for the year ended January 31, 19X5.

Preparing a merchandiser's balance sheet ***(Obj. 4)***

DE5-16 Use the data in Daily Exercise 5-15 to prepare Dell Computer's balance sheet at January 31, 19X5. Use the report format with all headings, and list accounts in proper order.

Computing the gross margin percentage and the rate of inventory turnover
(Obj. 5)

DE5-17 Refer to the Dell Computer situation in Daily Exercise 5-15. Compute Dell's gross margin percentage and rate of inventory turnover for 19X5. One year earlier, at January 31, 19X4, Dell's inventory balance was $220 million.

Contrasting accounting income and cash flows
(Obj. 4)

DE5-18 Lands' End, the catalog merchant, reported the following for the year ended January 31, 1997 (as adapted, with amounts in millions):

Cash payments for financing activities	**$ 28**	**Cash payments to suppliers**	**$ 573**
Cash collections from customers	**1,118**	**Selling, general, and administrative expenses**	**424**
Cash payments for investing activities	**18**	**Net sales revenue**	**1,119**
		Cost of sales	**609**

As an investor, you wonder which was greater, Lands' End's (a) gross margin, or (b) the company's excess of cash collections from customers over cash payments to suppliers? Compute both amounts to answer this question.

Computing cost of goods sold in a periodic inventory system ***(Obj. 6)***

DE5-19 At January 31, 1996, The May Department Stores Company had merchandise inventory of $2,134 million. During the year, May purchased inventory costing $8,472 million, including freight in. At January 31, 1997, May's inventory stood at $2,380 million.

1. Compute May's cost of goods sold as in the periodic inventory system.
2. Compare your cost-of-goods-sold figure to Exhibit 5-1, page 182. The two amounts should be equal. Are they?

Computing net sales, cost of goods sold, and gross margin in a periodic inventory system
(Obj. 6)

DE5-20 Bonnieux Chic, a boutique in Paris, France, had the following accounts in its accounting records at December 31, 19X7 (amounts in French francs, denoted as "F"):

Purchases	**F100,000**	**Freight in**	**F 5,000**
Sales discounts	**2,000**	**Purchase returns**	**3,000**
Inventory:		**Sales**	**200,000**
December 31, 19X6	**20,000**	**Purchase discounts**	**1,000**
December 31, 19X7	**30,000**	**Sales returns**	**4,000**

Compute the following for Bonnieux Chic:

1. Net sales revenue
2. Cost of goods sold
3. Gross margin

Computing inventory purchases
(Obj. 6)

DE5-21 The Gap, Inc., reported Cost of Goods Sold totaling $3,285 million. Ending inventory was $578 million, and beginning inventory was $483 million. How much inventory did The Gap purchase during the year?

Exercises

Evaluating a company's revenues, gross margin, operating income, and net income
(Obj. 1)

E5-1 Toys "Я" Us reported the following:

TOYS "Я" US, INC., AND SUBSIDIARIES
Consolidated Statements of Earnings (adapted)

(In millions)	**Fiscal Years Ended January 31, 1997**	**January 31, 1996**
Net sales	$9,932.4	$9,426.9
Costs and expenses:		
Cost of sales	6,892.5	6,592.3
Selling, advertising, general, and administrative	2,019.7	1,894.8
Depreciation	206.4	191.7
Other charges	59.5	396.6
Interest expense	98.6	103.3
Interest and other income	(17.4)	(17.4)
	9,259.3	9,161.3
Earnings before taxes on income	673.1	265.6
Taxes on income	245.7	117.5
Net earnings	$ 427.4	$ 148.1

TOYS "Я" US, INC., AND SUBSIDIARIES
Consolidated Balance Sheets (partial, adapted)

(In millions)	**January 31, 1997**	**January 31, 1996**
ASSETS		
Current Assets:		
Cash and cash equivalents	$ 760.9	$ 202.7
Accounts and other receivables	142.1	128.9
Merchandise inventories	2,214.6	1,999.5
Prepaid expenses and other current assets	42.0	87.8
Total Current Assets	$3,159.6	$2,418.9

REQUIRED

1. Is Toys "Я" Us a merchandising entity, a service business, or both? How can you tell? List the items in the Toys "Я" Us financial statements that influence your answer.
2. Compute Toys "Я" Us's gross margin for fiscal years 1997 and 1996. Did the gross margin increase or decrease in 1997? Is this a good sign or a bad sign about the company?
3. Write a brief memo to investors advising them of Toys "Я" Us's trend of sales, gross margin, and net income. Indicate whether the outlook for Toys "Я" Us is favorable or unfavorable, based on this trend. Use the following memo format:

Date:	____________________
To:	Investors
From:	Student Name
Subject:	Trend of sales, gross margin and net income for Toys "Я" Us

Journalizing purchase and sales transactions
(Obj. 2)

E5-2 Journalize, without explanations, the following transactions of The Gift House during the month of June:

June	3	Purchased $700 of inventory on account under terms of 2/10 n/eom (end of month) and FOB shipping point.
	7	Returned $300 of defective merchandise purchased on June 3.
	9	Paid freight bill of $30 on June 3 purchase.
	10	Sold inventory on account for $2,200. Payment terms on the remainder were 2/15 n/30. These goods cost The Gift House $1,300.
	12	Paid amount owed on credit purchase of June 3, less the discount and the return.
	16	Granted a sales allowance of $800 on the June 10 sale.
	23	Received cash from June 10 customer in full settlement of her debt, less the allowance and the discount.

Journalizing transactions from a purchase invoice
(Obj. 2)

E5-3 As the proprietor of Kendrick Tire Company, you receive the following invoice from a supplier:

ABC TIRE WHOLESALE DISTRIBUTORS, INC.
2600 Commonwealth Avenue
Boston, Massachusetts 02215

Invoice date: May 14, 19X3 **Payment terms:** 2/10 n/30

Sold to: Kendrick Tire Co.
4219 Crestwood Parkway
Lexington, Mass. 02173

Quantity Ordered	Description	Quantity Shipped	Price	Amount
6	P135–X4 Radials	6	$37.14	$ 222.84
8	L912 Belted-bias	8	41.32	330.56
14	R39 Truck tires	10	50.02	500.20
	Total			$1,053.60

Due date:	Amount:
May 24, 19X3	$1,032.53
May 25 through June 13, 19X3	$1,053.60

Paid:

REQUIRED

1. Record the May 15 purchase on account. Carry to the nearest cent throughout.
2. The R39 truck tires were ordered by mistake and were therefore returned to ABC. Journalize the return on May 19.
3. Record the May 22 payment of the amount owed.

E5-4 On April 30, Rapaport Jewelers purchased inventory of $5,000 on account from La Roche Fine Gems, a jewelry importer. Terms were 3/15 net 45. On receiving the goods, Rapaport checked the order and found $800 of unsuitable merchandise. Rapaport returned $800 of the merchandise to La Roche on May 4.

Journalizing purchase transactions (Obj. 2)

To pay the remaining amount owed, Rapaport had to borrow the net amount of the invoice from the bank. On May 14, Rapaport signed a short-term note payable to the bank and immediately paid the borrowed funds to La Roche. On June 14, Rapaport paid the bank the net amount of the invoice, which Rapaport had borrowed, plus 1% monthly interest (round to the nearest dollar).

REQUIRED

Record the indicated transactions in the journal of Rapaport Jewelers. Explanations are not required.

E5-5 Refer to the business situation in Exercise 5-4. Journalize the transactions of La Roche Fine Gems. La Roche's gross margin is 40%, so cost of goods sold is 60% of sales. Explanations are not required.

Journalizing sales transactions (Obj. 2)

E5-6 The Home Depot is one of the largest retailers in the United States, with over 400 full-service, warehouse-style stores. For a recent year, The Home Depot's accounting records carried the following accounts (adapted, with amounts in millions) at January 31, 19X6:

Making closing entries (Obj. 3)

Receivables	**$ 326**	**Selling expense**	**$ 2,784**
Interest revenue	**20**	**Sales revenue**	**15,470**
Accounts payable	**825**	**Interest expense**	**4**
Other expense	**516**	**Merchandise inventories**	**2,180**
Cost of goods sold	**11,185**	**General and administrative expense**	**269**
Owner withdrawals	**68**		

1. Journalize all of The Home Depot's closing entries at January 31, 19X6. Use an Owner Capital account.
2. Set up T-accounts for the Income Summary account and the Owner Capital account. Post to these accounts and take their ending balances. One year earlier, at January 31, 19X5, the Owner Capital balance was $3,442 million.

E5-7 The trial balance and adjustments columns of the work sheet of ColorMaster Tinting Supply at March 31, 19X6, follow.

Using work sheet data to make the closing entries (Obj. 3)

Account Title	Trial Balance Debit	Trial Balance Credit	Adjustments Debit	Adjustments Credit
Cash	2,000			
Accounts receivable	8,500		(a) 2,100	
Inventory	36,100			(b) 1,170
Supplies	13,000			(c) 8,600
Equipment	42,470			
Accumulated depreciation		11,250		(d) 2,250
Accounts payable		9,300		
Salary payable				(e) 1,200
Note payable, long-term		7,500		
Millie Fraser, capital		33,920		
Millie Fraser, withdrawals	45,000			
Sales revenue		233,000		(a) 2,100
Sales discounts	2,000			
Cost of goods sold	111,600		(b) 1,170	
Selling expense	21,050		(c) 5,200 (e) 1,200	
General expense	10,500		(c) 3,400 (d) 2,250	
Interest expense	2,750			
Total	294,970	294,970	15,320	15,320

Compute the adjusted balance for each account that must be closed. Then journalize Color Master's closing entries at March 31, 19X6. How much was ColorMaster's net income or net loss?

Preparing a multi-step income statement **(Obj. 4)**

E5-8 Use the data in Exercise 5-7 to prepare the multi-step income statement of ColorMaster Tinting Supply for the year ended March 31, 19X6.

Using the gross margin percentage and the rate of inventory turnover to evaluate profitability **(Obj. 5)**

E5-9 Refer to Exercise 5-8. After completing ColorMaster's income statement for the year ended March 31, 19X6, compute these ratios to evaluate ColorMaster's performance:

- Gross margin percentage
- Inventory turnover (Ending inventory one year earlier, at March 31, 19X5, was $30,500.)

Compare your figures with the 19X5 gross margin percentage of 49% and the inventory turnover rate of 3.16 for 19X5. Does the two-year trend suggest that ColorMaster's profits are increasing or decreasing?

Preparing a merchandiser's multi-step income statement to evaluate the business **(Obj. 4, 5)**

E5-10 Selected amounts from the accounting records of Alamo Tire Company are listed in alphabetical order.

Accounts payable	**$16,200**	**Owner's equity, May 31**	**$126,070**
Accumulated depreciation	**18,700**	**Sales discounts**	**9,000**
Cost of goods sold	**91,300**	**Sales returns**	**4,600**
General expenses	**23,500**	**Sales revenue**	**201,000**
Interest revenue	**1,500**	**Selling expenses**	**37,800**
Inventory, December 31, 19X6.	**21,000**	**Unearned sales revenue**	**6,500**
Inventory, December 31, 19X7.	**19,400**		

REQUIRED

1. Prepare the business's multi-step income statement for the year ended December 31, 19X7.
2. Compute the rate of inventory turnover for the year. Last year the turnover rate was 3.8. Does this two-year trend suggest improvement or deterioration in inventory turnover?

Preparing a single-step income statement to evaluate the business **(Obj. 4, 5)**

E5-11 Prepare Alamo Tire Company's single-step income statement for 19X7, using the data from Exercise 5-10. Compute the gross margin percentage, and compare it with last year's gross margin percentage of 58 percent. Does this two-year trend suggest better or worse profitability during the current year?

Contracting gross margin and cash flows **(Obj. 4)**

E5-12 Ford Motor Company is a business empire, with both automotive operations and financial services. During 1996, Ford's automotive operations made sales of $118 billion and had cost of goods sold totaling $109 billion. Ford's automotive assets totaled $263 billion at December 31, 1996. Total automotive liabilities were $68 billion.

During 1996, Ford's automotive operations paid $108 billion for inventory and collected $118 billion from customers. Ford's automotive operations spent over $8,573 billion for investing activities and more than $763 billion for financing activities.

REQUIRED

As an investor, you wonder which was greater, Ford's (a) gross margin on automotive sales or Ford's (b) excess of cash collections from customers over cash payments to suppliers. Compute both amounts to answer this question.

Computing cost of goods sold in a periodic inventory system **(Obj. 6)**

E5-13 The periodic inventory records of Alamo Tire Company include these accounts at December 31, 19X7:

Purchases of inventory	**$90,600**
Purchase discounts	**3,000**
Purchase returns and allowances	**2,000**
Freight in	**4,100**
Inventory	**19,400**

One year ago, at December 31, 19X6, Alamo's inventory balance stood at $21,000.

REQUIRED

Compute Alamo's cost of goods sold for 19X7.

Computing inventory and cost of goods sold amounts in a periodic inventory system **(Obj. 6)**

E5-14 Supply the missing income statement amounts in each of the following situations:

Sales	Sales Discounts	Net Sales	Beginning Inventory	Net Purchases	Ending Inventory	Cost of Goods Sold	Gross Margin
$95,300	(a)	$92,800	$32,500	$66,700	$39,400	(b)	$33,000
82,400	$2,100	(c)	27,450	43,000	(d)	$44,100	(e)
91,500	1,800	89,700	(f)	44,900	22,600	59,400	(g)
(h)	3,000	(i)	40,700	(j)	48,230	72,500	36,600

E5-15 For the year ended December 31, 19X9, House of Fabrics, a retailer of home-related products, reported net sales of $338 million and cost of goods sold of $154 million. The company's balance sheet at December 31, 19X8 and 19X9, reported inventories of $133 million and $129 million, respectively. How much were House of Fabrics' net purchases during 19X9?

Computing an actual company's net purchases **(Obj. 6)**

CONTINUING EXERCISE

This exercise completes the Alvin Deering Consultant situation begun in Exercise 2-15 of Chapter 2 and continued through Exercise 3-14 of Chapter 3 and Exercise 4-11 of Chapter 4.

E5-16 *Link Back to Chapters 2 through 4.* Alvin Deering's consulting practice includes a great deal of systems consulting business. Deering has begun selling accounting software. During January, the business completed these transactions:

Accounting for both merchandising and service operations **(Obj. 2, 3, 4)**

Jan.	2	Completed a consulting engagement and received cash of $5,800.
	2	Prepaid three months' office rent, $1,500.
	7	Purchased accounting software on account for merchandise inventory, $4,000.
	16	Paid employee salary, $1,400.
	18	Sold accounting software on account, $1,100 (cost $700).
	19	Consulted with a client for a fee of $900 on account.
	21	Paid on account, $2,000.
	24	Paid utilities, $300.
	28	Sold accounting software for cash, $600 (cost $400).
	31	Recorded these adjusting entries:
		Accrued salary expense, $1,400.
		Accounted for expiration of prepaid rent.
		Depreciation of office furniture, $200.

REQUIRED

1. Open the following T-accounts in the ledger: Cash; Accounts Receivable; Accounting Software Inventory; Prepaid Rent; Accumulated Depreciation; Accounts Payable; Salary Payable; Alvin Deering, Capital; Income Summary; Service Revenue; Sales Revenue; Cost of Goods Sold; Salary Expense; Rent Expense; Utilities Expense; and Depreciation Expense.
2. Journalize and post the January transactions. Key all items by date. Compute each account balance, and denote the balance as *Bal.* Journalize and post the closing entries. Denote each closing amount as *Clo.* After posting, prove the equality of debits and credits in the ledger.
3. Prepare the January income statement of Alvin Deering, Consultant. Use the single-step format.

Beyond the Numbers

BN5-1 Pharmacy Management Services, Inc. (PMSI), is a leading provider of products for workers' compensation insurance purposes. The company recently reported these figures (adapted):

Evaluating a company's profitability **(Obj. 1, 5)**

PHARMACY MANAGEMENT SERVICES, INC.
Statement of Operations (Adapted)
Years Ended July 31, 19X2 and 19X1

Amounts in Thousands	19X2	19X1
Sales	$106,116	$81,686
Cost of sales	76,424	60,982
Gross margin	29,692	20,704
Cost and expenses		
Selling, general and administrative	21,802	16,576
Depreciation and amortization	2,169	919
Restructuring charges	7,097	
	31,068	17,495
Operating income (loss)	(1,376)	3,209
Other items (summarized)	(635)	(1,315)
Net income (loss)	$ (2,011)	$ 1,894

REQUIRED

Evaluate PMSI's operations during 19X2 in comparison with 19X1. Consider sales, gross margin, operating income, and net income. Track the gross margin percentage and inventory turnover in both years. PMSI's inventories were as follows at December 31:

Year End	Amount (Thousands)
19X2	$ 7,766
19X1	12,163
19X0	10,177

In the annual report, PMSI's management describes the restructuring charges in 19X2 as a one-time event. How does this additional information affect your evaluation?

ETHICAL ISSUE

Greg Ogden Belting Company makes all sales of industrial conveyor belts under terms of FOB shipping point. The company usually receives orders for sales approximately one week before shipping inventory to customers. For orders received late in December, Greg Ogden, the owner, decides when to ship the goods. If profits are already at an acceptable level, Ogden delays shipment until January. If profits for the current year are lagging behind expectations, Ogden ships the goods during December.

REQUIRED

1. Under Ogden's FOB policy, when should the company record a sale?
2. Do you approve or disapprove of Ogden's manner of deciding when to ship goods to customers and record the sales revenue? If you approve, give your reason. If you disapprove, identify a better way to decide when to ship goods. (There is no accounting rule against Ogden's practice.)

Problems (GROUP A)

Explaining the perpetual inventory system **(Obj. 2)**

P5-1A EyeMasters is a regional chain of optical shops in the southwestern United States. The company offers a large selection of eyeglass frames, and EyeMasters stores provide while-you-wait service. EyeMasters has launched a vigorous advertising campaign to promote two-for-the-price-of-one frame sales.

REQUIRED

EyeMasters expects to grow rapidly and to increase its level of inventory. As the chief accountant of this company, you wish to install a perpetual inventory system. Write a one-paragraph business memo to the company president to explain how that system would work.

Use the following heading for your memo:

Date: ____________

To: **Company President**

From: **Chief Accountant**

Subject: How a perpetual inventory system works

Accounting for the purchase and sale of inventory **(Obj. 2)**

P5-2A Assume the following transactions occurred between Rexall Drug Stores and Johnson & Johnson (J&J) during June of the current year:

June 8 Johnson & Johnson sold $5,000 worth of merchandise to Rexall Drug Stores on terms of 2/10 n/30, FOB shipping point. Rexall received a 10% quantity discount and was liable for only the net amount after subtracting the discount. J&J prepaid freight charges of $200 and included this amount in the invoice total. (J&J's entry to record the freight payment debits Accounts Receivable and credits Cash.) These goods cost J&J $2,100.

11 Rexall returned $600 of the merchandise purchased on June 8. J&J issued a credit memo for this amount and returned the goods to inventory (J&J's cost, $250).

17 Rexall paid $2,000 of the invoice amount owed to J&J for the June 8 purchase, less the discount. This payment included none of the freight charge.

26 Rexall paid the remaining amount owed to J&J for the June 8 purchase.

REQUIRED

Journalize these transactions, first on the books of Rexall Drug Stores and second on the books of Johnson &Johnson.

P5-3A Rogers Furniture Company engaged in the following transactions during July of the current year:

Journalizing purchase and sale transactions
(Obj. 2)

July	2	Purchased inventory for cash, $800, less a quantity discount of $150.
	5	Purchased store supplies on credit terms of net eom, $450.
	8	Purchased inventory of $3,000 less a quantity discount of 10%, plus freight charges of $230. Credit terms are 3/15 n/30.
	9	Sold goods for cash, $1,200. Rogers' cost of these goods was $700.
	11	Returned $200 (net amount after the quantity discount) of the inventory purchased on July 8. It was damaged in shipment.
	12	Purchased inventory on credit terms of 3/10 n/30, $3,330.
	14	Sold inventory on credit terms of 2/10 n/30, $9,600, less a $600 quantity discount (cost, $5,000).
	16	Paid the electricity and water bills, $275.
	20	Received returned inventory from the July 14 sale, $400 (net amount after the quantity discount). Rogers shipped the wrong goods by mistake. Rogers' cost of the inventory received was $250.
	21	Borrowed the amount owed on the July 8 purchase. Signed a note payable to the bank for $2,655, which takes into account the return of inventory on July 11.
	21	Paid supplier for goods purchased on July 8 less the discount and the return.
	23	Received $6,860 cash in partial settlement of his account from the customer who purchased inventory on July 14. Granted the customer a 2% discount and credited his account receivable for $7,000.
	30	Paid for the store supplies purchased on July 5.

REQUIRED

1. Journalize the preceding transactions on the books of Rogers Furniture Company.
2. Compute the amount of the receivable at July 31 from the customer to whom Rogers sold inventory on July 14. What amount of cash discount applies to this receivable at July 31?

P5-4A Interstate Produce Company's trial balance pertains to December 31, 19X8.

Preparing a merchandiser's work sheet
(Obj. 3)

INTERSTATE PRODUCE COMPANY
Trial Balance
December 31, 19X8

Cash	$ 2,910	
Accounts receivable	6,560	
Inventory	101,760	
Store supplies	1,990	
Prepaid insurance	3,200	
Store fixtures	63,900	
Accumulated depreciation		$ 37,640
Accounts payable		29,770
Salary payable		
Interest payable		
Note payable, long-term		37,200
Camilo Pasquali, capital		63,120
Camilo Pasquali, withdrawals	36,300	
Sales revenue		286,370
Cost of goods sold	161,090	
Salary expense	46,580	
Rent expense	14,630	
Utilities expense	6,780	
Depreciation expense		
Insurance expense	5,300	
Store supplies expense		
Interest expense	3,100	
Total	$454,100	$454,100

Additional data at December 31, 19X8:

a. Insurance expense for the year, $6,090.
b. Store fixtures have an estimated useful life of ten years and are expected to be worthless when they are retired from service.

c. Accrued salaries at December 31, $1,260.
d. Accrued interest expense at December 31, $870.
e. Store supplies on hand at December 31, $760.
f. Inventory on hand at December 31, $99,650.

REQUIRED

Complete Interstate's accounting work sheet for the year ended December 31, 19X8. Key adjusting entries by letter.

Journalizing the adjusting and closing entries of a merchandising business ***(Obj. 3)***

P5-5A Refer to the data in Problem 5-4A.

REQUIRED

1. Journalize the adjusting and closing entries of Interstate Produce Company.
2. Determine the December 31 balance of Camilo Pasquali, Capital.

Preparing a multi-step income statement and a classified balance sheet ***(Obj. 3, 4)***

P5-6A *Link Back to Chapter 4 (Classified Balance Sheet).* Selected accounts of Callaway Entertainment Center are listed in alphabetical order.

Accounts payable	$127,300	Interest payable	$ 3,000
Accounts receivable	31,200	Inventory: July 31	187,300
Accumulated depreciation— store equipment	16,400	Note payable, long-term	160,000
		Salary payable	6,100
L. E. Callaway, capital, June 30	67,100	Sales discounts	8,300
		Sales returns and allowances	17,900
L. E. Callaway, withdrawals	11,000	Sales revenue	531,600
Cash	12,300	Selling expense	84,600
Cost of goods sold	360,900	Store equipment	126,000
General expense	75,800	Supplies	4,300
Interest expense	1,200	Unearned sales revenue	9,300

REQUIRED

1. Prepare the entity's *multi-step* income statement for the month ended July 31, 19X9.
2. Prepare Callaway's classified balance sheet in *report format* at July 31, 19X9. Show your computation of the July 31 balance of Capital.

P5-7A *Link Back to Chapter 4 (Classified Balance Sheet).*

REQUIRED

Preparing a single-step income statement and a classified balance sheet ***(Obj. 4)***

1. Use the data of Problem 5-6A to prepare Callaway Entertainment Center's *single-step* income statement for July 31, 19X9.
2. Prepare Callaway's classified balance sheet in *report format* at July 31, 19X9. Show your computation of the July 31 balance of L. E. Callway, Capital.

Using work sheet data to prepare financial statements and evaluate the business; multi-step income statement ***(Obj. 4, 5)***

P5-8A The trial balance and adjustments columns of the work sheet of Campeche Ceramics Company include the accounts and balances at September 30, 19X5 (top of page 221).

REQUIRED

1. Inventory on hand at September 30, 19X4, was $8,580. Without completing a formal accounting work sheet, prepare the company's multi-step income statement for the year ended September 30, 19X5.
2. Compute the gross margin percentage and the inventory turnover for 19X5. For 19X4, Campeche's gross margin percentage was 60% and the inventory turnover rate was 9.8 times. Does the two-year trend in these ratios suggest improvement or deterioration in profitability?

Account Title	Trial Balance Debit	Trial Balance Credit	Adjustments Debit	Adjustments Credit
Cash	7,300			
Accounts receivable	4,360		(a) 1,800	
Inventory	9,630		(b) 2,100	
Supplies	10,700			(c) 7,640
Equipment	99,450			
Accumulated depreciation		29,800		(d) 9,900
Accounts payable		13,800		
Salary payable				(f) 200
Unearned sales revenue		3,780	(e) 2,600	
Note payable, long-term		10,000		
Ruby Campeche, capital		58,360		
Ruby Campeche, drawing	35,000			
Sales revenue		212,000		(a) 1,800 (e) 2,600
Sales returns	3,100			
Cost of goods sold	95,600			(b) 2,100
Selling expense	40,600		(c) 7,640 (f) 200	
General expense	21,000		(d) 9,900	
Interest expense	1,000			
Total	327,740	327,740	24,240	24,240

P5-9A The following are selected amounts from the accounting records of Midas Auto Parts at June 30, 19X9:

Computing cost of goods sold and gross margin in a periodic inventory system; evaluating the business ***(Obj. 5, 6)***

Cash	**$ 13,600**
Purchases of inventory	**98,100**
Freight in	**4,300**
Sales revenue	**193,100**
Purchase returns and allowances	**1,400**
Salary payable	**1,800**
Gerald Midas, capital	**36,000**
Sales returns and allowances	**12,100**
Inventory: June 30, 19X8	**23,800**
June 30, 19X9	**28,500**
Selling expenses	**29,800**
Equipment	**44,700**
Purchase discounts	**1,300**
Accumulated depreciation—equipment	**6,900**
Sales discounts	**3,400**
General expenses	**16,300**
Accounts payable	**23,800**

REQUIRED

1. Show the computation of Midas Auto Parts' net sales, cost of goods sold, and gross margin for the year ended June 30, 19X9.
2. Gerald Midas, owner of the business, strives to earn a gross margin percentage of 40 percent. Did he achieve this goal?
3. Did the rate of inventory turnover reach the industry average of 3.4 times per year?

Problems (GROUP B)

P5-1B Wal-Mart Stores, Inc., is the largest retailer in the world, with over 2,700 stores in the United States. A key Wal-Mart advantage is its sophisticated perpetual inventory accounting system.

Explaining the perpetual inventory system ***(Obj. 2)***

REQUIRED

You are the manager of a Wal-Mart store in Kansas City, Missouri. Write a one-paragraph business memo to a new employee explaining how the company accounts for the purchase and sale of merchandise inventory. Use the following heading for your memo:

Date:	____________
To:	**New Employee**
From:	**Store Manager**
Subject:	**Wal-Mart's accounting system for inventories**

Accounting for the purchase and sale of inventory
(Obj. 2)

P5-2B Assume the following transactions occurred between Johnson & Johnson (J&J) and Eckerd, the drugstore chain, during February of the current year:

Feb. 6 Johnson &Johnson sold $6,000 worth of merchandise to Eckerd on terms of 2/10 n/30, FOB shipping point. Eckerd received a quantity discount of 10% and was liable for only the net amount after subtracting the discount. J&J prepaid freight charges of $500 and included this amount in the invoice total. (J&J's entry to record the freight payment debits Accounts Receivable and credits Cash.) These goods cost J&J $4,100.

10 Eckerd returned $900 of the merchandise purchased on February 6. J&J issued a credit memo for this amount and returned the goods to inventory (cost, $590).

15 Eckerd paid $3,000 of the invoice amount owed to J&J for the February 6 purchase, less the account. This payment included none of the freight charge.

27 Eckerd paid the remaining amount owed to J&J for the February 6 purchase.

REQUIRED

Journalize these transactions, first on the books of Eckerd and second on the books of Johnson & Johnson.

Journalizing purchase and sale transactions
(Obj. 2)

P5-3B Jastrow Distributing Company engaged in the following transactions during May of the current year:

May 3 Purchased office supplies for cash, $300.

7 Purchased inventory on credit terms of 3/10 net eom, $2,000.

8 Returned half the inventory purchased on May 7. It was not the inventory ordered.

10 Sold goods for cash, $450 (cost, $250).

13 Sold inventory on credit terms of 2/15 n/45, $3,900, less $600 quantity discount offered to customers who purchased in large quantities (cost, $1,800).

16 Paid the amount owed on account from the purchase of May 7, less the discount and the return.

17 Received defective inventory as a sales return from May 13 sale, $900, which is the net amount after the quantity discount. Jastrow's cost of the inventory received was $600.

18 Purchased inventory of $4,000 on account. Payment terms were 2/10 net 30.

26 Borrowed $3,920 from the bank to take advantage of the discount offered on the May 18 purchase. Signed a note payable to the bank for this amount.

28 Received cash in full settlement of this account from the customer who purchased inventory on May 13, less the discount and the return.

29 Purchased inventory for cash, $2,000, less a quantity discount of $400, plus freight charges of $160.

REQUIRED

1. Journalize the preceding transactions on the books of Jastrow Distributing Company.
2. The note payable signed on May 26 requires Jastrow to pay $30 interest expense. Was the decision to borrow funds to take advantage of the cash discount wise or unwise? Support your answer by comparing the discount to the interest paid.

Preparing a merchandiser's work sheet
(Obj. 3)

P5-4B Peking China Restaurant's trial balance on the following page pertains to December 31, 19X9.
Additional data at December 31, 19X9:

a. Rent expense for the year, $10,200.
b. Store fixtures have an estimated useful life of ten years and are expected to be worthless when they are retired from service.
c. Accrued salaries at December 31, $900.
d. Accrued interest expense at December 31, $360.
e. Inventory on hand at December 31, $73,200.

PEKING CHINA RESTAURANT Trial Balance December 31, 19X9		
Cash	$ 1,270	
Accounts receivable	4,430	
Inventory	73,900	
Prepaid rent	4,400	
Fixtures	22,100	
Accumulated depreciation		$ 8,380
Accounts payable		6,290
Salary payable		
Interest payable		
Note payable, long-term		18,000
Lei Ma, capital		55,920
Lei Ma, withdrawals	39,550	
Sales revenue		170,150
Cost of goods sold	67,870	
Salary expense	24,700	
Rent expense	7,700	
Advertising expense	4,510	
Utilities expense	3,880	
Depreciation expense		
Insurance expense	2,770	
Interest expense	1,660	
Total	$258,740	$258,740

Complete Peking China's accounting work sheet for the year ended December 31, 19X9. Key adjusting entries by letter.

REQUIRED

Journalizing the adjusting and closing entries of a merchandising business ***(Obj. 3)***

P5-5B Refer to the data in Problem 5-4B.

REQUIRED

1. Journalize the adjusting and closing entries.
2. Determine the December 31 balance of Lei Ma, Capital.

Preparing a multi-step income statement and a classified balance sheet ***(Obj. 4)***

P5-6B *Link Back to Chapter 4 (Classified Balance Sheet).* Selected accounts of HEC Grocery Supply are listed in alphabetical order.

Accounts payable	**$ 16,900**	**Interest expense**	**$ 400**
Accounts receivable	**43,700**	**Interest payable**	**1,100**
Accumulated depreciation—equipment	**38,000**	**Inventory: May 31**	**65,500**
		Note payable, long-term	**45,000**
H. E. Cameron, capital, April 30	**73,900**	**Salary payable**	**2,800**
		Sales discounts	**10,400**
H. E. Cameron, withdrawals	**9,000**	**Sales returns and allowances**	**18,000**
Cash	**7,800**	**Sales revenue**	**731,000**
Cost of goods sold	**362,000**	**Selling expenses**	**137,900**
Equipment	**146,000**	**Supplies**	**5,100**
General expenses	**116,700**	**Unearned sales revenue**	**13,800**

REQUIRED

1. Prepare the business's *multi-step* income statement for the month ended May 31, 19X9.
2. Prepare HEC's classified balance sheet in *report format* at May 31, 19X9. Show your computation of the May 31 balance of H. E. Cameron, Capital.

P5-7B *Link Back to Chapter 4 (Classified Balance Sheet).*

REQUIRED

Preparing a single-step income statement and a balance sheet ***(Obj. 4)***

1. Use the data of Problem 5-6B to prepare HEC Grocery Supply's *single-step* income statement for the month ended May 31, 19X9.
2. Prepare HEC's classified balance sheet in report format at May 31, 19X9. Show your computation of the May 31 balance of H. E. Cameron, Capital.

Using work sheet data to prepare financial statements and evaluate the business; multi-step income statement
(Obj. 4, 5)

P5-8B The trial balance and adjustments columns of the work sheet of Chopin Piano Company include the following accounts and balances at November 30, 19X4:

Account Title	Trial Balance Debit	Trial Balance Credit	Adjustments Debit	Adjustments Credit
Cash	24,000			
Accounts receivable	14,500		(a) 6,000	
Inventory	36,330		(b) 1,010	
Supplies	2,800			(c) 2,400
Furniture	39,600			
Accumulated depreciation		4,900		(d) 2,450
Accounts payable		12,600		
Salary payable				(f) 1,000
Unearned sales revenue		13,570	(e) 6,700	
Note payable, long-term		15,000		
F. Chopin, capital		60,310		
F. Chopin, drawing	42,000			
Sales revenue		174,000		(a) 6,000 (e) 6,700
Sales returns	6,300			
Cost of goods sold	72,170			(b) 1,010
Selling expense	28,080		(f) 1,000	
General expense	13,100		(c) 2,400 (d) 2,450	
Interest expense	1,500			
Total	280,380	280,380	19,560	19,560

REQUIRED

1. Inventory on hand at November 30, 19X3, was $32,650. Without entering the preceding data on a formal work sheet, prepare the company's multi-step income statement for the year ended November 30, 19X4.
2. Compute the gross margin percentage and the rate of inventory turnover for 19X4. For 19X3, Chopin's gross margin percentage was 58%, and inventory turnover was 1.8 times during the year. Does the two-year trend in these ratios suggest improvement or deterioration in profitability?

Computing cost of goods sold and gross margin in a periodic inventory system; evaluating the business
(Obj. 5, 6)

P5-9B Selected accounts from the accounting records of Dietz Appliance Company had these balances at November 30 of the current year:

Purchases of inventory	**$132,000**
Selling expenses	**8,800**
Furniture	**37,200**
Purchase returns and allowances	**900**
Salary payable	**300**
William Dietz, capital	**52,800**
Sales revenue	**194,600**
Sales returns and allowances	**3,200**
Inventory: November 30, 19X0	**41,700**
November 30, 19X1	**41,500**
Accounts payable	**9,500**
Cash	**3,700**
Freight in	**1,600**
Accumulated depreciation—furniture	**13,600**
Purchase discounts	**600**
Sales discounts	**2,100**
General expenses	**19,300**

REQUIRED

1. Show the computation of Dietz's net sales, cost of goods sold, and gross margin for the year ended November 30 of the current year.
2. William Dietz, owner of the company, strives to earn a gross margin percentage of 25 percent. Did he achieve this goal?
3. Did the rate of inventory turnover reach the industry average of 3.4 times per year?

Applying Your Knowledge

DECISION CASES

Using the financial statements to decide on a business expansion
(Obj. 4, 5)

CASE 1. *Link Back to Chapter 4 (Classified Balance Sheet, Current Ratio, Debt Ratio).* David Wheelis owns Heights Pharmacy, which has prospered during its second year of operation. In deciding whether to open another pharmacy in the area, Wheelis has prepared the current financial statements of the business (below and on page 226).

Wheelis recently read in an industry trade journal that a successful pharmacy meets all of these criteria:

a. Gross margin percentage is at least 50 percent.
b. Current ratio is at least 2.0.
c. Debt ratio is no higher than 0.50.
d. Inventory turnover rate is at least 3.40. (Heights Pharmacy's inventory one year ago, at December 31, 19X0, was $19,200.)

Basing his opinion on the entity's financial statement data, Wheelis believes the business meets all four criteria. He plans to go ahead with the expansion plan and asks your advice on preparing the pharmacy's financial statements in accordance with generally accepted accounting principles. When you point out that the statements are not properly prepared, he assures you that all amounts are correct.

HEIGHTS PHARMACY Income Statement Year Ended December 31, 19X1		
Sales revenue		$175,000
Gain on sale of land		24,600
Total revenue		199,600
Cost of goods sold		85,200
Gross margin		114,400
Operating expenses:		
Salary expense	$18,690	
Rent expense	12,000	
Interest expense	6,000	
Depreciation expense	4,900	
Utilities expense	2,330	
Supplies expense	1,400	
Total operating expense		45,320
Income from operations		69,080
Other expense:		
Sales discounts ($3,600) and returns ($7,100)		10,700
Net income		$ 58,380

HEIGHTS PHARMACY Statement of Owner's Equity Year Ended December 31, 19X1	
D. Wheelis, capital, December 31, 19X0	$30,000
Add increases in owner's equity:	
Net income	58,380
D. Wheelis, capital, December 31, 19X1	$88,380

HEIGHTS PHARMACY Balance Sheet December 31, 19X1	
Assets	
Current:	
Cash	$ 5,320
Accounts receivable	9,710
Inventory	30,100
Supplies	2,760
Store fixtures	63,000
Total current assets	110,890
Other:	
Withdrawals	45,000
Total assets	$155,890
Liabilities	
Current:	
Accumulated depreciation—store fixtures	$ 6,300
Accounts payable	10,310
Salary payable	900
Total current liabilities	17,510
Other:	
Note payable due in 90 days	50,000
Total liabilities	67,510
Owner's Equity	
D. Wheelis, capital	88,380
Total liabilities and owner's equity	$155,890

REQUIRED

1. Compute the four ratios based on the Heights Pharmacy financial statements prepared by Wheelis. Does the business appear to be ready for expansion?
2. Prepare a correct multi-step income statement, a correct statement of owner's equity, and a correct classified balance sheet in report format.
3. On the basis of the corrected financial statements, compute correct measures of the four criteria listed in the trade journal.
4. Make a recommendation about whether Wheelis should undertake the expansion.

Understanding the operating cycle of a merchandiser
(Obj. 1, 3)

CASE 2. Clark Staas has come to you for advice. Earlier this year, he opened a record store near a university. The store sells compact discs at very low prices and on special credit terms for students. Many of the students alternate school and work terms. Staas allows the students to buy on credit while they are on a school term, with the understanding that they will pay their account shortly after starting a work term.

Business has been very good. Staas is sure it is because of his competitive prices and the unique credit terms he offers. His problem is that he is short of cash, and his loan with the bank has grown significantly. The bank manager wishes to reduce Staas's line of credit because the banker is worried that Staas will get into financial difficulties.

REQUIRED

1. Explain to Staas why he is short of cash.
2. Staas has asked you to explain his problem to the bank manager and to assist in asking for more credit. What might you say to the bank manager to assist Staas?

Correcting an inventory error
(Obj. 6)

CASE 3. The employees of Northern Telecommunications made an error when they performed the periodic inventory count at year end, October 31, 19X8. Part of one warehouse was not counted, and therefore its inventory was not included in the company's total inventory.

REQUIRED

1. Indicate the effect of the inventory error on cost of goods sold, gross margin, and net income for the year ended October 31, 19X8.
2. Will the error affect cost of goods sold, gross margin, and net income in 19X9? If so, what will the effects be?

FINANCIAL STATEMENT CASES

Closing entries for a merchandising corporation; evaluating ratio data
(Obj. 3, 5)

CASE 1. This problem uses both the income statement (statement of income) and the balance sheet of NIKE, Inc., in Appendix A. It will aid your understanding of the closing process of a business with inventories.

REQUIRED

1. Journalize NIKE's closing entries for the year ended May 31, 1997. You may be unfamiliar with certain revenues and expenses, but treat them as either revenues or expenses. Close the Income Summary account to the Retained Earnings account. For this purpose, Retained Earnings is similar to the owner's Capital account.
2. What amount was closed to Retained Earnings? How is this amount labeled on the income statement?
3. Compute NIKE's gross margin (gross profit) percentage and inventory turnover rate for the year ended May 31, 1997.

Identifying items from a company's financial statements
(Obj. 3, 5)

CASE 2. Obtain the annual report of a company of your choosing. *Make sure that the company's balance sheet reports Inventory, Merchandise Inventory, or a similar asset category.* Answer the following questions about the company.

REQUIRED

1. What was the balance of total inventories reported on the balance sheet at the end of the current year? At the end of the preceding year? (If you selected a manufacturing company, you may observe more than one category of inventories. If so, name these categories and briefly explain what you think they mean.)
2. Give the company's journal entries to close Income Summary and Dividends.
3. Compute the company's gross margin percentage for the current year and for the preceding year. Did the gross margin percentage increase, decrease, or hold steady during the current year? Is that a favorable signal or an unfavorable signal about the company?
4. Compute the rate of inventory turnover for the current year. Would you expect this company's rate of inventory turnover to be higher or lower than that of a grocery chain such as Safeway or Kroger? Higher or lower than that of an aircraft manufacturer such as The Boeing Company? State your reasoning.

Team Project

With a small team of classmates, visit one or more actual merchandising (not service or manufacturing) businesses in your area. Interview a responsible official of the company to learn about its inventory policies and accounting system. Obtain answers to the following questions, write a report, and be prepared to make a presentation to the class if your instructor so directs:

1. What mechandise inventory does the business sell?
2. From whom does the business buy its inventory? Is the relationship with the supplier new or longstanding?
3. What are the FOB terms on inventory purchases? Who pays the freight, the buyer or the seller? Is freight a significant amount or is freight cost low? What percentage of total inventory cost is the freight?
4. What are the credit terms on inventory purchases—2/10 n/30, or other? Does the business pay early to get purchase discounts? If so, why? If not, why not?
5. Does the business get quantity discounts? What percentage is the discount?
6. How does the business actually pay its suppliers? Does it mail a check or pay electronically? What is the actual payment procedure?
7. Which type of inventory accounting system does the business use—perpetual or periodic? Is this system computerized?
8. How often does the business take a physical count of its inventory? When during the year is the count taken? Describe the count procedures followed by the company.
9. Does the owner or manager use the gross margin percentage and the rate of inventory turnover to evaluate the business? If not, show the manager how to use these ratios in decision making.
10. Ask any other questions that your group considers appropriate.

SUPPLEMENT to Chapter 5

Accounting for Merchandise in a Periodic Inventory System

Purchasing Merchandise in the Periodic Inventory System

Some businesses find it uneconomical to invest in a computerized (perpetual) inventory system that keeps daily records of inventory and cost of goods sold. For example, the owner of a small clothing store may decide that a perpetual inventory system probably costs more than it is worth. These types of business use a periodic system. Accountants make entries to the Inventory account only in response to the physical count at the end of the period.

Recording the Purchases of Inventory

Objective S2

Account for the purchase and sale of inventory

The periodic system uses the Inventory account. But purchases, purchase discounts, purchase returns and allowances, and transportation costs are recorded in separate accounts bearing these titles. Let's account for Austin Sound Stereo Center's purchase of the JVC goods in Exhibit 5S-1. The following entries record the purchase and payment on account within the discount period:

May 27	Purchases	707.00	
	Accounts Payable		707.00
	Purchased inventory on account.		
June 10	Accounts Payable	707.00	
	Cash ($707.00 × 0.97)		685.79
	Purchase Discounts ($707.00 × 0.03)		21.21
	Paid on account.		

EXHIBIT 5S-1
An Invoice

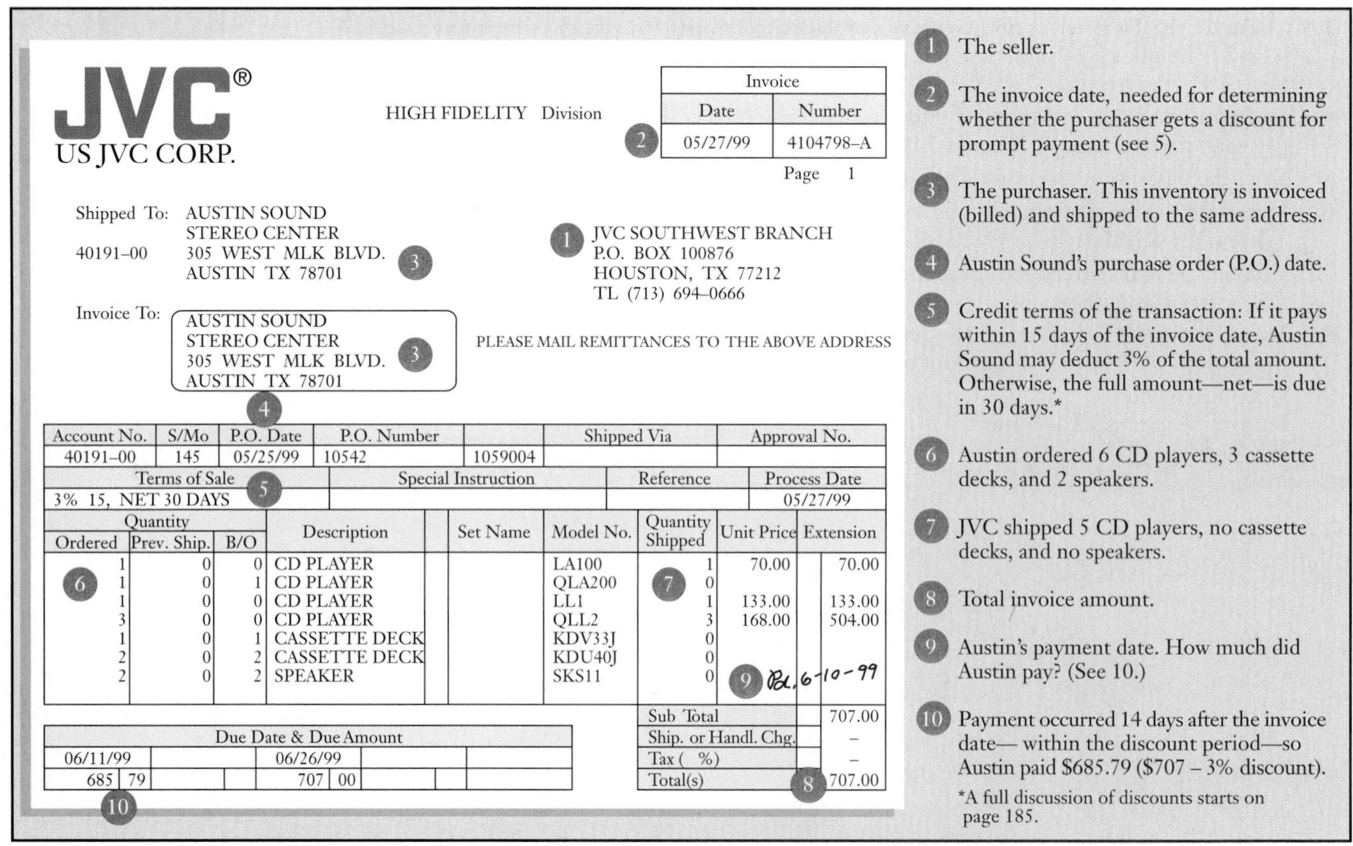

JVC®
US JVC CORP.

HIGH FIDELITY Division

Invoice	
Date	Number
05/27/99	4104798–A

Page 1

Shipped To: AUSTIN SOUND STEREO CENTER
40191–00 305 WEST MLK BLVD. AUSTIN TX 78701

JVC SOUTHWEST BRANCH
P.O. BOX 100876
HOUSTON, TX 77212
TL (713) 694–0666

Invoice To: AUSTIN SOUND STEREO CENTER 305 WEST MLK BLVD. AUSTIN TX 78701

PLEASE MAIL REMITTANCES TO THE ABOVE ADDRESS

Account No.	S/Mo	P.O. Date	P.O. Number		Shipped Via	Approval No.
40191–00	145	05/25/99	10542	1059004		

Terms of Sale	Special Instruction	Reference	Process Date
3% 15, NET 30 DAYS			05/27/99

Quantity Ordered	Quantity Prev. Ship.	Quantity B/O	Description	Set Name	Model No.	Quantity Shipped	Unit Price	Extension
1	0	0	CD PLAYER		LA100	1	70.00	70.00
1	0	1	CD PLAYER		QLA200	0		
1	0	0	CD PLAYER		LL1	1	133.00	133.00
3	0	0	CD PLAYER		QLL2	3	168.00	504.00
1	0	1	CASSETTE DECK		KDV33J	0		
2	0	2	CASSETTE DECK		KDU40J	0		
2	0	2	SPEAKER		SKS11	0	Pd. 6-10-99	

Due Date & Due Amount	
06/11/99	06/26/99
685 79	707 00

Sub Total	707.00
Ship. or Handl. Chg.	–
Tax (%)	–
Total(s)	707.00

1. The seller.
2. The invoice date, needed for determining whether the purchaser gets a discount for prompt payment (see 5).
3. The purchaser. This inventory is invoiced (billed) and shipped to the same address.
4. Austin Sound's purchase order (P.O.) date.
5. Credit terms of the transaction: If it pays within 15 days of the invoice date, Austin Sound may deduct 3% of the total amount. Otherwise, the full amount—net—is due in 30 days.*
6. Austin ordered 6 CD players, 3 cassette decks, and 2 speakers.
7. JVC shipped 5 CD players, no cassette decks, and no speakers.
8. Total invoice amount.
9. Austin's payment date. How much did Austin pay? (See 10.)
10. Payment occurred 14 days after the invoice date— within the discount period—so Austin paid $685.79 ($707 – 3% discount).

*A full discussion of discounts starts on page 185.

Recording Purchase Returns and Allowances

Suppose instead that prior to payment Austin Sound returned to JVC goods costing $70 and also received from JVC a purchase allowance of $10. Austin Sound would record these transactions as follows:

June 3	Accounts Payable	70.00	
	Purchase Returns and Allowances		70.00
	Returned inventory to seller.		
June 4	Accounts Payable	10.00	
	Purchase Returns and Allowances		10.00
	Received a purchase allowance.		

During the period, the business records the cost of all inventory bought in the Purchases account. The balance of Purchases is a *gross* amount because it does not include subtractions for purchase discounts, returns, or allowances. **Net purchases** is the remainder computed by subtracting the contra accounts from Purchases:

Net Purchases. Purchases less purchase discounts and purchase returns and allowances.

Purchases (*debit* balance account)
− Purchase Discounts (*credit* balance account)
− Purchase Returns and Allowances (*credit* balance account)
= Net purchases (a *debit* subtotal, not a separate account)

Recording Transportation Costs

Under the periodic system, costs to transport purchased inventory from seller to buyer are debited to a separate account, as shown for payment of a $60 freight bill:

June 1	Freight In	60.00	
	Cash		60.00
	Paid a freight bill.		

Recording the Sale of Inventory

Recording sales is streamlined in the periodic system. With no running record of inventory to maintain, we can record a $3,000 sale as follows:

June 5	Accounts Receivable	3,000	
	Sales Revenue		3,000
	Sale on account.		

No accompanying entry to Inventory and Cost of Goods Sold is required. Also, sales discounts and sales returns and allowances are recorded as shown for the perpetual system on pages 191–192, but with no entry to Inventory and Cost of Goods Sold.

Cost of Goods Sold

Objective S3

Compute cost of goods sold

Cost of goods sold (also called **cost of sales**) is the largest single expense of most businesses that sell merchandise, such as May Department Stores and Austin Sound. It is the cost of the inventory that the business has sold to customers. In a periodic system, cost of goods sold must be computed as in Exhibit 5S-2.

Exhibit 5S-3 summarizes the first half of this chapter by showing Austin Sound's net sales revenue, cost of goods sold—including net purchases and freight in—and gross margin on the income statement for the periodic system. (All amounts are assumed.)

Adjusting and Closing the Accounts in a Periodic Inventory System

Objective S4

Adjust and close the accounts of a merchandising business

A merchandising business adjusts and closes the accounts much as a service entity does. The steps of this end-of-period process are the same: If a work sheet is used, the trial

Concept Highlight

EXHIBIT 5S-2
Measuring Cost of Goods Sold in the Periodic Inventory System

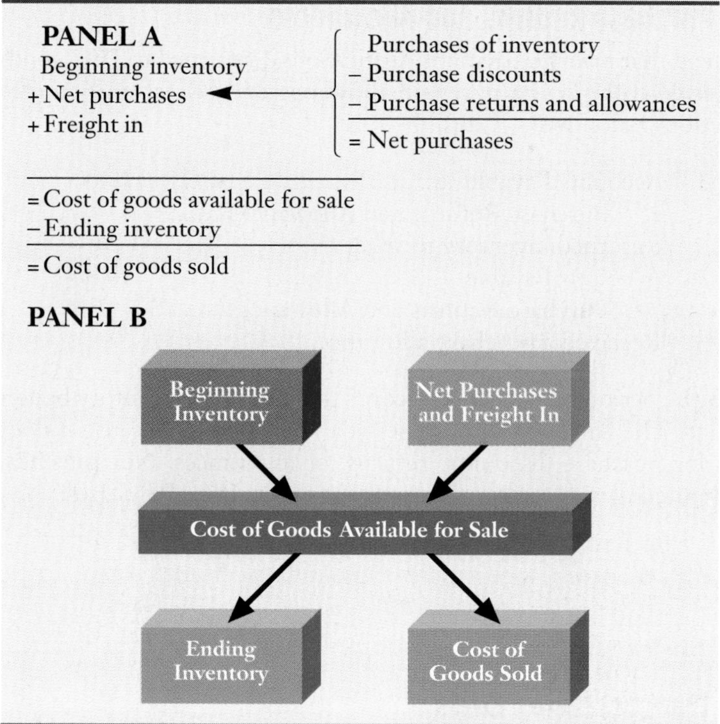

balance is entered and the work sheet completed to determine net income or net loss. The work sheet provides the data for journalizing the adjusting and closing entries and for preparing the financial statements.

At the end of the period, before any adjusting or closing entries, the Inventory account balance is still the cost of the inventory that was on hand at the end of the preceding period. It is necessary to remove this beginning balance and replace it with the cost of the inventory on hand at the end of the current period. Various techniques may be used to bring the inventory records up to date.

EXHIBIT 5S-3
Partial Income Statement

AUSTIN SOUND STEREO CENTER
Income Statement
Year Ended December 31, 19X6

PANEL A—Detailed Gross Margin Section

Sales revenue			$169,300	
Less: Sales discounts		$ (1,400)		
Sales returns and allowances		(2,000)	(3,400)	
Net sales				$165,900
Cost of goods sold:				
Beginning inventory			$ 38,600	
Purchases		$91,400		
Less: Purchase discounts	$(3,000)			
Purchase returns and allowances	(1,200)	(4,200)		
Net purchases			87,200	
Freight in			5,200	
Cost of goods available for sale			131,000	
Less: Ending inventory			(40,200)	
Cost of goods sold				90,800
Gross margin				$ 75,100

PANEL B—Gross Margin Section—Often Streamlined in Annual Reports to Outsiders

Net sales	$165,900
Cost of goods sold	90,800
Gross margin	$ 75,100

To illustrate a merchandiser's adjusting and closing process under the periodic inventory system, let's use Austin Sound's December 31, 19X6, trial balance in Exhibit 5S-4. All the new accounts—Inventory, Freight In, and the contra accounts—are highlighted for emphasis. Inventory is the only account that is affected by the new closing procedures. The additional data item (h) gives the ending inventory figure $40,200.

EXHIBIT 5S-4
Trial Balance

AUSTIN SOUND STEREO CENTER
Trial Balance
December 31, 19X6

Cash	$ 2,850	
Accounts receivable	4,600	
Note receivable, current	8,000	
Interest receivable		
Inventory	38,600	
Supplies	650	
Prepaid insurance	1,200	
Furniture and fixtures	33,200	
Accumulated depreciation		$ 2,400
Accounts payable		47,000
Unearned sales revenue		2,000
Wages payable		
Interest payable		
Note payable, long-term		12,600
C. Ernest, capital		25,900
C. Ernest, withdrawals	54,100	
Sales revenue		168,000
Sales discounts	1,400	
Sales returns and allowances	2,000	
Interest revenue		600
Purchases	91,400	
Purchase discounts		3,000
Purchase returns and allowances		1,200
Freight in	5,200	
Wage expense	9,800	
Rent expense	8,400	
Depreciation expense		
Insurance expense		
Supplies expense		
Interest expense	1,300	
Total	$262,700	$262,700

Additional data at December 31, 19X6:

a. Interest revenue earned but not yet collected, $400.
b. Supplies on hand, $100.
c. Prepaid insurance expired during the year, $1,000.
d. Depreciation, $600.
e. Unearned sales revenue earned during the year, $1,300.
f. Accrued wage expense, $400.
g. Accrued interest expense, $200.
h. Inventory on hand, $40,200.

Preparing and Using the Work Sheet in a Periodic Inventory System

This work sheet is slightly different from the one introduced in the Chapter 4 acetates following page 138—it contains four pairs of columns, not five.

The Exhibit 5S-5 work sheet is similar to the work sheets we have seen so far, but a few differences appear. In most accounting systems, a single operation combines trial balance amounts with the adjustments and extends the adjusted balances directly to the income statement and balance sheet columns. Therefore, to reduce clutter, the adjusted trial balance columns are omitted.

EXHIBIT 5S-5
Accounting Work Sheet

AUSTIN SOUND STEREO CENTER
Accounting Work Sheet (Periodic Inventory System)
Year Ended December 31, 19X6

	Trial Balance		Adjustments		Income Statement		Balance Sheet	
Account Title	**Debit**	**Credit**	**Debit**	**Credit**	**Debit**	**Credit**	**Debit**	**Credit**
Cash	2,850						2,850	
Accounts receivable	4,600						4,600	
Note receivable, current	8,000						8,000	
Interest receivable			(a) 400				400	
Inventory	38,600				38,600	40,200	40,200	
Supplies	650			(b) 550			100	
Prepaid insurance	1,200			(c) 1,000			200	
Furniture and fixtures	33,200						33,200	
Accumulated depreciation		2,400		(d) 600				3,000
Accounts payable		47,000						47,000
Unearned sales revenue		2,000	(e) 1,300					700
Wages payable				(f) 400				400
Interest payable				(g) 200				200
Note payable, long-term		12,600						12,600
C. Ernest, capital		25,900						25,900
C. Ernest, withdrawals	54,100						54,100	
Sales revenue		168,000		(e) 1,300		169,300		
Sales discounts	1,400				1,400			
Sales returns and allowances	2,000				2,000			
Interest revenue		600		(a) 400		1,000		
Purchases	91,400				91,400			
Purchase discounts		3,000				3,000		
Purchase returns and allowances		1,200				1,200		
Freight in	5,200				5,200			
Wage expense	9,800		(f) 400		10,200			
Rent expense	8,400				8,400			
Depreciation expense			(d) 600		600			
Insurance expense			(c) 1,000		1,000			
Supplies expense			(b) 550		550			
Interest expense	1,300		(g) 200		1,500			
	262,700	262,700	4,450	4,450	160,850	214,700	143,650	89,800
Net income					53,850			53,850
					214,700	214,700	143,650	143,650

ACCOUNT TITLE COLUMNS The trial balance lists a number of accounts without balances. Ordinarily, these accounts are affected by the adjusting process. Examples include Interest Receivable, Interest Payable, and Depreciation Expense. The accounts are listed in the order they appear in the ledger. If additional accounts are needed, they can be written in at the bottom, above net income.

TRIAL BALANCE COLUMNS Examine the Inventory account, $38,600 in the trial balance. This $38,600 is the cost of the beginning inventory. The work sheet is designed to replace this outdated amount with the new ending balance, which in our example is $40,200 [additional data item (h) in Exhibit 5S-4]. As we shall see, this task is accomplished later in the columns for the income statement and the balance sheet.

ADJUSTMENTS COLUMNS The adjustments are similar to those discussed in Chapters 3 and 4. They may be entered in any order desired. The debit amount of each entry should equal the credit amount, and total debits should equal total credits. You should review the adjusting data in Exhibit 5S-5 to reassure yourself that the adjustments are correct.

INCOME STATEMENT COLUMNS The income statement columns contain adjusted amounts for the revenues and the expenses. Sales Revenue, for example, is $169,300, which includes the $1,300 adjustment.

You may be wondering why the two inventory amounts appear in the income statement columns. The reason is that both beginning inventory and ending inventory enter the computation of cost of goods sold. *Placement of beginning inventory ($38,600) in the work sheet's income statement debit column has the effect of adding beginning inventory in computing cost of goods sold. Placing ending inventory ($40,200) in the credit column decreases cost of goods sold.*

Purchases and Freight In appear in the debit column because they are added in computing cost of goods sold. Purchase Discounts and Purchase Returns and Allowances appear as credits because they are subtracted in computing cost of good sold—$90,800 on the income statement in Exhibit 5S-6.

The income statement column subtotals on the work sheet indicate whether the business earned net income or incurred a net loss. If total credits are greater, the result is net income, as shown in Exhibit 5S-5. If total debits are greater, a net loss has occurred.

BALANCE SHEET COLUMNS The only new item on the balance sheet is inventory. The balance listed is the ending amount of $40,200, which is determined by a physical count of inventory on hand at the end of the period.

Preparing the Financial Statements of a Merchandising Business

Objective S5

Prepare a merchandiser's financial statements

Exhibit 5S-6 presents Austin Sound's financial statements. The *income statement* through gross margin repeats Exhibit 5S-3. This information is followed by the **operating expenses,** expenses other than cost of goods sold that are incurred in the entity's major line of business—merchandising. Wage expense is Austin Sound's cost of employing workers. Rent is the cost of obtaining store space. Insurance helps to protect the inventory. Store furniture and fixtures wear out; the expense is depreciation. Supplies expense is the cost of stationery, mailing, and the like, used in operations.

Many companies report their operating expenses in two categories.

- *Selling expenses* are those expenses related to marketing the company's products—sales salaries; sales commissions; advertising; depreciation, rent, utilities, and property taxes on store buildings; depreciation on store furniture; delivery expense; and so on.
- *General expenses* include office expenses, such as the salaries of office employees, and depreciation, rent, utilities, and property taxes on the home office building.

Gross margin minus operating expenses and plus any other operating revenues equals **operating income,** or **income from operations.** Many businesspeople view operating income as the most reliable indicator of a business's success because it measures the results of the entity's major ongoing activities.

EXHIBIT 5S-6
Financial Statements of Austin Sound Stereo Center

AUSTIN SOUND STEREO CENTER
Income Statement
Year Ended December 31, 19X6

Sales revenue			$169,300	
Less: Sales discounts		$ (1,400)		
Sales returns and allowances		(2,000)	(3,400)	
Net sales revenue				$165,900
Cost of goods sold:				
Beginning inventory			$ 38,600	
Purchases		$91,400		
Less: Purchases discounts	$(3,000)			
Purchase returns and allowances	(1,200)	(4,200)		
Net purchases			87,200	
Freight in			5,200	
Cost of goods available for sale			131,000	
Less: Ending inventory			(40,200)	
Cost of goods sold				90,800
Gross margin				75,100
Operating expenses:				
Wage expense			10,200	
Rent expense			8,400	
Insurance expense			1,000	
Depreciation expense			600	
Supplies expense			550	20,750
Income from operations				54,350
Other revenue and (expense):				
Interest revenue			1,000	
Interest expense			(1,500)	(500)
Net income				$ 53,850

AUSTIN SOUND STEREO CENTER
Statement of Owner's Equity
Year Ended December 31, 19X6

C. Ernest, capital, December 31, 19X5	$25,900
Add: Net income	53,850
	79,750
Less: Withdrawals	(54,100)
C. Ernest, capital, December 31, 19X6	$25,650

AUSTIN SOUND STEREO CENTER
Balance Sheet
December 31, 19X6

Assets			**Liabilities**	
Current:			Current:	
Cash		$ 2,850	Accounts payable	$47,000
Accounts receivable		4,600	Unearned sales revenue	700
Note receivable		8,000	Wages payable	400
Interest receivable		400	Interest payable	200
Inventory		40,200	Total current liabilities	48,300
Prepaid insurance		200	Long-term:	
Supplies		100	Note payable	12,600
Total current assets		56,350	Total liabilities	60,900
Plant:				
Furniture and fixtures	$33,200		**Owner's Equity**	
Less: Accumulated			C. Ernest, capital	25,650
depreciation	(3,000)	30,200	Total liabilities and	
Total assets		$86,550	owner's equity	$86,550

The last section of Austin Sound's income statement is **other revenue and expenses,** which is handled the same way in both inventory systems. This category reports revenues and expenses that are outside the company's main line of business.

Journalizing the Adjusting and Closing Entries in a Periodic Inventory System

Exhibit 5S-7 presents Austin Sound's adjusting entries. These entries follow the same pattern illustrated in Chapter 4 for a service entity.

The exhibit also gives Austin Sound's closing entries. The first closing entry closes the revenue accounts. Closing entries 2 and 3 are new. Entry 2 closes the beginning balance of the Inventory account ($38,600), along with Purchases and Freight In, into the Cost of Goods Sold account. Entry 3 sets up the ending balance of Inventory ($40,200) with a debit and also closes the Purchases contra accounts to Cost of Goods Sold.[1] Now Inventory and Cost of Goods Sold have their correct ending balances as follows:

Inventory

Jan. 1 Bal.	38,600	Dec. 31 Clo.	38,600
Dec. 31 Clo.	40,200		
Dec. 31 Bal.	40,200		

Cost of Goods Sold

Beg. inventory	38,600	Pur. discounts	3,000
Purchases	91,400	Pur. returns and allowances	1,200
Freight in	5,200	End. inventory	40,200
Bal.	90,800		

The entries to the Inventory account deserve additional explanation. Recall that before the closing process, Inventory still had the period's beginning balance. At the end of the period, this balance is one year old and must be replaced with the ending balance in order to prepare the financial statements at December 31, 19X6. Closing entries 2 and 3 give Inventory its correct ending balance of $40,200.

Closing entry 4 then closes the Sales contra accounts and Cost of Goods Sold along with the other expense accounts into Income Summary. Closing entries 5 and 6 complete the closing process. All data for the closing entries are taken from the income statement columns of the work sheet.

Study Exhibits 5S-5, 5S-6, and 5S-7 carefully because they illustrate the entire end-of-period process that leads to the financial statements. As you progress through this book, you may want to refer to these exhibits to refresh your understanding of the adjusting and closing process for a merchandising business.

Net sales, cost of goods sold, operating income, and net income are unaffected by the choice of inventory system. You can prove this by comparing Austin Sound's financial statements given in Exhibit 5S-6 with the corresponding statements in Exhibit 5-7. The only differences appear in the cost-of-goods-sold section of the income statement, and those differences are unimportant. In fact, virtually all companies report cost of goods sold in streamlined fashion, as shown for May Department Stores in Exhibit 5-1 and for Austin Sound in Exhibit 5-7.

[1]Some accountants make the inventory entries as adjustments rather than as part of the closing process. The adjusting-entry approach adds these adjustments (shifted out of the closing entries):

Adjusting Entries

Dec. 31	Cost of Goods Sold	38,600	
	Inventory (beginning balance)		38,600
31	Inventory (ending balance)	40,200	
	Cost of Goods Sold		40,200

When these entries are posted, the Inventory account will look exactly as shown here, except that the journal references will be "Adj." instead of "Clo." The financial statements are unaffected by the approach used for these inventory entries.

Concept Highlight

EXHIBIT 5S-7
Adjusting and Closing Entries

Journal

Adjusting Entries

	Date	Accounts	Debit	Credit
a.	Dec. 31	Interest Receivable	400	
		Interest Revenue		400
b.	31	Supplies Expense ($650 – $100)	550	
		Supplies		550
c.	31	Insurance Expense	1,000	
		Prepaid Insurance		1,000
d.	31	Depreciation Expense	600	
		Accumulated Depreciation		600
e.	31	Unearned Sales Revenue	1,300	
		Sales Revenue		1,300
f.	31	Wage Expense	400	
		Wages Payable		400
g.	31	Interest Expense	200	
		Interest Payable		200

Closing Entries

	Date	Accounts	Debit	Credit
1.	Dec. 31	Sales Revenue	169,300	
		Interest Revenue	1,000	
		Income Summary		170,300
2.	31	Cost of Goods Sold	135,200	
		Inventory (beginning balance)		38,600
		Purchases		91,400
		Freight In		5,200
3.	31	Inventory (ending balance)	40,200	
		Purchase Discounts	3,000	
		Purchase Returns and Allowances	1,200	
		Cost of Goods Sold		44,400
4.	31	Income Summary	116,450	
		Sales Discounts		1,400
		Sales Returns and Allowances		2,000
		Cost of Goods Sold ($135,200 – $44,400)		90,800
		Wage Expense		10,200
		Rent Expense		8,400
		Depreciation Expense		600
		Insurance Expense		1,000
		Supplies Expense		550
		Interest Expense		1,500
5.	31	Income Summary ($170,300 – $116,450)	53,850	
		C. Ernest, Capital		53,850
6.	31	C. Ernest, Capital	54,100	
		C. Ernest, Withdrawals		54,100

Learning Tip: Here is an easy way to remember the closing process. First look at the work sheet. Then

1. Debit all income statement accounts with a credit balance. Credit Income Summary for the sum of all these debits.
2. Credit all income statement accounts with a debit balance. Debit Income Summary for the sum of all these credits.
3. Take the balance in the Income Summary account. If the account has a debit balance, there is a net loss; credit Income Summary for that amount, and debit Capital. If Income Summary has a credit balance, there is a net income for the period; debit Income Summary for that amount, and credit Capital.
4. Look at the debit balance of Withdrawals in the balance-sheet column. Credit Withdrawals for its balance, and debit Capital for the same amount.

SUMMARY PROBLEM FOR YOUR REVIEW

The following trial balance pertains to Jan King Distributing Company:

JAN KING DISTRIBUTING COMPANY Trial Balance (Periodic Inventory System) December 31, 19X3		
Cash	$ 5,670	
Accounts receivable	37,100	
Inventory	60,500	
Supplies	3,930	
Prepaid rent	6,000	
Furniture and fixtures	26,500	
Accumulated depreciation		$ 21,200
Accounts payable		46,340
Salary payable		
Interest payable		
Unearned sales revenue		3,500
Note payable, long-term		35,000
Jan King, capital		23,680
Jan King, withdrawals	48,000	
Sales revenue		346,700
Sales discounts	10,300	
Sales returns and allowances	8,200	
Purchases	175,900	
Purchase discounts		6,000
Purchase returns and allowances		7,430
Freight in	9,300	
Salary expense	82,750	
Rent expense	7,000	
Depreciation expense		
Utilities expense	5,800	
Supplies expense		
Interest expense	2,900	
Total	$489,850	$489,850

Additional data at December 31, 19X3:

- **a.** Supplies used during the year, $2,580.
- **b.** Prepaid rent in force, $1,000.
- **c.** Unearned sales revenue still not earned, $2,400. The company expects to earn this amount during the next few months.
- **d.** Depreciation. The furniture and fixtures' estimated useful life is ten years, and they are expected to be worthless when they are retired from service.
- **e.** Accrued salaries, $1,300.
- **f.** Accrued interest expense, $600.
- **g.** Inventory on hand, $65,800.

REQUIRED

1. Enter the trial balance on an accounting work sheet and complete the work sheet.
2. Journalize the adjusting and closing entries at December 31. Post to the Income Summary account as an accuracy check on the entries affecting that account. The credit balance closed out of Income Summary should equal net income computed on the work sheet.
3. Prepare the company's multi-step income statement, statement of owner's equity, and balance sheet in account format. Draw arrows connecting the statements.
4. Compute the inventory turnover for 19X3. Turnover for 19X2 was 2.1. Would you expect Jan King Distributing Company to be more profitable or less profitable in 19X3 than in 19X2? Give your reason.

■ **SOLUTION**

REQUIREMENT 1

JAN KING DISTRIBUTING COMPANY
Accounting Work Sheet (Perpetual Inventory System)
Year Ended December 31, 19X3

Account Title	Trial Balance		Adjustments		Income Statement		Balance Sheet	
	Debit	Credit	Debit	Credit	Debit	Credit	Debit	Credit
Cash	5,670						5,670	
Accounts receivable	37,100						37,100	
Inventory	60,500				60,500	65,800	65,800	
Supplies	3,930			(a) 2,580			1,350	
Prepaid rent	6,000			(b) 5,000			1,000	
Furniture and fixtures	26,500						26,500	
Accumulated depreciation		21,200		(d) 2,650				23,850
Accounts payable		46,340						46,340
Salary payable				(e) 1,300				1,300
Interest payable				(f) 600				600
Unearned sales revenue		3,500	(c) 1,100					2,400
Note payable, long-term		35,000						35,000
Jan King, capital		23,680						23,680
Jan King, withdrawals	48,000						48,000	
Sales revenue		346,700		(c) 1,100		347,800		
Sales discounts	10,300				10,300			
Sales returns and allowances	8,200				8,200			
Purchases	175,900				175,900			
Purchase discounts		6,000				6,000		
Purchase returns and allowances		7,430				7,430		
Freight in	9,300				9,300			
Salary expense	82,750		(e) 1,300		84,050			
Rent expense	7,000		(b) 5,000		12,000			
Depreciation expense			(d) 2,650		2,650			
Utilities expense	5,800				5,800			
Supplies expense			(a) 2,580		2,580			
Interest expense	2,900		(f) 600		3,500			
	489,850	489,850	13,230	13,230	374,780	427,030	185,420	133,170
Net income					52,250			52,250
					427,030	427,030	185,420	185,420

REQUIREMENT 2

Adjusting Entries

19X3			
Dec. 31	Supplies Expense	2,580	
	Supplies		2,580
31	Rent Expense	5,000	
	Prepaid Rent		5,000
31	Unearned Sales Revenue ($3,500 – $2,400)	1,100	
	Sales Revenue		1,100
31	Depreciation Expense ($26,500/10)	2,650	
	Accumulated Depreciation		2,650
31	Salary Expense	1,300	
	Salary Payable		1,300
31	Interest Expense	600	
	Interest Payable		600

Closing Entries

19X3			
Dec. 31	Sales Revenue	347,800	
	Income Summary		347,800
31	Cost of Goods Sold	245,700	
	Inventory (beginning balance)		60,500
	Purchases		175,900
	Freight In		9,300
31	Inventory	65,800	
	Purchase Discounts	6,000	
	Purchase Returns and Allowances	7,430	
	Cost of Goods Sold		79,230
31	Income Summary	295,550	
	Sales Discounts		10,300
	Sales Returns and Allowances		8,200
	Cost of Goods Sold ($245,700 – $79,230)		166,470
	Salary Expense		84,050
	Rent Expense		12,000
	Depreciation Expense		2,650
	Utilities Expense		5,800
	Supplies Expense		2,580
	Interest Expense		3,500
31	Income Summary ($347,800 – $295,550)	52,250	
	Jan King, Capital		52,250
31	Jan King, Capital	48,000	
	Jan King, Withdrawals		48,000

Income Summary

Clo.	295,550	Clo.	347,800
Clo.	52,250	Bal.	52,250

REQUIREMENT 3

JAN KING DISTRIBUTING COMPANY
Income Statement
Year Ended December 31, 19X3

Sales revenue			$347,800	
Less: Sales discounts		$ (10,300)		
Sales returns and allowances		(8,200)	(18,500)	
Net sales revenue				$329,300
Cost of goods sold:				
Beginning inventory			$ 60,500	
Purchases		$175,900		
Less: Purchase discounts	$(6,000)			
Purchase returns and allowances	(7,430)	(13,430)		
Net purchases			162,470	
Freight in			9,300	
Cost of goods available for sale			232,270	
Less: Ending inventory			(65,800)	
Cost of goods sold				166,470
Gross margin				162,830
Operating expenses:				
Salary expense			84,050	
Rent expense			12,000	
Utilities expense			5,800	
Depreciation expense			2,650	
Supplies expense			2,580	107,080
Income from operations				55,750
Other expense:				
Interest expense				3,500
Net income				$ 52,250

JAN KING DISTRIBUTING COMPANY
Statement of Owner's Equity
Year Ended December 31, 19X3

Jan King, capital, December 31, 19X2	$23,680
Add: Net income	52,250
	75,930
Less: Withdrawals	(48,000)
Jan King, capital, December 31, 19X3	$27,930

JAN KING DISTRIBUTING COMPANY
Balance Sheet
December 31, 19X3

Assets			Liabilities	
Current:			Current:	
Cash		$ 5,670	Accounts payable	$ 46,340
Accounts receivable		37,100	Salary payable	1,300
Inventory		65,800	Interest payable	600
Supplies		1,350	Unearned sales revenue	2,400
Prepaid rent		1,000	Total current liabilities	50,640
Total current assets		110,920	Long-term:	
Plant:			Note payable	35,000
Furniture and fixtures	$26,500		Total liabilities	85,640
Less: Accumulated depreciation	(23,850)	2,650	**Owner's Equity**	
			Jan King, capital	27,930
Total assets		$113,570	Total liabilities and owner's equity	$113,570

REQUIREMENT 4

$$\text{Inventory turnover} = \frac{\text{Cost of goods sold}}{\text{Average inventory}} = \frac{\$166,470}{(\$60,500 + \$65,800)/2} = 2.6$$

The increase in the rate of inventory turnover from 2.1 to 2.6 suggests higher profits in 19X3 than in 19X2.

Supplement Exercises

Journalizing purchase and sales transactions
(Obj. S2)

E5S-1 Journalize, without explanations, the following transactions of The Gift House during June:

June 3	Purchased $700 of inventory under terms of 2/10 n/eom (end of month) and FOB shipping point.
7	Returned $300 of defective merchandise purchased on June 3.
9	Paid freight bill of $30 on June 3 purchase.
10	Sold inventory for $2,200, collecting cash of $400. Payment terms on the remainder were 2/15 n/30.
12	Paid amount owed on credit purchase of June 3, less the discount and the return.
16	Granted a sales allowance of $800 on the June 10 sale.
23	Received cash from June 10 customer in full settlement of her debt, less the allowance and the discount.

E5S-2 As the proprietor of Kendrick Tire Company, you receive the following invoice from a supplier:

Journalizing transactions from a purchase invoice
(Obj. S2)

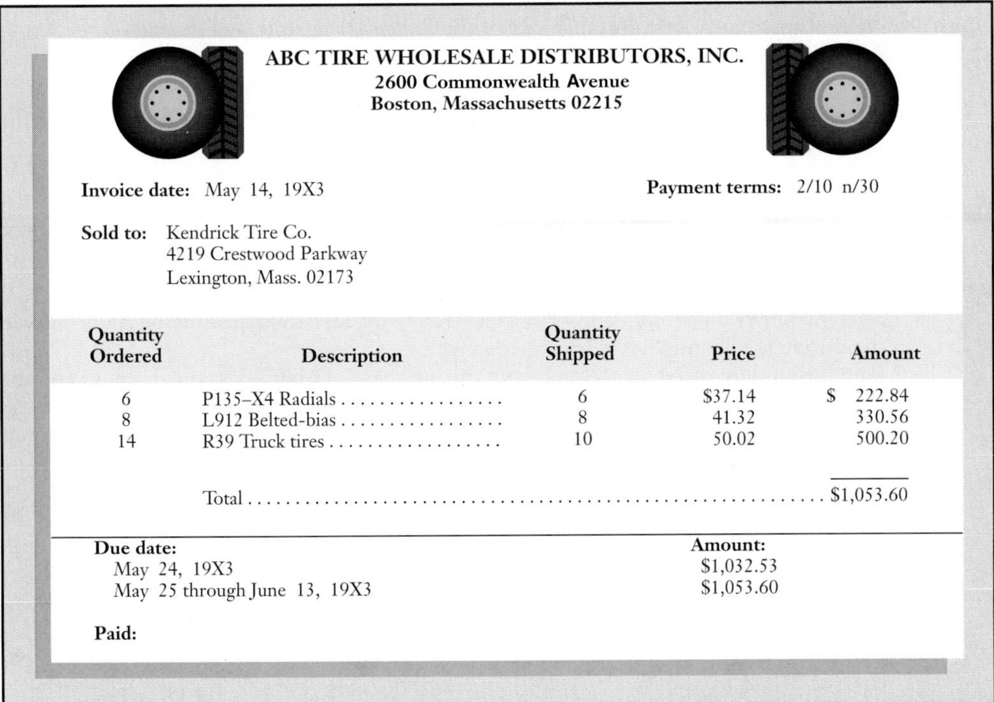

ABC TIRE WHOLESALE DISTRIBUTORS, INC.
2600 Commonwealth Avenue
Boston, Massachusetts 02215

Invoice date: May 14, 19X3 **Payment terms:** 2/10 n/30

Sold to: Kendrick Tire Co.
4219 Crestwood Parkway
Lexington, Mass. 02173

Quantity Ordered	Description	Quantity Shipped	Price	Amount
6	P135–X4 Radials	6	$37.14	$ 222.84
8	L912 Belted-bias	8	41.32	330.56
14	R39 Truck tires	10	50.02	500.20
	Total			$1,053.60

Due date:	Amount:
May 24, 19X3	$1,032.53
May 25 through June 13, 19X3	$1,053.60

Paid:

REQUIRED

1. Record the May 15 purchase on account. Carry to the nearest cent throughout.
2. The R 39 truck tires were ordered by mistake and were therefore returned to ABC. Journalize the return on May 19.
3. Record the May 22 payment of the amount owed.

E5S-3 On April 30, Rapaport Jewelers purchased inventory of $5,000 on account from La Roche Fine Gems, a jewelry importer. Terms were 3/15 net 45. On receiving the goods, Rapaport checked the order and found $800 of unsuitable merchandise. Therefore, Rapaport returned $800 of merchandise to La Roche on May 4.

Journalizing purchase transactions
(Obj. S2)

To pay the remaining amount owed, Rapaport had to borrow the net amount of the invoice from the bank. On May 14, Rapaport signed a short-term note payable to the bank and immediately paid the borrowed funds to La Roche. On June 14, Rapaport paid the bank the net amount of the invoice, which Rapaport had borrowed, plus 1% monthly interest (round to the nearest dollar).

REQUIRED

Record the indicated transactions in the journal of Rapaport Jewelers. Explanations are not required.

E5S-4 Refer to the business situation in Exercise 5S-3. Journalize the transactions of La Roche Fine Gems. Explanations are not required.

Journalizing sale transactions
(Obj. S2)

Note: Exercises 5-13 (page 216), 5-14 (page 216), and 5-15 (page 217) also pertain to the periodic inventory system.

Supplement Problems

P5S-1 The following transactions occurred between Glendale Medical Supply and a Revco Drug store during November of the current year:

Accounting for the purchase and sale of inventory
(Obj. S2)

Nov. 6 Glendale Medical Supply sold $5,000 worth of merchandise to Revco on terms of 2/10 n/30, FOB shipping point. Glendale prepaid freight charges of $300 and included this amount in the invoice total. (Glendale's entry to record the freight payment debits Accounts Receivable and credits Cash.)

10 Revco returned $900 of the merchandise purchased on November 6. Glendale issued a credit memo for this amount.

Nov. 15 Revco paid $3,000 of the invoice amount owed to Glendale for the November 6 purchase, less the discount. This payment included none of the freight charge.
27 Revco paid the remaining amount owed to Glendale for the November 6 purchase.

REQUIRED

Journalize these transactions, first on the books of the Revco Drug store and second on the books of Glendale Medical Supply.

Journalizing purchase and sale transactions
(Obj. S2)

P5S-2 Jastrow Distributing Company engaged in the following transactions during May of the current year:

May 3 Purchased office supplies for cash, $300.
7 Purchased inventory on credit terms of 3/10 net eom, $2,000.
8 Returned half the inventory purchased on May 7. It was not the inventory ordered.
10 Sold goods for cash, $450.
13 Sold inventory on credit terms of 2/15 n/45, $3,900, less $600 quantity discount offered to customers who purchased in large quantities.
16 Paid the amount owed on account from the purchase of May 7, less the discount and the return.
17 Received defective inventory returned from May 13 sale, $900, which is the net amount after the quantity discount.
18 Purchased inventory of $4,000 on account. Payment terms were 2/10 net 30.
26 Borrowed $3,920 from the bank to take advantage of the discount offered on May 18 purchase. Signed a note payable to the bank for this amount.
26 Paid supplier for goods purchased on May 18, less the discount.
28 Received cash in full settlement of this account from the customer who purchased inventory on May 13, less the discount and the return.
29 Purchased inventory for cash, $2,000 less a quantity discount of $400, plus freight charges of $160.

REQUIRED

1. Journalize the preceding transactions. Explanations are not required.
2. The note payable signed on May 26 requires the payment of $30 interest expense. Was the decision to borrow funds to take advantage of the cash discount wise or unwise? Support your answer by comparing the discount to the interest paid.

Journalizing purchase and sale transactions
(Obj. S2)

P5S-3 Rogers Furniture Company engaged in the following transactions during July of the current year:

July 2 Purchased inventory for cash, $800, less a quantity discount of $150.
5 Purchased store supplies on credit terms of net eom, $450.
8 Purchased inventory of $3,000, less a quantity discount of 10%, plus freight charges of $230. Credit terms are 3/15 n/30.
9 Sold goods for cash, $1,200.
11 Returned $200 (net amount after the quantity discount) of the inventory purchased on July 8. It was damaged in shipment.
12 Purchased inventory on credit terms of 3/10 n/30, $3,330.
14 Sold inventory on credit terms of 2/10 n/30, $9,600, less a $600 quantity discount.
16 Paid the electricity and water bills, $275.
20 Received returned inventory from July 14 sale, $400 (net amount after the quantity discount). Rogers shipped the wrong goods by mistake.
21 Borrowed the amount owed on the July 8 purchase. Signed a note payable to the bank for $2,655, which takes into account the return of inventory on July 11.
21 Paid supplier for goods purchased on July 8 less the discount and the return.
23 Received $6,860 cash in partial settlement of this account from the customer who purchased inventory on July 14. Granted the customer a 2% discount and credited this account receivable for $7,000.
30 Paid for the store supplies purchased on July 5.

REQUIRED

1. Journalize the preceding transactions. Explanations are not required.
2. Compute the amount of the receivable at July 31 from the customer to whom Rogers sold inventory on July 14. What amount of cash discount applies to this receivable at July 31?

P5S-4 The year-end trial balance of Bliss Sales Company pertains to March 31 of the current year.

Preparing a merchandiser's accounting work sheet, financial statements, and adjusting and closing entries ***(Obj. S3, S4, S5)***

BLISS SALES COMPANY
Trial Balance
March 31, 19XX

Cash	$ 7,880	
Notes receivable, current	12,400	
Interest receivable		
Inventory	130,050	
Prepaid insurance	3,600	
Notes receivable, long-term	62,000	
Furniture	6,000	
Accumulated depreciation		$ 4,000
Accounts payable		12,220
Sales commission payable		
Salary payable		
Unearned sales revenue		9,610
Mark Bliss, capital		172,780
Mark Bliss, withdrawals	66,040	
Sales revenue		440,000
Sales discounts	4,800	
Sales returns and allowances	11,300	
Interest revenue		8,600
Purchases	233,000	
Purchase discounts		3,100
Purchase returns and allowances		7,600
Freight in	10,000	
Sales commission expense	78,300	
Salary expense	24,700	
Rent expense	6,000	
Utilities expense	1,840	
Depreciation expense		
Insurance expense		
Total	$657,910	$657,910

Additional data at March 31, 19XX:

a. Accrued interest revenue, $1,030.
b. Insurance expense for the year, $3,000.
c. Furniture has an estimated useful life of six years. Its value is expected to be zero when it is retired from service.
d. Unearned sales revenue still unearned, $8,200.
e. Accrued salaries, $1,200.
f. Accrued sales commission expense, $1,700.
g. Inventory on hand, $133,200.

REQUIRED

1. Enter the trial balance on an accounting work sheet, and complete the work sheet for the year ended March 31 of the current year.
2. Prepare the company's multi-step income statement and statement of owner's equity for the year ended March 31 of the current year. Also prepare its balance sheet at that date. Long-term notes receivable should be reported on the balance sheet between current assets and plant assets in a separate section labeled Investments.
3. Journalize the adjusting and closing entries at March 31.
4. Post to the Mark Bliss, Capital account and to the Income Summary account as an accuracy check on the adjusting and closing process.

Note: Problems 5-9A (page 221) and 5-9B (page 224) also pertain to the periodic inventory system.

CHAPTER 6

Accounting Information Systems: Special Journals, Control Accounts, and Subsidiary Ledgers

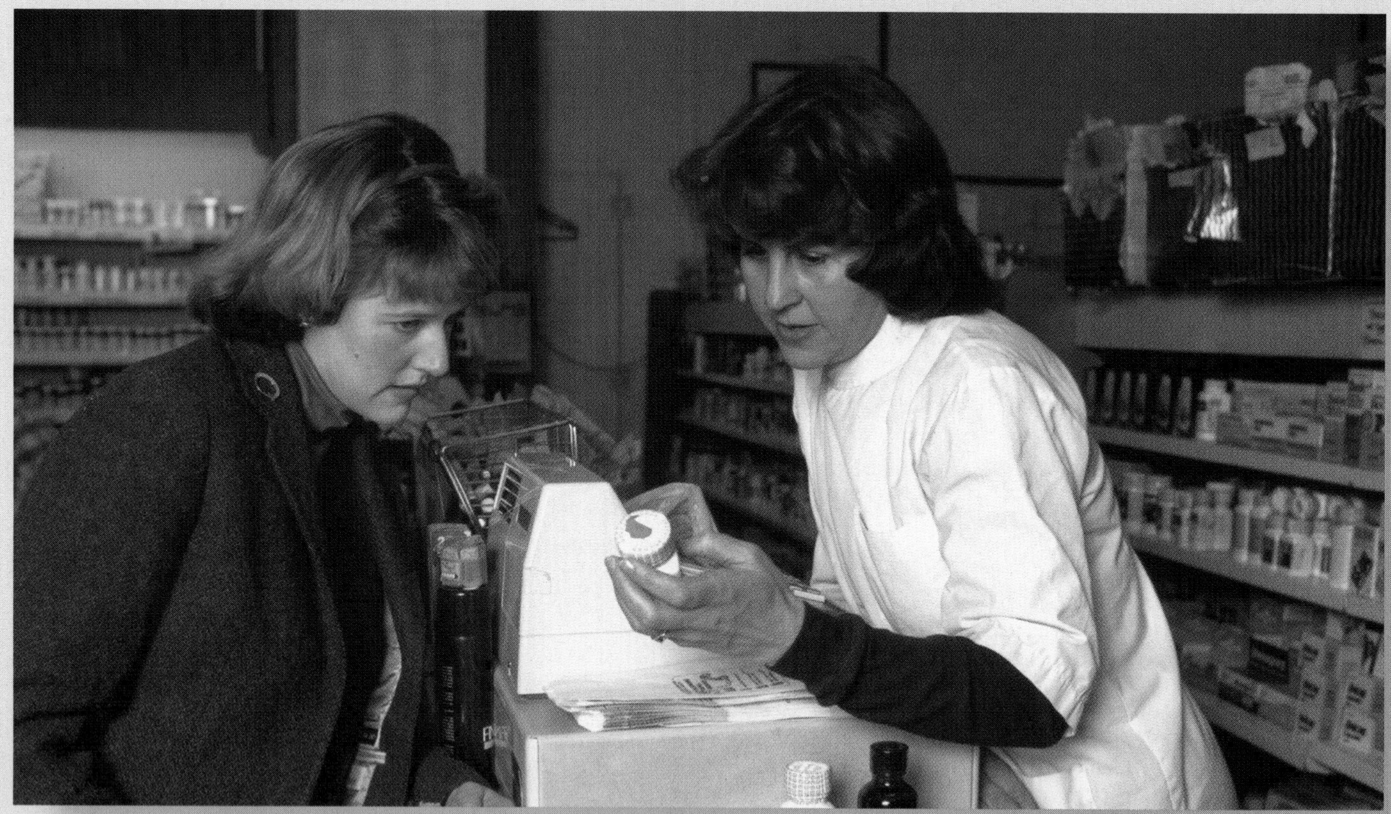

LEARNING OBJECTIVES

After studying this chapter, you should be able to

1. Describe the features of an effective accounting information system
2. Understand how computerized and manual accounting systems work
3. Understand how spreadsheets are used in accounting
4. Use the sales journal, the cash receipts journal, and the accounts receivable subsidiary ledger
5. Use the purchases journal, the cash disbursements journal, and the accounts payable subsidiary ledger

> *After 30 years in the pharmacy business, our office is finally organized, our accounts receivable figures are at our fingertips, our payroll is simple to compute, and our bills go out promptly—all thanks to this new computer system!*
>
> BOB AND MAUREEN HALLISEY,
> OWNERS OF HALLISEY'S PHARMACY

Bob and Maureen Hallisey, owners of Hallisey's Pharmacy in Old Saybrook, Connecticut, computerized their business ten years ago. For 20 years, they had used a manual accounting system. When asked, "Why did you computerize?" they replied, "For efficiency and speed."

The Halliseys began with a now-obsolete software package. Four years ago, their hardware failed. When they replaced it, they switched to new software called Business Works.

Now they can analyze their cash and track slow-paying customers on a daily basis. The new software also generates the end-of-year information for their financial statements. A key report shows sales by product. The Halliseys can set prices to achieve a target gross profit percentage on each product. The new accounting system has paid for itself many times over by helping the Halliseys make better business decisions.

Accounting Information System. The combination of personnel, records, and procedures that a business uses to meet its need for financial data.

Hallisey's Pharmacy has more than an accounting system. It has an accounting *information* system. An **accounting information system** is the combination of personnel, records, and procedures that a business uses to meet its need for financial data. Special management reports provided by an accounting information system, such as sales by product and cash-flow projections, provide valuable information for the Halliseys' business decisions.

We have already been using an accounting information system in this text. That simple accounting system consists of two basic components:

- A general journal
- A general ledger

The journal and the ledger we have been using are the *general* journal and the *general* ledger. Every accounting system has these components, but this simple system can efficiently handle only a few transactions per period. Accounting systems cope with heavy transaction loads in two ways: computerization and specialization. We *computerize* to journalize, post, and prepare reports faster and more reliably. *Specialization* comes when we deal with similar transactions in groups to speed the process. We will explore special journals in the second half of this chapter.

Features of an Effective Accounting Information System

Objective 1

Describe the features of an effective accounting information system

Several design features make accounting systems run efficiently. A good system—whether computerized or manual—includes four features: control, compatibility, flexibility, and a favorable cost/benefit relationship.

Control

Managers need *control* over operations. *Internal controls* are the methods and procedures used to authorize transactions and safeguard assets. For example, in companies such as Coca-Cola, Dow Chemical, and Kinko's, managers exert tight control over cash disbursements to avoid theft through unauthorized payments. Also, VISA, MasterCard, and Discover keep records of their accounts receivable to ensure that they receive collections on time.

Compatibility

A *compatible* system is one that works smoothly with the business's operations, personnel, and organizational structure. An example is Bank of America, which is organized as a network of branch offices. Bank of America's top managers want to know revenues in each region where the bank does business. They also want to analyze the bank's loans in different geographic regions. If revenues and loans in California are lagging, the managers can concentrate their efforts in that state. They may relocate some branch offices or hire new personnel to increase revenues and net income. A compatible accounting *information* system conforms to the needs of the business.

Flexibility

Organizations evolve. They develop new products, sell off unprofitable operations and acquire new ones, and adjust employee pay scales. Changes in the business often call for changes in the accounting system. A well-designed system is *flexible* if it accommodates changes without needing a complete overhaul. Consider Monsanto Company's acquisition of the pharmaceuticals firm Searle, including Searle's Nutrasweet division. Monsanto's accounting system had the flexibility to fold Searle's/Nutrasweet's financial statements into those of Monsanto.

Favorable Cost/Benefit Relationship

Achieving control, compatibility, and flexibility costs money. These costs reduce a company's net income, so managers often must settle for less than the perfect accounting system. They strive for a system that offers maximum benefits at a minimum cost—that is, a favorable *cost/benefit relationship.* Most small companies, such as Hallisey's Pharmacy, use off-the-shelf computerized accounting packages, and the very smallest businesses might not computerize at all. But large companies, such as the brokerage firm Merrill Lynch, have specialized needs for information. For them, customized programming is a must. The benefits—in terms of information tailored to the company's needs—far outweigh the cost of the system. The result? Better decisions.

■ Daily Exercise 6-1

Components of a Computerized Accounting System

Three components form the heart of a computerized accounting system:

1. Hardware
2. Software
3. Company personnel

Each component is critical to the system's success.

Hardware is the electronic equipment that includes computers, disk drives, monitors, printers, and the network that connects them. Most modern accounting systems require a **network,** the system of electronic linkages that allows different computers to share the same information. In a networked system, many computers can be connected to the main computer, or **server,** which stores the program and the data. With the right network, a Price Waterhouse auditor in London can access the data of a client located in Sydney, Australia. The result is a speedier audit for the client, often at lower cost than if the auditor had to perform all the work on site in Sydney.

Hardware. Electronic equipment that includes computers, disk drives, monitors, printers, and the network that connects them.

Network. The system of electronic linkages that allows different computers to share the same information.

Server. The main computer in a network, where the program and data are stored.

Software. Set of programs or instructions that drive the computer to perform the work desired.

Database. A computerized storehouse of information.

Software is the set of programs that drive the computer to perform the work desired. Accounting software accepts, edits (alters), and stores transaction data and generates the reports managers use to run the business. Many accounting software packages operate independently from the other computing activities of the system. For example, a company that is only partly computerized may use software programs to account for employee payrolls and sales and accounts receivable. The other parts of the accounting system may not be fully automated.

For large enterprises, such as Hershey Foods and Caterpillar Tractor, the accounting software is integrated within the overall company **database,** or computerized storehouse of information. Many business databases, or *management information systems,* include both accounting and nonaccounting data. In negotiating a union contract, the Union Pacific Railroad often needs to examine the relationship between the employment history and salary levels of company employees. Union Pacific's database provides the data managers need to negotiate effectively with their labor unions. During negotiations, both parties carry laptop computers to analyze the effects of decisions on the spot.

"For large enterprises, such as Hershey Foods and Caterpillar Tractor, the accounting software is integrated within the overall company database . . ."

Finally, properly trained personnel are critical to the success of any accounting information system.

■ Daily Exercise 6-2

■ Daily Exercise 6-3

The Three Stages of Data Processing: A Comparison of Computerized and Manual Accounting Systems

Objective 2

Understand how computerized and manual accounting systems work

Computerized accounting systems have replaced manual systems in many organizations—even small businesses such as Hallisey's Pharmacy. As we discuss the three stages of data processing, observe the differences between a computerized system and a manual system. The relationship among the three stages of data processing is shown in Exhibit 6-1.

Inputs represent data from source documents, such as sales receipts, bank deposit slips, and fax orders and other telecommunications. Inputs are usually grouped by type. For example, a firm would enter cash-sale transactions separately from credit sales and purchase transactions.

EXHIBIT 6-1
The Three Stages of Data Processing

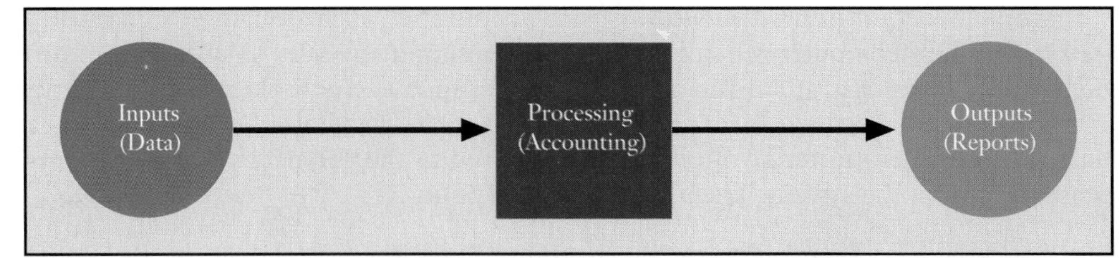

In a manual system, *processing* includes journalizing transactions, posting to the accounts, and preparing the financial statements. A computerized system also processes but without the intermediate steps (journal, ledger, and trial balance).

Outputs are the reports used for decision making, including the financial statements (income statement, balance sheet, and so on). The Halliseys are making better decisions—and prospering—because of the reports produced by their accounting system. From the computer's point of view, a trial balance is also a report. But a manual system would treat the trial balance as a *processing* step leading to the statements. Exhibit 6-2 is an overview of a computerized accounting system.

Designing an Accounting System: The Chart of Accounts

Recall from Chapter 2, p. 59, that the chart of accounts lists all the accounts and their account numbers.

Design of the accounting system begins with the chart of accounts. In the accounting system of a large, complex company such as Eastman Kodak, account numbers take on added importance. It is efficient to represent a complex account title, such as Accumulated Depreciation—Photographic Equipment, with a concise account number (for example, 12570).

Recall that asset accounts generally begin with the digit 1, liabilities with the digit 2, owner's equity accounts with the digit 3, revenues with 4, and expenses with 5. Exhibit 6-3 diagrams one structure for computerized accounts. Assets are divided into current assets, fixed assets (property, plant, and equipment), and other assets. Among the current assets, we illustrate only three general ledger accounts: Cash in Bank (Account No. 111), Accounts Receivable (No. 112), and Prepaid Insurance (No. 115).

The account numbers in Exhibit 6-3 get longer and more detailed as you move from top to bottom. For example, Customer A's account number is 1120001, in which 112 represents Accounts Receivable and 0001 refers to Customer A.

EXHIBIT 6-2
Overview of a Computerized Accounting System

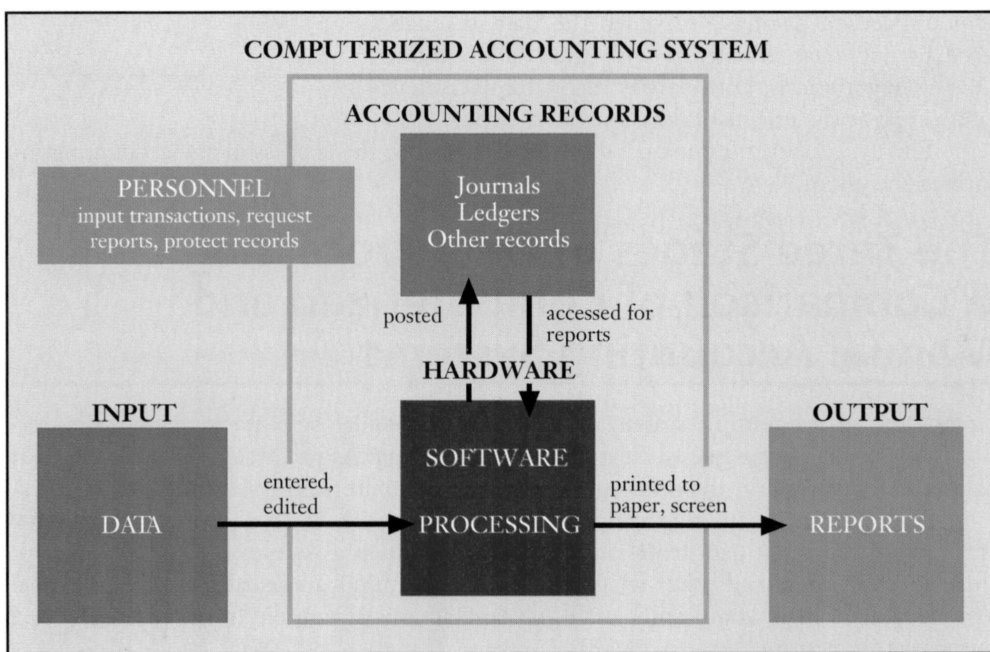

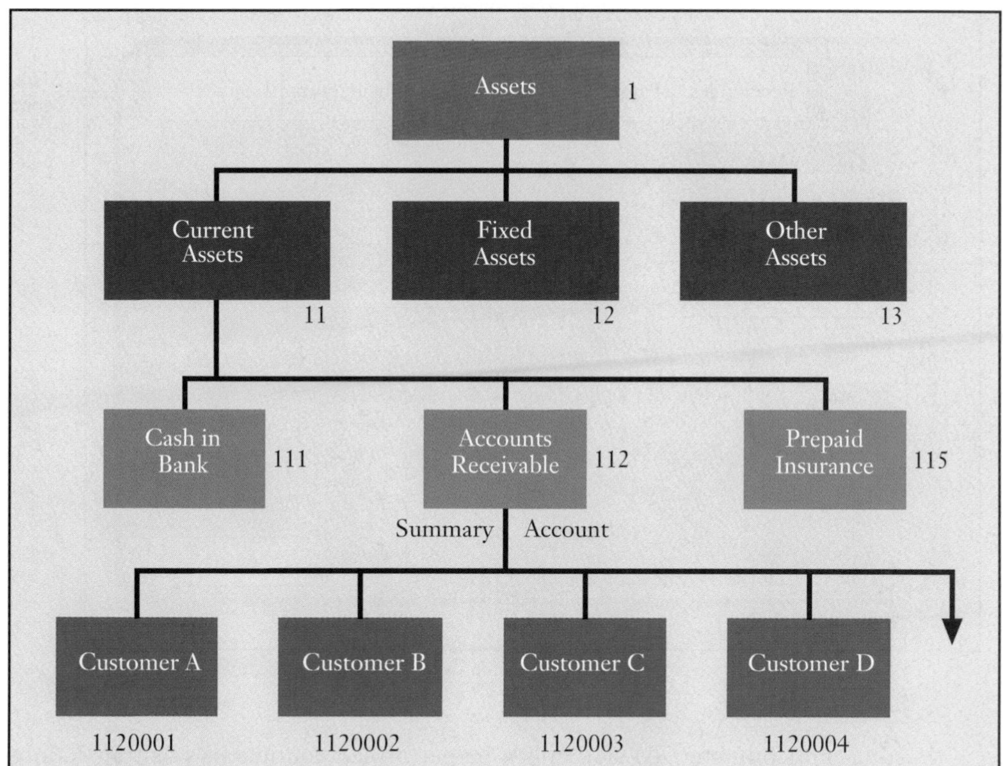

EXHIBIT 6-3
Structure for Computerized Accounts

Computerized accounting systems rely on account *number ranges* to translate accounts and their balances into properly organized financial statements and other reports. For example, the accounts numbered 101–399 (assets, liabilities, and owner's equity) are sorted to the balance sheet, while the accounts numbered 401–599 (revenues and expenses) go to the income statement.

■ Daily Exercise 6-4

Classifying Transactions: Computerized and Manual Systems

Recording transactions in an actual accounting system requires an additional step that we have skipped thus far. A business of any size must *classify* transactions by type for efficient handling. In a manual system, credit sales, purchases on account, cash receipts, and cash payments are treated as four separate categories, with each type entered into its own special journal. For example:

- Credit sales are recorded in a special journal called a *sales journal.*
- Cash receipts are entered into a *cash receipts journal.*
- Credit purchases of inventory and other assets are recorded in a *purchases journal.*
- Cash payments are entered in a *cash disbursements journal.*
- Transactions that do not fit any of the special journals, such as the adjusting entries at the end of the period, are recorded in the *general journal,* which serves as the "journal of last resort."

We discuss these journals in detail later in this chapter.

Menu-Driven Accounting Systems

Computerized systems are organized by function, or task. Access to functions is arranged in terms of menus. A **menu** is a list of options for choosing computer functions. In such a *menu-driven* system, you first access the most general group of functions, called the *main menu.* You then choose from one or more submenus until you finally reach the function you want.

Menu. A list of options for choosing computer functions.

Exhibit 6-4 illustrates one type of menu structure. The row at the top of the exhibit shows the main menu. The computer operator (or accountant) has chosen the General option (short for General Ledger), highlighed by the cursor. This action opened a submenu of four items—Transactions, Posting, Account Maintenance, and Closing. The Transactions option was then chosen (highlighted).

EXHIBIT 6-4
Main Menu of a Computerized Accounting System

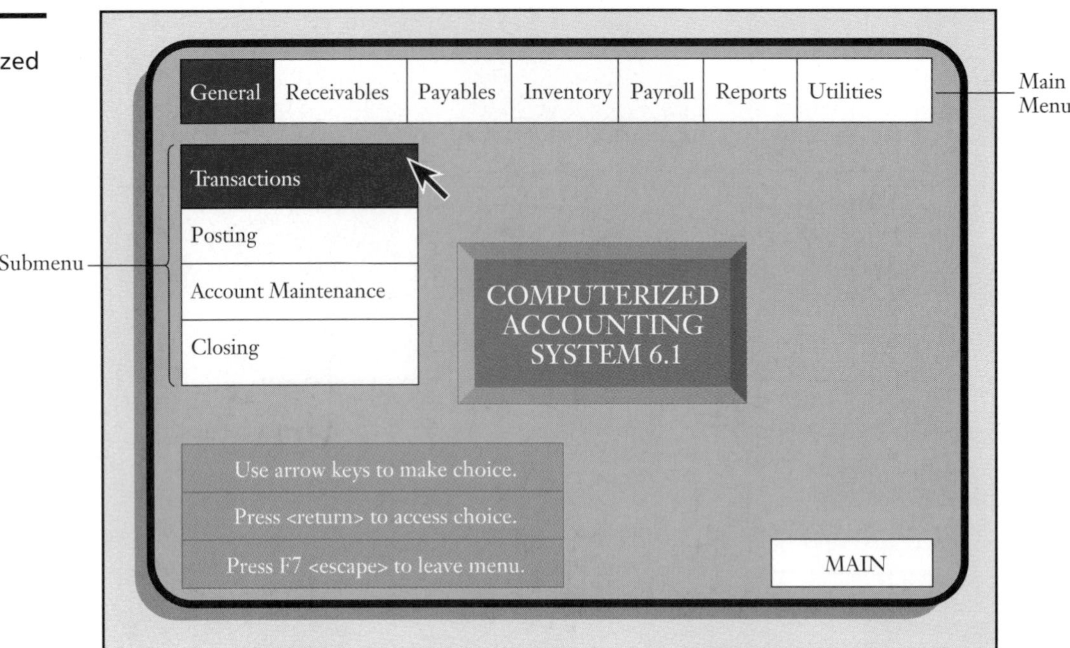

On-line Processing. Computerized processing of related functions, such as the recording and posting of transactions, on a continuous basis.

Batch Processing. Computerized accounting for similar transactions in a group or batch.

Posting in a computerized system can be performed continuously as transactions are being recorded (**on-line processing**) or later for a group or batch of similar transactions (**batch processing**). In either case, posting is automatic. Batch processing of accounting data allows accountants to check the entries for accuracy before posting them. In effect, the transaction data are "parked" in the computer to await posting, which simply updates the account balances.

Preparing Accounting Reports

Outputs—accounting reports—are the final stage of data processing. In a computerized system, the financial statements can be printed automatically. For example, the Reports option in the main menu gives the operator various report choices, which are expanded in the Reports submenu of Exhibit 6-5. In the exhibit, the operator is working with the financial statements, specifically the balance sheet, as shown by the highlighting.

EXHIBIT 6-5
Reports Submenu of a Computerized Accounting System

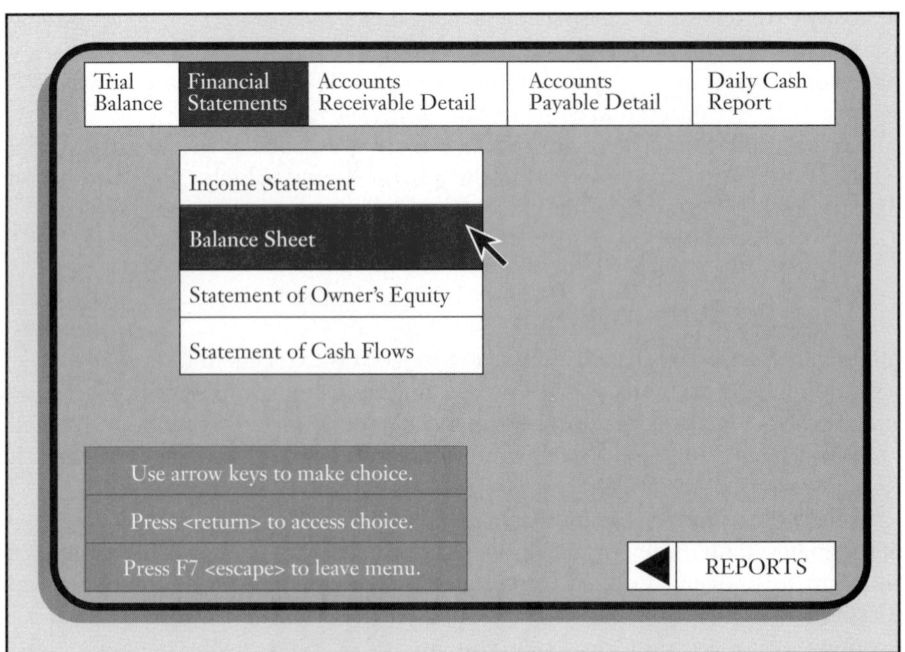

Computerized System	Manual System
1. Start with the account balances in the ledger at the beginning of the period.	1. Same.
2. Analyze and classify business transactions by type. Access appropriate menus for data entry.	2. Analyze and journalize transactions as they occur.
3. Computer automatically posts transactions as a batch or when entered on-line.	3. Post journal entries to the ledger accounts.
4. The unadjusted balances are available immediately after each posting.	4. Compute the unadjusted balance in each account at the end of the period.
5. The trial balance, if needed, can be accessed as a report.	5. Enter the trial balance on the work sheet, and complete the work sheet.
6. Enter and post the adjusting entries. Print the financial statements. Run automatic closing procedure after backing up the period's accounting records.	6. Prepare the financial statements. Journalize and post the adjusting entries. Journalize and post the closing entries.
7. The next period's opening balances are created automatically as a result of closing.	7. Prepare the postclosing trial balance. This trial balance becomes step 1 for the next period.

Concept Highlight

EXHIBIT 6-6
Comparison of the Accounting Cycle in a Computerized and a Manual System

Summary of the Accounting Cycle: Computerized and Manual

Exhibit 6-6 summarizes the accounting cycle in a computerized system and in a manual system. As you study the exhibit, compare and contrast the two types of systems.

Integrated Accounting Software

Computerized accounting packages are organized by **modules,** separate but integrated units that are compatible and that function together. Changes affecting one module will affect others. For example, entering and posting a credit-sale transaction will update two modules: Accounts Receivable/Sales and Inventory/Cost of Goods Sold. Accounting packages, such as Business Works, Peachtree, and DacEasy, come as an integrated system. The Halliseys in the chapter opening story chose Business Works.

Module. Separate compatible units of an accounting package that are integrated to function together.

Spreadsheets

Objective 3

Understand how spreadsheets are used in accounting

You may be preparing your homework assignments manually. Imagine preparing a work sheet for General Motors (GM). Each adjustment changes the company's financial statement totals. Consider computing GM's revenue amounts by hand. The task would be overwhelming. For even a small business with only a few departments, the computations are tedious, time-consuming, and therefore expensive. Also, errors are likely.

Spreadsheets are computer programs that link data by means of formulas and functions. These electronic work sheets were invented to update budgets. Spreadsheets are organized as a rectangular grid composed of *cells,* each defined by a row number and a column number. A cell can contain words (called labels), numbers, or formulas (relationships among cells). The *cursor,* or electronic highlighter, indicates which cell is active, and it can be moved around the spreadsheet. When the cursor is placed over any cell, information can be entered there for processing.

Spreadsheet. A computer program that links data by means of formulas and functions; an electronic work sheet.

Exhibit 6-7 shows a simple income statement on a spreadsheet screen. The labels were entered in cells A1 through A4. The dollar amount of revenues was entered in cell B2 and expenses in cell B3. A formula was placed in cell B4 as follows: =B2–B3. This formula subtracts expenses from revenues to compute net income in cell B4. If revenues in cell B2 increase to $110,000, net income in B4 automatically increases to $50,000. No other cells will change.

Spreadsheets are ideally suited to preparing a budget, which summarizes the financial goals of a business. Consider Procter & Gamble, whose Health-Care Sector has an annual advertising budget of several hundred million dollars. Suppose Procter & Gamble allocates $40 to $50 million for its Crest Complete toothbrush. Procter & Gamble's

EXHIBIT 6-7
A Spreadsheet Screen

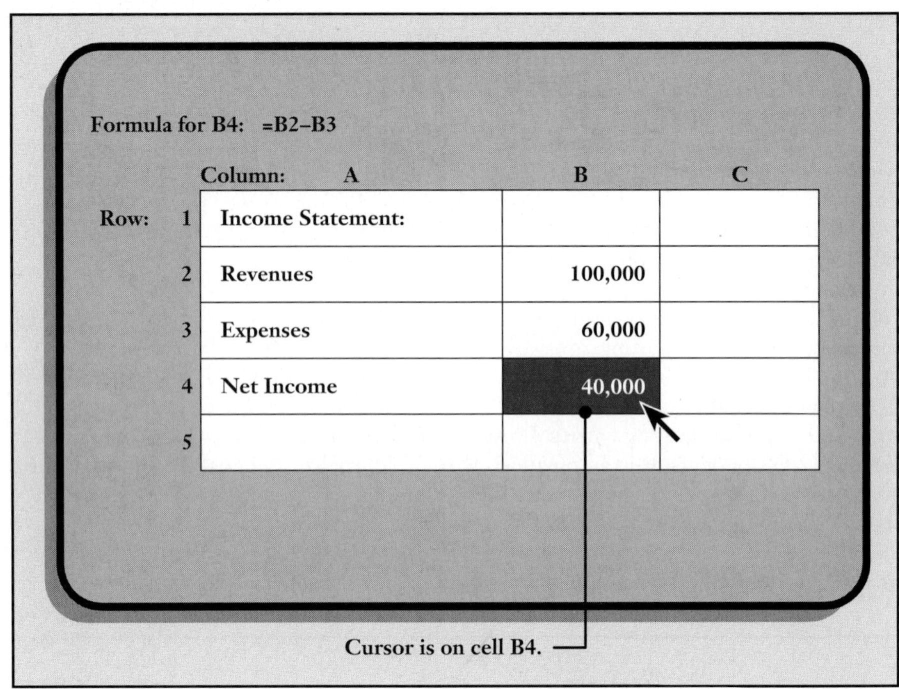

advertising expenses will increase. The company will also forecast an increase in sales revenue, cost of goods sold, and other expenses. A spreadsheet computes all these changes automatically in response to the advertising. The spreadsheet lets Procter & Gamble's managers track the profitability of each product. Armed with current data, the managers can make informed decisions. The result is higher profits.

Formula for B4: =B2–B3
Column: A B C
Row: 1 Income Statement:
2 Revenues 100,000
3 Expenses 60,000
4 Net Income 40,000
5
Cursor is on cell B4.

We can add or delete whole rows and columns of data and move blocks of numbers and words on a spreadsheet. The power of a spreadsheet is apparent when enormous amounts of data must be analyzed. Change only one number, and save hours of manual recalculation. Exhibit 6-8 shows the basic arithmetic operations in some popular spreadsheet programs such as Excel.

Special Journals

Exhibit 6-9 diagrams a typical accounting system for a merchandising business. The remainder of this chapter describes some of the more important aspects of the system described in Exhibit 6-9.

Special Accounting Journals

General Journal. Journal used to record all transactions that do not fit one of the special journals.

Special Journal. An accounting journal designed to record one specific type of transaction.

The journal entries illustrated so far in this book have been made in the general journal. The **general journal** is used to record all transactions that do not fit one of the special journals. In practice, it is inefficient to record all transactions in the general journal, so we use special journals. A **special journal** is an accounting journal designed to record one specific type of transaction, such as credit sales, in a sales journal.

EXHIBIT 6-8
Basic Arithmetic Operations in Excel Spreadsheets

Operation	Symbol
Addition	+
Subtraction	–
Multiplication	*
Division	/
Addition of a range of cells	=SUM(beginning cell:ending cell)
Examples:	
Add the contents of cells A2 through A9	=SUM(A2:A9)
Divide the contents of cell C2 by the contents of cell D1	=C2/D1

■ Daily Exercise 6-5

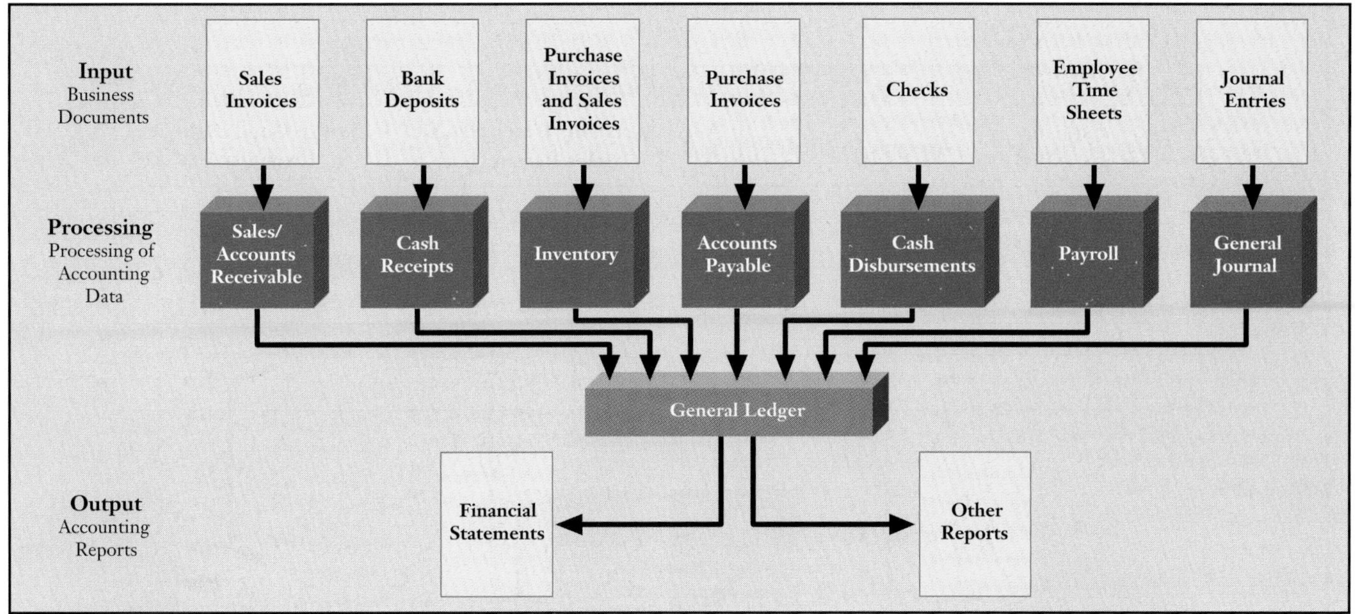

EXHIBIT 6-9
Overview of an Accounting System with Special Journals

Both manual systems and computerized systems must specialize by organizing transaction entry by type. Special journals and accounting modules accomplish that task. In a computerized system, accountants do not enter transaction data in these journals. Instead, they input data through various modules, such as the Accounts Receivable module for credit sales. But the underlying accounting principles are the same in manual and computerized systems.

In all likelihood, you will be working with a computerized system. We would rather you *not* view the process as a black box. To help you understand the basic accounting, over the next several pages we take you through the steps in a manual system.

Most of a business's transactions fall into one of five categories, so accountants use five different journals to record these transactions. This system reduces the time and cost otherwise spent journalizing, as we will see. The five categories of transactions, the related journal, and the posting abbreviations are as follows:

Transaction	Special Journal	Posting Abbreviation
1. Sale on account	Sales journal	S
2. Cash receipt	Cash receipts journal	C R
3. Purchase on account	Purchases journal	P
4. Cash disbursement	Cash disbursements journal	C D
5. All others	General journal	J

Adjusting and closing entries are entered in the general journal.

■ Daily Exercise 6-6

Learning Tip: Transactions are recorded in either the general journal or a special journal, but not in both.

Objective 4

Use the sales journal, the cash receipts journal, and the accounts receivable subsidiary ledger

Using the Sales Journal

Most merchandisers sell at least some of their inventory on account. These credit sales are entered in the **sales journal.** Credit sales of assets other than inventory—for example, buildings—occur infrequently and are recorded in the general journal.

Sales Journal. Special journal used to record credit sales.

Exhibit 6-10 illustrates a sales journal (Panel A) and the related posting to the ledgers (Panel B) of Austin Sound Stereo Center, the stereo shop introduced in Chapter 5. Each entry in the Accounts Receivable/Sales Revenue column of the sales journal in Exhibit 6-10 is a debit (Dr.) to Accounts Receivable and a credit (Cr.) to Sales Revenue, as the heading above this column indicates. For each transaction, the accountant enters the date, invoice number, customer account, and transaction amount. This streamlined way of recording sales on account saves a vast amount of time that, in a manual system, would be spent entering account titles and dollar amounts in the general journal.

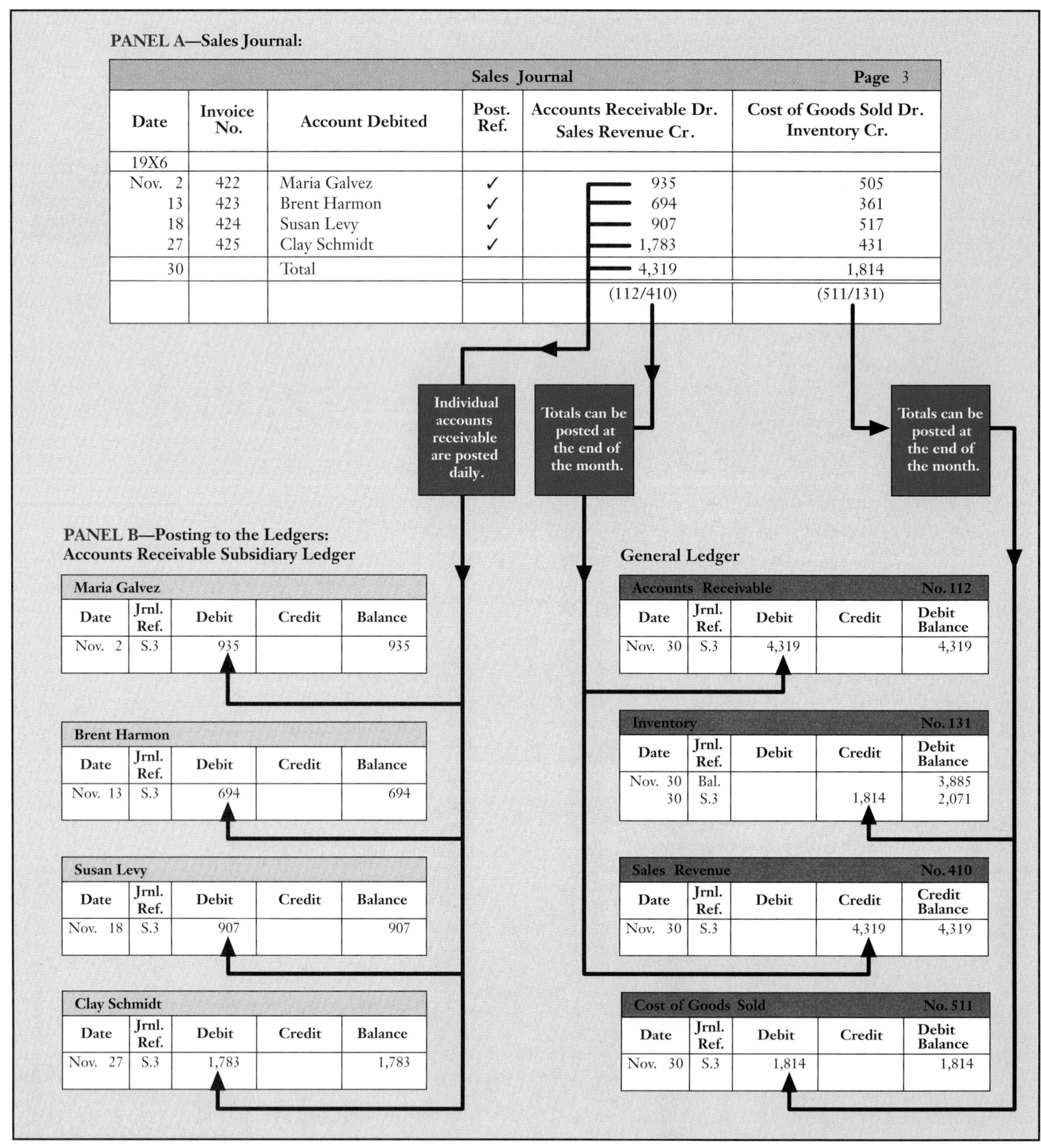

PANEL A—Sales Journal:

Sales Journal					Page 3
Date	Invoice No.	Account Debited	Post. Ref.	Accounts Receivable Dr. Sales Revenue Cr.	Cost of Goods Sold Dr. Inventory Cr.
19X6					
Nov. 2	422	Maria Galvez	✓	935	505
13	423	Brent Harmon	✓	694	361
18	424	Susan Levy	✓	907	517
27	425	Clay Schmidt	✓	1,783	431
30		Total		4,319	1,814
				(112/410)	(511/131)

Individual accounts receivable are posted daily.
Totals can be posted at the end of the month.
Totals can be posted at the end of the month.

PANEL B—Posting to the Ledgers:
Accounts Receivable Subsidiary Ledger

Maria Galvez

Date	Jrnl. Ref.	Debit	Credit	Balance
Nov. 2	S.3	935		935

Brent Harmon

Date	Jrnl. Ref.	Debit	Credit	Balance
Nov. 13	S.3	694		694

Susan Levy

Date	Jrnl. Ref.	Debit	Credit	Balance
Nov. 18	S.3	907		907

Clay Schmidt

Date	Jrnl. Ref.	Debit	Credit	Balance
Nov. 27	S.3	1,783		1,783

General Ledger

Accounts Receivable — No. 112

Date	Jrnl. Ref.	Debit	Credit	Debit Balance
Nov. 30	S.3	4,319		4,319

Inventory — No. 131

Date	Jrnl. Ref.	Debit	Credit	Debit Balance
Nov. 30	Bal.			3,885
30	S.3		1,814	2,071

Sales Revenue — No. 410

Date	Jrnl. Ref.	Debit	Credit	Credit Balance
Nov. 30	S.3		4,319	4,319

Cost of Goods Sold — No. 511

Date	Jrnl. Ref.	Debit	Credit	Debit Balance
Nov. 30	S.3	1,814		1,814

EXHIBIT 6-10
Sales Journal (Panel A) and Posting to the Ledgers (Panel B)

■ Daily Exercise 6-7
■ Daily Exercise 6-8

In recording credit sales in previous chapters, we did not keep a record of the names of credit-sale customers. In practice, the business must know the amount receivable from each customer. How else can the company keep track of who owes it money, when payment is due, and how much?

Consider the first transaction in Panel A. On November 2, Austin Sound sold stereo equipment on account to Maria Galvez for $935. The invoice number is 422. All this information appears on a single line in the sales journal. No explanation is necessary. The transaction's presence in the sales journal means that it is a credit sale, debited to Accounts Receivable—Maria Galvez and credited to Sales Revenue. To gain additional information about the transaction, we would look up the actual invoice.

Recall from Chapter 5 that Austin Sound uses a *perpetual* inventory system. At the time of recording the sale, Austin Sound also records the cost of the goods sold and the decrease in inventory. Many computerized accounting systems are programmed to read both the sales amount (from the bar code on the package of the item sold) and the cost of goods sold. A separate column of the sales journal holds the cost of goods sold and inventory amount—$505 for the sale to Maria Galvez. If Austin Sound used a *periodic* inventory system, it would not record cost of goods sold and the decrease in inventory at the time of sale. The sales journal would need only one column to debit Accounts Receivable and to credit Sales Revenue for the amount of the sale.

POSTING TO THE GENERAL LEDGER The ledger we have used so far is the **general ledger,** which holds the accounts reported in the financial statements. We will soon introduce other ledgers.

General Ledger. Ledger of accounts that are reported in the financial statements.

Posting from the sales journal to the general ledger can be done only once each month. In Exhibit 6-10 (Panel A), November's credit sales total $4,319. This column has two headings, Accounts Receivable and Sales Revenue. When the $4,319 is posted to these accounts in the general ledger, their account numbers are written beneath the total in the sales journal. In Panel B of Exhibit 6-10, the account number for Accounts Receivable is 112 and the account number for Sales Revenue is 410. Printing these account numbers beneath the credit-sales total in the sales journal signifies that the $4,319 has been posted to the two accounts.

The debit to Cost of Goods Sold and the credit to Inventory for the monthly total of $1,814 can also be posted at the end of the month. After posting, these accounts' numbers are entered beneath the total to show that Cost of Goods Sold and Inventory have been updated.

POSTING TO THE ACCOUNTS RECEIVABLE SUBSIDIARY LEDGER The $4,319 sum of the November debits to Accounts Receivable does not identify the amount receivable from any specific customer. A business may have thousands of customers. For example, the Consumers Digest Company, a Chicago-based firm that publishes the bimonthly magazine *Consumers Digest,* has 1.2 million customer accounts—one for each subscriber.

". . . Consumers Digest Company, a Chicago-based firm that publishes the bimonthly magazine Consumers Digest, *has 1.2 million customer accounts—one for each subscriber."*

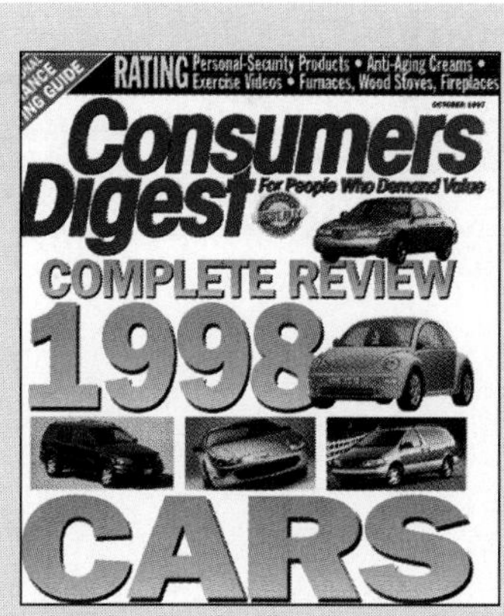

To streamline operations, businesses place the accounts of their individual credit customers in a subsidiary ledger, called the Accounts Receivable ledger. A **subsidiary ledger** is a record of accounts that provides supporting details on individual balances, the total of which appears in a general ledger account. The customer accounts are arranged in alphabetical order.

Amounts in the sales journal are posted to the subsidiary ledger *daily* to keep a current record of the amount receivable from each customer. Daily posting allows the business to answer customer inquiries promptly. Suppose Maria Galvez telephones Austin Sound on November 3 to ask how much money she owes. The subsidiary ledger readily provides that information, $935 in Exhibit 6-10, Panel B.

Subsidiary Ledger. Book of accounts that provides supporting details on individual balances, the total of which appears in a general ledger account.

When each transaction amount is posted to the subsidiary ledger, a check mark or some other notation is entered in the posting reference column of the sales journal (see Exhibit 6-10, Panel A).

JOURNAL REFERENCES IN THE LEDGERS When amounts are posted to the ledgers, the journal page number is printed in the account to identify the source of the data. All transaction data in Exhibit 6-10 originated on page 3 of the sales journal, so all journal references in the ledger accounts are S.3. The "S." indicates sales journal.

Trace all the postings in Exhibit 6-10. The most effective way to learn about accounting systems and special journals is to study the flow of data. The arrows indicate the direction of the information. The arrows also show the links between the individual customer accounts in the subsidiary ledger and the Accounts Receivable account. The Accounts Receivable debit balance in the general ledger should equal the sum of the individual customer balances in the subsidiary ledger, as follows:

General Ledger	
Accounts Receivable debit balance	$4,319

Subsidiary Ledger: Customer Accounts Receivable

Customer	Balance
Maria Galvez	$ 935
Brent Harmon	694
Susan Levy..	907
Clay Schmidt	1,783
Total accounts receivable......................................	$4,319

Control Account. An account whose balance equals the sum of the balances in a group of related accounts in a subsidiary ledger.

Accounts Receivable in the general ledger is a **control account.** Its balance equals the sum of the balances of a group of related accounts in a subsidiary ledger. The individual customer accounts are subsidiary accounts. They are said to be "controlled" by the Accounts Receivable account in the general ledger.

Additional data can be recorded in the sales journal. For example, a company may add a column to record sales terms, such as 2/10 n/30. The design of the journal depends on managers' needs for information.

Thinking It Over Suppose Austin Sound had 400 credit sales for the month. How many postings to the general ledger would be made from the sales journal? (Ignore Cost of Goods Sold and Inventory.) How many would there be if all sales transactions were routed through the general journal?

Answer: There are only two postings from the sales journal to the general ledger: one to Accounts Receivable and one to Sales Revenue. There would be 800 postings from the general journal: 400 to Accounts Receivable and 400 to Sales Revenue. This difference clearly shows the benefit of using a sales journal.

Using the Cash Receipts Journal

Cash Receipts Journal. Special journal used to record cash receipts.

Cash transactions are common in most businesses because cash receipts from customers are the lifeblood of business. To record repetitive cash receipt transactions, accountants use the **cash receipts journal.**

Exhibit 6-11, Panel A, illustrates the cash receipts journal. The related posting to ledgers is shown in Panel B. The exhibit illustrates November transactions for Austin Sound Stereo Center.

Every transaction recorded in this journal is a cash receipt, so the second column (after the date) is for debits to the Cash account. The next column is for debits to Sales Discounts on collections from customers. In a typical merchandising business, the main sources of cash are

- Collections on account
- Cash sales

The cash receipts journal has credit columns for Accounts Receivable and Sales Revenue. The journal also has a credit column for Other Accounts, which lists sources of cash other than cash sales and collections on account. This Other Accounts column is also used to record the names of customers from whom cash is received on account.

In Exhibit 6-11, cash sales occurred on November 6, 19, and 28. Observe the debits to Cash and the credits to Sales Revenue ($517, $853, and $1,802). Each sale entry is accompanied by a separate entry that debits Cost of Goods Sold and credits Inventory for the cost of the merchandise sold. The column for this entry is at the far right side of the cash receipts journal.

On November 11, Austin Sound borrowed $1,000 from First Bank. Cash is debited, and Note Payable to First Bank is credited in the Other Accounts column because no specific credit column is set up to account for borrowings. For this transaction, we print the account title, Note Payable to First Bank, in the Other Accounts/Account Title column.This entry records the source of cash.

On November 25, Austin Sound collected $762 of interest revenue. The account credited, Interest Revenue, is printed in the Other Accounts column. The November 11 and 25 transactions illustrate a key fact about business. Different entities have different

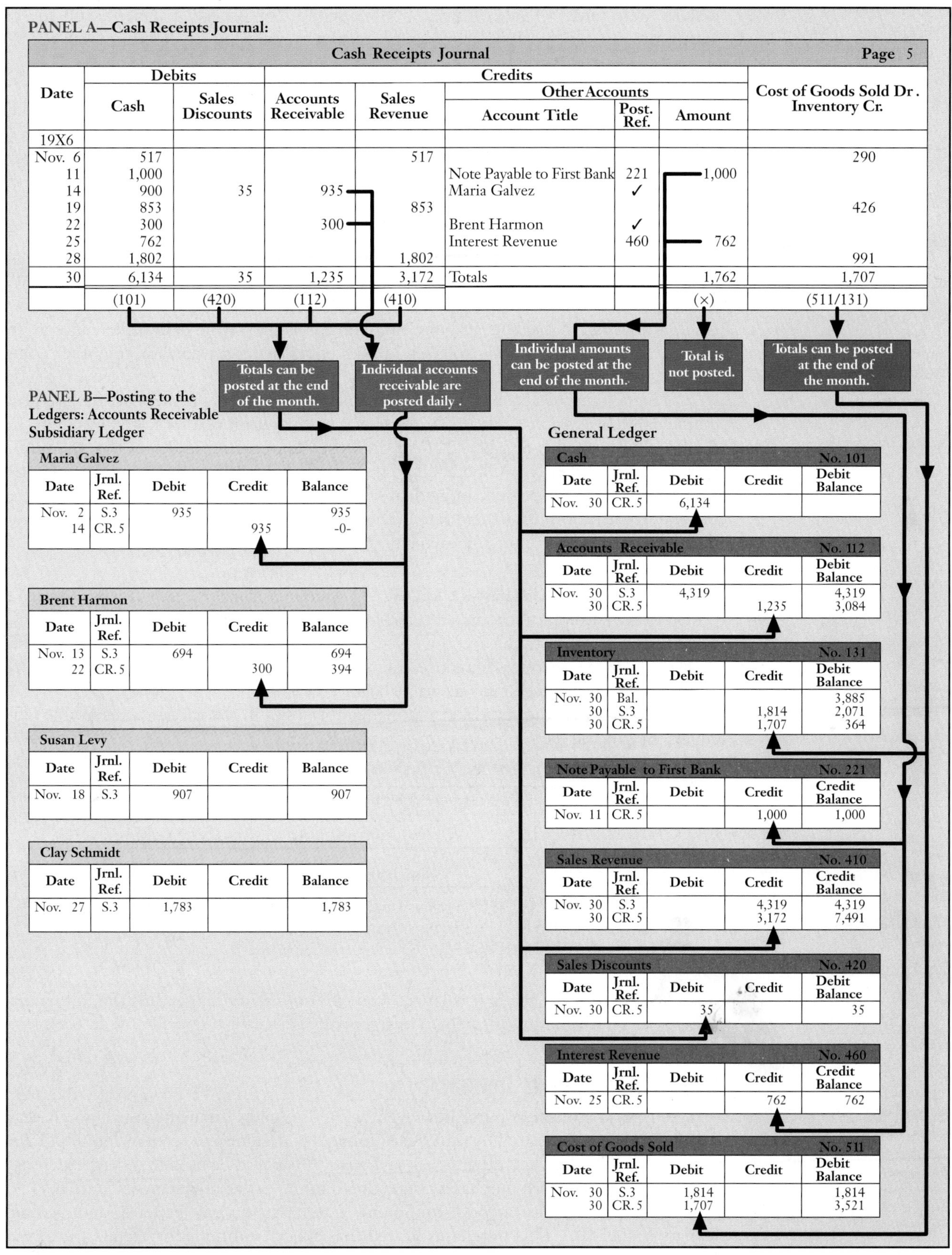

PANEL A—Cash Receipts Journal:

Cash Receipts Journal — Page 5

Date	Debits: Cash	Debits: Sales Discounts	Credits: Accounts Receivable	Credits: Sales Revenue	Other Accounts: Account Title	Post. Ref.	Other Accounts: Amount	Cost of Goods Sold Dr. Inventory Cr.
19X6								
Nov. 6	517			517				290
11	1,000				Note Payable to First Bank	221	1,000	
14	900	35	935		Maria Galvez	✓		
19	853			853				426
22	300		300		Brent Harmon	✓		
25	762				Interest Revenue	460	762	
28	1,802			1,802				991
30	6,134	35	1,235	3,172	Totals		1,762	1,707
	(101)	(420)	(112)	(410)			(×)	(511/131)

Totals can be posted at the end of the month.
Individual accounts receivable are posted daily.
Individual amounts can be posted at the end of the month.
Total is not posted.
Totals can be posted at the end of the month.

PANEL B—Posting to the Ledgers: Accounts Receivable Subsidiary Ledger

Maria Galvez

Date	Jrnl. Ref.	Debit	Credit	Balance
Nov. 2	S.3	935		935
14	CR. 5		935	-0-

Brent Harmon

Date	Jrnl. Ref.	Debit	Credit	Balance
Nov. 13	S.3	694		694
22	CR. 5		300	394

Susan Levy

Date	Jrnl. Ref.	Debit	Credit	Balance
Nov. 18	S.3	907		907

Clay Schmidt

Date	Jrnl. Ref.	Debit	Credit	Balance
Nov. 27	S.3	1,783		1,783

General Ledger

Cash — No. 101

Date	Jrnl. Ref.	Debit	Credit	Debit Balance
Nov. 30	CR. 5	6,134		

Accounts Receivable — No. 112

Date	Jrnl. Ref.	Debit	Credit	Debit Balance
Nov. 30	S.3	4,319		4,319
30	CR. 5		1,235	3,084

Inventory — No. 131

Date	Jrnl. Ref.	Debit	Credit	Debit Balance
Nov. 30	Bal.			3,885
30	S.3		1,814	2,071
30	CR. 5		1,707	364

Note Payable to First Bank — No. 221

Date	Jrnl. Ref.	Debit	Credit	Credit Balance
Nov. 11	CR. 5		1,000	1,000

Sales Revenue — No. 410

Date	Jrnl. Ref.	Debit	Credit	Credit Balance
Nov. 30	S.3		4,319	4,319
30	CR. 5		3,172	7,491

Sales Discounts — No. 420

Date	Jrnl. Ref.	Debit	Credit	Debit Balance
Nov. 30	CR. 5	35		35

Interest Revenue — No. 460

Date	Jrnl. Ref.	Debit	Credit	Credit Balance
Nov. 25	CR. 5		762	762

Cost of Goods Sold — No. 511

Date	Jrnl. Ref.	Debit	Credit	Debit Balance
Nov. 30	S.3	1,814		1,814
30	CR. 5	1,707		3,521

EXHIBIT 6-11 Cash Receipts Journal (Panel A) and Posting to the Ledgers (Panel B)

types of transactions; they design their special journals to meet their particular needs for information. In this case, the Other Accounts credit column is the catchall used to record all nonroutine cash receipt transactions.

On November 14, Austin Sound collected $900 from Maria Galvez. Referring to Exhibit 6-10, we see that on November 2, Austin Sound sold merchandise for $935 to

■ Daily Exercise 6-9

Galvez. The terms of sale allowed a $35 discount for prompt payment, and she paid within the discount period. Austin's cash receipt is recorded by debiting Cash for $900 and Sales Discounts for $35, and by crediting Accounts Receivable for $935. The customer's name appears in the Other Accounts/Account Title column.

Total debits should equal total credits in the cash receipts journal. This equality holds for each transaction and for the monthly totals. For the month, total debits ($6,134 + $35 = $6,169) equal total credits ($1,235 + $3,172 + $1,762 = $6,169). The debit to Cost of Goods Sold and the credit to Inventory are separate.

Learning Tip: Every entry in the cash receipts journal includes a debit to Cash. Cash sales are recorded here rather than in the sales journal.

POSTING TO THE GENERAL LEDGER The column totals can be posted monthly. To indicate their posting, the account number is written below the column total in the cash receipts journal. Note the account number for Cash (101) below the column total $6,134, and trace the posting to Cash in the general ledger. Likewise, the other column totals also are posted to the general ledger.

The column total for *Other Accounts* is *not* posted. Instead, these credits are posted individually. In Exhibit 6-11, the November 11 transaction reads "Note Payable to First Bank." This account's number (221) in the Post. Ref. column indicates that the transaction amount was posted individually. The letter x below the column indicates that the column total was *not* posted. Individual amounts can be posted to the general ledger at the end of the month. But their date in the ledger accounts should be their actual date in the journal, to facilitate tracing each amount back to the journal.

POSTING TO THE SUBSIDIARY LEDGER Amounts from the cash receipts journal are posted to the subsidiary accounts receivable ledger daily to keep the individual balances up to date. The postings to the accounts receivable ledger are credits. Trace the $935 posting to Maria Galvez's account. It reduces her balance to zero. The $300 receipt from Brent Harmon reduces his accounts receivable balance to $394.

After posting, the sum of the individual balances in the accounts receivable ledger equals the general ledger balance in Accounts Receivable.

General Ledger

Accounts Receivable debit balance	$3,084

Subsidiary Ledger: Customer Accounts Receivable

Customer	Balance
Brent Harmon	$ 394
Susan Levy...	907
Clay Schmidt	1,783
Total accounts receivable..................................	$3,084

Austin Sound's list of account balances from the subsidiary ledger aids the follow up on slow-paying customers. This helps a business manage cash.

Using the Purchases Journal

Objective 5

Use the purchases journal, the cash disbursements journal, and the accounts payable subsidiary ledger

Purchases Journal. Special journal used to record all purchases of inventory, supplies, and other assets on account.

A merchandising business purchases inventory and supplies frequently. Such purchases are usually made on account. The **purchases journal** is designed to account for all purchases of inventory, supplies, and other assets *on account*. It can also be used to record expenses incurred on account. Cash purchases are recorded in the cash disbursements journal.

Exhibit 6-12 illustrates Austin Sound's purchases journal (Panel A) and posting to ledgers (Panel B).[1] This purchases journal has special columns for credits to Accounts Payable and debits to Inventory, Supplies, and Other Accounts. A periodic inventory system would replace the Inventory column with a column titled "Purchases." The Other

[1]This is the only special journal that we illustrate with the credit column placed to the left and the debit columns to the right. This arrangement of columns focuses on Accounts Payable (which is credited for each entry to this journal) on the individual supplier to be paid.

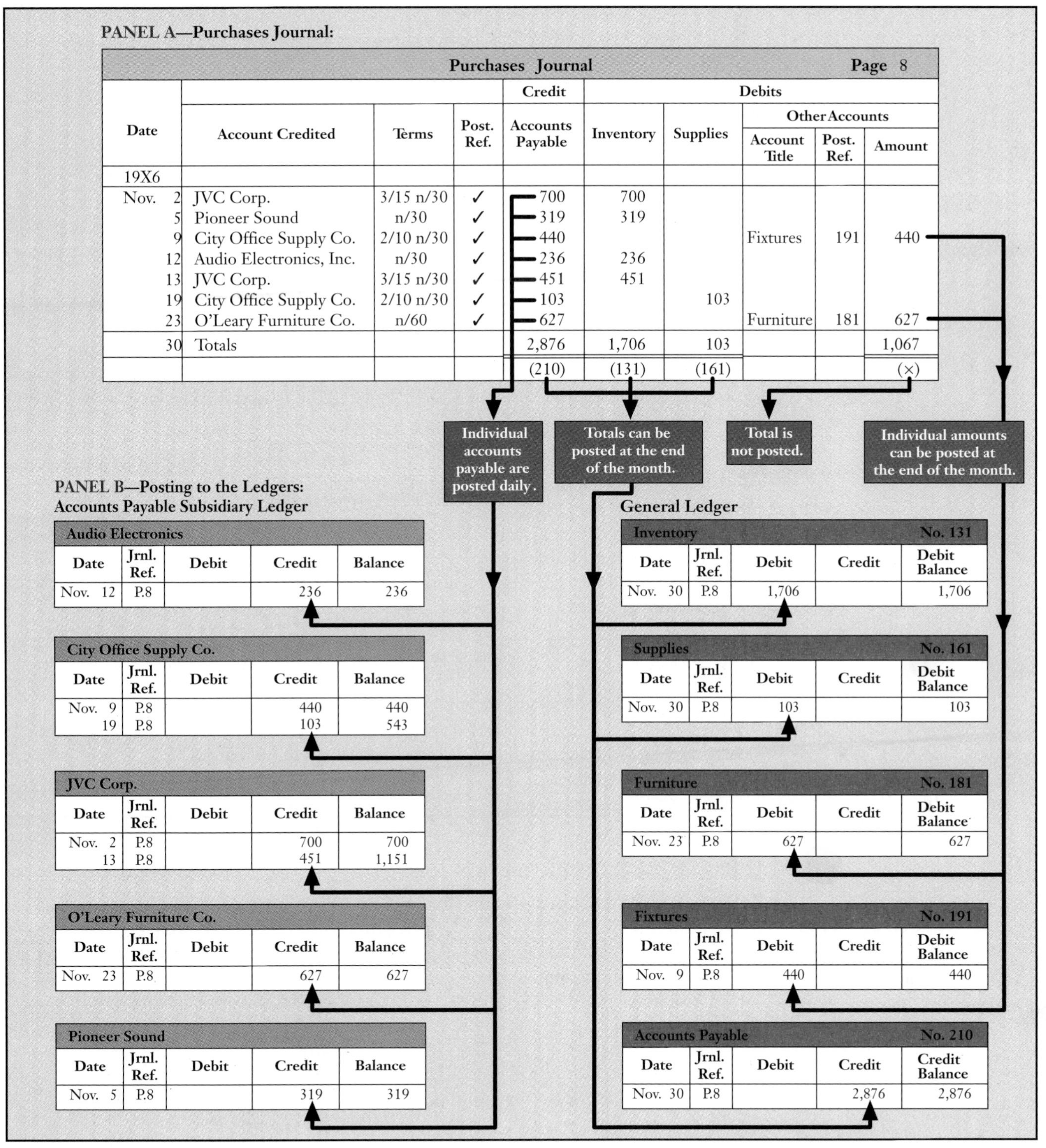

PANEL A—Purchases Journal:

Purchases Journal									Page 8
				Credit	Debits				
							Other Accounts		
Date	Account Credited	Terms	Post. Ref.	Accounts Payable	Inventory	Supplies	Account Title	Post. Ref.	Amount
19X6									
Nov. 2	JVC Corp.	3/15 n/30	✓	700	700				
5	Pioneer Sound	n/30	✓	319	319				
9	City Office Supply Co.	2/10 n/30	✓	440			Fixtures	191	440
12	Audio Electronics, Inc.	n/30	✓	236	236				
13	JVC Corp.	3/15 n/30	✓	451	451				
19	City Office Supply Co.	2/10 n/30	✓	103		103			
23	O'Leary Furniture Co.	n/60	✓	627			Furniture	181	627
30	Totals			2,876	1,706	103			1,067
				(210)	(131)	(161)			(×)

Individual accounts payable are posted daily.
Totals can be posted at the end of the month.
Total is not posted.
Individual amounts can be posted at the end of the month.

PANEL B—Posting to the Ledgers:

Accounts Payable Subsidiary Ledger

Audio Electronics				
Date	Jrnl. Ref.	Debit	Credit	Balance
Nov. 12	P.8		236	236

City Office Supply Co.				
Date	Jrnl. Ref.	Debit	Credit	Balance
Nov. 9	P.8		440	440
19	P.8		103	543

JVC Corp.				
Date	Jrnl. Ref.	Debit	Credit	Balance
Nov. 2	P.8		700	700
13	P.8		451	1,151

O'Leary Furniture Co.				
Date	Jrnl. Ref.	Debit	Credit	Balance
Nov. 23	P.8		627	627

Pioneer Sound				
Date	Jrnl. Ref.	Debit	Credit	Balance
Nov. 5	P.8		319	319

General Ledger

Inventory				No. 131
Date	Jrnl. Ref.	Debit	Credit	Debit Balance
Nov. 30	P.8	1,706		1,706

Supplies				No. 161
Date	Jrnl. Ref.	Debit	Credit	Debit Balance
Nov. 30	P.8	103		103

Furniture				No. 181
Date	Jrnl. Ref.	Debit	Credit	Debit Balance
Nov. 23	P.8	627		627

Fixtures				No. 191
Date	Jrnl. Ref.	Debit	Credit	Debit Balance
Nov. 9	P.8	440		440

Accounts Payable				No. 210
Date	Jrnl. Ref.	Debit	Credit	Credit Balance
Nov. 30	P.8		2,876	2,876

EXHIBIT 6-12
Purchases Journal (Panel A) and Posting to the Ledgers (Panel B)

Accounts columns accommodate purchases of items other than inventory and supplies. Accounts Payable is credited for all transactions recorded in the purchases journal.

On November 2, Austin Sound purchased stereo inventory costing $700 from JVC Corporation. The creditor's name (JVC Corporation) is entered in the Account Credited column. The purchase terms of 3/15 n/30 are also printed to help identify the due date and the discount available. Accounts Payable is credited for the transaction amount, and Inventory is debited.

Note the November 9 purchase of fixtures from City Office Supply. The purchases journal contains no column for fixtures, so the Other Accounts debit column is used. Because this was a credit purchase, the accountant enters the creditor name (City Office

Supply) in the Account Credited column and Fixtures in the Other Accounts/Account Title column. The total credits in the purchases journal ($2,876) equal the total debits ($1,706 + $103 + $1,067 = $2,876).

Learning Tip: Every transaction in the purchases journal will include a credit to Accounts Payable.

ACCOUNTS PAYABLE SUBSIDIARY LEDGER To pay debts efficiently, a company must know how much it owes particular creditors. The Accounts Payable account in the general ledger shows only a single total for the amount owed on account. It does not indicate the amount owed to each creditor. Companies keep an accounts payable subsidiary ledger that is similar to the accounts receivable subsidiary ledger that we used in conjunction with credit sales.

The accounts payable subsidiary ledger lists the creditors in alphabetical order, along with the amounts owed to them. Exhibit 6-12, Panel B, shows Austin Sound's accounts payable subsidiary ledger, which includes accounts for Audio Electronics, City Office Supply, and others. After the daily posting is done, the total of the individual balances in the subsidiary ledger equals the balance in the Accounts Payable control account in the general ledger.

POSTING FROM THE PURCHASES JOURNAL Posting from the purchases journal is similar to posting from the sales journal and the cash receipts journal. Exhibit 6-12, Panel B, illustrates the posting process.

Individual accounts payable in the *accounts payable subsidiary ledger* are posted daily, and column totals and other amounts can be posted to the *general ledger* at the end of the month. In the ledger accounts, P.8 indicates the source of the posted amounts—that is, purchases journal page 8.

Thinking It Over Contrast the number of *general ledger* postings from the purchases journal in Exhibit 6-12 with the number that would be required if the general journal were used to record the same seven transactions.

Answer: Use of the purchases journal requires only five *general ledger* postings—$2,876 to Accounts Payable, $1,706 to Inventory, $103 to Supplies, $440 to Fixtures, and $627 to Furniture. Without the purchases journal, there would have been 14 postings, two for each of the seven transactions.

Using the Cash Disbursements Journal

Cash Disbursements Journal. Special journal used to record cash payments by check. Also called the **check register** or **cash payments journal.**

Businesses make most cash disbursements by check. All payments by check are recorded in the **cash disbursements journal.** Other titles of this special journal are the *check register* and the *cash payments journal.* Like the other special journals, it has special columns for recording cash payments that occur frequently.

Exhibit 6-13, Panel A, illustrates the cash disbursements journal, and Panel B shows the postings to the ledgers of Austin Sound. This cash disbursements journal has two debit columns—one for Other Accounts and one for Accounts Payable. It has two credit columns—one for purchase discounts, which are credited to the Inventory account in a perpetual inventory system, and one for Cash. This special journal also has columns for the date and for the check number of each cash payment.

Suppose a business makes numerous cash purchases of inventory. What additional column would its cash disbursements journal need ? A column for Inventory, which would appear under the Debits heading, would streamline the information in the journal.

All entries in the cash disbursements journal include a credit to Cash. Payments on account are debits to Accounts Payable. On November 15, Austin Sound paid JVC on account, with credit terms of 3/15 n/30 (for details, see the first transaction in Exhibit 6-12). Paying within the discount period, Austin took the 3% discount and paid $679 ($700 less the $21 discount). The discount is credited to the Inventory account.

The Other Accounts column is used to record debits to accounts for which no special column exists. For example, on November 3, Austin Sound paid rent expense of $1,200.

As with all other journals, the total debits ($3,461 + $819 = $4,280) should equal the total credits ($21 + $4,259 = $4,280).

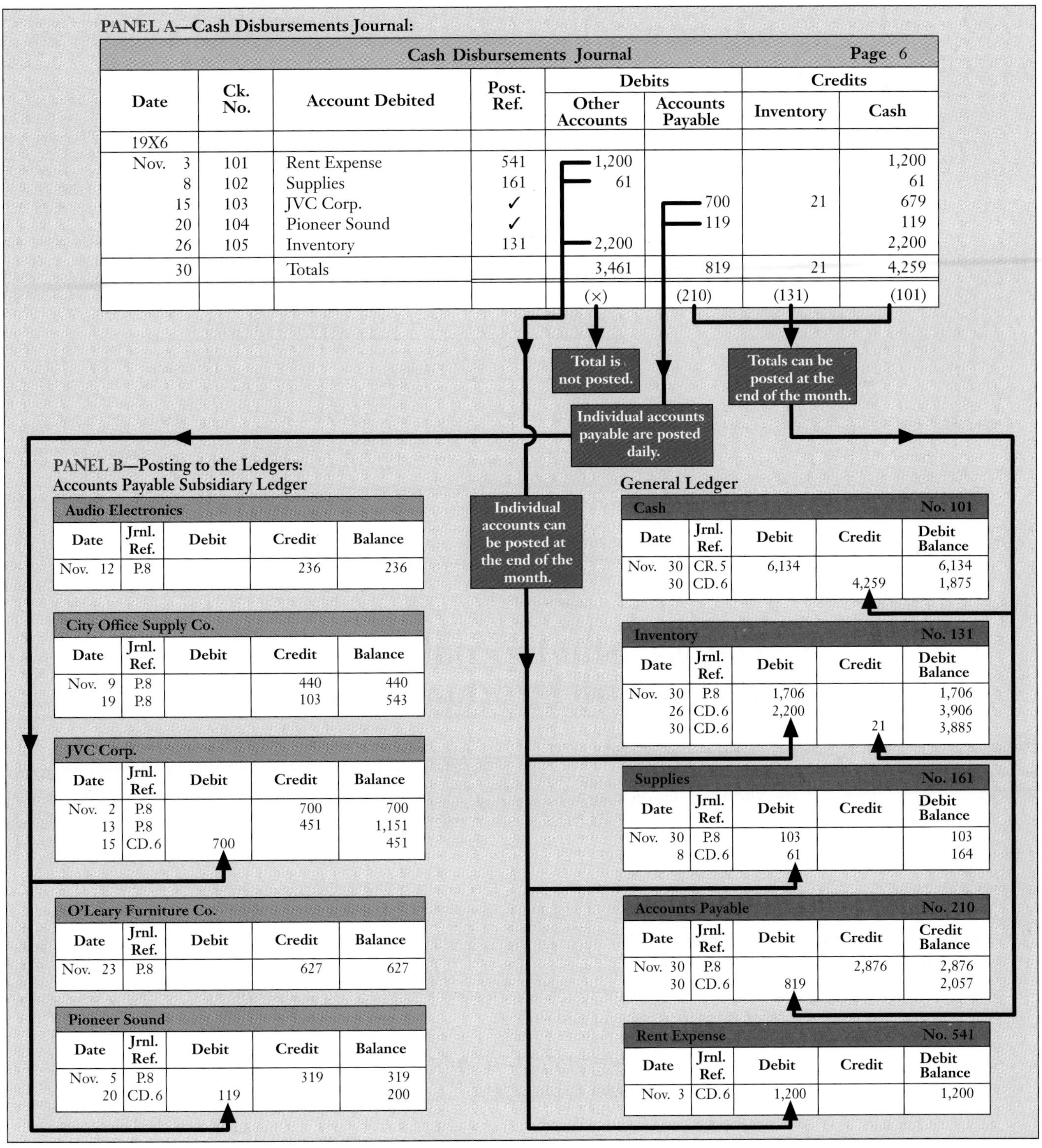

PANEL A—Cash Disbursements Journal:

Cash Disbursements Journal — Page 6

Date	Ck. No.	Account Debited	Post. Ref.	Debits: Other Accounts	Debits: Accounts Payable	Credits: Inventory	Credits: Cash
19X6							
Nov. 3	101	Rent Expense	541	1,200			1,200
8	102	Supplies	161	61			61
15	103	JVC Corp.	✓		700	21	679
20	104	Pioneer Sound	✓		119		119
26	105	Inventory	131	2,200			2,200
30		Totals		3,461	819	21	4,259
				(×)	(210)	(131)	(101)

Total is not posted.
Totals can be posted at the end of the month.
Individual accounts payable are posted daily.
Individual accounts can be posted at the end of the month.

PANEL B—Posting to the Ledgers:

Accounts Payable Subsidiary Ledger

Audio Electronics

Date	Jrnl. Ref.	Debit	Credit	Balance
Nov. 12	P.8		236	236

City Office Supply Co.

Date	Jrnl. Ref.	Debit	Credit	Balance
Nov. 9	P.8		440	440
19	P.8		103	543

JVC Corp.

Date	Jrnl. Ref.	Debit	Credit	Balance
Nov. 2	P.8		700	700
13	P.8		451	1,151
15	CD.6	700		451

O'Leary Furniture Co.

Date	Jrnl. Ref.	Debit	Credit	Balance
Nov. 23	P.8		627	627

Pioneer Sound

Date	Jrnl. Ref.	Debit	Credit	Balance
Nov. 5	P.8		319	319
20	CD.6	119		200

General Ledger

Cash — No. 101

Date	Jrnl. Ref.	Debit	Credit	Debit Balance
Nov. 30	CR.5	6,134		6,134
30	CD.6		4,259	1,875

Inventory — No. 131

Date	Jrnl. Ref.	Debit	Credit	Debit Balance
Nov. 30	P.8	1,706		1,706
26	CD.6	2,200		3,906
30	CD.6		21	3,885

Supplies — No. 161

Date	Jrnl. Ref.	Debit	Credit	Debit Balance
Nov. 30	P.8	103		103
8	CD.6	61		164

Accounts Payable — No. 210

Date	Jrnl. Ref.	Debit	Credit	Credit Balance
Nov. 30	P.8		2,876	2,876
30	CD.6	819		2,057

Rent Expense — No. 541

Date	Jrnl. Ref.	Debit	Credit	Debit Balance
Nov. 3	CD.6	1,200		1,200

EXHIBIT 6-13
Cash Disbursements Journal (Panel A) and Posting to the Ledgers (Panel B)

■ Daily Exercise 6-10
■ Daily Exercise 6-11
■ Daily Exercise 6-12

POSTING FROM THE CASH DISBURSEMENTS JOURNAL Posting from the cash disbursements journal is similar to posting from the cash receipts journal. Individual creditor amounts are posted daily, and column totals and Other Accounts can be posted at the end of the month. Exhibit 6-13, Panel B, illustrates the posting process.

Observe the effect of posting to the Accounts Payable account in the general ledger. The first posted amount in the Accounts Payable account (credit $2,876) originated in the purchases journal, page 8 (P.8). The second posted amount (debit $819) came from the cash disbursements journal, page 6 (CD.6). The resulting credit balance in Accounts Payable is $2,057. Also, see the Cash account; after posting, its debit balance is $1,875.

Amounts in the Other Accounts column are posted individually (for example, Rent Expense—debit $1,200). When each Other Accounts amount is posted to the general ledger, the account number is entered in the Post. Ref. column of the journal. The letter x below the column total signifies that the total is *not* posted.

To review their accounts payable, companies list the individual creditor balances in the accounts payable subsidiary ledger:

General Ledger

Accounts Payable credit balance	$2,057

Subsidiary Ledger: Creditor Accounts Payable

Creditor	Balance
Audio Electronics	$ 236
City Office Supply	543
JVC Corp.	451
O'Leary Furniture	627
Pioneer Sound	200
Total accounts payable	$2,057

This total agrees with the Accounts Payable balance in the general ledger in Exhibit 6-13.

The General Journal's Role in an Accounting Information System

Special journals save much time in recording repetitive transactions and posting to the ledgers. But some transactions do not fit into any of the special journals. Examples include the depreciation of buildings and equipment, the expiration of prepaid insurance, and the accrual of salary payable at the end of the period. Therefore,

> **Even the most sophisticated accounting system needs a general journal. The adjusting entries and the closing entries that we illustrated in Chapters 3 through 5 are recorded in the general journal.**

Accountants also record other transactions in the general journal. Many companies record their sales returns and allowances and their purchase returns in the general journal. Let's examine the *credit memorandum*, the document that leads to the entries for sales returns and allowances.

The Credit Memorandum—The Document for Recording Sales Returns and Allowances

Credit Memorandum or **Credit Memo.** A document issued by a seller to credit a customer's account for returned merchandise.

As we saw in Chapter 5, customers sometimes return merchandise to the seller, and sellers grant sales allowances to customers because of product defects and for other reasons. The effect of sales returns and sales allowances is the same—both decrease net sales in the same way a sales discount does. The document issued by the seller for a credit to the customer's Account Receivable is called a **credit memorandum,** or **credit memo,** because the company gives the customer credit for the returned merchandise. When a company issues a credit memo, it debits Sales Returns and Allowances and credits Accounts Receivable.

On November 27, Austin Sound sold four stereo speakers for $1,783 on account to Clay Schmidt. Later, Schmidt discovered a defect and returned the speakers. Austin Sound then issued to Schmidt a credit memo like the one in Exhibit 6-14.

To record the *sale return* and receipt of the defective speakers from the customer, Austin Sound would make the following entries in the general journal:

General Journal **Page 9**

Date	Accounts	Post Ref.	Debit	Credit
Dec. 1	Sales Returns and Allowances	430	1,783	
	Accounts Receivable—Clay Schmidt	112/✓		1,783
	Credit memo no. 27.			
Dec. 1	Inventory	131	431	
	Cost of Goods Sold	511		431
	Received defective goods from customer.			

Focus on the first entry. The debit side of the entry is posted to Sales Returns and Allowances. Its account number (430) is written in the posting reference column when $1,783 is posted. The credit side of the entry requires two $1,783 postings, one to Accounts Receivable, the control account in the general ledger (account number 112), and the other to Clay Schmidt's account in the accounts receivable subsidiary ledger. These credit postings explain why the document is called a *credit memo.*

Observe that the posting reference of the credit includes two notations. The account number (112) denotes the posting to Accounts Receivable in the general ledger. The check mark (✓) denotes the posting to Schmidt's account in the subsidiary ledger. Why are two postings needed? Because this is the general journal. Without specially designed columns, it is necessary to write both posting references on the same line.

A business with a high volume of sales returns, such as a department store chain, may use a special journal for sales returns and allowances.

The second entry records Austin Sound's receipt of the defective inventory from the customer. The speakers cost Austin Sound $431, and Austin Sound, like all other merchandisers, records its inventory at cost. Now let's see how Austin Sound records the return of the defective speakers to JVC, from whom Austin Sound purchased them.

The Debit Memorandum—The Business Document for Recording Purchase Returns and Allowances

Purchase returns occur when a business returns goods to the seller. The procedures for handling purchase returns are similar to those dealing with sales returns. The purchaser gives the merchandise back to the seller and receives either a cash refund or replacement goods.

When a business returns merchandise to the seller, it may also send a business document known as a **debit memorandum,** or **debit memo.** This document states that the

Debit Memorandum or **Debit Memo.** A document issued by a buyer when returning merchandise. The memo informs the seller that the buyer no longer owes the seller for the amount of the returned purchases.

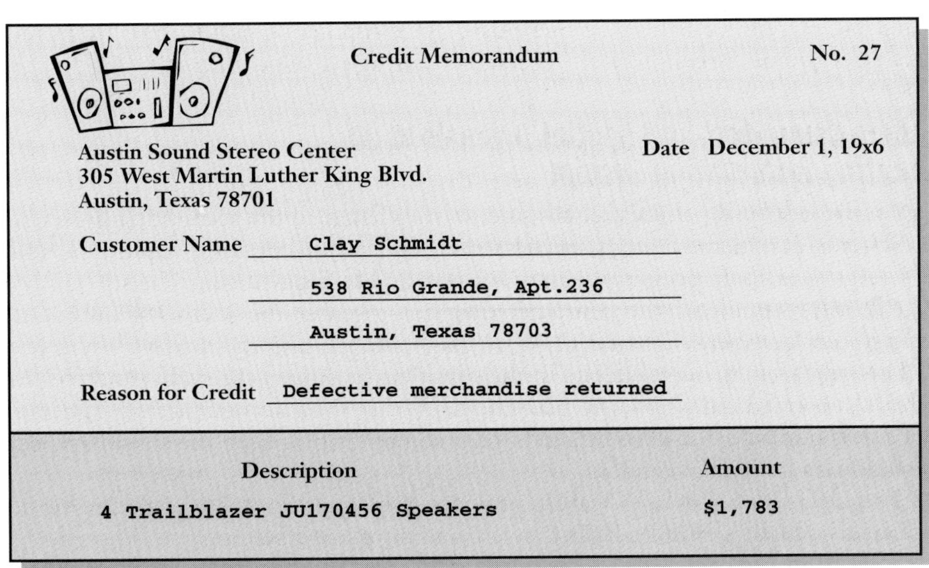
Credit Memorandum No. 27

Austin Sound Stereo Center
305 West Martin Luther King Blvd.
Austin, Texas 78701

Date December 1, 19x6

Customer Name Clay Schmidt
538 Rio Grande, Apt.236
Austin, Texas 78703

Reason for Credit Defective merchandise returned

Description	Amount
4 Trailblazer JU170456 Speakers	$1,783

EXHIBIT 6-14
Credit Memorandum Issued by Austin Sound Stereo Center

buyer no longer owes the seller for the amount of the returned purchases. The buyer debits the Accounts Payable to the seller and credits Inventory for the cost of the goods returned to the seller.

Many businesses record their purchase returns in the general journal. Austin Sound would record its return of defective speakers to JVC as follows:

General Journal **Page 9**

Date	Accounts	Post Ref.	Debit	Credit
Dec. 2	Accounts Payable—JVC Corp.........	210/✓	431	
	Inventory	131		431
	Debit memo no. 16.			

Balancing the Ledgers

At the end of the period, after all postings have been made, equality should exist between

1. *General ledger:*

   Total debits = Total credits of all account balances

2. *General ledger and Accounts receivable subsidiary ledger:*

   Balance of Accounts Receivable control account = Sum of individual customer account balances in the accounts receivable subsidiary ledger

3. *General ledger and Accounts payable subsidiary ledger:*

   Balance of Accounts Payable control account = Sum of individual creditor account balances in the accounts payable subsidiary ledger

The process of ensuring that these equalities exist is called *balancing the ledgers*, or *proving the ledgers*. It is an important control procedure because it helps ensure the accuracy of the accounting records.

Using Documents as Journals in a Manual Accounting System

Many small businesses streamline their accounting systems by using their business documents as the journals. This practice avoids the need to keep special journals and thereby saves money. For example, Austin Sound could keep sales invoices in a loose-leaf binder and let the invoices themselves serve as its sales journal. At the end of the period, the accountant simply totals the sales on account and posts the total as a debit to Accounts Receivable and a credit to Sales Revenue. Also, the accountant can post directly from the invoices to customer accounts in the accounts receivable ledger.

Blending Computers and Special Journals in an Accounting Information System

Computerizing special journals requires no drastic change in the accounting system's design. Systems designers create a special screen for each accounting application (module)—credit sales, cash receipts, credit purchases, and cash payments. The special screen for credit sales would ask the computer operator to enter the following information: date, customer number, customer name, invoice number, and the dollar amount of the sale. These data can generate debits to the subsidiary accounts receivable and files from which are generated monthly customer statements that show account activity and ending balance. For purchases on account, additional computer files keep the subsidiary ledger information on individual vendors.

The Decision Guidelines feature provides guidelines for some of the major decisions that accountants must make as they use an information system.

DECISION GUIDELINES — Using Special Journals and Control Accounts

DECISION	GUIDELINES
What are the main components of an accounting system?	Journals • General journal • Special journals Ledgers • General ledger • Subsidiary ledgers
Where to record • Sales on account? • Cash receipts? • Purchases on account? • Cash payments? • All other transactions?	Journals • Sales journal • Cash receipts journal • Purchases journal • Cash disbursements journal • General journal
How does the general ledger relate to the subsidiary ledgers?	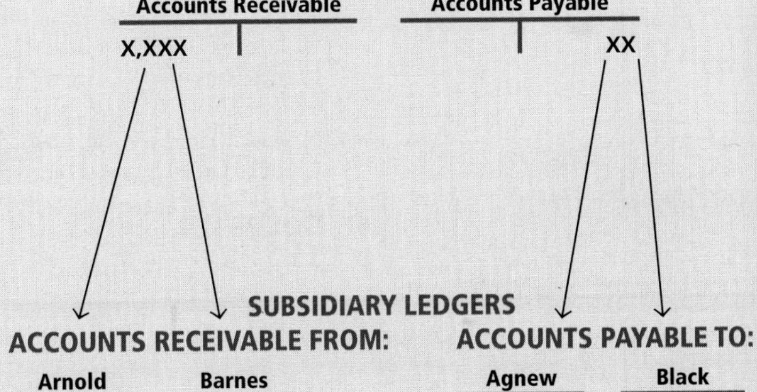
When to post from the journals to • General ledger? • Subsidiary ledgers?	—Monthly (or more often, if needed) —Daily
How to achieve control over • Accounts receivable? • Accounts payable?	Balance the ledgers, as follows: **General Ledger** / **Subsidiary Ledger** Accounts receivable = Sum of individual *customer* account balances Accounts payable = Sum of individual *creditor* account balances

SUMMARY PROBLEM FOR YOUR REVIEW

Riggs Company completed the following selected transactions during March:

Mar. 4 Received $500 from a cash sale to a customer (cost, $319).
6 Received $60 on account from Brady Lee. The full invoice amount was $65, but Lee paid within the discount period to gain the $5 discount.
9 Received $1,080 on a note receivable from Beverly Mann. This amount includes the $1,000 note receivable plus interest revenue.
15 Received $800 from a cash sale to a customer (cost, $522).
24 Borrowed $2,200 by signing a note payable to Interstate Bank.
27 Received $1,200 on account from Lance Albert. Payment was received after the discount period lapsed.

REQUIRED

The general ledger showed the following balances at February 28: Cash, $1,117; Accounts Receivable, $2,790; Note Receivable—Beverly Mann, $1,000; and Inventory, $1,819. The accounts receivable subsidiary ledger at February 28 contained debit balances as follows: Lance Albert, $1,840; Melinda Fultz, $885; Brady Lee, $65.

1. Record the transactions in the cash receipts journal, page 7.
2. Compute column totals at March 31. Show that total debits equal total credits in the cash receipts journal.
3. Post to the general ledger and the accounts receivable subsidiary ledger. Use complete posting references, including the following account numbers: Cash, 11; Accounts Receivable, 12; Note Receivable—Beverly Mann, 13; Inventory, 14; Note Payable—Interstate Bank, 22; Sales Revenue, 41; Sales Discounts, 42; Interest Revenue, 46; and Cost of Goods Sold, 51. Insert a check mark (✓) in the posting reference column for each February 28 account balance.
4. Show that the total of the customer balances in the subsidiary ledger equals the general ledger balance in Accounts Receivable.

SOLUTION

REQUIREMENTS 1 AND 2

Cash Receipts Journal — **Page 7**

	Debits		Credits					
					Other Accounts			
Date	**Cash**	**Sales Discounts**	**Accounts Receivable**	**Sales Revenue**	**Account Title**	**Post. Ref.**	**Amount**	**Cost of Goods Sold Debit Inventory Credit**
Mar. 4	500			500				319
6	60	5	65		Brady Lee	✓		
9	1,080				Note Receivable—Beverly Mann	13	1,000	
					Interest Revenue	46	80	
15	800			800				522
24	2,200				Note Payable—Interstate Bank	22	2,200	
27	1,200		1,200		Lance Albert	✓		
31	5,840	5	1,265	1,300	Total		3,280	841
	(11)	(42)	(12)	(41)			(✓)	(51/14)

Total Dr. = 5,845 Total Cr. = 5,845

REQUIREMENT 3

Accounts Receivable Ledger

Lance Albert

Date	Jrnl. Ref.	Debit	Credit	Balance
Feb. 28	✓			1,840
Mar. 27	CR.7		1,200	640

Melinda Fultz

Date	Jrnl. Ref.	Debit	Credit	Balance
Feb. 28	✓			885

Brady Lee

Date	Jrnl. Ref.	Debit	Credit	Balance
Feb. 28	✓			65
Mar. 6	CR.7		65	—

General Ledger

Cash No. 11

Date	Jrnl. Ref.	Debit	Credit	Balance
Feb. 28	✓			1,117
Mar. 31	CR.7	5,840		6,957

Accounts Receivable No. 12

Date	Jrnl. Ref.	Debit	Credit	Balance
Feb. 28	✓			2,790
Mar. 31	CR.7		1,265	1,525

Note Receivable—Beverly Mann No. 13

Date	Jrnl. Ref.	Debit	Credit	Balance
Feb. 28	✓			1,000
Mar. 9	CR.7		1,000	—

Inventory No. 14

Date	Jrnl. Ref.	Debit	Credit	Balance
Feb. 28	✓			1,819
Mar. 31	CR.7		841	978

Note Payable—Interstate Bank No. 22

Date	Jrnl. Ref.	Debit	Credit	Balance
Mar. 24	CR.7		2,200	2,200

Sales Revenue No. 41

Date	Jrnl. Ref.	Debit	Credit	Balance
Mar. 31	CR.7		1,300	1,300

Sales Discounts No. 42

Date	Jrnl. Ref.	Debit	Credit	Balance
Mar. 31	CR.7	5		5

Interest Revenue No. 46

Date	Jrnl. Ref.	Debit	Credit	Balance
Mar. 9	CR.7		80	80

Cost of Goods Sold No. 51

Date	Jrnl. Ref.	Debit	Credit	Balance
Mar. 31	CR.7	841		841

REQUIREMENT 4

General Ledger	
Accounts Receivable debit balance............	$1,525

Accounts Receivable Subsidiary Ledger:
Customer Accounts Receivable

Customer	Balance
Lance Albert	$ 640
Melinda Fultz...	885
Total accounts receivable..........................	$1,525

Summary of Learning Objectives

1. *Describe the features of an effective accounting information system.* An effective *accounting information system* captures and summarizes transactions quickly, accurately, and usefully. The four major aspects of a good accounting information system are (1) control over operations; (2) compatibility with the particular features of the business; (3) flexibility in response to changes in the business; and (4) a favorable cost/benefit relationship, with benefits outweighing costs.

2. *Understand how computerized and manual accounting systems work.* Computerized accounting systems process inputs faster than do manual systems and can generate more types of reports. The key components of a computerized accounting system are *hardware*, *software*, and company personnel. Account numbers play an important role in the operation of computerized systems, because computers classify accounts by account numbers. Both computerized and manual accounting systems require transactions to be classified by type.

Computerized systems use a *menu* structure to organize accounting functions. Posting, trial balances, financial statements, and closing procedures are carried out automatically in a computerized accounting system. Computerized accounting systems are integrated so that the system's different modules are updated together.

3. *Understand how spreadsheets are used in accounting.* *Spreadsheets* are electronic work sheets whose grid points, or cells, are linked by formulas. The numerical relationships in the spreadsheet are maintained whenever changes are made to the spreadsheet. Spreadsheets are ideally suited to detailed computations, as in budgeting.

4. *Use the sales journal, the cash receipts journal, and the accounts receivable subsidiary ledger.* Many accounting systems use *special journals* to record transactions by category. Credit sales are recorded in a *sales journal*, and cash receipts in a *cash receipts journal*. Posting goes to the *general ledger* and to the accounts receivable *subsidiary ledger*, which lists each customer and the amount receivable from that customer. The accounts receivable subsidiary ledger is the main device for ensuring that the company collects from customers.

5. *Use the purchases journal, the cash disbursements journal, and the accounts payable subsidiary ledger.* Credit purchases in a manual system are recorded in a *purchases journal*, and cash payments in a *cash disbursements journal*. Posting from these journals is to the general ledger and to the accounts payable subsidiary ledger. The accounts payable subsidiary ledger helps the company stay current in its payments to suppliers.

Accounting Vocabulary

accounting information system *(p. 246)*
batch processing *(p. 250)*
cash disbursements journal *(p. 260)*
cash payments journal *(p. 260)*
cash receipts journal *(p. 256)*
check register *(p. 260)*
control account *(p. 256)*
credit memorandum or credit memo *(p. 262)*
database *(p. 247)*
debit memorandum or debit memo *(p. 263)*
general journal *(p. 252)*
general ledger *(p. 255)*
hardware *(p. 247)*
menu *(p. 249)*
module *(p. 251)*
network *(p. 247)*
on-line processing *(p. 250)*
purchases journal *(p. 258)*
sales journal *(p. 253)*
server *(p. 247)*
software *(p. 247)*
special journal *(p. 252)*
spreadsheet *(p. 251)*
subsidiary ledger *(p. 255)*

Questions

1. Describe the four criteria of an effective accounting system.
2. Distinguish batch computer processing from on-line computer processing.
3. What accounting categories correspond to the account numbers 1, 2, 3, 4, and 5 in a typical computerized accounting system?
4. Why might the number 112 be assigned to Accounts Receivable and the number 1120708 to Carl Erickson, a customer?
5. Describe the function of menus in a computerized accounting system.
6. How do formulas in spreadsheets speed the process of budget preparation and revision?
7. Name four special journals used in accounting systems. For what type of transaction is each designed?
8. Describe the two advantages that special journals have over recording all transactions in the general journal.
9. What is a control account, and how is it related to a subsidiary ledger? Name two common control accounts.
10. Graff Company's sales journal has one amount column headed Accounts Receivable Dr. and Sales Revenue Cr. In this journal, 86 transactions are recorded. How many posting references appear in the journal? What does each posting reference represent?
11. The accountant for Bannister Company posted all amounts correctly from the cash receipts journal to the general ledger. However, she failed to post three credits to customer accounts in the accounts receivable subsidiary ledger. How would this error be detected?
12. At what two times is posting done from a special journal? What items are posted at each time?
13. What is the purpose of balancing the ledgers?
14. Posting from the journals of McKedrick Realty is complete. But the total of the individual balances in the accounts payable subsidiary ledger does not equal the balance in the Accounts Payable control account in the general ledger. Does this discrepancy necessarily indicate that the trial balance is out of balance? Explain.
15. Assume that posting is completed. The trial balance shows no errors, but the sum of the individual accounts payable does not equal the Accounts Payable control balance in the general ledger. What two errors could cause this problem?

Daily Exercises

Features of an effective information system
(Obj. 1)

DE6-1 Suppose you have just invested your life savings in a company that prints rubberized logos on T-shirts. The business is growing fast, and you need a better accounting information system. Consider the features of an effective system, as discussed on page 246. Which feature do you regard as most important? Why? Which feature must you consider if your financial resources are limited?

Components of a computerized accounting system
(Obj. 1)

DE6-2 Match each component of a computerized accounting system with its meaning.

Component		Meaning
A. Software	_____	Electronic linkages that allow different computers to share the same information
B. Network	_____	Electronic equipment
C. Server	_____	Programs that drive a computer
D. Hardware	_____	Main computer in a networked system

Accounting system vocabulary
(Obj. 1)

DE6-3 Complete the crossword puzzle on page 269.
Down:

1. Electronic computer equipment
2. A _______ible information system accommodates changes as the organization evolves
3. Programs that drive a computer
4. Managers need _______ over operations in order to authorize transactions and safeguard assets
5. The opposite of debits

Across:

3. Main computer in a networked system
6. Electronic linkage that allows different computers to share the same information
7. Cost-_______ relationship must be favorable

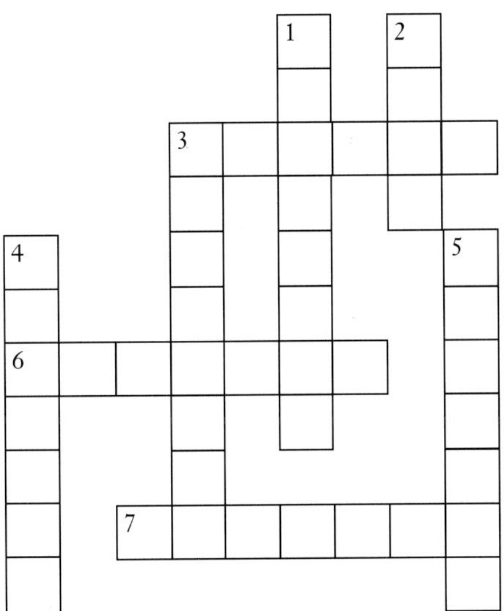

DE6-4 Use account numbers 11 through 16, 21, 22, 31, 32, 41, 51, and 52 to correspond to the following selected accounts from the general ledger of Mountainview Gift Shop. List the accounts and their account numbers in proper order, starting with the most liquid current asset.

Setting up a chart of accounts (Obj. 2)

Jeffrey Blois, capital	**Depreciation expense**
Cost of goods sold	**Cash**
Accounts payable	**Jeffrey Blois, withdrawals**
Inventory	**Prepaid insurance**
Sales revenue	**Accumulated depreciation**
Store fixtures	**Accounts receivable**
Note payable, long-term	

DE6-5 Refer to the spreadsheet screen in Exhibit 6-7, page 252. Suppose cells B1 through B4 are your business's actual income statement for the current year. You wish to develop your financial plan for the coming year. Assume that you expect revenues to increase by 10% and expenses to increase by 8 percent. Write the formulas in cells C2 through C4 to compute the amounts of expected revenues, expenses, and net income for the coming year.

Using a spreadsheet (Obj. 3)

DE6-6 Use the following abbreviations to indicate the journal in which you would record transactions a through n.

Using the journals (Obj. 4, 5)

J = General journal
S = Sales journal
CR = Cash receipts journal
P = Purchases journal
CD = Cash disbursements journal

Transactions:

_____ **a.** Payment of rent.
_____ **b.** Depreciation of computer equipment.
_____ **c.** Purchases of inventory on account.
_____ **d.** Collection of accounts receivable.
_____ **e.** Expiration of prepaid insurance.
_____ **f.** Sale on account.
_____ **g.** Payment on account.
_____ **h.** Cash purchase of inventory.
_____ **i.** Collection of dividend revenue earned on an investment.
_____ **j.** Prepayment of insurance.
_____ **k.** Borrowing money on a long-term note payable.
_____ **l.** Purchase of equipment on account.
_____ **m.** Cost of goods sold along with a credit sale.
_____ **n.** Cash sale of inventory.

Using the sales journal and the related ledgers
(Obj. 4)

DE6-7 ⟸ *Link Back to Chapter 5 (Gross Margin).* Use the sales journal and the related ledger accounts in Exhibit 6-10, page 254, to answer these questions about Austin Sound Stereo Center.

1. After these transactions, how much does Susan Levy owe Austin Sound? Where do you obtain this information? Be specific.
2. If there were no discounts, how much would Austin Sound hope to collect from all its customers? Where is this amount stored in a single figure?
3. How much gross margin did Austin Sound earn on credit sales during November? For this answer, ignore any sales discounts and any sales returns and allowances.
4. What amount did Austin Sound post to the Sales Revenue account? When did Austin Sound post to the Sales Revenue account? Assume a manual accounting system.

Using accounts receivable records
(Obj. 4)

DE6-8

1. A business that sells on account must have good accounts receivable records to ensure collection from customers. What is the name of the detailed record of amounts collectible from individual customers?
2. Where does the total amount receivable from all the customers appear? Be specific.
3. A key control feature of Austin Sound Stereo Center's accounting system lies in the agreement between the detailed records in question 1 above and the summary total in question 2. Use the data in Exhibit 6-10, page 254, to prove that Austin Sound's accounts receivable records are accurate.

Using cash receipts data
(Obj. 4)

DE6-9 The cash receipts journal of Austin Sound Stereo Center appears in Exhibit 6-11, page 257, along with the company's various ledger accounts. Use the data in Exhibit 6-11 to answer the following questions that Charles Ernest, owner of the business, might face.

1. How much were total cash receipts during November?
2. How much cash did Austin Sound collect on account from customers? How much in total discounts did customers earn by paying quickly? How much did Austin Sound's accounts receivable decrease because of collections from customers during November?
3. How much were cash sales during November?
4. How much did Austin Sound borrow during November? Where else could you look to determine whether Austin Sound has paid off part of the loan?

Using the purchases journal and the cash disbursements journal
(Obj. 5)

DE6-10 Refer to Austin Sound Stereo Center's purchases journal (Exhibit 6-12, page 259) and cash disbursements journal (Exhibit 6-13, page 261). Charles Ernest, the owner, has raised the following questions about the business.

1. How much did total credit purchases of inventory, supplies, fixtures, and furniture increase Austin Sound's accounts payable during November?
2. How much of the accounts payable did Austin Sound pay off during November? What amount of cash did Austin Sound pay on account? Explain the difference.
3. At November 30, after all purchases and all cash payments, how much does Austin Sound owe JVC Corporation? How much in total does Austin Sound owe on account? Prove that the total is correct.

Using the purchases journal and the cash disbursements journal
(Obj. 5)

DE6-11 ⟸ *Link Back to Chapters 1 and 2 (Recording transactions).* Use Austin Sound's purchases journal (Exhibit 6-12, page 259) and cash disbursements journal (Exhibit 6-13, page 261) to address these real-world questions faced by Charles Ernest, owner of the business.

1. Suppose it is December 1 and Ernest wishes to pay the full amount that Austin Sound owes on account. Examine the purchases journal (page 259) to determine whether Ernest can take any purchase discounts, and also consider the cash disbursements journal. Then make a general journal entry to record payment of the correct amount on December 1. Include an explanation.
2. Why do you think Austin Sound debited Rent Expense for the rent payment on November 3?
3. How much were Austin Sound's total purchases of inventory during November? How much were net purchases of inventory? What explains the difference? Which account holds these amounts?

Using all the journals
(Obj. 4, 5)

DE6-12 Answer the following questions about the November transactions of Austin Sound Stereo Center. You will need to refer to Exhibits 6-10 through 6-13, which begin on page 254.

1. Determine Austin Sound's gross sales revenue and net sales revenue for November. Indicate which ledger provides the data for your answer.
2. Did Austin Sound's interest revenue for November result from a cash receipt or from an accrual of interest? How can you tell?

3. How did Austin Sound purchase furniture—for cash or on account? Indicate the basis for your answer.
4. From whom did Austin Sound purchase supplies on account? How much in total does Austin Sound owe this company on November 30? Can Austin Sound take a discount when Austin Sound pays? Why or why not?
5. How much cash does Austin Sound have on hand at November 30? How much inventory does Austin Sound have after all transactions are recorded, including the cash receipts journal (Exhibit 6–11, page 257)? Indicate which exhibit provides each answer.

Exercises

Assigning account numbers (Obj. 2)

E6-1 Assign account numbers (from the list that follows) to the accounts of Monochrome Plastics. Identify the headings, which are *not* accounts and would not be assigned an account number.

Assets	Jean-Claude Dubet, Capital
Current Assets	Jean-Claude Dubet, Withdrawals
Property, Plant, and Equipment	Revenues
Accounts Payable	Depreciation Expense

Numbers from which to choose:

1	21
2	28
3	31
4	32
5	33
11	53
12	121
16	131
17	411

Using a trial balance (Obj. 2)

E6-2 The following accounts in the computerized accounting system of Monte Gilbert Company show some of the company's adjusted balances before closing:

Total assets	**?**
Current assets	**15,600**
Plant assets	**63,400**
Total liabilities	**?**
Current liabilities	**41,100**
Long-term liabilities	**?**
Monte Gilbert, capital	**8,600**
Monte Gilbert, withdrawals	**2,000**
Total revenues	**28,000**
Total expenses	**21,000**

Compute the missing amounts.

Using a spreadsheet to compute depreciation (Obj. 3)

E6-3 Equipment listed on a spreadsheet has a cost of $100,000; this amount is located in cell C4. The number of years of the asset's useful life is found in cell D1. Write the spreadsheet formula to express annual depreciation expense for the equipment.

Computing financial statement amounts with a spreadsheet (Obj. 3)

E6-4 The values of the following items are stored in the cells of a Fotomat Copy Center's spreadsheet:

Item	Cell
Total assets	B7
Current assets	B8
Fixed assets	B9
Total liabilities	B10
Current liabilities	B11
Long-term liabilities	B12

Write the spreadsheet formula to calculate the copy center's

a. Current ratio
b. Total owner's equity
c. Debt ratio

Using the sales and cash receipts journals
(Obj. 4)

E6-5 The sales and cash receipts journals of Epstein Carbonic Company include the following entries:

Sales Journal

Date	Account Debited	Post. Ref.	Accounts Receivable Dr. Sales Revenue Cr.	Cost of Goods Sold Dr. Inventory Cr.
Oct. 7	U. Mason	✓	930	550
10	T. Muecke	✓	3,800	1,970
10	E. Lovell	✓	690	410
12	B. Goebel	✓	5,470	3,340
31	Total		10,890	6,270

Cash Receipts Journal

	Debits		Credits					
					Other Accounts			
Date	Cash	Sales Discounts	Accounts Receivable	Sales Revenue	Account Title	Post. Ref.	Amount	Cost of Goods Sold Debit Inventory Credit
Oct. 16					U. Mason	✓		
19					E. Lovell	✓		
24	300			300				190
30					T. Muecke	✓		

Epstein Carbonic makes all credit sales on terms of 2/10 n/30. Complete the cash receipts journal for those transactions indicated. Also, total the journal and show that total debits equal total credits. Each cash receipt was for the full amount of the receivable.

Classifying postings from the cash receipts journal
(Obj. 4)

E6-6 The cash receipts journal of Appollo Oil Company follows.

Cash Receipts Journal **Page 7**

	Debits		Credits				
					Other Accounts		
Date	Cash	Sales Discounts	Accounts Receivable	Sales Revenue	Account Title	Post. Ref.	Amount
Dec. 2	794	16	810		Magna Co.	(a)	
9	491		491		Kamm, Inc.	(b)	
14	3,904			3,904			
19	4,480				Note Receivable	(c)	4,000
					Interest Revenue	(d)	480
30	314	7	321		J. T. Franz	(e)	
31	4,235			4,235			
31	14,218	23	1,622	8,139	Totals		4,480
	(f)	(g)	(h)	(i)			(j)

Appollo's general ledger includes the following selected accounts, along with their account numbers:

Number	Account	Number	Account
111	Cash	511	Sales revenue
112	Accounts receivable	512	Sales discounts
113	Note receivable	513	Sales returns
119	Land	521	Interest revenue

REQUIRED

Indicate whether each posting reference (a) through (j) should be a

- Checkmark (✓) for a posting to a customer account in the accounts receivable subsidiary ledger.
- Account number for a posting to an account in the general ledger. If so, give the account number.
- Letter (x) for an amount not posted.

Identifying transactions from postings to the accounts receivable subsidiary ledger
(Obj. 4)

E6-7 A customer account in the accounts receivable ledger of Memphis Masonry Company follows.

Christine Xavier

Date		Jrnl. Ref.	Dr.	Cr.	Balance Dr.	Balance Cr.
May 1	....				403	
6	....	S.5	1,180		1,583	
19	....	J.8		191	1,392	
21	....	CR.9		703	689	

Describe the three posted transactions.

REQUIRED

E6-8 During June, Escondido Sales Company completed the following *credit purchase* transactions:

Recording purchase transactions in the general journal and in the purchases journal
(Obj. 5)

June 4 Purchased inventory, $862, from McKee Co. Escondido uses a perpetual inventory system.
7 Purchased supplies, $107, from JJ Maine Corp.
19 Purchased equipment, $1,903, from Liston-Fry Co.
27 Purchased inventory, $2,210, from Milan, Inc.

Record these transactions first in the general journal—with explanations—and then in the purchases journal. Omit credit terms and posting references. Which procedure for recording transactions is quicker? Why?

Posting from the purchases journal, balancing the ledgers
(Obj. 5)

E6-9 The purchases journal of Acoustic Wave Company follows.

Purchases Journal — **Page 7**

Date	Account Credited	Terms	Post. Ref.	Account Payable Cr.	Inventory Dr.	Supplies Dr.	Other Accounts Dr. Acct. Title	Other Accounts Dr. Post. Ref.	Other Accounts Dr. Amt. Dr.
Sep. 2	Brotherton, Inc.	n/30		400	400				
5	Rolf Office Supply	n/30		175		175			
13	Brotherton, Inc.	2/10 n/30		847	847				
26	Marks Equipment Company	n/30		916			Equipment		916
30	Totals			2,338	1,247	175			916

REQUIRED

1. Open ledger accounts for Inventory, Supplies, Equipment, and Accounts Payable. Post to these accounts from the purchases journal. Use dates and posting references in the ledger accounts.
2. Open accounts in the accounts payable subsidiary ledger for Brotherton, Inc., Marks Equipment Company, and Rolf Office Supply. Post from the purchases journal. Use dates and journal references in the ledger accounts.
3. Balance the Accounts Payable control account in the general ledger with the total of the balances in the accounts payable subsidiary ledger.

E6-10 During February, PanAm Imports had the following transactions:

Using the cash disbursements journal
(Obj. 5)

Feb. 3 Paid $392 on account to Marquis Corp. net of an $8 discount for an earlier purchase of inventory.
6 Purchased inventory for cash, $1,267.
11 Paid $375 for supplies.
15 Purchased inventory on credit from Monroe Corporation, $774.
16 Paid $4,062 on account to LaGrange Associates; there was no discount.
21 Purchased furniture for cash, $960.
26 Paid $3,910 on account to Graff Software for an earlier purchase of inventory. The discount was $90.
28 Made a semiannual interest payment of $800 on a long-term note payable. The entire payment was for interest.

REQUIRED

1. Prepare a cash disbursements journal similar to the one illustrated in this chapter. Omit the check number (Ck. No.) and posting reference (Post. Ref.) columns.
2. Record the transactions in the journal. Which transaction should not be recorded in the cash disbursements journal? In what journal does it belong?
3. Total the amount columns of the journal. Determine that the total debits equal the total credits.

Using business documents to record transactions
(Obj. 5)

E6-11 *Link Back to Chapter 5 (Recording purchases, sales, and returns).* The following documents describe two business transactions.

Invoice

Date:	September 14, 19X0
Sold to:	BiWheel Bicycle Shop
Sold by:	Schwinn Company
Terms:	2/10 n/30

Items Purchased Bicycles

Quantity	Price	Total
4	$95	$380
1	70	70
5	60	300
Total		$750

Debit Memo

Date:	September 20, 19X0
Issued to:	Schwinn Company
Issued by:	BiWheel Bicycle Shop

Items Returned Bicycles

Quantity	Price	Total
1	$95	$ 95
1	70	70
Total		$165

Reason: Damaged in shipment

Use the general journal to record these transactions and BiWheel's cash payment on September 21. Record the transactions first on the books of BiWheel Bicycle Shop and, second, on the books of Schwinn Company, which makes and sells bicycles. Both BiWheel and Schwinn use a perpetual inventory system as illustrated in Chapter 5. Schwinn's cost of the bicycles sold to BiWheel was $400. Schwinn's cost of the returned merchandise was $80. Round to the nearest dollar. Explanations are not required. Set up your answer in the following format:

Date	BiWheel Journal Entries	Schwinn Journal Entries

CHALLENGE EXERCISE

Using the special journals
(Obj. 4, 5)

E6-12 *Link Back to Chapter 5 (Cost of Goods Sold, Gross Margin).*

1. Austin Sound Stereo Center's special journals in Exhibits 6-10 through 6-13 (pages 254–261) provide the owner with much of the data needed for preparation of the financial statements. Austin Sound uses the *perpetual* inventory system, so the amount of cost of goods sold is simply the ending balance in that account. Charles Ernest, the owner, needs to know the business's gross margin for November. Compute the gross margin.
2. Suppose Austin Sound used the *periodic* inventory system. In that case, the business must compute cost of goods sold by the formula:

Cost of goods sold:	
Beginning inventory	$ X*
+ Net purchases	XXX
= Cost of goods available for sale	X,XXX
– Ending inventory	(XX)
= Cost of goods sold	$ XX

Perform this calculation of cost of goods sold for Austin Sound. Does this computation of cost of goods sold agree with your answer to requirement 1?

Beyond the Numbers

Designing a special journal
(Obj. 4, 5)

BN6-1 Monarch Technology Associates creates and sells cutting-edge networking software. Monarch's quality control officer estimates that 20% of the company's sales and purchases of inventory are returned for additional debugging. Monarch needs special journals for

- Sales returns and allowances
- Purchase returns and allowances

*$0 for Austin Sound at November 1.

REQUIRED

1. Design the two special journals. For each journal, include a column for the appropriate business document.
2. Enter one transaction in each journal, using the Austin Sound transaction data illustrated on pages 254 and 257. Show all posting references, including those for column totals.

ETHICAL ISSUE

On a recent trip to Brazil, Carlos Santé, sales manager of Cyber Systems, Inc., took his wife along at company expense. Chelsea Brindley, vice president of sales and Santé's boss, thought his travel and entertainment expenses seemed excessive. Brindley approved the reimbursement, however, because she owed Santé a favor. Brindley, well aware that the company president routinely reviews all expenses recorded in the cash disbursements journal, had the accountant record Santé's wife's expenses in the general journal as follows:

Sales Promotion Expense..........	3,500	
Cash		3,500

REQUIRED

1. Does recording the transaction in the general journal rather than in the cash disbursements journal affect the amounts of cash and total expenses reported in the financial statements?
2. Why did Brindley want this transaction recorded in the general journal?
3. What is the ethical issue in this situation? What role does accounting play in this issue?

Problems (GROUP A)

Using a spreadsheet to prepare a partial balance sheet and evaluate financial positions
(Obj. 3)

P6-1A The following spreadsheet shows the assets section of the Ricoh Digital Products balance sheet:

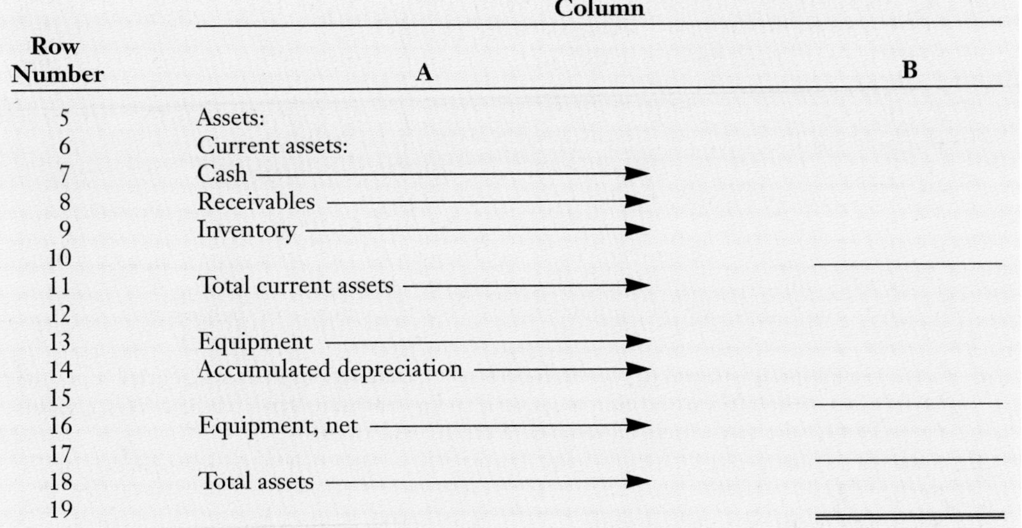

Row Number	Column A	Column B
5	Assets:	
6	Current assets:	
7	Cash ——→	
8	Receivables ——→	
9	Inventory ——→	
10		______
11	Total current assets ——→	
12		
13	Equipment ——→	
14	Accumulated depreciation ——→	
15		______
16	Equipment, net ——→	
17		______
18	Total assets ——→	
19		======

1. Write the word *number* in the cells (indicated by arrows) where numbers will be entered.
2. Write the appropriate formula in each cell that will need a formula. Symbols from which to choose are

+	add
–	subtract
*	multiply
/	divide

=SUM(beginning cell:ending cell)

3. Last year Ricoh used this spreadsheet to prepare the company's budgeted balance sheet for the current year. The budgeted balance sheet shows the company's goal for total current assets at the end of the year. It is now one year later, and Ricoh has prepared its actual year-end balance sheet. State how the owner of the company can use this balance sheet in decision making.

Using the sales, cash receipts, and general journals
(Obj. 4)

P6-2A The general ledger of Timken Watch Company includes the following accounts:

Cash	**111**
Accounts Receivable	**112**
Notes Receivable	**115**
Inventory	**131**
Equipment	**141**
Land	**142**
Sales Revenue	**411**
Sales Discounts	**412**
Sales Returns and Allowances	**413**
Interest Revenue	**417**
Gain on Sale of Land	**418**
Cost of Goods Sold	**511**

All credit sales are on the company's standard terms of 2/10 n/30. Transactions in October that affected sales and cash receipts were as follows:

Oct.	1	Sold inventory on credit to L. Ijiri, $2,000. Timken's cost of these goods was $1,114.
	5	As an accommodation to another company, sold new equipment for its cost of $770, receiving cash in this amount.
	6	Cash sales for the week totaled $2,107 (cost, $1,362).
	8	Sold merchandise on account to McNair Co., $2,830 (cost, $1,789).
	9	Sold land that cost $22,000 for cash of $40,000.
	11	Sold goods on account to Nickerson Builders, $6,099 (cost, $3,853).
	11	Received cash from L. Ijiri in full settlement of her account receivable from October 1.
	13	Cash sales for the week were $1,995 (cost $1,286).
	15	Sold inventory on credit to Montez and Montez, a partnership, $800 (cost, $517).
	18	Received inventory sold on October 8 to McNair Co. for $120. The goods we shipped were unsatisfactory. These goods cost Timken $73.
	19	Sold merchandise on account to Nickerson Builders, $3,900 (cost, $2,618).
	20	Cash sales for the week were $2,330 (cost, $1,574).
	21	Received $1,200 cash from McNair Co. in partial settlement of its account receivable. There was no discount.
	22	Received cash from Montez and Montez for its account receivable from October 15.
	22	Sold goods on account to Diamond Co., $2,022 (cost, $1,325).
	25	Collected $4,200 on a note receivable, of which $200 was interest.
	27	Cash sales for the week totaled $2,970 (cost, $1,936).
	27	Sold inventory on account to Littleton Corporation, $2,290 (cost, $1,434).
	28	Received goods sold on October 22 to Diamond Co. for $680. The goods were damaged in shipment. The salvage value of these goods was $96.
	30	Received $1,510 cash on account from McNair Co. There was no discount.

REQUIRED

1. Use the appropriate journal to record the preceding transactions in a sales journal (omit the Invoice No. column), a cash receipts journal, and a general journal. Timken Watch Company records sales returns and allowances in the general journal.
2. Total each column of the cash receipts journal. Determine that the total debits equal the total credits.
3. Show how postings would be made from the journals by writing the account numbers and checkmarks in the appropriate places in the journals.

Correcting errors in the cash receipts journal
(Obj. 4)

P6-3A The following cash receipts journal contains five entries. All five entries are for legitimate cash receipt transactions, but the journal contains some errors in recording the transactions. In fact, only one entry is correct, and each of the other four entries contains one error.

	Debits		Credits					
					Other Accounts			
Date	Cash	Sales Discounts	Accounts Receivable	Sales Revenue	Account Title	Post. Ref.	Amount	Cost of Goods Sold Debit Inventory Credit
9/3	711	34	745		Alcon Labs	✓		
9			346	346	Carl Ryther	✓		
10	22,000			22,000	Land	19		
19	73							44
30	1,060			1,133				631
	23,844	34	1,091	23,479	Totals			675
	(11)	(42)	(12)	(41)			(x)	

Cash Receipts Journal — Page 16

Total Dr. = $23,878 — Total Cr. = $24,570

REQUIRED

1. Identify the correct entry.
2. Identify the error in each of the other four entries.
3. Using the following format, prepare a corrected cash receipts journal.

Cash Receipts Journal — Page 16

	Debits		Credits					
					Other Accounts			
Date	Cash	Sales Discounts	Accounts Receivable	Sales Revenue	Account Title	Post. Ref.	Amount	Cost of Goods Sold Debit Inventory Credit
9/3					Alcon Labs	✓		
9					Carl Ryther	✓		
10					Land	19		
19								
30								
	24,190	34	1,091	1,133	Totals		22,000	
	(11)	(42)	(12)	(41)			(x)	(51/13)

Total Dr. = $24,224 — Total Cr. = $24,224

P6-4A The general ledger of Andino Luggage Company includes the following accounts:

Using the purchases, cash disbursements, and general journals ***(Obj. 5)***

Cash	**111**
Inventory	**131**
Prepaid Insurance	**161**
Supplies	**171**
Equipment	**189**
Accounts Payable	**211**
Rent Expense	**562**
Utilities Expense	**565**

Transactions in November that affected purchases and cash disbursements were as follows:

Nov. 1 Paid monthly rent, debiting Rent Expense for $1,350.
3 Purchased inventory on credit from Sylvania Co., $2,000. Terms were 2/15 n/45.
4 Purchased supplies on credit terms of 2/10 n/30 from Harmon Sales, $800.
7 Paid gas and water bills, $406.
10 Purchased equipment on account from Lancer Co., $1,050. Payment terms were 2/10 n/30.
11 Returned the equipment to Lancer Co. It was defective.
12 Paid Sylvania Co. the amount owed on the purchase of November 3.
12 Purchased inventory on account from Lancer Co., $1,100. Terms were 2/10 n/30.
14 Purchased inventory for cash, $1,585.
15 Paid an insurance premium, debiting Prepaid Insurance, $2,416.
16 Paid our account payable to Harmon Sales from November 4.
17 Paid electricity bill, $165.
20 Paid account payable to Lancer Co., from November 12.
21 Purchased supplies on account from Master Supply, $754. Terms were net 30.
22 Purchased inventory on credit terms of 1/10 n/30 from Linz Brothers, $3,400.

Nov. 26 Returned inventory purchased for $500 on November 22, to Linz Brothers.
30 Paid Linz Brothers the net amount owed from November 22, less the return on November 26.

REQUIRED

1. Use the appropriate journal to record the preceding transactions in a purchases journal, a cash disbursements journal (omit the Check No. column), and a general journal. Andino Luggage records purchase returns in the general journal.
2. Total each column of the special journals. Show that the total debits equal the total credits in each special journal.
3. Show how postings would be made from the journals by writing the account numbers and checkmarks in the appropriate places in the journals.

Using all the journals, posting, and balancing the ledgers
(Obj. 4, 5)

P6-5A Kent Sales Company, which uses the perpetual inventory system and makes all credit sales of 2/10 n/30, had these transactions during January:

Jan. 2 Issued invoice no. 191 for sale on account to L. E. Wooten, $2,350. Kent's cost of this inventory was $1,390.
3 Purchased inventory on credit terms of 3/10 n/60 from Delwood Plaza, $5,900.
4 Sold inventory for cash, $808 (cost, $510).
5 Issued check no. 473 to purchase furniture for cash, $1,087.
8 Collected interest revenue of $2,440.
9 Issued invoice no. 192 for sale on account to Cortez Co., $6,250 (cost, $3,300).
10 Purchased inventory for cash, $776, issuing check no. 474.
12 Received $2,303 cash from L. E. Wooten in full settlement of her account receivable, net of the discount, from the sale of January 2.
13 Issued check no. 475 to pay Delwood Plaza net amount owed from January 3.
13 Purchased supplies on account from Havrilla Corp., $689. Terms were net end-of-month.
15 Sold inventory on account to J. R. Wakeland, issuing invoice no. 193 for $743 (cost, $410).
17 Issued credit memo to J. R. Wakeland for $743 for defective merchandise returned to us by Wakeland. Also accounted for receipt of the inventory.
18 Issued invoice no. 194 for credit sale to L. E. Wooten, $1,825 (cost, $970).
19 Received $6,125 from Cortez Co. in full settlement of its account receivable from January 9.
20 Purchased inventory on credit terms of net 30 from Jasper Sales, $2,150.
22 Purchased furniture on credit terms of 3/10 n/60 from Delwood Plaza, $775.
22 Issued check no. 476 to pay for insurance coverage, debiting Prepaid Insurance for $1,345.
24 Sold supplies to an employee for cash of $86, which was Kent's cost.
25 Issued check no. 477 to pay utilities, $388.
28 Purchased inventory on credit terms of 2/10 n/30 from Havrilla Corp., $421.
29 Returned damaged inventory to Havrilla Corp., issuing a debit memo for $421.
29 Sold goods on account to Cortez Co., issuing invoice no. 195 for $567 (cost, $314).
30 Issued check no. 478 to pay Havrilla Corp. on account from January 13.
31 Received cash in full on account from L. E. Wooten on credit sale of January 18. There was no discount.
31 Issued check no. 479 to pay monthly salaries of $2,600.

REQUIRED

1. For Kent Sales Company, open the following general ledger accounts using the account numbers given:

Cash	**111**	**Sales Revenue**	**411**
Accounts Receivable	**112**	**Sales Discounts**	**412**
Supplies	**116**	**Sales Returns and Allowances**	**413**
Prepaid Insurance	**117**	**Interest Revenue**	**419**
Inventory	**118**	**Cost of Goods Sold**	**511**
Furniture	**151**	**Salary Expense**	**531**
Accounts Payable	**211**	**Utilities Expense**	**541**

2. Open these accounts in the subsidiary ledgers. Accounts receivable subsidiary ledger: Cortez Co., J. R. Wakeland, and L. E. Wooten. Accounts payable subsidiary ledger: Delwood Plaza, Havrilla Corp., and Jasper Sales.
3. Enter the transactions in a sales journal (page 8), a cash receipts journal (page 3), a purchases journal (page 6), a cash disbursements journal (page 9), and a general journal (page 4), as appropriate.
4. Post daily to the accounts receivable subsidiary ledger and to the accounts payable subsidiary ledger. On January 31, post to the general ledger.

5. Total each column of the special journals. Show that the total debits equal the total credits in each special journal.
6. Balance the total of the customer account balances in the accounts receivable subsidiary ledger against Accounts Receivable in the general ledger. Do the same for the accounts payable subsidiary ledger and Accounts Payable in the general ledger.

Problems (GROUP B)

P6-1B The following spreadsheet shows the income statement of Helmsley Wholesale Co.:

Using a spreadsheet to prepare an income statement and evaluate operations **(Obj. 3)**

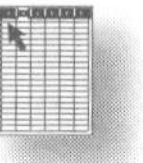

Row Number	Column A	Column B
5	Revenues:	
6	Service revenue ——→	
7	Rent revenue ——→	
8		———
9	Total revenue ——→	
10		
11	Expenses:	
12	Salary expense ——→	
13	Supplies expense ——→	
14	Rent expense ——→	
15	Depreciation expense ——→	
16		———
17	Total expenses ——→	
18		———
19	Net income ——→	
20		═══

REQUIRED

1. Write the word *number* in the cells (indicated by arrows) where numbers will be entered.
2. Write the appropriate formula in each cell that will need a formula. Symbols from which to choose are

+	add
–	subtract
*	multiply
/	divide

=SUM(beginning cell:ending cell)

3. Last year, Helmsley Wholesale Co. used this spreadsheet to prepare the company's budgeted income statement—which shows the company's net income goal—for the current year. It is now one year later, and Helmsley has prepared its actual income statement for the year. State how the owner of the company can use this income statement in decision making.

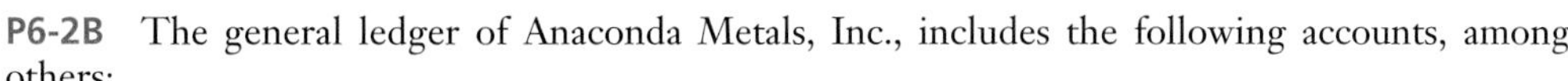

P6-2B The general ledger of Anaconda Metals, Inc., includes the following accounts, among others:

Using the sales, cash receipts, and general journals **(Obj. 4)**

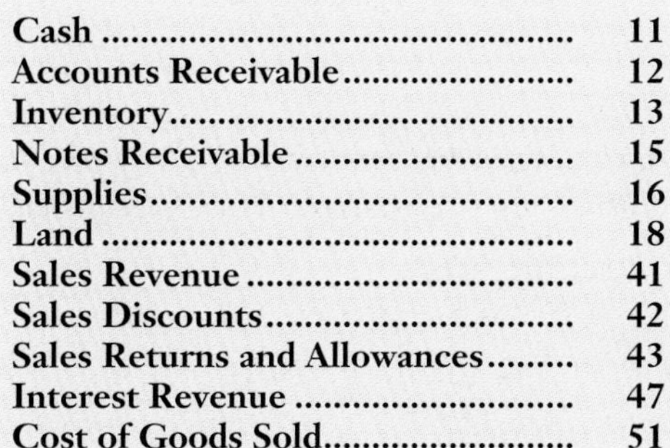

Account	No.
Cash	**11**
Accounts Receivable	**12**
Inventory	**13**
Notes Receivable	**15**
Supplies	**16**
Land	**18**
Sales Revenue	**41**
Sales Discounts	**42**
Sales Returns and Allowances	**43**
Interest Revenue	**47**
Cost of Goods Sold	**51**

All credit sales are on the company's standard terms of 2/10 n/30. Transactions in May that affected sales and cash receipts were as follows:

May	2	Sold inventory on credit to Ortez Co., $700. Anaconda's cost of these goods was $400.
	4	As an accommodation to a competitor, sold supplies at cost, $85, receiving cash.
	7	Cash sales for the week totaled $1,890 (cost, $1,640).

May 9 Sold merchandise on account to A. L. Prince, $7,320 (cost $5,110).
10 Sold land that cost $10,000 for cash of $10,000.
11 Sold goods on account to Sloan Electric, $5,104 (cost $3,520).
12 Received cash from Ortez Co. in full settlement of its account receivable from May 2.
14 Cash sales for the week were $2,106 (cost $1,530).
15 Sold inventory on credit to the partnership of Wilkie & Blinn, $3,650 (cost $2,260).
18 Received inventory sold on May 9 to A. L. Prince for $600. The goods shipped were unsatisfactory. These goods cost Anaconda $440.
20 Sold merchandise on account to Sloan Electric, $629 (cost, $450).
21 Cash sales for the week were $990 (cost, $690).
22 Received $4,000 cash from A. L. Prince in partial settlement of his account receivable.
25 Received cash from Wilkie & Blinn for its account receivable from May 15.
25 Sold goods on account to Olsen Co., $1,520 (cost, $1,050).
27 Collected $5,125 on a note receivable, of which $125 was interest.
28 Cash sales for the week totaled $3,774 (cost, $2,460).
29 Sold inventory on account to R. O. Bankston, $242 (cost, $170).
30 Received goods sold on May 25 to Olsen Co. for $40. The inventory was damaged in shipment. The salvage value of these goods was $10.
31 Received $2,720 cash on account from A. L. Prince.

REQUIRED

1. Anaconda records sales returns and allowances in the general journal. Use the appropriate journal to record the preceding transactions in a sales journal (omit the Invoice No. column), a cash receipts journal, and a general journal.
2. Total each column of the cash receipts journal. Show that the total debits equal the total credits.
3. Show how postings would be made from the journals by writing the account numbers and checkmarks in the appropriate places in the journals.

Correcting errors in the cash receipts journal
(Obj. 4)

P6-3B The following cash receipts journal contains five entries. All five entries are for legitimate cash receipt transactions, but the journal contains some errors in recording the transactions. In fact, only one entry is correct, and each of the other four entries contains one error.

Cash Receipts Journal **Page 22**

	Debits		Credits					
					Other Accounts			
Date	Cash	Sales Discounts	Accounts Receivable	Sales Revenue	Account Title	Post. Ref.	Amount	Cost of Goods Sold Debit Inventory Credit
5/6		600		600				290
7	429	22			Al Sperry	✓	451	
14	8,200				Note Receivable	15	7,700	
					Interest Revenue	45	500	
18				330				150
24	1,100		770					
	9,729	622	770	930	Totals		8,651	440
	(11)	(42)	(12)	(41)			(x)	(51/13)

Total Dr. = $10,351 Total Cr. = $10,351

REQUIRED

1. Identify the correct entry.
2. Identify the error in each of the other four entries.
3. Using the following format, prepare a corrected cash receipts journal.

Cash Receipts Journal								Page 22
	Debits		Credits					
					Other Accounts			
Date	Cash	Sales Discounts	Accounts Receivable	Sales Revenue	Account Title	Post. Ref.	Amount	Cost of Goods Sold Debit Inventory Credit
5/6								
7					Al Sperry	✓		
14					Note Receivable	15		
					Interest Revenue	45		
18								
24								
	10,329	22	1,221	930	Totals	8,200		
	(11)	(42)	(12)	(41)		(x)		

Total Dr. = $10,351 Total Cr. = $10,351

P6-4B The general ledger of Altigen Cellular includes the following accounts:

Using the purchases, cash disbursements, and general journals
(Obj. 5)

Cash	**111**
Inventory	**131**
Prepaid Insurance	**161**
Supplies	**171**
Furniture	**187**
Accounts Payable	**211**
Rent Expense	**564**
Utilities Expense	**583**

Transactions in August that affected purchases and cash disbursements were as follows:

Aug.	1	Purchased inventory on credit from Fort Worth Co., $1,900. Terms were 2/10 n/30.
	1	Paid monthly rent, debiting Rent Expense for $2,000.
	5	Purchased supplies on credit terms of 2/10 n/30 from Ross Supply, $450.
	8	Paid electricity bill, $588.
	9	Purchased furniture on account from A-1 Office Supply, $4,100. Payment terms were net 30.
	10	Returned the furniture to A-1 Office Supply. It was the wrong color.
	11	Paid Fort Worth Co. the amount owed on the purchase of August 1.
	12	Purchased inventory on account from Wynne, Inc., $4,400. Terms were 3/10 n/30.
	13	Purchased inventory for cash, $655.
	14	Paid a semiannual insurance premium, debiting Prepaid Insurance, $1,200.
	16	Paid our account payable to Ross Supply, from August 5.
	18	Paid gas and water bills, $196.
	21	Purchased inventory on credit terms of 1/10 n/45 from Software, Inc., $5,200.
	21	Paid account payable to Wynne, Inc. from August 12.
	22	Purchased supplies on account from Office Sales, Inc., $274. Terms were net 30.
	25	Returned to Software, Inc., $1,200 of the inventory purchased on August 21.
	31	Paid Software, Inc., the net amount owed from August 21 less the return on August 25.

REQUIRED

1. Altigen records purchase returns in the general journal. Use the appropriate journal to record the preceding transactions in a purchases journal, a cash disbursements journal (omit the Check No. column), and a general journal.
2. Total each column of the special journals. Show that the total debits equal the total credits in each special journal.
3. Show how postings would be made from the journals by writing the account numbers and checkmarks in the appropriate places in the journals.

P6-5B Lang Company, which uses the perpetual inventory system and makes all credit sales on terms of 2/10 n/30, completed the following transactions during July:

Using all the journals, posting, and balancing the ledgers
(Obj. 4, 5)

July	2	Issued invoice no. 913 for sale on account to N. J. Seiko, $4,100. Lang's cost of this inventory was $1,800.
	3	Purchased inventory on credit terms of 3/10 n/60 from Chicosky Co., $2,467.
	5	Sold inventory for cash, $1,077 (cost, $480).
	5	Issued check no. 532 to purchase furniture for cash, $2,185.

July	8	Collected interest revenue of $1,775.
	9	Issued invoice no. 914 for sale on account to Bell Co., $5,550 (cost, $2,310).
	10	Purchased inventory for cash, $1,143, issuing check no. 533.
	12	Received cash from N. J. Seiko in full settlement of her account receivable from the sale on July 2.
	13	Issued check no. 534 to pay Chicosky Co. the net amount owed from July 3. Round to the nearest dollar.
	13	Purchased supplies on account from Manley, Inc., $441. Terms were net end-of-month.
	15	Sold inventory on account to M. O. Brown, issuing invoice no. 915 for $665 (cost, $240).
	17	Issued credit memo to M. O. Brown for $665 for defective merchandise returned to us by Brown. Also accounted for receipt of the inventory.
	18	Issued invoice no. 916 for credit sale to N. J. Seiko, $357 (cost, $127).
	19	Received $5,439 from Bell Co. in full settlement of its account receivable from July 9. Bell earned a discount by paying early.
	20	Purchased inventory on credit terms of net 30 from Sims Distributing, $2,047.
	22	Purchased furniture on credit terms of 3/10 n/60 from Chicosky Co., $645.
	22	Issued check no. 535 to pay for insurance coverage, debiting Prepaid Insurance for $1,000.
	24	Sold supplies to an employee for cash of $54, which was Lang's cost.
	25	Issued check no. 536 to pay utilities, $453.
	28	Purchased inventory on credit terms of 2/10 n/30 from Manley, Inc., $675.
	29	Returned damaged inventory to Manley, Inc., issuing a debit memo for $675.
	29	Sold goods on account to Bell Co., issuing invoice no. 917 for $496 (cost, $220).
	30	Issued check no. 537 to pay Manley, Inc., in full on account from July 13.
	31	Received cash in full on account from N. J. Seiko on credit sale of January 18. There was no discount.
	31	Issued check no. 538 to pay monthly salaries of $2,347.

REQUIRED

1. For Lang Company, open the following general ledger accounts using the account numbers given:

Cash	**111**	**Sales Revenue**	**411**
Accounts Receivable	**112**	**Sales Discounts**	**412**
Supplies	**116**	**Sales Returns and Allowances**	**413**
Prepaid Insurance	**117**	**Interest Revenue**	**419**
Inventory	**118**	**Cost of Goods Sold**	**511**
Furniture	**151**	**Salary Expense**	**531**
Accounts Payable	**211**	**Utilities Expense**	**541**

2. Open these accounts in the subsidiary ledgers: Accounts receivable subsidiary ledger—Bell Co., M. O. Brown, and N. J. Seiko; accounts payable subsidiary ledger—Chicosky Co., Manley, Inc., and Sims Distributing.
3. Enter the transactions in a sales journal (page 7), a cash receipts journal (page 5), a purchases journal (page 10), a cash disbursements journal (page 8), and a general journal (page 6), as appropriate.
4. Post daily to the accounts receivable subsidiary ledger and to the accounts payable subsidiary ledger. On July 31, post to the general ledger.
5. Total each column of the special journals. Show that the total debits equal the total credits in each special journal.
6. Balance the total of the customer account balances in the accounts receivable subsidiary ledger against Accounts Receivable in the general ledger. Do the same for the accounts payable subsidiary ledger and Accounts Payable in the general ledger.

Applying Your Knowledge

DECISION CASES

Reconstructing transactions from amounts posted to the accounts receivable subsidiary ledger ***(Obj. 4)***

CASE 1. A fire destroyed certain accounting records of Premiere Art Supply. The owner, Jason Byrd, asks for your help in reconstructing the records. *He needs to know the beginning and ending balances of Accounts Receivable and the credit sales and cash receipts on account from customers during March.* All of Premiere's sales are on credit, with payment terms of 2/10 n/30. All cash receipts on account reached Premiere within the 10-day discount period, except as noted. Round all amounts to the nearest dollar. The only accounting record preserved from the fire is the accounts receivable subsidiary ledger, which follows.

Rachel Bouillet

Date	Item	Jrnl. Ref.	Debit	Credit	Balance
Mar. 8		S.6	2,378		2,378
16		S.6	903		3,281
18		CR.8		2,378	903
19		J.5		221	682
27		CR.8		682	–0–

Anna Fowler

Date	Item	Jrnl. Ref.	Debit	Credit	Balance
Mar. 1	Balance				1,096
5		CR.8		1,096	–0–
11		S.6	396		396
21		CR.8		396	–0–
24		S.6	3,944		3,944

Norris Associates

Date	Item	Jrnl. Ref.	Debit	Credit	Balance
Mar. 1	Balance				2,883
15		S.6	2,635		5,518
29		CR.8		2,883*	2,635

*Cash receipt did not occur within the discount period.

Suzuki, Inc.

Date	Item	Jrnl. Ref.	Debit	Credit	Balance
Mar. 1	Balance				440
3		CR.8		440	–0–
25		S.6	3,655		3,655
29		S.6	1,123		4,778

Understanding an accounting system ***(Obj. 4, 5)***

CASE 2. The external auditor must ensure that the amounts shown on the balance sheet for Accounts Receivable represent actual amounts that customers owe the company. Each customer account in the accounts receivable subsidiary ledger must represent an actual credit sale to the person indicated, and the customer's balance must not have been collected. This auditing concept is called *validity* or *validating the accounts receivable.*

The auditor must also ensure that all amounts that the company owes are included in Accounts Payable and other liability accounts. For example, all credit purchases of inventory made by the company and not yet paid should be included in the balance of the Accounts Payable account. This auditing concept is called *completeness.*

REQUIRED

Suggest how an auditor might test a customer's account receivable balance for validity. Indicate how the auditor might test the balance of the Accounts Payable account for completeness.

Team Projects

PROJECT 1: PREPARING A BUSINESS PLAN FOR A SERVICE ENTITY. List what you have learned thus far in the course. On the basis of what you have learned, refine your plan for promoting a rock concert (from Team Project 1 in Chapter 1) to include everything you believe you must do to succeed in this business venture.

PROJECT 2: PREPARING A BUSINESS PLAN FOR A MERCHANDISING ENTITY. As you work through Part 2 of this book (Chapters 7–12), you will be examining in detail the current assets, current liabilities, and plant assets of a business. Most of the organizations that form the context for business activity in the remainder of the book are merchandising entities. Therefore, in a group or individually—as directed by your instructor—develop a plan for beginning and operating an audio/video store or other type of business. Develop your plan in as much detail as you can. Remember that the business manager who attends to the most details delivers the best product at the lowest price for customers!

Internet Exercise KYNETICS SOFTWARE

Multi-Level Marketing is a marketing strategy in which consumer products and services are sold through individuals representing an organization. The independent representatives are compensated on the overall sales from their customers as well as the sales from their customers' customers and so on. Multi-level marketing is often referred to as a pyramid approach. This strategy has been successful for companies such as Mary Kay Cosmetics, Amway, and Excel Communications.

Many multi-level marketers (or network marketers) run their business on the side or as a part-time job. Consequently, they do not have the time necessary to establish and maintain a proper accounting system. This can lead to problems for the marketer in not following up on contacts on a timely basis, not maintaining the appropriate tax records, and not being able to track the sales activities of customers. Kynetics Software of San Carlos, California has created an accounting software package specifically designed for multi-level marketers.

REQUIRED

1. Go to *http://www.kynetics.com.* The site provides product information and ordering, testimonials, and a quick tour of its software, MLM Easy Money™.
2. Click on **Quick Tour.** After reading through the pages and examining the screens and reports, answer the following questions:
   a. Does the software appear to possess the four characteristics of an effective accounting information system—Control, Compatibility, Flexibility, and Favorable Cost/Benefit Relationship?
   b. Why do you think the software reports include a tax return report and income statement, but not a balance sheet or a statement of cash flows?
   c. An accounting information system includes more than computerized financial records. What information outside the accounting function does MLM Easy Money™ incorporate in its reports?
   d. Identify three features in the software that would help the user better manage his or her business.
   e. Does MLM Easy Money™ require extensive computer knowledge to run the program? Explain.
   f. From the **Testimonials,** what do selected MLM Easy Money™ customers have to say are the primary benefits of the software?

Comprehensive Problems for Part One, Chapters 1–6

PROBLEM 1. COMPLETING A MERCHANDISER'S ACCOUNTING CYCLE The end-of-month trial balance of St. James Technology at January 31 of the current year is on top of the next page. Additional data at January 31, 19XX:

a. Supplies consumed during the month, $1,500. Half is selling expense, and the other half is general expense.
b. Depreciation for the month: building, $4,000; fixtures, $4,800. One-fourth of depreciation is selling expense, and three-fourths is general expense.
c. Unearned sales revenue still unearned, $1,200.
d. Accrued salaries, a general expense, $1,150.
e. Accrued interest expense, $780.
f. Inventory on hand, $63,720. St. James uses the perpetual inventory system.

REQUIRED

1. Using four-column accounts, open the accounts listed on the trial balance, inserting their unadjusted balances. Date the balances of the following accounts January 1: Supplies; Building; Accumulated Depreciation—Building; Fixtures; Accumulated Depreciation—Fixtures; Unearned Sales Revenue; and Dirk St. James, Capital. Date the balance of Dirk St. James, Withdrawals, January 31. Also open the Income Summary, account number 33.
2. Enter the trial balance on an accounting work sheet, and complete the work sheet for the month ended January 31 of the current year. St. James Technology groups all operating expenses under two accounts, Selling Expense and General Expense. Leave two blank lines under Selling Expense and three blank lines under General Expense.
3. Prepare the company's multi-step income statement and statement of owner's equity for the month ended January 31 of the current year. Also prepare the balance sheet at that date in report form.

ST. JAMES TECHNOLOGY
Trial Balance
January 31, 19XX

Account Number	Account	Balance Debit	Balance Credit
11	Cash	$ 16,430	
12	Accounts receivable	19,090	
13	Inventory	65,400	
14	Supplies	2,700	
15	Building	188,170	
16	Accumulated depreciation—building		$ 36,000
17	Fixtures	45,600	
18	Accumulated depreciation—fixtures		5,800
21	Accounts payable		28,300
22	Salary payable		
23	Interest payable		
24	Unearned sales revenue		6,560
25	Note payable, long-term		87,000
31	Dirk St. James, capital		144,980
32	Dirk St. James, withdrawals	9,200	
41	Sales revenue		187,970
42	Sales discounts	7,300	
43	Sales returns and allowances	8,140	
51	Cost of goods sold	103,000	
54	Selling expense	21,520	
55	General expense	10,060	
56	Interest expense		
	Total	$496,610	$496,610

4. Journalize the adjusting and closing entries at January 31, using page 3 of the journal.
5. Post the adjusting and closing entries, using dates and posting references.
6. Compute St. James Technology's current ratio and debt ratio at January 31, and compare these values with the industry averages of 1.9 for the current ratio and 0.57 for the debt ratio. Compute the gross margin percentage and the rate of inventory turnover for the month (the inventory balance at the end of December was $47,100), and compare these ratio values with the industry average of 0.36 for the gross margin ratio and 1.7 for inventory turnover. Does St. James Technology appear to be stronger or weaker than the average company in the technology industry?

PROBLEM 2. COMPLETING THE ACCOUNTING CYCLE FOR A MERCHANDISING ENTITY *Note: This problem can be solved with or without special journals. See Requirement 2.* Anacomp Meter Company closes its books and prepares financial statements at the end of each month. Anacomp uses the perpetual inventory system. The company completed the following transactions during August:

Aug.	1	Issued check no. 682 for August office rent of $1,000. (Debit Rent Expense.)
	2	Issued check no. 683 to pay salaries of $1,240, which includes salary payable of $930 from July 31. Anacomp does *not* use reversing entries.
	2	Issued invoice no. 503 for sale on account to R. T. Loeb, $600. Anacomp's cost of this merchandise was $190.
	3	Purchased inventory on credit terms of 1/15 n/60 from Grant, Inc., $1,400.
	4	Received net amount of cash on account from Fullam Company, $2,156, within the discount period.
	4	Sold inventory for cash, $330 (cost, $104).
	5	Received from Park-Hee, Inc., merchandise that had been sold earlier for $550 (cost, $174).
	5	Issued check no. 684 to purchase supplies for cash, $780.
	6	Collected interest revenue of $1,100.
	7	Issued invoice no. 504 for sale on account to K. D. Skipper, $2,400 (cost, $759).
	8	Issued check no. 685 to pay Federal Company $2,600 of the amount owed at July 31. This payment occurred after the end of the discount period.
	11	Issued check no. 686 to pay Grant, Inc., the net amount owed from August 3.

Aug.	12	Received cash from R. T. Loeb in full settlement of her account receivable from August 2.
	16	Issued check no. 687 to pay salary expense of $1,240.
	19	Purchased inventory for cash, $850, issuing check no. 688.
	22	Purchased furniture on credit terms of 3/15 n/60 from Beaver Corporation, $510.
	23	Sold inventory on account to Fullam Company, issuing invoice no. 505 for $9,966 (cost, $3,152).
	24	Received half the July 31 amount receivable from K. D. Skipper—after the end of the discount period.
	25	Issued check no. 689 to pay utilities, $432.
	26	Purchased supplies on credit terms of 2/10 n/30 from Federal Company, $180.
	30	Returned damaged inventory to company from whom Anacomp made the cash purchase on August 19, receiving cash of $850.
	30	Granted a sales allowance of $175 to K. D. Skipper.
	31	Purchased inventory on credit terms of 1/10 n/30 from Suncrest Supply, $8,330.
	31	Issued check no. 690 to Lester Mednick, owner of the business, for personal withdrawal, $1,700.

REQUIRED

1. Open these accounts with their account numbers and July 31 balances in the various ledgers.

General Ledger:

101	Cash	$ 4,490
102	Accounts Receivable	22,560
104	Interest Receivable	
105	Inventory	41,800
109	Supplies	1,340
117	Prepaid Insurance	2,200
140	Note Receivable, Long-term	11,000
160	Furniture	37,270
161	Accumulated Depreciation	10,550
201	Accounts Payable	12,600
204	Salary Payable	930
207	Interest Payable	320
208	Unearned Sales Revenue	
220	Note Payable, Long-term	42,000
301	Lester Mednick, Capital	54,260
302	Lester Mednick, Withdrawals	
400	Income Summary	
401	Sales Revenue	
402	Sales Discounts	
403	Sales Returns and Allowances	
410	Interest Revenue	
501	Cost of Goods Sold	
510	Salary Expense	
513	Rent Expense	
514	Depreciation Expense	
516	Insurance Expense	
517	Utilities Expense	
519	Supplies Expense	
523	Interest Expense	

Accounts Receivable Subsidiary Ledger: Fullam Company, $2,200; R. T. Loeb, $0; Park-Hee, Inc., $11,590; K. D. Skipper, $8,770.

Accounts Payable Subsidiary Ledger: Beaver Corporation, $0; Federal Company, $12,600; Grant, Inc., $0; Suncrest Supply, $0.

2. Ask your professor for directions. Journalize the August transactions either in the general journal (page 9; explanations not required) or, as illustrated in this chapter, in a series of special journals: a sales journal (page 4), a cash receipts journal (page 11), a purchases journal (page 8), a cash disbursements journal (page 5), and a general journal (page 9). Anacomp makes all credit sales on terms of 2/10 n/30.
3. Post daily to the accounts receivable subsidiary ledger and the accounts payable subsidiary ledger. On August 31, post to the general ledger.
4. Prepare a trial balance in the Trial Balance columns of a work sheet, and use the following information to complete the work sheet for the month ended August 31:
   a. Accrued interest revenue, $100.
   b. Supplies on hand, $990.
   c. Prepaid insurance expired, $550.
   d. Depreciation expense, $230.

e. Accrued salary expense, $1,030.
f. Accrued interest expense, $320.
g. Unearned sales revenue, $450.*
h. Inventory on hand, $46,700.

5. Prepare Anacomp Meter Company's multi-step income statement and statement of owner's equity for August. Prepare the balance sheet at August 31.
6. Journalize and post the adjusting and closing entries.
7. Prepare a postclosing trial balance at August 31. Also, balance the total of the customer accounts in the accounts receivable subsidiary ledger against the Accounts Receivable balance in the general ledger. Do the same for the accounts payable subsidiary ledger and Accounts Payable in the general ledger.

*At August 31, $450 of unearned sales revenue needs to be recorded as a credit to Unearned Sales Revenue. Debit Sales Revenue. Also, the cost of this merchandise ($142) needs to be removed from Cost of Goods Sold and returned to Inventory.

CHAPTER 7

Internal Control, Managing Cash, and Making Ethical Judgments

LEARNING OBJECTIVES

After studying this chapter, you should be able to

1. Define internal control
2. Identify the characteristics of an effective system of internal control
3. Prepare a bank reconciliation and the related journal entries
4. Apply internal controls to cash receipts
5. Apply internal controls to cash disbursements, including petty cash transactions
6. Use a budget to manage cash
7. Make ethical judgments in business

> *If all employees were always accurate and ethical, internal controls would not be necessary. Our ineffective internal control system gave one dishonest employee the opportunity to embezzle cash over several years' time. From now on, we're going to make it a lot harder to steal anything!*
>
> JAN LARSEN, OWNER OF LARSEN & COMPANY

Jack Van Auken was a cashier at the Boulder, Colorado, office of the brokerage firm Larsen & Company. Van Auken's problems began when an auto accident forced him to miss work. Only then did owner Jan Larsen receive complaints from customers who had not received credit for their deposits. Larsen uncovered an embezzlement scheme that Van Auken had begun five years earlier.

The court found that Van Auken had stolen a total of $610,934 in a "rob-Peter-to-pay-Paul" scheme: Van Auken was transferring customer deposits into his own personal account and concealing the missing amounts with deposits from other customers. In this way, customer accounts always balanced as long as Van Auken could respond to customer inquiries. He simply explained that the account was temporarily out of balance. But while Van Auken was recovering in the hospital, his replacement was unable to explain the errors in customers' accounts. When all the evidence came to light, it pointed in the direction of the missing employee. Van Auken was sentenced to jail, and Larsen then understood why her dedicated cashier never took a vacation.

What went wrong at the Larsen & Company office? Jack Van Auken was able to control not only the cash received from customers, but also part of his company's accounting records. By manipulating the records, he was able to hide his theft for several years. Evidently, no one checked his work on a regular basis. Several procedures that we discuss in this chapter will explain how Larsen could have prevented this embezzlement. Such control systems cannot prevent all employee misconduct, but they can help to detect illegal behavior and thereby limit its effects.

Laws requiring internal control procedures have received much attention since the 1970s, when illegal payments, embezzlements, and other criminal business practices came to light. Concerned citizens wanted to know why the companies' internal controls had failed to alert top managers to these illegalities. "Where were the auditors?" people asked. To answer these growing worries, the U.S. Congress passed the Foreign Corrupt Practices Act in 1977. This act requires companies under SEC jurisdiction to maintain an appropriate system of internal control, whether or not they have foreign operations. The act also contains specific prohibitions against bribery and other corrupt practices.

This chapter discusses *internal control*—the organizational plan and integrated framework that managers use to protect company assets and keep the business under control. The chapter applies these control techniques mainly to cash (the most liquid asset) and provides a framework for making ethical judgments in business. Later chapters discuss how managers control other assets.

Internal Control

Objective 1

Define internal control

A key responsibility of a business's managers is to control operations. The owners and the top managers set the entity's goals, the managers lead the way, and the employees carry out the plan. Good managers must decide where the organization is headed over the next several years. But unless they control operations today, the entity may not stay in business long enough for managers to put their plans into effect.

Internal Control. Organizational plan and all the related measures adopted by an entity to safeguard assets, and encourage adherence to company policies, promote operational efficiency, and ensure accurate and reliable accounting records.

Internal control is the organizational plan and all the related measures that an entity adopts to

1. Safeguard assets,
2. Encourage adherence to company policies,
3. Promote operational efficiency (obtain the best outcome at the lowest cost), and
4. Ensure accurate and reliable accounting records.

■ Daily Exercise 7-1

Safeguarding assets is most important because all organizations need assets to conduct business. Internal controls are most effective when employees at all levels adopt the organization's goals, objectives, and ethical standards. Top managers should communicate these goals and standards to workers. Lee Iacocca, former president of Chrysler Corporation, instilled management's goals in Chrysler employees by getting out of the executive suite and spending time with assembly-line workers. (Japanese firms pioneered this style of participative management.) The result? Defects decreased dramatically, and Chrysler products became more competitive. Its sales of cars and trucks increased 14% in one year.

The only constant in business is that things are going to change. Companies take risks when they move into new industries. Although Larsen & Company is in the investment brokerage business, it also serves as a banker for its clients. Perhaps Larsen's lack of experience in the banking business contributed to the breakdown in internal controls that led to the embezzlement of $610,934. An effective system of internal control is designed to manage organizational change.

Exhibit 7-1 presents an excerpt from the Responsibility for Consolidated Financial Statements of Lands' End, Inc. The company's top managers take responsibility for the financial statements and for the related system of internal control. The second paragraph refers to a system of internal control, the protection of assets, and the prevention of fraudulent financial reporting. Let's examine in more detail how companies create an effective system of internal control.

EXHIBIT 7-1
Management Statement About Internal Controls—Lands' End, Inc.

Lands' End, Inc.—Responsibility for Consolidated Financial Statements

The management of Lands' End, Inc., and its subsidiaries has the responsibility for preparing the accompanying financial statements and for their integrity and objectivity. The statements were prepared in accordance with generally accepted accounting principles applied on a consistent basis. The consolidated financial statements include amounts that are based on management's best estimates and judgments. Management also prepared the other information in the annual report and is responsible for its accuracy and consistency with the consolidated financial statements.

Management of the company has established and maintains a system of internal control that provides for appropriate division of responsibility, reasonable assurance as to the integrity and reliability of the consolidated financial statements, the protection of assets from unauthorized use or disposition, and the prevention and detection of fraudulent financial reporting, and the maintenance of an active program of internal audits. Management believes that, as of February 2, 1996, the company's system of internal control is adequate to accomplish the objectives discussed herein.

Michael J. Smith
Chief Executive Officer

Stephen A. Orum
Chief Financial Officer

Source: Lands' End, Inc., *Annual Report 1996*, p. 20. Courtesy of Lands' End.

Establishing an Effective System of Internal Control

Objective 2

Identify the characteristics of an effective system of internal control

Whether the business is Larsen & Company, Lands' End, or a local department store, an effective system of internal controls has the following characteristics.

COMPETENT, RELIABLE, AND ETHICAL PERSONNEL Employees should be *competent, reliable*, and *ethical.* Paying top salaries to attract top-quality employees, training them to do their job well, and supervising their work all help a company build a competent staff.

ASSIGNMENT OF RESPONSIBILITIES In a business with a good internal control system, no important duty is overlooked. Each employee is assigned certain responsibilities. A model of such *assignment of responsibilities* appears in the corporate organizational chart in Exhibit 7-2. Notice that the corporation has a vice president of finance and accounting. Two other officers, the treasurer and the controller, report to that vice president. The treasurer is responsible for cash management. The **controller** is the chief accounting officer.

Controller. The chief accounting officer of a company.

Within this organization, the controller may be responsible for approving invoices (bills) for payment, and the treasurer may actually sign the checks. Working under the controller, one accountant may be responsible for property taxes, another accountant for income taxes. In sum, all duties are clearly defined and assigned to individuals who bear responsibility for carrying them out.

■ Daily Exercise 7-2

PROPER AUTHORIZATION An organization generally has a written set of rules that outlines approved procedures. Any deviation from standard policy requires *proper authorization.* For example, managers or assistant managers of retail stores must approve customer checks for amounts above the store's usual limit. Likewise, deans or department chairs of colleges and universities must authorize a junior to enroll in courses restricted to seniors.

SEPARATION OF DUTIES Smart management divides the responsibilities for transactions between two or more people or departments. *Separation of duties* limits the chances for fraud and promotes the accuracy of the accounting records. The Lands' End responsibility statement (Exhibit 7-1) refers to a *division of responsibility.* This crucial component of the internal control system may be divided into four parts:

1. *Separation of operations from accounting.* The entire accounting function should be completely separate from operating departments, such as manufacturing and sales, so that reliable records may be kept. For example, product inspectors, not machine operators, should count units produced by a manufacturing process. Accountants, not salespeople, should keep inventory records. Observe the separation of accounting from production and marketing in Exhibit 7-2.

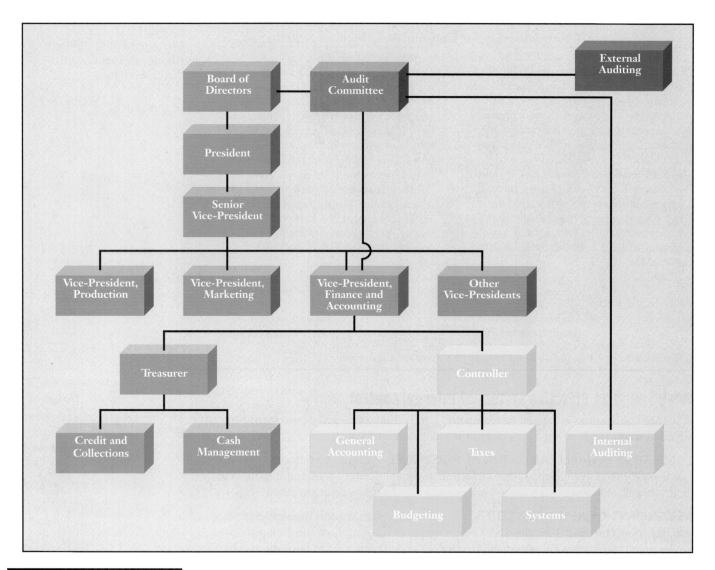

EXHIBIT 7-2
Organizational Chart of a Corporation

2. *Separation of the custody of assets from accounting.* Temptation and fraud are reduced if accountants do not handle cash and if cashiers do not have access to the accounting records. If one employee has both cash-handling and accounting duties, that person can steal cash and conceal the theft by making a bogus entry on the books. We see this component of internal control in Exhibit 7-2. The treasurer has custody of the cash, and the controller accounts for the cash. Neither person has both responsibilities. Jack Van Auken was able to apply one customer's cash deposit to another customer's account at Larsen & Company. Apparently, Van Auken, the cashier, controlled some data entered into the accounting system. This is a serious violation of the separation of duties.

Warehouse employees with no accounting duties should handle inventory. If they were allowed to account for the inventory, they could steal it and write it off as obsolete. A *write-off* is an entry that credits an asset account. This write-off could be recorded by debiting Loss on Inventory Obsolescence and crediting Inventory. A person with custody of assets should not have access to the computer programs. Similarly, the programmer should not have access to tempting assets such as cash.

3. *Separation of the authorization of transactions from the custody of related assets.* If possible, persons who authorize transactions should not handle the related asset. For example, the same person should not authorize the payment of a supplier's invoice and also sign the check to pay the bill. With both duties, the person can authorize payments to him- or herself and then sign the checks. When these duties are separated, only legitimate bills are paid.

4. *Separation of duties within the accounting function.* Different people should perform the various phases of accounting to minimize errors and opportunities for fraud. For example, different accountants should be responsible for recording cash receipts and cash disbursements. The employee who processes accounts payable and check requests should have nothing to do with the approval process.

■ Daily Exercise 7-3

INTERNAL AND EXTERNAL AUDITS To guarantee the accuracy of their accounting records, most companies undergo periodic audits. An **audit** is an examination of the company's financial statements and the accounting systems, controls, and records that produced them.

Audit. An examination of a company's financial statements and the accounting systems, controls, and records that produced them.

It is not economically feasible for auditors to examine all the transactions during a period, so they must rely on the accounting system to produce accurate records. To gauge the reliability of the company's accounting system, auditors evaluate its system of internal controls. Auditors also spot the weaknesses in the system and recommend corrections. Auditors offer *objectivity* in their reports, while managers immersed in operations may overlook their own weaknesses.

Audits can be internal or external. Exhibit 7-2 shows *internal auditors* as employees of the business reporting directly to the audit committee. Some organizations have the internal auditors report directly to a vice president. Throughout the year, the internal auditors examine various segments of the organization to ensure that employees follow company policies and that operations run efficiently. *External auditors* are entirely independent of the business. They are hired by a company to determine that the company's financial statements are prepared in accordance with generally accepted accounting principles. Both internal and external auditors are independent of the operations they examine, and both suggest improvements that help the business run more efficiently.

An auditor may find that an employee has both cash-handling and cash-accounting duties or may learn that a cash shortage has resulted from lax efforts to collect accounts receivable. Both internal and external auditors suggest improvements that help the business run more efficiently.

■ Daily Exercise 7-4
■ Daily Exercise 7-5

DOCUMENTS AND RECORDS Business *documents and records* vary considerably, from source documents such as invoices and purchase orders to special journals and subsidiary ledgers. Documents should be prenumbered. A gap in the numbered sequence calls attention to a missing document.

Prenumbering cash-sale receipts discourages theft by cashiers because the copies retained by the cashiers, which list the amount of the sale, can be checked against the actual amount of cash received. If the receipts are not prenumbered, the cashier can destroy the copy and pocket the cash received from the sale. However, if the receipts are prenumbered, the missing copy can easily be identified. In a computerized system, a permanent record of the sale is stored electronically when the transaction is completed.

In a bowling alley, for example, a key document is the score sheet. The manager can check on cashiers by comparing the number of games scored with the amount of cash received. By multiplying the number of games by the price per game and comparing the result with each day's cash receipts, the manager can see whether the business is collecting all the bowling revenue. If cash on hand is low, the cashier might be stealing.

ELECTRONIC DEVICES AND COMPUTER CONTROLS Businesses use electronic devices to help protect assets and control operations. For example, retailers such as Target Stores, Bradlees, and Dillard's control their inventories by attaching an electronic sensor to merchandise. The cashier removes the sensor when a sale is made. If a customer tries to remove from the store an item with the sensor attached, an alarm is activated. According to Checkpoint Systems, which manufactures electronic sensors, these devices reduce loss due to theft by as much as 50 percent.

". . . Target Stores, Bradlees, and Dillard's control their inventories by attaching an electronic sensor to merchandise."

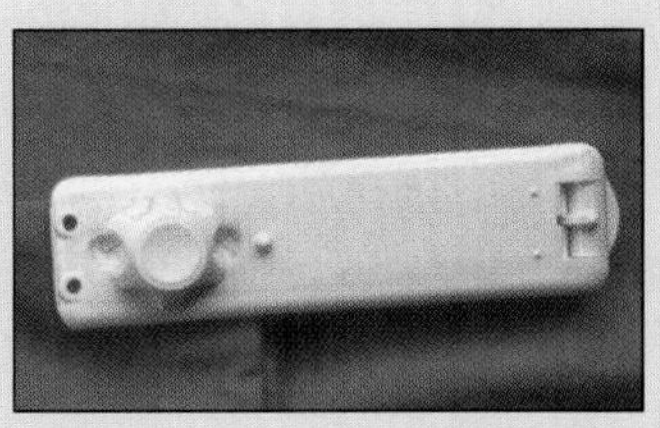

Accounting systems are relying less and less on documents and more and more on digital storage devices. Computers produce accurate records and enhance operational efficiency, but they do not automatically safeguard assets or encourage employees to behave in accordance with company policies. What computers have done is shift the internal controls to the people who write the programs. Programmers carry out the plans of managers and accountants. All the controls that apply to accountants apply to computer programmers as well.

Within a single company, each department may take steps to maintain control over its assets and accounting records. Consider a large company such as the retailer Saks Fifth Avenue. If the Saks system is well designed, each department can ensure that its transactions are processed correctly. Each department needs to maintain its own records. For example, the shoe department submits daily credit-sales totals for computer processing. The shoe department then expects a printout showing a total sales amount that agrees with the control total that it calculated.

The accounts receivable department relies on computer operators to post correctly to thousands of customer accounts. Proper posting can be ensured by devising customer account numbers so that the last digit is a mathematical function of the previous digits (for example, 1359, where $1 + 3 + 5 = 9$). Any miskeying of a customer account number would trigger an error message to the keyboarder, and the computer would not accept the number. Many companies now employ electronic data processing (EDP) auditors to ensure the integrity of their computer databases.

OTHER CONTROLS Businesses of all types keep cash and important business documents (such as contracts and titles to property) in *fireproof vaults.* They use *burglar alarms* to protect buildings and other property.

Retailers receive most of their cash from customers on the spot. To safeguard cash, they use *point-of-sale terminals* that serve as a cash register and record each transaction as it is entered into the machine. Several times each day, a supervisor removes the cash for deposit in the bank.

Employees who handle cash are in an especially tempting position. Many businesses purchase *fidelity bonds* on cashiers. The bond is an insurance policy that reimburses the company for any losses due to employee theft. Before issuing a fidelity bond, the insurance company investigates the employee's past to ensure a record of ethical conduct.

"General Electric, Eastman Kodak, and other large companies move employees from job to job—often at six-month intervals. Knowing that someone else will be doing their job next month also keeps employees honest."

Mandatory vacations and *job rotation* require that employees be trained to do a variety of jobs. General Electric, Eastman Kodak, and other large companies move employees from job to job—often at six-month intervals. This practice enhances morale by giving employees a broad view of the business and helping them decide where they want to specialize. Knowing that someone else will be doing their job next month also keeps employees honest. Had Larsen & Company moved Jack Van Auken from job to job and required him to take a vacation, his embezzlement would probably have been detected much earlier.

■ Daily Exercise 7-6

Thinking It Over Ralph works the late movie at Big-Hit Theater. Occasionally, he must both sell the tickets and take them as customers enter the theater. Standard procedure requires that Ralph tear the tickets, give one-half to the customer, and keep the other half. To control cash receipts, the theater manager compares each night's cash receipts with the number of ticket stubs on hand.

1. How could Ralph take money from the theater's cash receipts and hide the theft? What additional steps should the manager take to strengthen the control over cash receipts?
2. What is the internal control weakness in this situation? Explain the weakness.

Answers

1. Ralph could	Management could
• Issue no ticket and keep the customer's cash.	• Physically count the number of people watching a movie and compare that number to the number of ticket stubs retained.
• Destroy some tickets and keep the customer's cash.	• Account for all ticket stubs by serial number. Missing serial numbers raise questions.

2. The internal control weakness is lack of separation of duties. Ralph receives cash and also controls the tickets.

The Limitations of Internal Control

Unfortunately, most internal control measures can be circumvented or overcome. Systems designed to thwart an individual employee's fraud can be beaten by two or more employees working as a team—*colluding*—to defraud the firm. Consider the Big-Hit Theater. Ralph and a fellow employee could put together a scheme in which the ticket seller pockets the cash from ten customers and the ticket taker admits ten customers without tickets. To prevent this situation, the manager could take additional control measures, such as matching the number of people in the theater against the number of ticket stubs retained. But that would take time away from other duties. The stricter the internal control system, the more expensive and time-consuming it becomes.

A system of internal control that is too complex can strangle the business with red tape. Efficiency and control are hurt rather than helped. Just how tight should an internal control be? Managers must make sensible judgments. Investments in internal control must be judged in light of the costs and benefits.

Using the Bank Account as a Control Device

Cash is the most liquid asset because it is the medium of exchange. But cash can also be intangible, often consisting of electronic impulses in a bank's accounting system with no accompanying paper checks or deposit slips. Cash is easy to conceal, easy to move, and relatively easy to steal. As a result, most businesses use an elaborate system of internal controls to safeguard and manage their cash.

Keeping cash in a *bank account* is an important part of internal control because banks have established practices for safeguarding cash. Banks also provide depositors with detailed records of cash transactions. To take full advantage of these control features, the business should deposit all cash receipts in the bank account and make all cash payments through it (except petty cash disbursements, which we examine later in this chapter).

The documents used to control a bank account include the signature card, the deposit ticket, the check, the bank statement, and the bank reconciliation.

SIGNATURE CARD Banks require each person authorized to transact business through an account in that bank to sign a *signature card.* The bank compares the signatures on documents against the signature card to protect the bank and the depositor against forgery.

DEPOSIT TICKET Banks supply standard forms such as *deposit tickets.* The customer fills in the dollar amount and the date of deposit. As proof of the transaction, the customer retains either (1) a duplicate copy of the deposit ticket, or (2) a deposit receipt, depending on the bank's practice.

CHECK To draw money from an account, the depositor writes a **check,** which is a document instructing the bank to pay the designated person or business a specified amount of money. There are three parties to a check: the *maker,* who signs the check; the *payee,* to whom the check is paid; and the *bank* on which the check is drawn.

Check. Document that instructs a bank to pay the designated person or business a specified amount of money.

Most checks are serially numbered and preprinted with the name and address of the maker and the bank. The checks have places for the date, the name of the payee, the signature of the maker, and the amount. The bank name, bank identification number, and maker account number are usually printed in magnetic ink for machine processing.

Exhibit 7-3 shows a check drawn on the bank account of Business Research, Inc. The check has two parts, the check itself and the *remittance advice,* an optional attachment that tells the payee the reason for the payment. The maker (Business Research) retains a duplicate copy of the check for its recording in the check register (cash disbursements journal). Note that internal controls at Business Research require two signatures on checks.

BANK STATEMENT Most banks send monthly bank statements to their depositors. A **bank statement** is the document the bank uses to report what it did with the depositor's cash. The statement shows the bank account's beginning and ending cash balances for the period and lists the month's cash transactions conducted through the bank. Included with the statement are the maker's *canceled checks,* those checks the bank has paid on behalf of the depositor. The bank statement also lists any deposits and other changes in the account.

Bank Statement. Document the bank uses to report what it did with the depositor's cash. Shows the bank account's beginning and ending balances and lists the month's cash transactions conducted through the bank.

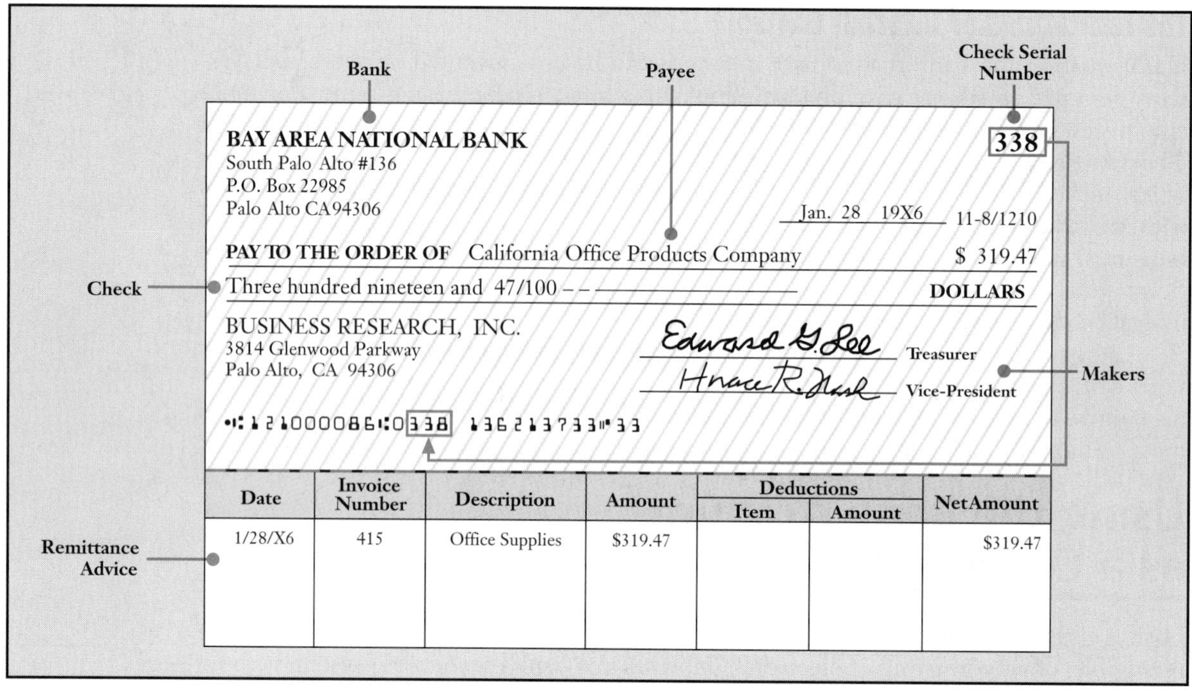

Date	Invoice Number	Description	Amount	Deductions: Item	Deductions: Amount	Net Amount
1/28/X6	415	Office Supplies	$319.47			$319.47

EXHIBIT 7-3
Check with Remittance Advice

Deposits appear in chronological order and checks in a logical order (usually by check serial number), along with the date each check cleared the bank.

Exhibit 7-4 is the bank statement of Business Research, Inc., for the month ended January 31, 19X6. Many banks send some individual depositors their statements on the first of the month, some on the second, and so on. This spacing eliminates the clerical burden of supplying all the statements at one time. Most businesses—like Business Research—receive their bank statements at the end of each calendar month.

Electronic Funds Transfer (EFT). System that transfers cash by electronic communication rather than by paper documents.

Electronic funds transfer (EFT) is a system that relies on electronic communications—not paper documents—to transfer cash. More and more businesses today rely on EFT for repetitive cash transactions. It is much cheaper for a company to pay employees by EFT (direct deposit) than by issuing hundreds of payroll checks. Also, many people make mortgage, rent, and insurance payments by prior arrangement with their bank and never write checks for those payments. The bank statement lists cash receipts by EFT among the deposits and cash payments by EFT among the checks and other bank charges.

The Bank Reconciliation

There are two records of a business's cash: (1) its Cash account in its own general ledger (Exhibit 7-5), and (2) the bank statement, which tells the actual amount of cash the business has in the bank. The balance in the business's Cash account rarely equals the balance shown on the bank statement.

The books and the bank statement may show different amounts, but both may be correct. The difference arises because of a time lag in recording certain transactions. When a firm writes a check, it immediately credits its Cash account. The bank, however, will not subtract the amount of the check from the business's balance until it receives the check for payment. This step may take days, even weeks, if the payee waits to cash the check. Likewise, the business immediately debits Cash for all cash receipts, but it may take a day or so for the bank to add these amounts to the business's bank balance.

Bank Reconciliation. Document explaining the reasons for the difference between a depositor's cash records and the depositor's cash balance in its bank account.

To ensure accuracy of the financial records, the firm's accountant must explain all differences between the firm's own cash records and the bank statement figures on a certain date. The result of this process is a document called the **bank reconciliation,** which is prepared by the company (not by the bank). Properly done, the bank reconciliation ensures that all cash transactions have been accounted for and that the bank and book records of cash are correct. Knowledge of where cash comes from, how it is spent, and the balance of cash available is vital to success in business.

Here are some common items that cause differences between the bank balance and the book balance.

ACCOUNT STATEMENT

Business Research, Inc.
3814 Glenwood Parkway
Palo Alto, CA 94306

CHECKING ACCOUNT 136–213733

CHECKING ACCOUNT SUMMARY AS OF 01/31/X6

BEGINNING BALANCE	TOTAL DEPOSITS	TOTAL WITHDRAWALS	SERVICE CHARGES	ENDING BALANCE
6,556.12	4,352.64	4,963.00	14.25	5,931.51

CHECKING ACCOUNT TRANSACTIONS

DEPOSITS	DATE	AMOUNT
Deposit	01/04	1,000.00
Deposit	01/04	112.00
Deposit	01/08	194.60
EFT—Collection of rent	01/17	904.03
Bank Collection	01/26	2,114.00
Interest	01/31	28.01

CHARGES	DATE	AMOUNT
Service Charge	01/31	14.25
Checks:		

CHECKS

Number	Date	Amount
656	01/06	100.00
332	01/12	3,000.00
333	01/12	150.00
334	01/10	100.00
335	01/06	100.00
336	01/31	1,100.00

DAILY BALANCE

Date	Balance	Date	Balance
12/31	6,556.12	01/17	5,264.75
01/04	7,616.12	01/20	4,903.75
01/06	7,416.12	01/26	7,017.75
01/08	7,610.72	01/31	5,931.51
01/10	7,510.72		
01/12	4,360.72		

OTHER CHARGES	DATE	AMOUNT
NSF	01/04	52.00
EFT—Insurance	01/20	361.00

MONTHLY SUMMARY

Withdrawals: 8 | Minimum Balance: 4,360.72 | Average Balance: 6,085.19

EXHIBIT 7-4
Bank Statement

1. Items recorded by the company but not yet recorded by the bank:
   a. **Deposits in transit** (outstanding deposits). The company has recorded these deposits, but the bank has not.
   b. **Outstanding checks.** The company has issued these checks and recorded them on its books, but the bank has not yet paid them.
2. Items recorded by the bank but not yet recorded by the company:
   a. **Bank collections.** Banks sometimes collect money on behalf of depositors. Many businesses have their customers pay directly to the company bank account. This practice, called a *lock-box system*, reduces the possibility of theft and also places the business's cash in circulation faster than if the cash had to be collected and deposited by company personnel. An example is a bank's collecting cash and interest on a note receivable for the depositor. The bank may notify the depositor of these bank collections on the bank's statement.
   b. *Electronic funds transfers.* The bank may receive or pay cash on behalf of the depositor. The bank statement will list the EFTs and may notify the depositor to record these transactions.
   c. *Service charge.* This is the bank's fee for processing the depositor's transactions. Banks commonly base the service charge on the account balance. The depositor learns the amount of the service charge from the bank statement.

Deposit in Transit. A deposit recorded by the company but not yet by its bank.

Outstanding Check. A check issued by the company and recorded on its books but not yet paid by its bank.

Bank Collection. Collection of money by the bank on behalf of a depositor.

EXHIBIT 7-5
Cash Records of Business Research, Inc.

General Ledger:

ACCOUNT Cash **No. 111**

Date	Item	Jrnl. Ref.	Debit	Credit	Balance
19X6					
Jan. 1	Balance	✓			6,556.12
2	Cash receipt	CR. 9	1,112.00		7,668.12
7	Cash receipt	CR. 9	194.60		7,862.72
31	Cash disbursements	CD. 17		6,160.14	1,702.58
31	Cash receipt	CR. 10	1,591.63		3,294.21

■ Daily Exercise 7-9

Cash Disbursements:

Check No.	Amount
332	$3,000.00
333	510.00
334	100.00
335	100.00
336	1,100.00
337	286.00
338	319.47
339	83.00
340	203.14
341	458.53
Total	$6,160.14

Nonsufficient Funds (NSF) Check. A "hot" check, one for which the maker's bank account has insufficient money to pay the check.

d. *Interest revenue on checking account.* Banks often pay interest to depositors who keep enough cash in their account. The bank notifies depositors of this interest on the bank statement.

e. **Nonsufficient funds (NSF) checks** received from customers. To understand how NSF checks (sometimes called *hot checks*) are handled, consider the route a check takes. The maker writes a check and gives the check to the payee, who deposits the check in his bank. The payee's bank adds the receipt amount to the payee's bank balance on the assumption that the check is good.

NSF checks are cash *receipts* that turn out to be worthless. If the maker's bank balance is insufficient to pay the check, the maker's bank refuses to pay the check and sends an NSF notice to the payee's bank. The payee's bank then subtracts the receipt amount from the payee's bank balance and notifies the payee of this NSF action. The payee may learn of NSF checks through the bank statement, which lists the NSF check as a charge (subtraction), as shown near the bottom of Exhibit 7-4.

Learning Tip: NSF checks are customer checks received by the company—not checks that the company has written.

f. *Checks collected, deposited, and returned to payee by the bank for reasons other than NSF.* Banks return checks to the payee if (1) the maker's account has closed, (2) the date is "stale" (some checks state "void after 30 days"), (3) the signature is not authorized, (4) the check has been altered, or (5) the check form is improper (for example, a counterfeit). Accounting for all returned checks is the same as for NSF checks.

g. *The cost of printed checks.* This charge is handled like a service charge.

3. Errors by either the company or the bank. For example, a bank may improperly charge (decrease) the bank balance of Business Research, Inc., for a check drawn by another company, perhaps Business Research Associates. Or a company may miscompute its bank balance on its own books. All errors must be corrected, and the corrections will be part of the bank reconciliation.

Objective 3

Prepare a bank reconciliation and the related journal entries

PREPARING THE BANK RECONCILIATION The steps in preparing the bank reconciliation are as follows:

1. Start with two figures, the balance shown on the bank statement *(balance per bank)* and the balance in the company's Cash account *(balance per books)*. These two amounts will probably disagree because of the differences discussed earlier.
2. Add to, or subtract from, the *bank* balance those items that appear on the books but not on the bank statement:
   a. Add *deposits in transit* to the bank balance. Deposits in transit are identified by comparing the deposits listed on the bank statement with the company's list of cash receipts. Deposits in transit show up as cash receipts on the books but not as deposits on the bank statement.
   b. Subtract *outstanding checks* from the bank balance. Outstanding checks are identified by comparing the canceled checks returned with the bank statement with the company's list of checks written for cash payments. Outstanding checks show up as cash payments on the books but not as paid checks on the bank statement. Outstanding checks are usually the most numerous items on a bank reconciliation.
3. Add to, or subtract from, the *book* balance those items that appear on the bank statement but not on the company books:
   a. Add to the book balance (1) *bank collections*, (2) *EFT cash receipts*, and (3) *interest revenue* earned on money in the bank. These items are identified by comparing the deposits listed on the bank statement with the company's list of cash receipts. They show up as cash receipts on the bank statement but not on the books.
   b. Subtract from the book balance (1) *EFT cash payments*, (2) *service charges*, (3) *cost of printed checks*, and (4) *other bank charges* (for example, charges for NSF or stale-date checks). These items are identified by comparing the other charges listed on the bank statement with the cash disbursements recorded on the company books. They show up as subtractions on the bank statement but not as cash payments on the books.
4. Compute the *adjusted bank balance* and the *adjusted book balance*. The two adjusted balances should be equal.
5. Journalize each item in step 3—that is, each item listed on the book portion of the bank reconciliation. These items must be recorded on the company books because they affect cash.
6. Correct all book errors and notify the bank of any errors it has made.

BANK RECONCILIATION ILLUSTRATED The bank statement in Exhibit 7-4 indicates that the January 31 bank balance of Business Research, Inc., is $5,931.51. However, the company's Cash account has a balance of $3,294.21, as shown in Exhibit 7-5. In following the steps outlined in the preceding section, the accountant finds these reconciling items:

1. The January 31 deposit of $1,591.63 (deposit in transit) does not appear on the bank statement. See the last item in the Company's Cash Account (Exhibit 7-5).
2. The bank erroneously charged to the Business Research, Inc., account a $100 check—number 656—written by Business Research Associates (a bank error).
3. Five company checks issued late in January and recorded in the cash disbursements journal have not been paid by the bank. The following checks are outstanding:

Check No.	Date	Amount
337	Jan. 17	$286.00
338	26	319.47
339	27	83.00
340	28	203.14
341	30	458.53

These checks are listed under cash disbursements in Exhibit 7-5.

4. The bank received $904.03 by EFT on behalf of Business Research, Inc. (an EFT receipt).
5. The bank collected on behalf of the company a note receivable, $2,114 (including interest revenue of $214). Business Research has not recorded this cash receipt (a bank collection).
6. The bank statement shows interest revenue of $28.01, which the company has earned on its cash balance (interest revenue).
7. Check number 333 for $150 paid to Brown Company on account was recorded as a cash payment of $510, creating a $360 understatement of the Cash balance in the books (a book error).
8. The bank service charge for the month was $14.25 (service charge).
9. The bank statement shows an NSF check for $52, which was received from customer L. Ross (NSF check).
10. Business Research pays insurance expense monthly by EFT. The company has not yet recorded this $361 payment (an EFT payment).

■ Daily Exercise 7-7

Exhibit 7-6 is the bank reconciliation based on the preceding data. Panel A lists the reconciling items, which are keyed by number to the reconciliation in Panel B.

Concept Highlight

EXHIBIT 7-6
Bank Reconciliation

PANEL A—Reconciling Items

1. Deposit in transit, $1,591.63.
2. Bank error, add $100 to bank balance.
3. Outstanding checks: no. 337, $286; no. 338, $319.47; no. 339, $83; no. 340, $203.14; no. 341, $458.53.
4. EFT receipt of rent revenue, $904.03.
5. Bank collection, $2,114, including interest revenue of $214.
6. Interest earned on bank balance, $28.01.
7. Book error, add $360 to book balance.
8. Bank service charge, $14.25.
9. NSF check from L. Ross, $52.
10. EFT payment of insurance expense, $361.

PANEL B—Bank Reconciliation

BUSINESS RESEARCH, INC.
Bank Reconciliation
January 31, 19X6

Bank			Books		
Balance, January 31		$5,931.51	Balance, January 31		$3,294.21
Add:			Add:		
1. Deposit of January 31 in transit		1,591.63	4. EFT receipt of rent revenue		904.03
2. Correction of bank error—Business Research Associates check 656 erroneously charged against company account		100.00	5. Bank collection of note receivable, including interest revenue of $214		2,114.00
		7,623.14	6. Interest revenue earned on bank balance		28.01
Less:			7. Correction of book error—overstated amount of check no. 333		360.00
3. Outstanding checks					6,700.25
No. 337	$286.00		Less:		
No. 338	319.47		8. Service charge	$ 14.25	
No. 339	83.00		9. NSF check	52.00	
No. 340	203.14		10. EFT payment of insurance expense	361.00	(427.25)
No. 341	458.53	(1,350.14)			
Adjusted bank balance		$6,273.00	Adjusted book balance		$6,273.00

Amounts agree.

■ Daily Exercise 7-10

Each reconciling item is treated in the same way in every situation. Here is a summary:

Bank Balance—always
- *Add* deposits in transit
- *Subtract* outstanding checks

Book Balance—always
- *Add* bank collections, interest revenue, and EFT receipts
- *Subtract* service charges, NSF checks, and EFT payments

JOURNALIZING TRANSACTIONS FROM THE RECONCILIATION The bank reconciliation does not directly affect the journals or the ledgers. The reconciliation is an accountant's tool, separate from the company's books.

The bank reconciliation acts as a control device. It signals the company to record the transactions listed as reconciling items in the books section of the reconciliation because the company has not yet recorded these items. For example, the bank collected the note receivable on behalf of the company, but the company has not yet recorded this cash receipt. In fact, the company learned of the cash receipt only when it received the bank statement.

Thinking It Over Why doesn't the company need to record the reconciling items on the bank side of the reconciliation?

Answer: Those items have already been recorded on the company books.

On the basis of the reconciliation in Exhibit 7-6, Business Research, Inc., makes the following entries. They are dated January 31 to bring the Cash account to the correct balance on that date. Numbers in parentheses correspond to the reconciling items listed in Exhibit 7-6, Panel A.

■ Daily Exercise 7-8

(4)	Jan. 31	Cash	904.03	
		Rent Revenue		904.03
		Receipt of monthly rent.		
(5)	31	Cash	2,114.00	
		Notes Receivable		1,900.00
		Interest Revenue		214.00
		Note receivable collected by bank.		
(6)	31	Cash	28.01	
		Interest Revenue		28.01
		Interest earned on bank balance.		
(7)	31	Cash	360.00	
		Accounts Payable—Brown Co.		360.00
		Correction of check no. 333.		
(8)	31	Miscellaneous Expense[1]	14.25	
		Cash		14.25
		Bank service charge.		
(9)	31	Accounts Receivable—L. Ross	52.00	
		Cash		52.00
		NSF check returned by bank.		
(10)	31	Insurance Expense	361.00	
		Cash		361.00
		Payment of monthly insurance.		

These entries bring the business's books up to date.

The entry for the NSF check (entry 9) needs explanation. Upon learning that L. Ross's $52 check was not good, Business Research credits Cash to bring the Cash account up to date. Because Business Research still has a receivable from Ross, it debits Accounts Receivable—L. Ross and pursues collection from him.

■ Daily Exercise 7-11

[1]Note: Miscellaneous Expense is debited for the bank service charge because the service charge pertains to no particular expense category.

Working It Out The bank statement balance is $4,500 and shows a service charge of $15, interest earned of $5, and an NSF check for $300. Deposits in transit total $1,200; outstanding checks are $575. The bookkeeper recorded as $152 a check of $125 in payment of an account payable.

1. What is the adjusted bank balance?
2. Prepare the journal entries needed to update the company's (not the bank's) books.

Answers

1. $5,125 ($4,500 + $1,200 – $575)
2.

Miscellaneous Expense	15	
Cash		15
Cash.......................................	5	
Interest Revenue		5
Accounts Receivable	300	
Cash		300
Cash.......................................	27	
Accounts Payable		27

How Owners and Managers Use the Bank Reconciliation

The bank reconciliation becomes a powerful control device in the hands of a business owner or manager, as the following example illustrates.

Randy Vaughn is a CPA in Houston, Texas. He owns several small apartment complexes that are managed by his aunt. His accounting practice keeps him busy, so he has little time to devote to his apartment investments. Vaughn's aunt signs up tenants, collects the monthly rent checks, arranges custodial and maintenance work, hires and fires employees, writes the checks, and performs the bank reconciliation. In short, she does it all. This concentration of duties in one person is terrible from an internal control standpoint. Vaughn's aunt could be stealing from him, and as a CPA he is aware of this possibility.

Vaughn trusts his aunt because she is a member of the family. Nevertheless, he exercises some loose controls over her management of his apartments. Vaughn periodically drops by his properties to see whether the custodial/maintenance staff is keeping them in good condition.

To control cash, Vaughn uses the bank statement and the bank reconciliation. On an irregular basis, he examines the bank reconciliation that his aunt has performed. He matches every check that cleared the bank to the journal entry on the books. Vaughn would know immediately if his aunt is writing checks to herself. Vaughn sometimes prepares his own bank reconciliation to see whether he agrees with his aunt's work. If his aunt is stealing cash and concealing it by manipulating the bank reconciliation, this would come to light. To keep his aunt on her toes, Vaughn lets her know that he periodically audits her work.

Vaughn has a simple method for controlling cash receipts. He knows the occupancy level of his apartments. He also knows the monthly rent he charges. He multiplies the number of apartments—say 20—by the monthly rent (which averages $500 per unit) to arrive at expected monthly rent revenue of $10,000. By tracing the $10,000 revenue to the bank statement, Vaughn can tell that his rent money went into his bank account.

■ Daily Exercise 7-12
■ Daily Exercise 7-13

Control activities such as these are critical in small businesses. With only a few employees, a separation of duties may not be feasible. The owner must oversee the operations of the business, or the assets will slip away, as they did for Larsen & Company in the chapter opening story.

The Cash account of Bain Company at February 28, 19X3, is as follows:

Cash			
Feb. 1 Balance	3,995	Feb. 3	400
6	800	12	3,100
15	1,800	19	1,100
23	1,100	25	500
28	2,400	27	900
Feb. 28 Balance	4,095		

Bain Company receives this bank statement on February 28, 19X3 (as always, negative amounts are in parentheses):

BANK STATEMENT FOR FEBRUARY 19X3		
Beginning balance		$3,995
Deposits:		
Feb. 7	$ 800	
15	1,800	
24	1,100	3,700
Checks (total per day):		
Feb. 8	$ 400	
16	3,100	
23	1,100	(4,600)
Other items:		
Service charge		(10)
NFS check from M. E. Crown		(700)
Bank collection of note receivable for the company		1,000*
EFT—monthly rent expense		(330)
Interest on account balance		15
Ending balance		$3,070

*Includes interest of $119.

Additional data: Bain Company deposits all cash receipts in the bank and makes all cash disbursements by check.

REQUIRED

1. Prepare the bank reconciliation of Bain Company at February 28, 19X3.
2. Record the entries based on the bank reconciliation.

SOLUTION

REQUIREMENT 1

BAIN COMPANY Bank Reconciliation February 28, 19X3		
Bank:		
Balance, February 28, 19X3		$3,070
Add: Deposit of February 28 in transit		2,400
		5,470
Less: Outstanding checks issued on Feb. 25 ($500) and Feb. 27 ($900)		(1,400)
Adjusted bank balance, February 28, 19X3		$4,070
Books:		
Balance, February 28, 19X3		$4,095
Add: Bank collection of note receivable, including interest of $119		1,000
Interest earned on bank balance		15
		5,110
Less: Service charge	$ 10	
NSF check	700	
EFT—Rent expense	330	(1,040)
Adjusted book balance, February 28, 19X3		$4,070

REQUIREMENT 2

Feb. 28	Cash	1,000	
	Note Receivable ($1,000 – $119)		881
	Interest Revenue		119
	Note receivable collected by bank.		
28	Cash	15	
	Interest Revenue		15
	Interest earned on bank balance.		
28	Miscellaneous Expense	10	
	Cash		10
	Bank service charge.		
28	Accounts Receivable—M. E. Crown	700	
	Cash		700
	NSF check returned by bank.		
28	Rent Expense	330	
	Cash		330
	Monthly rent expense.		

Internal Control over Cash Receipts

Objective 4

Apply internal controls to cash receipts

Internal control over cash receipts ensures that all cash receipts are deposited in the bank and that the company's accounting record is correct. Many businesses receive cash over the counter and through the mail. Each source of cash receipts calls for its own security measures.

CASH RECEIPTS OVER THE COUNTER The point-of-sale terminal (cash register) offers management control over the cash received in a store. Consider a Macy's store. First, the terminal should be positioned so that customers can see the amounts the cashier enters into the computer. No person willingly pays more than the marked price for an item, so the customer helps prevent the sales clerk from overcharging and pocketing the excess over actual prices. Also, company policy should require issuance of a receipt to make sure each sale is recorded by the cash register.

Second, the cash drawer opens only when the sales clerk enters an amount on the keypad, and a roll of tape locked inside the machine records each sale and cash transaction. At the end of the day, a manager proves the cash by comparing the total amount in the cash drawer against the tape's total. This step helps prevent outright theft by the clerk. For security reasons, the clerk should not have access to the tape.

Third, pricing merchandise at "uneven" amounts—say, \$3.95 instead of \$4.00—means that the clerk generally must make change, which in turn means having to get into the cash drawer. This requires entering the amount of the sale on the keypad and so onto the register tape—another way to prevent fraud.

■ Daily Exercise 7-14
■ Daily Exercise 7-15

At the end of the day, the cashier or other employee with cash-handling duties deposits the cash in the bank. The tape then goes to the accounting department as the basis for an entry in the accounting records. These security measures, coupled with periodic on-site inspection by a manager, discourage theft.

CASH RECEIPTS BY MAIL All incoming mail should be opened by a mailroom employee. This person should compare the amount of the check received with the attached remittance advice (the slip of paper that lists the amount of the check). If no advice was sent, the mailroom employee should prepare one and enter the amount of each receipt on a control tape. At the end of the day, this control tape is given to a responsible official, such as the controller, for verification. Cash receipts should be given to the cashier, who combines them with any cash received over the counter and prepares the bank deposit.

Assigning a mailroom employee as the first person to handle postal cash receipts is just another application of a good internal control procedure—in this case, separation of duties. If the accountants opened postal cash receipts, they could easily hide a theft.

The mailroom employee forwards the remittance advices to the accounting department. These provide the data for entries in the cash books and postings to customers' accounts in the accounts receivable ledger. As a final step, the controller compares the three records of the day's cash receipts: (1) the control tape total from the mailroom, (2) the bank deposit amount from the cashier, and (3) the debit to Cash from the accounting department.

Many companies use a lock-box system to separate cash duties and establish control over cash receipts. Customers send their checks directly to an address that is essentially a bank account. Internal control over the cash is enhanced because company personnel do not handle the cash. The lock-box system improves efficiency because the cash goes to work for the company immediately.

■ Daily Exercise 7-16

CASH SHORT AND OVER A difference often exists between actual cash receipts and the day's record of cash received. Usually, the difference is small and results from honest errors. When the recorded cash balance exceeds cash on hand, a *cash short* situation exists. When actual cash exceeds the recorded cash balance, there is a *cash over* situation. Suppose the cash register tapes of Macy's indicated sales revenue of \$25,000, but the cash received was \$24,980. To record the day's sales, the store would make this entry:

Cash	24,980	
Cash Short and Over.........	20	
Sales Revenue		25,000
Daily cash sales.		

As the entry shows, Cash Short and Over is debited when cash receipts are less than sales revenue. This account is credited when cash receipts exceed sales. A debit balance in Cash Short and Over appears on the income statement as Miscellaneous Expense, a credit balance as Other Revenue.

The Cash Short and Over balance should be small. The debits and credits for cash shorts and overs collected over an accounting period tend to cancel each other. A large balance signals the accountant to investigate. For example, too large a debit balance may mean an employee is stealing. Cash Short and Over, then, also acts as an internal control device.

Exhibit 7-7 summarizes the controls over cash receipts.

Thinking It Over The bookkeeper in your company has stolen cash received from customers. The bookkeeper prepared fake documents to indicate that the customers had returned merchandise. What internal control feature could have prevented this theft?

Answer: The bookkeeper should not have had access to cash.

Concept Highlight

EXHIBIT 7-7
Internal Controls over Cash Receipts

Element of Internal Control	Internal Controls over Cash Receipts
Competent, reliable, ethical personnel	Companies carefully screen employees for undesirable personality traits. They commit time and effort to training programs.
Assignment of responsibilities	Specific employees are designated as cashiers, supervisors of cashiers, or accountants for cash receipts.
Proper authorization	Only designated employees, such as department managers, can approve check receipts above a certain amount and allow customers to purchase on credit.
Separation of duties	Cashiers and mailroom employees who handle cash do not have access to the accounting records. Accountants who record cash receipts have no opportunity to handle cash.
Internal and external audits	Internal auditors examine company transactions for agreement with management policies. External auditors examine the internal controls over cash receipts to determine whether the accounting system produces accurate amounts for revenues, receivables, and other items related to cash receipts.
Documents and records	Customers receive receipts as transaction records. Bank statements list cash receipts for deposits. Customers who pay by mail include a remittance advice showing the amount of cash they sent to the company.
Electronic devices and computer controls	Cash registers serve as transaction records. Each day's receipts are matched with customer remittance advices and with the day's deposit ticket from the bank.
Other controls	Cashiers are bonded. Cash is stored in vaults and banks. Employees are rotated among jobs and are required to take vacations.

Internal Control over Cash Disbursements *(Payments)*

Objective 5

Apply internal controls to cash disbursements, including petty cash transactions

Exercising control over cash disbursements (payments) is at least as important as controlling cash receipts.

Controls over Payment by Check

Payment by check is an important control over cash disbursements. First, the check acts as a source document. Second, to be valid, the check must be signed by an authorized official so that each payment by check draws the attention of management. Before signing the check, the manager should study the evidence supporting the payment.

To illustrate the internal control over cash disbursements, suppose the business is buying inventory for sale to customers. Let's examine the process leading up to the cash payment.

CONTROLS OVER PURCHASING The purchasing process—outlined in Exhibit 7-8—starts when the sales department identifies the need for merchandise and prepares a *purchase request* (or *requisition*). A separate purchasing department specializes in locating the best buys and mails a *purchase order* to the supplier, the outside company that sells the needed goods. When the supplier ships the goods to the requesting business, the supplier also mails the *invoice*, or bill, which is notification of the need to pay. As the goods arrive, the receiving department checks the goods for any damage and lists the merchandise received on a document called the *receiving report*. The accounting department combines all the foregoing documents, checks them for accuracy and agreement, and forwards this *disbursement packet* to designated officers for approval and payment. The packet includes the purchase request, purchase order, invoice, and receiving report, as shown in Exhibit 7-9.

We introduced purchase orders and invoices in Chapter 5, page 185.

CONTROLS OVER APPROVAL OF PAYMENTS Before approving the disbursement, the controller and the treasurer should examine the packet to determine that the accounting department has performed the following control steps:

Business Document	Prepared by	Sent to
Purchase request (requisition)	Sales department	Purchasing department
Purchase order	Purchasing department	Outside company that sells the needed merchandise (supplier or vendor)
Invoice (bill)	Outside company that sells the needed merchandise (supplier or vendor)	Accounting department
Receiving report	Receiving department	Accounting department
Disbursement packet	Accounting department	Officer who signs the check

EXHIBIT 7-8
Purchasing Process

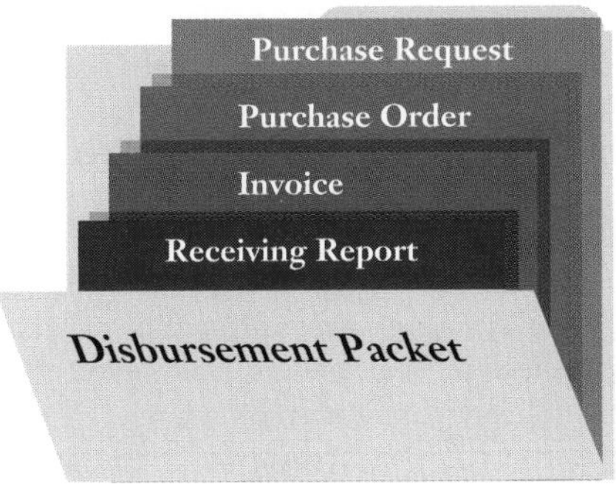

EXHIBIT 7-9
Disbursement Packet

1. The invoice is compared with a copy of the purchase order and purchase request to ensure that the business pays cash only for the goods that it ordered.
2. The invoice is compared with the receiving report to ensure that cash is paid only for the goods that were actually received.
3. The mathematical accuracy of the invoice is proved.

The use of **vouchers,** documents that authorize cash disbursements, improves the internal control over disbursements. As further security and control over disbursements, many firms require two signatures on a check, as we saw in Exhibit 7-3. To avoid document alteration, some firms also use machines that indelibly stamp the amount on the check. After payment, the check signer can punch a hole through the disbursement packet. This hole denotes that the invoice has been paid and discourages dishonest employees from running the documents through the system for a duplicate payment. We discuss the voucher system in more detail in the appendix to this chapter.

Voucher. Document authorizing a cash disbursement.

■ Daily Exercise 7-17

Information technology is streamlining cash disbursement procedures in many businesses. For example, the CPA firm of Deloitte & Touche is revamping the payment system of Bank of America. Exhibit 7-10 summarizes the internal controls over cash disbursements.

Thinking It Over Talon Computer Concepts processes payroll checks for small businesses. Clients give their employee time cards to Talon each week, and Talon programmers write computer programs to meet the clients' payrolls. Talon computer operators process and deliver the checks to the clients for distribution to employees. Identify two employee functions of Talon's cash disbursements system that should be separated. Give your reason.

Answer: The programmers should not also be computer operators. Any person who performed both functions could write the program to process checks to himself or herself or to a fictitious employee and then pocket the printed checks.

Petty Cash Disbursements

It would be uneconomical for a business to write a separate check for an executive's taxi fare, a box of pencils needed right away, or the delivery of a special package across town. Therefore, companies keep a small amount of cash on hand to pay for such minor amounts. This fund is called **petty cash.**

Petty Cash. Fund containing a small amount of cash that is used to pay for minor expenditures.

Concept Highlight

EXHIBIT 7-10
Internal Controls over Cash Disbursements

Element of Internal Control	Internal Controls over Cash Disbursements
Competent, reliable, ethical personnel	Cash disbursements are entrusted to high-level employees, with larger amounts paid by the treasurer or assistant treasurer.
Assignment of responsibilities	Specific employees approve purchase documents for payment. Executives examine approvals, then sign checks.
Proper authorization	Large expenditures must be authorized by the company owner or board of directors to ensure agreement with organizational goals.
Separation of duties	Computer operators and other employees who handle checks have no access to the accounting records. Accountants who record cash disbursements have no opportunity to handle cash.
Internal and external audits	Internal auditors examine company transactions for agreement with management policies. External auditors examine the internal controls over cash disbursements to determine whether the accounting system produces accurate amounts for expenses, assets, and other items related to cash disbursements.
Documents and records	Suppliers issue invoices that document the need to pay cash. Bank statements list cash payments (checks and EFT disbursements) for reconciliation with company records. Checks are prenumbered in sequence to account for payments.
Electronic devices, computer controls, and other controls	Blank checks are stored in a vault and controlled by a responsible official with no accounting duties. Machines stamp the amount on a check in indelible ink. Paid invoices are punched to avoid duplicate payment.

Even though the individual amounts paid through the petty cash fund may be small, such expenses occur so often that the total amount over an accounting period may grow quite large. Thus the business needs to set up these controls over petty cash:

1. Designate an employee to administer the fund as its custodian.
2. Keep a specific amount of cash on hand.
3. Support all fund disbursements with a petty cash ticket.
4. Replenish the fund through normal cash disbursement procedures.

The petty cash fund is opened when a payment is approved for a predetermined amount and a check for that amount is issued to Petty Cash. Assume that on February 28, the business decides to establish a petty cash fund of $200. The custodian cashes the check and places the currency and coin in the fund, which may be a cash box, safe, or other device. The petty cash custodian is responsible for controlling the fund. Starting the fund is recorded as follows:

Feb. 28	Petty Cash	200	
	Cash in Bank		200
	To open the petty cash fund.		

For each petty cash disbursement, the custodian prepares a *petty cash ticket* like the one illustrated in Exhibit 7-11.

Observe the signatures (or initials, for the custodian) that identify the recipient of petty cash and the fund custodian. Requiring both signatures reduces unauthorized cash disbursements. The custodian keeps all the petty cash tickets in the fund. The sum of the cash plus the total of the ticket amounts should equal the opening balance at all times—in this case, $200. Also, the Petty Cash account keeps its prescribed $200 balance at all times. Maintaining the Petty Cash account at this balance, supported by the fund (cash plus tickets totaling the same amount), is a characteristic of an **imprest system.** In an imprest system, the amount of cash for which the custodian is responsible is clearly identified. This is the system's main internal control feature.

Imprest System. A way to account for petty cash by maintaining a constant balance in the petty cash account, supported by the fund (cash plus disbursement tickets) totaling the same amount.

Disbursements reduce the amount of cash in the fund, so periodically the fund must be replenished. Suppose that on March 31, the fund has $118 in cash and $82 in tickets. A check for $82 is issued, made payable to Petty Cash. The fund custodian cashes

EXHIBIT 7-11
Petty Cash Ticket

PETTY CASH TICKET

Date Mar. 25, 19X6 No. 47
Amount $23.00
For Box of floppy diskettes
Debit Office Supplies, Acct. No. 145
Received by Lewis Wright Fund Custodian MAR

this check for currency and coins and puts the money in the fund to return its actual cash to $200. The petty cash tickets identify the accounts to be debited: Office Supplies for $23, Delivery Expense for $17, and Miscellaneous Selling Expense for $42. The entry to record replenishment of the fund is

Mar. 31	Office Supplies	23	
	Delivery Expense	17	
	Miscellaneous Selling Expense	42	
	Cash in Bank		82
	To replenish the petty cash fund.		

If this cash payment exceeds the sum of the tickets—that is, if the fund comes up short, Cash Short and Over is debited for the missing amount. If the sum of the tickets exceeds the payment, Cash Short and Over is credited. Replenishing the fund does *not* affect the Petty Cash account. Petty Cash keeps its $200 balance at all times.

Whenever petty cash runs low, the fund is replenished. It *must* be replenished on the balance-sheet date. Otherwise, the reported balance for Petty Cash will be overstated by the amount of the tickets in the fund. The income statement will understate the expenses listed on those tickets.

Learning Tip: No journal entries are made for petty cash disbursements until the fund is replenished. At that time, all petty cash payments will be recorded in a summary entry. This procedure avoids the need to journalize many small payments.

Petty Cash is debited only when the fund is started (see the February 28 entry) or when its amount is changed. In our illustration, suppose the business decides to raise the fund amount from $200 to $250 because of increased demand for petty cash. This step would require a $50 debit to Petty Cash.

■ Daily Exercise 7-18

Using a Budget to Manage Cash

Objective 6

Use a budget to manage cash

Owners and managers control their organizations with the help of budgets. A **budget** is a quantitative expression of a plan that helps managers coordinate the entity's activities. Cash receives the most attention in the budgeting process because all transactions ultimately affect cash. In this section, we introduce *cash budgeting* as a way to manage this important asset. (We discuss budgeting in greater detail in Chapters 23 and 24.)

Budget. A quantitative expression of a plan that helps managers coordinate the entity's activities.

How does MCI decide when to invest in new telecommunications equipment? How will the company decide how much to spend? Will borrowing be needed, or can MCI finance the purchase with internally generated cash? Similarly, by what process do you decide how much to spend on your education? On an automobile? On a house? All these decisions depend to some degree on the information that a cash budget provides.

A cash budget helps a business manage its cash by expressing the plan for the receipt and disbursement of cash during a future period.

To prepare for the future, a company must determine how much cash it will need and then figure out whether its operations will bring in the needed cash. Preparation of a cash budget includes four steps:

1. Start with the entity's cash balance at the beginning of the period. The beginning balance tells how much cash is left over from the preceding period.

2. Add the budgeted cash receipts and subtract the budgeted cash payments. This is the most challenging part of the budgeting process because managers must predict the cash effects of all transactions of the budget period, including
   a. Revenue and expense transactions (from the income statement)
   b. Asset acquisition and sale transactions (from the statement of cash flows)
   c. Liability and stockholders' equity transactions (from the statement of cash flows)

   Foresight is imperfect, so the actual figure will not always turn out as expected. It is important to develop *realistic* estimates of the cash receipts and payments during the budget period.
3. The beginning balance plus the expected receipts minus the expected payments equals the expected cash balance at the end of the period.
4. Compare the expected cash balance to the desired, or *budgeted*, cash balance at the end of the period. Owners and managers know the minimum amount of cash they need (the budgeted balance) to keep the entity running. If there is excess cash, they can invest. If the expected cash balance falls below the budgeted balance, the company must obtain additional financing to reach the desired cash balance.

Let's consider the benefits of budgeting cash. Suppose MCI's cash budget reveals a cash shortage during June of the coming year. The budget gives MCI managers an early warning of the need for additional cash. Managers can arrange financing in advance and probably get a lower interest rate and better payment terms than if they are forced to borrow money under rushed conditions. In short, the cash budget helps managers make decisions in an orderly manner. A budget serves the same purpose for individuals.

Exhibit 7-12 shows a hypothetical cash budget for The Gap, Inc., for the year ended January 31, 19X2. Study it carefully because at some point in your career or personal affairs you will use a cash budget.

Learning Tip: The cash budget is entirely separate from net income or net loss on the income statement. Thus, net income does not appear on the cash budget.

EXHIBIT 7-12
Cash Budget (Hypothetical)

■ Daily Exercise 7-19

THE GAP, INC.
Cash Budget
Year Ended January 31, 19X2

		(In millions)	
(1)	Cash balance, February 1, 19X1		$ 203
	Estimated cash receipts:		
(2)	Collections from customers	$ 2,858	
(3)	Interest and dividends on investments	6	
(4)	Sale of store fixtures	5	2,869
			3,072
	Estimated cash disbursements:		
(5)	Purchases of inventory	$(1,906)	
(6)	Operating expenses	(561)	
(7)	Expansions of existing stores	(206)	
(8)	Opening of new stores	(349)	
(9)	Payment of long-term debt	(145)	
(10)	Payment to owners of the business	(219)	(3,386)
(11)	Cash available (needed) before new financing		(314)
(12)	Budgeted cash balance, January 31, 19X2		(200)
(13)	Cash available for additional investments, or (New financing needed)		$ (514)

The cash budget has sections for cash receipts and cash disbursements. The budget is prepared *before* the period's transactions and can take any form that helps people make decisions. The cash budget is an internal document, so it is not bound by generally accepted accounting principles.

The Gap's hypothetical cash budget in Exhibit 7-12 begins with the company's actual cash balance at the beginning of the period. At February 1, 19X1, The Gap had cash of $203 million (line 1). The budgeted cash receipts and disbursements are expected to create a need for additional financing during the year (line 13).

Observe that the budget requires $206 million to expand existing stores (line 7) and $349 million to open new stores (line 8). Without these investing transactions, The Gap would not have needed additional cash. But long-term investments, such as new stores, keep the company competitive.

Assume that managers of The Gap wish to maintain a cash balance of at least $200 million (line 12). Because the year's activity is expected to leave the company with a *negative* cash balance of $314 million (line 11), The Gap's managers must arrange $514 million of financing (line 13). Line 11 of the cash budget identifies the amount of cash available or needed. Line 12 lists the minimum cash balance to maintain at all times. *Add* lines 11 and 12 to arrive at the amount of new financing needed. To meet this need for new financing, The Gap can either borrow or raise the money from outside investors.

"Because the year's activity is expected to leave the company with a negative cash balance of $314 million (line 11), The Gap's managers must arrange $514 million of financing (line 13)."

Managers also use budgets to evaluate performance. As the year progresses, managers compare actual figures with the budgeted amounts. Suppose it is now March 15 of the new year, and sales and collections from customers are lagging behind expectations for the first quarter of the year. Knowledge of the slowdown in sales alerts top management of The Gap to take action.

■ Daily Exercise 7-20

Working It Out Suppose line 11 of Exhibit 7-12 showed cash available of $150 million. How much new financing must The Gap line up?

Answer: $50 million ($150 million available – $200 million needed = new financing of $50 million).

International Focus

Managing cash is a complex process. International transactions add to the complexity of managing cash. When a U.S. company buys goods internationally, it may pay cash in a foreign currency, such as Canadian dollars or Mexican pesos. Consider the perfume department in a Macy's store. Macy's purchases Cartier perfume from the French manufacturer. Cartier may demand that Macy's pay for the perfume in French francs. Now Macy's has to buy the francs in order to pay its accounts payable to the French company. Francs and other foreign currencies change in value from day to day. In settling up, Macy's may have a gain or a loss on its foreign-currency transactions. We show how to account for foreign-currency transactions in Chapter 16.

Reporting Cash on the Balance Sheet

Cash is the first current asset listed on the balance sheet of most companies. Even small businesses have several bank accounts and one or more petty cash funds, but companies usually combine all cash amounts into a single total called "Cash and Cash Equivalents" on the balance sheet.

Cash equivalents include liquid assets such as time deposits and certificates of deposit, which are interest-bearing accounts that can be withdrawn with no penalty after a short period of time. Although they are slightly less liquid than cash, they are sufficiently similar to be reported along with cash. For example, the balance sheet of Intel Corporation recently reported the following:

INTEL CORPORATION Balance Sheet (Adapted) December 31, 1996	
	(In millions)
Assets	
Current assets:	
Cash and cash equivalents	$ 4,165
Short-term investments	3,829
Accounts receivable	3,723
Inventories	1,293
Other current assets	674
Total current assets	$13,684

Source: Intel Corporation. *Annual Report 1996*, p. 19.

Cash that is restricted and unavailable for immediate use should not be reported as a current asset if the company does not expect to spend the cash within a year or within the company's operating cycle, if longer than a year. For example, some banks require their depositors to maintain a *compensating balance* on deposit in the bank in order to borrow from the bank.

Ethics and Accounting

In a recent *Wall Street Journal* article, a young Russian entrepreneur stated that he was getting ahead in business by breaking laws. "Older people have an ethics problem," he said. "By that I mean they *have* ethics." Conversely, Roger Smith, former chairman of General Motors, said, "Ethical practice is, quite simply, good business." Smith has been in business long enough to see the danger in unethical behavior. Sooner or later unethical conduct comes to light, as was true in our chapter opening story. Moreover, ethical behavior wins out in the end because it is the right thing to do.

Corporate and Professional Codes of Ethics

Most large companies have a code of ethics designed to encourage employees to behave ethically and responsibly. However, a set of general guidelines may not be specific enough to identify misbehavior, and a list of do's and don'ts can lead to the false view that anything is okay if it's not specifically forbidden. There is no easy answer. But most businesses do not tolerate unethical conduct by employees.

Accountants have additional incentives to behave ethically. As professionals, they are expected to maintain higher standards than society in general. Their ability to attract business depends entirely on their reputation. Most independent accountants are members of the American Institute of Certified Public Accountants and must abide by the *AICPA Code of Professional Conduct*. Accountants who are members of the Institute of Management Accountants are bound by the *Standards of Ethical Conduct for Management Accountants*. These documents set minimum standards of conduct for members. Unacceptable actions can result in expulsion from the organization, which makes it difficult for the person to remain in the accounting profession.

See Chapter 19, page 837.

Objective 7

Make ethical judgments in business

Ethical Issues in Accounting

In many situations, the ethical choice is easy. For example, stealing cash is obviously unethical and illegal. In our chapter opening story, the cashier's actions landed him in jail. In other cases, the choices are more difficult. But, in every instance, ethical judgments boil down to a personal decision: What should I do in a given situation? Let's consider three ethical issues in accounting. The first two are easy to resolve. The third issue is more difficult.

SITUATION 1 Sonja Kleberg is preparing the income tax return of a client who has had a particularly good year—higher income than expected. On January 2, the client pays for newspaper advertising and asks Sonja to backdate the expense to the preceding year. The tax deduction would help the client more in the year just ended than in the current year. Backdating would decrease taxable income of the earlier year and lower the client's tax payments. After all, there is a difference of only two days between January 2 and December 31. This client is important to Kleberg. What should she do?

She should refuse the request because the transaction took place in January of the new year.

What internal control device could prove that Kleberg behaved unethically if she backdated the transaction in the accounting records? An IRS audit and documents and records—the date of the cash payment could prove that the expense occurred in January rather than in December.

SITUATION 2 Jack Mellichamp's software company owes $40,000 to Bank of America. The loan agreement requires Mellichamp's company to maintain a current ratio (current assets divided by current liabilities) of 1.50 or higher. It is late in the year, and the bank will review Mellichamp's situation early next year. At present, the company's current ratio is 1.40. At this level, Mellichamp is in violation of his loan agreement. He can increase the current ratio to 1.53 by paying off some current liabilities right before year end. Is it ethical to do so?

For a review of the current ratio, see Chapter 4, page 153.

Yes, because the action is a real business transaction.

However, paying off the liabilities is only a delaying tactic. It will hold off the creditors for now, but time will tell whether the business can improve its underlying operations.

SITUATION 3 Emilia Gomez, an accountant for the Democratic Party, discovers that her supervisor, Myles Packer, made several errors last year. Campaign contributions received from foreign citizens, which are illegal, were recorded as normal. It is not clear whether the errors were deliberate or accidental. Gomez is deciding what to do. She knows that Packer evaluates her job performance, and lately her work has been marginal. What should Gomez do?

■ Daily Exercise 7-21

The answer is uncertain.

To make her decision, Gomez could follow the framework outlined in the Decision Guidelines feature.

DECISION GUIDELINES — Framework for Making Ethical Judgments

Weighing tough ethical judgments requires a decision framework. Consider these six questions as general guidelines. Then apply them to Emilia Gomez's situation.

QUESTION	DECISION GUIDELINES
1. What are the facts?	1. *Determine the facts.* They are given above.
2. What is the ethical issue, if any?	2. *Identify the ethical issues.* The root word of ethical is *ethics,* which Webster's dictionary defines as "the discipline dealing with what is good and bad and with moral duty and obligation." Gomez's ethical dilemma is to decide what she should do with the information she has uncovered.
3. What are the options?	3. *Specify the alternatives.* For Emilia Gomez, three reasonable alternatives include (a) reporting the errors to Packer, (b) reporting the errors to Packer's boss, and (c) doing nothing.
4. Who is involved in the situation?	4. *Identify the people involved.* Individuals who could be affected include Gomez, Packer, the Democratic Party, and Gomez's co-workers who observe her behavior.

(continued)

DECISION GUIDELINES ***(continued)***

5. What are the possible consequences?	5. *Assess the possible outcomes.* (a) If Gomez reports the errors to Packer, he might penalize her, or he might reward her for careful work. Reporting the errors would preserve her integrity and probably would lead to return of the money to the donors. But the Democratic Party could suffer embarrassment if this situation were made public. (b) If Gomez reports to Packer's boss—going over Packer's head—her integrity would be preserved. Her relationship with Packer would surely be strained, and it might be difficult for them to work together in the future. Gomez might be rewarded for careful work. But if Packer's boss has colluded with Packer in recording the campaign contribution, Gomez could be penalized. If the error is corrected and outsiders notified, the Democratic Party would be embarrassed. Others observing this situation would be affected by the outcome. (c) If Gomez does nothing, she would avoid a confrontation with Packer or his boss. They might or might not discover the error. If they discover it, they might or might not correct it. All might criticize Gomez for not bringing the error to their attention. Fellow accountants might or might not learn of the situation.
6. What shall I do?	6. *Make the decision.* The best choice is not obvious. Gomez must balance the likely effects on the various people against the dictates of her own conscience. Even though this framework does not provide an easy decision, it identifies the relevant factors. Reporting the error to Packer is preferable because he is Gomez's supervisor. Moreover, Gomez must protect her reputation and consider the interests of outsiders who depend on an honest accounting to preserve the integrity of political campaigns.

Ethics and External Controls

There is another dimension to most ethical issues: *external controls*, which refer to the discipline placed on business conduct by outsiders who interact with the company.

- In situation 1, for example, Sonja Kleberg could give in to the client's request to backdate the advertising expense. But this action would be both dishonest and illegal. These external controls arise from the business's interaction with the taxing authorities. An IRS audit of Kleberg's client could uncover her action.
- In situation 2, the external controls arise from Jack Mellichamp's relationship with the bank that lent money to his software company. As long as the loan agreement is in effect, the company must maintain a current ratio of 1.50 or higher. Paying off current liabilities to improve the current ratio would be a short-term solution to Mellichamp's problem. Over the long run, his business must generate more current assets through operations. His business will almost certainly need to borrow in the future and will probably face similar loan restrictions. Managers are wise to focus on long-term solutions to their problems if they hope to succeed in business.
- The primary external control in situation 3 results from the laws of the United States and their enforcement through the U.S. legal system. Campaign contributions are public information, and sooner or later the public will learn that the Democratic Party received illegal campaign contributions. It would be in the party's best interest to

admit its mistake and correct the errors as quickly as possible—by returning the illegal contributions to the donors. The situation will probably lead to tighter party controls that will keep the mistake from being repeated. This is why organizations have codes of conduct and why, as Roger Smith put it, "Ethical practice is . . . good business."

Thinking It Over Can you identify the external control in the chapter opening story? How did it impose discipline on the cashier?

Answer: The external control was the monthly statement that Larsen & Company sends each client. When customers saw their account balances underreported on the monthly statements, they called in to ask why. Jack Van Auken must have spent half his time explaining the out-of-balance conditions of clients' accounts. Sooner or later he was bound to get caught. That's how external controls work.

SUMMARY PROBLEM FOR YOUR REVIEW

Grudnitski Company established a $300 petty cash fund. James C. Brown is the fund custodian. At the end of the first week, the petty cash fund contains the following:

a. Cash: $171 **b.** Petty cash tickets:

No.	Amount	Issued to	Signed by	Account Debited
44	$14	B. Jarvis	B. Jarvis and JCB	Office Supplies
45	9	S. Bell	S. Bell	Miscellaneous Expense
47	43	R. Tate	R. Tate and JCB	—
48	33	L. Blair	L. Blair and JCB	Travel Expense

REQUIRED

1. Identify the four internal control weaknesses revealed in the given data.
2. Prepare the general journal entries to record:
   a. Establishment of the petty cash fund.
   b. Replenishment of the fund. Assume that petty cash ticket no. 47 was issued for the purchase of office supplies.
3. What is the balance in the Petty Cash account immediately before replenishment? Immediately after replenishment?

SOLUTION

REQUIREMENT 1

The four internal control weaknesses are

a. Petty cash ticket no. 46 is missing. Coupled with weakness (b), this omission raises questions about the administration of the petty cash fund and about how the petty cash funds were used.

b. The $171 cash balance means that $129 has been disbursed ($300 – $171 = $129). However, the total amount of the petty cash tickets is only $99 ($14 + $9 + $43 + $33). The fund, then, is $30 short of cash ($129 – $99 = $30). Was petty cash ticket no. 46 issued for $30? The data in the problem offer no hint that helps answer this question. In practice, management would investigate the problem.

c. The petty cash custodian (JCB) did not sign petty cash ticket no. 45. This omission may have been an oversight on his part. However, it raises the question of whether he authorized the disbursement. Both the fund custodian and the recipient of cash should sign the ticket.

d. Petty cash ticket no. 47 does not indicate which account to debit. What did Tate do with the money, and what account should be debited? At worst, the funds have been stolen. At best, reconstructing the transaction from memory is haphazard. With no better choice available, debit Miscellaneous Expense.

REQUIREMENT 2

Petty cash journal entries:

a. Entry to establish the petty cash fund:

Petty Cash	300	
Cash in Bank..........		300

b. Entry to replenish the fund:

Office Supplies ($14 + $43)	57	
Miscellaneous Expense	9	
Travel Expense	33	
Cash Short and Over	30	
Cash in Bank		129

REQUIREMENT 3

The balance in Petty Cash is *always* its specified balance, in this case $300, as shown by posting the preceding entries to the account:

Petty Cash		
(a)	300	

The entry to establish the fund—entry (a)—debits Petty Cash. The entry to replenish the fund—entry (b)—neither debits nor credits Petty Cash.

Summary of Learning Objectives

1. ***Define internal control.*** *Internal control* is the organizational plan and all the related measures that an entity adopts to safeguard assets, encourage adherence to company policies, promote operational efficiency, and ensure accurate and reliable accounting records.

2. ***Identify the characteristics of an effective system of internal control.*** An effective internal control system includes these features: *competent, reliable, and ethical personnel; clear-cut assignment of responsibilities; proper authorization; separation of duties; internal and external audits; documents and records;* and *electronic devices and computer controls.* Many companies also make use of fireproof vaults, point-of-sale terminals, fidelity bonds, mandatory vacations, and job rotation. Effective computerized internal control systems must meet the same basic standards that good manual systems do.

3. ***Prepare a bank reconciliation and the related journal entries.*** The *bank account* helps to control and safeguard cash. Businesses use the *bank statement* and the *bank reconciliation* to account for banking transactions.

4. ***Apply internal controls to cash receipts.*** To control cash receipts over the counter, companies use point-of-sale terminals that customers can see, and require that cashiers provide customers with receipts. A tape inside the machine records each sale and cash transaction. Pricing with uneven amounts means that cashiers must open the drawer to make change, which requires the transaction to be recorded on tape.

To control cash receipts by mail, a mailroom employee should be charged with opening the mail, comparing the enclosed amount with the remittance advice, and preparing a control tape. This is an essential separation of duties—the accounting department should not open the mail. At the end of the day, the controller compares the three records of the day's cash receipts: the control tape total from the mailroom, the bank deposit amount from the cashier, and the debit to Cash from the accounting department.

5. ***Apply internal controls to cash disbursements, including petty cash transactions.*** To control payments by check, checks should be issued and signed only when a *disbursement packet* including the purchase request, purchase order, invoice (bill), and receiving report (with all appropriate signatures) has been prepared. To control petty cash disbursements, the custodian of the fund should require a completed petty cash ticket for all disbursements.

6. ***Use a budget to manage cash.*** A budget is a quantitative expression of a plan that helps managers coordinate the entity's activities. To prepare for the future, a company must determine how much cash it will need, then decide whether its operations will bring in the needed cash. If not, then the company knows to arrange financing early. If operations will bring in an excess of cash, the company can be on the lookout for investment activities.

7. ***Make ethical judgments in business.*** To make ethical decisions, people should proceed in six steps: (1) Determine the facts. (2) Identify the ethical issues. (3) Specify the alternatives. (4) Identify the people involved. (5) Assess the possible outcomes. (6) Make the decision.

Accounting Vocabulary

audit *(p. 293)*
bank collection *(p. 297)*
bank reconciliation *(p. 296)*
bank statement *(p. 295)*
budget *(p. 309)*
check *(p. 295)*
controller *(p. 291)*
deposit in transit *(p. 297)*
electronic funds transfer (EFT) *(p. 296)*
imprest system *(p. 308)*
internal control *(p. 290)*
nonsufficient funds (NSF) check *(p. 298)*
outstanding check *(p. 297)*
petty cash *(p. 307)*
voucher *(p. 307)*

Questions

1. Which of the features of effective internal control is the most fundamental? Why?
2. What is the title of the federal act that affects internal control? What requirement does it place on management?
3. Which company employees bear primary responsibility for a company's financial statements and for maintaining the company's system of internal control? How do these people carry out this responsibility?

4. Identify seven features of an effective system of internal control.
5. Separation of duties may be divided into four parts. What are they?
6. How can internal control systems be circumvented?
7. Are internal control systems designed to be foolproof and perfect? What is a fundamental constraint in planning and maintaining systems?
8. Briefly state how each of the following serves as an internal control measure over cash: bank account, signature card, deposit ticket, and bank statement.
9. What is the remittance advice of a check? What purpose does it serve?
10. Each of the items in the following list must be accounted for in the bank reconciliation. Next to each item, enter the appropriate letter from the following possible treatments: (a) bank side of reconciliation—add the item; (b) bank side of reconciliation—subtract the item; (c) book side of reconciliation—add the item; (d) book side of reconciliation—subtract the item.

    ________ Outstanding check
    ________ NSF check
    ________ Bank service charge
    ________ Cost of printed checks
    ________ Bank error that decreased bank balance
    ________ Deposit in transit
    ________ Bank collection
    ________ Customer check returned because of unauthorized signature
    ________ Book error that increased balance of Cash account

11. What purpose does a bank reconciliation serve?
12. Suppose a company has six bank accounts, two petty cash funds, and three certificates of deposit that can be withdrawn on demand. How many cash amounts would this company likely report on its balance sheet?
13. What role does a cash register play in an internal control system?
14. Describe internal control procedures for cash received by mail.
15. What documents make up the disbursement packet? Describe three procedures that use the disbursement packet to ensure that each payment is appropriate.
16. What balance does the Petty Cash account have at all times? Does this balance always equal the amount of cash in the fund? When are the two amounts equal? When are they unequal?
17. Describe how a budget helps a company manage its cash.
18. Suppose the cash budget indicates an excess of $20,000 cash receipts over cash disbursements for the period. Will the business need additional financing? What is the business likely to do with the extra cash?
19. Why should accountants adhere to a higher standard of ethical conduct than many other members of society?
20. "Our managers know that they are expected to meet budgeted profit figures. We don't want excuses. We want results." Discuss the ethical implications of this policy.
21. Why should the same employee not write the computer programs for cash disbursements, sign checks, and mail the checks to payees?

Daily Exercises

DE7-1 Internal controls are designed to safeguard assets, encourage employees to follow company policies, promote operational efficiency, and ensure accurate records. Which of these four goals of internal controls is most important? Stated differently, which goal must the internal controls accomplish for the business to survive? Give your reason.

Definition of internal control **(Obj. 1)**

DE7-2 Give the title of the chief accounting officer and the title of the chief financial officer in an organzation. What are the responsibilities of each person? How does separating their duties provide good internal control?

Aspects of internal control **(Obj. 1)**

DE7-3 Explain in your own words why separation of duties is often described as the cornerstone of internal control for safeguarding assets. Describe what can happen if the same person has custody of an asset and also accounts for the asset.

Characteristics of an effective system of internal control **(Obj. 2)**

DE7-4 Examine the organization chart in Exhibit 7-2, page 292. What is the main duty of the internal auditors? To whom do the internal auditors report? Why don't the internal auditors report directly to the treasurer? After all, the treasurer is responsible for cash management.

Characteristics of an effective system of internal control **(Obj. 2)**

DE7-5 How do internal auditors differ from external auditors? How does an internal audit differ from an external audit? How are the two types of audits similar?

Characteristics of an effective system of internal control **(Obj. 2)**

DE7-6 Review the characteristics of an effective system of internal control that begin on page 291. Then identify two things that Larsen & Company in the chapter opening story could have done to make it harder for Jack Van Auken, the cashier, to steal from the company and hide the theft. Explain how each new measure taken by Larsen & Company would have accomplished its goal.

Characteristics of an effective system of internal control **(Obj. 2)**

DE7-7 Draw a simple diagram with three boxes and two arrows to show the relationships among (a) the bank statement, (b) the bank reconciliation, and (c) the accounting records. Use the arrows to show the flow of data.

Bank reconciliation **(Obj. 3)**

Aspects of a bank reconciliation
(Obj. 3)

DE7-8 Answer the following questions pertaining to the bank reconciliation:

1. What is the difference between a bank statement and a bank reconciliation?
2. Is the bank reconciliation a journal, a ledger, an account, or a financial statement? If not, what is it?
3. Which side of the bank reconciliation generates data for new journal entries in the company's accounting records?

Identifying reconciling items from bank documents
(Obj. 3)

DE7-9 Compare Business Research, Inc.'s general ledger Cash account in Exhibit 7-5, page 298, with the bank statement that the company received in Exhibit 7-4, page 297.

1. Trace each cash receipt from the Cash account (Exhibit 7-5) to a deposit on the bank statement (Exhibit 7-4). Which deposit is in transit on January 31? Give its date and dollar amount.
2. Trace each of Business Research's checks from the cash disbursements record in Exhibit 7-5 to the bank statement in Exhibit 7-4. List all outstanding checks by check number and dollar amount.
3. On which side of the bank reconciliation do deposits in transit and outstanding checks appear—the bank side or the book side? Are they added or subtracted on the bank reconciliation?

Preparing a bank reconciliation
(Obj. 3)

DE7-10 The Cash account of Cabletron Concepts reported a balance of $1,500 at May 31. Included were outstanding checks totaling $900 and a May 31 deposit of $200 that did not appear on the bank statement. The bank statement, which came from Cornerstone Bank, listed a May 31 balance of $2,490. Included in the bank balance was a May 30 collection of $300 on account from Ben Jones, a Cabletron customer who pays the bank directly. The bank statement also shows a $20 service charge and $10 of interest revenue that Cabletron earned on its bank balance.

Prepare Cabletron's bank reconciliation at May 31.

Recording transactions from a bank reconciliation
(Obj. 3)

DE7-11 After preparing Cabletron Concepts' bank reconciliation in Daily Exercise 7-10, make Cabletron's general journal entries for transactions that arise from the bank reconciliation. Include an explanation with each entry.

Internal controls and the bank reconciliation
(Obj. 2, 3)

DE7-12 Who in an organization should prepare the bank reconciliation? Should it be someone with cash-handling duties, someone with accounting duties, or someone with both duties? Does it matter? Give your reason.

Using a bank reconciliation as a control device
(Obj. 3)

DE7-13 Louise Goldsmith owns Goldsmith Financial Services. She fears that a trusted employee has been stealing from the company. This employee receives cash from customers and also prepares the monthly bank reconciliation. To check up on the employee, Goldsmith prepares her own bank reconciliation, as follows:

GOLDSMITH FINANCIAL SERVICES
Bank Reconciliation
August 31, 19X7

BANK		BOOKS	
Balance, August 31	$3,000	Balance, August 31	$2,100
Add:		Add:	
Deposits in transit	400	Bank collections	800
		Interest revenue	10
Less:		Less:	
Outstanding checks	(1,100)	Service charge	(30)
Adjusted bank balance	$2,300	Adjusted book balance	$2,880

Does it appear that the employee has stolen from the company? If so, how much? Explain your answer. Which side of the bank reconciliation shows the company's true cash balance?

Controls over cash register receipts
(Obj. 4)

DE7-14 Consider the men's sportswear department of a Macy's department store. What could a dishonest salesperson do if he had access to the record of transactions that were conducted through his cash register? How does Macy's keep employees from behaving in this manner?

Control over cash receipts
(Obj. 4)

DE7-15 Max Emhart sells electrical appliances at Watson Electric Company in Joplin, Missouri. Company procedure requires Emhart to write a customer receipt for all sales. The receipt forms are prenumbered. Emhart is having personal financial problems and takes $500 that he received from a customer. To hide his theft, Emhart simply destroys the company copy of the sales receipt that he gave the customer. What will alert Murray Watson, the owner, that something is wrong? What will this knowledge lead Watson to do?

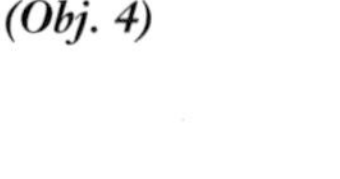

DE7-16 Review the internal controls over cash receipts by mail, discussed on page 297. Briefly describe how the final step in the process, performed by the controller, establishes that

Control over cash receipts by mail **(Obj. 4)**

1. The cash receipts went into the bank.
2. The business's customers received credit for their payments.

How does a lock-box system protect cash from theft?

DE7-17 Answer the following questions about internal control over cash disbursements.

Internal control over payments by check **(Obj. 5)**

1. Payment of cash disbursements by check carries two basic controls over cash. What are they?
2. Suppose a purchasing agent receives the goods that he purchases and also approves payment for the goods. How could a dishonest purchasing agent cheat his company? How do companies avoid this internal control weakness?

DE7-18

Control over petty cash **(Obj. 5)**

1. Describe how an *imprest* petty cash system works. What is the main control feature of an imprest system?
2. Fort Howard Home Products maintains an imprest $300 petty cash fund, which is under the control of Leah Hassan. At November 30, the fund holds $120 cash and petty cash tickets for travel expense, $80; office supplies, $60; and delivery expense, $40.
   Journalize Fort Howard's (a) establishment of the petty cash fund on November 1, and (b) replenishment of the fund on November 30.
3. Draw a T-account for Petty Cash, and post to the account. What is Petty Cash's account balance at all times?

DE7-19

Preparing a cash budget **(Obj. 6)**

1. Return to The Gap's cash budget in Exhibit 7-12, page 310. Suppose The Gap were to postpone the opening of new stores until 19X3. In that case, how much additional financing would The Gap need for the year ended January 31, 19X2?
2. Now suppose The Gap were to postpone both the expansions of existing stores and the opening of new stores until 19X3. How much new financing would The Gap need, or how much cash would the company have available for additional investments during the year ended January 31, 19X2?

DE7-20 Florida Progreso Growers is a major food cooperative. Suppose the company begins 1999 with cash of $6 million. Florida Progreso estimates cash receipts during 1999 will total $147 million. Planned disbursements for the year will require cash of $154 million. To meet daily cash needs, Florida Progreso must maintain a cash balance of at least $5 million.

Preparing a cash budget **(Obj. 6)**

Prepare Florida Progreso's cash budget for 1999. Identify two ways Florida Progreso can obtain the new financing.

DE7-21 Lane Gibbs, an accountant for Entergy Associates, discovers that his supervisor, Jules Duquet, made several errors last year. Overall, the errors overstated Entergy's net income by 20 percent. It is not clear whether the errors were deliberate or accidental. What should Gibbs do?

Making an ethical judgment **(Obj. 7)**

Exercises

E7-1 Consider this excerpt from a *Wall Street Journal* article:

Correcting an internal control weakness **(Obj. 2)**

> TOKYO—Sumitomo Corp., a Japanese trading company, said unauthorized trades by its former head of copper trading caused losses that may total $1.8 billion. Sumitomo said it learned of the damage when Yasuo Hamanaka called a superior and confessed to making unauthorized trades that led to the losses over a 10-year period. Mr. Hamanaka, according to a Sumitomo statement, admitted to concealing the losses by falsifying Sumitomo's books and records.

What internal control weakness at Sumitomo Corp. allowed this loss to grow so large? How could the company have avoided and/or limited the size of the loss?

E7-2 The following situations suggest either a strength or a weakness in internal control. Identify each as *strength* or *weakness*, and give the reason for your answer.

Identifying internal control strengths and weaknesses **(Obj. 2)**

a. Top managers delegate all internal control measures to the accounting department.
b. The accounting department orders merchandise and approves invoices for payment.
c. The operator of a computer has no other accounting or cash-handling duties.

d. Cash received over the counter is controlled by the sales clerk, who rings up the sale and places the cash in the register. The sales clerk matches the total recorded on the control tape stored in the register to each day's cash sales.

e. Cash received by mail goes straight to the accountant, who debits Cash and credits Accounts Receivable from the customer.

f. The vice president who signs checks does not examine the disbursement packet because the accounting department has matched the invoice with other supporting documents.

Identifying internal controls **(Obj. 2)**

E7-3 Identify the missing internal control characteristic in the following situations:

a. Business is slow at White Water Park on Tuesday, Wednesday, and Thursday nights. To reduce expenses, the owner decides not to use a ticket taker on those nights. The ticket seller (cashier) is told to keep the tickets as a record of the number sold.

b. The manager of a discount store wants to speed the flow of customers through check-out. She decides to reduce the time that cashiers spend making change, so she prices merchandise at round dollar amounts—such as $8.00 and $15.00—instead of the customary amounts—$7.95 and $14.95.

c. Grocery stores such as Kroger and Winn Dixie purchase large quantities of their merchandise from a few suppliers. At another grocery store, the manager decides to reduce paperwork. He eliminates the requirement that a receiving department employee prepare a receiving report, which lists the quantities of items received from the supplier.

d. When business is brisk, Stop-n-Shop and many other retail stores deposit cash in the bank several times during the day. The manager at another convenience store wants to reduce the time that employees spend delivering cash to the bank, so he starts a new policy. Cash will build up over Saturdays and Sundays, and the total two-day amount will be deposited on Sunday evening.

e. While reviewing the records of Pay Less Pharmacy, you find that the same employee orders merchandise and approves invoices for payment.

Explaining the role of internal control **(Obj. 2)**

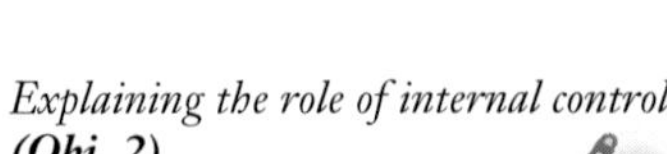

E7-4 The following questions pertain to internal control. Consider each situation separately.

1. Separation of duties is an important consideration if a system of internal control is to be effective. Why is this so?
2. Cash may be a relatively small item on the financial statements. Nevertheless, internal control over cash is very important. Why is this true?
3. Ling Ltd. requires that all documents supporting a check be canceled (stamped Paid) by the person who signs the check. Why do you think this practice is required? What might happen if it were not?
4. Many managers think that safeguarding assets is the most important objective of internal control systems, while auditors emphasize internal control's role in ensuring reliable accounting data. Explain why managers are more concerned about safeguarding assets and auditors are more concerned about the quality of the accounting records.

Classifying bank reconciliation items **(Obj. 3)**

E7-5 The following items may appear on a bank reconciliation:

1. Service charge.
2. Deposits in transit.
3. NSF check.
4. Bank collection of a note receivable on our behalf.
5. Book error: We debited Cash for $200. The correct debit was $2,000.
6. Outstanding checks.
7. Bank error: The bank charged our account for a check written by another customer.

Classify each item as (a) an addition to the bank balance, (b) a subtraction from the bank balance, (c) an addition to the book balance, or (d) a subtraction from the book balance.

Preparing a bank reconciliation **(Obj. 3)**

E7-6 D. J. Hunter's checkbook lists the following:

Date	Check No.	Item	Check	Deposit	Balance
9/1					$ 525
4	622	La Petite France Bakery	$ 19		506
9		Dividends received		$ 116	622
13	623	General Tire Co.	43		579
14	624	Exxon Oil Co.	58		521
18	625	Cash	50		471
26	626	Fellowship Bible Church	25		446
28	627	Bent Tree Apartments	275		171
30		Paycheck		1,800	1,971

Hunter's September bank statement shows the following:

Balance				$525
Add: Deposits				116
Deduct checks:	No.	Amount		
	622	$19		
	623	43		
	624	68*		
	625	50		(180)
Other charges:				
Printed checks			$ 8	
Service charge			12	(20)
Balance				$441

*This is the correct amount for check number 624.

REQUIRED

Prepare Hunter's bank reconciliation at September 30.

Preparing a bank reconciliation
(Obj. 3)

E7-7 Louis Nicosia operates four 7-11 stores. He has just received the monthly bank statement at October 31 from City National Bank, and the statement shows an ending balance of $3,840. Listed on the statement are an EFT rent collection of $400, a service charge of $12, two NSF checks totaling $74, and a $9 charge for printed checks. In reviewing his cash records, Nicosia identifies outstanding checks totaling $467 and an October 31 deposit in transit of $1,788. During October, he recorded a $290 check for the salary of a part-time employee by debiting Salary Expense and crediting Cash for $29. Nicosia's Cash account shows an October 31 cash balance of $5,117. Prepare the bank reconciliation at October 31.

Making journal entries from a bank reconciliation
(Obj. 3)

E7-8 Using the data from Exercise 7-7, make the journal entries that Nicosia should record on October 31. Include an explanation for each entry.

Applying internal controls to the bank reconciliation
(Obj. 2, 3)

E7-9 A grand jury indicted the manager of a Broken Spoke restaurant for stealing cash from the company. Over a three-year period, the manager allegedly took almost $100,000 and attempted to cover the theft by manipulating the bank reconciliation.

REQUIRED

What is the most likely way that a person would manipulate a bank reconciliation to cover a theft? Be specific. What internal control arrangement could have avoided this theft?

Evaluating internal control over cash receipts
(Obj. 4)

E7-10 A cash register is located in each department of a Saks Fifth Avenue store. The register display shows the amount of each sale, the cash received from the customer, and any change returned to the customer. The machine also produces a customer receipt but keeps no record of transactions. At the end of the day, the clerk counts the cash in the register and gives it to the cashier for deposit in the company bank account.

REQUIRED

Write a memo to convince the store manager that there is an internal control weakness over cash receipts. Identify the weakness that gives an employee the best opportunity to steal cash, and state how to prevent such a theft.

Petty cash, cash short and over
(Obj. 5)

E7-11 Record the following selected transactions of Rapid Transit Service in general journal format (explanations are not required):

April 1 Established a petty cash fund with a $300 balance.
2 Journalized the day's cash sales. Cash register tapes show a $2,869 total, but the cash in the register is $2,873.
10 The petty cash fund has $129 in cash and $161 in petty cash tickets issued to pay for Office Supplies ($111), Delivery Expense ($13), and Entertainment Expense ($37). Replenished the fund and recorded the expenses.

Accounting for petty cash
(Obj. 5)

E7-12 The Sisters of Charity in San Diego created a $400 imprest petty cash fund. During the first month of use, the fund custodian authorized and signed petty cash tickets as follows:

Petty Cash Ticket No.	Item	Account Debited	Amount
1	Delivery of pledge cards to donors	Delivery Expense	$ 22.19
2	Mail package	Postage Expense	52.80
3	Newsletter	Supplies Expense	134.14
4	Key to closet	Miscellaneous Expense	2.85
5	Wastebasket	Miscellaneous Expense	13.78
6	Computer diskettes	Supplies Expense	85.37

REQUIRED

1. Make the general journal entries that first would create the petty cash fund and then would show its replenishment. Include explanations.
2. Describe the items in the fund immediately before replenishment.
3. Describe the items in the fund immediately after replenishment.

Preparing a cash budget
(Obj. 6)

E7-13 Suppose Sprint Corporation, the long-distance telephone company, is preparing its cash budget for 19X4. The company ended 19X3 with $126 million, and top management foresees the need for a cash balance of at least $125 million to pay all bills as they come due in 19X4.

Collections from customers are expected to total $11,813 million during 19X4, and payments for the cost of services and products should reach $6,166 million. Operating expense payments are budgeted at $2,744 million.

During 19X4, Sprint expects to invest $1,826 million in new equipment, $275 million in the company's cellular division, and to sell older assets for $116 million. Debt payments scheduled for 19X4 will total $597 million. The company forecasts net income of $890 million for 19X4 and plans to pay $338 million to its owners.

REQUIRED

Prepare Sprint's cash budget for 19X4. Will the budgeted level of cash receipts leave Sprint with the desired ending cash balance of $125 million, or will the company need additional financing?

Evaluating the ethics of conduct by government legislators
(Obj. 7)

E7-14 Approximately 300 current and former members of the U.S. House of Representatives—on a regular basis—wrote $250,000 of checks without having the cash in their accounts. Later investigations revealed that no public funds were involved. The House bank was a free-standing institution that recirculated House members' cash. In effect, the delinquent check writers were borrowing money from each other on an interest-free, no-service-charge basis. Nevertheless, the House closed its bank after the events became public.

REQUIRED

Suppose you are a new congressional representative from your state. Apply the decision guidelines for ethical judgments outlined in the Decision Guidelines feature on pages 313–314 to decide whether you would write NSF checks on a regular basis through the House bank.

CHALLENGE EXERCISE

Preparing and using a cash budget
(Obj. 6)

E7-15 Among its many products, International Paper Company makes paper for J.C. Penney shopping bags, the labels on Del Monte canned foods, and *Redbook* magazine. Marianne Parrs, the Chief Financial Officer, is responsible for International Paper's cash budget for 19X5. The budget will help Parrs determine the amount of long-term borrowing needed to end the year with a cash balance of $300 million. Parrs' assistants have assembled budget data for 19X5, which the computer printed in alphabetical order. Not all of the following data items are used in preparing the cash budget.

Receipts Are Positive Amounts, Disbursements In Parentheses	(In millions)
Acquisition of other companies	$ (1,168)
Actual cash balance, December 31, 19X4	270
Borrowing	?
Budgeted total assets before borrowing	23,977
Budgeted total current assets before borrowing	5,873
Budgeted total current liabilities before borrowing	4,863
Budgeted total liabilities before borrowing	16,180
Budgeted total stockholders' equity before borrowing	7,797
Collections from customers	19,467
Payments to owners	(237)
Investments by owners	516
Net income	1,153
Other cash receipts	111
Payment of long-term and short-term debt	(950)
Payment of operating expenses	(2,349)
Purchases of inventory	(14,345)
Purchase of property and equipment	(1,518)

REQUIRED

Link Back to Chapter 4 (Current Ratio and Debt Ratio).

1. Prepare the cash budget to determine the amount of borrowing International Paper needs during 19X5.
2. Compute International Paper's expected current ratio and debt ratio at December 31, 19X5, both before and after borrowing on long-term debt. Assume you are the chief loan officer at a bank. Based on these figures, and on the budgeted levels of assets and liabilities, would you lend the requested amount to International Paper? Give the reason for your decision.

Beyond the Numbers

Correcting an internal control weakness **(*Obj. 1, 5*)**

BN7-1 This case is based on a situation experienced by one of the authors. Alpha Construction Company, headquartered in Chattanooga, Tennessee, built a Roadway Inn Motel in Cleveland, 35 miles east of Chattanooga. The construction foreman, whose name was Slim, moved into Cleveland in March to hire the 40 workers needed to complete the project. Slim hired the construction workers, had them fill out the necessary tax forms, and sent the employment documents to the home office, which opened a payroll file for each employee.

Work on the motel began on April 1 and ended September 1. Each Thursday evening, Slim filled out a time card that listed the hours worked by each employee during the five-day work week ended at 5 P.M. on Thursday. Slim faxed the time sheets to the home office, which prepared the payroll checks on Friday morning. Slim drove to the home office after lunch on Friday, picked up the payroll checks, and returned to the construction site. At 5 P.M. on Friday, Slim distributed the payroll checks to the workers.

a. Describe in detail the internal control weakness in this situation. Specify what negative result(s) could occur because of the internal control weakness.

b. Describe what you would do to correct the internal control weakness.

Internal control over cash disbursements, ethical considerations **(*Obj. 5, 7*)**

BN7-2 Tracie Kenan, the owner of Tracie's Dress Shop, has delegated management of the business to Meg Grayson, a friend. Kenan drops by the business to meet customers and checks up on cash receipts, but Grayson buys the merchandise and handles cash disbursements. Business has been brisk lately, and cash receipts have kept pace with the apparent level of sales. However, for a year or so, the amount of cash on hand has been too low. When asked about this, Grayson explains that designers are charging more for dresses than in the past. During the past year, Grayson has taken two expensive vacations, and Kenan wonders how Grayson could afford these trips on her $35,000 annual salary and commissions.

REQUIRED

List at least three ways Grayson could be defrauding Kenan's business of cash. In each instance, also identify how Kenan can determine whether Grayson's actions are ethical. Limit your answers to the dress shop's cash disbursements. The business pays all suppliers by check (no EFTs).

ETHICAL ISSUE

Julie Fraser owns apartment buildings in Michigan and Ohio. Each property has a manager who collects rent, arranges for repairs, and runs advertisements in the local newspaper. The property managers transfer cash to Fraser monthly and prepare their own bank reconciliations. The manager in Detroit has been stealing large sums of money. To cover the theft, he understates the amount of the outstanding checks on the monthly bank reconciliation. As a result, each monthly bank reconciliation appears to balance. However, the balance sheet reports more cash than Fraser actually has in the bank. In negotiating the sale of the Detroit property, Fraser is showing the balance sheet to prospective investors.

REQUIRED

1. Identify two parties other than Fraser who can be harmed by this theft. In what ways can they be harmed?
2. Discuss the role accounting plays in this situation.

Problems (GROUP A)

Identifying the characteristics of an effective internal control system **(*Obj. 1, 2*)**

P7-1A Century One Real Estate Development Company prospered during the lengthy economic expansion of the 1980s. Business was so good that the company used very few internal controls. The decline in the local real estate market in the early 1990s, however, caused Century One to experience a shortage of cash. Dave Campbell, the company owner, is looking for ways to save money.

REQUIRED

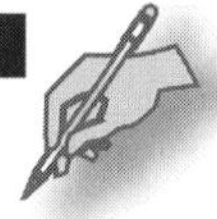

As a consultant for the company, write a memo to convince Campbell of the company's need for a system of internal control. Be specific in telling him how an internal control system could save the company money. Include the definition of internal control, and briefly discuss each characteristic of an effective internal control system, beginning with competent, reliable, and ethical personnel.

Correcting internal control weaknesses **(*Obj. 2, 4, 5*)**

P7-2A Each of the following situations has an internal control weakness.

a. In evaluating the internal control over cash disbursements, an auditor learns that the purchasing agent is responsible for purchasing diamonds for use in the company's manufacturing process, approving the invoices for payment, and signing the checks. No supervisor reviews the purchasing agent's work.

b. Todd Wagoner owns a firm that performs engineering services. His staff consists of 12 professional engineers, and he manages the office. Often, his work requires him to travel to meet with clients. During the past six months, he has observed that when he returns from a business trip, the engineering jobs in the office have not progressed satisfactorily. He learns that when he is away, several of his senior employees take over office management and neglect their engineering duties. One employee could manage the office.

c. Amy Fariss has been an employee of Griffith's Shoe Store for many years. Because the business is relatively small, Fariss performs all accounting duties, including opening the mail, preparing the bank deposit, and preparing the bank reconciliation.

d. Most large companies have internal audit staffs that continuously evaluate the business's internal control. Part of the auditor's job is to evaluate how efficiently the company is running. For example, is the company purchasing inventory from the least expensive wholesaler? After a particularly bad year, Campbell Design Company eliminates its internal audit department to reduce expenses.

e. CPA firms, law firms, and other professional organizations use paraprofessional employees to perform routine tasks. For example, an accounting paraprofessional might examine documents to assist a CPA in conducting an audit. In the CPA firm of Dunham & Lee, Cecil Dunham, the senior partner, turns over a significant portion of his high-level audit work to his paraprofessional staff.

REQUIRED

1. Identify the missing internal control characteristic in each situation.
2. Identify the business's possible problem.
3. Propose a solution to the problem.

Using the bank reconciliation as a control device
(Obj. 3)

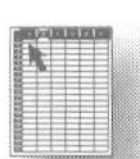

P7-3A The cash receipts and the cash disbursements of Fuddruckers for April 19X4 are as follows:

Cash Receipts (Posting reference is CR)		Cash Disbursements (Posting reference is CD)	
Date	**Cash Debit**	**Check No.**	**Cash Credit**
Apr. 2	$ 4,174	3113	$ 891
8	407	3114	147
10	559	3115	1,930
16	2,187	3116	664
22	1,854	3117	1,472
29	1,060	3118	1,000
30	337	3119	632
Total	$10,578	3120	1,675
		3121	100
		3122	2,413
		Total	$10,924

Assume that the Cash account of Fuddruckers shows the following information at April 30, 19X4:

Cash

Date	Item	Jrnl. Ref.	Debit	Credit	Balance
Apr. 1	Balance				7,911
30		CR. 6	10,578		18,489
30		CD. 11		10,924	7,565

On April 30, 19X4, Fuddruckers received the bank statement shown on the top of the following page. Additional data for the bank reconciliation include the following:

a. The EFT deposit was a receipt of monthly rent. The EFT debit was a monthly insurance payment.
b. The unauthorized-signature check was received from S. M. Holt.
c. The $1,368 bank collection of a note receivable on April 22 included $185 interest revenue.
d. The correct amount of check number 3115, a payment on account, is $1,390. (Fuddruckers's accountant mistakenly recorded the check for $1,930.)

REQUIRED

1. Prepare the Fuddruckers bank reconciliation at April 30, 19X4.
2. Describe how a bank account and the bank reconciliation help the Fuddruckers managers control the business's cash.

BANK STATEMENT FOR APRIL 19X4		
Beginning balance		$ 7,911
Deposits and other Credits:		
Apr. 1	$ 326 EFT	
4	4,174	
9	407	
12	559	
17	2,187	
22	1,368 BC	
23	1,854	10,875
Checks and other Debits		
Apr. 7	$ 891	
13	1,390	
14	903 US	
15	147	
18	664	
21	219 EFT	
26	1,472	
30	1,000	
30	20 SC	(6,706)
Ending balance		$12,080

Explanations: EFT—electronic funds transfer, BC—bank collection, US—unauthorized signature, SC—service charge.

Preparing a bank reconciliation and the related journal entries
(Obj. 3)

P7-4A The August 31 bank statement of Valu-D Company has just arrived from United Bank. To prepare the Valu-D bank reconciliation, you gather the following data:

a. Valu-D's Cash account shows a balance of $4,366.14 on August 31.

b. The bank statement includes two charges for returned checks from customers. One is a $395.00 check received from Shoreline Express and deposited on August 20, returned by Shoreline's bank with the imprint "Unauthorized Signature." The other is an NSF check in the amount of $146.67 received from Lipsey, Inc. This check was deposited on August 17.

c. Valu-D pays rent ($750) and insurance ($290) each month by EFT.

d. The following Valu-D checks are outstanding at August 31:

Check No.	Amount
237	$ 46.10
288	141.00
291	578.05
293	11.87
294	609.51
295	8.88
296	101.63

e. The bank statement includes a deposit of $1,191.17, collected by the bank on behalf of Valu-D. Of the total, $1,011.81 is collection of a note receivable, and the remainder is interest revenue.

f. The bank statement shows that Valu-D earned $38.19 of interest on its bank balance during August. This amount was added to Valu-D's account by the bank.

g. The bank statement lists a $10.50 subtraction for the bank service charge.

h. On August 31, the Valu-D treasurer deposited $316.15, but this deposit does not appear on the bank statement.

i. The bank statement includes a $300.00 deposit that Valu-D did not make. The bank had erroneously credited the Valu-D account for another bank customer's deposit.

j. The August 31 bank balance is $5,484.22.

REQUIRED

1. Prepare the bank reconciliation for Valu-D Company at August 31.
2. Record the entries necessary to bring the book balance of Cash into agreement with the adjusted book balance on the reconciliation. Include an explanation for each entry.

Identifying internal control weakness in cash receipts
(Obj. 4)

P7-5A VisiCalc, Inc., makes all sales of its spreadsheet software on credit. Cash receipts arrive by mail, usually within 30 days of the sale. Lynn Tatum opens envelopes and separates the checks from the accompanying remittance advices. Tatum forwards the checks to another employee, who makes the daily bank deposit but has no access to the accounting records. Tatum sends the remittance advices, which show the amount of cash received, to the accounting department for entry in the accounts. Tatum's only other duty is to grant sales allowances to customers. (Recall that a *sales allowance* decreases the amount that the customer must pay.) When she receives a customer check for less than the full amount of the invoice, she records the sales allowance and forwards the document to the accounting department.

REQUIRED

You are a new employee of VisiCalc, Inc. Write a memo to the company president identifying the internal control weakness in this situation. State how to correct the weakness.

Accounting for petty cash transactions **(Obj. 5)**

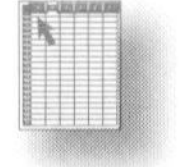

P7-6A Suppose that on June 1, Kahn Audio-Video opens a district office in Nashville and creates a petty cash fund with an imprest balance of $400. During June, Mel McHugh, the fund custodian, signs the following petty cash tickets:

Petty Cash Ticket Number	Item	Amount
1	Postage for package received	$ 18.40
2	Decorations and refreshments for office party	13.19
3	Two boxes of floppy disks	20.82
4	Typewriter ribbons	27.13
5	Dinner money for sales manager entertaining a customer	50.00
6	Plane ticket for executive business trip to Memphis	169.00
7	Delivery of package across town	6.30

On June 30, prior to replenishment, the fund contains these tickets plus cash of $91.51. The accounts affected by petty cash disbursements are Office Supplies Expense, Travel Expense, Delivery Expense, Entertainment Expense, and Postage Expense.

REQUIRED

1. Explain the characteristics and the internal control features of an imprest fund.
2. Make the general journal entries to create the fund and to replenish it. Include explanations. Also, briefly describe what the custodian does on these dates.
3. Make the entry on July 1 to increase the fund balance to $500. Include an explanation, and briefly describe what the custodian does.

Preparing a personal cash budget **(Obj. 6)**

P7-7A Suppose you are preparing your personal cash budget for 1999. During 1999, assume that you can expect to earn $3,000 from your summer job and $1,800 for work in the college cafeteria. Also, your family always gives you gifts totaling around $300 during the year. A scholarship from your home church adds $500 each year while you are in college.

Assume your family pays your college costs except for room and board. Planned expenditures for 1999 include apartment rent of $175 per month for 12 months and annual food costs of $5,000. Gas and other auto expenses usually run about $50 per month. You need to have a little fun, so entertainment will eat up $125 per month.

You need to keep a little cash in reserve for auto repairs and other emergencies, so you maintain a cash reserve of $500 at all times. To start 1999, you have this cash reserve plus $100.

Will you need a loan during 1999? To answer this question, prepare your personal cash budget for the year based on the data given.

Using cash-flow information to prepare a cash budget **(Obj. 6)**

P7-8A Louis Lipschitz, Chief Financial Officer of Toys "Я" Us, Inc., is responsible for the company's budgeting process. Suppose Lipschitz's staff is preparing the company's cash budget for 19X7. A key input to the budgeting process is last year's statement of cash flows, which provides the following data for 19X6. Cash receipts appear as positive amounts; cash disbursements are negative amounts, denoted within parentheses.

TOYS "Я" US, INC.
Cash-Flow Data for 19X6

(In millions)	19X6	(In millions)	19X6
Collections from customers	$9,414	Long-term debt repayments	$ (9)
Interest revenue	17	Investments by owners	16
Purchases of inventory	(6,750)	Payments to owners	(200)
Operating expenses	(2,431)	**Cash and Cash Equivalents**	
Purchases of plant assets	(535)	Beginning of year 19X6	$370
Short-term borrowings	210	End of year 19X6	$203
Long-term borrowings	82		

1. Prepare the Toys "Я" Us cash budget for 19X7. Date the budget simply "19X7" and denote the beginning and ending cash balances as "beginning" and "ending." Round to the nearest million dollars. Assume the company expects 19X7 to be the same as 19X6, but with the following changes:
   a. In 19X7, the company expects a 12% increase in collections from customers and a 10% increase in purchases of inventory.
   b. Lipschitz plans to end the year with a cash balance of $500 million.
2. Based on the cash budget you prepared, how much additional financing does it appear that Toys "Я" Us will need beyond the borrowings already scheduled for 19X7?

REQUIRED

Making an ethical judgment
(Obj. 7)

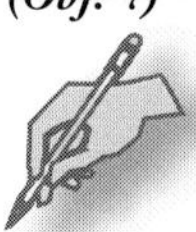

P7-9A Jana Sauer is executive vice president of Global Loan Associates in Baton Rouge, Louisiana. Active in community affairs, Sauer serves on the board of directors of Navpress Publishing Company. Navpress is expanding rapidly and is considering relocating its plant. At a recent meeting, board members decided to try to buy 15 acres of land on the edge of town. The owner of the property is Kyle Lewie, a customer of Global Loan. Lewie is completing a bitter divorce, and Sauer knows that Lewie is eager to sell his property. In view of Lewie's difficult situation, Sauer believes he would accept almost any offer for the land. Realtors have appraised the property at $5 million.

REQUIRED

Apply the ethical judgment framework outlined in the Decision Guidelines feature (pages 313–314) to help Sauer decide what her role should be in Navpress's attempt to buy the land from Lewie.

Problems (GROUP B)

Identifying the characteristics of an effective internal control system
(Obj. 1, 2)

REQUIRED

P7-1B An employee of Mirage Oil Company recently stole thousands of dollars of the company's cash. The company has decided to install a new system of internal controls.

As a consultant for Mirage Oil Company, write a memo to the president explaining how a separation of duties helps to safeguard assets.

Identifying internal control weaknesses
(Obj. 2, 4, 5)

P7-2B Each of the following situations has an internal control weakness.

a. Luann Sorelle employs three professional interior designers in her design studio. She is located in an area with a lot of new construction, and her business is booming. Ordinarily, Sorelle does all the purchasing of draperies, fabrics, and labor needed to complete jobs. During the summer, she takes a long vacation, and in her absence she allows each designer to purchase materials and labor. On her return, Sorelle observes that expenses are much higher and net income much lower than in the past.
b. Discount stores such as Target and Sam's receive a large portion of their sales revenue in cash, with the remainder in credit-card sales. To reduce expenses, a store manager ceases purchasing fidelity bonds on the cashiers.
c. The office supply company from which Champs Sporting Goods purchases cash receipt forms recently notified Champs that the last shipped receipts were not prenumbered. Alex Champion, the owner, replied that he did not use the receipt numbers, so the omission is not important.
d. Flowers Computer Programs is a software company that specializes in programs with accounting applications. The company's most popular program prepares the journal, accounts receivable subsidiary ledger, and general ledger. In the company's early days, the owner and eight employees wrote the computer programs, sold the products to stores such as ComputerLand and ComputerCraft, and performed the general management and accounting of the company. As the company has grown, the number of employees has increased dramatically. Recently, the development of a new software program stopped while the programmers redesigned Flowers's accounting system. Flowers's accountants could have performed this task.
e. Lydia Pink, a widow with no known sources of outside income, has been a trusted employee of Stone Products Company for 15 years. She performs all cash-handling and accounting duties, including opening the mail, preparing the bank deposit, accounting for all aspects of cash and accounts receivable, and preparing the bank reconciliation. She has just purchased a new Lexus and a new home in an expensive suburb. Grant Chavez, the owner of the company, wonders how she can afford these luxuries on her salary.

REQUIRED

1. Identify the missing internal control characteristics in each situation.
2. Identify the business's possible problem.
3. Propose a solution to the problem.

Using the bank reconciliation as a control device
(Obj. 3)

P7-3B The cash receipts and the cash disbursements of Xircom Resources for March 19X5 are as follows:

Cash Receipts (Posting reference is CR)		**Cash Disbursements (Posting reference is CD)**	
Date	**Cash Debit**	**Check No.**	**Cash Credit**
Mar. 4	$2,716	1413	$ 1,465
9	544	1414	1,004
11	1,655	1415	450
14	896	1416	8
17	367	1417	775
25	890	1418	88
31	2,038	1419	4,126
Total	$9,106	1420	970
		1421	200
		1422	2,267
		Total	$11,353

The Cash account of Xircom Resources shows the following information on March 31, 19X5:

Cash

Date	Item	Jrnl. Ref.	Debit	Credit	Balance
Mar. 1	Balance				15,188
31		CR. 10	9,106		24,294
31		CD. 16		11,353	12,941

On March 31, 19X5, Xircom Resources received this bank statement:

BANK STATEMENT FOR MARCH 19X5

Beginning balance		$15,188
Deposits and other Credits:		
Mar. 1	$ 625 EFT	
5	2,716	
10	544	
11	1,655	
15	896	
18	367	
25	890	
31	1,000 BC	8,693
Checks and other Debits:		
Mar. 8	$ 441 NSF	
9	1,465	
13	1,004	
14	450	
15	8	
19	340 EFT	
22	775	
29	88	
31	4,216	
31	25 SC	(8,812)
Ending balance		$15,069

Explanations: BC—bank collection, EFT—electronic funds transfer, NSF—nonsufficient funds check, SC—service charge.

Additional data for the bank reconciliation:

a. The EFT deposit was a receipt of monthly rent. The EFT debit was payment of monthly insurance.

b. The NSF check was received late in February from Jay Andrews.

c. The $1,000 bank collection of a note receivable on March 31 included $122 interest revenue.

d. The correct amount of check number 1419, a payment on account, is $4,216. (The Xircom Resources accountant mistakenly recorded the check for $4,126.)

REQUIRED

1. Prepare the bank reconciliation of Xircom Resources at March 31, 19X5.
2. Describe how a bank account and the bank reconciliation help Xircom managers control the business's cash.

Preparing a bank reconciliation and the related journal entries
(Obj. 3)

P7-4B The May 31 bank statement of Merrill College has just arrived from Central Bank. To prepare the Merrill bank reconciliation, you gather the following data.

a. The May 31 bank balance is $19,530.82.

b. The bank statement includes two charges for returned checks from customers. One is an NSF check in the amount of $67.50 received from Harley Doherty, a student, recorded on the books by a debit to Cash, and deposited on May 19. The other is a $195.03 check received from Maria Shell and deposited on May 21. It was returned by Shell's bank with the imprint "Unauthorized Signature."

c. The following Merrill checks are outstanding at May 31:

Check No.	Amount
616	$403.00
802	74.25
806	36.60
809	161.38
810	229.05
811	48.91

d. A few students pay monthly fees by EFT. The May bank statement lists a $200 deposit for student fees.

e. The bank statement includes two special deposits: $899.14, which is the amount of dividend revenue the bank collected from General Electric Company on behalf of Merrill, and $16.86, the interest revenue the college earned on its bank balance during May.

f. The bank statement lists a $6.25 subtraction for the bank service charge.

g. On May 31, the Merrill treasurer deposited $381.14, but this deposit does not appear on the bank statement.

h. The bank statement includes a $410.00 deduction for a check drawn by Marimont Freight Company. Merrill promptly notified the bank of its error.

i. Merrill's Cash account shows a balance of $18,521.55 on May 31.

REQUIRED

1. Prepare the bank reconciliation for Merrill College at May 31.
2. Record the entries necessary to bring the book balance of Cash into agreement with the adjusted book balance on the reconciliation. Include an explanation for each entry.

Identifying internal control weakness in cash receipts
(Obj. 4)

P7-5B Long Island Lighting makes all sales on credit. Cash receipts arrive by mail, usually within 30 days of the sale. Brad Copeland opens envelopes and separates the checks from the accompanying remittance advices. Copeland forwards the checks to another employee, who makes the daily bank deposit but has no access to the accounting records. Copeland sends the remittance advices, which show the amount of cash received, to the accounting department for entry in the accounts. Copeland's only other duty is to grant sales allowances to customers. (Recall that a *sales allowance* decreases the amount that the customer must pay.) When he receives a customer check for less than the full amount of the invoice, he records the sales allowance and forwards the document to the accounting department.

REQUIRED

You are a new employee of Long Island Lighting. Write a memo to the company president identifying the internal control weakness in this situation. State how to correct the weakness.

Accounting for petty cash transactions
(Obj. 5)

P7-6B Suppose that on April 1, Compak Computers creates a petty cash fund with an imprest balance of $500. During April, Melanie Ford, the fund custodian, signs the following petty cash tickets:

Petty Cash Ticket Number	Item	Amount
101	Office supplies	$86.89
102	Cab fare for executive	25.00
103	Delivery of package across town	37.75
104	Dinner money for sales manager entertaining a customer	80.00
105	Inventory	85.70
106	Decorations for office party	19.22
107	Six boxes of floppy disks	44.37

On April 30, prior to replenishment, the fund contains these tickets plus $113.66. The accounts affected by petty cash disbursements are Office Supplies Expense, Travel Expense, Delivery Expense, Entertainment Expense, and Freight in.

REQUIRED

1. Explain the characteristics and the internal control features of an imprest fund.
2. Make the general journal entries to create the fund and to replenish it. Include explanations. Also, briefly describe what the custodian does on these dates.

Preparing a personal cash budget
(Obj. 6)

P7-7B Suppose you are preparing your personal cash budget for the year 2000. During 2000, assume that you can expect to earn $3,600 from your summer job and $1,200 for work in the college cafeteria. Also, your family always gives you gifts totaling around $800 during the year. A scholarship from your home church adds $1,000 each year while you are in college.

Assume your family pays your college costs except for room and board. Planned expenditures for 2000 include apartment rent of $150 per month for 12 months and annual food costs of $4,800. Gas and other auto expenses usually run about $50 per month. You need to have a little fun, so entertainment will eat up $100 per month.

You need to keep a little cash in reserve for auto repairs and other emergencies, so you maintain a cash reserve of $300 at all times. To start 2000, you have this cash reserve plus $200.

Will you need a loan during 2000? To answer this question, prepare your personal cash budget for the year based on the data given.

Using cash-flow information to prepare a cash budget
(Obj. 6)

P7-8B Louis Lipschitz, Chief Financial Officer of Toys "Я" Us, Inc., is responsible for the company's budgeting process. Suppose Lipschitz's staff is preparing the Toys "Я" Us cash budget for 19X9. A key input to the budgeting process is last year's statement of cash flows, which provides the following data for 19X8. Cash receipts appear as positive amounts; cash disbursements are negative amounts, denoted within parentheses.

TOYS "Я" US, INC.
Cash-Flow Data for 19X8

(In millions)	19X8
Collections from customers	$8,089
Interest revenue	24
Purchases of inventory	(5,597)
Operating expenses	(1,859)
Purchases of plant assets	(614)
Short-term borrowings	119
Long-term borrowings	41
Long-term debt repayments	(1)
Investments by owners	30
Payments to owners	(183)
Cash and Cash Equivalents	
Beginning of year 19X8	$ 764
End of year 19X8	$ 792

REQUIRED

1. Prepare the Toys "Я" Us cash budget for 19X9. Date the budget simply "19X9" and denote the beginning and ending cash balances as "beginning" and "ending." Round to the nearest million dollars. Assume the company expects 19X9 to be similar to 19X8, but with the following changes:
   a. In 19X9, the company expects a 10% increase in collections from customers and an 8% increase in purchases of inventory.
   b. Lipschitz plans to end the year with a cash balance of $500 million.
2. Based on the cash budget you prepared, how much additional cash does it appear that Toys "Я" Us will have available for additional investments during 19X9?

Making an ethical judgment
(Obj. 7)

P7-9B Tri State Bank in Cairo, Illinois, has a loan receivable from Magellan Manufacturing Company. Magellan is six months late in making payments to the bank, and Lane Kidwell, a Tri State vice president, is assisting Magellan to restructure its debt. With unlimited access to Magellan's records, Kidwell learns that the company is depending on landing a manufacturing contract from Loew's Brothers, another Tri State Bank client. Kidwell also serves as Loew's loan officer at the bank. In this capacity, he is aware that Loew's is considering declaring bankruptcy. No one else outside Loew's Brothers knows this. Kidwell has been a great help to Magellan Manufacturing, and Magellan's owner is counting on his expertise in loan workouts to carry the company through this difficult process. To help the bank collect on this large loan, Kidwell has a strong motivation to help Magellan survive.

REQUIRED

Apply the ethical judgment framework outlined in the chapter to help Lane Kidwell plan his next action.

Applying Your Knowledge

DECISION CASE

Using the bank reconciliation to detect a theft
(Obj. 3)

First Union Company has poor internal control over its cash transactions. Recently Penelope Gann, the owner, has suspected Bert Bell, the cashier, of stealing. Here are some details of the business's cash position at September 30.

a. The Cash account shows a balance of $19,702. This amount includes a September 30 deposit of $3,794 that does not appear on the September 30 bank statement.

b. The September 30 bank statement shows a balance of $16,624. The bank statement lists a $200 credit for a bank collection, an $8 debit for the service charge, and a $36 debit for an NSF check. The First Union accountant has not recorded any of these items on the books.

c. At September 30, the following checks are outstanding:

Check No.	Amount
154	$116
256	150
278	353
291	190
292	206
293	145

d. The cashier handles all incoming cash and makes bank deposits. He also reconciles the monthly bank statement. Here is his September 30 reconciliation:

Balance per books, September 30..........		$19,702
Add: Outstanding checks		560
Bank collection		200
		20,462
Less: Deposits in transit........................	$3,794	
Service charge	8	
NSF check..................................	36	3,838
Balance per bank, September 30...........		$16,624

Gann has requested that you determine whether the cashier has stolen cash from the business and, if so, how much. She also asks you to identify how the cashier has attempted to conceal the theft. To make this determination, perform your own bank reconciliation using the format illustrated in the chapter. There are no bank or book errors. Gann also asks you to evaluate the internal controls and to recommend any changes needed to improve them.

FINANCIAL STATEMENT CASES

Internal controls and cash
(Obj. 1, 3)

CASE 1. Study the NIKE responsibility statement (labeled FINANCIAL REPORTING) and the audit opinion (labeled REPORT OF INDEPENDENT ACCOUNTANTS) of the NIKE, Inc., financial statements given at the end of Appendix A. Answer the following questions about the company's internal controls and cash position.

REQUIRED

1. What is the name of NIKE's outside auditing firm (independent accountants)? What office of this firm signed the audit report? How long after the NIKE year end did the auditors issue their opinion?
2. Who bears primary responsibility for the financial statements? How can you tell?
3. Does it appear that the NIKE internal controls are adequate? How can you tell?
4. What standard of auditing did the outside auditors use in examining the NIKE financial statements? By what accounting standards were the statements evaluated?
5. By how much did the company's cash balance (including cash equivalent) change during fiscal year 1997? The statement of cash flows tells why this change occurred. How much did each type of activity—operating, investing, financing, and other—contribute to this change? Account for the full amount of the change from the preceding year.

Audit opinion, management responsibility, internal controls, and cash
(Obj. 1, 2, 3)

CASE 2. Obtain the annual report of a company of your choosing. Study the audit opinion and the management statement of responsibility (if present) in conjunction with the financial statements. Then answer these questions.

REQUIRED

1. What is the name of the company's outside auditing firm? What office of this firm signed the audit report? How long after the company's year end did the auditors issue their opinion?
2. Who bears primary responsibility for the financial statements? How can you tell?
3. Does it appear that the company's internal controls are adequate? Give your reason.
4. What standard of auditing did the outside auditors use in examining the company's financial statements? By what accounting standards were the statements evaluated?
5. By how much did the company's cash position (including cash equivalents) change during the current year? The statement of cash flows tells why this increase or decrease occurred. Which type of activity—operating, investing, or financing—contributed most to the change in the cash balance?

Team Project

You are promoting a rock concert in your area. Assume each member of your team invests $10,000 of their hard-earned money in this venture. It is April 1, and the concert will be performed on June 30. Your promotional activities begin immediately, and ticket sales start on May 1. You expect to sell all the business's assets, pay all the liabilities, and distribute all remaining cash to the group members by July 31.

REQUIRED

Write an internal control manual that will help to safeguard the assets of the business. The starting point of the manual is to assign responsibilities among the group members. Authorize individuals, including group members and any outsiders that you need to hire, to perform specific jobs. Separate duties among the group and any employees.

APPENDIX to Chapter 7

The Voucher System

The voucher system for recording cash payments improves a business's internal control over cash disbursements by formalizing the process of approving and recording invoices for payment. The voucher system uses (1) vouchers, (2) a voucher register (similar to a purchases journal), (3) an unpaid voucher file, (4) a check register (similar to a cash disbursements journal), and (5) a paid voucher file. The improvement in internal control comes from recording all disbursements through the voucher register. In a voucher system, all expenditures must be approved before payment can be made. This approval takes the form of a voucher. The larger the business, the more likely it is to need strict control over disbursements. The voucher system helps supply this control.

A voucher is a document authorizing a cash disbursement. The accounting department prepares vouchers. Exhibit 7A-1 illustrates the voucher of Bliss Wholesale Company. In addition to places for writing in the *payee*, *due date*, *terms*, *description*, and *invoice amount*, the voucher includes a section for designated officers to sign their approval for payment. The back of the voucher has places for recording the *account debited*, *date paid*, and *check number*. You should locate these nine items in Exhibit 7A-1.

Exhibit 7A-2 lists the various business documents used to ensure that the company receives the goods it ordered and pays only for the goods it has actually received. Exhibit 7A-3 shows how a voucher added to the other documents can provide the evidence for a cash disbursement. The amounts on all these documents should agree.

Front of Voucher

Voucher No. 326

BLISS WHOLESALE COMPANY

Payee Van Heusen, Inc.
Address 4619 Shotwell Avenue
Brooklyn, NY 10564

Due Date March 7
Terms 2/10, n/30

Date	Invoice No.	Description	Amount
Mar. 1	6380	144 men's shirts stock no. X14	$1,764

Approved Jane Trent (Controller) Approved Bob Kraft (Treasurer)

Back of Voucher

Voucher No. 326
Payee Van Heusen, Inc.
Invoice Amount $1,800
Discount 36
Net Amount $1,764

Due Date Mar. 7
Date Paid Mar. 6
Check No. 694

Account Distribution		
Account Debited	**Acct. No.**	**Amount**
Inventory	105	1,800
Store Supplies	145	
Salary Expense	538	
Advertising Expense	542	
Utilities Expense	548	
Delivery Expense	544	
Total		$1,800

EXHIBIT 7A-1
Voucher

EXHIBIT 7A-2
Purchasing Process

Business Document	Prepared by	Sent to
Purchase request	Sales department	Purchasing department
Purchase order	Purchasing department	Outside company that sells the needed merchandise (supplier or vendor)
Invoice	Outside company that sells the needed merchandise (supplier or vendor)	Accounting department
Receiving report	Receiving department	Accounting department
Voucher	Accounting department	Officer who signs the check

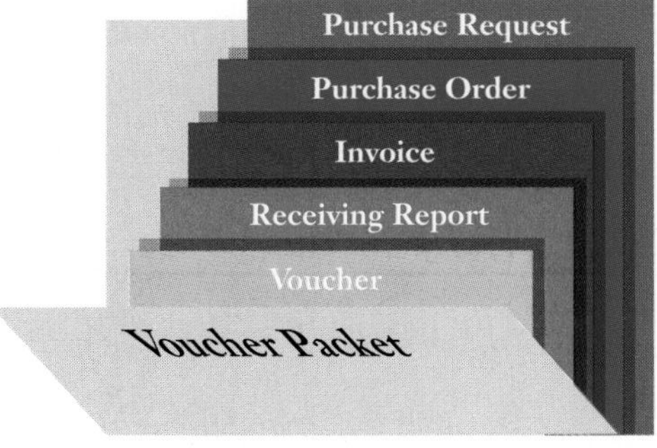

EXHIBIT 7A-3
Voucher Packet

CHAPTER 8

Accounts and Notes Receivable

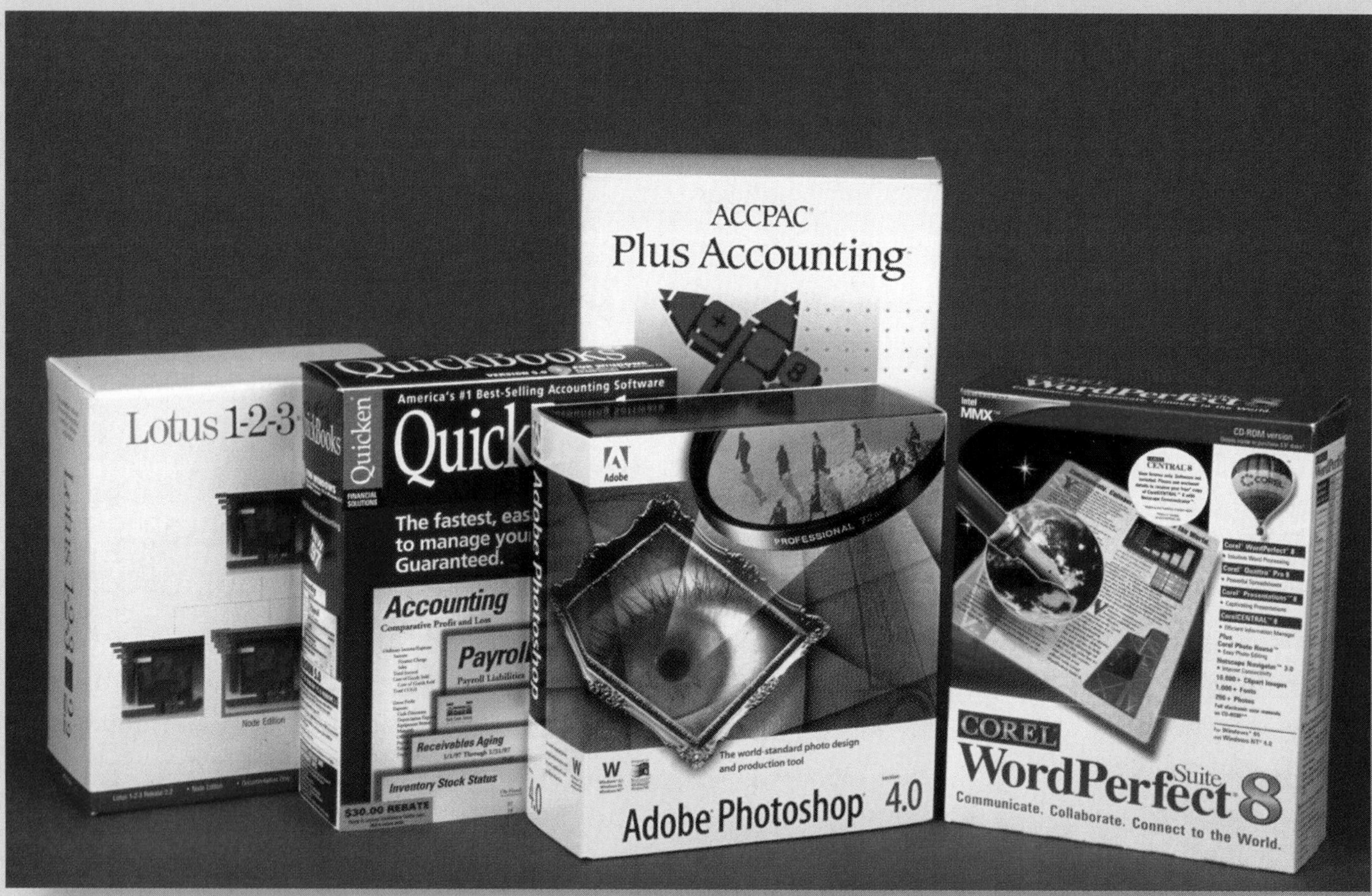

LEARNING OBJECTIVES

After studying this chapter, you should be able to

1. Design internal controls for receivables
2. Use the allowance method to account for uncollectibles and estimate uncollectibles by the percent of sales and aging methods
3. Use the direct write-off method to account for uncollectibles
4. Account for notes receivable
5. Report receivables on the balance sheet
6. Use the acid-test ratio and days' sales in receivables to evaluate a company's financial position
7. Report cash flows from receivables transactions on the statement of cash flows

> "*Time* is *money. The longer a receivable goes unpaid, the more difficult and expensive it is to collect, and the less it is worth. Effective credit and collection policies and procedures improve net income by reducing write-offs of accounts receivable, increasing cash flow, and improving customer relations.*"
>
> JAMES R. BOHMANN, SENIOR VICE PRESIDENT OF CORPORATE DEVELOPMENT, PAYCO AMERICAN CORP. (WORLD'S LARGEST PUBLICLY HELD RECEIVABLE MANAGEMENT FIRM)

Ultimax, Inc., designs computer software packages. The company grew rapidly during the early 1990s. Between 1990 and 1995, sales increased by 93% and net income increased by 16%, but top managers failed to notice the bulging balances in accounts receivable.

When hard times hit Ultimax, managers took a closer look at current assets. They found that the company's receivables had grown 150% from 1990 to 1995. They also found that Ultimax's days' sales in receivables—the average number of days it takes to collect receivables—increased from 124 days to 160 days. The results were a severe cash shortage, and a drain on profits.

Ultimax instituted a new system for managing receivables, including tougher credit and collection policies. These efforts paid off: By 1997, Ultimax had reduced its days' sales in receivables to 98 days.

Like most other assets, accounts receivable can represent good news or bad news: Good news because receivables represent a claim to the customer's cash; bad news when the business fails to collect the cash. In the case of Ultimax, receivables got out of hand, and profits suffered. Why would the company's sales almost double but its net income increase so modestly? Because Ultimax was not managing its receivables very well. Too much of Ultimax's resources were tied up in accounts receivable—an asset that earns no income. Cash was not flowing into the business quickly enough. To develop profitable computer software packages, Ultimax had to borrow money, and the related interest expense was draining profits.

In this chapter, we discuss the role of the credit department in deciding the customers to which the business will sell on account. We explain receivables, including how to account for them when they appear to be uncollectible, and internal control over receivables. We also cover notes receivable and introduce several measures that help a business manage customer accounts, including *days' sales in receivables.*

A receivable arises when a business (or person) sells goods or services to a second business (or person) on credit. A receivable is the seller's claim against the buyer for the amount of the transaction. Each credit transaction involves at least two parties:

Creditor. The party to a credit transaction who sells goods or a service and obtains a receivable.

Debtor. The party to a credit transaction who makes a purchase and has a payable.

- The **creditor** sells goods or a service and obtains a receivable.
- The **debtor** makes the purchase and has a payable.

This chapter focuses on accounting for receivables by the seller (the creditor).

Receivables: An Introduction

The Types of Receivables

Receivables. Monetary claims against a business or individual.

Receivables are monetary claims against businesses and individuals. The two major types of receivables are accounts receivable and notes receivable. A business's *accounts receivable* are the amounts to be collected from its customers. Accounts receivable, which are *current assets,* are sometimes called *trade receivables.*

As we saw in Chapter 6, the Accounts Receivable account in the general ledger serves as a *control account.* It summarizes the total amounts receivable from all customers. Companies also keep a *subsidiary ledger* of accounts receivable with a separate account for each customer, illustrated as follows:

■ Daily Exercise 8-1

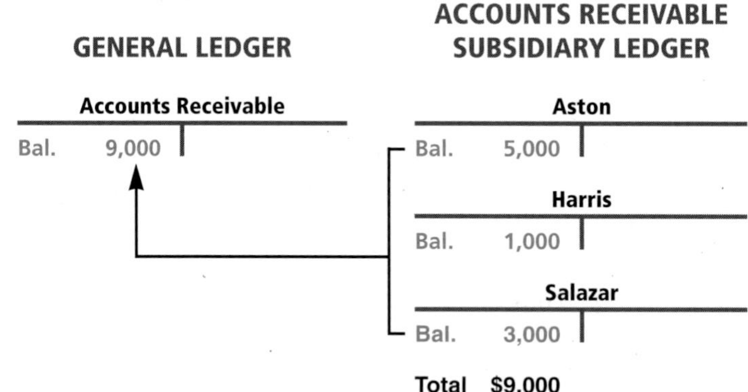

Notes receivable are more formal than accounts receivable. The debtor in a note receivable arrangement promises in writing to pay the creditor a definite sum at a specific future date—the *maturity* date. The terms of these notes usually extend for at least 60 days. A written document known as a *promissory note* serves as evidence of the receivable. The note may require the debtor to pledge *security* for the loan: The borrower promises that the lender may claim certain assets if the borrower fails to pay the amount due at maturity.

Notes receivable due within one year or less are current assets. Those notes due beyond one year are *long-term receivables.* Some notes receivable are collected in periodic installments. The portion due within one year is a current asset, and the remaining amount a long-term asset. General Motors may hold a $6,000 note receivable from you, but only the $1,500 you owe this year is a current asset to GM.

EXAMPLE COMPANY Balance Sheet Date				
Assets			**Liabilities**	
Current:			Current:	
Cash		$X,XXX	Accounts payable	$X,XXX
Accounts receivable	$X,XXX		Notes payable, short-term	X,XXX
Less Allowance for			Accrued current liabilities	X,XXX
uncollectible accounts	(XXX)	X,XXX	Total current liabilities	X,XXX
Notes receivable, short-term		X,XXX		
Inventories		X,XXX		
Prepaid expenses		X,XXX		
Total		X,XXX	Long-term:	
			Notes payable, long-term	X,XXX
Investments and long-term receivables:			Total liabilities	X,XXX
Investments in other companies		X,XXX		
Notes receivable, long-term		X,XXX		
Other receivables		X,XXX		
Total		X,XXX		
Plant assets:			**Owner Equity**	
Property, plant, and equipment		X,XXX	Capital	X,XXX
Total assets		$X,XXX	Total liabilities and owner equity	$X,XXX

EXHIBIT 8-1
Balance Sheet with Receivables Highlighted for Emphasis

Other receivables is a miscellaneous category that includes loans to employees and subsidiary companies. Usually, these are long-term receivables, but they are current assets if receivable within one year or less. Long-term notes receivable and other receivables are often reported on the balance sheet after current assets and before plant assets, as illustrated in Exhibit 8-1. The receivables are highlighted for emphasis.

The Decision Guidelines feature identifies the main issues in controlling, managing, and accounting for receivables. These guidelines serve as a framework for the remainder of the chapter.

Establishing Internal Control over the Collection of Receivables

Objective 1

Design internal controls for receivables

Businesses that sell on credit receive most of their cash receipts by mail. Internal control over collections of cash on account is an important part of the overall internal control system. Chapter 7 detailed control procedures over cash receipts. However, a critical element of internal control deserves emphasis here: the separation of cash-handling and cash-accounting duties. Consider the following case.

> Butler Supply Co. is a family-owned office supply business that takes pride in the loyalty of its workers. Most company employees have been with the Butlers for at least five years. The company makes 90% of its sales on account.
>
> The office staff consists of a bookkeeper and a supervisor. The bookkeeper maintains the general ledger and the accounts receivable subsidiary ledger. He also makes the daily bank deposit. The supervisor prepares monthly financial statements and any special reports the Butlers require. She also takes sales orders from customers and serves as office manager.

Can you identify the internal control weakness here? The bookkeeper has access to the general ledger and the accounts receivable subsidiary ledger, and also has custody of the cash. The bookkeeper could take a customer check and write off the customer's account as uncollectible.[1] Unless the supervisor or some other manager reviews the bookkeeper's work regularly, the theft may go undetected. In small businesses like Butler Supply Co., such a review may not be performed routinely.

[1]The bookkeeper would need to forge the endorsements of the checks and deposit them in a bank account he controls.

DECISION GUIDELINES — Controlling, Managing, and Accounting for Receivables

It is easy to lose sight of the big picture—the main issues—in controlling, managing, and accounting for receivables. Most of this chapter relates to one or more of the following issues.

The main issues in *controlling* and *managing* the collection of receivables, along with a related plan of action, are as follows:

ISSUE	ACTION
Extend credit only to creditworthy customers, the ones most likely to pay us.	Run a credit check on prospective customers.
Separate cash-handling, credit, and accounting duties to keep employees from stealing the cash collected from customers.	Design the internal control system to separate duties.
Pursue collection from customers to maximize cash flow.	Keep a close eye on collections from customers.

The main issues in *accounting* for receivables, and the related plans of action, are as follows:

ISSUE	ACTION
Measure and report receivables on the balance sheet at their *net realizable value,* the amount we expect to collect. This is necessary to report assets accurately.	Estimate the amount of uncollectible receivables. Report receivables at their net realizable value (accounts receivable – allowance for uncollectibles).
Measure and report the expense associated with failure to collect receivables, which we call *uncollectible-account expense,* on the income statement. This helps to report net income at a reasonable amount.	Measure the expense of failing to collect from our customers.

How can this control weakness be corrected? The supervisor could open incoming mail and make the daily bank deposit. The bookkeeper should not be allowed to handle cash. Only the remittance advices would be forwarded to the bookkeeper to indicate which customer accounts to credit. By removing cash-handling duties from the bookkeeper and keeping the accounts receivable subsidiary ledger away from the supervisor, the company would separate duties and strengthen internal control. These actions would reduce an employee's opportunity to steal cash and then cover it up with a false credit to a customer account.

■ Daily Exercise 8-2

Using a bank lock box achieves the same separation of duties. Customers can be instructed to send their payments directly to Butler Supply's bank, which will record the cash receipts and deposit the cash into the company's bank account. The bank then forwards the remittance advices to Butler Supply's bookkeeper, who credits the appropriate customer accounts.

We examined the lock-box system in detail in Chapter 7, page 297.

Managing the Collection of Receivables: The Credit Department

A customer who uses a credit card to acquire goods or services is buying on account. This transaction creates a receivable for the seller. Most companies with a high proportion of sales on account have a separate credit department. This department evaluates customers who apply for credit cards by using standard formulas—which include the applicant's income and credit history, among other factors—for deciding the customers to which the store will sell on account. The extension of credit requires a balancing act. The company wants to avoid losing sales to good customers who demand time to pay. It also wants to avoid losses from selling to deadbeats.

After approving a customer, the credit department monitors customer payment records. Customers with a history of paying on time may receive higher credit limits. Those who fail to pay on time have their limits reduced or eliminated. The goal is to collect from customers quickly enough to keep cash circulating. The credit department also assists the accounting department in measuring collection losses on customers who do not pay.

For good internal control over cash collections of receivables, it is critical that the credit department have no access to cash. For example, if a credit employee handles cash, he can pocket the money received from a customer. He can then label the customer's account as uncollectible, and the accounting department writes off the account receivable; as discussed in the next section. The company stops billing the customer, and the credit employee has covered up the embezzlement. If the customer places another order with the company, the credit employee can reinstate the account and repeat the cycle of theft.

■ Daily Exercise 8-3

Accounting for Uncollectible Accounts (Bad Debts): The Allowance Method

Selling on credit creates both a benefit and a cost.

- *The benefit:* Customers who are unwilling or unable to pay cash immediately may make a purchase on credit, and company revenues and profits rise as sales increase.
- *The cost:* The company will be unable to collect from some of its credit customers. Accountants label this cost **uncollectible-account expense, doubtful-account expense,** or **bad-debt expense.**

Uncollectible-Account Expense. Cost to the seller of extending credit. Arises from the failure to collect from credit customers. Also called **doubtful-account expense,** or **bad-debt expense.**

The extent of uncollectible-account expense varies from company to company. In certain businesses, a six-month-old receivable of $1 is worth only 67 cents, and a five-year-old receivable of $1 is worth only 4 cents. Uncollectible-account expense depends on the credit risks the business is willing to accept. At Albany Ladder, a $23 million construction-equipment and supply firm headquartered in Albany, New York, 85% of company sales are on account. Albany's receivables grow in proportion to sales. Bad debts cost Albany Ladder about $100,000 a year, or about 1 to 1½% of total sales. Albany undertakes careful credit screening and rigorous collection activity. It takes Albany Ladder an average of 70 days to collect its receivables.

"Bad debts cost Albany Ladder about $100,000 a year, or about 1 to 1½% of total sales."

Many small retail businesses appear to accept more risk than large stores such as Sears, J.C. Penney, and Macy's. Why? Extending credit increases sales. Moreover, small businesses often have personal ties to customers, who are more likely to pay their accounts when they know the proprietor personally.

For a firm that sells on credit, uncollectible-account expense is as much a part of doing business as salary expense and utilities expense. Uncollectible-Account Expense—an operating expense—must be measured, recorded, and reported. To do so, accountants use the allowance method or, in certain limited cases, the direct write-off method (which we discuss on page 344).

THE ALLOWANCE METHOD To present the most accurate financial statements possible, accountants in firms with large credit sales use the **allowance method** to measure bad debts. This method records collection losses on the basis of estimates instead of waiting to see which customers the business will not collect from.

Allowance Method. A method of recording collection losses on the basis of estimates, instead of waiting to see which customers the company will not collect from.

Smart owners and managers know that not every customer will pay in full. But at the time of sale, managers do not know which customers will not pay. If they did, they wouldn't sell on credit to those customers!

Rather than try to guess which accounts will go bad, managers estimate the total bad-debt expense for the period on the basis of the company's collection experience. The business records Uncollectible-Account Expense for the estimated amount and sets up **Allowance for Uncollectible Accounts** (or **Allowance for Doubtful Accounts**), a contra account related to Accounts Receivable. This allowance account shows the amount of the receivables that the business expects *not* to collect.

Allowance for Uncollectible Accounts. A contra account, related to accounts receivable, that holds the estimated amount of collection losses. Also called **Allowance for Doubtful Accounts.**

Subtracting the uncollectible allowance amount from Accounts Receivable yields the net amount that the company does expect to collect, as shown here (using assumed numbers):

Balance sheet (partial):	
Accounts receivable	$10,000
Less Allowance for uncollectible accounts	(900)
Accounts receivable, net	$ 9,100

Customers owe this company $10,000, of which the business expects to collect $9,100. The company estimates that it will not collect $900 of its accounts receivable.

Another way to report these receivables follows the pattern used by Ultimax, Inc., Intel Corporation, and other companies, as follows:

Accounts receivable, net of allowance of $900	$9,100

■ Daily Exercise 8-4

The income statement reports Uncollectible-Account Expense among the operating expenses, as follows (using assumed figures):

Income statement (partial):	
Expenses:	
Uncollectible-account expense	$2,000

Estimating Uncollectibles

Objective 2

Use the allowance method to account for uncollectibles and estimate uncollectibles by the percent of sales and aging methods

The more accurate the estimate of uncollectible accounts, the more reliable the information in the financial statements. How are bad-debt estimates made? The most logical way to estimate uncollectibles is to examine the business's past records. There are two basic ways to estimate uncollectibles:

- *Percentage of sales method*
- *Aging of accounts receivable method*

Both approaches work under the allowance method.

Percent of Sales Method. A method of estimating uncollectible receivables that calculates uncollectible-account expense. Also called the **income statement approach.**

PERCENT OF SALES The **percent of sales method** computes uncollectible-account expense as a percentage of net credit sales. This method is also called the **income statement approach** because it focuses on the amount of expense to be reported on the income statement. Uncollectible-account expense is recorded as an adjusting entry at the end of the period. Assume it is December 31, 19X3 and the accounts have these balances *before the year-end adjustments:*

Accounts Receivable	
120,000	

Allowance for Uncollectible Accounts	
	500

Customers owe the business $120,000, and the Allowance for Uncollectible Accounts is too low. The $500 balance in the Allowance account is left over from the preceding period. Prior to any adjustments, the net receivable amount is $119,500 ($120,000 – $500), which is more than the business expects to collect from customers.

Based on prior experience, the credit department estimates that uncollectible-account expense is 1.5% of net credit sales, which were $500,000 for 19X3. The adjusting entry to record uncollectible-account expense for the year and to update the allowance is

19X3			
Dec. 31	Uncollectible-Account Expense ($500,000 × 0.015)	7,500	
	Allowance for Uncollectible Accounts		7,500
	Recorded expense for the year.		

The accounting equation shows that the transaction to record the expense decreases the business's assets by the amount of the expense:

Assets	=	Liabilities	+	Owner's Equity	−	Expenses
−7,500	=	0			−	7,500

Now the accounts are ready for reporting in the 19X3 financial statements.

Accounts Receivable		Allowance for Uncollectible Accounts	
120,000			500
			7,500
			8,000

■ Daily Exercise 8-5

Customers still owe the business $120,000, but now the allowance for uncollectible account is realistic. The balance sheet will report accounts receivable at the net amount of $112,000 ($120,000 – $8,000). The income statement will report the period's uncollectible-account expense of $7,500, along with the other operating expenses for the period.

AGING OF ACCOUNTS RECEIVABLE The second popular method for estimating uncollectible accounts is **aging of accounts receivable.** This method is also called the **balance-sheet approach** because it focuses on accounts receivable. In the aging method, individual accounts receivable from specific customers are analyzed according to the length of time they have been receivable from the customer.

Aging of Accounts Receivable. A way to estimate bad debts by analyzing individual accounts receivable according to the length of time they have been receivable from the customer. Also called **balance-sheet approach.**

Computerized accounting packages prepare a report for aging accounts receivable. The computer accesses customer data and sorts accounts by customer number and by date of invoice. For example, the credit department of Schmidt Builders Supply groups its accounts receivable into 30-day periods, as Exhibit 8-2 shows.

Schmidt's total balance of accounts receivable is $112,000. Of this amount, the aging schedule indicates that the company will *not* collect $3,769. The allowance for uncollectible accounts is not up-to-date. Schmidt's accounts appear as follows *before the year-end adjustment*:

Accounts Receivable		Allowance for Uncollectible Accounts	
112,000			1,100

The aging method is designed to bring the balance of the allowance account to the needed amount ($3,769) determined by the aging schedule in Exhibit 8-2 (see the lower right corner for the final result).

EXHIBIT 8-2
Aging the Accounts Receivable of Schmidt Builders Supply

	Age of Account								
Customer Name	1–30 Days		31–60 Days		61–90 Days		Over 90 Days		Total Balance
T-Bar-M Co.	$20,000								$ 20,000
Chicago Pneumatic Parts	10,000								10,000
Sarasota Pipe Corp.			$13,000		$10,000				23,000
Oneida, Inc.					3,000		$1,000		4,000
Other accounts*	39,000		12,000		2,000		2,000		55,000
Totals	$69,000		$25,000		$15,000		$3,000		$112,000
Estimated percent uncollectible	× 0.1%		× 1%		× 5%		× 90%		
Allowance for Uncollectible Accounts balance	$69	+	$250	+	$750	+	$2,700	+	$3,769

*Each of the "Other accounts" would appear individually.

To update the allowance, Schmidt makes this adjusting entry at the end of the period:

19X8			
Dec. 31	Uncollectible-Account Expense	2,669	
	Allowance for Uncollectible Accounts ($3,769 – $1,100)		2,669
	Recorded expense for the year.		

Again, the recording of the expense decreases the business's assets by the amount of the expenses. The accounting equation for the expense transaction is

Assets	=	Liabilities	+	Owner's Equity	–	Expenses
–2,669	=	0			–	2,669

Now the balance sheet can report the amount that Schmidt expects to collect from customers, $108,231 ($112,000 – $3,769), as follows:

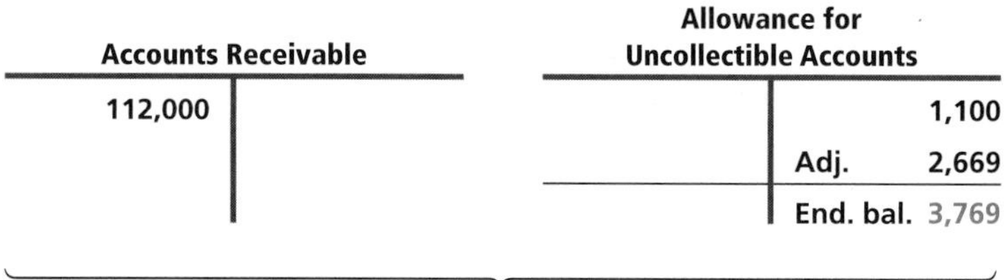

Net accounts receivable, 108,231

As with the percent of sales method, the income statement reports the uncollectible-account expense.

Using the Percent of Sales and the Aging Methods Together

In practice, companies use the percent of sales and the aging of accounts methods together.

- For *interim statements* (monthly or quarterly), companies use the percent of sales method because it is easier to apply. The percent of sales method focuses on the amount of uncollectible-account *expense.* But that is not enough.
- At the end of the year, these companies use the aging method to ensure that Accounts Receivable is reported at *expected realizable value*—that is, the expected amount to be collected. The aging method focuses on the amount of the receivables—the *asset*—that is uncollectible.
- Using the two methods together provides good measures of both the expense and the asset. Exhibit 8-3 summarizes and compares the two methods.

Concept Highlight

EXHIBIT 8-3
Comparing the Percent of Sales and Aging Methods for Estimating Uncollectibles

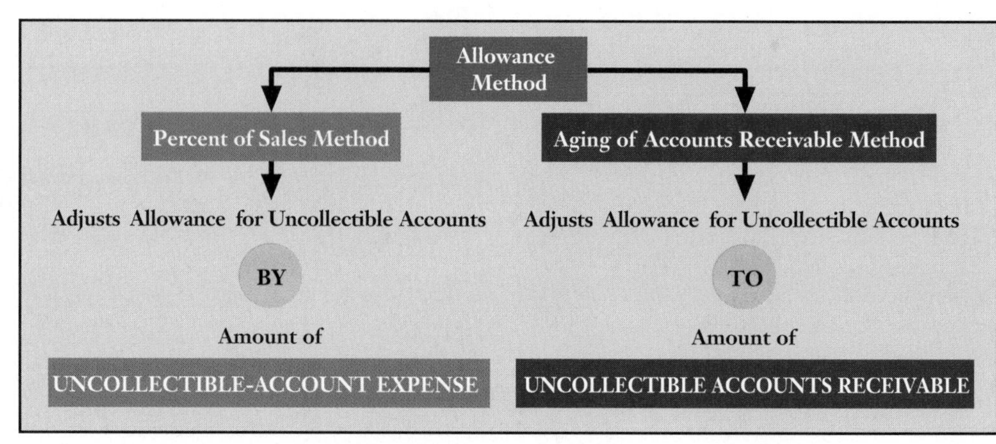

- Daily Exercise 8-8
- Daily Exercise 8-9
- Daily Exercise 8-10

Writing Off Uncollectible Accounts

Early in 19X9, Schmidt Builders Supply collects on most of its $112,000 accounts receivable and records the cash receipts as follows:

19X9			
Jan.–Mar.	Cash	92,000	
	Accounts Receivable		92,000
	Collected on account.		

Cash increases, and Accounts Receivable decreases by the same amount. Total assets are unchanged.

Assets	=	Liabilities	+	Owner's Equity
+92,000 −92,000	=	0	+	0

Suppose Schmidt's credit department determines that Schmidt cannot collect a total of $1,200 from customers Abbott and Smith. Schmidt's accountant then writes off Schmidt's receivables from the two delinquent customers with the following entry:

19X9			
Mar. 31	Allowance for Uncollectible Accounts	1,200	
	Accounts Receivable—Abbott		900
	Accounts Receivable—Smith		300
	Wrote off uncollectible accounts.		

The accounting equation shows that the write-off of uncollectible accounts has no effect on total assets or any other account.

Assets	=	Liabilities	+	Owner's Equity
+1,200 −1,200	=	0	+	0

Because the write-off entry affects no expense account, it *does not affect net income.* The write-off has no effect on net receivables either, as shown for Schmidt Builders Supply in Exhibit 8-4.

Thinking It Over If the write-off of specific uncollectible accounts affects neither an expense account nor the net amount of receivables, then why go to the trouble of writing off the uncollectible accounts of specific customers?

Answer: The business has decided that the uncollectible accounts are worthless. It is appropriate to eliminate these accounts from the accounts receivable records. Getting rid of worthless customer accounts alerts the credit department not to waste time pursuing collections from these customers. The credit department files their names in a database. If they later apply for credit, the credit department will think twice about selling to them on account.

- Daily Exercise 8-6
- Daily Exercise 8-7

Concept Highlight

EXHIBIT 8-4

Net Receivables Before and After the Write-Off of Uncollectible Accounts Are the Same

	Before Write-Off		After Write-Off
Accounts receivable ($112,000 – $92,000)	$20,000	($20,000 – $1,200)	$18,800
Less Allowance for uncollectible accounts	(3,769)	($3,769 – $1,200)	(2,569)
Accounts receivable, net	$16,231	← same →	$16,231

The Direct Write-Off Method

Objective 3

Use the direct write-off method to account for uncollectibles

Direct Write-off Method. A method of accounting for uncollectible receivables, in which the company waits until the credit department decides that a customer's account receivable is uncollectible, and then debits Uncollectible-Account Expense and credits the customer's Account Receivable.

■ Daily Exercise 8-11

■ Daily Exercise 8-12

There is an alternative way to account for uncollectible receivables. This method does *not* use an allowance account. Under the **direct write-off method** of accounting for uncollectible receivables, the company waits until it decides that a customer's account receivable is uncollectible. Then the accountant debits Uncollectible-Account Expense and credits the customer's Account Receivable to write off the account, as follows (using assumed data):

19X9			
Jan. 2	Uncollectible-Account Expense...........	2,000	
	Accounts Receivable—Jones.........		2,000
	Wrote off a bad account.		

This method is defective for two reasons:

1. It does not set up an allowance for uncollectibles. As a result, it always reports the receivables at their full amount, which is more than the business expects to collect. Assets are overstated on the balance sheet.

2. It may not match the uncollectible-account expense of each period against the revenue of the period in which the sale was made. In this example, the company made the sale to Jones in 19X1 and should have recorded the uncollectible-account expense during 19X1 to measure net income properly. By recording the expense in 19X2, the company overstates net income in 19X1 and understates net income in 19X2.

According to the matching principle (Chapter 3, page 95), expenses incurred must be matched against revenue earned during the period. Thus the direct write-off method is acceptable only when the amount of uncollectibles is so low that there is no material difference between bad-debt amounts determined by the allowance method and the direct write-off method.

Recoveries of Uncollectible Accounts

When an account receivable is written off as uncollectible, the receivable does not die. The customer still has an obligation to pay. However, the company ceases its collection effort and writes off the account. Such accounts are filed for use in future credit decisions. Some companies turn them over to an attorney for collection in the hope of recovering part of the receivable. To record a recovery, the accountant (1) reverses the write-off and (2) records the collection as follows (using assumed data):

(1) Accounts Receivable—Rolf................................	1,300	
Allowance for Uncollectible Accounts.........		1,300
Reinstated Rolf's account receivable.		
(2) Cash..	1,300	
Accounts Receivable—Rolf.........................		1,300
Collected on account.		

Credit-Card and Bankcard Sales

Credit-card sales are common in retailing. American Express and Discover are popular credit cards. Customers present credit cards to pay for purchases. The credit-card company then pays the seller the transaction amount and bills the customer, who then pays the credit-card company.

Credit cards offer customers the convenience of buying without having to pay the cash immediately. An American Express customer receives a monthly statement from American Express, detailing each of the customer's credit-card transactions. The customer can then write a single check to cover the entire month's credit-card purchases.

Retailers also benefit from credit-card sales. They do not have to check a customer's credit rating. The company that issued the card has already done so. Retailers do not have to keep an accounts receivable subsidiary ledger account for each customer, and they do not have to collect cash from customers. Further, retailers receive cash more quickly from the credit-card companies than they would from the customers themselves.

Of course, these services to the seller do not come free. The seller receives less than 100% of the face value of the invoice. The credit-card company takes a discount ranging between 1 and 5% on the sale to cover its services. Suppose a friend treats you to lunch at the Russian Tea Room (the seller) and pays the bill—$100—with a Discover card. The seller's entry to record the $100 Discover card sale, subject to the credit-card company's 3% discount, is

Accounts Receivable—Discover	97	
Credit-Card Discount Expense	3	
Sales Revenue		100
Recorded credit-card sales.		

On collection of the discounted value, the seller records the following:

Cash	97	
Accounts Receivable—Discover		97
Collected from Discover.		

Bankcard Sales

Most banks issue their own cards, known as *bankcards*, which operate much like American Express and Discover credit cards. VISA and MasterCard are the two main types of bankcards. However, when a business makes a sale and the customer pays with a VISA card—a bankcard sale—the seller receives cash at the point of the sale. The amount of the cash received is less than the full amount of the sale because the bank deducts its fee. For example, suppose a Shell gas station sells $150 of fuel to a family vacationing in their motor home. The customer pays with a VISA card, and the bank that issued the card charges a 2% fee to Shell. The Shell station records the bankcard sale as follows:

Cash	147	
Credit-Card Discount Expense ($150 × 0.02)	3	
Sales Revenue		150
Recorded a bankcard sale.		

■ Daily Exercise 8-13

Credit Balances in Accounts Receivable

Occasionally, customers overpay their accounts or return merchandise for which they have already paid. The result is a credit balance in the customer's account receivable. For example, Diamond Company's subsidiary ledger contains 213 accounts, with balances as shown:

210 accounts with *debit* balances totaling	$185,000
Less: 3 accounts with *credit* balances totaling	(2,800)
Net total of all balances	$182,200

Diamond Company should *not* report the asset Accounts Receivable at the net amount—$182,200. Why not? The credit balance—the $2,800—is a liability. Like any other liability, customer credit balances are debts. A balance sheet that does not indicate this liability would be misleading. Therefore, Diamond Company would report the following on its balance sheet:

Assets		Liabilities	
Current:		Current:	
Accounts receivable	$185,000	Credit balances in customer accounts receivable	$2,800

CPC International, Inc., is the food-products company that produces Skippy peanut butter, Hellmann's mayonnaise, and Mazola corn oil. The company balance sheet at December 31, 19X7, reported the following:

	Millions
Notes and accounts receivable [total]	$549.9
Allowance for uncollectible accounts	(12.5)

REQUIRED

1. How much of the December 31, 19X7, balance of notes and accounts receivable did CPC expect to collect? Stated differently, what was the expected realizable value of these receivables?
2. Journalize, without explanations, 19X8 entries for CPC International, assuming
   a. Total estimated Uncollectible-Account Expense was $19.2 million for the first three quarters of the year, based on the percent of sales method.
   b. Write-offs of accounts receivable totalled $23.6 million.
   c. December 31, 19X8, aging of receivables, which indicates that $15.3 million of the total receivables of $582.7 million is uncollectible. Post all three entries to Allowance for Uncollectible Accounts.
3. Show how CPC International's receivables and related allowance will appear on the December 31, 19X8, balance sheet.
4. What is the expected realizable value of receivables at December 31, 19X8? How much is uncollectible-account expense for 19X8?

SOLUTION

REQUIREMENT 1

	Millions
Expected realizable value of receivables ($549.9 – $12.5)	$537.4

REQUIREMENT 2

	Millions	
a. Uncollectible-Account Expense	19.2	
Allowance for Uncollectible Accounts		19.2
b. Allowance for Uncollectible Accounts	23.6	
Accounts Receivable		23.6
c. Uncollectible-Account Expense ($15.3 – $8.1)	7.2	
Allowance for Uncollectible Accounts		7.2

Allowance for Uncollectible Accounts

19X8 Write-offs	23.6	Dec. 31, 19X7 Bal.	12.5
		19X8 Expense	19.2
		Bal. before adj.	8.1
		Dec. 31, 19X8 Adj.	7.2
		Dec. 31, 19X8 Bal.	15.3

REQUIREMENT 3

	Millions
Notes and accounts receivable	$582.7
Allowance for uncollectible accounts	(15.3)

REQUIREMENT 4

	Millions
Expected realizable value of receivables at December 31, 19X8 ($582.7 – $15.3)	$567.4
Uncollectible-account expense for 19X8 ($19.2 + $7.2)	26.4

Notes Receivable: An Overview

As we pointed out earlier in this chapter, notes receivable are more formal arrangements than accounts receivable. Often the debtor signs a promissory note, which serves as evidence of the debt. Let's define the special terms used to discuss notes receivable.

- **Promissory note:** A written promise to pay a specified amount of money at a particular future date.

- **Maker of the note:** The person or business that signs the note and promises to pay the amount required by the note agreement; the maker of the note is the *debtor*.
- **Payee of the note:** The person or business to whom the maker promises future payment; the payee of the note is the *creditor*.
- **Principal amount,** or **principal:** The amount loaned out by the payee and borrowed by the maker of the note.
- **Interest:** The revenue to the payee for loaning out the principal and the expense to the maker for borrowing the principal.
- **Interest period:** The period of time during which interest is to be computed. It extends from the original date of the note to the maturity date. Also called the **note period, note term,** or simply **time.**
- **Interest rate:** The percentage rate that is multiplied by the principal amount to compute the amount of interest on the note.
- **Maturity date:** The date on which final payment of the note is due. Also called the **due date.**
- **Maturity value:** The sum of principal and interest due at the maturity date of the note.

Exhibit 8-5 illustrates a promissory note. Study it carefully.

Identifying a Note's Maturity Date

Some notes specify the maturity date, as shown in Exhibit 8-5. Other notes state the period of the note, in days or months. When the period is given in months, the note's maturity date falls on the same day of the month as the date the note was issued. For example, a six-month note dated February 16 matures on August 16.

When the period is given in days, the maturity date is determined by counting the days from the date of issue. A 120-day note dated September 14, 19X2, matures on January 12, 19X3, as shown here:

Month	Number of Days	Cumulative Total
Sep. 19X2	30 – 14 = 16	16
Oct. 19X2	31	47
Nov. 19X2	30	77
Dec. 19X2	31	108
Jan. 19X3	12	120

In counting the days remaining for a note, remember to count the maturity date and to omit the date the note was issued.

Computing Interest on a Note

The formula for computing interest is

$$\text{Principal} \times \text{Interest Rate} \times \text{Time} = \text{Amount of Interest}$$

EXHIBIT 8-5
A Promissory Note

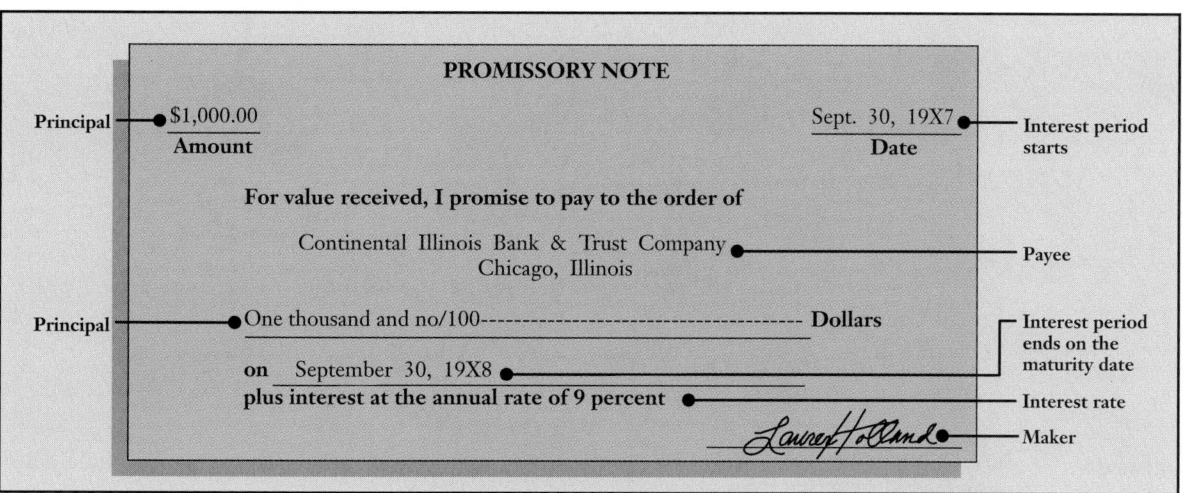
PROMISSORY NOTE

$1,000.00
Amount

Sept. 30, 19X7
Date

For value received, I promise to pay to the order of

Continental Illinois Bank & Trust Company
Chicago, Illinois

One thousand and no/100---------------------------------- Dollars

on September 30, 19X8
plus interest at the annual rate of 9 percent

Lauren Holland

■ Daily Exercise 8-14

Using the data in Exhibit 8-5, Continental Illinois Bank computes its interest revenue for one year on its note receivable as:

$$\begin{array}{ccccccc} \textbf{Principal} & & \textbf{Interest Rate} & & \textbf{Time} & & \textbf{Amount of Interest} \\ \$1{,}000 & \times & 0.09 & \times & 1\ (\text{yr.}) & = & \$90 \end{array}$$

The maturity value of the note is $1,090 ($1,000 principal + $90 interest). The time element is one (1) because interest is computed over a one-year period.

When the interest period of a note is stated in months, we compute the interest based on the 12-month year. Interest on a $2,000 note at 15% for three months is computed as

$$\begin{array}{ccccccc} \textbf{Principal} & & \textbf{Rate} & & \textbf{Time} & & \textbf{Interest} \\ \$2{,}000 & \times & 0.15 & \times & 3/12 & = & \$75 \end{array}$$

When the interest period is stated in days, we sometimes compute interest based on a 360-day year rather than on a 365-day year.[2] The interest on a $5,000 note at 12% for 60 days is computed as

$$\begin{array}{ccccccc} \textbf{Principal} & & \textbf{Interest Rate} & & \textbf{Time} & & \textbf{Amount of Interest} \\ \$5{,}000 & \times & 0.12 & \times & 60/360 & = & \$100 \end{array}$$

Learning Tip: Interest rates are usually stated as an annual rate. Therefore, the time in the formula for computing interest should also be expressed in terms of a year.

■ Daily Exercise 8-15

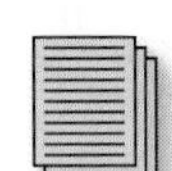

Working It Out Practice calculating interest on

1. A $30,000, 12½%, 180-day note
2. An $8,500, 9%, 6-month note

Answers

1. ($30,000 × 0.125 × 180/360) = $1,875
2. ($8,500 × 0.09 × 6/12) = $383

Accounting for Notes Receivable

Recording Notes Receivable

Objective 4

Account for notes receivable

Consider the loan agreement shown in Exhibit 8-5. After Lauren Holland signs the note and presents it to the bank, Continental Bank gives her $1,000 cash. At maturity, Holland pays the bank $1,090 ($1,000 principal plus $90 interest). The bank's entries are

Sep. 30, 19X7	Note Receivable—L. Holland	1,000	
	Cash		1,000
	To lend money.		
Sep. 30, 19X8	Cash	1,090	
	Note Receivable—L. Holland		1,000
	Interest Revenue ($1,000 × 0.09 × 1)		90
	To collect at maturity.		

Some companies sell merchandise in exchange for notes receivable. This arrangement occurs often when the payment term extends beyond the customary accounts receivable period, which generally ranges from 30 to 60 days.

[2]A 360-day year eliminates some rounding, which is consistent with our use of whole-dollar amounts throughout this book.

Suppose that on October 20, 19X3, General Electric sells household appliances for $15,000 to Dorman Builders. Dorman signs a 90-day promissory note at 10% annual interest. General Electric's entries to record the sale and collection from Dorman are

Oct. 20, 19X3	Note Receivable—Dorman Builders	15,000	
	Sales Revenue		15,000
	To record sale.		

Jan. 18, 19X4	Cash	15,375	
	Note Receivable—Dorman Builders		15,000
	Interest Revenue ($15,000 × 0.10 × 90/360)		375
	To record collection at maturity.		

■ Daily Exercise 8-16

A company may accept a note receivable from a trade customer who fails to pay an account receivable within the customary 30 to 60 days. The customer signs a promissory note—that is, becomes the **maker of the note**—and gives it to the creditor, who becomes the **payee.**

Maker of a Note. The person or business that signs the note and promises to pay the amount required by the note agreement; the debtor.

Payee of a Note. The person or business to whom the maker of a note promises future payment; the creditor.

Suppose Interlogic, Inc., sees that it will not be able to pay off its account payable to Hoffman Supply, which is due in 15 days. Hoffman may accept a one-year, $2,400 note receivable, with 9% interest, from Interlogic on October 1, 19X1. Hoffman's entry is

Oct. 1, 19X1	Note Receivable—Interlogic, Inc.	2,400	
	Accounts Receivable—Interlogic, Inc.		2,400
	To receive a note on account from a customer.		

Accruing Interest Revenue

Notes receivable may be outstanding at the end of an accounting period. The interest revenue, earned on the note during the year is part of that year's earnings. Recall that interest revenue is earned over time, not just when cash is received.

We saw in Chapter 3 on page 103 that accrued revenue creates an asset because the revenue has been earned but not received.

Let's continue with the Hoffman Supply note receivable from Interlogic, Inc. Hoffman Supply's accounting period ends December 31. How much of the total interest revenue does Hoffman earn in 19X1? How much in 19X2?

Hoffman will earn three months' interest in 19X1—for October, November, and December. In 19X2, Hoffman will earn nine months' interest—for January through September. At December 31, 19X1, Hoffman Supply will make the following adjusting entry to accrue interest revenue:

Dec. 31, 19X1	Interest Receivable ($2,400 × 0.09 × 3/12)	54	
	Interest Revenue		54
	To accrue interest revenue earned in 19X1 but not yet received.		

Then, on the maturity date, Hoffman Supply records collection of principal and interest as follows:

Sep. 30, 19X2	Cash [$2,400 + ($2,400 × 0.09)]	2,616	
	Note Receivable—Interlogic, Inc.		2,400
	Interest Receivable ($2,400 × 0.09 × 3/12)		54
	Interest Revenue ($2,400 × 0.09 × 9/12)		162
	To collect note receivable on which interest has been previously accrued.		

■ Daily Exercise 8-17

■ Daily Exercise 8-18

The entries to accrue interest revenue earned in 19X1 and to record collection in 19X2 assign the correct amount of interest to each year, in keeping with the revenue principle.

Discounting a Note Receivable

A payee of a note receivable (the person to whom money is owed) may need the cash before the maturity date of the note. When this occurs, the payee may sell the note. A note receivable is a *negotiable instrument*, which means that it is readily transferable from one party to another and may be sold. Selling a note is called **discounting a note receivable.** This practice is prevalent with long-term notes receivable secured by real estate as collateral. A bank that has lent money may discount the note receivable to a company such as the Federal National Mortgage Association (known as Fannie Mae). The net result is that the banks can quickly replenish their funds for lending.

Discounting a Note Receivable. Selling a note receivable before its maturity date.

Computers can be used to discount notes. A spreadsheet may handle the accounting (if the accounting software package does not include a special function for discounting). Companies such as Fannie Mae that discount notes on a regular basis would have a standard program to compute the proceeds.

The price Fannie Mae pays for a note receivable depends mainly on the interest rate that Fannie Mae seeks to earn on its investment. Fannie Mae pays cash now—at a discounted price—to receive a larger amount at a later date. This is the concept of *present value:* Less money today grows to a larger sum in the future.

A payee may also discount a short-term note receivable, one with a maturity of one year or less. There are several ways to compute the price to be received. Fundamentally, the price is determined by present-value concepts. But the transaction between the seller and the buyer of the note can take any form agreeable to the two parties. Here we illustrate one procedure used for discounting short-term notes receivable. To receive cash immediately, the seller is willing to accept a lower price than the note's maturity value.

We discuss these concepts in detail in Chapter 15.

To illustrate discounting a note receivable, let's return to the example of General Electric (GE) and Dorman Builders. The maturity date of the 90-day, 10% Dorman note is January 18, 19X4. Suppose GE discounts the Dorman note at First City National Bank on December 9, 19X3, when the note is 50 days old. The bank applies a 12% annual interest rate in computing the discounted value of the note. The bank will use a discount rate that is higher than the interest rate on the note in order to earn some interest on the note. GE may be willing to accept this higher rate in order to get cash quickly. The discounted value, called the *proceeds*, is the amount GE receives from the bank. The proceeds can be computed in five steps, as shown in Exhibit 8-6. At maturity the bank collects $15,375 from the maker of the note and earns $205 interest revenue from holding the note. GE's entry to record discounting (selling) the note is

Dec. 9, 19X3	Cash	15,170	
	Note Receivable—Dorman Builders...........		15,000
	Interest Revenue ($15,170 – $15,000).........		170
	To discount a note receivable.		

When the proceeds from discounting a note receivable are less than the principal amount of the note, the payee records a debit to Interest Expense for the amount of the

Concept Highlight

EXHIBIT 8-6
Discounting (Selling) a Note Receivable

Step	Computation	
1. Compute the original amount of interest on the note receivable.	$15,000 × 0.10 × 90/360	= $ 375
2. Maturity value of the note = principal + interest	$15,000 + $375	= $15,375
3. Determine the period (number of days, months, or years) the bank will hold the note (the discount period).	Dec. 9, 19X3 to Jan. 18, 19X4 =	40 days
4. Compute the bank's discount on the note. This is the bank's interest revenue from holding the note.	$15,375 × 0.12 × 40/360	= $ 205
5. Seller's proceeds from discounting the note receivable* = Maturity value of the note − Bank's discount on the note	$15,375 – $205	= $15,170

*(Buyer's cost of purchasing)

The authors thank Doug Hamilton for suggesting this exhibit.

difference. For example, GE could discount the note receivable for cash proceeds of $14,980. The entry to record this discounting transaction is

■ Daily Exercise 8-19

Dec. 9, 19X3	Cash	14,980	
	Interest Expense	20	
	Note Receivable—Dorman Builders		15,000
	To discount a note receivable.		

Working It Out On January 5, Mayberry Department Stores received a $5,000, 90-day, 10% note from Barney Fife. Mayberry sold the Fife note on January 25 by discounting it to a bank at 12 percent. Prepare the journal entry to record the discounted note on January 25.

Answers

1. Maturity value = $5,000 + ($5,000 × 10% × 90/360) = $5,125
2. Discount period = 90 – 20 = 70 days
3. Discount = $5,125 × 12% × 70/360 = $120
4. Proceeds = $5,125 – $120 = $5,005
5. Journal entry:

Cash	5,005	
Note Receivable—Barney Fife		5,000
Interest Revenue		5

■ Daily Exercise 8-20

Contingent Liabilities on Discounted Notes Receivable

A **contingent liability** is a potential liability that will become an actual liability only if a particular event does occur. Discounting a note receivable creates a contingent liability for the endorser. If the maker of the note (Dorman, in our example) fails to pay the maturity value to the new payee (the bank), then the original payee (GE, the note's original endorser) is legally obligated to pay the bank the amount due.[3] Now we see why the liability is "potential." If Dorman pays the bank, then GE can forget the note. But if Dorman dishonors the note—fails to pay it—then GE has an actual liability.

Contingent Liability. A potential liability that will become an actual liability only if a particular event does occur.

GE's contingent liability exists from the time of the endorsement to the note's maturity date. In our example, the contingent liability exists from December 9, 19X3—when GE endorsed the note—to the January 18, 19X4, maturity date.

Contingent liabilities are not included with actual liabilities on the balance sheet. After all, they are not real debts. However, financial statement users should be alerted that the business has *potential* debts. Many businesses report contingent liabilities in a footnote to the financial statements. GE's end-of-period balance sheet might carry this note:

> As of December 31, 19X3, the Company is contingently liable on notes receivable discounted in the amount of $15,000.

Dishonored Notes Receivable

If the maker of a note does not pay a note receivable at maturity, the maker is said to **dishonor,** or **default on,** the note. Because the term of the note has expired, the note agreement is no longer in force, and no one will buy it. However, the payee still has a claim against the note's maker and usually transfers the claim from the note receivable account to Accounts Receivable. The payee records interest revenue earned on the note and debits Accounts Receivable for the full maturity value of the note.

Dishonor of a Note. Failure of a note's maker to pay a note receivable at maturity. Also called **default on a note.**

[3]The discounting agreement between the endorser and the purchaser may be "without recourse," which means that the endorser has no liability if the note is dishonored at maturity. Under such an arrangement, there is no contingent liability.

Suppose Rubinstein Jewelers had a six-month, 10% note receivable for $1,200 from D. Hatachi, and on the February 3 maturity date, Hatachi defaulted. Rubinstein Jewelers would record the default as follows:

Feb. 3	Accounts Receivable—D. Hatachi [$1,200 + ($1,200 × 0.10 × 6/12)]	1,260	
	Note Receivable—D. Hatachi		1,200
	Interest Revenue ($1,200 × 0.10 × 6/12)		60
	To record dishonor of note receivable.		

Rubinstein would pursue collection from Hatachi as a default on a promissory note. Rubinstein may treat accounts receivable such as this as a special category to highlight them for added collection efforts. If the account receivable later proves uncollectible, Rubinstein would then write off the account against Allowance for Uncollectible Accounts in the manner previously discussed. (Note that all notes receivable bear interest until they are proved dead.)

Reporting Receivables and Allowances: Actual Company Reports

Objective 5

Report receivables on the balance sheet

Let's look at how some well-known companies report their receivables and related allowances for uncollectibles on the balance sheet. All accounts receivable, notes receivable, and allowance accounts appear on the balance sheet, but the terminology and setup vary.

Intel Corporation, maker of the Pentium® processor, reported accounts receivable under Current Assets (in millions):

Accounts receivable, net of allowance for doubtful accounts of $68	$3,723

To compute Intel's total amount of accounts receivable, add the allowance to the net accounts receivable amount: $68 + $3,723 = $3,791. Customers actually owe Intel $3,791 million, of which the company expects to collect $3,723 million.

General Electric Company reports a single amount for its current receivables in the body of the balance sheet and uses a note to give the details (amounts in millions):

Current receivables (note 8)		$4,872
Note 8:	Current Receivables:	
	Customers' accounts and notes	$3,989
	Associated companies	49
	Nonconsolidated affiliates	21
	Other	927
		4,986
	Less allowance for losses	(114)
		$4,872

Intel and GE report their receivables as *current assets*. National Can Corporation had some long-term receivables that it reported as other assets (amounts in millions of dollars):

Other (long-term) Assets:	
Notes and accounts receivable, less allowances	$37

■ Daily Exercise 8-21
■ Daily Exercise 8-22

National Can disclosed its allowance for doubtful accounts in a note as follows:

> Notes and accounts receivable included in other assets are net of allowances for doubtful accounts of $17.

Working It Out

1. How much did customers owe National Can Corporation?
2. How much did National Can expect to collect?
3. How much did National Can expect *not* to collect?

Answers

1. \$54 million = (\$37 million net + \$17 million allowance for doubtful accounts)
2. \$37 million
3. \$17 million

Using Accounting Information for Decision Making

Objective 6

Use the acid-test ratio and days' sales in receivables to evaluate a company's financial position

The balance sheet lists assets in their order of relative liquidity (closeness to cash):

- Cash comes first because it is the medium of exchange and can be used to purchase any item or pay any bill.
- Short-term investments (covered in a later chapter) come next because they can be sold for cash whenever the owner wishes.
- Current receivables are less liquid than short-term investments because the receivables must be collected.
- Merchandise inventory is less liquid than receivables because the goods must be sold.

The balance sheet of AMR Corporation (parent company of American Airlines) provides an example in Exhibit 8-7. Focus on the current assets at December 31, 1996.

Acid-Test (or Quick) Ratio

Acid-Test Ratio. Ratio of (the sum of cash plus short-term investments plus net current receivables) to total current liabilities. Tells whether the entity could pay all its current liabilities if they came due immediately. Also called the **quick ratio.**

In making decisions, owners and managers use some ratios based on the relative liquidity of assets. In Chapter 4, for example, we discussed the current ratio, which indicates the company's ability to pay current liabilities with current assets. A more stringent measure of the company's ability to pay current liabilities is the **acid-test** (or **quick**) **ratio.** The

EXHIBIT 8-7
An Actual Company's Balance Sheet

AMR CORPORATION (Parent Company of American Airlines)
Balance Sheet (Adapted)

(In millions)	December 31, 1996	1995
Assets		
Current Assets		
Cash	\$ 68	\$ 82
Short-term investments	1,743	819
Receivables, less allowance for uncollectible accounts (1996—\$17; 1995—\$18)	1,382	1,153
Inventories	633	589
Other current assets	644	494
Total current assets	4,470	3,137
Equipment and Property, less accumulated depreciation	13,305	13,565
Other Assets	2,722	2,854
Total Assets	\$20,497	\$19,556
Liabilities		
Current Liabilities		
Total current liabilities	\$ 5,566	\$ 4,632
Long-Term Debt and Other Long-Term Liabilities	9,263	11,204
Commitments and Contingencies		
Owners' Equity	5,668	3,720
Total Liabilities and Owners' Equity	\$20,497	\$19,556

acid test ratio tells whether the entity could pay all its current liabilities if they came due immediately:

For AMR Corporation (Exhibit 8-7)
(Dollar amounts in millions)

$$\text{Acid-test ratio} = \frac{\text{Cash} + \begin{matrix}\text{Short-term}\\\text{investments}\end{matrix} + \begin{matrix}\text{Net current}\\\text{receivables}\end{matrix}}{\text{Total current liabilities}} \qquad \frac{\$68 + \$1{,}743 + \$1{,}382}{\$5{,}566} = 0.57$$

The higher the acid-test ratio, the better the business is able to pay its current liabilities. AMR's acid-test ratio of 0.57 means that AMR has $0.57 of quick assets to pay each $1 of current liabilities—a fairly risky position.

What is an acceptable acid-test ratio value? The answer depends on the industry. Automobile dealers can operate smoothly with an acid-test ratio of 0.20. Several things make this possible: Car dealers have almost no current receivables. The acid-test ratio values for most department stores cluster about 0.80, while travel agencies average 1.10. In general, an acid-test ratio of 1.00 is considered safe.

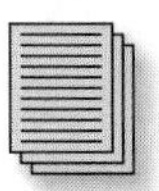

Working It Out Use the data in Exhibit 8-7 to compute AMR Corporation's current ratio at December 31, 1996. Then compare AMR's current ratio and acid-test ratio. Why is the current ratio higher?

Answer

$$\text{Current ratio} = \frac{\text{Total current assets}}{\text{Total current liabilities}} = \frac{\$4{,}470}{\$5{,}566} = 0.80$$

$$\text{Acid-test ratio} = \qquad 0.57$$

The current ratio is higher because assets in the numerator include inventory and other current assets, which are excluded from the acid-test ratio.

Days' Sales in Receivables

Days' Sales in Receivables. Ratio of average net accounts receivable to one day's sales. Tells how many days' sales it takes to collect the average level of receivables. Also called the **collection period.**

After a business makes a credit sale, the next critical event in the business cycle is collection of the receivable. Several financial ratios center on receivables. **Days' sales in receivables,** also called the **collection period,** indicates how many days it takes to collect the average level of receivables. The shorter the collection period, the more quickly the organization can use cash for operations. The longer the collection period, the less cash is available to pay bills and expand. Days' sales in receivables can be computed in two steps, as follows:[4]

For AMR Corporation (Exhibit 8-7)
(Dollar amounts in millions)

$$1.\ \text{One day's sales} = \frac{\text{Net sales}}{365\text{ days}} \qquad \frac{\$17{,}753^*}{365} = \$48.6\text{ per day}$$

$$2.\ \begin{matrix}\text{Days' sales in}\\\text{average accounts}\\\text{receivable}\end{matrix} = \frac{\begin{matrix}\text{Average net}\\\text{accounts receivable}\end{matrix}}{\text{One day's sales}} = \frac{\left(\begin{matrix}\text{Beginning net}\\\text{receivables}\end{matrix} + \begin{matrix}\text{Ending net}\\\text{receivables}\end{matrix}\right) \div 2}{\text{One day's sales}} = \frac{(\$1{,}153 + \$1{,}382)/2}{\$48.6} = 26\text{ days}$$

*Taken from AMR Corporation's 1996 income statement, not reproduced here.

The length of the collection period depends on the credit terms of the company's sales. For example, sales on net 30 terms should be collected within approximately 30 days. When there is a discount, such as 2/10 net 30, the collection period may be shorter. Terms of net 45 or net 60 result in longer collection periods.

We discussed sales discounts in Chapter 5, page 186.

[4]Days' sales in average receivables can also be computed in one step:

$$\begin{matrix}\text{Days' sales in}\\\text{average receivables}\end{matrix} = \frac{\text{Average net receivables}}{\text{Net sales}} \times 365$$

Thinking It Over AMR Corporation's collection period averaged 26 days during 1996. Why is it so short? To answer, consider when people pay for airline tickets.

Answer: Generally, people pay for airline tickets before they travel. This causes the airlines' days' sales in receivables to be low.

A company watches its collection period closely. Whenever the collection period lengthens, the business must find other sources of financing, such as borrowing. During recessions, customers pay more slowly, and a longer collection period may be unavoidable.

■ Daily Exercise 8-23
■ Daily Exercise 8-24

Learning Tip: Investors and creditors do not evaluate a company on the basis of one or two ratios. Instead, they perform a thorough analysis of all the information available on a company. Then they stand back from the data and ask, "What is our overall impression of the strength of this business?" Chapter 18 discusses a wide range of ratios used for decision making.

Reporting Receivables Transactions on the Statement of Cash Flows

Objective 7

Report cash flows from receivables transactions on the statement of cash flows

Receivables are assets, which appear on the balance sheet. As we have seen, receivables transactions affect cash, so their effects must also be reported on another financial statement, the statement of cash flows.

Each amount listed on the statement of cash flows (also called the cash-flow statement) in Exhibit 8-8 is either a cash receipt, which is a positive amount, or a cash payment, which is a negative amount (denoted by parentheses). The largest amount is the cash receipt for collections from customers, which is most companies' main source of cash.

Four basic receivables transactions affect the business's cash:

Cash Transaction	Account Affected (Besides Cash)
• Collection from customers →	Accounts receivable
• Receipts of cash interest →	Interest revenue (or Interest receivable if the interest was accrued earlier)
• Lending money →	Note receivable
• Collection of a note receivable →	Note receivable

The statement of cash flows reports cash flows under three types of activities:

1. Operating activities 2. Investing activities 3. Financing activities

The cash flows listed under **operating activities** relate to revenue and expense transactions. Collections from customers occur after the business makes a sale to earn the sales revenue. Receipts of cash interest follow the earning of interest revenue. Therefore, the statement of cash flows in Exhibit 8-8 reports collections from customers and receipts of cash interest as operating activities.

Operating Activities. Activities that relate to a business's revenue and expense transactions.

Investing activities include buying and selling long-term assets, as well as lending money on notes receivable and collecting the notes receivable. The statement of cash flows in Exhibit 8-8 reports lending money and collecting the notes receivable as investing activities.

Investing Activities. Activities that relate to the purchase and sale of a business's long-term assets.

EXHIBIT 8-8
Reporting the Effects of Receivables Transactions on the Statement of Cash Flows

EXAMPLE COMPANY Statement of Cash Flows (Partial) Year Ended December 31, 19XX	
Cash flows from *operating* activities:	
Collections from customers	$15,000
Receipts of interest	350
Cash flows from *investing* activities:	
Loaned out money on notes receivable	$ (500)
Collected on notes receivable	200

Financing Activities. Activities by which the company gets the cash needed to launch and sustain the business.

■ Daily Exercise 8-25

We discuss **financing activities,** by which the company gets the cash needed to launch and sustain the business, in later chapters. For now, focus on the operating activities and the investing activities that relate to the business's receivables. In future chapters, we will preview the other cash flows that make up the statement of cash flows. Then, preparation of the statement should come to you easily when we discuss it in detail in Chapter 17.

DECISION GUIDELINES — Accounting for Receivables Transactions

DECISION	GUIDELINES
Accounts Receivable	
How much of our receivables will we collect?	Less than the full amount of the receivables because we will be unable to collect from some customers.
How to report receivables at their net realizable value?	**1.** Use the *allowance method* to account for uncollectible receivables. Set up the allowance for Uncollectible Accounts. **2.** Estimate uncollectibles by the **a.** *Percent of sales method* (income statement approach) (p. 340) **b.** *Aging of receivables method* (balance-sheet approach) (p. 341) **3.** Write off uncollectible receivables as they are deemed uncollectible (p. 343). **4.** Net accounts receivable = Accounts Receivable − Allowance for Uncollectible Accounts (p. 343)
Is there another way to account for uncollectible receivables?	The *direct write-off method* simply debits Uncollectible Accounts Expense and credits an individual customer's Account Receivable to write-off an uncollectible account. This method uses no allowance for uncollectibles and thus reports receivables at their full amount. It is generally accepted only when uncollectibles are insignificant.
Notes Receivable	Notes receivable, an asset, earn interest revenue.
What other accounts accompany notes receivable?	• If the interest revenue has been collected in cash, then debit *Cash* and credit *Interest Revenue.* • If the interest revenue has not been collected, then it must be accrued. Debit *Interest Receivable* and credit *Interest Revenue.*
How to compute the interest on a note receivable?	Principal × Interest Rate × Time = Amount of Interest Interest is a function of time. If the time element is zero, there can be no interest on the note receivable.
Receivables in General What are two key decision aids that use receivables to evaluate a company's financial position?	• Acid-test ratio = $\dfrac{\text{Cash} + \text{Short-term investments} + \text{Net current receivables}}{\text{Total current liabilities}}$ • $\text{Days' sales in average receivables} = \dfrac{\text{Average net accounts receivable}}{\text{One day's sales}}$
How to report receivables on the balance sheet?	Accounts (or Notes) Receivable .... $XXX Less: Allowance for uncollectible accounts .... (X) Net accounts receivable .... $ XX
How to report receivables transactions on the statement of cash flows?	Cash flows from *operating* activities: Collection from customers .... $ XX Receipts of interest .... XX Cash flows from *investing* activities: Loaned out money on notes receivable .... $ (XX) Collected on notes receivable XX

Computers and Accounts Receivable

Accounting for receivables by a large company like M & M Mars requires tens of thousands of postings to customer accounts each month for credit sales and cash collections. Manual accounting methods cannot keep up.

As we saw in Chapter 6, Accounts Receivable can be set up on a computerized system. The order entry and shipping systems interface with the billing system, which credits Sales Revenue and debits Accounts Receivable. The computer then creates a sales invoice for each customer. At the same time, the computer prints out the sales for the period. Finally, computerized posting to the general ledger and accounts receivable subsidiary ledger occurs.

"Accounting for receivables . . . M & M Mars requires tens of thousands of postings to customer accounts each month for credit sales and cash collections."

SUMMARY PROBLEM FOR YOUR REVIEW

Suppose Exxon, Inc., engaged in the following transactions:

19X4
Apr. 1 Loaned $8,000 to Bland Co., a service station. Received a one-year, 10% note.
June 1 Discounted the Bland note at the bank at a discount rate of 12 percent.
Nov. 30 Loaned $6,000 to Flores, Inc., a regional distributor of Exxon products, on a three-month, 11% note.

19X5
Feb. 28 Collected the Flores note at maturity.

Exxon's accounting period ends on December 31.

REQUIRED

Explanations are not needed.

1. Record the 19X4 transactions on April 1, June 1, and November 30 on Exxon's books.
2. Make any adjusting entries needed on December 31, 19X4.
3. Record the February 28, 19X5, collection of the Flores note.
4. Which transaction creates a contingent liability for Exxon? When does the contingency begin? When does it end?
5. Write a footnote that Exxon could use in its 19X4 financial statements to report the contingent liability.

SOLUTION

REQUIREMENT 1

19X4			
Apr. 1	Note Receivable—Bland Co.	8,000	
	Cash		8,000
June 1	Cash	7,920*	
	Interest Expense	80	
	Note Receivable—Bland Co.		8,000
Nov. 30	Note Receivable—Flores, Inc.	6,000	
	Cash		6,000

*Computation of proceeds:

Principal	$8,000
+ Interest ($8,000 × 0.10 × 12/12)	800
= Maturity value	8,800
– Discount ($8,800 × 0.12 × 10/12)	(880)
= Proceeds	$7,920

REQUIREMENT 2

	Adjusting Entries		
19X4			
Dec. 31	Interest Receivable ($6,000 × 0.11 × 1/12)	55	
	Interest Revenue		55

REQUIREMENT 3

19X5			
Feb. 28	Cash [$6,000 + ($6,000 × 0.11 × 3/12)]	6,165	
	Note Receivable—Flores, Inc.		6,000
	Interest Receivable		55
	Interest Revenue ($6,000 × 0.11 × 2/12)		110

REQUIREMENT 4

Discounting the Bland note receivable creates a contingent liability for Exxon. The contingency exists from the date of discounting the note receivable (June 1) to the maturity date of the note (April 1, 19X5).

REQUIREMENT 5

Note XX—Contingent liabilities: At December 31, 19X4, the company is contingently liable on notes receivable discounted in the amount of $8,000 plus accrued interest.

Summary of Learning Objectives

1. *Design internal controls for receivables.* Companies that sell on credit receive most customer collections in the mail. Good *internal control* over mailed-in cash receipts means separating cash-handling duties from cash-accounting duties.

2. *Use the allowance method to account for uncollectibles and estimate uncollectibles by the percent of sales and aging methods.* Uncollectible receivables are accounted for by the allowance method or the direct write-off method. The *allowance method* matches expenses to sales revenue and also results in a more realistic measure of net accounts receivable. The *percent of sales method* and the *aging of accounts receivable method* are the two main approaches to estimating bad debts under the allowance method.

3. *Use the direct write-off method to account for uncollectibles.* The *direct write-off method* is easy to apply, but it fails to match the uncollectible-account expense to the corresponding sales revenue. Also, Accounts Receivable are reported at their full amount, which is misleading because it suggests that the company expects to collect all its accounts receivable.

4. *Account for notes receivable.* *Notes receivable* are formal credit agreements. Interest earned by the creditor is computed by multiplying the note's principal amount by the interest rate times the length of the interest period.

Because notes receivable are negotiable, they may be sold. Selling a note receivable—called *discounting a note*—creates a *contingent liability* for the note's payee.

5. *Report receivables on the balance sheet.* All accounts receivable, notes receivable, and allowance accounts appear in the balance sheet. However, companies use various formats and terms to report these assets.

6. *Use the acid-test ratio and days' sales in receivables to evaluate a company's financial position.* The *acid-test ratio* measures ability to pay current liabilities from the most liquid current assets. *Days' sales in receivables* indicates how long it takes to collect the average level of receivables.

7. *Report cash flows from receivables transactions on the statement of cash flows.* Receivables transactions are reported under operating activities or investing activities on the statement of cash flow.

Accounting Vocabulary

acid-test ratio *(p. 353)*
aging of accounts receivable *(p. 341)*
Allowance for Doubtful Accounts *(p. 339)*
Allowance for Uncollectible Accounts *(p. 339)*
allowance method *(p. 339)*
bad-debt expense *(p. 339)*
balance-sheet approach *(p. 341)*
collection period *(p. 354)*
contingent liability *(p. 351)*
creditor *(p. 336)*
days' sales in receivables *(p. 354)*
debtor *(p. 336)*
default on a note *(p. 351)*
direct write-off method *(p. 344)*
discounting a note receivable *(p. 350)*
dishonor of a note *(p. 351)*
doubtful-account expense *(p. 339)*
due date *(p. 347)*
financing activities *(p. 356)*
income statement approach *(p. 340)*
interest *(p. 347)*
interest period *(p. 347)*
interest rate *(p. 347)*
investing activities *(p. 355)*
maker of a note *(p. 349)*
maturity date *(p. 347)*
maturity value *(p. 347)*
note period *(p. 347)*
note term *(p. 347)*
operating activities *(p. 355)*
payee of a note *(p. 349)*
percent of sales method *(p. 340)*
principal *(p. 347)*
principal amount *(p. 347)*
promissory note *(p. 346)*
quick ratio *(p. 353)*
receivables *(p. 336)*
time *(p. 347)*
uncollectible-account expense *(p. 339)*

Questions

1. Name the two parties to a receivable/payable transaction. Which party has the receivable? Which has the payable? The asset? The liability?
2. List three categories of receivables. State how each category is classified for reporting on the balance sheet.
3. Many businesses receive most of their cash on credit sales through the mail. Suppose you own a business so large that you must hire employees to handle cash receipts and perform the related accounting duties. What internal control feature should you use to ensure that the cash received from customers is not taken by a dishonest employee?
4. Name the two methods of accounting for uncollectible receivables. Which method is easier to apply? Which method is consistent with generally accepted accounting principles?
5. Which of the two methods of accounting for uncollectible accounts—the allowance method or the direct write-off method—is preferable? Why?
6. Identify the accounts debited and credited to account for uncollectibles under (a) the allowance method, and (b) the direct write-off method.
7. What is another term for Allowance for Uncollectible Accounts? What are two other terms for Uncollectible-Account Expense?
8. Which entry decreases net income under the allowance method of accounting for uncollectibles: the entry to record uncollectible-account expense or the entry to write off an uncollectible-account receivable?
9. Identify and briefly describe the two ways to estimate bad-debt expense and uncollectible accounts.
10. Briefly describe how a company may use both the percent of sales method and the aging method to account for uncollectibles.
11. How does a credit balance arise in a customer's account receivable? How does the company report this credit balance on its balance sheet?
12. Use the terms *maker, payee, principal amount, maturity date, promissory note,* and *interest* in an appropiate sentence or two describing a note receivable.
13. Name three situations in which a company might receive a note receivable. For each situation, show the account debited and the account credited to record receipt of the note.
14. For each of the following notes receivable, compute the amount of interest revenue earned during 19X6:

	Principal	Interest Rate	Interest Period	Maturity Date
Note 1	$ 10,000	9%	60 days	11/30/19X6
Note 2	50,000	10%	3 months	9/30/19X6
Note 3	100,000	8%	1½ years	12/31/19X7
Note 4	15,000	12%	90 days	1/15/19X7

15. Suppose you hold a 180-day, $5,000 note receivable that specifies 10% interest. After 60 days, you discount the note at 12 percent. How much cash do you receive?
16. How does a contingent liability differ from an ordinary liability? How does discounting a note receivable create a contingent liability? When does the contingency cease to exist?
17. When the maker of a note dishonors the note at maturity, what accounts does the payee debit and credit?
18. Why does the payee of a note receivable usually need to make adjusting entries for interest at the end of the accounting period?
19. Show three ways to report Accounts Receivable of $100,000 and Allowance for Uncollectible Accounts of $2,800 on the balance sheet or in the related notes.
20. Why is the acid-test ratio a more stringent measure of the ability to pay current liabilities than the current ratio?
21. Which measure of days' sales in receivables is preferable, 30 or 40? Give your reason.
22. What is most companies' most important cash flow related to receivables? Under what category does the company report this cash flow? Why?
23. List four receivable-related cash flows under their respective categories as they would appear on the statement of cash flows.

Daily Exercises

Accounts receivable records **(*Obj. 1*)**

DE8-1 Examine the Accounts Receivable T-accounts on page 336, and answer these questions:

1. Which account (and which amount) will appear on the company's balance sheet? Suppose the company has cash of $4,000. Show how the balance sheet will report cash and the other item on page 336.
2. Who are Aston, Harris, and Salazar? What do their accounts indicate that these three persons are obligated to do?

Internal control over the collection of receivables **(*Obj. 1*)**

DE8-2 Return to the Accounts Receivable T-accounts on page 336. Suppose Gary Bauer is the accountant responsible for these records. What duty will a good internal control system withhold from Bauer? Why?

Internal control over the credit department **(*Obj. 1*)**

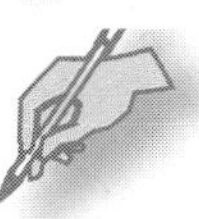

DE8-3 What duty must be withheld from a company's credit department in order to safeguard its cash? If this duty is granted to the credit department, what can a dishonest credit department employee do to hurt the company?

Applying the allowance method to account for uncollectibles **(*Obj. 2*)**

DE8-4 The allowance method of accounting for uncollectible receivables uses two accounts in addition to Accounts Receivable. Identify the two accounts and indicate which financial statement reports each account. Which of these is a contra account? Make up reasonable amounts to show how to report the contra account under its companion account on the balance sheet.

Applying the allowance method (percent of sales) to account for uncollectibles **(Obj. 2)**

DE8-5 During its first year of operations, Zurich Film Production Company had net sales of $600,000, all on account. Industry experience suggests that Zurich's bad debts will amount to 1% of net credit sales. At December 31, 19X7, Zurich's accounts receivable total $90,000. The company uses the allowance method to account for uncollectibles.

1. Make Zurich's journal entry for uncollectible-account expense using the percent of sales method.
2. Show how Zurich should report accounts receivable on its balance sheet at December 31, 19X7. Follow the reporting format illustrated at the top of page 340.

Applying the allowance method (percent of sales) to account for uncollectibles **(Obj. 2)**

DE8-6 ◄ *Link Back to Chapter 5 (Recording Sales Transactions).* This exercise continues the situation of Daily Exercise 8-5, in which Zurich Film Production Company ended the year 19X7 with accounts receivable of $90,000 and an allowance for uncollectible accounts of $6,000.

During 19X8, Zurich Film Production Company completed the following transactions:

1. Net credit sales, $800,000 (ignore cost of goods sold).
2. Collections on account, $780,000.
3. Write-offs of uncollectibles, $5,000.
4. Uncollectible-account expense, 1% of net credit sales.

Journalize the foregoing 19X8 transactions for Zurich Film Production Company.

Applying the allowance method (percent of sales) to account for uncollectibles **(Obj. 2)**

DE8-7 Use the solution to Daily Exercise 8-7 to answer these questions about Zurich Film Production Company:

1. Start with Accounts Receivable's beginning balance ($90,000), and then post to the Accounts Receivable T-account. How much do Zurich's customers owe the company at December 31, 19X8?
2. Start with the Allowance account's beginning balance ($6,000), and then post to the Allowance for Uncollectible Accounts T-account. How much of the receivables at December 31, 19X8, does Zurich expect *not* to collect?
3. At December 31, 19X8, how much cash does Zurich expect to collect on its accounts receivable?

Applying the allowance method (aging of accounts receivables) to account for uncollectibles **(Obj. 2)**

DE8-8 ◄ *Link Back to Chapter 5 (Recording Sales Transactions).* Guardian Medical Group started 19X8 with accounts receivable of $100,000 and an allowance for uncollectible accounts of $3,000. The 19X8 credit sales were $700,000, and cash collections on account totaled $720,000. During 19X8, Guardian wrote off uncollectible accounts receivable of $6,000. At December 31, 19X8, the aging of accounts receivable indicated that Guardian will *not* collect $2,000 of its accounts receivable.

Journalize Guardian's (a) credit sales (ignore cost of goods sold), (b) cash collections on account, (c) write-offs of uncollectible receivables, and (d) uncollectible-account expense for the year. Prepare a T-account for Allowance for Uncollectible Accounts to show your computation of uncollectible-account expense for the year.

Applying the allowance method (aging of accounts receivable) to account for uncollectibles **(Obj. 2)**

DE8-9 Perform the following operations for the receivables of Guardian Medical Group at December 31, 19X8.

1. Start with the beginning balances for these T-accounts:
   - Accounts Receivable, $100,000
   - Allowance for Uncollectible Accounts, $3,000

   Post the following 19X8 transactions to the T-accounts:
   a. Net credit sales of $700,000
   b. Collections on account, $720,000
   c. Write-offs of uncollectible accounts, $6,000
   d. Uncollectible-account expense (allowance method), $5,000
2. What are the ending balances of Accounts Receivable and Allowance for Uncollectible Accounts?
3. Show how Guardian will report accounts receivable on its balance sheet at December 31, 19X8. Follow the reporting format at the top of page 340.

Applying the allowance method (aging of accounts receivables) to account for uncollectibles **(Obj. 2)**

DE8-10 Interstate Energy Company accounts include the following balances at December 31, 19X9, before the year-end adjustments:

Accounts Receivable	
104,000	

Allowance for Uncollectible Accounts	
	1,000

The aging of accounts receivable yields these data:

	Age of Accounts Receivable				
	0–30 Days	31–60 Days	61–90 Days	Over 90 Days	Total Receivables
Amount receivable	$70,000	$20,000	$10,000	$4,000	$104,000
Percent uncollectible	× 1%	× 2%	× 5%	× 25%	

1. Journalize Interstate's entry to record uncollectible-account expense for the year and to adjust the allowance account to its correct balance at December 31, 19X9.
2. What caused Allowance for Uncollectible Accounts to have the unadjusted debit balance that appears in the preceding T-account?

Contrasting the allowance method and the direct write-off method of accounting for uncollectibles
(Obj. 2, 3)

DE8-11 Return to the Schmidt Builders Supply example of accounting for uncollectibles that begins under the heading "Writing Off Uncollectible Accounts" on page 343. Suppose Schmidt's past experience indicates that Schmidt will fail to collect 2% of net credit sales, which totaled $100,000 during the three-month period January through March of 19X9.

Record Schmidt's uncollectible-account expense for January through March under

a. The allowance method
b. The direct write-off method (You need not identify individual customer accounts. Use the data given for Abbott and Smith on page 343.)

Which method of accounting for uncollectibles is better? What makes this preferred method better?

Applying the direct write-off method to account for uncollectibles
(Obj. 3)

DE 8-12 Howard Woolf is a CPA in Corpus Christi, Texas. Woolf will accept a client only after performing a careful credit check on the person's payment history. As a result, Woolf experiences a very low rate of uncollectible receivables from clients. Therefore, Woolf appropriately uses the direct write-off method to account for his uncollectible receivables.

1. During June, Woolf earned service revenue of $15,000, all on account. He wrote off $300 of old receivables as uncollectible. His other expenses for June totaled $6,200. How much were Woolf's total expenses and his net income for June? Prepare Woolf's income statement for June of the current year.
2. At May 31, Woolf's accounts receivable were $6,000. During May, Woolf collected $12,000 from clients on account. What is Woolf's balance of Accounts Receivable at June 30? Does he expect to collect all of this amount? Why or why not?

Recording credit-card sales
(Obj. 3)

DE 8-13 Gas stations do a large volume of business by customer credit cards and bankcards. Suppose the Exxon station on West Paces Ferry Road in Atlanta, Georgia, had these transactions on a busy Saturday in July:

American Express credit-card sales....................	$3,000
VISA bankcard sales..	8,000

Suppose American Express charges merchants 4% and VISA charges 2 percent. Record these sale transactions for the Exxon station.

Identifying key items for a note receivable
(Obj. 4)

DE 8-14 Examine the promissory note in Exhibit 8-5, page 347. Answer the following questions about the note:

1. When does interest on the note start running? When does the interest stop running?
2. Who is the debtor? Who is the creditor?
3. Which party to the note has a note receivable? Which party has a note payable? Which party has interest revenue? Which party has interest expense?
4. When must Lauren Holland pay off the note?
5. How much interest must Holland pay on the maturity date of the note? How much cash must Holland pay in total at maturity?

Computing notes receivable amounts
(Obj. 4)

DE 8-15

1. Compute the amount of interest during 19X7, 19X8, and 19X9 for the following note receivable:

   On April 30, 19X7, City National Bank of Cincinnati lent $1,000,000 to Marjorie Redwine on a two-year, 9% note.

2. Which party has a
   a. Note receivable?
   b. Note payable?
   c. Interest revenue?
   d. Interest expense?
3. How much in total would Redwine pay City National Bank if Redwine paid off the note early—say, on November 30, 19X7?

Accounting for a note receivable
(Obj. 4)

DE 8-16 Metzger Bank lent $100,000 to Jean Nowlin on a 90-day, 8% note. Record the following for Metzger Bank:

a. Lending the money on May 19.
b. Collecting the principal and interest at maturity. Specify the date. For convenience, use a 360-day year.

Explanations are not required.

Accruing interest receivable and collecting a note receivable
(Obj. 4)

DE 8-17 Return to the promissory note in Exhibit 8-5, page 347. The accounting year of Continental Illinois Bank & Trust Company ends on December 31, 19X7. Journalize Continental Bank's (a) lending money on the note receivable at September 30, 19X7, (b) accrual of interest at December 31, 19X7, and (c) collection of principal and interest at September 30, 19X8, the maturity date of the note. Carry amounts to the nearest cent.

Reporting receivables amounts
(Obj. 5)

DE 8-18 Using your answers to Daily Exercise 8-17 for Continental Illinois Bank & Trust Company, and carrying amounts to the nearest cent, show how the bank will report

a. Note receivable and interest receivable on its classified balance sheet at December 31, 19X7.
b. Whatever needs to be reported on its income statement for the year ended December 31, 19X7.
c. Whatever needs to be reported for the note and related interest on its classified balance sheet at December 31, 19X8. You may ignore Cash.
d. Whatever needs to be reported on its income statement for the year ended December 31, 19X8.

Discounting a note receivable
(Obj. 4)

DE 8-19 General Telecom installs telephone systems and receives its pay in the form of notes receivable. General Telecom installed a system for the city of Akron, Ohio, receiving a nine-month, 8%, $500,000 note receivable on May 31, 19X1. To obtain cash quickly, General Telecom discounted the note with Great Lakes Bank on June 30, 19X1. The bank charged a discount rate of 9 percent.

Compute General Telecom's cash proceeds from discounting the note. Follow the five-step procedure outlined in Exhibit 8-6, page 350.

Accounting for a discounted note receivable
(Obj. 4)

DE 8-20 ◄ *Link Back to Chapter 5 (Recording a Sale).* Use your answers to Daily Exercise 8-19 to journalize General Telecom's transactions as follows:

May 31	Sold a telecommunications system, receiving a 9-month, 8%, $500,000 note from the city of Akron. General Telecom's cost of the system was $450,000.
June 30	Received cash for interest revenue for one month.
June 30	Discounted the note to Great Lakes Bank at a discount rate of 9 percent.

Reporting receivables
(Obj. 5)

DE 8-21 Examine the actual-company receivables shown on page 352 and in Exhibit 8-7, page 353. Complete the following table to show the amounts (in millions of dollars) that each company will report on its balance sheet:

Company	Total Current Receivables	−	Allowance for Uncollectibles	=	Net Realizable Value
Intel Corporation	$		$ ( )		$
General Electric					
National Can					
AMR Corporation (1996 only)............................					

How much does AMR Corporation expect to collect from its customers?

Reporting receivables and other accounts in the financial statements
(Obj. 5)

DE 8-22 ◄ *Link Back to Chapters 1–3 (Debit/Credit Balances; Income Statement).* Sprint Corporation, the telecommunications company, included the following items in its financial statements (amounts in millions):

Service revenue	$14,045	Unearned revenues..........................	$ 200
Other assets	355	Allowance for doubtful accounts	117
Receivables, long-term....................	1,527	Cash	1,151
Cost of services sold and other expenses......................	12,861	Accounts receivable..........................	2,581
Notes payable	3,281	Accounts payable	1,027

1. Classify each item as (a) income statement or balance sheet, and as (b) debit balance or credit balance.
2. How much net income did Sprint report for the year?
3. Show how Sprint reported receivables on its classified balance sheet. Follow the reporting format at the top of page 340.

Using the acid-test ratio and days' sales in receivables to evaluate an actual company ***(Obj. 6)***

DE 8-23 Cabletron Systems, a cable TV company, reported the following items at February 28, 19X7 (amounts in millions, with 19X6 amounts also given as needed):

Accounts payable	$ 69	Accounts receivable:	
Cash	215	February 28, 19X7	$ 235
Allowance for uncollectible		February 28, 19X6	160
accounts:		Cost of goods sold	575
February 28, 19X7	15	Short-term investments	165
February 29, 19X6	7	Other current assets	93
Inventories:		Other current liabilities	145
February 28, 19X7	198	Net sales revenue	1,406
February 28, 19X6	161	Long-term assets	416
Long-term liabilities	11		

Compute Cabletron's (a) acid-test ratio and (b) days' sales in average receivables for 19X7. Evaluate each ratio value as strong or weak. Assume Cabletron sells its goods on terms of net 45.

Computing key ratios for an actual company ***(Obj. 6)***

DE 8-24 *Link Back to Chapter 4 (Current Ratio and Debt Ratio) and Chapter 5 (Gross Margin Percentage and Inventory Turnover).* Using the data in Daily Exercise 8-23, compute for Cabletron Systems the following ratios for 19X7:

a. Current ratio
b. Debt ratio
c. Gross margin percentage
d. Rate of inventory turnover

Reporting cash flows from receivables transactions ***(Obj. 7)***

DE 8-25 In 1999, Vulcan Steel Company, headquartered in Birmingham, Alabama, lent $100,000 to Taladego Mines to help Taladega extract iron ore from the ground. Later in 1999, Vulcan collected from Taladega half of the note, plus 8% interest for half the year. In addition, Vulcan received cash of $700,000 from customers on account.

Show how Vulcan Steel Company will report these cash flows on its statement of cash flows for the year ended December 31, 1999. Include a complete heading for the statement and show cash payments in parentheses, as in Exhibit 8-8, page 355.

Exercises

Controlling cash receipts from customers ***(Obj. 1)***

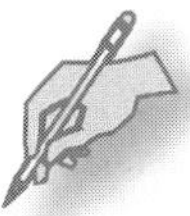

E8-1 As a recent college graduate, you land your first job in the customer collections department of Lowes & Kellogg, a partnership. Grant Kellogg, one of the owners, has asked you to propose a system to ensure that cash received by mail from customers is handled properly. Draft a short memorandum identifying the essential element in your proposed plan, and state why this element is important. Refer to Chapter 7 if necessary. Use this format for your memo:

Date:	______________
To:	Grant Kellogg
From:	Student Name
RE:	Essential element of internal control over collections from customers

Identifying and correcting an internal control weakness ***(Obj. 1)***

E8-2 *Link Back to Chapter 7 (Internal Control Over Cash Receipts).* Suppose Nestlé, the Swiss chocolate company, is opening a district office in Minneapolis. Gunther Oswald, the office manager, is designing the internal control system for the office. Oswald proposes the following procedures for credit checks on new customers, sales on account, cash collections, and write-offs of uncollectible receivables:

- The credit department will run a credit check on all customers who apply for credit.
- Sales on account are the responsibility of the Nestlé salespersons. Credit sales above $50,000 (which is a reasonable limit) require the approval of the credit manager.
- Cash receipts come into the credit department, which separates the cash received from the customer remittance slips. The credit department lists all cash receipts by name of customer and the amount of cash received. The cash goes to the treasurer for deposit in the bank. The remittance slips go to the accounting department for posting to individual customer accounts in the accounts receivable subsidiary ledger. Each day's listing of cash receipts goes to the controller for his end-of-day comparison with the daily deposit slip and the day's listing of the total dollar

amount posted to customer accounts from the accounting department. The three amounts must agree.

- The credit department reviews customer accounts receivable monthly. Late-paying customers are notified that their accounts are past due. After 90 days, the credit department turns over past-due accounts to the company attorney for collection. After 180 days, the credit department writes off a customer account as uncollectible.

Identify the internal control weakness in this situation, and propose a way to strengthen the controls.

Using the allowance method for bad debts
(Obj. 2, 5)

E8-3 On September 30, SaveTime Delivery Service had a $28,000 debit balance in Accounts Receivable. During October, the company had sales of $137,000, which included $90,000 in credit sales. October collections were $91,000, and write-offs of uncollectible receivables totaled $1,070. Other data include

- September 30 credit balance in Allowance for Uncollectible Accounts, $1,600.
- Uncollectible-account expense, estimated as 2% of credit sales.

REQUIRED

1. Prepare journal entries to record sales, collections, uncollectible-account expense by the allowance method (using the percent of sales method), and write-offs of uncollectibles during October.
2. Show the ending balances in Accounts Receivable, Allowance for Uncollectible Accounts, and *net* accounts receivable at October 31. How much does SaveTime expect to collect?
3. Show how SaveTime will report Accounts Receivable on its October 31 balance sheet.

Using the direct write-off method for bad debts
(Obj. 3)

E8-4 Refer to Exercise 8-3.

REQUIRED

1. Record uncollectible-account expense for October by the direct write-off method.
2. What amount of accounts receivable would SaveTime report on its October 31 balance sheet under the direct write-off method? Does SaveTime expect to collect the full amount?

Using the aging method to estimate bad debts
(Obj. 2, 5)

E8-5 At December 31, 19X7, the accounts receivable balance of First Arkansas Company is $269,000. The allowance for uncollectible accounts has a $3,910 credit balance. Accountants for First Arkansas prepare the following aging schedule for its accounts receivable:

	Age of Accounts			
Total Balance	**1–30 Days**	**31–60 Days**	**61–90 Days**	**Over 90 Days**
$269,000	$107,000	$78,000	$69,000	$15,000
Estimated percent uncollectible	0.3%	1.2%	6.0%	50%

REQUIRED

1. Journalize the adjusting entry for doubtful accounts on the basis of the aging schedule. Show the T-account for the allowance.
2. Show how First Arkansas will report Accounts Receivable on its December 31 balance sheet.

Reporting bad debts by the allowance method
(Obj. 2, 5)

E8-6 At December 31, 19X5, Gateway 5000, Inc., has an accounts receivable balance of $137,000. Sales revenue for 19X5 is $950,000, including credit sales of $600,000. For each of the following situations, prepare the year-end adjusting entry to record uncollectible-account expense. Show how the accounts receivable and the allowance for uncollectible accounts are reported on the balance sheet.

a. Allowance for Uncollectible Accounts has a credit balance of $1,600 before adjustment. Gateway estimates that uncollectible-account expense for the year is ½ of 1% of credit sales.
b. Allowance for Uncollectible Accounts has a debit balance before adjustment of $1,700. Gateway estimates that $3,900 of the accounts receivable will prove uncollectible.

Recording notes receivable and accruing interest revenue
(Obj. 4)

E8-7 Record the following transactions in the journal of Key Elements, Inc.:

Nov.	1	Loaned $50,000 cash to Jay Merck on a one-year, 9% note.
Dec.	3	Sold goods to Baylor, Inc., receiving a 90-day, 12% note for $3,750.
	16	Received a $2,000, six-month, 12% note on account from EMC Co.
	31	Accrued interest revenue on all notes receivable.

Recording bankcard sales and a note receivable, and accruing interest revenue (Obj. 4)

E8-8 Record the following transactions in Postino Company's journal:

19X6	
Feb. 12	Recorded VISA bankcard sales of $30,000, less a 2% discount.
Apr. 1	Loaned $8,000 to Lee Franz on a one-year, 10% note.
Dec. 31	Accrued interest revenue on the Franz note.
19X7	
Apr. 1	Received the maturity value of the note from Franz.

Recording notes receivable, discounting a note, and reporting the contingent liability in a note (Obj. 4)

E8-9 Rider Systems, Inc., sells on account. When a customer account becomes three months old, Rider converts the account to a note receivable and immediately discounts the note to a bank. During 19X4, Rider completed these transactions:

Aug. 29	Sold goods on account to V. Moyer, $3,900.
Dec. 1	Received a $3,900, 60-day, 10% note from V. Moyer in satisfaction of his past-due account receivable.
1	Sold the Moyer note by discounting it to a bank for $3,600.

REQUIRED

1. Record the transactions in Rider Systems' journal.
2. Write the financial statement note to disclose the contingent liability at December 31.

Evaluating ratio data (Obj. 6)

E8-10 Goldstein-Migel Co., a department store, reported the following amounts in its 19X6 financial statements. The 19X5 figures are given for comparison.

	19X6		19X5	
Current assets:				
Cash		$ 4,000		$ 9,000
Short-term investments		23,000		11,000
Accounts receivable	$80,000		$74,000	
Less Allowance for uncollectibles	7,000	73,000	6,000	68,000
Inventory		192,000		189,000
Prepaid insurance		2,000		2,000
Total current assets		294,000		279,000
Total current liabilities		$114,000		$107,000
Net sales		$703,000		$732,000

REQUIRED

1. Determine whether Goldstein-Migel's acid-test ratio improved or deteriorated from 19X5 to 19X6. How does Goldstein-Migel's acid-test ratio compare with the industry average of 0.85?
2. Compare the days' sales in receivables measure for 19X6 with the company's credit terms of net 30. What action, if any, should Goldstein-Migel take?

Analyzing a company's financial statements (Obj. 6)

E8-11 Wal-Mart Stores, Inc., is the largest retailer in the United States. Recently, Wal-Mart reported these figures (in millions of dollars):

	19X9	19X8
Net sales	$43,887	$32,602
Receivables at end of year	419	305

The Wal-Mart financial statements include no uncollectible-account expense or allowance for uncollectibles.

REQUIRED

1. Compute Wal-Mart's average collection period on receivables during 19X9.
2. Why are Wal-Mart's receivables so low? How can Wal-Mart have $419 million of receivables at January 31, 19X9, and no significant allowance for uncollectibles?

Reporting investments and receivables transactions on the statement of cash flows (Obj. 7)

E8-12 Arden, Inc., is a manufacturer of cosmetics, specializing in products for sensitive skin. During 19X7, Kmart and Target offered Arden products for the first time, so 19X7 was Arden's best year ever. Net income reached $80 million on sales of $430 million, and Arden collected $440 million from customers.

The increased volume of sales and collections left Arden with excess cash during the year, so the company loaned out $18 million on notes receivable. Arden collected $16 million on notes receivable during the year. At December 31, 19X7, Arden's interest revenue for the year totaled $1 million. Arden collected $2 million of interest during 19X7.

REQUIRED

Show what Arden, Inc., will report on its 19X7 cash flow statement as a result of these transactions.

CHALLENGE EXERCISE

Evaluating credit-card sales for profitability
(Obj. 2)

E8-13 Crossroads Appliance Mart sells on store credit and manages its own receivables. Average experience each year for the past three years has been as follows:

	Cash	Credit	Total
Sales	$200,000	$150,000	$350,000
Cost of goods sold	120,000	90,000	210,000
Uncollectible-account expense	—	4,000	4,000
Other expenses	34,000	27,000	61,000

Larry Salomon, the owner, is considering whether to accept bankcards (VISA, MasterCard). Typically, accepting bankcards increases total sales by 10 percent. But VISA and MasterCard charge approximately 1% of sales. If Salomon switches to bankcards, he can save $2,000 on accounting and other expenses. He figures that *cash* customers will continue buying in the same volume regardless of the type of credit the store offers.

REQUIRED

Should Crossroads Appliance start selling on bankcards? Show the computations of net income under the present plan and under the bankcard plan.

Beyond the Numbers

Computing receivables amounts to report on the balance sheet
(Obj. 5)

BN8-1 Bristol Office Supply's statement of cash flows reported the following for the year ended June 30, 19X9:

BRISTOL OFFICE SUPPLY
Statement of Cash Flows
Year Ended June 30, 19X9

Cash flows from operating activities:	
Collections from customers on account..........	$300,000
Receipts of interest	6,000
Cash flows from investing activities:	
Loaned out money on notes receivable...........	$ (50,000)
Collected on notes receivable..........................	60,000

Bristol's balance sheet one year earlier—at June 30, 19X8—reported Accounts Receivable of $40,000 and Notes Receivable of $20,000. Credit sales for the year ended June 30, 19X9, totaled $310,000, and the company collects all of its accounts receivable because uncollectibles rarely occur.

Bristol Office Supply needs a loan and the owner is preparing Bristol's balance sheet at June 30, 19X9. To complete the balance sheet, the owner needs to know the balances of Accounts Receivable and Notes Receivable at June 30, 19X9. Supply the needed information; T-accounts are helpful.

ETHICAL ISSUE

E-Z Finance Company is in the consumer loan business. It borrows from banks and loans out the money at higher interest rates. E-Z's bank requires E-Z to submit quarterly financial statements in order to keep its line of credit. E-Z's main asset is Notes Receivable. Therefore, Uncollectible-Account Expense and Allowance for Uncollectible Accounts are important accounts.

Alicia Johnston, the company's owner, likes net income to increase in a smooth pattern, rather than increase in some periods and decrease in other periods. To report smoothly increasing net income, Johnston underestimates Uncollectible-Account Expense in some periods. In other periods, Johnston overestimates the expense. She reasons that the income overstatements roughly offset the income understatements over time.

REQUIRED

Is E-Z's practice of smoothing income ethical? Why or why not?

Problems (GROUP A)

Controlling cash receipts from customers ***(Obj. 1)***

P8-1A Dental Laboratory Service prepares crowns, dentures, and other dental appliances. All work is performed on account, with regular monthly billing to participating dentists. Melany Rank, accountant for Dental Laboratory Service, receives and opens the mail. Company procedure requires her to separate customer checks from the remittance slips, which list the amounts she posts as credits to customer accounts receivable. Rank deposits the checks in the bank. She computes each day's total amount posted to customer accounts and matches this total to the bank deposit slip. This procedure is intended to ensure that all receipts are deposited in the bank.

REQUIRED

As a consultant hired by Dental Laboratory Service, write a memo to management evaluating the company's internal controls over cash receipts from customers. If the system is effective, identify its strong features. If the system has flaws, propose a way to strengthen the controls. Use the memorandum format given in Exercise 8-1, page 363.

Accounting for uncollectibles by the direct write-off and allowance methods ***(Obj. 2, 3, 5)***

P8-2A On May 31, Schlotzky, Inc., had a $219,000 debit balance in Accounts Receivable. During June, the company had sales revenue of $789,000, which included $640,000 in credit sales. Other data for June include

- Collections on accounts receivable, $581,400.
- Write-offs of uncollectible receivables, $8,900.

REQUIRED

1. Record uncollectible-account expense for June by the direct write-off method. Post to Accounts Receivable and Uncollectible-Account Expense and show their balances at June 30.
2. Record uncollectible-account expense and write-offs of customer accounts for June by the allowance method. Show all June activity in Accounts Receivable, Allowance for Uncollectible Accounts, and Uncollectible-Account Expense. The May 31 unadjusted balance in Allowance for Uncollectible Accounts was $2,800 (credit), as the company closes its books at the end of each calendar quarter. Uncollectible-Account Expense was estimated at 2% of credit sales.
3. What amount of uncollectible-account expense would Schlotzky report on its June income statement under the two methods? Which amount better matches expense with revenue? Give your reason.
4. What amount of *net* accounts receivable would Schlotzky report on its June 30 balance sheet under the two methods? Which amount is more realistic? Give your reason.

Using the percent of sales and aging methods for uncollectibles ***(Obj. 2, 5)***

P8-3A The June 30, 19X4, balance sheet of A-1 Healthcare, Inc., reports the following:

Accounts Receivable	$143,000
Allowance for Uncollectible Accounts (credit balance)	3,200

At the end of each quarter, A-1 estimates uncollectible-account expense to be 1½% of credit sales. At the end of the year, the company ages its accounts receivable and adjusts the balance in Allowance for Uncollectible Accounts to correspond to the aging schedule. During the second half of 19X4, A-1 completed the following selected transactions:

Aug. 9	Made a compound entry to write off the following uncollectible accounts: Clif, Inc., $235; Matz Co., $188; and L. Norris, $706.
Sep. 30	Recorded uncollectible-account expense based on credit sales of $130,000.
Oct. 18	Wrote off as uncollectible the $767 account receivable from Bliss Co. and the $430 account receivable from Micro Data.
Dec. 31	Recorded uncollectible-account expense based on the aging of accounts receivable.

Total Balance	Age of Accounts			
	1–30 Days	31–60 Days	61–90 Days	Over 90 Days
$129,400	$74,600	$31,100	$14,000	$9,700
Estimated percent uncollectible	0.1%	0.4%	5.0%	30.0%

REQUIRED

1. Record the transactions in the journal.
2. Open the Allowance for Uncollectible Accounts, and post entries affecting that account. Keep a running balance.
3. Most companies report two-year comparative financial statements. If A-1's Accounts Receivable balance was $118,000 and the Allowance for Uncollectible Accounts stood at $2,700 at December 31, 19X3, show how the company will report its accounts receivable on a comparative balance sheet for 19X4 and 19X3.

Using the percent of sales and aging methods for uncollectibles
(Obj. 2, 5)

P8-4A ⟸ *Link Back to Chapter 4 (Closing Entries).* Masters Company completed the following transactions during 19X1 and 19X2:

19X1	
Dec. 31	Estimated that uncollectible-account expense for the year was ¾ of 1% on credit sales of $300,000, and recorded that amount as expense.
31	Made the closing entry for uncollectible-account expense.
19X2	
Jan. 17	Sold inventory to Mary Lee, $652, on credit terms of 2/10 n/30. Ignore cost of goods sold.
June 29	Wrote off the Mary Lee account as uncollectible after repeated efforts to collect from her.
Aug. 6	Received $250 from Mary Lee, along with a letter stating her intention to pay her debt in full within 30 days. Reinstated her account in full.
Sept. 4	Received the balance due from Mary Lee.
Dec. 31	Made a compound entry to write off the following accounts as uncollectible: Bernard Klaus, $737; Louis Mann, $348; and Millie Burnett, $622.
31	Estimated that uncollectible-account expense for the year was ⅔ of 1% on credit sales of $420,000, and recorded that amount as expense.
31	Made the closing entry for uncollectible-account expense.

REQUIRED

1. Open general ledger accounts for Allowance for Uncollectible Accounts and Uncollectible-Account Expense. Keep running balances.
2. Record the transactions in the general journal, and post to the two ledger accounts.
3. The December 31, 19X2, balance of Accounts Receivable is $139,000. Show how Accounts Receivable would be reported at that date.
4. This requirement is entirely independent of requirements 1 through 3. Assume that Masters Company begins aging accounts receivable on December 31, 19X2. The balance in Accounts Receivable is $139,000, the credit balance in Allowance for Uncollectible Accounts is $543, and the company estimates that $2,600 of its accounts receivable will prove uncollectible.
   a. Make the adjusting entry for uncollectibles.
   b. Show how Accounts Receivable will be reported on the December 31, 19X2, balance sheet.

Accounting for notes receivable, including discounting notes and accruing interest revenue
(Obj. 4)

P8-5A A company received the following notes during 19X3. Notes (1), (2), and (3) were discounted on the dates and at the rates indicated.

Note	Date	Principal Amount	Interest Rate	Term	Date Discounted	Discount Rate
(1)	July 12	$10,000	10%	3 months	Aug. 12	15%
(2)	Aug. 4	6,000	11%	90 days	Aug. 30	13%
(3)	Oct. 21	8,000	15%	60 days	Nov. 3	18%
(4)	Nov. 30	12,000	12%	6 months	—	—
(5)	Dec. 7	9,000	10%	30 days	—	—
(6)	Dec. 23	15,000	9%	1 year	—	—

REQUIRED

As necessary in requirements 1 through 5, identify each note by number, compute interest using a 360-day year for those notes with terms specified in days or years, round all interest amounts to the nearest dollar, and present entries in general journal form. Explanations are not required.

1. Determine the due date and maturity value of each note.
2. For each discounted note, determine the discount and proceeds from sale of the note.
3. Journalize the discounting of notes (1) and (2).
4. Journalize a single adjusting entry at December 31, 19X3, to record accrued interest revenue on notes (4), (5), and (6).
5. Journalize the collection of principal and interest on note (5).

Accounting for notes receivable, discounted notes, dishonored notes, and accrued interest revenue
(Obj. 4)

P8-6A ⟸ *Link Back to Chapter 4 (Closing Entries).* Record the following selected transactions in the general journal of Well Point Instrument Company. Explanations are not required.

19X6	
Dec. 19	Received a $2,000, 60-day, 12% note on account from Claude Bernard.
31	Made an adjusting entry to accrue interest on the Bernard note.
31	Made an adjusting entry to record uncollectible-account expense in the amount of 1% of credit sales of $474,500.
31	Made a compound closing entry for interest revenue and uncollectible-account expense.

19X7

Feb. 17 Collected the maturity value of the Bernard note.
Mar. 22 Sold merchandise to Idaho Power Co., receiving $1,400 cash and a 90-day, 10% note for $6,000. Ignore cost of goods sold.
May 3 Discounted the Idaho Power Co. note to First National Bank at 15 percent.
June 1 Loaned $10,000 cash to Linz Brothers, receiving a 6-month, 11% note.
Oct 31 Received a $1,500, 60-day, 12% note from Ned Pierce on his past-due account receivable.
Dec. 1 Collected the maturity value of the Linz Brothers note.
30 Ned Pierce dishonored his note at maturity; wrote off the note receivable as uncollectible, debiting Allowance for Uncollectible Accounts.
31 Wrote off as uncollectible the account receivable of Al Bynum, $435, and Ray Sharp, $276.

P8-7A Assume that Del Monte Foods, famous for its canned vegetables, completed the following selected transactions:

Journalizing uncollectibles, notes receivable, discounting notes, and accrued interest revenue
(Obj. 4)

19X5

Nov. 1 Sold goods to Safeway Co., receiving a $24,000, three-month, 8% note. Ignore cost of goods sold.
Dec. 31 Made an adjusting entry to accrue interest on the Safeway note.
31 Made an adjusting entry to record uncollectible-account expense based on an aging of accounts receivable. The aging analysis indicates that $197,400 of accounts receivable will not be collected. Prior to this adjustment, the credit balance in Allowance for Uncollectible Accounts is $189,900.

19X6

Feb. 1 Collected the maturity value of the Safeway note.
23 Received a 90-day, 15%, $4,000 note from Bliss Co. on account.
Mar. 31 Discounted the Bliss Co. note to Lakewood Bank, receiving cash of $3,925.
June 23 Sold merchandise to Lear Corp., receiving a 60-day, 10% note for $9,000. Ignore cost of goods sold.
Aug. 22 Lear Corp. dishonored (failed to pay) its note at maturity; converted the maturity value of the note to an account receivable.
Nov. 16 Loaned $8,500 cash to McNeil, Inc., receiving a 90-day, 12% note.
Dec. 5 Collected in full from Lear Corp.
31 Accrued the interest on the McNeil, Inc., note.

REQUIRED

Record the transactions in the journal of Del Monte Foods. Explanations are not required.

P8-8A *Link Back to Chapter 4 (Current Ratio).* The comparative financial statements of Pinnacle East, Inc., for 19X9, 19X8, and 19X7 include the following selected data:

Using ratio data to evaluate a company's financial position
(Obj. 6)

	19X9	19X8	19X7
		(In millions)	
Balance sheet:			
Current assets:			
Cash	$ 76	$ 80	$ 60
Short-term investments	140	174	122
Receivables, net of allowance for doubtful accounts of $6, $6, and $5, respectively	257	265	218
Inventories	429	341	302
Prepaid expenses	21	27	46
Total current assets	923	887	748
Total current liabilities	$ 503	$ 528	$ 413
Income statement:			
Sales revenue	$5,189	$4,995	$4,206
Cost of sales	2,734	2,636	2,418

REQUIRED

1. Compute these ratios for 19X9 and 19X8:
   a. Current ratio
   b. Acid-test ratio
   c. Days' sales in receivables
2. Write a memo explaining to top management which ratio values showed improvement from 19X8 to 19X9 and which ratio values showed deterioration. Which item in the financial statements caused some ratio values to improve and others to deteriorate? Discuss whether this factor conveys a favorable or an unfavorable impression about the company.

Reporting cash flows related to receivables; computing net income
(Obj. 7)

P8-9A ◀ *Link Back to Chapter 5 (Income Statement)* Ford Motor Company is one of the world's largest companies. During some years, Ford earns more net income from lending money than it does from making automobiles. Therefore, Ford's receivables are its largest asset. This problem will sharpen your understanding of the reporting of cash flows.

At December 31, 19X6, end of the company's year, Ford reported the following items (adapted) in its financial statements (amounts in billions):

Net sales	$118	Notes receivable	$162
Cash	4	Loaned out money on notes receivable	109
Cash receipts of interest (same as interest revenue)	30	Total current liabilities	33
Inventories	7	Current receivable, net	4
Cost of goods sold	109	Collections on notes receivable	85
Collections from customers	147	All other expenses	35

REQUIRED

1. Show how Ford Motor Company could have reported the relevant items from this list on its statement of cash flows for the year ended December 31, 19X6. Include a heading for the statement. Not all items are reported on the cash-flow statement.
2. Compute Ford's net income for the year. Was all the net income received in cash? How can you tell?

Problems (GROUP B)

Controlling cash receipts from customers
(Obj. 1)

P8-1B Oshman's Sporting Goods distributes merchandise to sporting goods stores. All sales are on credit, so virtually all cash receipts arrive in the mail. Menachem Fultz, the company president, has just returned from a trade association meeting with new ideas for the business. Among other things, Fultz plans to institute stronger internal controls over cash receipts from customers.

REQUIRED

Assume you are Menachem Fultz, the company president. Write a memo to employees outlining a set of procedures to ensure that all cash receipts are deposited in the bank and that the total amounts of each day's cash receipts are posted as credits to customer accounts receivable. Use the memorandum format given in Exercise 8-1, page 363.

Accounting for uncollectibles by the direct write-off and allowance methods
(Obj. 2, 3, 5)

P8-2B On February 28, Dudley Curry Co. had a $75,000 debit balance in Accounts Receivable. During March, the company had sales revenue of $509,000, which included $445,000 in credit sales. Other data for March include

- Collections on accounts receivable, $431,600.
- Write-offs of uncollectible receivables, $3,500.

REQUIRED

1. Record uncollectible-account expense for March by the direct write-off method. Post to Accounts Receivable and Uncollectible-Account Expense and show their balances at March 31.
2. Record uncollectible-account expense and write-offs of customer accounts for March by the allowance method. Show all March activity in Accounts Receivable, Allowance for Uncollectible Accounts, and Uncollectible-Account Expense. The February 28 unadjusted balance in Allowance for Uncollectible Accounts was $800 (debit), as the company closes its books at the end of each calendar quarter. Uncollectible-Account Expense was estimated at 2% of credit sales.
3. What amount of uncollectible-account expense would Dudley Curry Co. report on its March income statement under the two methods? Which amount better matches expense with revenue? Give your reason.
4. What amount of *net* accounts receivable would Dudley Curry Co. report on its March 31 balance sheet under the two methods? Which amount is more realistic? Give your reason.

Using the percent of sales and aging methods for uncollectibles
(Obj. 2, 5)

P8-3B The June 30, 19X9, balance sheet of The Headliners Club, Inc., reports the following:

Accounts Receivable	$265,000
Allowance for Uncollectible Accounts (credit balance)	7,100

At the end of each quarter, The Headliners Club estimates uncollectible-account expense to be 2% of credit sales. At the end of the year, the company ages its accounts receivable and adjusts the balance in Allowance for Uncollectible Accounts to correspond to the aging schedule. During the second half of 19X9, The Headliners Club completed the following selected transactions:

July 14	Made a compound entry to write off the following uncollectible accounts: C. H. Harris, $766; Graphics, Inc., $2,413; and B. McQueen, $134.
Sep. 30	Recorded uncollectible-account expense based on credit sales of $141,400.

Nov. 22	Wrote off the following accounts receivable as uncollectible: Monet Corp., $1,345; Blocker, Inc., $2,109; and M Street Plaza, $755.
Dec. 31	Recorded uncollectible-account expense based on the aging of accounts receivable.

	Age of Accounts			
Total Balance	1–30 Days	31–60 Days	61–90 Days	Over 90 Days
$296,600	$161,500	$86,000	$34,000	$15,100
Estimated percent uncollectible	0.2%	0.5%	4.0%	50.0%

REQUIRED

1. Record the transactions in the journal.
2. Open the Allowance for Uncollectible Accounts, and post entries affecting that account. Keep a running balance.
3. Most companies report two-year comparative financial statements. If The Headliners Club Accounts Receivable balance was $271,400 and the Allowance for Uncollectible Accounts stood at $8,240 at December 31, 19X8, show how the company will report its accounts receivable in a comparative balance sheet for 19X9 and 19X8.

Using the percent of sales and aging methods for uncollectibles ***(Obj. 2, 5)***

P8-4B *Link Back to Chapter 4 (Closing Entries).* Reynaldo Company completed the following selected transactions during 19X1 and 19X2:

19X1	
Dec. 31	Estimated that uncollectible-account expense for the year was ⅔ of 1% on credit sales of $450,000, and recorded that amount as expense.
31	Made the closing entry for uncollectible-account expense.
19X2	
Feb. 4	Sold inventory to Gary Carter, $1,521, on credit terms of 2/10 n/30. Ignore cost of goods sold.
July 1	Wrote off Gary Carter's account as uncollectible after repeated efforts to collect from him.
Oct. 19	Received $521 from Gary Carter, along with a letter stating his intention to pay his debt in full within 30 days. Reinstated his account in full.
Nov. 15	Received the balance due from Gary Carter.
Dec. 31	Made a compound entry to write off the following accounts as uncollectible: Kris Moore, $899; Marie Mandue, $530; and Grant Frycer, $1,272.
31	Estimated that uncollectible-account expense for the year was ⅔ of 1% on credit sales of $540,000, and recorded the expense.
31	Made the closing entry for uncollectible-account expense.

REQUIRED

1. Open general ledger accounts for Allowance for Uncollectible Accounts and Uncollectible-Account Expense. Keep running balances.
2. Record the transactions in the general journal, and post to the two ledger accounts.
3. The December 31, 19X2, balance of Accounts Receivable is $164,500. Show how Accounts Receivable would be reported at that date.
4. This requirement is entirely independent of requirements 1 through 3. Assume that Reynaldo Company begins aging its accounts receivable on December 31, 19X2. The balance in Accounts Receivable is $164,500, the credit balance in Allowance for Uncollectible Accounts is $299, and the company estimates that $3,545 of its accounts receivable will prove uncollectible.
   - **a.** Make the adjusting entry for uncollectibles.
   - **b.** Show how Accounts Receivable will be reported on the December 31, 19X2, balance sheet.

Accounting for notes receivable, including discounting notes and accruing interest revenue ***(Obj. 4)***

P8-5B A company received the following notes during 19X5. Notes (1), (2), and (3) were discounted on the dates and at the rates indicated.

Note	Date	Principal Amount	Interest Rate	Term	Date Discounted	Discount Rate
(1)	July 15	$ 6,000	10%	6 months	Oct. 15	12%
(2)	Aug. 19	9,000	12%	90 days	Aug. 30	15%
(3)	Sept. 1	8,000	15%	120 days	Nov. 2	20%
(4)	Oct. 30	7,000	12%	3 months	—	—
(5)	Nov. 19	15,000	10%	60 days	—	—
(6)	Dec. 1	12,000	9%	1 year	—	—

REQUIRED

As necessary in requirements 1 through 5, identify each note by number, compute interest using a 360-day year for those notes with terms specified in days or years, round all interest amounts to the nearest dollar, and present entries in general journal form. Explanations are not required.

1. Determine the due date and maturity value of each note.
2. For each discounted note, determine the discount and proceeds from sale of the note.
3. Journalize the discounting of notes (1) and (2).
4. Journalize a single adjusting entry at December 31, 19X5, to record accrued interest revenue on notes (4), (5), and (6).
5. Journalize the collection of principal and interest on note (4).

Accounting for notes receivable, discounted notes, dishonored notes, and accrued interest revenue
(Obj. 4)

P8-6B ◄ *Link Back to Chapter 4 (Closing Entries).* Record the following selected transactions in the general journal of Aetna Systems. Explanations are not required.

19X2	
Dec. 21	Received a $3,600, 30-day, 10% note on account from Myron Blake.
31	Made an adjusting entry to accrue interest on the Blake note.
31	Made an adjusting entry to record uncollectible-account expense in the amount of ¾ of 1% on credit sales of $604,800.
31	Made a compound closing entry for interest revenue and uncollectible-account expense.

19X3	
Jan. 20	Collected the maturity value of the Blake note.
Apr. 19	Sold merchandise to city of Akron, receiving $500 cash and a 120-day, 12% note for $5,000. Ignore cost of goods sold.
May 1	Discounted the city of Akron note to First National Bank at 15 percent.
Sept. 14	Loaned $6,000 cash to Allstate Investors, receiving a three-month, 13% note.
30	Received a $1,675, 60-day, 16% note from Matt Kurtz on his past-due account receivable.
Nov. 29	Matt Kurtz dishonored his note at maturity; wrote off the note as uncollectible, debiting Allowance for Uncollectible Accounts.
Dec. 14	Collected the maturity value of the Allstate Investors note.
31	Wrote off as uncollectible the accounts receivable of Ty Larson, $1,005; and Terry Gee, $140.

Journalizing uncollectibles notes receivable, discounting notes, and accrued interest revenue
(Obj. 4)

P8-7B Assume that Sherwin Williams, a major paint manufacturer, completed the following selected transactions:

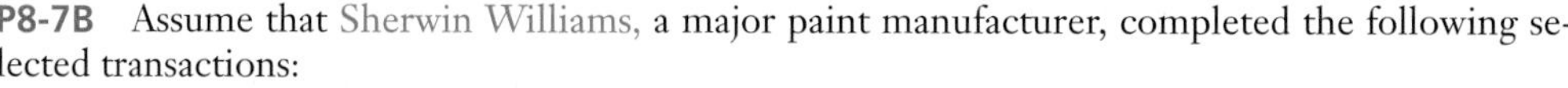

19X4	
Dec. 1	Sold goods to Central Paint Co., receiving a $17,000, three-month, 10% note. Ignore cost of goods sold.
31	Made an adjusting entry to accrue interest on the Central Paint Co. note.
31	Made an adjusting entry to record uncollectible-account expense based on an aging of accounts receivable. The aging analysis indicates that $355,800 of accounts receivable will not be collected. Prior to this adjustment, the credit balance in Allowance for Uncollectible Accounts is $346,100.

19X5	
Feb. 18	Received a 90-day, 10%, $5,000 note from Altex Co. on account.
Mar. 1	Collected the maturity value of the Central Paint Co. note.
8	Discounted the Altex note to First State Bank, receiving cash of $4,894.
July 21	Sold merchandise to Logos, Inc., receiving a 60-day, 9% note for $4,000. Ignore cost of goods sold.
Sep. 19	Logos, Inc., dishonored its note at maturity; converted the maturity value of the note to an account receivable.
Nov. 11	Loaned $40,000 cash to Consolidated, Inc., receiving a 90-day, 9% note.
Dec. 2	Collected in full from Logos, Inc.
31	Accrued the interest on the Consolidated, Inc., note.

REQUIRED

Record the transactions in the journal of Sherwin Williams. Explanations are not required.

P8-8B ⇐ *Link Back to Chapter 4 (Current Ratio).* The comparative financial statements of Mainline Sales Company for 19X8, 19X7, and 19X6 include the following selected data:

Using ratio data to evaluate a company's financial position
(Obj. 6)

	19X8	19X7	19X6
		(In millions)	
Balance sheet:			
Current assets:			
Cash	$ 27	$ 26	$ 22
Short-term investments	93	101	69
Receivables, net of allowance for doubtful accounts of $7, $6, and $4, respectively	146	154	127
Inventories	438	383	341
Prepaid expenses	32	31	25
Total current assets	736	695	584
Total current liabilities	$ 440	$ 446	$ 388
Income statement:			
Sales revenue	$2,671	$2,505	$1,944
Cost of sales	1,380	1,360	963

REQUIRED

1. Compute these ratios for 19X8 and 19X7:
   a. Current ratio **b.** Acid-test ratio **c.** Days' sales in receivables
2. Write a memo explaining to top management which ratio values showed improvement from 19X7 to 19X8 and which ratio values deteriorated. Which item in the financial statements caused some ratio values to improve and others to deteriorate? Discuss whether this factor conveys a favorable or an unfavorable sign about the company.

P8-9B ⇐ *Link Back to Chapter 5 (Merchandiser's Income Statement).* The Home Depot, Inc., is the world's largest home improvement retailer. One of the company's great strengths is its cash flow from operations. The Home Depot has been able to grow rapidly without having to borrow heavily. This problem will sharpen your understanding of the reporting of cash flows.

Reporting cash flows related to receivables; computing net income
(Obj. 7)

At January 31, 19X7, end of the company's fiscal year, The Home Depot reported the following items (adapted) in its financial statements (amounts in millions):

Net sales	$19,536	Notes receivable	$39,518
Cash	146	Loaned out money on notes receivable	1,342
Cash receipts of interest (same as interest revenue)	26	Merchandise inventories	2,708
Buildings	2,470	Accounts receivable, net	388
Cost of goods sold	14,101	Collections on notes receivable	16,539
Collections from customers	19,473	All other expenses	4,523

1. Show how The Home Depot could have reported the relevant items from this list on its statement of cash flows for the year ended January 31, 19X7. Include a heading for the statement.
2. Compute The Home Depot's net income for the year. Was all the net income received in cash? How can you tell?

Applying Your Knowledge

DECISION CASES

CASE 1. SunItaly Corporation performs service either for cash or on notes receivable. The business uses the direct write-off method to account for bad debts. Ann Adolfo, the owner, has prepared the company's financial statements. The most recent comparative income statements, for 19X8 and 19X7, are as follows:

Uncollectible accounts and evaluating a business
(Obj. 2, 3)

	19X8	19X7
Total revenue	$220,000	$195,000
Total expenses	157,000	143,000
Net income	$ 63,000	$ 52,000

On the basis of the increase in net income, Adolfo seeks to expand operations. She asks you to invest $50,000 in the business. You and Adolfo have several meetings, at which you learn that notes receivable from customers were $200,000 at the end of 19X6 and $400,000 at the end of 19X7.

Also, total revenues for 19X8 and 19X7 include interest at 15% on the year's beginning notes receivable balance. Total expenses include uncollectible-account expense of $2,000 each year, based on the direct write-off method. Adolfo estimates that uncollectible-account expense would be 5% of sales revenue if the allowance method were used.

REQUIRED

1. Prepare for SunItaly Corporation a comparative single-step income statement that identifies service revenue, interest revenue, uncollectible-account expense, and other expenses, all computed in accordance with generally accepted accounting principles.
2. Is SunItaly's future as promising as Adolfo's income statement makes it appear? Give the reason for your answer.

Estimating the collectibility of accounts receivable
(Obj. 2)

CASE 2. Assume that you work in the corporate loan department of Bank of San Remo. Jake Butler, owner of Butler Builders, a manufacturer of mobile homes, has come to you seeking a loan for $1 million to expand operations. Butler proposes to use accounts receivable as collateral for the loan and has provided you with the following information from the most recent financial statements:

	19X9	19X8	19X7
		(In thousands)	
Sales	$1,475	$1,589	$1,502
Cost of goods sold	876	947	905
Gross profit	599	642	597
Other expenses	518	487	453
Net profit or (loss) before taxes	$ 81	$ 155	$ 144
Accounts receivable	$ 458	$ 387	$ 374
Allowance for uncollectible accounts	23	31	29

REQUIRED

1. Analyze the information Butler has provided. Would you grant the loan on the basis of this information? Give your reason.
2. What additional information would you request from Butler? Give your reason.
3. Assume that Butler provided you with the information requested in requirement 2. What would make you change the decision you made in requirement 1?

FINANCIAL STATEMENT CASES

CASE 1. Use data from the balance sheet and income statement of NIKE, Inc., in Appendix A.

REQUIRED

Analyzing accounts receivable and uncollectibles
(Obj. 2, 6)

1. How much did customers owe NIKE at May 31, 1997? Of this amount, how much did NIKE expect to collect? How much did NIKE expect *not* to collect?
2. Assume that during fiscal year 1997, NIKE recorded doubtful-account expense equal to 1% of revenues. Starting with the beginning balance, analyze the Allowance for Doubtful Accounts to determine the amount of accounts receivable that NIKE wrote off as uncollectible during the year. For this analysis, insert the beginning and ending credit balances in the Allowance T-account. Then post the credit to the Allowance for the amount of doubtful-account expense for 1997. Finally, solve for the debit amount that represents write-offs for the year.
3. Compute NIKE's acid-test ratio at May 31, 1997. If all the current liabilities came due immediately, could NIKE pay them?

CASE 2. Obtain the annual report of a company of your choosing.

REQUIRED

Analyzing accounts receivable, uncollectibles, and notes receivable
(Obj. 2, 4)

1. How much did customers owe the company at the end of the current year? Of this amount, how much did the company expect to collect? How much did the company expect *not* to collect?
2. Assume that during the current year the company recorded doubtful-account expense equal to 1% of net sales. Starting with the beginning balance, analyze the Allowance for Doubtful Accounts to determine the amount of the receivable write-offs during the current year.
3. If the company does not have notes receivable, you may skip this requirement. If notes receivable are present at the end of the current year, assume that their interest rate is 9 percent. Assume also that no new notes receivable arose during the following year. Journalize these transactions which took place during the following year:
   a. Received cash for 75% of the interest revenue earned during the year.
   b. Accrued the remaining portion of the interest revenue earned during the year.
   c. At year end collected half the notes receivable.

Team Project (Notes Receivable of the Bank)

Shannon Billings and Monica Salazar worked for several years as sales representatives for Xerox Corporation. During this time, they became close friends as they acquired expertise with the company's full range of copier equipment. Now they see an opportunity to put their experience to work and fulfill lifelong desires to establish their own business. Taft Community College, located in their city, is expanding, and there is no copy center within five miles of the campus. Business in the area is booming—office buildings and apartments are springing up, and the population of this section of the city is growing.

Billings and Salazar want to open a copy center, similar to a Kinko's, near the campus. A small shopping center across the street from the college has a vacancy that would fit their needs. Billings and Salazar each have $35,000 to invest in the business, but they forecast the need for $50,000 to renovate the store. Xerox Corporation will lease two large copiers to them at a total monthly rental of $6,000. With enough cash to see them through the first six months of operation, they are confident they can make the business succeed. The two women work very well together, and both have excellent credit ratings. Billings and Salazar must borrow $100,000 to start the business, advertise its opening, and keep it running for its first six months.

REQUIRED

Assume the roles of Billings and Salazar, the partners who will own Taft Copy Center.

1. As a group, visit a copy center to familiarize yourselves with its operations. If possible, interview the manager or another employee. Then write a loan request that Billings and Salazar will submit to a bank with the intent of borrowing $100,000 to be paid back over three years. The loan will be a personal loan to the partnership of Billings and Salazar, not to Taft Copy Center. The request should specify all the details of Billings' and Salazar's plan that will motivate the bank to grant the loan. Include a budgeted income statement for the first six months of the copy center's operation.
2. As a group, interview a loan officer in a bank. Have the loan officer evaluate your loan request. Write a report, or make a presentation to your class—as directed by your instructor—to reveal the loan officer's decision.

Internet Exercise SEARS

Sears is the nation's second largest retailer. Over the past several years, Sears has aggressively extended its credit-card program. Today, Sears has more than 50 million credit-card holders. But this growth in credit-card receivables has not come without problems. Recently, delinquencies have risen, and Sears admitted to illegally collecting money from credit-card holders in bankruptcy. Despite these setbacks, Sears derives half of its profits from the credit-card group.

How have these recent events been reflected in Sears' financial statements?

REQUIRED

1. Go to Sears' home page at **http://www.sears.com.**
2. Click on the **About Our Company** icon. Here the visitor can explore many facets of Sears' business, including its grand history, job opportunities, and financial offerings.
3. Click on **Investor Relations** and locate the most recent annual report. Answer the following questions relating to Sears' credit-card receivables.
   a. What is the credit-card receivable balance at the end of the most recent year?
   b. What is the related allowance for bad debts at the end of the most recent year?
   c. In the Analysis of Consolidated Operations section of the annual report, Sears' management presents detailed data of Sears credit-card activities. What is Sears' provision for uncollectible accounts (that is, bad debt expense) for the most recent year?
   d. Calculate Sears' days' sales in average net credit-card receivables for the most recent year. Use data from the income statement (Merchandise sales and services) and the balance sheet (Credit-card receivables, net) to compute this ratio. Why is Sears' days' sales in receivables ratio so high?

CHAPTER 9

Accounting for Merchandise Inventory

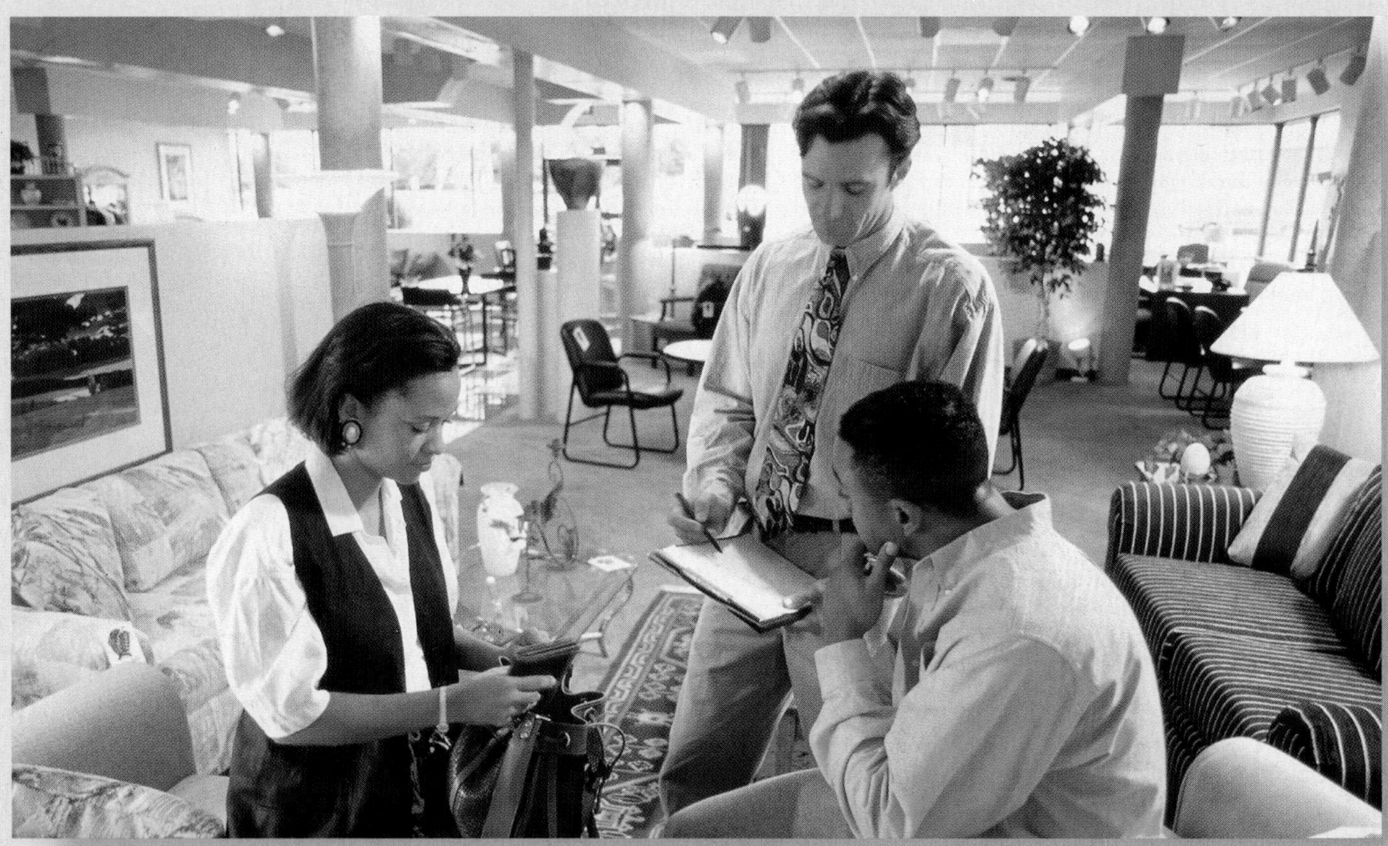

LEARNING OBJECTIVES

After studying this chapter, you should be able to

1. Account for inventory by the periodic and perpetual systems
2. Apply the inventory costing methods: specific unit cost, weighted-average cost, FIFO, and LIFO
3. Identify the income effects and the tax effects of the inventory costing methods
4. Apply the lower-of-cost-or-market rule to inventory
5. Determine the effects of inventory errors on cost of goods sold and net income
6. Estimate ending inventory by the gross margin method
7. Report inventory transactions on the statement of cash flows

> *"Over the past few years, we have been focusing on building net income, and our record-breaking 1997 profits show that our efforts have paid off. But when we took a hard look at our inventory costing method, we were amazed to find that we could eventually save millions of dollars in taxes just by switching accounting methods."*
>
> —BRAD STREET, CONTROLLER OF HUNTINGTON GALLERIES

Huntington Galleries, a Maryland-based furniture retailer, reported net income of $53.9 million for 1997, up 20% from the previous year (Exhibit 9-1). The reported figures continued the company's pattern of uninterrupted growth in profits. Wall Street responded favorably to the announcement, and Huntington's stock price rose $0.75.

Lori Huntington, chief executive officer of Huntington Galleries, attributed the strong performance to a demand for the company's high-end line of furniture during the second half of the year. In a report filed with the SEC, Huntington disclosed that the company switched from the *FIFO method* to the *LIFO method* of accounting for inventories. Brad Street, the controller of Huntington Galleries, explained that the company changed inventory methods to save on income taxes. He estimated that the switch in inventory methods will save Huntington Galleries $1.3 million over the next two years.

EXHIBIT 9-1
Financial Statements of Huntington Galleries

HUNTINGTON GALLERIES
Income Statement
Year Ended December 31, 1997
(In thousands)

Net sales		$165,900
Cost of goods sold		90,800
Gross margin		75,100
Operating expenses:		
Wage expense	$10,200	
Rent expense	8,400	
Insurance expense	1,000	
Depreciation expense	600	
Supplies expense	500	20,700
Operating income		54,400
Other revenue and (expense):		
Interest revenue	$ 1,000	
Interest expense	(1,500)	(500)
Net income		$ 53,900

HUNTINGTON GALLERIES
Balance Sheet
December 31, 1997
(In thousands)

Assets			Liabilities	
Current:			Current:	
Cash		$ 2,800	Accounts payable	$43,200
Short-term investments		1,600	Unearned sales revenue	700
Note receivable		11,000	Wages payable	400
Interest receivable		400	Interest payable	200
Inventory		40,200	Income tax payable	3,800
Prepaid expenses		300	Total current liabilities	48,300
Total current assets		56,300	Long term:	
Plant:			Note payable	12,600
Store fixtures			Total liabilities	60,900
and equipment	$33,200		**Owners' Equity**	
Less: Accumulated depreciation	(3,000)	30,200	Owners' capital	25,600
			Total liabilities and	
Total assets		$86,500	owners' equity	$86,500

Merchandising Company. A company that resells products that it bought from suppliers.

The experience of Huntington Galleries underscores the importance of *merchandise inventory*. Huntington is a **merchandising company**—a company that resells products that it bought from suppliers. As Huntington's balance sheet shows, inventory is the lifeblood of a merchandising entity—the entity's major current asset. What is the entity's major expense? It is *cost of goods sold* or *cost of sales*, the cost of the inventory that the business has sold to customers. For example, Wal-Mart Stores, Inc., reported cost of goods sold at $83.7 billion and operating, selling, and administrative expenses at $16.8 billion in 1997. For many merchandising companies, cost of goods sold is greater than all other expenses combined. This is the case at Huntington Galleries, as the company's income statement shows.

If the business buys inventory that is in demand, it will be able to sell the goods at a profit. But there is much more to merchandising than buying and selling.

Accounting plays an important role in merchandising. The most obvious role is the recordkeeping required to stay abreast of quantities on hand in order to meet customer demand. Beyond that, there are several different methods of accounting for the cost of inventories. The chapter opening story refers to the FIFO and LIFO inventory methods, which you will learn about shortly. *FIFO* stands for "first-in, first-out." *LIFO* stands for "last-in, first-out." These popular methods have some distinct characteristics that managers, investors, and creditors need to understand. For example, FIFO and LIFO result in different amounts of reported income and different amounts of income tax. Huntington Galleries' switch from FIFO to LIFO will save the company $1.3 million in income taxes. In short, accounting for inventory goes far beyond recordkeeping.

We begin this chapter with the basic concept of accounting for inventories. Then we examine different inventory systems (perpetual and periodic), the different inventory methods (FIFO, LIFO, and average), and several related topics.

The Basic Concept of Inventory Accounting

The basic concept of accounting for inventory can be illustrated as follows. Suppose Huntington Galleries

- Buys three chairs for $300 each and marks them up $200
- Sells two chairs for the retail price of $500 each

Huntington's balance sheet and income statement then report the following:

Balance Sheet (partial)	
Current assets:	
Cash	$XXX
Short-term investments	XXX
Accounts receivable	XXX
Inventory (1 chair @ $300)	300
Prepaid expenses	XXX

Income Statement (partial)	
Sales revenue	
(2 chairs @ $500)	$1,000
Cost of goods sold	
(2 chairs @ $300)	600
Gross margin	$ 400

As we saw in Chapter 5, **gross margin,** also called **gross profit,** is the excess of sales revenue over cost of goods sold. It is called *gross* margin because operating expenses have not yet been subtracted. Gross margin minus all the operating expenses equals *net* income.

Gross Margin or **Gross Profit.** Excess of sales revenue over cost of goods sold.

In practice, accounting for inventory is usually more complex than our simple example would suggest. Complexity arises from several sources. The following sections describe alternative ways to account for inventories.

■ Daily Exercise 9-1

Objective 1

Account for inventory by the periodic and perpetual systems

Inventory Systems

There are two main types of inventory accounting systems: the periodic system and the perpetual system. The **periodic inventory system** is used by businesses that sell relatively inexpensive goods. Convenience stores without optical-scanning cash registers do not keep a daily running record of every loaf of bread and every six pack of drinks they buy and sell. Instead, these stores count their inventory periodically—at least once a year—to determine the quantities on hand in order to prepare the annual financial statements.

We described these methods briefly in Chapter 5, pages 184.

Periodic Inventory System. An inventory accounting system in which the business does not keep a continuous record of the inventory on hand. Instead, at the end of the period, the business makes a physical count of the on-hand inventory on hand and uses this information to prepare the financial statements.

Under the **perpetual inventory system,** the business maintains a running record of inventory on hand, usually on computer. This system achieves control over goods such as automobiles, jewelry, and furniture. The loss of one item would be significant, and this justifies the cost of a perpetual system. Because the cost of computers has come down, many small businesses now use perpetual inventory systems for all types of goods.

Even under a perpetual system the business still counts the inventory on hand annually. The physical count establishes the correct amount of ending inventory and serves as a check on the perpetual records. The following chart compares the periodic and perpetual systems:

Perpetual Inventory System. An accounting inventory system in which the business keeps a continuous record for each inventory item to show the inventory on hand at all times.

Periodic Inventory System	Perpetual Inventory System
• Does not keep a running record of all goods bought and sold	• Keeps a running record of all goods bought and sold
• Inventory counted at least once a year	• Inventory counted once a year
• Used for inexpensive goods	• Used for all types of goods

Perpetual Inventory System

Perpetual inventory records can be a computer printout like the Huntington Galleries record shown in Exhibit 9-2. The quantities of goods on hand are updated daily, as inventory transactions occur. Many companies keep their perpetual records in terms of quantities only. Others keep perpetual inventory records both in quantities and dollar cost as shown in Exhibit 9-8, page 391.

ENTRIES UNDER THE PERPETUAL SYSTEM In the perpetual system, the business records purchases of inventory by debiting the Inventory account. When the business makes a sale, two entries are needed. The company records the sale in the usual manner—debits Cash or Accounts Receivable and credits Sales Revenue for the sale price of the goods. The company also debits Cost of Goods Sold (which is an expense account) and credits Inventory for cost. The debit to Inventory (for purchases) and the credit to Inventory (for sales) serve to keep an up-to-date record of the cost of inventory on hand. The Inventory account and the Cost of Goods Sold account carry a current balance during the period.

Exhibit 9-3 illustrates the accounting for inventory transactions in a perpetual system (and in a periodic system as well) at Huntington Galleries. Panel A gives the journal entries and the T-accounts, and Panel B presents the income statement and balance-sheet effects. All amounts are assumed.

In Exhibit 9-3, Panel A, the first entry to Inventory summarizes a lot of detail. The cost of the inventory, $560,000, is the *net* amount of the purchases, determined as follows (using assumed amounts):

Net Purchases	
Purchase price of the inventory (including freight in)	$600,000
– Purchase returns for damaged or otherwise unsuitable goods returned to the seller	(25,000)
– Purchase allowances granted by the seller	(5,000)
– Purchase discounts for early payment	(10,000)
= Net purchases of inventory	$560,000

Throughout the remainder of the book, we often refer to net purchases simply as Purchases, as in Exhibit 9-3.

EXHIBIT 9-2
Perpetual Inventory Record—Quantities Only Huntington Galleries

Item: Early American Chair

Date	Quantity Received	Quantity Sold	Quantity on Hand
Nov. 1			10
5		6	4
7	25		29
12		13	16
26	25		41
30		21	20
Totals	50	40	20

PANEL A—Recording in the Journal and Posting to the T-accounts

Perpetual System

1. Credit purchases of $560,000:

Inventory	560,000	
Accounts Payable		560,000

2. Credit sales of $900,000 (cost $540,000):

Accounts Receivable	900,000	
Sales Revenue		900,000
Cost of Goods Sold	540,000	
Inventory		540,000

3. End-of-period entries:
No entries required. Both Inventory and Cost of Goods Sold are-up-to date.

INVENTORY AND COST OF GOODS SOLD ACCOUNTS

Inventory		Cost of Goods Sold	
100,000*	540,000	540,000	
560,000			
120,000			

*Beginning inventory was $100,000.

Periodic System

1. Credit purchases of $560,000:

Purchases	560,000	
Accounts Payable		560,000

2. Credit sales of $900,000:

Accounts Receivable	900,000	
Sales Revenue		900,000

3. End-of-period entries to update Inventory and record Cost of Goods Sold:

a. Transfer the cost of beginning inventory ($100,000) to Cost of Goods Sold:

Cost of Goods Sold	100,000	
Inventory (beginning balance)		100,000

b. Record the cost of ending inventory ($120,000) based on a physical count:

Inventory (ending balance)	120,000	
Cost of Goods Sold		120,000

c. Transfer the cost of purchases to Cost of Goods Sold:

Cost of Goods Sold	560,000	
Purchases		560,000

INVENTORY AND COST OF GOODS SOLD ACCOUNTS

Inventory		Cost of Goods Sold	
100,000*	100,000	100,000	120,000
120,000		560,000	
		540,000	

*Beginning inventory was $100,000.

PANEL B—Reporting in the Financial Statements

Perpetual System

Income Statement (partial)

Sales revenue	$900,000
Cost of goods sold	540,000
Gross margin	$360,000

Ending Balance Sheet (partial)

Current assets:

Cash	$ XXX
Short-term investments	XXX
Accounts receivable	XXX
Inventories	120,000
Prepaid expenses	XXX

Periodic System

Sales revenue		$900,000
Cost of goods sold:		
Beginning inventory	$100,000	
Purchases	560,000	
Cost of goods available for sale	660,000	
Less: Ending inventory	(120,000)	
Cost of goods sold		540,000
Gross margin		$360,000

Current assets:

Cash	$ XXX
Short-term investments	XXX
Accounts receivable	XXX
Inventories	120,000
Prepaid expenses	XXX

■ Daily Exercise 9-2
■ Daily Exercise 9-3
■ Daily Exercise 9-4

EXHIBIT 9-3
Recording and Reporting Inventory Transactions of Huntington Galleries—Perpetual and Periodic Systems (amounts assumed)

The cost of the goods purchased by Huntington Galleries during the year was $560,000. This is based on a general principle:

The cost of an asset =	**The sum of all the costs incurred to bring the asset to its intended purpose, net of all discounts**

Therefore, the buyer's cost of transporting goods from the supplier (freight in) is part of the purchase cost of the inventory. These transportation charges are *not* recorded as an expense.

At the end of the period, no adjusting entries are required. Both Inventory and Cost of Goods Sold are up-to-date.

Periodic Inventory System

In the periodic inventory system, the business does not keep a continuous record of the inventory on hand. Instead, at the end of the period, the business makes a physical count of the inventory on hand and computes the cost of ending inventory. This inventory figure appears on the balance sheet and is used to compute cost of goods sold.

The periodic system is also called the *physical system* because it relies on the actual physical count of inventory. To use the periodic system effectively, the company's owner must be able to control inventory by visual inspection. For example, when a customer inquires about quantities on hand, the owner or manager should be able to eyeball the goods in the store.

ENTRIES UNDER THE PERIODIC SYSTEM In the periodic system (Exhibit 9-3, Panel A), the business records purchases of inventory as an expense in the Purchases account. Throughout the period, the Inventory account carries the beginning balance left over from the end of the preceding period. At the end of the period, the Inventory account must be updated for the financial statements. A journal entry removes the beginning balance, crediting Inventory and debiting Cost of Goods Sold. A second journal entry sets up the ending balance, based on the physical count. The debit is to Inventory, and the credit to Cost of Goods Sold. The final entry in this sequence transfers the amount of Purchases to Cost of Goods Sold. These end-of-period entries can be made during the closing process.

After the process is complete, Inventory has its correct balance of $120,000, and Cost of Goods Sold shows $540,000, regardless of which inventory system the company uses.

Comparing the Perpetual and Periodic Inventory Systems

Compare the entries under both inventory systems in Exhibit 9-3 step by step. First, study the perpetual system all the way through. On the income statement, the perpetual system reports cost of goods sold on a single line. Then study the periodic system, which reports a more detailed computation of cost of goods sold. Both inventory systems report the same amounts for inventory on the balance sheet and cost of goods sold on the income statement.

Thinking It Over Answer the following questions about various features of the perpetual inventory system and the periodic inventory system.

1. Do the perpetual and periodic inventory systems result in the same or different dollar amounts for Inventory and Cost of Goods Sold to be reported in the financial statements? Explain.
2. a. Which inventory system records the cost of inventory purchased as an asset and then records the cost of inventory sold as expense?
   b. Which inventory system records the cost of inventory purchased as an expense (name the expense account) and then records the cost of inventory on hand at the end of the period as an asset?
3. Suppose your company produces microchips for use in manufacturing computer circuit boards. Technology is advancing rapidly, and you require monthly financial statements to remain competitive. Which inventory system should you use?

Answers

1. Both inventory systems result in the same amounts for Inventory and Cost of Goods Sold because the facts are the same regardless of the inventory system.
2. a. The *perpetual inventory system* records the cost of inventory purchased as an asset and then the cost of goods sold as an expense.
   b. The *periodic inventory system* records the cost of inventory purchased as an expense (the Purchases account) and then records the cost of inventory on hand at the end of the period as an asset.
3. You should use the *perpetual inventory system* because it gives up-to-date inventory information that can be used to prepare the financial statements at any time.

Cost of Goods Sold (Cost of Sales) and Gross Margin (Gross Profit)

Exhibit 9-3 illustrates the measurement of cost of goods sold (cost of sales) in the two inventory systems. In a perpetual system, cost of sales is simply the sum of all the amounts posted to the Cost of Goods Sold account throughout the period (see Exhibit 9-3, Panel A). By contrast, the periodic system measures cost of sales only at the end of the period after a physical count of the inventory is done and the closing process is complete.

Using the periodic system, the cost-of-goods-sold computation from Exhibit 9-3 is as follows:

Cost of Goods Sold	
Beginning inventory	$100,000
+ Purchases (including freight in)	560,000
= Cost of goods available for sale	660,000
− Ending inventory	(120,000)
= Cost of goods sold	$540,000

The business began the period with $100,000 of inventory. During the period, it purchased goods costing $560,000. The sum of the beginning inventory plus the purchases equals the **cost of goods available for sale** during the period, $660,000. Goods available are either in ending inventory, $120,000, or they were sold during the period. Cost of goods sold during the year was thus $660,000 – $120,000 = $540,000. Learn this model now because you will use it throughout your business career.

Cost of Goods Available for Sale. Beginning inventory plus purchases during a period.

How Owners and Managers Use the Cost-of-Goods-Sold Model

Suppose you are the general manager of Huntington Galleries. You are planning for the next period and preparing a budget to guide your buying. You have examined the new lines of furniture offered by Drexel, Hickory, and Lane, your three main suppliers, and you've decided which sofas and chairs to purchase for the upcoming season. Now you must decide how much inventory to purchase.

How will you make the purchasing decision? The amount of inventory to purchase depends on three factors: budgeted cost of goods sold, budgeted ending inventory, and the beginning inventory with which you started the period. A rearrangement of the cost-of-goods-sold formula helps you budget purchases as follows (all budgeted amounts are assumed for the next period):

Computation of Budgeted Purchases	
Cost of goods sold (based on the budget for the next period)	$600,000
+ Ending inventory (based on the budget for the next period)	150,000
= Cost of goods available for sale, as budgeted	750,000
− Beginning inventory (actual amount left over from the prior period)	(120,000)
= Purchases (how much inventory you need to buy in the current period)	$630,000

Business owners and managers use this formula to determine how much to spend on inventory, regardless of whether the business uses a perpetual or a periodic inventory system. The power of the cost-of-goods-sold model lies in the key information it captures: beginning and ending inventory levels, purchases, and cost of goods sold.

Gross Margin (Gross Profit)

As we saw earlier, *gross margin*, or *gross profit*, is sales revenue minus cost of goods sold. A company's gross margin is one of its most important statistics. It reveals the company's success in selling its goods at a profit, before deducting operating expenses. "Gross" margin means *before operating expenses.* By contrast, "net" income means *after subtracting all expenses.* A humorous example illustrates the importance of earning a gross profit:

> Johnny and Susie operate a lemonade stand near a busy corner. Heading home from work on a hot day, Lee Jones, a neighbor, asks, "How much do you charge for a glass of lemonade?" "Ten cents," answers Johnny, so Jones replies, "Pour me a big glass." While sipping the lemonade, Jones probes more deeply, "How much does a glass of lemonade cost you?" "About a quarter," answers Susie. Jones then asks, "How can you make money selling lemonade for a dime if it costs you a quarter?" Johnny and Susie shoot back, "Volume. We'll make a profit if we have enough volume."

Businesses must sell their merchandise at a profit, or they will go bankrupt. For this reason, owners and managers keep a close eye on the business's gross margin. Investors and creditors watch gross margin too. An increase in a company's gross margin means higher net income. A sharp downturn in the gross margin is cause for alarm.

Computing the Cost of Inventory

The Huntington Galleries inventory record in Exhibit 9-2 follows the common practice of recording quantities only. The company can multiply the quantity of 20 chairs on hand at November 30 by the unit cost of each chair to compute the value of the ending inventory for the balance sheet, as follows:

Quantity of Inventory on Hand	×	**Unit Cost**	=	**Cost of Inventory on Hand**
20 chairs	×	$300	=	$6,000

DETERMINING THE QUANTITY OF INVENTORY Many businesses—even those that use the perpetual system—physically count their inventory, often on the last day of the fiscal year. If you have worked at a grocery store or some other type of retail business, you will recall the process of "taking inventory." Some entities shut the business down to get a good count of inventory on hand.

Complications may arise in determining the inventory quantity. Suppose the business has purchased some goods that are in transit when the inventory is counted. Even though these items are not physically present, they should be included in the inventory count if title to the goods has passed to the purchaser. When title passes from seller to purchaser, the purchaser becomes the legal owner of the goods.

Recall from Chapter 5 (page 188) that FOB terms determine when title passes from seller to buyer.

Consignment. Transfer of goods by the owner (consignor) to another business (consignee) that, for a fee, sells the inventory on the owner's behalf. The consignee does not take title to the consigned goods.

Another complication in counting inventory arises from consigned goods. In a **consignment** arrangement, the owner of the inventory (the *consignor*) transfers the goods to another business (the *consignee*). For a fee, the consignee sells the inventory for the owner. The consignee does *not* take title to the consigned goods and therefore should not include them in its own inventory. Consignments are common in retailing. Suppose Huntington Galleries is the consignee for a line of beds in its stores. Should Huntington include this consigned merchandise in its inventory count? No, because Huntington Galleries does not own the beds. Instead, the bed manufacturer—the consignor—includes the consigned goods in its inventory. *A rule of thumb is to include in inventory only what the business owns.*

DETERMINING THE UNIT COST OF INVENTORY As we've seen, *inventory cost* is the price the business pays to acquire the inventory—not the selling price of the goods. Suppose Huntington Galleries purchases furniture polish for $10 and sells it for $15. The inventory is reported at its cost of $10 per unit, multiplied by the number of units owned, not at its selling price of $15.

Inventory cost includes invoice price, less any purchase discount, plus sales tax, tariffs, transportation charges, insurance while in transit, and all other costs incurred to make the goods ready for sale. *Net purchases* means the net cost of inventory acquired for resale, after subtracting any purchase discounts and purchase returns and allowances. As we stated earlier, we use the terms *purchases* and *net purchases* interchangeably.

Inventory Costing Methods

Determining the unit cost of inventory is easy when the unit cost remains constant during the period. But the unit cost often changes. For example, during times of inflation, prices rise. The chair that cost Huntington Galleries $300 in January may cost $315 in June and $322 in October. Suppose Huntington sells 40 chairs in November. How many of the chairs cost $300, how many cost $315, and how many cost $322? To compute the cost of goods sold and the cost of inventory on hand, the accountant must have some way to assign the business's cost to each item sold. The four costing methods that GAAP allows are

1. Specific unit cost
2. Weighted-average cost
3. First-in, first-out (FIFO) cost
4. Last-in, first-out (LIFO) cost

A company can use any of these methods. Many companies use different methods for different categories of inventory. Here we use the periodic inventory system to illustrate the four inventory costing methods. We illustrate the methods under the perpetual method later in this chapter.

Objective 2

Apply the inventory costing methods: specific unit cost, weighted-average cost, FIFO, and LIFO

SPECIFIC UNIT COST Some businesses deal in inventory items that differ from unit to unit, such as automobiles, jewels, and real estate. These businesses usually cost their inventory at the specific unit cost of the particular unit. For instance, a Chevrolet dealer may have two vehicles in the showroom—a "stripped-down" model that cost $14,000 and a "loaded" model that cost $17,000. If the dealer sells the loaded model for $19,700, cost of goods sold is $17,000, the cost of the specific unit. The gross margin on this sale is $2,700 ($19,700 – $17,000). If the stripped-down auto is the only unit left in inventory at the end of the period, ending inventory is $14,000, the dealer's cost of the specific unit on hand.

The **specific-unit-cost method** is also called the **specific identification method.** This method is not practical for inventory items that have common characteristics, such as bushels of wheat, gallons of paint, or boxes of laundry detergent.

Specific-Unit-Cost Method. Inventory cost method based on the specific cost of particular units of inventory. Also called the **specific identification method.**

The weighted-average cost, FIFO (first-in, first-out) cost, and LIFO (last-in, first-out) cost methods are fundamentally different from the specific-unit-cost method. These methods do not assign to inventory the specific cost of particular units. Instead, they assume different flows of costs into and out of inventory, as illustrated in Exhibit 9-4. Panel A gives the illustrative data for all three inventory cost methods.

WEIGHTED-AVERAGE COST The **weighted-average cost method,** often called the *average-cost method*, is based on the weighted-average cost of inventory during the period. Weighted-average cost is determined as follows:

Weighted-Average Cost Method. Inventory costing method based on the weighted-average cost of inventory during the period. Weighted-average cost is determined by dividing the cost of goods available for sale by the number of units available. Also called the **average-cost method.**

- Determine the weighted-average cost by dividing the cost of goods available for sale (beginning inventory plus purchases) by the number of units available for sale (beginning inventory plus purchases).
- Compute the ending inventory and cost of goods sold by multiplying the number of units by the weighted-average cost per unit.

To illustrate the costing methods, suppose the business has 60 units of inventory available for sale during the period.

- Ending inventory consists of 20 units.
- Cost of goods sold is based on 40 units.

EXHIBIT 9-4
Inventory and Cost of Goods Sold under Three Costing Methods:
Weighted-Average (Panel B)
FIFO (Panel C)
LIFO (Panel D)

- Daily Exercise 9-5
- Daily Exercise 9-6
- Daily Exercise 9-7

PANEL A—Illustrative Data

Beginning inventory (10 units @ $1,000 per unit)		$10,000
Purchases:		
No. 1 (25 units @ $1,400 per unit)	$35,000	
No. 2 (25 units @ $1,800 per unit)	45,000	
Total purchases		80,000
Cost of goods available for sale (60 units)		90,000
Ending inventory (20 units @ $? per unit)		(?)
Cost of goods sold (40 units @ $? per unit)		$?

PANEL B—Ending Inventory and Cost of Goods Sold

Weighted-Average Cost Method

Cost of goods available for sale—see Panel A (60 units @ average cost of $1,500* per unit)	$90,000
Ending inventory (20 units @ $1,500 per unit)	(30,000)
Cost of goods sold (40 units @ $1,500 per unit)	$60,000

$$*\frac{\text{Cost of goods available for sale, \$90,000}}{\text{Number of units available for sale, 60}} = \text{Average cost per unit, \$1,500}$$

PANEL C—Ending Inventory and Cost of Goods Sold

FIFO Cost Method

Cost of goods available for sale (60 units—see Panel A)		$90,000
Ending inventory (cost of the *last* 20 units available):		
20 units @ $1,800 per unit (from purchase No. 2)		(36,000)
Cost of goods sold (cost of the *first* 40 units available):		
10 units @ $1,000 per unit (all of beginning inventory)	$10,000	
25 units @ $1,400 per unit (all of purchase No. 1)	35,000	
5 units @ $1,800 per unit (from purchase No. 2)	9,000	
Cost of goods sold		$54,000

PANEL D—Ending Inventory and Cost of Goods Sold

LIFO Cost Method

Cost of goods available for sale (60 units—see Panel A)		$90,000
Ending inventory (cost of the *first* 20 units available):		
10 units @ $1,000 per unit (all of beginning inventory)	$(10,000)	
10 units @ $1,400 per unit (from purchase No. 1)	(14,000)	
Ending inventory		(24,000)
Cost of goods sold (cost of the *last* 40 units available):		
25 units @ $1,800 per unit (all of purchase No. 2)	$45,000	
15 units @ $1,400 per unit (from purchase No. 1)	21,000	
Cost of goods sold		$66,000

First-In, First-Out (FIFO) Inventory Costing Method. Inventory costing method by which the first costs into inventory are the first costs out to cost of goods sold. Ending inventory is based on the costs of the most recent purchases.

Last-In, First-Out (LIFO) Inventory Costing Method. Inventory costing method by which the last costs into inventory are the first costs out to cost of goods sold. This method leaves the oldest costs—those of beginning inventory and the earliest purchases of the period—in ending inventory.

Panel A of Exhibit 9-4 gives the data for computing ending inventory and cost of goods sold, and Panel B shows the weighted-average cost computations.

FIRST-IN, FIRST-OUT (FIFO) COST Under the **first-in, first-out (FIFO) method,** the company must keep a record of the cost of each inventory unit purchased. The unit costs for ending inventory may differ from the unit costs used to compute the cost of goods sold. Under FIFO,

- The first costs into inventory are the first costs out to cost of goods sold—hence the name *first-in, first-out.*
- Ending inventory is based on the costs of the most recent purchases.

In our example in Exhibit 9-4, the FIFO cost of ending inventory is $36,000. Cost of goods sold is $54,000. Panel A gives the data, and Panel C shows the FIFO computations.

LAST-IN, FIRST-OUT (LIFO) COST The **last-in, first-out (LIFO) method** also depends on the costs of particular inventory purchases. LIFO is the opposite of FIFO. Under LIFO,

	FIFO		LIFO		Weighted-Average	
Sales revenue (assumed)		$100,000		$100,000		$100,000
Cost of goods sold:						
Goods available for sale (from Exhibit 9-4)	$90,000		$90,000		$90,000	
Ending inventory	(36,000)		(24,000)		(30,000)	
Cost of goods sold		54,000		66,000		60,000
Gross margin		$ 46,000		$ 34,000		$ 40,000

Summary of Income Effects—When inventory unit costs are *increasing*

FIFO	LIFO	Weighted-average
Highest ending inventory Lowest cost of goods sold Highest gross margin	Lowest ending inventory Highest cost of goods sold Lowest gross margin	Results fall between the extremes of FIFO and LIFO

Summary of Income Effects—When inventory unit costs are *decreasing*

FIFO	LIFO	Weighted-average
Lowest ending inventory Highest cost of goods sold Lowest gross margin	Highest ending inventory Lowest cost of goods sold Highest gross margin	Results fall between the extremes of FIFO and LIFO

Concept Highlight

EXHIBIT 9-5
Income Effects of FIFO, LIFO, and Weighted-Average Inventory Methods

- Daily Exercise 9-8
- Daily Exercise 9-9

- The last costs into inventory are the first costs out to cost of goods sold.
- Ending inventory is based on the oldest costs—those of beginning inventory and plus the earliest purchases of the period.

Exhibit 9-4 shows that the LIFO cost of ending inventory is $24,000. Cost of goods sold is $66,000. Again, Panel A gives the data, and Panel D shows the LIFO computations.

Learning Tip: Remember that the terms *FIFO* and *LIFO* describe not which goods are left but rather which goods are sold. FIFO assumes that goods in first are sold first; therefore, the last goods in are left in ending inventory. LIFO assumes that the last goods in are sold first; therefore, the first goods in are left in ending inventory.

Income Effects of FIFO, LIFO, and Weighted-Average Cost

In our example, the cost of inventory rose during the accounting period from $1,000 per unit to $1,400 and finally to $1,800 (Exhibit 9-4, Panel A). When inventory unit costs change, the different costing methods produce different cost of goods sold and ending inventory figures, as Exhibit 9-4 shows (Panels B, C, and D). When inventory unit costs are *increasing*,

- FIFO ending inventory is *highest* because it is priced at the most recent costs, which are the highest.
- LIFO ending inventory is *lowest* because it is priced at the oldest costs, which are the lowest.

When inventory unit costs are *decreasing*,

- FIFO ending inventory is lowest.
- LIFO ending inventory is highest.

Exhibit 9-5 summarizes the income effects of the three inventory methods, using the data from Exhibit 9-4. Study the exhibit carefully, focusing on ending inventory, cost of goods sold, and gross margin.

The Income Tax Advantage of LIFO

Objective 3

Identify the income effects and the tax effects of the inventory costing methods

When prices are rising, the LIFO method results in the *lowest taxable income* and thus the *lowest income taxes*. Using the gross margin data of Exhibit 9-5, we have the following:

■ Daily Exercise 9-10

	FIFO	LIFO	Weighted-Average
Gross margin	$46,000	$34,000	$40,000
Operating expenses (assumed)	26,000	26,000	26,000
Income before income tax	$20,000	$ 8,000	$14,000
Income tax expense (40%)	$ 8,000	$ 3,200	$ 5,600

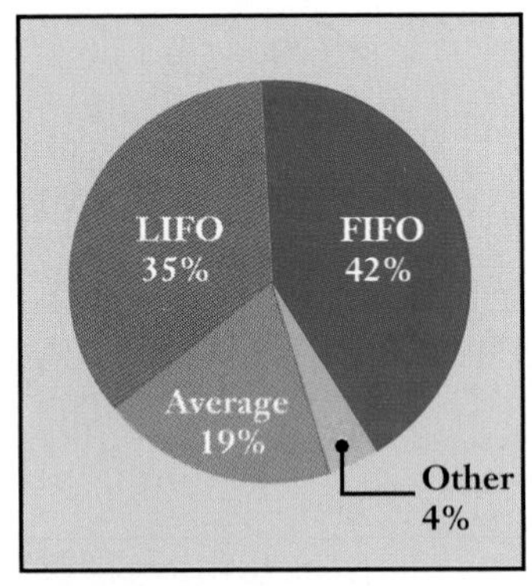

EXHIBIT 9-6
Use of the Various Inventory Costing Methods

Income tax expense is lowest under LIFO ($3,200) and highest under FIFO ($8,000). The most attractive feature of LIFO is reduced income tax payments, which is why Huntington Galleries in our chapter opening story switched from the FIFO to the LIFO method.

The 1970s and early 1980s were marked by high inflation, so many companies changed to LIFO for its tax advantage. Exhibit 9-6, based on an American Institute of Certified Public Accountants (AICPA) survey of 600 companies, indicates that FIFO and LIFO are the most popular inventory costing methods.

GAAP and Practical Considerations: A Comparison of Inventory Methods

We may ask three questions to judge the three major inventory costing methods.

1. How well does each method match inventory expense—the cost of goods sold—to sales revenue on the income statement?
2. Which method reports the most up-to-date inventory amount on the balance sheet?
3. What effects do the methods have on income taxes?

MATCHING OF EXPENSE WITH REVENUE ON THE INCOME STATEMENT LIFO best matches the current value of cost of goods sold with current revenue by assigning to this expense the most recent inventory costs. Therefore, LIFO produces the cost of goods sold figure that is closest to what it would cost the company to replace the goods that were sold. In this sense, LIFO produces the best measure of net income. In contrast, FIFO matches the oldest inventory costs against the period's revenue—a poor matching of current expense with current revenue.

CURRENT INVENTORY COST ON THE BALANCE SHEET FIFO reports the most current inventory costs on the balance sheet. LIFO can result in misleading inventory costs on the balance sheet because the oldest prices are left in ending inventory.

INCOME TAX As we saw earlier, LIFO results in the lowest income tax payments when prices are rising. Tax payments are highest under FIFO. When inventory prices are decreasing, tax payments are highest under LIFO and lowest under FIFO. The weighted-average cost method produces amounts between the extremes of LIFO and FIFO.

Inventory Profit. Difference between gross margin figured on the FIFO basis and gross margin figured on the LIFO basis.

FIFO PRODUCES INVENTORY PROFITS FIFO is sometimes criticized because it overstates income by so-called inventory profit during periods of inflation. Briefly, **inventory profit** is the difference between gross margin figured on the FIFO basis and gross margin figured on the LIFO basis. Exhibit 9-5 illustrates inventory profit. The $12,000 difference between FIFO and LIFO gross margins ($46,000 – $34,000 at the top of this page) results from the difference in cost of goods sold. This $12,000 amount is called *FIFO inventory profit* because it results from using the FIFO method during a period of rising prices.

LIFO ALLOWS OWNERS AND MANAGERS TO MANAGE REPORTED INCOME—UP OR DOWN LIFO is often criticized because it allows managers to manage net income. When inventory prices are rising rapidly and a company wants to show less income for the year (in order to pay less in taxes), managers can buy a large amount of inventory before the end of the year. Under LIFO, these high inventory costs immediately become expense—as cost of goods sold. As a result, the income statement reports a lower net income. Conversely, if the business is having a bad year, management may wish to increase reported income. To do so, managers can delay a large purchase of high-cost inventory until the next period. This high-cost inventory is not expensed as cost of goods sold in the current year. Thus management avoids decreasing the current year's reported income. In the process, the company draws down inventory quantities, a practice known as *LIFO liquidation.*

LIFO LIQUIDATION When the LIFO method is used and inventory quantities fall below the level of the previous period, the situation is called **LIFO liquidation.** To compute cost of goods sold, the company must dip into older layers of inventory cost. Under LIFO and during a period of rising inventory costs, that action shifts older, lower costs into cost of goods sold. The result is higher net income than the company would have reported if no LIFO liquidation had occurred. Managers try to avoid LIFO liquidation because it increases reported income and income taxes. Owens-Corning, the world's leading supplier of glass fiber materials, reported that LIFO liquidations added $2.7 million to its net income.

LIFO Liquidation. Occurs when the LIFO inventory method is used and inventory quantities fall below the level of the previous period.

"Owens-Corning, the world's leading supplier of glass fiber materials, reported that LIFO liquidations added $2.7 million to its net income."

INTERNATIONAL PERSPECTIVE Many companies manufacture their inventory in foreign countries, and companies that value inventory by the LIFO method often must use another accounting method for their inventories in foreign countries. Why? LIFO is allowed in the United States, but other countries are not bound by U.S. accounting practices. Australia and the United Kingdom, for example, do not permit the use of LIFO. Virtually all countries permit FIFO and the weighted-average cost method. Exhibit 9-7 lists a sampling of countries and whether or not they permit LIFO.

■ Daily Exercise 9-11

HIGHER INCOME OR LOWER TAXES? A company may want to report the highest income, and (as we've seen) FIFO meets this need when prices are rising. But the company also pays the highest income taxes under FIFO. When prices are falling, LIFO reports the highest income.

Which inventory method is better—LIFO or FIFO? There is no single answer to this question. Different companies have different motives for the inventory method they choose. Polaroid Corporation uses FIFO, J.C. Penney Company uses LIFO, and Motorola, Inc., uses weighted-average cost. Still other companies use more than one method. The Black & Decker Corporation, best known for its power tools and small appliances, uses both LIFO and FIFO. The following excerpt is from a Black & Decker annual report (amount in millions):

Inventories................................ $390

Notes to Consolidated Financial Statements
Note 1: Summary of Accounting Policies
Inventories: The cost of United States inventories is based on the last-in, first-out (LIFO) method; all other inventories are based on the first-in, first-out (FIFO) method. The cost of . . . inventories stated under the LIFO method represents approximately 40% of the value of total inventories.

EXHIBIT 9-7
LIFO Use by Country

Country	LIFO Permitted?	Country	LIFO Permitted?
Australia	No	Netherlands	Yes
Brazil	Yes	Nigeria	No
Canada	Yes	Singapore	No
France	Yes	South Africa	Yes
Germany	Yes	Sweden	No
Hong Kong	No	Switzerland	No
Japan	Yes	United Kingdom	No
Mexico	Yes	United States	Yes

SUMMARY PROBLEM FOR YOUR REVIEW — MID-CHAPTER

Suppose a division of IBM Corporation that handles computer components has these inventory records for January 19X6:

Date	Item	Quantity	Unit Cost	Sale Price
Jan. 1	Beginning inventory	100 units	$ 8	
6	Purchase	60 units	9	
13	Sale	70 units		$20
21	Purchase	150 units	9	
24	Sale	210 units		22
27	Purchase	90 units	10	
30	Sale	30 units		25

Company accounting records reveal that operating expense for January was $1,900.

REQUIRED

1. Prepare the January income statement, showing amounts for FIFO, LIFO, and weighted-average cost. Label the bottom line "Operating income." (Round the weighted-average cost per unit to three decimal places and all other figures to whole-dollar amounts.) Show your computations, and use the periodic inventory model in Exhibit 9-4 to compute cost of goods sold.
2. Suppose you are the financial vice president of IBM. Which inventory method will you use if your motive is to (state the reason for each answer)
   - a. Minimize income taxes?
   - b. Report the highest operating income?
   - c. Report operating income between the extremes of FIFO and LIFO?
   - d. Report inventory on the balance sheet at the most current cost?
   - e. Attain the best measure of net income for the income statement?

SOLUTION

REQUIREMENT 1

IBM CORPORATION
Income Statement for Component
Month Ended January 31, 19X6

	FIFO		LIFO		Weighted-Average	
Sales revenue		$6,770		$6,770		$6,770
Cost of goods sold:						
Beginning inventory	$ 800		$ 800		$ 800	
Net purchases	2,790		2,790		2,790	
Cost of goods available for sale	3,590		3,590		3,590	
Ending inventory	(900)		(720)		(808)	
Cost of goods sold		2,690		2,870		2,782
Gross margin		4,080		3,900		3,988
Operating expenses		1,900		1,900		1,900
Operating income		$2,180		$2,000		$2,088

Computations

Sales revenue:	(70 × $20) + (210 × $22) + (30 × $25)	= $6,770
Beginning inventory:	100 × $8	= $800
Purchases:	(60 × $9) + (150 × $9) + (90 × $10)	= $2,790
Ending inventory—FIFO:	90* × $10	= $900
LIFO:	90 × $8	= $720
Weighted-average:	90 × $8.975**	= $808 (rounded from $807.75)

*Number of units in ending inventory = 100 + 60 − 70 + 150 − 210 + 90 − 30 = 90
**$3,590/400 units† = $8.975 per unit
†Number of units available = 100 + 60 + 150 + 90 = 400

REQUIREMENT 2

a. Use LIFO to minimize income taxes. Operating income under LIFO is lowest when inventory unit costs are increasing, as they are in this case (from $8 to $10). (If inventory costs were decreasing, income and income taxes under FIFO would be lowest.)

b. Use FIFO to report the highest operating income. Income under FIFO is highest when inventory unit costs are increasing, as in this situation.

c. Use weighted-average cost to report an operating income amount between the FIFO and LIFO extremes. This is true both in this situation and in others when inventory unit costs are increasing or decreasing.

d. Use FIFO to report inventory on the balance sheet at the most current cost. Under FIFO, the oldest inventory costs are expensed as cost of goods sold, leaving in ending inventory the most recent (most current) costs of the period.

e. Use LIFO to attain the best measure of net income. LIFO produces the best matching of current expense with current revenue. The most recent (most current) inventory costs are expensed as cost of goods sold.

Perpetual Inventory Records under FIFO, LIFO, and Weighted-Average Costing

Many companies keep their perpetual inventory records in quantities only, as illustrated in Exhibit 9-2. Other companies keep perpetual records in both quantities and dollar costs. Here we show how the four inventory costing methods are applied in a *perpetual* inventory system.

FIFO Huntington Galleries uses the FIFO inventory method. Exhibit 9-8 shows Huntington's perpetual inventory record for the Early American chairs—in both quantities and dollar costs for the month of November.

To prepare financial statements at November 30, Huntington can take the ending inventory cost ($6,400) straight to the balance sheet. Cost of goods sold for the November income statement is $12,350. Here is Huntington's computation of cost of goods sold during November, with data taken from the perpetual record in Exhibit 9-8:

■ Daily Exercise 9-12

Cost of Goods Sold (Early American Chairs)—November	
Beginning inventory	$ 3,000
+ Purchases	15,750
= Cost of goods available for sale	18,750
− Ending inventory	(6,400)
= Cost of goods sold	$12,350

Some companies combine elements of the perpetual and periodic inventory systems—the perpetual system for control and preparation of the financial statements, and the periodic system for analysis.

Learning Tip: The total in the Received column of Exhibit 9-8 represents total purchases. The total in the Sold column represents cost of goods sold. The total in the Balance column represents the cost of the inventory on hand. Remember to use *cost,* not *sale price,* in the Sold column.

EXHIBIT 9-8
Perpetual Inventory Record—FIFO Cost

Huntington Galleries

Item: Early American Chair

	Received			Sold			Balance		
Date	Qty.	Unit Cost	Total	Qty.	Unit Cost	Total	Qty.	Unit Cost	Total
Nov. 1							10	$300	$3,000
5				6	$300	$ 1,800	4	300	1,200
7	25	$310	$ 7,750				4	300	1,200
							25	310	7,750
12				4	300	1,200			
				9	310	2,790	16	310	4,960
26	25	320	8,000				16	310	4,960
							25	320	8,000
30				16	310	4,960			
				5	320	1,600	20	320	6,400
Totals	50		$15,750	40		$12,350	20	$ 320	$6,400

LIFO Few companies keep perpetual inventory records at LIFO cost. The recordkeeping is expensive, and LIFO liquidations can occur during the year. To avoid these problems, LIFO companies can keep perpetual inventory records in terms of quantities only, as illustrated in Exhibit 9-2. For financial statements, they then apply LIFO costs at the end of the period. Other companies maintain perpetual inventory records at FIFO cost and then convert the FIFO amounts to LIFO costs for the financial statements. This topic is covered in intermediate accounting courses.

WEIGHTED-AVERAGE COST Perpetual inventory records can be kept at weighted-average cost. Most companies that use this method compute the weighted-average cost for the entire period. They apply this cost to both ending inventory and cost of goods sold. These procedures parallel those used in the periodic inventory system (Exhibit 9-4).

The use of computer software to account for inventory eases the computation of the average cost per unit each time additional goods are purchased. The new average unit cost is then applied to each subsequent sale until more goods are purchased, at which time another new average cost is computed.

Working It Out Examine Exhibit 9-8. What was Huntington Galleries' weighted-average unit cost during November? How much were ending inventory and cost of goods sold at weighted-average cost? What was the cost of goods available for sale?

Answer

$$\text{Weighted-average unit cost} = \frac{\text{Cost of goods available for sale}}{\text{Units available for sale}}$$

$$= \frac{\text{Cost of beginning inventory} + \text{Cost of purchases}}{\text{Units of beginning inventory} + \text{Units purchased}}$$

$$= \frac{\$3{,}000 + \$15{,}750}{10 \text{ units} + 50 \text{ units}} = \frac{\$18{,}750}{60 \text{ units}} = \$312.50$$

Ending inventory	=	**20 units**	×	**\$312.50**	=	**\$ 6,250**
Cost of goods sold	=	**40 units**	×	**\$312.50**	=	**12,500**
Cost of goods available for sale					=	**\$18,750**

Accounting Principles and Their Relevance to Inventories

Several of the generally accepted accounting principles have special relevance to inventories. Among them are the consistency principle, the disclosure principle, the materiality concept, and accounting conservatism.

Consistency Principle

Consistency Principle. A business should use the same accounting methods and procedures from period to period.

The **consistency principle** states that businesses should use the same accounting methods and procedures from period to period. Consistency makes it possible to compare a company's financial statements from one period to the next.

Suppose you are analyzing a company's net income pattern over a two-year period. The company switched from LIFO to FIFO during that time. Its net income increased dramatically but only as a result of the change in inventory method. If you did not know of the change, you might believe that the company's income increased because of improved operations, which is not the case.

The consistency principle does not require that all companies within an industry use the same accounting method. Nor does it mean that a company may *never* change its accounting methods. However, a company making an accounting change must disclose the effect of the change on net income. Sun Company, Inc., an oil company, disclosed the following in a note to its annual report:

EXCERPT FROM NOTE 6 OF THE SUN COMPANY FINANCIAL STATEMENTS
... Sun changed its method of accounting for the cost of crude oil and refined product inventories ... from the FIFO method to the LIFO method. Sun believes that the use of the LIFO method better matches current costs with current revenues. . . . The change decreased the 19X1 net loss ... by $3 million. . . .

Disclosure Principle

The **disclosure principle** holds that a company's financial statements should report enough information for outsiders to make knowledgeable decisions about the company. In short, the company should report *relevant*, *reliable*, and *comparable* information about its economic affairs. With respect to inventories, the disclosure principle means disclosing the method or methods in use. Without knowledge of the inventory method, a banker could gain an unrealistic impression of a company and thus make an unwise lending decision. For example, suppose the banker is comparing two companies—one using LIFO and the other FIFO. The FIFO company reports higher net income, but only because it uses a particular inventory method. Without knowledge of the accounting methods the companies are using, the banker could loan money to the wrong business or refuse a loan to a promising customer.

Disclosure Principle. A business's financial statements must report enough information for outsiders to make knowledgeable decisions about the company.

Materiality Concept

The **materiality concept** states that a company must perform strictly proper accounting *only* for items and transactions that are significant to the business's financial statements. Information is significant—or, in accounting terminology, *material*—when its inclusion and correct presentation in the financial statements would cause a statement user to change a decision because of that information. Immaterial—nonsignificant—items justify less-than-perfect accounting. The inclusion and proper presentation of immaterial items would not affect a statement user's decision. The materiality concept frees accountants from having to compute and report every last item in strict accordance with GAAP. Thus, the materiality concept reduces the cost of recording accounting information.

Materiality Concept. A company must perform strictly proper accounting only for items and transactions that are significant to the business's financial statements.

How does a business decide where to draw the line between the material and the immaterial? This decision rests to a great degree on how large the business is. The fast-food chain Wendy's, for example, has close to $500 million in assets. Management would likely treat as immaterial a $100 loss of inventory due to spoilage. A loss of this amount is immaterial to Wendy's total assets and net income, so company accountants may not report the loss separately. Will this accounting treatment affect anyone's decision about Wendy's? Probably not, so it doesn't matter whether the loss is reported separately or simply embedded in cost of goods sold.

Accounting Conservatism

Conservatism in accounting means reporting items in the financial statements at amounts that lead to the gloomiest immediate financial results. Conservatism comes into play when there are alternative ways to account for an item. What advantage does conservatism give a business? Managers must be optimistic to be good leaders. This optimism sometimes causes them to look on the bright side of operations, and they may overstate a company's income and asset values. Many accountants regard conservatism as a counterbalance to managers' optimistic tendencies. The goal is for financial statements to present realistic figures.

Conservatism. Reporting the least favorable figures in the financial statements.

Conservatism appears in accounting guidelines such as

- "Anticipate no gains, but provide for all probable losses."
- "If in doubt, record an asset at the lowest reasonable amount and a liability at the highest reasonable amount."
- When there's a question, debit an expense account rather than an asset."

Conservatism directs accountants to decrease the accounting value of an asset if it appears unrealistically high—even if no transaction occurs. Assume that a company paid $35,000 for inventory that has become obsolete and whose current value is only $12,000. Conservatism dictates that the inventory be *written down* (that is, decreased) to $12,000.

Lower-of-Cost-or-Market Rule

Objective 4

Apply the lower-of-cost-or-market rule to inventory

Lower-of-Cost-or-Market (LCM) Rule. Requires that an asset be reported in the financial statements at whichever is lower—its historical cost or its market value (current replacement cost for inventory).

The **lower-of-cost-or-market rule** (abbreviated as LCM) shows accounting conservatism in action. LCM requires that inventory be reported in the financial statements at whichever is lower—the inventory's historical cost or its market value. For inventories, *market value* generally means *current replacement cost* (that is, how much the business would have to pay now to purchase the amount of inventory that it has on hand). If the replacement cost of inventory falls below its historical cost, the business must write down the value of its goods because of the likelihood of incurring a loss on the inventory. GAAP requires this departure from historical cost accounting. The business reports ending inventory at its LCM value on the balance sheet. All this can be done automatically by a computerized accounting system. How is the write-down accomplished?

Suppose a business paid $3,000 for inventory on September 26. By December 31, its value has fallen. The inventory can now be replaced for $2,200. Market value is below cost, and the December 31 balance sheet reports this inventory at its LCM value of $2,200.

Exhibit 9-9 presents the effects of LCM on the income statement and the balance sheet. The exhibit shows that the lower of (a) cost or (b) market value is the relevant amount for valuing inventory on the balance sheet. Now examine the income statement in Exhibit 9-9. What expense absorbs the impact of the $800 inventory write-down? Cost of goods sold is debited when inventory is credited as follows in a perpetual inventory system:

Cost of Goods Sold (cost, $3,000 – market, $2,200)	800	
Inventory		800

Companies often disclose LCM in notes to their financial statements, as shown here for CBS, Inc., the television broadcasting conglomerate:

NOTE 1: STATEMENT OF SIGNIFICANT ACCOUNTING POLICIES
Inventories. Inventories are stated at the *lower of cost* (principally based on average cost) *or market value.* [Emphasis added.]

EXHIBIT 9-9
Lower-of-Cost-or-Market (LCM) Effects

■ Daily Exercise 9-13

Balance Sheet

Current assets:		
Cash	$ XXX	
Short-term investments	XXX	
Accounts receivable	XXX	
Inventories, at market (which is lower than $3,000 cost)	2,200	
Prepaid expenses	XXX	
Total current assets	$X,XXX	

Income Statement

Sales revenue		$20,000
Cost of goods sold:		
Beginning inventory (LCM = Cost)	$ 2,800	
Net purchases	11,000	
Cost of goods available for sale	13,800	
Ending inventory—		
Cost = $3,000		
Replacement cost (market value) = $2,200		
LCM = Market	(2,200)	
Cost of goods sold		11,600
Gross margin		$ 8,400

Effects of Inventory Errors

Objective 5

Determine the effects of inventory errors on cost of goods sold and net income

Businesses count their inventories at the end of the period. In the process of counting the items, applying unit costs, and computing amounts, errors may arise. As the period 1 segment of Exhibit 9-10 shows, an error in the ending inventory amount creates errors in the amounts for cost of goods sold and gross margin. Compare period 1, when ending inventory is overstated and cost of goods sold is understated, each by $5,000, with period 3, which is correct. Period 1 should look exactly like period 3.

Recall that one period's ending inventory is the next period's beginning inventory. Thus the error in ending inventory carries over into the next period; note the amounts in color in Exhibit 9-10.

■ Daily Exercise 9-14

Because ending inventory is *subtracted* in computing cost of goods sold in one period and the same amount is *added* as beginning inventory to compute next period's cost of goods sold, the error's effect cancels out at the end of the second period. The overstatement of cost of goods sold in period 2 counterbalances the understatement in cost of goods sold for period 1. Thus the total gross margin amount for the two periods is the correct $100,000 figure whether or not there is an error. As a result, owner's equity at the end of period 2 is correct. These effects are summarized in Exhibit 9-11.

Inventory errors cannot be ignored simply because they counterbalance, however. Suppose you are analyzing trends in the business's operations. Exhibit 9-10 shows a drop in gross margin from period 1 to period 2, followed by an increase in period 3. But that picture of operations is untrue because of the accounting error. The correct gross margin is $50,000 for each period. Providing accurate information for decision making requires that all inventory errors be corrected.

■ Daily Exercise 9-15

EXHIBIT 9-10
Inventory Errors: An Example

	Period 1		Period 2		Period 3	
	Ending Inventory Overstated by $5,000		Beginning Inventory Overstated by $5,000		Correct	
Sales revenue		$100,000		$100,000		$100,000
Cost of goods sold:						
Beginning inventory	$10,000		$15,000		$10,000	
Net purchases	50,000		50,000		50,000	
Cost of goods available for sale	60,000		65,000		60,000	
Ending inventory	(15,000)		(10,000)		(10,000)	
Cost of goods sold		45,000		55,000		50,000
Gross margin		$ 55,000		$ 45,000		$ 50,000
			$100,000			

Source: The authors thank Carl High for this example.

Concept Highlight

EXHIBIT 9-11
Effects of Inventory Errors

	Period 1			Period 2		
Inventory Error	Cost of Goods Sold	Gross Margin and Net Income	Ending Owner's Equity	Cost of Goods Sold	Gross Margin and Net Income	Ending Owner's Equity
Period 1 Ending inventory overstated	Understated	Overstated	Overstated	Overstated	Understated	Correct
Period 1 Ending inventory understated	Overstated	Understated	Understated	Understated	Overstated	Correct

Ethical Issues in Inventory Accounting

No area of accounting has a deeper ethical dimension than inventory. Owners and managers of companies whose profits do not meet expectations are sometimes tempted to "cook the books" to increase reported income. The increase in reported income may lead investors and creditors into thinking the business is more successful than it really is.

What do managers hope to gain from the fraudulent accounting? In some cases, they are trying to keep their jobs. In other cases, their bonuses are tied to reported income: The higher the company's net income, the higher the managers' bonuses. In still other cases, the business may need a loan. Financial statements that report high profits and large inventory values are more likely to impress lenders than low net income and lagging inventory amounts.

There are two main schemes for cooking the books. The easiest, and the most obvious, is simply to overstate ending inventory. In the preceding section on the effects of inventory errors, we saw how an error in ending inventory affects net income. A company can intentionally overstate its ending inventory. Such an error understates cost of goods sold and overstates net income and owner's equity, as shown in the accounting equation. The upward-pointing arrows indicate an overstatement—reporting more assets and equity than are actually present:

Assets	=	Liabilities	+	Owners' Equity
↑	=	0	+	↑

■ Daily Exercise 9-16

Remember that an inventory error has an offsetting effect in the next period. This means that managers who misstate ending inventory can only hope to "buy some time" by hyping reported income in the short term. Next period's net income will be lower as a result of this period's error. As with all other deceptions, an inventory misstatement comes back to haunt the business.

The second way of using inventory to cook the books involves sales. Sales schemes are more complex than simple inventory overstatements. Datapoint Corporation and MiniScribe, both computer-related concerns, were charged with creating fictitious sales to boost their reported profits.

"Datapoint is alleged to have hired drivers to transport its inventory around San Antonio so that the goods could not be physically counted."

Datapoint is alleged to have hired drivers to transport its inventory around San Antonio so that the goods could *not* be physically counted. Datapoint's logic seemed to be that excluding the goods from ending inventory would imply that the goods had been sold. The faulty reasoning broke down when the trucks returned the goods to Datapoint's warehouse. Datapoint had far too much in sales returns. What would you think of a company with $10 million in sales and $4 million of the goods were returned by customers?

MiniScribe is alleged to have cooked its books by shipping boxes of bricks labeled as computer parts to its distributors right before year end. The accounting equations show how the scheme affected MiniScribe's reported figures (assuming sales of $10 million and cost of goods sold of $6 million):

	Assets	=	Liabilities	+	Owners' Equity
Sales	10	=	0	+	10
Cost of goods sold	−6	=	0	−	6
Net effect	4	=	0	+	4

The bogus transactions increased the company's assets and equity by $4 million—but only temporarily.

The distributors refused to accept the goods and returned them to MiniScribe—but in the next accounting period. In the earlier period, MiniScribe recorded sales revenue and temporarily reported millions of dollars of sales and income that did not exist. Again, the scheme boomeranged in the next period when MiniScribe had to record the sales returns. In virtually every area, accounting imposes a discipline that works to keep every business honest in its financial reporting.

Estimating Inventory

Objective 6

Estimate ending inventory by the gross margin method

Often a business must *estimate* the value of its inventory. Because of cost and inconvenience, few companies physically count their inventories at the end of each month, yet they may need monthly financial statements. Suppose the company does not use the perpetual inventory system and thus cannot determine ending inventory by looking at the Inventory account.

A fire may destroy inventory, and to file an insurance claim, the business must estimate the value of its loss. In this case, the business needs to know the value of ending inventory but cannot count it. A widely used method for estimating ending inventory is the *gross margin method.*

Gross Margin (Gross Profit) Method

The **gross margin method,** also known as the *gross profit method,* is a way of estimating inventory on the basis of the familiar cost-of-goods-sold model (amounts assumed for illustration):

Gross Margin Method. A way to estimate inventory on the basis of the cost-of-goods-sold model: Beginning inventory + Net purchases = Cost of goods available for sale. Cost of goods available for sale − Cost of goods sold = Ending inventory. Also called the **gross profit method.**

	Beginning inventory	**$10**
+	**Purchases**	**50**
=	**Cost of goods available for sale**	**60**
−	Ending inventory	(20)
=	Cost of goods sold	$40

Rearranging *ending inventory* and *cost of goods sold* makes the model useful for estimating ending inventory and is illustrated in the following equation and in Exhibit 9-12 (amounts assumed for illustration):

	Beginning inventory	**$10**
+	**Purchases**	**50**
=	**Cost of goods available for sale**	**60**
−	Cost of goods sold	(40)
=	Ending inventory	$20

Suppose a fire destroys your business's inventory. To collect insurance, you must estimate the cost of the ending inventory. Beginning inventory and purchases amounts may be taken directly from the accounting records. Sales Revenue less Sales Returns and Allowances and Sales Discounts indicates net sales up to the date of the fire. Using the entity's normal *gross margin percent* (that is, gross margin divided by net sales revenue), you can estimate cost of goods sold. The last step is to subtract cost of goods sold from goods available to estimate ending inventory. Exhibit 9-12 illustrates the gross margin method.

Accountants, managers, and auditors use the gross margin method to test the overall reasonableness of an ending inventory amount that has been determined by a physical count. This method helps to detect large errors.

■ Daily Exercise 9-17

EXHIBIT 9-12
Gross Margin Method of Estimating Inventory *(amounts assumed)*

Beginning inventory		$14,000
Purchases		66,000
Cost of goods available for sale		80,000
Cost of goods sold:		
Sales revenue	$100,000	
Less Estimated gross margin of 40%	(40,000)	
Estimated cost of goods sold		(60,000)
Estimated cost of *ending inventory*		$20,000

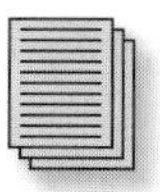

Working It Out Beginning inventory is $70,000, net purchases total $298,000, and net sales are $480,000. With a normal gross margin rate of 40% of sales, how much is ending inventory?

Answer:

Beginning inventory		$ 70,000
Net purchases		298,000
Cost of goods available for sale		368,000
Cost of goods sold:		
Net sales revenue	$480,000	
Less Estimated gross margin of 40%	(192,000)	
Estimated cost of goods sold		(288,000)
Estimated cost of ending inventory		$ 80,000

Internal Control over Inventory

Internal control over inventory is important because inventory is such an important asset. Successful companies take great care to protect their inventory. Elements of good internal control over inventory include

1. Physically counting inventory at least once each year, regardless of which inventory accounting system is used
2. Storing inventory to protect it against theft, damage, and decay
3. Giving access to inventory only to personnel who do *not* have access to the accounting records
4. Keeping perpetual inventory records for high-unit-cost merchandise
5. Keeping enough inventory on hand to prevent shortage situations, which lead to lost sales
6. Not keeping too large an inventory stockpiled, thus avoiding the expense of tying up money in unneeded items
7. Purchasing inventory in economical quantities

The annual physical count of inventory (item 1) is necessary because the only way to be certain of the amount of inventory on hand is to count it. Errors arise in even the best accounting systems, and the count is needed to establish the correct value of the inventory. When an error is detected, the records are brought into agreement with the physical count.

Keeping inventory handlers away from the accounting records (item 3) is an essential separation of duties, discussed in Chapter 7. An employee with access to both inventory and the accounting records can steal the goods and make an entry to conceal the theft. For example, the employee could increase the amount of an inventory write-down to make it appear that goods became obsolete when in fact they were stolen.

Computerized inventory systems allow companies to minimize both the amount of inventory on hand and the chances of running out of stock (items 5 and 6). In an increasingly competitive business environment, companies cannot afford to tie up cash in too much inventory. Many manufacturing companies use *just-in-time (JIT) inventory systems*, which require suppliers to deliver materials just in time to be used in the production process. JIT systems help minimize the amount of money a company has tied up in inventory.

Reporting Inventory Transactions on the Statement of Cash Flows

Objective 7

Report inventory transactions on the statement of cash flows

Let's return once again to the Huntington Galleries example. In addition to the income statement and the balance sheet, Huntington publishes a statement of cash flows at the end of the year. A company's inventory transactions are among its most important activities. Huge amounts of cash are involved in inventory transactions.

Examine the Huntington Galleries income statement and balance sheet in Exhibit 9-1 on page 378. The income statement shows Huntington's revenues, expenses, and net income—the company's operating results for 1997. The balance sheet reports the company's assets, liabilities, and owners' equity—financial position—at the end of the year.

EXHIBIT 9-13
Statement of Cash Flows for Huntington Galleries

HUNTINGTON GALLERIES Statement of Cash Flows (partial) Year Ended December 31, 1997	
Cash flows from operating activities:	**(Amounts in Thousands)**
Cash receipts:	
Collections from customers	$164,100
Receipts of interest	800
Cash payments:	
Payments for inventory	(91,600)
Payments to other suppliers	(21,700)
Payments of operating expenses	(18,100)
Cash provided by operating activities	$ 33,500

But how much cash did Huntington spend on inventory during the year? And how much cash did the company collect from customers? Did operations provide a net cash inflow, as they should for a successful company? Or were operating activities a drain on cash? Only the statement of cash flows answers these questions. Exhibit 9-13 highlights Huntington's inventory-related transactions on its statement of cash flows for 1997:

- Collections from customers
- Payments for inventory

Inventory-related transactions are *operating activities* because the purchase and sale of merchandise are at the very core of a company's operations. Huntington Galleries is no exception. Collections from customers and payments for inventory are its two largest operating cash flows. As we saw in Chapter 8, collections from customers are also related to receivables. A merchandiser makes sales on account and then collects cash for the receivables.

■ Daily Exercise 9-18

The cash-flow statement reports that Huntington collected $164.1 million from customers and paid $91.6 million for inventory during the year. Exhibit 9-13 also reports other operating cash flows for completeness. Altogether, Huntington's operations provided a net total of $33.5 million of cash during 1997. We will reexamine the reporting of cash flows in Chapter 17.

This chapter has discussed various aspects of controlling and accounting for inventory, cost of goods sold, and gross margin. The Decision Guidelines feature summarizes some basic decision guidelines that are helpful in managing a business's inventory operations.

DECISION GUIDELINES — Guidelines for Inventory Management

DECISION	GUIDELINES	SYSTEM OR METHOD
Which inventory system to use?	• Expensive merchandise • Cannot control inventory by visual inspection	→ Perpetual system
	• Can control inventory by visual inspection	→ Periodic system
Which costing method to use?	Unique inventory items	→ Specific unit cost
	• Most current cost of ending inventory • Maximizes reported income when costs are rising	→ FIFO
	• Most current measure of cost of goods sold and net income • Minimizes income tax when costs are rising	→ LIFO
	• Middle-of-the-road approach for income tax and reported income	→ Weighted-average

(continued)

DECISION GUIDELINES *(continued)*

How to estimate the cost of ending inventory?	• The cost-of-goods-sold model provides the framework →	Gross margin (gross profit) method

SUMMARY PROBLEM FOR YOUR REVIEW

Mesa Hardware Company began 19X8 with 60,000 units of inventory that cost $36,000. During 19X8, Mesa purchased merchandise on account for $352,500 as follows:

Purchase 1 (100,000 units costing)..........	$ 65,000
Purchase 2 (270,000 units costing)..........	175,500
Purchase 3 (160,000 units costing)..........	112,000

Cash payments on account for inventory totaled $326,000 during the year.

Mesa's sales during 19X8 consisted of 520,000 units of inventory for $660,000, all on account. The company uses the FIFO inventory method.

Cash collections from customers were $630,000. Operating expenses totaled $240,500, of which Mesa paid $211,000 in cash. Mesa credited Accrued Liabilities for the remainder.

REQUIRED

1. Make summary journal entries to record Mesa Hardware's transactions for the year, assuming the company uses a perpetual inventory system.
2. Determine the FIFO cost of Mesa's ending inventory at December 31, 19X8, two ways:
   a. Use a T-account.
   b. Multiply the number of units by the unit cost.
3. Use the cost-of-goods-sold model to show how Mesa would compute cost of goods sold for 19X8 under the periodic inventory system.
4. Prepare Mesa Hardware's income statement for 19X8. Show totals for the gross margin and net income.
5. Show how Mesa would report its inventory transactions on the statement of cash flows for 19X8.

SOLUTION

REQUIREMENT 1

Inventory ($65,000 + $175,500 + $112,000)..........	352,500	
Accounts Payable..........		352,500
Accounts Payable..........	326,000	
Cash..........		326,000
Accounts Receivable..........	660,000	
Sales Revenue..........		660,000
Cost of Goods Sold..........	339,500	
Inventory.......... [$36,000 + $65,000 + $175,500 + $63,000 (90,000 units × $0.70)] ($112,000 ÷ 160,000 units = $0.70 per unit)		339,500
Cash..........	630,000	
Accounts Receivable..........		630,000
Operating Expenses..........	240,500	
Cash..........		211,000
Accrued Liabilities..........		29,500

REQUIREMENT 2

a.

Inventory	
36,000	339,500
352,500	
49,000	

b.

Number of units in ending inventory (60,000 + 100,000 + 270,000 + 160,000 − 520,000)..............	70,000
Unit cost of ending inventory at FIFO ($112,000 ÷ 160,000)..............	× $ 0.70
FIFO cost of ending inventory..............	$49,000

REQUIREMENT 3

Cost of goods sold (periodic inventory system):

Beginning inventory	$ 36,000
Purchases	352,500
Cost of goods available for sale	388,500
Less ending inventory	(49,000)
Cost of goods sold	$339,500

REQUIREMENT 4

MESA HARDWARE COMPANY
Income Statement
Year Ended December 31, 19X8

Sales revenue	$660,000
Cost of goods sold	339,500
Gross margin	320,500
Operating expenses	240,500
Net income	$ 80,000

REQUIREMENT 5

MESA HARDWARE COMPANY
Statement of Cash Flows (partial)
Year Ended December 31, 19X8

Cash flows from operating activities:	
Cash receipts:	
Collections from customers	$630,000
Cash payments:	
Payments for inventory	(326,000)

Summary of Learning Objectives

1. ***Account for inventory by the periodic and perpetual systems.*** Accounting for inventory plays an important part in merchandisers' accounting systems because selling inventory is the heart of their business. Inventory is generally the largest current asset on their balance sheet, and inventory expense—called *cost of goods sold*—is usually the largest expense on the income statement.

Merchandisers can choose between two inventory systems. In a *periodic inventory system,* the business does not keep a running record of the inventory on hand. Instead, at the end of the period, the business counts the inventory on hand and then updates its records. In a *perpetual inventory system,* the business keeps a continuous record for each inventory item to show the inventory on hand at all times. A physical count of inventory is needed in both systems for control purposes.

2. ***Apply the inventory costing methods: specific unit cost, weighted-average cost, FIFO, and LIFO.*** Businesses multiply the quantity of inventory items by their unit cost to determine inventory cost. There are four inventory costing methods: *specific unit cost; weighted-average cost; first-in, first out (FIFO) cost;* and *last-in, first-out (LIFO) cost.* Only businesses that sell items that may be identified individually, such as automobiles and jewels, use the specific-unit-cost method. Most other companies use the other methods. FIFO reports ending inventory at the most current cost. LIFO reports cost of goods sold at the most current cost.

3. ***Identify the income effects and the tax effects of the inventory costing methods.*** When inventory costs are increasing, LIFO produces the highest cost of goods sold and the lowest income, thus minimizing income taxes. FIFO results in the highest income. The weighted-average cost method gives results between the extremes of FIFO and LIFO.

4. ***Apply the lower-of-cost-or-market rule to inventory.*** The *lower-of-cost-or-market (LCM) rule*—an example of accounting *conservatism*—requires that businesses report inventory on the balance sheet at the lower of its cost or current replacement value. Companies can disclose LCM in notes to their financial statements.

5. ***Determine the effects of inventory errors on cost of goods sold and net income.*** Although inventory overstatements in one period are counterbalanced by inventory understatements in the next period, effective decision making depends on accurate inventory information.

6. ***Estimate ending inventory by the gross margin method.*** The *gross margin method* is a technique for estimating the cost of inventory. It comes in handy for preparing interim financial statements and for estimating the cost of inventory destroyed by fire or other casualties.

7. ***Report inventory transactions on the statement of cash flows.*** Inventory-related cash flows are operating activities.

Accounting Vocabulary

average-cost method *(p. 385)*
conservatism *(p. 393)*
consignment *(p. 384)*
consistency principle *(p. 392)*
cost of goods available for sale *(p. 383)*
disclosure principle *(p. 393)*
first-in, first-out (FIFO) inventory costing method *(p. 386)*
gross margin *(p. 379)*
gross margin method *(p. 397)*
gross profit *(p. 379)*
gross profit method *(p. 397)*
inventory profit *(p. 388)*
last-in, first-out (LIFO) inventory costing method *(p. 386)*
LIFO liquidation *(p. 389)*
lower-of-cost-or-market (LCM) rule *(p. 394)*
materiality concept *(p. 393)*
merchandising company *(p. 378)*
periodic inventory system *(p. 379)*
perpetual inventory system *(p. 380)*
specific identification method *(p. 385)*
specific-unit-cost method *(p. 385)*
weighted-average cost method *(p. 385)*

Questions

1. Why is merchandise inventory so important to a retailer or wholesaler?
2. Suppose your company deals in expensive jewelry. Which inventory system should you use to achieve good internal control over the inventory? If your business is a hardware store that sells low-cost goods, which inventory system would you be likely to use? Why would you choose this system?
3. Identify the accounts debited and credited in the standard purchase and sale entries under (a) the perpetual inventory system, and (b) the periodic inventory system.
4. What is the role of the physical count of inventory in (a) the periodic inventory system, and (b) the perpetual inventory system?
5. If beginning inventory is $10,000, purchases total $85,000, and ending inventory is $12,700, how much is cost of goods sold?
6. If beginning inventory is $32,000, purchases total $119,000, and cost of goods sold is $127,000, how much is ending inventory?
7. What role does the cost principle play in accounting for inventory?
8. What two items determine the cost of ending inventory?
9. Briefly describe the four generally accepted inventory cost methods. During a period of rising prices, which method produces the highest reported income? Which produces the lowest reported income?
10. Which inventory costing method produces the ending inventory valued at the most current cost? Which method produces the cost-of-goods-sold amount valued at the most current cost?
11. What is the most attractive feature of LIFO? Does LIFO have this advantage during periods of increasing prices or during periods of decreasing prices?
12. Which two inventory costing methods are used the most in practice?
13. What is inventory profit? Which method produces it?
14. Identify the chief criticism of LIFO.
15. How does the consistency principle affect accounting for inventory?
16. Briefly describe the influence that the concept of conservatism has on accounting for inventory.
17. Manley Company's inventory has a cost of $48,000 at the end of the year, and the current replacement cost of the inventory is $51,000. At which amount should the company report the inventory on its balance sheet? Suppose the current replacement cost of the inventory is $45,000 instead of $51,000. At which amount should Manley report the inventory? What rule governs your answers to these questions?
18. Gabriel Company accidentally overstated its ending inventory by $10,000 at the end of period 1. Is gross margin of period 1 overstated or understated? Is gross margin of period 2 overstated, understated, or unaffected by the period 1 error? Is total gross margin for the two periods overstated, understated, or correct? Give the reason for your answers.
19. Identify an important method of estimating inventory amounts. What familiar model underlies this estimation method?
20. A fire destroyed the inventory of Olivera Company, but the accounting records were saved. The beginning inventory was $22,000, purchases for the period were $71,000, and sales were $140,000. Olivera's customary gross margin is 45% of sales. Use the gross margin method to estimate the cost of the inventory destroyed by the fire.
21. True or false? A company that sells inventory of low unit cost needs no internal controls over the goods. Any inventory loss would probably be small.
22. What are likely to be the two largest cash flows for a merchandising entity?

Daily Exercises

Basic concept of accounting for inventory ***(Obj. 1)***

DE9-1 Karas Enterprises purchased 1,000 units of inventory for $60 each and marked up the goods by $40 per unit. Karas then sold 800 units. For these transactions, show what Karas would report on its balance sheet at December 31, 19X0 and on its income statement for the year ended December 31, 19X0. Include a complete heading for each statement.

Accounting for inventory under the perpetual and the periodic systems ***(Obj. 1)***

DE9-2 Study Exhibit 9-3, page 381, and answer these questions:

1. What was Huntington Galleries' cost of the inventory that Huntington purchased during the year?
2. How much were Huntington's sales for the year? How much were cost of goods sold and the gross margin? What was the cost of ending inventory?
3. Which inventory system (perpetual or periodic) generates higher profits? Give the reason for your answer.

DE9-3 Magnum Auto Parts purchased inventory costing $100,000 and sold half the goods for $120,000, with all transactions on account.

Accounting for inventory transactions: perpetual system ***(Obj. 1)***

Journalize these two transactions under the perpetual inventory system. How much gross margin did Magnum earn on these sales? Which statement reports the gross margin?

DE9-4 Use the data in Daily Exercise 9-3 to record Magnum Auto Parts' purchase and sale transactions under the periodic inventory system. Why can't you measure Magnum's gross margin under the periodic system? What additional information is needed to compute cost of goods sold and the gross margin?

Accounting for inventory transactions: periodic system ***(Obj. 1)***

DE9-5 Study Exhibit 9-4, page 386, and answer these questions.

Applying the FIFO, LIFO, and weighted-average cost methods ***(Obj. 2)***

1. In Panel A, are the company's inventory costs stable, increasing, or decreasing during the period? Cite specific figures to support your answer.
2. Which inventory method results in the *highest* amount for ending inventory (give this figure)? Explain why this method produces the highest amount for ending inventory.
3. Does this method result in the highest, or the lowest, cost of goods sold? Explain why this occurs.
4. Does this method result in the highest, or the lowest, gross margin? Explain your answer.

DE9-6 Study Exhibit 9-4, page 386, and answer these questions.

Applying the FIFO, LIFO, and weighted-average cost methods ***(Obj. 2)***

1. In Panel A, are the company's inventory costs stable, increasing, or decreasing during the period? Cite specific figures to support your answer.
2. Which inventory method results in the *lowest* amount for ending inventory (give this figure)? Explain why this method produces the lowest amount for ending inventory.
3. Does this method result in the highest, or the lowest, cost of goods sold? Explain why this occurs.
4. Does this method result in the highest, or the lowest, gross margin? Explain your answer.

DE9-7 Return to Exhibit 9-4, page 386, and assume that the business sold 30 units of inventory during the period (instead of 40 units as in the exhibit). Compute ending inventory and cost of goods sold for each of the following costing methods:

Applying the weighted-average, FIFO, and LIFO methods ***(Obj. 2)***

a. Weighted-average b. FIFO c. LIFO

Follow the computational format illustrated in the exhibit.

DE9-8 IKON Data Systems markets the ink used in laser printers. IKON started the year with 100 containers of ink (weighted-average cost of $9.14 each; FIFO cost of $9 each, LIFO cost of $8 each). During the year, IKON purchased 800 containers of ink at $13 and sold 700 units for $20 each, with all transactions on account. IKON paid operating expenses throughout the year, a total of $4,000.

Applying the weighted-average, FIFO, and LIFO methods ***(Obj. 2)***

Journalize IKON's purchases, sales, and operating expense transactions using the following format. IKON uses the perpetual inventory method to account for laser-printer ink.

	DEBIT/CREDIT AMOUNTS		
Accounts	**Weighted-Average***	**FIFO**	**LIFO**

*Round weighted-average unit cost to the nearest cent.

DE9-9 This exercise uses the data from Daily Exercise 9-8. It can follow Daily Exercise 9-8, or it can be solved independently.

Income effects of the inventory costing methods ***(Obj. 3)***

Prepare IKON Data Systems' income statement for the current year ended December 31 under the weighted-average, FIFO, and LIFO inventory costing methods. Include a complete statement heading, and use a format similar to that illustrated for Daily Exercise 9-8 for the three inventory methods.

DE9-10 This exercise should be used in conjunction with Daily Exercise 9-9.

Income tax effects of the inventory costing methods ***(Obj. 3)***

Assume IKON Data Systems in Daily Exercise 9-9 is a corporation subject to a 40% income tax. Compute IKON's income tax expense under the weighted-average, FIFO, and LIFO inventory costing methods. Which method would you select in order to (a) maximize reported income, and (b) minimize income tax expense? Format your answer as shown on page 388.

Income and tax effects of LIFO
(Obj. 3)

DE9-11 NIKE, Inc., the athletic-clothing company, uses the LIFO method to account for inventory. Suppose Nike is having an unusually good year, with net income far above expectations. Assume Nike's inventory costs are rising rapidly. What can Nike's managers do immediately before the end of the year to decrease reported profits and thereby save on income taxes? Explain how this action decreases reported income.

Income effects of the inventory methods; using a perpetual inventory record
(Obj. 3)

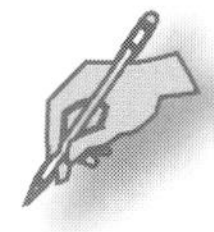

DE9-12 Examine the perpetual inventory record in Exhibit 9-8, page 391. Answer these questions about Huntington Galleries' inventories.

1. Which costing method does Huntington use? Prove your answer by citing cost data from the exhibit. Focus on the November 12 sale.
2. Huntington Galleries sold the chairs in the exhibit for $500 each. How much did Huntington report for sales revenue, cost of goods sold, and gross margin? On which financial statement did Huntington Galleries report these figures?

Applying the lower-of-cost-or-market rule to inventory
(Obj. 4)

DE9-13 Huntington Galleries uses the perpetual inventory record for early American chairs in Exhibit 9-8, page 391. At December 31, 1997, Brad Street, controller of the company, applied the lower-of-cost-or-market rule to Huntington's inventories. Street determined that the current replacement cost (current market value) of the chairs was $5,800. Show how Street reported this inventory on the balance sheet and the cost of goods sold on the income statement.

Assessing the effect of an inventory error—one year only
(Obj. 5)

DE9-14 Examine Huntington Galleries' financial statements in Exhibit 9-1, on page 378. Suppose Huntington's reported cost of inventory at December 31, 1997, is overstated by $3 million ($3,000 thousand, as in the statements). What are Huntington's correct amounts for (a) inventory, (b) cost of goods sold, (c) gross margin, and (d) net income?

Assessing the effect of an inventory error on two years' statements
(Obj. 5)

DE9-15 Maggie Lang, staff accountant of Crestar Stores, learned that Crestar's $4 million cost of inventory at the end of last year was understated by $1.5 million. She notified the company president of the accounting error and the need to alert Crestar's lenders that last year's reported net income was incorrect. Michael LeVan, president of Crestar, explained to Lang that there is no need to report the error to lenders because the error will counterbalance this year. This year's error will affect this year's net income in the opposite direction of last year's error. Even with no correction, LeVan reasons, net income for both years combined will be the same whether or not Crestar corrects its error.

1. Was last year's reported net income of $6.0 million overstated, understated, or correct? What was the correct amount of net income last year?
2. Is this year's net income of $6.8 million overstated, understated, or correct? What is the correct amount of net income for the current year?
3. Whose perspective is better, Lang's or LeVan's? Give your reason. Consider the trend of reported net income both without the correction and with the correction.

Ethical implications of inventory actions
(Obj. 3, 4, 5)

DE9-16 Determine whether each of the following actions in buying, selling, and accounting for inventories is ethical or unethical. Give your reason for each answer.

1. DTE Photo Film purchased lots of inventory shortly before year end to increase the LIFO cost of goods sold and decrease reported income for the year.
2. Edison Electrical Products delayed the purchase of inventory until after December 31, 19X9, in order to keep 19X9's cost of goods sold from growing too large. The delay in purchasing inventory helped net income of 19X9 to reach the level of profit demanded by the company's investors.
3. Dover Sales Company deliberately overstated ending inventory in order to report higher profits (net income).
4. Brazos River Corporation consciously overstated purchases to produce a high figure for cost of goods sold (low amount of net income). The real reason was to decrease the company's income tax payments to the government.
5. In applying the lower-of-cost-or-market rule to inventories, Fort Wayne Industries recorded an excessively low market value for ending inventory. This allowed the company to keep from paying income tax for the year.

Estimating ending inventory by the gross margin method
(Obj. 6)

DE9-17 Answer the following questions.

1. Nextel Chemical Company began the year with inventory of $500,000. Inventory purchases for the year totaled $1,600,000. Nextel managers estimate that cost of goods sold for the year will be $1,800,000. How much is Nextel's estimated cost of ending inventory? Use the gross margin method.

2. Nextel Mining, a related company, began the year with inventory of $500,000 and purchased $1,600,000 of goods during the year (the same as in requirement 1). Sales for the year are $3,000,000, and Nextel's gross margin percentage is 40% of sales. Compute Nextel's estimated cost of ending inventory by the gross margin method. Compare this answer to your answer in Requirement 1; they should be the same. Focus on the computation of estimated cost of goods sold to explain why the two answers are the same.

DE9-18

Reporting inventory transactions on the statement of cash flows
(Obj. 7)

1. Journalize the following transactions for The Coca-Cola Company:

   - Sales on account, $18.0 billion
   - Collections on account, $17.8 billion

Which amount is reported on the statement of cash flows? How would you classify this item—as an operating cash flow, an investing cash flow, or a financing cash flow? Give the reason for your answer.

2. Journalize these transactions of The Coca-Cola Company:

   - Cash purchases of inventory, $7.0 billion
   - Cost of goods sold (perpetual inventory system), $6.9 billion

Which amount is reported on the statement of cash flows? Is it an operating cash flow, an investing cash flow, or a financing cash flow? Give your reason.

Exercises

Accounting for inventory under the perpetual and periodic systems
(Obj. 1)

E9-1 Accounting records for Le Gap Sportswear yield the following data for the year ended December 31, 19X5 (amounts in thousands)

Inventory, December 31, 19X4	$ 370
Purchases of inventory (on account)	2,933
Sales of inventory—80% on account; 20% for cash (cost $2,821)	4,395
Inventory at FIFO cost, December 31, 19X5	?

REQUIRED

1. Journalize Le Gap's inventory transactions for the year two ways—first under the perpetual system, then under the periodic system. Show all amounts in thousands. Use Exhibit 9-3 on page 381 as a model.
2. Report ending inventory, sales, cost of goods sold, and gross margin on the appropriate financial statement (amounts in thousands). Show the computation of cost of goods sold in the periodic system.

Budgeting inventory purchases
(Obj. 1)

E9-2 Toys "Я" Us is budgeting for the fiscal year ended January 31, 1997. During the preceding year ended January 31, 1996, sales totaled $9,427 million and cost of goods sold was $6,592 million. Inventory stood at $1,752 million at January 31, 1995, and at January 31, 1996, inventory stood at $1,999 million.

During the upcoming 1997 year, suppose Toys "Я" Us expects sales and cost of goods sold to increase by 8 percent. The company budgets next year's ending inventory at $2,110 million.

REQUIRED

How much inventory should Toys "Я" Us purchase during the upcoming year in order to reach its budgeted figures? Round to the nearest $1 million.

Determining ending inventory and cost of goods sold by four methods
(Obj. 2)

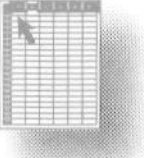

E9-3 Abba Medical Supply's inventory records for pacemaker switches indicate the following at October 31:

Oct. 1	Beginning inventory	7 units @ $160
8	Purchase	4 units @ 160
15	Purchase	11 units @ 170
26	Purchase	5 units @ 176

The physical count of inventory at October 31 indicates that eight units are on hand, and there are no consignment goods.

REQUIRED

Compute ending inventory and cost of goods sold, using each of the following methods:

1. Specific unit cost, assuming five $170 units and three $160 units are on hand
2. Weighted-average cost (round weighted-average unit cost to three decimal places)
3. First-in, first-out
4. Last-in, first-out

Recording inventory transactions
(Obj. 1, 2)

E9-4 Use the data in Exercise 9-3 to journalize the following, first for the perpetual inventory system, then for the periodic system:

a. Total October purchases in one summary entry. All purchases were on credit.

b. Total October sales in a summary entry. Assume that the selling price was $300 per unit and that all sales were on credit. Abba Medical Supply uses LIFO.

c. October 31 end-of-period entries for inventory in the periodic system. Abba Medical Supply uses LIFO. Post to the Cost of Goods Sold T-account to show how this amount is determined. Label each item in the account. How does the balance for Cost of Goods Sold compare to the Cost of Goods Sold amount recorded under the perpetual system?

Computing the tax advantage of LIFO over FIFO
(Obj. 3)

E9-5 Use the data in Exercise 9-3 to illustrate the income tax advantage of LIFO over FIFO, assuming that sales revenue is $8,000, operating expenses are $1,100, and the income tax rate is 30 percent. How much in taxes would Abba Medical Supply save by using the LIFO method?

Determining amounts for the income statement: periodic system
(Obj. 1)

E9-6 Supply the missing income statement amounts for each of the following companies:

Company	Net Sales	Beginning Inventory	Net Purchases	Ending Inventory	Cost of Goods Sold	Gross Margin
A	$92,800	$12,500	$62,700	$19,400	(a)	$37,000
B	(b)	27,450	93,000	(c)	$94,100	51,200
C	94,700	(d)	54,900	22,600	59,400	(e)
D	98,600	10,700	(f)	8,200	(g)	47,100

Prepare the income statement for company D, which uses the periodic inventory system. Include a complete heading. Company D's operating expenses for the year were $32,100.

Measuring profitability
(Obj. 3)

E9-7 *Link Back to Chapter 5 (Gross Margin Percentage and Inventory Turnover).* Refer to the data in Exercise 9-6. Which company is likely to be the most profitable, based on its gross margin percentage and rate of inventory turnover?

Suppose you are a financial analyst, and a client has asked you to recommend an investment in one of these companies. Write a memo outlining which company you recommend, and explain your reasoning.

Determining ending inventory and cost of goods sold in a perpetual system
(Obj. 1, 2)

E9-8 Piazza Music World carries a large inventory of guitars, keyboards, and other musical instruments. Because each item is expensive, Piazza uses a perpetual inventory system. Company records indicate the following for a particular line of Casio keyboards:

Date	Item	Quantity	Unit Cost
May 1	Balance	5	$90
6	Sale	3	
8	Purchase	11	95
17	Sale	4	
30	Sale	1	

REQUIRED

Determine the amounts that Piazza should report for ending inventory and cost of goods sold by the FIFO method. Prepare the perpetual inventory record for Casio keyboards, using Exhibit 9-8 as a model.

Change from LIFO to FIFO
(Obj. 3)

E9-9 Magna Enterprises is considering a change from the LIFO inventory method to the FIFO method. Managers are concerned about the effect of this change on income tax expense and reported net income. If the change is made, it will become effective on March 1. Inventory on hand at February 28 is $63,000. During March, Magna managers expect sales of $260,000, net purchases between $159,000 and $182,000, and operating expenses of $83,000. Inventories at March 31 are budgeted as follows: FIFO, $85,000; LIFO, $78,000.

REQUIRED

Create a spreadsheet model to compute estimated net income four ways: Assume net purchases at $159,000 and $182,000 for March under both FIFO and LIFO. Format your answer as follows:

MAGNA ENTERPRISES
Estimated Income under FIFO and LIFO
March 19XX

	FIFO	LIFO	FIFO	LIFO
Sales	$260,000	$260,000	$260,000	$260,000
Cost of goods sold				
Beginning inventory	63,000	63,000	63,000	63,000
Net purchases	159,000	159,000	182,000	182,000
Cost of goods available				
Ending inventory	85,000	78,000	85,000	78,000
Cost of goods sold				
Gross margin				
Operating expenses	83,000	83,000	83,000	83,000
Net income	$	$	$	$

Managing income taxes under the LIFO method
(Obj. 3)

E9-10 Deitrick Enterprises is nearing the end of its best year ever. With three weeks until year end, it appears that net income for the year will have increased by 70% over last year. Jim Deitrick, the principal stockholder and president, is pleased with the year's success but unhappy about the huge increase in income taxes that the business will have to pay.

He asks you, the financial vice president, to come up with a way to decrease the business's income tax burden. Inventory quantities are a little lower than normal because sales have been especially strong during the last few months. Deitrick Enterprises uses the LIFO inventory method, and inventory costs have risen dramatically during the latter part of the year.

REQUIRED

Write a memorandum to Jim Deitrick to explain how Deitrick Enterprises can decrease its income taxes for the current year. Deitrick is a man of integrity, so your plan must be completely honest.

Identifying income, tax, and other effects of the inventory methods
(Obj. 3)

E9-11 This exercise tests your understanding of the four inventory methods. In the space provided, write the name of the inventory method that best fits the description. Assume that the cost of inventory is rising.

FI **a.** Maximizes reported income.
LI **b.** Enables a company to buy high-cost inventory at year end and thereby decrease reported income.
LI **c.** Reported income and income taxes rise when the company liquidates older, low-cost, layers of inventory.
LI **d.** Matches the most current cost of goods sold against sales revenue.
LI **e.** Results in an old measure of the cost of ending inventory.
LI **f.** Generally associated with saving income taxes.
FI **g.** Results in a cost of ending inventory that is close to the current cost of replacing the inventory.
SPEC. COST **h.** Used to account for automobiles, jewelry, and art objects.
FI **i.** Associated with inventory profits.
W.A **j.** Provides a middle-ground measure of ending inventory and cost of goods sold.

Applying the lower-of-cost-or-market rule to inventories: perpetual system
(Obj. 1, 4)

E9-12 Hillis Corporation, which uses a perpetual inventory system, has these account balances at December 31, 19X7, prior to releasing the financial statements for the year:

Inventory		Cost of Goods Sold		Sales Revenue	
Beg. bal. 12,489					
End. bal. 18,028		Bal. 110,161			Bal. 225,000

A year ago, when Hillis prepared its 19X6 financial statements, the replacement cost of ending inventory was $13,051. Hillis has determined that the replacement cost of the December 31, 19X7, ending inventory is $16,840.

REQUIRED

Prepare Hillis Corporation's 19X7 income statement through gross margin to show how Hillis would apply the lower-of-cost-or-market rule to its inventories. Include a complete heading for the statement.

Applying the lower-of-cost-or-market rule to inventories: periodic system ***(Obj. 1, 4)***

E9-13 Brunswick Tool Company uses a periodic inventory system and reports inventory at the lower of FIFO cost or market. Prior to releasing its March 19X4 financial statements, Brunswick's preliminary income statement appears as follows:

BRUNSWICK TOOL COMPANY Income Statement (partial)		
Sales revenue		$89,000
Cost of goods sold:		
Beginning inventory	$17,200	
Net purchases	51,700	
Cost of goods available for sale	68,900	
Ending inventory	(23,800)	
Cost of goods sold		45,100
Gross margin		$43,900

Brunswick has determined that the current replacement cost of ending inventory is $19,800. Adjust the preceding income statement to apply the lower-of-cost-or market rule to Brunswick's inventory. Also show the relevant portion of Brunswick's balance sheet. The replacement cost of Brunswick's beginning inventory was $18,600.

Correcting an inventory error ***(Obj. 5)***

E9-14 Malzone Auto Supply reported the following comparative income statement for the years ended September 30, 19X9 and 19X8:

MALZONE AUTO SUPPLY Income Statements Years Ended September 30, 19X9 and 19X8				
	19X9		**19X8**	
Sales revenue		$137,300		$121,700
Cost of goods sold:				
Beginning inventory	$14,000		$12,800	
Net purchases	72,000		66,000	
Cost of goods available	86,000		78,800	
Ending inventory	(16,600)		(14,000)	
Cost of goods sold		69,400		64,800
Gross margin		67,900		56,900
Operating expenses		30,300		26,100
Net income		$ 37,600		$ 30,800

During 19X9, accountants for the company discovered that ending 19X8 inventory was overstated by $2,000. Prepare the corrected comparative income statement for the two-year period, complete with a heading for the statement. What was the effect of the error on net income for the two years combined? Explain your answer.

Estimating ending inventory by the gross margin method ***(Obj. 6)***

E9-15 Gobel Aviation Supply began January with inventory of $42,000. The business made net purchases of $37,600 and had net sales of $60,000 before a fire destroyed the company's inventory. For the past several years, Gobel's gross margin on sales has been 40 percent. Estimate the cost of the inventory destroyed by the fire. Identify another reason managers use the gross margin method to estimate inventory cost on a regular basis.

CHALLENGE EXERCISES

Inventory policy decisions ***(Obj. 2, 3)***

E9-16 For each of the following situations, identify the inventory method that you would use, or, given the use of a particular method, state the strategy that you would follow to accomplish your goal.

a. Company management, like that of IBM, prefers a middle-of-the-road inventory policy that avoids extremes.

b. Inventory costs are increasing, and the company prefers to report high income. (Give the reason for your choice of method.)

c. Suppliers of your inventory are threatening a labor strike, and it may be difficult for your company to obtain inventory. This situation could increase your income taxes.

d. Inventory costs are decreasing, and your company's board of directors wants to minimize income taxes.

e. Inventory costs are increasing. Your company uses LIFO and is having an unexpectedly good year. It is near year end, and you need to keep net income from increasing too much.

f. Inventory costs have been stable for several years, and you expect costs to remain stable for the indefinite future. (Give the reason for your choice of method.)

LIFO liquidation
(Obj. 2)

E9-17 Whirlpool Corporation, the world's leading manufacturer of major home appliances, reported these figures for 19X1 (in millions of dollars):

WHIRLPOOL CORPORATION
Income Statement (adapted)

Net revenues	$6,757
Cost of products sold	4,967
Operating expenses	1,397
Other expense (net)	93
Earnings before income taxes	300
Income taxes	130
Net earnings	$ 170

Note 4 of the financial statements disclosed:
Liquidation of prior years' LIFO inventory layers increased net earnings $8 million.

REQUIRED

1. Explain what the LIFO liquidation means and why it affects net earnings.
2. Would Whirlpool management be pleased or displeased at the increase in income due to the LIFO liquidation? Give your reason.
3. Prepare a revised income statement for Whirlpool Corporation if no LIFO liquidation had occurred. The income tax rate was 43.33 percent.

Evaluating a company's profitability
(Obj. 7)

E9-18 Pharmacy Management Services, Inc. (PMSI), is a leading provider of products for workers' compensation insurance purposes. The company recently reported these figures.

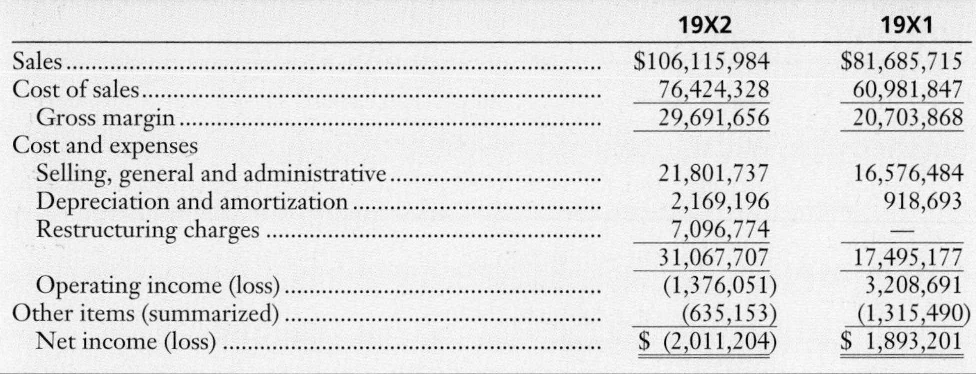

PHARMACY MANAGEMENT SERVICES, INC., AND SUBSIDIARIES
Consolidated Statements of Operations
Years Ended July 31, 19X2 and 19X1

	19X2	19X1
Sales	$106,115,984	$81,685,715
Cost of sales	76,424,328	60,981,847
Gross margin	29,691,656	20,703,868
Cost and expenses		
Selling, general and administrative	21,801,737	16,576,484
Depreciation and amortization	2,169,196	918,693
Restructuring charges	7,096,774	—
	31,067,707	17,495,177
Operating income (loss)	(1,376,051)	3,208,691
Other items (summarized)	(635,153)	(1,315,490)
Net income (loss)	$ (2,011,204)	$ 1,893,201

REQUIRED

Evaluate PMSI's operations during 19X2 in comparison with 19X1. Consider sales, gross margin, operating income, and net income. In the annual report, PMSI's management describes the restructuring charges in 19X2 as a one-time event that is not expected to recur. How does this additional information affect your evaluation?

Reporting inventory transactions on the statement of cash flows, income statement, and balance sheet
(Obj. 7)

E9-19 *Link Back to Chapter 5 (Income Statement and Balance Sheet).* Campbell Soup Company uses a perpetual inventory system and the LIFO method to determine the cost of its inventory. During a recent year, Campbell Soup reported the following items (adapted) in its financial statements (listed in alphabetical order, and with amounts given in millions of dollars)

Collections from customers..........	$7,255	Payments for inventory..........	$4,150
Cost of goods sold	4,264	Revenues, total	7,288
Other expenses..............................	2,326	Total assets.............................	6,315
Owners' equity.............................	2,468	Total liabilities	3,847

REQUIRED

1. Prepare as much of Campbell Soup Company's statement of cash flows for the year ended July 31, 19X5, as you can. Include a complete heading.
2. Prepare Campbell Soup Company's summary income statement for the year ended July 31, 19X5, complete with a heading.
3. Prepare Campbell Soup Company's summary balance sheet at July 31, 19X5, complete with a heading.

Beyond the Numbers

Assessing the impact of the inventory costing method on the financial statements
(Obj. 2, 3, 4)

BN9-1 The inventory costing method a company chooses can affect the financial statements and thus the decisions of the people who use those statements.

REQUIRED

1. A leading accounting researcher stated that one inventory costing method reports the most recent costs in the income statement, while another method reports the most recent costs in the balance sheet. What did the researcher mean?
2. Conservatism is an accepted accounting concept. Would you want management to be conservative in accounting for inventory if you were a shareholder of the company? Give your reason.
3. Elgin Ltd. follows conservative accounting and writes the value of its inventory of bicycles down to market, which has declined below cost. The following year, an unexpected cycling craze results in a demand for bicycles that far exceeds supply, and the market price increases above the previous cost. What effect will conservatism have on the income of Elgin during each year?

ETHICAL ISSUE

During 19X6, Arrow Carpet Company changed to the LIFO method of accounting for inventory. Suppose that during 19X7, Arrow changes back to the FIFO method and the following year switches back to LIFO again.

REQUIRED

1. What would you think of a company's ethics if it changed accounting methods every year?
2. What accounting principle would changing methods every year violate?
3. Who can be harmed when a company changes its accounting methods too often? How?

Problems (GROUP A)

Accounting for inventory in a perpetual system
(Obj. 1, 2)

P9-1A Toys "Я" Us purchases inventory in crates of merchandise, so each unit of inventory is a crate of toys. Assume you are dealing with a single department in the Toys "Я" Us store in Knoxville, Tennessee. The fiscal year of Toys "Я" Us ends each January 31.

Assume the department began fiscal year 19X5 with an inventory of 20 units that cost a total of $1,200. During the year, the department purchased merchandise on account as follows:

April (30 units @ $65)..................	$ 1,950
August (50 units @ $65)...............	3,250
November (90 units @ $70)..........	6,300
Total purchases	$11,500

Cash payments on account during the year totaled $11,390.

During fiscal year 19X5, the department sold 180 units of merchandise for $16,400, of which $5,300 was for cash and the balance was on account. Toys "Я" Us uses the LIFO method for inventories. Department operating expenses for the year were $3,630. The department paid two-thirds in cash and accrued the rest.

1. Make summary journal entries to record the department's transactions for the year ended January 31, 19X5. Toys "Я" Us uses a perpetual inventory system.
2. Determine the LIFO cost of the store's ending inventory at January 31, 19X5. Use a T-account.
3. Prepare the department's income statement for the year ended January 31, 19X5. Include a complete heading, and show totals for the gross margin and net income.

REQUIRED

P9-2A Condensed versions of a Texaco convenience store's most recent income statement and balance sheet reported the following figures. The business uses a periodic inventory system.

Using the cost-of-goods-sold model to budget operations
(Obj. 1)

TEXACO CONVENIENCE STORE
Balance Sheet
December 31, 19X4

Assets	Thousands	Liabilities and Capital	Thousands
Cash	$ 70	Accounts payable	$ 35
Inventories	35	Note payable	280
Land and buildings, net	360	Total liabilities	315
		Owner, capital	150
Total assets	$465	Total liabilities and capital	$465

TEXACO CONVENIENCE STORE
Income Statement
Year Ended December 31, 19X4

	Thousands
Sales	$800
Cost of sales	660
Gross margin	140
Operating expenses	80
Net income	$ 60

The owner is budgeting for 19X5. He expects sales and cost of sales to increase by 10 percent. To meet customer demand for the increase in sales, ending inventory will need to be $40 thousand at December 31, 19X5. The owner can lower operating expenses by doing some of the work himself. He hopes to earn a net income of $80 thousand next year.

1. A key variable the owner can control is the amount of inventory he purchases. Show how to determine the amount of purchases he should make in 19X5 (amounts in thousands).
2. Prepare the store's budgeted income statement for 19X5 to reach the target net income of $80 thousand.

REQUIRED

P9-3A An American Tourister outlet store began August 19X8 with 50 units of inventory that cost $40 each. The sale price of these units was $70. During August, the store completed these inventory transactions:

Using the perpetual and periodic inventory systems
(Obj. 1, 2)

		Units	Unit Cost	Unit Sale Price
Aug. 3	Sale	16	$40	$70
8	Purchase	80	41	72
11	Sale	34	40	70
19	Sale	9	41	72
24	Sale	35	41	72
30	Purchase	18	42	73
31	Sale	6	41	72

1. The preceding data are taken from the store's perpetual inventory records. Which cost method does the store use?
2. Determine the store's cost of goods sold for August under the
   a. Perpetual inventory system **b.** Periodic inventory system
3. Compute gross margin for August.

REQUIRED

P9-4A BullsEye Electric Co. began March with 73 units of inventory that cost $23 each. During the month, BullsEye made the following purchases:

Computing inventory by three methods
(Obj. 2, 3)

March 4	113 @ $27
12	81 @ 29
19	167 @ 32
25	44 @ 35

The company uses the periodic inventory system, and the physical count at March 31 indicates that ending inventory consists of 51 units.

REQUIRED

1. Determine the ending inventory and cost-of-goods-sold amounts for the March financial statements under (a) weighted-average cost, (b) FIFO cost, and (c) LIFO cost. Round weighted-average cost per unit to the nearest cent, and round all other amounts to the nearest dollar.
2. How much income tax would BullsEye Electric save during the month by using LIFO versus FIFO? The income tax rate is 40 percent.

Preparing an income statement directly from the accounts
(Obj. 2, 3)

P9-5A The records of Ridgewood Golf Shop include the following accounts at December 31 of the current year:

Inventory

Jan. 1	Balance {700 units @ $7.00}	4,900	

Purchases

Jan. 6	300 units @ $7.05	2,115	
Mar. 19	1,100 units @ 7.35	8,085	
June 22	8,400 units @ 7.50	63,000	
Oct. 4	500 units @ 8.50	4,250	
Dec. 31	Balance	77,450	

Sales Revenue

	Feb. 5	1,000 units @ $12.00	12,000
	Apr. 10	700 units @ 12.10	8,470
	July 31	1,800 units @ 13.25	23,850
	Sep. 4	3,500 units @ 13.50	47,250
	Nov. 27	3,100 units @ 15.00	46,500
	Dec. 31	Balance	138,070

REQUIRED

1. Prepare a partial income statement through gross margin under the weighted-average cost, FIFO cost, and LIFO cost methods. Ridgewood uses a periodic inventory system.
2. Which inventory method would you use to minimize income tax?

Applying the lower-of-cost-or-market rule to inventories
(Obj. 4)

P9-6A Hypermart has recently been plagued with lackluster sales. The rate of inventory turnover has dropped, and some of the company's merchandise is gathering dust. At the same time, competition has forced Hypermart's suppliers to lower the prices that Hypermart will pay when it replaces its inventory. It is now December 31, 19X9, and the current replacement cost of Hypermart's ending inventory is $800,000 below what Hypermart actually paid for the goods, which was $4,900,000. Before any adjustments at the end of the period, Hypermart's Cost of Goods Sold account has a balance of $29,600,000.

What action should Hypermart take in this situation, if any? Give any journal entry required. At what amount should Hypermart report Inventory on the balance sheet? At what amount should the company report Cost of Goods Sold on the income statement? Discuss the accounting principle or concept that is most relevant to this situation.

Correcting inventory errors over a three-year period
(Obj. 5)

P9-7A The Schlecte Glass Company books show these data (in thousands):

	19X6		19X5		19X4	
Net sales revenue		$360		$285		$244
Cost of goods sold:						
Beginning inventory	$ 65		$ 55		$ 70	
Net purchases	195		135		130	
Cost of goods available	260		190		200	
Less ending inventory	(70)		(65)		(55)	
Cost of goods sold		190		125		145
Gross margin		170		160		99
Operating expenses		113		109		76
Net income		$ 57		$ 51		$ 23

In early 19X7, a team of internal auditors discovered that the ending inventory for 19X4 had been overstated by $5 thousand and that the ending inventory for 19X6 had been understated by $6 thousand. The ending inventory at December 31, 19X5, was correct.

REQUIRED

1. Show corrected income statements for the three years.

2. State whether each year's net income and owners' equity amounts are understated or overstated. Ignore income tax because Schlecte is a proprietorship. For each incorrect figure, indicate the amount of the understatement or overstatement.

Estimating ending inventory by the gross margin method; preparing the income statement
(Obj. 6)

P9-8A Rolex Quartz Company estimates its inventory by the gross margin method when preparing monthly financial statements. For the past two years, the gross margin has averaged 40% of net sales. The company's inventory records reveal the following data amounts in thousands:

Inventory, July 1	$ 367
Transactions during July:	
Purchases	3,789
Purchase discounts	26
Purchase returns	12
Sales	6,430
Sales returns	25

REQUIRED

1. Estimate the July 31 inventory, using the gross margin method.
2. Prepare the July income statement through gross margin for the Rolex Quartz Company.

Reporting inventory transactions on the statement of cash flows, income statement, and balance sheet
(Obj. 7)

P9-9A *Link Back to Chapter 5 (Merchandiser's Income Statement and Balance Sheet).* Lands' End, Inc., uses a perpetual inventory system and the LIFO method to determine the cost of its inventory. During a recent year, Lands' End reported the following items (adapted) in its financial statements (listed in alphabetical order, and with amounts given in millions of dollars):

Collections from customers	$1,028	Other revenues	$ 4
Cost of goods sold	588	Owner's equity	201
Long-term liabilities	7	Payments for inventory	575
Net sales revenue	1,032	Property, plant & equipment	99
Other assets	2	Total current assets	222
Other expenses	417	Total current liabilities	115

REQUIRED

1. Prepare as much of the Lands' End statement of cash flows for the year ended January 31, 19X6, as you can. Include a complete heading.
2. Prepare a single-step income statement for Lands' End for the year ended January 31, 19X6, complete with a heading.
3. Prepare the Lands' End balance sheet at January 31, 19X6, complete with a heading.

Problems (GROUP B)

Accounting for inventory: perpetual system
(Obj. 1, 2)

P9-1B The May Department Stores Company operates more than 300 department stores in the United States, including Lord & Taylor, Hecht's, Foleys, Robinson-May, Kaufmanns, and Filene's. Assume you are dealing with one department in a Lord & Taylor store in Washington, D.C. The company's fiscal year ends each January 31. Also assume the department began fiscal year 19X6 with an inventory of 50 units that cost $1,500. During the year, the department purchased merchandise on account as follows:

March (60 units @ $32)	$1,920
August (40 units @ $34)	1,360
October (180 units @ $35)	6,300
Total purchases	$9,580

Cash payments on account during the year totaled $9,110.

During fiscal year 19X6, the department sold 300 units of merchandise for $13,400, of which $4,700 was for cash and the balance was on account. The May Company uses the LIFO method for inventories.

Operating expenses for the year were $2,430. The department paid two-thirds in cash and accrued the rest.

REQUIRED

1. Make summary journal entries to record the department's transactions for the year ended January 31, 19X6. The company uses a perpetual inventory system.
2. Determine the LIFO cost of the department's ending inventory at January 31, 19X6. Use a T-account.
3. Prepare the department's income statement for the year ended January 31, 19X6. Show totals for the gross margin and net income.

Using the cost-of-goods-sold model to budget operations
(Obj. 1)

P9-2B Condensed versions of an Exxon convenience store's most recent income statement and balance sheet reported the following figures. The business is organized as a proprietorship, so it pays no corporate income tax. It uses a periodic inventory system.

EXXON CONVENIENCE STORE Income Statement Year Ended December 31, 19X7	
	Thousands
Sales	$900
Cost of sales	720
Gross margin	180
Operating expenses	90
Net income	$ 90

EXXON CONVENIENCE STORE
Balance Sheet
December 31, 19X7

Assets	Thousands	Liabilities and Capital	Thousands
Cash	$ 40	Accounts payable	$ 30
Inventories	70	Note payable	190
Land and buildings, net	270	Total liabilities	220
		Owner, capital	160
Total assets	$380	Total liabilities and capital	$380

The owner is budgeting for 19X8. He expects sales and cost of sales to increase by 5 percent. To meet customer demand for the increase in sales, ending inventory will need to be $80 thousand at December 31, 19X8. The owner can lower operating expenses by doing some of the work himself. He hopes to earn a net income of $100 thousand next year.

REQUIRED

1. A key variable the owner can control is the amount of inventory he purchases. Show how to determine the amount of purchases the owner should make in 19X8.
2. Prepare the store's budgeted income statement for 19X8 to reach the target net income of $100 thousand.

Using the periodic and perpetual inventory systems
(Obj. 1, 2)

P9-3B Kendrick Tire Co. began March with 50 units of inventory that cost $19 each. The sale price of each unit was $36. During March, Kendrick completed these inventory transactions:

			Units	Unit Cost	Unit Sale Price
March	2	Purchase	12	$20	$37
	8	Sale	27	19	36
	13	Sale	23	19	36
			1	20	37
	17	Purchase	24	20	37
	22	Sale	31	20	37
	29	Purchase	24	21	39

REQUIRED

1. The preceding data are taken from Kendrick's perpetual inventory records. Which cost method does Kendrick use?
2. Determine Kendrick's cost of goods sold for March under the
   a. Perpetual inventory system **b.** Periodic inventory system
3. Compute gross margin for March.

Computing inventory by three methods
(Obj. 2, 3)

P9-4B An AT&T Phone Center began December with 140 units of inventory that cost $79 each. During December, the store made the following purchases:

Dec.	3	217 @ $81
	12	95 @ 82
	18	210 @ 84
	24	248 @ 87

The store uses the periodic inventory system, and the physical count at December 31 indicates that ending inventory consists of 229 units.

REQUIRED

1. Determine the ending inventory and cost-of-goods-sold amounts for the December financial statements under the weighted-average, FIFO, and LIFO cost methods. Round weighted-average cost per unit to the nearest cent, and round all other amounts to the nearest dollar.
2. How much income tax would AT&T save during December for this one store by using LIFO versus FIFO? The income tax rate is 40 percent.

Preparing an income statement directly from the accounts
(Obj. 2, 3)

P9-5B The records of Sav-On Office Supply include the following accounts for one of its products at December 31 of the current year:

Inventory

Jan.	1	Balance	300 units @ $3.00 100 units @ 3.15	1,215

Purchases			
Feb. 6	800 units @ $3.15	2,520	
May 19	600 units @ 3.35	2,010	
Aug. 12	460 units @ 3.50	1,610	
Oct. 4	800 units @ 3.70	2,960	
Dec. 31 Balance		9,100	

Sales Revenue			
	Mar. 12	500 units @ $4.10	2,050
	June 9	1,100 units @ 4.20	4,620
	Aug. 21	300 units @ 4.50	1,350
	Nov. 2	600 units @ 4.50	2,700
	Dec. 18	100 units @ 4.80	480
	Dec. 31 Balance		11,200

REQUIRED

1. Prepare a partial income statement through gross margin under the weighted-average, FIFO, and LIFO cost methods. Round weighted-average cost to the nearest cent and all other amounts to the nearest dollar. Sav-On uses a periodic inventory system.
2. Which inventory method would you use to report the highest net income?

Applying the lower-of-cost-or-market rule to inventories
(Obj. 4)

P9-6B Kmart has recently been plagued with lackluster sales. The rate of inventory turnover has dropped, and some of the company's merchandise is gathering dust. At the same time, competition has forced some of Kmart's suppliers to lower the prices that Kmart will pay when it replaces its inventory. It is now December 31, 19X9. Assume the current replacement cost of a Kmart store's ending inventory is $500,000 below what Kmart paid for the goods, which was $3,900,000. Before any adjustments at the end of the period, assume the store's Cost of Goods Sold account has a balance of $22,400,000.

What action should Kmart take in this situation, if any? Give any journal entry required. At what amount should Kmart report Inventory on the balance sheet? At what amount should the company report Cost of Goods Sold on the income statement? Discuss the accounting principle or concept that is most relevant to this situation.

Correcting inventory errors over a three-year period
(Obj. 5)

P9-7B Assume the accounting records of Heitmiller Steak House show these data (in thousands):

	19X3		19X2		19X1	
Net sales revenue		$210		$165		$170
Cost of goods sold:						
Beginning inventory	$ 15		$ 25		$ 40	
Net purchases	135		100		90	
Cost of goods available	150		125		130	
Less ending inventory	(30)		(15)		(25)	
Cost of goods sold		120		110		105
Gross margin		90		55		65
Operating expenses		74		38		46
Net income		$ 16		$ 17		$ 19

In early 19X4, a team of internal auditors discovered that the ending inventory for 19X1 had been understated by $4 thousand and that the ending inventory for 19X3 had been overstated by $3 thousand. The ending inventory at December 31, 19X2, was correct.

REQUIRED

1. Show corrected income statements for the three years.
2. State whether each year's net income as reported here and the related owners' equity amounts are understated or overstated. Ignore income tax because Heitmiller is organized as a proprietorship. For each incorrect figure, indicate the amount of the understatement or overstatement.

Estimating ending inventory by the gross margin method; preparing the income statement
(Obj. 6)

P9-8B Canon Color Labs estimates its inventory by the gross margin method when preparing monthly financial statements. For the past two years, gross margin has averaged 25% of net sales. Assume further that the company's inventory records for stores in the southeastern region reveal the following data (amounts in thousands):

Inventory, March 1	$ 292
Transactions during March:	
Purchases........................	6,585
Purchase discounts.........	149
Purchase returns	8
Sales................................	8,657
Sales returns....................	17

REQUIRED

1. Estimate the March 31 inventory using the gross margin method.
2. Prepare the March income statement through gross margin for the Canon Color Labs stores in the southeastern region.

Reporting inventory transactions on the statement of cash flows, income statement, and balance sheet **(Obj. 7)**

P9-9B *Link Back to Chapter 5 (Merchandiser's Income Statement and Balance Sheet).* The Gap, Inc., uses a perpetual inventory system and the FIFO method to determine the cost of its inventory. During a recent year, The Gap reported the following items (as adapted) in its financial statements (listed in alphabetical order, and with amounts given in millions of dollars):

Collections from customers	$5,284	Other revenues..................................	$ 20
Cost of goods sold	3,285	Owners' equity..................................	1,654
Long-term liabilities	198	Payments for inventory.....................	3,292
Net sales revenue..............................	5,284	Property, plant, and equipment.........	1,136
Other assets	162	Total current assets	1,329
Other expenses	1,566	Total current liabilities......................	775

REQUIRED

1. Prepare as much of The Gap's statement of cash flows for the year ended January 31, 19X7, as you can. Include a complete heading.
2. Prepare The Gap's single-step income statement for the year ended January 31, 19X7, complete with a heading.
3. Prepare The Gap's balance sheet at January 31, 19X7, complete with a heading.

Applying Your Knowledge

DECISION CASE

Assessing the impact of a year-end purchase of inventory **(Obj. 2, 3)**

Whitewater Sporting Goods is nearing the end of its first year of operations. The company made inventory purchases of $745,000 during the year, as follows:

January	1,000	units @	$100.00	=	$100,000
July	4,000		121.25		485,000
November	1,000		160.00		160,000
Totals	6,000				$745,000

Sales for the year will be 5,000 units for $1,200,000 revenue. Expenses other than cost of goods sold and income taxes will be $200,000. The president of the company is undecided about whether to adopt the FIFO method or the LIFO method for inventories.

The company has storage capacity for 5,000 additional units of inventory. Inventory prices are expected to stay at $160 per unit for the next few months. The president is considering purchasing 1,000 additional units of inventory at $160 each before the end of the year. He wishes to know how the purchase would affect net income under both FIFO and LIFO. The income tax rate is 40 percent.

REQUIRED

1. To aid company decision making, prepare income statements under FIFO and under LIFO, both without and with the year-end purchase of 1,000 units of inventory at $160 per unit.
2. Compare net income under FIFO without and with the year-end purchase. Make the same comparison under LIFO. Under which method does the year-end purchase affect net income?
3. Under which method can a year-end purchase be made in order to manage net income?

FINANCIAL STATEMENT CASES

Analyzing inventories **(Obj. 2)**

CASE 1. The notes are an important part of a company's financial statements, giving valuable details that would clutter the tabular data presented in the statements. This case will help you learn to use a company's inventory notes. Refer to the NIKE, Inc., statements and related notes in Appendix A and answer the following questions.

1. How much was the NIKE merchandise inventory at May 31, 1997? At May 31, 1996?
2. How does NIKE value its inventories? Which cost methods does the company use?
3. What three categories of inventories did NIKE have on May 31, 1997? Give the title and amount of each category. Briefly describe each category in your own words. (NIKE has three various categories of inventory because NIKE manufactures the inventory it sells.)
4. By rearranging the cost-of-goods-sold formula, you can determine purchases, which are not disclosed in the NIKE statements. How much were the company's inventory purchases during the year ended May 31, 1997? For this computation, use total inventories.

REQUIRED

CASE 2. Obtain the annual report of a company. Make sure that *Inventories* are included among its current assets. Answer these questions about the company.

Analyzing inventories ***(Obj. 2)***

REQUIRED

1. How much were the company's total inventories at the end of the current year? At the end of the preceding year?
2. How does the company value its inventories? Which cost method or methods does the company use?
3. Depending on the nature of the company's business, would you expect the company to use a periodic inventory system or a perpetual system? Give your reason.
4. By rearranging the cost-of-goods-sold formula, you can solve for net purchases, which are not disclosed. Show how to compute the company's net purchases during the current year. Examine the company's note entitled Inventories, Merchandise inventories, or a similar term. If the company discloses several categories of inventories, use the beginning and ending balances of total inventories for the computation of net purchases.

Team Project

Link Back to Chapter 5 (Gross Margin Percentage and Inventory Turnover). Obtain the annual reports of ten companies, two from each of five different industries.

REQUIRED

1. Identify the inventory method used by each company.
2. Compute each company's gross margin percentage and rate of inventory turnover for the most recent two years. If annual reports are unavailable or do not provide enough data for multiple-year computations, you can gather financial statement data from *Moody's Industrial Manual* or from the company's home page on the Internet.
3. For the industries of the companies you are analyzing, obtain the industry averages for gross margin percentage and inventory turnover from Robert Morris Associates, *Annual Statement Studies;* Dun and Bradstreet, *Industry Norms and Key Business Ratios;* or Leo Troy, *Almanac of Business and Industrial Financial Ratios.*
4. How well does each of your companies compare to the other company in its industry? How well do your companies compare to the average for their industry? What insight about your companies can you glean from these ratios?
5. Write a memo to summarize your findings, stating whether your group would invest in each of the companies it has analyzed.

CHAPTER 10

Accounting for Plant Assets, Intangible Assets, and Related Expenses

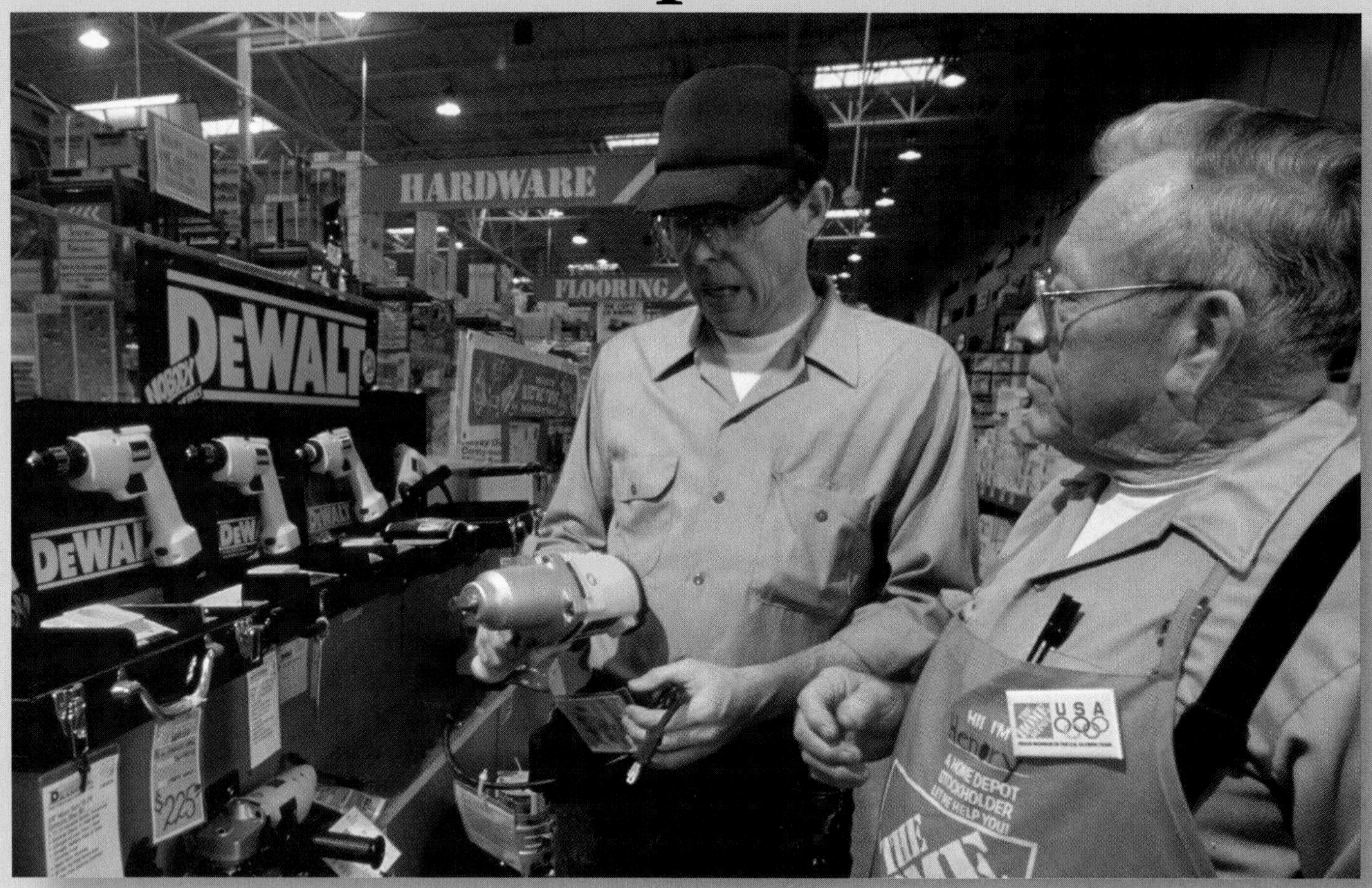

LEARNING OBJECTIVES

After studying this chapter, you should be able to

1. Determine the cost of a plant asset
2. Account for depreciation
3. Select the best depreciation method for income tax purposes
4. Account for the disposal of a plant asset
5. Account for natural resource assets and depletion
6. Account for intangible assets and amortization
7. Report plant asset transactions on the statement of cash flows

> *"The Home Depot is one of the really great retailing companies of all time, and it is still in a very powerful growth mode."*
>
> —CS First Boston

Founded in 1978 in Atlanta, Georgia, The Home Depot is the world's largest home improvement retailer and ranks among the ten largest retailers in the United States. The company has experienced major growth in the last decade, and the company plans to continue expanding. An excerpt from the annual report makes The Home Depot's strategy clear:

> The Home Depot's business strategy is to offer a broad assortment of high-quality merchandise at low "Day-In, Day-Out" warehouse prices and provide exceptional customer service through highly-trained and knowledgeable associates. The average Home Depot store includes approximately 105,000 square feet of indoor selling space, with an additional 20,000 to 28,000 square feet in the outside garden center. *Source:* The Home Depot® *1996 Annual Report.*

How did The Home Depot develop the reputation for being in a "very powerful growth mode"? By opening new stores at a rapid pace. The Home Depot's balance sheet (Exhibit 10-1) shows the effect of the company's growth. During the most recent year, total assets increased from $7.4 billion to $9.3 billion (line 20)—an increase of 26 percent. Much of the growth in assets shows up in Property and equipment (lines 7–15), collectively labeled *plant assets*, which we examine in this chapter.

We introduced plant assets in Chapter 3, page 99.

This chapter also covers *intangible assets*, those assets without physical form, such as Cost in excess of the fair value of net assets acquired—better known as *goodwill*. This is the next-to-last asset reported on Home Depot's balance sheet (line 18). Finally, we discuss natural resource assets (such as oil, gas, timber, and gravel). The expenses that relate to plant assets, natural resources, and intangible assets are *depreciation*, *depletion*, and *amortization*.

Chapter 10 concludes our coverage of asset topics, except for long-term investments, which we discuss in Chapter 16. By the time you complete this chapter, you should feel comfortable with your understanding of the various assets of a business and how companies manage, control, and account for them.

Types of Assets

Plant Assets. Long-lived tangible assets, such as land, buildings, and equipment, used in the operation of a business. Also called **fixed assets.**

Long-lived assets used in the operation of a business and not held for sale as investments can be divided into two categories: plant assets and intangible assets. **Plant assets,** or **fixed assets,** are long-lived assets that are tangible—for instance, land, buildings, and equipment. Their physical form provides their usefulness. The expense associated with plant assets is called *depreciation*. Of the plant assets, land is unique. Its cost is *not* depreciated—expensed over time—because its usefulness does not decrease as does that of other assets. Most companies report plant assets under the heading Property, plant, and equipment on the balance sheet.

We introduced the concept of depreciation in Chapter 3, page 99.

EXHIBIT 10-1
The Home Depot Balance Sheet (partial, adapted)

■ Daily Exercise 10-1

THE HOME DEPOT, INC.
Balance Sheet (Adapted, Assets Only)
Amounts in Millions

			January 31, 1997
		Assets	
		Current Assets:	
	1	Cash and cash equivalents	$ 146
	2	Short-term investments	413
	3	Receivables, net	388
	4	Merchandise inventories	2,708
	5	Other current assets	54
	6	Total Current Assets	3,709
Plant Assets		Property and Equipment, at cost:	
Plant Assets	7	Land	1,855
Plant Assets	8	Buildings	2,470
Plant Assets	9	Furniture, fixtures, and equipment	1,084
Plant Assets	10	Leasehold improvements	340
Plant Assets	11	Construction in progress	284
Plant Assets	12	Capital leases	117
	13		6,150
	14	Less Accumulated depreciation	(713)
	15	Net Property and equipment	5,437
	16	Long-term investments	8
	17	Notes receivable	40
Intangibles	18	Cost in excess of the fair value of net assets acquired, net of accumulated amortization of $15	87
	19	Other assets	61
	20	Total Assets	$9,342

Asset Account on the Balance Sheet	Related Expense Account on the Income Statement
Plant Assets	
Land	None
Buildings, Machinery, and Equipment, Furniture and Fixtures, and Land Improvements	Depreciation
Natural Resources	Depletion
Intangibles	Amortization

Concept Highlight

EXHIBIT 10-2
Terminology Used in Accounting for Plant Assets and Intangible Assets

Intangible assets do not have any physical form. They are useful not because of their physical characteristics, but because of the special rights they carry. Patents, copyrights, and trademarks are intangible assets. Accounting for intangibles is similar to accounting for plant assets that have a physical form.

Intangible Assets. Assets with no physical form. Valuable because of the special rights they carry. Examples are patents and copyrights.

Accounting for intangibles has its own terminology. Different names apply to the individual plant assets and their corresponding expense accounts, as shown in Exhibit 10-2.

In the first half of the chapter, we illustrate how to identify the cost of a plant asset and how to expense its cost. In the second half, we discuss the disposal of plant assets and how to account for natural resources and intangible assets. Unless stated otherwise, we describe accounting in accordance with generally accepted accounting principles for financial statement reporting, as distinguished from reporting to the IRS for income tax purposes.

Measuring the Cost of Plant Assets

Objective 1

Determine the cost of a plant asset

The *cost principle* directs a business to carry an asset on the balance sheet at the amount paid for the asset. The general rule for measuring the cost of any asset (repeated from Chapter 9, page 385) is

The cost of an asset = The sum of all the costs incurred to bring the asset to its intended purpose, net of all discounts

The *cost of a plant asset* is the purchase price, applicable taxes, purchase commissions, and all other amounts paid to acquire the asset and to ready it for its intended use. In Chapter 9, we applied this principle to determine the cost of inventory. Because the types of costs differ for various categories of plant assets, we discuss the major groups individually.

Land

The cost of land includes its purchase price (cash plus any note payable given), brokerage commission, survey fees, legal fees, and any back property taxes that the purchaser pays. Land cost also includes any expenditures for grading and clearing the land and for demolishing or removing any unwanted buildings.

The cost of land does *not* include the cost of fencing, paving, sprinkler systems, and lighting. These separate plant assets—called *land improvements*—are subject to depreciation.

Suppose The Home Depot signs a $300,000 note payable to purchase 20 acres of land for a new store site. Home Depot also pays $10,000 in back property tax, $8,000 in transfer taxes, $5,000 for removal of an old building, a $1,000 survey fee, and $260,000 to pave the parking lot, all in cash. What is the cost of this land?

Purchase price of land		$300,000
Add related costs:		
Back property taxes	$10,000	
Transfer taxes	8,000	
Removal of building	5,000	
Survey fee	1,000	
Total related costs		24,000
Total cost of land		$324,000

Note that the cost of paving the lot, $260,000, is *not* included, because the pavement is a land improvement. The Home Depot's entry to record purchase of the land is

Land	324,000	
Note Payable		300,000
Cash		24,000

We would say that The Home Depot *capitalized* the cost of the land at $324,000. This means that the company debited an asset account (Land) for $324,000.

Learning Tip: Remember that land is not depreciated because it does not wear out.

■ Daily Exercise 10-2

Buildings

The cost of constructing a building includes architectural fees, building permits, contractors' charges, and payments for material, labor, and overhead. The time between the first expenditure for a new building and its completion can be many months, even years, and the number of related expenditures may be numerous. If the company constructs its own assets, the cost of the building may also include the cost of interest on money borrowed to finance the construction. (We discuss this topic in the next section of this chapter.)

When an existing building (new or old) is purchased, its cost includes the purchase price, brokerage commission, sales and other taxes, and cash or credit expenditures for repairing and renovating the building for its intended purpose.

Machinery and Equipment

The cost of machinery and equipment includes its purchase price (less any discounts), transportation charges, insurance while in transit, sales and other taxes, purchase commission, installation costs, and any expenditures to test the asset before it is placed in service. After the asset is up and running, insurance, taxes, and maintenance costs are recorded as expenses.

Land and Leasehold Improvements

For a Home Depot store, the cost to pave a parking lot ($260,000) is not part of the cost of the land. Instead, the $260,000 would be recorded in a separate account entitled Land improvements. This account includes costs for such other items as driveways, signs, fences, and sprinkler systems. Although these assets are located on the land, they are subject to decay, and their cost should therefore be depreciated. Also, the cost of a new building constructed on the land is a debit to the asset account Building.

The Home Depot leases some of its store buildings, warehouses, and vehicles. The company also customizes some of these assets to meet its special needs. For example, The Home Depot may paint its logo on a rental truck and install a special lift on the truck. These improvements are assets of The Home Depot even though the company does not own the truck. The cost of improvements to leased assets appear on the company's balance sheet as *leasehold improvements* (see, for example, line 10 of Home Depot's balance sheet on page 420). The cost of leasehold improvements should be depreciated over the term of the lease. Some companies refer to the depreciation on leasehold improvements as *amortization*, which is the same basic concept as depreciation.

Construction in Progress and Capital Leases

The Home Depot's balance sheet includes two additional categories of plant assets: Construction in progress (line 11) and Capital leases (line 12).

"For The Home Depot, construction in progress is a plant asset because the company expects to use the asset in its operations."

CONSTRUCTION IN PROGRESS *Construction in progress* is an asset, such as a warehouse, that the company is constructing for its own use. On the balance sheet date, the construction is incomplete and the warehouse is not ready for use. However, the construction costs are assets because The Home Depot expects the warehouse, when completed, to render future benefits for the company. For The Home Depot, construction in progress is a plant asset because the company expects to use the asset in its operations.

CAPITAL LEASES A *capital lease* is a lease arrangement similar to an installment purchase of the leased asset. Companies report assets rented through capital leases as assets even though they do not own the assets. Why? Because their lease payments secure the use of the asset over the term of the lease. For example, The Home Depot has long-term capital leases on some of its store buildings. The Home Depot could report the cost of these assets either under Buildings or under Capital leases. Either way, the asset shows up on the balance sheet as a plant asset. Chapter 15 on long-term liabilities goes into capital leases in more detail.

A capital lease is different from an *operating lease*, which is an ordinary rental agreement, such as an apartment lease or the rental of a Hertz automobile. The lessee (the renter) records rent expense when making a payment under an operating lease.

■ Daily Exercise 10-3

Capitalizing the Cost of Interest

The Home Depot constructs some of its plant assets and finances part of the construction with borrowed money, on which The Home Depot must pay interest. A company should generally include its interest cost as part of the cost of a self-constructed asset, such as a building or equipment that takes a long time to build. The practice of including interest as part of an asset's cost is called *capitalizing interest.* To **capitalize a cost** means to record it as part of an asset's cost. In accounting, we debit a capitalized cost to an asset (versus an expense) account.

Capitalize a Cost. To record a cost as part of an asset's cost, rather than as an expense.

Capitalizing interest cost is an exception to the normal practice of recording interest as an expense. Ordinarily, a company that borrows money records interest expense. But on assets that the business builds for its own use, the company should capitalize some of its interest cost. The logic goes like this: If The Home Depot buys a building from a construction company, the price of the building will include the builder's interest cost that was used to finance the construction. To place self-constructed assets on the same footing, it makes sense to capitalize any interest incurred to finance the construction.

The amount of interest to capitalize is based on the average accumulated construction expenditures for the asset. The interest to capitalize should not exceed the company's actual interest cost. The following equation shows the amount of interest to capitalize:

$$\textbf{Interest cost to capitalize} = \textbf{The lesser of} \begin{cases} \textbf{Interest cost based on the average accumulated construction expenditures} \\ \textbf{or} \\ \textbf{Actual interest cost on borrowed money during the period} \end{cases}$$

Suppose on January 2, 19X7, The Home Depot borrows \$1,000,000 on a one-year, 10% note payable to build a warehouse. The entry to record the borrowing is

19X7			
Jan. 2	Cash	1,000,000	
	Note Payable		1,000,000
	Borrowed money for construction of building.		

The company spends the money on construction during 19X7.

19X7			
Jan.–Dec.	Building (or Construction in Progress)	1,000,000	
	Cash		1,000,000
	Incurred construction cost.		

Total interest for the year is \$1,000,000 × 0.10 = \$100,000. Assume The Home Depot's average accumulated expenditures on the construction project during 19X7 are \$600,000. The company should capitalize \$60,000 (\$600,000 × 0.10) of its total \$100,000 interest as part of the building's cost. The Home Depot's entry to accrue the interest at year end is as follows.

19X7			
Dec. 31	Building (or Construction in Progress) ($600,000 × 0.10)	60,000	
	Interest Expense	40,000	
	Interest Payable ($1,000,000 × 0.10)		100,000
	Accrued interest on construction loan.		

The last entry capitalizes $60,000 of interest as part of the cost of the building. The remaining $40,000 of interest is expensed as usual. In January 19X8, The Home Depot will pay off the note and the interest payable.

■ Daily Exercise 10-4
■ Daily Exercise 10-5

What is The Home Depot's cost of the building? The building's cost is $1,060,000, construction cost ($1,000,000) plus the capitalized amount of interest ($60,000). The Home Depot will then depreciate the asset's total cost of $1,060,000.

Thinking It Over How much interest expense would The Home Depot report on its income statement for 19X7?

Answer: $40,000, the amount recorded as interest expense.

Lump-Sum (or Basket) Purchases of Assets

Businesses often purchase several assets as a group, or in a "basket," for a single lump-sum amount. For example, a company may pay one price for land and an office building. The company must identify the cost of each asset. The total cost is divided among the assets according to their relative sales (or market) values. This allocation technique is called the *relative-sales-value method.*

Suppose Xerox Corporation purchases land and a building in Kansas City for a midwestern sales office. The building sits on two acres of land, and the combined purchase price of land and building is $2,800,000. An appraisal indicates that the land's market (sales) value is $300,000 and that the building's market (sales) value is $2,700,000.

An accountant first figures the ratio of each asset's market value to the total market value. Total appraised value is $2,700,000 + $300,000 = $3,000,000. Thus the land, valued at $300,000, is 10% of the total market value. The building's appraised value is 90% of the total:

Asset	Market (Sales) Value		Total Market Value		Percentage
Land	$ 300,000	÷	$3,000,000	=	10%
Building	2,700,000	÷	3,000,000	=	90%
Total	$3,000,000				100%

The percentage for each asset is then multiplied by the total purchase price to determine its cost in the purchase:

Asset	Total Purchase Price		Percentage		Allocated Cost
Land	$2,800,000	×	0.10	=	$ 280,000
Building	$2,800,000	×	0.90	=	2,520,000
Total			1.00		$2,800,000

If Xerox pays cash, the entry to record the purchase of the land and building is

Land	280,000	
Building	2,520,000	
Cash		2,800,000

Working It Out How would a business divide a $120,000 lump-sum purchase price for land, building, and equipment with estimated market values of $40,000, $95,000, and $15,000, respectively?

Answer: To answer this question, we must first determine total estimated market value: $40,000 + $95,000 + $15,000 = $150,000 total estimated market value. Second, we divide the estimated market value for each *individual* asset by the total market value. This gives us each asset's percentage of the total.

	Estimated Market Value	Percentage of Total
Land	$ 40,000	$40,000 / $150,000 = 26.7%
Building	95,000	$95,000 / $150,000 = 63.3%
Equipment	15,000	$15,000 / $150,000 = 10.0%
Total	$150,000	100.0%

Third, we determine each asset's part of the purchase price by multiplying the percentage for each asset by the total purchase price.

	Allocation of Purchase Price
Land ($120,000 × 0.267)	$ 32,040
Building ($120,000 × 0.633)	75,960
Equipment ($120,000 × 0.10)	12,000
Total	$120,000

■ Daily Exercise 10-6

Capital Expenditures versus Revenue Expenditures

When a company makes a plant asset expenditure, it must decide whether to debit an asset account or an expense account. In this context, *expenditure* refers to either a cash purchase or a credit purchase of goods or services related to the asset. Examples of these expenditures range from General Motors' purchase of robots for use in an assembly plant to a motorist's replacing the windshield wipers on a Chevrolet.

Expenditures that increase the asset's capacity or efficiency or extend its useful life are called **capital expenditures.** For example, the cost of a major overhaul that extends a taxi's useful life is a capital expenditure. Repair work that generates a capital expenditure is called a **major repair,** or an **extraordinary repair.** The amount of the capital expenditure, said to be capitalized, is debited to an asset account. For an extraordinary repair on a taxi, we would debit the asset account Automobile.

Other expenditures that do not extend the asset's capacity, which merely maintain the asset or restore it to working order, are called **revenue expenditures.** These costs are expenses, which are matched against revenue. Examples include the costs of repainting a taxi, repairing a dented fender, and replacing tires. Revenue expenditures are debited to an expense account. For the **ordinary repairs,** or betterments, on the taxi, we would debit Repair Expense.

The distinction between capital and revenue expenditures is often a matter of opinion. Does the cost extend the life of the asset (a capital expenditure), or does it only maintain the asset in good order (a revenue expenditure)? When doubt exists, companies tend to debit an expense, for two reasons. First, many expenditures are minor in amount, and most companies have a policy of debiting expense for all expenditures below a specific minimum, such as $1,000. Second, the income tax motive favors debiting all borderline expenditures to expense in order to create an immediate tax deduction. Higher expenses mean lower net income, which in turn means lower tax payments. Capital expenditures are not immediate tax deductions.

Exhibit 10-3 illustrates the distinction between capital expenditures and revenue expenditures (expense) for several delivery-truck expenditures. Note also the difference between extraordinary and ordinary repairs.

Treating a capital expenditure as a revenue expenditure, or vice versa, creates errors in the financial statements. Suppose a company makes a capital expenditure and erroneously expenses this cost. A capital expenditure should have been debited to an asset account. This accounting error overstates expenses and understates net income on the

Capital Expenditure. Expenditure that increases the capacity or efficiency of an asset or extends its useful life. Capital expenditures are debited to an asset account.

Major Repair or Extraordinary Repair. Repair work that generates a capital expenditure.

Revenue Expenditure. Expenditure that merely maintains an asset or restores the asset to working order. Revenue expenditures are expensed (matched against revenue).

Ordinary Repair. Repair work that creates a revenue expenditure, debited to an expense account.

EXHIBIT 10-3
Delivery-Truck Expenditures—Capital Expenditure or Revenue Expenditure

Debit an Asset Account for Capital Expenditures	Debit Repair and Maintenance Expense for Revenue Expenditures
Extraordinary repairs:	Ordinary repairs:
Major engine overhaul	Repair of transmission or other mechanism
Modification of body for new use of truck	Oil change, lubrication, and so on
Addition to storage capacity of truck	Replacement tires, windshield, and the like
	Paint job

income statement. On the balance sheet, the equipment account is understated, and so is owners' (or stockholders') equity, as follows:

Income Statement

Revenues	CORRECT
Expenses	OVERSTATED
Net income	UNDERSTATED

Balance Sheet

Current assets	CORRECT	Total liabilities	CORRECT
Plant assets	UNDERSTATED	Owners' equity	UNDERSTATED
Total assets	UNDERSTATED	Total liabilities and owners' equity	UNDERSTATED

■ Daily Exercise 10-7

Capitalizing the cost of an ordinary repair creates the opposite error. Expenses are then understated, and net income is overstated on the income statement. And the balance sheet reports overstated amounts for assets and for owners' equity.

Measuring the Depreciation of Plant Assets

See Chapter 3, page 95, for a discussion of the matching principle.

The allocation of a plant asset's cost to expense over the period the asset is used is called *depreciation.* Depreciation accounting is designed to match the asset's expense against the revenue generated over the asset's life, as the matching principle directs. Exhibit 10-4 shows the depreciation process for the purchase of a Boeing 737 jet by United Airlines. The primary purpose of depreciation accounting is to measure income accurately.

Suppose The Home Depot buys a computer for use in its accounting system. Home Depot believes it will get four years of service from the computer, which will then be worthless. Using the straight-line depreciation method (which we discuss later in this chapter), The Home Depot expenses one-quarter of the asset's cost in each of its four years of use.

EXHIBIT 10-4
Depreciation and the Matching of Expense with Revenue

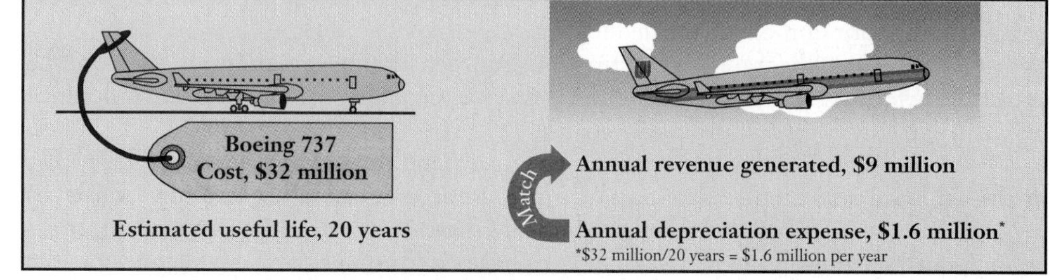

Let's contrast what depreciation accounting is with what it is *not.*

1. *Depreciation is not a process of valuation.* Businesses do not record depreciation based on appraisals of their plant assets made at the end of each period. Instead, businesses allocate the asset's cost to the periods of its useful life based on a specific depreciation method, as discussed later in this chapter.
2. *Depreciation does not mean that the business sets aside cash to replace an asset when it is fully depreciated.* Establishing such a cash fund is a decision entirely separate from depreciation. *Accumulated depreciation* is that portion of the plant asset's cost that has already been recorded as an expense. Accumulated depreciation does not represent a growing amount of cash.

We learned in Chapter 3, p. 100, that *accumulated depreciation* is the sum of all depreciation expense from the date a plant asset was acquired. Depreciation *expense* is the depreciation amount for the current period only.

The Causes of Depreciation

No asset (other than land) has an unlimited useful life. For some plant assets, physical *wear and tear* from operations and from the elements is the primary cause of depreciation. For example, physical deterioration takes its toll on the usefulness of trucks that move Home Depot merchandise from warehouses to the company's stores. The store fixtures used to display merchandise are also subject to physical wear and tear.

Assets such as computers, other electronic equipment, and airplanes may be *obsolete* before they physically deteriorate. An asset is obsolete when another asset can do the job better or more efficiently. Thus an asset's useful life may be much shorter than its physical life. Accountants usually depreciate computers over a short period of time—perhaps four years—even though they know the computers will remain in working condition much longer. Whether wear and tear or obsolescence causes depreciation, the asset's cost is depreciated over its expected useful life.

Measuring Depreciation

To measure depreciation for a plant asset, we must know the asset's

1. Cost
2. Estimated useful life
3. Estimated residual value

We have already discussed cost, which is the purchase price paid to acquire the asset. This is a known amount. The other two factors must be estimated.

Estimated useful life is the length of service the business expects to get from the asset—an estimate of how long the asset will be useful. Useful life may be expressed in years, units of output, miles, or another measure. For example, the useful life of a building is stated in years. The useful life of a bookbinding machine may be stated as the number of books the machine is expected to bind—that is, its expected units of output. A reasonable measure of a delivery truck's useful life is the total number of miles the truck is expected to travel. Companies base such estimates on past experience and information from industry magazines and government publications.

Estimated Useful Life. Length of service that a business expects to get from an asset. May be expressed in years, units of output, miles, or another measure.

Estimated residual value—also called **scrap value** or **salvage value**—is the expected cash value of an asset at the end of its useful life. For example, a business may believe that a machine's useful life will be seven years. After that time, the company expects to sell the machine as scrap metal. The amount the business believes it can get for the machine is the estimated residual value. In computations of depreciation, estimated residual value is *not* depreciated because the business expects to receive this amount from disposing of the asset. The full cost of a plant asset is depreciated if the asset is expected to have no residual value. The plant asset's cost minus its estimated residual value is called the **depreciable cost.**

Estimated Residual Value. Expected cash value of an asset at the end of its useful life. Also called **scrap value,** or **salvage value.**

Depreciable Cost. The cost of a plant asset minus its estimated residual value.

Of the factors entering the computation of depreciation, only one factor is known—cost. The other two factors—useful life and residual value—must be estimated. Depreciation, then, is an estimated amount.

Objective 2

Account for depreciation

Depreciation Methods

Four methods exist for computing depreciation: straight-line, units-of-production, declining-balance, and sum-of-years'-digits. These four methods allocate different amounts of depreciation expense to each period. However, they all result in the same total

EXHIBIT 10-5
Data for Depreciation Computations for a Home Depot Truck

Data Item		Amount
Cost of truck		$41,000
Less: Estimated residual value		(1,000)
Depreciable cost		$40,000
Estimated useful life:		
Years	5 years	
Units of production	100,000 units [miles]	

amount of depreciation, the asset's depreciable cost over the life of the asset. Exhibit 10-5 presents the data we will use to illustrate depreciation computations for a Home Depot truck by the three most widely used methods. We omit the sum-of-years'-digits method because so few companies use it.

Straight-Line (SL) Depreciation Method. Depreciation method in which an equal amount of depreciation expense is assigned to each year (or period) of asset use.

STRAIGHT-LINE METHOD In the **straight-line (SL) method,** an equal amount of depreciation expense is assigned to each year (or period) of asset use. Depreciable cost is divided by useful life in years to determine the annual depreciation expense. The equation for SL depreciation, applied to the Home Depot truck data from Exhibit 10-5, is

$$\textbf{Straight-line depreciation per year} = \frac{\textbf{Cost} - \textbf{Residual value}}{\textbf{Useful life, in years}}$$

$$= \frac{\$41{,}000 - \$1{,}000}{5}$$

$$= \$8{,}000$$

The entry to record this depreciation is

Depreciation Expense	8,000	
Accumulated Depreciation		8,000

Assume that the truck was purchased on January 1, 19X1, and that Home Depot's fiscal year ends on December 31. A *straight-line depreciation schedule* is presented in Exhibit 10-6. The final column in Exhibit 10-6 shows the asset's *book value*, which is its cost less accumulated depreciation. Book value is also called *carrying amount* or *carrying value*.

We introduced book value in Chapter 3, page 101.

As an asset is used, accumulated depreciation increases, and the book value decreases. (Compare the Accumulated Depreciation column and the Book Value column.) An asset's final book value is its *residual value* ($1,000 in Exhibit 10-6). At the end of its useful life, the asset is said to be *fully depreciated.*

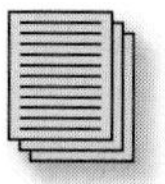

Working It Out An asset with cost of $10,000, useful life of five years, and residual value of $2,000 was purchased on January 1. What was the SL depreciation for the first year? For the second year? For the fifth year?

Answer

$$\text{SL depreciation per year} = \frac{\text{Cost} - \text{Residual value}}{\text{Useful life, in years}}$$

$$= \frac{\$10{,}000 - \$2{,}000}{5}$$

$$= \$1{,}600 \text{ per year } \textit{every year}$$

Units-of-Production (UOP) Depreciation Method. Depreciation method by which a fixed amount of depreciation is assigned to each unit of output produced by a plant asset.

UNITS-OF-PRODUCTION (UOP) METHOD In the **units-of-production (UOP) method,** a fixed amount of depreciation is assigned to each *unit of output*, or service, produced by the plant asset. Depreciable cost is divided by useful life, in units of production, to determine this amount. This per-unit depreciation expense is then multiplied by the number of units produced each period to compute depreciation for the period. The

Date	Asset Cost	Depreciation for the Year: Depreciation Rate		Depreciable Cost		Depreciation Expense	Accumulated Depreciation	Asset Book Value
1- 1-19X1	$41,000							$41,000
12-31-19X1		0.20*	×	$40,000	=	$8,000	$ 8,000	33,000
12-31-19X2		0.20	×	40,000	=	8,000	16,000	25,000
12-31-19X3		0.20	×	40,000	=	8,000	24,000	17,000
12-31-19X4		0.20	×	40,000	=	8,000	32,000	9,000
12-31-19X5		0.20	×	40,000	=	8,000	40,000	1,000

*1/5 year = 0.20 per year

EXHIBIT 10-6
Straight-Line Depreciation Schedule for a Home Depot Truck

UOP depreciation equation for the Home Depot truck data in Exhibit 10-5, in which the units are miles, is

$$\textbf{Units-of-production depreciation per unit of output} = \frac{\textbf{Cost} - \textbf{Residual value}}{\textbf{Useful life, in units of production}}$$

$$= \frac{\$41{,}000 - \$1{,}000}{100{,}000 \text{ miles}}$$

$$= \$0.40 \text{ per mile}$$

Assume that the truck is expected to be driven 20,000 miles during the first year, 30,000 during the second, 25,000 during the third, 15,000 during the fourth, and 10,000 during the fifth. The UOP depreciation schedule for this asset is shown in Exhibit 10-7.

The amount of UOP depreciation each period varies with the number of units the asset produces. In our example, the total number of units produced is 100,000, the measure of this asset's useful life. Therefore, UOP depreciation does not depend directly on time as do the other methods.

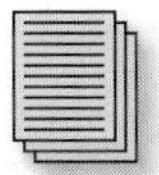

Working It Out The asset in the preceding Working It Out produced 3,000 units in the first year, 4,000 in the second, 4,500 in the third, 2,500 in the fourth, and 2,000 units in the last year. Its estimated useful life is 16,000 miles. What was UOP depreciation for each year?

Answer

$$\text{Depreciation per unit} = \frac{\text{Cost} - \text{Residual value}}{\text{Useful life, in units of production}}$$

$$= \frac{\$10{,}000 - \$2{,}000}{16{,}000 \text{ miles}}$$

$$= \$0.50 \text{ per mile}$$

Yr. 1: $1,500 (3,000 × $0.50)
Yr. 2: $2,000 (4,000 × $0.50)
Yr. 3: $2,250 (4,500 × $0.50)
Yr. 4: $1,250 (2,500 × $0.50)
Yr. 5: $1,000 (2,000 × $0.50)

EXHIBIT 10-7
Units-of-Production Depreciation Schedule for a Home Depot Truck

Date	Asset Cost	Depreciation for the Year: Depreciation Per Unit		Number of Units		Depreciation Expense	Accumulated Depreciation	Asset Book Value
1- 1-19X1	$41,000							$41,000
12-31-19X1		$0.40	×	20,000	=	$ 8,000	$ 8,000	33,000
12-31-19X2		0.40	×	30,000	=	12,000	20,000	21,000
12-31-19X3		0.40	×	25,000	=	10,000	30,000	11,000
12-31-19X4		0.40	×	15,000	=	6,000	36,000	5,000
12-31-19X5		0.40	×	10,000	=	4,000	40,000	1,000

Accelerated Depreciation Method. A depreciation method that writes off a relatively larger amount of the asset's cost near the start of its useful life than does the straight-line method.

Double-Declining-Balance (DDB) Depreciation Method. An accelerated depreciation method that computes annual depreciation by multiplying the asset's decreasing book value by a constant percentage, which is 2 times the straight-line rate.

DOUBLE-DECLINING BALANCE METHOD An **accelerated depreciation method** writes off a relatively larger amount of the asset's cost near the start of its useful life than the straight-line method does. One of the accelerated depreciation methods, **double-declining-balance (DDB) depreciation** computes annual depreciation by multiplying the asset's decreasing book value by a constant percentage, which is 2 times the straight-line depreciation rate. DDB amounts are computed as follows.

First, compute the straight-line depreciation rate per year. For example, a five-year truck has a straight-line depreciation rate of 1/5, or 20 percent. A ten-year asset has a straight-line rate of 1/10, or 10%, and so on.

Second, compute the DDB rate: Multiply the straight-line rate by 2. The DDB rate for a ten-year asset is 20% per year (10% × 2 = 20%). For a five-year asset, such as the Home Depot truck in Exhibit 10-5, the DDB rate is 40% (20% × 2 = 40%).

Third, compute the year's DDB depreciation. Multiply the asset's book value (cost less accumulated depreciation) at the beginning of each year by the DDB rate. Ignore the asset's residual value in computing depreciation, except during the last year. The first-year depreciation for the truck in Exhibit 10-5 is

$$\text{DDB depreciation for the first year} = \text{Asset book value at the beginning of the period} \times \text{DDB rate}$$

$$= \$41{,}000 \times 0.40$$

$$= \$16{,}400$$

The same approach is used to compute DDB depreciation for all later years, except for the final year.

Fourth, determine the final year's depreciation amount, the amount needed to reduce the asset's book value to its residual value. In the DDB depreciation schedule in Exhibit 10-8, the fifth and final year's depreciation is $4,314—the $5,314 book value less the $1,000 residual value. The residual value should not be depreciated but should remain on the books until the asset's disposal.

Many companies change to the straight-line method during the next-to-last year of the asset's life. Under this plan, annual depreciation for 19X4 and 19X5 is $3,928. Look at Exhibit 10-8. Depreciable cost at the end of 19X3 is $7,856 (book value of $8,856 less residual value of $1,000). Depreciable cost can be spread evenly over the last two years of the asset's life ($7,856 ÷ 2 remaining years = $3,928 per year).

The DDB method differs from the other methods in two ways: (1) The asset's residual value is ignored initially. In the first year, depreciation is computed on the asset's full cost. (2) The final year's calculation is changed in order to bring the asset's book value to the residual value.

Learning Tip: Depreciation expense in the final year is whatever amount is needed to reduce the asset's book value to the residual value.

EXHIBIT 10-8
Double-Declining-Balance Depreciation Schedule for a Home Depot Truck

		Depreciation for the Year						
Date	**Asset Cost**	**DDB Rate**		**Asset Book Value**		**Depreciation Expense**	**Accumulated Depreciation**	**Asset Book Value**
1- 1-19X1	$41,000							$41,000
12-31-19X1		0.40	×	$41,000	=	$16,400	$16,400	24,600
12-31-19X2		0.40	×	24,600	=	9,840	26,240	14,760
12-31-19X3		0.40	×	14,760	=	5,904	32,144	8,856
12-31-19X4		0.40	×	8,856	=	3,542	35,686	5,314
12-31-19X5						4,314*	40,000	1,000

*Last-year depreciation is the amount needed to reduce asset book value to the residual value ($5,314 – $1,000 = $4,314).

Working It Out What is the DDB depreciation for each year for the asset in the Working It Out on page 428?

Answers: DDB rate = 1/5 × 2 = 40%

Yr. 1: $4,000 ($10,000 × 40%)
Yr. 2: $2,400 [($10,000 – $4,000 = $6,000) × 40%]
Yr. 3: $1,440 [($6,000 – $2,400 = $3,600) × 40%]
Yr. 4: $160 ($3,600 – $1,440 – $2,000*)

*An asset's cost is not depreciated below its residual value.

Comparing the Depreciation Methods

Let's compare the three methods we've just discussed in terms of the yearly amount of depreciation:

Amount of Depreciation Per Year

Year	Straight-Line	Units-of-Production	Accelerated Method Double-Declining-Balance
1	$ 8,000	$ 8,000	$16,400
2	8,000	12,000	9,840
3	8,000	10,000	5,904
4	8,000	6,000	3,542
5	8,000	4,000	4,314
Total	$40,000	$40,000	$40,000

■ Daily Exercise 10-8
■ Daily Exercise 10-9

The yearly amount of depreciation varies by method, but the total $40,000 depreciable cost is the same under all the methods.

Generally accepted accounting principles direct a business to match an asset's expense against the revenue that asset produces. For a plant asset that generates revenue evenly over time, the straight-line method best meets the matching principle. During each period the asset is used, an equal amount of depreciation is recorded.

The units-of-production method best fits those assets that wear out because of physical use, not obsolescence. Depreciation is recorded only when the asset is used, and the more units the asset generates in a given year, the greater the depreciation expense.

The accelerated method (DDB) applies best to those assets that generate greater revenue early in their useful lives. The greater expense recorded under the accelerated method in the earlier periods is matched against those periods' greater revenue.

Exhibit 10-9 graphs annual depreciation amounts for the straight-line, units-of-production, and accelerated (DDB) depreciation methods. The graph of straight-line depreciation is flat because annual depreciation is the same in all periods. Units-of-production depreciation follows no particular pattern because annual depreciation depends on the use of the asset. The greater the use, the greater the amount of depreciation. Accelerated depreciation is greatest in the asset's first year and less in the later years.

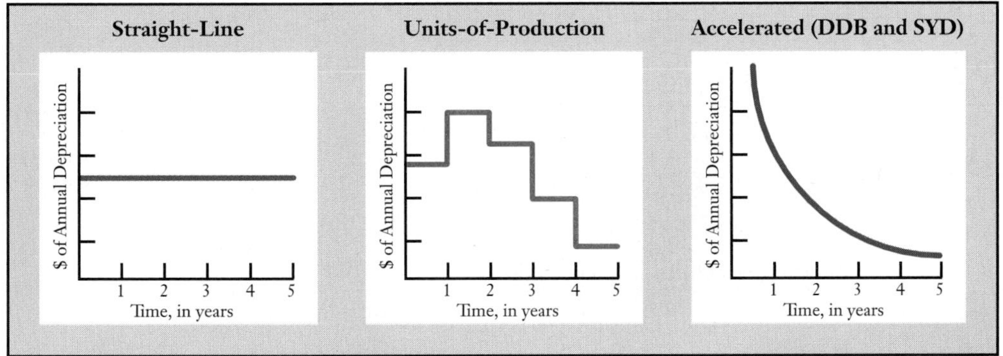

Concept Highlight

EXHIBIT 10-9
Depreciation Patterns through Time

A recent survey of 600 companies, conducted by the American Institute of CPAs, indicated that the straight-line method is most popular. Exhibit 10-10 shows the percentages of companies that use each depreciation method.

EXHIBIT 10-10
Use of the Depreciation Methods by 600 Companies

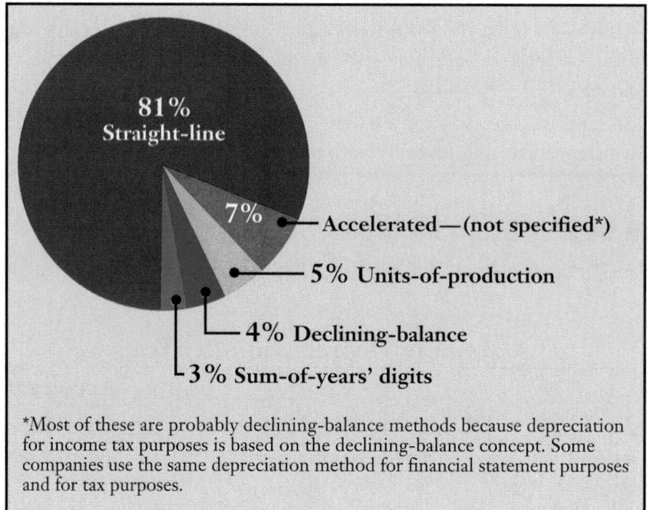

*Most of these are probably declining-balance methods because depreciation for income tax purposes is based on the declining-balance concept. Some companies use the same depreciation method for financial statement purposes and for tax purposes.

SUMMARY PROBLEM FOR YOUR REVIEW — MID-CHAPTER

Hubbard Company purchased equipment on January 1, 19X5, for $44,000. The expected useful life of the equipment is ten years or 100,000 units of production, and its residual value is $4,000. Under three depreciation methods, the annual depreciation expense and the balance of accumulated depreciation at the end of 19X5 and 19X6 are as follows:

	Method A		Method B		Method C	
Year	Annual Depreciation Expense	Accumulated Depreciation	Annual Depreciation Expense	Accumulated Depreciation	Annual Depreciation Expense	Accumulated Depreciation
19X5	$4,000	$4,000	$8,800	$ 8,800	$1,200	$1,200
19X6	4,000	8,000	7,040	15,840	5,600	6,800

REQUIRED

1. Identify the depreciation method used in each instance, and show the equation and computation for each. (Round off to the nearest dollar.)
2. Assume continued use of the same method through year 19X7. Determine the annual depreciation expense, accumulated depreciation, and book value of the equipment for 19X5 through 19X7 under each method, assuming 12,000 units of production in 19X7.

SOLUTION

REQUIREMENT 1

Method A: Straight-Line

Depreciable cost = $44,000 − $4,000 = $40,000
Each year: $40,000/10 years = $4,000

Method B: Double-Declining-Balance

$$\text{Rate} = \frac{1}{10 \text{ years}} \times 2 = 10\% \times 2 = 20\%$$

19X5: 0.20 × $44,000 = $8,800
19X6: 0.20 × ($44,000 − $8,800) = $7,040

Method C: Units-of-Production

$$\text{Depreciation per unit} = \frac{\$44{,}000 - \$4{,}000}{100{,}000 \text{ units}} = \$0.40$$

19X5: $0.40 × 3,000 units = $1,200
19X6: $0.40 × 14,000 units = $5,600

REQUIREMENT 2

Method A: Straight-Line

Year	Annual Depreciation Expense	Accumulated Depreciation	Book Value
Start			$44,000
19X5	$4,000	$ 4,000	40,000
19X6	4,000	8,000	36,000
19X7	4,000	12,000	32,000

Method B: Double-Declining-Balance

Year	Annual Depreciation Expense	Accumulated Depreciation	Book Value
Start			$44,000
19X5	$8,800	$ 8,800	35,200
19X6	7,040	15,840	28,160
19X7	5,632	21,472	22,528

Method C: Units-of-Production

Year	Annual Depreciation Expense	Accumulated Depreciation	Book Value
Start			$44,000
19X5	$1,200	$ 1,200	42,800
19X6	5,600	6,800	37,200
19X7	4,800	11,600	32,400

Computations for 19X7:

Straight-line	**$40,000/10 years = $4,000**
Double-declining-balance	**0.20 × $28,160 = $5,632**
Units-of-production	**$0.40 × 12,000 units = $4,800**

The Relationship Between Depreciation and Income Taxes

Objective 3

Select the best depreciation method for income tax purposes

Most companies use the straight-line depreciation method for reporting to their stockholders and creditors on their financial statements. But companies keep a separate set of depreciation records for computing their income taxes. For income tax purposes, most companies use an accelerated depreciation method.

Suppose you are a business manager. The IRS allows an accelerated depreciation method, which most managers prefer to straight-line depreciation. Why? Because it provides the most depreciation expense as quickly as possible, thus decreasing your immediate tax payments. You can then apply the cash you save to fit your business needs. This is the strategy most businesses follow.

To understand the relationships between cash flow (cash provided by operations), depreciation, and income tax, recall our earlier depreciation example for a Home Depot truck: First-year depreciation is $8,000 under straight-line and $16,400 under double-declining-balance. Now for illustrative purposes, let's assume that DDB is permitted for income tax reporting and apply this to a Home Depot store that has a truck with the same depreciation schedule as before. This store has $400,000 in cash sales and $300,000 in cash operating expenses during the truck's first year and an income tax rate of 30 percent. The cash flow analysis appears in Exhibit 10-11.

Exhibit 10-11 highlights several important business relationships. Compare the amount of cash provided by operations before income tax. Both columns show $100,000. If there were no income taxes, the total cash provided by operations would be the same regardless of the depreciation method used. Depreciation is a noncash expense (an expense that requires no outlay of cash) and thus does not affect cash from operations.

EXHIBIT 10-11
Cash-Flow Advantage of Accelerated Depreciation over Straight-Line Depreciation for Income Tax Purposes

	Income Tax Rate (30%)	
	SL	Accelerated
Cash revenues	$400,000	$400,000
Cash operating expenses	300,000	300,000
Cash provided by operations before income tax	100,000	100,000
Depreciation expense (a noncash expense)	8,000	16,400
Income before income tax	92,000	83,600
Income tax expense (30%)	27,600	25,080
Net income	$ 64,400	$ 58,520
Cash-flow analysis:		
Cash provided by operations before income tax	$100,000	$100,000
Income tax expense	27,600	25,080
Cash provided by operations	$ 72,400	$ 74,920
Extra cash available for investment if DDB is used ($74,920 – $72,400)		$2,520
Assumed earnings rate on investment of extra cash		× 0.10
Cash advantage of using DDB over SL		$ 252

■ Daily Exercise 10-10

EXHIBIT 10-12
Details of the Modified Accelerated Cost Recovery System (MACRS) Depreciation Method

Class Identified by Asset Life (years)	Representative Assets	Depreciation Method
3	Race horses	DDB
5	Automobiles, light trucks	DDB
7	Equipment	DDB
10	Equipment	DDB
15	Sewage-treatment plants	150% DB
20	Certain real estate	150% DB
27½	Residential rental property	SL
39	Nonresidential rental property	SL

Depreciation, however, is a tax-deductible expense. The higher the depreciation expense, the lower the before-tax income and thus the lower the income tax payment. Therefore, accelerated depreciation helps conserve cash for use in the business. Exhibit 10-11 indicates that the business will have $2,520 more cash at the end of the first year if it uses accelerated depreciation instead of SL ($74,920 versus $72,400). If the company invests this money to earn a return of 10% during the second year, it will be better off by $252 ($2,520 × 10% = $252). The cash advantage of using the accelerated method is the $252 additional revenue.

The Tax Reform Act of 1986 created a special depreciation method—used only for income tax purposes—called the *Modified Accelerated Cost Recovery System (MACRS)*. Under this method, assets are grouped into one of eight classes identified by asset life, as shown in Exhibit 10-12. Depreciation for the first four classes is computed by the double-declining-balance method. Depreciation for 15- and 20-year assets is computed by the 150%-declining-balance method. Under this method, the annual depreciation rate is computed by multiplying the straight-line rate by 1.50 (rather than by 2.00, as for DDB). For a 20-year asset, the straight-line rate is 0.05 (1/20 = 0.05), so the annual MACRS depreciation rate is 0.075 (0.05 × 1.50 = 0.075). Most real estate is depreciated by the straight-line method.

Depreciation for Partial Years

Companies purchase plant assets as needed. They do not wait until the beginning of a year or a month. Therefore, companies must develop policies to compute depreciation for partial years. Suppose the County Line Bar-B-Q Restaurant in Denver purchases a building on April 1 for $500,000. The building's estimated life is 20 years, and its estimated residual value is $80,000. The restaurant company's fiscal year ends on December 31. How does the company compute depreciation for the year ended December 31?

Date	Asset Cost	DDB Rate		Asset Book Value, Beginning		Fraction of the Year		Depreciation Expense	Accumulated Depreciation	Asset Book Value, Ending
		Depreciation for the Year								
10- 4-19X1	$500,000									$500,000
12-31-19X1		1/20 × 2 = 0.10	×	$500,000	×	3/12	=	$12,500	$ 12,500	487,500
12-31-19X2		0.10	×	487,500	×	12/12	=	48,750	61,250	438,750
12-31-19X3		0.10	×	438,750	×	12/12	=	43,875	105,125	394,875

EXHIBIT 10-13
Annual DDB Depreciation for Partial Years

Many companies compute partial-year depreciation by first computing a full year's depreciation. They then multiply that amount by the fraction of the year that they held the asset. Assuming the straight-line method, the year's depreciation for the restaurant building is $15,750, computed as follows:

$$\textbf{Full-year depreciation:} \quad \frac{\$500{,}000 - \$80{,}000}{20} = \$21{,}000$$

$$\textbf{Partial-year depreciation:} \quad \$21{,}000 \times 9/12 = \$15{,}750$$

What if the company bought the asset on April 18? A widely used policy directs businesses to record no depreciation on assets purchased after the 15th of the month and to record a full month's depreciation on an asset bought on or before the 15th. Thus the company would record no depreciation for April on an April 18 purchase. In that case, the year's depreciation would be $14,000 ($21,000 × 8/12).

How is partial-year depreciation computed under the other depreciation methods? Suppose County Line Bar-B-Q acquires the building on October 4 and uses the double-declining-balance method. For a 20-year asset, the DDB rate is 10% (1/20 = 5%; 5% × 2 = 10%). The annual depreciation computations for 19X1, 19X2, and 19X3 are shown in Exhibit 10-13.

Most companies use computerized systems to account for fixed assets. They identify each asset with a unique identification number and indicate the asset's cost, estimated life, residual value, and depreciation method. The system will automatically calculate the depreciation expense for each period. Both Accumulated Depreciation and book value are automatically updated.

■ Daily Exercise 10-11

Changing the Useful Life of a Depreciable Asset

As we have discussed, a business must estimate the useful life of a plant asset to compute depreciation on that asset. This prediction is the most difficult part of accounting for depreciation. After the asset is put into use, the business may refine its estimate on the basis of experience and new information. The Walt Disney Company made such a change, called a *change in accounting estimate.* Disney recalculated depreciation on the basis of revised useful lives of several of its theme park assets. The following note in Walt Disney's financial statements reports this change in accounting estimate:

"The Walt Disney Company made . . . a change in accounting estimate. Disney recalculated depreciation on the basis of revised useful lives of several of its theme park assets."

Note 5
. . . [T]he Company extended the estimated useful lives of certain theme park ride and attraction assets based upon historical data and engineering studies. The effect of this change was to decrease depreciation by approximately $8 million (an increase in net income of approximately $4.2 million . . .).

Such accounting changes are common because no business has perfect foresight. Generally accepted accounting principles require the business to report the nature, reason, and effect of the change on net income, as the Disney example shows. To *record* a

change in accounting estimate, the remaining book value of the asset is spread over its adjusted remaining useful life. The adjusted useful life may be longer or shorter than the original useful life. With computer-based systems, depreciation calculations resulting from revised useful lives or revised residual values are automatic.

Assume that a Disney World hot dog stand cost $40,000 and that the company originally believed the asset had an eight-year useful life with no residual value. Using the straight-line method, the company would record $5,000 depreciation each year ($40,000/8 years = $5,000). Suppose Disney used the asset for two years. Accumulated depreciation reached $10,000, leaving a remaining depreciable book value (cost *less* accumulated depreciation *less* residual value) of $30,000 ($40,000 – $10,000). From its experience with the asset during the first two years, management believes the asset will remain useful for an additional ten years. The company would compute a revised annual depreciation amount and record it as follows:

Asset's remaining depreciable book value	÷	(New) Estimated useful life remaining	=	(New) Annual depreciation
$30,000	÷	**10 years**	=	**$3,000**

The yearly depreciation entry based on the new estimated useful life is

■ Daily Exercise 10-12

Depreciation Expense—Hot Dog Stand	3,000	
Accumulated Depreciation—Hot Dog Stand		3,000

The equation for revised straight-line depreciation is

$$\text{Revised SL depreciation} = \frac{\text{Cost} - \text{Accumulated depreciation} - \text{New residual value}}{\text{Estimated remaining useful life in years}}$$

Thinking It Over

1. Suppose The Home Depot was having a bad year—net income below expectations and lower than last year's income. For depreciation purposes, Home Depot extended the estimated useful lives of its depreciable assets. How would this accounting change affect Home Depot's (a) depreciation expense, (b) net income, and (c) owners' equity?
2. Suppose The Home Depot's accounting change turned a loss year into a profitable year. Without the accounting change, the company would have reported a net loss for the year, but the accounting change enabled The Home Depot to report net income. Under GAAP, Home Depot's annual report must disclose the accounting change and its effect on net income. Would investors evaluate The Home Depot as better or worse in response to these disclosures?

Answers

1. An accounting change that lengthens the estimated useful lives of depreciable assets (a) decreases depreciation expense, and (b, c) increases net income and owners' equity.
2. There is evidence that companies cannot fool investors. With enough information—such as the knowledge of an accounting change disclosed in the annual report—investors can process the information correctly. In this case, investment advisers would *probably* subtract the amount of additional income caused by the accounting change from Home Depot's reported net income. Investors could then use the remaining net *loss* figure to evaluate Home Depot's lack of progress during the year. Investors would probably view The Home Depot as worse for having made this accounting change. For this reason, and because the ethics behind such an accounting change are questionable, The Home Depot's managers would not engage in this type of activity.

Using Fully Depreciated Assets

A *fully depreciated asset* is an asset that has reached the end of its *estimated* useful life. No more depreciation is recorded for the asset. If the asset is no longer suitable for its purpose, it is disposed of, as discussed in the next section. However, the company may be in a cash bind and thus be unable to replace the asset. Or the asset's useful life may have been underestimated at the outset. Foresight is not perfect. In any event, companies sometimes continue using fully depreciated assets. The asset account and its related accumulated depreciation account remain in the ledger even though no additional depreciation is recorded for the asset.

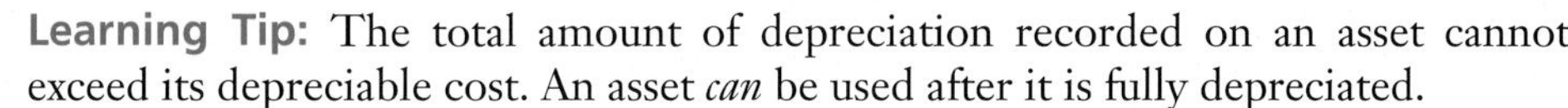

Learning Tip: The total amount of depreciation recorded on an asset cannot exceed its depreciable cost. An asset *can* be used after it is fully depreciated.

Disposal of Plant Assets

Objective 4

Account for the disposal of a plant asset

Eventually, a plant asset ceases to serve a company's needs. The asset may have become worn out, obsolete, or, for some other reason, no longer useful to the business. In general, a company disposes of a plant asset by selling it or exchanging it. If the asset cannot be sold or exchanged, then the asset is junked. Whatever the method of disposal, the business should bring depreciation up to date to measure the asset's final book value properly.

To account for disposal, credit the asset account and debit its related accumulated depreciation account. Suppose the final year's depreciation expense has just been recorded for a machine that cost $6,000 and is estimated to have zero residual value. The machine's accumulated depreciation thus totals $6,000. Assuming that this asset cannot be sold or exchanged, the entry to record its disposal is

Accumulated Depreciation—Machinery	6,000	
Machinery		6,000
To dispose of fully depreciated machine.		

If assets are junked before being fully depreciated, the company records a loss equal to the asset's book value. Suppose Wal-Mart store fixtures that cost $4,000 are disposed of in this manner. Accumulated depreciation is $3,000, and book value is therefore $1,000. Disposal of these store fixtures records a loss equal to the book value of the asset that is junked, as follows:

Accumulated Depreciation—Store Fixtures.........	3,000	
Loss on Disposal of Store Fixtures	1,000	
Store Fixtures..		4,000
To dispose of store fixtures.		

Loss accounts such as Loss on Disposal of Store Fixtures decrease net income. Losses are reported on the income statement.

Selling a Plant Asset

Suppose a business sells furniture (a plant asset) on September 30, 19X4, for $5,000 cash. The furniture cost $10,000 when purchased on January 1, 19X1, and has been depreciated on a straight-line basis. Managers estimated a ten-year useful life and no residual value. Prior to recording the sale of the furniture, accountants must update depreciation. Because the business uses the calendar year as its accounting period, partial-year depreciation must be recorded for the asset's expense from January 1, 19X4, to the sale date. The straight-line depreciation entry at September 30, 19X4, is

Sep. 30	Depreciation Expense ($10,000/10 years × 9/12).........	750	
	Accumulated Depreciation—Furniture		750
	To update depreciation.		

After this entry is posted, the Furniture account and the Accumulated Depreciation—Furniture account appear as follows. The furniture book value is $6,250 ($10,000 – $3,750).

Furniture

Jan. 1, 19X1	10,000	

Accumulated Depreciation—Furniture

	Dec. 31, 19X1	1,000
	Dec. 31, 19X2	1,000
	Dec. 31, 19X3	1,000
	Sep. 30, 19X4	750
	Balance	3,750

Book Value = $6,250

Suppose the business sells the furniture for $5,000 cash. The loss on the sale is $1,250, determined as follows:

Cash received from sale of the asset		$5,000
Book value of asset sold:		
Cost	$10,000	
Less Accumulated depreciation up to date of sale	(3,750)	6,250
Gain (loss) on sale of the asset		($1,250)

The entry to record sale of the furniture for $5,000 cash is

Sep. 30	Cash	5,000	
	Accumulated Depreciation—Furniture	3,750	
	Loss on Sale of Furniture	1,250	
	Furniture		10,000
	To sell furniture.		

When recording the sale of a plant asset, the business must remove the balances in the asset account (Furniture, in this case) and its related accumulated depreciation account and also record a gain or a loss if the amount of cash received differs from the asset's book value. In our example, cash of $5,000 is less than the book value of the furniture, $6,250. The result is a loss of $1,250.

If the sale price had been $7,000, the business would have had a gain of $750 (Cash, $7,000 – asset book value, $6,250). The entry to record this transaction would be

Sep. 30	Cash	7,000	
	Accumulated Depreciation—Furniture	3,750	
	Furniture		10,000
	Gain on Sale of Furniture		750
	To sell furniture.		

■ Daily Exercise 10-13

A gain is recorded when an asset is sold for a price greater than the asset's book value. A loss is recorded when the sale price is less than book value. Gains increase net income, and losses decrease net income. Gains and losses are reported on the income statement, as shown for Wal-Mart Stores, Inc., in the following Thinking It Over.

Learning Tip: When an asset is sold, a gain or loss on the sale is determined by comparing the proceeds from the sale to the asset's book value:

- Proceeds > Book value = Gain
- Proceeds < Book value = Loss

Thinking It Over Suppose Wal-Mart's comparative income statement for two years included these items:

	19X2	19X1
	(In billions)	
Net sales	$42.0	$40.0
Income from operations	$ 0.2	$ 1.0
Gain on sale of store facilities	1.2	
Net income	$ 1.4	$ 1.0

Which was a better year for Wal-Mart—19X2 or 19X1?

Answer: From a *sales* standpoint, 19X2 was better because sales and net income were higher. But from an *income from operations* standpoint, 19X1 was the better year. In 19X1, merchandising operations—Wal-Mart's main business—generated $1 billion of income from operations. In 19X2, merchandising produced only $0.2 billion of operating income. Most of the company's income in 19X2 came from selling store facilities. A business cannot hope to continue on this path very long. This example illustrates why investors and creditors are interested in the sources of a company's profits, not just the final amount of net income.

Exchanging Plant Assets

Businesses often exchange (trade in) their old plant assets for similar assets that are newer and more efficient. For example, Domino's pizzeria may decide to trade in a five-year-old delivery car for a newer model. To record the exchange, the business must remove from the books the balances for the asset being exchanged and its related accumulated depreciation account.

In many cases, the business simply carries forward the book value of the old asset plus any cash payment as the cost of the new asset. For example, assume the pizzeria's old delivery car cost $9,000 and has accumulated depreciation of $8,000. The car's book value is $1,000. If the pizzeria trades in the old automobile and pays cash of $10,000, the cost of the new delivery car is $11,000. The pizzeria should first record depreciation expense up to the date of the exchange. Then the business records the exchange transaction as follows:

Delivery Auto (new)	11,000	
Accumulated Depreciation (old)	8,000	
Delivery Auto (old)		9,000
Cash		10,000
Traded in old delivery car for new auto.		

Under certain conditions, the business can have a loss on an exchange. Gains on the exchange of assets are not as common because accounting conservatism favors losses, not gains.

Internal Control of Plant Assets

Internal control of plant assets includes provisions for safeguarding the assets and an adequate accounting system. To see the need for controlling plant assets, consider the following situation. The home office and top managers of Symington Wayne Corporation are located in New Jersey. The company manufactures gas pumps in Canada, then sells them in Europe. The company's top managers and owners rarely see the manufacturing plant and therefore cannot control plant assets by on-the-spot management. What features does their internal control system need?

Recall from Chapter 7 the importance of a strong system of internal controls within a business.

Safeguarding plant assets includes

1. Assigning responsibility for custody of the assets.
2. Separating custody of assets from accounting for the assets. (This separation of duties is a cornerstone of internal control in almost every area.)
3. Setting up security measures—for instance, armed guards and restricted access to plant assets—to prevent theft.
4. Protecting assets from the elements (rain, snow, and so on).
5. Having adequate insurance against fire, storm, and other casualty losses.
6. Training operating personnel in the proper use of the assets.
7. Keeping a regular maintenance schedule.

Plant assets are controlled in much the same way that high-priced inventory is controlled—with the help of subsidiary records. For plant assets, companies use a plant asset ledger. Each plant asset is represented by a control record describing the asset and listing its location and the employee responsibile for it. These details aid in safeguarding the asset. The control record also shows the asset's cost, useful life, and other accounting data. Exhibit 10-14 could be an example for the display racks in a Home Depot store.

The control record provides the data for computing depreciation on the asset. It serves as a subsidiary record of accumulated depreciation. The asset balance ($190,000) and accumulated depreciation amount ($45,000) agree with the balances in the respective general ledger accounts (Store Fixtures and Accumulated Depreciation—Store Fixtures).

EXHIBIT 10-14
Plant Asset Ledger Record

Asset Display racks **Location** Paint department
Employee responsible for the asset Department manager

Cost $190,000 **Purchased From** Industrial Furniture Co.
Depreciation Method SL
Useful Life 10 years **Residual Value** $10,000
General Ledger Account Store Fixtures

Date	Explanation	Asset			Accumulated Depreciation		
		Dr.	Cr.	Bal.	Dr.	Cr.	Bal.
Jul. 3, 19X4	Purchase	190,000		190,000			
Dec. 31, 19X4	Depreciation					9,000	9,000
Dec. 31, 19X5	Depreciation					18,000	27,000
Dec. 31, 19X6	Depreciation					18,000	45,000

Accounting for Natural Resources and Depletion

Objective 5

Account for natural resource assets and depletion

Natural resources such as iron ore, petroleum (oil), natural gas, and timber are plant assets of a special type. An investment in natural resources could be described as an investment in inventories in the ground (oil) or on top of the ground (timber). As plant assets (such as machines) are expensed through depreciation, so natural resource assets are expensed through depletion. **Depletion expense** is that portion of the cost of natural resources that is used up in a particular period. Depletion expense is computed in the same way as units-of-production depreciation:

Depletion Expense. The portion of a natural resource's cost that is used up in a particular period. Depletion expense is computed just as units-of-production depreciation is.

$$\text{Depletion per unit} = \frac{\text{Cost} - \text{Residual value}}{\text{Estimated total units of natural resource}}$$

An oil well may cost $100,000 and contain an estimated 10,000 barrels of oil. The well has no residual value. The depletion rate would thus be $10 per barrel ($100,000/10,000 barrels). If 3,000 barrels are extracted during the year, depletion expense is $30,000 (3,000 barrels × $10 per barrel). The depletion entry for the year is

Depletion Expense (3,000 barrels × $10).........	30,000	
Accumulated Depletion—Oil..................		30,000

If 4,500 barrels are removed the next year, that period's depletion is $45,000 (4,500 barrels × $10 per barrel). Accumulated Depletion is a contra account similar to Accumulated Depreciation.

Natural resource assets can be reported on the balance sheet as follows:

■ Daily Exercise 10-14

Property, Plant, and Equipment:		
Land..................		$120,000
Buildings..................	$ 800,000	
Equipment..................	160,000	
	960,000	
Less: Accumulated depreciation..................	410,000	550,000
Oil..................	$340,000	
Less: Accumulated depletion..................	75,000	265,000
Total property, plant, and equipment..........		$935,000

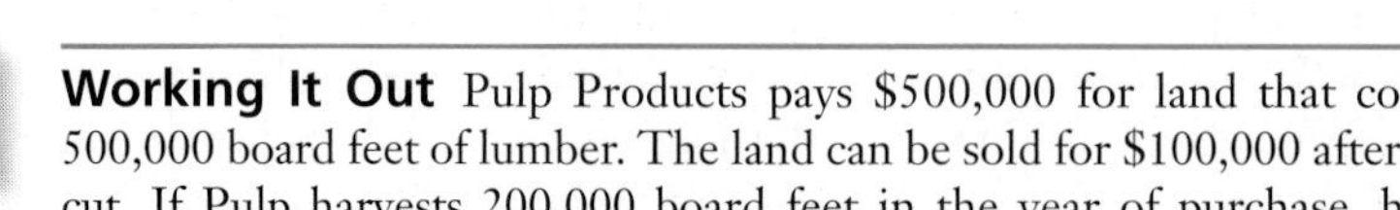

Working It Out Pulp Products pays $500,000 for land that contains an estimated 500,000 board feet of lumber. The land can be sold for $100,000 after the timber has been cut. If Pulp harvests 200,000 board feet in the year of purchase, how much depletion should be recorded?

Answer:

(Cost – Residual)	÷	Total	=	Depletion rate	×	Production	=	Depletion
($500,000 – $100,000)	÷	500,000	=	$0.80 per foot	×	200,000	=	$160,000

Accounting for Intangible Assets and Amortization

Objective 6

Account for intangible assets and amortization

As we saw earlier in the chapter, *intangible assets* are long-lived assets that are not physical in nature. Instead, these assets are special rights to current and expected future benefits from patents, copyrights, trademarks, and so on.

The acquisition cost of an intangible asset is debited to an asset account. The intangible is expensed through **amortization,** the systematic reduction of a lump-sum amount. Amortization applies to intangible assets in the same way depreciation applies to plant assets and depletion applies to natural resources. All three methods of expensing assets are conceptually the same.

Amortization. The systematic reduction of a lump-sum amount. Expense that applies to intangible assets in the same way depreciation applies to plant assets and depletion applies to natural resources.

Amortization is generally computed on a straight-line basis over the asset's estimated useful life—up to a maximum of 40 years, according to GAAP. But obsolescence often cuts an intangible asset's useful life shorter than its legal life. Amortization expense for an intangible asset is written off directly against the asset account rather than held in an accumulated amortization account. The residual value of most intangible assets is zero.

Assume that a business purchases a patent on a special manufacturing process. Legally, the patent may run for 20 years. The business realizes, however, that new technologies will limit the patented process's life to four years. If the patent cost $80,000, each year's amortization expense is $20,000 ($80,000/4). The balance sheet reports the patent at its acquisition cost less amortization expense to date. After one year, the patent has a $60,000 balance ($80,000 – $20,000), after two years a $40,000 balance, and so on.

A brief discussion of specific intangible assets follows.

- **Patents** are federal government grants giving the holder the exclusive right for 20 years to produce and sell an invention. The invention may be a product or a process—for example, Sony compact disc players and the Dolby noise-reduction process. Like any other asset, a patent may be purchased. Suppose a company pays $170,000 to acquire a patent on January 1, and the business believes the expected useful life of the patent is only five years. Amortization expense is $34,000 per year ($170,000/5 years). The company's acquisition and amortization entries for this patent are

Patent. A federal government grant giving the holder the exclusive right to produce and sell an invention for 20 years.

Jan. 1	Patents	170,000	
	Cash		170,000
	To acquire a patent.		
Dec. 31	Amortization Expense—Patents ($170,000/5)	34,000	
	Patents		34,000
	To amortize the cost of a patent.		

- **Copyrights** are exclusive rights to reproduce and sell a book, musical composition, film, or other work of art. Copyrights also protect computer software programs, such as Microsoft's Windows and Lotus's 1–2–3 spreadsheet. Issued by the federal government, copyrights extend 50 years beyond the author's (composer's, artist's, or programmer's) life. The cost of obtaining a copyright from the government is low, but a company may pay a large sum to purchase an existing copyright from the owner. For example, a publisher may pay the author of a popular novel $1 million or more for the book's copyright. The useful life of a copyright is usually no longer than two or three years, so each period's amortization amount is a high proportion of the copyright's cost.

Copyright. Exclusive right to reproduce and sell a book, musical composition, film, other work of art, or computer program. Issued by the federal government, copyrights extend 50 years beyond the author's life.

- **Trademarks** and **trade names** (or **brand names**) are distinctive identifications of products or services. The "eye" symbol that flashes across our television screens is the trademark that identifies the CBS television network. You are probably also familiar with NBC's peacock trademark. Seven-Up, Pepsi, Egg McMuffin, and Rice-a-Roni

Trademarks, Trade Names, or **Brand Names.** Distinctive identifications of a product or service.

are everyday trade names. Advertising slogans that are legally protected include United Airlines' "Fly the friendly skies" and Avis Rental Car's "We try harder."

The cost of a trademark or trade name is amortized over its useful life, not to exceed 40 years. The cost of advertising and promotions that use the trademark or trade name is not a part of the asset's cost, but rather a debit to the Advertising Expense account.

Franchises, Licenses. Privileges granted by a private business or a government to sell a product or service in accordance with specified conditions.

- **Franchises** and **licenses** are privileges granted by a private business or a government to sell a product or service in accordance with specified conditions. The Dallas Cowboys football organization is a franchise granted to its owner, Jerry Jones, by the National Football League. McDonald's restaurants and Holiday Inns are popular franchises. Consolidated Edison Company (ConEd) holds a New York City franchise right to provide electricity to residents. The acquisition costs of franchises and licenses are amortized over their useful lives rather than over legal lives, subject to the 40-year maximum.

"The Dallas Cowboys football organization is a franchise granted to its owner, Jerry Jones, by the National Football League."

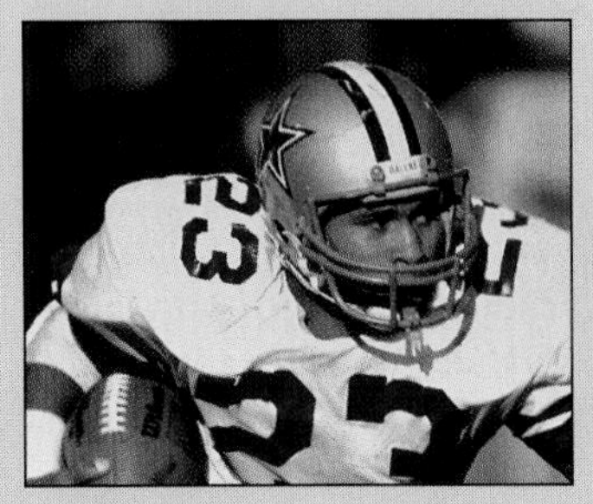

Leasehold. Prepayment of rent that a lessee (renter) makes to secure the use of an asset from a lessor (landlord).

- A **leasehold** is a prepayment of rent that a lessee (renter) makes to secure the use of an asset from a lessor (landlord). For example, Wal-Mart leases many of its store buildings from other entities. Often, leases require the lessee to make this prepayment in addition to monthly rental payments. The lessee debits the monthly lease payments to the Rent Expense account. The prepayment, however, is prepaid rent recorded in an intangible asset account titled Leaseholds. This amount is amortized over the life of the lease by debiting Rent Expense and crediting Leaseholds.

Goodwill. Excess of the cost of an acquired company over the sum of the market values of its net assets (assets minus liabilities).

- The term *goodwill* in accounting has a rather different meaning than the everyday term, "goodwill among men." In accounting, **goodwill** is defined as the excess of the cost of an acquired company over the sum of the market values of its net assets (assets minus liabilities). Recently, Wal-Mart Stores, Inc., has been expanding into Mexico. Suppose Wal-Mart acquired Mexana Company at a cost of $10 million. The sum of the market values of Mexana's assets was $9 million, and its liabilities totaled $1 million. In this case, Wal-Mart paid $2 million for goodwill, computed as follows:

Purchase price paid for Mexana Company..............		$10 million
Sum of the market values of Mexana Company's assets..............	$9 million	
Less: Mexana Company's liabilities..............	(1 million)	
Market value of Mexana Company's net assets..............		8 million
Excess is called *goodwill*..............		$ 2 million

Wal-Mart's entry to record the acquisition of Mexana Company, including its goodwill, would be

Assets (Cash, Receivables, Inventories, Plant Assets, all at market value)..............	9,000,000	
Goodwill..............	2,000,000	
Liabilities..............		1,000,000
Cash..............		10,000,000

Note that Wal-Mart has acquired both Mexana's assets *and* its liabilities.

Goodwill has special features, which include the following points:

1. Goodwill is recorded, at its cost, only when it is purchased in the acquisition of another company. Even though a favorable location, a superior product, or an outstanding reputation may create goodwill for a company, that entity never records goodwill for its own business. Instead, goodwill is recorded *only* by the acquiring company. A purchase transaction provides objective evidence of the value of the goodwill.
2. According to GAAP, goodwill is amortized over a period not to exceed 40 years. In reality, the goodwill of many entities increases in value. Nevertheless, the Accounting Principles Board specified in *Opinion No. 17* that the cost of all intangible assets

■ Daily Exercise 10-15
■ Daily Exercise 10-16

must be amortized as expense. The Opinion prohibits a lump-sum write-off of the cost of goodwill upon acquisition.

INTERNATIONAL ACCOUNTING FOR GOODWILL Companies in The Netherlands (such as Royal Dutch Shell and Phillips), in Great Britain (such as British Petroleum and British Airways), and in other European nations do not have to record goodwill when they purchase another business. Instead, they may record the cost of goodwill as a decrease in owners' equity. These companies never have to amortize the cost of goodwill, so their net income is higher than a U.S. company's would be. Not surprisingly, U.S. companies often cry "foul" when bidding against a European firm to acquire another business. Why? Americans claim the Europeans can pay higher prices because their income never takes a hit for amortization expense.

Thinking It Over How could companies around the world be placed on the same accounting basis?

Answer: If all companies worldwide followed the same accounting rules, they would be reporting income and other amounts computed similarly. But this is not the case. Companies must follow the accounting rules of their own nation, and there are differences, as the goodwill situation illustrates. This is why international investors keep abreast of accounting methods used in different nations—for much the same reason that U.S. investors care whether a company uses LIFO or FIFO for inventories. An international body, the International Accounting Standards Committee, has a set of accounting standards, but the organization has no enforcement power.

RESEARCH AND DEVELOPMENT COSTS Accounting for research and development (R&D) costs is one of the most difficult issues the accounting profession has faced. R&D is the lifeblood of companies such as Procter & Gamble, General Electric, Intel, and Boeing. At these and many other companies, R&D is vital to the development of new products and processes. Thus it can be argued that the cost of R&D activities is one of these companies' most valuable (intangible) assets. But, in general, they do not report R&D assets on their balance sheets.

■ Daily Exercise 10-17

GAAP requires companies to expense R&D costs as they incur the costs. Only in limited circumstances may the company capitalize the R&D cost as an asset. For example, assume that a company incurs R&D costs under a contract guaranteeing that the company will recover the costs from a customer. In this case, it is clear that the R&D cost is an asset, and the company records an intangible R&D asset when it incurs the cost. But this is the exception to the general rule.

In other situations, it is often unclear whether the R&D cost is an asset (with future benefit) or an expense (with no future benefit). The Financial Accounting Standards Board (FASB) could have let each company make the decision whether to capitalize or expense its R&D costs. Instead, the FASB decided to standardize accounting practice by requiring that R&D costs be expensed as incurred.

Ethical Issues in Accounting for Plant Assets and Intangibles

The main ethical issue in accounting for plant assets and intangibles is whether to capitalize or expense a particular cost. In this area, companies have split personalities. On the one hand, they all want to save on taxes. This motivates companies to expense all the costs they can in order to decrease their taxable income. On the other hand, most companies also want their financial statements to look as good as they can, with high net income and high reported amounts for assets.

In most cases, a cost that is capitalized or expensed for tax purposes must be treated the same way for reporting to stockholders and creditors in the financial statements. What, then, is the ethical path? Accountants should follow the general guidelines for capitalizing a cost: Capitalize all costs that provide a future benefit for the business, and expense all other costs, as outlined in the Decision Guidelines feature.

Many companies have gotten into trouble by capitalizing costs they should have expensed. They made their financial statements look better than the facts warranted. But there

We discussed accounting conservatism in Chapter 9, page 393.

are very few cases of companies getting into trouble by following the general guidelines, or even by erring on the side of expensing questionable costs. This is another example of accounting conservatism in action. It works.

DECISION GUIDELINES — Accounting for Plant Assets and Related Expenses

DECISION	GUIDELINES
Capitalize or expense a cost?	General rule: Capitalize all costs that provide *future* benefit for the business. Expense all costs that provide *no future* benefit.
Capitalize or expense:	
• Cost associated with a new asset?	Capitalize all costs that bring the asset to its intended use.
• Cost associated with an existing asset?	Capitalize only those costs that add to the asset's usefulness or its useful life. Expense all other costs as maintenance or repairs.
• Interest cost incurred to finance the asset's acquisition?	Capitalize interest cost only on assets constructed by the business for its own use. Expense all other interest cost.
Which depreciation method to use:	
• For financial reporting?	Use the method that best matches depreciation expense against the revenues produced by the asset.
• For income tax?	Use the method that produces the fastest tax deductions (MACRS). A company can use different depreciation methods for financial reporting and for income tax purposes. In the United States, this practice is considered both legal and ethical.

Reporting Plant Asset Transactions on the Statement of Cash Flows

Objective 7

Report plant asset transactions on the statement of cash flows

Two main types of plant asset transactions appear on the statement of cash flows: acquisitions and sales. Acquisitions and sales are *investing* activities. A company invests in plant assets by paying cash or by incurring a liability. The cash payments for plant and equipment are investing activities that appear on the statement of cash flows. The sale of plant assets results in a cash receipt, as illustrated in Exhibit 10-15, which excerpts data from the cash-flow statement of The Home Depot, Inc.

Let's examine these investing activities in more detail. During the fiscal year ended January 31, 1997, The Home Depot paid $1,194 million for property and equipment. The cash-flow statement reports this cash payment as Capital expenditures, a common description. During the year, the company sold property and equipment, receiving cash of $22 million. The Home Depot labels the cash received as Proceeds from sales of plant assets. The $22 million is the amount of cash received from the sale of plant assets. It is neither the cost nor the book value of the assets sold. If the cash received from the sale differs from the asset's book value, the company reports a gain or a loss on the sale in the income statement, as discussed on pages 437 and 438.

■ Daily Exercise 10-18

EXHIBIT 10-15
Reporting Plant Asset Transactions on the Statement of Cash Flows

THE HOME DEPOT, INC.
Statement of Cash Flows (partial, adapted)
Fiscal Year Ended January 31, 1997

	(In millions)
Cash Flows From Investing Activities:	
Capital expenditures (same as Purchases of plant assets)	$(1,194)
Proceeds from sales of plant assets	22

Working It Out Test your ability to use the cash-flow statement.

1. Make an entry in the journal to record The Home Depot's capital expenditures during the year.
2. Suppose the book value of the property and equipment that The Home Depot sold was $32 million. The assets' cost was $53 million, and their accumulated depreciation was $21 million. Record the company's transaction to sell the property and equipment. Also write a sentence to explain why the sale transaction resulted in a loss for The Home Depot.

Answers

		(In millions)	
1.	Property and Equipment	1,194	
	Cash		1,194
	Made capital expenditures.		
2.	Cash	22	
	Accumulated Depreciation	21	
	Loss on Sale of Property and Equipment	10	
	Property and Equipment		53
	Sold property and equipment.		

The company sold for $22 million assets that had a book value of $32 million. The result of the sale was a loss of $10 million ($32 million – $22 million).

SUMMARY PROBLEM FOR YOUR REVIEW

The following figures appear in the Answers to the Mid-Chapter Summary Problem, requirement 2, on page 433.

	Method A: Straight-Line			Method B: Double-Declining-Balance		
Year	Annual Depreciation Expense	Accumulated Depreciation	Book Value	Annual Depreciation Expense	Accumulated Depreciation	Book Value
Start			$44,000			$44,000
19X5	$4,000	$ 4,000	40,000	$8,800	$ 8,800	35,200
19X6	4,000	8,000	36,000	7,040	15,840	28,160
19X7	4,000	12,000	32,000	5,632	21,472	22,528

Hubbard Company purchased equipment on January 1, 19X5. Management has depreciated the equipment by using the double-declining-balance method. On July 1, 19X7, the company sold the equipment for $27,000 cash.

REQUIRED

1. Suppose the income tax authorities permitted a choice between the two depreciation methods shown. Which method would you select for income tax purposes? Why?
2. Record Hubbard's depreciation for 19X7 and the sale of the equipment on July 1, 19X7.

SOLUTION

REQUIREMENT 1

For tax purposes, most companies select the accelerated method because it results in the most depreciation in the earliest years of the equipment's life. Accelerated depreciation minimizes taxable income and income tax payments in the early years of the asset's life, thereby maximizing the business's cash at the earliest possible time.

REQUIREMENT 2

To record depreciation to date of sale and sale of Hubbard's equipment:

19X7			
July 1	Depreciation Expense—Equipment ($5,632 × 1/2 year)	2,816	
	Accumulated Depreciation—Equipment		2,816
	To update depreciation.		
July 1	Cash	27,000	
	Accumulated Depreciation—Equipment ($15,840 + $2,816)	18,656	
	Equipment		44,000
	Gain on Sale of Equipment		1,656
	To record sale of equipment.		

Summary of Learning Objectives

1. *Determine the cost of a plant asset.* Plant assets are long-lived tangible assets, such as land, buildings, and equipment, used in the operation of a business. The cost of a plant asset is the purchase price plus applicable taxes, purchase commissions, and all other amounts paid to acquire the asset and to prepare it for its intended use.

2. *Account for depreciation.* Businesses may account for depreciation (the allocation of a plant asset's cost to expense over its useful life) by four methods: the *straight-line method*, the *units-of-production method*, the *double-declining-balance method*, or the *sum-of-the-years'-digits method.* In practice, the last method is not used much. All these methods require accountants to estimate the asset's useful life and residual value.

3. *Select the best depreciation method for income tax purposes.* Most companies use an accelerated depreciation method for income tax purposes. Accelerated depreciation results in higher expenses, lower taxable income, and lower tax payments early in the asset's life.

4. *Account for the disposal of a plant asset.* Before disposing of, selling, or trading in a plant asset, the company must update the asset's depreciation. Disposal is then recorded by removing the book balances from both the asset account and its related accumulated depreciation account. Sales often result in a gain or loss, which is reported on the income statement. When exchanging a plant asset, the company often carries forward the book value of the old asset plus any cash payment as the cost of the new asset, and thus records no gain or loss on the exchange.

5. *Account for natural resource assets and depletion.* The cost of natural resources, a special category of long-lived assets, is expensed through *depletion.* Depletion is computed on a units-of-production basis. Accumulated Depletion is a contra account similar to Accumulated Depreciation.

6. *Account for intangible assets and amortization.* *Intangible assets* are assets that have no physical form. They give their owners a special right to current and expected future benefits. The major types of intangible assets are patents, copyrights, trademarks, franchises and licenses, leaseholds, and goodwill.

The cost of intangibles is expensed through *amortization,* which is the same concept as depreciation. Amortization on intangibles is computed on a straight-line basis over a maximum of 40 years. However, the useful life of an intangible is often shorter than its legal life.

7. *Report plant asset transactions on the statement of cash flows.* Two main types of plant asset investing transactions appear on the statement of cash flows. They are acquisitions and sales of plant assets.

Accounting Vocabulary

accelerated depreciation method *(p. 430)*
amortization *(p. 441)*
brand names *(p. 441)*
capital expenditure *(p. 425)*
capitalize a cost *(p. 423)*
copyright *(p. 441)*
depletion expense *(p. 440)*
depreciable cost *(p. 427)*
double-declining-balance (DDB) depreciation method *(p. 430)*
estimated residual value *(p. 427)*
estimated useful life *(p. 427)*
extraordinary repair *(p. 425)*
fixed assets *(p. 420)*
franchises *(p. 442)*
goodwill *(p. 442)*
intangible asset *(p. 421)*
leasehold *(p. 442)*
licenses *(p. 442)*
major repair *(p. 425)*
ordinary repair *(p. 425)*
patent *(p. 441)*
plant assets *(p. 420)*
revenue expenditure *(p. 425)*
salvage value *(p. 427)*
scrap value *(p. 427)*
straight-line (SL) depreciation method *(p. 428)*
trademark *(p. 441)*
trade name *(p. 441)*
units-of-production (UOP) depreciation method *(p. 428)*

Questions

1. To what types of long-lived assets do the following expenses apply: depreciation, depletion, and amortization?
2. Describe how to measure the cost of a plant asset. Would an ordinary cost of repairing the asset after it is placed in service be included in the asset's cost?
3. Suppose land is purchased for $100,000. How do you account for the $8,000 cost of removing an unwanted building?
4. When assets are purchased as a group for a single price and no individual asset cost is given, how is each asset's cost determined?
5. Distinguish a capital expenditure from a revenue expenditure. Explain the title "revenue expenditure," which is curious in that a revenue expenditure is a debit to an expense account.
6. Are ordinary repairs capital expenditures or revenue expenditures? Which type of expenditures are extraordinary repairs?
7. Define depreciation. Present the common misconceptions about depreciation.
8. Which depreciation method does each of the following graphs characterize—straight-line, units-of-production, or accelerated?

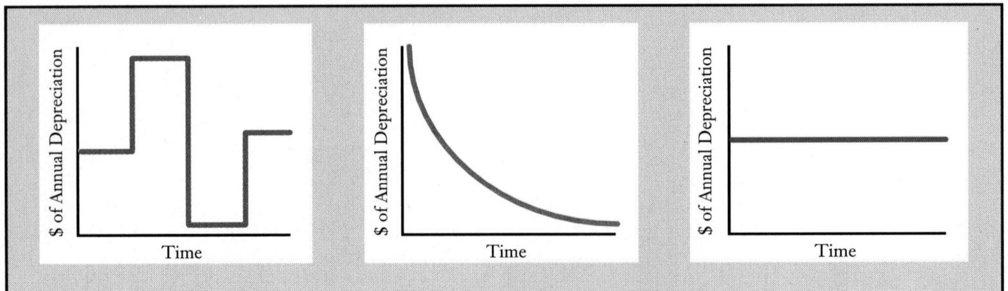

9. Which of the depreciation methods results in the most depreciation in the first year of the asset's life?
10. Explain the concept of accelerated depreciation. Which other depreciation method is used in the definition of double-declining-balance depreciation?
11. The level of business activity fluctuates widely for Harwood Delivery Service, reaching its peak around Christmas each year. At other times, business is slow. Which depreciation method is most appropriate for the company's fleet of Ford Aerostar minivans?
12. Oswalt Computer Service Center uses the most advanced computers available to keep a competitive edge over other service centers. To maintain this advantage, Oswalt replaces its computers before they are worn out. Describe the major factors affecting the useful life of a plant asset, and indicate which factor seems most relevant to Oswalt's computers.
13. Which depreciation method does not consider estimated residual value in computing depreciation during the early years of the asset's life?
14. Which type of depreciation method is best from an income tax standpoint? Why?
15. How does depreciation affect income taxes? How does depreciation affect cash provided by operations?
16. Describe how to compute depreciation for less than a full year and how to account for depreciation for less than a full month.
17. Ragland Company paid $10,000 for office furniture. The company expected the furniture to remain in service for six years and to have a $1,000 residual value. After two years' use, Ragland believes the furniture will last an additional six years. How much depreciation will Ragland record for each year, before and after the accounting change, assuming straight-line depreciation and no change in the estimated residual value?
18. When a company sells a plant asset before the year's end, what must it record before accounting for the sale?
19. Describe how to determine whether a company experiences a gain or a loss when an old plant asset is exchanged for a new one. Does GAAP favor the recognition of gains or losses? Which accounting concept underlies your answer?
20. Identify seven elements of internal control designed to safeguard plant assets.
21. What expense applies to natural resources? By which depreciation method is this expense computed?
22. How do intangible assets differ from most other assets? Why are they assets at all? What expense applies to intangible assets?
23. Why is the cost of patents and other intangible assets often expensed over a shorter period than the legal life of the asset?
24. Your company has just purchased another company for $400,000. The market value of the other company's net assets is $325,000. What is the $75,000 excess called? What type of asset is it? What is the maximum period over which its cost is amortized under generally accepted accounting principles?
25. IBM Corporation is recognized as a world leader in the manufacture and sale of computers. The company's past success created vast amounts of business goodwill. Would you expect to see this goodwill reported on IBM's financial statements? Why or why not?
26. What two plant asset transactions do companies report as investing activities on the statement of cash flows? Show how to report these cash flows from investing activities.

Daily Exercises

Cost and book value of a company's plant assets **(Obj. 1)**

DE10-1 Examine the balance sheet of The Home Depot in Exhibit 10-1 at the beginning of this chapter. Answer these questions about the company:

1. When does The Home Depot's fiscal year end? Why does the company's fiscal year end on this date?
2. What is The Home Depot's largest category of assets—current assets, property and equipment, or other category?
3. What was The Home Depot's cost of property and equipment at January 31, 1997? What was the book value of property and equipment on this date?

Measuring the cost of a plant asset **(Obj. 1)**

DE10-2 Page 421 of this chapter lists the costs included for the acquisition of land. First is the purchase price of the land, which is obviously included in the cost of the land. The reasons for including the related costs are not so obvious. For example, property tax is ordinarily an expense, not part of the cost of an asset. State why the related costs listed on page 421 are included as part of the cost of the land. After the land is ready for use, will these related costs be capitalized or expensed?

Understanding leases **(Obj. 1)**

DE10-3 A lessee (who is renting an asset such as a building) makes periodic lease payments to the lessor (who owns the building). The lessee does not have a legal title to the building. Nevertheless, under certain conditions the lessee may account for the building as though the lessee owned an asset. How can a lease be fundamentally like an asset to the lessee? What type of lease does the lessee account for as an asset?

Capitalizing interest cost **(Obj. 1)**

DE10-4 Interest is the cost of renting money. Interest is normally an expense to the borrower and revenue to the lender. Let's focus on the interest cost of the borrower. Under what conditions can interest cost be capitalized (treated as an asset) by the borrower? Use The Home Depot as an example to illustrate how the borrower can account for interest as an asset rather than an expense.

Capitalizing interest cost **(Obj. 1)**

DE10-5 Suppose Ohio Edison, the utility company, is constructing power-generating equipment for use in its operations. To finance construction, Ohio Edison borrows $500,000 on notes payable on January 2, 19X9. During 19X9, Ohio Edison incurs interest cost equal to 10% of its construction loan. The company's average accumulated construction expenditures for the year total $200,000.

1. Make the journal entry to accrue Ohio Edison's interest cost at December 31, 19X9.
2. At December 31, 19X9, what is the balance in the Equipment (or Construction in Progress) account?

Lump-sum purchase of assets
(Obj. 1)

DE10-6 Return to the Working It Out feature on pages 424 and 425. Suppose at the time of your acquisition, the land has a current market value of $80,000, the building's market value is $60,000, and the equipment's market value is $20,000. Journalize the lump-sum purchase of the three assets for a total cost of $120,000. You sign a note payable for this amount.

Capitalizing versus expensing plant asset costs
(Obj. 1)

DE10-7 Steitz Aviation repaired one of its McDonnell Douglas DC10 aircraft at a cost of $1 million, which Steitz paid in cash. The Steitz accountant erroneously capitalized this cost as part of the cost of the plane.

1. Journalize both the incorrect entry the accountant made to record this transaction and the correct entry that the accountant should have made.
2. Show the effects of the accounting error on Steitz Aviation's income statement and balance sheet, using the format illustrated on page 426.

Computing depreciation by three methods—first year only
(Obj. 2)

DE10-8 At the beginning of the year, Steitz Aviation purchased a used Boeing 737 aircraft at a cost of $21,000,000. Steitz expects the plane to remain useful for five years (1 million miles) and to have a residual value of $6,000,000. Steitz expects the plane to be flown 150,000 miles the first year and 250,000 miles the last year.

1. Compute Steitz's first-year depreciation on the plane using the following methods:
   a. Straight-line **b.** Units-of-production **c.** Double-declining-balance
2. Show the airplane's book value at the end of the first year under each depreciation method.

Computing depreciation by three methods—final year only
(Obj. 2)

DE10-9 At the beginning of 19X7, Steitz Aviation purchased a used Boeing 737 aircraft at a cost of $21,000,000. Steitz expects the plane to remain useful for five years (1 million miles) and to have a residual value of $6,000,000. Steitz expects the plane to be flown 150,000 miles the first year and 250,000 miles the fifth year. Compute Steitz's fifth-year depreciation on the plane using the following methods:

a. Straight-line
b. Units-of-production
c. Double-declining-balance (you must compute depreciation for all five years)

Selecting the best depreciation method for income tax purposes
(Obj. 3)

DE10-10 This exercise uses the Steitz Aviation data from Daily Exercise 10-8. Assume Steitz Aviation is trying to decide which depreciation method to use for income tax purposes.

1. Which depreciation method offers the tax advantage for the first year? Describe the nature of the tax advantage.
2. How much income tax will Steitz save for the first year of the airplane's use as compared to using the straight-line depreciation method? Steitz's income tax rate is 40 percent. Ignore any earnings from investing the extra cash.

Partial-year depreciation
(Obj. 2)

DE10-11 On March 31, 19X8, Steitz Aviation purchased a used Boeing 737 aircraft at a cost of $21,000,000. Steitz expects the plane to remain useful for five years (1,000,000 miles) and to have a residual value of $6,000,000. Steitz expects the plane to be flown 100,000 miles during the remainder of the first year ended December 31, 19X8. Compute Steitz's depreciation for the year ended December 31, 19X8, on the plane using the following methods:

a. Straight-line **b.** Units-of-production **c.** Double-declining-balance

Computing and recording depreciation after a change in useful life of the asset
(Obj. 2)

DE10-12 Return to the example of the Disney World hot dog stand on page 436. Suppose that after using the hot dog stand for three years, the Walt Disney Company determines that the asset will remain useful for only three more years. Record Disney's depreciation on the hot dog stand for year 4 by the straight-line method.

Recording a gain or loss on disposal under two depreciation methods
(Obj. 4)

DE10-13 Return to the Home Depot delivery-truck depreciation example in Exhibits 10-6 and 10-8. Suppose The Home Depot sold the truck on December 31, 19X2, for $20,000 cash, after using the truck for two full years. Depreciation for 19X2 has already been recorded.

1. Make a separate journal entry to record The Home Depot's sale of the truck under
   a. Straight-line depreciation (Exhibit 10-6, page 429).
   b. Double-declining-balance depreciation (Exhibit 10-8, page 430).
2. Why is there such a big difference between the gain or loss on disposal under the two depreciation methods?

Accounting for the depletion of a company's natural resources
(Obj. 5)

DE10-14 Texaco, the giant oil company, holds huge reserves of oil and gas assets. At the end of 19X5, Texaco's cost of mineral assets totaled approximately $22 billion, representing 2.4 billion barrels of oil and gas reserves in the ground.

1. Which depreciation method do Texaco and other oil companies use to compute their annual depletion expense for the minerals removed from the ground?

2. Suppose Texaco removed 0.6 billion barrels of oil during 19X6. Record Texaco's depletion expense for 19X6.
3. At December 31, 19X5, Texaco's Accumulated Depletion account stood at $15.0 billion. If Texaco did not add any new oil and gas reserves during 19X6, what would be the book value of the company's oil and gas reserves at December 31, 19X6? Cite a specific figure from your answer to illustrate why exploration activities are so important for companies such as Texaco.

Accounting for goodwill
(Obj. 6)

DE10-15 Media-related companies such as newspapers and radio and television stations have little in the way of tangible plant assets. Instead, their main asset is goodwill. When one media company buys another, goodwill is often the most costly asset acquired. Blair Newspapers paid $800,000 to acquire *The Thrifty Nickel,* an advertising paper headquartered in Texas. At the time of Blair's acquisition, *The Thrifty Nickel*'s balance sheet reported total assets of $1,300,000 and liabilities of $900,000. The fair market value of *The Thrifty Nickel*'s assets was $1,200,000.

1. How much goodwill did Blair purchase as part of the acquisition of *The Thrifty Nickel*?
2. Make Blair's summary journal entry to record the acquisition of *The Thrifty Nickel.*
3. What is the maximum useful life of the goodwill under GAAP? If Blair amortizes the goodwill over the maximum useful life, how much amortization expense will Blair record each year?

Analyzing a company's goodwill
(Obj. 6)

DE10-16 Examine the balance sheet of The Home Depot in Exhibit 10-1 at the beginning of this chapter. Answer these questions about the company:

1. What account title does The Home Depot use for goodwill?
2. What was the book value of The Home Depot's goodwill at January 31, 1997? What was the amount of accumulated amortization on the goodwill? What was The Home Depot's cost of its goodwill on this date?
3. One year earlier, on January 31, 1996, The Home Depot had Goodwill at cost of $98 million, less Accumulated Amortization of $11 million, for a book value of $87 million. During the year ended January 31, 1997, The Home Depot sold no companies and thus sold none of its goodwill. Use your answer to requirement 2 to answer these questions:
   a. How much goodwill did The Home Depot purchase during the year ended January 31, 1997?
   b. How much amortization expense on its goodwill did the company record during the year?

Accounting for patents and research and development cost
(Obj. 6)

DE10-17 This exercise summarizes the accounting for patents, which like copyrights, trademarks, and franchises, provide the owner with a special right or privilege. It also covers research and development costs.

Suppose Oracle Software paid $700,000 to research and develop a new software program. Oracle also paid $300,000 to acquire a patent on the new software. After readying the software for production, Oracle's sales revenue for the first year totaled $1,300,000. Cost of goods sold was $200,000, and operating (chiefly selling) expenses were $400,000. All these transactions occurred during 19X6. Oracle expects the patent to have a useful life of three years.

1. Prepare Oracle Software's income statement for the year ended December 31, 19X6, complete with a heading.
2. Considering the makeup of Oracle's expenses, what should the company's outlook for future profits be on the new software program?

Reporting investing activities on the statement of cash flows
(Obj. 7)

DE10-18 During fiscal year 19X8, Kodan, Inc., a pharmaceutical company, purchased another company for $2 million. Kodan financed this purchase by paying cash of $1 million and borrowing the remainder. Also during fiscal 19X8, Kodan made capital expenditures of $4 million to expand its manufacturing plant. During the year, older equipment wore out, and Kodan sold the equipment, receiving cash of $0.3 million and suffering a loss of $0.2 million on the disposal. Overall, Kodan reported a net loss of $1.4 million during fiscal 19X8.

Show what Kodan, Inc., would report for cash flows from investing activities on its statement of cash flows for the year ended September 30, 19X8.

Exercises

Determining the cost of plant assets
(Obj. 1)

E10-1 Shannon Miller, Inc., purchased land, paying $90,000 cash as a down payment and signing a $120,000 note payable for the balance. In addition, Miller paid delinquent property tax of $2,000, title insurance costing $2,500, and a $5,400 charge for leveling the land and removing an unwanted building. The company constructed an office building on the land at a cost of $810,000. It also paid $63,000 for a fence around the boundary of the property, $10,400 for the company sign near the entrance to the property, and $6,000 for special lighting of the grounds. Determine the cost of the company's land, land improvements, and building.

Measuring the cost of an asset; capitalizing interest
(Obj. 1)

E10-2 Garcia Brick Co. manufactures brick and other building materials in Reynosa, Arizona. During 19X7, Garcia constructed its own factory building with financing from Maricopa Bank of Reynosa. The 11% loan was for $1,300,000. During the year, Garcia spent $980,000 on construction of the building, expecting to complete construction during January 19X8. Garcia's average accumulated expenditures during 19X7 were $640,000. At year end, Garcia accrued the interest for one year.

REQUIRED

1. How much should Garcia record as the cost of the building in 19X7? What other account could Garcia use in place of the Factory Building account while the building is being constructed?
2. Record all of Garcia's transactions during 19X7.

Allocating cost to assets acquired in a lump-sum purchase
(Obj. 1)

E10-3 Advantage Leasing Company bought three used machines in a $40,000 lump-sum purchase. An independent appraiser valued the machines as follows:

Machine No.	Appraised Value
1	$14,000
2	18,000
3	16,000

Advantage paid half in cash and signed a note payable for the remainder. Record the purchase in the journal, identifying each machine's individual cost in a separate Machine account. Round decimals to three places.

Distinguishing capital expenditures from expenses
(Obj. 1)

E10-4 Classify each of the following expenditures as a capital expenditure or a revenue expenditure (expense) related to machinery: (a) purchase price; (b) sales tax paid on the purchase price; (c) transportation and insurance while machinery is in transit from seller to buyer; (d) installation; (e) training of personnel for initial operation of the machinery; (f) special reinforcement to the machinery platform; (g) income tax paid on income earned from the sale of products manufactured by the machinery; (h) major overhaul to extend useful life by three years; (i) ordinary recurring repairs to keep the machinery in good working order; (j) lubrication of the machinery before it is placed in service; and (k) periodic lubrication after the machinery is placed in service.

Explaining the concept of depreciation
(Obj. 2)

E10-5 Louise Gaines has just slept through the class in which Professor Shepard explained the concept of depreciation. Because the next test is scheduled for Wednesday, Gaines telephones Leah Nichols to get her notes from the lecture. Nichols' notes are concise: "Depreciation—Sounds like Greek to me." Gaines next tries Ray Mellichamp, who says he thinks depreciation is what happens when an asset wears out. Sally Bower is confident that depreciation is the process of building up a cash fund to replace an asset at the end of its useful life. Explain the concept of depreciation for Gaines. Evaluate the explanations of Mellichamp and Bower. Be specific.

Determining depreciation amounts by three methods
(Obj. 2, 3)

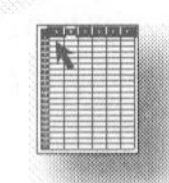

E10-6 Lancer Furniture bought a delivery truck on January 2, 19X1, for $13,000. The truck was expected to remain in service four years and to last 100,000 miles. At the end of its useful life, Lancer officials estimated that the truck's residual value would be $3,000. The truck traveled 34,000 miles the first year, 28,000 the second year, 18,000 the third year, and 20,000 the fourth year. Prepare a schedule of *depreciation expense* per year for the truck under the three depreciation methods. After two years under the double-declining-balance method, the company switched to the straight-line method. Show your computations.

Which method tracks the wear and tear on the truck most closely? Which method would Lancer prefer to use for income tax purposes? Explain in detail why Lancer prefers this method.

Selecting the best depreciation method for income tax purposes
(Obj. 3)

E10-7 Beth Spencer Co. paid $140,000 for equipment that is expected to have a seven-year life. In this industry, the residual value of equipment is approximately 10% of the asset's cost.

Select the appropriate MACRS depreciation method for income tax purposes. Then determine the extra amount of cash that Spencer Co. can invest by using MACRS depreciation, versus straight-line, during the first two years of the equipment's life. Ignore any interest Spencer can earn by investing the extra cash.

Changing a plant asset's useful life
(Obj. 2)

E10-8 Manhattan Shirt Co. purchased a building for $900,000 and depreciated it on a straight-line basis over a 40-year period. The estimated residual value was $100,000. After using the building for 15 years, Manhattan realized that wear and tear on the building would force the company to replace it before 40 years. Starting with the sixteenth year, Manhattan began depreciating the building over a revised total life of 30 years, and increased the estimated residual value to $200,000. Record depreciation expense on the building for years 15 and 16.

Analyzing the effect of a sale of a plant asset; DDB depreciation
(Obj. 4)

E10-9 On January 2, 19X7, Gulf Coast Products purchased store fixtures for $8,700 cash, expecting the fixtures to remain in service five years. Gulf Coast has depreciated the fixtures on a double-declining-balance basis, with $1,000 estimated residual value. On September 30, 19X8, Gulf Coast sold the fixtures for $4,950 cash. Record both the depreciation expense on the fixtures for 19X8, and the sale of the fixtures on September 30, 19X8.

Measuring a plant asset's cost, using UOP depreciation, and trading in a used asset
(Obj. 1, 2, 4)

E10-10 Granite Shoals Corporation, based in Branson, Missouri, is a large trucking company that operates throughout the midwestern United States. Granite Shoals uses the units-of-production (UOP) method to depreciate its trucks because its managers believe UOP depreciation best measures the wear and tear on the trucks. Granite Shoals trades in used trucks often to keep driver morale high and to maximize fuel efficiency. Consider these facts about one Mack truck in the company's fleet.

When acquired in 19X6, the tractor/trailer rig cost $285,000 and was expected to remain in service for ten years, or 1,000,000 miles. Estimated residual value was $85,000. The truck was driven 75,000 miles in 19X6, 120,000 miles in 19X7, and 210,000 miles in 19X8. After 40,000 miles in 19X9, the company traded in the Mack truck for a less-expensive Freightliner rig. Granite Shoals paid cash of $80,000. Determine Granite Shoals' cost of the new truck. Journal entries are not required.

Recording natural resource assets and depletion
(Obj. 5)

E10-11 Grand Teton Mines paid $298,500 for the right to extract ore from a 200,000-ton mineral deposit. In addition to the purchase price, Grand Teton also paid a $500 filing fee, a $1,000 license fee to the state of Wyoming, and $60,000 for a geological survey of the property. Because the company purchased the rights to the minerals only, the company expected the asset to have zero residual value when fully depleted. During the first year of production, Grand Teton removed 35,000 tons of ore. Make general journal entries to record (a) purchase of the mineral rights (debit Mineral Asset), (b) payment of fees and other costs, and (c) depletion for first-year production.

Recording intangibles, amortization, and a change in the asset's useful life
(Obj. 6)

E10-12 ***Part 1.*** Karolyi Corporation, which manufactures high-speed printers, has recently paid $1.52 million for a patent on a new laser printer. Although it gives legal protection for 20 years, the patent is expected to provide Karolyi with a competitive advantage for only eight years. Assuming the straight-line method of amortization, make journal entries to record (a) the purchase of the patent, and (b) amortization for year 1.

Part 2. After using the patent for four years, Karolyi learns at an industry trade show that another company is designing a more efficient printer. On the basis of this new information, Karolyi decides, starting with year 5, to amortize the remaining cost of the patent over two additional years, giving the patent a total useful life of six years. Record amortization for year 5.

Measuring goodwill
(Obj. 6)

E10-13 Campbell Soup Company's 19X5 statement of cash flows includes the following:

	19X5
Cash Flows from Investing Activities:	Millions
Businesses acquired..................................	$(1,255)

Campbell's Note 15 to the balance sheet, includes the following for Intangible Assets:

	19X5	19X4
Purchase price in excess of net	Millions	
assets of businesses acquired.............	$1,716	$542
Less: Accumulated amortization..........	(133)	(90)

REQUIRED

1. What title does Campbell Soup Company use to describe its goodwill? How well does Campbell's title agree with the text definition of goodwill?
2. How much did Campbell Soup Company pay to acquire other businesses during 19X5? How much of the purchase price was for goodwill? How much did Campbell pay for the other assets of the businesses it acquired? What other assets besides goodwill was Campbell Soup Company acquiring?

Measuring and recording goodwill
(Obj. 6)

E10-14 PepsiCo, Inc., has aggressively acquired other companies, such as Kentucky Fried Chicken, Frito-Lay, Pizza Hut, and Taco Bell. Assume that PepsiCo, Inc., purchased Chip-O Company for $12 million cash. The market value of Chip-O's assets is $14 million, and Chip-O Company has liabilities of $11 million.

REQUIRED

1. Compute the cost of the goodwill purchased by PepsiCo.
2. Record the purchase of Chip-O Company by PepsiCo.
3. Record PepsiCo's amortization of goodwill for year 1, assuming the straight-line method and a useful life of ten years.

Interpreting a cash-flow statement ***(Obj. 7)***

E10-15 Prior to its purchase by Boeing, McDonnell Douglas was one of the world's largest makers of commercial and military aircraft. The following items are excerpted from the company's 19X4 annual report:

MCDONNELL DOUGLAS Statement of Cash Flows	
Year Ended December 31 (Millions of dollars)	**19X4**
Investing Activities	
Property, plant and equipment acquired	$(112)
Proceeds from sale of assets	24
Other, including discontinued operations	62

Explain in detail each investing activity.

CHALLENGE EXERCISES

Capitalizing versus expensing; measuring the effect of an error ***(Obj. 1)***

E10-16 Mirage Sportswear is a catalog merchant in France—similar to L. L. Bean and Lands' End in the United States. The company's assets consist mainly of inventory, a warehouse, and automated shipping equipment. Assume that early in year 1, Mirage purchased equipment at a cost of 3 million francs (F3 million). Management expects the equipment to remain in service five years. Because the equipment is so specialized, estimated residual value is negligible. Mirage uses the straight-line depreciation method. Through an accounting error, Mirage accidentally expensed the entire cost of the equipment at the time of purchase. The company is family-owned and operated as a partnership, so it pays no income tax.

REQUIRED

Prepare a schedule to show the overstatement or understatement in the following items at the end of each year over the five-year life of the equipment.

1. Total current assets
2. Equipment, net
3. Net income
4. Owner's equity

Reconstructing transactions from the financial statements ***(Obj. 2, 4)***

E10-17 Ford Motor Company's comparative balance sheet reported these amounts (in millions of dollars):

	December 31,	
	19X1	**19X0**
Property:		
Land, plant, and equipment	$35,726.3	$34,825.1
Less accumulated depreciation	(19,422.0)	(18,486.8)
Net land, plant, and equipment	16,304.3	16,338.3
Unamortized special tools	6,218.0	5,869.5
Net property	$22,522.3	$22,207.8

Ford's income statement for 19X1 reported the following expenses (in millions):

Depreciation	$2,455.8
Amortization of special tools	1,822.1

Unamortized special tools refer to the remaining asset balance after amortization expense has been subtracted. Ford does not use an accumulated amortization account for special tools.

REQUIRED

1. There were no disposals of special tools during 19X1. Compute the cost of new acquisitions of special tools.
2. Assume that during 19X1, Ford sold land, plant, and equipment for $92 million and that this transaction produced a gain of $9 million. What was the book value of the assets sold?

3. Use the answer to requirement 2 to compute the cost of land, plant, and equipment acquired during 19X1. For convenience, work with net land, plant, and equipment.

Beyond the Numbers

Plant assets and intangible assets (Obj. 1, 6)

BN10-1 The following questions are unrelated except that they all apply to fixed assets and intangible assets:

a. The manager of Garden Ridge Corporation regularly buys plant assets and debits the cost to Repairs and Maintenance Expense. Why would he do that, since he knows this action violates GAAP?

b. The manager of Onassis Company regularly debits the cost of repairs and maintenance of plant assets to Plant and Equipment. Why would she do that, since she knows she is violating GAAP?

c. It has been suggested that, because many intangible assets have no value except to the company that owns them, they should be valued at $1.00 or zero on the balance sheet. Many accountants disagree with this view. Which view do you support? Why?

ETHICAL ISSUE

Village Oak Apartments purchased land and a building for the lump sum of $2.2 million. To get the maximum tax deduction, Village Oak managers allocated 90% of the purchase price to the building and only 10% to the land. A more realistic allocation would have been 70% to the building and 30% to the land.

REQUIRED

1. Explain the tax advantage of allocating too much to the building and too little to the land.
2. Was Village Oak's allocation ethical? If so, state why. If not, why not? Identify who was harmed.

Problems (GROUP A)

Identifying the elements of a plant asset's cost (Obj. 1, 2)

P10-1A Alameda Construction Company incurred the following costs in acquiring land, making land improvements, and constructing and furnishing its own sales building.

a.	Purchase price of four acres of land, including an old building that will be used for a garage (land market value is $280,000; building market value is $40,000)	$300,000
b.	Landscaping (additional dirt and earth moving)	8,100
c.	Fence around the boundary of the land	17,650
d.	Attorney fee for title search on the land	600
e.	Delinquent real estate taxes on the land to be paid by Alameda	5,900
f.	Company signs at front of the company property	1,800
g.	Building permit for the sales building	350
h.	Architect's fee for the design of the sales building	19,800
i.	Masonry, carpentry, roofing, and other labor to construct the sales building	709,000
j.	Concrete, wood, and other materials used in the construction of the sales building	214,000
k.	Renovation of the garage building	41,800
l.	Interest cost on construction loan for sales building, based on average accumulated expenditures	9,000
m.	Landscaping (trees and shrubs)	6,400
n.	Parking lot and concrete walks on the property	29,750
o.	Lights for the parking lot, walkways, and company signs	7,300
p.	Supervisory salary of construction supervisor (85% to sales building; 9% to fencing, parking lot, and concrete walks; and 6% to garage building renovation)	40,000
q.	Office furniture for the sales building	107,100
r.	Transportation and installation of furniture	1,800

Alameda depreciates buildings over 40 years, land improvements over 20 years, and furniture over 8 years, all on a straight-line basis with zero residual value.

REQUIRED

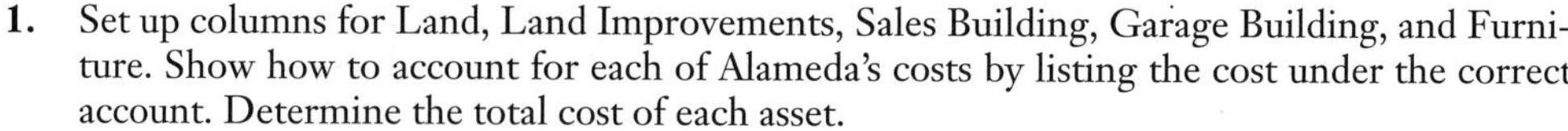

1. Set up columns for Land, Land Improvements, Sales Building, Garage Building, and Furniture. Show how to account for each of Alameda's costs by listing the cost under the correct account. Determine the total cost of each asset.
2. Assuming that all construction was complete and the assets were placed in service on May 4, record depreciation for the year ended December 31. Round figures to the nearest dollar.

Recording plant asset transactions, exchange, and disposal
(Obj. 1, 2, 4)

P10-2A Central Forwarding provides local freight service in Des Moines, Iowa. The company's balance sheet includes the following assets under Property, Plant, and Equipment: Land, Buildings, and Motor-Carrier Equipment. Central has a separate accumulated depreciation account for each of these assets except land. Assume that Central Forwarding completed the following transactions:

Jan. 5	Traded in motor-carrier equipment with book value of $47,000 (cost of $130,000) for similar new equipment with a cash cost of $176,000. Central received a trade-in allowance of $70,000 on the old equipment and paid the remainder in cash.
July 2	Sold a building that cost $550,000 and that had accumulated depreciation of $247,500 through December 31 of the preceding year. Depreciation is computed on a straight-line basis. The building has a 30-year useful life and a residual value of $55,000. Central received $100,000 cash and a $600,000 note receivable.
Oct. 26	Purchased land and a building for a single price of $300,000. An independent appraisal valued the land at $115,000 and the building at $230,000.
Dec. 31	Recorded depreciation as follows: Motor-carrier equipment has an expected useful life of five years and an estimated residual value of 5% of cost. Depreciation is computed on the double-declining-balance method. Depreciation on buildings is computed by the straight-line method. The new building carries a 40-year useful life and a residual value equal to 10% of its cost.

REQUIRED

Record the transactions in Central Forwarding's journal.

Explaining the concept of depreciation
(Obj. 2)

P10-3A The board of directors of Ultramar Corporation is reviewing the 19X8 annual report. A new board member—a professor with little business experience—questions the company accountant about the depreciation amounts. The professor wonders why depreciation expense has decreased from $200,000 in 19X6 to $184,000 in 19X7 to $172,000 in 19X8. She states that she could understand the decreasing annual amounts if the company had been disposing of properties each year, but that has not occurred. Further, she notes that growth in the city is increasing the values of company properties. Why is the company recording depreciation when the property values are increasing?

REQUIRED

Write a paragraph or two to explain the concept of depreciation to the professor and to answer her questions. In particular, which depreciation method does Ultramar appear to be using?

Computing depreciation by three methods and the cash-flow advantage of accelerated depreciation for tax purposes
(Obj. 2, 3)

P10-4A On January 3, 19X1, Zivley Corporation paid $224,000 for equipment used in manufacturing automotive supplies. In addition to the basic purchase price, the company paid $700 transportation charges, $100 insurance for the goods in transit, $12,100 sales tax, and $3,100 for a special platform on which to place the equipment in the plant. Zivley management estimates that the equipment will remain in service five years and have a residual value of $20,000. The equipment will produce 50,000 units the first year, with annual production decreasing by 5,000 units during each of the next four years (that is, 45,000 units in year 2; 40,000 units in year 3; and so on). In trying to decide which depreciation method to use, Martha Zivley has requested a depreciation schedule for each of three depreciation methods (straight-line, units-of-production, and double-declining-balance).

REQUIRED

1. For each of the generally accepted depreciation methods, prepare a depreciation schedule showing asset cost, depreciation expense, accumulated depreciation, and asset book value.
2. Zivley reports to stockholders and creditors in the financial statements using the depreciation method that maximizes reported income in the early years of asset use. For income tax purposes, however, the company uses the depreciation method that minimizes income tax payments in those early years. Consider the first year Zivley uses the equipment. Identify the depreciation methods that meet Zivley's objectives, assuming the income tax authorities permit the use of any of the methods.

3. Assume that cash provided by operations before income tax is $180,000 for the equipment's first year. The combined federal and state income tax rate is 40 percent. For the two depreciation methods identified in requirement 2, compare the net income and cash provided by operations (cash flow). Show which method gives the net-income advantage and which method gives the cash-flow advantage. Ignore the earnings rate in the cash-flow analysis.

Analyzing plant asset transactions from a company's financial statements
(Obj. 2, 4, 7)

P10-5A IBM is the world's largest computer company. After a few lean years, Big Blue, as the company is called, has rebounded strongly with some new products and improving profits. The following excerpts come from IBM's 19X5 financial statements:

INTERNATIONAL BUSINESS MACHINES CORPORATION
Balance Sheet (Adapted)

(Dollars in millions) **At December 31:**	**19X5**	**19X4**
Assets		
Current assets:		
Cash	$ 1,746	$ 1,240
Cash equivalents	5,513	6,682
Marketable securities	442	2,632
Notes and accounts receivable—trade, net of allowances	16,450	14,018
Sales-type leases receivable	5,961	6,351
Other accounts receivable	991	1,164
Inventories	6,323	6,334
Prepaid expenses and other current assets	3,265	2,917
Total current assets	40,691	41,338
Plant, rental machines, and other property	43,981	44,820
Less: Accumulated depreciation	27,402	28,156
Plant, rental machines, and other property—net	16,579	16,664
Software, less accumulated amortization (19X5, $11,276; 19X4, $10,793)	2,419	2,963
Investments and sundry assets	20,603	20,126
Total assets	$80,292	$81,091

INTERNATIONAL BUSINESS MACHINES CORPORATION
Statement of Cash Flows (Excerpts)

(Dollars in millions) **For the year ended December 31:**	**19X5**	**19X4**
Cash flow from investing activities:		
Payments for plant, rental machines, and other property	$(4,744)	$(3,078)
Proceeds from disposition of plant, rental machines, and other property	1,561	900

REQUIRED

1. At December 31, 19X5, what was IBM's cost of its plant assets? What was the amount of accumulated depreciation? What percentage of the cost has been used up?
2. IBM's depreciation expense for 19X5 was $3,955 million. Why is the amount of depreciation expense so different from accumulated depreciation at December 31, 19X5?
3. How much did IBM pay for plant assets during 19X5? Prepare a T-account for Plant Assets at cost to determine whether IBM bought or sold more plant assets during the year.
4. How much cash did IBM receive for the sale of plant assets during 19X5? If the plant assets that IBM sold had a book value of $1,222 million, did IBM have a gain or a loss on the sale of plant assets? How much was the gain or loss?
5. IBM's balance sheet reports Software. What category of asset is software?

Accounting for natural resources, intangibles, and the related expenses
(Obj. 5, 6)

P10-6A ***Part 1.*** Georgia-Pacific Corporation is one of the world's largest forest products companies. The company's balance sheet includes the assets Natural Gas, Oil, and Coal.

Suppose Georgia-Pacific paid $2.8 million cash for the right to work a mine with an estimated 100,000 tons of coal. Assume the company paid $60,000 to remove unwanted buildings from the land and $45,000 to prepare the surface for mining. Further, assume that Georgia-Pacific signed a $30,000 note payable to a company that will return the land surface to its original condition after the lease ends. During the first year, Georgia-Pacific removed 35,000 tons of coal, which it sold on account for $37 per ton. Operating expenses for the first year totaled $240,000, all paid in cash.

REQUIRED

1. Record all of Georgia-Pacific's transactions for the year.
2. Prepare the company's income statement for its coal operations for the first year. Evaluate the profitability of the coal operations.

Part 2. Collins Foods International, Inc., is the majority owner of Sizzler Restaurants. The company's balance sheet reports the asset Cost in Excess of Net Assets of Purchased Businesses. Assume that Collins purchased this asset as part of the acquisition of another company, which carried these figures:

Book value of assets	$2.4 million
Market value of assets	3.1 million
Liabilities	2.2 million

REQUIRED

1. What is another title for the asset Cost in Excess of Net Assets of Purchased Businesses?
2. Make the journal entry to record Collins's purchase of the other company for $2.7 million cash.
3. Assume Collins amortizes Cost in Excess of Net Assets of Purchased Businesses over 20 years. Record the straight-line amortization for one year.

Reporting plant asset transactions on the statement of cash flows
(Obj. 7)

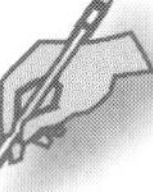

P10-7A At the end of 1997, The Coca-Cola Company had total assets of $16.9 billion and total liabilities of $9.6 billion. Included among the assets were property, plant, and equipment with a cost of $5.8 billion and accumulated depreciation of $2.0 billion.

Assume that Coca-Cola completed the following selected transactions during 1998: The company earned total revenues of $19.1 billion and incurred total expenses of $15.2 billion, which included depreciation of $0.5 billion. During the year, Coca-Cola paid $1.1 billion for new property, plant, and equipment and sold old plant assets for $0.2 billion. The cost of the assets sold was $0.6 billion, and their accumulated depreciation was $0.4 billion.

REQUIRED

1. Show how Coca-Cola would report property, plant, and equipment on the balance sheet at December 31, 1998. What was the book value of property, plant, and equipment?
2. Show how Coca-Cola would report investing activities on its statement of cash flows for 1998.
3. Explain how to determine whether Coca-Cola had a gain or loss on the sale of old plant assets during the year. What was the amount of the gain or loss, if any?

Problems (GROUP B)

Identifying the elements of a plant asset's cost
(Obj. 1, 2)

P10-1B Potomac Electric Company incurred the following costs in acquiring land and a garage, making land improvements, and constructing and furnishing a district office building:

a.	Purchase price of 3½ acres of land, including an old building that will be used as a garage for company vehicles (land market value is $700,000; building market value is $100,000)	$640,000
b.	Delinquent real estate taxes on the land to be paid by Potomac Electric..........	3,700
c.	Landscaping (additional dirt and earth moving)	3,550
d.	Title insurance on the land acquisition..................	1,000
e.	Fence around the boundary of the land..................	44,100
f.	Building permit for the office building..................	200
g.	Architect's fee for the design of the office building..................	45,000
h.	Company signs near front and rear approaches to the company property........	23,550
i.	Renovation of the garage	23,800
j.	Concrete, wood, and other materials used in the construction of the district office building..................	814,000
k.	Masonry, carpentry, roofing, and other labor to construct the district office building..................	734,000
l.	Interest cost on construction loan for the district office building, based on average accumulated expenditures..................	3,400
m.	Parking lots and concrete walks on the property	17,450

n.	Lights for the parking lot, walkways, and company signs	$ 8,900
o.	Supervisory salary of construction supervisor (90% to district office building; 6% to fencing, parking lot, and concrete walks; and 4% to garage renovation)	55,000
p.	Office furniture for the district office building	123,500
q.	Transportation of furniture from seller to the office building	1,300
r.	Landscaping (trees and shrubs)	9,100

Potomac Electric depreciates buildings over 40 years, land improvements over 20 years, and furniture over 8 years, all on a straight-line basis with zero residual value.

REQUIRED

1. Set up columns for Land, Land Improvements, District Office Building, Garage, and Furniture. Show how to account for each of Potomac's costs by listing the cost under the correct account. Determine the total cost of each asset.
2. Assuming that all construction was complete and the assets were placed in service on March 19, record depreciation for the year ended December 31. Round figures to the nearest dollar.

Recording plant asset transactions, exchange, and disposal
(Obj. 1, 2, 4)

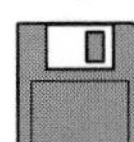

P10-2B Boyd & Yankovitz surveys American television-viewing trends. The company's balance sheet reports the following assets under Property and Equipment: Land, Buildings, Office Furniture, Communication Equipment, and Televideo Equipment. The company has a separate accumulated depreciation account for each of these assets except land. Assume that Boyd & Yankovitz completed the following transactions:

Jan. 4	Traded in communication equipment with book value of $11,000 (cost of $96,000) for similar new equipment with a cash cost of $88,000. The seller gave Boyd & Yankovitz a trade-in allowance of $20,000 on the old equipment, and Boyd & Yankovitz paid the remainder in cash.
Aug. 29	Sold a building that had cost $475,000 and had accumulated depreciation of $353,500 through December 31 of the preceding year. Depreciation is computed on a straight-line basis. The building has a 30-year useful life and a residual value of $47,500. Boyd & Yankovitz received $150,000 cash and a $450,000 note receivable.
Nov. 10	Purchased used communication and televideo equipment from the Gallup polling organization. Total cost was $80,000 paid in cash. An independent appraisal valued the communication equipment at $75,000 and the televideo equipment at $25,000.
Dec. 31	Recorded depreciation as follows: Equipment is depreciated by the double-declining-balance method over a five-year life with zero residual value. Record depreciation on the equipment purchased on January 4 and on November 10 separately.

REQUIRED

Record the transactions in the journal of Boyd & Yankovitz.

Explaining the concept of depreciation
(Obj. 2)

P10-3B The board of directors of High Tumblers Gymnastics Center is having its regular quarterly meeting. Accounting policies are on the agenda, and depreciation is being discussed. A new board member, an attorney, has some strong opinions about two aspects of depreciation policy. Bryce Dodson argues that depreciation must be coupled with a fund to replace company assets. Otherwise, there is no substance to depreciation, he argues. He also challenges the five-year estimated life over which High Tumblers is depreciating company computers. He states that the computers will last much longer and should be depreciated over at least ten years.

REQUIRED

Write a paragraph or two to explain the concept of depreciation to Dodson and to answer his arguments.

Computing depreciation by three methods and the cash-flow advantage of accelerated depreciation for tax purposes
(Obj. 2, 3)

P10-4B On January 2, 19X1, Quantum Construction Company purchased a used dump truck at a cost of $63,000. Before placing the truck in service, the company spent $2,200 painting it, $800 replacing tires, and $4,000 overhauling the engine. Quantum management estimates that the truck will remain in service for six years and have a residual value of $16,000. The truck's annual mileage is expected to be 18,000 miles in each of the first four years and 14,000 miles in each of the next two years. In deciding which depreciation method to use, George Farouk, the general manager, requests a depreciation schedule for each of the depreciation methods (straight-line, units-of-production, and double-declining-balance).

REQUIRED

1. Prepare a depreciation schedule for each depreciation method, showing asset cost, depreciation expense, accumulated depreciation, and asset book value.

2. Quantum reports to creditors in the financial statements using the depreciation method that maximizes reported income in the early years of asset use. For income tax purposes, however, the company uses the depreciation method that minimizes income tax payments in those early years. Consider the first year that Quantum uses the truck. Identify the depreciation methods that meet the general manager's objectives, assuming the income tax authorities permit the use of any of the methods.
3. Cash provided by operations before income tax is $150,000 for the truck's first year. The combined federal and state income tax rate is 40 percent. For the two depreciation methods identified in requirement 2, compare the net income and cash provided by operations (cash flow). Show which method gives the net-income advantage and which method gives the cash-flow advantage. Ignore the earnings rate in the cash-flow analysis.

Analyzing plant asset transactions from a company's financial statements
(Obj. 2, 4, 7)

P10-5B Curtiss-Wright Corporation is a medium-sized manufacturer of high-tech parts used in commercial and military aircraft. The following excerpts come from Curtiss-Wright's 19X5 financial statements:

CURTISS-WRIGHT CORPORATION
Balance Sheet (Adapted)

	December 31,	
(In thousands)	**19X5**	**19X4**
Assets		
Current assets:		
Cash and cash equivalents	$ 8,865	$ 4,245
Short-term investments	69,898	72,200
Receivables, net	36,277	32,467
Inventories	29,111	24,889
Prepaid expenses and other current assets	9,474	10,542
Total current assets	153,625	144,343
Property, plant, and equipment, at cost:		
Land	4,504	4,655
Buildings and improvements	79,352	78,680
Machinery, equipment, and other	114,195	119,653
	198,051	202,988
Less Accumulated depreciation	(141,782)	(142,550)
Property, plant, and equipment, net	56,269	60,438
Prepaid pension costs	31,128	28,092
Other assets	5,179	5,821
Total assets	$246,201	$238,694

CURTISS-WRIGHT CORPORATION
Statements of Cash Flows (Excerpts)

	For the Years Ended December 31,	
(In thousands)	**19X5**	**19X4**
Cash flows from investing activities:		
Proceeds from sales and disposals of plant assets	$3,290	$1,326
Additions to property, plant, and equipment	(6,985)	(4,609)

REQUIRED

Answer these questions about Curtiss-Wright's plant assets.

1. At December 31, 19X5, what was Curtiss-Wright's cost of its plant assets? What was the amount of accumulated depreciation? What was the book value of the plant assets? Does book value measure how much Curtiss-Wright could sell the assets for? Why or why not?
2. Curtiss-Wright's depreciation expense for 19X5 was $9,512 thousand. Why is the amount of depreciation expense so different from accumulated depreciation at December 31, 19X5?
3. How much did Curtiss-Wright pay for plant assets during 19X5? Prepare a T-account for Plant Assets at cost to determine whether Curtiss-Wright bought or sold more plant assets during the year.

4. How much cash did Curtiss-Wright receive for the sale of plant assets during 19X5? If the plant assets sold by the company had a book value of $3,071,000, did Curtiss-Wright experience a gain or a loss on the sale of plant assets? How much was the gain or loss?

Accounting for natural resources, intangibles, and the related expenses ***(Obj. 5, 6)***

P10-6B ***Part 1.*** Continental Pipeline Company operates a pipeline that provides natural gas to Atlanta; Washington, D.C.; Philadelphia; and New York City. The company's balance sheet includes the asset Oil Properties.

Suppose Continental paid $7 million cash for oil and gas reserves with an estimated 500,000 barrels of oil. Assume the company paid $350,000 for additional geological tests of the property and $110,000 to prepare the surface for drilling. Prior to production, the company signed a $65,000 note payable to have a building constructed on the property. The building will be abandoned when the oil is depleted, so its cost is debited to the Oil Properties account and included in depletion charges. During the first year of production, Continental removed 82,000 barrels of oil, which it sold on credit for $19 per barrel. Operating expenses related to this project totaled $185,000 for the first year, all paid in cash.

REQUIRED

1. Record all of Continental's transactions for the year.
2. Prepare the company's income statement for this oil and gas project for the first year. Evaluate the profitability of the project.

Part 2. United Telecommunications, Inc. (United Telecom) provides communication services in Florida, North Carolina, New Jersey, Texas, and other states. The company's balance sheet reports the asset Cost of Acquisitions in Excess of the Fair Market Value of the Net Assets of Subsidiaries. Assume that United Telecom purchased this asset as part of the acquisition of another company, which carried these figures:

Book value of assets	$640,000
Market value of assets.................	920,000
Liabilities..................................	405,000

REQUIRED

1. What is another title for the asset Cost of Acquisitions in Excess of the Fair Market Value of the Net Assets of Subsidiaries?
2. Make the journal entry recording United Telecom's purchase of the other company for $1,650,000 cash.
3. Assume United Telecom amortizes Cost of Acquisitions in Excess of the Fair Market Value of the Net Assets of Subsidiaries over 20 years. Record the straight-line amortization for one year.

Reporting plant asset transactions on the statement of cash flows ***(Obj. 7)***

P10-7B At the end of 1997, Sprint Corporation, the telecommunications company, had total assets of $18.2 billion and total liabilities of $9.1 billion. Included among the assets were property, plant, and equipment with a cost of $23.2 billion and accumulated depreciation of $11.7 billion.

Assume that Sprint completed the following selected transactions during 1998: The company earned total revenues of $13.9 billion and incurred total expenses of $13.2 billion, which included depreciation of $1.5 billion. During the year, Sprint paid $2.1 billion for new property, plant, and equipment, and sold old plant assets for $0.2 billion. The cost of the assets sold was $0.6 billion, and their accumulated depreciation was $0.4 billion.

REQUIRED

1. Show how Sprint Corporation would report property, plant, and equipment on the balance sheet at December 31, 1998.
2. Show how Sprint would report investing activities on its statement of cash flows for 1998.
3. Explain how to determine whether Sprint had a gain or a loss on the sale of old plant assets. What was the amount of the gain or loss, if any?

Applying Your Knowledge

DECISION CASE

Measuring profitability based on different inventory and depreciation methods ***(Obj. 2, 3)***

Link Back to Chapter 9 (Inventory Methods). Suppose you are considering investing in two businesses, Waldorf Sales Company, and Seattle Supply Company. The two companies are virtually identical, and both began operations at the beginning of the current year. During the year, each company purchased inventory as follows:

Jan. 4	10,000 units at $4 =	$ 40,000
Apr. 6	5,000 units at 5 =	25,000
Aug. 9	7,000 units at 6 =	42,000
Nov. 27	10,000 units at 7 =	70,000
Totals	32,000	$177,000

During the first year, both companies sold 25,000 units of inventory.

In early January, both companies purchased equipment costing $150,000 that had a ten-year estimated useful life and a $20,000 residual value. Waldorf uses the inventory and depreciation methods that maximize reported income (FIFO and straight-line). By contrast, Seattle uses the inventory and depreciation methods that minimize income tax payments (LIFO and double-declining-balance). Both companies' trial balances at December 31 included the following:

Sales revenue...........................	$370,000
Operating expenses................	80,000

REQUIRED

1. Prepare both companies' income statements.
2. Write an investment newsletter to address the following questions for your clients: Which company appears to be more profitable? Which company has more cash to invest in promising projects? If prices continue rising in both companies' industries over the long term, which company would you prefer to invest in? Why?

FINANCIAL STATEMENT CASES

Plant assets and intangible assets
(Obj. 2, 3, 4, 7)

CASE 1. Refer to the NIKE, Inc., financial statements in Appendix A, and answer the following questions.

REQUIRED

1. Which depreciation method or methods does NIKE use for reporting to stockholders and creditors in the financial statements? What type of depreciation method does the company probably use for income tax purposes? Why is this method preferable for tax purposes?
2. Depreciation expense is embedded in the selling and administrative expense amounts listed on the income statement. The statement of cash flows gives the amount of depreciation expense. What was the amount of depreciation for fiscal year 1997? Record depreciation expense for the year.
3. The statement of cash flows also reports purchases of assets and the proceeds (sale prices) received on disposal of plant assets. How much were NIKE's plant asset acquisitions during fiscal year 1997? Journalize NIKE's acquisition of plant assets.
4. How much cash did NIKE receive on the sale of plant assets during fiscal 1997? Assume the plant assets that were sold had a cost of $35,200 thousand and accumulated depreciation of $10,445 thousand. Record the sale of these plant assets. How much was the gain or loss on the sale of plant assets during the year?
5. In what category of the statement of cash flows are capital expenditures reported? What words does NIKE use to describe its capital expenditures?

Plant assets and intangible assets
(Obj. 2, 3, 4, 7)

CASE 2. Obtain the annual report of a company of your choosing. Answer these questions about the company. Concentrate on the current year in the annual report you select.

REQUIRED

1. Which depreciation method or methods does the company use for reporting to stockholders and creditors in the financial statements? Does the company disclose the estimated useful lives of plant assets for depreciation purposes? If so, identify the useful lives.
2. Depreciation and amortization expenses are often combined because they are similar. Many income statements embed depreciation and amortization in other expense amounts. To learn the amounts of these expenses, it often becomes necessary to examine the statement of cash flows. Where does your company report depreciation and amortization? What were these expenses for the current year? (*Note*: The company you selected may have no amortization—only depreciation.)
3. How much did the company spend to acquire plant assets during the current year? Journalize the acquisitions in a single entry.
4. How much did the company receive on the sale of plant assets? Assume a particular cost and accumulated depreciation of the plant assets sold. Journalize the sale of the plant assets, assuming that the sale resulted in a $700,000 loss.
5. What categories of intangible assets does the company report? What is their reported amount?

Team Project

Visit a local business.

REQUIRED

1. List all its plant assets.
2. If possible, interview the manager. Gain as much information as you can about the business's plant assets. For example, try to determine the assets' costs, the depreciation method the company is using, and the estimated useful life of each asset category. If an interview is impossible, then develop your own estimates of the assets' costs, useful lives, and book values, assuming an appropriate depreciation method.
3. Determine whether the business has any intangible assets. If so, list them and gain as much information as possible about their nature, cost, and estimated useful lives.
4. Write a detailed report of your findings and be prepared to present your results to the class.

CHAPTER 11

Current Liabilities and Payroll Accounting

LEARNING OBJECTIVES

After studying this chapter, you should be able to

1. Account for current liabilities of known amount
2. Account for current liabilities that must be estimated
3. Identify and report contingent liabilities
4. Compute payroll amounts
5. Make basic payroll entries
6. Use a payroll system
7. Report current liabilities on the balance sheet

> *"Airlines with frequent-flier programs must record as a current liability the cost of flying those who will use frequent-flier miles over the next year. When the airline is in partnership with another organization (such as a hotel chain), the problem of determining the current liability becomes more complex."*
>
> JOSEPH D. WESSELKAMPER, CPA, PRESIDENT OF JOSEPH D. WESSELKAMPER & ASSOCIATES, INC.

First came the airlines' frequent-flier programs: Fly so many miles on a particular airline, and receive a free ticket to the destination of your choice. Now some hotels—first Marriotts, then Holiday Inns and Sheratons—are offering their guests *airline* mileage on such carriers as American, United, and Delta.

For example, Holiday Inn Worldwide offers its guests 2.5 frequent-flier miles per dollar spent on Holiday Inn rooms. Why would Holiday Inn make such an offer? To encourage travelers to stay at one of its hotels. To the hotel company, the cost is promotion expense. Why would an airline like American Airlines allow the hotels to make this offer? To generate revenue—the airlines charge the hotels approximately \$0.015 per mile credited to a customer's account.

The arrangement between Holiday Inn and the airlines illustrates the challenge of accounting for liabilities. In this case, the airlines have an obligation to provide travel that the hotels have paid for in advance. The airline receives cash in advance, which creates an obligation to provide future transportation—a current liability. AMR Corporation (the parent company of American Airlines) reports this obligation as Air Traffic Liability, one of the current liabilities shown on its balance sheet in Exhibit 11-1, line 4.

AMR Corporation accounts for the liabilities and revenues arising from its frequent-flier program as follows (adapted from AMR's annual report):

> ***Frequent Flier Program*** American sells mileage credits to participating companies in its frequent flier program. Such revenues [are] deferred [as Air Traffic Liability] and recognized [as revenue when] the transportation is provided.

In this chapter, we explain how to account for all types of current liabilities. The first half of the chapter concentrates on current liabilities, and the second half on payroll accounting, which generates some specific current liabilities.

Objective 1

Account for current liabilities of known amount

Current Liabilities of Known Amount

Recall that *current liabilities* are obligations due within one year or within the company's normal operating cycle if it is longer than one year. Obligations due beyond that period of time are classified as *long-term liabilities.*

We discussed current liabilities and long-term liabilities in Chapter 4, page 150.

Current liabilities fall into two categories: liabilities of a known amount and those whose amount must be estimated. We look first at current liabilities of known amount.

Accounts Payable

Amounts owed to suppliers for products or services purchased on open account are *accounts payable*. Accounts payable do not bear interest expense for the debtor. We have seen many accounts payable examples in preceding chapters. For example, a business may purchase inventories and office supplies on an account payable. AMR Corporation reported Accounts payable of $817 million at December 31, 19X5 (see line 1 of Exhibit 11-1).

Current liabilities arising from many similar transactions are well suited to computerized accounting. One of a merchandiser's most common transactions is the credit purchase of inventory, recorded as follows with assumed amounts:

Inventory............................	600	
Accounts Payable		600
Purchase on account.		

EXHIBIT 11-1
How AMR Reports Its Current and Contingent Liabilities

AMR CORPORATION
(Parent Company of American Airlines)
Balance Sheet (partial; adapted)

	(In millions)	December 31, 19X5
	Liabilities	
	Current Liabilities	
1	Accounts payable	$ 817
2	Salaries and wages payable	729
3	Accrued liabilities payable	1,331
4	Air traffic liability	1,466
5	Current maturities of long-term debt	228
6	Current obligations under capital leases	122
7	Total current liabilities	4,693
8	**Commitments and Contingencies**	—

A computer makes it easy to integrate the accounts payable and perpetual inventory systems. When merchandise dips below a predetermined level, the computer automatically prepares a purchase request. After the order is placed and the goods are received, clerks enter inventory and accounts payable data into the system. The computer then increases Inventory and Accounts Payable to account for the purchase. For payments, the computer debits Accounts Payable and credits Cash, as follows:

Accounts Payable.........	400	
Cash		400
Paid on account.		

The program may also update account balances and print journals, ledger accounts, and the financial statements.

Short-Term Notes Payable

Short-term notes payable, a common form of financing, are promissory notes payable due within one year. Companies often issue short-term notes payable to borrow cash or to purchase inventory or plant assets. In addition to recording the note payable and its eventual payment, the business must also pay interest expense and accrue interest expense and interest payable at the end of the period. The following entries are typical of this liability:

Short-Term Note Payable. Promissory note payable due within one year, a common form of financing.

Recall from Chapter 3, page 103, that all adjusting entries for accrued expenses require a debit to an expense and a credit to a payable.

19X1			
Sep. 30	Inventory	8,000	
	Note Payable, Short-Term......................		8,000
	Purchased inventory by issuing a one-year, 10% note payable.		
19X1			
Dec. 31	Interest Expense ($8,000 × 0.10 × 3/12).........	200	
	Interest Payable		200
	Adjusting entry to accrue interest expense at year end.		

The balance sheet at December 31, 19X1, will report the Note Payable of $8,000 and the related Interest Payable of $200 as current liabilities. The 19X1 income statement will report interest expense of $200, as illustrated.

Balance Sheet at December 31, 19X1

Assets	**Liabilities**	
	Current liabilities:	
	Note payable, short-term.........	$8,000
	Interest payable.........................	200

Income Statement for the Year Ended December 31, 19X1

Revenues:	
Expenses:	
Interest expense.........	$200

The following entry records the note's payment at maturity:

19X2			
Sep. 30	Note Payable, Short-Term................................	8,000	
	Interest Payable	200	
	Interest Expense ($8,000 × 0.10 × 9/12)	600	
	Cash [$8,000 + ($8,000 × 0.10)]		8,800
	Paid a note payable and interest at maturity.		

- Daily Exercise 11-1
- Daily Exercise 11-2
- Daily Exercise 11-3

The cash payment entry must separate the total interest on the note between the portion accrued at the end of the previous period ($200) and the current period's expense ($600).

The face amount of notes payable and their interest rates and payment dates can be stored for electronic data processing. Computer programs calculate interest, print the interest checks, journalize the transactions, and update account balances.

Short-Term Notes Payable Issued at a Discount

Discounting a Note Payable. A borrowing arrangement in which the bank subtracts the interest amount from a note's face value. The borrower receives the net amount.

In another common borrowing arrangement, a company may **discount a note payable** at the bank. The bank subtracts the interest amount from the note's face value, and the borrower receives the net amount. At maturity, the borrower pays back the full face value, which includes all of the interest.

Suppose Procter & Gamble discounts a $100,000, 60-day note payable to its bank at 12 percent. The company will receive $98,000—that is, the $100,000 face value less interest of $2,000 ($100,000 × 0.12 × 60/360). Assume that this transaction occurs on November 25, 19X1. Procter & Gamble's entries to record discounting the note are as follows:

19X1			
Nov. 25	Cash ($100,000 – $2,000)	98,000	
	Discount on Note Payable ($100,000 × 0.12 × 60/360)	2,000	
	Note Payable, Short-Term		100,000
	Discounted a $100,000, 60-day, 12% note payable to borrow cash.		

Note Payable		Discount on Note Payable	
	Nov. 25 100,000	Nov. 25 2,000	

Net liability, $98,000

The T-accounts show that Discount on Note Payable is a contra account to the liability Note Payable, Short-Term. For this reason, Discount on Notes Payable is journalized as a *debit*. A balance sheet prepared immediately after this transaction would report the note payable at its net amount of $98,000, as follows:

Balance Sheet	
Current liabilities:	
Note payable, short-term	$100,000
Less: Discount on note payable	(2,000)
Note payable, short-term, net	$ 98,000

Thinking It Over How much did Procter & Gamble (P&G) borrow from the bank—$98,000 or $100,000? How much will P&G pay back? How much interest expense will P&G record for the borrowing arrangement?

Answers: P&G borrowed $98,000, the amount of cash the company received. They will pay back $100,000 at maturity. Their interest expense will be $2,000 ($100,000 paid back – $98,000 borrowed).

The accrued interest at year end must be recorded, as it would for any note payable. The adjusting entry at December 31 records interest for 36 days as follows:

19X1			
Dec. 31	Interest Expense ($100,000 × 0.12 × 36/360)	1,200	
	Discount on Note Payable		1,200
	Adjusting entry to accrue interest expense at year end.		

For a discounted note, this entry credits Discount on Notes Payable instead of Interest Payable. Crediting the Discount reduces the contra account's balance and increases the net amount of the note payable. After the adjusting entry, only $800 of the Discount remains.

Note Payable			
		Nov. 25	100,000

Discount on Note Payable			
Nov. 25	2,000	Dec. 31	1,200
Bal.	800		

Net liability, $99,200

The carrying amount of the note payable increases to $99,200, as follows:

Balance Sheet	
Current liabilities:	
Note payable, short-term	$100,000
Less: Discount on note payable ($2,000 – $1,200)	(800)
Note payable, short-term, net	$ 99,200

At maturity, the business records the final amount of interest expense and the payment of the note:

19X2			
Jan. 24	Interest Expense ($100,000 × 0.12 × 24/360).........	800	
	Discount on Note Payable.............................		800
	To record interest expense.		
Jan. 24	Note Payable, Short-Term	100,000	
	Cash..		100,000
	To pay note payable at maturity.		

After these entries, the balances in the Note Payable and Discount accounts are zero.

Note Payable	
100,000	100,000

Discount on Note Payable	
2,000	1,200
	800

■ Daily Exercise 11-4

Learning Tip: In Chapter 8, we discussed discounting a note *receivable*, which means to sell the note receivable in order to receive the cash immediately. Here we are discounting a note *payable*, which means to borrow a lesser amount of money (a discounted amount) and pay back the face value of the note payable later.

Sales Tax Payable

Every state except Delaware, Montana, New Hampshire, and Oregon, levies a sales tax on retail sales. Retailers charge their customers the sales tax in addition to the price of the item sold. Because the retailers owe the state the sales tax collected, the account Sales Tax Payable is a current liability. For example, ShowBiz Pizza Time, Inc. (known for its family restaurant/entertainment centers, such as Chuck E. Cheese), reported sales tax payable of $737,712 as a current liability.

". . . ShowBiz Pizza Time, Inc. (known for its family restaurant/entertainment centers, such as Chuck E. Cheese), reported sales tax payable of $737,712 as a current liability."

States do not levy sales tax on the sales of manufacturers, such as Procter & Gamble and General Motors. Such companies sell their products to wholesalers and retailers rather than to final consumers. Therefore, manufacturers have no sales tax liability.

Suppose one Saturday's sales at a ShowBiz Pizza Time totaled $10,000. The business collected an additional 5% in sales tax, which would equal $500 ($10,000 × 0.05). The business would record that day's sales as follows:

Cash ($10,000 × 1.05)	10,500	
Sales Revenue		10,000
Sales Tax Payable ($10,000 × 0.05)		500
To record cash sales and the related sales tax.		

Cash		Sales Tax Payable		Sales Revenue	
10,500			500		10,000

Companies forward the collected sales tax to the taxing authority at regular intervals, at which time they debit Sales Tax Payable and credit Cash. Observe that Sales Tax Payable does *not* correspond to any sales tax expense that the business is incurring. Nor does this liability arise from the purchase of any asset. Rather, the obligation arises because the business is collecting money for the government.

Many companies consider it inefficient to credit Sales Tax Payable when recording sales. Rather, they record the sales in an amount that includes the tax. Then, prior to paying tax to the state, they make a single entry for the entire period's transactions to bring Sales Revenue and Sales Tax Payable to their correct balances.

Suppose a company made July sales of $100,000, subject to a tax of 6 percent. Its summary entry to record the month's sales could be as follows:

July 31	Cash ($100,000 × 1.06)	106,000	
	Sales Revenue		106,000
	To record sales for the month.		

The entry to adjust Sales Revenue and Sales Tax Payable to their correct balances would then be

July 31	Sales Revenue [$106,000 – ($106,000 ÷ 1.06)].........	6,000	
	Sales Tax Payable...		6,000
	To record sales tax.		

Companies that follow this procedure need to make an adjusting entry at the end of the period in order to report the correct amounts of revenue and sales tax liability on their financial statements.

Current Portion of Long-Term Debt

Current Portion of Long-Term Debt. Amount of the principal that is payable within one year. Also called **current maturity.**

Some long-term notes payable and long-term bonds payable must be paid in installments. The **current portion of long-term debt,** or **current maturity,** is the amount of the principal that is payable within one year. At the end of each year, a company reclassifies (from long-term debt to a current liability) the amount of its long-term debt that must be paid during the upcoming year.

AMR's balance sheet (Exhibit 11-1, page 464) reports Current maturities of long-term debt, the next-to-last current liability (line 5). On its full balance sheet, AMR reports Long-term debt immediately after total current liabilities. *Long-term debt* refers to the notes payable that are payable later than one year beyond the balance sheet date.

The liabilities for the current portion of long-term debt (line 5) do *not* include any accrued interest payable. The account, Current Maturities of Long-Term Debt, represents only the *principal amount owed.* Interest Payable is a separate account for a different liability—the interest that must be paid. AMR includes interest payable under the current liability caption Accrued liabilities payable (line 3).

AMR Corporation reports Current obligations under capital leases as its last current liability (line 6). This liability, which is similar to current maturities of long-term debt, is next year's lease payment on leases that AMR has capitalized as an asset. (On its full balance sheet, AMR also reports a long-term liability for Obligations under capital leases. In Chapter 10, we saw that companies record assets they acquire through capital leases. We cover capital lease liabilities in Chapter 15.)

Working It Out Suppose AMR Corporation owes $600 million on long-term notes payable at December 31, 19X5. The borrowing agreement requires AMR to pay $228 million of the long-term debt on September 30, 19X6. AMR will pay $300 million during 19X7 and the remaining $72 million during 19X8. Show how AMR will report long-term debt on its balance sheet at December 31, 19X5.

Answer

	Millions
Current liabilities:	
Current maturities of long-term debt........................	$228*
Long-term liabilities:	
Long-term debt ($300 + $72, or $600 – $228)..........	372

*This appears on the AMR Corporation balance sheet, as shown in Exhibit 11-1, page 464.

Accrued Expenses (Accrued Liabilities)

An **accrued expense** is an expense incurred but not yet paid by the company. Therefore, it is also a liability, which explains why accrued expenses are sometimes called **accrued liabilities.** Accrued expenses typically occur with the passage of time, such as AMR Corporation's interest payable on its long-term debt. By contrast, an account payable results from a particular transaction in which the company purchased a good or a service.

Accrued Expense. An expense incurred but not yet paid by the company. Also called **accrued liability.**

We introduced accrued expenses in Chapter 3, page 101.

Like most other companies, AMR Corporation reports several categories of accrued liabilities on its balance sheet: Salaries and wages payable (line 2 in Exhibit 11-1); and Accrued liabilities payable (line 3). Salaries and wages payable are the company's accrued liabilities for salaries and wages payable at the end of the period. This caption also includes other payroll-related liabilities, such as taxes withheld from employee paychecks. Accrued liabilities payable includes the company's current liabilities for such items as interest payable and income tax payable. We illustrated the accounting for interest payable under the caption Short-term notes payable on page 465. The following section, plus the second half of this chapter, covers the accounting for accrued salaries and wages and other payroll liabilities.

Payroll Liabilities

Payroll, also called **employee compensation,** is a major expense of many businesses. For service organizations—such as CPA firms, real-estate brokers, and travel agents—payroll is *the* major expense. Service organizations sell their personnel's services, so employee compensation is their primary cost of doing business, just as cost of goods sold is the largest expense for a merchandising company.

Payroll. A major expense of many businesses. Also called **employee compensation.**

Employee compensation takes different forms:

- *Salary* is pay stated at a yearly, monthly, or weekly rate.
- *Wages* are employee pay amounts that are stated at an hourly figure.
- *Commissions* are computed as a percentage of the sales the employee has made.
- *Bonus* is an amount over and above regular compensation.

Journalizing all these forms of compensation follows the same pattern, which is illustrated in Exhibit 11-2 below (using assumed figures).

Salary (or other payroll) expense, which represents employees' *gross pay* (that is, pay before subtractions for taxes and other deductions), creates several liabilities for the company. Salary payable to employees, which is their *net* (take-home) *pay,* is the largest payroll liability. *Employee Income Tax Payable* is the employees' income tax that has been

EXHIBIT 11-2
Accounting for Payroll Expenses and Liabilities

Salary Expense (or Wage Expense or Commission Expense)..........	10,000	
Employee Income Tax Payable		1,200
FICA Tax Payable..		800
Employee Union Dues Payable		140
Salary Payable to Employees [take-home pay]		7,860
To record salary expense.		

withheld from their paychecks. *FICA Tax Payable* is the employees' Social Security tax, which also is withheld from paychecks. (FICA stands for the Federal Insurance Contributions Act, which created the Social Security tax.) The company owes these liabilities to the U.S. government. In our example in Exhibit 11-2, employees have authorized the company to withhold union dues, which are payable to the union.

In addition to salaries and wages, companies must pay some employer payroll taxes and expenses for employee fringe benefits. Accounting for these expenses, which is similar to the illustration in Exhibit 11-2, is covered in more detail in the second half of this chapter.

Unearned Revenues

Unearned revenues are also called *deferred revenues, revenues collected in advance*, and *customer prepayments.* All these account titles indicate that the business has received cash from its customers before it has earned the revenue. The company has an obligation to provide goods or services to the customer. The chapter opening story provides an illustration of AMR Corporation's unearned revenue. Let's consider another example.

As we saw in Chapter 3, page 104, an unearned revenue is a liability because it represents an obligation to provide a good or service.

The Dun & Bradstreet (D&B) Corporation provides credit evaluation services to businesses that subscribe to the D&B reports. Finance companies pay D&B in advance to have D&B investigate the credit histories of potential customers. By receiving cash before earning the revenue, D&B incurs a liability to provide future service. The liability account is called Unearned Subscription Revenue (which could also be titled Unearned Subscription Income).

Assume that D&B charges $450 for a finance company's three-year subscription. D&B's cash-receipt entry would be

19X1			
Jan. 1	Cash	450	
	Unearned Subscription Revenue		450
	Received cash in advance.		

After receiving the cash on January 1, 19X1, D&B owes its customers service that D&B will perform over three years. D&B's liability appears in its Unearned Subscription Revenue account as follows:

Unearned Subscription Revenue	
	450

During 19X1, D&B performs one-third of the total service and earns $150 ($450 × 1/3) of the subscription revenue. At December 31, 19X1, D&B makes the following adjusting entry to decrease (debit) the liability Unearned Subscription Revenue and increase (credit) Subscription Revenue:

19X1			
Dec. 31	Unearned Subscription Revenue	150	
	Subscription Revenue ($450 × 1/3)		150
	Earned revenue that was collected in advance.		

After this entry is posted, the two accounts appear as follows:

Unearned Subscription Revenue			
Dec. 31	150	Jan. 1	450
		Bal.	300

Subscription Revenue			
		Dec. 31	150

At December 31, 19X1, D&B has earned $150 of the revenue. D&B still owes its customer $300 in total liabilities:

- $150 for the service D&B will perform during 19X2. This is a current liability.
- $150 for the service D&B will perform during 19X3. This is a long-term liability.

D&B's financial statements would report the following at the end of the first year:

■ Daily Exercise 11-5

Balance Sheet at December 31, 19X1	
Current liabilities:	
Unearned subscription revenue	$150
Long-term liabilities:	
Unearned subscription revenue	$150

Income Statement for the Year Ended December 31, 19X1	
Revenues:	
Subscription revenue	$150

The journal entries and the financial statements for 19X2 and 19X3 follow this same pattern.

Current Liabilities That Must Be Estimated

Objective 2

Account for current liabilities that must be estimated

A business may know that a liability exists but not know the exact amount. The liability may not simply be ignored. The unknown amount of a liability must be estimated, recorded in the accounts, and reported on the balance sheet.

Estimated current liabilities vary among companies. As a first example, let's look at Estimated Warranty Payable, a liability account common among merchandisers.

Estimated Warranty Payable

Many merchandising companies guarantee their products against defects under *warranty* agreements. The warranty period may extend for any length of time. Ninety-day warranties and one-year warranties are common. The automobile companies—BMW, General Motors, and Toyota, for example—accrue liabilities for their three-year, 30,000-mile warranties.

The matching principle demands that the company record the *warranty expense* in the same period that the business recognizes sales revenue, regardless of when the company pays for warranty claims. Offering the warranty—and incurring warranty expense—is a part of generating revenue through sales. At the time of the sale, the company does not know which products are defective. The exact amount of warranty expense cannot be known with certainty, so the business must estimate its warranty expense and the related liability at the time of sale.

For a review of the matching principle, see Chapter 3, page 95.

Assume that Whirlpool Corporation, which manufactures appliances for Sears and other companies, made sales of $200,000,000, subject to product warranties. If, in past years, between 2% and 4% of products proved defective, Whirlpool management could estimate that 3% of the products it sells this year will require repair or replacement during the one-year warranty period. The company would record warranty expense of $6,000,000 ($200,000,000 × 0.03) for the period:

Warranty Expense	6,000,000	
Estimated Warranty Payable		6,000,000
To accrue warranty expense.		

Assume that defective merchandise totals $5,800,000. Whirlpool may either repair or replace it. Corresponding entries are as follows:

Estimated Warranty Payable	5,800,000	
Cash		5,800,000
To *repair* defective products sold under warranty.		

Estimated Warranty Payable	5,800,000	
Inventory		5,800,000
To *replace* defective products sold under warranty.		

Whirlpool's expense is $6,000,000 on the income statement regardless of the amount of the cash payment or the cost of the replacement inventory. After paying these warranty claims, Whirlpool's Estimated Warranty Payable account appears as follows:

Estimated Warranty Payable

Debit	Credit
5,800,000	6,000,000
	Bal. 200,000

In future periods, Whirlpool may debit the liability Estimated Warranty Payable for the remaining $200,000. However, *when* the company repairs or replaces defective merchandise has no bearing on when the company records warranty expense. Whirlpool records warranty expense in the same period as the sale. The company reports its estimated warranty payable on the balance sheet under the current-liability caption Accrued liabilities payable, as illustrated in Exhibit 11-1 (line 3).

■ Daily Exercise 11-6
■ Daily Exercise 11-7

Working It Out Maxim Company made sales of $400,000 and the company estimated warranty repairs at 5% of the sales. Maxim's actual warranty outlays were $19,000. Record the sales (ignore cost of goods sold), the warranty expense, and the warranty outlays. Assuming a beginning balance of zero for Estimated Warranty Payable, how much is Maxim's estimated warranty payable at the end of the period?

Answer

Accounts Receivable	400,000	
Sales Revenue		400,000
Warranty Expense ($400,000 × 0.05)	20,000	
Estimated Warranty Payable		20,000
Estimated Warranty Payable	19,000	
Cash		19,000

Estimated Warranty Payable

Debit	Credit
19,000	20,000
	Bal. 1,000

Estimated Vacation Pay Liability

Most companies grant paid vacations to their employees. The employees receive this benefit when they take their vacation, but they earn the benefit by working the other days of the year. Two-week vacations are common. To properly match expense with revenue, the company accrues the vacation pay expense and liability for each of the 50 workweeks of the year. Then, the company records payment during the two-week vacation period. Employee turnover and terminations force companies to estimate their vacation pay liability.

Suppose a company's January payroll is $100,000 and vacation pay adds 4% (2 weeks of annual vacation divided by 50 workweeks each year). Experience indicates that only 90% of the available vacations will be taken, so the January vacation pay estimate is $3,600 ($100,000 × 0.04 × 0.90). In January, the company records vacation pay as follows:

Jan. 31	Vacation Pay Expense	3,600	
	Estimated Vacation Pay Liability		3,600

Each month thereafter, the company makes a similar entry.

If an employee takes a two-week vacation during August, his or her $2,000 salary is recorded as follows:

Aug. 31	Estimated Vacation Pay Liability	2,000	
	Cash		2,000

Income Tax Payable (for a Corporation)

Corporations pay income tax in the same way that individual taxpayers do. Corporations file their income tax returns with the Internal Revenue Service after the end of the year, so they must estimate their income tax payable for reporting on the balance sheet. During the year, corporations make quarterly tax payments to the government. A corporation would record the payment of $100,000 of income tax expense for the third quarter as follows:

Sept. 30	Income Tax Expense	100,000	
	Cash		100,000
	To pay quarterly income tax.		

The corporation's entry to accrue $40,000 of income tax expense at year end is

Dec. 31	Income Tax Expense	40,000	
	Income Tax Payable......................		40,000
	To accrue income tax at year end.		

The corporation will pay off this tax liability during the next year, when it files its tax return with the Internal Revenue Service.

Objective 3

Identify and report contingent liabilities

Contingent Liabilities

A *contingent liability* is not an actual liability. Instead, it is a potential liability that depends on a *future* event arising out of past events. For example, AMR Corporation, the parent company of American Airlines, faces a possible loss if its pilots walk off the job in a threatened labor strike. The future event is the negotiation between the airline and the pilots' labor union. The past event was American Airlines' signing a labor agreement with its pilots. The airline thus faces a contingent liability, which may or may not become an actual liability.

We introduced contingent liabilities in Chapter 8, page 351.

It would be unethical for the airline to withhold knowledge of the labor negotiations from anyone considering investing in the business. A person or business could be misled into thinking the company is stronger financially than it really is. The *disclosure principle* (see Chapter 9) requires a company to report any information deemed relevant to outsiders. The goal is to give people relevant, reliable information for decision making. The Financial Accounting Standards Board (FASB) separates contingencies into two categories:

1. Contingent losses and related liabilities
2. Contingent gains and related assets

Businesses do not record contingent gains and their related assets. Accountants record only actual gains. But accountants record some contingent losses as though they had already occurred.

The FASB provides these guidelines to account for contingent losses (or expenses) and their related liabilities:

1. Record a liability if it is *probable*—likely—that the loss (or expense) will occur and the *amount can be reasonably estimated.* Warranty expense and vacation pay expense are examples.
2. Report the contingency in a financial statement note if it is *reasonably possible* that a loss (or expense) will occur. The remainder of this section discusses contingencies of this type.
3. There is no need to report a contingent loss that is *remote*—unlikely to occur. Instead, wait until an actual transaction clears up the situation. For example, suppose Del Monte Foods conducts business in Nicaragua, and the Nicaraguan government issues a mild threat to confiscate the assets of all foreign companies. Del Monte will neither record a loss nor report the contingency if the probability of a loss is considered remote.

Sometimes, the contingent liability has a definite amount. Recall from Chapter 8 that the payee of a discounted note receivable has a contingent liability. If the maker of the note pays at maturity, the contingent liability ceases to exist. However, if the maker defaults, the payee, who sold the note, has a liability to pay off the note to the purchaser.

Another contingent liability of known amount arises when one company *cosigns a note payable* for another company. In this case, company A guarantees that company B will pay a note payable owed to another party. This practice obligates the guarantor (company A) to pay the note and interest if, and only if, the primary debtor (company B) fails to pay. Thus the guarantor has a contingent liability until the note becomes due. If the primary debtor pays off the note, the contingent liability ceases to exist. If the primary debtor fails to pay, the guarantor's contingent liability becomes actual.

The amount of a contingent liability may be hard to determine. For example, companies face lawsuits, which may cause possible obligations of amounts to be determined by the courts.

Short Presentation. A way to report contingent liabilities in the body of the balance sheet, after total liabilities but with no amount given. An explanatory note accompanies the presentation.

Contingent liabilities may be reported in two ways. In what is called a **short presentation,** the contingent liability appears in the body of the balance sheet, after total liabilities, but with no amounts given. In general, an explanatory note accompanies a short presentation. Sears, Roebuck and Company reported contingent liabilities this way:

	Millions
Total liabilities....................................	$27,830.7
Contingent liabilities (note 10)..........	—

Note 10: Various legal actions and governmental proceedings are pending against Sears, Roebuck and Co. and its subsidiaries. The consequences of these matters are not presently determinable but, in the opinion of management, the ultimate liability resulting, if any, will not have a material effect on the company.

AMR Corporation's balance sheet in Exhibit 11-1, line 8, includes a short presentation of contingencies. AMR's notes explain the contingencies in more detail.

Many companies use a second method of reporting, presenting only a note to describe contingent liabilities. International Business Machines Corporation (IBM) mentioned its contingent liabilities in a half-page supplementary note labeled *litigation.*

"International Business Machines Corporation (IBM) mentions its contingent liabilities in a half-page supplementary note labeled litigation.*"*

FASB GUIDELINES The line between a contingent liability and a real liability may be hard to draw. As a practical guide, the FASB says to record an actual liability if (1) it is probable that the business has suffered a loss, and (2) its amount can be reasonably estimated. If both of these conditions are met, the FASB reasons that the obligation has passed from contingent to real, even if its amount must be estimated. Suppose that at the balance sheet date, a hospital has lost a court case for uninsured malpractice, but the amount of damages is uncertain. The hospital estimates that the liability will fall between $1.0 and $2.5 million. In this case, the hospital must record a loss or expense and a liability for $1.0 million. The income statement will report the loss, and the balance sheet the liability. Also, the hospital must disclose in a note the possibility of an additional $1.5 million loss.

■ Daily Exercise 11-8

Ethical Issues in Accounting for Current and Contingent Liabilities

Accounting for current liabilities poses ethical and legal challenges. Business owners and managers want their company to look as successful as possible. They like to report high levels of net income on the income statement. Why? Because high net income makes the company look profitable and helps the company raise money from investors. And high net income leads to large bonuses for managers. Owners want their balance sheet to report high asset values and low liability amounts, which make the company look safe to lenders and help the company borrow money at low interest rates. The following illustrates the relationships among expenses, net income, and liabilities:

- Low expenses ⟶ High net income
- Low accrued expenses ⟶ Low accrued liabilities
- Low liabilities ⟶ High owner's equity

Owners and managers may be tempted to overlook some accrued expenses at the end of the accounting period. For example, a company can fail to accrue warranty expense or employee vacation pay. This failure will cause total expenses to be understated and net income to be overstated on the income statement. It will also cause the balance sheet to understate total liabilities and overstate owner's equity.

Contingent liabilities also pose an ethical challenge. Because contingencies are not real liabilities, they are easy to overlook. But a contingent liability can be very important, especially if it threatens a company's existence. A business with a contingent liability walks a tightrope between (1) disclosing enough information to enable outsiders to evaluate the company realistically, and (2) giving away too much information. For example, a company that is a defendant in a lawsuit may believe that it is 50% guilty. On the one hand, if this belief were disclosed in the financial statements, the lawsuit's outcome could be affected. On the other hand, suppose the company withholds the information and people invest in the company. If the company then loses the lawsuit and goes out of business, the investors are likely to lose all their money. They can blame the company's management for failing to give them enough information.

A basic element of an audit performed by independent CPAs is the search for unrecorded liabilities. Auditors perform extensive tests to ensure that a company's balance sheet reports the full amount of its actual liabilities. The audit also looks for contingent liabilities. The goal of the audit is to give outsiders the information they need to reach a reasonable conclusion about the company's operating performance, financial position, and cash flows.

Ethical business owners and managers do not play games with their accounting. Falsifying financial statements can ruin one's reputation. It can also land a person in a federal or state prison.

At this half-way point of the chapter, review what you have learned by studying the following Decision Guidelines.

DECISION GUIDELINES — Accounting for Current and Contingent Liabilities, Including Payroll

DECISION	GUIDELINES
What are the two main issues in accounting for current liabilities?	• *Recording* the liability and the asset acquired or the expense incurred • *Reporting* the liability on the balance sheet
What are the two basic categories of current liabilities?	• Current liabilities of *known amount:* Accounts payable; Short-term notes payable; Sales tax payable; Current portion of long-term debt; Accrued expenses (accrued liabilities); Payroll liabilities; Salary, wages, commission, and bonus payable; Unearned revenues • Current liabilities that *must be estimated:* Estimated warranty payable Estimated vacation pay liability Income tax payable (for a corporation)

(continued)

DECISION GUIDELINES ***(continued)***

How to account for contingent (potential) liabilities?	Report contingent liabilities either • *Short* (with no dollar amount) on the balance sheet, along with an explanatory note, or • With only the explanatory *note*
What is the ethical and legal challenge in accounting for current and contingent liabilities?	• Ensure that the balance sheet (and the related notes) reports the *full amount of all* the business's current and contingent liabilities

SUMMARY PROBLEM FOR YOUR REVIEW — MID-CHAPTER

This problem consists of three independent parts.

REQUIRED

1. A Wendy's hamburger restaurant made cash sales of $4,000 subject to a 5% sales tax. Record the sales and the related sales tax. Also record Wendy's payment of the tax to the state government.
2. At April 30, 19X2, H. J. Heinz Company reported its 6% long-term debt as follows:

Current Liabilities (in part)	
Portion of long-term debt due within one year	$ 14,000,000
Interest payable ($200,000,000 × 0.06 × 5/12)	5,000,000
Long-Term Debt and Other Liabilities (in part)	
Long-term debt	$186,000,000

The company pays interest on its long-term debt on November 30 each year.

Show how Heinz Company would report its liabilities on the year-end balance sheet at April 30, 19X3. Assume that the current maturity of its long-term debt is $16 million.

3. What distinguishes a contingent liability from an actual liability?

SOLUTION

1.

Cash ($4,000 × 1.05)	4,200	
Sales Revenue		4,000
Sales Tax Payable ($4,000 × 0.05)		200
To record cash sales and related sales tax.		
Sales Tax Payable	200	
Cash		200
To pay sales tax to the state government.		

2. H. J. Heinz Company balance sheet at April 30, 19X3:

Current Liabilities (in part)	
Portion of long-term debt due within one year	$ 16,000,000
Interest payable ($186,000,000 × 0.06 × 5/12)	4,650,000
Long-Term Debt and Other Liabilities (in part)	
Long-term debt	$170,000,000

3. A contingent liability is a *potential* liability, which may or may not become an actual liability.

Accounting for Payroll

Payroll costs are so important to most businesses that they adopt special systems to account for their labor costs. This section covers the basics of accounting for payroll.

Objective 4

Compute payroll amounts

Businesses often pay employees at a base rate for a set number of hours—called *straight time*. For working any additional hours—called *overtime*—the employee receives a higher rate.

Lucy Childres is an accountant for MicroAge Electronics Company. Lucy earns \$600 per week straight time. The company work week runs 40 hours, so Lucy's hourly straight-time pay is \$15 (\$600/40). Her company pays her *time and a half* for overtime. That rate is 150% (1.5 times) the straight-time rate. Thus Lucy earns \$22.50 for each hour of overtime she works (\$15.00 × 1.5 = \$22.50). For working 42 hours during a week, she earns \$645, computed as follows:

Straight-time pay for 40 hours	\$600
Overtime pay for 2 overtime hours: 2 × \$22.50	45
Total pay	\$645

Gross Pay and Net Pay

Before withholding taxes were introduced in 1943, employees brought home all they earned. For example, back in 1940, Lucy Childres would have taken home the full \$645 that she made. Payroll accounting was straightforward. Those days are long past.

The federal government, most state governments, and even some city governments require employers to act as collection agents for employee taxes, which are deducted from employee checks. Insurance companies, labor unions, and other organizations may also receive pieces of employees' pay. Amounts withheld from an employee's check are called *deductions*.

Gross pay is the total amount of salary, wages, commissions, or any other employee compensation before taxes and other deductions. **Net pay**—or "take-home pay"—equals gross pay minus all deductions. As Exhibit 11-3 shows, net pay is the amount the employee actually takes home.

Gross Pay. Total amount of salary, wages, commissions, or any other employee compensation before taxes and other deductions.

Net Pay. Gross pay minus all deductions. The amount of compensation that the employee actually takes home.

Many companies also pay employee *benefits*, which are a form of employee compensation. Examples include health and life insurance premiums paid directly to the insurance companies. Other examples include retirement pay and health insurance premiums paid during the retirement years, benefits that the employee does not receive immediately in cash. Payroll accounting has become quite complex. Let's turn now to a discussion of payroll deductions.

Payroll Deductions

Payroll deductions that are withheld from employees' pay fall into two categories: (1) *required deductions*, which include employee income tax and social security tax; and (2) *optional deductions*, which include union dues, insurance premiums, charitable contributions, and other amounts that are withheld at the employee's request. After they are withheld, payroll deductions become the liability of the employer, who assumes responsibility for paying the outside party. For example, the employer pays the government the employee income tax withheld and pays the union the employee union dues withheld.

■ Daily Exercise 11-9

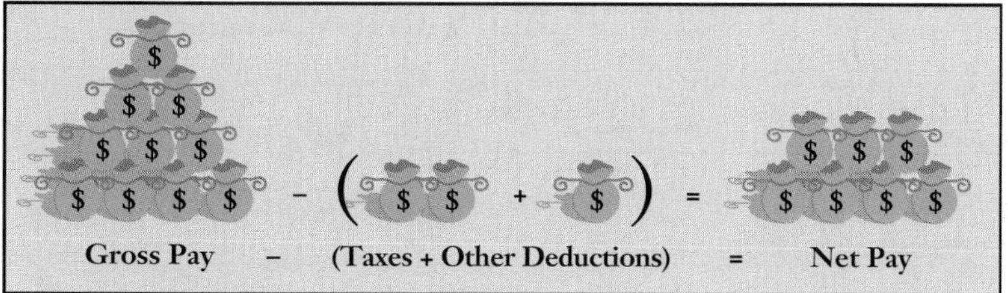

Concept Highlight

EXHIBIT 11-3
Gross Pay and Net Pay

Required Payroll Deductions

EMPLOYEE INCOME TAX In the United States, the law requires most employers to withhold income tax from their employees' salaries and wages. Income tax is one of the largest sources of national tax revenues. Employee income tax generates 36% of tax receipts in the United States, 38% in Sweden, and 41% in Canada.

Withheld Income Tax. Income tax deducted from employees' gross pay.

The amount of income tax deducted from gross pay is called **withheld income tax.** For many employees, income tax is the largest deduction. The amount withheld depends on the employee's gross pay and on the number of *withholding allowances* the employee claims.

All employees file a Form W-4 with their employer to indicate the number of allowances claimed for withholding purposes. Each allowance lowers the amount of tax withheld from the employee's paycheck. By varying the number of withholding allowances, the employee can adjust the amount of taxes withheld. An unmarried taxpayer can claim only one allowance; a childless married couple, up to two allowances; a married couple with one child, up to three allowances; and so on. Exhibit 11-4 shows a W-4 for R. C. Dean, who claims four allowances (line 5).

The employer sends its employees' withheld income tax to the government. The amount of the income tax withheld determines how often the employer submits tax payments. The employer must remit the taxes to the government at least quarterly. Every business must account for payroll taxes on a calendar-year basis regardless of its fiscal year.

The employer accumulates taxes in the Employee Income Tax Payable account. The word *payable* indicates that the account is the employer's liability to the government, even though the employees are the people taxed.

EMPLOYEE SOCIAL SECURITY (FICA) TAX The *Federal Insurance Contributions Act (FICA)*, also known as the Social Security Act, created the Social Security Tax. The Social Security program provides retirement, disability, and medical benefits. The law requires employers to withhold **Social Security (FICA) tax** from employees' pay. The FICA tax has two components:

Social Security Tax. Federal Insurance Contributions Act (FICA) tax, which is withheld from employees' pay. Also called **FICA tax.**

1. Old age, survivors', and disability insurance (OASDI)
2. Health insurance (Medicare)

The amount of tax withheld from employees' pay varies from year to year. As of 1997, the OASDI portion of the tax applies to the first $65,400 of employee earnings in a year. The taxable amount of earnings is adjusted annually depending on the rate of inflation in the U.S. economy. The OASDI tax rate is 6.2 percent. Therefore, the maximum OASDI tax that an employee paid in 1997 was $4,055 ($65,400 × 0.062).

EXHIBIT 11-4
Form W-4

Cut here and give the certificate to your employer. Keep the top portion for your records.

Form **W-4** — Department of the Treasury, Internal Revenue Service

Employee's Withholding Allowance Certificate

► For Privacy Act and Paperwork Reduction Act Notice, see reverse.

OMB No. 1545-0010 — **1997**

1 Type or print your first name and middle initial: R. C. — Last name: Dean — 2 Your social security number: 344 86 4529

Home address (number and street or rural route): 4376 Palm Drive — 3 ☐ Single ☒ Married ☐ Married, but withhold at higher Single rate. Note: *If married, but legally separated, or spouse is a nonresident alien, check the Single box.*

City or town, state, and ZIP code: Fort Lauderdale, FL 33317 — 4 If your last name differs from that on your social security card, check here and call 1-800-772-1213 for more information . . . . ► ☐

5 Total number of allowances you are claiming (from line G above or from the worksheets on page 2 if they apply) . — 5: 4

6 Additional amount, if any, you want withheld from each paycheck . . . . — 6: $

7 I claim exemption from withholding for 1994 and I certify that I meet **BOTH** of the following conditions for exemption:
- Last year I had a right to a refund of **ALL** Federal income tax withheld because I had **NO** tax liability; **AND**
- This year I expect a refund of **ALL** Federal income tax withheld because I expect to have **NO** tax liability.

If you meet both conditions, enter "EXEMPT" here . . . . ► 7

Under penalties of perjury, I certify that I am entitled to the number of withholding allowances claimed on this certificate or entitled to claim exempt status.

Employee's signature ► R. C. Dean — **Date** ► 7-22 , 19 97

8 Employer's name and address (Employer: Complete 8 and 10 only if sending to the IRS): Blumenthal's, Crescent Square Shopping Center, Fort Lauderdale, FL 33310 — 9 Office code (optional): 14 — 10 Employer identification number: 83 19475

The Medicare portion of the FICA tax applies to all employee earnings. This tax rate is 1.45 percent. An employee thus pays a combined FICA tax rate of 7.65% (6.2% + 1.45%) of the first $65,400 of annual earnings, plus 1.45% of earnings above $65,400. **To ease the computational burden and focus on the concepts, we assume that the FICA tax is 8% of the first $65,000 of employee earnings each year. (Use these numbers when you complete this chapter's assignment material, unless instructed otherwise.)** For each employee who earns $65,000 or more, the employer withholds $5,200 ($65,000 × 0.08) from the employee's pay and sends that amount to the federal government. The employer records this employee tax in the account FICA Tax Payable.

Assume that Rex Jennings, an employee, earned $63,500 prior to December. Jennings' salary for December is $6,000. How much FICA tax will be withheld from his December paycheck? The computation is as follows:

Employee earnings subject to the tax in one year	$65,000
Employee earnings prior to the current pay period.........	63,500
Current pay subject to FICA tax......................................	$ 1,500
FICA tax rate...	× 0.08
FICA tax to be withheld from current pay	$ 120

Optional Payroll Deductions

As a convenience to employees, many companies make payroll deductions and disburse cash according to employee instructions. Union dues, insurance payments, payroll savings plans, and gifts to charities are examples. The account Employees' Union Dues Payable holds employee deductions for union membership.

Many employers offer *cafeteria plans* that allow workers to select from a menu of insurance coverage. Suppose Xerox Corporation provides each employee with $250 of insurance coverage each month. One employee may use the monthly allowance to purchase only life insurance. Another employee may select only disability coverage. A third worker may choose a combination of life insurance and disability coverage. Cafeteria plans are popular because they add flexibility to a worker's total compensation package.

Employer Payroll Taxes

Employers must bear the expense of at least three payroll taxes: (1) Social Security (FICA) tax, (2) state **unemployment compensation tax,** and (3) federal **unemployment compensation tax.**

Unemployment Compensation Tax. Payroll tax paid by employers to the government, which uses the money to pay unemployment benefits to people who are out of work.

Employer FICA Tax

In addition to being responsible for collecting the employee's contribution to Social Security, the employer also must pay into the program. The employer's Social Security tax is the same as the amount withheld from employee pay. Thus the Social Security system is funded by equal contributions from employees and employers. Using our 8% and $65,000 annual pay figures, the maximum annual employer tax on each employee is $5,200 ($65,000 × 0.08). The liability account the employer uses for this payroll tax is the same FICA Tax Payable account used for the amount withheld from employee pay. Both the tax rate and the amount of earnings that are subject to the tax change from time to time as Congress passes new legislation.

State and Federal Unemployment Compensation Taxes

■ Daily Exercise 11-10

These two payroll taxes are products of the Federal Unemployment Tax Act (FUTA). **In recent years, employers have paid a combined tax of 6.2% on the first $7,000 of each employee's annual earnings.** The proportion paid to the state is 5.4%, and 0.8% is paid to the federal government. The government then uses the money to pay unemployment benefits to people who are out of work. The employer uses the accounts Federal Unemployment Tax Payable and State Unemployment Tax Payable. Exhibit 11-5 shows a typical disbursement of payroll costs by an employer company.

■ Daily Exercise 11-11

EXHIBIT 11-5
Typical Breakdown of Payroll Costs for One Employee

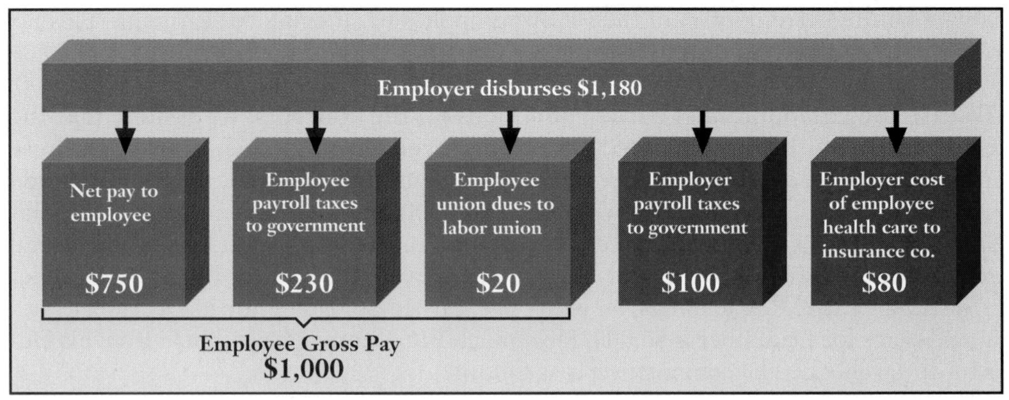

Payroll Entries

Objective 5

Make basic payroll entries

Exhibit 11-6 summarizes an employer's entries to record a monthly payroll of $10,000. All amounts are assumed for illustration only.

Entry A in Exhibit 11-6 records the employer's *salary expense*. The *gross salary* of all employees, $10,000, is their monthly pay before any deductions. The federal government imposes the income tax and FICA tax. Most states and some cities also levy income taxes, which are accounted for in like manner. The union dues are optional. Employees' take-home (net) pay is $7,860. One important point about this payroll transaction is that the employees pay their own income and FICA taxes and union dues. The employer serves merely as a collecting agent and sends these amounts to the government and the union.

Entry B records the employer's *payroll taxes*. In addition to the employee's FICA tax ($800 in entry A), the employer must also pay the $800 FICA tax shown in entry B. The other two employer payroll taxes are state and federal unemployment taxes. Employees make no payments for unemployment taxes.

Entry C records employee *benefits* paid by the employer. The company in the exhibit pays health and life insurance premiums for its employees, a common practice. Also, the employer funds pensions (that is, pays cash into a pension plan) for the benefit of employees when they retire. In the exhibit, the employer's pension expense for the month is $500, and the total employer expense for benefits is $1,500. **The total payroll expense of the employer in Exhibit 11-6 is $12,920 (salary expense of $10,000 + payroll tax expense of $1,420 + benefits expense of $1,500).**

Concept Highlight

EXHIBIT 11-6
Payroll Accounting by the Employer

■ Daily Exercise 11-12

A. Salary Expense		
Salary Expense (or Wage Expense or Commission Expense)	10,000	
Employee Income Tax Payable		1,200
FICA Tax Payable ($10,000 × 0.08)		800
Employee Union Dues Payable		140
Salary Payable to Employees [take-home pay]		7,860
To record *salary expense.*		
B. Payroll Tax Expense		
Payroll Tax Expense	1,420	
FICA Tax Payable ($10,000 × 0.08)		800
State Unemployment Tax Payable ($10,000 × 0.054)		540
Federal Unemployment Tax Payable ($10,000 × 0.008)		80
To record employer's *payroll taxes.*		
C. Benefits Expense		
Health Insurance Expense for Employees	800	
Life Insurance Expense for Employees	200	
Pension Expense	500	
Employee Benefits Payable		1,500
To record employee *benefits* payable by employer.		

Total Payroll Expense ($12,920) = Salary Expense ($10,000) + Payroll Tax Expense ($1,420) + Benefits Expense ($1,500)

Learning Tip: Benefits are expenses of the employer. They do not represent amounts withheld from the employees' paycheck.

A company's payments to people who are not employees—outsiders called independent contractors—are *not* company payroll expenses. Consider two CPAs, Fermi and Scott. Fermi is a corporation's chief financial officer. Scott is the corporation's outside auditor. Fermi is an employee of the corporation, and his compensation is a debit to Salary Expense. Scott, however, performs auditing service for many clients, and the corporation debits Auditing Expense when it pays her. **Any payment for services performed by a person outside the company is a debit to an expense account other than payroll.**

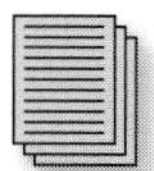

Working It Out Record the payroll and payroll taxes for the following information:

Gross salary (subject to all taxes)	$190,000
Employees' federal income tax withheld	35,800
Life insurance paid by employees	2,000
FICA tax rate	8%
State unemployment tax rate	5.4%
Federal unemployment tax rate	0.8%

- Daily Exercise 11-13
- Daily Exercise 11-14

Answer

Payroll Entry:

Salary Expense	190,000	
FICA Tax Payable ($190,000 × .08)		15,200
Life Insurance Premium Payable		2,000
Employee Income Tax Payable		35,800
Salary Payable		137,000

Payroll Tax Entry:

Payroll Tax Expense	26,980	
FICA Tax Payable		15,200
State Unemployment Tax Payable ($190,000 × .054)		10,260
Federal Unemployment Tax Payable ($190,000 × .008)		1,520

The Payroll System

Objective 6

Use a payroll system

Good business means paying employees accurately and on time. Also, companies have the legal responsibility to handle employees' and their own payroll taxes, as we have seen. These demands require companies to process a great deal of payroll data. To make payroll accounting accurate and timely, accountants have developed the *payroll system.*

The components of the payroll system are

- A payroll register
- A special payroll bank account
- Payroll checks
- An earnings record for each employee

Payroll Register

Each pay period, the company organizes the payroll data in a special journal called the *payroll register* or *payroll journal.* This register lists each employee and the figures the business needs to record payroll amounts. The payroll register, which resembles the cash disbursements journal (or check register), also serves as a check register by providing a place to record each payroll check.

We introduced the cash disbursements journal in Chapter 6, page 256.

A payroll register similar to that for Blumenthal's in Exhibit 11-7 is used by companies such as Marriott Corp. The *Gross Pay* section has columns for straight-time pay, overtime pay, and total gross pay for each employee. Columns under the *Deductions* heading vary from company to company, but every employer must deduct federal income tax and FICA tax. (State income tax is left out for convenience.) Additional column headings depend on which optional deductions the business handles. In Exhibit 11-7, the

EXHIBIT 11-7
Blumenthal's Payroll Register

Week ended December 31, 19X7													
		a	*b*	*c*	*d*	*e*	*f*	*g*	*h*	*i*	*j*	*k*	*l*
		Gross pay			Deductions					Net Pay		Account Debited	
Employee Name	Hours	Straight-Time	Overtime	Total	Federal Income Tax	FICA Tax	Union Dues	United Way Charities	Total	(c − h) Amount	Check No.	Office Salary Expense	Sales Salary Expense
Chen, W. L.*	40	500.00		500.00	71.05	40.00	5.00	2.50	118.55	381.45	1621	500.00	
Dean, R. C.	46	400.00	90.00	490.00	59.94	39.20		2.00	101.14	388.86	1622		490.00
Ellis, M.	41	560.00	21.00	581.00	86.14	46.48	5.00		137.62	443.38	1623	581.00	
Trimble, E. A.†	40	1,360.00		1,360.00	463.22			15.00	478.22	881.78	1641		1,360.00
Total		12,940.00	714.00	13,654.00	3,167.76	861.94	85.00	155.00	4,269.70	9,384.30		4,464.00	9,190.00

*W. L. Chen earned gross pay of $500. His net pay was $381.45, paid with check number 1621. Chen is an office worker, so his salary is debited to Office Salary Expense.

†The business deducted no FICA tax from E. A. Trimble. She has already earned more than $65,000. Any employee whose earnings exceed this annual maximum pays no additional FICA tax during that year.

Note: For simplicity we ignore the additional tax for Medicare benefits.

employer deducts employee payroll taxes, union dues, and gifts to United Way, and then sends the amounts to the proper parties. The business may add deduction columns as needed. The *Net Pay* section lists each employee's net (take-home) pay and the number of the check issued to him or her. The last two columns indicate the *Account Debited* for the employee's gross pay. (The company has office workers and salespeople.)

The payroll register in Exhibit 11-7 gives the employer the information needed to record salary expense for the pay period. Using the total amounts for columns (d) through (l), the employer records total salary expense as follows:

Dec. 31	Office Salary Expense	4,464.00	
	Sales Salary Expense	9,190.00	
	Employee Income Tax Payable		3,167.76
	FICA Tax Payable		861.94
	Employee Union Dues Payable		85.00
	Employee United Way Payable		155.00
	Salary Payable to Employees		9,384.30

A company may include additional information on its payroll register. The payroll register of American Airlines, for example, lists such data as year-to-date totals, hourly rates, and insurance codes.

■ Daily Exercise 11-15

Payroll Bank Account

After the payroll has been recorded, the company books include a credit balance in Salary Payable to Employees for net pay of $9,384.30. (See column (i) in Exhibit 11-7.) How the business pays this liability depends on its payroll system. Many companies disburse paychecks to employees from a special *payroll bank account*. The employer draws a check for net pay ($9,384.30 in our illustration) on its regular bank account and deposits this check in the special payroll bank account. Or, as Marriott Corp. does, the company may wire the net pay amount into the payroll bank account. Then the company writes paychecks to employees out of the payroll account. When the paychecks clear the bank, the payroll account has a zero balance, ready for the activity of the next pay period. Disbursing paychecks from a separate bank account isolates net pay for analysis and control, as we discuss later in the chapter.

Other payroll disbursements—for withheld taxes, union dues, and so on—are neither as numerous nor as frequent as weekly or monthly paychecks. The employer pays taxes, union dues, and charities from its regular bank account.

Payroll Checks

Most companies pay employees by check. A *payroll check* is like any other check except that its perforated attachment lists the employee's gross pay, payroll deductions, and net pay. These amounts are taken from the payroll register. Exhibit 11-8 shows payroll check number 1622, issued to R. C. Dean for net pay of $388.86 earned during the week ended December 31, 19X7. To enhance your ability to use payroll data, trace all amounts on the check attachment to the payroll register in Exhibit 11-7.

Increasingly, companies are paying employees by electronic funds transfer, as Marriott Corp. does. The employee can authorize the company to make all deposits directly to his or her bank. With no check to write and deliver to the employee, the company saves time and money. As evidence of the deposit, most companies, including American Airlines, issue a voided check to employees. The employee avoids the trouble of receiving, endorsing, and depositing the paycheck.

Earnings Record

The employer must file payroll tax returns with the federal and state governments. Exhibit 11-9 is the Form 941 that Blumenthal's filed with the Internal Revenue Service for the quarter ended December 31, 19X7. These forms must be filed no later than one month after the end of a quarter.

Line 13 of the exhibit shows that Blumenthal's payroll taxes for the quarter totaled $35,200. Line 14 indicates that during the quarter Blumenthal's paid the full tax bill, so the balance due on line 15 was zero. There are heavy penalties for paying these taxes late.

EXHIBIT 11-8
Payroll Check

Blumenthal's 1622
Payroll Account
Fort Lauderdale, FL

12/31 19 X7

Pay to the
Order of R. C. Dean $ 388.86

Three hundred eighty-eight & 86/100 - Dollars

Republic Bank
Fort Lauderdale,
Florida 33310

Anna Figaro
Treasurer

• A111900031A 0787C50000454C

Pay			Deductions					Net Pay	Check No.
Straight-time	Overtime	Gross	Income Tax	FICA	Union Dues	United Way	Total		
400.00	90.00	490.00	59.94	39.20		2.00	101.14	388.86	1622

The employer must also provide the employee with a wage and tax statement, Form W-2, at the end of the year. Therefore, employers maintain an *earnings record* for each employee. Exhibit 11-10 is a five-week excerpt from the earnings record of employee R. C. Dean.

The employee earnings record is not a journal or a ledger, and it is not required by law. It is an accounting tool—like the work sheet—that the employer uses to prepare payroll tax reports to the Internal Revenue Service.

Exhibit 11-11 is the Wage and Tax Statement, Form W-2, for employee R. C. Dean. The employer prepares this statement and gives copies to the employee and to the Internal Revenue Service (IRS). Dean uses the W-2 to prepare his personal income tax return. To ensure that Dean is paying income tax on all his income from that job, the IRS matches Dean's income as reported on his tax return with his earnings as reported on the W-2.

Recording Cash Disbursements for Payroll

Up to this point, we have talked about the recording of payroll expenses. We now turn to the disbursement of cash that occurs when companies actually *pay* these liabilities. Most employers must make at least three entries to record payroll cash disbursements: one for net pay to employees, one for payroll taxes to the government and payroll deductions, and one for employee benefits.

Net Pay to Employees

When the employer pays employees, the company debits Salary Payable to Employees and credits Cash. Using the data in Exhibit 11-7, the company would make the following entry to record the cash payment (column (i)) for the December 31 weekly payroll:

Dec. 31	Salary Payable to Employees.........	9,384.30	
	Cash..		9,384.30

Payroll Taxes and Payroll Deductions to the Government

The employer must send to the government two sets of payroll taxes: those withheld from employees' pay and those paid by the employer. On the basis of Exhibit 11-7,

Form **941** (Rev. January 1998) Department of the Treasury Internal Revenue Service

Employer's Quarterly Federal Tax Return

▶ See separate instructions for information on completing this return.

Please type or print.

Enter state code for state in which deposits were made ONLY if different from state in address to the right ▶ F L (see page 3 of instructions).

BLUMENTHAL'S
CRESCENT SQUARE SHOPPING CENTER
FORT LAUDERDALE, FL 33310-1234

OMB No. 1545-0029

T
FF
FD
FP
I
T

If address is different from prior return, check here ▶ ☐ — IRS Use

If you do not have to file returns in the future, check here ▶ ☐ and enter date final wages paid ▶

If you are a seasonal employer, see **Seasonal employers** on page 1 of the instructions and check here ▶ ☐

1	Number of employees in the pay period that includes March 12th . ▶	1			19
2	Total wages and tips, plus other compensation			2	113,654
3	Total income tax withheld from wages, tips, and sick pay			3	18,168
4	Adjustment of withheld income tax for preceding quarters of calendar year			4	—
5	Adjusted total of income tax withheld (line 3 as adjusted by line 4—see instructions)			5	18,168
6	Taxable social security wages	6a	110,774	× 12.4% (.124) = 6b	13,736
	Taxable social security tips	6c		× 12.4% (.124) = 6d	
7	Taxable Medicare wages and tips	7a	113,654	× 2.9% (.029) = 7b	3,296
8	Total social security and Medicare taxes (add lines 6b, 6d, and 7b). Check here if wages are not subject to social security and/or Medicare tax ▶ ☐			8	17,032
9	Adjustment of social security and Medicare taxes (see instructions for required explanation) Sick Pay $ ______ ± Fractions of Cents $ ______ ± Other $ ______ =			9	—
10	Adjusted total of social security and Medicare taxes (line 8 as adjusted by line 9—see instructions)			10	17,032
11	**Total taxes** (add lines 5 and 10)			11	35,200
12	Advance earned income credit (EIC) payments made to employees			12	—
13	Net taxes (subtract line 12 from line 11). **This should equal line 17, column (d) below (or line D of Schedule B (Form 941))**			13	35,200
14	Total deposits for quarter, including overpayment applied from a prior quarter			14	35,200
15	**Balance due** (subtract line 14 from line 13). See instructions			15	–0–
16	**Overpayment,** if line 14 is more than line 13, enter excess here ▶ $ ______ and check if to be: ☐ Applied to next return **OR** ☐ Refunded.				

- **All filers:** If line 13 is less than $500, you need not complete line 17 or Schedule B (Form 941).
- **Semiweekly schedule depositors:** Complete Schedule B (Form 941) and check here ▶ ☐
- **Monthly schedule depositors:** Complete line 17, columns (a) through (d), and check here ▶ ☐

17 Monthly Summary of Federal Tax Liability. Do not complete if you were a semiweekly schedule depositor.

(a) First month liability	(b) Second month liability	(c) Third month liability	(d) Total liability for quarter
35,017	35,336	34,967	35,200

Sign Here Under penalties of perjury, I declare that I have examined this return, including accompanying schedules and statements, and to the best of my knowledge and belief, it is true, correct, and complete.

Signature ▶ Anna Figaro   Print Your Name and Title ▶ Anna Figaro, Treasurer   Date ▶ 1/30/98

For Privacy Act and Paperwork Reduction Act Notice, see page 4 of separate instructions. Cat. No. 17001Z Form **941** (Rev. 1-98)

EXHIBIT 11-9
Payroll Tax Return

EMPLOYEE NAME AND ADDRESS:	SOCIAL SECURITY NO.: 344-86-4529
	MARITAL STATUS: MARRIED
DEAN, R. C.	WITHHOLDING EXEMPTIONS: 4
4376 PALM DRIVE	PAY RATE: $400 PER WEEK
FORT LAUDERDALE, FL 33317	JOB TITLE: SALESPERSON

		Gross Pay				Deductions					Net Pay	
Week Ended	Hrs.	Straight-Time	Over-time	Total	To Date	Federal Income Tax	FICA Tax	Union Dues	United Way Charity	Total	Amount	Check No.
Dec. 3	40	400.00		400.00	21,340.00	42.19	32.00		2.00	76.19	323.81	1525
Dec. 10	40	400.00		400.00	21,740.00	42.19	32.00		2.00	76.19	323.81	1548
Dec. 17	44	400.00	60.00	460.00	22,200.00	54.76	36.80		2.00	93.56	366.44	1574
Dec. 24	48	400.00	120.00	520.00	22,720.00	66.75	41.60		2.00	110.35	409.65	1598
Dec. 31	46	400.00	90.00	490.00	23,210.00	59.94	39.20		2.00	101.14	388.86	1622
Total		20,800.00	2,410.00	23,210.00		1,946.72	1,856.80		104.00	3,907.52	19,302.48	

EXHIBIT 11-10
Employee Earnings Record for 19X7

columns (d) through (g), the business would record a series of cash payment entries summarized as follows (employer tax amounts are assumed):

Dec. 31	Employee Income Tax Payable	3,167.76	
	FICA Tax Payable ($861.94 × 2)	1,723.88	
	Employee Union Dues Payable	85.00	
	Employee United Way Payable	155.00	
	State Unemployment Tax Payable	104.62	
	Federal Unemployment Tax Payable	15.50	
	Cash..		5,251.76

EXHIBIT 11-11
Employee Wage and Tax Statement, Form W-2

a Control number 22222	Void ☐ For Official Use Only ▶ OMB No. 1545-0008		
b Employer's identification number 83-19475		1 Wages, tips, other compensation 23,210.00	2 Federal income tax withheld 1,946.72
c Employer's name, address, and ZIP code Blumenthal's Crescent Square Shopping Center Fort Lauderdale, FL 33310-1234		3 Social security wages 23,210.00	4 Social security tax withheld 1,439.02
		5 Medicare wages and tips 23,210.00	6 Medicare tax withheld 417.78
		7 Social security tips	8 Allocated tips
d Employee's social security number 344-86-4529		9 Advance EIC payment	10 Dependent care benefits
e Employee's name (first, middle initial, last) R. C. Dean		11 Nonqualified plans	12 Benefits included in box 1
4376 Palm Drive Fort Lauderdale, FL 33317 f Employee's address and ZIP code		13 See Instrs. for box 13	14 Other
		15 Statutory employee ☐ Deceased ☐ Pension plan ☐ Legal rep. ☐ 942 emp. ☐ Subtotal ☐ Deferred compensation ☐	

16 State	Employer's state I.D. No.	17 State wages, tips, etc.	18 State income tax	19 Locality name	20 Local wages, tips, etc.	21 Local income tax

Cat. No. 10134D Department of the Treasury—Internal Revenue Service

Form **W-2** Wage and Tax Statement **1997**

Copy A For Social Security Administration

For Paperwork Reduction Act Notice, see separate instructions.

Benefits

The employer might pay for employees' insurance coverage and pension plan. If the total cash payment for these benefits is $1,927.14, this entry for payments to third parties will be

■ Daily Exercise 11-16

Dec. 31	Employee Benefits Payable	1,927.14	
	Cash		1,927.14

POSTRETIREMENT BENEFITS Employees receive some benefits, such as medical insurance, during their working years. The employer accrues this expense as it occurs to achieve a proper matching of the expense against the revenues generated by the employee's labor. Many employers also provide *postretirement benefits*—medical insurance and other benefits for retired workers.

The accounting profession has struggled to identify the appropriate accounting for the expense of postretirement benefits. Should the expense be recorded after the employee has retired, when the employer pays these expenses? Or should the expense be recorded during the employee's working years? The FASB requires that companies accrue the expense for postretirement benefits during the working years because that is when the employee's effort produces revenues. The matching principle controls this decision. Most of the liability for postretirement benefits is long-term because it accumulates over the years that an employee works to earn the postretirement medical insurance.

Pensions, which pay employees during retirement, are another postretirement benefit. Companies also accrue this expense and the related long-term liability during the employee's working years. We discuss accounting for pensions in Chapter 15, which is devoted to long-term liabilities.

Internal Control over Payroll

The internal controls over cash disbursements discussed in Chapter 7 apply to payroll. In addition, companies adopt special controls in payroll accounting. The large number of transactions and the many different parties involved increase the risk of a control failure. Accounting systems feature two types of special controls over payroll: controls for efficiency and controls for safeguarding payroll disbursements.

Controls for Efficiency

For companies with many employees, reconciling the bank account can be time-consuming because of the large number of outstanding payroll checks. For example, a March 30 payroll check would probably not have time to clear the bank before a bank statement on March 31. This check and others in a March 30 payroll would be outstanding. Identifying a large number of outstanding checks for the bank reconciliation increases accounting expense. To limit the number of outstanding checks, many companies use two payroll bank accounts. They make payroll disbursements from one payroll account one month and from the other payroll account the next month, and reconcile each account every other month. In this system, a March 30 paycheck has until April 30 to clear the bank before the account is reconciled. Outstanding checks are essentially eliminated, the time it takes to prepare the bank reconciliation is reduced, and accounting expense decreases. Also, many companies' checks become void if not cashed within a certain period of time. This constraint, too, limits the number of outstanding checks.

Payroll transactions are ideally suited for computer processing. Employee pay rates and withholding data are stored on computer. Each payroll period, computer operators enter the number of hours worked by each employee. The computer performs the calculations, prints the payroll register and paychecks, and updates the employee earnings records. The program also computes payroll taxes and prepares quarterly reports to government agencies. Expense and liability accounts are automatically updated for the payroll transactions. The payroll register is in a computer database form, which allows users to generate a wide variety of reports. At the end of an accounting period, the computerized payroll system automatically computes the amounts for the general ledger system, including any accruals of salary expense incurred but not paid.

Controls for Safeguarding Payroll Disbursements

Owners and managers of small businesses can monitor their payroll disbursements by personal contact with their employees. Large corporations cannot do so. These businesses must establish controls to ensure that payroll disbursements are made only to legitimate employees and for the correct amounts. A particular danger is that payroll checks may be written to a fictitious employee and cashed by a dishonest employee. To guard against this and other crimes, large businesses adopt strict internal control policies.

The duties of hiring and firing employees should be separated from the duties of accounting for payroll and distributing paychecks. Requiring an identification badge bearing an employee's photograph also helps internal control. Issuing paychecks only to employees with badges ensures that only actual employees receive pay.

A formal timekeeping system helps ensure that employees have actually worked the number of hours claimed. Having employees punch time cards at the start and end of the workday proves their attendance—as long as management makes sure that no employee punches in and out for others. Some companies have their workers fill in weekly or monthly time sheets.

■ Daily Exercise 11-17

Again we see that the key to good internal control is separation of duties. The responsibilities of the personnel department, the payroll department, the accounting department, time-card management, and paycheck distribution should be separate.

Thinking It Over Centurion Homes of Omaha, Nebraska, builds houses with four construction crews. The foremen hire—and fire—workers and keep their hourly records. Each Friday morning, the foremen telephone their workers' hours to the home office, where accountants prepare the weekly paychecks. Around noon, the foremen pick up the paychecks. They return to the construction site and pay the workers at day's end. What is the internal control weakness in this situation? Propose a way to improve the internal controls.

Answer: Construction workers often have limited contact with the home office. The foremen control most of the payroll information, so they can forge the payroll records of fictitious employees and pocket their pay. To improve internal control, Centurion could hire and fire all workers through the home office. This practice would establish the identity of all workers listed in the payroll records. Another way to improve the internal controls would be to have a home-office employee distribute paychecks on a surprise basis. Any unclaimed checks would arouse suspicion toward the foreman. This system would probably prevent foremen from cheating the company.

Reporting Payroll Expense and Liabilities

Objective 7

Report current liabilities on the balance sheet

At the end of its fiscal year, the company reports the amount of *payroll liability* owed to all parties—employees, state and federal governments, unions, and so forth. Payroll liability is *not* the payroll expense for the year. The liability at year end is the amount of the expense that is still unpaid. Payroll expense appears on the income statement, payroll liability on the balance sheet. Kellogg Company, makers of Kellogg's Corn Flakes, Pop Tarts, and Eggo Waffles, reported salaries and wage payable of $78 million as a current liability on its year-end balance sheet, as shown in Exhibit 11-12. However, Kellogg's payroll expense for the year far exceeded $78 million. (Exhibit 11-12 also presents other current liabilities we have discussed.)

EXHIBIT 11-12
Partial Kellogg Company Balance Sheet

Current Liabilities	Millions
Current maturities of long-term debt	$ 1.9
Notes payable	210.0
Accounts payable	313.8
Accrued liabilities:	
Income taxes payable	104.1
Salaries and wages payable	78.0
Advertising and promotion payable	228.0
Other	135.2
Total current liabilities	**$1,071.0**

■ Daily Exercise 11-18

Exhibit 11-13 summarizes the current liabilities we have discussed in the chapter.

The following Decision Guidelines feature summarizes some of the more important payroll decisions that a business must consider.

Amount of Liability Known When Recorded	Amount of Liability Estimated When Recorded
Trade accounts payable	Warranty payable
Short-term notes payable	Income tax payable
Sales tax payable	Vacation pay liability
Current portion of long-term debt	
Accrued expenses payable:	
Interest payable	
Payroll liabilities (salary payable, wages payable, and commissions payable)	
Payroll taxes payable (employee and employer)	
Unearned revenues (revenues collected in advance of being earned)	

EXHIBIT 11-13
Categories of Current Liabilities

■ Daily Exercise 11-19

DECISION GUIDELINES — Accounting for Payroll

DECISION	GUIDELINES
What are the key elements of a payroll accounting system?	• Employee's Withholding Allowance Certificate, Form W-4 • Payroll register • Payroll bank account and payroll checks • Employer's quarterly tax returns, such as Form 941 • Employee earnings record • Employee wage and tax statement, Form W-2
What are the key terms in the payroll area?	Gross pay (Total amount earned by the employee) – *Payroll deductions* **a.** Withheld income tax **b.** FICA (Social Security) tax—equal amount also paid by employer **c.** Optional deductions (insurance, savings, charitable contributions, union dues) = *Net (take-home) pay*
What is the employer's total payroll expense?	Gross pay + Employer's payroll taxes **a.** FICA (Social Security) tax—equal amount also paid by employee **b.** State and federal unemployment taxes + Benefits for employees **a.** Insurance (health, life, and disability) **b.** Pension (and other retirement) benefits **c.** Club memberships and other = Employer's total payroll costs
Where to report payroll costs?	• Payroll expenses on the income statement • Payroll liabilities on the balance sheet

SUMMARY PROBLEM FOR YOUR REVIEW

Beth Denius, Limited, a clothing store, employs one salesperson, Alan Kingsley. His straight-time salary is $360 per week. He earns time and a half for hours worked in excess of 40 per week. The owner, Beth Denius, withholds income tax (11.0%) and FICA tax (8.0%) from Kingsley's pay. She pays the following employer payroll taxes: FICA (8.0%) and state and federal unemployment (5.4% and 0.8%, respectively). In addition, Denius contributes to a pension plan an amount equal to 10% of Kingsley's gross pay.

During the week ended December 26, 19X4, Kingsley worked 48 hours. Prior to this week, Kingsley had earned $5,470.

REQUIRED

1. Compute Kingsley's gross pay and net pay for the week.
2. Record the following payroll entries that Denius would make:
   a. Expense for Kingsley's salary, including overtime pay
   b. Employer payroll taxes
   c. Expense for employee benefits
   d. Payment of cash to Kingsley
   e. Payment of all payroll taxes
   f. Payment for employee benefits
3. How much total payroll expense did Denius incur for the week? How much cash did the business spend on its payroll?

REQUIREMENT 1

Gross pay:	Straight-time pay for 40 hours		$360.00
	Overtime pay:		
	Rate per hour ($360/40 × 1.5)	$ 13.50	
	Hours (48 – 40)	× 8	108.00
	Total gross pay		$468.00
Net pay:	Gross pay		$468.00
	Less: Withheld income tax ($468 × 0.11)	$ 51.48	
	Withheld FICA tax ($468 × 0.08)	37.44	88.92
	Net pay		$379.08

REQUIREMENT 2

		Debit	Credit
a.	Sales Salary Expense	468.00	
	Employee Income Tax Payable		51.48
	FICA Tax Payable		37.44
	Salary Payable to Employee		379.08
b.	Payroll Tax Expense	66.45	
	FICA Tax Payable ($468 × 0.08)		37.44
	State Unemployment Tax Payable ($468 × 0.054)		25.27
	Federal Unemployment Tax Payable (468 × 0.008)		3.74
c.	Pension Expense ($468 × 0.10)	46.80	
	Employee Benefits Payable		46.80
d.	Salary Payable to Employee	379.08	
	Cash		379.08
e.	Employee Income Tax Payable	51.48	
	FICA Tax Payable ($37.44 × 2)	74.88	
	State Unemployment Tax Payable	25.27	
	Federal Unemployment Tax Payable	3.74	
	Cash		155.37
f.	Employee Benefits Payable	46.80	
	Cash		46.80

REQUIREMENT 3

Denius incurred *total payroll expense* of $581.25 (gross salary of $468.00 + payroll taxes of $66.45 + benefits of $46.80). See entries (a–c).

Denius *paid cash* of $581.25 on payroll (Kingsley's net pay of $379.08 + payroll taxes of $155.37 + benefits of $46.80). See entries (d) through (f).

Summary of Learning Objectives

1. *Account for current liabilities of known amount.* *Current liabilities* may be divided into those of *known amount* and those that must be *estimated*. Trade accounts payable, short-term notes payable, and the related liability for accrued expenses are current liabilities of known amount.

2. *Account for current liabilities that must be estimated.* Current liabilities that must be estimated include warranties payable and corporations' income tax payable.

3. *Identify and report contingent liabilities.* *Contingent liabilities* are not actual liabilities but potential liabilities that may arise in the future. Contingent liabilities, like current liabilities, may be of known amount or an indefinite amount. A business that faces a lawsuit not yet decided in court has a contingent liability of indefinite amount.

4. *Compute payroll amounts.* *Payroll* accounting handles the expenses and liabilities arising from compensating employees. Employers must withhold income and FICA taxes from employees' pay and send these *employee payroll* taxes to the government. In addition, many employers allow their employees to pay for insurance and union dues and to make gifts to charities through payroll deductions. An employee's net pay is the gross pay less all payroll taxes and optional deductions.

5. *Make basic payroll entries.* An *employer's* payroll expenses include FICA and unemployment taxes, which are separate from the payroll taxes borne by the employees. Also, most employers provide their employees with fringe benefits, such as insurance coverage and retirement pensions.

6. *Use a payroll system.* A *payroll system* consists of a payroll register, a payroll bank account, payroll checks, and an earnings record for each employee. Good *internal controls* over payroll disbursements help the business to conduct payroll accounting efficiently and to safeguard the company's cash. The cornerstone of internal control is the separation of duties.

7. *Report current liabilities on the balance sheet.* The company reports on the balance sheet all current liabilities that it owes: current liabilities of known amount, including payroll liabilities; and current liabilities that must be estimated.

Accounting Vocabulary

accrued expense *(p. 469)*
accrued liability *(p. 469)*
current portion of long-term debt *(p. 468)*
current maturity *(p. 468)*
discounting a note payable *(p. 466)*
employee compensation *(p. 469)*
FICA tax *(p. 478)*
gross pay *(p. 477)*
net pay *(p. 477)*
payroll *(p. 469)*
short presentation *(p. 474)*
short-term note payable *(p. 465)*
Social Security tax *(p. 478)*
unemployment compensation tax *(p. 479)*
withheld income tax *(p. 478)*

Questions

1. Give a more descriptive account title for each of the following current liabilities: Accrued Interest, Accrued Salaries, Accrued Income Tax.
2. What distinguishes a current liability from a long-term liability? What distinguishes a contingent liability from an actual liability?
3. A company purchases a machine by signing a $21,000, one-year, 10% note payable on July 31. Interest is to be paid at maturity. What two current liabilities related to this purchase does the company report on its December 31 balance sheet? What is the amount of each current liability?
4. A company borrowed cash by discounting a $15,000, six-month, 8% note payable to the bank, receiving cash of $14,400. (a) Show how the amount of cash was computed. Also, identify (b) the total amount of interest expense to be recognized on this note and (c) the amount of the borrower's cash payment at maturity.
5. Explain why sales tax that is paid by consumers is a liability of the store that sold the merchandise.
6. What is meant by the term *current portion of long-term debt*, and how is this item reported in the financial statements?
7. At the beginning of the school term, what type of account is the tuition that your college or university collects from students? What type of account is the tuition at the end of the school term?
8. Patton Company warrants its products against defects for three years from date of sale. During the current year, the company made sales of $300,000. Store management estimated that warranty costs on those sales would total $18,000 over the three-year warranty period. Ultimately, the company paid $22,000 cash on warranties. What was the company's warranty expense for the year? What accounting principle governs this answer?
9. Identify two contingent liabilities of a definite amount and two contingent liabilities of an indefinite amount.
10. Describe two ways to report contingent liabilities.
11. Why is payroll expense relatively more important to a service business such as a CPA firm than it is to a merchandising company such as Kmart?
12. Two persons are studying Allen Company's manufacturing process. One person is Allen's factory supervisor, and the other person is an outside consultant who is an expert in the industry. Which person's salary is the payroll expense of Allen Company? Identify the expense account that Allen would debit to record the pay of each person.
13. What are two elements of an employer's payroll expense in addition to salaries, wages, commissions, and overtime pay?
14. What determines the amount of income tax that is withheld from employee paychecks?
15. What are FICA taxes? Who pays them? What are the funds used for?
16. Identify two required deductions and four optional deductions from employee paychecks.
17. Identify three employer payroll taxes.
18. Who pays state and federal unemployment taxes? What are these funds used for?
19. Briefly describe a payroll accounting system's components and their functions.
20. How much Social Security tax has been withheld from the pay of an employee who has earned $72,288 during the current year? How much Social Security tax must the employer pay for this employee?
21. Briefly describe the two principal categories of internal controls over payroll.
22. Why do some companies use two special payroll bank accounts?
23. Identify three internal controls designed to safeguard payroll cash.

Daily Exercises

Accounts payable and notes payable
(Obj. 1)

DE11-1 Describe the similarities and the differences between an account payable and a short-term note payable. If necessary, review notes receivable in Chapter 8.

Accounting for a note payable
(Obj. 1)

DE11-2 Return to the $8,000 purchase of inventory on a short-term note payable that begins on page 465. Assume that the purchase of inventory occurred on April 30, 19X1, instead of September 30, 19X1. Journalize the company's (a) purchase of inventory, (b) accrual of interest expense on December 31, 19X1, and (c) payment of the note plus interest on April 30, 19X2.

Reporting a short-term note payable and the related interest in the financial statements
(Obj. 1)

DE11-3 This exercise should be done in conjunction with Daily Exercise 11-2.

1. Refer to the data in Daily Exercise 11-2. Show what the company would report for the note payable on its balance sheet at December 31, 19X1, and on its income statement for the year ended on that date.
2. What one item will the financial statements for the year ended December 31, 19X2, report? Identify the financial statement, the item, and its amount.

Accounting for a discounted note payable
(Obj. 1)

DE11-4 Accounting for a discounted note payable is illustrated for a $100,000 note at the top of page 466.

1. Why did Procter & Gamble (P&G) sign the note payable? What did P&G receive?
2. Suppose P&G signed the note payable on December 16, 19X1, instead of November 25, 19X1. Make P&G's adjusting entry to accrue interest expense at December 31, 19X1.
3. Show how P&G would report the note payable on its balance sheet at December 31, 19X1.
4. Journalize P&G's interest expense and payment of the note payable at maturity.

Accounting for unearned revenue
(Obj. 1)

DE11-5 The chapter opening story describes the airlines' sale of frequent-flier miles to hotel chains such as Holiday Inn and Marriott. Suppose American Airlines sells 1,000,000 American AAdvantage frequent-flier miles to Marriott for $0.015 per mile. During the next six months, Marriott customers use 200,000 of the American AAdvantage miles for free trips on American Airlines.

1. Using American Airlines' actual account title for the unearned revenue (see Exhibit 11-1, page 464), journalize American's (a) receipt of cash from Marriott, and (b) provision of transportation services for the Marriott customers. American Airlines labels its revenue as Passenger Revenues.
2. Post to the unearned revenue (Air Traffic Liability) T-account. How much does American Airlines owe the Marriott customers after the preceding transactions?

Accounting for warranty expense and estimated warranty payable
(Obj. 2)

DE11-6 Chrysler Corporation, the automaker, warranties its automobiles for three years or 36,000 miles, whichever comes first. Suppose Chrysler's experience indicates that the company can expect warranty costs during the three-year period to add up to 5% of sales.

Assume that Four Corners Dodge in Durango, Colorado made sales of $500,000 during 19X7, its first year of operations. Four Corners Dodge received cash for 30% of the sales and notes receivable for the remainder. Payments to satisfy customer warranty claims totaled $22,000 during 19X7.

1. Record the sales, warranty expense, and warranty payments for Four Corners Dodge. Ignore any reimbursement Four Corners Dodge may receive from Chrysler Corporation.
2. Post to the Estimated Warranty Payable T-account. At the end of 19X7, how much in estimated warranty payable does Four Corners Dodge owe its customers? Why must the warranty payable amount be estimated?

Applying GAAP; reporting warranties in the financial statements
(Obj. 2)

DE11-7 Refer to the data given in Daily Exercise 11-6.

What amount of warranty expense will Four Corners Dodge report during 19X7? Which accounting principle addresses this situation? Does the warranty expense for the year equal the year's cash payments for warranties? Explain how the accounting principle works for measuring warranty expense.

Interpreting a company's contingent liabilities
(Obj. 3)

DE11-8 Harley-Davidson, Inc., the motorcycle manufacturer, included the following note in its annual report:

> *NOTES TO CONSOLIDATED FINANCIAL STATEMENTS*
> *7 (In Part): Commitments And Contingencies*
> The Company self-insures its product liability losses in the United States up to $3 million (catastrophic coverage is maintained for individual claims in excess of $3 million up to $25 million). Outside the United States, the Company is insured for product liability up to $25 million per individual claim and in the aggregate.

1. Why are these *contingent* (versus real) liabilities?
2. In the United States, how can the contingent liability become a real liability for Harley-Davidson? What are the limits to the company's product liabilities in the United States? Explain how these limits work.
3. How can a contingency outside the United States become a real liability for the company? How does Harley-Davidson's potential liability differ for claims outside the United States?

Assessing the importance of payroll expenses **(Obj. 4)**

DE11-9 Consider the operations of a McDonald's restaurant, Ford Motor Company, and a large law firm. Rank these businesses in terms of the percentage of labor cost to the company's total expenses—from most important to least important. Give the reason for your ranking.

Daily Exercise 11-10 begins a sequence of exercises that ends with Daily Exercise 11-12.

Computing an employee's total pay **(Obj. 4)**

DE11-10 Examine the payroll situation of Lucy Childres on page 477.

1. Compute Childres's total pay for working 50 hours during the first week of February.
2. Childres is single, and her income tax withholding is 12% of total pay. Her only payroll deductions are payroll taxes. Compute Childres's net pay for the week. (Use an 8% FICA tax rate.)

Computing total payroll expense of an employer **(Obj. 4)**

DE11-11 Return to the Lucy Childres payroll situation in Daily Exercise 11-10. Childres's employer, MicroAge Computing, pays all the standard payroll taxes plus benefits for employee pensions (10% of total pay), health insurance ($60 per employee per month), and disability insurance ($8 per employee per month).

Compute MicroAge's total expense of employing Lucy Childres for the 50 hours that she worked during the first week of February. Carry amounts to the nearest cent.

Making payroll entries **(Obj. 5)**

DE11-12 After solving Daily Exercises 11-10 and 11-11, journalize for MicroAge Computing the following expenses related to the employment of Lucy Childres:

a. Salary expense
b. Employer payroll taxes
c. Benefits

Use Exhibit 11-6, page 480, to format your journal entries. Carry all amounts to the nearest cent.

Computing payroll amounts late in the year **(Obj. 4)**

DE11-13 Suppose you have worked for an accounting firm all year and you earn a monthly salary of $7,000. Your withheld income taxes consume 15% of your gross pay. In addition to payroll taxes, which are required, you elect to contribute 5% monthly to your pension plan. Your employer also deducts $200 monthly for your co-pay of the health insurance premium.

Compute your net pay for October. Use an 8% FICA tax rate on the first $65,000 of income.

Making basic payroll entries **(Obj. 5)**

DE11-14 Exhibit 11-5, page 480, shows the breakdown of an employer's total payroll cost of $1,180 for one employee. Journalize the employer's (a) salary expense (use a single Payroll Tax Payable account), (b) payroll taxes (use a single Payroll Tax Payable account), and (c) cost of health insurance. Follow the pattern of the entries in Exhibit 11-6, page 480.

Using a payroll system **(Obj. 6)**

DE11-15 Refer to the payroll register in Exhibit 11-7, page 482.

1. How much was the company's total salary expense for the week? What accounts were debited? How much was debited to each account?
2. How much did *employees* pay this week for
   a. Withheld federal income tax?
   b. Withheld FICA tax?
3. How much expense did the *employer* have this week for
   a. Employee federal income tax?
   b. FICA tax?
4. How much cash did the employees take home for their work this week?
5. Which employees earned less than $65,000, and which employees earned more than $65,000 this year? How can you tell?

Using a payroll system to compute total payroll expense **(Obj. 6)**

DE11-16 Study the Employee Earnings Record for R. C. Dean in Exhibit 11-10, page 486. In addition to the amounts shown in the exhibit, the employer also paid all payroll taxes plus (a) an amount equal to 6% of gross pay into Dean's pension retirement account, and (b) health insurance for Dean at a cost of $110 per month.

Compute the employer's total payroll expense for employee R. C. Dean during 19X7. Carry all amounts to the nearest cent.

Internal controls over payroll disbursements
(Obj. 6)

DE11-17 ◄ *Link Back to Chapter 7 (Internal Controls).*

1. Explain how the use of two payroll bank accounts (one account the first month, the other account the next month) makes accounting for the payroll of a large company more efficient. Identify another control for efficiency in the payroll area.
2. What are some of the important elements of good internal control to safeguard payroll disbursements?

Reporting current and contingent liabilities
(Obj. 7)

DE11-18 Study the payroll register of Blumenthal's in Exhibit 11-7, page 482. Assume Blumenthal's will pay this payroll on January 2, 19X8. In addition to the payroll liabilities shown in the exhibit, Blumenthal's has the following liabilities at December 31, 19X7:

Accounts payable	$38,140	Current portion of long-term debt	$10,000
Employer FICA tax payable	862	Interest payable	1,116
Long-term debt	80,000	Contingent liabilities	—
Unearned revenue	4,430		

Prepare the current liabilities section of Blumenthal's balance sheet at December 31, 19X7. List current liabilities in descending order starting with the largest first. Also list each of the payroll liabilties from Exhibit 11-7, rounded to the nearest dollar. Show the total of current liabilities. Report the contingent liabilities "short" on the balance sheet.

Interpreting the current liabilities of a company
(Obj. 7)

DE11-19 Refer to AMR Corporation's current liabilities in Exhibit 11-1, page 464.

1. Explain in your own words each of the company's current liabilities.
2. When will AMR pay these liabilities? When is the latest date that AMR will pay the liabilities? How can you tell?

Exercises

Recording sales tax two ways
(Obj. 1)

E11-1 Make general journal entries to record the following transactions of Delta Resorts Company for a two-month period. Explanations are not required.

March 31	Recorded cash sales of $100,000 for the month, plus sales tax of 5% collected on behalf of the state of Idaho. Recorded sales tax in a separate account.
April 6	Sent March sales tax to the state.

Journalize these transactions a second time. Record the sales tax initially in the Sales Revenue account.

Accounting for warranty expense and the related liability
(Obj. 2)

E11-2 The accounting records of Nicor Steel Company included the following balances at the end of the period:

Estimated Warranty Payable		Sales Revenue		Warranty Expense	
	Beg. bal. 3,100		161,000		

In the past, Nicor's warranty expense has been 5% of sales. During the current period, the business paid $10,400 to satisfy the warranty claims of customers.

REQUIRED

1. Record Nicor's warranty expense for the period and the company's cash payments during the period to satisfy warranty claims. Explanations are not required.
2. What ending balance of Estimated Warranty Payable will Nicor report on its balance sheet?

Recording note payable transactions
(Obj. 1)

E11-3 Record the following note payable transactions of Vanderbilt, Inc., in the company's general journal. Explanations are not required.

19X2	
Apr. 1	Purchased equipment costing $10,000 by issuing a one-year, 8% note payable.
Dec. 31	Accrued interest on the note payable.
19X3	
Apr. 1	Paid the note payable at maturity.

Discounting a note payable
(Obj. 1)

E11-4 On September 1, 19X4, Milwaukee Signal Company discounted a six-month, $12,000 note payable to the bank at 7 percent.

REQUIRED

1. Prepare general journal entries to record (a) issuance of the note, (b) accrual of interest at December 31, and (c) payment of the note at maturity in 19X5. Explanations are not required.
2. Show how Milwaukee would report the note on the December 31, 19X4, balance sheet.

E11-5 Carnegie Fire Prevention is a defendant in lawsuits brought against the marketing and distribution of its products. Damages of $2.4 million are claimed against Carnegie, but the company denies the charges and is vigorously defending itself. In a recent press conference, the president of the company said management does not believe that any actual liabilities resulting from the lawsuits will significantly affect the company's financial position.

Reporting a contingent liability **(Obj. 3)**

REQUIRED

Prepare a partial balance sheet to show how Carnegie Fire Prevention would report this contingent liability in a short presentation. Total actual liabilities are $6.3 million. Also, write the disclosure note to describe the contingency.

E11-6 Refer to the Carnegie Fire Prevention situation in Exercise 11-5. Suppose Carnegie's attorneys believe it is probable that a judgment of $1.6 million will be rendered against the company.

Accruing a contingency **(Obj. 3)**

REQUIRED

Describe how to report this situation in the Carnegie Fire Prevention financial statements. Journalize any entry required under GAAP. Explanations are not required.

E11-7 *Link Back to Chapter 4 (Current Ratio).* The top management of UAW Carbide examines the following company accounting records at December 29, immediately before the end of the year:

Reporting current liabilities **(Obj. 7)**

Total current assets................	$ 480,000
Noncurrent assets	730,000
	$1,210,000
Total current liabilities..........	$ 250,000
Noncurrent liabilities............	300,000
Owners' equity......................	660,000
	$1,210,000

UAW's borrowing agreements with creditors require the company to keep a current ratio of 2.0 or better. How much in current liabilities should UAW pay off within the next two days in order to comply with its borrowing agreements?

E11-8 Bill Kosub is manager of the men's department of Filene's Department Store in Boston. He earns a base monthly salary of $750 plus an 8% commission on his personal sales. Through payroll deductions, Kosub donates $25 per month to a charitable organization, and he authorizes Filene's to deduct $22.50 monthly for his family's health insurance. Tax rates on Kosub's earnings are 10% for income tax and 8% of the first $65,000 for FICA subject to the maximum. During the first 11 months of the year, he earned $62,140. Compute Kosub's gross pay and net pay for December, assuming his sales for the month are $80,000.

Computing net pay **(Obj. 4)**

E11-9 Karen O'Conner works for a 7-Eleven store for straight-time earnings of $6 per hour, with time-and-a-half compensation for hours in excess of 40 per week. O'Conner's payroll deductions include withheld income tax of 7% of total earnings, FICA tax of 8% of total earnings, and a weekly deduction of $5 for a charitable contribution to United Fund. Assuming she worked 48 hours during the week, (a) compute her gross pay and net pay for the week, and (b) make a general journal entry to record the store's wage expense for O'Conner's work, including her payroll deductions. Explanations are not required. Round all amounts to the nearest cent.

Computing and recording gross pay and net pay **(Obj. 4, 5)**

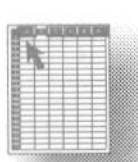

E11-10 Federated Retailers incurred salary expense of $92,000 for December. The store's payroll expense includes employer FICA tax of 8% in addition to state unemployment tax of 5.4% and federal unemployment tax of 0.8%. Of the total salaries, $88,400 is subject to FICA tax, and $9,100 is subject to unemployment tax. Also, the store provides the following benefits for employees: health insurance (cost to the store, $2,062.15), life insurance (cost to the store, $351.07), and pension benefits (cost to the store, 5% of salary expense). Record Federated's payroll taxes and its expenses for employee benefits. Explanations are not required.

Recording a payroll **(Obj. 4, 5)**

E11-11 Suppose Union Planters Cotton Co-Op borrowed $4,000,000 on December 31, 19X0, by issuing 9% long-term debt that must be paid in four equal annual installments plus interest each January 2. Insert the appropriate amounts to show how Union Planters Co-Op would report its long-term debt.

Reporting current and long-term liabilities **(Obj. 7)**

	December 31,			
	19X1	19X2	19X3	19X4
Current liabilities:				
Current portion of long-term debt.............	$____	$____	$____	$____
Interest payable	____	____	____	____
Long-term liabilities:				
Long-term debt..	____	____	____	____

Reporting current and long-term liabilities
(Obj. 7)

E11-12 Assume that Wilson Sporting Goods completed these selected transactions during December 19X6:

a. Champs, a chain of sporting goods stores, ordered $15,000 of tennis and golf equipment. With its order, Champs sent a check for $15,000 in advance. Wilson will ship the goods on January 3, 19X7.

b. The December payroll of $195,000 is subject to employee withheld income tax of 9%, FICA tax of 8% (employee and employer), state unemployment tax of 5.4%, and federal unemployment tax of 0.8 percent. On December 31, Wilson pays employees but accrues all tax amounts.

c. Sales of $1,000,000 are subject to estimated warranty cost of 1.4 percent.

d. On December 1, Wilson signed a $100,000 note payable that requires annual payments of $20,000 plus 9% interest on the unpaid balance each December 1.

REQUIRED

Classify each liability as current or long-term, and report the amount that would appear for each item on Wilson's balance sheet at December 31, 19X6. Show total current liabilities.

CHALLENGE EXERCISES

Accounting for and reporting current liabilities
(Obj. 1, 7)

E11-13 *Link Back to Chapter 4 (Current Ratio).* The balance sheets of PepsiCo, Inc., for two years reported these figures:

	Billions	
	19X2	**19X1**
Total current assets................	$ 4.6	$ 4.1
Noncurrent assets	14.2	13.0
	$18.8	$17.1
Total current liabilities..........	$ 3.7	$ 4.8
Noncurrent liabilities...........	9.5	7.4
Stockholders' equity.............	5.6	4.9
	$18.8	$17.1

During 19X2, PepsiCo reclassified $3.4 billion of current liabilities as long-term.

REQUIRED

1. Compute PepsiCo's current ratio as reported at the end of each year. Describe the trend that you observe.
2. Assume that PepsiCo had not reclassified $3.4 billion of current liabilities as long-term during 19X2. Recompute the current ratio at the end of 19X2. Why do you think PepsiCo reclassified the liabilities as long-term?

Analyzing current liability accounts
(Obj. 1, 7)

E11-14 PepsiCo, Inc., reported short-term debt payable and salary payable (adapted, in millions), as follows:

	December 31,	
	19X2	**19X1**
Current liabilities (partial):		
Short-term debt payable	$707	$228
Salary payable................................	327	334

Assume that during 19X2, PepsiCo borrowed $1,237 million on short-term debt. Also assume that PepsiCo paid $4,100 million for salaries during 19X2.

REQUIRED

1. Compute PepsiCo's payment of short-term debt during 19X2.
2. Compute PepsiCo's salary expense during 19X2.

Beyond the Numbers

BN11-1 The Boeing Company, manufacturer of jet aircraft, is the defendant in numerous lawsuits claiming unfair trade practices. Boeing has strong incentives not to disclose these contingent liabilities. However, GAAP requires that companies report their contingent liabilities.

REQUIRED

1. Why would a company prefer not to disclose its contingent liabilities?
2. Describe how a bank could be harmed if a company seeking a loan did not disclose its contingent liabilities?
3. What is the ethical tightrope that companies must walk when they report their contingent liabilities?

BN11-2 The following questions are not related.

Unearned revenues, warranties, and contingent liabilities (Obj. 1, 2, 3)

1. A friend comments that he thought liabilities represented amounts owed by a company. He asks why unearned revenues are shown as a current liability. How would you respond?
2. A warranty is like a contingent liability in that the amount to be paid is not known at year end. Why are warranties payable shown as a current liability, while contingent liabilities are reported in the notes to the financial statements?
3. Auditors have procedures for determining whether they have discovered all of a company's contingent liabilities. These procedures differ from the procedures used for determining that accounts payable are stated correctly. How would an auditor identify a client's contingent liabilities?

ETHICAL ISSUE

Ling-Temco-Vought, Inc. (LTV), manufacturer of aircraft and aircraft-related electronic devices, borrowed heavily during the 1970s to exploit the advantage of financing operations with debt. At first, LTV was able to earn operating income much higher than its interest expense and was therefore quite profitable. However, when the business cycle turned down, LTV's debt burden pushed the company to the brink of bankruptcy. Operating income was less than interest expense.

REQUIRED

Is it unethical for managers to saddle a company with a high level of debt? Or is it just risky? Who could be hurt by a company's taking on too much debt? Discuss.

Problems (GROUP A)

P11-1A The following transactions of TransAmerica Electric occurred during 19X2 and 19X3.

Journalizing liability-related transactions (Obj. 1, 2)

19X2	
Feb. 3	Purchased equipment for $10,200, signing a six-month, 8% note payable.
28	Recorded the week's sales of $51,000, one-third for cash, and two-thirds on credit. All sales amounts are subject to a 5% state sales tax.
Mar. 7	Sent the last week's sales tax to the state.
Apr. 30	Borrowed $100,000 on a four-year, 9% note payable that calls for annual installment payments of $25,000 principal plus interest.
Aug. 3	Paid the six-month, 8% note at maturity.
Sep. 14	Discounted a $6,000, 60-day, 7% note payable to the bank, receiving cash for the net amount after interest was deducted from the note's maturity value.
Nov. 13	Recorded interest on the 7% discounted note and paid off the note at maturity.
30	Purchased inventory at a cost of $7,200, signing a three-month, 9% note payable for that amount.
Dec. 31	Accrued warranty expense, which is estimated at 3% of sales of $145,000.
31	Accrued interest on all outstanding notes payable. Made a separate interest accrual entry for each note payable.
19X3	
Feb. 28	Paid off the 9% inventory note, plus interest, at maturity.
Apr. 30	Paid the first installment and interest for one year on the long-term note payable.

REQUIRED

Record the transactions in the company's general journal. Explanations are not required.

P11-2A Kristy Arabian Farm provides riding lessons for girls ages 8 through 15. Most students are beginners, and none of the girls owns her own horse. K. K. Kristy, the owner of the farm, uses horses stabled at her farm and owned by the Kultgens. Most of the horses are for sale, but the economy has been bad for several years and horse sales have been slow. The Kultgens are happy that Kristy uses their horses in exchange for rooming and boarding them. Because of a recent financial setback, Kristy cannot afford insurance. She seeks your advice about her business's exposure to liabilities.

Identifying contingent liabilities (Obj. 3)

REQUIRED

Write a memorandum to inform Kristy of specific contingent liabilities arising from the business. It will be necessary to define a contingent liability because she is a professional horse trainer, not a businessperson. Propose a way for Kristy to limit her exposure to these liabilities.

P11-3A The partial monthly records of Pfizer Food Company show the following figures:

Computing and recording payroll amounts (Obj. 4, 5)

Employee Earnings	
(a) Straight-time earnings................	$?
(b) Overtime pay..............................	5,109
(c) Total employee earnings	?

Deductions and Net Pay	
(d) Withheld income tax	$ 9,293
(e) FICA tax	6,052
(f) Charitable contributions	?
(g) Medical insurance	1,373
(h) Total deductions	17,603
(i) Net pay	64,813
Accounts Debited	
(j) Salary Expense	$31,278
(k) Wage Expense	?
(l) Sales Commission Expense	27,931

REQUIRED

1. Determine the missing amounts on lines (a), (c), (f), and (k).
2. Prepare the general journal entry to record Pfizer's payroll for the month. Credit Payrolls Payable for net pay. No explanation is required.

Computing and recording payroll amounts
(Obj. 4, 5)

P11-4A Mary Cheney is a commercial lender at Swiss Credit Bank in New York City. During 19X2, she worked for the bank all year at a $5,195 monthly salary. She also earned a year-end bonus equal to 12% of her annual salary.

Cheney's federal income tax withheld during 19X2 was $822 per month. Also, there was a one-time withholding of $2,487 on her bonus check. State income tax withheld came to $61 per month, and the city of New York withheld income tax of $21 per month. In addition, Cheney paid one-time withholdings of $64 (state) and $19 (city) on the bonus. The FICA tax withheld was 8% of the first $65,000 in annual earnings. Cheney authorized the following payroll deductions: United Fund contribution of 1% of total earnings and life insurance of $17 per month.

Swiss Credit Bank incurred payroll tax expense on Cheney for FICA tax of 8% of the first $65,000 in annual earnings. The bank also paid state unemployment tax of 5.4% and federal unemployment tax of 0.8% on the first $7,000 in annual earnings. The bank provided Cheney with the following benefits: health insurance at a cost of $48 per month, and pension benefits to be paid to Cheney during her retirement. During 19X2, Swiss Credit Bank's cost of Cheney's pension program was $4,083.

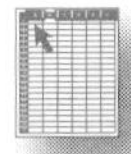

REQUIRED

1. Compute Cheney's gross pay, payroll deductions, and net pay for the full year of 19X2. Round all amounts to the nearest dollar.
2. Compute Swiss Credit Bank's total 19X2 payroll cost for Cheney.
3. Prepare Swiss Credit Bank's summary general journal entries to record its expense for the following:
   a. Cheney's total earnings for the year, her payroll deductions, and her net pay. Debit Salary Expense and Executive Bonus Compensation as appropriate. Credit liability accounts for the payroll deductions and Cash for net pay.
   b. Employer payroll taxes for Cheney. Credit liability accounts.
   c. Benefits provided to Cheney. Credit a liability account.

   Explanations are not required.

Journalizing, posting, and reporting liabilities
(Obj. 1, 2, 3, 4, 5, 7)

P11-5A The Comerica Financial Services general ledger at September 30, 19X7, the end of the company's fiscal year, includes the following account balances before adjusting entries. Parentheses indicate a debit balance.

Note Payable, Short-Term	$ 21,000
Discount on Notes Payable	(1,680)
Accounts Payable	88,240
Current Portion of Long-Term Debt Payable	______
Interest Payable	______
Salary Payable	______
Employee Payroll Taxes Payable	______
Employer Payroll Taxes Payable	______
Estimated Vacation Pay Liability	2,105
Unearned Rent Revenue	3,900
Long-Term Debt Payable	100,000
Contingent Liabilities	______

The additional data needed to develop the adjusting entries at September 30 are as follows:

a. The $21,000 short-term note payable was issued on August 31, matures one year from date of issuance, and was discounted at 8 percent.

b. The long-term debt is payable in annual installments of $50,000, with the next installment due on January 31, 19X8. On that date, Comerica Financial will also pay one year's interest at 6.6 percent. Interest was last paid on January 31. (Make the adjusting entry to shift the current installment of the long-term debt to a current liability.)
c. Gross salaries for the last payroll of the fiscal year were $4,319. Of this amount, employee payroll taxes payable were $958, and salary payable was $3,361.
d. Employer payroll taxes payable were $755.
e. Comerica estimates that vacation pay is 4% of gross salaries.
f. On August 1, the company collected six months' rent of $3,900 in advance.
g. At September 30, Comerica is the defendant in a $500,000 lawsuit, which the company hopes to win. However, the outcome is uncertain. Report this contingent liability "short" on the balance sheet, and write the note to give more details.

REQUIRED

1. Open the listed accounts, inserting their unadjusted September 30 balances.
2. Journalize and post the September 30 adjusting entries to the accounts opened. Key adjusting entries by letter.
3. Prepare the liability section of Comerica Financial's balance sheet at September 30. Show total current liabilities.

Using payroll register, recording a payroll
(Obj. 6)

P11-6A Assume that payroll records of a district sales office of Comp USA provided the following information for the weekly pay period ended December 26, 19X3:

Employee	Hours Worked	Weekly Earnings Rate	Federal Income Tax	Health Insurance	United Way Contribution	Earnings through Previous Week
Mel Black	43	$ 400	$ 94	$ 9	$ 7	$17,060
Leroy Dixon	46	480	121	5	5	22,365
Karol Stastny	47	1,200	319	16	30	64,247
Lisa Trent	40	240	32	4	2	3,413

Black and Trent work in the office, and Dixon and Stastny work in sales. All employees are paid time and a half for hours worked in excess of 40 per week. For convenience, round all amounts to the nearest dollar. Show your computations. Explanations are not required for journal entries.

REQUIRED

1. Enter the appropriate information in a payroll register similar to Exhibit 11-7. In addition to the deductions listed, the employer also takes out FICA tax: 8% of the first $65,000 of each employee's annual earnings.
2. Record the payroll information in the general journal.
3. Assume that the first payroll check is number 178, paid to Black. Record the check numbers in the payroll register. Also, prepare the general journal entry to record payment of net pay to the employees.
4. The employer's payroll taxes include FICA of 8% of the first $65,000 of each employee's annual earnings. The employer also pays unemployment taxes of 6.2% (5.4% for the state and 0.8% for the federal government) on the first $7,000 of each employee's annual earnings. Record the employer's payroll taxes in the general journal.

Reporting current liabilities
(Obj. 7)

P11-7A Following are pertinent facts about events during the current year at Osaka Engine Company:

a. On August 31, Osaka signed a six-month, 6% note payable to purchase a machine costing $50,000. The note requires payment of principal and interest at maturity.
b. Sales of $909,000 were covered by Osaka's product warranty. At January 1, estimated warranty payable was $11,300. During the year, Osaka recorded warranty expense of $27,900 and paid warranty claims of $30,100.
c. On October 31, Osaka received rent of $2,400 in advance for a lease on a building. This rent will be earned evenly over four months.
d. On November 30, Osaka discounted a $10,000 note payable to InterBank Savings. The interest rate on the one-year note is 8 percent.
e. December sales totaled $104,000 and Osaka collected sales tax of 9 percent. The sales tax will be sent to the state of Washington early in January.
f. Osaka owes $75,000 on a long-term note payable. At December 31, 6% interest for the year plus $25,000 of this principal are payable within one year.

REQUIRED

For each item, indicate the account and the related amount to be reported as a current liability on Osaka's December 31 balance sheet.

Problems (GROUP B)

Journalizing liability-related transactions
(Obj. 1, 2)

P11-1B The following transactions of UniSys Medical Products occurred during 19X4 and 19X5:

19X4	
Jan. 9	Purchased equipment at a cost of $20,000, signing a six-month, 8% note payable for that amount.
29	Recorded the week's sales of $22,200, three-fourths on credit, and one-fourth for cash. Sales amounts are subject to an additional 6% state sales tax.
Feb. 5	Sent the last week's sales tax to the state.
28	Borrowed $200,000 on a four-year, 9% note payable that calls for annual installment payments of $50,000 principal plus interest.
July 9	Paid the six-month, 8% note at maturity.
Oct. 22	Discounted a $5,000, 90-day, 7% note payable to the bank, receiving cash for the net amount after interest was deducted from the note's maturity value.
Nov. 30	Purchased inventory for $3,100, signing a six-month, 10% note payable.
Dec. 31	Accrued warranty expense, which is estimated at 3% of sales of $650,000.
31	Accrued interest on all outstanding notes payable. Made a separate interest accrual entry for each note payable.
19X5	
Jan. 20	Paid off the 7% discounted note payable. Made a separate entry for the interest.
Feb. 28	Paid the first installment and interest for one year on the long-term note payable.
May 31	Paid off the 10% note plus interest on maturity.

REQUIRED

Record the transactions in the company's general journal. Explanations are not required.

Identifying contingent liabilities
(Obj. 3)

P11-2B Crossroads Nissan is one of the largest Nissan dealers in the southwestern United States. The dealership sells new and used cars and operates a body shop and a service department. Roger Beech, the general manager, is considering changing insurance companies because of a disagreement with Doug Stillwell, agent for the Travelers Insurance Company. Travelers is doubling Crossroads' liability insurance cost for the next year. In discussing insurance coverage with you, a trusted business associate, Stillwell brings up the subject of contingent liabilities.

REQUIRED

Write a memorandum to inform Crossroads Nissan of specific contingent liabilities arising from the business. In your discussion, define a contingent liability.

Computing and recording payroll amounts
(Obj. 4, 5)

P11-3B The partial monthly records of Gillette Boat Company show the following figures:

Employee Earnings	
(a) Straight-time earnings	$16,431
(b) Overtime pay	?
(c) Total employee earnings	?
Deductions and Net Pay	
(d) Withheld income tax	$ 2,403
(e) FICA tax	?
(f) Charitable contributions	340
(g) Medical insurance	668
(h) Total deductions	5,409
(i) Net pay	17,936
Accounts Debited	
(j) Salary Expense	$?
(k) Wage Expense	8,573
(l) Sales Commission Expense	2,077

REQUIRED

1. Determine the missing amounts on lines (b), (c), (e), and (j).
2. Prepare the general journal entry to record Gillette's payroll for the month. Credit Payrolls Payable for net pay. No explanation is required.

Computing and recording payroll amounts
(Obj. 4, 5)

P11-4B Natacha St. Hill is a vice president of Wells Fargo Bank's leasing operations in San Francisco. During 19X6, she worked for the company all year at a $5,625 monthly salary. She also earned a year-end bonus equal to 10% of her salary.

St. Hill's federal income tax withheld during 19X6 was $737 per month. Also, there was a one-time federal withholding tax of $1,007 on her bonus check. State income tax withheld came to $43 per month, and there was a one-time state withholding tax of $27 on the bonus. The FICA tax withheld was 8.0% of the first $65,000 in annual earnings. St. Hill authorized the following payroll deductions: United Fund contribution of 1% of total earnings and life insurance of $19 per month.

Wells Fargo Bank incurred payroll tax expense on St. Hill for FICA tax of 8% of the first $65,000 in annual earnings. The bank also paid state unemployment tax of 5.4% and federal unemployment tax of 0.8% on the first $7,000 in annual earnings. In addition, the bank provides St. Hill with health insurance at a cost of $35 per month and pension benefits. During 19X6, Wells Fargo Bank paid $7,178 into St. Hill's pension program.

REQUIRED

1. Compute St. Hill's gross pay, payroll deductions, and net pay for the full year 19X6. Round all amounts to the nearest dollar.
2. Compute Wells Fargo Bank's total 19X6 payroll cost for St. Hill.
3. Prepare Wells Fargo Bank's summary general journal entries to record its expense for the following:
   a. St. Hill's total earnings for the year, her payroll deductions, and her net pay. Debit Salary Expense and Executive Bonus Compensation as appropriate. Credit liability accounts for the payroll deductions and Cash for net pay.
   b. Employer payroll taxes on St. Hill. Credit liability accounts.
   c. Benefits provided to St. Hill. Credit a liability account. Explanations are not required.

Journalizing, posting, and reporting liabilities
(Obj. 1, 2, 3, 4, 5, 7)

P11-5B The general ledger of Inland Bankshares at June 30, 19X3, the end of the company's fiscal year, includes the following account balances before adjusting entries. Parentheses indicate a debit balance.

Account	Balance
Notes Payable, Short-Term	$ 15,000
Discount on Notes Payable	(600)
Accounts Payable	105,520
Current Portion of Long-Term Debt Payable	
Interest Payable	
Salary Payable	
Employee Payroll Taxes Payable	
Employer Payroll Taxes Payable	
Estimated Vacation Pay Liability	7,620
Unearned Rent Revenue	6,000
Long-Term Debt Payable	120,000
Contingent Liabilities	

The additional data needed to develop the adjusting entries at June 30 are as follows:

a. The $15,000 short-term note payable was issued on January 31. It matures six months from date of issuance and was discounted at 8 percent.
b. The long-term debt is payable in annual installments of $40,000 with the next installment due on July 31. On that date, Inland will also pay one year's interest at 7 percent. Interest was last paid on July 31 of the preceding year. (Make the adjusting entry to shift the current installment of the long-term debt to a current liability.)
c. Gross salaries for the last payroll of the fiscal year were $5,044. Of this amount, employee payroll taxes payable were $1,088, and salary payable was $3,956.
d. Employer payroll taxes payable were $876.
e. Inland estimates that vacation pay expense is 4% of gross salaries.
f. On February 1, the company collected one year's rent of $6,000 in advance.
g. At June 30, Inland is the defendant in a $300,000 lawsuit, which the company hopes to win. However, the outcome is uncertain. Report this contingent liability in the appropriate manner.

REQUIRED

1. Open the listed accounts, inserting their unadjusted June 30 balances.
2. Journalize and post the June 30 adjusting entries to the accounts opened. Key adjusting entries by letter.
3. Prepare the liability section of the balance sheet at June 30.

Using a payroll register, recording a payroll
(Obj. 6)

P11-6B Assume that the payroll records of a district sales office of Pinnacle Golf Corporation provided the following information for the weekly pay period ended December 21, 19X5:

Employee	Hours Worked	Hourly Earnings Rate	Federal Income Tax	Union Dues	United Way Contributions	Earnings through Previous Week
Morgan Gray	42	$28	$278	$6	$35	$67,474
James English	47	8	56	4	4	23,154
Louise French	40	11	72	—	4	4,880
Roberto Garza	41	22	188	6	8	64,600

Gray and Garza are salesmen. English and French work in the office. All employees are paid time and a half for hours worked in excess of 40 per week. For convenience, round all amounts to the nearest dollar. Show your computations. Explanations are not required for journal entries.

REQUIRED

1. Enter the appropriate information in a payroll register similar to Exhibit 11-7. In addition to the deductions listed, the employer also takes out FICA tax: 8% of the first $65,000 of each employee's annual earnings.
2. Record the payroll information in the general journal.
3. Assume that the first payroll check is number 319, paid to Morgan Gray. Record the check numbers in the payroll register. Also, prepare the general journal entry to record payment of net pay to the employees.
4. The employer's payroll taxes include FICA tax of 8% of the first $65,000 of each employee's earnings. The employer also pays unemployment taxes of 6.2% (5.4% for the state and 0.8% for the federal government on the first $7,000 of each employee's annual earnings). Record the employer's payroll taxes in the general journal.

Reporting current liabilities ***(Obj. 7)***

P11-7B Following are pertinent facts about events during the current year at Adaptec, Inc.:

a. Sales of $430,000 were covered by Adaptec's product warranty. At January 1, estimated warranty payable was $8,100. During the year, Adaptec recorded warranty expense of $22,300 and paid warranty claims of $23,600.
b. On September 30, Adaptec signed a six-month, 9% note payable to purchase equipment costing $30,000. The note requires payment of principal and interest at maturity.
c. On September 30, Adaptec discounted a $50,000 note payable to Lake Air National Bank. The interest rate on the one-year note is 8 percent.
d. On November 30, Adaptec received rent of $5,100 in advance for a lease on a building. This rent will be earned evenly over three months.
e. December sales totaled $38,000, and Adaptec collected an additional state sales tax of 7 percent. This amount will be sent to the state of Arizona early in January.
f. Adaptec owes $100,000 on a long-term note payable. At December 31, 6% interest since July 31 and $20,000 of this principal are payable within one year.

REQUIRED

For each item, indicate the account and the related amount to be reported as a current liability on Adaptec's December 31 balance sheet.

Applying Your Knowledge

DECISION CASE

Identifying internal control weaknesses and their solution ***(Obj. 6)***

Capital City Homebuilders is a construction company in Frankfort, Kentucky. The owner and manager, Jonathan Echols, oversees all company operations. He employs 15 work crews, each made up of six to ten members. Construction supervisors, who report directly to Echols, lead the crews. Most supervisors are longtime employees, so Echols trusts them. Echols's office staff consists of an accountant and an office manager.

Because employee turnover is high in the construction industry, supervisors hire and fire their own crew members. Supervisors notify the office of all personnel changes. Also, supervisors forward to the office the employee W-4 forms, which the crew members fill out. Each Thursday, the supervisors submit weekly time sheets for their crews, and the accountant prepares the payroll. At noon on Friday, the supervisors come to the office to get paychecks for distribution to the workers at 5 P.M.

Capital City's accountant prepares the payroll, including the payroll checks, which are written on a single payroll bank account. Echols signs all payroll checks after matching the employee name to the time sheets submitted by the foremen. Often the construction workers wait several days to cash their paychecks. To verify that each construction worker is a bona fide employee, the accountant matches the employee's endorsement signature on the back of the canceled payroll check with the signature on that employee's W-4 form.

REQUIRED

1. Identify one *efficiency* weakness in Capital City's payroll accounting system. How can the business correct this weakness?
2. Identify one way that a supervisor can defraud Capital City Homebuilders under the present system.
3. Discuss a control feature that Capital City Homebuilders can use to *safeguard* against the fraud you identified in requirement 2.

FINANCIAL STATEMENT CASES

Current and contingent liabilities
(Obj. 1, 2, 3)

CASE 1. Details about a company's current and contingent liabilities appear in a number of places in the annual report. Use NIKE's financial statements to answer the following questions.

REQUIRED

1. Give the breakdown of NIKE's current liabilities at May 31, 1997. Give the June 1997 entry to record the payment of accounts payable that NIKE owed at May 31, 1997.
2. How much was NIKE's long-term debt at May 31, 1997? Of this amount, how much was due within one year? How much was payable beyond one year in the future?
3. The balance sheet lists a $53,923 thousand liability for "Income Taxes Payable." Was income tax expense for the year, as reported on the income statement, equal to, less than, or greater than this amount? Why is one amount greater than the other?
4. In what two places does NIKE report contingent liabilities? Start with the balance sheet. What events caused NIKE's contingent liabilities?

Current and contingent liabilities and payroll
(Obj. 1, 2, 3)

CASE 2. Obtain the annual report of a company of your choosing. Details about the company's current and contingent liabilities and payroll costs may appear in a number of places in the annual report. Use the statements of the company you select to answer the following questions. Concentrate on the current year in the annual report.

REQUIRED

1. Give the breakdown of the company's current liabilities at the end of the current year. Journalize the payment in the following year of Accounts Payable reported on the balance sheet.
2. How much of the company's long-term debt at the end of the current year was reported as a current liability? Do the notes to the financial statements identify the specific items of long-term debt coming due within the next year? If so, identify the specific liabilities.
3. Identify the current liability for income tax at the end of the current year. Give its amount, and record its payment in the next year.
4. Does the company report any unearned revenue? If so, identify the item and give its amount.
5. Where does the company report contingent liabilities—on the face of the balance sheet or in a note? Give important details about the company's contingent liabilities at the end of the current year.

Team Projects

PROJECT 1. In recent years, the airline industry has dominated headlines as airline companies have adjusted to government deregulation of fares and routes. Fare wars, bankruptcies, and new "no-frills" carriers are signs of an industry fighting to survive. Many airlines cannot fill the planes they own. Fierce competition has resulted in bargain fares that fail to cover the airlines' operating costs. And the government has repeatedly raised fuel and excise taxes.

To date, the consumer has been the big winner. As competing airlines lower fares to fill seats, consumers have learned to shop around for the lowest rates. The carriers have also lured customers with frequent-flyer programs, which award free flights to passengers who accumulate specified miles of travel. Some years ago, the business community (and the accounting profession) recognized that unredeemed frequent-flyer mileage represents a liability that airlines must include on their balance sheets.

Industry executives believe that to succeed, airlines must reduce operating costs and offer various levels of service at different prices—just as the hotel chains do.

Southwest Airlines, a profitable, no-frills carrier based in Dallas, has been a notable exception to this industry's ills. Southwest controls costs by flying to smaller, less expensive airports; using only one model of aircraft; serving no meals; increasing staff efficiency; and having a shorter aircraft turnaround time on the ground between flights. The fact that most of the cities served by Southwest have predictable weather maximizes its on-time arrival record.

Industry executives predict that, in the long run, the weaker airlines will go out of business. The supply of passenger seats will adjust to match consumer demand better. The resulting decrease in competition will put an end to the bargain fares.

With a partner or group, lead your class in a discussion of the following questions, or write a report as directed by your instructor.

REQUIRED

1. Many of the aircraft purchased by airlines in the "booming" 1980s now sit idle. When purchased, the aircraft represented major amounts of depreciable assets for those companies. What accounting considerations arise when a company is strapped with significant amounts of nonproductive equipment? How might an airline achieve more flexibility in the number of aircraft in service?

2. Frequent-flyer programs have grown into significant obligations for airlines. Why should a liability be recorded for those programs? Discuss how you might calculate the amount of this liability. Can you think of other industries that offer similar incentives that create a liability?
3. One of Southwest Airlines' strategies for success is shortening stops at airport gates between flights. The company's chairman has stated, "What [you] produce is lower fares for the customers because you generate more revenue from the same fixed cost in that airplane." Look up fixed cost in the index of this book. What is the "fixed cost" of an airplane? How can better utilization of assets improve a company's profits?

PROJECT 2. Consider three different businesses:

a. A bank
b. A magazine publisher
c. A department store

For each business, list all of its liabilities—both current and long-term. If necessary, study Chapter 15 on long-term liabilities. Then compare the three lists to identify what liabilities the three businesses have in common. Also identify the liabilities that are unique to each type of business.

Comprehensive Problems for Part Two

COMPARING TWO BUSINESSES

Suppose you created a software package that is now being sold worldwide. You recently sold the business to a large company. Now you are ready to invest in a small resort property. Several locations look promising: Jekyll Island, Georgia; Bar Harbor, Maine; and Palm Springs, California. Each place has its appeal, but Jekyll Island wins out. The main allure is that prices there are low, so a dollar will stretch further. Two small resorts are available. The property owners provide the following data:

	Island Resorts	Ocean Hideaway
Cash	$ 34,100	$ 63,800
Accounts receivable	20,500	18,300
Inventory	74,200	68,400
Land	270,600	669,200
Buildings	1,800,000	1,960,000
Accumulated depreciation—buildings	(105,000)	(822,600)
Furniture and fixtures	750,000	933,000
Accumulated depreciation—furniture and fixtures	(225,000)	(535,300)
Total assets	$2,619,400	$2,354,800
Total liabilities	$1,124,300	$1,008,500
Owners' equity	1,495,100	1,346,300
Total liabilities and owners' equity	$2,619,400	$2,354,800

Income statements for the last three years report total net income of $531,000 for Island Resorts and $283,000 for Ocean Hideaway.

INVENTORIES Island Resorts uses the FIFO inventory method, and Ocean Hideaway uses the LIFO method. If Island Resorts had used LIFO, its reported inventory would have been $7,000 lower. If Ocean Hideaway had used FIFO, its reported inventory would have been $6,000 higher. Three years ago, there was little difference between the LIFO and FIFO amounts for either company.

PLANT ASSETS Island Resorts uses the straight-line depreciation method and an estimated useful life of 40 years for buildings and ten years for furniture and fixtures. Estimated residual values are $400,000 for buildings, and $0 for furniture and fixtures. Island's buildings are three years old.

Ocean Hideaway uses the double-declining-balance method and depreciates buildings over 30 years with an estimated residual value of $460,000. The furniture and fixtures, now three years old, are being depreciated over ten years with an estimated residual value of $85,000.

ACCOUNTS RECEIVABLE Island Resorts uses the direct write-off method for uncollectibles. Ocean Hideaway uses the allowance method. The Island Resorts owner estimates that $2,000 of the company's receivables are doubtful. Prior to the current year, uncollectibles were insignificant. Ocean Hideaway receivables are already reported at net realizable value.

REQUIRED

1. Puzzled at first by how to compare the two resorts, you decide to convert Island Resorts' balance sheet to the accounting methods and the estimated useful lives used by Ocean Hideaway. Round all depreciation amounts to the nearest $100. The necessary revisions will not affect Island's total liabilities.
2. Convert Island Resorts' total net income for the last three years to reflect the accounting methods used by Ocean Hideaway. Round all depreciation amounts to the nearest $100.
3. Compare the two resorts' finances after you have revised Island Resorts' figures. Which resort looked better at the outset? Which looks better when they are placed on equal footing?

CHAPTER 12

Accounting for Partnerships

LEARNING OBJECTIVES

After studying this chapter, you should be able to

1. Identify the characteristics of a partnership
2. Account for partners' initial investments in a partnership
3. Allocate profits and losses to the partners by different methods
4. Account for the admission of a new partner to the business
5. Account for the withdrawal of a partner from the business
6. Account for the liquidation of a partnership
7. Prepare partnership financial statements

> *For my accounting practice to grow, I had to join forces with at least one other professional. Forming a partnership with Ann Campi helped me achieve my business goals. But the partnership also raised questions I never faced when I was on my own.*
>
> BLAKE WILLIS, PARTNER, WILLIS & CAMPI, CERTIFIED PUBLIC ACCOUNTANTS

Blake Willis's accounting practice grew rapidly. After three years, the firm's revenue topped $150,000, and net income reached $90,000. After taking the business this far while working alone, Willis faced a tough decision. Should he continue as a sole proprietorship, or would it be better to incorporate the business? He decided instead to take on a partner and form a partnership.

Willis's closest friend at The University of Georgia, Ann Campi, had recently moved back to Savannah, Georgia. Like Willis, Campi had majored in accounting at Georgia. For the past three years, she had worked as a consultant for an accounting firm in Washington, D.C. Together, the pair formed the partnership of Willis & Campi, Certified Public Accountants. Willis would specialize in tax matters, and Campi would attract consulting clients.

The partnership form of business introduced some complexities that Willis's proprietorship had avoided. How much cash should Campi contribute to the business? She was buying into the client base developed by Willis. How should the partners divide profits and losses? How should a partner who leaves the firm be compensated for his or her share of the business? Willis and Campi had to iron out these and many other details.

Partnership. An association of two or more persons who co-own a business for profit.

A **partnership** is an association of two or more persons who co-own a business for profit. This definition derives from the Uniform Partnership Act, which nearly every state in the United States has adopted to regulate partnership practice.

Forming a partnership is easy. It requires no permission from government authorities and involves no legal procedures. When two persons decide to go into business together, a partnership is automatically formed.

A partnership brings together the assets, talents, and experience of the partners. Business opportunities closed to an individual may open up to a partnership. Suppose neither Willis nor Campi has enough money individually to buy a small office building in which to practice. They may be able to afford it together in a partnership. They may pool their talents and know-how. Their partnership can thus offer a fuller range of accounting services than either person could offer alone.

Partnerships come in all sizes. Many partnerships have fewer than ten partners. Some medical and law firms have 20 or more partners. The largest CPA firms have over 1,500 partners. Exhibit 12-1 lists the eight largest CPA firms in the United States, the number of partners in each firm, and their revenues in 1996.

Characteristics of a Partnership

Objective 1

Identify the characteristics of a partnership

Starting a partnership is voluntary. A person cannot be forced to join a partnership, and partners cannot be forced to accept another person as a partner. Although the partnership agreement may be oral, a written agreement between the partners reduces the chance of a misunderstanding. The following characteristics distinguish partnerships from sole proprietorships and corporations.

Partnership Agreement. The contract between partners that specifies such items as the name, location, and nature of the business; the name, capital investment, and duties of each partner; and the method of sharing profits and losses among the partners. Also called **articles of partnership.**

THE WRITTEN PARTNERSHIP AGREEMENT A business partnership is like a marriage. To be successful, the partners must cooperate. But business partners do not vow to remain together for life. Business partnerships come and go. To make certain that each partner fully understands how the partnership operates and to lower the chances that any partner might misunderstand how the business is run, partners may draw up a **partnership agreement,** also called the **articles of partnership.** This agreement is a contract between the partners, so transactions involving the agreement are governed by contract law. The articles of partnership should make the following points clear:

1. Name, location, and nature of the business
2. Name, capital investment, and duties of each partner
3. Method of sharing profits and losses among the partners
4. Withdrawals of assets allowed to the partners
5. Procedures for settling disputes between the partners
6. Procedures for admitting new partners
7. Procedures for settling up with a partner who withdraws from the business
8. Procedures for liquidating the partnership—selling the assets, paying the liabilities, and disbursing any remaining cash to the partners

Dissolution. Ending of a partnership.

Mutual Agency. Every partner can bind the business to a contract within the scope of the partnership's regular business operations.

LIMITED LIFE A partnership has a life limited by the length of time that all partners continue to own the business. If Blake Willis of the chapter opening story withdraws from the business, the partnership of Willis & Campi will cease to exist. A new partnership may emerge to continue the same business, but the old partnership will have been dissolved. **Dissolution** is the ending of a partnership. The addition of a new partner dissolves the old partnership and creates a new partnership.

MUTUAL AGENCY **Mutual agency** in a partnership means that every partner can bind the business to a contract within the scope of the partnership's regular business op-

Rank 1996	Firm	City	Number of Partners	1996 Revenue (Billions)
1	Arthur Andersen & Co., S.C.	Chicago	1,575	$4.5
2	Ernst & Young	New York	1,933	3.6
3	Deloitte & Touche	Wilton, Conn.	1,556	2.9
4	KPMG Peat Marwick	New York	1,515	2.5
5	Coopers & Lybrand	New York	1,241	2.1
6	Price Waterhouse	New York	963	2.0
7	Grant Thornton	New York	285	0.8
8	McGladrey & Pullen	Davenport, Iowa	388	0.3

Source: Accounting Today, March 17–April 6, 1997, page 28.

EXHIBIT 12-1
The Eight Largest Accounting Partnerships in the United States

erations. If Ann Campi enters into a contract with a business to provide accounting service, then the firm of Willis & Campi—not just Campi—is bound to provide that service. If Campi signs a contract to purchase lawn services for her home, however, the partnership will not be bound to pay. Contracting for personal services is not a regular business operation of the partnership.

UNLIMITED LIABILITY Each partner has an **unlimited personal liability** for the debts of the partnership. When a partnership cannot pay its debts with business assets, the partners must use their personal assets to meet the debt. Proprietors also have unlimited personal liability for the debts of their business.

Unlimited Personal Liability. When a partnership (or a proprietorship) cannot pay its debts with business assets, the partners (or the proprietor) must use personal assets to meet the debt.

Suppose the Willis & Campi firm has had an unsuccessful year and the partnership's liabilities exceed its assets by $20,000. Willis and Campi must pay this amount with their personal assets. Because each partner has unlimited liability, if a partner is unable to pay his or her part of the debt, the other partner (or partners) must make payment. If Campi can pay only $5,000 of the liability, Willis must pay $15,000.

Unlimited liability and mutual agency are closely related. A dishonest partner or a partner with poor judgment may commit the partnership to a contract under which the business loses money. In turn, creditors may force *all* the partners to pay the debt from personal assets. Hence, a business partner should be chosen with care.

Partners can avoid unlimited personal liability for partnership obligations by forming a *limited partnership*. In this form of business organization, one or more *general partners* assume the unlimited liability for business debts. In addition, the partnership has another class of owners, *limited partners*, who can lose only as much as their investment in the business. In this sense, limited partners have limited liability similar to the limited liability enjoyed by the stockholders of a corporation. Some of the large accounting firms in Exhibit 12-1 have reorganized as limited partnerships.

CO-OWNERSHIP OF PROPERTY Any asset—cash, inventory, machinery, and so on—that a partner invests in the partnership becomes the joint property of all the partners. Also, each partner has a claim to his or her share of the business's profits.

NO PARTNERSHIP INCOME TAXES A partnership pays no income tax on its business income. Instead, the net income of the partnership is divided and becomes the taxable income of the partners. Suppose Willis & Campi, Certified Public Accountants, earned net income of $200,000, shared equally by the partners. The firm would pay no income tax *as a business entity.* Willis and Campi, however, would each pay income tax as individuals on their $100,000 shares of partnership income.

PARTNERS' OWNER'S EQUITY ACCOUNTS Accounting for a partnership is much like accounting for a proprietorship. We record buying and selling goods and services, collecting and paying cash for a partnership just as we do for a proprietorship. But because a partnership has more than one owner, the partnership must have more than one owner's equity account. Every partner in the business—whether the firm has two or 2,000 partners—has an individual owner's equity account. Often these accounts carry the name of the particular partner and the word *capital.* For example, the owner's equity account for Blake Willis would read "Willis, Capital." Similarly, each partner has a

■ Daily Exercise 12-1

Partnership Advantages

Versus Proprietorships:

1. Can raise more capital.
2. Brings together the expertise of more than one person.
3. 1 + 1 > 2 in a good partnership. If the partners work well together, they can add more value than by working alone.

Versus Corporations:

4. Less expensive to organize than a corporation, which requires a charter from the state.
5. No taxation of partnership income, which is taxed to the partners as individuals.

Partnership Disadvantages

1. Partnership agreement may be difficult to formulate. Each time a new partner is admitted or a partner withdraws, the business needs a new partnership agreement.
2. Relationships among partners may be fragile.
3. Mutual agency and unlimited personal liability create personal obligations for each partner.

Concept Highlight

EXHIBIT 12-2
Advantages and Disadvantages of Partnerships
■ Daily Exercise 12-2

withdrawal account. If the number of partners is large, the general ledger may contain the single account Partners' Capital, or Owners' Equity. A subsidiary ledger can be used for individual partner accounts.

Exhibit 12-2 lists the advantages and disadvantages of partnerships (compared with proprietorships and corporations).

Learning Tip: A partnership is really a "multiple proprietorship." Most features of a proprietorship also apply to a partnership—in particular, limited life and unlimited liability.

Different Types of Partnerships

There are two basic types of partnerships: general partnerships and limited partnerships.

General Partnerships

General Partnership. A form of partnership in which each partner is an owner of the business, with all the privileges and risks of ownership.

A **general partnership** is the basic form of partnership organization. Each partner is an owner of the business with all the privileges and risks of ownership. The general partners share the profits, losses, and the risks of the business. The partnership *reports* its income to the governmental tax authorities (the Internal Revenue Service in the United States), but the partnership itself pays *no* income tax. The profits and losses of the partnership pass through the business to the partners, who then pay personal income tax on their income.

Limited Partnerships

Limited Partnership. A partnership with at least two classes of partners: a general partner and limited partners.

A **limited partnership** has at least two classes of partners. There must be at least one *general partner*, who takes primary responsibility for the management of the business. The general partner also takes the bulk of the risk of failure in the event the partnership goes bankrupt (liabilities exceed assets). In real-estate limited partnerships, the general partner often invests little cash in the business. Instead, the general partner's contribution is his or her skill in managing the organization. Usually, the general partner is the last owner to receive a share of partnership profits and losses. But the general partner may earn all excess profits after satisfying the limited partners' demands for income.

The *limited partners* are so named because their personal obligation for the partnership's liabilities is limited to the amount they have invested in the business. Usually, the limited partners have invested the bulk of the partnership's assets and capital. They therefore usually have first claim to partnership profits and losses, but only up to a specified limit. In exchange for their limited liability, their potential for profits usually has an upper limit as well.

Limited Liability Partnership. A form of partnership in which each partner's personal liability for the business's debts is limited to a certain amount. Also called **LLP's.**

Most of the large accounting firms are organized as **limited liability partnerships,** or **LLPs,** which means that each partner's personal liability for the business's debts is limited to a certain amount. The LLP must carry a large insurance policy to protect the public in case the partnership is found guilty of malpractice. Medical, legal, and other firms of professionals can also be organized as LLPs.

S CORPORATIONS An **S Corporation** is a corporation that is taxed in the same way that a partnership is taxed. Therefore, S corporations are often discussed in conjunction with partnerships. This form of business organization derives its name from Subchapter S of the U.S. Internal Revenue Code.

S Corporation. A corporation taxed in the same way as a partnership.

An ordinary (Subchapter C) corporation is subject to double taxation. First, the corporation pays corporate income tax on its income. Then, when the corporation pays dividends to the stockholders, they pay personal income tax on their dividend income. An S corporation pays no corporate income tax. Instead, the corporation's income flows through directly to the stockholders (the owners), who pay personal income tax on their share of the S corporation's income. The one-time taxation of an S corporation's income is an important advantage over an ordinary corporation. Thus from a tax standpoint, an S corporation operates like a partnership.

To qualify as an S corporation, the company can have no more than 75 stockholders, all of whom must be citizens or residents of the United States. Accounting for an S corporation resembles that of accounting for a partnership because the allocation of corporate income follows the same procedure used by partnerships.

Initial Investments by Partners

Objective 2

Account for partners' initial investments in a partnership

Let's see how to account for the multiple owner's equity accounts—and learn how they appear on the balance sheet—by examining how to account for the startup of a partnership.

Partners in a new partnership may invest assets and liabilities in the business. These contributions are entered in the books in the same way that a proprietor's assets and liabilities are recorded. Subtraction of each partner's liabilities from his or her assets yields the amount to be credited to that partner's capital account. Often the partners hire an independent firm to appraise their assets and liabilities at current market value at the time a partnership is formed. This outside evaluation assures an objective accounting for what each partner brings into the business.

Assume that Dave Benz and Joan Hanna form a partnership to manufacture and sell computer software. The partners agree on the following values based on an independent appraisal:

Benz's contributions

- Cash, $10,000; inventory, $70,000; and accounts payable, $85,000 (The appraiser believes that the current market values for these items equal Benz's values.)
- Accounts receivable, $30,000, less allowance for doubtful accounts of $5,000
- Computer equipment—cost, $800,000; accumulated depreciation, $200,000; current market value, $450,000

Hanna's contributions

- Cash, $5,000
- Computer software: cost, $18,000; market value, $100,000

The partnership records receipt of the partners' initial investments at the current market values of the assets and liabilities because, in effect, the partnership is buying the assets and assuming the liabilities at their current market values. The partnership entries are as follows:

Benz's investment

June 1	Cash	10,000	
	Accounts Receivable	30,000	
	Inventory	70,000	
	Computer Equipment	450,000	
	Allowance for Doubtful Accounts		5,000
	Accounts Payable		85,000
	Benz, Capital ($560,000 – $90,000)		470,000
	To record Benz's investment in the partnership.		

BENZ AND HANNA Balance Sheet June 1, 19X5				
Assets			**Liabilities**	
Cash		$ 15,000	Accounts payable	$ 85,000
Accounts receivable	$30,000			
Less Allowance for doubtful accounts	(5,000)	25,000	**Capital**	
Inventory		70,000	Benz, capital	470,000
Computer equipment		450,000	Hanna, capital	105,000
Computer software		100,000	Total liabilities	
Total assets		$660,000	and capital	$660,000

EXHIBIT 12-3
Partnership Balance Sheet

Hanna's investment

June 1	Cash	5,000	
	Computer Software	100,000	
	Hanna, Capital		105,000
	To record Hanna's investment in the partnership.		

The initial partnership balance sheet reports the amounts shown in Exhibit 12-3. Note that the asset and liability sections on the balance sheet are the same for a proprietorship and a partnership.

■ Daily Exercise 12-3
■ Daily Exercise 12-4

Sharing Partnership Profits and Losses

Objective 3

Allocate profits and losses to the partners by different methods

Allocating profits and losses among partners is one of the most challenging aspects of managing a partnership. If the partners have not drawn up an agreement or if the agreement does not state how the partners will divide profits and losses, then, by law, the partners must share profits and losses equally. If the agreement specifies a method for sharing profits but not losses, then losses are shared in the same proportion as profits. For example, a partner who was allocated 75% of the profits would likewise absorb 75% of any losses.

In some cases, an equal division is not fair. One partner may perform more work for the business than the other partner, or one partner may make a larger capital contribution. In the preceding example, Joan Hanna might agree to work longer hours for the partnership than Dave Benz to earn a greater share of profits. Benz could argue that he should share in more of the profits because he contributed more net assets ($470,000) than Hanna did ($105,000). Hanna might contend that her computer software program is the partnership's most important asset and that her share of the profits should be greater than Benz's share. Agreeing on a fair sharing of profits and losses in a partnership may be difficult. We now discuss options available in determining partners' shares.

Sharing Based on a Stated Fraction

Partners may agree to any profit-and-loss-sharing method they desire. They may, for example, state a particular fraction of the total profits and losses that each individual partner will share. Suppose the partnership agreement of Lou Cagle and Justin Dean allocates two-thirds of the business profits and losses to Cagle and one-third to Dean. If net income for the year is $90,000 and all revenue and expense accounts have been closed, the Income Summary account has a credit balance of $90,000:

■ Daily Exercise 12-5

Income Summary		
	Bal.	90,000

The entry to close this account and allocate the profit to the partners' capital accounts is

		Debit	Credit
Dec. 31	Income Summary	90,000	
	Cagle, Capital ($90,000 × 2/3)		60,000
	Dean, Capital ($90,000 × 1/3)		30,000
	To allocate net income to partners.		

Consider the effect of this entry. Does Cagle get cash of $60,000 and Dean cash of $30,000? No. The increase in the partners' capital accounts cannot be linked to any particular asset, including cash. Instead, the entry indicates that Cagle's ownership in *all* the assets of the business increased by $60,000 and Dean's by $30,000.

If the year's operations resulted in a net loss of $66,000, the Income Summary account would have a debit balance of $66,000. In that case, the closing entry to allocate the loss to the partners' capital accounts would be

		Debit	Credit
Dec. 31	Cagle, Capital ($66,000 × 2/3)	44,000	
	Dean, Capital ($66,000 × 1/3)	22,000	
	Income Summary		66,000
	To allocate net loss to partners.		

■ Daily Exercise 12-6

Just as a profit of $90,000 did not mean that the partners received cash of $60,000 and $30,000, so the loss of $66,000 does not mean that the partners must contribute cash of $44,000 and $22,000. A profit or loss will increase or decrease each partner's capital account, but cash may not change hands.

Sharing Based on Capital Contributions

Profits and losses are often allocated in proportion to the partners' capital contributions in the business. Suppose that Jenny Aycock, Erika Barber, and Sue Cordoba are partners in ABC Company. Their capital accounts have the following balances at the end of the year, before the closing entries:

Aycock, Capital	$ 40,000
Barber, Capital	60,000
Cordoba, Capital	50,000
Total capital balances	$150,000

Assume that the partnership earned a profit of $120,000 for the year. To allocate this amount on the basis of capital contributions, compute each partner's percentage share of the partnership's total capital balance by dividing each partner's contribution by the total capital amount. These figures, multiplied by the $120,000 profit amount, yield each partner's share of the year's profits:

Aycock:	($40,000/$150,000) × $120,000 =	$ 32,000
Barber:	($60,000/$150,000) × $120,000 =	48,000
Cordoba:	($50,000/$150,000) × $120,000 =	40,000
	Net income allocated to partners =	$120,000

The closing entry to allocate the profit to the partners' capital accounts is

		Debit	Credit
Dec. 31	Income Summary	120,000	
	Aycock, Capital		32,000
	Barber, Capital		48,000
	Cordoba, Capital		40,000
	To allocate net income to partners.		

After this closing entry, the partners' capital balances are

Aycock, Capital ($40,000 + $32,000)	$ 72,000
Barber, Capital ($60,000 + $48,000)	108,000
Cordoba, Capital ($50,000 + $40,000)	90,000
Total capital balances after allocation of net income	$270,000

Sharing Based on Capital Contributions and on Service

One partner, regardless of his or her capital contribution, may put more work into the business than the other partners do. Even among partners who log equal service time, one person's superior experience and knowledge may command a greater share of income. To reward the harder-working or more valuable person, the profit-and-loss-sharing method may be based on a combination of contributed capital *and* service to the business. The Chicago-based law firm Baker & McKenzie, for example, which has nearly 500 partners, takes seniority into account in determining partner compensation.

Assume that Debbie Randolph and Nancy Scott formed a partnership in which Randolph invested $60,000 and Scott invested $40,000, a total of $100,000. Scott devotes more time to the partnership and earns the larger salary. Accordingly, the two partners have agreed to share profits as follows:

1. The first $50,000 of partnership profits is to be allocated on the basis of partners' capital contributions to the business.
2. The next $60,000 of profits is to be allocated on the basis of service, with Randolph receiving $24,000 and Scott receiving $36,000.
3. Any remaining amount is to be allocated equally.

If net income for the first year is $125,000, the partners' shares of this profit are computed as follows:

	Randolph	Scott	Total
Total net income			$125,000
Sharing of first $50,000 of net income, based on capital contributions:			
Randolph ($60,000/$100,000 × $50,000)	$30,000		
Scott ($40,000/$100,000 × $50,000)		$20,000	
Total			50,000
Net income remaining for allocation			75,000
Sharing of next $60,000, based on service:			
Randolph	24,000		
Scott		36,000	
Total			60,000
Net income remaining for allocation			15,000
Remainder shared equally:			
Randolph ($15,000 × 1/2)	7,500		
Scott ($15,000 × 1/2)		7,500	
Total			15,000
Net income remaining for allocation			$ –0–
Net income allocated to the partners	$61,500	$63,500	$125,000

On the basis of this allocation, the closing entry is

■ Daily Exercise 12-7

Dec. 31	Income Summary	125,000	
	Randolph, Capital		61,500
	Scott, Capital		63,500
	To allocate net income to partners.		

Sharing Based on Salaries and on Interest

Partners may be rewarded for their service and their capital contributions to the business in other ways. In one sharing plan, the partners are allocated salaries plus interest on their capital balances. Assume that Randy Lewis and Gerald Clark form an oil-exploration partnership. At the beginning of the year, their capital balances are $80,000 and $100,000, respectively. The partnership agreement allocates annual salaries of $43,000 to Lewis and $35,000 to Clark. After salaries are allocated, each partner earns 8% interest on his beginning capital balance. Any remaining net income is divided equally. Partnership profit of $96,000 will be allocated as follows:

	Lewis	Clark	Total
Total net income			$96,000
First, salaries:			
Lewis	$43,000		
Clark		$35,000	
Total			78,000
Net income remaining for allocation			18,000
Second, interest on beginning capital balances:			
Lewis ($80,000 × 0.08)	6,400		
Clark ($100,000 × 0.08)		8,000	
Total			14,400
Net income remaining for allocation			3,600
Third, remainder shared equally:			
Lewis ($3,600 × 1/2)	1,800		
Clark ($3,600 × 1/2)		1,800	
Total			3,600
Net income remaining for allocation			$ -0-
Net income allocated to the partners	$51,200	$44,800	$96,000

In the preceding illustration, net income exceeded the sum of salary and interest. If the partnership profit is less than the allocated sum of salary and interest, a negative remainder will occur at some stage in the allocation process. Even so, the partners use the same method for allocation purposes. For example, assume that Lewis and Clark Partnership earned only $82,000:

■ Daily Exercise 12-8

	Lewis	Clark	Total
Total net income			$82,000
First, salaries:			
Lewis	$43,000		
Clark		$35,000	
Total			78,000
Net income remaining for allocation			4,000
Second, interest on beginning capital balances:			
Lewis ($80,000 × 0.08)	6,400		
Clark ($100,000 × 0.08)		8,000	
Total			14,400
Net income remaining for allocation			(10,400)
Third, remainder shared equally:			
Lewis ($10,400 × 1/2)	(5,200)		
Clark ($10,400 × 1/2)		(5,200)	
Total			(10,400)
Net income remaining for allocation			$ -0-
Net income allocated to the partners	$44,200	$37,800	$82,000

A net loss would be allocated to Lewis and Clark in the same manner outlined for net income. The sharing procedure would begin with the net loss and then allocate salary, interest, and any other specified amounts to the partners.

Thinking It Over Are these salaries and interest amounts business expenses in the usual sense? Explain your answer.

Answer: No, partners do not work for their own business to earn a salary, as an employee does. They do not loan money to their own business to earn interest. Their goal is for the partnership to earn a profit. Therefore, salaries and interest in partnership agreements are simply ways of expressing the allocation of profits and losses to the partners. For example, the salary component of partner income rewards service to the partnership. The interest component rewards a partner's investment of cash or other assets in the business. But the partners' salary and interest amounts are *not* salary expense and interest expense in the partnership's accounting or tax records.

We see that partners may allocate profits and losses on the basis of a stated fraction, contributed capital, service, interest on capital, or any combination of these factors. Each partnership shapes its profit-and-loss-sharing ratio to fit its own needs.

Partner Drawings

Like anyone else, partners need cash for personal living expenses. Partnership agreements usually allow partners to withdraw cash or other assets from the business. Drawings from a partnership are recorded exactly as for a proprietorship. Assume that both Randy Lewis and Gerald Clark are allowed a monthly withdrawal of $3,500. The partnership records the March withdrawals with this entry:

Mar. 31	Lewis, Drawing	3,500	
	Clark, Drawing	3,500	
	Cash		7,000
	Monthly partner withdrawals of cash.		

During the year, each partner's drawing account accumulates 12 such amounts, a total of $42,000 ($3,500 × 12) per partner. At the end of the period, the general ledger shows the following account balances immediately after net income has been closed to the partners' capital accounts. Assume these beginning balances for Lewis and Clark at the start of the year and that $82,000 of profit has been allocated on the basis of the preceding illustration.

Lewis, Capital

Debit		Credit	
		Jan. 1 Bal.	80,000
		Dec. 31 Net. inc.	44,200

Clark, Capital

Debit		Credit	
		Jan. 1 Bal.	100,000
		Dec. 31 Net. inc.	37,800

Lewis, Drawing

Debit		Credit
Dec. 31 Bal.	42,000	

Clark, Drawing

Debit		Credit
Dec. 31 Bal.	42,000	

The drawing accounts must be closed at the end of the period, exactly as for a proprietorship: The closing entry credits each partner's drawing account and debits each capital account.

We covered this closing entry in Chapter 4, page 147.

Learning Tip: The amount of the drawings does not depend on the partnership's income or loss for the year.

Objective 4

Account for the admission of a new partner to the business

Admission of a Partner

A partnership lasts only as long as its partners remain in the business. The addition of a new member or the withdrawal of an existing member dissolves the partnership. We turn now to a discussion of how partnerships dissolve—and how new partnerships arise.

Often a new partnership is formed to carry on the former partnership's business. In fact, the new partnership may retain the dissolved partnership's name. Price Waterhouse, for example, is an accounting firm that retires and hires partners during the year. Thus the former partnership dissolves and a new partnership begins many times. But the business retains the name and continues operations. Other partnerships may dissolve and then re-form under a new name. Let's look now at the ways that a new member may gain admission into an existing partnership.

Admission by Purchasing a Partner's Interest

A person may become a member of a partnership by gaining the approval of the other partner (or partners) for entrance into the firm *and* by purchasing a present partner's interest in the business. Let's assume that Roberta Fisher and Benitez Garcia have a partnership that carries these figures:

Cash	$ 40,000	Total liabilities	$120,000
Other assets	360,000	Fisher, capital	110,000
		Garcia, capital	170,000
Total assets	$400,000	Total liabilities and capital	$400,000

Business is going so well that Fisher receives an offer from Barry Dynak, an outside party, to buy her $110,000 interest in the business for $150,000. Fisher agrees to sell out to Dynak, and Garcia approves Dynak as a new partner. The firm records the transfer of capital interest in the business with this entry:

Apr. 16	Fisher, Capital	110,000	
	Dynak, Capital		110,000
	To transfer Fisher's equity in the business to Dynak.		

The debit side of the entry closes Fisher's capital account because she is no longer a partner in the firm. The credit side opens Dynak's capital account because Fisher's equity has been transferred to Dynak. The entry amount is Fisher's capital balance ($110,000) and not the $150,000 price that Dynak paid Fisher to buy into the business. The full $150,000 goes to Fisher, including the $40,000 difference between her capital balance and the price received from Dynak. In this example, the partnership receives no cash because the transaction was between Dynak and Fisher, not between Dynak and the partnership. Suppose Dynak pays Fisher less than Fisher's capital balance. The entry on the partnership books is not affected. Fisher's equity is transferred to Dynak at book value ($110,000).

The old partnership has dissolved. Garcia and Dynak draw up a new partnership agreement with a new profit-and-loss-sharing ratio and continue business operations. If Garcia does not accept Dynak as a partner, Dynak gets no voice in management of the firm. However, under the Uniform Partnership Act, the purchaser shares in the profits and losses of the firm and in its assets at liquidation.

Admission by Investing in the Partnership

As Ann Campi did in our chapter opening story, a person may be admitted as a partner by investing directly in the partnership rather than by purchasing an existing partner's interest. The new partner contributes assets—for example, cash, inventory, or equipment—to the business. Assume that the partnership of Robin Ingel and Michael Jay has the following assets, liabilities, and capital:

Cash	$ 20,000	Total liabilities	$ 60,000
Other assets	200,000	Ingel, capital	70,000
		Jay, capital	90,000
Total assets	$220,000	Total liabilities and capital	$220,000

Laura Kahn offers to invest equipment and land (Other Assets) with a market value of $80,000 to persuade the existing partners to take her into the business. Ingel and Jay agree to dissolve the existing partnership and to start up a new business, giving Kahn one-third interest—[$80,000/($70,000 + $90,000 + $80,000) = 1/3]—in exchange for the contributed assets. Notice that Kahn is buying into the partnership at book value because her one-third investment ($80,000) equals one-third of the new partnership's total capital ($240,000). The entry to record Kahn's investment is

July 18	Other Assets	80,000	
	Kahn, Capital		80,000
	To admit L. Kahn as a partner with a one-third interest in the business.		

After this entry, the partnership books show

Cash	$ 20,000	Total liabilities	$ 60,000
Other assets ($200,000 + $80,000)	280,000	Ingel, capital	70,000
		Jay, capital	90,000
		Kahn, capital	80,000
Total assets	$300,000	Total liabilities and capital	$300,000

■ Daily Exercise 12-9
■ Daily Exercise 12-10

Kahn's one-third interest in the partnership does not necessarily entitle her to one-third of the profits. The sharing of profits and losses is a separate element in the partnership agreement.

ADMISSION BY INVESTING IN THE PARTNERSHIP—BONUS TO THE OLD PARTNERS

The more successful a partnership, the higher the payment the partners may demand from a person entering the business. Partners in a business that is doing quite well might require an incoming person to pay them a bonus. The bonus increases the current partners' capital accounts.

Suppose that Hiro Nagasawa and Ralph Osburn's partnership has earned above-average profits for ten years. The two partners share profits and losses equally. The partnership balance sheet carries these figures:

Cash	$ 40,000	Total liabilities	$100,000
Other assets	210,000	Nagasawa, capital	70,000
		Osburn, capital	80,000
Total assets	$250,000	Total liabilities and capital	$250,000

The partners agree to admit Glen Parker to a one-fourth interest with his cash investment of $90,000. Parker's capital balance on the partnership books is only $60,000, computed as follows:

Partnership capital before Parker is admitted ($70,000 + $80,000)	$150,000
Parker's investment in the partnership	90,000
Partnership capital after Parker is admitted	$240,000
Parker's capital in the partnership ($240,000 × 1/4)	$ 60,000
Bonus to the old partners ($90,000 – $60,000)	$ 30,000

■ Daily Exercise 12-11

In effect, Parker had to buy into the partnership at a price ($90,000) above the book value of his one-fourth interest ($60,000). Parker's extra investment of $30,000 creates a *bonus* for the existing partners. The entry on the partnership books to record Parker's investment is

Mar. 1	Cash..	90,000	
	Parker, Capital..		60,000
	Nagasawa, Capital ($30,000 × 1/2)..........................		15,000
	Osburn, Capital ($30,000 × 1/2)..............................		15,000
	To admit G. Parker as a partner with a one-fourth interest in the business.		

Parker's capital account is credited for his one-fourth interest in the partnership. The *bonus* is allocated to the partners on the basis of their profit-and-loss ratio.

The new partnership's balance sheet reports these amounts:

Cash ($40,000 + $90,000).....	$130,000	Total liabilities	$100,000
Other assets..........................	210,000	Nagasawa, capital	
		($70,000 + $15,000)...........	85,000
		Osburn, capital	
		($80,000 + $15,000)...........	95,000
		Parker, capital.......................	60,000
Total assets............................	$340,000	Total liabilities and capital	$340,000

■ Daily Exercise 12-12

Working It Out Mia and Susan are partners with capital balances of $25,000 and $75,000, respectively. They share profits and losses in a 30:70 ratio. Mia and Susan admit Tab to a 10% interest in a new partnership when Tab invests $20,000 in the business.

1. Journalize the partnership's receipt of cash from Tab.
2. What is each partner's capital in the new partnership?

Answers

1.

Cash...	20,000	
Tab, Capital		12,000
Mia, Capital ($8,000 × 0.30)		2,400
Susan, Capital ($8,000 × 0.70)		5,600
To admit Tab with a 10% interest in the business.		

Partnership capital before Tab is admitted ($25,000 + $75,000)..........	$100,000
Tab's investment in the partnership..	20,000
Partnership capital after Tab is admitted	$120,000
Tab's capital in the partnership ($120,000 × 1/10)...............................	$ 12,000
Bonus to the old partners ($20,000 – $12,000).....................................	$ 8,000

2. Partners' capital balances:

Mia, capital ($25,000 + $2,400)..............	$ 27,400
Susan, capital ($75,000 + $5,600)...........	80,600
Tab, capital...	12,000
Total partnership capital.........................	$120,000

ADMISSION BY INVESTING IN THE PARTNERSHIP—BONUS TO THE NEW PARTNER A potential new partner may be so important that the existing partners offer him or her a partnership share that includes a bonus. A law firm may strongly desire a former governor or other official as a partner because of the person's reputation and connections. A restaurant owner may want to go into partnership with a famous sports personality, movie star, or model. The growing chain Planet Hollywood, for example, opened its first restaurant in 1991 in New York City. Planet Hollywood, whose majority owner is Robert Earl, has prospered

"Planet Hollywood, whose majority owner is Robert Earl, has prospered with the help of celebrity partners Sylvester Stallone, Arnold Schwarzenegger, Bruce Willis, and Don Johnson."

with the help of celebrity partners Sylvester Stallone, Arnold Schwarzenegger, Bruce Willis, and Don Johnson.

Suppose that Allan Page and Olivia Franco have a law partnership. The firm's balance sheet appears as follows:

■ Daily Exercise 12-13

Cash	$140,000	Total liabilities	$120,000
Other assets	360,000	Page, capital	230,000
		Franco, capital	150,000
Total assets	$500,000	Total liabilities and capital	$500,000

Page and Franco admit Martin Schiller, a former attorney general, as a partner with a one-third interest in exchange for his cash investment of $100,000. At the time of Schiller's admission, the firm's capital is $380,000 (Page, $230,000, plus Franco, $150,000). Page and Franco share profits and losses in the ratio of two-thirds to Page and one-third to Franco. The computation of Schiller's equity in the partnership is

Partnership capital before Schiller is admitted ($230,000 + $150,000)	$380,000
Schiller's investment in the partnership	100,000
Partnership capital after Schiller is admitted	$480,000
Schiller's capital in the partnership ($480,000 × 1/3)	$160,000
Bonus to the new partner ($160,000 − $100,000)	$ 60,000

In this case, Schiller bought into the partnership at a price ($100,000) below the book value of his interest ($160,000). The bonus of $60,000 went to Schiller from the other partners. The capital accounts of Page and Franco are debited for the $60,000 difference between the new partner's equity ($160,000) and his investment ($100,000). The existing partners share this decrease in capital as though it were a loss, on the basis of their profit-and-loss ratio. The entry to record Schiller's investment is

Aug. 24	Cash	100,000	
	Page, Capital ($60,000 × 2/3)	40,000	
	Franco, Capital ($60,000 × 1/3)	20,000	
	Schiller, Capital		160,000
	To admit M. Schiller as a partner with a one-third interest in the business.		

The new partnership's balance sheet reports these amounts:

Cash ($140,000 + $100,000)	$240,000	Total liabilities	$120,000
Other assets	360,000	Page, capital ($230,000 − $40,000)	190,000
		Franco, capital ($150,000 − $20,000)	130,000
		Schiller, capital	160,000
Total assets	$600,000	Total liabilities and capital	$600,000

Working It Out John and Ron are partners with capital balances of $30,000 and $40,000, respectively. They share profits and losses in a 25:75 ratio. John and Ron admit Lou to a 20% interest in a new partnership when Lou invests $10,000 in the business.

1. Journalize the partnership's receipt of cash from Lou.
2. What is each partner's capital in the new partnership?

Answers

1.	Cash	10,000	
	John, Capital ($6,000 × 0.25)	1,500	
	Ron, Capital ($6,000 × 0.75)	4,500	
	Lou, Capital		16,000
	To admit Lou with a 20% interest in the business.		

Partnership capital before Lou is admitted ($30,000 + $40,000)	$70,000
Lou's investment in the partnership	10,000
Partnership capital after Lou is admitted	$80,000
Lou's capital in the partnership ($80,000 × 0.20)	$16,000
Bonus to the new partner ($16,000 − $10,000)	$ 6,000

2. Partners' capital balances:

John, capital ($30,000 − $1,500)	$28,500
Ron, capital ($40,000 − $4,500)	35,500
Lou, capital	16,000
Total partnership capital	$80,000

Withdrawal of a Partner

Objective 5

Account for the withdrawal of a partner from the business

A partner may withdraw from the business for many reasons, including retirement or a dispute with the other partners. The withdrawal of a partner dissolves the old partnership. The partnership agreement should contain a provision to govern how to settle with a withdrawing partner. In the simplest case, illustrated on page 517, a partner may withdraw and sell his or her interest to another partner in a personal transaction. The only entry needed to record this transfer of equity debits the withdrawing partner's capital account and credits the purchaser's capital account. The dollar amount of the entry is the capital balance of the withdrawing partner, regardless of the price paid by the purchaser. The accounting when one current partner buys a second partner's interest is the same as when an outside party buys a current partner's interest.

If the partner withdraws in the middle of an accounting period, the partnership books should be updated to determine the withdrawing partner's capital balance. The business must measure net income or net loss for the fraction of the year up to the withdrawal date and allocate profit or loss according to the existing ratio. After the books have been closed, the business then accounts for the change in partnership capital.

The withdrawing partner may receive his or her share of the business in partnership assets other than cash. The question arises as to what value to assign the partnership assets—book value or current market value? The settlement procedure may specify an independent appraisal of assets to determine their current market value. If market values have changed, the appraisal will result in revaluing the partnership assets. Thus the partners share in any market value changes that their efforts caused.

Suppose that Keith Isaac is retiring in midyear from the partnership of Green, Henry, and Isaac. After the books have been adjusted for partial-period income but before the asset appraisal, revaluation, and closing entries, the balance sheet reports the following:

Cash		$ 39,000	Total liabilities	$ 80,000
Inventory		44,000	Green, capital	54,000
Land		55,000	Henry, capital	43,000
Building	$95,000		Isaac, capital	21,000
Less Accum. depr.	(35,000)	60,000	Total liabilities and	
Total assets		$198,000	capital	$198,000

An independent appraiser revalues the inventory at $38,000 (down from $44,000) and the land at $101,000 (up from $55,000). The partners share the differences between these assets' market values and their prior book values on the basis of their profit-and-loss ratio. The partnership agreement has allocated one-fourth of the profits to Susan

Green, one-half to Charles Henry, and one-fourth to Isaac. (This ratio may be written 1:2:1 for one part to Green, two parts to Henry, and one part to Isaac.) For each share that Green or Isaac has, Henry has two. The entries to record the revaluation of the inventory and land are

July 31	Green, Capital ($6,000 × 1/4)	1,500	
	Henry, Capital ($6,000 × 1/2)	3,000	
	Isaac, Capital ($6,000 × 1/4)	1,500	
	Inventory ($44,000 – $38,000)		6,000
	To revalue the inventory and allocate the loss to the partners.		
31	Land ($101,000 – $55,000)	46,000	
	Green, Capital ($46,000 × 1/4)		11,500
	Henry, Capital ($46,000 × 1/2)		23,000
	Isaac, Capital ($46,000 × 1/4)		11,500
	To revalue the land and allocate the gain to the partners.		

After the revaluations, the partnership balance sheet reports the following:

Cash		$ 39,000	Total liabilities	$ 80,000
Inventory		38,000	Green, capital	
Land		101,000	($54,000 – $1,500 + $11,500)	64,000
Building	$95,000		Henry, capital	
Less Accum. depr.	(35,000)	60,000	($43,000 – $3,000 + $23,000)	63,000
			Isaac, capital	
			($21,000 – $1,500 + $11,500)	31,000
Total assets		$238,000	Total liabilities and capital	$238,000

The books now carry the assets at current market value, which becomes the new book value, and the capital accounts have been adjusted accordingly. As the balance sheet shows, Isaac has a claim to $31,000 in partnership assets. How is his withdrawal from the business accounted for?

Withdrawal at Book Value

If Keith Isaac withdraws by receiving cash equal to the book value of his owner's equity, the entry will be

July 31	Isaac, Capital	31,000	
	Cash		31,000
	To record withdrawal of K. Isaac from the business.		

■ Daily Exercise 12-14

This entry records the payment of partnership cash to Isaac and the closing of his capital account upon his withdrawal from the business.

Withdrawal at Less than Book Value

The withdrawing partner may be so eager to leave the business that he or she is willing to take less than his or her equity. This situation has occurred in real-estate and oil-drilling partnerships. Assume that Keith Isaac withdraws from the business and agrees to receive partnership cash of $10,000 and the new partnership's note for $15,000. This $25,000 settlement is $6,000 less than Isaac's $31,000 equity in the business. The remaining partners share this $6,000 difference—which is a bonus to them—according to their profit-and-loss ratio. However, because Isaac has withdrawn from the partnership, a new agreement—and a new profit-and-loss ratio—must be drawn up. In forming a new partnership, Henry and Green may decide on any ratio that they see fit. Let's assume they agree that Henry will earn two-thirds of partnership profits and losses and Green one-third. The entry to record Isaac's withdrawal at less than book value is

July 31	Isaac, Capital	31,000	
	Cash		10,000
	Note Payable to K. Isaac		15,000
	Green, Capital ($6,000 × 1/3)		2,000
	Henry, Capital ($6,000 × 2/3)		4,000
	To record withdrawal of K. Isaac from the business.		

Isaac's account is closed, and Henry and Green may or may not continue the business as a new partnership.

■ Daily Exercise 12-15

Withdrawal at More than Book Value

The settlement with a withdrawing partner may allow him or her to take assets of greater value than the book value of that partner's capital. Also, the remaining partners may be so eager for the withdrawing partner to leave the firm that they pay him or her a bonus to withdraw from the business. In either case, the partner's withdrawal causes a decrease in the book equity of the remaining partners. This decrease is allocated to the partners on the basis of their profit-and-loss ratio.

The accounting for this situation follows the pattern illustrated for withdrawal at less than book value—with one exception. The remaining partners' capital accounts are debited because the withdrawing partner receives more than his or her book equity.

■ Daily Exercise 12-16

Working It Out Linda is withdrawing from the partnership of Linda, Jacob, and Karla. The partners share profits and losses in a 1:2:3 ratio for Linda, Jacob, and Karla, respectively. After the revaluation of assets, Linda's capital balance is $50,000, and the other partners agree to pay her $60,000. Journalize the payment to Linda and her withdrawal from the partnership.

Answer

Linda, Capital	50,000	
Jacob, Capital [($60,000 – $50,000) × 2/5]	4,000	
Karla, Capital [($60,000 – $50,000) × 3/5]	6,000	
Cash		60,000
To record withdrawal of Linda from the business.		

Death of a Partner

Like any other form of partnership withdrawal, death of a partner dissolves a partnership. The partnership accounts are adjusted to measure net income or loss for the fraction of the year up to the date of death, then closed to determine the partners' capital balances on that date. Settlement with the deceased partner's estate is based on the partnership agreement. The estate commonly receives partnership assets equal to the partner's capital balance. The partnership closes the deceased partner's capital account with a debit. This entry credits a payable to the estate.

Alternatively, a remaining partner may purchase the deceased partner's equity. The deceased partner's equity is debited, and the purchaser's equity is credited. The amount of this entry is the ending credit balance in the deceased partner's capital account.

Objective 6

Account for the liquidation of a partnership

Liquidation of a Partnership

Liquidation. The process of going out of business by selling the entity's assets and paying its liabilities. The final step in liquidation of a business is the distribution of any remaining cash to the owner(s).

Admission of a new partner or withdrawal or death of an existing partner dissolves the partnership. However, the business may continue operating with no apparent change to outsiders such as customers and creditors. In contrast, business **liquidation** is the process of going out of business by selling the entity's assets and paying its liabilities. The final step in liquidation of a business is the *distribution of the remaining cash to the owners.* Before the business is liquidated, its books should be adjusted and closed. After closing, only asset, liability, and partners' capital accounts remain open.

Liquidation of a partnership includes three basic steps:

1. Sell the assets. Allocate the gain or loss to the partners' capital accounts on the basis of the profit-and-loss ratio.
2. Pay the partnership liabilities.
3. Disburse the remaining cash to the partners on the basis of their capital balances.

In practice, the liquidation of a business can stretch over weeks or months. Selling every asset and paying every liability of the entity takes time. After the 80 partners of Shea & Gould, one of New York's best-known law firms, voted to dissolve their partnership, the firm remained open for an extra year to collect bills and pay off liabilities.

To avoid excessive detail in our illustrations, we include only two asset categories—Cash and Noncash Assets—and a single liability category—Liabilities. Our examples assume that the business sells the noncash assets in a single transaction and pays the liabilities in a single transaction.

Assume that Jane Aviron, Elaine Bloch, and Mark Crane have shared profits and losses in the ratio of 3:1:1. (This ratio is equal to 3/5, 1/5, 1/5, or a 60%, 20%, 20% sharing ratio.) They decide to liquidate their partnership. After the books are adjusted and closed, the general ledger contains the following balances:

Cash	$ 10,000	Liabilities	$ 30,000
Noncash assets	90,000	Aviron, capital	40,000
		Bloch, capital	20,000
		Crane, capital	10,000
Total assets	$100,000	Total liabilities and capital	$100,000

Sale of Noncash Assets at a Gain

Assume that the Aviron, Bloch, and Crane partnership sells its noncash assets (shown on the balance sheet as $90,000) for cash of $150,000. The partnership realizes a gain of $60,000, which is allocated to the partners on the basis of their profit-and-loss-sharing ratio. The entry to record this sale and allocation of the gain is

Oct. 31	Cash	150,000	
	Noncash Assets		90,000
	Aviron, Capital ($60,000 × 0.60)		36,000
	Bloch, Capital ($60,000 × 0.20)		12,000
	Crane, Capital ($60,000 × 0.20)		12,000
	To sell noncash assets at a gain.		

The partnership must next pay off its liabilities:

Oct. 31	Liabilities	30,000	
	Cash		30,000
	To pay liabilities.		

In the final liquidation transaction, the remaining cash is disbursed to the partners. *The partners share in the cash according to their capital balances.* (In contrast, *gains and losses* on the sale of assets are shared by the partners on the basis of their profit-and-loss-sharing ratio.) The amount of cash left in the partnership is $130,000—the $10,000 beginning balance plus the $150,000 cash sale of assets minus the $30,000 cash payment of liabilities. The partners divide the remaining cash according to their capital balances:

Oct. 31	Aviron, Capital ($40,000 + $36,000)	76,000	
	Bloch, Capital ($20,000 + $12,000)	32,000	
	Crane, Capital ($10,000 + $12,000)	22,000	
	Cash		130,000
	To disburse cash in liquidation.		

	Cash	+	Noncash Assets	=	Liabilities	+	Capital Aviron (60%)	+	Capital Bloch (20%)	+	Capital Crane (20%)
Balance before sale of assets	$ 10,000		$ 90,000		$ 30,000		$ 40,000		$ 20,000		$ 10,000
Sale of assets and sharing of gain	150,000		(90,000)				36,000		12,000		12,000
Balances	160,000		–0–		30,000		76,000		32,000		22,000
Payment of liabilities	(30,000)				(30,000)						
Balances	130,000		–0–		–0–		76,000		32,000		22,000
Disbursement of cash to partners	(130,000)						(76,000)		(32,000)		(22,000)
Balances	$ –0–		$ –0–		$ –0–		$ –0–		$ –0–		$ –0–

EXHIBIT 12-4
Partnership Liquidation—Sale of Assets at a Gain

■ Daily Exercise 12-17
■ Daily Exercise 12-18

A convenient way to summarize the transactions in a partnership liquidation is given in Exhibit 12-4.

After the disbursement of cash to the partners, the business has no assets, liabilities, or owners' equity. All the balances are zero. By the accounting equation, partnership assets *must* equal partnership liabilities plus partnership capital.

Learning Tip: Upon liquidation, gains on the sale of assets are divided according to the *profit-and-loss ratio.* The final cash disbursement is based on *capital balances.*

Sale of Noncash Assets at a Loss

Liquidation of a business often includes the sale of noncash assets at a loss. When this occurs, the partners' capital accounts are debited as they share the loss in their profit-and-loss-sharing ratio. Otherwise, the accounting follows the pattern illustrated for the sale of noncash assets at a gain.

Thinking It Over The liquidation of the Dirk & Cross partnership included the sale of assets at a $150,000 loss. Lorraine Dirk's capital balance of $45,000 was less than her $60,000 share of the loss. Allocation of losses to the partners created a $15,000 deficit (debit balance) in Dirk's capital account. Identify ways that the partnership could deal with the negative balance (a capital deficiency) in Dirk's capital account.

Answer: Two possibilities are

1. Dirk could contribute assets to the partnership in an amount equal to her capital deficiency.
2. Joseph Cross, Dirk's partner, could absorb her capital deficiency by decreasing his own capital balance.

Partnership Financial Statements

Objective 7

Prepare partnership financial statements

Partnership financial statements are much like those of a proprietorship. However, a partnership income statement includes a section showing the division of net income to the partners. For example, the partnership of Leslie Gray and DeWayne Hayward might report its statements for the year ended December 31, 19X6, as shown in Panel A of Exhibit 12-5. A proprietorship's statements are presented in Panel B for comparison.

Large partnerships may not find it feasible to report the net income of every partner. Instead, the firm may report the allocation of net income to active and retired partners and average earnings per partner. For example, Exhibit 12-6 shows how the CPA firm Main Price & Anders reported its earnings.

(dollars in thousands)

PANEL A—Partnership

GRAY & HAYWARD CONSULTING Income Statement Year Ended December 31, 19X6		
Revenues		$ 460
Expenses		(270)
Net income		$ 190
Allocation of net income:		
To Gray	$114	
To Hayward	76	$ 190

GRAY & HAYWARD CONSULTING Statement of Owners' Equity Year Ended December 31, 19X6	Gray	Hayward
Capital, December 31, 19X5	$ 50	$ 40
Additional investments	10	—
Net income	114	76
Subtotal	174	116
Drawings	(72)	(48)
Capital, December 31, 19X6	$102	$ 68

GRAY & HAYWARD CONSULTING Balance Sheet December 31, 19X6	
Assets	
Cash and other assets	$170
Owners' Equity	
Gray, capital	$102
Hayward, capital	68
Total capital	$170

PANEL B—Proprietorship

GRAY CONSULTING Income Statement Year Ended December 31, 19X6	
Revenues	$ 460
Expenses	(270)
Net income	$ 190

GRAY CONSULTING Statement of Owners' Equity Year Ended December 31, 19X6	
Capital, December 31, 19X5	$ 90
Additional investment	10
Net income	190
Subtotal	290
Drawings	(120)
Capital, December 31, 19X6	$170

GRAY CONSULTING Balance Sheet December 31, 19X6	
Assets	
Cash and other assets	$170
Owner's Equity	
Gray, capital	$170

Concept Highlight

EXHIBIT 12-5
Financial Statements of a Partnership and a Proprietorship

■ Daily Exercise 12-19
■ Daily Exercise 12-20

MAIN PRICE & ANDERS Combined Statement of Earnings Year Ended August 31, 19X7	
Dollar amounts in thousands	
Fees for professional services	$914,492
Earnings for the year	$297,880
Allocation of earnings:	
To partners active during the year—	
Resigned, retired, and deceased partners	$ 19,901
Partners active at year end	253,270
To retired and deceased partners—retirement and death benefits	8,310
Not allocated to partners—retained for specific partnership purposes	16,399
	$297,880
Average earnings per partner active at year end (1,336 partners)	$ 223

EXHIBIT 12-6
Reporting Net Income for a Large Partnership

The following Decision Guidelines feature summarizes the main points of accounting for partnerships.

DECISION GUIDELINES — Accounting for Partnerships

DECISION	GUIDELINES
How to organize the business?	A partnership offers both advantages and disadvantages in comparison with proprietorships and corporations. (See Exhibit 12–2, page 510.)
On what matters should the partners agree?	See the list on page 508, under the heading "The Written Partnership Agreement."
At what value does the partnership record assets and liabilities?	Current market value on the date of acquisition, because, in effect, the partnership is buying its assets at their current market value.
How are partnership profits and losses shared among the partners?	• Equally if there is no profit-and-loss-sharing agreement. • As provided in the partnership agreement. Can be based on the partners' **a.** Stated fractions **b.** Capital contributions **c.** Service to the partnership **d.** Salaries and interest on their capital contributions
What happens when a partner withdraws from the partnership?	The old partnership ceases to exist. The remaining partners may or may not form a new partnership.
How are new partners admitted to the partnership?	• *Purchase a partner's interest.* The old partnership is dissolved. The remaining partners may admit the new partner to the partnership. If not, the new partner gets no voice in the management of the firm but shares in the profits and losses of the partnership. Close the withdrawing partner's Capital account, and open a Capital account for the new partner. Carry over the old partner's Capital balance to the Capital account of the new partner. • *Invest in the partnership.* Buying in at book value creates no bonus to any partner. Buying in at a price above book value creates a bonus to the old partners. Buying in at a price below book value creates a bonus for the new partner.
How to account for the withdrawal of a partner from the business?	• First, adjust and close the books up to the date of the partner's withdrawal from the business. • Second, appraise the assets and the liabilities at their current market value. • Third, account for the partner's withdrawal **a.** At book value (no change in remaining partners' Capital balances) **b.** At less than book value (increase the remaining partners' Capital balances) **c.** At more than book value (decrease the remaining partners' Capital balances)
What happens if the partnership goes out of business?	Liquidate the partnership, as follows: **a.** Adjust and close the partnership books up to the date of liquidation. **b.** Sell the partnership's assets. Allocate gain or loss to the partners' Capital accounts based on their profit-and-loss ratio. **c.** Pay the partnership liabilities. **d.** Disburse any remaining cash to the partners based on their Capital balances.
How do partnership financial statements differ from those of a proprietorship?	• The partnership income statement reports the allocation of net income or net loss to the partners. • The partnership balance sheet (or a separate schedule) reports the Capital balance of each partner. • The statement of cash flows is the same for a partnership as for a proprietorship.

SUMMARY PROBLEM FOR YOUR REVIEW

The partnership of Taylor & Uvalde is considering admitting Steven Vaughn as a partner on January 1, 19X8. The partnership general ledger includes the following balances on that date:

Cash	$ 9,000	Total liabilities	$ 50,000
Other assets	110,000	Taylor, capital	45,000
		Uvalde, capital	24,000
Total assets	$119,000	Total liabilities and capital	$119,000

Ross Taylor's share of profits and losses is 60%, and Thomas Uvalde's share is 40 percent.

REQUIRED (ITEMS 1 AND 2 ARE INDEPENDENT)

1. Suppose that Vaughn pays Uvalde $31,000 to acquire Uvalde's interest in the business. Taylor approves Vaughn as a partner.
   - **a.** Record the transfer of owner's equity on the partnership books.
   - **b.** Prepare the partnership balance sheet immediately after Vaughn is admitted as a partner.
2. Suppose that Vaughn becomes a partner by investing $31,000 cash to acquire a one-fourth interest in the business.
   - **a.** Compute Vaughn's capital balance, and record his investment in the business.
   - **b.** Prepare the partnership balance sheet immediately after Vaughn is admitted as a partner. Include the heading.
3. Which way of admitting Vaughn to the partnership increases its total assets? Give your reason.

SOLUTION

REQUIREMENT 1

a.

Date	Accounts	Debit	Credit
Jan. 1	Uvalde, Capital	24,000	
	Vaughn, Capital		24,000
	To transfer Uvalde's equity in the partnership to Vaughn.		

b. The balance sheet for the partnership of Taylor and Vaughn is identical to the balance sheet given for Taylor and Uvalde in the problem, except that Vaughn's name replaces Uvalde's name in the title and in the listing of Capital accounts.

REQUIREMENT 2

a. Computations of Vaughn's capital balance:

Partnership capital before Vaughn is admitted ($45,000 + $24,000)	$69,000
Vaughn's investment in the partnership	31,000
Partnership capital after Vaughn is admitted	$100,000
Vaughn's capital in the partnership ($100,000 × 1/4)	$ 25,000

Date	Accounts	Debit	Credit
Jan. 1	Cash	31,000	
	Vaughn, Capital		25,000
	Taylor, Capital [($31,000 – $25,000) × 0.60]		3,600
	Uvalde, Capital[($31,000 – $25,000) × 0.40]		2,400
	To admit Vaughn as a partner with a one-fourth interest in the business.		

b.

TAYLOR, UVALDE, & VAUGHN
Balance Sheet
January 1, 19X8

Cash ($9,000 + $31,000)	$ 40,000	Total liabilities	$ 50,000
Other assets	110,000	Taylor, capital ($45,000 + $3,600)	48,600
		Uvalde, capital ($24,000 + $2,400)	26,400
		Vaughn, capital	25,000
Total assets	$150,000	Total liabilities and capital	$150,000

REQUIREMENT 3

Vaughn's investment in the partnership increases its total assets by the amount of his contribution. Total assets of the business are $150,000 after his investment, compared with $119,000 before. In contrast, Vaughn's purchase of Uvalde's interest in the business is a personal transaction between the two individuals. It does not affect the assets of the partnership regardless of the amount Vaughn pays Uvalde.

Summary of Learning Objectives

1. ***Identify the characteristics of a partnership.*** A *partnership* is a business co-owned by two or more persons for profit. The characteristics of this form of business organization are its *ease of formation*, *limited life*, *mutual agency*, *unlimited liability*, and *no partnership income taxes*. In a *limited partnership*, the limited partners have limited personal liability for the obligations of the business.

A written *partnership agreement*, or *articles of partnership*, establishes procedures for admission of a new partner, withdrawals of a partner, and the sharing of profits and losses among the partners. When a new partner is admitted to the firm or an existing partner withdraws, the old partnership is *dissolved*, or ceases to exist. A new partnership may or may not emerge to continue the business.

2. ***Account for partners' initial investments in a partnership.*** Accounting for a partnership is similar to accounting for a proprietorship. However, a partnership has more than one owner. Each partner has an individual capital account and a withdrawal account.

3. ***Allocate profits and losses to the partners by different methods.*** Partners share net income or loss in any manner they choose. Common sharing agreements base the *profit-and-loss ratio* on a stated fraction, partners' capital contributions, and/or their service to the partnership. Some partnerships call the cash drawings of partners *salaries* and *interest*, but these amounts are not expenses of the business. Instead, they are merely ways of allocating partnership net income to the partners.

4. ***Account for the admission of a new partner to the business.*** An outside person may become a partner by purchasing a current partner's interest or by investing in the partnership. In some cases, the new partner must pay the current partners a bonus to join. In other situations, the new partner may receive a bonus to join.

5. ***Account for the withdrawal of a partner from the business.*** When a partner withdraws, partnership assets may be reappraised. Partners share any gain or loss on the asset revaluation on the basis of their profit-and-loss ratio. The withdrawing partner may receive payment equal to, greater than, or less than his or her capital book value, depending on the agreement with the other partners.

6. ***Account for the liquidation of a partnership.*** In *liquidation*, a partnership goes out of business by selling the assets, paying the liabilities, and disbursing any remaining cash to the partners.

7. ***Prepare partnership financial statements.*** Partnership *financial statements* are similar to those of a proprietorship. However, the partnership income statement commonly reports the allocation of net income to the partners, and the balance sheet has a Capital account for each partner.

Accounting Vocabulary

articles of partnership *(p. 508)*
dissolution *(p. 508)*
general partnership *(p. 510)*
limited partnership *(p. 510)*
limited liability partnership *(p. 510)*
liquidation *(p. 523)*
LLP's *(p. 510)*
mutual agency *(p. 508)*
partnership *(p. 508)*
partnership agreement *(p. 508)*
S Corporation *(p. 511)*
unlimited personal liability *(p. 509)*

Questions

1. What is another name for a partnership agreement? List eight items that the agreement should specify.
2. Ron Montgomery, who is a partner in M&N Associates, commits the firm to a contract for a job within the scope of its regular business operations. What term describes Montgomery's ability to obligate the partnership?
3. If a partnership cannot pay a debt, who must make the payment? What term describes this obligation of the partners?
4. How is the income of a partnership taxed?
5. Identify the advantages and disadvantages of the partnership form of business organization.
6. Rex Randall and Ken Smith's partnership agreement states that Randall gets 60% of profits and Smith gets 40 percent. If the agreement does not discuss the treatment of losses, how are losses shared? How do the partners share profits and losses if the agreement specifies no profit-and-loss-sharing ratio?
7. What determines the amount of the credit to a partner's Capital account when the partner contributes assets other than cash to the business?
8. Do partner withdrawals of cash for personal use affect the sharing of profits and losses by the partner? If so, explain how. If not, explain why not.
9. Name two events that can cause the dissolution of a partnership.
10. Briefly describe how to account for the purchase of an existing partner's interest in the business.
11. Jeff Malcolm purchases Nona Brown's interest in the Brown & Kareem partnership. What right does Malcolm obtain from the purchase? What is required for Malcolm to become Paula Kareem's partner?
12. Sal Assissi and Cal Carter each have capital of $75,000 in their business. They share profits in the ratio of 55:45. Kathy Denman acquires a one-fifth share in the partnership by investing cash of $50,000. What are the capital balances of the three partners immediately after Denman is admitted?
13. When a partner resigns from the partnership and receives assets greater than his or her capital balance, how is the excess shared by the other partners?
14. Distinguish between dissolution and liquidation of a partnership.
15. Name the three steps in liquidating a partnership.
16. The partnership of Ralls and Sauls is in the process of liquidation. How do the partners share (a) gains and losses on the sale of noncash assets, and (b) the final cash disbursement?
17. Compare and contrast the financial statements of a proprietorship and a partnership.
18. Summarize the situations in which partnership allocations are based on (a) the profit-and-loss-sharing ratio, and (b) the partners' capital balances.

Daily Exercises

Partnership characteristics
(Obj. 1)

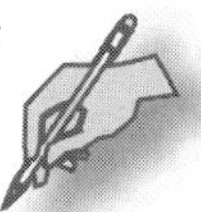

DE12-1 Sandy Saxe and Ira Weiss are forming a business to imprint T-shirts. Saxe suggests that they organize as a partnership in order to avoid the unlimited personal liability of a proprietorship. According to Saxe, partnerships are not very risky.

Saxe explains to Weiss that if the business does not succeed, each partner can withdraw from the business, taking the same assets that he or she invested at its beginning. Saxe states that the main disadvantage of the partnership form of organization is double taxation: First, the partnership pays a business income tax; second, each partner also pays personal income tax on his or her share of the business's profits.

Correct the errors in Saxe's explanation.

Partnership characteristics
(Obj. 1)

DE12-2 After studying the characteristics of a partnership, write two short paragraphs, as follows.

1. Explain the *advantages* of a partnership over a proprietorship and a corporation.
2. Explain the *disadvantages* of a partnership over a proprietorship and a corporation.

A partner's investment in a partnership
(Obj. 2)

DE12-3 Val Dierks invests a building in a partnership with Lena Marx. Dierks purchased the building in 1997 for $300,000. Accumulated depreciation to the date of forming the partnership is $80,000. A real estate appraiser states that the building is now worth $400,000. Dierks wants $400,000 capital in the new partnership, but Marx objects. Marx believes that Dierks's capital contribution into the partnership should be measured by the book value of his building.

Marx and Dierks seek your advice. Which value of the building is appropriate for measuring Dierks's capital, book value or current market value? State the reason for your answer. Give the partnership's journal entry to record Dierks's investment in the business.

Investments by partners
(Obj. 2)

DE12-4 Duane Warner and Eli Broad are forming the partnership Sun Florida Development to develop a theme park near Panama City. Warner contributes cash of $2 million and land valued at $30 million. When Warner purchased the land in 1996, its cost was $8 million. The partnership will assume Warner's $3 million note payable on the land. Broad invests cash of $10 million and construction equipment that he purchased for $7 million (accumulated depreciation to date, $3 million). The equipment's market value is equal to its book value.

1. Before recording any journal entries, compute the partnership's total assets, total liabilities, and total owners' equity immediately after organizing.
2. Journalize the partnership's receipt of assets and liabilities from Warner and from Broad. Record each asset at its current market value with no entry to accumulated depreciation.
3. Use your journal entries to prove the correctness of total owners' equity from requirement 1.

Partners' profits, losses, and capital balances
(Obj. 3)

DE12-5 Examine the Benz and Hanna balance sheet in Exhibit 12-3, page 512. Note that Benz invested far more in the partnership than Hanna. Suppose the two partners fail to agree upon a profit-and-loss-sharing ratio. For the first month (June 19X5), the partnership lost $20,000.

1. How much of this loss goes to Benz? How much goes to Hanna?
2. Assume the partners withdrew no cash or other assets during June. What is each partner's capital balance at June 30? Prepare a T-account for each partner's capital to answer this question.

Partners' profits, drawings, and capital balances; closing entries
(Obj. 3)

DE12-6 *Link Back to Chapter 4 (Closing Entries).* Return to the Benz and Hanna balance sheet in Exhibit 12-3, page 512. The partnership earned $115,000 during the year ended May 31, 19X6, its first year of operation. The partners share profits and losses based on their capital balances at the beginning of the year. During the first year, Benz withdrew $80,000 cash from the business and Hanna's drawings totaled $60,000.

1. Journalize the entries for (a) partner withdrawals of cash, (b) closing the business's profits into the partners' capital accounts at May 31, 19X6, and (c) closing the partners' drawing accounts.
2. Post to the partners' capital accounts after inserting their beginning amounts. What is the amount of total partnership capital at May 31, 19X6?

Allocating partnership profits based on capital contributions and service
(Obj. 3)

DE12-7 Day, Flagg, and Garcia have capital balances of $20,000, $30,000, and $50,000, respectively. The partners share profits and losses as follows:

a. The first $40,000 is divided based on the partners' capital balances.
b. The next $40,000 is based on service, equally shared by Day and Garcia.
c. The remainder is divided equally.

Compute each partner's share of the business's $110,000 net income for the year.

DE12-8 Susan Lin and Chan Tran have capital balances of $30,000 and $40,000, respectively. The partners share profits and losses as follows:

Allocating partnership profits based on salaries and interest **(Obj. 3)**

a. Lin receives a salary of $15,000 and Tran a salary of $10,000.
b. The partners earn 8% interest on their capital balances.
c. The remainder is shared equally.

Compute each partner's share of the year's net income of $50,000.

DE12-9 Study the Ingel and Jay partnership balance sheet near the bottom of page 517. Christa Lee pays $125,000 to purchase Michael Jay's interest in the partnership.

Admitting a partner who purchases an existing partner's interest **(Obj. 4)**

1. Journalize the partnership's transaction to admit Lee to the partnership. What happens to the $35,000 difference between Lee's payment and Jay's capital balance?
2. Must Robin Ingel accept Christa Lee as a full partner? What right does Lee have after purchasing Jay's interest in the partnership?

DE12-10 Return to the partnership balance sheet of Ingel and Jay near the bottom of page 517. Anthony Klaiber invests cash of $40,000 to acquire a one-fifth interest in the partnership.

Admitting a partner who invests in the business **(Obj. 4)**

1. Does Klaiber's investment provide a bonus to the partners? Show calculations to support your answer.
2. Journalize the partnership's receipt of the $40,000 from Klaiber.

DE12-11 Study the partnership balance sheet of Nagasawa and Osburn on page 518. Suppose Beth Quixote invests $190,000 to purchase a one-half interest in the new partnership of Nagasawa, Osburn, and Quixote (NOQ).

Journalize the partnership's receipt of cash from Quixote.

Admitting a new partner; bonus to the existing partners **(Obj. 4)**

DE12-12 This exercise uses the data given in Daily Exercise 12-11. After recording the partnership's receipt of cash from Quixote in Daily Exercise 12-11, prepare the balance sheet of the new partnership of NOQ Partners at June 30, 19X9. Include a complete heading.

Preparing a partnership balance sheet **(Obj. 7)**

DE12-13 Refer to the partnership balance sheet of Page and Franco near the top of page 520. Assume Haenni invests $120,000 to acquire a 30% interest in the new partnership of Page, Franco, and Haenni.

Journalize the partnership's receipt of cash from Haenni.

Admitting a new partner; bonus to the new partner **(Obj. 4)**

DE12-14 Examine the Green, Henry, and Isaac balance sheet near the bottom of page 521.

Withdrawal of a partner **(Obj. 5)**

1. The partners share profits and losses as follows: 25% to Green, 50% to Henry, and 25% to Isaac. Suppose Susan Green is withdrawing from the business, and the partners agree that no appraisal of assets is needed. How much in assets can Green take from the partnership? Give the reason for your answer, including an explanation of why the profit-and-loss-sharing ratio is not used for this determination.
2. Henry and Isaac plan to form a new partnership to continue the business. If Green demands cash for her full settlement upon withdrawing from the business, how can Henry and Isaac come up with the cash to pay Green? Identify two ways.

DE12-15 Return to the Green, Henry, and Isaac partnership balance sheet near the bottom of page 521. Suppose Henry is retiring from the business and the partners agree to revalue the assets at their current market value. A real-estate appraiser issues his professional opinion that the current market value (replacement cost) of the building is $150,000, and that the building is half used up. The book values of all other assets approximate their current market value.

Journalize (a) the revaluation of the building and its accumulated depreciation, (b) borrowing $40,000 on a note payable in order to pay Henry, and (c) payment of $40,500 to Henry upon his retirement from the business on July 31.

Withdrawal of a partner at more than book value; asset revaluation **(Obj. 5)**

DE12-16 This exercise uses the data given in Daily Exercise 12-15 with one modification. Assume Henry is retiring from the partnership and agrees to take cash of $60,500.

Journalize the payment of $60,500 to Henry upon his withdrawal from the partnership.

Withdrawal of a partner at less than book value **(Obj. 5)**

DE12-17 Use the data in Exhibit 12-4, page 525. Suppose the partnership of Aviron, Bloch, and Crane liquidates by selling all noncash assets for $80,000.

Complete the liquidation schedule as shown in Exhibit 12-4.

Liquidation of a partnership at a loss **(Obj. 6)**

DE12-18 This exercise builds on the solution to Daily Exercise 12-17. After completing the liquidation schedule in Daily Exercise12-17, journalize the partnership's (a) sale of noncash assets for $80,000 (use a single account for Noncash Assets), (b) payment of liabilities, and (c) disbursement of cash to the partners. Include an explanation with each entry.

Liquidation entries for a partnership **(Obj. 6)**

Preparing a partnership balance sheet
(Obj. 7)

DE12-19 This exercise uses the Green, Henry, and Isaac balance sheet, after revaluation of inventory and land, given in the middle of page 522. Furthermore, assume Isaac has withdrawn from the partnership at less than book value, as recorded at the top of page 523.

Prepare the balance sheet of the new partnership of Green and Henry on July 31.

Preparing a partnership income statement
(Obj. 7)

DE12-20 The partnership of Teter and Lund had these balances at September 30, 19X8:

Cash	$20,000	Service revenue..........	$140,000
Liabilities	40,000	Teter, capital	30,000
Lund, capital..........	10,000	Total expenses............	50,000
Other assets	60,000		

Teter gets two-thirds of profits and losses, and Lund one-third.

Prepare the partnership's income statement for the year ended September 30, 19X8.

Exercises

Organizing a business as a partnership
(Obj. 1)

E12-1 Lana Kendall, a friend from college, approaches you about forming a partnership to export software. Since graduating, Kendall has worked for the Export-Import Bank, developing important contacts among government officials and business leaders in Eastern Europe. Kendall believes she is in a unique position to capitalize on the growing market in Eastern Europe for American computers. With expertise in finance, you would have responsibility for accounting and finance in the partnership.

Discuss the advantages and disadvantages of organizing the export business as a partnership rather than a proprietorship. Comment on how partnership income is taxed.

Recording a partner's investment
(Obj. 2)

E12-2 Sylvester Gato has been operating an apartment-location service as a proprietorship. He and Tim Vanderploeg have decided to reorganize the business as a partnership. Gato's investment in the partnership consists of cash, $13,100; accounts receivable, $10,600, less allowance for uncollectibles, $800; office furniture, $2,700, less accumulated depreciation, $1,100; a small building, $55,000, less accumulated depreciation, $27,500; accounts payable, $3,300; and a note payable to the bank, $10,000.

To determine Gato's equity in the partnership, he and Vanderploeg hire an independent appraiser. This outside party provides the following market values of the assets and liabilities that Gato is contributing to the business: cash, accounts receivable, office furniture, accounts payable, and note payable—the same as Gato's book value; allowance for uncollectible accounts, $2,900; building, $71,000; and accrued expenses payable (including interest on the note payable), $1,200.

REQUIRED

Make the entry on the partnership books to record Gato's investment.

Computing partners' shares of net income and net loss
(Obj. 3)

E12-3 Beth Vines and Chad Horton form a partnership, investing $40,000 and $70,000, respectively. Determine their shares of net income or net loss for each of the following situations:

a. Net loss is $52,000, and the partners have no written partnership agreement.

b. Net income is $44,000, and the partnership agreement states that the partners share profits and losses on the basis of their capital contributions.

c. Net loss is $77,000, and the partnership agreement states that the partners share profits on the basis of their capital contributions.

d. Net income is $110,000. The first $60,000 is shared on the basis of partner capital contributions. The next $45,000 is based on partner service, with Vines receiving 30% and Horton receiving 70 percent. The remainder is shared equally.

Computing partners' capital balances
(Obj. 3)

E12-4 Beth Vines withdrew cash of $52,000 for personal use, and Chad Horton withdrew cash of $50,000 during the year. Using the data from situation (d) in Exercise 12-3, journalize the entries to close (a) the income summary account, and (b) the partners' drawing accounts. Explanations are not required. Indicate the amount of increase or decrease in each partner's capital balance. What was the overall effect on partnership capital?

Admitting a new partner
(Obj. 4)

E12-5 Jason Kraft is admitted to a partnership. Prior to his admission, the partnership books show Grant Boyd's capital balance at $100,000 and Alison Terrell's capital balance at $50,000. Compute each partner's equity on the books of the new partnership under the following plans:

a. Kraft pays $80,000 for Terrell's equity. Kraft's payment is not an investment in the partnership but instead goes directly to Terrell.

b. Kraft invests $50,000 to acquire a one-fourth interest in the partnership.

c. Kraft invests $90,000 to acquire a one-fourth interest in the partnership.

E12-6 Make the partnership journal entry to record the admission of Kraft under plans (a), (b), and (c) in Exercise 12-5. Explanations are not required.

Recording the admission of a new partner **(Obj. 4)**

E12-7 After the books are closed, Brandon & Holmes's partnership balance sheet reports capital of $60,000 for Brandon and $80,000 for Holmes. Brandon is withdrawing from the firm. The partners agree to write down partnership assets by $30,000. They have shared profits and losses in the ratio of one-third to Brandon and two-thirds to Holmes. The partnership agreement states that a withdrawing partner will receive assets equal to the book value of his owner's equity.

Withdrawal of a partner **(Obj. 5)**

1. How much will Brandon receive? Holmes will continue to operate the business as a proprietorship.
2. What is Holmes's beginning capital on the proprietorship books?

E12-8 Lana Brown is retiring from the partnership of Brown, Green, and White on May 31. The partner capital balances are Brown, $36,000; Green, $51,000; and White, $22,000. The partners agree to have the partnership assets revalued to current market values. The independent appraiser reports that the book value of the inventory should be decreased by $8,000, and the book value of the land should be increased by $32,000. The partners agree to these revaluations. The profit-and-loss ratio has been 5:3:2 for Brown, Green, and White, respectively. In retiring from the firm, Brown receives $25,000 cash and a $25,000 note from the partnership.

Withdrawal of a partner **(Obj. 5)**

REQUIRED

Journalize (a) the asset revaluations, and (b) Brown's withdrawal from the firm.

E12-9 Marsh, Ng, and Orsulak are liquidating their partnership. Before selling the noncash assets and paying the liabilities, the capital balances are Marsh, $23,000; Ng, $14,000; and Orsulak, $11,000. The partnership agreement divides profits and losses equally.

Liquidation of a partnership **(Obj. 6)**

REQUIRED

1. After selling the noncash assets and paying the liabilities, the partnership has cash of $48,000. How much cash will each partner receive in final liquidation?
2. After selling the noncash assets and paying the liabilities, the partnership has cash of $45,000. How much cash will each partner receive in final liquidation?

E12-10 Prior to liquidation, the accounting records of Pratt, Qualls, and Ramirez included the following balances and profit-and-loss-sharing percentages:

Liquidation of a partnership **(Obj. 6)**

					Capital	
	Cash +	Noncash Assets	= Liabilities +	Pratt (40%) +	Qualls (30%) +	Ramirez (30%)
Balances before sale of assets	$8,000	$57,000	$19,000	$20,000	$15,000	$11,000

The partnership sold the noncash assets for $73,000, paid the liabilities, and disbursed the remaining cash to the partners. Complete the summary of transactions in the liquidation of the partnership. Use the format illustrated in Exhibit 12-4.

E12-11 The partnership of Foust, Gray, and Hart is dissolving. Business assets, liabilities, and partners' capital balances prior to dissolution follow. The partners share profits and losses as follows: Cory Foust, 25%; Betty Gray, 55%; and Clyde Hart, 20 percent.

Liquidation of a partnership **(Obj. 6)**

REQUIRED

Create a spreadsheet or solve manually—as directed by your instructor—to show the ending balances in all accounts after the noncash assets are sold for $136,000 and for $90,000. Determine the unknown amounts:

	A	B	C	D	E	F
1			FOUST, GRAY, AND HART			
2			Sale of Noncash Assets			
3			(For $136,000)			
4						
5		Noncash		Foust	Gray	Hart
6	Cash	Assets	Liabilities	Capital	Capital	Capital
7	$ 6,000	$126,000	$77,000	$12,000	$37,000	$6,000
8	136,000	(126,000)		?	?	?
9						
10	$142,000	$ 0	$77,000	$?	$?	$?
11						
12				($A8–$B7)*.25		
13						
14						
15			(For $90,000)			
16		Noncash		Foust	Gray	Hart
17	Cash	Assets	Liabilities	Capital	Capital	Capital
18	$ 6,000	$126,000	$77,000	$12,000	$37,000	$6,000
19	90,000	(126,000)		?	?	?
20						
21	$ 96,000	$ 0	$77,000	$?	$?	$?
22						
23				($A19–$B18)*.25		
24						

Identify two ways the partners can deal with the negative ending balance in Hart's capital account.

CHALLENGE EXERCISE

Preparing a partnership balance sheet (Obj. 7)

E12-12 On October 31, 19X9, Jill Justine and Don Gabriel agree to combine their proprietorships as a partnership. Their balance sheets on October 31 are as follows:

	Justine's Business		Gabriel's Business	
	Book Value	Current Market Value	Book Value	Current Market Value
Assets				
Cash	$ 3,700	$ 3,700	$ 4,000	$ 4,000
Accounts receivable (net)	22,000	20,200	8,000	6,300
Inventory	51,000	46,000	34,000	35,100
Plant assets (net)	121,800	103,500	53,500	57,400
Total assets	$198,500	$173,400	$99,500	$102,800
Liabilities and Capital				
Accounts payable	$ 23,600	$ 23,600	$ 9,100	$ 9,100
Accrued expenses payable	2,200	2,200	1,400	1,400
Notes payable	55,000	55,000		
Justine, capital	117,700	?		
Gabriel, capital			89,000	?
Total liabilities and capital	$198,500	$173,400	$99,500	$102,800

REQUIRED

Prepare the partnership balance sheet at October 31, 19X9.

Beyond the Numbers

Partnership issues (Obj. 1, 5)

BN12-1 The following questions relate to issues faced by partnerships.

1. The text suggests that a written partnership agreement should be drawn up between the partners in a partnership. One benefit of an agreement is that it provides a mechanism for

resolving disputes between the partners. List five areas of dispute that might be resolved by a partnership agreement.

2. The statement has been made that "If you must take on a partner, make sure the partner is richer than you are." Why is this statement valid?
3. Willis, Boone, & Hill is a law partnership. Andrew Hill is planning to retire from the partnership and move to Canada. What options are available to Hill to enable him to convert his share of the partnership assets to cash?

ETHICAL ISSUE

Cindy Nguyen and Dan Tiedeman operate The Party Center, a party supply store in Charlotte, North Carolina. The partners split profits and losses equally, and each takes an annual salary of $50,000. To even out the work load, Tiedeman does the buying and Nguyen serves as the accountant. From time to time, they use small amounts of store merchandise for personal use. In preparing for a large private party at her home, Nguyen took engraved invitations, napkins, placemats, and other goods that cost $1,000. She recorded the transaction as follows:

Cost of Goods Sold..........	1,000	
Inventory..................		1,000

1. How should Nguyen have recorded this transaction?
2. Discuss the ethical dimensions of Nguyen's action.

Problems (GROUP A)

Writing a partnership agreement (Obj. 1)

P12-1A Elizabeth Palomin and John Arendale are discussing the formation of a partnership to install payroll accounting systems. Palomin is skilled in systems design, and she is convinced that her designs will draw large sales volumes. Arendale is a super salesperson and has already lined up several clients.

REQUIRED

Write a partnership agreement to cover all elements essential for the business to operate smoothly. Make up names, amounts, profit-and-loss-sharing percentages, and so on as needed.

Investments by partners (Obj. 2, 7)

P12-2A On June 30, Abe Treacy and Megan Kell formed a partnership. The partners agreed to invest equal amounts of capital. Treacy invested his proprietorship's assets and liabilities (credit balances in parentheses).

	Treacy's Book Value	Current Market Value
Accounts receivable..........	$ 7,200	$ 7,200
Allowance for doubtful accounts	(–0–)	(1,050)
Inventory..........	22,340	24,100
Prepaid expenses..........	1,700	1,700
Office equipment..........	45,900	27,600
Accumulated depreciation..........	(15,300)	–0–
Accounts payable..........	(19,100)	(19,100)

On June 30, Kell invested cash in an amount equal to the current market value of Treacy's partnership capital. The partners decided that Treacy would earn two-thirds of partnership profits because he would manage the business. Kell agreed to accept one-third of the profits. During the remainder of the year, the partnership earned $60,000. Treacy's drawings were $35,200, and Kell's drawings were $23,000.

REQUIRED

1. Journalize the partners' initial investments.
2. Prepare the partnership balance sheet immediately after its formation on June 30.
3. Journalize the December 31 entries to close the Income Summary account and the partners' drawing accounts.

Admitting a new partner (Obj. 4)

P12-3A Englewood Consulting Associates is a partnership, and its owners are considering admitting Hilda Newton as a new partner. On March 31 of the current year, the capital accounts of the three existing partners and their shares of profits and losses are as follows:

	Capital	Profit-and-Loss Share
Jim Zook..........	$ 40,000	15%
Richard Land..........	100,000	30
Jennifer Lim..........	160,000	55

REQUIRED

Journalize the admission of Newton as a partner on March 31 for each of the following independent situations:

1. Newton pays Lim $145,000 cash to purchase Lim's interest in the partnership.
2. Newton invests $60,000 in the partnership, acquiring a one-sixth interest in the business.
3. Newton invests $60,000 in the partnership, acquiring a one-fifth interest in the business.
4. Newton invests $40,000 in the partnership, acquiring a 10% interest in the business.

Computing partners' shares of net income and net loss
(Obj. 3, 7)

P12-4A Larry Collins, Elinor Davis, and Paul Chiu have formed a partnership. Collins invested $15,000, Davis $18,000, and Chiu $27,000. Collins will manage the store, Davis will work in the store half-time, and Chiu will not work in the business.

REQUIRED

1. Compute the partners' shares of profits and losses under each of the following plans:
   - **a.** Net loss is $42,900, and the articles of partnership do not specify how profits and losses are shared.
   - **b.** Net loss is $60,000, and the partnership agreement allocates 40% of profits to Collins, 25% to Davis, and 35% to Chiu. The agreement does not discuss the sharing of losses.
   - **c.** Net income is $92,000. The first $40,000 is allocated on the basis of salaries, with Collins receiving $28,000 and Davis receiving $12,000. The remainder is allocated on the basis of partner capital contributions.
   - **d.** Net income for the year ended January 31, 19X8, is $180,000. The first $75,000 is allocated on the basis of partner capital contributions, and the next $36,000 is based on service, with Collins receiving $28,000 and Davis receiving $8,000. Any remainder is shared equally.

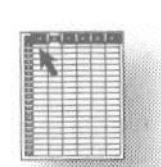

2. Revenues for the year ended January 31, 19X8, were $870,000, and expenses were $690,000. Under plan (d), prepare the partnership income statement for the year.

Withdrawal of a partner
(Obj. 4, 5)

P12-5A Personal Financial Services is a partnership owned by three individuals. The partners share profits and losses in the ratio of 28% to Dan Smythe, 38% to Max Lark, and 34% to Emily Spahn. At December 31, 19X7, the firm has the following balance sheet:

Cash		$ 12,000	Total liabilities	$ 75,000
Accounts receivable	$ 22,000			
Less allowance for uncollectibles	(4,000)	18,000	Smythe, capital	83,000
Building	$310,000		Lark, capital	50,000
Less accumulated depreciation	(70,000)	240,000	Spahn, capital	62,000
Total assets		$270,000	Total liabilities and capital	$270,000

Lark withdraws from the partnership on December 31, 19X7, to establish his own consulting practice.

REQUIRED

Record Lark's withdrawal from the partnership under the following plans:

1. Lark gives his interest in the business to Terry Boyd, his nephew.
2. In personal transactions, Lark sells his equity in the partnership to Bea Patell and Al Bruckner, who each pay Lark $40,000 for half his interest. Smythe and Spahn agree to accept Patell and Bruckner as partners.
3. The partnership pays Lark cash of $15,000 and gives him a note payable for the remainder of his book equity in settlement of his partnership interest.
4. Lark receives cash of $10,000 and a note for $70,000 from the partnership.
5. The partners agree that the building is worth only $280,000 and that its accumulated depreciation should remain at $70,000. After the revaluation, the partnership settles with Lark by giving him cash of $14,100 and a note payable for the remainder of his book equity.

Liquidation of a partnership
(Obj. 6)

P12-6A The partnership of Monet, Blair, & Trippi has experienced operating losses for three consecutive years. The partners—who have shared profits and losses in the ratio of Mindy Monet, 10%; Burt Blair, 30%; and Toni Trippi, 60%—are considering the liquidation of the business. They ask you to analyze the effects of liquidation under various possibilities regarding the sale of the noncash assets. They present the following condensed partnership balance sheet at December 31, end of the current year:

Cash	$ 27,000	Liabilities	$131,000
Noncash assets	202,000	Monet, capital	21,000
		Blair, capital	39,000
		Trippi, capital	38,000
Total assets	$229,000	Total liabilities and capital	$229,000

REQUIRED

1. Prepare a summary of liquidation transactions (as illustrated in Exhibit 12-4) for each of the following situations:
   a. The noncash assets are sold for $212,000.
   b. The noncash assets are sold for $182,000.
2. Make the journal entries to record the liquidation transactions in requirement 1b.

Liquidation of a partnership (Obj. 6)

P12-7A *Link Back to Chapter 4 (Closing Entries).* BP&O is a partnership owned by Bell, Pastena, and O'Donnell, who share profits and losses in the ratio of 5:3:2. The adjusted trial balance of the partnership (in condensed form) at September 30, end of the current fiscal year, follows.

BP&O
Adjusted Trial Balance
September 30, 19XX

Cash	$ 10,000	
Noncash assets	177,000	
Liabilities		$135,000
Bell, capital		57,000
Pastena, capital		44,000
O'Donnell, capital		21,000
Bell, drawing	45,000	
Pastena, drawing	37,000	
O'Donnell, drawing	18,000	
Revenues		211,000
Expenses	181,000	
Totals	$468,000	$468,000

REQUIRED

1. Prepare the September 30 entries to close the revenue, expense, income summary, and drawing accounts.
2. Insert the opening capital balances in the partner capital accounts, post the closing entries to the capital accounts, and determine each partner's ending capital balance.
3. The partnership liquidates on September 30 by selling the noncash assets for $132,000. Using the ending balances of the partner capital accounts computed in requirement 2, prepare a summary of liquidation transactions (as illustrated in Exhibit 12–4).

Problems (GROUP B)

Writing a partnership agreement (Obj. 1)

P12-1B Dolores Sanchez and Leticia Gaitan are discussing the formation of a partnership to import dresses from Guatemala. Sanchez is especially artistic, so she will travel to Central America to buy merchandise. Gaitan is a super salesperson and has already lined up several large stores to which she can sell the dresses.

REQUIRED

Write a partnership agreement to cover all elements essential for the business to operate smoothly. Make up names, amounts, profit-and-loss-sharing percentages, and so on as needed.

Investments by partners (Obj. 2, 7)

P12-2B Jo Ringle and Mel LeBlanc formed a partnership on March 15. The partners agreed to invest equal amounts of capital. LeBlanc invested his proprietorship's assets and liabilities (credit balances in parentheses):

	LeBlanc's Book Value	Current Market Value
Accounts receivable	$ 12,000	$ 12,000
Allowance for doubtful accounts	(740)	(1,360)
Inventory	43,850	31,220
Prepaid expenses	2,400	2,400
Store equipment	36,700	26,600
Accumulated depreciation	(9,200)	(–0–)
Accounts payable	(22,300)	(22,300)

On March 15, Ringle invested cash in an amount equal to the current market value of LeBlanc's partnership capital. The partners decided that LeBlanc would earn 70% of partnership profits because he would manage the business. Ringle agreed to accept 30% of profits. During the period ended December 31, the partnership earned $80,000. Ringle's drawings were $32,000, and LeBlanc's drawings were $36,000.

REQUIRED

1. Journalize the partners' initial investments.
2. Prepare the partnership balance sheet immediately after its formation on March 15.
3. Journalize the December 31 entries to close the Income Summary account and the partners' drawing accounts.

Admitting a new partner
(Obj. 4)

P12-3B Red River Resort is a partnership, and its owners are considering admitting Greg Lake as a new partner. On July 31 of the current year, the capital accounts of the three existing partners and their shares of profits and losses are as follows:

	Capital	Profit-and-Loss Ratio
Ellen Urlang..........	$48,000	1/6
Amy Sharp.............	64,000	1/3
Bob Hayes	88,000	1/2

REQUIRED

Journalize the admission of Lake as a partner on July 31 for each of the following independent situations.

1. Lake pays Hayes $50,000 cash to purchase one-half of Hayes's interest.
2. Lake invests $50,000 in the partnership, acquiring a one-fifth interest in the business.
3. Lake invests $40,000 in the partnership, acquiring a one-eighth interest in the business.
4. Lake invests $30,000 in the partnership, acquiring a 15% interest in the business.

Computing partners' shares of net income and net loss
(Obj. 3, 7)

P12-4B Robin Dewey, Kami Karlin, and Dean DeCastro have formed a partnership. Dewey invested $20,000; Karlin, $40,000; and DeCastro, $60,000. Dewey will manage the store, Karlin will work in the store three-quarters of the time, and DeCastro will not work in the business.

REQUIRED

1. Compute the partners' shares of profits and losses under each of the following plans:
   a. Net income is $87,000, and the articles of partnership do not specify how profits and losses are shared.
   b. Net loss is $47,000, and the partnership agreement allocates 45% of profits to Dewey, 35% to Karlin, and 20% to DeCastro. The agreement does not discuss the sharing of losses.
   c. Net income is $104,000. The first $50,000 is allocated on the basis of salaries of $34,000 for Dewey and $16,000 for Karlin. The remainder is allocated on the basis of partner capital contributions.
   d. Net income for the year ended September 30, 19X4, is $91,000. The first $30,000 is allocated on the basis of partner capital contributions. The next $30,000 is based on service, with $20,000 going to Dewey and $10,000 going to Karlin. Any remainder is shared equally.
2. Revenues for the year ended September 30, 19X4, were $572,000, and expenses were $481,000. Under plan (d), prepare the partnership income statement for the year.

Withdrawal of a partner
(Obj. 4, 5)

P12-5B Airborne Systems is a partnership owned by three individuals. The partners share profits and losses in the ratio of 30% to Eve Koehn, 40% to Earl Neiman, and 30% to Ivana Marcus. At December 31, 19X6, the firm has the following balance sheet:

Cash		$ 25,000	Total liabilities	$103,000
Accounts receivable	$ 16,000			
Less allowance for uncollectibles	(1,000)	15,000		
Inventory		92,000	Koehn, capital..........................	38,000
Equipment.........................	130,000		Nieman, capital.........................	49,000
Less accumulated			Marcus, capital.........................	42,000
depreciation	(30,000)	100,000	Total liabilities and	
Total assets.........................		$232,000	capital	$232,000

Koehn withdraws from the partnership on this date.

REQUIRED

Record Koehn's withdrawal from the partnership under the following plans:

1. Koehn gives her interest in the business to Lynn Albelli, her cousin.

2. In personal transactions, Koehn sells her equity in the partnership to Matt Bullock and Shelley Jones, who each pay Koehn $15,000 for half her interest. Neiman and Marcus agree to accept Bullock and Jones as partners.
3. The partnership pays Koehn cash of $5,000 and gives her a note payable for the remainder of her book equity in settlement of her partnership interest.
4. Koehn receives cash of $20,000 and a note payable for $20,000 from the partnership.
5. The partners agree that the equipment is worth $150,000 and that accumulated depreciation should remain at $30,000. After the revaluation, the partnership settles with Koehn by giving her cash of $10,000 and inventory for the remainder of her book equity.

Liquidation of a partnership (Obj. 6)

P12-6B The partnership of Whitney, Kosse, & Itasca has experienced operating losses for three consecutive years. The partners—who have shared profits and losses in the ratio of Fran Whitney, 15%; Walt Kosse, 60%; and Emil Itasca, 25%—are considering the liquidation of the business. They ask you to analyze the effects of liquidation under various possibilities regarding the sale of the noncash assets. They present the following condensed partnership balance sheet at December 31, end of the current year:

Cash	$ 7,000	Liabilities	$ 63,000
Noncash assets	163,000	Whitney, capital	24,000
		Kosse, capital	66,000
		Itasca, capital	17,000
		Total liabilities and	
Total assets	$170,000	capital	$170,000

REQUIRED

1. Prepare a summary of liquidation transactions (as illustrated in the Exhibit 12-4) for each of the following situations:
   a. The noncash assets are sold for $175,000.
   b. The noncash assets are sold for $141,000.
2. Make the journal entries to record the liquidation transactions in requirement 1b.

Liquidation of a partnership (Obj. 6)

P12-7B *Link Back to Chapter 4 (Closing Entries).* RMG & Company is a partnership owned by Ryan, Morales, and Goldberg, who share profits and losses in the ratio of 1:3:4. The adjusted trial balance of the partnership (in condensed form) at June 30, end of the current fiscal year, follows.

RMG & COMPANY
Adjusted Trial Balance
June 30, 19XX

Cash	$ 24,000	
Noncash assets	116,000	
Liabilities		$100,000
Ryan, capital		22,000
Morales, capital		41,000
Goldberg, capital		62,000
Ryan, drawing	14,000	
Morales, drawing	35,000	
Goldberg, drawing	54,000	
Revenues		108,000
Expenses	90,000	
Totals	$333,000	$333,000

REQUIRED

1. Prepare the June 30 entries to close the revenue, expense, income summary, and drawing accounts.
2. Insert the opening capital balances in the partners' capital accounts, post the closing entries to the capital accounts, and determine each partner's ending capital balance.
3. The partnership liquidates on June 30 by selling the noncash assets for $100,000. Using the ending balances of the partners' capital accounts computed in requirement 2, prepare a summary of liquidation transactions (as illustrated in Exhibit 12–4).

Applying Your Knowledge

DECISION CASE

Settling disagreements among partners ***(Obj. 3)***

Becky Jones invested $20,000 and Imelda Nichols invested $10,000 in a public relations firm that has operated for ten years. Neither partner has made an additional investment. They have shared profits and losses in the ratio of 2:1, which is the ratio of their investments in the business. Jones manages the office, supervises the 16 employees, and does the accounting. Nichols, the moderator of a television talk show, is responsible for marketing. Her high profile generates important revenue for the business. During the year ended December 19X4, the partnership earned net income of $87,000, shared in the 2:1 ratio. On December 31, 19X4, Jones's capital balance was $150,000, and Nichols's capital balance was $100,000.

REQUIRED

Respond to each of the following situations.

1. What explains the difference between the ratio of partner capital balances at December 31, 19X4, and the 2:1 ratio of partner investments and profit sharing?
2. Nichols believes that the profit-and-loss-sharing ratio is unfair. She proposes a change, but Jones insists on keeping the 2:1 ratio. What two factors may underlie Nichols's unhappiness?
3. During January 19X5, Jones learned that revenues of $18,000 were omitted from the reported 19X4 income. She brings this omission to Nichols's attention, pointing out that Jones's share of this added income is two-thirds, or $12,000, and Nichols's share is one-third, or $6,000. Nichols believes that they should share this added income on the basis of their capital balances—60%, or $10,800, to Jones and 40%, or $7,200, to herself. Which partner is correct? Why?
4. Assume that the 19X4 $18,000 omission was an account payable for an operating expense. On what basis would the partners share this amount?

FINANCIAL STATEMENT CASE

KPMG Peat Marwick is an international accounting firm. Summary data from the partnership's *1997 Annual Report* follow.

(Dollars in millions, except where indicated)	Years Ended June 30				
	1997	1996	1995	1994	1993
Revenues					
Assurance	$1,234	$1,122	$1,064	$1,093	$1,070
Consulting	1,007	775	658	473	349
Tax	743	628	567	515	557
Total Revenues	$2,984	$2,525	$2,289	$2,081	$1,976
Operating Summary					
Revenues	$2,984	$2,525	$2,289	$2,081	$1,976
Personnel Costs	1,215	1,004	887	805	726
Other Costs	1,212	1,030	967	898	829
Income to Partners	$ 557	$ 491	$ 435	$ 378	$ 421
Statistical Data					
Average Number of Partners	1,494	1,428	1,413	1,449	1,453

REQUIRED

1. What percentages of total revenues did KPMG earn by performing assurance services (similar to audit), consulting services, and tax services during 1993? What were the percentages in 1997? Which type of services grew the most from 1993 to 1997?
2. Compute the average revenue per partner in 1997. Assume each partner works 2,000 hours per year. On average, how much does each partner charge a client for one hour of time?
3. How much net income did each KPMG partner earn, on average, in 1997? For people who enjoy accounting, consulting, and tax work, do you see why accounting is a popular major in college?

Team Project

Visit a business partnership in your area, and interview one or more of the partners. Obtain answers to the following questions and ask your instructor for directions. As directed by your instructor, either (a) prepare a written report of your findings, or (b) make a presentation to your class.

1. Why did you organize the business as a partnership? What advantages does the partnership form of organization offer the business? What are the disadvantages of the partnership form of organization?
2. Is the business a general partnership, or is it a limited partnership?
3. Do the partners have a written partnership agreement? What does the agreement cover? Obtain a copy if possible.
4. Who manages the business? Do all partners participate in day-to-day management, or is management the responsibility of only certain partners?
5. If there is no written agreement, what is the mechanism for making key decisions?
6. Have you ever admitted a new partner? If so, when did it occur? What are the partnership's procedures for admitting a new partner?
7. Has a partner ever withdrawn from the business? If so, when? What are the partnership's procedures for settling up with a withdrawing partner?
8. If possible, learn how the partnership divides profits and losses among the partners.
9. Ask for any additional insights that the partner whom you interview can provide about the business.

Internet Exercise ANDERSON WORLDWIDE

The world largest accounting firms are organized as partnerships. Known as the Big Six (or Five or Four or Three—depending on the results of recent mergers), these firms provide more than the traditional auditing and tax work. Today, these accounting firms call themselves professional services firms and they provide every conceivable business service: from business process reengineering to identifying CEO candidates for its clients. What began as green-eye shaded accountants pouring over a client's accounting records has evolved into a $20+ billion industry.

The largest of the accounting firms is Arthur Andersen. Founded in Chicago by its namesake, Arthur Andersen, back in 1913, the firm has expanded to over 50,000 people in 76 countries.

REQUIRED

1. Go to **http://www.arthurandersen.com.** This is the home page for Arthur Andersen.
2. Click on **About Arthur Andersen.** This section allows you to learn more about the firm as well as the history of accounting. Note, to fully enjoy the history of accounting pages, your Web browser needs to have the Shockwave for Director plug-in. After exploring this section, answer the following questions:
   a. Why does Arthur Andersen *not* publish financial statements? In fact, none of the large accounting firms publish financial statements.
   b. What are the two main groups that comprise Andersen Worldwide? How much in revenues did Andersen Worldwide earn last year?
   c. Which business does Arthur Andersen cite as the most important?
   d. How do accounting professors across the country rank Arthur Andersen?

CHAPTER 13

Corporate Organization, Paid-in Capital, and the Balance Sheet

LEARNING OBJECTIVES

After studying this chapter, you should be able to

1. Identify the characteristics of a corporation
2. Record the issuance of stock
3. Prepare the stockholders' equity section of a corporation's balance sheet
4. Account for cash dividends
5. Use different stock values in decision making
6. Evaluate a company's return on assets and return on stockholders' equity
7. Account for a corporation's income tax

> *"Going public is a good way for a company to raise needed capital. Being publicly traded gets the company more attention in the financial pages and in brokerage-firm research reports. This allows the company, when it's doing well, to raise money easily and cheaply."*
>
> MALCOLM P. APPELBAUM,
> PRIVATE EQUITY INVESTOR,
> WAND PARTNERS, INC.

Based in Glendale, California, IHOP Corporation develops, franchises, and operates International House of Pancakes family restaurants. There are almost 600 IHOPs in 35 states, Canada, and Japan—with big concentrations of IHOP restaurants in California, New York, New Jersey, Florida, and Texas.

IHOP still serves up stacks of great pancakes, but now you can buy the stock as well. When IHOP Corp. went public, the company offered 6.2 million shares at $10 each. The shares got off to a strong start and have performed well. IHOP's stock lately has traded at about $36 per share. *Sources:* Adapted from "Stacked Stock," *Forbes*, July 6, 1992, p. 128, and "Looking at IHOP: Not Just Pancakes," *New York Times*, November 6, 1992.

What does it mean to "go public," as IHOP did? A corporation *goes public* when it issues its stock to the general public. A common reason for going public is to raise money for expansion. By offering its stock to the public, a company can hope to raise more money than if the stockholders are limited to a few insiders. In its public offering of stock, IHOP hoped to receive cash of $62 million (6.2 million shares of stock at $10 each). The investors who bought IHOP's stock at $10 have done well. IHOP stock is now worth over $36 per share. The opportunity to profit from buying a good stock makes corporations an attractive form of business organization.

Objective 1

Identify the characteristics of a corporation

Corporations: An Overview

The corporation is the dominant form of business organization in the United States. International House of Pancakes is an example. Although proprietorships and partnerships are more numerous, corporations transact more business and are larger in terms of total assets, sales revenue, and number of employees. Most well-known companies, such as NIKE, CBS, General Motors, and IBM, are corporations. Their full names include *Corporation* or *Incorporated* (abbreviated *Corp.* and *Inc.*) to indicate that they are corporations—for example, CBS, Inc., and General Motors Corporation.

Characteristics of a Corporation

Why is the corporate form of business so attractive? We now look at the features that distinguish corporations from proprietorships and partnerships, and some of the advantages and disadvantages of corporations.

SEPARATE LEGAL ENTITY A corporation is a business entity formed under state law. The state grants a **charter,** which is a document that gives a business the state's permission to form a corporation. Neither a proprietorship nor a partnership requires state approval to do business, because in the eyes of the law the business is the same as the owner(s).

Charter. Document that gives the state's permission to form a corporation.

From a legal perspective, a corporation is a distinct entity, an artificial person that exists apart from its owners, who are called **stockholders** or **shareholders.** The corporation has many of the rights that a person has. For example, a corporation may buy, own, and sell property. Assets and liabilities in the business belong to the corporation rather than to its owners. The corporation may enter into contracts, sue, and be sued.

Stockholder. A person who owns the stock of a corporation. Also called **shareholder.**

The owners' equity of a corporation is divided into shares of **stock.** The corporate charter specifies how much stock the corporation can issue (sell).

Stock. Shares into which the owners' equity of a corporation is divided.

CONTINUOUS LIFE AND TRANSFERABILITY OF OWNERSHIP Most corporations have *continuous lives* regardless of changes in the ownership of their stock. The stockholders of IHOP or any corporation may transfer stock as they wish. They may sell or trade the stock to another person, give it away, bequeath it in a will, or dispose of it in any other way. The transfer of the stock does not affect the continuity of the corporation. In contrast, proprietorships and partnerships terminate when their ownership changes.

NO MUTAL AGENCY *Mutual agency* is an arrangement whereby all owners act as agents of the business. A contract signed by one owner is binding for the whole company. Mutual agency operates in partnerships but *not* in corporations. A stockholder of IHOP Corp. cannot commit the corporation to a contract (unless he or she is also an officer in the business). For this reason, a stockholder need not exercise the care that partners must in selecting co-owners of the business.

We introduced the idea of mutual agency, which applies only to partnerships, in Chapter 12, page 508.

LIMITED LIABILITY OF STOCKHOLDERS Stockholders have **limited liability** for corporation debts. That is, they have no personal obligation for corporation liabilities. The most that a stockholder can lose on an investment in a corporation's stock is the amount invested. In contrast, proprietors and partners are personally liable for all the debts of their businesses.

Limited Liability. No personal obligation of a stockholder for corporation debts. A stockholder can lose no more on an investment in a corporation's stock than the cost of the investment.

The combination of limited liability and no mutual agency means that persons can invest limited amounts in a corporation without fear of losing all their personal wealth if the business fails. This feature enables a corporation to raise more capital from a wider group of investors than proprietorships and partnerships can.

SEPARATION OF OWNERSHIP AND MANAGEMENT Stockholders own the business, but a *board of directors*—elected by the stockholders—appoints corporate officers to manage the business. Thus stockholders may invest $1,000 or $1 million in the corporation without having to manage the business or disrupt their personal affairs.

Management's goal is to maximize the firm's value for the stockholders' benefit. However, the separation between owners—stockholders—and management can create problems. Corporate officers may decide to run the business for their own benefit and not to the stockholders' advantage. Stockholders may find it difficult to lodge an effective protest against management policy because of the distance between them and management.

CORPORATE TAXATION Corporations are separate taxable entities. They pay a variety of taxes not borne by proprietorships or partnerships, including an annual franchise tax levied by the state. The franchise tax is paid to keep the corporate charter in force and enables the corporation to continue in business. Corporations also pay federal and state income taxes.

Corporate earnings are subject to **double taxation.** First, corporations pay income taxes on corporate income. Then, stockholders pay personal income tax on the cash dividends (distributions) they receive from corporations. Proprietorships and partnerships pay no business income tax. Instead, the tax falls solely on the owners.

Double Taxation. Corporations pay their own income taxes on corporate income. Then, the stockholders pay personal income tax on the cash dividends that they receive from corporations.

GOVERNMENT REGULATION Because stockholders have only limited liability for corporation debts, outsiders doing business with the corporation can look no further than the corporation itself for any claims that may arise against the business. To protect persons who loan money to a corporation or who invest in its stock, both federal agencies and the states monitor corporations. This *government regulation* consists mainly of ensuring that corporations disclose the information that investors and creditors need to make informed decisions. For many corporations, government regulation is expensive.

Exhibit 13-1 summarizes the advantages and disadvantages of the corporate form of business organization.

■ Daily Exercise 13-1

Organization of a Corporation

The process of creating a corporation begins when its organizers, called the *incorporators*, obtain a charter from the state. The charter includes the authorization for the corporation to issue a certain number of shares of stock, which are shares of ownership in the corporation. The incorporators pay fees, sign the charter, and file required documents with the state. The corporation then comes into existence. The incorporators agree to a set of **bylaws,** which act as the constitution for governing the corporation.

The ultimate control of the corporation rests with the stockholders. The stockholders elect the members of the **board of directors,** which sets policy for the corporation and appoints the officers. The board elects a **chairperson,** who usually is the most powerful person in the corporation. The board also designates the **president,** who is the chief operating officer in charge of day-to-day operations. Most corporations also have vice presidents in charge of sales, manufacturing, accounting and finance, and other key areas. Often, the president and one or more vice presidents are also elected to the board of directors. Exhibit 13-2 shows the authority structure in a corporation.

Bylaws. Constitution for governing a corporation.

Board of Directors. Group elected by the stockholders to set policy for a corporation and to appoint its officers.

Chairperson. Elected by a corporation's board of directors, usually the most powerful person in the corporations.

President. Chief operating officer in charge of managing the day-to-day operations of a corporation.

Concept Highlight

EXHIBIT 13-1
Advantages and Disadvantages of a Corporation

Advantages	Disadvantages
1. Can raise more capital than a proprietorship or partnership	1. Separation of ownership and management
2. Continuous life	2. Corporate taxation
3. Ease of transferring ownership	3. Government regulation
4. No mutual agency of stockholders	
5. Limited liability of stockholders	

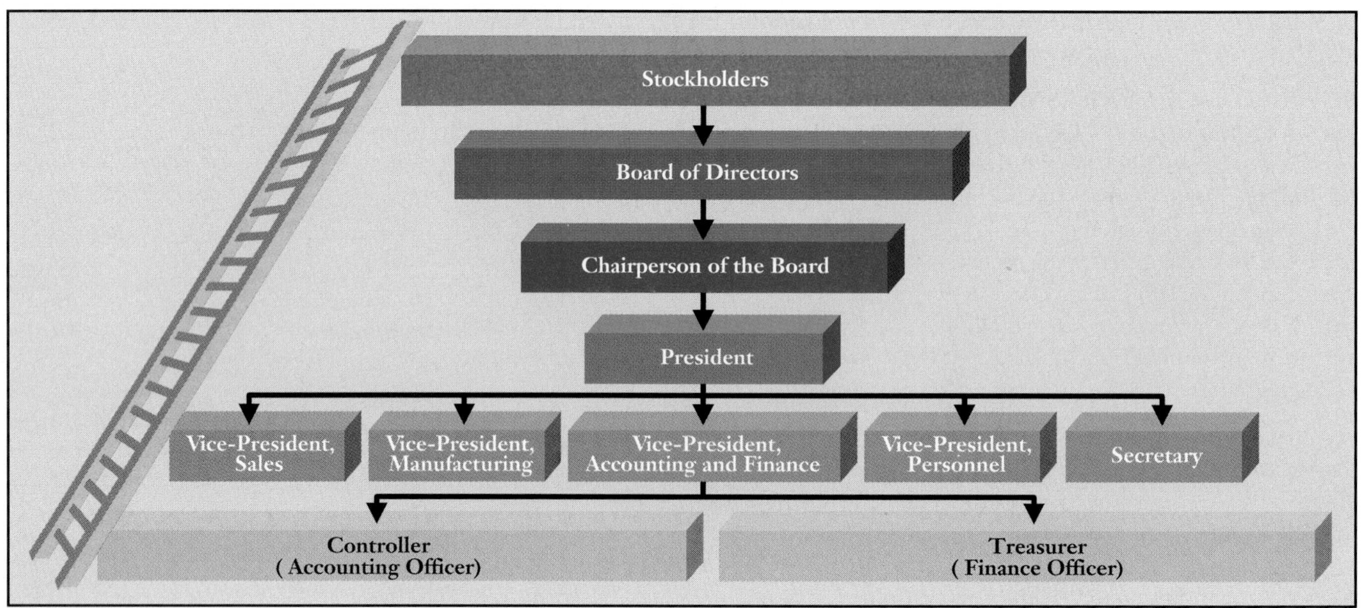

EXHIBIT 13-2
Authority Structure in a Corporation

■ Daily Exercise 13-2

Capital Stock

A corporation issues *stock certificates* to its owners in exchange for their investments in the business. Because stock represents the corporation's capital, it is often called *capital stock*. The basic unit of capital stock is called a *share*. A corporation may issue a stock certificate for any number of shares it wishes—one share, 100 shares, or any other number—but the total number of *authorized* shares is limited by charter. Exhibit 13-3 depicts an actual stock certificate for 288 shares of Central Jersey Bancorp common stock. The certificate shows the company's name, the stockholder's name, the number of shares, and the par value of the stock (discussed later in this chapter).

Outstanding Stock. Stock in the hands of stockholders.

Stock in the hands of a stockholder is said to be **outstanding.** The total number of shares of stock outstanding at any time represents 100% ownership of the corporation.

EXHIBIT 13-3
Stock Certificate

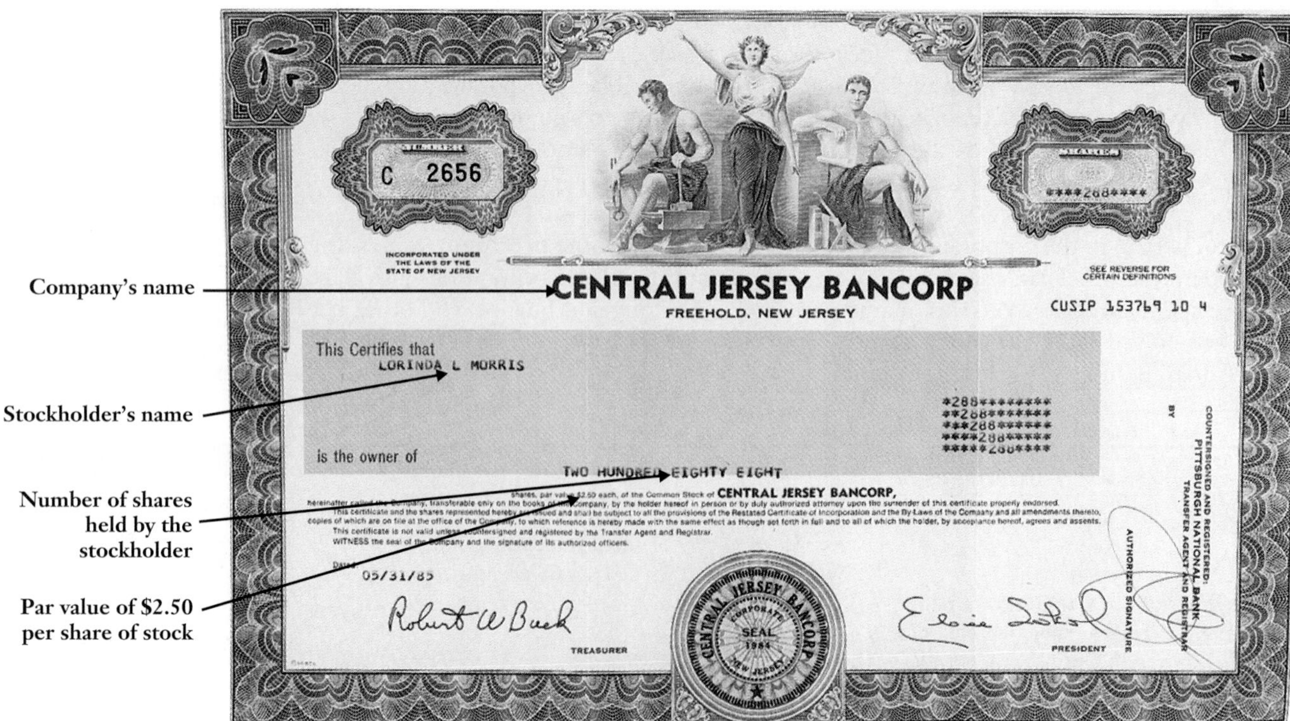

Stockholders' Equity

The balance sheet of a corporation reports assets and liabilities in the same way as a proprietorship or a partnership. However, owners' equity of a corporation—called **stockholders' equity**—is reported differently. State laws require corporations to report the sources of their capital. The two most basic sources of capital are

Stockholders' Equity. Owners' equity of a corporation.

- **Paid-in capital** (also called **contributed capital**), which represents investments by the stockholders in the corporation
- **Retained earnings,** which is capital that the corporation has earned through profitable operations

Paid-in Capital. A corporation's capital from investments by the stockholders. Also called **contributed capital.**

Retained Earnings. A corporation's capital that is earned through profitable operation of the business.

Exhibit 13-4 outlines a summarized version of the balance sheet of Wal-Mart Stores, Inc., to show how to report these categories of stockholders' equity.

Paid-in Capital Is Received from the Stockholders

Common stock is paid-in capital. It is regarded as the permanent capital of the business because it is *not* subject to withdrawal by the stockholders. An investment of cash or any other asset in a corporation increases the corporation's assets and stockholders' equity. Wal-Mart's entry for receipt of $20,000 cash and issuance of Wal-Mart stock to a stockholder is

Common Stock. The most basic form of capital stock. In a corporation, the common stockholders are the owners of the business.

Oct. 20	Cash	20,000	
	Common Stock..........		20,000
	Issued stock.		

Retained Earnings Are Earned from the Customers

Profitable operations produce income, which increases stockholders' equity through a separate account called Retained Earnings. At the end of the year, the net income (or net loss) balance of the Income Summary account is closed to Retained Earnings. For example, if Wal-Mart's net income is $3,000 million, Income Summary will have a $3,000 million credit balance. Wal-Mart's closing entry will debit Income Summary to transfer net income to Retained Earnings as follows (in millions of dollars):

Dec. 31	Income Summary..	3,000	
	Retained Earnings.....................................		3,000
	To close *net income* to Retained Earnings.		

If operations produce a net *loss* rather than net income, the Income Summary account will have a debit balance. Income Summary must be credited to close it. With a $60,000 loss, the closing entry is

Dec. 31	Retained Earnings...	60,000	
	Income Summary......................................		60,000
	To close *net loss* to Retained Earnings.		

NEGATIVE RETAINED EARNINGS IS CALLED A DEFICIT A large loss may cause a debit balance in the Retained Earnings account. This condition—called a Retained

EXHIBIT 13-4
Summarized Balance Sheet of Wal-Mart Stores, Inc. (Amounts in Millions)

Assets	$39,604	Liabilities	$22,461
		Stockholders' Equity	
		Paid-in capital:	
		Common stock.........................	375
		Retained earnings........................	16,768
		Total stockholders' equity..........	17,143
		Total liabilities and	
Total assets..........	$39,604	stockholders' equity	$39,604

■ Daily Exercise 13-3

Deficit. Debit balance in the Retained Earnings account.

Earnings **deficit**—is reported on the balance sheet as a negative amount in stockholders' equity. HAL, INC., which owns Hawaiian Airlines, Inc., reported this deficit:

Stockholders' Equity	(in millions)
Paid-in capital: Common stock..........	$ 50
Deficit..	(193)
Total stockholders' equity	$(143)

HAL's deficit was so large that it produced a negative amount of stockholders' equity. This situation is unusual for a going concern.

Corporations May Pay Dividends to the Stockholders

Dividends. Distributions by a corporation to its stockholders.

Legal Capital. The portion of stockholders' equity that cannot be used for dividends.

If the corporation has been profitable and has sufficient cash, a distribution of cash may be made to the stockholders. Such distributions—called **dividends**—are similar to a withdrawal by the owner from a proprietorship or by a partner from a partnership. Dividends decrease both the assets and the retained earnings of the business. Most states prohibit the practice of using paid-in capital for dividends. Accountants use the term **legal capital** to refer to the portion of stockholders' equity that *cannot* be used for dividends.

Some people think of Retained Earnings as a fund of cash. It is not, because Retained Earnings is an element of stockholders' equity. *Remember that cash and other property dividends are paid out of assets, not out of retained earnings.*

Stockholders' Rights

The ownership of stock entitles stockholders to four basic rights, unless specific rights are withheld by agreement with the stockholders:

1. *Vote.* The right to participate in management by voting on matters that come before the stockholders. This is the stockholder's sole right to a voice in the management of the corporation. A stockholder is entitled to one vote for each share of stock owned.

2. *Dividends.* The right to receive a proportionate part of any dividend. Each share of stock in a particular class receives an equal dividend.

3. *Liquidation.* The right to receive a proportionate share (based on number of shares held) of any assets remaining after the corporation pays its liabilities in liquidation.

4. *Preemption.* The right to maintain one's proportionate ownership in the corporation. Suppose you own 5% of a corporation's stock. If the corporation issues 100,000 new shares of stock, it must offer you the opportunity to buy 5% (5,000) of the new shares. This right, called the *preemptive right*, is usually withheld from the stockholders.

Classes of Stock

Corporations issue different types of stock to appeal to a wide variety of investors. The stock of a corporation may be either common or preferred and either par or no-par.

Common and Preferred Stock

Every corporation issues *common stock*, the most basic form of capital stock. Unless designated otherwise, the word *stock* is understood to mean "common stock." Common stockholders have the four basic rights of stock ownership, unless a right is specifically withheld. For example, some companies issue Class A common stock, which usually carries the right to vote, and Class B common stock, which may be nonvoting. (Classes of common stock may also be designated Series A, Series B, and so on.) The general ledger has a separate account for each class of common stock. In describing a corporation, we would say the common stockholders are the owners of the business.

Investors who buy common stock take the ultimate risk with a corporation. The corporation makes no promises to pay them. If the corporation succeeds, it will pay dividends to its stockholders, but if net income and cash are too low, the stockholders may receive no dividends. The stock of successful corporations increases in value, and investors enjoy the benefit of selling the stock at a gain. But stock prices can decrease, leaving the investors holding worthless stock certificates. Because common stockholders take a risky investment position, they demand increases in stock prices, high dividends, or both. If the corporation does not deliver, the stockholders sell the stock, and its market price falls.

Preferred stock gives its owners certain advantages over common stockholders. These benefits include the priority to receive dividends before the common stockholders and the priority to receive assets before the common stockholders if the corporation liquidates. Corporations pay a fixed amount of dividends on preferred stock. Investors usually buy preferred stock to earn those dividends.

Owners of preferred stock also have the four basic stockholder rights, unless a right is specifically denied. Often the right to vote is withheld from preferred stockholders. Companies may issue different classes of preferred stock. (Class A and Class B or Series A and Series B, for example). Each class is recorded in a separate account. Preferred stock is rarer than you might think. A recent survey of 600 corporations revealed that only 145 of them (24%) had some preferred stock outstanding (Exhibit 13-5). All corporations have common stock. Exhibit 13-6 summarizes the similarities and differences among common stock, preferred stock, and long-term debt.

EXHIBIT 13-5
Preferred Stock

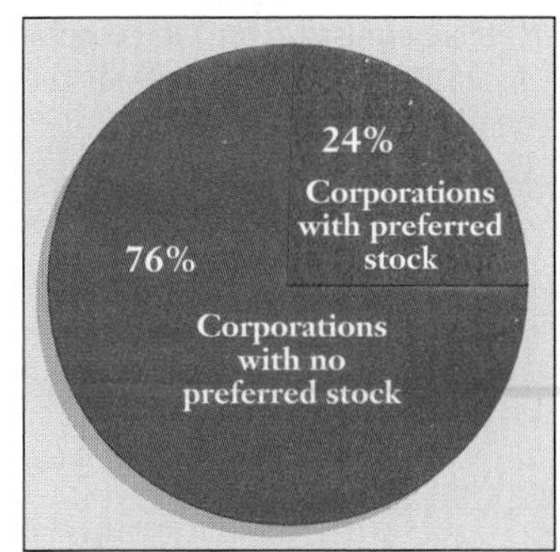

Preferred Stock. Stock that gives its owners certain advantages over common stockholders, such as the priority to receive dividends before the common stockholders and the priority to receive assets before the common stockholders if the corporation liquidates.

Par Value, Stated Value, and No-Par Stock

Stock may be par-value stock or no-par stock. **Par value** is an arbitrary amount assigned by a company to a share of its stock. Most companies set the par value of their common stock quite low to avoid legal difficulties from issuing their stock below par. Most states require companies to maintain a minimum amount of stockholders' equity for the protection of creditors, and this minimum is often called the corporation's legal capital. For corporations with par-value stock, *legal capital* is the par value of the shares issued.

Par value. Arbitrary amount assigned to a share of stock.

■ Daily Exercise 13-4

The common stock par value of Kimberly Clark, best known for its Kleenex tissues, is $1.25 per share. Of 600 million shares of stock, Kimberly Clark has issued 284.3 million shares. J.C. Penney's common stock par value is 50¢ per share, and Sprint Corporation's common stock par value is $2.50 per share. Par value of preferred stock is often higher; some preferred stocks have par values of $25 and $10. Par value is used to compute dividends on preferred stock, as we shall see.

"The common stock par value of Kimberly Clark, best known for its Kleenex tissues, is $1.25 per share."

No-par stock does not have par value. Kimberly Clark has 20 million shares of preferred stock authorized with no par value. But some no-par stock has a **stated value,** which makes it similar to par-value stock. The stated value is an arbitrary amount that accountants treat as though it were par value.

Stated Value. Similar to par value.

Issuing Stock

Objective 2
Record the issuance of stock

Large corporations such as Coca-Cola, Xerox, and British Petroleum need huge quantities of money to operate. They cannot expect to finance all their operations through

EXHIBIT 13-6
Comparison of Common Stock, Preferred Stock, and Long-Term Debt

	Common Stock	Preferred Stock	Long-Term Debt
Investment risk	High	Medium	Low
Corporate obligation to repay principal	No	No	Yes
Dividends/interest	Dividends	Dividends	Tax-deductible interest expense
Corporate obligation to pay dividends/interest	Only after declaration	Only after declaration	At fixed dates
Fluctuations in market value under normal conditions	High	Medium	Low

Authorization of Stock. Provision in a corporate charter that gives the state's permission for the corporation to issue—that is, to sell—a certain number of shares of stock.

borrowing. They need capital that they raise by issuing stock. The charter that the incorporators receive from the state includes an **authorization of stock**—that is, a provision giving the state's permission for the business to issue (to sell) a certain number of shares of stock. Corporations may sell the stock directly to the stockholders or use the service of an *underwriter*, such as the brokerage firms Merrill Lynch and Dean Witter. An underwriter agrees to buy all the stock it cannot sell to its clients.

The corporation need not issue all the stock that the state authorizes. Management may hold some stock back and issue it later if the need for additional capital arises. The stock that the corporation issues to stockholders is called *issued stock*. Only by issuing stock—not by receiving authorization—does the corporation increase the asset and stockholders' equity amounts on its balance sheet.

The price that the stockholder pays to acquire stock from the corporation is called the *issue price*. Often, the issue price far exceeds the stock's par value because the par value was intentionally set quite low. The company's earnings record, prospects for success, and general business conditions determine the stock's issue price. Investors will not pay more than market value for the stock. In the following sections, we show how companies account for the issuance of stock.

Issuing Common Stock

Companies often advertise the issuance of their stock to attract investors. The *Wall Street Journal* is the most popular medium for the advertisements, which are also called *tombstones*. Exhibit 13-7 is a reproduction of IHOP's tombstone, which appeared in the *Wall Street Journal*, with the data given in the chapter opening story.

The lead underwriter of IHOP's public offering was The First Boston Corporation. Twenty-one other domestic brokerage firms and investment bankers sold IHOP's stock to their clients. Outside the United States, six investment bankers assisted with the offering. Altogether, IHOP hoped to raise approximately $62 million of capital. As it turned out, IHOP issued only 3.2 million of the shares and received cash of approximately $32 million.

ISSUING COMMON STOCK AT PAR Suppose IHOP's common stock carried a par value of $10 per share. The stock issuance entry of 3.2 million shares would be

Jan. 8	Cash (3,200,000 × $10)	32,000,000	
	Common Stock.....................		32,000,000
	Issued common stock at par.		

The amount invested in the corporation, $32 million in this case, is paid-in capital, or contributed capital, of IHOP. The credit to Common Stock records an increase in the corporation's paid-in capital.

ISSUING COMMON STOCK AT A PREMIUM Many corporations set par value at a low amount, then issue common stock for a price above par value. The amount above par is called a *premium*. IHOP's common stock has a par value of $0.01 (1 cent) per share. The $9.99 difference between issue price ($10) and par value ($0.01) is a premium. This sale of stock increases the corporation's paid-in capital by the full $10, the total issue price of the stock. Both the par value of the stock and the premium are part of paid-in capital.

A premium on the sale of stock is not gain, income, or profit to the corporation, because the entity is dealing with its own stockholders. This situation illustrates one of the fundamentals of accounting: *A company neither earns a profit nor incurs a loss when it sells its stock to, or buys its stock from, its own stockholders.*

With a par value of $0.01, IHOP's entry to record the issuance of the stock is

■ Daily Exercise 13-5

July 23	Cash (3,200,000 × $10)	32,000,000	
	Common Stock (3,200,000 × $0.01).........		32,000
	Paid-in Capital in Excess of Par— Common (3,200,000 × $9.99)		31,968,000
	Issued common stock at a premium.		

EXHIBIT 13-7
Announcement of Public Offering of IHOP Stock

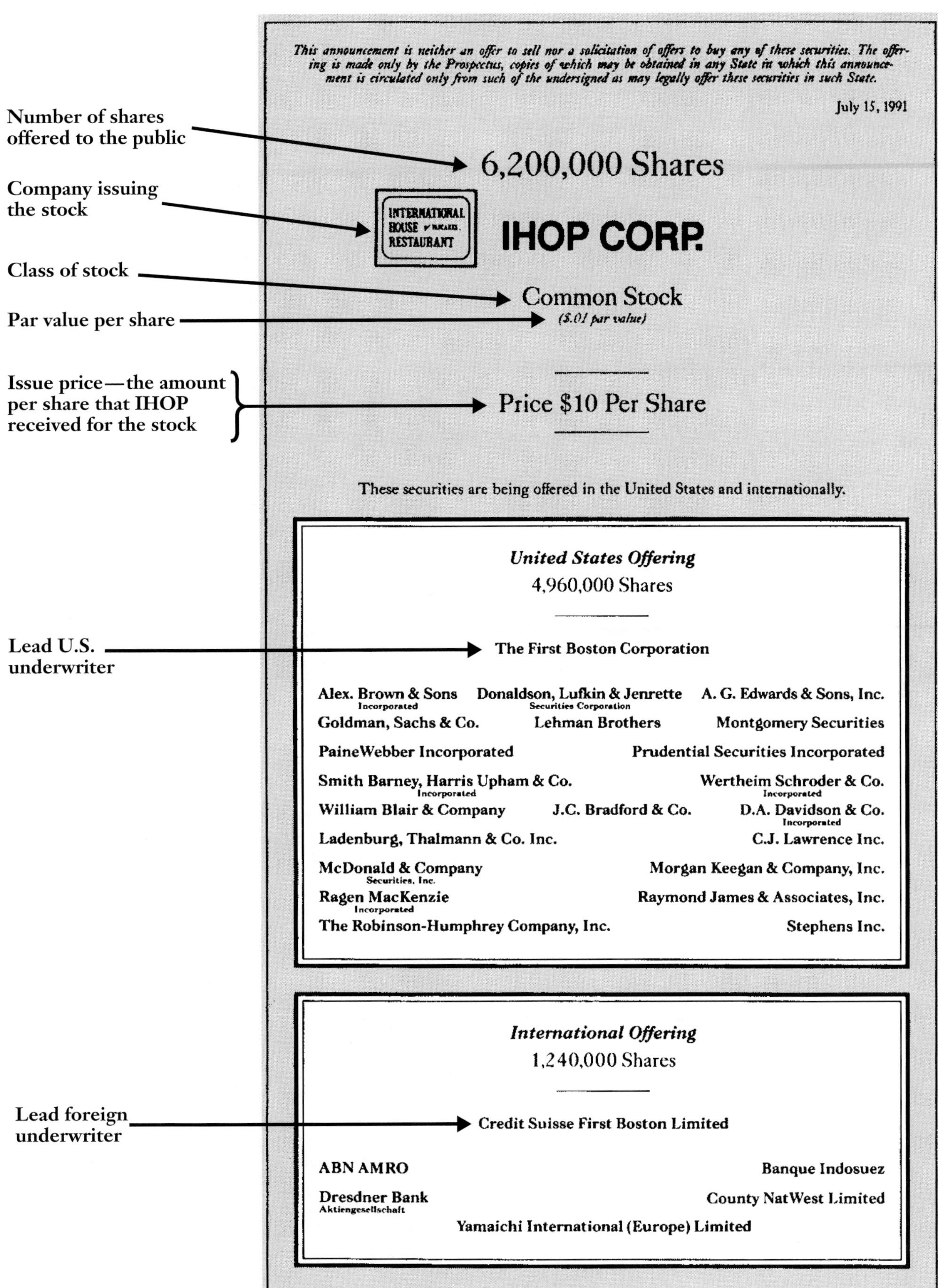

This announcement is neither an offer to sell nor a solicitation of offers to buy any of these securities. The offering is made only by the Prospectus, copies of which may be obtained in any State in which this announcement is circulated only from such of the undersigned as may legally offer these securities in such State.

July 15, 1991

6,200,000 Shares

INTERNATIONAL HOUSE OF PANCAKES RESTAURANT

IHOP CORP.

Common Stock
($.01 par value)

Price $10 Per Share

These securities are being offered in the United States and internationally.

United States Offering
4,960,000 Shares

The First Boston Corporation

Alex. Brown & Sons Incorporated — **Donaldson, Lufkin & Jenrette Securities Corporation** — **A. G. Edwards & Sons, Inc.**
Goldman, Sachs & Co. — **Lehman Brothers** — **Montgomery Securities**
PaineWebber Incorporated — **Prudential Securities Incorporated**
Smith Barney, Harris Upham & Co. Incorporated — **Wertheim Schroder & Co. Incorporated**
William Blair & Company — **J.C. Bradford & Co.** — **D.A. Davidson & Co. Incorporated**
Ladenburg, Thalmann & Co. Inc. — **C.J. Lawrence Inc.**
McDonald & Company Securities, Inc. — **Morgan Keegan & Company, Inc.**
Ragen MacKenzie Incorporated — **Raymond James & Associates, Inc.**
The Robinson-Humphrey Company, Inc. — **Stephens Inc.**

International Offering
1,240,000 Shares

Credit Suisse First Boston Limited

ABN AMRO — **Banque Indosuez**
Dresdner Bank Aktiengesellschaft — **County NatWest Limited**
Yamaichi International (Europe) Limited

Account titles that could be used in place of Paid-in Capital in Excess of Par—Common are *Additional Paid-in Capital—Common* and *Premium on Common Stock.* Since both par value and premium amounts increase the corporation's capital, they appear in the stockholders' equity section of the balance sheet.

At the end of the year, IHOP Corp. would report stockholders' equity on its balance sheet as follows, assuming that the corporate charter authorizes 40,000,000 shares of common stock and the balance of retained earnings is $26,000,000.

■ Daily Exercise 13-6
■ Daily Exercise 13-7

Stockholders' Equity	
Paid-in capital:	
Common stock, $0.01 par, 40 million shares authorized, 3.2 million shares issued	$ 32,000
Paid-in capital in excess of par	31,968,000
Total paid-in capital	32,000,000
Retained earnings	26,000,000
Total stockholders' equity	$58,000,000

We determine the dollar amount reported for common stock by multiplying the total number of shares *issued* (3.2 million) by the par value per share. The *authorization* reports the maximum number of shares the company may issue under its charter.

All of the transactions recorded in this section include a receipt of cash by the corporation as it issues new stock to its stockholders. These transactions are different from the vast majority of stock transactions reported each day in the financial press. In those transactions, one stockholder sells his or her stock to another investor, and the corporation makes no formal journal entry because its paid-in capital is unchanged.

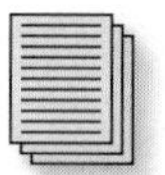

Working It Out IHOP Corp. actually had total liabilities of $92 million on the balance sheet date just given. What was IHOP's debt ratio?

Answer: The debt ratio is 0.61:

$$\frac{\textbf{Total liabilities}}{\textbf{Total assets}} = \frac{\$92{,}000{,}000}{\$92{,}000{,}000 + \$58{,}000{,}000} = 0.61$$

ISSUING NO-PAR COMMON STOCK When a company issues stock that has no par value, there can be no premium. A recent survey of 600 companies revealed that they had 69 issues of no-par stock.

When a company issues no-par stock, it debits the asset received and credits the stock account. Glenwood Corporation, which manufactures skateboards, issues 3,000 shares of no-par common stock for $20 per share. The stock issuance entry is

Aug. 14	Cash (3,000 × $20)	60,000	
	Common Stock		60,000
	Issued no-par common stock.		

Regardless of the stock's price, Cash is debited and Common Stock is credited for the amount of cash received. There is no Paid-in Capital in Excess of Par for true no-par stock.

Glenwood Corporation's charter authorizes Glenwood to issue 10,000 shares of no-par stock, and the company has $46,000 in retained earnings. The corporation reports stockholders' equity on the balance sheet as follows:

Stockholders' Equity	
Paid-in capital:	
Common stock, no-par, 10,000 shares authorized, 3,000 shares issued	$ 60,000
Retained earnings	46,000
Total stockholders' equity	$106,000

ISSUING NO-PAR COMMON STOCK WITH A STATED VALUE Accounting for no-par stock with a stated value is identical to accounting for par-value stock. The premium account for no-par common stock with a stated value is entitled Paid-in Capital in Excess of Stated Value—Common.

■ Daily Exercise 13-8

ISSUING COMMON STOCK FOR ASSETS OTHER THAN CASH When a corporation issues stock in exchange for assets other than cash, it records the assets received at their current market value and credits the capital accounts accordingly. The assets' prior book value does not matter because the stockholder will demand stock equal to the market value of the asset given. Kahn Corporation issued 15,000 shares of its $1 par common stock for equipment worth $4,000 and a building worth $120,000. Kahn's entry is

Nov. 12	Equipment..	4,000	
	Building..	120,000	
	Common Stock (15,000 × $1)...............		15,000
	Paid-in Capital in Excess of Par— Common ($124,000 – $15,000).........		109,000
	Issued common stock in exchange for equipment and a building.		

Working It Out How did this transaction affect Kahn Corporation's cash? Total assets? Paid-in capital? Retained earnings? Total stockholders' equity?

■ Daily Exercise 13-9

Answer

	Cash	Total Assets	Paid-in Capital	Retained Earnings	Total Stockholders' Equity
Effect	None	Increase $124,000	Increase $124,000	None	Increase $124,000

Issuing Preferred Stock

Accounting for preferred stock follows the pattern we illustrated for common stock. The charter of Brown-Forman Corporation, a distilling company, authorizes issuance of 1,177,948 shares of 4%, $10 par preferred stock. [The 4% refers to the annual cash dividend rate on the stock. Each Brown-Forman preferred stockholder receives an annual cash dividend of $0.40 ($10 par × 0.04). Note that the dividend is computed based on the *par value.*] Assume that on July 31 the company issued all the shares at a price equal to the par value. The issuance entry is

July 31	Cash..	11,779,480	
	Preferred Stock (1,177,948 × $10)		11,779,480
	Issued preferred stock at par.		

If Brown-Forman had issued the preferred stock at a premium, the entry would have also credited an account titled Paid-in Capital in Excess of Par—Preferred. A corporation lists separate accounts for Paid-in Capital in Excess of Par on Preferred Stock and on Common Stock to differentiate the two classes of equity.

Accounting for no-par preferred stock follows the pattern illustrated for no-par common stock. When reporting stockholders' equity on the balance sheet, a corporation lists preferred stock, common stock, and retained earnings—in that order.

Ethical Considerations in Accounting for the Issuance of Stock

Issuance of stock for *cash* poses no serious ethical challenge. The company simply receives cash and issues the stock to the shareholders, giving them stock certificates as evidence of their purchase.

Issuing stock for assets other than cash can pose an ethical challenge, however. The company issuing the stock often wishes to record a large amount for the noncash asset received (such as land or a building) and for the stock that it is issuing. Why? Because large asset and stockholders' equity amounts on the balance sheet make the business look more prosperous and more creditworthy. The motivation to look good can inject a subtle bias into the amount recorded for stock issued in return for assets other than cash.

As we discussed on page 553, a company is supposed to record an asset received at its current market value. But one person's perception of a particular asset's market value can differ from another person's perception. One person may appraise land at a market value of $400,000. Another may honestly believe the land is worth only $300,000. A company receiving land in exchange for its stock must decide whether to record the land received and the stock issued at $300,000, at $400,000, or at some amount in between.

The ethical course of action is to record the asset at its current fair market value, as determined by a good-faith estimate of market value from independent appraisers. It is rare for a public corporation to be found guilty of *understating* the asset values on its balance sheet, but companies have been embarrassed by *overstating* their asset values. Investors who rely on the financial statements may be able to prove that an overstatement of asset values caused them to pay too much for the company's stock. In this case, a court of law may render a judgment against the company. For this reason, companies often tend to value assets conservatively in order to avoid an overstatement of their book value.

Donations Received by a Corporation

Corporations occasionally receive gifts, or *donations*. For example, city council members may offer a company free land to encourage it to locate in their city. Cities in the southern United States have lured some companies away from the North with such offers. The free land is a donation. For example, J.C. Penney Co. and American Airlines moved corporate headquarters from New York City to the Dallas–Fort Worth area because of concessions granted by the Texas cities. Also, a stockholder may make a donation to the corporation in the form of cash, land or other assets, or stock.

A donation increases the corporation's assets, but the donor (giver) receives no ownership interest in the company in return. A donation increases the corporation's revenue and thus affects income and retained earnings. The corporation records a donation by debiting the asset received at its current market value and by crediting Revenue from Donations, which is reported as Other Revenue on the income statement. But a donation received from a government entity is recorded as a credit to Donated Capital. For example, American Airlines would debit Land and credit Donated Capital for the value of any land it receives from a city or county government. Donated capital is a separate category of paid-in capital listed on the balance sheet after Common Stock and Paid-in Capital in Excess of Par.

■ Daily Exercise 13-10

Objective 3

Prepare the stockholders' equity section of a corporation's balance sheet

Review of Accounting for Paid-in Capital

Let's review the first half of this chapter by showing the stockholders' equity section of Medina Corporation's balance sheet in Exhibit 13-8. All amounts are assumed for the il-

EXHIBIT 13-8
Part of Medina Corporation's Balance Sheet

■ Daily Exercise 13-11
■ Daily Exercise 13-12
■ Daily Exercise 13-13

Stockholders' Equity	
Paid-in capital:	
Preferred stock, 5%, $100 par, 5,000 shares authorized, 400 shares issued	$ 40,000
Paid-in capital in excess of par—preferred	14,000
Common stock, $10 par, 20,000 shares authorized, 4,500 shares issued	45,000
Paid-in capital in excess of par—common	72,000
Donated capital	20,000
Total paid-in capital	191,000
Retained earnings	85,000
Total stockholders' equity	$276,000

lustration. Note the two sections of stockholders' equity: paid-in capital and retained earnings. Also observe the order of the equity accounts:

- Preferred stock at par value
- Paid-in capital in excess of par on preferred stock
- Common stock at par value
- Paid-in capital in excess of par on common stock
- Donated capital

Many companies combine several accounts, such as Paid-in Capital in Excess of Par—Common, plus Donated Capital, and report the sum as **Additional Paid-in Capital** on the balance sheet. However, they are careful not to include Paid-in Capital in Excess of Par—Preferred because that paid-in capital belongs to the preferred stockholders.

Additional Paid-in Capital. The sum of paid-in capital in excess of par—common plus donated capital and other accounts combined for reporting on the balance sheet.

Thinking It Over Examine Medina Corporation's stockholders' equity in Exhibit 13-8, and answer these questions.

1. How much did Medina's preferred stockholders pay into the corporation?
2. How much did the common stockholders pay into Medina Corporation?
3. What did the stockholders get for their payments into the company?
4. How does the donated capital differ from the other paid-in capital accounts?

Answers

1. \$54,000 (\$40,000 + \$14,000)
2. \$117,000 (\$45,000 + \$72,000)
3. The stockholders received stock, which represents their ownership in the assets of the corporation.
4. Donated capital represents a donation to the company for which the donor received no ownership interest in the assets of the company. The stock accounts and the paid-in capital in excess of par represent what the stockholders paid for their ownership in the company's assets.

Now review the Decision Guidelines feature to solidify your understanding of stockholders' equity as it is reported on the balance sheet.

DECISION GUIDELINES — Reporting Stockholders' Equity on the Balance Sheet

DECISION	GUIDELINES
What are the two main segments of stockholders' equity?	• Paid-in capital • Retained earnings
Which is more permanent, paid-in capital or retained earnings?	Paid-in capital is more permanent because corporations use their retained earnings for declaring dividends to the stockholders.
How are paid-in capital and retained earnings	
• Similar?	• Both represent the stockholders' equity (ownership) in the assets of the corporation.
• Different?	• Paid-in capital and retained earnings come from different *sources:* **a.** Paid-in capital comes from the corporation's stockholders, who invested in the company. **b.** Retained earnings comes from the corporation's customers. It was earned by the company's profitable operations.
What are the main categories of paid-in capital?	• Preferred stock • Common stock • Paid-in capital in excess of par on **a.** Preferred stock **b.** Common stock • Donated capital

1. Test your understanding of the first half of this chapter by answering whether each of the following statements is true or false:
   a. A stockholder may bind the corporation to a contract.
   b. The policy-making body in a corporation is called the board of directors.
   c. The owner of 100 shares of preferred stock has greater voting rights than the owner of 100 shares of common stock.
   d. Par-value stock is worth more than no-par stock.
   e. Issuance of 1,000 shares of $5 par-value stock at $12 increases contributed capital by $12,000.
   f. The issuance of no-par stock with a stated value is fundamentally different from issuing par-value stock.
   g. A corporation issues its preferred stock in exchange for land and a building with a combined market value of $200,000. This transaction increases the corporation's owners' equity by $200,000 regardless of the assets' prior book value.

2. The brewery Adolph Coors Company has two classes of common stock. Only the Class A common stockholders are entitled to vote. The company's balance sheet included the following presentation:

Shareholders' Equity	
Capital stock	
Class A common stock, voting, $1 par value, authorized and issued 1,260,000 shares	$ 1,260,000
Class B common stock, nonvoting, no-par value, authorized and issued 46,200,000 shares	11,000,000
	12,260,000
Additional paid-in capital	2,011,000
Retained earnings	872,403,000
	$886,674,000

REQUIRED

1. Record the issuance of the Class A common stock. Assume that the additional paid-in capital amount is related to the Class A common stock. Use the Coors account titles.
2. Record the issuance of the Class B common stock. Use the Coors account titles.
3. Rearrange the Coors stockholders' equity section to correspond to the following format:

Shareholders' Equity	
Paid-in capital:	
Class A common stock	$
Paid-in capital in excess of par—Class A common stock	
Class B common stock	
Total paid-in capital	
Retained earnings	
Total shareholders' equity	$

4. What is the total paid-in capital of the company?
5. How did Coors withhold the voting privilege from the Class B common stockholders?

SOLUTIONS

1. Answers to true/false statements:

a. False	b. True	c. False	d. False
e. True	f. False	g. True	

2. a.

Cash	3,271,000	
Class A Common Stock		1,260,000
Additional Paid-in Capital		2,011,000
To record issuance of Class A common stock at a premium.		

b.	Cash	11,000,000	
	Class B Common Stock		11,000,000
	To record issuance of Class B common stock.		

c. **Shareholders' Equity**

Paid-in capital:	
Class A common stock, voting, $1 par value, authorized and issued 1,260,000 shares	$ 1,260,000
Paid-in capital in excess of par—Class A common stock	2,011,000
Class B common stock, nonvoting, no par value, authorized and issued 46,200,000 shares	11,000,000
Total paid-in capital	14,271,000
Retained earnings	872,403,000
Total shareholders' equity	$886,674,000

d. Total paid-in capital is $14,271,000, as shown in the answer to (c).

e. The voting privilege was withheld from stockholders by specific agreement with them.

Accounting for Cash Dividends

Corporations share the company's wealth with their owners, the stockholders, through dividends. Corporations declare dividends from retained earnings and pay the dividends with cash. The corporation must have enough retained earnings to declare the dividend and enough cash to pay the dividend.

Dividend Dates

A corporation must declare a dividend before paying it. The board of directors alone has the authority to declare a dividend. The corporation has no obligation to pay a dividend until the board declares one, but once declared, the dividend becomes a legal liability of the corporation. Three relevant dates for dividends are

1. *Declaration date.* On the declaration date, the board of directors announces the intention to pay the dividend. The declaration creates a liability for the corporation. Declaration is recorded by debiting Retained Earnings and crediting Dividends Payable.
2. *Date of record.* The corporation announces the record date, which follows the declaration date by a few weeks, as part of the declaration. The corporation makes no journal entry on the date of record because no transaction occurs. Nevertheless, much work takes place behind the scenes to properly identify the stockholders of record on this date because the stock is being traded continuously. Only the people who own the stock on the date of record receive the dividend.
3. *Payment date.* Payment of the dividend usually follows the record date by two to four weeks. Payment is recorded by debiting Dividends Payable and crediting Cash.

Dividends on Preferred and Common Stock

Objective 4

Account for cash dividends

Declaration of a cash dividend is recorded by debiting Retained Earnings and crediting Dividends Payable as follows:[1]

June 19	Retained Earnings	XXX	
	Dividends Payable		XXX
	Declared a cash dividend.		

Payment of the dividend, which usually follows declaration by a few weeks, is recorded by debiting Dividends Payable and crediting Cash:

July 2	Dividends Payable	XXX	
	Cash		XXX
	Paid the cash dividend.		

■ Daily Exercise 13-14

[1]In Chapters 1–4, we debited the Dividends account, which is closed to Retained Earnings. Many businesses debit Retained Earnings directly, as shown here.

EXHIBIT 13-9
Division of a Dividend between Preferred Stock and Common Stock

Case A: Total dividend of $150,000	
Preferred dividend (9,000 shares × $1.75 per share)	$ 15,750
Common dividend ($150,000 – $15,750)	134,250
Total dividend	$150,000
Case B: Total dividend of $20,000	
Preferred dividend (9,000 shares × $1.75 per share)	$ 15,750
Common dividend ($20,000 – $15,750)	4,250
Total dividend	$ 20,000
Case C: Total dividend of $8,000	
Preferred dividend (the full $8,000 goes to preferred because the annual preferred dividend is $15,750)	$ 8,000
Common dividend (none because the total dividend did not cover the preferred dividend for the year)	-0-
Total dividend	$ 8,000

If Pine Industries' annual dividend is large enough to cover the preferred dividend for the year (Cases A and B), the preferred stockholders receive their regular dividend, and the common stockholders receive the remainder. But if the year's dividend falls below the amount of the annual preferred dividend (Case C), the preferred stockholders receive the entire dividend, and the common stockholders receive nothing that year.

Dividends Payable is a current liability. When a company has issued both preferred and common stock, the preferred stockholders receive their dividends first. The common stockholders receive dividends only if the total declared dividend is large enough to pay the preferred stockholders first.

In addition to its common stock, Pine Industries, Inc., has 9,000 shares of preferred stock outstanding. Preferred dividends are paid at the annual rate of $1.75 per share. Exhibit 13-9 shows the division between preferred and common for three amounts of the total annual dividend declared by Pine Industries.

This example illustrates an important relationship between preferred stock and common stock. To an investor, the preferred stock is safer because it receives dividends first. However, the earnings potential from an investment in common stock is much greater than from an investment in preferred stock. Preferred dividends are usually limited to the specified amount, but there is no upper limit on the amount of common dividends.

When a company has more than one class of preferred stock or common stock, the division of dividends among the various classes of stock follows this same pattern: the preferred stock with the most senior rights gets the first dividends, and so on.

We noted that preferred stockholders enjoy the advantage of priority over common stockholders in receiving dividends. The dividend preference is stated as a percentage rate or a dollar amount. For example, preferred stock may be "6% preferred," which means that owners of the preferred stock receive an annual dividend of 6% of the par value of the stock. If par value is $100 per share, preferred stockholders receive an annual cash dividend of $6 per share (6% of $100). The preferred stock may be "$3 preferred," which means that stockholders receive an annual dividend of $3 per share regardless of the preferred stock's par value. The dividend rate on no-par preferred stock is stated in a dollar amount per share.

■ Daily Exercise 13-15

Dividends on Cumulative and Noncumulative Preferred Stock

The allocation of dividends may be complex if the preferred stock is *cumulative*. Corporations sometimes fail to pay a dividend to their preferred stockholders. This occurrence is called *passing the dividend*, and the passed dividends are said to be *in arrears*. The owners of **cumulative preferred stock** must receive all dividends in arrears plus the current year's dividend before the corporation pays dividends to the common stockholders.

Cumulative Preferred Stock. Preferred stock whose owners must receive all dividends in arrears before the corporation pays dividends to the common stockholders.

The preferred stock of Pine Industries is cumulative. Suppose the company passed the 19X4 preferred dividend of $15,750. Before paying dividends to its common stockholders in 19X5, the company must first pay preferred dividends of $15,750 for both 19X4 and 19X5, a total of $31,500. *Preferred stock is cumulative in the eyes of the law unless it is labeled as noncumulative.*

Assume that Pine Industries passes its 19X4 preferred dividend. In 19X5, the company declares a $50,000 dividend. The entry to record the declaration is

Sep. 6	Retained Earnings	50,000	
	Dividends Payable, Preferred ($15,750 × 2)		31,500
	Dividends Payable, Common ($50,000 – $31,500)		18,500
	Declared a cash dividend.		

If the preferred stock is *noncumulative*, the corporation is not obligated to pay dividends in arrears. Suppose that the Pine Industries preferred stock was noncumulative and the company passed the 19X4 preferred dividend of $15,750. The preferred stockholders would lose the 19X4 dividend forever. Of course, the common stockholders would not receive a 19X4 dividend either. Before paying any common dividends in 19X5, the company would have to pay the 19X5 preferred dividend of $15,750.

Having dividends in arrears on cumulative preferred stock is *not* a liability for the corporation. (A liability for dividends arises only after the board of directors declares the dividend.) Nevertheless, a corporation must report cumulative preferred dividends in arrears. This information alerts common stockholders as to how much in cumulative preferred dividends must be paid before any dividends will be paid on the common stock. This information gives the common stockholders an idea about the likelihood of receiving dividends and satisfies the disclosure principle.

Dividends in arrears are often disclosed in notes, as follows (all dates and amounts assumed). Observe the two references to Note 3 in this section of the balance sheet. The "6%" after "Preferred stock" is the dividend rate.

Preferred stock, 6%, $50 par, 2,000 shares issued (Note 3)	$100,000
Retained earnings (Note 3)	414,000

Note 3—Cumulative preferred dividends in arrears. At December 31, 19X2, dividends on the company's 6% preferred stock were in arrears for 19X1 and 19X2, in the amount of $12,000 (6% × $100,000 × 2 years).

Convertible Preferred Stock

Convertible preferred stock may be exchanged by the preferred stockholders, if they choose, for another class of stock in the corporation. For example, the Pine Industries preferred stock may be converted into the company's common stock. A note to Pine's balance sheet describes the conversion terms as follows:

Convertible Preferred Stock. Preferred stock that may be exchanged by the preferred stockholders, if they choose, for another class of stock in the corporation.

> The . . . preferred stock is convertible at the rate of 6.51 shares of common stock for each share of preferred stock outstanding.

If you owned 100 shares of Pine's convertible preferred stock, you could convert it into 651 (100 × 6.51) shares of Pine common stock. Under what condition would you exercise the conversion privilege? You would do so if the market value of the common stock that you could receive from conversion exceeded the market value of the preferred stock that you presently hold. This way, you as an investor could increase your personal wealth.

Different Values of Stock

Objective 5

Use different stock values in decision making

There are several different *stock values* in addition to par value. Market value, redemption value, liquidation value, and book value are used for various investor decisions.

Market Value

Market Value. Price for which a person could buy or sell a share of stock.

A stock's **market value,** or *market price*, is the price for which a person could buy or sell a share of the stock. The issuing corporation's net income, financial position, and future prospects and the general economic conditions determine market value. Daily newspapers report the market price of many stocks. Corporate annual reports report the high and the low market values of the company's common stock for each quarter of the year. *In almost all cases, stockholders are more concerned about the market value of a stock than about any of the other values discussed next.* In the chapter opening story, IHOP's most recent stock price was quoted at 36, which means that the stock could be sold for, or bought for, $36 per share. The purchase of 100 shares of IHOP stock would cost $3,600 ($36.00 × 100), plus a commission. If you were selling 100 shares of IHOP stock, you would receive cash of $3,600 less a commission. The commission is the fee an investor pays to a stockbroker for buying or selling the stock. The price of a share of IHOP stock has fluctuated from $10 at issuance to a recent high of $44.75.

Learning Tip: If you buy stock in IBM from another investor, IBM gets no cash. The transaction is a sale between investors. IBM records only the change in stockholder name.

Redemption Value

Preferred stock that requires the company to redeem (pay to retire) the stock at a set price is called *redeemable preferred stock.* The company is *obligated* to redeem the preferred stock. The price the corporation agrees to pay for the stock, which is set when the stock is issued, is called the *redemption value.* Some preferred stock is *callable*, which means that the company may call (pay to retire) the stock if it wishes. The preferred stock of Pine Industries, Inc., is "callable at the option of the Company at $25 per share."

Beginning in 2001, Pine is "required to redeem annually 6,765 shares of the preferred stock ($169,125 annually)." Pine's annual redemption payment to the preferred stockholders will include this redemption value plus any dividends in arrears. In the year 2000, Pine Industries' preferred stock ceases to be owners' equity and becomes a liability. Starting in 2001, Pine must start paying off the preferred stock as though it were debt.

■ Daily Exercise 13-16

Thinking It Over Suppose you are a banker and Pine Industries asks you for a large long-term loan in the year 2000. If you overlook Pine's obligation to pay off its preferred stock, what error are you likely to make in evaluating the loan request?

Answer: By ignoring Pine's obligation to pay off its preferred stock, you may lend money to Pine on too-favorable terms. For example, you may be willing to lend more money to Pine Industries than the company is able to pay back. Or you may give Pine too much time to pay you back. In either case, you run the risk of failing to collect the loan.

Liquidation Value

The *liquidation value*, which applies only to preferred stock, is the amount the corporation agrees to pay the preferred stockholder per share if the company liquidates. Dividends in arrears are added to liquidation value in determining the payment to the preferred stockholders if the company liquidates. Some companies report their preferred stock at its liquidation value on the balance sheet. Consider the BF Goodrich Company, which makes chemicals and aerospace components and sells tires under the Michelin label. BF Goodrich has 2.2 million shares of convertible preferred stock that is stated at "a liquidation value of $50 per share." The balance in BF Goodrich's preferred stock account is thus $110 million (2.2 million shares × $50).

Book Value

Book Value. Amount of owners' equity on the company's books for each share of its stock.

The **book value** of a stock is the amount of owners' equity on the company's books for each share of its stock. Corporations often report this amount in their annual reports. If the company has only common stock outstanding, its book value is computed by dividing total stockholders' equity by the number of shares *outstanding.* A company with stockholders' equity of $180,000 and 5,000 shares of common stock outstanding has a book value of $36 per share ($180,000/5,000 shares).

If the company has both preferred and common stock outstanding, the preferred stockholders have the first claim to owners' equity. Ordinarily, preferred stock has a specified liquidation or redemption value. The book value of preferred stock is its redemption value plus any cumulative dividends in arrears on the stock. Its book value *per share* equals the sum of redemption value and any cumulative dividends in arrears divided by the number of preferred shares *outstanding*. After the corporation figures the book value of the preferred shares, it computes the common stock book value per share. The corporation divides the common equity (total stockholders' equity minus preferred equity) by the number of common shares outstanding.

The company balance sheet reports the following amounts:

Stockholders' Equity	
Paid-in capital:	
Preferred stock, 6%, $10 par, 5,000 shares authorized, 5,000 shares issued (redemption value $13 per share)	$ 50,000
Paid-in capital in excess of par—preferred	14,000
Common stock, $1 par, 20,000 shares authorized, 15,000 shares issued	15,000
Paid-in capital in excess of par—common	172,000
Donated capital	40,000
Total paid-in capital	291,000
Retained earnings	122,000
Total stockholders' equity	$413,000

Suppose that four years' (including the current year) cumulative preferred dividends are in arrears. The book-value-per-share computations for this corporation are as follows:

Preferred	
Redemption value (5,000 shares × $13)	$ 65,000
Cumulative dividends ($50,000 × 0.06 × 4)	12,000
Stockholders' equity allocated to preferred	$ 77,000
Book value per share ($77,000/5,000 shares)	$ 15.40
Common	
Total stockholders' equity	$413,000
Less stockholders' equity allocated to preferred	(77,000)
Stockholders' equity allocated to common	$336,000
Book value per share ($336,000/15,000 shares)	$ 22.40

■ Daily Exercise 13-17

If the preferred stock has no specified redemption value, then we would use the sum of par value plus paid-in capital in excess of par–preferred, $64,000, plus cumulative dividends to compute the book value of the preferred stock.

BOOK VALUE AND DECISION MAKING How is book value per share used in decision making? Companies negotiating the purchase of a corporation may wish to know the book value of its stock. The book value of stockholders' equity may figure into the negotiated purchase price of a corporation whose stock is not publicly traded. Also, a corporation may buy out a retiring executive or other stockholder, agreeing to pay the book value of the person's stock in the company.

Some investors have traditionally compared the book value of a share of a company's stock with the stock's market value. The idea was that a stock selling below its book value was underpriced and thus a good buy. The relationship between book value and market value is far from clear. Some investors believe that a company whose stock sells at a price below book value must be experiencing financial difficulty.

Book value is a product of the accounting system, which is based on historical costs. Market value, conversely, depends on investors' subjective outlook for dividends and increases in the stock's value. Exhibit 13-10 contrasts the book values and ranges of market

■ Daily Exercise 13-18

EXHIBIT 13-10
Book Value and Market Value for Three Companies

	Year-End Book Value	52-Week Market-Value Range
IHOP Corp.	$11.55	$19.25–$ 37.38
Toys "Я" Us	12.57	$24.38–$ 37.63
IBM	40.47	$56.25–$109.44

values for the common stocks of three well-known companies. For all three companies, the market value of stock exceeds its book value—a mark of success.

Evaluating Operations: Rate of Return on Total Assets and Rate of Return on Common Stockholders' Equity

Objective 6

Evaluate a company's return on assets and return on stockholders' equity

Investors and creditors are constantly evaluating managers' ability to earn profits. Investors search for companies whose stocks are likely to increase in value. Investment decisions often include a comparison of companies. But a comparison of IHOP's net income with the net income of a new company in the restaurant industry simply is not meaningful. IHOP's profits may run into the millions of dollars, which far exceed a new company's net income. To compare companies of different size, investors use some standard profitability measures, including rate of return on total assets and rate of return on stockholders' equity.

Return on Assets

Rate of Return on Total Assets. The sum of net income plus interest expense divided by average total assets. This ratio measures the success a company has in using its assets to earn income for the persons who finance the business. Also called **return on assets.**

The **rate of return on total assets,** or simply **return on assets,** measures a company's success in using its assets to earn income for the persons who are financing the business. Creditors have loaned money to the corporation and thus earn interest. The stockholders have invested in the corporation's stock and therefore own the company's net income. The sum of interest expense and net income is the return to the two groups that have financed the corporation's assets, and this is the numerator of the return-on-assets ratio. The denominator is average total assets. Return on assets is computed as follows, using data from the 1996 annual report of IHOP Corp. (dollar amounts in thousands of dollars):

$$\text{Rate of return on total assets} = \frac{\text{Net income} + \text{Interest expense}}{\text{Average total assets}}$$

$$= \frac{\$18{,}604 + \$11{,}691}{(\$252{,}057 + \$328{,}889)/2} = \frac{\$30{,}295}{\$290{,}473} = 0.104$$

Net income and interest expense are taken from the income statement. Average total assets is computed from the beginning and ending balance sheets.

Investors use return on assets to compare companies in terms of how well their management earns a return for the people who finance the corporation. By relating the sum of net income and interest expense to average total assets, they have a standard measure that describes the profitability of all types of companies. Brokerage companies such as Merrill Lynch and Paine Webber often single out particular industries as likely sources of good investments. For example, brokerage analysts may believe that the health-care industry is in a growth phase. These analysts would identify specific health-care companies whose profitabilities are likely to lead the industry and so be sound investments. Return on assets is one measure of profitability.

What is a good rate of return on total assets? There is no single answer to this question because rates of return vary widely by industry. For example, high technology companies earn much higher returns than do utility companies, groceries, and manufacturers of consumer goods such as toothpaste.

Return on Equity

Rate of Return on Common Stockholders' Equity. Net income minus preferred dividends, divided by average common stockholders' equity. A measure of profitability. Also called **return on equity.**

Rate of return on common stockholders' equity, often called **return on equity,** shows the relationship between net income and average common stockholders' equity. The numerator is net income minus preferred dividends. Preferred dividends are subtracted because the preferred stockholders have the first claim on the company's net income. The denominator is average *common stockholders' equity*—total stockholders' equity minus preferred equity. IHOP's rate of return on common stockholders' equity for 1996 is computed as follows (dollar amounts in thousands of dollars):

$$\text{Rate of return on common stockholders' equity} = \frac{\text{Net income} - \text{Preferred dividends}}{\text{Average common stockholders' equity}}$$

$$= \frac{\$18,604 - \$0}{(\$108,297 + \$129,357)/2} = \frac{\$18,604}{\$118,827} = 0.157$$

IHOP Corp. has no preferred stock, so preferred dividends are zero. With no preferred stock outstanding, average *common* stockholders' equity is the same as average *total* equity—the average of the beginning and ending amounts.

■ Daily Exercise 13-19

IHOP's return on equity (15.7%) is higher than its return on assets (10.4%). This difference results from the interest-expense component of return on assets. Companies such as IHOP borrow at one rate (say, 7%) and invest the funds to earn a higher rate (say, 16%). Borrowing at a lower rate than the return on investments is called *using leverage.* During good times, leverage produces high returns for stockholders. However, too much leverage can make it difficult to pay the interest on the debt. The company's creditors are guaranteed a fixed rate of return on their loans. But because the stockholders have no guarantee that the corporation will earn net income, their investments are riskier. Consequently, stockholders demand a higher rate of return than do creditors, which explains why *return on equity should exceed return on assets.* If return on assets is higher than return on equity, the company is in trouble. Interest expense should always be lower than the amount the company earns on its investments.

Investors and creditors use return on common stockholders' equity in much the same way they use return on total assets—to compare companies. The higher the rate of return, the more successful the company. IHOP's 15.7% return on common stockholders' equity would be considered good in most industries. Investors also compare a company's return on stockholders' equity with interest rates available in the market. If interest rates are almost as high as return on equity, many investors will lend their money to earn interest. They choose to forgo the extra risk of investing in stock when the rate of return on equity is too low.

■ Daily Exercise 13-20

Accounting for Income Taxes by Corporations

Objective 7

Account for a corporation's income tax

Corporations pay income tax in the same way that individuals do. Corporate and personal tax rates differ, however. At this writing, the federal tax rate on most corporate income is 35 percent. Most states also levy their own income taxes on corporations, so most corporations have a combined federal and state income tax rate of approximately 40 percent.

To account for income tax, the corporation measures for each period:

- Income tax expense, an expense on the income statement
- Income tax payable, a liability on the balance sheet

Accounting for income tax by a corporation follows the general principles that govern accounting for all other transactions. Let's return to IHOP Corp. In 19X6, IHOP reported income before tax (also called pretax accounting income) of approximately \$30 million on its income statement. IHOP's combined income tax rate was 40 percent. Assume IHOP's income tax expense and income tax payable are the same. Then IHOP would record income tax for the year as follows (amounts in millions):

19X6			
Dec. 31	Income Tax Expense (\$30 × 0.40)..........	12	
	Income Tax Payable		12
	Recorded income tax for the year.		

IHOP's 19X6 financial statements would report these figures (adapted, in millions):

Income statement	
Income before income tax..........	$ 30
Income tax expense.....................	(12)
Net income	$ 18

Balance sheet	
Current liabilities:	
Income tax payable	$12

Early in 19X7, IHOP would pay its income tax payable when the company files its 19X6 income tax return with the Internal Revenue Service.

In general, income tax expense and income tax payable can be computed as follows:[2]

Income tax *expense* = **Income before income tax (from the income statement)** × **Income tax rate**

Income tax *payable* = **Taxable income (from the income tax return filed with the IRS** × **Income tax rate**

The income statement and the income tax return are entirely separate documents:

- The income statement reports the results of operations that we have been working with throughout this course.
- The income tax return is filed with the Internal Revenue Service to determine how much tax the company must pay the government.

For most companies, income tax expense and income tax payable differ. Certain items of revenue and expense enter into the determination of income at different times for the purposes of measuring income for accounting purposes and for measuring taxable income for income tax purposes. The most important difference between income before income tax and taxable income occurs when a corporation uses the straight-line method to compute depreciation for the financial statements and an accelerated depreciation method for the tax return and the payment of taxes. The tax depreciation method is called the *modified accelerated cost recovery system*, abbreviated as MACRS. For any one year, MACRS depreciation listed on the tax return may differ from accounting depreciation on the income statement.

We learned in Chapter 10, page 434, that the MACRS depreciation method is similar to the double-declining-balance method.

Continuing with the IHOP illustration, suppose for 19X7 that IHOP Corp. has

- Pretax accounting income of $40 million on the income statement
- Taxable income of $35 million on the company's income tax return

IHOP will record income tax for 19X7 as follows (dollar amounts in millions and an income tax rate of 40%):

19X7			
Dec. 31	Income Tax Expense ($40 × 0.40)	16	
	Income Tax Payable ($35 × 0.40)		14
	Deferred Tax Liability		2
	Recorded income tax for the year.		

IHOP's 19X7 financial statements would report these figures (adapted, in millions):

Income statement	
Income before income tax..........	$ 40
Income tax expense.....................	(16)
Net income	$ 24

Balance sheet	
Current liabilities:	
Income tax payable	$14
Long-term liabilities:	
Deferred tax liability	2*

*Assumes the beginning balance of Deferred tax liability was zero.

[2]The authors thank Jean Marie Hudson for suggesting this presentation.

Early in 19X8, IHOP would pay its income tax payable of $14 million because this is a current liability. Deferred tax liability, however, is usually long-term, and the company may pay this liability over a longer period.

■ Daily Exercise 13-21

The Decision Guidelines feature provides an overview of the second half of the chapter.

DECISION GUIDELINES

Dividends, Stock Values, Evaluating Operations, & Accounting for Income Tax

DECISION	GUIDELINES
Dividends	
Whether to declare a cash dividend?	• Must have enough retained earnings to declare the dividend. • Must have enough cash to pay the dividend.
What happens with a dividend?	• The corporation's board of directors declares the dividend. Then the dividend becomes a liability of the corporation. • The date of record fixes who will receive the dividend. • Payment of the dividend occurs later.
Who receives the dividend?	• Preferred stockholders first receive their dividends at a specified rate. • Common stockholders receive the remainder.
Stock Values	
How much to pay for a stock?	Its market value.
What unique values apply to preferred stock?	• Redemption value—the amount the corporation must pay to redeem (retire) the stock • Liquidation value—the amount the corporation agrees to pay if the company liquidates
What is book value's role in decision making?	Sometimes used to help determine the market value of a stock that is not traded on a stock exchange.
Evaluating Operations	
How to evaluate the operations of a corporation?	There are many ways. Two measures that relate earnings to the amount that stockholders have invested include • Rate of return on assets • Rate of return on common stockholders' equity For a healthy company, return on stockholders' equity should exceed return on assets.
Accounting for Income Tax	
What are the three main accounts?	• Income tax expense • Income tax payable, a current liability • Deferred tax liability, usually a long-term liability
How to measure	
• Income tax expense?	Income before income tax (from the income statement) × Income tax rate
• Income tax payable?	Taxable income (from the income tax return filed with the Internal Revenue Service) × Income tax rate
• Deferred tax liability?	Difference between income tax expense and income tax payable for any one year

SUMMARY PROBLEM FOR YOUR REVIEW

1. Use the following accounts and related balances to prepare the classified balance sheet of Whitehall, Inc., at September 30, 19X4. Use the account format of the balance sheet.

Common stock, $1 par, 50,000 shares authorized, 20,000 shares issued	$ 20,000	Long-term note payable	$ 73,000
Dividends payable	4,000	Inventory	85,000
Cash	9,000	Property, plant, and equipment, net	225,000
Accounts payable	28,000	Revenue from donations	18,000
Retained earnings	75,000	Accounts receivable, net	23,000
Paid-in capital in excess of par—common	115,000	Preferred stock, $3.75, no-par, 10,000 shares authorized, 2,000 shares issued	24,000
		Accrued liabilities	3,000

2. The balance sheet of Trendline Corporation reported the following at March 31, 19X6, the end of its fiscal year. Note that Trendline reports paid-in capital in excess of par or stated value after the stock accounts.

Stockholders' Equity	
Preferred stock, 4%, $10 par, 10,000 shares authorized (redemption value, $110,000)	$100,000
Common stock, no-par, $5 stated value, 100,000 shares authorized	250,000
Paid-in capital in excess of par:	
Common stock	231,500
Retained earnings	395,000
Total stockholders' equity	$976,500

REQUIRED

1. Is the preferred stock cumulative or noncumulative? How can you tell?
2. What is the total amount of the annual preferred dividend?
3. How many shares of preferred and common stock has the company issued?
4. Compute the book value per share of the preferred and the common stock. No prior year preferred dividends are in arrears, but Trendline has not declared the current-year dividend.

SOLUTION

WHITEHALL, INC.
Balance Sheet
September 30, 19X4

Assets		**Liabilities**		
Current:		Current:		
Cash	$ 9,000	Accounts payable		$ 28,000
Accounts receivable, net	23,000	Dividends payable		4,000
Inventory	85,000	Accrued liabilities		3,000
Total current assets	117,000	Total current liabilities		35,000
Property, plant and equipment, net	225,000	Long-term note payable		73,000
		Total liabilities		108,000
		Stockholders' Equity		
		Paid-in capital:		
		Preferred stock, $3.75, no-par, 10,000 shares authorized, 2,000 shares issued	$ 24,000	
		Common stock, $1 par, 50,000 shares authorized, 20,000 shares issued	20,000	
		Paid-in capital in excess of par—common	115,000	
		Total paid-in capital	159,000	
		Retained earnings	75,000	
		Total stockholders' equity		234,000
Total assets	$342,000	Total liabilities and stockholders' equity		$342,000

REQUIRED

1. The preferred stock is cumulative because it is not specifically labeled otherwise.
2. Total annual preferred dividend: $4,000 ($100,000 × 0.04).
3. Preferred stock issued: 10,000 shares ($100,000/$10 par value).
   Common stock issued: 50,000 shares ($250,000/$5 stated value).
4. Book values per share of preferred and common stock:

Preferred:	
Redemption value	$110,000
Cumulative dividend for current year ($100,000 × 0.04)	4,000
Stockholders' equity allocated to preferred	$114,000
Book value per share ($114,000/10,000 shares)	$ 11.40
Common:	
Total stockholders' equity	$976,500
Less stockholders' equity allocated to preferred	(114,000)
Stockholders' equity allocated to common	$862,500
Book value per share ($862,500/50,000 shares)	$ 17.25

Summary of Learning Objectives

1. ***Identify the characteristics of a corporation.*** A corporation is a separate legal and business entity. *Continuous life*, the *ease of raising large amounts of capital and transferring ownership*, and *limited liability* are among the advantages of the corporate form of organization. An important disadvantage is *double taxation*. Corporations pay *income taxes*, and stockholders pay tax on dividends. *Stockholders* are the owners of the corporations. They elect a *board of directors*, which elects a chairperson and appoints the officers to manage the business.

2. ***Record the issuance of stock.*** Corporations may issue different classes of stock: *par value, no-par value, common*, and *preferred*. Stock is usually issued at a *premium*—an amount above par value.

3. ***Prepare the stockholders' equity section of a corporation's balance sheet.*** The balance sheet carries the capital raised through stock issuance under the heading Paid-in Capital or Contributed Capital in the stockholders' equity section.

4. ***Account for cash dividends.*** Only when the board of directors declares a *dividend* does the corporation incur the liability to pay dividends. Preferred stock has priority over common stock as to dividends, which may be stated as a percentage of par value or as a dollar amount per share. In addition, preferred stock has a claim to dividends in arrears if it is *cumulative*. *Convertible* preferred stock may be exchanged for the corporation's common stock.

5. ***Use different stock values in decision making.*** A stock's *market value* is the price for which a share may be bought or sold. *Redemption value, liquidation value*, and *book value*—the amount of owners' equity per share of company stock—are other values that may apply to stock.

6. ***Evaluate a company's return on assets and return on stockholders' equity.*** *Return on assets* and *return on stockholders' equity* are two standard measures of profitability. A healthy company's return on equity will exceed its return on assets.

7. ***Account for a corporation's income tax.*** Corporations pay income tax and must account for the income tax expense and income tax payable. A difference between the expense and the payable creates another account, Deferred Tax Liability.

Accounting Vocabulary

additional paid-in capital *(p. 555)*
authorization of stock *(p. 550)*
board of directors *(p. 545)*
book value *(p. 560)*
bylaws *(p. 545)*
chairperson *(p. 545)*
charter *(p. 544)*
common stock *(p. 547)*
contributed capital *(p. 547)*
convertible preferred stock *(p. 559)*
cumulative preferred stock *(p. 558)*
deficit *(p. 548)*
dividends *(p. 548)*
double taxation *(p. 545)*
legal capital *(p. 548)*
limited liability *(p. 544)*
market value *(p. 559)*
outstanding stock *(p. 546)*
paid-in capital *(p. 547)*
par value *(p. 549)*
preferred stock *(p. 549)*
president *(p. 545)*
rate of return on common stockholders' equity *(p. 562)*
rate of return on total assets *(p. 562)*
retained earnings *(p. 547)*
return on assets *(p. 562)*
return on equity *(p. 562)*
shareholder *(p. 544)*
stated value *(p. 549)*
stock *(p. 544)*
stockholder *(p. 544)*
stockholders' equity *(p. 547)*

Questions

1. Why is a corporation called a creature of the state?
2. Identify the characteristics of a corporation.
3. Explain why corporations face a tax disadvantage.
4. Briefly outline the steps in the organization of a corporation.
5. How are the structures of a partnership and a corporation similar, and how are they different?

6. Name the four rights of a stockholder. Is preferred stock automatically nonvoting? Explain how a right may be withheld from a stockholder.
7. Dividends on preferred stock may be stated as a percentage rate or a dollar amount. What is the annual dividend on these preferred stocks: 4%, $100 par; $3.50, $20 par; and 6%, no-par with $50 stated value?
8. Which event increases the assets of the corporation: authorization of stock or issuance of stock? Explain.
9. Suppose H. J. Heinz Company issued 1,000 shares of its 3.65%, $100 par preferred stock for $120. How much would this transaction increase the company's paid-in capital? How much would it increase Heinz's retained earnings? How much would it increase Heinz's annual cash dividend payments?
10. Give two alternative account titles for Paid-in Capital in Excess of Par—Common Stock.
11. How does issuance of 1,000 shares of no-par stock for land and a building, together worth $150,000, affect paid-in capital?
12. Rank the following accounts in the order they would appear on the balance sheet: Common Stock, Preferred Stock, Retained Earnings, Dividends Payable. Also, give each account's balance sheet classification.
13. Briefly discuss the three important dates for a dividend.
14. Mancini, Inc., has 3,000 shares of its $2.50, $10 par preferred stock outstanding. Dividends for 19X1 and 19X2 are in arrears, and the company has declared no dividends on preferred stock for the current year, 19X3. Assume that Mancini declares total dividends of $35,000 at the end of 19X3. Show how to allocate the dividends to preferred and common if preferred is (a) cumulative, or (b) noncumulative.
15. As a preferred stockholder, would you rather own cumulative or noncumulative preferred? If all other factors are the same, would the corporation rather the preferred stock be cumulative or noncumulative? Give your reason.
16. How are cumulative preferred dividends in arrears reported in the financial statements? When do dividends become a liability of the corporation?
17. Distinguish between the market value of stock and the book value of stock. Which is more important to investors?
18. How is book value per share of common stock computed when the company has both preferred stock and common stock outstanding?
19. Why should a healthy company's rate of return on stockholders' equity exceed its rate of return on total assets?
20. Explain the difference between the income tax expense and the income tax payable of a corporation.

Daily Exercises

Characteristics of a corporation
(Obj. 1)

DE13-1 Suppose you are forming a business and you need some outside money from other investors. Assume you have decided to organize the business as a corporation that will issue stock to raise the needed funds. Briefly discuss your most important reason for organizing as a corporation rather than as a partnership. If you had decided to organize as a partnership, what would be your most important reason for not organizing as a corporation?

Authority structure in a corporation
(Obj. 1)

DE13-2 Consider the authority structure in a corporation, as diagrammed in Exhibit 13-2, page 546.

1. What group holds the ultimate power in a corporation?
2. Who is the most powerful person in the corporation?
3. Who is in charge of day-to-day operations?
4. Who manages the accounting?
5. Who has primary responsibility for the corporation's cash?

Similarities and differences between the balance sheets of a corporation and a proprietorship
(Obj. 1)

DE13-3 Examine the summarized balance sheet of Wal-Mart Stores, Inc., in Exhibit 13-4, page 547. Suppose Wal-Mart Stores were a proprietorship owned by Sam Walton. How would the Wal-Mart proprietorship balance sheet differ from the one given in Exhibit 13-4? How would the proprietorship balance sheet be similar to the one given in Exhibit 13-4?

Characteristics of preferred and common stock
(Obj. 1)

DE13-4 Answer the following questions about the characteristics of a corporation's stock.

1. Which stockholders are the real owners of a corporation?
2. Which right clearly distinguishes a stockholder from a creditor (who has lent money to the corporation)?
3. What privileges do preferred stockholders enjoy that common stockholders do not have?
4. Which class of stockholders would expect to reap greater benefits from a highly profitable corporation? Why?

Effect of a stock issuance on net income
(Obj. 2)

DE13-5 Study IHOP's July 23 stock issuance entry given on page 550, and answer these questions about the nature of the IHOP transaction.

1. IHOP received $32,000,000 for the issuance of its stock. The par value of the IHOP stock was only $32,000. Was the excess amount of $31,968,000 a profit to IHOP? If not, what was it?
2. Suppose the par value of the IHOP stock had been $1 per share, $5 per share, or $10 per share. Would a change in the par value of the company's stock affect IHOP's net income? Give the reason for your answer.

DE13-6 The Coca-Cola Company reported the following on its balance sheet at December 31, 1997 (adapted, amounts in millions, except for par value):

Issuing stock and interpreting stockholders' equity ***(Obj. 2)***

Common stock, $0.25 par value	
Authorized: 5,600 shares	
Issued: 3,443 shares	$ 861
Paid-in capital in excess of par	1,527
Retained earnings	17,869

1. Assume Coca-Cola issued all of its stock during 1997. Journalize the company's issuance of the stock for cash.
2. Was Coca-Cola's main source of stockholders' equity paid-in capital or profitable operations? How can you tell?

DE13-7 At December 31, 1997, The Coca-Cola Company reported the following on its comparative balance sheet, which included 1996 amounts for comparison (adapted, with all amounts except par value in millions):

Issuing stock and analyzing retained earnings ***(Obj. 2)***

	December 31,	
	1997	**1996**
Common stock $0.25 par value		
Authorized: 5,600 shares		
Issued: 3,443 shares in 1997	$ 861	
3,433 shares in 1996		$ 858
Paid-in capital in excess of par	1,527	1,058
Retained earnings	17,869	15,127

1. How much did Coca-Cola's total paid-in capital increase during 1997? What caused total paid-in capital to increase? How can you tell?
2. Journalize Coca-Cola's issuance of stock for cash during 1997.
3. Did Coca-Cola have a profit or a loss for 1997? How can you tell?

DE13-8 Steitz Corporation has three classes of stock: Common, $1 par; Preferred Class A, $10 par; and Preferred Class B, no-par.
Journalize Steitz's issuance of

Issuing stock ***(Obj. 2)***

a. 1,000 shares of common stock for $40 per share
b. 1,000 shares of class A preferred stock for a total of $25,000
c. 1,000 shares of class B preferred stock for $18 per share

Explanations are not required.

DE13-9 This exercise shows the similarity and the difference between two ways to acquire plant assets.

Issuing stock to finance the purchase of assets ***(Obj. 2)***

Case A—Issue stock and buy the assets in separate transactions:

> Data Warehouse, Inc., issued 10,000 shares of its $5 par common stock for cash of $700,000. In a separate transaction, Data Warehouse then used the cash to purchase a warehouse building for $600,000 and equipment for $100,000. Journalize the two transactions.

Case B—Issue stock to acquire the assets:

> Data Warehouse issued 10,000 shares of its $5 par common stock to acquire a warehouse building valued at $600,000 and equipment worth $100,000. Journalize this transaction.

Compare the balances in all accounts after making both sets of entries. Are the account balances similar or different?

DE13-10 Suppose Lands' End received two donations as follows:

Accounting for receipt of two donations ***(Obj. 3)***

a. Land worth $8,400,000 received from the city of Dodgeville, Wisconsin
b. A company recreation center valued at $2,000,000 received from the founder of the company

REQUIRED

1. Journalize Lands' End's receipt of both donations.
2. Which donation affected the company's
   a. Total assets? c. Total stockholders' equity?
   b. Total paid-in capital? d. Net income?
   Was each effect an increase or a decrease?

Preparing the stockholders' equity section of a balance sheet **(Obj. 3)**

DE13-11 The financial statements of Landa Computer, Inc., reported the following accounts (adapted, in millions except for par value):

Net sales	**$1,031.5**	**Paid-in capital in excess of par**	**$ 26.2**
Accounts payable	**62.4**	**Cost of goods sold**	**588.0**
Retained earnings	**166.2**	**Common stock $0.01 par, 40.2 shares issued**	**0.4**
Other current liabilities	**52.3**	**Inventory**	**165.0**
Operating expenses	**412.9**	**Long-term debt**	**7.6**
Donated capital	**8.4**		

Prepare the stockholders' equity section of the Landa Computer balance sheet. Net income has already been closed to Retained Earnings.

Using stockholders' equity data **(Obj. 3)**

DE13-12 *Link Back to Chapter 1 (Accounting Equation, Income Statement).* Use the Landa Computer data in Daily Exercise 13-11 to compute Landa's

a. Net income b. Total liabilities c. Total assets

Reporting stockholders' equity on the balance sheet **(Obj. 3)**

DE13-13 Telex Corporation began operations in 19X3 with a charter that authorized the company to issue 10,000 shares of 5%, $10 par preferred stock and 100,000 shares of no-par common stock. During 19X3 through 19X8, Telex issued 3,000 shares of the preferred stock for $25 per share, and 50,000 shares of its common stock for $6 per share. At December 31, 19X8, Telex had retained earnings of $110,000. During 19X9, Telex earned net income of $70,000 and declared cash dividends of $15,000.

Show how Telex Corporation reported stockholders' equity on its balance sheet at December 31, 19X9.

Accounting for cash dividends **(Obj. 4)**

DE13-14 Augusta Company earned net income of $90,000 during the year ended December 31, 19X6. On December 15, Augusta declared the annual cash dividend on its 6% preferred stock (10,000 shares with total par value of $100,000) and a $0.50 per share cash dividend on its common stock (50,000 shares with total par value of $250,000). Augusta then paid the dividends on January 4, 19X7.

Journalize for Augusta Company:

a. Declaring the cash dividends on December 15
b. Closing net income to Retained Earnings on December 31, 19X6
c. Paying the cash dividends on January 4, 19X7

Did Retained Earnings increase or decrease during 19X6? By how much?

Dividing cash dividends between preferred and common stock **(Obj. 4)**

DE13-15 Refer to the stockholders' equity of Medina Corporation in Exhibit 13-8, page 554. Answer these questions about Medina's dividends.

1. How much in dividends must Medina declare each year before the common stockholders receive cash dividends for the year?
2. Suppose Medina declares cash dividends of $10,000 for 19X5. How much of the dividends go to preferred? How much goes to common?
3. Is Medina's preferred stock cumulative or noncumulative? How can you tell?
4. Suppose Medina passed the preferred dividend in 19X6 and 19X7. In 19X8, Medina declares cash dividends of $10,000. How much of the dividends go to preferred? How much goes to common?

Similarities and differences between preferred stock and common stock **(Obj. 5)**

DE13-16 For the following list of characteristics of capital stock, indicate whether each characteristic applies to preferred and common stock:

a. Stated dividend
b. Voting rights
c. Preemptive right
d. Priority to receive assets in the event of liquidation
e. Cumulative
f. Callable
g. Redemption value

DE13-17 Refer to the stockholders' equity of Medina Corporation in Exhibit 13-8, page 554. Medina's preferred stock has a redemption value of $150 per share, and Medina has not declared preferred dividends for three years (including the current year). Compute the book value of Medina's (a) preferred stock, and (b) common stock.

Book value per share of preferred and common stock
(Obj. 5)

DE13-18 Answer the following questions about various stock values.

Explaining the use of different stock values for decision making
(Obj. 5)

1. Suppose you are an investor considering the purchase of Coca-Cola common stock as an investment. You have called your stockbroker to inquire about the stock. Which stock value are you most concerned about and why?
2. Suppose you are the general manager of a small company that is considering going public, as IHOP Corp. did in the chapter opening story. Which stock value are you most concerned about and why?
3. How is the book value of a stock used in decision making?

DE13-19 Give the formula for computing (a) rate of return on total assets, and (b) rate of return on common stockholders' equity. Then answer these questions about the rate-of-return computations.

Computing and explaining return on assets and return on equity
(Obj. 6)

1. Why is interest expense added to net income to compute return on assets?
2. Why are preferred dividends subtracted from net income to compute return on common stockholders' equity?

DE13-20 The Coca-Cola Company has earned extraordinarily high rates of return on its assets and its stockholders' equity in recent years. Coca-Cola's 1996 financial statements reported the following items—with 1995 figures given for comparison (adapted, in millions):

Computing return on assets and return on equity for a leading company
(Obj. 6)

	1996	1995
Balance sheet		
Total current assets	$ 5,910	$ 5,450
Total long-term assets	10,251	9,591
Total assets	$16,161	$15,041
Total liabilities	$10,005	$ 9,649
Total stockholders' equity (all common)	6,156	5,392
Total liabilities and equity	$16,161	$15,041
Income statement		
Net sales	$18,546	
Cost of goods sold	6,738	
Gross margin	11,808	
Selling, administrative, and general expenses	7,893	
Interest expense	286	
All other expenses, net	137	
Net income	$ 3,492	

Compute Coca-Cola's rate of return on total assets and rate of return on common stockholders' equity for 1996. Do these rates of return look high or low?

DE13-21 Pappadeaux Pizza had income before income tax of $100,000 and taxable income of $80,000 for 19X9, the company's first year of operations. The income tax rate is 40 percent.

Accounting for a corporation's income tax
(Obj. 7)

1. Make the entry to record Pappadeaux's income taxes for 19X9.
2. Show what Pappadeaux Pizza will report on its 19X9 income statement starting with income before income tax. Also show what Pappadeaux will report for current and long-term liabilities on its December 31, 19X9, balance sheet. Assume the beginning balance of Deferred Tax Liability was zero.

Exercises

E13-1 Kathy Whittle and Angela Lane are opening a limousine service to be named K & A Transportation Enterprises. They need outside capital, so they plan to organize the business as a corporation. They come to you for advice. Write a memorandum informing them of the steps in forming a corporation. Identify specific documents used in this process, and name the different parties involved in the ownership and management of a corporation.

Organizing a corporation
(Obj. 1)

Issuing stock
(Obj. 2)

E13-2 Exhibition Software completed the following stock issuance transactions:

June	19	Issued 1,000 shares of $1.50 par common stock for cash of $10.50 per share.
July	3	Sold 300 shares of $4.50, no-par Class A preferred stock for $12,000 cash.
	11	Received inventory valued at $23,000 and equipment with market value of $11,000. Issued 3,300 shares of the $1.50 par common stock.
	15	Issued 1,000 shares of 5%, no-par Class B preferred stock with stated value of $50 per share. The issue price was cash of $60 per share.

REQUIRED

1. Journalize the transactions. Explanations are not required.
2. How much paid-in capital did these transactions generate for Exhibition Software?

Issuing stock and preparing the stockholders' equity section of the balance sheet
(Obj. 2, 3)

E13-3 The charter for Greenlawn, Inc., authorizes the company to issue 100,000 shares of $3, no-par preferred stock and 500,000 shares of common stock with $1 par value. During its start-up phase, Greenlawn completed the following transactions:

July	6	Issued 500 shares of common stock to the promoters who organized the corporation, receiving cash of $15,000.
	12	Issued 300 shares of preferred stock for cash of $18,000.
	14	Issued 800 shares of common stock in exchange for land valued at $24,000.
	31	Earned a small profit for July and closed the $4,000 net income into Retained Earnings.

REQUIRED

1. Record the transactions in the general journal.
2. Prepare the stockholders' equity section of the Greenlawn balance sheet at July 31.

Recording issuance of stock
(Obj. 2)

E13-4 The balance sheet of Baldridge Corporation, as adapted, reported the following stockholders' equity. Baldridge has two separate classes of preferred stock, labeled Series A and Series B. All dollar amounts, except for per-share amounts, are given in thousands.

Stockholders' Equity	
Preferred stock, $1 par, authorized 4,000,000 shares (Note 7)	
Series A	$ 50
Series B	370
Common stock, $0.10 par, authorized 20,000,000, [issued and] outstanding 9,000,000 shares	900
Capital in excess of par	75,000

Note 7. Preferred Stock:

	Shares [Issued and] Outstanding
Series A	50,000
Series B	370,000

REQUIRED

The Series A preferred stock was issued for $5 cash per share, the Series B preferred was issued for $10 cash per share, and the common was issued for cash of $72,370. Make the summary journal entries to record issuance of all the Baldridge stock. Explanations are not required. After you record these entries, what is the balance of Capital in Excess of Par?

Recording issuance of no-par stock
(Obj. 2)

E13-5 Oriental Rug Co., located in Memphis, Tennessee, imports European furniture and Oriental rugs. The corporation issued 5,000 shares of no-par common stock for $10 per share. Record issuance of the stock if the stock (a) is true no-par stock, and (b) has stated value of $2 per share.

Stockholders' equity section of a balance sheet
(Obj. 3)

E13-6 The charter of Elsimate Company authorizes the issuance of 5,000 shares of Class A preferred stock, 1,000 shares of Class B preferred stock, and 10,000 shares of common stock. During a two-month period, Elsimate completed these stock-issuance transactions:

Jan.	23	Issued 1,000 shares of $1 par common stock for cash of $12.50 per share.
Feb.	2	Sold 300 shares of $4.50, no-par Class A preferred stock for $20,000 cash.
	12	Received inventory valued at $25,000 and equipment with market value of $16,000 for 3,300 shares of the $1 par common stock.
	17	Issued 1,000 shares of 5%, no-par Class B preferred stock with stated value of $50 per share. The issue price was cash of $60 per share.

REQUIRED

Prepare the stockholders' equity section of the Elsimate balance sheet for the transactions given in this exercise. Retained earnings has a balance of $46,000.

E13-7 Lynn Corp. recently organized. The company issued common stock to an attorney in exchange for his patent with a market value of $40,000. In addition, Lynn received cash both for 2,000 shares of its $50 par preferred stock at $80 per share and for 26,000 shares of its no-par common stock at $15 per share. The city of Atlanta donated 50 acres of land to the company as a plant site. The market value of the land was $400,000. Retained earnings at the end of the first year was $70,000. Without making journal entries, determine the total paid-in capital created by these transactions.

Paid-in capital for a corporation
(Obj. 2)

E13-8 Colleen Kennedy, Inc., has the following selected account balances at June 30, 19X7. Prepare the stockholders' equity section of the company's balance sheet.

Stockholders' equity section of a balance sheet
(Obj. 3)

Inventory	**$112,000**	**Common stock, no-par with $1 stated value, 500,000 shares authorized, 120,000 shares issued**	**$120,000**
Machinery and equipment	**109,000**	**Accumulated depreciation—machinery and equipment**	**62,000**
Preferred stock, 5%, $20 par, 20,000 shares authorized, 5,000 shares issued	**100,000**	**Retained earnings**	**119,000**
Paid-in capital in excess of par—preferred stock	**88,000**	**Cost of goods sold**	**81,000**

E13-9 Mannheim Corporation has the following stockholders' equity:

Dividing dividends between preferred and common stock
(Obj. 4)

Preferred stock, 7%, $10 par, 100,000 shares authorized, 20,000 shares issued	**$ 200,000**
Common stock, $0.50 par, 500,000 shares authorized, 300,000 shares issued	**150,000**
Paid-in capital in excess of par—common	**600,000**
Total paid-in capital	**$ 950,000**
Retained earnings	**150,000**
Total stockholders' equity	**$1,100,000**

First, determine whether preferred stock is cumulative or noncumulative. Then compute the amount of dividends to preferred and to common for 19X8 and 19X9 if total dividends are $10,000 in 19X8 and $60,000 in 19X9.

E13-10 The following elements of stockholders' equity are adapted from the balance sheet of Baldridge Corporation. All dollar amounts, except the dividends per share, are given in thousands.

Computing dividends on preferred and common stock
(Obj. 4)

Stockholders' Equity	
Preferred stock, cumulative, $1 par (Note 7)	
Series A, 50,000 shares issued	$ 50
Series B, 370,000 shares issued	370
Common stock, $0.10 par, 9,000,000 shares issued	900

Note 7. Preferred Stock:

Designated Annual Cash Dividend per Share	
Series A	$0.20
Series B	1.30

The Series A preferred has preference over the Series B preferred, and the company has paid all preferred dividends through 19X4.

REQUIRED

Compute the dividends to both series of preferred stock and to common for 19X5 and 19X6 if total dividends are $0 in 19X5 and $1,100,000 in 19X6.

E13-11 The balance sheet of Gamma Corporation reported the following:

Book value per share of preferred and common stock
(Obj. 5)

Redeemable preferred stock; 100 shares issued and outstanding, redemption value $6,000	**$ 4,800**
Common stockholders' equity, 10,000 shares issued and outstanding	**216,000**
Total stockholders' equity	**$220,800**

Assume that Gamma has paid preferred dividends for the current year and all prior years (no dividends in arrears). Compute the book value per share of the preferred stock and the common stock.

E13-12 Refer to Exercise 13-11. Compute the book value per share of the preferred stock and the common stock if three years' preferred dividends (including dividends for the current year) are in arrears. The preferred stock dividend rate is 6 percent. Round book value to the nearest cent.

Book value per share of preferred and common stock; preferred dividends in arrears
(Obj. 5)

Evaluating profitability
(Obj. 6)

E13-13 DuBois Furniture, Inc., reported these figures for 19X7 and 19X6:

	19X7	19X6
Income statement:		
Interest expense	$ 17,400,000	$ 7,100,000
Net income	12,000,000	18,700,000
Balance sheet:		
Total assets	351,000,000	317,000,000
Preferred stock, $1.30, no-par, 100,000 shares issued and outstanding	2,500,000	2,500,000
Common stockholders' equity	164,000,000	151,000,000
Total stockholders' equity	166,500,000	153,500,000

Compute rate of return on total assets and rate of return on common stockholders' equity for 19X7. Do these rates of return suggest strength or weakness? Give your reason.

Accounting for income tax by a corporation
(Obj. 7)

E13-14 Temple Construction Company was chartered in Texas during 19X0. Temple has income before income tax of $420,000 in 19X0. Taxable income is $380,000 for 19X0. Texas has no corporate income tax, and the federal income tax rate is 35 percent. Record Temple's income tax for the year. Show what Temple will report on its 19X0 income statement starting with income before income tax. Also show what Temple will report for current and long-term liabilities on its December 31, 19X0, balance sheet.

CHALLENGE EXERCISE

Accounting for stockholders' equity transactions
(Obj. 2, 4)

E13-15 Wal-Mart Stores, Inc., reported these comparative stockholders' equity data (amounts in millions except par value):

	January 31, 19X2	January 31, 19X1
Common stock ($0.10 par value)	$ 115	$ 114
Capital in excess of par value	626	416
Retained earnings	6,249	4,836

During 19X2, Wal-Mart completed these transactions:

a. Net income, $1,608.
b. Cash dividends declared and paid, $195.
c. Issuance of stock for cash, $211.

REQUIRED

1. Give the journal entries to show how Wal-Mart accounted for these 19X2 transactions.
2. For each stockholders' equity account, start with the January 31, 19X1, balance and work toward the balance at January 31, 19X2 to show how your journal entries accounted for the changes in the Wal-Mart accounts.

Beyond the Numbers

Characteristics of corporations' capital stock
(Obj. 2, 5)

BN13-1 Answering the following questions will enhance your understanding of the capital stock of corporations.

1. Why do you think capital stock and retained earnings are shown separately in the shareholders' equity section?
2. Lynn Liu, major shareholder of L-S, Inc., proposes to sell some land she owns to the company for common shares in L-S. What problem does L-S, Inc., face in recording the transaction?
3. Preferred shares generally are preferred with respect to dividends and on liquidation. Why would investors buy common stock when preferred stock is available?
4. What does it mean if the liquidation value of a company's preferred stock is greater than its market value?
5. If you owned 100 shares of stock in Carta Corporation and someone offered to buy the stock for its book value, would you accept the offer? Why or why not?

ETHICAL ISSUE

Note: This case is based on an actual situation.

George Campbell paid $50,000 for a franchise that entitled him to market Success Associates software programs in the countries of the European Common Market. Campbell intended to sell individual franchises for the major language groups of western Europe—German, French, English, Spanish, and Italian. Naturally, investors considering buying a franchise from Campbell asked to see the financial statements of his business.

Believing the value of the franchise to be greater than $50,000, Campbell sought to capitalize his own franchise at $500,000. The law firm of McDonald & LaDue helped Campbell form a corporation chartered to issue 500,000 shares of common stock with par value of $1 per share. Attorneys suggested the following chain of transactions:

a. A third party borrows $500,000 and purchases the franchise from Campbell.
b. Campbell pays the corporation $500,000 to acquire all its stock.
c. The corporation buys the franchise from the third party, who repays the loan.

In the final analysis, the third party is debt-free and out of the picture. Campbell owns all the corporation's stock, and the corporation owns the franchise. The corporation's balance sheet lists a franchise acquired at a cost of $500,000. This balance sheet is Campbell's most valuable marketing tool.

REQUIRED

1. What is unethical about this situation?
2. Who can be harmed? How can they be harmed? What role does accounting play?

Problems (GROUP A)

Organizing a corporation **(Obj. 1)**

P13-1A Barry Camp and Mark Wible are opening an Office Depot store in a shopping center in Santa Fe, New Mexico. The area is growing, and no competitors are located nearby. Their most basic decision is how to organize the business. Camp thinks the partnership form is best. Wible favors the corporate form of organization. They seek your advice.

REQUIRED

Write a memo to Camp and Wible to make them aware of the advantages and the disadvantages of organizing the business as a corporation. Use the following format for your memo:

Date:	______________
To:	**Barry Camp and Mark Wible**
From:	**Student Name**
Subject:	**Advantages and disadvantages of the corporation form of business organization**

Journalizing corporation transactions and preparing the stockholders' equity section of the balance sheet **(Obj. 2, 3)**

P13-2A The partners who own Engell & Blatt wished to avoid the unlimited personal liability of the partnership form of business, so they incorporated the partnership as E&B Exploration, Inc. The charter from the state of Louisiana authorizes the corporation to issue 10,000 shares of 6%, $100 par preferred stock and 250,000 shares of no-par common stock. In its first month, E&B Exploration completed the following transactions:

Jan. 3	Issued 5,100 shares of common stock to Engell and 3,800 shares to Blatt, both for cash of $10 per share.
7	Received land valued at $160,000 as a donation from the city of Lafayette.
12	Issued 1,000 shares of preferred stock to acquire a patent with a market value of $110,000.
22	Issued 1,500 shares of common stock to other investors for $15 cash per share.

REQUIRED

1. Record the transactions in the general journal.
2. Prepare the stockholders' equity section of the E&B Exploration, Inc., balance sheet at January 31. The ending balance of Retained Earnings is $40,300.

Issuing stock and preparing the stockholders' equity section of the balance sheet **(Obj. 2, 3)**

P13-3A Kluzewski Corporation was organized in 19X8. At December 31, 19X8, Kluzewski's balance sheet reported the following stockholders' equity:

Preferred stock, 5%, $10 par, 50,000 shares authorized, none issued	**$ —**
Common stock, $2 par, 100,000 shares authorized, 10,000 shares issued	**20,000**
Paid-in capital in excess of par—common	**30,000**
Retained earnings (Deficit)	**(5,000)**
Total stockholders' equity	**$45,000**

REQUIRED

Answer the following questions, making journal entries as needed.

1. What does the 5% mean for the preferred stock? After Kluzewski issues preferred stock, how much in cash dividends will Kluzewski expect to pay on 1,000 shares?

2. At what price per share did Kluzewski issue the common stock during 19X8?
3. Were first-year operations profitable? Give your reason.
4. During 19X9, the company completed the following selected transactions. Journalize each transaction. Explanations are not required.
   a. Issued for cash 5,000 shares of preferred stock at par value.
   b. Issued for cash 1,000 shares of common stock at a price of $7 per share.
   c. Issued 20,000 shares of common stock to acquire a building valued at $140,000.
   d. Net income for the year was $50,000, and the company declared no dividends. Make the closing entry for net income.
5. Prepare the stockholders' equity section of the Kluzewski Corporation balance sheet at December 31, 19X9.

Stockholders' equity section of the balance sheet
(Obj. 3)

P13-4A Stockholders' equity information for two independent companies, The Yankee Group, Inc., and Alltell Corp. is as follows:

- ***The Yankee Group, Inc.*** The Yankee Group is authorized to issue 50,000 shares of $5 par common stock. All the stock was issued at $12 per share. The company incurred a net loss of $41,000 in 19X1. It earned net income of $60,000 in 19X2 and $90,000 in 19X3. The company declared no dividends during the three-year period.
- ***Alltell Corp.*** Alltell's charter authorizes the company to issue 10,000 shares of $2.50 preferred stock with par value of $50, and 120,000 shares of no-par common stock. Alltell issued 1,000 shares of the preferred stock at $54 per share. It issued 40,000 shares of the common stock for a total of $220,000. The company's retained earnings balance at the beginning of 19X3 was $72,000, and net income for the year was $90,000. During 19X3, the company declared the specified dividend on preferred and a $0.50 per share dividend on common. Preferred dividends for 19X2 were in arrears.

REQUIRED

For each company, prepare the stockholders' equity section of its balance sheet at December 31, 19X3. Show the computation of all amounts. Entries are not required.

Analyzing the stockholders' equity of an actual corporation
(Obj. 3, 4)

P13-5A The purpose of this problem is to familiarize you with financial statement information. U and I Group, which makes food products and livestock feeds, included the following stockholders' equity on its year-end balance sheet at February 28, 19X8:

Stockholders' Equity	($ Thousands)
Voting Preferred stock, 5.5% cumulative—par value $23 per share; authorized 100,000 shares in each class:	
Class A—issued 75,473 shares	$ 1,736
Class B—issued 92,172 shares	2,120
Common stock—par value $5 per share; authorized 5,000,000 shares; issued 2,870,950 shares	14,355
Paid-in Capital in Excess of Par—Common	5,548
Retained earnings	8,336
	$32,095

REQUIRED

1. Identify the different issues of stock U and I has outstanding.
2. Give the summary entries to record issuance of all the U and I stock. Assume that all the stock was issued for cash. Explanations are not required.
3. Assume that preferred dividends are in arrears for 19X8.
   a. Write Note 5 of the February 28, 19X8, financial statements to disclose the dividends in arrears.
   b. Record the declaration of a $450,000 dividend on February 28, 19X9. An explanation is not required.

Preparing a corporation balance sheet; measuring profitability
(Obj. 3, 6)

P13-6A *Link Back to Chapter 1 (Accounting Equation).* The following accounts and related balances of Borzhov, Inc., are arranged in no particular order.

Accounts receivable, net	**$46,000**	**Interest expense**	**$ 6,100**
Paid-in capital in excess of par—common	**19,000**	**Property, plant, and equipment, net**	**261,000**
Accrued liabilities	**26,000**	**Common stock, $1 par, 500,000 shares authorized, 236,000 shares issued**	**236,000**
Long-term note payable	**42,000**		
Inventory	**81,000**		

Dividends payable	$ 9,000	Prepaid expenses	$ 10,000
Retained earnings	?	Revenue from donation	6,000
Accounts payable	31,000	Common stockholders' equity, June 30, 19X1	222,000
Trademark, net	9,000	Net income	31,000
Preferred stock, $0.10, no-par, 10,000 shares authorized and issued	27,000	Total assets, June 30, 19X1	404,000
		Cash	13,000

REQUIRED

1. Prepare the company's classified balance sheet in the account format at June 30, 19X2. Use the accounting equation to compute Retained Earnings.
2. Compute rate of return on total assets and rate of return on common stockholders' equity for the year ended June 30, 19X2.
3. Do these rates of return suggest strength or weakness? Give your reason.

Computing dividends on preferred and common stock
(Obj. 4)

P13-7A AIG Financial Services has 10,000 shares of $3.50, no-par preferred stock and 50,000 shares of no-par common stock outstanding. AIG declared and paid the following dividends during a three-year period: 19X1, $20,000; 19X2, $100,000; and 19X3, $215,000.

REQUIRED

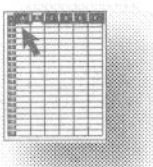

1. Compute the total dividends to preferred stock and to common stock for each of the three years if
   a. Preferred is noncumulative.
   b. Preferred is cumulative.
2. For case (1b), record the declaration of the 19X3 dividends on December 28, 19X3, and the payment of the dividends on January 17, 19X4.

Analyzing the stockholders' equity of an actual corporation
(Obj. 4, 5)

P13-8A The balance sheet of Elsimate, Inc., reported the following:

Stockholders' Investment [same as stockholders' equity]	
Redeemable nonvoting preferred stock, no-par (redemption value, $358,000)	$320,000
Common stock, $1.50 par value, authorized 75,000 shares; issued 36,000 shares	54,000
[Additional] paid-in capital	231,000
Retained earnings	119,000
Total stockholders' investment	$724,000

Notes to the financial statements indicate that 8,000 shares of $2.60 preferred stock with a stated value of $40 per share were issued and outstanding. Preferred dividends are in arrears for three years, including the current year. The additional paid-in capital was contributed by the common stockholders. On the balance sheet date, the market value of the Elsimate common stock was $7.50 per share.

REQUIRED

1. Is the preferred stock cumulative or noncumulative? How can you tell?
2. What is the amount of the annual preferred dividend?
3. Which class of stockholders controls the company? Give your reason.
4. What is the total paid-in capital of the company?
5. What was the total market value of the common stock?
6. Compute the book value per share of the preferred stock and the common stock.

Computing and recording a corporation's income tax
(Obj. 7)

P13-9A The accounting (not the income tax) records of MRI Intelligence Systems, Inc., provide the income statement for 19X3.

Total revenue		**$680,000**
Expenses:		
Cost of goods sold	**$290,000**	
Operating expenses	**180,000**	
Total expenses before tax		**470,000**
Income before income tax		**$210,000**

The operating expenses include depreciation of $40,000 computed under the straight-line method. In calculating taxable income on the tax return, MRI uses the modified accelerated cost recovery system (MACRS). MACRS depreciation was $50,000 for 19X3. The corporate income tax rate is 35 percent.

REQUIRED

1. Compute taxable income for the year.
2. Journalize the corporation's income tax for 19X3.
3. Prepare the corporation's single-step income statement for 19X3.

Problems (GROUP B)

Organizing a corporation
(Obj. 1)

P13-1B Helen Monroe and Rita Cheng are opening a Shoney's Restaurant in Columbia, South Carolina. There are no competing family restaurants in the immediate vicinity. Their most fundamental decision is how to organize the business. Monroe thinks the partnership form is best for their business. Cheng favors the corporate form of organization. They seek your advice.

REQUIRED

Write a memo to Monroe and Cheng to make them aware of the advantages and the disadvantages of organizing the business as a corporation. Use the following format for your memo:

Date:	________________
To:	**Helen Monroe and Rita Cheng**
From:	**Student Name**
Subject:	**Advantages and disadvantages of the corporate form of business organization**

Journalizing corporation transactions and preparing the stockholders' equity section of the balance sheet
(Obj. 2, 3)

P13-2B The partnership of Sanchez & Mundo needed additional capital to expand into new markets, so the business incorporated as Tiempo Grande, Inc. The charter from the state of Arizona authorizes Tiempo Grande to issue 50,000 shares of 6%, $100-par preferred stock and 100,000 shares of no-par common stock. In its first month, Tiempo Grande completed the following transactions:

Dec.	2	Issued 9,000 shares of common stock to Sanchez and 12,000 shares to Mundo, both for cash of $5 per share.
	8	Received a parcel of land valued at $112,000 as a donation from the city of Tucson.
	10	Issued 400 shares of preferred stock to acquire a patent with a market value of $50,000.
	27	Issued 12,000 shares of common stock to other investors for cash of $96,000.

REQUIRED

1. Record the transactions in the general journal.
2. Prepare the stockholders' equity section of the Tiempo Grande, Inc., balance sheet at December 31. The ending balance of Retained Earnings is $57,100.

Issuing stock and preparing the stockholders' equity section of the balance sheet
(Obj. 2, 3)

P13-3B Manitowoc, Inc., was organized in 19X7. At December 31, 19X7, Manitowoc's balance sheet reported the following stockholders' equity:

Preferred stock, 6%, $50 par, 100,000 shares authorized, none issued	**$ —**
Common stock, $1 par, 500,000 shares authorized, 60,000 shares issued	**60,000**
Paid-in capital in excess of par—common	**40,000**
Retained earnings—Deficit	**(25,000)**
Total stockholders' equity	**$75,000**

REQUIRED

Answer the following questions, making journal entries as needed.

1. What does the 6% mean for the preferred stock? After Manitowoc issues preferred stock, how much in cash dividends will Manitowoc expect to pay on 1,000 shares?
2. At what price per share did Manitowoc issue the common stock during 19X7?
3. Were first-year operations profitable? Give your reason.
4. During 19X8, the company completed the following selected transactions. Journalize each transaction. Explanations are not required.
   a. Issued for cash 1,000 shares of preferred stock at par value.
   b. Issued for cash 2,000 shares of common stock at a price of $3 per share.
   c. Issued 50,000 shares of common stock to acquire a building valued at $100,000.
   d. Net income for the year was $65,000, and the company declared no dividends. Make the closing entry for net income.
5. Prepare the stockholders' equity section of the Manitowoc, Inc., balance sheet at December 31, 19X8.

Stockholders' equity section of the balance sheet
(Obj. 3)

P13-4B The following summaries for Omega Fotographic, Inc., and Homeowners Insurance Company provide the information needed to prepare the stockholders' equity section of the company balance sheet. The two companies are independent.

- ***Omega Fotographic, Inc.*** Omega Fotographic is authorized to issue 50,000 shares of $1 par common stock. All the stock was issued at $12 per share. The company incurred net losses of $50,000 in 19X1 and $14,000 in 19X2. It earned net income of $23,000 in 19X3 and $71,000 in 19X4. The company declared no dividends during the four-year period.
- ***Homeowners Insurance Company.*** Homeowners Insurance Company's charter authorizes the company to issue 50,000 shares of 5%, $10 par preferred stock and 500,000 shares of no-par common stock. Homeowners Insurance issued 1,000 shares of the preferred stock at $15 per share. It issued 100,000 shares of the common stock for $400,000. The company's retained earnings balance at the beginning of 19X4 was $120,000. Net income for 19X4 was $60,000, and the company declared the specified preferred dividend for 19X4. Preferred dividends for 19X3 were in arrears.

REQUIRED

For each company, prepare the stockholders' equity section of its balance sheet at December 31, 19X4. Show the computation of all amounts. Entries are not required.

Analyzing the stockholders' equity of an actual corporation
(Obj. 3, 4)

P13-5B The purpose of this problem is to familiarize you with financial statement information. Bethlehem Steel Corporation, a large steel company, reported the following stockholders' equity on its balance sheet at December 31, 19X5:

Stockholders' Equity	($ Millions)
Preferred stock—	
Authorized 20,000,000 shares in each class; issued:	
$5.00 Cumulative Convertible Preferred Stock, at $50.00 stated value, 2,500,000 shares	$ 125
$2.50 Cumulative Convertible Preferred Stock, at $25.00 stated value, 4,000,000 shares	100
Common stock—$8 par value—	
Authorized 80,000,000 shares; issued 48,308,516 shares	621
Retained earnings	529
	$1,375

Note that Bethlehem reports no Paid-in Capital in Excess of Par or Stated Value. Instead, the company reports those items in the stock accounts.

REQUIRED

1. Identify the different issues of stock Bethlehem has outstanding.
2. Which class of stock did Bethlehem issue at par or stated value, and which class did it issue above par or stated value?
3. Assume preferred dividends are in arrears for 19X5.
   a. Write Note 6 of the December 31, 19X5, financial statements to disclose the dividends in arrears.
   b. Journalize the declaration of a $60 million dividend at December 31, 19X6. An explanation is not required.

Preparing a corporation balance sheet; measuring profitability
(Obj. 3, 6)

P13-6B ◄ *Link Back to Chapter 1 (Accounting Equation).* The following accounts and related balances of Columbia Manufacturing are arranged in no particular order.

Common stock, $5 par, 100,000 shares authorized, 22,000 shares issued	**$110,000**	**Retained earnings**	**$?**
Dividends payable	**3,000**	**Inventory**	**181,000**
Total assets, November 30, 19X6	**581,000**	**Property, plant, and equipment, net**	**278,000**
Net income	**36,200**	**Prepaid expenses**	**13,000**
Common stockholders' equity, November 30, 19X6	**383,000**	**Patent, net**	**37,000**
Interest expense	**12,800**	**Accrued liabilities**	**17,000**
Additional paid-in capital—common	**140,000**	**Long-term note payable**	**104,000**
Accounts payable	**31,000**	**Accounts receivable, net**	**102,000**
		Preferred stock, 4%, $10 par, 25,000 shares authorized, 3,700 shares issued	**37,000**
		Cash	**32,000**

REQUIRED

1. Prepare the company's classified balance sheet in the account format at November 30, 19X7. Use the accounting equation to compute Retained Earnings.
2. Compute rate of return on total assets and rate of return on common stockholders' equity for the year ended November 30, 19X7.
3. Do these rates of return suggest strength or weakness? Give your reason.

Computing dividends on preferred and common stock
(Obj. 4)

P13-7B Nevada Airline Corporation has 5,000 shares of 5%, $10 par value preferred stock and 100,000 shares of $1.50 par common stock outstanding. During a three-year period, Nevada declared and paid cash dividends as follows: 19X1, $1,500; 19X2, $15,000; and 19X3, $26,000.

REQUIRED

1. Compute the total dividends to preferred stock and to common stock for each of the three years if
   a. Preferred is noncumulative.
   b. Preferred is cumulative.
2. For case (1b), record the declaration of the 19X3 dividends on December 22, 19X3, and the payment of the dividends on January 14, 19X4.

Analyzing the stockholders' equity of an actual corporation
(Obj. 4, 5)

P13-8B The balance sheet of Oak Manufacturing, Inc., reported the following:

Stockholders' Investment [same as stockholders' equity]	($ Thousands)
Cumulative preferred stock	$ 45
Common stock, $1 par, authorized 40,000,000 shares; issued 16,000,000 shares	16,000
[Additional] paid-in capital	176,000
Retained earnings	(77,165)
Total stockholders' investment	$114,880

Notes to the financial statements indicate that 9,000 shares of $1.60 preferred stock with a stated value of $5 per share were issued and outstanding. The preferred stock has a redemption value of $25 per share, and preferred dividends are in arrears for two years, including the current year. The additional paid-in capital was contributed by the common stockholders. On the balance sheet date, the market value of the Oak Manufacturing common stock was $7.50 per share.

REQUIRED

1. Is the preferred stock cumulative or noncumulative? How can you tell?
2. What is the amount of the annual preferred dividend?
3. What is the total paid-in capital of the company?
4. What was the total market value of the common stock?
5. Compute the book value per share of the preferred stock and the common stock.

Computing and recording a corporation's income tax
(Obj. 7)

P13-9B The accounting (not the income tax) records of Solomon Energy Corporation provide the income statement for 19X7.

Total revenue		**$930,000**
Expenses:		
Cost of goods sold	**$430,000**	
Operating expenses	**270,000**	
Total expenses before tax		**700,000**
Income before income tax		**$230,000**

The operating expenses include depreciation of $50,000 computed on the straight-line method. In calculating taxable income on the tax return, Solomon uses the modified accelerated cost recovery system (MACRS). MACRS depreciation was $80,000 for 19X7. The corporate income tax rate is 40 percent.

REQUIRED

1. Compute taxable income for the year.
2. Journalize the corporation's income tax for 19X7.
3. Prepare the corporation's single-step income statement for 19X7.

Applying Your Knowledge

DECISION CASE

Evaluating alternative ways of raising capital
(Obj. 2, 3)

Ron Buck and Sue Ladd have written a spreadsheet program that they believe will rival Excel and Lotus. They need additional capital to market the product, and they plan to incorporate the business. They are considering alternative capital structures for the corporation. Their primary goal is to raise as much capital as possible without giving up control of the business. The partners plan to invest the software program and receive 110,000 shares of the corporation's common stock. The partners have been offered $110,000 for the rights to the software program.

The corporation's plans for a charter include an authorization to issue 5,000 shares of preferred stock and 500,000 shares of $1 par common stock. Buck and Ladd are uncertain about the most desirable features for the preferred stock. Prior to incorporating, the partners are discussing their plans with two investment groups. The corporation can obtain capital from outside investors under either of the following plans:

- ***Plan 1.*** Group 1 will invest $105,000 to acquire 1,000 shares of $5, no-par preferred stock and $70,000 to acquire 70,000 shares of common stock. Each preferred share receives 50 votes on matters that come before the stockholders.
- ***Plan 2.*** Group 2 will invest $160,000 to acquire 1,400 shares of 6%, $100 par nonvoting, noncumulative preferred stock.

Assume that the corporation is chartered.

REQUIRED

1. Journalize the issuance of common stock to Buck and Ladd. Explanations are not required.
2. Journalize the issuance of stock to the outsiders under both plans. Explanations are not required.
3. Assume that net income for the first year is $150,000 and total dividends are $30,000. Prepare the stockholders' equity section of the corporation's balance sheet under both plans.
4. Recommend one of the plans to Buck and Ladd. Give your reasons.

FINANCIAL STATEMENT CASE

Analyzing stockholders' equity ***(Obj. 2, 3)***

CASE 1. The NIKE, Inc., financial statements appear in Appendix A. Answer the following questions about the company's stock.

REQUIRED

1. How can you tell from NIKE's balance sheet that NIKE treats its Redeemable Preferred Stock as a liability and not as stockholders' equity? Why is the preferred stock a liability?
2. Examine NIKE's balance sheet. Which stockholders' equity account increased the most during the year ended May 31, 1997 (fiscal year 1997)? Did this increase occur because of paid-in capital that NIKE received from its stockholders? If so, explain. If not, identify what caused the big increase in stockholders' equity.
3. During fiscal year 1997, NIKE's stockholders converted $1,000 of NIKE's Class A Common Stock into NIKE's Class B Common Stock. Make NIKE's journal entry to record this transaction. Only the two stock accounts were affected.
4. Did NIKE issue any Class B Common Stock during fiscal year 1997 over and above the stock that NIKE issued for the conversion of Class A common into Class B common? How can you tell?

Team Project

Competitive pressures are the norm in business. Lexus automobiles (made in Japan) have cut into the sales of Mercedes-Benz (a German company), Jaguar Motors (a British company), General Motors' Cadillac Division, and Ford's Lincoln Division (both U.S. companies). Dell, Gateway, and Compaq computers have siphoned business away from Apple and IBM. Foreign steelmakers have reduced the once-massive U.S. steel industry to a fraction of its former size.

Indeed, corporate downsizing has occurred on a massive scale. During the past few years, each company or industry mentioned here has pared down plant and equipment, laid off employees, or restructured operations.

REQUIRED

1. Identify all the stakeholders of a corporation and the stake each group has in the company. A *stakeholder* is a person or a group who has an interest (that is, a stake) in the success of the organization.
2. Identify several measures by which a corporation may be considered deficient and which may indicate the need for downsizing. How can downsizing help to solve this problem? Discuss how each measure can indicate the need for downsizing.
3. Debate the downsizing issue. One group of students takes the perspective of the company and its stockholders, and another group of students takes the perspective of other stakeholders of the company.

APPENDIX A

NIKE, Inc. Annual Report (Excerpts)

FINANCIALS 1997

FINANCIAL HISTORY

(in thousands, except per share data and financial ratios)

YEAR ENDED MAY 31,	1997	1996	1995	1994
Revenues	$9,186,539	$6,470,625	$4,760,834	$3,789,668
Gross margin	3,683,546	2,563,879	1,895,554	1,488,245
Gross margin %	40.1%	39.6%	39.8%	39.3%
Net income	795,822	553,190	399,664	298,794
Net income per common share	2.68	1.88	1.36	0.99
Average number of common and common equivalent shares	297,000	293,608	294,012	301,824
Cash dividends declared per common share	0.38	0.29	0.24	0.20
Cash flow from operations	323,120	339,672	254,913	576,463
Price range of common stock				
High	76.375	52.063	20.156	18.688
Low	47.875	19.531	14.063	10.781
At May 31:				
Cash and equivalents	$ 445,421	$ 262,117	$ 216,071	$ 518,816
Inventories	1,338,640	931,151	629,742	470,023
Working capital	1,964,002	1,259,881	938,393	1,208,444
Total assets	5,361,207	3,951,628	3,142,745	2,373,815
Long-term debt	296,020	9,584	10,565	12,364
Redeemable Preferred Stock	300	300	300	300
Common shareholders' equity	3,155,838	2,431,400	1,964,689	1,740,949
Year-end stock price	57.500	50 .188	19.719	14.750
Market capitalization	16,633,047	14,416,792	5,635,190	4,318,800
Financial Ratios:				
Return on equity	28.5%	25.2%	21.6%	17.7%
Return on assets	17.1%	15.6%	14.5%	13.1%
Inventory turns	4.8	5.0	5.2	4.3
Current ratio at May 31	2.1	1.9	1.8	3.2
Price/Earnings ratio at May 31	21.5	26.6	14.5	14.9
Geographic Revenues:				
United States	$5,529,132	$3,964,662	$ 2,997,864	$2,432,684
Europe	1,833,722	1,334,340	980,444	927,269
Asia/Pacific	1,245,217	735,094	515,652	283,421
Canada, Latin America, and other	578,468	436,529	266,874	146,294
Total Revenues	$9,186,539	$6,470,625	$4,760,834	$3,789,668

All per common share data has been adjusted to reflect the 2-for-1 stock splits paid October 23, 1996, October 30, 1995 and October 5, 1990. The Company's Class B Common Stock is listed on the New York and Pacific Exchanges and trades under the symbol NKE. At May 31, 1997, there were approximately 300,000 shareholders. Years 1993 and prior have been restated to reflect the implementation of Statement of Financial Accounting Standard No. 109 – Accounting for Income Taxes (see Notes 1 and 6 to the Consolidated Financial Statements).

1973 1974 1975 1976 1977 1978 1980 1981 1982 1983 1984 19
2000 2001 2002 2003 2004 2005 2006 2007 2008 2009 20

1993	1992	1991	1990	1989	1988
$3,930,984	$3,405,211	$3,003,610	$2,235,244	$1,710,803	$1,203,440
1,543,991	1,316,122	1,153,080	851,072	635,972	400,060
39.3%	38.7%	38.4%	38.1%	37.2%	33.2%
365,016	329,218	287,046	242,958	167,047	101,695
1.18	1.07	0.94	0.80	0.56	0.34
308,252	306,408	304,268	302,672	300,576	301,112
0.19	0.15	0.13	0.10	0.07	0.05
265,292	435,838	11,122	127,075	169,441	19,019
22.563	19.344	13.625	10.375	4.969	3.313
13.750	8.781	6.500	4.750	2.891	1.750
$ 291,284	$ 260,050	$ 119,804	$ 90,449	$ 85,749	$ 75,357
592,986	471,202	586,594	309,476	222,924	198,470
1,165,204	964,291	662,645	561,642	419,599	295,937
2,186,269	1,871,667	1,707,236	1,093,358	824,216	707,901
15,033	69,476	29,992	25,941	34,051	30,306
300	300	300	300	300	300
1,642,819	1,328,488	1,029,582	781,012	558,597	408,567
18.125	14.500	9.938	9.813	4.750	3.031
5,499,273	4,379,574	2,993,020	2,942,679	1,417,381	899,741
24.5%	27.9%	31.7%	36.3%	34.5%	27.4%
18.0%	18.4%	20.5%	25.3%	21.8%	16.7%
4.5	3.9	4.1	5.2	5.1	5.0
3.6	3.3	2.1	3.1	2.9	2.2
15.3	13.5	10.5	12.2	8.6	9.0
$2,528,848	$2,270,880	$2,141,461	$1,755,496	$1,362,148	$ 900,417
1,085,683	919,763	664,747	334,275	241,380	233,402
178,196	75,732	56,238	29,332	32,027	21,058
138,257	138,836	141,164	116,141	75,248	48,563
$3,930,984	$3,405,211	$3,003,610	$2,235,244	$1,710,803	$1,203,440

FINANCIAL REPORTING

Management of NIKE, Inc. is responsible for the information and representations contained in this report. The financial statements have been prepared in conformity with the generally accepted accounting principles we considered appropriate in the circumstances and include some amounts based on our best estimates and judgments. Other financial information in this report is consistent with these financial statements.

The Company's accounting systems include controls designed to reasonably assure that assets are safeguarded from unauthorized use or disposition and which provide for the preparation of financial statements in conformity with generally accepted accounting principles. These systems are supplemented by the selection and training of qualified financial personnel and an organizational structure providing for appropriate segregation of duties.

An Internal Audit department reviews the results of its work with the Audit Committee of the Board of Directors, presently consisting of three outside directors of the Company. The Audit Committee is responsible for recommending to the Board of Directors the appointment of the independent accountants and reviews with the independent accountants, management and the internal audit staff, the scope and the results of the annual examination, the effectiveness of the accounting control system and other matters relating to the financial affairs of the Company as they deem appropriate. The independent accountants and the internal auditors have full access to the Committee, with and without the presence of management, to discuss any appropriate matters.

REPORT OF INDEPENDENT ACCOUNTANTS

Portland, Oregon
June 27, 1997
To the Board of Directors and
Shareholders of NIKE, Inc.

In our opinion, the accompanying consolidated balance sheet and the related consolidated statements of income, of cash flows and of shareholders' equity present fairly, in all material respects, the financial position of NIKE, Inc. and its subsidiaries at May 31, 1997 and 1996, and the results of their operations and their cash flows for each of the three years in the period ended May 31, 1997, in conformity with generally accepted accounting principles. These financial statements are the responsibility of the Company's management; our responsibility is to express an opinion on these financial statements based on our audits. We conducted our audits of these statements in accordance with generally accepted auditing standards which require that we plan and perform the audit to obtain reasonable assurance about whether the financial statements are free of material misstatement. An audit includes examining, on a test basis, evidence supporting the amounts and disclosures in the financial statements, assessing the accounting principles used and significant estimates made by management, and evaluating the overall financial statement presentation. We believe that our audits provide a reasonable basis for the opinion expressed above.

Price Waterhouse LLP

NIKE, INC. CONSOLIDATED STATEMENT OF INCOME

(in thousands, except per share data)

YEAR ENDED MAY 31,	1997	1996	1995
Revenues	$9,186,539	$6,470,625	$4,760,834
Costs and expenses:			
Costs of sales	5,502,993	3,906,746	2,865,280
Selling and administrative	2,303,704	1,588,612	1,209,760
Interest expense (Notes 4 and 5)	52,343	39,498	24,208
Other income/expense, net (Notes 1, 9 and 10)	32,277	36,679	11,722
	7,891,317	5,571,535	4,110,970
Income before income taxes	1,295,222	899,090	649,864
Income taxes (Note 6)	499,400	345,900	250,200
Net income	$ 795,822	$ 553,190	$ 399,664
Net income per common share (Note 1)	$ 2.68	$ 1.88	$ 1.36
Average number of common and common equivalent shares (Note 1)	297,000	293,608	294,012

The accompanying notes to consolidated financial statements are an integral part of this statement.

NIKE, INC. CONSOLIDATED BALANCE SHEET

(in thousands)

MAY 31,	1997	1996
Assets		
Current Assets:		
Cash and equivalents	$ 445,421	$ 262,117
Accounts receivable, less allowance for doubtful accounts of $57,233 and $43,372	1,754,137	1,346,125
Inventories (Note 2)	1,338,640	931,151
Deferred income taxes (Note 6)	135,663	93,120
Prepaid expenses (Note 1)	157,058	94,427
Total current assets	3,830,919	2,726,940
Property, plant and equipment, net (Notes 3 and 5)	922,369	643,459
Identifiable intangible assets and goodwill (Note 1)	464,191	474,812
Deferred income taxes and other assets (Notes 1 and 6)	143,728	106,417
Total assets	$5,361,207	$3,951,628
Liabilities and Shareholders' Equity		
Current Liabilities:		
Current portion of long-term debt (Note 5)	$ 2,216	$ 7,301
Notes payable (Note 4)	553,153	445,064
Accounts payable (Note 4)	687,121	455,034
Accrued liabilities	570,504	480,407
Income taxes payable	53,923	79,253
Total current liabilities	1,866,917	1,467,059
Long-term debt (Notes 5 and 13)	296,020	9,584
Deferred income taxes and other liabilities (Notes 1 and 6)	42,132	43,285
Commitments and contingencies (Notes 11 and 14)	—	—
Redeemable Preferred Stock (Note 7)	300	300
Shareholders' equity (Note 8):		
Common Stock at stated value:		
Class A convertible – 101,711 and 102,240 shares outstanding	152	153
Class B – 187,559 and 185,018 shares outstanding	2,706	2,702
Capital in excess of stated value	210,650	154,833
Foreign currency translation adjustment	(31,333)	(16,501)
Retained earnings	2,973,663	2,290,213
Total shareholders' equity	3,155,838	2,431,400
Total liabilities and shareholders' equity	$5,361,207	$3,951,628

The accompanying notes to consolidated financial statements are an integral part of this statement.

986 1987 1988 1989 1990 1991 1992 1993 1994 1996 1997 19
011 2012 2013 2014 2015 2016 2017 2018 2019 2020 2021 20

NIKE, INC. CONSOLIDATED STATEMENT OF CASH FLOWS

(in thousands)

YEAR ENDED MAY 31,	1997	1996	1995
Cash provided (used) by operations:			
Net income	$795,822	$553,190	$399,664
Income charges (credits) not affecting cash:			
Depreciation	138,038	97,179	71,113
Deferred income taxes and purchased tax benefits	(47,146)	(73,279)	(24,668)
Amortization and other	30,291	32,685	14,966
Changes in certain working capital components:			
Increase in inventories	(416,706)	(301,409)	(69,676)
Increase in accounts receivable	(485,595)	(292,888)	(301,648)
Increase in other current assets	(56,928)	(20,054)	(10,276)
Increase in accounts payable, accrued liabilities and income taxes payable	365,344	344,248	175,438
Cash provided by operations	323,120	339,672	254,913
Cash provided (used) by investing activities:			
Additions to property, plant and equipment	(465,908)	(216,384)	(154,125)
Disposals of property, plant and equipment	24,294	12,775	9,011
Increase in other assets	(43,829)	(26,376)	(9,499)
(Decrease) increase in other liabilities	(10,833)	(9,651)	3,239
Acquisition of subsidiaries:			
Identifiable intangible assets and goodwill	—	—	(345,901)
Net assets acquired	—	—	(84,119)
Cash used by investing activities	(496,276)	(239,636)	(581,394)
Cash provided (used) by financing activities:			
Additions to long-term debt	300,500	5,044	2,971
Reductions in long-term debt including current portion	(5,190)	(30,352)	(39,804)
Increase in notes payable	92,926	47,964	263,874
Proceeds from exercise of options	26,282	21,150	6,154
Repurchase of stock	—	(18,756)	(142,919)
Dividends – common and preferred	(100,896)	(78,834)	(65,418)
Cash provided (used) by financing activities	313,622	(53,784)	24,858
Effect of exchange rate changes on cash	(166)	(206)	(1,122)
Effect of May 1996 cash flow activity for certain subsidiaries (Note 1)	43,004	—	—
Net increase (decrease) in cash and equivalents	183,304	46,046	(302,745)
Cash and equivalents, beginning of year	262,117	216,071	518,816
Cash and equivalents, end of year	$445,421	$262,117	$216,071
Supplemental disclosure of cash flow information:			
Cash paid during the year for:			
Interest (net of amount capitalized)	$ 44,000	$ 32,800	$ 20,200
Income taxes	543,100	359,300	285,400

The accompanying notes to consolidated financial statements are an integral part of this statement.

1973 1974 1975 1976 1977 1978 1980 1981 1982 1983 1984

2000 2001 2002 2003 2004 2005 2006 2007 2008 2009

NIKE, INC. CONSOLIDATED STATEMENT OF SHAREHOLDERS' EQUITY

(in thousands)	Common Stock				Capital In Excess Of Stated Value	Foreign Currency Translation Adjustment	Retained Earnings	Total
	Class A		Class B					
	Shares	Amount	Shares	Amount				
Balance at May 31, 1994	26,679	$159	46,521	$2,704	$108,284	$(15,123)	$1,644,925	$1,740,949
Stock options exercised			241	2	8,954			8,956
Conversion to Class B Common Stock	(784)	(4)	784	4				—
Repurchase of Class B Common Stock			(2,130)	(13)	(4,801)		(138,106)	(142,920)
Stock issued pursuant to contractual obligations			134	1	9,999			10,000
Translation of statements of non-U.S. operations						16,708		16,708
Net income							399,664	399,664
Dividends on Redeemable Preferred Stock							(30)	(30)
Dividends on Common Stock							(68,638)	(68,638)
Balance at May 31, 1995	25,895	155	45,550	2,698	122,436	1,585	1,837,815	1,964,689
Stock options exercised			756	3	32,848			32,851
Conversion to Class B Common Stock	(655)	(2)	655	2				—
Repurchase of Class B Common Stock			(200)	(1)	(451)		(18,304)	(18,756)
Two-for-one Stock Split October 30, 1995	25,880		45,748					
Translation of statements of non-U.S. operations						(18,086)		(18,086)
Net income							553,190	553,190
Dividends on Redeemable Preferred Stock							(30)	(30)
Dividends on Common Stock							(82,458)	(82,458)
Balance at May 31, 1996	51,120	153	92,509	2,702	154,833	(16,501)	2,290,213	2,431,400
Stock options exercised			1,475	3	55,817			55,820
Conversion to Class B Common Stock	(279)	(1)	279	1				—
Two-for-one Stock Split October 23, 1996	50,870		93,296					
Translation of statements of non-U.S. operations						(14,832)		(14,832)
Net income							795,822	795,822
Dividends on Redeemable Preferred Stock							(30)	(30)
Dividends on Common Stock							(108,249)	(108,249)
Net income for the month ended May 1996, due to the change in fiscal year-end of certain non-U.S. operations (Note 1)							(4,093)	(4,093)
Balance at May 31, 1997	101,711	$152	187,559	$2,706	$210,650	($31,333)	$2,973,663	$3,155,838

The accompanying notes to consolidated financial statements are an integral part of this statement.

NIKE, INC. NOTES TO CONSOLIDATED FINANCIAL STATEMENTS

NOTE 1 – SUMMARY OF SIGNIFICANT ACCOUNTING POLICIES:

Basis of consolidation:

The consolidated financial statements include the accounts of the Company and its subsidiaries. All significant intercompany transactions and balances have been eliminated. Prior to fiscal year 1997, certain of the Company's non-U.S. operations reported their results of operations on a one month lag which allowed more time to compile results. Beginning in the first quarter of fiscal year 1997, the one month lag was eliminated. As a result, the May 1996 charge from operations for these entities of $4,093,000 was recorded to retained earnings in the first quarter of the current year.

Recognition of revenues:

Revenues recognized include sales plus fees earned on sales by licensees.

Advertising:

Advertising production costs are expensed the first time the advertisement is run. Media (TV and print) placement costs are expensed in the month the advertising appears. Total advertising and promotion expenses were $978,251,000, $642,498,000 and $495,006,000 for the years ended May 31, 1997, 1996 and 1995, respectively. Included in prepaid expenses and other assets was $111,925,000 and $69,340,000 at May 31, 1997 and 1996, respectively, relating to prepaid advertising and promotion expenses.

Cash and equivalents:

Cash and equivalents represent cash and short-term, highly liquid investments with original maturities three months or less.

Inventory valuation:

Inventories are stated at the lower of cost or market. Cost is determined using the last-in, first-out (LIFO) method for substantially all U.S. inventories. Non-U.S. inventories are valued on a first-in, first-out (FIFO) basis.

Property, plant and equipment and depreciation:

Property, plant and equipment are recorded at cost. Depreciation for financial reporting purposes is determined on a straight-line basis for buildings and leasehold improvements and principally on a declining balance basis for machinery and equipment, based upon estimated useful lives ranging from two to thirty years.

Identifiable intangible assets and goodwill:

At May 31, 1997 and 1996, the Company had patents, trademarks and other identifiable intangible assets with a value of $219,186,000 and $209,586,000, respectively. The Company's excess of purchase cost over the fair value of net assets of businesses acquired (goodwill) was $326,252,000 and $327,555,000 at May 31, 1997 and 1996, respectively.

Identifiable intangible assets and goodwill are being amortized over their estimated useful lives on a straight-line basis over five to forty years. Accumulated amortization was $81,247,000 and $62,329,000 at May 31, 1997 and 1996, respectively. Amortization expense, which is included in other income/expense, was $19,765,000, $21,772,000 and $13,176,000 for the years ended May 31, 1997, 1996 and 1995, respectively. Intangible assets are periodically reviewed by the Company for impairments where the fair value is less than the carrying value.

Other liabilities:

Other liabilities include amounts with settlement dates beyond one year, and are primarily composed of long-term deferred endorsement payments of $15,815,000 and $21,674,000 at May 31, 1997 and 1996, respectively. Deferred payments to endorsers relate to amounts due beyond contract termination, which are discounted at various interest rates and accrued over the contract period.

Endorsement contracts:

Accounting for endorsement contracts is based upon specific contract provisions. Generally, endorsement payments are expensed uniformly over the term of the contract after giving recognition to periodic performance compliance provisions of the contracts. Contracts requiring prepayments are included in prepaid expenses or other assets depending on the length of the contract.

Foreign currency translation:

Adjustments resulting from translating foreign functional currency financial statements into U.S. dollars are included in the foreign currency translation adjustment in shareholders' equity.

Derivatives:

The Company enters into foreign currency contracts in order to reduce the impact of certain foreign currency fluctuations. Firmly committed transactions and the related receivables and payables may be hedged with forward exchange contracts or purchased options. Anticipated, but not yet firmly committed, transactions may be hedged through the use of purchased options. Premiums paid on purchased options and any gains are included in prepaid expenses or accrued liabilities and are recognized in earnings when the transaction being hedged is recognized. Gains and losses arising from foreign currency forward and option contracts, and cross-currency swap transactions are recognized in income or expense as offsets of gains and losses resulting from the underlying hedged transactions. Cash flows from risk management activities are classified in the same category as the cash flows from the related investment, borrowing or foreign exchange activity. See Note 14 for further discussion.

Income taxes:

Income taxes are provided currently on financial statement earnings of non-U.S. subsidiaries expected to be repatriated. The Company intends to determine annually the amount of undistributed non-U.S. earnings to invest indefinitely in its non-U.S. operations.

The Company accounts for income taxes using the asset and liability method. This approach requires the recognition of deferred tax liabilities and assets for the expected future tax consequences of temporary differences between the carrying amounts and the tax bases of other assets and liabilities. See Note 6 for further discussion.

Net income per common share:

Net income per common share is computed based on the weighted average number of common and common equivalent (stock option) shares outstanding for the periods reported.

On October 23, 1996 and October 30, 1995, the Company issued additional shares in connection with two-for-one stock splits effected in the form of a 100% stock dividend on outstanding Class A and Class B common stock. The per common share amounts in the Consolidated Financial Statements and accompanying notes have been adjusted to reflect these stock splits.

Management estimates:

The preparation of financial statements in conformity with generally accepted accounting principles requires management to make estimates, including estimates relating to assumptions that affect the reported amounts of assets and liabilities and disclosure of contingent assets and liabilities at the date of financial statements and the reported amounts of revenues and expenses during the reporting period. Actual results could differ from these estimates.

Reclassifications:

Certain prior year amounts have been reclassified to conform to fiscal 1997 presentation. These changes had no impact on previously reported results of operations or shareholders' equity.

5 1986 1987 1988 1989 1990 1991 1992 1993 1994 1996 1997
0 2011 2012 2013 2014 2015 2016 2017 2018 2019 2020 2021

NOTE 2 – INVENTORIES:

Inventories by major classification are as follows:

(in thousands)

MAY 31,	1997	1996
Finished goods	$1,248,401	$874,700
Work-in-progress	50,245	28,940
Raw materials	39,994	27,511
	$1,338,640	$931,151

The excess of replacement cost over LIFO cost was $20,716,000 at May 31, 1997, and $16,023,000 at May 31,1996.

NOTE 3 – PROPERTY, PLANT AND EQUIPMENT:

Property, plant and equipment includes the following:

(in thousands)

MAY 31,	1997	1996
Land	$ 90,792	$ 75,369
Buildings	241,062	246,602
Machinery and equipment	735,739	572,396
Leasehold improvements	206,593	83,678
Construction in process	151,561	69,660
	1,425,747	1,047,705
Less accumulated depreciation	503,378	404,246
	$ 922,369	$ 643,459

Capitalized interest expense was $2,765,000, $858,000 and $261,000 for the fiscal years ended May 31, 1997, 1996 and 1995 respectively.

NOTE 5 – LONG-TERM DEBT:

Long-term debt includes the following:

(in thousands)

MAY 31,	1997	1996
6.375% Medium term notes, payable December 1, 2003	$199,211	$ —
4.30% Japanese yen notes, payable June 26, 2011	92,373	—
9.43% capital warehouse lease	—	7,485
Other	6,652	9,400
Total	298,236	16,885
Less current maturities	2,216	7,301
	$296,020	$ 9,584

In December of 1996, the Company filed a $500 million shelf registration with the Securities and Exhange Commission and issued $200 million seven-year notes, maturing December 1, 2003. The proceeds were subsequently exchanged for Dutch Guilders and loaned to a European subsidiary. Interest on the loan is paid semi-annually. The Company entered into swap transactions reducing the effective interest rate to 5.64% as well as to hedge the foreign currency exposure related to the repayment of the intercompany loan. In June of 1997, the Company issued an additional $100 million medium term notes under this program with maturities of June 16, 2000 and June 17, 2002.

In June of 1996, the Company's Japanese subsidiary borrowed 10.5 billion yen in a private placement with a maturity of June 26, 2011. Interest is paid semi-annually. The agreement provides for early retirement after year ten.

The Company's long-term debt ratings are A+ by Standard and Poor's Corporation and A1 by Moody's Investor Service.

Amounts of long-term maturities in each of the five fiscal years 1998 through 2002, respectively, are $2,216,000, $1,891,000, $2,187,000, $188,000 and $47,000.

NOTE 7 – REDEEMABLE PREFERRED STOCK:

NIAC is the sole owner of the Company's authorized Redeemable Preferred Stock, $1 par value, which is redeemable at the option of NIAC at par value aggregating $300,000. A cumulative dividend of $.10 per share is payable annually on May 31 and no dividends may be declared or paid on the Common Stock of the Company unless dividends on the Redeemable Preferred Stock have been declared and paid in full. There have been no changes in the Redeemable Preferred Stock in the three years ended May 31, 1997. As the holder of the Redeemable Preferred Stock, NIAC does not have general voting rights but does have the right to vote as a separate class on the sale of all or substantially all of the assets of the Company and its subsidiaries, on merger, consolidation, liquidation or dissolution of the Company or on the sale or assignment of the NIKE trademark for athletic footwear sold in the United States.

NOTE 11 – COMMITMENTS AND CONTINGENCIES:

The Company leases space for its offices, warehouses and retail stores under leases expiring from one to twenty years after May 31, 1997. Rent expense aggregated $84,109,000, $52,483,000 and $43,506,000 for the years ended May 31, 1997, 1996 and 1995, respectively. Amounts of minimum future annual rental commitments under non-cancellable operating leases in each of the five fiscal years 1998 through 2002 are $76,319,000, $65,315,000, $53,776,000, $46,125,000, $42,274,000, respectively, and $326,198,000 in later years.

Lawsuits arise during the normal course of business. In the opinion of management, none of the pending lawsuits will result in a significant impact on the consolidated results of operations or financial position.

APPENDIX B

Present-Value Tables and Future-Value Tables

This appendix provides present-value tables and future-value tables (more complete than those in the Chapter 15 appendix and in Chapter 26).

EXHIBIT B-1
Present Value of $1

	Present Value										
Periods	1%	2%	3%	4%	5%	6%	7%	8%	9%	10%	12%
1	0.990	0.980	0.971	0.962	0.952	0.943	0.935	0.926	0.917	0.909	0.893
2	0.980	0.961	0.943	0.925	0.907	0.890	0.873	0.857	0.842	0.826	0.797
3	0.971	0.942	0.915	0.889	0.864	0.840	0.816	0.794	0.772	0.751	0.712
4	0.961	0.924	0.888	0.855	0.823	0.792	0.763	0.735	0.708	0.683	0.636
5	0.951	0.906	0.883	0.822	0.784	0.747	0.713	0.681	0.650	0.621	0.567
6	0.942	0.888	0.837	0.790	0.746	0.705	0.666	0.630	0.596	0.564	0.507
7	0.933	0.871	0.813	0.760	0.711	0.665	0.623	0.583	0.547	0.513	0.452
8	0.923	0.853	0.789	0.731	0.677	0.627	0.582	0.540	0.502	0.467	0.404
9	0.914	0.837	0.766	0.703	0.645	0.592	0.544	0.500	0.460	0.424	0.361
10	0.905	0.820	0.744	0.676	0.614	0.558	0.508	0.463	0.422	0.386	0.322
11	0.896	0.804	0.722	0.650	0.585	0.527	0.475	0.429	0.388	0.350	0.287
12	0.887	0.788	0.701	0.625	0.557	0.497	0.444	0.397	0.356	0.319	0.257
13	0.879	0.773	0.681	0.601	0.530	0.469	0.415	0.368	0.326	0.290	0.229
14	0.870	0.758	0.661	0.577	0.505	0.442	0.388	0.340	0.299	0.263	0.205
15	0.861	0.743	0.642	0.555	0.481	0.417	0.362	0.315	0.275	0.239	0.183
16	0.853	0.728	0.623	0.534	0.458	0.394	0.339	0.292	0.252	0.218	0.163
17	0.844	0.714	0.605	0.513	0.436	0.371	0.317	0.270	0.231	0.198	0.146
18	0.836	0.700	0.587	0.494	0.416	0.350	0.296	0.250	0.212	0.180	0.130
19	0.828	0.686	0.570	0.475	0.396	0.331	0.277	0.232	0.194	0.164	0.116
20	0.820	0.673	0.554	0.456	0.377	0.312	0.258	0.215	0.178	0.149	0.104
21	0.811	0.660	0.538	0.439	0.359	0.294	0.242	0.199	0.164	0.135	0.093
22	0.803	0.647	0.522	0.422	0.342	0.278	0.226	0.184	0.150	0.123	0.083
23	0.795	0.634	0.507	0.406	0.326	0.262	0.211	0.170	0.138	0.112	0.074
24	0.788	0.622	0.492	0.390	0.310	0.247	0.197	0.158	0.126	0.102	0.066
25	0.780	0.610	0.478	0.375	0.295	0.233	0.184	0.146	0.116	0.092	0.059
26	0.772	0.598	0.464	0.361	0.281	0.220	0.172	0.135	0.106	0.084	0.053
27	0.764	0.586	0.450	0.347	0.268	0.207	0.161	0.125	0.098	0.076	0.047
28	0.757	0.574	0.437	0.333	0.255	0.196	0.150	0.116	0.090	0.069	0.042
29	0.749	0.563	0.424	0.321	0.243	0.185	0.141	0.107	0.082	0.063	0.037
30	0.742	0.552	0.412	0.308	0.231	0.174	0.131	0.099	0.075	0.057	0.033
40	0.672	0.453	0.307	0.208	0.142	0.097	0.067	0.046	0.032	0.022	0.011
50	0.608	0.372	0.228	0.141	0.087	0.054	0.034	0.021	0.013	0.009	0.003

EXHIBIT B-1
(cont'd)

Present Value											
14%	15%	16%	18%	20%	25%	30%	35%	40%	45%	50%	Periods
0.877	0.870	0.862	0.847	0.833	0.800	0.769	0.741	0.714	0.690	0.667	1
0.769	0.756	0.743	0.718	0.694	0.640	0.592	0.549	0.510	0.476	0.444	2
0.675	0.658	0.641	0.609	0.579	0.512	0.455	0.406	0.364	0.328	0.296	3
0.592	0.572	0.552	0.516	0.482	0.410	0.350	0.301	0.260	0.226	0.198	4
0.519	0.497	0.476	0.437	0.402	0.328	0.269	0.223	0.186	0.156	0.132	5
0.456	0.432	0.410	0.370	0.335	0.262	0.207	0.165	0.133	0.108	0.088	6
0.400	0.376	0.354	0.314	0.279	0.210	0.159	0.122	0.095	0.074	0.059	7
0.351	0.327	0.305	0.266	0.233	0.168	0.123	0.091	0.068	0.051	0.039	8
0.308	0.284	0.263	0.225	0.194	0.134	0.094	0.067	0.048	0.035	0.026	9
0.270	0.247	0.227	0.191	0.162	0.107	0.073	0.050	0.035	0.024	0.017	10
0.237	0.215	0.195	0.162	0.135	0.086	0.056	0.037	0.025	0.017	0.012	11
0.208	0.187	0.168	0.137	0.112	0.069	0.043	0.027	0.018	0.012	0.008	12
0.182	0.163	0.145	0.116	0.093	0.055	0.033	0.020	0.013	0.008	0.005	13
0.160	0.141	0.125	0.099	0.078	0.044	0.025	0.015	0.009	0.006	0.003	14
0.140	0.123	0.108	0.084	0.065	0.035	0.020	0.011	0.006	0.004	0.002	15
0.123	0.107	0.093	0.071	0.054	0.028	0.015	0.008	0.005	0.003	0.002	16
0.108	0.093	0.080	0.060	0.045	0.023	0.012	0.006	0.003	0.002	0.001	17
0.095	0.081	0.069	0.051	0.038	0.018	0.009	0.005	0.002	0.001	0.001	18
0.083	0.070	0.060	0.043	0.031	0.014	0.007	0.003	0.002	0.001		19
0.073	0.061	0.051	0.037	0.026	0.012	0.005	0.002	0.001	0.001		20
0.064	0.053	0.044	0.031	0.022	0.009	0.004	0.002	0.001			21
0.056	0.046	0.038	0.026	0.018	0.007	0.003	0.001	0.001			22
0.049	0.040	0.033	0.022	0.015	0.006	0.002	0.001				23
0.043	0.035	0.028	0.019	0.013	0.005	0.002	0.001				24
0.038	0.030	0.024	0.016	0.010	0.004	0.001	0.001				25
0.033	0.026	0.021	0.014	0.009	0.003	0.001					26
0.029	0.023	0.018	0.011	0.007	0.002	0.001					27
0.026	0.020	0.016	0.010	0.006	0.002	0.001					28
0.022	0.017	0.014	0.008	0.005	0.002						29
0.020	0.015	0.012	0.007	0.004	0.001						30
0.005	0.004	0.003	0.001	0.001							40
0.001	0.001	0.001									50

EXHIBIT B-2
Present Value of Annuity of $1

Periods	Present Value 1%	2%	3%	4%	5%	6%	7%	8%	9%	10%	12%
1	0.990	0.980	0.971	0.962	0.952	0.943	0.935	0.926	0.917	0.909	0.893
2	1.970	1.942	1.913	1.886	1.859	1.833	1.808	1.783	1.759	1.736	1.690
3	2.941	2.884	2.829	2.775	2.723	2.673	2.624	2.577	2.531	2.487	2.402
4	3.902	3.808	3.717	3.630	3.546	3.465	3.387	3.312	3.240	3.170	3.037
5	4.853	4.713	4.580	4.452	4.329	4.212	4.100	3.993	3.890	3.791	3.605
6	5.795	5.601	5.417	5.242	5.076	4.917	4.767	4.623	4.486	4.355	4.111
7	6.728	6.472	6.230	6.002	5.786	5.582	5.389	5.206	5.033	4.868	4.564
8	7.652	7.325	7.020	6.733	6.463	6.210	5.971	5.747	5.535	5.335	4.968
9	8.566	8.162	7.786	7.435	7.108	6.802	6.515	6.247	5.995	5.759	5.328
10	9.471	8.983	8.530	8.111	7.722	7.360	7.024	6.710	6.418	6.145	5.650
11	10.368	9.787	9.253	8.760	8.306	7.887	7.499	7.139	6.805	6.495	5.938
12	11.255	10.575	9.954	9.385	8.863	8.384	7.943	7.536	7.161	6.814	6.194
13	12.134	11.348	10.635	9.986	9.394	8.853	8.358	7.904	7.487	7.103	6.424
14	13.004	12.106	11.296	10.563	9.899	9.295	8.745	8.244	7.786	7.367	6.628
15	13.865	12.849	11.938	11.118	10.380	9.712	9.108	8.559	8.061	7.606	6.811
16	14.718	13.578	12.561	11.652	10.838	10.106	9.447	8.851	8.313	7.824	6.974
17	15.562	14.292	13.166	12.166	11.274	10.477	9.763	9.122	8.544	8.022	7.120
18	16.398	14.992	13.754	12.659	11.690	10.828	10.059	9.372	8.756	8.201	7.250
19	17.226	15.678	14.324	13.134	12.085	11.158	10.336	9.604	8.950	8.365	7.366
20	18.046	16.351	14.878	13.590	12.462	11.470	10.594	9.818	9.129	8.514	7.469
21	18.857	17.011	15.415	14.029	12.821	11.764	10.836	10.017	9.292	8.649	7.562
22	19.660	17.658	15.937	14.451	13.163	12.042	11.061	10.201	9.442	8.772	7.645
23	20.456	18.292	16.444	14.857	13.489	12.303	11.272	10.371	9.580	8.883	7.718
24	21.243	18.914	16.936	15.247	13.799	12.550	11.469	10.529	9.707	8.985	7.784
25	22.023	19.523	17.413	15.622	14.094	12.783	11.654	10.675	9.823	9.077	7.843
26	22.795	20.121	17.877	15.983	14.375	13.003	11.826	10.810	9.929	9.161	7.896
27	23.560	20.707	18.327	16.330	14.643	13.211	11.987	10.935	10.027	9.237	7.943
28	24.316	21.281	18.764	16.663	14.898	13.406	12.137	11.051	10.116	9.307	7.984
29	25.066	21.844	19.189	16.984	15.141	13.591	12.278	11.158	10.198	9.370	8.022
30	25.808	22.396	19.600	17.292	15.373	13.765	12.409	11.258	10.274	9.427	8.055
40	32.835	27.355	23.115	19.793	17.159	15.046	13.332	11.925	10.757	9.779	8.244
50	39.196	31.424	25.730	21.482	18.256	15.762	13.801	12.234	10.962	9.915	8.305

EXHIBIT B-2
(cont'd)

Present Value											
14%	15%	16%	18%	20%	25%	30%	35%	40%	45%	50%	Periods
0.877	0.870	0.862	0.847	0.833	0.800	0.769	0.741	0.714	0.690	0.667	1
1.647	1.626	1.605	1.566	1.528	1.440	1.361	1.289	1.224	1.165	1.111	2
2.322	2.283	2.246	2.174	2.106	1.952	1.816	1.696	1.589	1.493	1.407	3
2.914	2.855	2.798	2.690	2.589	2.362	2.166	1.997	1.849	1.720	1.605	4
3.433	3.352	3.274	3.127	2.991	2.689	2.436	2.220	2.035	1.876	1.737	5
3.889	3.784	3.685	3.498	3.326	2.951	2.643	2.385	2.168	1.983	1.824	6
4.288	4.160	4.039	3.812	3.605	3.161	2.802	2.508	2.263	2.057	1.883	7
4.639	4.487	4.344	4.078	3.837	3.329	2.925	2.598	2.331	2.109	1.922	8
4.946	4.772	4.607	4.303	4.031	3.463	3.019	2.665	2.379	2.144	1.948	9
5.216	5.019	4.833	4.494	4.192	3.571	3.092	2.715	2.414	2.168	1.965	10
5.553	5.234	5.029	4.656	4.327	3.656	3.147	2.752	2.438	2.185	1.977	11
5.660	5.421	5.197	4.793	4.439	3.725	3.190	2.779	2.456	2.197	1.985	12
5.842	5.583	5.342	4.910	4.533	3.780	3.223	2.799	2.469	2.204	1.990	13
6.002	5.724	5.468	5.008	4.611	3.824	3.249	2.814	2.478	2.210	1.993	14
6.142	5.847	5.575	5.092	4.675	3.859	3.268	2.825	2.484	2.214	1.995	15
6.265	5.954	5.669	5.162	4.730	3.887	3.283	2.834	2.489	2.216	1.997	16
6.373	6.047	5.749	5.222	4.775	3.910	3.295	2.840	2.492	2.218	1.998	17
6.467	6.128	5.818	5.273	4.812	3.928	3.304	2.844	2.494	2.219	1.999	18
6.550	6.198	5.877	5.316	4.844	3.942	3.311	2.848	2.496	2.220	1.999	19
6.623	6.259	5.929	5.353	4.870	3.954	3.316	2.850	2.497	2.221	1.999	20
6.687	6.312	5.973	5.384	4.891	3.963	3.320	2.852	2.498	2.221	2.000	21
6.743	6.359	6.011	5.410	4.909	3.970	3.323	2.853	2.498	2.222	2.000	22
6.792	6.399	6.044	5.432	4.925	3.976	3.325	2.854	2.499	2.222	2.000	23
6.835	6.434	6.073	5.451	4.937	3.981	3.327	2.855	2.499	2.222	2.000	24
6.873	6.464	6.097	5.467	4.948	3.985	3.329	2.856	2.499	2.222	2.000	25
6.906	6.491	6.118	5.480	4.956	3.988	3.330	2.856	2.500	2.222	2.000	26
6.935	6.514	6.136	5.492	4.964	3.990	3.331	2.856	2.500	2.222	2.000	27
6.961	6.534	6.152	5.502	4.970	3.992	3.331	2.857	2.500	2.222	2.000	28
6.983	6.551	6.166	5.510	4.975	3.994	3.332	2.857	2.500	2.222	2.000	29
7.003	6.566	6.177	5.517	4.979	3.995	3.332	2.857	2.500	2.222	2.000	30
7.105	6.642	6.234	5.548	4.997	3.999	3.333	2.857	2.500	2.222	2.000	40
7.133	6.661	6.246	5.554	4.999	4.000	3.333	2.857	2.500	2.222	2.000	50

EXHIBIT B-3
Future Value of $1

Periods	Future Value 1%	2%	3%	4%	5%	6%	7%	8%	9%	10%	12%	14%	15%
1	1.010	1.020	1.030	1.040	1.050	1.060	1.070	1.080	1.090	1.100	1.120	1.140	1.150
2	1.020	1.040	1.061	1.082	1.103	1.124	1.145	1.166	1.188	1.210	1.254	1.300	1.323
3	1.030	1.061	1.093	1.125	1.158	1.191	1.225	1.260	1.295	1.331	1.405	1.482	1.521
4	1.041	1.082	1.126	1.170	1.216	1.262	1.311	1.360	1.412	1.464	1.574	1.689	1.749
5	1.051	1.104	1.159	1.217	1.276	1.338	1.403	1.469	1.539	1.611	1.762	1.925	2.011
6	1.062	1.126	1.194	1.265	1.340	1.419	1.501	1.587	1.677	1.772	1.974	2.195	2.313
7	1.072	1.149	1.230	1.316	1.407	1.504	1.606	1.714	1.828	1.949	2.211	2.502	2.660
8	1.083	1.172	1.267	1.369	1.477	1.594	1.718	1.851	1.993	2.144	2.476	2.853	3.059
9	1.094	1.195	1.305	1.423	1.551	1.689	1.838	1.999	2.172	2.358	2.773	3.252	3.518
10	1.105	1.219	1.344	1.480	1.629	1.791	1.967	2.159	2.367	2.594	3.106	3.707	4.046
11	1.116	1.243	1.384	1.539	1.710	1.898	2.105	2.332	2.580	2.853	3.479	4.226	4.652
12	1.127	1.268	1.426	1.601	1.796	2.012	2.252	2.518	2.813	3.138	3.896	4.818	5.350
13	1.138	1.294	1.469	1.665	1.886	2.133	2.410	2.720	3.066	3.452	4.363	5.492	6.153
14	1.149	1.319	1.513	1.732	1.980	2.261	2.579	2.937	3.342	3.798	4.887	6.261	7.076
15	1.161	1.346	1.558	1.801	2.079	2.397	2.759	3.172	3.642	4.177	5.474	7.138	8.137
16	1.173	1.373	1.605	1.873	2.183	2.540	2.952	3.426	3.970	4.595	6.130	8.137	9.358
17	1.184	1.400	1.653	1.948	2.292	2.693	3.159	3.700	4.328	5.054	6.866	9.276	10.76
18	1.196	1.428	1.702	2.026	2.407	2.854	3.380	3.996	4.717	5.560	7.690	10.58	12.38
19	1.208	1.457	1.754	2.107	2.527	3.026	3.617	4.316	5.142	6.116	8.613	12.06	14.23
20	1.220	1.486	1.806	2.191	2.653	3.207	3.870	4.661	5.604	6.728	9.646	13.74	16.37
21	1.232	1.516	1.860	2.279	2.786	3.400	4.141	5.034	6.109	7.400	10.80	15.67	18.82
22	1.245	1.546	1.916	2.370	2.925	3.604	4.430	5.437	6.659	8.140	12.10	17.86	21.64
23	1.257	1.577	1.974	2.465	3.072	3.820	4.741	5.871	7.258	8.954	13.55	20.36	24.89
24	1.270	1.608	2.033	2.563	3.225	4.049	5.072	6.341	7.911	9.850	15.18	23.21	28.63
25	1.282	1.641	2.094	2.666	3.386	4.292	5.427	6.848	8.623	10.83	17.00	26.46	32.92
26	1.295	1.673	2.157	2.772	3.556	4.549	5.807	7.396	9.399	11.92	19.04	30.17	37.86
27	1.308	1.707	2.221	2.883	3.733	4.822	6.214	7.988	10.25	13.11	21.32	34.39	43.54
28	1.321	1.741	2.288	2.999	3.920	5.112	6.649	8.627	11.17	14.42	23.88	39.20	50.07
29	1.335	1.776	2.357	3.119	4.116	5.418	7.114	9.317	12.17	15.86	26.75	44.69	57.58
30	1.348	1.811	2.427	3.243	4.322	5.743	7.612	10.06	13.27	17.45	29.96	50.95	66.21
40	1.489	2.208	3.262	4.801	7.040	10.29	14.97	21.72	31.41	45.26	93.05	188.9	267.9
50	1.645	2.692	4.384	7.107	11.47	18.42	29.46	46.90	74.36	117.4	289.0	700.2	1,084

EXHIBIT B-4

Future Value of Annuity $1

	Future Value												
Periods	**1%**	**2%**	**3%**	**4%**	**5%**	**6%**	**7%**	**8%**	**9%**	**10%**	**12%**	**14%**	**15%**
1	1.000	1.000	1.000	1.000	1.000	1.000	1.000	1.000	1.000	1.000	1.000	1.000	1.000
2	2.010	2.020	2.030	2.040	2.050	2.060	2.070	2.080	2.090	2.100	2.120	2.140	2.150
3	3.030	3.060	3.091	3.122	3.153	3.184	3.215	3.246	3.278	3.310	3.374	3.440	3.473
4	4.060	4.122	4.184	4.246	4.310	4.375	4.440	4.506	4.573	4.641	4.779	4.921	4.993
5	5.101	5.204	5.309	5.416	5.526	5.637	5.751	5.867	5.985	6.105	6.353	6.610	6.742
6	6.152	6.308	6.468	6.633	6.802	6.975	7.153	7.336	7.523	7.716	8.115	8.536	8.754
7	7.214	7.434	7.662	7.898	8.142	8.394	8.654	8.923	9.200	9.487	10.09	10.73	11.07
8	8.286	8.583	8.892	9.214	9.549	9.897	10.26	10.64	11.03	11.44	12.30	13.23	13.73
9	9.369	9.755	10.16	10.58	11.03	11.49	11.98	12.49	13.02	13.58	14.78	16.09	16.79
10	10.46	10.95	11.46	12.01	12.58	13.18	13.82	14.49	15.19	15.94	17.55	19.34	20.30
11	11.57	12.17	12.81	13.49	14.21	14.97	15.78	16.65	17.56	18.53	20.65	23.04	24.35
12	12.68	13.41	14.19	15.03	15.92	16.87	17.89	18.98	20.14	21.38	24.13	27.27	29.00
13	13.81	14.68	15.62	16.63	17.71	18.88	20.14	21.50	22.95	24.52	28.03	32.09	34.35
14	14.95	15.97	17.09	18.29	19.60	21.02	22.55	24.21	26.02	27.98	32.39	37.58	40.50
15	16.10	17.29	18.60	20.02	21.58	23.28	25.13	27.15	29.36	31.77	37.28	43.84	47.58
16	17.26	18.64	20.16	21.82	23.66	25.67	27.89	30.32	33.00	35.95	42.75	50.98	55.72
17	18.43	20.01	21.76	23.70	25.84	28.21	30.84	33.75	36.97	40.54	48.88	59.12	65.08
18	19.61	21.41	23.41	25.65	28.13	30.91	34.00	37.45	41.30	45.60	55.75	68.39	75.84
19	20.81	22.84	25.12	27.67	30.54	33.76	37.38	41.45	46.02	51.16	63.44	78.97	88.21
20	22.02	24.30	26.87	29.78	33.07	36.79	41.00	45.76	51.16	57.28	72.05	91.02	102.4
21	23.24	25.78	28.68	31.97	35.72	39.99	44.87	50.42	56.76	64.00	81.70	104.8	118.8
22	24.47	27.30	30.54	34.25	38.51	43.39	49.01	55.46	62.87	71.40	92.50	120.4	137.6
23	25.72	28.85	32.45	36.62	41.43	47.00	53.44	60.89	69.53	79.54	104.6	138.3	159.3
24	26.97	30.42	34.43	39.08	44.50	50.82	58.18	66.76	76.79	88.50	118.2	158.7	184.2
25	28.24	32.03	36.46	41.65	47.73	54.86	63.25	73.11	84.70	98.35	133.3	181.9	212.8
26	29.53	33.67	38.55	44.31	51.11	59.16	68.68	79.95	93.32	109.2	150.3	208.3	245.7
27	30.82	35.34	40.71	47.08	54.67	63.71	74.48	87.35	102.7	121.1	169.4	238.5	283.6
28	32.13	37.05	42.93	49.97	58.40	68.53	80.70	95.34	113.0	134.2	190.7	272.9	327.1
29	33.45	38.79	45.22	52.97	62.32	73.64	87.35	104.0	124.1	148.6	214.6	312.1	377.2
30	34.78	40.57	47.58	56.08	66.44	79.06	94.46	113.3	136.3	164.5	241.3	356.8	434.7
40	48.89	60.40	75.40	95.03	120.8	154.8	199.6	259.1	337.9	442.6	767.1	1,342	1,779
50	64.46	84.58	112.8	152.7	209.3	290.3	406.5	573.8	815.1	1,164	2,400	4,995	7,218

Glossary

Absorption Costing: The costing method that assigns both variable and fixed manufacturing costs to products *(p. 968).*

Accelerated Depreciation Method: A depreciation method that writes off a relatively larger amount of the asset's cost near the start of its useful life than does the straight-line method *(p. 430).*

Account Payable: A liability backed by the general reputation and credit standing of the debtor *(p. 13).*

Account Receivable: A promise to receive cash from customers to whom the business has sold goods or for whom the business has performed services *(p. 13).*

Account: The detailed record of the changes that have occurred in a particular asset, liability, or owner's equity during a period. The basic summary device of accounting *(p. 44).*

Accounting Cycle: Process by which companies produce an entity's financial statements for a specific period *(p. 138).*

Accounting Equation: The most basic tool of accounting, presenting the resources of the business and the claims to those resources: Assets = Liabilities + Owner's Equity *(p. 12).*

Accounting Information System: The combination of personnel, records, and procedures that a business uses to meet its need for financial data *(p. 246).*

Accounting: The information system that measures business activities, processes that information into reports, and communicates the results to decision makers *(p. 6).*

Accounting Rate of Return: A measure of profitability computed by dividing the average annual operating income from an asset by the average amount invested in the asset *(p. 1136).*

Accounts Receivable Turnover: Ratio of net credit sales to average net accounts receivable. Measures ability to collect cash from credit customers *(p. 788).*

Accrual-Basis Accounting: Accounting that records the impact of a business event as it occurs, regardless of whether the transaction affected cash *(p. 92).*

Accrued Expense: An expense that the business has incurred but not yet paid. Also called **accrued liability** *(pp. 102, 469).*

Accrued Revenue: A revenue that has been earned but not yet received in cash *(p. 103).*

Accumulated Depreciation: The cumulative sum of all depreciation expense recorded for an asset *(p. 100).*

Acid-Test Ratio: Ratio of (the sum of cash plus short-term investments plus net current receivables) to total current liabilities. Tells whether the entity could pay all its current liabilities if they came due immediately. Also called the **quick ratio** *(pp. 353, 784).*

Activity-Based Costing (ABC): A system that focuses on activities as the fundamental cost objects and uses the costs of those activities as building blocks for compiling costs *(p. 1079).*

Additional Paid-in Capital: The sum of paid-in capital in excess of par—common plus donated capital and other accounts combined for reporting on the balance sheet *(p. 555).*

Adjusted Trial Balance: A list of all the ledger accounts with their adjusted balances, useful in preparing the financial statements *(p. 106).*

Adjusting Entry: Entry made at the end of the period to assign revenues to the period in which they are earned and expenses to the period in which they are incurred. Adjusting entries help measure the period's income and bring the related asset and liability accounts to correct balances for the financial statements *(p. 97).*

Aging of Accounts Receivable: A way to estimate bad debts by analyzing individual accounts receivable according to the length of time they have been receivable from the customer. Also called **balance-sheet approach** *(p. 341).*

Allowance for Uncollectible Accounts: A contra account, related to accounts receivable, that holds the estimated amount of collection losses. Also called **Allowance for Doubtful Accounts** *(p. 339).*

Allowance Method: A method of recording collection losses on the basis of estimates, instead of waiting to see which customers the company will not collect from *(p. 339).*

Amortization: The systematic reduction of a lump-sum amount. Expense that applies to intangible assets in the same way depreciation applies to plant assets and depletion applies to natural resources *(p. 441).*

Annuity: A stream of equal periodic amounts *(p. 1138).*

Appraisal Costs: Costs incurred to detect poor-quality goods or services *(p. 1095).*

Appropriation of Retained Earnings: Restriction of retained earnings that is recorded by a formal journal entry *(p. 595).*

Asset: An economic resource that is expected to be of benefit in the future *(p. 12).*

Audit: An examination of a company's financial statements and the accounting systems, controls, and records that produced them *(p. 293).*

Authorization of Stock: Provision in a corporate charter that gives the state's permission for the corporation to issue—that is, to sell—a certain number of shares of stock *(p. 550).*

Available-for-Sale Securities: Stock investments other than trading securities in which the investor cannot exercise significant influence over the investee *(p. 675).*

Balance Sheet: List of an entity's assets, liabilities, and owner's equity as of a specific date. Also called the **statement of financial position** *(p. 20).*

Bank Collection: Collection of money by the bank on behalf of a depositor *(p. 297).*

Bank Reconciliation: Document explaining the reasons for the difference between a depositor's cash records and the depositor's cash balance in its bank account *(p. 296).*

Bank Statement: Document the bank uses to report what it did with the depositor's cash. Shows the bank account's beginning and ending balances and lists the month's cash transactions conducted through the bank *(p. 295)*.

Batch Processing: Computerized accounting for similar transactions in a group or batch *(p. 250)*.

Benchmarking: The practice of comparing a company to a standard set by other companies, with a view toward improvement *(pp. 779, 1045)*.

Board of Directors: Group elected by the stockholders to set policy for a corporation and to appoint its officers *(p. 545)*.

Bonds Payable: Groups of notes payable (bonds) issued to multiple lenders called bondholders *(p. 626)*.

Book Value: Amount of owners' equity on the company's books for each share of its stock *(p. 560)*.

Book Value (of a Plant Asset): The asset's cost minus accumulated depreciation *(p. 101)*.

Book Value Per Share of Common Stock: Common stockholders' equity divided by the number of shares of common stock outstanding *(p. 793)*.

Brand Names: Distinctive identifications of a product or service *(p. 441)*.

Break-Even Point: The sales level at which operating income is zero: Total revenues equal total expenses *(p. 957)*.

Budget: Quantitative expression of a plan of action that helps managers coordinate and implement the plan *(pp. 309, 818)*.

Bylaws: Constitution for governing a corporation *(p. 545)*.

Callable Bonds: Bonds that the issuer may call or pay off at a specified price whenever the issuer wants *(p. 641)*.

Capital Budgeting: A formal means of analyzing long-term investment decisions. Describes budgetting for the acquisition of capital assets *(p. 1134)*.

Capital Charge: The amount that stockholders and lenders charge a company for the use of their money *(p. 794)*.

Capital Expenditure: Expenditure that increases the capacity or efficiency of an asset or extends its useful life. Capital expenditures are debited to an asset account *(p. 425)*.

Capital Expenditures Budget: A company's plan for purchases of property, plant, equipment, and other long-term assets *(p. 995)*.

Capital Lease: Lease agreement that meets any one of four criteria: (1) The lease transfers title of the leased asset to the lessee. (2) The lease contains a bargain purchase option. (3) The lease term is 75% or more of the estimated useful life of the leased asset. (4) The present value of the lease payments is 90% or more of the market value of the leased asset *(p. 645)*.

Capitalize a Cost: To record a cost as part of an asset's cost, rather than as an expense *(p. 423)*.

Cash-Basis Accounting: Accounting that records transactions only when cash is received or paid *(p. 92)*.

Cash Budget: Details how the business expects to go from the beginning cash balance to the desired ending balance. Also called the statement of budgeted cash receipts and disbursements *(p. 1001)*.

Cash Disbursements Journal: Special journal used to record cash payments by check. Also called the **check register** or **cash payments journal** *(p. 260)*.

Cash Equivalents: Highly liquid short-term investments that can be converted into cash with little delay *(p. 715)*.

Cash Flows: Cash receipts and cash payments (disbursements) *(p. 714)*.

Cash Receipts Journal: Special journal used to record cash receipts *(p. 256)*.

Certified Management Accountant (CMA): A licensed accountant who works for a single company *(p. 8)*.

Certified Public Accountant (CPA): A licensed accountant who serves the general public rather than one particular company *(p. 8)*.

Chairperson: Elected by a corporation's board of directors, usually the most powerful person in the corporations *(p. 545)*.

Chart of Accounts: List of all the accounts and their account numbers in the ledger *(p. 59)*.

Charter: Document that gives the state's permission to form a corporation *(p. 544)*.

Check: Document that instructs a bank to pay the designated person or business a specified amount of money *(p. 295)*.

Closing Entries: Entries that transfer the revenue, expense, and owner withdrawal balances from these respective accounts to the capital account *(p. 146)*.

Closing the Accounts: Step in the accounting cycle at the end of the period that prepares the accounts for recording the transactions of the next period. Closing the accounts consists of journalizing and posting the closing entries to set the balances of the revenue, expense, and owner withdrawal accounts to zero *(p. 145)*.

Common-Size Statement: A financial statement that reports only percentages (no dollar amounts); a type of vertical analysis *(p. 778)*.

Common Stock: The most basic form of capital stock. In a corporation, the common stockholders are the owners of the business *(p. 547)*.

Comprehensive Income: Company's change in total stockholders' equity from all sources other than from the owners of the business *(p. 602)*.

Conservatism: Reporting the least favorable figures in the financial statements *(p. 393)*.

Consignment: Transfer of goods by the owner (consignor) to another business (consignee) that, for a fee, sells the inventory on the owner's behalf. The consignee does not take title to the consigned goods *(p. 384)*.

Consistency Principle: A business should use the same accounting methods and procedures from period to period *(p. 392)*.

Consolidated Statements: Financial statements of the parent company plus those of majority-owned subsidiaries as if the combination were a single legal entity *(p. 682)*.

Constraint: A factor that restricts production or sale of a product *(p. 1128)*.

Contingent Liability: A potential liability that will become an actual liability only if a particular event does occur *(p. 351)*.

Continuous Improvement: A philosophy requiring employees to continually look for ways to improve performance *(p. 836)*.

Contra Account: An account that always has a companion account and whose normal balance is opposite that of the companion account *(p. 100)*.

Contract Interest Rate: Interest rate that determines the amount of cash interest the borrower pays and the investor receives each year. Also called the **stated interest rate** *(p. 628)*.

Contribution Margin: The excess of sales revenue over variable expenses *(p. 954)*.

Contribution Margin Income Statement: Income statement that groups variable and fixed expenses separately, and highlights the contribution margin *(p. 954)*.

Contribution Margin per Unit: Excess of the sales revenue per unit (sale price) over the variable expense per unit *(p. 958)*.

Contribution Margin Ratio: The ratio of contribution margin to sales revenue *(p. 958).*

Control Account: An account whose balance equals the sum of the balances in a group of related accounts in a subsidiary ledger *(p. 256).*

Controller: The chief accounting officer of a company *(p. 291).*

Controlling: Acting to implement planning decisions and then evaluating the performance of operations and employees *(p. 818).*

Conversion Costs: Costs of converting direct materials into finished products, usually direct labor plus manufacturing overhead *(pp. 825, 908).*

Convertible Bonds: Bonds (or notes) that may be converted into the common stock of the issuing company at the option of the investor *(p. 642).*

Convertible Preferred Stock: Preferred stock that may be exchanged by the preferred stockholders, if they choose, for another class of stock in the corporation *(p. 559).*

Copyright: Exclusive right to reproduce and sell a book, musical composition, film, other work of art, or computer program. Issued by the federal government, copyrights extend 50 years beyond the author's life *(p. 441).*

Corporation: A business owned by stockholders; it begins when the state approves its articles of incorporation. A corporation is a legal entity, an "artificial person," in the eyes of the law *(p. 9).*

Cost Behavior: Describes how costs change as a cost driver changes *(p. 950).*

Cost-Benefit Analysis: The weighing of costs against benefits to aid decision making *(p. 819).*

Cost Object: Anything for which a separate measurement of costs is desired *(p. 822).*

Cost of Capital: A weighted average of the returns demanded by a company's stockholders and lenders *(p. 794).*

Cost of Goods Available for Sale: Beginning inventory plus purchases during a period *(p. 383).*

Cost of Goods Manufactured: The (manufacturing) cost of the goods that were (finished)—that is, the cost of the units that completed the production process this period. This is the manufacturer's counterpart to the merchandiser's purchases *(p. 829).*

Cost of Goods Sold: The cost of the inventory that the business has sold to customers, the largest single expense of most merchandising businesses. Also called **cost of sales** *(p. 182).*

Cost-Volume-Profit (CVP) Analysis: Expresses the relationships among costs, volume, and profit or loss *(p. 950).*

Credit Memorandum or Credit Memo: A document issued by a seller to credit a customer's account for returned merchandise *(p. 262).*

Credit: The right side of an account *(p. 47).*

Creditor: The party to a credit transaction who sells goods or a service and obtains a receivable *(p. 336).*

Cumulative Preferred Stock: Preferred stock whose owners must receive all dividends in arrears before the corporation pays dividends to the common stockholders *(p. 558).*

Current Asset: An asset that is expected to be converted to cash, sold, or consumed during the next 12 months, or within the business's normal operating cycle if longer than a year *(p. 150).*

Current Liability: A debt due to be paid with cash or with goods and services within one year or within the entity's operating cycle if the cycle is longer than a year *(p. 150).*

Current Portion of Long-Term Debt: Amount of the principal that is payable within one year. Also called **current maturity** *(p. 468).*

Current Ratio: Total current assets divided by total current liabilities. Measures the ability to pay current liabilities from current assets *(pp. 153, 783).*

Customer Service: Support provided for customers after the sale *(p. 822).*

Database: A computerized storehouse of information *(p. 247).*

Days' Sales in Receivables: Ratio of average net accounts receivable to one day's sales. Tells how many days' sales remain in Accounts Receivable awaiting collection. Also called the **collection period** *(pp. 354, 788).*

Debentures: Unsecured bonds, backed only by the good faith of the borrower *(p. 626).*

Debit Memorandum or Debit Memo: A document issued by a buyer when returning merchandise. The memo informs the seller that the buyer no longer owes the seller for the amount of the returned purchases *(p. 263).*

Debit: The left side of an account *(p. 47).*

Debt Ratio: Ratio of total liabilities to total assets. Tells the proportion of a company's assets that it has financed with debt *(pp. 154, 789).*

Debtor: The party to a credit transaction who makes a purchase and has a payable *(p. 336).*

Deficit: Debit balance in the Retained Earnings account *(p. 548).*

Depletion Expense: The portion of a natural resource's cost that is used up in a particular period. Depletion expense is computed just as units-of-production depreciation is *(p. 440).*

Deposit in Transit: A deposit recorded by the company but not yet by its bank *(p. 297).*

Depreciable Cost: The cost of a plant asset minus its estimated residual value *(p. 427).*

Depreciation: The allocation of a plant asset's cost to expense over its useful life *(p. 99).*

Design: Detailed engineering of products and services, or processes for producing them *(p. 822).*

Direct Cost: A cost that can be specifically traced to a cost object *(p. 822).*

Direct Labor: The compensation of employees who physically convert materials into the company's products; labor costs that are directly traceable to finished products *(p. 824).*

Direct Materials: Materials that become a physical part of a finished product and whose costs are separately and conveniently traceable through the manufacturing process to a finished product *(p. 824).*

Direct Method: Format of the operating activities section of the statement of cash flows that lists the major categories of operating cash receipts (collections from customers and receipts of interest and dividends) and cash disbursements (payments to suppliers, to employees, for interest and income taxes) *(p. 718).*

Direct Write-off Method: A method of accounting for uncollectible receivables, in which the company waits until the credit department decides that a customer's account receivable is uncollectible, and then debits Uncollectible-Account Expense and credits the customer's Account Receivable *(p. 344).*

Disclosure Principle: A business's financial statements must report enough information for outsiders to make knowledgeable decisions about the company *(p. 393).*

Discount (on a Bond): Excess of a bond's maturity (par value) over its issue price. Also called a **bond discount** *(p. 627).*

Discounting a Note Payable: A borrowing arrangement in which the bank subtracts the interest amount from a note's face value. The borrower receives the net amount *(p. 466)*.

Discounting a Note Receivable: Selling a note receivable before its maturity date *(p. 350)*.

Discount Rate: Management's minimum desired rate of return on an investment. Also called the **Hurdle rate, required rate of return,** and **cost of capital** *(p. 1138)*.

Dishonor of a Note: Failure of a note's maker to pay a note receivable at maturity. Also called **default on a note** *(p. 351)*.

Dissolution: Ending of a partnership *(p. 508)*.

Distribution: Delivery of products or services to customers *(p. 822)*.

Dividend Yield: Ratio of dividends per share of stock to the stock's market price per share. Tells the percentage of a stock's market value that the company pays to stockholders as dividends *(p. 792)*.

Dividends: Distributions by a corporation to its stockholders *(p. 548)*.

Double Taxation: Corporations pay their own income taxes on corporate income. Then, the stockholders pay personal income tax on the cash dividends that they receive from corporations *(p. 545)*.

Double-Declining-Balance (DDB) Depreciation Method: An accelerated depreciation method that computes annual depreciation by multiplying the asset's decreasing book value by a constant percentage, which is 2 times the straight-line rate *(p. 430)*.

Earnings Per Share (EPS): Amount of a company's net income per share of its outstanding common stock *(pp. 601, 791)*.

Economic Value Added (EVA): Combines the concepts of accounting income and corporate finance to measure whether the company's operations have increased stockholder wealth *(p. 794)*.

Efficiency Variance: Measures whether the quantity of materials or labor used to make the actual number of outputs is within the standard allowed for that number of outputs. This is computed as the difference in quantities (actual quantity of input used minus standard quantity of input allowed for the actual number of outputs), multiplied by the standard unit price of the input *(p. 1048)*.

Efficient Capital Market: A capital market in which market prices fully reflect all information available to the public *(p. 795)*.

Electronic Funds Transfer (EFT): System that transfers cash by electronic communication rather than by paper documents *(p. 296)*.

Entity: An organization or a section of an organization that, for accounting purposes, stands apart from other organizations and individuals as a separate economic unit *(p. 10)*.

Equity Method for Investments: The method used to account for investments in which the investor has 20–50% of the investee's voting stock and can significantly influence the decisions of the investee. The investment account is debited for ownership in the investee's net income and credited for ownership in the investee's dividends *(p. 679)*.

Equivalent Units: A measure of the amount of work done during a period, expressed in terms of fully complete units of output. Also called **equivalent units of production** *(p. 909)*.

Estimated Residual Value: Expected cash value of an asset at the end of its useful life. Also called scrap value, or salvage value *(p. 427)*.

Estimated Useful Life: Length of service that a business expects to get from an asset. May be expressed in years, units of output, miles, or another measure *(p. 427)*.

Expense: Decrease in owner's equity that occurs from using assets or increasing liabilities in the course of delivering goods or services to customers *(p. 13)*.

External Failure Costs: Costs incurred when poor-quality goods or services are not detected until after delivery to customers *(p. 1095)*.

Extraordinary Item: A gain or loss that is both unusual for the company and infrequent. Also called **extraordinary gains and losses** *(p. 599)*.

Financial Accounting Standards Board (FASB): The private organization that determines how accounting is practiced in the United States *(p. 8)*.

Financial Accounting: The branch of accounting that focuses on information for people outside the firm *(p. 7)*.

Financial Budget: Projects cash inflows and outflows, the period-ending balance sheet, and the statement of cash flows *(p. 995)*.

Financial Statements: Business documents that report on a business in monetary amounts, providing information to help people make informed business decisions *(p. 6)*.

Financing Activities: Activities by which the company gets the cash needed to launch and sustain the business *(p. 356)*.

Financing Activity: Activity that obtains the funds from investors and creditors needed to launch and sustain the business; a section of the statement of cash flows *(p. 716)*.

Finished Goods Inventory: Completed goods that have not yet been sold *(p. 821)*.

First-In, First-Out (FIFO) Inventory Costing Method: Inventory costing method by which the first costs into inventory are the first costs out to cost of goods sold. Ending inventory is based on the costs of the most recent purchases *(p. 386)*.

First-In, First-Out (FIFO) Process Costing Method: A process costing method that assigns to each period's equivalent units of production that period's costs per equivalent unit *(p. 917)*.

Fixed Asset: Another name for property, plant, and equipment *(p. 150)*.

Fixed Cost: Cost that does not change in total despite wide changes in volume *(p. 951)*.

Flexible Budget Variance: The difference between what the company actually spent at the actual level of output and what it should have spent to obtain the actual level of output. This is computed as the difference between the actual amount and a flexible budget amount *(p. 1040)*.

Flexible Budget: A summarized budget that can easily be computed for several different volume levels. Flexible budgets separate variable costs from fixed costs; it is the variable costs that put the "flex" in the flexible budget *(p. 1036)*.

Foreign-Currency Exchange Rate: The measure of one currency against another currency *(p. 687)*.

Franchises, Licenses: Privileges granted by a private business or a government to sell a product or service in accordance with specified conditions *(p. 442)*.

Full Product Costs: The costs of all resources that are used throughout the value chain for a product *(p. 823)*.

General Journal: Journal used to record all transactions that do not fit one of the special journals *(p. 252)*.

General Ledger: Ledger of accounts that are reported in the financial statements *(p. 255)*.

General Partnership: A form of partnership in which each partner is an owner of the business, with all the privileges and risks of ownership *(p. 510)*.

Generally Accepted Accounting Principles (GAAP): Accounting guidelines, formulated by the Financial Accounting Standards Board, that govern how accountants measure, process, and communicate financial information *(p. 10)*.

Goodwill: Excess of the cost of an acquired company over the sum of the market values of its net assets (assets minus liabilities) *(p. 442)*.

Gross Margin: Excess of sales revenue over cost of goods sold. Also called **gross profit** *(pp. 183, 379)*.

Gross Margin Method: A way to estimate inventory on the basis of the cost-of-goods-sold model: Beginning inventory + Net purchases = Cost of goods available for sale. Cost of goods available for sale − Cost of goods sold = Ending inventory. Also called the **gross profit method** *(p. 397)*.

Gross Margin Percentage: Gross margin divided by net sales revenue. A measure of profitability. Also called **gross profit percentage** *(p. 201)*.

Gross Pay: Total amount of salary, wages, commissions, or any other employee compensation before taxes and other deductions *(p. 477)*.

Hardware: Electronic equipment that includes computers, disk drives, monitors, printers, and the network that connects them *(p. 247)*.

Hedging: Protecting oneself from losing money in one transaction by engaging in a counterbalancing transaction *(p. 689)*.

Held-to-Maturity Securities: Investment in bonds, notes, and other debt securities that the investor expects to hold until their maturity date *(p. 683)*.

Horizontal Analysis: Study of percentage changes in comparative financial statements *(p. 773)*.

Imprest System: A way to account for petty cash by maintaining a constant balance in the petty cash account, supported by the fund (cash plus disbursement tickets) totaling the same amount *(p. 308)*.

Income Statement: Summary of an entity's revenues, expenses, and net income or net loss for a specific period. Also called the **statement of operations** or the **statement of earnings** *(p. 19)*.

Income Summary: A temporary "holding tank" account into which revenues and expenses are transferred prior to their final transfer to the capital account *(p. 146)*.

Indirect Cost: A cost that cannot be specifically traced to a cost object *(p. 822)*.

Indirect Labor: Labor costs that are difficult to trace to specific products *(p. 825)*.

Indirect Materials: Materials whose costs cannot conveniently be directly traced to particular finished products *(p. 825)*.

Indirect Method: Format of the operating activities section of the statement of cash flows that starts with net income and shows the reconciliation from net income to operating cash flows. Also called the **reconciliation method** *(p. 718)*.

Intangible Assets: Assets with no physical form. Valuable because of the special rights they carry. Examples are patents and copyrights *(p. 421)*.

Internal Control: Organizational plan and all the related measures adopted by an entity to safeguard assets, and encourage adherence to company policies, promote operational efficiency, and ensure accurate and reliable accounting records *(p. 290)*.

Internal Failure Costs: Costs incurred when the company detects and corrects poor-quality goods or services before delivery to customers *(p. 1095)*.

Internal Rate of Return (IRR): The rate of return (based on discounted cash flows) that a company can expect to earn on a project. The discount rate that makes the net present value of the project's cash flows equal to zero *(p. 1141)*.

Inventoriable Product Costs: All costs of a product that are regarded as an asset for external financial reporting. Must conform to GAAP *(p. 823)*.

Inventory Profit: Difference between gross margin figured on the FIFO basis and gross margin figured on the LIFO basis *(p. 388)*.

Inventory Turnover: Ratio of cost of goods sold to average inventory. Measures the number of times a company sells its average level of inventory during a year *(pp. 201, 786)*.

Investing Activities: Activities that relate to the purchase and sale of a business's long-term assets *(p. 355)*.

Investing Activity: Activity that increases and decreases the long-term assets available to the business; a section of the statement of cash flows *(p. 716)*.

Invoice: A seller's request for cash from the purchaser *(p. 185)*.

Journal: The chronological accounting record of an entity's transactions *(p. 49)*.

Just-In-Time (JIT) Costing: A standard costing system that starts with output completed and then assigns manufacturing costs to units sold and to inventories. Also called **backflush costing** *(p. 1093)*.

Just-In-Time (JIT): A system in which a company schedules production just in time to satisfy needs. Materials are purchased and finished goods are completed only as needed to satisfy customer demand *(p. 834)*.

Last-In, First-Out (LIFO) Inventory Costing Method: Inventory costing method by which the last costs into inventory are the first costs out to cost of goods sold. This method leaves the oldest costs—those of beginning inventory and the earliest purchases of the period—in ending inventory *(p. 386)*.

Lease: Rental agreement in which the tenant (lessee) agrees to make rent payments to the property owner (lessor) to obtain the use of the asset *(p. 644)*.

Ledger: The book of accounts *(p. 44)*.

Legal Capital: The portion of stockholders' equity that cannot be used for dividends *(p. 548)*.

Lessee: Tenant in a lease agreement *(p. 644)*.

Lessor: Property owner in a lease agreement *(p. 644)*.

Liability: An economic obligation (a debt) payable to an individual or an organization outside the business *(p. 12)*.

Life-Cycle Budget: A budget that predicts a product's revenues and costs over its entire life cycle *(p. 1098)*.

LIFO Liquidation: Occurs when the LIFO inventory method is used and inventory quantities fall below the level of the previous period *(p. 389)*.

Limited Liability Partnership: A form of partnership in which each partner's personal liability for the business's debts is limited to a certain amount. Also called **LLPs** *(p. 510)*.

Limited Liability: No personal obligation of a stockholder for corporation debts. A stockholder can lose no more on an investment in a corporation's stock than the cost of the investment *(p. 544)*.

Limited Partnership: A partnership with at least two classes of partners: a general partner and limited partners *(p. 510)*.

Liquidation: The process of going out of business by selling the entity's assets and paying its liabilities. The final step in liquidation of a business is the distribution of any remaining cash to the owner(s) *(p. 523)*.

Liquidity: Measure of how quickly an item can be converted to cash *(p. 150)*.

Long-Term Asset: An asset other than a current asset *(p. 150).*

Long-Term Investment: A noncurrent asset, a separate asset category reported on the balance sheet between current assets and plant assets *(p. 675).*

Long-Term Liability: A liability other than a current liability *(p. 150).*

Long-Term Solvency: Ability to generate enough cash to pay long-term debts as they mature *(p. 772).*

Lower-of-Cost-or-Market (LCM) Rule: Requires that an asset be reported in the financial statements at whichever is lower—its historical cost or its market value (current replacement cost for inventory) *(p. 394).*

Major Repair or Extraordinary Repair: Repair work that generates a capital expenditure *(p. 425).*

Maker of a Note: The person or business that signs the note and promises to pay the amount required by the note agreement; the debtor *(p. 349).*

Management Accounting: The branch of accounting that focuses on information for internal decision makers of a business, such as top executives *(p. 7).*

Management by Exception: Directs management's attention to important differences between actual and budgeted amounts *(p. 1011).*

Manufacturing Company: A company that uses labor, plant, and equipment to convert raw materials into new finished products *(p. 820).*

Manufacturing Overhead: All manufacturing costs other than direct materials and direct labor. Also called **factory overhead** or **indirect manufacturing cost** *(p. 824).*

Margin of Safety: Excess of expected sales over break-even sales. Drop in sales a company can absorb before incurring an operating loss *(p. 964).*

Market Interest Rate: Interest rate that investors demand in order to loan their money. Also called the **effective interest rate** *(p. 628).*

Market Value: Price for which a person could buy or sell a share of stock *(p. 559).*

Market-Value Method for Investments: Used to account for all trading investments. These investments are reported at their current market value *(p. 675).*

Marketing: Promotion of products or services *(p. 822).*

Master Budget: The set of budgeted financial statements and supporting schedules for the entire organization. This comprehensive budget includes the operating budget, the capital expenditures budget, and the financial budget *(p. 995).*

Matching Principle: The basis for recording expenses. Directs accountants to identify all expenses incurred during the period, to measure the expenses, and to match them against the revenues earned during that same span of time *(p. 95).*

Materiality Concept: A company must perform strictly proper accounting only for items and transactions that are significant to the business's financial statements *(p. 393).*

Materials Inventory: Raw materials for use in the manufacturing process *(p. 821).*

Menu: A list of options for choosing computer functions *(p. 249).*

Merchandising Company: A company that buys ready-made inventory for resale to customers *(pp. 378, 820).*

Method: A depreciation method that writes off a relatively larger amount of the asset's cost near the start of its useful life than does the straight-line method *(p. 430).*

Minority Interest: A subsidiary company's equity that is held by stockholders other than the parent company *(p. 682).*

Mixed Cost: Cost that is part variable and part fixed *(p. 952).*

Module: Separate compatible units of an accounting package that are integrated to function together *(p. 251).*

Mortgage: Borrower's promise to transfer the legal title to certain assets to the lender if the debt is not paid on schedule *(p. 643).*

Multi-step Income Statement: Format that contains subtotals to highlight significant relationships. In addition to net income, it presents gross margin and operating income *(p. 200).*

Mutual Agency: Every partner can bind the business to a contract within the scope of the partnership's regular business operations *(p. 508).*

Net Income: Excess of total revenues over total expenses. Also called **net earnings** or **net profit** *(p. 17).*

Net Loss: Excess of total expenses over total revenues *(p. 17).*

Net Pay: Gross pay minus all deductions. The amount of compensation that the employee actually takes home *(p. 477).*

Net Present Value (NPV): The decision model that brings cash inflows and outflows back to a common time period by discounting these expected future cash flows to their present value, using a minimum desired rate of return *(p. 1137).*

Net Purchases: Purchases less purchase discounts and purchase returns and allowances *(pp. 204, 229).*

Net Sales: Sales revenue less sales discounts and sales returns and allowances *(p. 182).*

Network: The system of electronic linkages that allows different computers to share the same information *(p. 247).*

Non-Value-Added Activities: Activities that do not increase customer value *(p. 1091).*

Nonsufficient Funds (NSF) Check: A "hot" check, one for which the maker's bank account has insufficient money to pay the check *(p. 298).*

Note Payable: A written promise of future payment *(p. 13).*

Note Receivable: A written promise for future collection of cash *(p. 13).*

Off Balance Sheet Financing: Acquisition of assets or services with debt that is not reported on the balance sheet *(p. 647).*

On-line Processing: Computerized processing of related functions, such as the recording and posting of transactions, on a continuous basis *(p. 250).*

Operating Activities: Activities that relate to a business's revenue and expense transactions *(p. 355).*

Operating Activity: Activity that creates revenue or expense in the entity's major line of business; a section of the statement of cash flows. Operating activities affect the income statement *(p. 715).*

Operating Budget: Sets the expected revenues and expenses—and thus operating income—for the period *(p. 995).*

Operating Cycle: Time span during which cash is paid for goods and services, which are then sold to customers from whom the business collects cash *(p. 150).*

Operating Expenses: Expenses, other than cost of goods sold, that are incurred in the entity's major line of business. Examples include rent, depreciation, salaries, wages, utilities, property tax, and supplies expense *(p. 198).*

Operating Income: Gross margin minus operating expenses plus any other operating revenues. Also called **income from operations** *(p. 198).*

Operating Lease: Usually a short-term or cancelable rental agreement *(p. 645).*

Opportunity Cost: The benefit that can be obtained from the next-best course of action *(p. 1131)*.

Ordinary Repair: Repair work that creates a revenue expenditure, debited to an expense account *(p. 425)*.

Other Expense: Expense that is outside the main operations of a business, such as a loss on the sale of plant assets *(p. 198)*.

Other Revenue: Revenue that is outside the main operations of a business, such as a gain on the sale of plant assets *(p. 198)*.

Outsourcing: A make-or-buy decision, where managers must decide whether to buy a component product or service, or to produce it in-house *(p. 1129)*.

Outstanding Check: A check issued by the company and recorded on its books but not yet paid by its bank *(p. 297)*.

Outstanding Stock: Stock in the hands of stockholders *(p. 546)*.

Overhead Flexible Budget Variance: The difference between the actual overhead cost and the flexible budget overhead for the actual number of outputs *(p. 1054)*.

Owner Withdrawals: Amounts removed from the business by an owner *(p. 13)*.

Owner's Equity: The claim of a business owner to the assets of the business. Also called **capital** *(p. 12)*.

Paid-in Capital: A corporation's capital from investments by the stockholders. Also called **contributed capital** *(p. 547)*.

Par Value: Arbitrary amount assigned to a share of stock *(p. 549)*.

Partnership Agreement: The contract between partners that specifies such items as the name, location, and nature of the business; the name, capital investment, and duties of each partner; and the method of sharing profits and losses among the partners. Also called **articles of partnership** *(p. 508)*.

Partnership: An association of two or more persons who co-own a business for profit *(pp. 9, 508)*.

Patent: A federal government grant giving the holder the exclusive right to produce and sell an invention for 20 years *(p. 441)*.

Payback: The length of time it will take to recover, in net cash inflows from operations, the dollars of a capital outlay *(p. 1134)*.

Payee of a Note: The person or business to whom the maker of a note promises future payment; the creditor *(p. 349)*.

Payroll: A major expense of many businesses. Also called **employee compensation** *(p. 469)*.

Pension: Employee compensation that will be received during retirement *(p. 647)*.

Percent of Sales Method: A method of estimating uncollectible receivables that calculates uncollectible-account expense. Also called the **income statement approach** *(p. 340)*.

Period Costs: Operating costs that are expensed in the period in which they are incurred *(p. 823)*.

Periodic Inventory System: An inventory accounting system in which the business does not keep a continuous record of the inventory on hand. Instead, at the end of the period the business makes a physical count of the on-hand inventory and uses this information to prepare the financial statements *(pp. 184, 379)*.

Permanent Accounts: Accounts that are not closed at the end of the period—asset, liability, and capital accounts. Also called **real accounts** *(p. 146)*.

Perpetual Inventory System: The accounting inventory system in which the business keeps a running record of inventory and cost of goods sold *(pp. 184, 380)*.

Petty Cash: Fund containing a small amount of cash that is used to pay for minor expenditures *(p. 307)*.

Planning: Choosing goals and deciding how to achieve them *(p. 818)*.

Plant Assets: Long-lived tangible assets, such as land, buildings, and equipment, used in the operation of a business. Also called **fixed assets** *(pp. 99, 420)*.

Postclosing Trial Balance: List of the ledger accounts *(p. 148)*.

Posting: Transferring of amounts from the journal to the ledger *(p. 51)*.

Preferred Stock: Stock that gives its owners certain advantages over common stockholders, such as the priority to receive dividends before the common stockholders and the priority to receive assets before the common stockholders if the corporation liquidates *(p. 549)*.

Premium: Excess of a bond's issue price over its maturity (par) value. Also called **bond premium** *(p. 627)*.

Prepaid Expense: Advance payments of expenses. A category of miscellaneous assets that typically expire or are used up in the near future. Examples include prepaid rent, prepaid insurance, and supplies *(p. 97)*.

Present Value: Amount a person would invest now to receive a greater amount at a future date *(p. 628)*.

President: Chief operating officer in charge of managing the day-to-day operations of a corporation *(p. 545)*.

Prevention Costs: Costs incurred to avoid poor-quality goods or services *(p. 1095)*.

Price Variance: Measures how well the business keeps unit prices of material and labor units within standards. This is computed as the difference in prices (actual unit price minus standard unit price) of an input, multiplied by the actual quantity of the input *(p. 1047)*.

Price/Earnings Ratio: Ratio of the market price of a share of common stock to the company's earnings per share. Measures the value that the stock market places on $1 of a company's earnings *(p. 792)*.

Prime Costs: Direct costs of the manufacturing process, usually direct materials plus direct labor *(p. 825)*.

Prior-period Adjustment: A correction to retained earnings for an error of an earlier period *(p. 603)*.

Product Life Cycle: The time from research and development through the product's sales and on to the end of customer service *(p. 1097)*.

Production Cost Report: Summarizes the operations of a processing department for a period *(p. 922)*.

Production or Purchases: Resources used to produce a product or service, or the purchase of finished merchandise *(p. 822)*.

Production Volume Variance: The difference between the manufacturing overhead cost in the flexible budget for actual outputs and the standard overhead allocated to production *(p. 1055)*.

Proprietorship: A business with a single owner *(p. 9)*.

Purchases Journal: Special journal used to record all purchases of inventory, supplies, and other assets on account *(p. 258)*.

Rate of Return on Common Stockholders' Equity: Net income minus preferred dividends, divided by average common stockholders' equity. A measure of profitability. Also called **return on stockholders' equity** *(pp. 562, 791)*.

Rate of Return on Net Sales: Ratio of net income to net sales. A measure of profitability. Also called **return on sales** *(p. 790)*.

Rate of Return on Total Assets: The sum of net income plus interest expense divided by average total assets. This ratio measures the success a company has in using its assets to earn income for the persons who finance the business. Also called **return on assets** *(pp. 562, 790)*.

Receivables: Monetary claims against a business or individual *(p. 336)*.

Reconciliation Method: Another name for the indirect method *(p. 733)*.

Relevant Information: Expected future data that differ among alternative courses of action *(p. 1122)*.

Relevant Range: A band of volume in which a specific relationship exists between cost and volume *(p. 953)*.

Research and Development (R&D): The process of researching and developing new or improved products or services, or the processes for producing them *(p. 821)*.

Responsibility Accounting: A system for evaluating the performance of each responsibility center and its manager *(p. 1009)*.

Responsibility Center: A part or subunit of an organization whose manager is accountable for specific activities *(p. 1009)*.

Retained Earnings: A corporation's capital that is earned through profitable operation of the business *(p. 547)*.

Revenue Expenditure: Expenditure that merely maintains an asset or restores the asset to working order. Revenue expenditures are expensed (matched against revenue) *(p. 425)*.

Revenue Principle: The basis for recording revenues; tells accountants when to record revenue and the amount of revenue to record *(p. 94)*.

Revenue: Amounts earned by delivering goods or services to customers. Revenues increase owner's equity *(p. 13)*.

Reversing Entry: An entry that switches the debit and the credit of a previous adjusting entry. The reversing entry is dated the first day of the period after the adjusting entry *(p. 178)*.

S Corporation: A corporation taxed in the same way as a partnership *(p. 511)*.

Sales Discount: Reduction in the amount receivable from a customer, offered by the seller as an incentive for the customer to pay promptly. A contra account to Sales Revenue *(p. 191)*.

Sales Journal: Special journal used to record credit sales *(p. 253)*.

Sales Mix: Combination of products that make up total sales *(p. 965)*.

Sales Returns and Allowances: Decreases in the seller's receivable from a customer's return of merchandise or from granting the customer an allowance from the amount owed to the seller. A contra account to Sales Revenue *(p. 191)*.

Sales Revenue: The amount that a merchandiser earns from selling its inventory. Also called **sales** *(p. 182)*.

Sales Volume Variance: The difference arising only because the number of units actually sold differs from the number of units expected to be sold according to the static budget. This is computed as the difference between a flexible budget amount and a static budget amount *(p. 1040)*.

Segment of the Business: One of various separate divisions of a company *(p. 599)*.

Sensitivity Analysis: A what-if technique that asks what a result will be if a predicted amount is not achieved or if an underlying assumption changes *(p. 1005)*.

Server: The main computer in a network, where the program and data are stored *(p. 247)*.

Service Company: A company that provides intangible services, rather than tangible products *(p. 820)*.

Short Presentation: A way to report contingent liabilities in the body of the balance sheet, after total liabilities but with no amount given. An explanatory note accompanies the presentation *(p. 474)*.

Short-Term Investment: A current asset; an investment that is readily convertible to cash and that the investor intends either to convert to cash within one year or to use to pay a current liability. Also called a **marketable security** *(p. 675)*.

Short-Term Liquidity: Ability to meet current payments as they come due *(p. 772)*.

Short-Term Note Payable: Promissory note payable due within one year, a common form of financing *(p. 465)*.

Single-Step Income Statement: Format that groups all revenues together and then lists and deducts all expenses together without drawing any subtotals *(p. 200)*.

Social Security Tax: Federal Insurance Contributions Act (FICA) tax, which is withheld from employees' pay. Also called **FICA tax** *(p. 478)*.

Software: Set of programs or instructions that drive the computer to perform the work desired *(p. 247)*.

Special Journal: An accounting journal designed to record one specific type of transaction *(p. 252)*.

Specific-Unit-Cost Method: Inventory cost method based on the specific cost of particular units of inventory. Also called the **specific identification method** *(p. 385)*.

Spreadsheet: A computer program that links data by means of formulas and functions; an electronic work sheet *(p. 251)*.

Standard Cost: A carefully predetermined cost that usually is expressed on a per-unit basis *(p. 1044)*.

Stated Value: Similar to par value *(p. 549)*.

Statement of Cash Flows: Reports cash receipts and cash disbursements classified according to the entity's major activities: operating, investing, and financing *(pp. 20, 714)*.

Statement of Owner's Equity: Summary of the changes in an entity's owner's equity during a specific period *(p. 20)*.

Statement of Stockholders' Equity: Reports the changes in all categories of stockholders' equity during the period *(p. 605)*.

Static Budget: The budget prepared for only one level of volume. Also called the **master budget** *(p. 1036)*.

Stock Dividend: A proportional distribution by a corporation of its own stock to its stockholders *(p. 585)*.

Stock Split: An increase in the number of outstanding shares of stock coupled with a proportionate reduction in the par value of the stock *(p. 588)*.

Stock: Shares into which the owners' equity of a corporation is divided *(p. 544)*.

Stockholder: A person who owns stock in a corporation. Also called a **shareholder** *(pp. 9, 544)*.

Stockholders' Equity: Owners' equity of a corporation *(p. 547)*.

Straight-Line (SL) Depreciation Method: Depreciation method in which an equal amount of depreciation expense is assigned to each year (or period) of asset use *(p. 428)*.

Strategy: A set of business goals and the tactics to achieve them *(p. 1122)*.

Strong Currency: A currency that is rising relative to other nations' currencies *(p. 687)*.

Subsidiary Ledger: Book of accounts that provides supporting details on individual balances, the total of which appears in a general ledger account *(p. 255)*.

Sunk Cost: A past cost that cannot be changed regardless of which future action is taken *(p. 1131)*.

Target Costing: A cost management technique that helps managers set goals for cost savings through product design *(p. 1099)*.

Temporary Accounts: The revenue and expense accounts that relate to a particular accounting period and are closed at the end of the period. For a proprietorship, the owner withdrawal account is also temporary. Also called **nominal accounts** *(p. 146).*

Term Bonds: Bonds that all mature at the same time for a particular issue *(p. 626).*

Throughput Time: The time between receipt of raw materials and completion of finished products *(pp. 834, 1091).*

Time-Period Concept: Ensures that accounting information is reported at regular intervals *(p. 95).*

Times-Interest-Earned Ratio: Ratio of income from operations to interest expense. Measures the number of times that operating income can cover interest expense. Also called the **interest-coverage ratio** *(p. 789).*

Time Value of Money: The fact that income can be earned by investing money for a period of time *(p. 1137).*

Total Quality Management (TQM): A philosophy of delighting customers by providing them with superior products and services. Involves improving quality and eliminating defects and waste throughout the value chain *(p. 835).*

Trademarks, Trade Names, or Brand Names: Distinctive identifications of a product or service *(p. 441).*

Trading on the Equity: Earning more income on borrowed money than the related interest expense, thereby increasing the earnings for the owners of the business. Also called **leverage** *(pp. 644, 791).*

Trading Securities: Investments that are to be sold in the very near future with the intent of generating profits on price changes *(p. 675).*

Transaction: An event that affects the financial position of a particular entity and can be reliably recorded *(p. 14).*

Transferred-In Costs: Costs incurred in a previous process that are carried forward as part of the product's cost when it moves to the next process *(p. 920).*

Treasury Stock: A corporation's own stock that it has issued and later reacquired *(p. 589).*

Trial Balance: A list of all the ledger accounts with their balances *(p. 54).*

Trigger Points: Points in operations that prompt entries in the accounting records in just-in-time costing *(p. 1093).*

Uncollectible-Account Expense: Cost to the seller of extending credit. Arises from the failure to collect from credit customers. Also called **doubtful-account expense,** or **bad-debt expense** *(p. 339).*

Underwriter: Organization that purchases the bonds from an issuing company and resells them to its clients or sells the bonds for a commission, agreeing to buy all unsold bonds *(p. 626).*

Unearned Revenue: A liability created when a business collects cash from customers in advance of doing work for the customer. The obligation is to provide a product or a service in the future. Also called **deferred revenue** *(p. 104).*

Unemployment Compensation Tax: Payroll tax paid by employers to the government, which uses the money to pay unemployment benefits to people who are out of work *(p. 479).*

Units-of-Production (UOP) Depreciation Method: Depreciation method by which a fixed amount of depreciation is assigned to each unit of output produced by a plant asset *(p. 428).*

Unlimited Personal Liability: When a partnership (or a proprietorship) cannot pay its debts with business assets, the partners (or the proprietor) must use personal assets to meet the debt *(p. 509).*

Value Chain: Sequence of activities that adds value to a firm's products or services. Includes R&D, design, production, or purchases, marketing, distribution, and customer service *(p. 821).*

Value Engineering (VE): Designing products that achieve cost targets and meet specified quality and performance standards *(p. 1099).*

Variable Costing: The costing method that assigns only variable manufacturing costs to products *(p. 968).*

Variable Costs: Costs that change in total in direct proportion to changes in volume of activity *(p. 950).*

Variance: The difference between an actual amount and the corresponding budgeted amount. A variance is labeled as favorable if it increases operating income and unfavorable if it decreases operating income *(p. 1036).*

Vertical Analysis: Analysis of a financial statement that reveals the relationship of each statement item to the total, which is 100 percent *(p. 776).*

Voucher: Document authorizing a cash disbursement *(p. 307).*

Weak Currency: A currency that is falling relative to other nations' currencies *(p. 687).*

Weighted-Average Cost Method: Inventory costing method based on the weighted-average cost of inventory during the period. Weighted-average cost is determined by dividing the cost of goods available for sale by the number of units available. Also called the **average-cost method** *(p. 385).*

Weighted-Average Process Costing Method: A process costing method that costs all equivalent units of work with a weighted average of that period's and the previous period's costs per equivalent unit *(p. 923).*

Withheld Income Tax: Income tax deducted from employees' gross pay *(p. 478).*

Work in Process Inventory: Goods that are partway through the manufacturing process but not yet complete *(p. 821).*

Work Sheet: A columnar document designed to help move data from the trial balance to the financial statements *(p. 138).*

Working Capital: Current assets minus current liabilities; measures a business's ability to meet its short-term obligations with its current assets *(p. 783).*

Company Index

Real companies are in bold type

a

ABC Company, 513–14
Adolph Coors Company, 556–57
Albany Ladder, 339
American Airlines, 105, 182, 353, 463–64, 473, 492, 554
American Brands, 8
American Express, 344
AMR Corporation, 353–54, 355, 362, 464–65, 468–69, 473–74, 494
Amway, 284
Anacomp Meter Company, 285–87
Apple Computer, 581
Arden, Inc., 365–66
Arthur Andersen & Company, 3, 509, 541
Atlanta Braves, 182
Austin Sound Stereo Center, 185–92, 194–99, 201–2, 204, 211, 228–36, 253–62, 270–71

b

Bain Company, 303–4
Baker & McKenzie, 514
Bank of America, 246, 307, 313
Barnes & Noble, Inc., 194
BDO Seidman, 3
Best Buy, 181
Beth Denius, Limited, 490
Bethlehem Steel Corporation, 579
BF Goodrich Company, 560
B.G. Graphics, 46
Big-Hit Theatre, 294–95
Black & Decker Corporation, 389
Bloomingdale's, 154
Blumenthal's, 481–86
BMW, 471
Boeing Company, 8, 227, 443, 452, 496
Bradlees, 293
British Airways, 443
British Petroleum, 443, 549–50
Brown-Forman Corporation, 553
Brun Sales Company, 192–93
Burger King, Inc., 145
Business Research, Inc., 295–96, 298–302
Business Research Associates, 298–302
Butler Supply Co., 337–38

c

Cabletron Systems, 363
Campbell Soup Company, 410, 451
Campus Apartment Locators, 23–25
Cartier, 311
Caterpillar Tractor, 247
CBS, Inc., 394, 544
Central Jersey Bancorp, 546
Centurion Homes, 488
Checkpoint Systems, 293
Chrysler Corporation, 290, 492
Coca-Cola Company, 10, 74, 246, 405, 456, 549–50, 569, 571
Collins Foods International, Inc., 456
Compaq, 581
Consolidated Edison Company (ConEd), 442
Consumer's Digest Company, 255
Continental Pipeline Company, 459
Coopers & Lybrand, 3, 509
County Line Bar-B-Q Restaurant, 434–35
CPC International, Inc., 346
Curtiss-Wright Corporation, 458–59

d

Dallas Cowboys, 442
Datapoint Corporation, 396
Dean Witter, 550
Dell Computer Corporation, 212, 581
Del Monte Foods, 322, 369, 473
Deloitte & Touche, 3, 307, 509
Delta Airlines, 463
Diamond Company, 345
Dillard's, 293
Dirk & Cross Partnership, 525
Discover, 246, 344
Dolby Noise-Reduction Systems, 441
Domino's Pizza, 439
Dorman Builders, 349, 350–51
Dow Chemical Company, 246
Dun & Bradstreet (D&B) Corporation, 470–71

e

Eastman Kodak, 248, 294
Eckerds, 222
Ernst & Young, 3, 509
Excel Communications, 284
Exxon, Inc., 32, 181, 357–58, 413–14
EyeMasters, 218

f

Famous-Barr, 181
Federated Department Stores, 154
Filene's, 181
First Boston Corporation, 550
Foley's, 181
Ford Motor Company, 95, 182, 216, 370, 493, 581

g

The Gap, Inc., 211, 213, 310–11, 416
Garcia Brick Co., 450
Gary Lyon, CPA, 14–22, 45–55, 57–60, 93–95, 96–104, 108–10, 138–44, 145–50, 151, 153, 177–79, 182
Gateway International, 581
General Electric Company (GE), 294, 349, 350–51, 352, 362, 443
General Motors Corporation (GM), 251, 312, 336, 425, 467, 471, 544, 581
Georgia-Pacific Corporation, 455–56
Glenwood Corporation, 552
Granite Shoals Corporation, 451
Grant Thornton, 3, 509
Greg Ogden Belting Company, 218
Grudnitski Company, 315–16

h

HAL, Inc., 548
Hallisey's Pharmacy, 245–46, 247, 248, 251
Harley-Davidson, Inc., 492–93
Hasbro, 211
Hawaiian Airlines, Inc., 95, 548
Hecht's, 181
Helping Hand, 5–7, 11, 12
Hershey Foods, 182, 247
H.J. Heinz Company, 476

Hoffman Supply, 349
Holiday Inns, 442, 463–64, 492
The Home Depot, Inc., 215, 373, 419–20, 421–24, 426–31, 433–34, 436, 439–40, 444–45, 447, 448
H & R Block Tax Services, 3
Hubbard Company, 432–33, 445
Huntington Galleries, 377–88, 391–92, 398–99

i

IBM Corporation, 151–53, 155, 200, 390–91, 447, 455, 474, 544, 581
IHOP Corporation (International House of Pancakes), 543–44, 550–52, 560, 562–65, 568
Intel Corporation, 73, 116–17, 211, 312, 340, 352, 362, 443
Interlogic, Inc., 349
International Paper Company, 322
It's Just Lunch, 91–92, 93, 111

j

Jaguar Motors, Ltd., 581
Jan King Distributing Company, 237–40
J.C. Penney Company, 94, 322, 339, 389, 549, 554
Johnson & Johnson, 101, 218, 222
Joseph D. Wesselkamper & Associates, Inc., 463
JVC Corporation, 185–92, 228–29, 259–60, 263–64

k

Kahn Corporation, 553
Kaufmann's, 181
Kellogg Company, 488
Kendrick Tire Company, 214, 241, 414
Kimberly Clark, 549
Kinko's, 246
Kmart, 150, 184, 415, 491
KPMG Peat Marwick, 3, 509, 540
Kroger, 227, 320
Kynetics Software, 284

l

Lands' End, Inc., 31, 43, 44–45, 67, 161, 212, 290–91, 413, 569–70
Larsen & Company, 289–94
Lewis and Clark Partnership, 515–16
Lexus, 581
The Limited, Inc., 311
Ling-Temco-Vought, Inc. (LTV), 497
Liz Claiborne, Inc., 210–11
Lord & Taylor, 181, 182, 210
Lotus, 441
L.S. Ayres, 181

m

McDonald's Corporation, 13, 97, 442, 493
McDonnell Douglas, 452
McGladrey & Pullen, 3, 509
Macy's, 304–5, 311, 318, 339
Main, Price & Anders, CPAs, 525–26
Marriott Corp., 463, 481, 483, 492
Mary Kay Cosmetics, 284
MasterCard, 246, 345, 366
Mattel, 211
Maxim Company, 472
May Department Stores Company, 181–84, 200–202, 203, 210, 212–13, 235, 413
MCI, 309–10
Medina Corporation, 554–55
Mercedes-Benz, 581
Merrill Lynch, 247, 550, 562
Mesa Hardware Company, 400–401
Mexana Company, 442
MicroAge Electronics Company, 477
Microsoft, 441
MiniScribe, 396
M & M Mars, 357
Monsanto, 246
Motorola, Inc., 137, 150, 176, 389

n

National Can Corporation, 352–53, 362
Nautica, 184
Nestlé, 363–64
NIKE, Inc., 38–39, 41, 86, 131, 175, 200, 226–27, 331–32, 374, 404, 416–17, 460, 503, 544, 581

o

Occidental Petroleum, 97
Owens-Corning, 389

p

Paine Webber, 562
Payco American Corp., 335
PepsiCo, Inc., 451, 496
Pharmacy Management Services, Inc. (PMSI), 217–18, 409
Philip Morris, 8
Phillips Petroleum Company, 443
Pine Industries, 558–60
Planet Hollywood, 519–20
Plaza Hotel, 92
Price Waterhouse, 3, 247, 509, 517
Procter & Gamble, 251–52, 443, 466–67, 492

r

Randy Vaughn, CPA, 302
Rexall Drug Stores, 218
Ricoh Digital Products, 275
Riggs Company, 265–67
RJR Nabisco, 8
Robinsons-May, 181
Royal Dutch Shell, 443
Rubenstein Jewelers, 352
Rutgers Accounting Web (RAW), 40

s

Safeway Stores, 182, 227
St. James Technology, 284–85
Saks Fifth Avenue, 294
Sam's Clubs, 327
Sara Nichols, Attorney, 62–66
Schmidt Builders Supply, 341–43
Schwinn Company, 374
Searle, 246
Sears, Roebuck & Co., 150, 181, 339, 375, 471
Shea & Gould, 524
Shea's Research Service, 55–56
Sheraton, 463
Sherwin Williams, 372
ShowBiz Pizza Time, Inc., 467–68
Sony, 182, 441
Southwest Airlines, 503
Sprint Corporation, 160, 162, 322, 362–63, 459, 549
State Service Company, 112–15, 142–43, 156–58
Stop-n-Shop, 320
Storage USA, 117
Strawbridge's, 181
Sumitomo Corporation, 319
Sun Company, Inc., 392–93
Symington Wayne Corporation, 439

t

Talon Computer Concepts, 307
Target Stores, 293, 327
Taylor & Uvalde, 528
Texaco, 411, 448–49
Tomassini Computer Service Center, 68–70
Tonka, 211
Top Cut Meats, 13
Toyota, 11, 471
Toys "Я" Us, Inc., 30–31, 211, 213–14, 326, 330, 405, 410–11

u

U and I Group, 576

Ultimax, Inc., 335–36, 340

Union Pacific Railroad, 247

United Airlines, 463

United Telecommunications, Inc., 459

USJVC Corporation. *See* **JVC Corporation**

V

VISA, 246, 345, 366

W

Wal-Mart Stores, Inc., 181, 184, 200–202, 221–22, 365, 378, 437–38, 442, 547, 568, 574

Walt Disney Company, 435–36

Wand Partners, Inc., 543

Wendy's, 393

Whirlpool Corporation, 409, 471–72

Whitehall, Inc., 566–67

Willis & Campi, Certified Public Accountants, 507–10

Winn Dixie, 320

X

Xerox Corporation, 105, 424–25, 479, 549–50

Y

Yankelovich-Clancy-Shulman, 59

Subject Index

a

Accelerated depreciation method, 430, 433–34
Account(s). *See also specific accounts*
  adjustments to, 96–106
  after posting, 54, 66
  in chart of accounts, 59–60
  defined, 44–45
  increases and decreases in, 47–49
  normal balance of, 60
  posting to, 52–54, 62–66
  on work sheet, 139, 141
Accountants
  certified management (CMAs), 2, 8
  certified public accountants (CPAs), 8
Account format
  of balance sheet, 153
  four column, 58–59
  T-accounts, 46–47
Accounting
  for business transactions, 14–18
  careers in, 1–3
  computers and. *See* Computerized accounting systems
  concepts and principles of. *See* Generally accepted accounting principles (GAAP)
  data, flow of, 51–54
  defined, 6
  development of, 8
  ethical issues of, 8–9
  public *vs.* private, 2
  separation of duties, 292–93
Accounting cycle
  completing, 143–49
  decision guidelines, 155–56
  defined, 138
  for merchandising operations, 205
  summary of computerized and manual, 251
Accounting equation, 12–14, 47, 49, 61
Accounting information
  in decision making, 67, 353–55
  users of, 6–7
Accounting information systems. *See also* Computerized accounting systems
  blending computers and special journals, 264
  comparison of computerized and manual, 247–51
  defined, 246
  features of, 246–47
  general journal role in, 262–67
  with special journals, 253
Accounting organizations, 3, 509
Accounting period, 93–94
Accounting ratios, 153–55. *See also* Ratios
Accounting work sheet. *See* Work sheet
Account number ranges, 249
Accounts payable, 13
Accounts Payable account
  as current liability, 150
  defined, 45
Accounts payable subsidiary ledger, 260, 264
Accounts receivable. *See also* Notes receivable
  aging, 341–42
  in computerized accounting system, 357
  credit balances in, 345
  as current asset, 336, 352
  defined, 13
Accounts Receivable account
  about, 44
  as control account, 336
  as current asset, 150
  validating, 283
Accounts receivable subsidiary ledger, 255, 264, 336
Accrual-basis accounting
  adjusting entries and, 144
  vs. cash-basis accounting, 92–93
  decision guidelines, 111
  ethical issues in, 111
  for merchandisers, 202–3
Accrued expense. *See also* Payroll
  adjusting entries to, 101–3, 106
  defined, 102, 469
  reversing entries for, 177
Accrued liability, 45. *See also* Accrued expense
Accrued revenue, adjusting entries to, 103–4, 106
Accumulated deficit, 547–48
Accumulated Depletion account, 440
Accumulated depreciation, 427
Accumulated Depreciation account, 100–101, 110, 436, 437–38
Acid-test ratio, 353–54
Additional paid-in capital, 555
Additional Paid-in Capital—Common account, 552
Adjusted bank balance, 299
Adjusted trial balance
  about, 106–8
  contra accounts on, 110
  decision guidelines, 111–12
  preparing financial statements from, 108–10, 138–42
  work sheet column, 138–40, 141
Adjusting entries
  about, 96–105
  accrual-basis accounting and, 144
  to accrued expense, 101–3, 106
  to accrued revenue, 103–4, 106
  decision guidelines, 111–12
  defined, 92
  to depreciation, 106
  examples of, 107, 112–15
  journalizing for merchandisers, 198–99
  journalizing in periodic inventory system, 235–36
  to prepaid expenses, 97–99, 106, 133–34
  process summary, 105–6
  recording, 144–45
  reversing entries and, 177, 178–79
  summary of, 106
  to trial balance, 92
  to unearned revenue, 104–5, 106
  on work sheet, 141
Adjustments
  to accounts, 96–106
  work sheet column, 138, 140–41, 195, 233
Advertising Expense account, 442
Aging of accounts receivable, 341
AICPA Code of Professional Conduct, 9, 312
Allowance for Doubtful Accounts account, 339
Allowance for Uncollectible Accounts account, 339
Allowances. *See also* Purchase returns and allowances
  about, 191–92
  recording, 229, 262–64
  reporting on, 352–53
Allowances account, 191–92
American Institute of Certified Public Accountants (AICPA)
  about, 8
  Code of Professional Conduct, 312
  inventory costing method survey of, 388
  survey on depreciation, 432
Amortization
  accounting for, 441–43
  defined, 441
  as depreciation on leasehold improvements, 422
  plant assets and, 420
Amortization Expense account, 441
Andersen, Arthur, 541
Appelbaum, Malcolm P., 543
Articles of partnership, 508, 534–35

Asset(s)
classification of, 150
as debit/credit, 47
in debt ratio, 154
defined, 12
fully depreciated, 428
lump-sum (basket) purchase of, 424–25
separation of custody, 292
types of, 420–21
for uncollectible accounts, 342
on work sheet, 139, 141
Asset accounts
in chart of accounts, 248
charts of, for different business types, 87–88
types of, 44–45
Auditing, 2, 283, 293
Auditors
for electronic data processing, 294
external, 293
internal, 2, 293
Authorization
proper, 291
of stock, 550
Available-for-Sale Investments, 150
Average cost method. *See* Weighted-average cost method

b

Backdating, 313
Bad debts. *See* Uncollectible accounts
Balance of account, normal, 60–61
Balance per bank, 299
Balance per books, 299
Balance sheet. *See also* Classified balance sheet
with acid-test ratio, 353
cash reporting on, 311–12
comparison of inventory methods, 388
contra accounts on, 110
with current and contingent liabilities, 464
defined, 20, 341
examples of, 21, 110, 144, 151
formats of, 153
with intangible assets, 420
with inventory, 379
with lower-of-cost-or-market effects, 394
for merchandisers, 197, 234
normal balance of accounts, 61
order of preparation, 110
for partnerships, 512, 526
with payroll liabilities, 488
with plant assets, 420
with receivables, 337
relationship to other financial statements, 110
with stockholders' equity, 547, 552, 554, 555, 561
with unearned revenues, 471
work sheet column, 140–42, 196, 233
Balancing the ledgers, 264
Bank account
as control device, 295–302
for payroll, 483
Bankcard sales, 345
Bank charges, 299
Bank collections, 297, 299
Bank reconciliation
about, 296–99
illustrated, 299–300
journalizing transactions from, 300–302
preparing, 299
using, 302
Bank statements, 295–96
Basket purchase of assets, 424–25
Batch processing, 250
Benefits, 487
Benefits expenses, 480
Bill (invoice), 185, 186, 306
Board of directors, 545
Bohman, James R., 335
Bond(s), fidelity, 294
Bonus, 469
Bookkeeping, 6
Books. *See* Ledger
Books, adjusting. *See* Adjusting entries
Book value
defined, 101
example of, 428
of stock, 560–62
Brand names, 441–42
Budget(s)
for cash management, 309–11
defined, 309–10
in private accounting, 2
Building account
about, 44
as fixed asset, 150
Buildings, 422
Burglar alarms, 294
Business decisions. *See* Decision making
Business income, adjusting process, 111–12
Business organizations, types of, 9–10
Business transactions, 14–18
Bylaws, 545

c

Cafeteria plans, 479
Calendar year, 94
Callable preferred stock, 560
Campi, Ann, 507–10
Canceled checks, 295
Capital. *See also* Owners' equity
defined, 12
legal, 548
paid-in, 547, 554–55
Capital account
about, 45
closing entries to, 146–48, 199
normal balance of, 62
Capital balance, on liquidation, 525
Capital contributions, partner sharing based on, 513–15
Capital expenditures
defined, 425
vs. revenue expenditures, 425–26
Capitalizing a cost
decision guidelines, 444
defined, 423
ethical issues of, 443–44
Capitalizing interest, 423–24
Capital leases, 423
Capital stock, 546
Careers in accounting, 1–3
Carrying amount, 428. *See also* Book value
Carrying value. *See* Book value; Carrying amount
Cash
balance sheet reporting, 311–12
safeguarding, 295
Cash account
about, 44
balance per books, 299
as current assets, 150
in reconciliation, 296, 298
Cash-basis accounting, *vs.* accrual-basis accounting, 92–93
Cash budget, 309–11
Cash disbursements
internal control over, 306–9
for payroll, 484–87
on statement of cash flows, 20
Cash disbursements journal, 260–62, 332
Cash dividends, accounting for, 557–59
Cash flows, 202–3. *See also* Statement of cash flows
Cash over situation, 305, 309
Cash payments. *See* Cash disbursements
Cash payments journal, 260–62
Cash receipts, 304–6
Cash receipts journal, 256–58
Cash registers, 294, 304–5
Cash sales
operating cycle for, 183
recording, 189–90
Cash Short and Over account, 305
Cash short situation, 305, 309
Certified management accountants (CMAs), 2, 8
Certified public accountants (CPAs), 8
Chairperson, 545
Change, in accounting estimate, 435
Charitable gifts, 479
Charter, corporate, 544
Chart of accounts
designing, 248–49
for different business types, 87–88
examples of, 59
in ledger, 59–60
Check register (cash disbursements journal), 260–62, 332
Checks
controls over payment by, 306
cost of printing, 298, 299

defined, 295
nonsufficient funds (NSF), 298
outstanding, 297, 299
payroll, 483, 484
with remittance advice, 296
returned, 298
Chief operating officer, 545
Classified balance sheet, 60–61, 151–53
Closing entries
about, 146–48
journalizing, 145, 147
journalizing for merchandisers, 198–99
journalizing in periodic inventory system, 235–36
posting, 145
reversing entries and, 177
Closing the accounts, 137, 145–48
Code of ethics, 9, 312
Collection period, 354–55
Collusion, 295
Combined statement of earnings, for partnerships, 526
Comer, Gary, 45
Commission, 469
Common stock
about, 548–49
dividends on, 557–58
issuing, 550–53
as paid-in capital, 547
Common stockholders' equity, rate of return on, 562–63
Compatibility of information systems, 246
Compensation, employee. *See* Payroll
Computerized accounting systems. *See also* Accounting information systems; Spreadsheets
accounts receivable and, 357
account structure for, 249
auditors of, 294
comparison with manual system, 247–51
components of, 247
controls in, 293–94
cost/benefit relationships of, 246–47
error elimination by, 54
general journal and, 246
general ledger and, 246
integrated accounting software, 251–52
inventory systems, 184, 398
main menu example, 250
overview of, 248
payroll calculations with, 487
reports submenu example, 250
software, defined, 247
Conservatism, 393–94
Consignment, 384
Consistency principle, 392–93
Consolidated statements, financial position, 152
Construction in progress, 422
Contingent liability
about, 473–74
on balance sheet, 464
decision guidelines, 475–76
defined, 351
disclosure principle and, 473
on discounted notes receivable, 351
ethical issues for, 474–75
Continuous life of corporations, 544
Contra accounts, 100, 110
Contra asset account, 100
Contributed capital (paid-in capital), 547, 554–55
Control
internal. *See* Internal control
over operations, 246
for payroll disbursements, 488
for payroll efficiency, 487
Control account
Accounts Receivable account as, 336
decision guidelines, 265
defined, 256
Controller, 291
Convertible preferred stock, 559
Co-ownership of partnership property, 509
Copyrights, 441
Corporate taxation, 473, 545, 563–65
Corporation
advantages and disadvantages of, 545
authority structure in, 546
capital stock of, 546
characteristics of, 544–45
compared to other entities, 545
decision guidelines, 565
defined, 9–10
dividends of. *See* Dividends
donations to, 554
income taxes on, 473, 545, 563–65
manufacturing, 88
merchandising, 88
organizational chart of, 292
organization of, 545
partnership advantages *vs.*, 510
stock, classes of, 548–49
stock, issuing, 549–53
Correcting entries, 149–50
Cost accounting, 2
Cost/benefit relationships, 246–47
Costing methods, for inventory, 385–87
Cost of asset, 382, 421
Cost of goods
available for sale, 383
overstatement of, 395
Cost of Goods Sold account, 190–91, 194, 195, 198–99, 204, 380–82, 383
Cost of goods sold (cost of sales)
computing, 229
defined, 182
in gross margin method, 397
matching principle and, 95
measuring, 383–84
in merchandising company, 378
in periodic inventory system, 203–4, 230
recording, 189–92
Cost of sales. *See* Cost of goods sold (cost of sales)
Cost principle, 11
Credit
expanded rules of, 62
rules of, 47
Credit balance
in accounts receivable, 345
example of, 54
Credit-balance accounts, 60
Credit-card sales, 344–45
Credit department, 338–39
Credit memorandum, 262–63
Creditors, 336
Cumulative preferred stock, 558
Current asset. *See also* Accounts receivable
accounts receivable as, 336, 352
in current ratio, 153–54
defined, 150
Current liability. *See also* Payroll
Accounts Payable account as, 150
in current ratio, 153–54
decision guidelines, 475–76
defined, 150
with estimation mandatory, 471–73
ethical issues for, 474–75
Interest Payable accounts as, 150
of known amount, 464
Notes Payable account as, 150
Salary Payable accounts as, 150
Unearned Revenue accounts as, 150
Current maturity, 468
Current portion of long-term debt, 468
Current ratio, 153–55
Current replacement cost, 394
Customer prepayment. *See* Unearned revenue

d

Data, flow of, 51–54
Database, 247
Data processing, stages of, 248. *See also* Accounting information systems; Computerized accounting systems
Date of record, 557
Days' sales in receivables, 354–55
Debit
expanded rules of, 62
rules of, 47
Debit balance, 54
Debit-balance accounts, 60
Debit memorandum, 263–64
Debt, long term, 468. *See also* Uncollectible accounts
Debtor, 336
Debt ratio, 154–55
Decision making. *See also* Ratios
accounting information for, 67, 353–55
with accounting ratios, 153–55
guidelines, 23
for merchandisers, 200–202
Declaration date of dividend, 557
Deductions, on payroll, 477, 478–79, 481–82, 484–85

Default on a note, 351
Deferrals, 97–101
Deferred revenue. *See* Unearned revenue
Deficit, 547–48
Depletion, 420
Depletion expense, 440
Deposits in transit, 297, 299
Deposit ticket, 295
Depreciable asset, changing useful life of, 435–37
Depreciable cost, 427
Depreciation
  about, 426–27
  accelerated method of, 430, 433–34
  accumulated, 100–101, 110, 427, 436, 437–38
  adjusting entries to, 106
  causes of, 427
  comparing methods of, 431–32
  defined, 99
  double-declining balance (DDB) method of, 430
  as estimated figure, 111
  full-year, 435
  generally accepted accounting principles (GAAP) for, 431
  income taxes and, 433–34
  measuring, 427
  methods of, 427–30
  for partial years, 434–35
  of plant assets, 99–101, 426–32
  plant assets and, 420
  straight-line (SL) method of, 428, 429, 433–34
  sum-of-years'-digits method of, 427–28
  units-of-production method of, 428–29
Depreciation Expense account, 436
Design
  of chart of accounts, 248–49
  of information systems, 2
Development costs, 443
Direct write-off method, 344
Disbursement packet, 306
Disclosure principle, 393, 473
Discount
  from purchase prices, 185–87
  sales, 191–92
Discounted notes receivable, contingent liabilities on, 351
Discounting
  notes payable, 466
  notes receivable, 350, 467
Discount on Notes Payable account, 466–67
Dishonored notes receivable, 351
Dissolution, of partnership, 508
Dividends
  cash, 557–59
  on cumulative and noncumulative preferred stock, 558–59
  dates for, 557
  defined, 548
  on preferred and common stock, 557–58
  to stockholders, 548
Documents
  internal control over, 293
  as journals in manual accounting, 264
Donated Capital account, 554
Donations to corporations, 554
Double-declining balance (DDB) depreciation method, 430
Double-entry accounting, 46–49
Double taxation, 545
Doubtful-account expense, 339
Drawing, on partnerships, 516
Duties, separation of, 291–93, 488

e

Earl, Robert, 519
Earnings record, 483–85
EDGAR (Electronic Data Gathering, Analysis, and Retrieval System), 41
Efficiency, payroll controls for, 487
Electronic control devices, 293
Electronic data processing auditors, 294
Electronic funds transfer (EFT)
  in bank reconciliation, 297
  cash payments, 299
  cash receipts, 299
  defined, 296
Employee earnings record, 484, 486
Employee Income Tax Payable account, 469–70
Employees
  benefits of, 477, 487
  compensation of. *See* Payroll
  internal control and, 291
  net pay to, 484
Employee Social Security (FICA) tax, 478–79
Employee Union Dues Payable account, 479
Employee Wage and Tax Statement (Form W-2), 484, 486
Employee Withholding Allowance Certificate (Form W-4), 478
Employer Earnings Record (Form 941), 483–85
Employer FICA tax, 479
Employer payroll taxes, 479
Ending inventory, in gross margin method, 397
Entity concept, 10–11
Equipment, 422
Equipment account
  about, 45
  as fixed asset, 150
Errors
  in bank reconciliation, 298–302
  correction in trial balance, 54–55
  elimination by computerized accounting systems, 54
  inventory, effects of, 395
Estimated residual value, 427
Estimated useful life
  defined, 427
  ethical issues of, 111
  surpassing, 436
Estimated vacation pay liability, 472
Estimated warranty payable, 471–72
Ethical issues
  in accounting, 8–9, 312–15
  in accrual accounting, 111
  for current and contingent liabilities, 474–75
  in inventory accounting, 396–97
  in plant assets and intangibles accounting, 443–44
  in stock issuance, 553–54
Expected realizable value, 342
Expenditures, capital *vs.* revenue expenditures, 425–26
Expense accounts
  about, 45
  in chart of accounts, 248
  closing entries, 145
Expenses
  about, 60–62
  accrued, 101–3, 106, 177, 469
  cash-basis recording of, 93
  defined, 13
  depletion, 440
  examples of use, 62–66
  matching against revenue, 95
  payroll, reporting, 488–89
  prepaid, 44, 97–99, 106, 133–34
  for uncollectible accounts, 342
  on work sheet, 141
External auditors, 293
External controls, and ethics, 314–15
Extraordinary repair, 425

f

FASB. *See* Financial Accounting Standards Board (FASB)
Federal Insurance Contributions Act (FICA), 470, 478
Federal National Mortgage Association (Fannie Mae), 350
Federal unemployment compensation tax, 479
Fidelity bonds, 294
FIFO. *See* First-in, first-out (FIFO) method
Financial accounting, 7
Financial Accounting Standards Board (FASB)
  about, 8
  on contingencies, 473
  contingent liability guidelines of, 474
  generally accepted accounting principles (GAAP), 10
  on postretirement benefits, 487
  on research and development costs, 443
  on World Wide Web, 40–41
Financial ratios. *See* Ratios
Financial statements. *See also specific statements*
  about, 18–22
  defined, 6
  headings for, 20
  for merchandisers, 197–99, 200–202, 233–36

order of preparation, 108, 110
for partnerships, 525–26
preparing from adjusted trial balance, 108–10, 138–42
preparing from work sheet, 143–44
for proprietorships, 525–26
relationships among, 20–22, 110
reporting inventory transactions, 381
work sheet to prepare. *See* Work sheet
Financing activities, 356
Fireproof vaults, 294
First-in, first-out (FIFO) method
comparison with other methods, 387
decision guidelines, 399
defined, 386
illustrated, 386
income effects of, 387
perpetual inventory records for, 391–92
Fiscal year, 94
Fixed assets, 150, 420. *See also* Plant asset(s)
Flexibility, of information systems, 246
FOB (free on board) terms, 187–89
Foreign Corrupt Practices Act, 290
Form 941, 483–85
Form W-2, 484, 486
Form W-4, 478
Four-column account format, 58–59
Fraction, partner sharing based on, 512–13
Franchises, 442
Freight-in costs, 188–89
Freight-out costs, 189
Frequent-flier programs, 463–64
Fully depreciated assets, 428, 436–37
Full-year depreciation, 435
Furniture and Fixtures account, 45, 150, 437–38

g

GAAP. *See* Generally accepted accounting principles (GAAP)
Gain(s), on sale of noncash assets, 524–25
General expenses, for merchandisers, 233
General journal
accounting information system role of, 262–67
computerization of, 246
defined, 252
General ledger
balancing, 264
cash accounts in, 298
computerization of, 246
posting from cash disbursements journal, 261–62
posting from cash receipts journal, 258
posting from purchases journal, 260
posting from sales journal, 255, 256
stock classes in, 548
Generally accepted accounting principles (GAAP)
accrual basis and, 93
for amortization, 441
for change in accounting estimate, 435–36
defined, 10
for depreciation, 431
for goodwill, 442
inventory methods and, 388–89
materiality concept and, 393
relevance to inventories, 392–94
for research and development costs, 443
reversing entries and, 177
General partners, 509, 510
Gifts, to corporations, 554
Going-concern concept, 11–12
Going public, 544
Goodwill
about, 420, 442–43
defined, 442
Government regulation, of corporations, 545
Gross margin (gross profit)
defined, 183, 379
detailed in income statement, 230
measuring, 384
Gross margin (gross profit) method, 397, 399
Gross margin (gross profit) percentage, 201, 397
Gross pay
about, 469
decision guidelines, 489
defined, 477
on payroll register, 481–82
Gross profit. *See* Gross margin (gross profit)
Gross profit percentage, 201, 397
Gross salary, 480

h

Hallisey, Bob, 245
Hallisey, Maureen, 245
Hardware, 247
Health insurance (Medicare), 478–79
Held-to-maturity investments, 150
Historical cost, 11

i

Iacocca, Lee, 290
Illusory profit, 388
Imprest system, 308
Income. *See* Net income; Operating income
Income statement
adjusting entries and, 92
comparison of inventory methods, 388
on corporations, 473, 545, 563–65
defined, 19
with detailed gross margin section, 230
examples of, 21, 109, 144
with inventory, 379, 390–91
listing expenses on, 109
with lower-of-cost-or-market effects, 394
for merchandisers, 197, 198, 234
multi-step and single-step formats, 200
order of preparation, 108
for partnerships, 526
relationship to other financial statements, 20, 110
statement of earnings compared to, 182
work sheet column, 139–42, 195–96, 233
Income statement approach, 340
Income summary, 146
Income Summary account, 146–47, 198–99
Income tax
comparison of inventory methods, 388, 389
on corporations, 563–65
depreciation and, 433–34
LIFO advantages for, 387–88
partnerships and, 509
Income Tax Expense account, 473
Income Tax Payable account, 473
Inflation, 12
Information systems design, 2. *See also* Accounting information systems
Inputs, 247
Institute of Management Accountants (IMA)
about, 8
Standards of Ethical Conduct, 9, 312
Insurance expenses, 480
Intangible assets
about, 420
accounting for, 441–43
defined, 421
terminology of, 421
Integrated accounting software, 251–52
Interest
capitalizing cost of, 423–24
computing for notes, 347–48
partner sharing based on, 515–16
Interest Expense account, 198
Interest Payable account, 45, 150, 468
Interest period, 347
Interest rate, 347
Interest revenue
on checking accounts, 298, 299
on notes receivable, 349
Interest Revenue account, 198
Interim statements, 342
Internal auditors, 2, 293
Internal control
about, 290–95
with bank account, 295–302
defined, 246
employees and, 291
for inventory, 398
over cash disbursements, 306–9
over cash receipts, 304–6
over documents, 293
over payroll, 487–88, 502
over plant assets, 439
over receivables collection, 337–38
Internal Revenue Code, Subchapter S, 511
Internal Revenue Service (IRS)
corporations filing with, 564
earnings records filed with, 483–84
partnership income, reporting to, 510

International accounting
goodwill, 443
inventory methods, 389
transactions, 311
Internet, 40–41. *See also* World Wide Web
Inventory account
as current asset, 150
in merchandising business, 194
in perpetual inventory system, 186–91, 380–82
relationship with Cost of Goods Sold account, 204
Inventory accounting, ethical issues in, 396–97
Inventory(ies)
about, 182
adjusting based on physical count, 194
basic accounting concepts, 379
comparison of methods, 388–89
computing cost of, 384–85
costing methods, 385–87
decision guidelines, 399–400
errors, effects of, 395
estimating, 397–98
ethical issues of accounting, 396–97
generally accepted accounting principles (GAAP) and, 392–94
internal control over, 398
purchases in periodic inventory system, 203–4
recording purchase of, 228
recording sale of, 229
selling, 189–92
system types, 379–83
transactions on statement of cash flows, 398–99
Inventory liquidation, 389
Inventory profit, 388
Inventory systems, 184
Inventory turnover, 201–2
Investing activities, 355
Investment(s), in partnerships, 511–12
Invoice, 185, 186, 306
Issued stock, 550
Issue price, 550

j

Job rotation, 294
Johnson, Don, 520
Johnson, Kenneth J., 137
Journal(s). *See also* General journal
cash disbursements, 260–62, 332
cash payments, 260–62
cash receipts, 256–58
decision guidelines, 265
defined, 49
documents as, 264
posting from, 51, 57–58
purchases, 258–60
recording inventory transactions, 381
sales, 253–56
special accounting, 252–53
Journal entries
correcting, 149–50
posting to ledger, 51
Journalizing
about, 52–54
from bank reconciliation, 300–302
closing entries, 145, 147
delaying, 144
details of, 56–59
examples of, 62–66
merchandisers' adjusting and closing entries, 198–99
for periodic inventory system, 235–36, 382
for perpetual inventory system, 380–82
steps of, 49–51
Journal references, in ledgers, 57, 255–56
Just-in-time (JIT) inventory systems, 398

l

La Comb, Charlotte, 43
Land, 421–22
Land account
about, 44
as fixed asset, 150
Land improvements, 421
Last-in, first-out (LIFO) method
comparison of methods, 387
decision guidelines, 399
defined, 386
illustrated, 386
income effects of, 387
income tax advantage of, 387–88
perpetual inventory records for, 392
Leasehold, 442
Leasehold improvements, 422
Ledger
balancing, 264
chart of accounts in, 59–60
defined, 44
details of, 56–59
journal references in, 255–56
posting to, 51, 57–58
subsidiary, 255, 258, 260
Ledger account, 107
Legal capital, 548
Legal Revenue account, 134
Leverage, 563
Liability account
about, 45
in chart of accounts, 248
charts of, for different business types, 87–88
Liability(ies). *See also* Accounts payable; Notes payable
accrued, 45
classification of, 150–51
contingent. *See* Contingent liability
current. *See* Current liability
as debit/credit, 47
in debt ratio, 154
defined, 12
limited, 10, 544–45
long term. *See* Long-term liability
payroll, reporting, 488–89
unearned revenue as, 150
unlimited personal, 509
on work sheet, 139, 141
Licenses, 442
LIFO method. *See* Last-in, first-out (LIFO) method
Limited liability, of stockholders, 544–45
Limited liability partnerships (LLPs), 510
Limited life, of partnership, 508
Limited partnership, 509, 510
Limited personal liability, 10
Liquidation
about, 93–94
defined, 523
stockholders and, 548
Liquidation value, 560
Lock-box systems, 297, 305
Long-term assets, 150. *See also* Intangible assets; Plant asset(s)
Long-term debt. *See* Long-term liability
Long-term liability
about, 150–51
vs. current liability, 464
current portion of, 468
Long-term receivables, 336
Loss(es)
net, 17, 20, 92, 139
partnership sharing of, 512–16
sale of noncash partnership assets, 525
Loss on Disposal of Store Fixtures account, 437
Lower-of-cost-or-market rule (LCM), 394
Lump-sum (basket) purchase of assets, 424–25

m

McGinty, Andrea, 91, 111
Machinery and equipment, 422
Mail cash receipts, 305
Major repair, 425
Maker of note, 295, 347
Management accounting, 7
Management consulting, 2
Management information system, 247
Mandatory vacations, 294
Manufacturing company, chart of accounts, 88
Market value (market price), 394, 559–60, 560–61
Matching principle, 95, 487
Materiality concept, 393
Maturity date of note, 347
Maturity value of note, 347
Medicare, 478–79
Menu, 249
Menu-driven accounting systems, 249–50
Merchandise
purchasing in periodic inventory systems, 228–29

purchasing in perpetual inventory system, 185–89
return of, 187, 191–92
Merchandise inventory, 378. *See also* Inventory(ies)
Merchandising business
accrual accounting and cash flows for, 202–3
adjusting and closing accounts for, 194–96, 229–33
chart of accounts, 88
defined, 375
financial statements of, 197–99, 233–36
journalizing adjusting and closing entries, 198–99
operating cycle of, 183
work sheet of, 194–96
Merchandising operations
about, 182–83
decision guidelines, 205
ethical issues for, 218
Miscellaneous Expense account, 109
Modified Accelerated Cost Recovery System (MACRS), 434, 564
Multi-step income statement, 200
Mutual agency
corporations and, 544
in partnership, 508–9

n

Natural resources, 440
Neely, Bill, 46
Negative retained earnings, 547–48
Negotiable instruments, 350. *See also* Notes receivable
Net assets, 13
Net book value. *See* Book value
Net earnings. *See* Net income
Net income
adjusting entries and, 92
defined, 17
on income statement, 20
on work sheet, 139
Net loss
adjusting entries and, 92
defined, 17
on income statement, 20
on work sheet, 139
Net profit. *See* Net income
Net purchases, 204, 385. *See also* Purchase
Net sales, 182
Net (take-home) pay, 469, 477, 482–83, 484, 489
Network, 247
Nominal (temporary) account, 145
Noncumulative preferred stock, 559
Nonsufficient funds (NSF) checks, 298
No-par stock, 549, 552–53
Normal balance of account, 60
Note period, 347
Notes
interest period of, 347
interest rate of, 347
Notes payable
cosigning, 474
defined, 13
long term, 150
short term, 465–67
Notes Payable, Short-Term account, 465–66
Notes Payable account
about, 45
as current liability, 150
Notes receivable
about, 346–48
accounting for, 348–52
vs. accounts receivable, 336
defined, 13
discounting, 350, 467
interest revenue on, 349
selling, 349–51
Notes Receivable account
about, 44
as current asset, 150

o

Objectivity principle, 11
Obsolescence, 427
Office Equipment account, 45
Office Supplies account, 44
Old age, survivors', and disability insurance (OASDI), 478
On-line processing, 250
Operating activities, 355
Operating cycle, 150, 183
Operating expenses
defined, 198
for merchandisers, 233
Operating income
defined, 198
for merchandisers, 233
Operating leases, 423
Operations
merchandising, 203
separation from accounting, 291
Organizational chart, example of, 292
Other assets, 150
Other expense, 198, 235
Other receivables, 337
Other revenue, 198, 235
Outputs, 248. *See also* Financial statements
Outstanding checks, 297, 299
Outstanding deposits, 297, 299
Outstanding stock, 546
Overstatement
of asset values, 554
of cost of goods, 395
Over-the-counter cash receipts, 304–5
Overtime pay, 477
Owners' equity. *See also* Stockholders' equity
about, 13–14
as debit/credit, 47
defined, 12
statement of. *See* Statement of owners' equity
on work sheet, 139, 141
Owners' Equity account
about, 45
in chart of accounts, 87, 248
of partners, 509–10
revenues and expenses, 60–66
Ownership, of corporations, 544
Owners' Withdrawals account, 110
Owner withdrawals, 13

p

Paid-in capital (contributed capital), 547, 554–55
Paid-in Capital in Excess of Par—Common account, 550, 552–53
Paid voucher file, 332
Partial-year depreciation, 434–35
Partners' Capital account, 510
Partner sharing
based on capital contributions, 513–15
based on capital contributions and on service, 514
based on salaries and interest, 515–16
based on stated fraction, 512–13
Partnership
admission of partner, 516–21
advantages and disadvantages of, 510
characteristics of, 508
combined statement of earnings, 526
compared to other entities, 10
corporation advantages *vs.*, 510
death of partner, 523
defined, 9, 508
drawing on, 516
financial statements, 525–26
guidelines, 257
initial investments in, 511–12
sharing profits and losses, 512–16
types of, 510–11
Partnership agreement, 508, 534–35
Partnership liquidation
about, 523–24
sale of noncash assets at a gain, 524–25
sale of noncash assets at a loss, 525
Partnership withdrawals
about, 521–22
at book value, 522
at less than book value, 522–23
at more than book value, 523
Par value, issuing stock at, 549, 550–52
Passing the dividend, 558
Patents, 441
Payables. *See* Accounts payable; Notes payable
Payee of note, 295, 347
Payment date, 557
Payments, control over approval, 306–7
Payroll
accounting for, 477

bank account for, 483
cash disbursements for, 484–87
controls for disbursements, 488
cost breakdown, 480
decision guidelines, 475–76, 489
deductions, 477, 478–79, 481–82, 484–85
defined, 469
employer taxes, 479
entries, 480–81
expense reporting, 488–89
internal control over, 487–88, 502
liabilities, 469–70
liability reporting, 488–89
optional deductions, 479
required deductions, 478–79
Payroll checks, 483, 484
Payroll journal, 481–83
Payroll register, 481–83
Payroll savings plans, 479
Payroll system, 481–84
Payroll tax, 480, 484–85. *See also* Employer Earnings Record (Form 941)
Pension, 487
Pension expenses, 480
Percent of sales method, 340, 342
Periodic inventory system
adjusting and closing accounts in, 229–33
decision guidelines, 399
defined, 184, 379
journalizing adjusting and closing entries, 235–36
measurements in, 203–4
perpetual inventory system compared with, 255, 382–83
purchasing merchandise in, 228–29
relationship of accounts in, 204
work sheets for, 232–33
Permanent (real) accounts, 145–46
Perpetual inventory system
about, 380–82
decision guidelines, 399
defined, 184, 379–80
under FIFO method, 391–92
under LIFO method, 392
periodic inventory system compared with, 255, 382–83
purchasing merchandise in, 185–89
under weight-average cost method, 392
Petty cash
defined, 307
disbursements, 307–9
Petty Cash account, 308–9
Petty cash ticket, 308, 309
Phantom profit, 388
Physical system. *See* Periodic inventory system
Plant asset(s)
on balance sheet, 420
decision guidelines, 444
defined, 99, 420
depreciation of, 99–101, 426–32
ethical issues, 443–44
exchanging, 439
internal control over, 439
measuring cost of, 421–25
measuring depreciation of, 426–32
selling, 437–38
on statement of cash flows, 444–45
terminology of, 421
Point-of-sale terminals, 294, 304–5
Postclosing trial balance, 148–49
Posting
to accounts, 52–54, 62–66
from cash disbursements journal, 261–62
from cash receipts journal, 258
closing entries, 145
in general ledger, 255, 258, 260, 261–62
inventory transactions, 381
to ledger, 51, 57–58
from purchases journal, 260
from sales journal, 255
to subsidiary ledger, 255, 258, 260
Postretirement benefit, 487
Preemptive right of stockholders, 548
Preferred stock
defined, 549
dividends on, 557–58, 558–59
issuing, 553
redemption value of, 560
values of, 560–61
Preferred Stock account, 553
Premium, stock issued at, 550–52
Premium on Common Stock account, 552
Prenumbered documents, 293
Prepaid Advertising account, 133
Prepaid expenses
adjusting entries to, 97–99, 106, 133–34
alternative accounting for, 133
defined, 44
recorded initially as expense, 133–34
Prepaid Expenses account
about, 44
as current asset, 150
Prepaid Insurance account, 44, 133
Prepaid Legal Cost account, 133
Prepaid Rent account, 44, 97–98, 133–34
Prepaids, 97–101
Present value, 350
President of corporation, 545
Price(s)
discount from purchase, 185–87
issue, 550
market, 394, 559–60, 560–61
Pricing with uneven amounts, 305
Principal, of note, 347
Principles. *See* Generally accepted accounting principles (GAAP)
Private accountants, 2
Proceeds, of notes receivable, 350
Processing, 248
Professional codes of conduct, 9, 312
Profit
gross. *See* Gross margin (gross profit)
inventory, 388
net. *See* Net income
partnership sharing of, 512–16
Profit-and-loss ratio, on liquidation, 525
Promissory note, 44, 336, 346, 347
Proper authorization, 291
Property, co-ownership in partnership, 509
Property, plant, and equipment. *See* Plant asset(s)
Proprietorship
compared to other entities, 10, 508
defined, 9
financial statements for, 525–26
partnership advantages *vs.*, 510
service, 87
Proving the ledgers, 264
Public accountants
about, 2–3
certified public accountants (CPAs), 8
Purchase
lump-sum (basket) purchase of assets, 424–25
net, 204, 385
Purchase discounts, 185–87, 189, 228
Purchase invoice, 185
Purchase order, 306
Purchase price, discount from, 185–87
Purchase requests, 306
Purchase returns and allowances, 187, 189, 229, 263–64
Purchase Returns and Allowances account, 229
Purchases journal, 258–60
Purchasing
controls over, 306
overview of, 307

q

Quantity discounts, 185–86
Quick ratio, 353–54

r

Rate of return on common stockholders' equity, 562–63
Rate of return on total assets, 562
Ratios
accounting ratios, 153–55
acid-test ratio, 353–54
current ratio, 153–55
debt ratio, 154–55
gross margin percentage, 201, 397
inventory turnover, 201–2
profit-and-loss ratio, 525
rate of return on common stockholders' equity, 562–63
rate of return on total assets, 562
Real (permanent) account, 145–46
Receivables. *See also* Accounts receivable
about, 336–39
days' sales in, 354–55
decision guidelines, 338
defined, 336
reporting on, 352–53, 355–56
transactions, 356
Receiving report, 306

Recording of transactions. *See* Transaction recording
Records, internal control over, 293
Redeemable preferred stock, 560
Regulation, government, 545
Relative-sales-value method, 424
Reliability (objectivity) principle, 11
Remittance advice, 295, 296
Rent Expense account, 98
Repairs, 425
Replacement cost, current, 394
Reported income, managing, 388–89
Reports
  balance sheet format, 153
  preparing accounting reports, 250
Requisitions, 306
Research and development (R&D) costs, 443
Residual, 13
Residual value, 427, 428
Responsibilities
  assignment of, 291
  division of, 291, 292
Retained earnings, 547–48
Returned checks, 298
Return on assets, 562
Return on equity, 562–63
Returns
  merchandise, 187, 191–92
  purchase, 187, 189, 229, 263–64
  sales, 191–92
Revenue(s)
  about, 60–62
  accrual-basis recording of, 93
  accrued, 103–4, 106
  defined, 13, 45
  examples of use, 62–66
  matching expenses against, 95
  other, 198, 235
  prepaid revenue recorded initially as, 134
  recording, 94–95
  sales, 182
  service, 15–16
  unearned, 104–5, 106
  on work sheet, 141
Revenue account
  about, 45
  in chart of accounts, 248
  closing entries, 145
Revenue collected in advance. *See* Unearned revenue
Revenue expenditures
  vs. capital expenditures, 425–26
  defined, 425
Revenue from Donations account, 554
Revenue principle, 94–95
Reversing entries, 177–79

S

Salary
  defined, 469
  partner sharing based on, 515–16
Salary expense, 480
Salary Expense account, 102–3
Salary Payable account, 45, 103, 150, 483
Sale of inventory, 229. *See also* Sales revenue
Sales discounts, 191–92
Sales invoice, 185
Sales journal, 253–56
Sales on account
  about, 190
  operating cycle of, 183
Sales Returns account, 191
Sales returns and allowances, 191–92, 262–63
Sales revenue, 182
Sales Revenue account, 190–91
Sales schemes, 396–97
Sales tax payable, 467–68
Salvage (scrap) value, 427
Schwarzenegger, Arnold, 520
S Corporations, 511
Securities. *See* Stock
Securities and Exchange Commission (SEC), 290
Security, for loans, 336
Selling expenses, 233
Separation of duties, 291–93, 488
Server, 247
Service, partnership sharing based on, 514
Service charge, 297, 299
Service partnership, 87
Service proprietorship, 87
Service revenue, 15–16
Shareholder, 9, 544
Short presentation, 474
Short-term notes payable
  defined, 465–66
  issued at discount, 466–67
Signature card, 295
Single-step income statement, 200
Social Security Act, 478
Social Security (FICA) Tax, 470, 478–79
Software. *See also* Computerized accounting systems
  database, 247
  defined, 247
  integrated accounting, 251–52
  spreadsheets, 251–52
Sole proprietorship. *See* Proprietorship
Special accounting journal, 252–53
Special journals
  about, 252–62
  with computers in accounting information system, 264
Specific-unit-cost method, 385, 399
Spreadsheets, 251–52
Stable-monetary-unit concept, 12
Stallone, Sylvester, 520
Standards, of professional conduct, 9, 312. *See also* Financial Accounting Standards Board (FASB)
Standards of Ethical Conduct, 9
Stated fraction, partnership sharing based on, 512–13
Stated-value stock, 549
Statement of budgeted cash receipts and disbursements, 309–11
Statement of cash flows
  categories in, 203
  defined, 20
  examples of, 21, 22
  inventory transactions on, 398–99
  plant asset transactions on, 444–45
  receivables transactions on, 355–56
Statement of earnings, 182. *See also* Income statement
Statement of financial position. *See* Balance sheet
Statement of operations. *See* Income statement
Statement of owners' equity
  about, 19–20
  examples of, 21, 109, 144
  for merchandisers, 197, 234
  order of preparation, 110
  for partnerships, 526
  relationship to other financial statements, 110
Statements, financial. *See* Financial statements
State unemployment compensation tax, 479
Stock. *See also* Common stock; Preferred stock
  classes of, 548–49
  comparison of types, 549
  defined, 544
  different values of, 559–62
  ethical considerations for issuance, 553–54, 574
  issuing, 549–53
  par value, 549, 550–52
  public offering of, 544, 551
Stock certificates, 546
Stockholder
  defined, 9, 544
  limited liability of, 544–45
  rights of, 548
Stockholders' equity. *See also* Owners' equity
  about, 547–48
  on balance sheet, 548
  rate of return on, 562–63
  reporting on balance sheet, 555
Stockholder's Equity account, charts of, 88
Stocks, decision guidelines, 565
Straight-line (SL) depreciation method, 428, 433–34
Straight-line (SL) depreciation schedule, 428, 429
Straight-time pay, 477
Subsidiary ledger
  defined, 255
  posting from cash receipts journal, 258
  posting from purchases journal, 260
  posting from sales journal, 255
Sum-of-years'-digits depreciation method, 427–28
Supplies account, 96, 98–99

Supplies Expense account, 98–99

T-account
  about, 46–47
  alternatives to, 58–59
  posting inventory transactions, 381
Take-home pay, 469, 477, 482–83, 484, 489
Tax accounting, 2
Taxation. *See also* Income tax
  of corporations, 473, 545, 563–65
  double, 545
  employer payroll taxes, 479
  unemployment compensation, 479
Taxes Payable account, 45
Tax Reform Act, 434
Temporary (nominal) account, 145, 146
Time-and-a-half pay, 477
Timekeeping systems, 488
Time (note period), 347
Time-period concept, 95–96
Tombstones, 550–51
Trademarks and trade names, 441–42
Trade receivables, 336
Transaction(s)
  classifying, 249
  defined, 14
  international, 311
  journalizing from bank reconciliation, 300–302
  separation of authorization, 292
Transaction analysis
  decision guidelines, 66–67
  examples of, 62–66
  journalizing and, 52–54
Transaction recording
  account increases and decreases, 47–49
  decision guidelines, 66–67
  steps of, 49–51
Transportation costs
  alternative procedures for, 189
  recording, 187–89, 229
Trial balance
  about, 54–55
  adjusted. *See* Adjusted trial balance
  adjusting entries to, 92
  examples of, 55, 56, 66, 96
  illustrated, 142–43
  merchandiser adjusting and closing process, 231
  merchandisers example, 195
  postclosing, 148–49
  unadjusted, 96–97
  work sheet column, 138–40, 195, 233
Turnover, of inventory, 201–2

u

Unadjusted trial balance, 96–97
Unclassified balance sheet, 151
Uncollectible-account expense, 339
Uncollectible accounts
  allowance method for, 339–40
  estimating, 340–42
  recoveries of, 344
  writing off, 343, 344
Understatement of asset values, 554
Underwriter, 550
Unearned Legal Revenue account, 134
Unearned revenue
  about, 470–71
  adjusting entries to, 104–5, 106
  alternative accounting for, 134
  defined, 104
  recorded initially as revenue, 134
Unearned Revenue account, as current liability, 150
Unearned Service Revenue account, 104–5
Unemployment compensation tax, 479
Unethical sales schemes, 396–97
Uniform Partnership Act, 508, 517
Union dues, 479
Unit of output, 428
Units-of-production (UOP) depreciation method, 428–29
Unlimited personal liability, 509
Unpaid voucher file, 332
Useful life, 435–37. *See also* Estimated useful life

v

Vacation pay, 472
Validity, 283
Vaults, fireproof, 294
Voting, by stockholders, 548
Voucher, 307
Voucher register, 332
Voucher system, 332–33

w

Wage and Tax Statement (Form W-2), 484, 486
Wages, 469
Wall Street Journal, 550
Warranty expense, 471
Wear and tear, 427
Weighted-average cost method
  comparison with other methods, 387
  decision guidelines, 399
  defined, 385
  illustrated, 386
  income effects of, 387
  perpetual inventory records for, 392
Wesselkamper, Joseph D., 463
Willis, Blake, 507–10
Willis, Bruce, 520
Withdrawals, owner, 13
Withdrawals, partnership, 521–23
Withdrawals account
  about, 45
  closing entries to, 146–48
Withheld income tax, 478
Withholding allowances, 478
Work sheet
  about, 138–42
  account title column, 194–95, 233
  adjusted trial balance column, 138–40, 141
  adjustments column, 138, 140–41, 195, 233
  balance sheet column, 140–42, 196, 233
  example of, 106
  in periodic inventory system, 232–33
  preparing financial statements from, 143–44
  recording adjusting entries, 144–45
  trial balance column, 138–40, 195, 233
World Wide Web, 40–41. *See also* Internet
Write-offs, 292, 343–44

Check Figures

Check Figures—Chapter 1

DE1-1	No check figure
DE1-2	No check figure
DE1-3	No check figure
DE1-4	No check figure
DE1-5	$3,000
DE1-6	No check figure
DE1-7	Capital $57,500
DE1-8	No check figure
DE1-9	No check figure
DE1-10	Capital $55,800
DE1-11	No check figure
DE1-12	No check figure
DE1-13	2. $52,900
DE1-14	No check figure
DE1-15	Net income $40,000
DE1-16	End. cap. $17,000
DE1-17	Total assets $24,000
DE1-18	No check figure
E1-1	No check figure
E1-2	No check figure
E1-3	No check figure
E1-4	A $146,200
	B 11,900
	C 21,900
E1-5	No check figure
E1-6	1. $13,000
	2. $34,000
	3. $(19,000)
E1-7	No check figure
E1-8	End. cap. $85,300
E1-9	2. $5,100
E1-10	2. Total assets $21,750
E1-11	1. Net income $96,200
	2. $84,100
E1-12	1. Net income $148 mil.
E1-13	Decr. in cash $3 mil.
E1-14	Red $20,000
	White $165,000
	Blue $150,000
BN1-1	No check figure
BN1-2	No check figure
P1-1A	2. End. cap. $97,600
P1-2A	1. Total assets $59,000
P1-3A	1. Total assets $94,000
P1-4A	No check figure
P1-5A	1. Net income $43,000
	3. Total assets $96,000
P1-6A	2. Net income $4,240
	4. Total assets $39,920
P1-1B	2. End. cap. $63,000
P1-2B	1. Total assets $70,000
P1-3B	1. Total assets $150,000
P1-4B	No check figure
P1-5B	1. Net income $70,000
	3. Total assets $275,000
P1-6B	2. Net income $2,100
	4. Total assets $29,750
Decision Case 1	No check figure
Decision Case 2	No check figure
Financial Statement Case 1	1. $445,421,200
	1997 $5,361,207,000

Check Figures—Chapter 2

DE2-1	2. $2,000
DE2-2	No check figure
DE2-3	No check figure
DE2-4	No check figure
DE2-5	No check figure
DE2-6	No check figure
DE2-7	No check figure
DE2-8	No check figure
DE2-9	No check figure
DE2-10	2. Cr. bal. $500
DE2-11	3. a. $3,000
	b. $3,000
DE2-12	3. Totals $78,000
DE2-13	Totals $40 bil.
DE2-14	1. Total dr. $13,500
	Total cr. $14,900
	2. Total dr. $14,200
	Total cr. $52,000
DE2-15	No check figure
DE2-16	Cash dr. $80,000
	Equip. dr. $30,000
E2-1	No check figure
E2-2	2. $3 bil.
	4. Incr. $1 bil.
E2-3	No check figure
E2-4	Total dr. $228,600
E2-5	No check figure
E2-6	2. Totals $48,700
E2-7	3. Totals $35,850
E2-8	No check figure
E2-9	Totals $57,400
E2-10	Totals $120,100
E2-11	Totals $75,800
E2-12	Cash $6,700
E2-13	Totals $19,900
E2-14	3. Total dr. $37,000
E2-15	4. Totals $18,400
E2-16	a. $10,000 c. $53,000
	b. $63,000 d. $6,000
E2-17	a, d, e. Dr. = Cr.
	b. Dr. < Cr. c. Dr. > Cr.
BN2-1	No check figure
P2-1A	No check figure
P2-2A	No check figure
P2-3A	3. Totals $45,500
P2-4A	3. Totals $52,900
P2-5A	1. Totals $62,500
	2. Net income $7,640
P2-6A	Totals $57,900
P2-7A	1. Net income $100
	Total assets $51,600
P2-1B	No check figure
P2-2B	No check figure
P2-3B	3. Totals $32,100
P2-4B	3. Totals $40,300
P2-5B	1. Totals $68,000
	2. Net income $4,870
P2-6B	Totals $99,800
P2-7B	1. Net income $2,800
	Total assets $92,400
Decision Case 1	3. Totals $16,800
	4. Net income $4,850
Decision Case 2	No check figure
Financial Statement Case 1	No check figure

Check Figures—Chapter 3

DE3-1	Cash basis
	1998 $15,000
	1999 –0–
DE3-2	No check figure
DE3-3	2. $400,000
DE3-4	$160,000
DE3-5	Net income $44 mil.
DE3-6	1. 1997 $200,000
DE3-7	1. Prepaid Rent $2,500
	2. Supplies $100
DE3-8	3. $35,000
DE3-9	3. Aug. 31 $80
	Sept. 30 $160
DE3-10	3. Aug. 31 $80
	Sept. 30 $160
DE3-11	No check figure
DE3-12	Prepaid rent on the B/S $2,000
DE3-13	2c. Service rev. $7,400
DE3-14	No check figure
DE3-15	2. Total assets 45,925
DE3-16	2. Net income $3,525
E3-1	No check figure
E3-2	No check figure
E3-3	No check figure
E3-4	1. Insur. exp. $1,500
	2. Payments $600
	3. End. prepaid $600
	4. Payments $700
E3-5	No check figure
E3-6	Net. income over by $2,300
E3-7	No check figure
E3-8	Accts. rec. $1,350
E3-9	(a) Accts. Rec. 600
	Serv. Rev. 600
E3-10	(a) Accts. Rec. 600
	Serv. Rev. 600
E3-11	Net inc. $6,850
	Total assets $28,800
E3-12	Net income $72,000
E3-13	End. capital $141,000
E3-14	Net income $1,690
	Total assets $16,790
E3-15	$5,200
E3-16	$4,700
BN3-1	No check figure
P3-1A	Cash net loss $2,600
	Accrual net inc. $833
P3-2A	No check figure

P3-3A a. Rent Exp. 1,600
Prepaid Rent 1,600
P3-4A a. Accts. Rec. 340
Serv. Rev. 340
P3-5A Totals $50,730
P3-6A Net income $46,030
Total assets $62,810
P3-7A 2. Net income $7,600
Total assets $45,900
P3-1B Cash net loss $1,650
Accrual net inc. $900
P3-2B No check figure
P3-3B a. Salary Exp. 3,200
Salary Pay. 3,200
P3-4B a. Accts. Rec. 5,830
Service Rev. 5,830
P3-5B Totals $66,500
P3-6B Net income $69,470
Total assets $120,030
P3-7B 2. Net income $7,450
Total assets $43,050
Decision Case 1 Your bid price $180,000
End. O/E $189,400
Decision Case 2 No check figure
Financial Statement Case 1 No check figure
E3A-1 Acct. bals. should be the same:
Supplies $1,360
Supplies Exp. $5,730
E3A-2 Acct. bals. should be the same:
Unearned Service Rev. $3,700
Service Rev. $9,050
P3A-1 End. bals.: Prepaid Rent $1,500
Unearned Service
Rev. $2,400

Check Figures—Chapter 4

DE4-1 No check figure
DE4-2 No check figure
DE4-3 No check figure
DE4-4 No check figure
DE4-5 No check figure
DE4-6 3. a. $31,575
b. -0-
DE4-7 1. $31,575
DE4-8 No check figure
DE4-9 All balances -0-
DE4-10 No check figure
DE4-11 No check figure
DE4-12 Supp. Exp. -0-
Software $15,000
DE4-13 No check figure
DE4-14 a. $40.695 mil.
d. $40,437 mil.
e. $25,504 mil.
DE4-15 Totals $16,953 mil.
DE4-16 1. $1.31
2. 50%
DE4-17 Lyon current ratio
2. 07; debt ratio 0.31
E4-1 Adjusted trial balance total $50,520;
Net income $2,140;
Balance sheet total $45,150
E4-2 No check figure
E4-3 No check figure
E4-4 Totals $42,150
E4-5 End. cap. $33,900
E4-6 End. cap. $69,700
E4-7 End. cap. $65,000
E4-8 2. Net income $6,300
E4-9 Total assets $49,600
E4-10 No check figure
E4-11 2. Total assets $16,790
E4-12 Net income $56,800

P4-1A Adjusted trial balance
total $131,520
Net income $14,820
Balance sheet total $124,800
P4-2A 2. Net income $29,740
Total assets $162,660
P4-3A 2. Net income $72,000
Total assets $119,000
P4-4A 2. Totals $136,000
P4-5A 3. Net income $7,990
Total assets $101,080
P4-6A 1. Total assets $78,200
P4-7A d. Net income overstated by $480
P4-1B Adjusted trial
balance total $194,330
Net income $16,670
Balance sheet total $184,740
P4-2B 2. Net income $84,630
Total assets $247,680
P4-3B 2. Net income $67,000
Total assets $108,000
P4-4B 2. Totals $153,000
P4-5B 3. Net income $25,750
Total assets $104,320
P4-6B 1. Total assets $108,800
P4-7B Net income overstated by $3,540
Decision Case 1 Net income $53,540
Total assets $58,390
End. capital $35,120
Decision Case 2 No check figure
Financial Statement Case 1 3. Current ratio
1997 2.05; debt
ratio 1997 0.41
Team Project 1. Net income $2,450
2. Total assets $2,590
P4A-1 3. and 4. Balances:
Salary Pay. 0
Salary Exp. $120

Check Figures—Chapter 5

DE5-1 a. $3,774 mil.
DE5-2 May Revenues; Austin Net sales rev.
$165,000
DE5-3 No check figure
DE5-4 Cost $24,500
DE5-5 Gross margin $8,500
DE5-6 No check figure
DE5-7 c. Dr. Cash $23,250
DE5-8 a. $72,000
b. $69,840
DE5-9 c. Cr. Cash $69,840
DE5-10 a. $780,120
b. $440,120
DE5-11 No check figure
DE5-12 End cap. $25,650
DE5-13 No check figure
DE5-14 No check figure
DE5-15 Net inc. $149 mil.
DE5-16 Total assets $1,594 mil.
DE5-17 Gross margin% 21.2%
Invy T/O 10.7 times
DE5-18 a. $510 mil.
b. $545 mil.
DE5-19 COGS $8,226 mil.
DE5-20 1. F 194,000
2. F 91,000
DE5-21 $3,380 mil.
E5-1 Gross margin 1997 $3,039.9 mil.
E5-2 June 23 Dr. Cash $1,372
E5-3 May 22 Cr. Cash $542.33
E5-4 June 14 Cr. Cash $4,115
E5-5 May 14, Dr. Cash $4,074
E5-6 2. End. cap. $4,106 mil.
E5-7 Net inc. $73,980

E5-8 Net inc. $73,980
E5-9 Gross margin% 19X6 52%
Invy: T/O 19X6 3.45 times
E5-10 Net inc. $36,300
E5-11 Net inc. $36,300
E5-12 a. $9 bil.
b. $10 bil.
E5-13 $91,300
E5-14 d. $26,350
f. $37,100
h. $112,100
E5-15 $150 mil.
E5-16 3. Net inc. $3,500
BN5-1 Gross margin% 19X2 28%
Invy T/O 19X2 7.7 times
P5-1A No check figure
P5-2A June 26 Dr. Cash $2,100
P5-3A 2. Rec. $1,600; no disct.
P5-4A Net inc. $36,240
B/S total $212,490
P5-5A 2. End. cap. $63,060
P5-6A 1. Net loss $17,100
2. Total assets $344,700
P5-7A 1. Net loss $17,100
2. Total assets $344,700
P5-8A 1. Net inc. $39,460
2. Gross margin% 19X5 56%
Invy. T/O 19X5 9.2 times
P5-9A 1. Gross margin $82,600
P5-1B No check figure
P5-2B Feb. 27 Dr. Cash $2,000
P5-3B May 29 Cr. Cash $1,760
P5-4B Net inc. $50,390
B/S total $142,450
P5-5B 2. End. cap. $66,760
P5-6B 1. Net inc. $85,600
2. Total assets $230,100
P5-7B 1. Net inc. $85,600
2. Total assets $230,100
P5-8B 1. Net inc. $60,710
2. Gross margin% 61%
Invy: T/O 2.03 times
P5-9B 1. Gross margin $57,000
Decision Case 1 2. Net inc. $58,380
Total assets $104,590
Decision Case 2 No check figure
Decision Case 3 No check figure
Financial Statement Case 1 2. Net inc.
$795,822,000
E5S-1 June 23, Dr. Cash $980
E5S-2 May 22 Dr. Cash $542.33
E5S-3 June 14 Cr. Cash $4,115
E5S-4 May 14 Dr. Cash $4,074
P5S-1 No check figure
P5S-2 No check figure
P5S-3 2. Rec. $1,600; no disct.
P5S-4 2. Net inc. $88,050
Total assets $218,110

Check Figures—Chapter 6

DE6-1 No check figure
DE6-2 No check figure
DE6-3 No check figure
DE6-4 No check figure
DE6-5 Net income $40,000
DE6-6 No check figure
DE6-7 1. $907
DE6-8 3. Accounts receivable $4,319
DE6-9 2. Collections $1,200
DE6-10 3. Accounts payable $2,057
DE6-11 3. Net purchases $3,885
DE6-12 5. Cash $1,875
Inventory $ 364
E6-1 No check figure
E6-2 LT liability $24,300

E6-3	No check figure
E6-4	No check figure
E6-5	Total cash $5,687.60
E6-6	No check figure
E6-7	No check figure
E6-8	No check figure
E6-9	3. Accounts payable $2,338
E6-10	Total cash $11,766
E6-11	Sept. 14 BiWheels Cr. Cash $573
E6-12	1. $3,935 2. $3,521
BN6-1	No check figure
P6-1A	No check figure
P6-2A	1. Total sales $19,941 Total cash $59,826
P6-3A	3. Total cash $24,190
P6-4A	1. Total accounts payable $9,104 Total cash $12,631
P6-5A	End. balances Cash $979; Accounts receivable $567; Inventory $2,165; Accounts payable $2,925; Sales revenue $12,543; COGS $6,484
P6-1B	No check figure
P6-2B	1. Total sales $19,165 Total cash $34,953
P6-3B	3. Total cash $10,329
P6-4B	1. Total accounts payable $16,324 Total cash $15,179
P6-5B	End. balances Cash $2,758; Accounts receivable $496; Inventory $646; Accounts payable $2,692; Sales revenue $12,245; COGS $4,937
Decision Case 1	Cash receipt on account $7,774
Decision Case 2	No check figure
Comprehensive Problem 1	Net income $29,400 Total assets $283,610
Comprehensive Problem 2	Net income $2,027 Total assets $117,727

Check Figures—Chapter 7

DE7-1	No check figure
DE7-2	No check figure
DE7-3	No check figure
DE7-4	No check figure
DE7-5	No check figure
DE7-6	No check figure
DE7-7	No check figure
DE7-8	No check figure
DE7-9	No check figure
DE7-10	Adj. bal. $1,790
DE7-11	No check figure
DE7-12	No check figure
DE7-13	$580 was stolen
DE7-14	No check figure
DE7-15	No check figure
DE7-16	No check figure
DE7-17	No check figure
DE7-18	No check figure
DE7-19	1. New financing needed $165 mil. 2. Cash available $41 mil.
DE7-20	New financing needed $6 mil.
DE7-21	No check figure
E7-1	No check figure
E7-2	No check figure
E7-3	No check figure
E7-4	No check figure
E7-5	Adj. bal. $1,941
E7-6	Adj. bal. $5,161
E7-7	Cash short $10
E7-8	No check figure
E7-9	No check figure
E7-10	No check figure
E7-11	Cash short $10
E7-12	No check figure
E7-13	New financing needed $16 mil.
E7-14	No check figure
E7-15	1. New financing needed $503 mil. 2. After: current ratio 1.31
BN7-1	No check figure
BN7-2	No check figure
P7-1A	No check figure
P7-2A	No check figure
P7-3A	Adj. bal. $8,657
P7-4A	Adj. bal. $4,003.33
P7-5A	No check figure
P7-6A	Cash short $3.65
P7-7A	New financing needed $3,500
P7-8A	New financing needed $28 mil.
P7-9A	No check figure
P7-1B	No check figure
P7-2B	No check figure
P7-3B	Adj. bal. $13,670
P7-4B	Adj. bal. $19,368.77
P7-5B	No check figure
P7-6B	Cash short $7.41
P7-7B	New financing needed $1,600
P7-8B	Cash available $702 mil.
P7-9B	No check figure
Decision Case	Adj. bank $19,258 Adj. book $19,858
Financial Statement Case 1	5. Increase in cash $183,304,000

Check Figures—Chapter 8

DE8-1	No check figure
DE8-2	No check figure
DE8-3	No check figure
DE8-4	No check figure
DE8-5	Accts. receiv., net $84,000
DE8-6	No check figure
DE8-7	3. $96,000
DE8-8	d. $5,000
DE8-9	3. Accts. receiv., net $72,000
DE8-10	1. $3,600
DE8-11	No check figure
DE8-12	1. Net inc. $8,500 2. $8,700
DE8-13	No check figure
DE8-14	5. $1,090
DE8-15	3. $1,052,500
DE8-16	No check figure
DE8-17	c. Cr. Interest rev. $67.50
DE8-18	d. Interest. rev. $67.50
DE8-19	5. $498,200
DE8-20	June 30 Dr. Cash $498,200
DE8-21	AMR $1,382 mil.
DE8-22	2. $1,184 mil.
DE8-23	a. 2.80 b. 48 days
DE8-24	a. 4.16 c. 0.59 b. 0.17 d. 3.2 times
DE8-25	No check figure
E8-1	No check figure
E8-2	No check figure
E8-3	3. Accts. receiv., net $23,600
E8-4	2. $25,930
E8-5	2. Accts. receiv., net $256,103
E8-6	a. Accts. receiv., net $132,400 b. Accts. receiv., net $133,100
E8-7	Dec. 31 Cr. Interest Rev. $795
E8-8	4/1/X7 Dr. Cash $8,800
E8-9	No check figure
E8-10	1. A/T ratio .88 2. Days' sales 37
E8-11	1. 3 days
E8-12	No check figure
E8-13	Net inc.: w/o Bankcards $75,000 w/Bankcards $93,150
BN8-1	Accts. receiv. $50,000 Note receiv. $10,000
P8-1A	No check figure
P8-3A	3. Accts. receiv., net 19X4 $125,591
P8-4A	3. Accts. receiv., net $135,657
P8-5A	4. $210
P8-6A	12/1/X7 Dr. Cash $10,550
P8-7A	12/31/X6 Cr. Interest Rev. $128
P8-8A	19X9 a. 168 b. .94 c. 18 days
P8-9A	2. Net inc. $4 bil.
P8-1B	No check figure
P8-2B	4. Accts. receiv., net: Direct method $84,900 Allow. method $80,300
P8-3B	3. Accts. receiv., net 19X9 $286,937
P8-4B	3. Accts. receiv., net $160,601
P8-5B	4. $405
P8-6B	12/14/X3 Dr. Cash $6,195
P8-7B	3/1/X5 Cr. Interest Rev. $283
P8-8B	19X8 a. 1.67 b. .60 c. 20 days
P8-9B	2. Net inc. $938 mil.
Decision Case 1	Net inc. 19X8 $57,000 19X7 $45,750
Decision Case 2	No check figure
Financial Statement Case 1	2. $78,004,390 3. 1.18

Check Figures—Chapter 9

DE9-1	I/S GM $32,000
DE9-2	2. End. inv. $120,000
DE9-3	GM $70,000
DE9-4	No check figure
DE9-5	No check figure
DE9-6	No check figure
DE9-7	COGS a. $45,000 b. $38,000 c. $52,000
DE9-8	COGS: Wtd. avg. $8,799; FIFO $8,700; LIFO $9,100
DE9-9	Net inc.: Wtd. avg. $1,201; FIFO $1,300; LIFO $900
DE9-10	Inc. tax exp.: Wtd. avg. $480; FIFO $520; LIFO $360
DE9-11	No check figure
DE9-12	2. GM $7,650
DE9-13	COGS $12,950
DE9-14	d. $50,900
DE9-15	3. Correct net inc. Last yr. $7.5 mil.; This yr. $5.3 mil.
DE9-16	No check figure
DE9-17	1. & 2. $300,000
DE9-18	No check figure
E9-1	1. COGS $2,821,000
E9-2	Purchase $7,230 mil.
E9-3	COGS 1. $3,180; 2. $3,174; 3. $3,120; 4. $3,230
E9-4	COGS $3,230
E9-5	LIFO tax adv. $33
E9-6	(a) $55,800; (d) $27,100; (f) $49,000
E9-7	A GM% 39.9%; Inv. T/O 3.5 times

E9-8 COGS $735
E9-9 FIFO net inc. $40,000 @ pur. of $159,000
E9-10 No check figure
E9-11 No check figure
E9-12 GM $113,651
E9-13 GM $39,900
E9-14 Net inc.: 19X8 $28,800; 19X9 $39,600
E9-15 $43,600 destroyed
E9-16 No check figure
E9-17 w/o liquidation, net earnings $162 mil. cost of products sold $4,981 mil.
E9-18 No check figure
E9-19 Net inc. $698 mil.
BN9-1 No check figure
P9-1A 3. Net inc. $670
P9-2A 1. $731,000
2. GM $154,000
P9-3A 3. Gross margin $3,050
P9-4A COGS: Wtd. avg. $12,473; FIFO $12,199; LIFO $12,790
P9-5A GM: Wtd. avg. $62,461; FIFO $62,970; LIFO $62,030
P9-6A COGS $30,400,000
P9-7A Net inc.: 19X4 $18,000; 19X5 $56,000; 19X6 $63,000
P9-8A 2. GM $2,562,000
P9-9A Net inc. $31 mil.
P9-1B 3. Net inc. $790
P9-2B 1. $766,000
2. GM $189,000
P9-3B 3. GM $1,394
P9-4B COGS: Wtd. avg. $56,609; FIFO $55,720; LIFO $57,374
P9-5B GM: Wtd. avg. $2,435 FIFO $2,587; LIFO $2,289
P9-6B COGS $22,900,000
P9-7B Net inc.: 19X1 $23,000; 19X2 $13,000; 19X3 $13,000
P9-8B 2. GM $2,160,000
P9-9B Net inc. $453 mil.
Decision Case 1 Net inc. w/pur. FIFO $249,000 LIFO $189,750
Financial Statement Case 1 4. Pur. $5,910,482,000

Check Figures—Chapter 10

DE10-1 Book val. $5,437 million
DE10-2 No check figure
DE10-3 No check figure
DE10-4 No check figure
DE10-5 2. $220,000
DE10-6 Dr. Land $60,000
DE10-7 No check figure
DE10-8 Book value: S/L $18 million; UOP $18.75 mil.; DDB $12.6 mil.
DE10-9 S/L $3 million; UOP $3.75 million; DDB -0-
DE10-10 2. $2.16 mil.
DE10-11 S/L $2.25 mil.; UOP $1.5 mil.; DDB $6.3 mil.
DE10-12 $8,333
DE10-13 a. Loss $5,000
b. Gain $5,240
DE10-14 Book value $1.5 bil.
DE10-15 3. Amortiz. $12,500
DE10-16 3. b. Amortiz. $4 million
DE10-17 1. Net loss $100,000
DE10-18 No check figure
E10-1 Land $219,900
Land improv. $ 79,400
Building $810,000
E10-2 1. $1,050,400
E10-3 Machine 1 $11,680
E10-4 No check figure
E10-5 No check figure
E10-6 Depr. 19X4: S/L $2,500; UOP $2,000; DDB $125
E10-7 $32,571
E10-8 Depr. Yr 16 $26,667
E10-9 Gain on sale $1,296
E10-10 $276,000
E10-11 (c) Depletion $63,000
E10-12 1. b. Amortiz. $190,000
2. Amortiz. $380,000
E10-13 2. Cost of Goodwill $1,174 mil. Payment for other assets $81 mil.
E10-14 3. Amortiz. $900,000
E10-15 No check figure
E10-16 4. O/E: Yr. 1 F2.4 mil. under; Yr. 2 F1.8 mil. over
E10-17 1. $2,170.6 mil.
3. $2,504.8 mil.
BN10-1 No check figure
P10-1A 1. Land $277,100; Land Improv. $66,500; Sales Bldg. $986,150; Garage Bldg. $81,700
P10-2A Dec. 31 Depr.: Motor Carrier Equip. $61,200; Bldg. (old) $80,000; Bldg. (new) $750
P10-3A No check figure
P10-4A 1. Depr. 19X1: S/L $44,000; UOP $55,000; DDB $96,000
P10-5A 1. % used up 62.3%
4. Gain $339 mil.
P10-6A Part 1. 2. Net inc. $27,750
Part 2. 3. Amortiz. $90,000
P10-7A 1. BV $4.2 bil.
3. Gain (loss) $0.0
P10-1B 1. Land $568,250; Land improv. $106,400; Dist. Office Bldg. $1,646,100; Garage $106,000; Furniture $124,800
P10-2B Dec. 31 Depr.: Comm. Equip. (old) $31,600; Comm. Equip. (new) $4,000; Televideo Equip. $1,333; Bldg. $1,920,000
P10-4B 1. Depr. 19X1: S/L $9,000; UOP $9,720; DDB $23,333
P10-5B 1. Book value $56,269,000
4. Gain $219,000
P10-6B Part 1. 2. Net inc. $138,900
Part 2. 3. Amortiz. $56,750
P10-7B 1. Book value $11.9 bil.
3. Gain (loss) $0.0
Decision Case 1. Net inc.: Waldorf $149,000; Seattle $111,000
Financial Statement Case 1 4. Loss $461,000

Check Figures—Chapter 11

DE11-1 No check figure
DE11-2 Int. pay. $533
DE11-3 I/S Int. exp. $533
DE11-4 3. Note pay., net $98,500
DE11-5 2. $12,000
DE11-6 2. $3,000
DE11-7 Warr. exp. $25,000
DE11-8 No check figure
DE11-9 No check figure
DE11-10 2. $660
De11-11 Total exp. $1,041.65
DE11-12 1. Salary exp. $825
2. Payroll tax exp. $117.15
3. Empl. benefit pay. $99.50
DE11-13 Net pay $5,240
DE11-14 a. Salary exp. $1,000
DE11-15 4. $9,384.30
DE11-16 $28,213.40
DE11-17 No check figure
DE11-18 Total current liabil. $68,202
DE11-19 No check figure
E11-1 No check figure
E11-2 2. $750
E11-3 4/1/X3 Cr. Cash $10,800
E11-4 2. Note pay., net $11,860
E11-5 No check figure
E11-6 No check figure
E11-7 Pay off $20,000
E11-8 Net pay $6,158.70
E11-9 a. Net pay $260.20
E11-10 Payroll tax exp. $7,636.20 Benefits Pay. $6,513.22
E11-11 19X1 Current portion $1,000,000; Int. pay. $360,000; LT debt $3,000,000
E11-12 Total current liabil. $110,590
E11-13 2. Current ratio w/o reclassif. 0.65
E11-14 1. $758 mil.
2. $4,093 mil.
BN11-1 No check figure
BN11-2 No check figure
P11-1A 12/31/X2 Interest exp. $6,000 + $54
P11-2A No check figure
P11-3A k. $23,207
P11-4A 1. Net pay $50,301 2. $80,114
P11-5A 3. Total current liabil. $172,204
P11-6A 2. Cr. Salary Pay. $1,982
4. Dr. Payroll Tax Exp. $177
P11-7A d. Note pay., net $9,267
P11-1B 12/31/X4 Interest exp. $15,000 + $68 + $26
P11-2B No check figure
P11-3B j. $12,695
P11-4B 1. Net pay. $57,685
2. $87,482
P11-5B 3. Total current liabil. $185,880
P11-6B Cr. Sal. Pay. $2,201
4. Dr. Payroll Tax Exp. $127
P11-7B c. Note pay., net $47,000
Decision Case No check figure
Financial Statement Case 1 No check figure
Comparing Two Businesses Island revised total assets $2,237,900 O/E $1,113,600 Island revised net income for last 3 yrs. $149,500

Check Figures—Chapter 12

DE12-1 No check figure
DE12-2 No check figure

DE12-3 No check figure
DE12-4 3. Total owner's equity $43 mil.
DE12-5 2. Benz $460,000
Hanna $95,000
DE12-6 2. $550,000
DE12-7 D $38,000;
F $22,000;
G $50,000
DE12-8 L $27,100;
T $22,900
DE12-9 No check figure
DE12-10 1. No bonus
DE12-11 Bonus to old partners N
and O $20,000
DE12-12 Total owner's equity $340,000
DE12-13 Bonus to Haenni $30,000
DE12-14 No check figure
DE12-15 c. Cr. G, Cap. $5,000
I, Cap. $5,000
DE12-16 Dr. G, Cap. $5,000
I, Cap. $5,000
DE12-17 Cash to: A, $34,000;
B, $18,000; C, $8,000
DE12-18 Dr.: A, Cap. $34,000; B, Cap. $18,000;
C, Cap. $8,000
DE12-19 Total assets $228,000
Total owners' equity $133,000
DE12-20 Net incr. to: T $60,000;
L $30,000
E12-1 No check figure
E12-2 Cr. G, Cap. $78,900
E12-3 d. Net inc. to: V $37,818
H $72,182
E12-4 Overall, partnership
cap. increased $8,000
E12-5 c. K, Cap. $60,000
B, Cap. $115,000;
T, Cap. $65,000
E12-6 No check figure
E12-7 1. $50,000
2. $60,000
E12-8 b. Dr. B. Cap. $48,000;
G, Cap. $1,200; W, Cap. $800
E12-9 a. M $23,000; N $14,000;
O $11,000
E12-10 Cash to: P $26,000;
Q $19,000; R $15,800
E12-11 Sale for $136,000;
F, Cap. $14,500;
G, Cap. $42,500;
H, Cap. $8,000
E12-12 Total assets $276,200;
J, Cap. $92,600
G, Cap. $92,300
BN12-1 No check figure
P12-1A No check figure
P12-2A 2. Total assets $100,000
T, Cap. $40,450;
K, Cap. $40,450
P12-3A 3. Cr. N, Cap. $72,000
4. Cr. N, Cap. $34,000
P12-4A 1. d. Net inc. to:
Collins $69,750;
Davis $53,500;
Chiu $56,750
P12-5A 5. Dr. L, Cap. $38,600
P12-6A 1. a. Cash to:
M $22,000;
B $42,000;
T $44,000
P12-7A 3. Cash to:
B $4,500;
P $2,500;
O $0
P12-1B No check figure
P12-2B 2. Total assets $119,420
R, Cap. $48,560
L, Cap. $48,560
P12-3B 3. Cr. L, Cap. $30,000
4. Cr. L, Cap. $34,500
P12-4B 1. d. Net inc. to:
Dewey $35,333
Karlin $30,333
DeCastro $25,334
P12-5B 5. Dr. K, Cap. $44,000
P12-6B 1. a. Cash to:
W $25,800;
K $73,200;
I $20,000
P12-7B 3. Cash to:
R $8,250;
M $6,750;
G $9,000
Decision Case No check figure
Financial Statement Case 2. $999 per hour
3. $372,825

Check Figures—Chapter 13

DE13-1 No check figure
DE13-2 No check figure
DE13-3 No check figure
DE13-4 No check figure
DE13-5 No check figure
DE13-6 1. Dr. Cash $2,388 mil.
DE13-7 1. $472 mil.
DE13-8 Sum of all dr. to Cash $83,000
DE13-9 All acct. bals. should be the same for cases A and B
DE13-10 No check figure
DE13-11 Total S/E $201.2 mil.
DE13-12 c. $323.5 mil.
DE13-13 Total S/E $540,000
DE13-14 R/E incr. by $59,000
DE13-15 4. Pfd. $6,000, Com. $4,000
DE13-16 No check figure
DE13-17 a. $165 b. $46.67
DE13-18 No check figure
DE13-19 No check figure
DE13-20 ROA 24.2%
ROE 60.5%
DE13-21 2. Net inc. $60,000; Inc. tax pay. $32,000; Def. tax liabil. $8,000
E13-1 No check figure
E13-2 2. $116,500
E13-3 2. Total S/E $61,000
E13-4 Cap. in X/S of Par $75,000
E13-5 No check figure
E13-6 Total S/E $179,500
E13-7 Total PIC $990,000
E13-8 Total S/E $427,000
E13-9 Pfd. $18,000
Com. $42,000
E13-10 Pfd. A $20,000
Pfd. B $962,000; Com. $118,000
E13-11 BV: Pfd. $60; Com. $21.48
E13-12 BV: Pfd. $68.64; Com. $21.39
E13-13 ROA .088; ROE .075
E13-14 Net inc. $273,000; Inc. tax pay. $133,000; Def. tax liabil. $14,000
E13-15 No check figure
BN13-1 No check figure
P13-1A No check figure
P13-2A 2. Total S/E $421,800
P13-3A 5. Total S/E $292,000
P13-4A Total S/E: Yankee $709,000;
Alltell $411,000
P13-5A No check figure
P13-6A 1. Total assets $420,000; Total S/E $312,000
P13-7A 1. b. Pfd. $35,000
Com. $180,000
P13-8A 6. BV: Pfd. $52.55; Com. $8.43
P13-9A 1. $200,000
3. Net inc. $136,500
P13-1B No check figure
P13-2B 2. Total S/E $420,100
P13-3B 5. Total S/E $296,000
P13-4B Total S/E: Omega $630,000;
Homeown. $594,000
P13-5B No check figure
P13-6B 1. Total assets $643,000; Total S/E $488,000
P13-7B 1. b. Pfd. $2,500;
Com. $23,500
P13-8B 5. BV: Pfd. $28.20;
Com. $7.16
P13-9B 1. $200,000
3. Net inc. $138,000
Decision Case 3. Total S/E:
Plan 1 $405,000;
Plan 2 $390,000
Financial Statement Case No check figure